Family Law for the Paralegal

CONCEPTS AND APPLICATIONS

Third Edition

Mary E. Wilson
Northern Essex Community College

PEARSON

Boston   Columbus   Indianapolis   New York   San Francisco   Amsterdam
Cape Town   Dubai   London   Madrid   Milan   Munich   Paris   Montréal   Toronto   Delhi
Mexico City   São Paulo   Sydney   Hong Kong   Seoul   Singapore   Taipei   Tokyo

Editorial Director: Andrew Gilfillan
Executive Editor: Gary Bauer
Editorial Assistant: Lynda Cramer
Director of Marketing: David Gesell
Marketing Manager: Thomas Hayward
Product Marketing Manager: Kaylee Carlson
Marketing Assistant: Les Roberts
Program Manager: Tara Horton
Project Manager Team Lead: Bryan Pirrmann
Project Manager: Patricia Gutierrez
Operations Specialist: Deidra Smith
Creative Director: Diane Ernsberger
Art Director: Diane Six
Cover Designer: Melissa Welch, Studio Montage
Cover Images: Image Source/Getty Images
Manager, Product Strategy: Sara Eilert
Product Strategy Manager: Anne Rynearson
Team Lead, Media Development & Production: Rachel Collett
Media Project Manager: Maura Barclay
Full-Service Project Management: Revathi Viswanathan/Lumina Datamatics, Inc.
Printer/Binder: Edwards Brothers Malloy Jackson Rd
Cover Printer: Phoenix Color/Hagerstown
Text Font: Minion Pro

Credits and acknowledgments borrowed from other sources and reproduced, with permission, in this textbook appear on appropriate page within text.

Acknowledgements of third party content appear on page with the borrowed material, which constitutes an extension of this copyright page.

Library of Congress Cataloging-in-Publication Data

Wilson, Mary E. (Writer on law), author.
  Family law for the paralegal : concepts and applications / Mary E. Wilson, Northern Essex Community College. — Third edition.
    pages cm
  Includes bibliographical references and index.
  ISBN 978-0-13-377971-4 — ISBN 0-13-377971-8
  1. Domestic relations—United States.   2. Legal assistants—United States—Handbooks, manuals, etc.
I. Title.
  KF505.W555 2015
  346.7301'5—dc23
                                                        2015036211

ISBN-10:   0-13-377971-8
ISBN-13: 978-0-13-377971-4

Dedication

This book is dedicated to:

My partner in life and in this work, Richard A. Tauson,
who encourages me to accept uncertainty and embrace adventure

My mother, Florence Ruth Purcell Wilson,
who remains an abiding source of love and inspiration

My father, the Honorable Robert Gardiner Wilson Jr.,
who set the bar high

My professors, the late Honorable John E. Fenton Jr. and John G. Schuler, who made a difference,

and

My students, past, present, and future, who keep me learning and who make it all worthwhile

BRIEF CONTENTS

CONTENTS

CHAPTER 3   Marriage 69

CHAPTER 9   Child Custody   306

CHAPTER 10   Child Support   361

CHAPTER 12   Property Division   435

PREFACE

FROM THE AUTHOR

Welcome to *Family Law for the Paralegal: Concepts and Applications*, 3rd edition. As you embark on your study of family law, I want to share a few thoughts with you about the nature, purpose, and scope of this text.

One of its primary purposes is to introduce you to basic principles of family law and procedure. Although the focus is on traditional terminology and generic topics, an effort is made to alert you to the considerable variation that exists in both law and procedure from jurisdiction to jurisdiction. Each chapter provides opportunities for you to consider issues through the lens of your own state and the facts of a particular case.

Another major purpose of this text is to foster development of your practical skills and self-confidence so that you are better prepared to transition to the workforce well equipped to carry out your responsibilities as a valued member of a family law team or as a resource in a general practice that addresses domestic relations cases as well as other matters. The text focuses specifically on the role of a family law paralegal afforded the opportunity to be involved in all phases of legal representation, including, for example, interviewing clients, maintaining client contact in emotionally charged contexts, preparing discovery requests, drafting pleadings, conducting research, engaging in creative problem solving, and preparing for and assisting at trial.

Every effort has been made to ensure that the material provided is current and accurate, including URL addresses. However, sources of information and the law continually evolve and the success of a client's case may ultimately turn on a recently decided case or a newly passed statute. Practical applications and exercises throughout the text emphasize the need to continually update your knowledge base particularly with respect to the governing law and procedure where you are employed.

This is an exciting time to be learning about the rapidly evolving field of family law in general and in your particular jurisdiction. As you will see, family law is no longer solely about who is to blame for the breakup of a traditional marriage or who gets the kids and the house. You may well be surprised and challenged by the range of topics it encompasses. Now take a deep breath and enjoy your adventure in family law!

Mary E. Wilson

TEXTBOOK FEATURES

This text is designed to effectively meet the needs of two primary audiences: *students* who want an interesting, readable text that presents course content in a manner designed to build their knowledge base, strengthen their skills, and enhance their job prospects and performance; and *instructors* who want to employ diverse teaching strategies but who often lack the time or the resources to develop course materials that will promote conceptual, critical-thinking, problem-solving, interpersonal, and technical job skills. To this end, each chapter includes the following features that introduce, explain, and apply basic family law concepts:

Narrative Features

Chapter Opening Scenarios.   The scenarios are designed to pique the reader's interest and place chapter content in context. Each scenario anticipates one or more of the exercises at the end of the chapter.

Learning Objectives.   The objectives essentially introduce the basic content and organization of the chapter.

Paralegal Applications.   Each chapter includes a number of real-world applications and exercises designed to reinforce substantive content, illustrate applications in the workplace, and promote critical thinking and class discussion. Many expose students to ideas, concepts, beliefs, and points of view different from their own.

Paralegal Practice and Drafting Tips.   Tips contain nuggets of information that enhance job performance by giving paralegals an "edge" in the workplace. Theyprovide a level of practical detail and exposure to jurisdictional variations and unique twists on content not usually available in texts or reached in class lectures.

Cases.   The text contains a broad selection of excerpts from current and landmark cases, most with accompanying questions designed to promote case analysis, application of legal concepts, critical-thinking skills, and lively class discussion. A majority of the featured opinions can be accessed in their entirety on the companion website for this text at *www.pearsonhighered.com/careersresources/*.

Exhibits.   Each chapter includes a series of exhibits that summarize and visually illustrate a variety of concepts, forms, statutes, terms, principles, etc., that reinforce chapter content. Many of the exhibits highlight multistate variations in approaches to specific family law topics and issues.

End-of-Chapter Concept Reinforcement and Developing Your Paralegal Skills Exercises

Key Terms.   A list of chapter-specific key terms appears at the end of each chapter. Definitions are provided in margins for emphasis as well as in a Glossary at the end of the text for easy reference.

Review Questions.   Each chapter includes a series of questions to focus and reinforce content review.

Focus on the Job.   An extensive hypothetical is provided at the end of each chapter that builds on the opening scenario and calls for students individually, in pairs, or in small groups to complete a work assignment, such as drafting a pleading, preparing a discovery request, or conducting an interview.

Focus on Ethics.   Attention to ethical concerns permeates the text. In particular, each chapter includes an end-of-chapter exercise that requires the student to analyze, discuss, and/or recommend a response to a situation with reference to specific codes of paralegal conduct.

Focus on Case Law.   This Focus requires the student to address a particular case in some fashion (IRAC, brief, oral or written responses to a series of questions, etc.).

Focus on State Law and Procedure.   This activity gives students an opportunity to relate chapter content to their home states by locating a form, statute, case, etc., and completing a related assignment.

Focus on Technology.   This focus provides a list and brief description of selected websites related to the chapter content along with one or more online assignments.

Internet Links/Website References.   The third edition of this text identifies about 400 URLs for forms, statutes, cases, and resources related to chapter content, many of which provide information relating to all fifty states. In addition, Appendix B identifies websites of general interest by topic and Appendix C provides URLs for each state for students and instructors wanting to access state forms and/or statutes. All of the URLs were operational as of November 2015.

HIGHLIGHTS OF THE THIRD EDITION

- The marriage chapter has been retitled and revised to include a description of the road to marriage equality, a review of the landmark 2015 *Obergefell* decision, and a projection of its impact particularly on family law practices—content unavailable in any other family law paralegal text on the market as this edition goes to print.
- Revisions have been made in the parenthood, adoption, and custody chapters to reflect the significant effect of marriage equality on the establishment of legal parenthood and parental rights especially for married and unmarried gays and lesbians.
- A segment is now included on the appointment and role of guardians *ad litem* (GALs), particularly in family law cases involving minor children.
- A description of the ways in which the Internet has revolutionized many aspects of the adoption process has been added.
- Chapter 2 introduces the "new" Uniform Premarital and Marital Agreements Act recommended by the Uniform Commission on Uniform State Laws for adoption in all states (in lieu of the Uniform Premarital Agreement Act). The UPMAA reflects the current trend with respect to the standards to be used when assessing the enforceability of premarital (as well as postmarital) agreements.
- Recent decisions have been incorporated in various formats including U.S. Supreme Court decisions in *Obergefell* (marriage equality), *Elonis* (free speech and cyberstalking), and *Caputo* (posthumous reproduction) and state decisions reflecting new trends in various areas of family law (such as the impact of cohabitation on spousal support and property division, modification of child support based on incarceration, the parental

privilege as a defense to alleged child abuse, establishment of parental rights for heterosexual, gay, and lesbian parents, etc.).

- The overall organization of the text has been improved by placing the four child-related chapters in sequence.
- Narrative flow is streamlined by placing most Paralegal Practice Tips in the margins while leaving Paralegal Applications, Cases, and Exhibits in the narrative with related text.
- Each chapter now includes an introductory paragraph describing the basic contents of the chapter.
- New opportunities to learn more about:

Techniques for locating hidden assets

Discovery of electronically stored information (ESI) and in particular social media as targets

The complexities of international adoption, the Hague Convention, and international custody disputes

The effective illustration of property division proposals and settlements

Trends in alimony reform across the country

And more…

CHAPTER ORGANIZATION AND ADDITIONAL NEW COVERAGE

Chapter 1 Introduction to a Family Law Practice

This chapter focuses on the evolving nature and scope of a family law practice, the role of a paralegal, and ethical principles that guide a paralegal's conduct. It specifically discusses three tasks commonly performed by paralegals: billing, client intake, and research. Attention is given to the impact of technology on the practice of family law, primary legal research resources used by family law paralegals, and various kinds of fee agreements. Website references emphasize codes of ethics and related articles/opinions, cases, fee agreement forms, and letters of engagement. New material has been added identifying other areas of substantive law often implicated in family law cases.

Chapter 2 Cohabitation and Premarital Agreements

The initial focus of this chapter is on cohabitation: its definition and prevalence, the devices that cohabitants use to establish their respective rights and responsibilities including cohabitation agreements, and the equitable remedies potentially available when their relationships end. The focus then shifts to the purpose, nature, and enforcement of premarital agreements. The requirements for valid agreements (substantive and procedural fairness, etc.) are identified and illustrated. A comprehensive sample agreement is provided with extensive drafting tips and references to jurisdictional variations. Various approaches to enforceability of both pre- and postmarital agreements are described and illustrated including the UPAA, UPMAA, fairness, and conscionability approaches. Excerpts from seminal cases are provided. New material is added on trends in enforceability of pre- and postmarital agreements and state approaches to so-called palimony agreements.

Chapter 3 Marriage

This chapter focuses on the right to marry and its regulation by the states and federal government. It reviews various forms of marriage (ceremonial, common law, covenant, and putative) and other legally recognized relationships (civil unions and domestic partnerships) and their associated rights and benefits. Highlighted are key milestones in the road to marriage equality (DOMA, *Goodridge, Lawrence, Windsor*, etc.) with particular attention to the 2015 *Obergefell* decision and its implications for the practice of family law. A Table of state statutes governing marriage is provided. Website references emphasize forms, cases, and statutory variations across the country.

Chapter 4 Annulment

This chapter focuses on the nature, purpose, and effects of annulment of void and voidable "marriages." The differences between annulment and divorce are identified. The primary focus is on grounds for annulment based on: technical requirements for a valid marriage; legal capacity to marry; consent/intent to marry; and physical factors. The nature of annulment actions is described addressing issues such as standing, defenses, and conflicts of law. Consequences of annulment for parties, children, and third parties are identified. Included are a Complaint form, excerpts from representative cases, and website references focusing on variations in state laws. A new Exhibit summarizes various grounds for annulment with examples and likely effects.

Chapter 5 The Divorce Process

This chapter provides an overview of the divorce process along with descriptions of the paralegal's role at each stage from the client's first contact with the firm through postdivorce activities. Particular attention is given to jurisdictional issues, fault and no-fault grounds for divorce, defenses, and alternative dispute resolution options. A skeletal outline of the divorce process helps guide the chapter flow. Selected forms are included along with more than fifty website references reflecting variations in state laws, rules, forms, and cases. The Focus on Case Law remains an Indiana case involving a defendant in the military serving overseas.

Chapter 6 Discovery and Financial Statements

This chapter focuses on the nature, purpose, and scope of discovery in the family law context. It reviews strengths and weaknesses of the three primary means of conducting discovery: informal discovery initiatives, the five formal discovery methods, and financial affidavits. Particular attention is given to two areas of heightened importance in contemporary family law cases: (1) the search for hidden assets and (2) the accessing of electronically stored information (ESI). The roles of the client, the paralegal, and the court in discovery are featured. New material has been added with respect to uncovering hidden assets, discovery of ESI through both formal and informal methods, the targeting of social media sites as sources, and related issues concerning the admissibility of ESI evidence and ethical challenges for members of the family law team.

Chapter 7 Parenthood

This chapter now logically precedes the other chapters specifically related to children including adoption, custody, and child support. It reviews the primary ways of establishing and, in some cases, disestablishing parenthood: presumptions, acknowledgments, and adjudications. Traditional paternity actions (with forms) are reviewed as well as establishment of parentage through adoption, contractual/ co-parenting agreements, and application of equitable theories. New case examples are provided involving heterosexual, gay, and lesbian parents, disestablishment of paternity and maternity, and common law fraud actions as an alternative remedy for paternity fraud. The more complex material on assisted reproductive technology has been reduced. However, given its heightened potential significance in a post *Obergefell* era, coverage still is given to surrogacy agreements, cryopreservation, and posthumous reproduction including the *Caputo* case that reached the U.S. Supreme Court in 2012. The Focus on Case Law includes a new option in the form of a case decided by the Maine Supreme Court in 2014, which opens the door to a child having three legal parents. The chapter includes over two dozen website references primarily to forms related to establishment of parenthood.

Chapter 8 Adoption

This chapter focuses on the creation of family relationships through adoption. The emphasis is on types of adoption (including agency and independent adoptions, open and closed adoptions, and stepparent adoptions), the common steps in the adoption process, and the rights of various individuals in the adoption context (married and unmarried, heterosexual, and gay). New material addresses circumstances warranting termination of parental rights, the impact of marriage equality on second/co-parent adoptions, the challenges of international adoption, when consents are required and can be revoked, grounds for challenging adoptions, and the dramatic impact of the Internet on all aspects of the process. Attention is given to jurisdictional variations and the role played by the paralegal. Tips, exercises, and website recommendations focus on putative father registries and forms, safe haven laws, consent forms, open records laws, reunion registries, ICPA interstate adoption information, etc.

Chapter 9 Child Custody

The focus of this chapter is on custody in divorce and third party actions involving stepparents, grandparents, and *de facto* parents with new case illustrations. Featured topics include where and when custody and visitation are sought, types of custody, jurisdictional issues, standards and factors considered by the courts when making custody decisions, the nature and purpose of parenting plans, and when and how awards can be modified and enforced. Exhibits, cases, exercises, and websites focus on the functions of paralegals in custody cases, parental rights of gays and lesbians, the nature of parent education programs, factors considered when determining the best interests of children, circumstances in which modifications may be warranted, and variations in custody laws across the country. The primary additions include material on the impact of marriage equality and a substantial segment on the appointment and role of guardians *ad litem* (GALs) primarily in custody cases.

Chapter 10 Child Support

This chapter examines the duty of child support: when it arises, who has it, how long it lasts, and how it differs from the duty of spousal support. The basics of establishing, modifying, and enforcing child support awards are reviewed with attention to related jurisdictional issues and variations among the states. The role played by the federal government in shaping child support policies is described with emphasis on UIFSA and Title IV-D. Particular attention is given to child support guidelines and factors considered by the courts when establishing and modifying support orders. Methods of enforcing orders are discussed and illustrated.

Chapter 11 Spousal Support

This chapter focuses on spousal support trends with emphasis on short-term forms of alimony (transitional, rehabilitative, restitutional), durational limits, pre- and postmarital contributions, and compensation for "lost opportunity." Distinctions between spousal support, child support, and property division are highlighted. Particular attention is given to factors courts consider when making alimony decisions, key features of alimony provisions in separation agreements, and approaches to modification, termination, and enforcement of spousal support awards. The role of the paralegal is discussed. Practice tips, exercises, and website recommendations highlight jurisdictional variations in statutes, forms, and resources some with state-by-state links. New material addresses questions such as the nature of transitional alimony, when cohabitation warrants termination of spousal support, and when a change in circumstances warrants a modification.

Chapter 12 Property Division

This chapter examines the five phases of the property division process with references to variations in state law and procedure and the role of the paralegal in each phase: definition of property; classification of property as separate or marital; identification of property subject to division; valuation; and division of the property including both assets and liabilities according to a community property or equitable distribution approach in the absence of an agreement. New case excerpts and exercises focus on treatment of particular assets (such as pets, business goodwill, professional degrees, and personal injury awards) as well as factors sometimes considered by the courts including fault, contribution, appreciation, and premarital cohabitation. A Property Division Exhibit in a particular case is provided.

Chapter 13 Separation Agreements

This chapter focuses on separation agreements: what they are, the purposes they serve, how they are developed, their basic components, and how they are approved, modified, and enforced by the courts. In this edition, the material on the characteristics of effective separation agreements is expanded and examples are provided. The distinction between a merged and surviving agreement is described and illustrated. The role played by a paralegal from initial client contact through enforcement of an agreement is highlighted. A sample of an agreement (updated in each edition) is provided with extensive drafting tips. Several paralegal practice tips and website references feature jurisdictional variations.

Chapter 14 Family Violence

This chapter first focuses on family violence in intimate partner relationships: its nature, extent, and selected remedies available to victims including civil and criminal actions, protective orders, and guardianships. It then considers the common types, extent, and consequences of child abuse. Specific topics highlighted include the impact of abuse on custody determinations, state responses to reports of abuse, recognizing when a client is a victim or perpetrator of abuse, and related ethical duties of attorneys and paralegals. Case excerpts include a 2015 U.S. Supreme Court cyber-stalking case, the use of the battered woman's syndrome as a defense in a criminal action, and a parental privilege case. State variations and resources are referenced addressing topics such as mandated reporter laws and definitions of various forms of abuse. Websites point to forms for reporting abuse or seeking protection, CHINS-related forms, and forms that comply with the Indian Child Welfare Act.

SUPPLEMENTS

COMPANION WEBSITE FOR STUDENTS

Students can access a wealth of textbook-related resources at *www.pearsonhighered.com/careersresources/*. This online companion website includes the following for each chapter: learning objectives; links to cases and forms (such as motions, pleadings, and discovery requests); and additional useful resources and supplementary material.

INSTRUCTOR SUPPLEMENTS

Instructor's Manual With Test Bank

The Instructor's Manual contains chapter objectives, chapter overviews, a model syllabus, lecture outlines, supplementary class activities, and suggested answers to end-of-chapter assignments. This also contains a Word document version of the test bank.

TestGen

This computerized test generation system gives you maximum flexibility in creating and administering tests on paper, electronically, or online. It provides state-of-the-art features for viewing and editing test bank questions, dragging a selected question into a test you are creating, and printing sleek, formatted tests in a variety of layouts. Select test items from test banks included with TestGen for quick test creation, or write your own questions from scratch. TestGen's random generator provides the option to display different text or calculated number values each time questions are used.

PowerPoint Presentation Package

Our presentations offer clear, straightforward outlines and notes to use for class lectures or study materials. Photos, illustrations, charts, and tables from the book are included in the presentations when applicable.

To access supplementary materials online, instructors need to request an instructor access code. Go to *www.pearsonhighered.com/irc*, where you can register for an instructor access code. Within 48 hours after registering, you will receive a confirming email, including an instructor access code. Once you have received your code, go to the site and log on for full instructions on downloading the materials you wish to use.

ALTERNATE VERSIONS

eBooks

This text is also available in multiple eBook formats. These are an exciting new choice for students looking to save money. As an alternative to purchasing the printed textbook, students can purchase an electronic version of the same content. With an eTextbook, students can search the text, make notes online, print out reading assignments that incorporate lecture notes, and bookmark important passages for later review. For more information, visit your favorite online eBook reseller or visit *www.mypearsonstore.com*.

ACKNOWLEDGMENTS

Primary thanks go to my husband and partner, Richard Tauson. Ric has been my number-one supporter and most constructive critic. His long hours of research, attention to detail, manuscript preparation, and review were invaluable. His patience, and that of friends and family, make many things possible.

Much appreciation is due the Commonwealth of Massachusetts Trial Court Law Library—Lawrence Division—and the Northern Essex Community College Library (most especially Librarians Gail Stuart and Louise Bevilacqua). Thanks also go to Kelly Sullivan, esq. for helpful advice and Hugh Sims for technical assistance. I also want to thank my paralegal program colleagues for providing input and encouragement, as well as my family law students at Northern Essex for their enthusiastic pilot-testing of several of the Paralegal Applications, research assignments, ethics exercises, and drafting projects.

Finally, I want to thank personnel at Pearson for their guidance, assistance, patience and support, especially Gary Bauer, Tara Horton, and Patricia Gutierrez, and, from Lumina Datamatics, Revathi Viswanathan and Jennifer (Gray) Vittorioso. Thanks also are due the following reviewers for their helpful suggestions regarding one or more editions of this text:

Richard Q. Barrett, *Simpson College*
Heidi Getchell-Bastien, *Northern Essex Community College*
Carol Brady, *Milwaukee Area Technical College*
Patricia Greer, *Berkeley College*
Erma Hart, *Wharton County Junior College*
Annette R. Heim, *University of North Carolina–Charlotte*
Warren C. Hodges, *Forsyth Technical Community College*
Jennifer Jenkins, *South College*
Tracy Kaiser, *Manor College*
Heidi K. Koeneman, *Ivy Tech Community College, Fort Wayne*
Sharee Laidlaw, *Salt Lake Community College*
Sondi A. Lee, *Camden County College*
Genia Lee, *McNeese State University*
Elaine S. Lerner, *Kaplan University*
June Peterson-Gleason, *College of Lake County*
Beth R. Pless, *Northeast Wisconsin Technical College*
Annalinda Ragazzo, *Bryant and Stratton College*
Cheryl Reinhart, *Pulaski Technical College*
Joan Stevens, *Loyola University of Chicago*
Laura Tolsma, *Lansing Community College*
Buzz Wheeler, *Highline Community College*
And, most especially, Julia O. Tryk, *Cuyahoga Community College*

ABOUT THE AUTHOR

MARY E. WILSON is a graduate of Suffolk University Law School in Boston, Massachusetts. In addition to her law degree, she earned a Master's Degree in Education from Boston University and a Bachelor's Degree from Middlebury College in English and Psychology. She is a member of the American Bar Association Family Law Section and is admitted to the practice of law in Massachusetts and New Hampshire. Having retired as a full professor in 1997, she is an adjunct faculty member at Northern Essex Community College in Haverhill and Lawrence, Massachusetts, where she has taught courses in the paralegal and criminal justice programs. In her more than thirty-five years of teaching at both public and private institutions, she has designed and taught a variety of behavioral science, education, and law courses. She has also directed a statewide training program for foster parents and social workers through the Massachusetts Community College system and has authored training manuals on child discipline and working with abused and neglected children. A former department chair, she has also served as a director and dean at Northern Essex.

Exhibits (EX), Cases (CA), and Paralegal Applications (PA)

Chapter 1
Introduction to a Family Law Practice

Chapter 2
Cohabitation and Premarital Agreements

Chapter 6
Discovery and Financial Statements

Chapter 7
Parenthood

Chapter 10
Child Support

Chapter 11
Spousal Support

Chapter 12
Property Division

chapter 1

INTRODUCTION TO A FAMILY LAW PRACTICE

© Stephen Coburn/Shutterstock

Annamaria Santiago did well in her paralegal coursework in college and graduated with honors. This morning she starts work at a law firm that specializes in family law. While driving to the office, she recalls how each chapter of her family law textbook began with a factual scenario related to the content of the chapter and ended with challenging exercises based on that scenario. Now those challenges will involve real people and their well-being, and she will be called upon to use her skills to deal with them. As her feelings of anxiety and excitement build, she recalls her father once telling her that the Chinese expression for "crisis" is made up of two characters. One means danger and the other, opportunity. That expression captures how she feels today. She is apprehensive but also knows she has an opportunity to become one of the "experienced and trusted" paralegals about whom she has read, provided she remains mindful of her responsibilities and ethical duties.

LEARNING OBJECTIVES

After reading this chapter and completing related assignments, you should be able to:

- describe the nature and scope of a contemporary family law practice

- identify ways in which technology has impacted the practice of family law

- describe the role of a paralegal in a family law practice

- identify the major objectives of an initial client interview

- distinguish among various kinds of fee agreements

- list primary legal research resources used by family law paralegals

- identify basic ethical principles that guide the professional conduct of family law paralegals

Family law
the body of law that governs the rights and responsibilities of individuals in the formation, continuation, and dissolution of marriages and other "family" relationships

Introduction

Welcome to the study of family law. In general, **family law** is the body of law governing the rights and responsibilities of individuals in the formation, continuation, and dissolution of marriages and other "family" relationships. Because it addresses issues at the core of people's personal lives, it is a challenging and sometimes heartbreaking area of practice. But given that approximately half of all marriages end in divorce and nearly 40% of all children under the age of eighteen are being raised in one-parent households, family law is an essential area. It tests the skills and integrity of practitioners and provides potentially rewarding opportunities for creative and constructive problem solving. Members of family law teams are in a position to help shape and improve the lives of both adults and children, and paralegals are invaluable members of those teams.

In this first chapter, you will learn about the evolving nature and scope of family law, the role of a paralegal in a family law practice, and the ethical principles that guide the paralegal's conduct. In addition, you will briefly explore three tasks commonly performed by paralegals: billing, client intake, and research.

The Evolving Nature and Scope of a Family Law Practice

Because its development tends to track many of the social, political, and economic issues of the day, family law has gradually yet dramatically evolved in its nature and scope over the last five decades. Some of the most significant changes include the following:

- From a layman's perspective, the family law legal landscape has been most noticeably (and controversially) altered by the U.S. Supreme Court's historic redefinition of marriage in June 2015. For centuries marriage was defined as the legal union of one man and one woman, and the right to heterosexual marriage enjoyed sustained constitutional protection. As the millennium approached, however, the national debate about the rights of homosexuals generally, and same-sex partners in particular, began to increasingly focus on demands for equal protection and freedom from discrimination based on sexual orientation in the family law context. States, municipalities, private employers, and eventually the federal government as well, came to recognize the rights of same-sex partners, extending to them a variety of benefits and legal statuses. Today, marriage equality is the law of the land, and the reverberations of that development are being felt in many areas of substantive law. We will explore its impact on family law in particular throughout this text.

- A "traditional" pre-1970s family law practice focused primarily on proving fault in divorce and alimony actions involving heterosexual spouses. Today, family law cases involve both heterosexual and same-sex spouses, no-fault grounds for divorce are available in every state, alimony awards are less and less common, and the courts pay minimal attention to fault unless the "misconduct" has economic consequences for the marital unit. Although divorce is still their bread and butter, most contemporary family law practices generally have become more multidimensional and address diverse topics such as premarital planning, division of marital property, legal parentage of children, rights of unmarried same-sex partners, adoption, and family violence.

- The practice of family law has gradually become less adversarial. The courts commonly encourage parties to resolve their differences through mediation and negotiation rather than litigation, often resulting in mutual agreements and uncontested final hearings in which increasing numbers of parties proceed *pro se*. Given high divorce rates, many couples now elect to execute premarital agreements or, in the alternative, to postpone or forgo marriage entirely, sometimes negotiating cohabitation or "living-together" agreements.

- Gender stereotypes have largely been abandoned in theory if not entirely in practice. Today, men are no longer cast solely in the role of breadwinner and women in the roles of homemaker and primary caretaker of the children. Both partners are viewed as making economic and noneconomic contributions to the marriage. Alimony is gender neutral by law, and marital assets usually are divided equally or on the basis of principles of fairness depending on the jurisdiction.

Pro se
[Latin: for himself or on his or her own behalf] [adj. or adv.] representing one's self in a legal proceeding without the aid of an attorney

- Divorcing parents now are at least initially perceived as having equal rights to custody of the children of their marriage. Historically the right of those parents to raise their children as they see fit has been staunchly protected by judges and legislators. However, that protection has begun to erode as the courts have chosen, in some circumstances, to recognize "rights" of third parties. Individuals such as grandparents, "psychological" parents, co-parents, and others are increasingly seeking and being granted an opportunity to play a significant parenting role in children's lives even if against the wishes of the "actual" parents.

- Five decades ago, babies were produced as a result of a man and a woman engaging in sexual relations. Since then, advances in reproductive technology initially led to artificial insemination and surrogate parenting arrangements. Now the horizon appears limitless. Among other options, we have *in vitro* fertilization, cryopreserved embryos, postmortem reproduction, and cytoplasmic egg donation in which genetic material is transferred from one woman's eggs to another's, creating two genetic mothers.

- Up until the 1970s, creation and enforcement of substantive family law and policy were primarily left to the states. However, since that time, the federal government has assumed a leadership role in creating national standards, rules, and regulations impacting family law in areas such as taxes, jurisdiction, paternity, child support enforcement, bankruptcy, adoption, and family violence. In addition to being partially shaped by federal law, family law is also increasingly influenced by model acts promulgated by the National Conference of Commissioners on Uniform State Laws for consideration by the states. These acts promote uniform legislation and policy in many areas, such as premarital agreements, parentage, assisted conception, marital property, custody, and child support.

- Electronic technology has dramatically altered the practice of law and the ways in which law firms create, receive, obtain, store, and retrieve information. Wireless laptops, smartphones, personal digital assistants (PDAs), voice mail, and fax machines were just a beginning. The "paperless" office is becoming a reality. To compete in a digital age and properly serve clients, members of the family law team must be aware of the potential of technology and its advantages and disadvantages. A full discussion of this topic is beyond the scope of this text, but Paralegal Application 1.1 identifies some of the implications of technological advances for a family law practice.

PARALEGAL PRACTICE TIP

www.uniformlaws.org is the website for the National Conference of Commissioners on Uniform State Laws. All of the Uniform Acts can be accessed at this site along with Enactment Status Maps and information about pending related legislation that can be viewed by state.

Paralegal **Application 1.1**

The Impact of Technology on a Family Law Practice: Some Examples

- Some jurisdictions now manage dockets electronically and permit electronic filing. This will likely be the standard in the not-too-distant future.
- Most states have developed websites with interactive computer programs, enabling family law team members to complete complaints, financial statements, child support guidelines worksheets, and other documents online.
- Under federal and state law, subject to evolving procedural rules, data retained in electronic form by a party is discoverable if not protected by privilege or other consideration. Parties have an obligation to preserve evidence and may be judicially sanctioned for willfully destroying relevant electronic files and documents, such as financial records and e-mails.
- Servers and freestanding storage media, such as flash drives and disks, are gradually replacing cumbersome file cabinets since digitally stored data is far more conveniently organized, accessible, compact, and transportable. Commercial companies now provide

(Continued)

comprehensive data backup and protection systems that automatically encrypt and store information in secure remote locations accessible from anywhere by the user. Lawyers in some states such as California may maintain a virtual law office in "the cloud" where communications with the client and storage of all information in the client's case are managed solely via the Internet using a third-party secure server.

- To a significant extent, facsimiles, e-mail, and texting are replacing the U.S. mail and the telephone.
- Computer "forensics" experts are becoming as commonplace as traditional private investigators as they "cybersleuth" to gather information to support a client's case.
- Software products designed to support law practices now allow attorneys to manage caseloads, client lists, documents, and billing far more efficiently.
- Valuation of various types of property is facilitated by such online resources as *www.zillow.com* for real estate and *www.nada.com* (National Automobile Dealers Association) and *www.kbb.com* (Kelley Bluebook) for vehicles.
- Offices of secretaries of state and registries of deeds now have websites on which the ownership of property and operation of businesses within a state can be researched online.
- At trial, attorneys are increasingly using PowerPoint and other media presentations to highlight elements of their clients' cases such as proposed parenting schedules or the dissipation of marital assets over time. Some are created by paralegals and attorneys and others by litigation graphics and trial strategy firms that specialize in developing persuasive multimedia demonstrations.
- The family law team can now perform most research online, eliminating the need to maintain costly and extensive in-house libraries.

PARALEGAL PRACTICE TIP

Paralegals need to be aware of their firm's records maintenance, retention, and destruction policies as well as applicable federal or state rules with respect to client files. Technically, the "file" is the property of the client, but in the age of digital technology, what constitutes the "file" and where is it located? If the client wants to receive a copy of his or her file in electronic form, the firm may be required to deliver it in digital format. See the New Hampshire Bar Association Ethics Committee Opinion #2005–06/3 on this topic available at *www.nhbar.org*.

Substantive law

laws that relate to rights and obligations/duties rather than to technical rules and procedures

As you progress through the upcoming chapters, you will see that family law does not exist in an isolated legal vacuum. Family law cases often involve other areas of **substantive law** such as the following:

- **Criminal law:** One or both of the parties may have a criminal record or be engaged in an illegal enterprise that has led to the breakdown of the marriage and diminished marital assets through forfeitures and legal fees.
- **Property law:** The parties, individually or jointly, may own a considerable amount of real estate and personal property that may be subject to division when they divorce.
- **Contract law:** One party may have entered contracts during the marriage for which the other may potentially be liable.
- **Tort law:** One or both of the parties may have committed a tort against the other (or a third party) such as a fraud, assault, or intentional infliction of emotional distress.
- **Juvenile law:** The parties may have a child who has been designated a child/person in need of services (CHINS/PINS).
- **Bankruptcy law:** A party may be threatening to declare bankruptcy in an effort to deprive the other of a fair share of the marital assets.
- **Constitutional law:** One of the parties may be claiming a constitutionally protected right to abort a fetus she is carrying despite the strenuous opposition of the other party.
- **Evidence law:** The case may trigger questions about the admissibility of evidence obtained through "fraudulent friending," electronic communications received in error, installation of spyware on a spouse's computer, or a tracking feature on a phone or Global Positioning System (GPS) device attached to a party's vehicle.

- **Tax law:** One of the parties may have totally controlled the parties' finances and have filed fraudulent joint tax returns during the marriage resulting in taxes and penalties for which the "innocent spouse" may potentially be held liable.
- **Corporate/business law:** A party may own or have an interest in a business and the nature of ownership as well as the value of the assets and liabilities of the business may need to be determined in anticipation of a property division settlement.
- **Immigration law:** The legal residency status of one of the parties may potentially be impacted by the pending divorce.

The Role of a Paralegal in a Family Law Practice

The National Association of Legal Assistants (NALA) defines paralegals as a distinguishable group of persons who through formal education, training, and experience have knowledge and expertise regarding the legal system and substantive and **procedural law** which qualify them to do work of a legal nature under the supervision of an attorney.[1]

The role of a paralegal in a family law practice is shaped by four primary forces:

- **The size of the practice:** In a small practice, the paralegal may be called upon to function as a legal assistant, a secretary, and a receptionist. In a larger practice, the paralegal is more likely to be utilized more fully as a true legal support person.
- **The style and expectations of the supervising attorney:** Some attorneys have high expectations of paralegals and delegate a wide range of responsibilities. Others provide close supervision and delegate only the most fundamental tasks.
- **The scope of the practice:** Although the major focus of most family law practices continues to be on divorce, as a member of a family law team a paralegal may have an opportunity to address a broad range of matters including, for example, establishment of paternity, enforceability of premarital agreements, awarding of grandparent visitation, termination of parental rights, and issues raised by same-sex relationships. Some family law practitioners specialize in particular aspects of family law such as alternative dispute resolution, appellate law, child support enforcement, international adoption, or matters involving the care and protection of children.
- **The skill of the paralegal:** Initially, entry-level paralegals are likely to focus on completing standardized forms, writing routine correspondence, drafting basic discovery requests, scheduling meetings, and preparing invoices. Experienced paralegals perform more demanding and complex tasks such as organizing trial notebooks, searching for hidden assets, preparing pretrial memoranda, and drafting appellate briefs.

The job description of a paralegal in a family law practice is, in many respects, like a generic paralegal job description. The sample description provided in Exhibit 1.1 presumes a highly skilled paralegal and a family law attorney willing to delegate responsibilities and provide appropriate supervision. Paralegal Application 1.2 provides a series of practical suggestions designed to supplement the formal job description and improve the paralegal's efficiency, productivity, and job satisfaction.

PARALEGAL PRACTICE TIP

The NALA-based definition, adopted in the state of South Dakota Rules of Professional Conduct, can be located at *www.legis.state.sd.us*.

procedural law
the technical rules for bringing and defending actions before a court or administrative agency

PARALEGAL PRACTICE TIP

Job descriptions can be deceiving, and no single job description applies in all settings. When interviewing for a position, an applicant should try to get a sense of how paralegals actually are treated and utilized in the practice. Do they function as legal assistants or legal secretaries? Knowing in advance can help promote realistic expectations and enhance later job satisfaction.

EXHIBIT 1.1 Paralegal Job Description

The following functions are performed by paralegals under the direction and supervision of a licensed attorney. The terms "draft" and "prepare" refer to a preliminary writing to be approved and signed by the attorney, if required.

- Develop office management systems: record keeping, filing, billing, calendaring of meetings and court dates, etc.
- Screen potential clients for conflicts of interest
- Participate in initial and follow-up interviews with clients and record notes in memoranda for the supervising attorney and the file
- Prepare letters of engagement (or nonengagement) and fee agreements as directed
- Maintain communication with the client throughout the period of representation
- Gather preliminary information and documents essential to the case
- Prepare release and authorization forms necessary to obtain copies of documents such as employment records, income tax returns, financial records, medical records, police reports, and social service agency records and reports
- Research legal issues and assist in drafting briefs and memoranda
- Draft initial complaints/petitions and responsive pleadings such as answers and counterclaims, along with accompanying documents (such as affidavits) for review, approval, signature(s), filing, and service
- Draft motions for temporary orders and other forms of relief, along with supporting affidavits and proposed orders, if required
- Assist the client in gathering data on income, expenses, assets, and liabilities and in preparing financial statements
- Draft and edit successive versions of stipulations/agreements between the parties
- File pleadings and other documents with appropriate transmittal letters and copies as directed and arrange for service, if necessary
- Check calendars and schedule hearings as required and then mark all appropriate calendars
- Schedule meetings as directed with mediators, clients, opposing counsel, witnesses, experts, etc.
- Draft discovery requests and review responses received from opposing parties
- Review discovery requests received from opposing parties and help draft responses
- Monitor deadlines to confirm that all are met by the paralegal, the supervising attorney, and the opposition
- Compile property inventories and documentation of values and proof of ownership
- Facilitate activity and payment of accountants, appraisers, **Guardians *ad litem***, experts, private investigators, and other agents as needed
- Assist with preparation of trial materials such as pretrial memoranda, exhibits, trial notebooks, PowerPoints, and other media presentations
- Assist with preparation and orientation of witnesses (including clients) as directed
- Draft any necessary post-trial materials such as **Qualified Domestic Relations Orders (QDROs)**, deeds, and other documents transferring assets as ordered
- Draft post-trial pleadings, motions, etc., such as notices of appeal, motions to enforce judgment, and requests for modification, as warranted
- Draft letters concluding representation, including the attorney's opinion as to the tax-deductible portion of fees paid (i.e., the amount attributable to the provision of tax advice and analysis)

PARALEGAL PRACTICE TIP

In some states, if the attorney actually drafts a document and the client files it, the document must be marked "prepared by counsel" in order to avoid a lack of candor before the court.

Guardian *ad litem* (GAL)
a person, usually a lawyer, appointed by the court to conduct an investigation and/or represent a party who is a minor or otherwise unable to represent himself or herself in a legal proceeding; the guardian's role may be limited to investigation of a particular matter, such as custody

Qualified Domestic Relations Order (QDRO)
a court order directing the administrator of a pension plan to pay a specified portion of a current or former employee's pension to an alternate payee to satisfy a support or other marital obligation

Paralegal Application 1.2

Tips for Effective Job Performance and Satisfaction

There are many tasks effective family law paralegals perform that do not appear in formal job descriptions but that have the potential to significantly improve job performance and satisfaction. These tasks include the following among others:

- Maintain checklists regarding the tasks commonly performed and use them to guide and double-check your work. Several examples of lists are provided throughout this text addressing such topics as the common elements of separation or marital agreements, the materials to be filed with a complaint/petition for divorce, the steps to be followed when serving or responding to various types of discovery requests, and the kinds of property subject to division upon divorce. There are many useful resources containing other examples of checklists as well as models of common correspondence. See, for example, Mark Chinn, *Forms, Checklists and Procedures for the Family Lawyer*, published by the American Bar Association (ABA).

- Maintain lists of key governing statutes, court rules, and case law on a variety of commonly encountered issues, particularly those that establish standards for the court as it makes decisions. For example, what is the standard in the jurisdiction for assessing a custodial parent's request to relocate to another state or country with his or her child? Under what circumstances will a court "impute" income to a party who is understating income on a financial statement? Such lists are very useful when drafting pretrial memoranda or appellate briefs or when considering the kinds of information to include in motions and supporting affidavits.

- Develop your own "tickler" (reminder) system with respect to various dates (of hearings, client meetings, pretrial conferences, etc.) and deadlines (for filing answers, initiating appeals, responding to discovery requests, etc.). Suggested characteristics of a good tickler system are discussed at *www.tba.org /tickler-and-calendar-systems*.

- Keep models/templates of various kinds of motions, pleadings, discovery requests, and types of correspondence (transmittal letters, confirmation of hearings and appointments, letters of engagement, etc.). Many forms are now available on disks accompanying practice manuals and online through court-sponsored sites and the like. These resources can save you significant time and prevent reinvention of the wheel, BUT remember to verify which forms and formats are mandatory and/or currently in use and to tailor each document to the specific facts of the client's case.

- Proofread and never solely rely on computer spell- and grammar-check. Accuracy is essential. Errors reflect poorly on the paralegal and the attorney and can have costly consequences. For example, use of an incorrect address can result in a failure of proper service of a complaint or published notice. If not detected, transposition of figures on a financial statement can impact the amount of a property settlement. For example, the value of a stock portfolio worth \$849,456 may be incorrectly listed at \$489,456, and a client receives "50%" of the lower rather than the higher figure. If the error is discovered at a later date, the "injured" client may seek relief from the divorce judgment and pursue a malpractice claim against his or her attorney.

- When given an assignment, make a note of the date you receive it and the date by which it is to be completed. Listen carefully and be sure you understand instructions. Repeat them if necessary. If warranted, ask for feedback as you move forward with the task. It is a strength rather than a weakness to recognize your limitations and when you need guidance and supervision.

- When overwhelmed with a multiplicity of tasks to be performed, prioritize them with your supervisor.

- Be respectful of colleagues, both in and out of the office.

- Learn the names of court personnel and others you communicate with in your professional capacity and address them by name.

- Be alert to the unique practices and procedures of the various courts and agencies the firm deals with on a regular basis and to any idiosyncrasies of contact persons in those settings.

- Maintain high standards of professional ethics. If something doesn't feel right, check it out; it probably isn't!

- Keep your skills current, and participate in continuing legal education programs (preferably with the encouragement and financial support of your employer).

- Be aware of your own personal biases, and remember, everyone is entitled to representation. Personal, moral, or religious beliefs should not compromise competent advocacy. If you perceive a personal conflict, bring it to the attention of your supervisor.

- Be prepared for the often physically and emotionally draining nature of the job. Family law is perhaps the most stressful area of legal practice. Much too often, hearts are broken, dreams are shattered, children are used as pawns by angry combatants, finances are exhausted, and no one is a "winner." To maintain a healthy perspective in the midst of such emotional chaos, be sure to "have a life" apart from the job!

THE FAMILY LAW PARALEGAL'S ROLE IN THE CLIENT INTAKE PROCESS

A paralegal is often a prospective client's first contact with a family law practice. This contact typically occurs by telephone when the client calls to schedule a meeting with the attorney. The initial interview (sometimes called an initial consultation or intake interview) is occasionally conducted over the telephone, but most often involves a face-to-face meeting in which the participants essentially screen each other. Occasionally, the meeting will be taped with the consent of the client, but many attorneys find that taping inhibits the openness and free flow of the interview. However it is conducted, it is an important meeting because it sets the tone for a future working relationship. Paralegal Application 1.3 provides a checklist identifying the primary objectives of an initial meeting with a prospective client.

Paralegal **Application 1.3**

Initial Client Intake Interview Checklist

The primary objectives of an initial client intake interview are to:

- identify the nature of the client's need for services
- establish whether or not any conflict of interest exists that would prohibit or restrict representation
- discuss the client's goals and expectations for the representation, and indicate what the firm can and cannot do with respect to those goals
- determine whether or not the attorney is able and willing to represent the client and whether or not the client wants to retain the attorney
- discuss the scope of representation and potential fees, costs, and payment terms
- introduce the primary members of the family law team and describe their respective roles, emphasizing the paralegal's greater accessibility and the cost efficiency of having them perform certain tasks and maintain routine communication with the client
- describe the nature and scope of attorney-client confidentiality and privilege
- identify any urgent deadlines or emergency situations needing immediate attention
- confirm and/or gather basic information called for in an initial Client Intake Form
- agree on a course of action and plan for follow-up, including execution of a fee agreement, completion of a comprehensive client questionnaire tailored to the subject matter of the representation, and identification of materials to be gathered

Given the purposes of an initial intake interview, it is advisable that an attorney conduct it, at least in part. The kinds of decisions needing to be made, such as whether or not to accept the case, setting the fee, and determining an appropriate course of action, are all decisions that the attorney must make. It is difficult, if not impossible, for a paralegal to accomplish the same purposes without engaging in the **unauthorized practice of law**. A common compromise approach is to divide the meeting into two parts: The attorney conducts the first part and makes the legal decisions while the paralegal takes notes, observes the client, and records any follow-up activity needed and/or requested by either the client or the attorney. The paralegal should listen to the client's words and also observe his or her body language,

Unauthorized practice of law (UPL)
engaging in the practice of law without a license

being alert to potential "red flags." For example, are there any signs of deception? Does it appear the client intends to lie in court regarding assets or conduct? Does the client give any indication of being a victim or perpetrator of abuse? Is the client uncertain about the course of action he or she wants to pursue (e.g., divorce or reconciliation)? If the client and attorney agree on the terms, purposes, and scope of the representation, the paralegal may then be asked to conduct the second portion of the meeting, which is essentially an information-gathering session.

Interviewing, even if only to collect data, is a skill that usually develops with practice and experience. The paralegal may want to consult some of the many resources available on basic interviewing techniques and structuring interviews in the legal context. Research can be helpful, but good interviewing flows primarily from strong interpersonal skills that allow the paralegal to exercise:

- an unconditional positive regard (a nonjudgmental respect and acceptance) for the client
- an ability to focus on, listen to, and hear the client
- a capacity to empathize with the client while maintaining an appropriate professional demeanor (See Paralegal Application 1.4.)

PARALEGAL PRACTICE TIP

Some attorneys use a comprehensive client questionnaire to guide the initial interview, but such forms may be overwhelming for the client, detract from the spontaneity of the meeting, and force attention on "nitty-gritty" items usually best left to follow-up by the paralegal and the client. An example of a generic Client Intake Form, suitable for use in a family law case, is available on the companion website for this text at *www.pearsonhighered.com /careersresources/* in the material related to Chapter 1 under Forms.

Paralegal Application 1.4

Basic Interviewing Tips for Paralegals

- Determine how the client would like to be addressed, for example, by his or her first name or by a professional title such as Dr.
- Communicate with the client in plain English and avoid the use of "legalese" unless the client has a legal background.
- Adopt a style you are comfortable with and then tailor it as much as possible to the client's communication style. Each client is different. Some will feel free to present a spontaneous, open-ended narrative but will eventually need a degree of structure in the form of focused questions. Others will need to be encouraged, reassured, and drawn out.
- Focus on the client and maintain eye contact as much as possible unless the client is from a background that views direct visual contact as hostile or threatening (including certain Native American tribes). Be sensitive to the fact that in some cultures, it is especially difficult for people to discuss "private failures" that bring shame to the family.
- Use a basic interview format as a guide, but be flexible, allowing the client to tell his or her story without interruption. The gaps can always be filled in later.
- Assuming the interview is not taped, strike a balance between focusing on the client and note taking.

Note taking can be distracting and convey the message that the client is being ignored. It helps to explain to the client the purpose of note taking and to develop a personal shorthand for abbreviating common terms.
- Be prepared for a variety of emotions to be expressed in the context of the interview, given the emotionally charged nature of issues commonly addressed in a family law practice.
- Be empathetic when appropriate, but try to keep focused on the progression of the interview. If it appears the client might benefit from a referral to a mental health professional or other resource, suggest that possibility to the supervising attorney.
- Avoid the temptation to interject your own life story. A certain amount of small talk is appropriate at the outset to establish an initial rapport, but remember, the client may be paying by the hour and will not appreciate the banter when the bill arrives!
- If the firm is going to represent a client you find offensive or threatening, remain objective in the context of the interview but later bring your concerns to the attention of your supervisor. If the client becomes extremely hostile or assaultive, remove yourself to a safe location if possible and call for assistance.

Letter of engagement
a letter from an attorney to a client confirming that the attorney agrees to represent the client in a particular legal matter

Letter of nonengagement
a letter from an attorney to an individual confirming that the attorney will NOT be representing that individual with respect to a particular legal matter

After the initial interview, the paralegal will customarily perform the following tasks:

- Draft a **letter of engagement** or a **letter of nonengagement** (or declination) if the attorney does not accept the case. Attorneys elect to decline cases for one or more reasons that may include:
  - the prospective client's inability to pay
  - the likelihood that the person is raising frivolous or baseless claims
  - the person's unrealistic expectations or stated intent to "do whatever is necessary" to prevail, including concealing assets and lying under oath in court
  - the existence of a conflict of interest
  - a case complexity that calls for a level of skill and expertise far beyond that of the attorney such that accepting the case would violate the attorney's ethical duty to provide competent representation
- Prepare an interview summary for the supervising attorney, including highlights, issues, concerns, and follow-up matters
- Prepare a fee agreement based on the attorney's instructions and make arrangements to have it signed by both the client and the attorney
- Open a client file and ensure that the client's name is promptly added to the firm's master client list to facilitate future conflicts checks
- Send the client any documents needing to be completed and/or signed, such as:
  - a client questionnaire
  - a financial statement
  - release forms authorizing the attorney to seek and receive information concerning the client from third parties such as hospitals, doctors, accountants, social service agencies, and the Internal Revenue Service

FEE AGREEMENTS AND BILLING

Fee Agreements

One of the major sources of malpractice actions and tension between attorneys and clients relates to fees and costs. Fee agreements are designed to help prevent such problems. A **fee agreement** is a contract between an attorney and a client, and a failure of either party to comply with its terms may give rise to an action for breach of contract or malpractice. An effective fee agreement:

Fee agreement
a contract between an attorney and a client regarding payment for the attorney's professional services

- is executed at the outset of the representation
- describes the rights and responsibilities of both the attorney and the client
- is written in plain terms and in the language of the client if he or she is non-English speaking
- clearly describes the scope of the legal services to be performed (and the tasks that will not be performed, if appropriate)
- specifies the fees to be charged for professional employees working on the client's case including the lead attorney, associate attorneys, and paralegals

- identifies the kinds of costs the client will be responsible for, such as filing fees, phone calls, travel, postage, and copying charges
- spells out the circumstances under which the attorney may terminate the representation

Exhibit 1.2 identifies the most common types of fee agreements used by attorneys. A developing trend in legal representation, and particularly with respect to family law matters, is toward "unbundling" legal services provided to parties proceeding in part *pro se*. This option affords the client the benefit of legal services when needed at reduced overall expense. When permitted, rather than comprehensive representation, the client retains the attorney to perform certain discrete tasks for a fee. In order to prevent abuse, confusion, and misunderstanding, fee agreements in such cases (**limited-scope agreements**) must be carefully drafted to specify the precise tasks to be performed, such as researching a specific issue or drafting a particular document to be filed under the client's signature. The agreement should also indicate any major blocks of services, such as trial preparation, court appearances, or postdivorce services the attorney will not perform.

EXHIBIT 1.2 Types of Fees

Flat fee	A fixed dollar amount is charged to handle a specific legal matter, such as negotiating and drafting of a premarital agreement.
Hourly rate	The attorney charges the client for each hour worked on the case (usually billing in tenths of an hour) plus fees (filing, recording, etc.), costs (phone, postage, copying, etc.), and other expenses such as travel.
Retainer (1)	This term is sometimes used in general to describe the contract between the attorney and the client, particularly with respect to fees.
Retainer (2)	The client advances a lump-sum payment to an attorney for deposit in a client trust fund account. The attorney withdraws funds from the retainer as the client incurs fees and costs. If the retainer is exhausted and the representation has not yet concluded, the client is asked to provide an additional amount or to continue payments on some other basis. Any unused portion of a retainer is returned to the client at the conclusion of the representation.
Retainer (3)	Occasionally, an attorney is paid a retainer for the purpose of making him- or herself readily available to the client whenever needed. A retainer of this type, in effect, pays the attorney for declining other employment.
Contingent fee	The attorney is paid a certain percentage of the amount recovered by the client in a settlement or court judgment (plus fees and costs). Common in personal injury cases, contingent fees based on results obtained usually are not permitted in divorce cases, as they have a tendency to fuel litigation and discourage settlement or reconciliation. Limited exceptions to this general rule may apply when, for example, reconciliation is no longer a possibility or an attorney is retained for the sole purpose of recovering a debt owed to a client in the form of unpaid alimony or delinquent child support payments.
Split fee	The dividing of a fee between attorneys is permissible under certain circumstances (e.g., the total fee is in reasonable proportion to the work performed, and the client consents).[2] Dividing a fee for legal services with a nonattorney is not permitted.

PARALEGAL PRACTICE TIP

Attorneys and paralegals often spend far more time working on cases than is eventually billed to clients. The decision as to how much time is ultimately charged to a client's account is made by the attorney.

Billing

Billing is viewed by some practitioners as a burden but clearly a necessary one. If not properly managed, it is a potential source of malpractice actions. Keeping accurate track of time spent on a case and for what specific purpose needs to become an automatic function, an integral part of each attorney's and paralegal's *modus operandi*. The costs of paralegal services are recoverable as a component of overall attorneys' fees if those costs are reasonable, for appropriate services, and properly documented.[4] Therefore, paralegals are required to keep track of the time they spend working on client files. This is customarily accomplished through the use of time sheets (commonly electronic) that include the client's name, file/docket number, date, time spent, and nature of services performed. These records provide the documentation necessary to support client billing.

LEGAL RESEARCH IN A FAMILY LAW PRACTICE

PARALEGAL PRACTICE TIP

In the event that the reader has not yet completed a course in legal research and writing, a list and brief description of "Major Research Resources and Related Terminology" is available at *www.pearsonhighered.com/careersresources/* in the companion website material for Chapter 1 of this text under Resources.

One of the most important functions a family law paralegal performs is legal research. Research is not merely a job requirement; it is an ethical obligation and a failure to conduct adequate research may expose an attorney to liability for malpractice. For example, in a case in which it upheld a lower court's award of $100,000 to an attorney's former client, the California Supreme Court held that "Even as to doubtful matters, an attorney is expected to perform sufficient research to enable him to make an informed and intelligent judgment on behalf of his client."[5]

Paralegals are often surprised to learn that consistent with an ethical duty of candor before the court, attorneys have an obligation to bring to its attention not only controlling primary authority that supports the client's position but also contradictory dispositive primary authority if opposing counsel fails to do so.[6] In the face of unfavorable controlling authority, every effort must be made to distinguish the facts of the client's particular case from the facts of "controlling" case law.

Several cases and statutes are referenced in this text that are "good law" as of the spring of 2015. However, because the law is constantly evolving, the reader is reminded that attorneys and paralegals must always verify that they are referencing appropriate governing law, using up-to-date forms, and following currently applicable rules and procedures. This means shephardizing cases and statutes and regularly checking pocket parts, advance sheets, and legal publications. It should also be noted that various websites are highlighted throughout the book. Several of these sites contain links to laws on a variety of topics on a state-by-state basis. A list of websites of particular interest is available in Appendix B. Appendix C provides URLs where basic family law statutes and forms for the fifty states can be found. These lists were current as of spring 2015. Although there is a significant amount of useful material available free on the Internet, the reader is reminded that much of it is anonymous, unregulated, and unmonitored. **Caution needs to be exercised.**

PARALEGAL PRACTICE TIP

Information located on the Internet that is referenced in documents submitted to the court needs to be cited. Rule 18 of the *Bluebook* provides rules for citing Internet sources.

In doing their research, paralegals draw on a rich variety of resources. Paralegal Application 1.5 provides a description of the basic components of a paralegal's family law library. Paralegal Application 1.6 provides a brief introduction to a common research topic: jurisdiction.

Paralegal **Application 1.5**

The Paralegal's Basic Family Law Library

The legal materials most often utilized by a family law paralegal on a day-to-day basis are the following:

- **State statutory codes**, primarily those sections governing domestic relations matters such as marriage, divorce, custody, child support, spousal support, property division, adoption, and related jurisdictional requirements
- **Court rules** governing domestic relations practice and procedure
- **Case law** contained in state, regional, and Supreme Court reporters with "pocket parts." Most states and regions also have digests containing brief summaries of court opinions.
- **Practice manuals** providing a wealth of information about substantive law and procedure as well as forms and useful checklists
- **Form books** containing forms for use in a variety of actions

- **A legal dictionary**, such as the current edition of *Black's Law Dictionary*
- **A citation manual**, such as the *Bluebook*
- **Legal newspapers** often published weekly by state bar associations and available in libraries and by subscription. They provide current information on recent cases, legislative developments, legal trends and publications, state and local bar association activities, etc.

Codes, Rules of Procedure, and reporters are available in law and college libraries, many law offices, and online through law libraries and commercial databases such as Lexis-Nexis, WESTLAW, and Loislaw. In some states, they may also be available through state-sponsored public sites at no cost, although the commercial databases are generally more likely to be accurate and up to date.

Paralegal **Application 1.6**

A Common Research Challenge—Jurisdictional Issues

Virtually, every case involves a consideration of jurisdictional issues. There are two primary meanings of **jurisdiction** in the legal context:

1. A geographical location, such as a country, circuit, state, or county, in which a certain body of law is governing or a particular procedure is required. The potential impact of jurisdiction on the rights and interests of family law clients can be significant. For example, will fault grounds for divorce be available? Will marital property be divided equally or equitably? Will alimony be a potential option? Can a particular person adopt or be adopted? How will same-sex relationships be treated in various contexts?

2. The authority of a court to hear a case and issue enforceable orders concerning:

   - A particular type of legal matter = **subject matter jurisdiction**
   - A particular person = **personal jurisdiction**
   - A particular property or thing = *in rem* **jurisdiction**.

In a majority of cases, these issues are relatively straightforward. For example, the parties to a divorce and their children all live in one state and all of their property is located in that state. However, some cases are jurisdictionally complex. They may involve multiple parties and property located in several different states. Where a document is prepared, a property is located, or an action is brought may determine the outcome of that case. Attorneys often assign paralegals to research jurisdictional issues and gather information necessary for the attorney to make informed recommendations and decisions. Paralegals do not need to understand all the subtle intricacies of jurisdictional issues, but they need to be able to ask the right questions, know where to look for possible answers, and recognize the kinds of facts that will be necessary to support a client's position.

Jurisdiction

(1) a geographical area in which a certain law or procedure is governing; (2) the authority of a court to issue enforceable orders concerning a particular type of legal matter, person, or thing

(Continued)

Subject matter jurisdiction
the authority of a court to hear and decide a particular type of claim or controversy

Personal jurisdiction
the authority of a court to issue and enforce orders binding a particular individual; sometimes called *in personam* jurisdiction

In rem **jurisdiction**
[Latin: against a thing] the authority a court has over a property or thing (rather than over persons) located within its jurisdictional borders

Types of jurisdiction are reviewed in greater depth in Chapter 5, and jurisdictional variations are highlighted throughout the text as they relate to specific chapter topics.

Ethical Rules That Guide the Paralegal's Professional Conduct

Ethics
the standards or rules of conduct to which members of a profession are expected to conform

Ethics are standards or rules of conduct to which members of a profession are expected to conform. *Black's Law Dictionary* (8th edition) specifically defines legal ethics as "The minimum standards of appropriate conduct within the legal profession involving the duties that its members owe one another, their clients, and the courts." Across the country, there exist a number of paralegal codes and guidelines for practice, sometimes called canons or rules of professional responsibility. Some related to paralegals are written by attorneys for attorneys, such as the American Bar Association's Model Guidelines for the Utilization of Paralegal Services and similar rules promulgated by state bar associations. Some are written, at least in part, by paralegals under the auspices of professional paralegal associations at the local, state, or national level, such as the National Federation of Paralegal Associations (NFPA) or the National Association of Legal Assistants (NALA). (See Appendix A.)

PARALEGAL PRACTICE TIP

The ABA Model Guidelines for Utilization of Paralegal Services can be found at *www.americanbar.org*.

PARALEGAL PRACTICE TIP

The Model Code of Ethics and Professional Responsibility and Guidelines for Enforcement promulgated by the National Federation of Paralegal Associations can be found at *www.paralegals.org*.

Codes of ethics specifically applicable to paralegals do not exist in every state. However, each state does have a code governing the conduct of attorneys practicing law within its jurisdictional boundaries. These codes are backed by sanctions, such as suspension or disbarment. Sanctions may be imposed as a result of the attorney's own direct actions or due to the actions of paralegals and others employed by the attorney under the **doctrine of** *respondeat superior*. Under this doctrine, the lawyer may be held vicariously liable for acts of the paralegal performed within the scope of employment provided:

Doctrine of *respondeat superior*
[Latin: let the superior make answer] the doctrine under which an attorney is held vicariously liable for the acts of his or her employees performed within the scope of employment

- the lawyer knows of or ratifies the conduct, or
- the lawyer has supervisory authority over the paralegal, knows of the conduct at a time when the consequences of the harm could be avoided, and fails to take remedial action, or
- the lawyer fails to exercise adequate supervision over the paralegal

PARALEGAL PRACTICE TIP

If paralegals "hold themselves out" as attorneys or as possessing a higher level of legal skills, they may be held to that higher standard in a civil action.

Codes of conduct for paralegals commonly are not backed by sanctions, although organizations such as the NFPA urge a move in that direction. However, paralegals may be sanctioned by a state in some circumstances, particularly those involving the unauthorized practice of law. (See Case 1.1.) Even if not sanctioned by the state for ethical violations, paralegals may lose their jobs and their professional reputations or be sued for actions taken outside of the scope of employment that result in harm to a client. In addition, a paralegal is not insulated as an employee from potential criminal liability if he or she knowingly participates in criminal activity such as embezzling client funds from a trust account.

The vast majority of law firms maintain **malpractice** insurance to cover negligence of attorneys and other employees within the scope of their employment. Malpractice complaints in the area of family law typically involve:

- failure to properly advise a client
- failure to investigate the nature and extent of marital assets
- failure to protect pension or retirement rights
- failure to draft appropriate terms for a property settlement agreement or proposed divorce decree
- failure to give proper notice
- failure to timely perfect an appeal
- failure to ensure the payment of money or the transfer of property[7]

Clearly, no matter how hard members of a family law team work, few family law cases can be described as "total victories," and occasionally mistakes are made. Dissatisfied clients sometimes seek redress but are not necessarily successful, absent particularly egregious promises or conduct on the part of the attorney. An attorney who acts in good faith and in an honest belief that his or her advice and acts are well founded and in the best interest of the client usually will not be held liable for a mere error of judgment or for a mistake in a point of law which has not yet been clearly settled.[8]

Malpractice
intentional or negligent professional misconduct of an attorney that may occur in the form of a failure to properly supervise a paralegal

PARALEGAL PRACTICE TIP
Some states require attorneys to notify clients in writing if they do not maintain a certain level of malpractice insurance.

CASE **1.1** *Columbus Bar Association v. Thomas*, 109 Ohio St. 3d 89, 2006 Ohio 1930, 846 N.E.2d 31 (2006)

BACKGROUND

William Thomas was employed by attorney James Watson for several years as a paralegal/legal assistant. In 2002, Attorney Watson was recovering at home for several months after sustaining a serious injury. During that period, he relied on his legal assistant to perform duties subject to his supervision and approval. Thomas, who was not licensed to practice law in Ohio, exceeded the authority granted to him and acted independently on behalf of Richard Zahner in a divorce case. He prepared and filed an answer and counterclaim as well as a motion for a restraining order and a supporting affidavit. Zahner denied that the signature on the affidavit was his although Thomas had notarized it by using Attorney Watson's notary seal and signing Watson's name. Without Watson's knowledge, authority, or approval, Thomas also drafted a letter to Zahner describing the domestic relations process and giving legal advice on his case. He signed the attorney's name on the letter. In response to Watson's instructions, he also prepared objections to a magistrate's order in the case but did not obtain Watson's approval of the filing or specific authorization to sign it on his behalf.

While working for Watson during 1997, Thomas also assisted a relative, Inez Faulkes, with preparation of her will and, following her death, prepared legal documents regarding her estate using Watson's signature but without his knowledge or review.

Based on these facts, the Board on the Unauthorized Practice of Law of the Ohio Supreme Court found that Thomas had engaged in the unauthorized practice of law and also found that he had not cooperated in the board proceedings. Based on lack of cooperation, the flagrancy of the violations, and harm to third parties, the board recommended a $10,000 civil penalty representing $5,000 for each count (Zahner and Faulkes cases). (No. UPL 05–01)

(Continued)

PARALEGAL PRACTICE TIP

The giving of legal advice to a client involves an exercise of professional judgment based on knowledge of the law. It includes advising a client about his or her rights and responsibilities, recommending a course of action, or predicting an outcome. For example, if a client asks what a counterclaim for divorce is, the paralegal can provide a definition (based on an established source such as a legal dictionary) but cannot advise the client as to whether or not and why he or she should file a counterclaim.[9]

PARALEGAL PRACTICE TIP

Do not allow yourself to be seduced by your skills or your job, however tempting it may be, especially when pressured by a person for assistance. Preparing documents for an uncontested divorce without the supervision of an attorney constitutes the unauthorized practice of law. "Common sense dictates that the drafting of even a simple complaint or an uncomplicated petition for dissolution of marriage requires at least some degree of legal knowledge or skill."[10]

FROM THE OPINION

We agree that respondent engaged in the unauthorized practice of law. Section 2(B)(1)(g), Article IV, Ohio Constitution confers on this court original jurisdiction regarding admission to the practice of law, the discipline of persons so admitted, and all other matters relating to the practice of law. A person who is not admitted to the practice of law pursuant to the Supreme Court Rules for the Government of the Bar engages in the unauthorized practice of law when he or she provides legal services to another in this state. . . .

The practice of law is not limited to appearances in court. It also embraces the preparation of papers that are to be filed in court on another's behalf and that are otherwise incident to a lawsuit. . . .

We have specifically held that a lay employee engages in the unauthorized practice of law by preparing legal documents for another to be filed in domestic-relations court without a licensed attorney's oversight. *Cleveland Bar Assn. v. Para-Legals, Inc.*, 106 Ohio St. 3d 455, 2005 Ohio 5519, 835 N.E.2d 1240. Providing legal counsel by a layperson in preparing another person's will also constitutes the unauthorized practice of law. . . . Further, unauthorized practice occurs when a layperson renders legal advice in the pursuit of managing another person's legal actions and proceedings before courts of law. . . .

Rules prohibiting the unauthorized practice of law are "intended to protect Ohio citizens from the dangers of faulty legal representation rendered by persons not trained in, examined on, or licensed to practice by the laws of this state." *Disciplinary Counsel v. Pavlik* (2000), 89 Ohio St.3d 458, 461, 2000 Ohio 219, 732 N.E.2d 985. Thus, although laypersons may assist lawyers in preparing legal papers to be filed in court and managing pending claims, those activities must be carefully supervised and approved by a licensed practitioner. . . . Because respondent lacked this professional oversight, his actions with respect to Zahner and Faulkes violated the prohibitions against the unauthorized practice of law.

To discourage such practices, we agree that a civil penalty is warranted, but we find the recommended $10,000 civil penalty to be excessive. Respondent did not appear before the board; however, he did cooperate during relator's investigation by being deposed twice and candidly admitting many of the facts underlying relator's complaint. From this testimony, we are convinced that respondent did not understand, despite his years of experience as a legal assistant, the extent to which he had overstepped the bounds of that role. We find what the panel and board conceded was possible: that respondent believed, although he was seriously mistaken, that he had Watson's permission to prepare and sign documents on his behalf.

Respondent is enjoined from engaging in acts constituting the unauthorized practice of law, including preparing and filing in court papers to determine the legal rights of others and offering legal advice to others about how to protect those rights. We also order respondent to pay a civil penalty of $5,000 pursuant to Gov. Bar R. VII(8)(B) and VII(19)(D)(1)(c). Costs are taxed to the respondent.

Judgment accordingly.

SIDEBAR

What do you think of the Ohio Supreme Court's decision in this case? Was the court too hard on the legal assistant? Too lenient? Should the attorney have been sanctioned for a failure to properly supervise his employee? The full opinion in this case is available at *http://www.pearsonhighered.com/careersresources/* in the companion website material for this text related to Chapter 1 under Cases.

Because of its importance, the topic of paralegal ethics is sometimes covered in a separate semester-long course. In this text, an effort is made to weave ethical considerations into all of the chapters, each of which includes a Focus on Ethics exercise. Paralegal Application 1.7 provides an initial introduction to paralegal dos and don'ts likely to be relevant in the family law context.

Paralegal **Application 1.7**

Paralegal Ethics in a Nutshell

- The paralegal may participate in an initial interview with a prospective client under an attorney's direction **BUT** may not solicit clients, accept or reject cases on behalf of the firm, or set any fee for representation.
- The paralegal may be paid a reasonable fee for services and receive bonuses and profit-sharing plan benefits unrelated to a specific case **BUT** may not split legal fees with an attorney.
- The paralegal can provide to a client factual information that is a matter of public record (such as a court's order or the content of a statute) and may relay advice from the attorney to the client **BUT** may not give legal advice to or counsel a client, as that would constitute the unauthorized practice of law (the practice of law without a license).
- The paralegal may communicate with opposing counsel as directed by the supervisor **BUT** may not communicate directly with an opposing party who is represented by counsel unless that party's counsel consents to the contact.
- The paralegal may assist in maintaining a relationship with a client, **BUT** the attorney must maintain control over the relationship.
- The paralegal may complete tasks delegated by an attorney (such as drafting pleadings and discovery requests), **BUT** the tasks must be performed under the supervision of the attorney, be subject to the attorney's review and approval, and merge with the attorney's work product.
- In a majority of states, the paralegal's name may appear in a firm's letterhead or on the paralegal's business card, **BUT** the paralegal's title and nonattorney status must be clearly indicated and the paralegal may not be a partner with a lawyer when any of the activities of the partnership include the practice of law.
- The paralegal should communicate to the supervising attorney confidential information provided by the client **BUT** must not reveal those confidences to anyone else in or outside of the firm, not even a spouse or a parent. The confidentiality rule extends to ALL communication relating to representation of a client. Special care needs to be exercised when utilizing cell phones, e-mail, and fax machines or leaving files open on a desk or on a computer screen where passersby may see them.

- The paralegal may perform work on a case in which the firm represents multiple parties in a particular matter (sometimes called joint or common representation) if permitted under governing rules of professional conduct **BUT** otherwise must avoid conflicts of interest and bring them to the attention of the attorney.
- The paralegal may prepare and sign basic correspondence as directed by a supervisor (such as transmittal cover letters or letters confirming appointments) **BUT** may not sign actual **pleadings** (informing an adverse party of the nature of a claim or defense) or **motions** (applications to the court for an order) filed with the court and requiring the attorney's signature. The attorney's signature is a certification that the attorney has read the pleading and that, to the best of his or her knowledge, it is filed in good faith, that there are grounds to support it, that it is supported by existing law (or by a good-faith argument for extension, modification, or reversal of existing law), and that it is not filed for the purpose of delaying the underlying action or harassing the opposing party.
- The paralegal may assist and "represent" clients at a variety of administrative hearings (such as before the Social Security or Veterans Administration or a workman's compensation board)[11] **BUT** generally may not represent a client in court. The family law paralegal may assist an attorney in court with the court's permission and provided the paralegal is introduced and his or her role clearly indicated. However, some states allow paralegals to appear in court with clients in uncontested matters or domestic violence cases.
- The paralegal must seek to maintain a high level of competence **BUT** should not perform tasks for which he or she is unqualified. The client is entitled to competent representation.

Pleading
a formal statement, usually written, setting forth the claims and defenses of parties to a lawsuit

Motion
a written or oral request that a court issue a particular ruling or order

CONFLICTS OF INTEREST

An attorney (and by extension members of the family law team) has a duty of undivided loyalty to the client. Any situation that interferes with that duty and the exercise of independent judgment may place a client at a disadvantage and impair the capacity of team members to competently and zealously advocate for the client. Situations that constitute **conflicts of interest** arise in a variety of contexts. When a conflict exists, disqualifying one attorney or paralegal in a firm from working on a case, the disqualification may be imputed to the entire firm. However, sometimes disqualification may not be necessary if an "**ethical wall**" can be created around the employee who creates the conflict. With respect to paralegals, the NFPA Model Code defines an "ethical wall" as a "screening method implemented in order to protect a client from a conflict of interest. An ethical wall generally includes, but is not limited to, the following elements: (1) prohibit the paralegal from having any connection with the matter; (2) ban discussions with or the transfer of documents to or from the paralegal; (3) restrict access to files; and (4) educate all members of the firm, corporation, or entity as to the separation of the paralegal (both organizationally and physically) from the pending matter."[12] Paralegal Application 1.8 presents some examples of ethical dilemmas involving conflicts of interest encountered by paralegals in a family law practice.

Paralegal **Application 1.8**

Paralegal Ethical Dilemmas Involving Conflicts of Interest

- At law firm A, Mikayla worked on Charlie Morgan's criminal case. He was charged with statutory rape and was eventually acquitted following a brief trial. During the representation, she was privy to a considerable amount of confidential information about Charlie. Two months after his acquittal, she got a job nearer to her home as a paralegal at firm B. In her first week there, she became aware that her new employer was representing Ava Morgan, Charlie's wife, in her action for divorce. Although not the same matter, the divorce action was substantially related to the criminal case, as Ava was suing her husband for divorce on the grounds of adultery with a series of young women. The paralegal's duty to the earlier client did not end when the relationship or prior employment ended. In such circumstances, the paralegal should promptly bring the conflict to the supervisor's attention, because it may not be apparent in a conflicts check against the firm's master client list. In this set of facts and especially in a small firm, it is unlikely the conflict can be overcome (even with creation of an "ethical wall" around the paralegal), and the disqualification may extend to other members of the firm as well. However, if the nature of the later action had been totally unrelated to the earlier representation (such as drafting of a bill of sale for an automobile) and the former client consented, the paralegal's new employer might be permitted to represent the former client's adversary.

- Brooke's supervisor has just agreed to represent Jackie Notar, a single mother of a two-year-old daughter named Shayla. Shayla's dad, Scott, is seeking sole custody of the child. Jackie has told her attorney that she is living alone and never uses drugs despite Scott's claims to the contrary. Brooke is aware through an acquaintance of Jackie that she is living with a new boyfriend and that drugs and drug paraphernalia are openly present in the home and frequently used by the couple in front of the child. Brooke believes strongly that Jackie is not a fit mother for Shayla and that Scott appears to be a great dad. Brooke nevertheless has a duty of loyalty to Jackie. If her bias against Jackie is so strong that it interferes with her work performance, Brooke must bring the conflict to the supervising attorney's attention.

- Against his own better judgment, Hank develops an intimate relationship with a client, Liz, after working closely with her for almost a year. Liz initially was heartbroken when her husband sued her for divorce. Hank tried to comfort and reassure her that there is life after divorce. He hopes that her new life will be with him. However, that hope soon may be dashed because Liz's husband is seeking to reconcile with his wife. Hank's interests are now potentially at odds

(Continued)

with Liz's in light of their personal relationship. If the personal relationship interferes with his capacity to work on her case, Hank must bring the situation to his supervisor's attention. Paralegals should strive to avoid even the appearance of impropriety in their professional lives. It is therefore generally ill-advised to engage in personal relationships with clients.

- Dennis invests his modest savings in a start-up computer company owned by a client of the firm where he is employed. The client, Bonnie, is in the midst of a bitter divorce and doesn't want her husband to benefit in any way from her company.

Bonnie has told both Dennis and his supervisor that she intends to run the company into the ground so that her husband never sees a dime from it. A conflict arises if the business relationship compromises undivided loyalty to the client and creates competing interests, as it appears to do in this instance. Some "business relationships" with clients do not create conflicts of interest. For example, no conflict is created if Bonnie owns the only insurance company in the small town where they both live and work and Dennis insures his automobile through that company.

CONFIDENTIALITY

Clients need to feel free to communicate with members of the family law team, particularly their attorneys, without fear that the information they share will be revealed to others to their disadvantage. The protection of communications between attorney and client arises in two areas of law, each of which is governed by its own rules:

- The **attorney-client privilege** (and **work product** doctrine) in the law of evidence applies in proceedings in which the lawyer is called as a witness or is required to produce evidence relating to a client. The "privilege" belongs to the client and prevents the attorney from disclosing attorney-client communications subject to limited exceptions. It is based on state and federal rules of evidence.
- The **rule of attorney-client confidentiality** is established in codes of professional ethics. It refers to the attorney's duty not to reveal any information relating to representation of the client, not merely "confidences" or "secrets." It is not restricted to testimonial disclosures of client information in court proceedings. Some firms require employees to sign agreements in which they promise not to reveal client information. Violation of the agreement may result in loss of employment and, in some states, criminal sanctions. The duty is triggered even if the individual came in only for a consultation and later retains another attorney.

For the duty and the privilege to apply, the client must have communicated information to the attorney (or his or her paralegal) in confidence for the purpose of obtaining legal advice from a person acting as a legal professional.

Although members of the family law team are obligated to maintain client confidentiality, there are exceptions to this general rule established by court rules and codes of ethics on a state-by-state basis. The attorney usually may reveal confidential information:

- if the client consents to the release of information, preferably in a writing that sets forth what can be released, when, to whom, and under what circumstances
- if the attorney reasonably believes the client is about to engage in conduct that will result in serious bodily harm or death or the wrongful execution of another. There is a strong movement toward also including serious financial harm, such as the depletion of a company's retirement fund
- if a third person, such as a parent or friend, who is not a member of the family law team is present when the client "confides" in his or her attorney or paralegal, or when communication with the attorney is overheard in a restaurant or crowded elevator

Attorney-client privilege
the client's right to refuse to disclose and to prevent the attorney from disclosing confidential communications between the client and the attorney unless the communication concerns future commission of a serious crime; the privilege is established by statute and/or rules of evidence

Work product
written or oral material prepared for or by an attorney in preparation for litigation either planned or in progress, not subject to discovery absent a court's finding of special need

Rule of attorney-client confidentiality
the duty of an attorney not to reveal any information relating to representation of a client; the rule is an ethical rule established in codes of professional conduct

- to the extent necessary to establish a claim or defense on behalf of the lawyer, for example, in litigation between the attorney and the client in a malpractice action or a suit for nonpayment of fees
- if necessary to rectify a client fraud in which the lawyer's services were used without his or her knowledge

Paralegal **Application 1.9**

Ethics and E-mail

E-mail has tremendous potential for facilitating communication between counsel and members of the family law team and their clients. Messages are transmitted over a variety of networks in a largely open environment and often include attachments such as financial statements or agreements. As such, they are vulnerable to misuse, alteration, and interception. They may also run afoul of the attorney's duty to protect the confidentiality of client communications. The paralegal needs to be aware of relevant ethical rules and the firm's policy with respect to e-mail communications. The firm may, for example:

- prohibit e-mail communication with clients

- utilize encryption software to help ensure the security of communications
- include boilerplate language on every e-mail (and facsimile) stating that the message is private and confidential and intended only for the recipient and that if it is received by another in error, it should be returned to the sender and may not be copied or destroyed. Language of this nature is required in some states
- advise clients of the risks and benefits of communication by e-mail and have them sign a waiver consenting to communication by that means if they wish to do so

Can you think of other ways of protecting e-mail communications?

Paralegal **Application 1.10**

Ethics and Firm Websites

The U.S. Supreme Court has held that the public has a right to learn about the availability and cost of legal services and that attorneys have a constitutional right to advertise, although that advertising may be subject to reasonable regulation by the states.[13] For example, it is reasonable for a state to require that the advertising not be false or misleading (e.g., it should not guarantee results). Although they may advertise to the general public, attorneys ordinarily are not permitted to solicit business directly from strangers (e.g., persons who are neither relatives nor existing clients). The distinction between advertising and solicitation relates to the fact that personal contact tends to subject prospective clients to undue pressure when they are most vulnerable (hence the phrase "ambulance chasing").

The majority of law firms today maintain websites (sometimes developed by paralegals) that are designed in part to market their services to prospective clients. They customarily provide a description of the firm including areas of specialization, background information on the attorneys employed by the firm and their respective areas of expertise, and sometimes informational material on legal topics. It is important to be sure that the content that appears on such sites complies with applicable state bar regulations and any laws governing advertising and solicitation. Sites that invite inquiries must also be careful not to inadvertently or unintentionally create attorney-client relationships with responders.

CHAPTER **SUMMARY**

This chapter provides a beginning, a preview of what is ahead in future chapters. It introduces the reader to the nature and scope of contemporary family law, the body of law governing formation, continuation, and dissolution of marriage and other "family" relationships. Forces impacting its evolution since the 1970s are identified such as the gradual extension of rights to same-sex couples and establishment of marriage equality across the nation in 2015, a decreased emphasis on fault and litigation, the impact of technology, the abandonment of rigid gender stereotypes, and the increased role of the federal government in specific areas such as child support enforcement. The chapter also orients the reader to the role of a paralegal in a family law practice in general and specifically with respect to tasks involving fees and billing, client intake and interviewing, and research. Because ethical issues permeate the practice of family law, a broad range of paralegal ethical dos and don'ts is reviewed in this chapter and each subsequent chapter addresses at least one ethical dilemma encountered by paralegals in the family law context. Readers are encouraged to internalize basic ethical principles in the interest of their employers and clients as well their own professional integrity and success.

The chapters ahead focus on the body of substantive and procedural law governing specific family-related matters such as premarital planning, parentage, custody, divorce, support, property division, and family violence. As you progress in this course, always keep in mind that the law is continually evolving. Members of the family law team, including paralegals, have an ethical duty to maintain their competence through continuing education programs and other strategies designed to keep their knowledge and skills up to date.

Family law is a challenging field of practice that provides rich professional opportunities for paralegals. It tests interviewing, research, drafting, organizational, computer, and problem-solving skills. It poses challenging ethical dilemmas. Last, but not least, it stretches to the maximum the emotional stamina of members of the family law team.

CONCEPT REVIEW AND REINFORCEMENT

KEY **TERMS**

Attorney-client privilege
Conflict of interest
Doctrine of *respondeat superior*
Ethical wall
Ethics
Family law
Fee agreement
Guardian *ad litem* (GAL)
In rem jurisdiction

Jurisdiction
Letter of engagement
Letter of nonengagement
Limited-scope agreement
Malpractice
Motion
Personal jurisdiction
Pleading
Pro se

Procedural law
Qualified Domestic Relations Order (QDRO)
Rule of attorney-client confidentiality
Subject matter jurisdiction
Substantive law
Unauthorized practice of law
Work product

REVIEW **QUESTIONS**

1. Define family law and list at least five ways in which it has evolved since the 1970s.
2. Identify a minimum of three ways in which technology is influencing the practice of family law.
3. Describe the role of a paralegal in a family law practice.
4. Identify the primary purposes of an initial client interview and describe the potential role played by the paralegal.

5. Describe the characteristics of an effective fee agreement and identify the various types of fee agreements that may be used in divorce cases.
6. List the kinds of resources included in a paralegal's basic family law library.
7. Identify at least five ethical "dos" that should guide the professional conduct of paralegals.
8. Distinguish between the attorney-client privilege and the ethical rule of attorney-client confidentiality.

DEVELOPING YOUR PARALEGAL SKILLS

FOCUS ON **THE JOB**

This activity provides students with an opportunity to role-play an initial client interview.

The Facts

Maria Petrocelli has decided to divorce her husband, Tony, after a troubled fifteen-year marriage. Attorney Schornstein has agreed to represent her in this matter and has scheduled an initial intake interview. Attorney Schornstein's paralegal will participate in the interview.

The Assignment

Your class should be divided into groups of three. One student in each group will play the role of Attorney Schornstein, another the client, Maria Petrocelli, and the third will function as the attorney's paralegal. Role-play

an initial interview assuming that: Maria has discovered her spouse is having an affair and she thinks she wants a divorce; the parties have one child, a five-year old son named Damien; and Maria is employed as a radiologist and her husband, Sal, is a stay-at-home dad. The "client" can fill in the rest of the details. In conducting the interview, apply the information you have learned thus far about interviewing and the purposes of an initial client intake interview. Refer to Paralegal Applications 1.3 and 1.4 for guidance.

FOCUS ON **ETHICS**

This focus on ethics asks you to consider some of the ethical issues that arise when documents including confidential information are accidentally sent to opposing counsel by facsimile.

The Ethical Dilemma

Assume that you are a paralegal working for Attorney Chen on a divorce case involving William and Elizabeth Beauregard. Attorney Chen represents Elizabeth, who is convinced that William is attempting to conceal marital assets. His attorney, Hugh Woodford, telephones you to say that his paralegal will be faxing a copy of William's financial statement for Attorney Chen's information. When you go to the fax machine, you discover that the paralegal apparently accidentally faxed not only the promised statement but also a note from William that reads: "H——This is the revised statement and the version I want to give her. I took a few accounts out and upped my expenses! She'll never know the difference. WB"

What ethical concerns arise in this situation? What do you think you should do? Would your response be the same if the wife had found the note at home and brought it in to

Attorney Chen? Do you find any guidance in the ethical canons for paralegals promulgated by the National Association of Legal Assistants (see Appendix A)? Does your state's bar association or code of professional responsibility for attorneys address circumstances like this? Present your responses to these questions in a one- to two-page paper.

Note: Rule 4.4(b) of the *ABA Model Rules of Professional Conduct* (2013 edition) states, "A lawyer who receives a document or electronically stored information relating to the representation of the lawyer's client and knows or reasonably should know that the document or electronically stored information was inadvertently sent shall promptly notify the sender." An earlier version of the rule and related ethics opinions had provided that the receiving attorney should not read inadvertently sent information and should notify the sender and follow his or her instructions with respect to disposition of the material (in the interest of respecting attorney-client confidentiality). Each state has its own professional conduct rules and virtually all are based on the *ABA Model Rules* in whole or part. The *ABA Model Rules* can be found at *www.americanbar.org*. Information on state rules can also be found at this site.

FOCUS ON **CASE LAW**

This activity requires you to brief a case that addresses the topic of whether or not attorneys can charge fees for services provided by paralegals.

The Assignment

Read the court's opinion in *McMackin v. McMackin*, 651 A.2d 778 (1993) and then brief the case using the format

provided on the resource website for this text or one prescribed by your instructor. The case can be found at *www.pearsonhighered.com/careersresources/* in the resource website material for this text related to Chapter 1 under Cases. The format appears under Resources.

FOCUS ON **STATE LAW AND PROCEDURE**

This activity requires the student to locate the rules governing the ethical conduct of attorneys and paralegals in his or her state in the context of a particular fact pattern.

The Assignment

Attorney Niskala has recently moved to your state and joined the small family law firm where you are employed.

She is a very conscientious attorney and wants to be certain she abides by the rules governing attorney conduct in your state, including any rules relating to the utilization and supervision of paralegals. She also wants to learn whether there are any rules of ethics governing the conduct of paralegals. She has asked you to research these questions and report your results to her in a one-page internal memo. You can use the following format:

Memorandum

To: Attorney Niskala

From: *Your Name, Paralegal*

Re: *The topic of the assignment*

Date: *Insert date*

Description of the assignment: *What is it that you have been asked to do?*

Results of Research: *What did you find and where?*

FOCUS ON **TECHNOLOGY**

Note that there is a companion website for this text which can be accessed at *www.pearsonhighered.com/careersresources/*. Select this text by title or discipline from among those available on the site. The reader is urged to make frequent use of the companion website which contains useful links to full opinions of many of the cases featured in the text; a selection of illustrative forms and statutes; and a variety of resources such as sample motions, discovery requests, and checklists. The material is organized by chapter, and a document will appear in the material for the chapter of the text in which it is mentioned unless otherwise indicated.

Websites of Interest

In addition to the links provided throughout the chapter, this activity provides a series of useful websites for reference along with technology-related assignments for completion.

www.americanbar.org

This is the website for the American Bar Association (ABA). The Model Code of Professional Responsibility, Model Guidelines for Utilization of Paralegal Services, and links to state ethics rules can be located at this site.

www.family.findlaw.com

This site can be used to access a wide range of information related to divorce and other family law matters, such as child custody, child support, paternity, grandparents' rights, adoption, and domestic violence. Links to many state statutes and forms are provided.

www.legalethics.com

This site provides summaries of and links to recently published articles on a number of topics related to legal ethics. It also provides links to other ethics-related sites.

www.nala.org

This is the site of the National Association of Legal Assistants (NALA).

www.paralegals.org

This is the site of the National Federation of Paralegal Associations (NFPA).

Assignments

1. Find out if your state's statutory code is available at no cost on the Internet. If so, what is the address (URL, or Uniform Resource Locator) where it can be accessed? Appendix C and *www.findlaw.com* may be useful resources as you complete this task.

2. Assume that you are assigned to create the home page for the website of the firm where you are employed. Locate the rules governing legal advertising in your state, if any, to guide your plan. Then create a design after having visited at least five websites of other attorneys practicing in your state.

3. Go to the website for the National Association of Legal Assistants at *www.nala.org* to locate that association's criteria for certification as a paralegal. Would you qualify?

4. Visit the site of the ABA's Standing Committee on Paralegals located at *www.americanbar.org*. List what you think are the five most useful resources available at this site.

5. Using a search engine such as Google, Bing, or Yahoo, conduct a search of "paralegals in your state" and then compile a list of what you consider to be the five most informative results of the search.

6. Assume you have been hired by an attorney just establishing a legal practice. As one of your first assignments related to office management procedures, she asks you to research the features of effective conflicts checking systems. Do a search and compile a list of recommended features. You might begin your search at *www.tba.org*, the website of the Tennessee Bar Association.

PORTFOLIO PRODUCTS

1. Brief of the *McMackin* case on fees for paralegal services
2. Report on ethics issues that arise in a hypothetical fact pattern
3. Memorandum on codes of ethics in a specific jurisdiction

© Image Source/Getty Images

chapter 2

COHABITATION AND PREMARITAL AGREEMENTS

LEARNING OBJECTIVES

After reading this chapter and completing related assignments, you should be able to:

- define cohabitation

- identify various kinds of devices cohabiting partners can use to create and protect their rights

- explain what a cohabitation agreement is

- identify forms of relief potentially available to cohabiting partners if their relationship terminates

- describe the nature and purpose of a premarital agreement

- identify commonly accepted legal requirements for a valid premarital agreement

- list the kinds of provisions a basic premarital agreement contains

- identify trends regarding the enforceability of premarital agreements

- describe the paralegal's potential role with respect to cases involving cohabitation and premarital agreements

Tran and Malia are both in their sixties. They have been seeing each other for six months and enjoy their relationship tremendously. They have decided to live together, and they intend to remain intimate partners for the rest of their lives. Each of them is semiretired after a successful career, and each has been self-supporting for some time. Tran thinks they will marry eventually, but he just wants them to live together for now. Malia has said, "Whatever you want is fine with me."

Introduction

A broad objective of this chapter and the next is to introduce the reader to the dramatic evolution that is taking place in contemporary society around legal recognition of marital and nonmarital intimate relationships. In this chapter, our primary focus is on issues related to two kinds of couples: those who choose to live together and not get married and those who plan to marry in the relatively near future. Increasingly parties in such circumstances proactively seek to establish and protect their rights and obligations with respect to each other. We will first consider cohabitation: its definition and prevalence, the devices that cohabitants may use to establish their respective rights and responsibilities including cohabitation or living-together agreements, and the remedies potentially available to former cohabitants when their relationships end. Our focus will then shift to the purpose, nature, and enforcement of premarital agreements—agreements executed by persons about to marry in hopes of minimizing problems if their upcoming marriage later ends in a divorce or legal separation.

Cohabitation

Cohabitation
two unmarried people living together, commonly in an intimate relationship

With the changes that have taken place in the landscape of family and social life in this country, cohabitation has become a mainstream behavior for many American couples. **Cohabitation** is broadly defined as two unmarried persons living together in an intimate relationship. Although the term traditionally has been used to refer to heterosexual couples, it encompasses both opposite- and same-sex relationships.

In the United States, a number of agencies and organizations gather data about cohabiting couples. However, we have no uniform definition of cohabitation or any national legal registration system that encompasses two people living together in an intimate relationship as a nonmarital "family unit." Thus far, the best measure demographers have developed to gauge the living arrangements of U.S. residents is the Census Bureau's data on household types and relationships. Some of the available data sources tell us the following:

- A Census Bureau survey has estimated married-couple households in the United States at just under 50%—a new minority.[1]
- In 2010, fewer than 22% of all households were "traditional" households (a married couple with one or more minor children under the age of eighteen).[2]
- In 1960, an estimated 450,000 unmarried couples lived together. Today that figure has risen to over 7.5 million couples.[3]
- According to the UCLA Williams Institute on Sexual Orientation Law and Public Policy, which tracks the demographics of gay and lesbian Americans, prior to the nationalization of marriage equality in June 2015, roughly one million same-sex couples lived together in the United States, 360,000 of whom were married. The Institute estimates that an additional 70,000 who had been living in states that previously did not recognize same-sex marriage will marry within three years (i.e., by June 2018).[4] For a variety of reasons, many gay couples, like heterosexual couples, will choose to continue to cohabit rather than marry.
- Approximately 75% of cohabiters say they plan to marry their partners, and roughly half marry within five years of moving in together; approximately 40% break up within five years; and about 10% remain in an unmarried relationship for five years or longer.[5]

Cohabitation "is now a multifaceted and multigenerational phenomenon. It includes young men and women who are sharing living space with a dating partner in order to save money, more committed couples who are testing the strength of their relationship, engaged couples who are planning to eventually marry, committed couples who view their relationship as marital but have chosen to avoid marriage for practical reasons such as the potential loss of alimony or a surviving-spouse entitlement, and many couples whose motives are mixed or who disagree about the nature of their relationship."[6] It provides an option for people who do not want the personal commitment and responsibilities that come with marriage or the emotional and financial costs that come with divorce. For couples who cannot legally marry in the state where they reside (such as first cousins in some states), it may be their only option.

No longer criminalized in most states, cohabitation has helped liberate both women and men from the constraints of rigid gender roles and the social pressure to marry. However, it is important to remember that there are distinct differences between marriage and cohabitation, and the legal effect of these differences is not always fully appreciated by couples who choose to cohabit. To appreciate the difficulties such couples may encounter, review the comparison between marriage and cohabitation provided in Exhibit 2.1 and then consider the hypothetical that follows.

PARALEGAL PRACTICE TIP

A wealth of data about types of households can be accessed at *www.census.gov/acs*. This is the site for the U.S. Census Bureau's American Community Survey.

PARALEGAL PRACTICE TIP

Visit *www.ncsl.org* to find a report on the status of state laws regarding the marriage of first cousins, which is banned in approximately half of the states. Search for "Marriages Between First Cousins."

PARALEGAL PRACTICE TIP

In 1960, virtually all states criminalized nonmarital cohabitation. Although the ban still exists in some jurisdictions, if challenged, such statutes likely would be found unconstitutional. As of 2015, the still-existing Michigan statute appears in the state penal code with other "Indecency and Immorality" offenses. It provides that "Any man or woman, not being married to each other, who lewdly and lasciviously associates and cohabits together, and any man or woman, married or unmarried, who is guilty of open and gross lewdness and lascivious behavior, is guilty of a misdemeanor. . . ."[7] After an unsuccessful effort in 2003, in 2007 North Dakota repealed its law, which provided that a person was guilty of a misdemeanor "if he or she lives openly and notoriously with a person of the opposite sex as a married couple without being married to the other person." N.D. Cent. Code 12.1–20–10 (1997).

EXHIBIT 2.1 Marriage and Cohabitation—A Comparison

MARRIAGE	COHABITATION
To enter a marriage, the parties must satisfy certain requirements that vary state to state but customarily include a minimum age for marrying without parental consent, a license, and a ceremony.	In states where cohabitation is legal, parties may freely elect to cohabit without satisfying any formal requirements.
A marriage is terminated by formal legal process.	A period of cohabitation can be terminated without legal process.
In virtually all states, children born during a marriage are presumed to be offspring of the husband and wife, and each spouse owes them a duty of support for however long the law requires. This presumption is gradually being extended to same-sex spouses in some contexts (e.g., artificial insemination).	There is generally no presumption of paternity/parentage when a child is born to a female partner in a cohabiting couple and, therefore, there is no parallel duty of child support during or after the period of cohabitation.
After termination of a marriage, both parents of minor children generally have custody and visitation rights absent a finding of unfitness.	Absent establishment of paternity/parentage, a former partner has no custody or visitation rights following termination of a period of cohabitation with the legal parent of a child.
Division of property upon termination of marriage is governed by state law absent an enforceable premarital agreement (or postmarital agreement, where permitted).	Division of property may be based on an agreement of the parties, sometimes embodied in the provisions of a cohabitation agreement. In the event of a disagreement, absent evidence of "true" ownership of property, or an enforceable express agreement, a party may seek equitable relief through the courts in most states.
In most states, spousal support may be awarded to a former spouse based on one party's need and the other party's ability to pay.	Absent a statute or contractual agreement to the contrary, a cohabiting partner will not be ordered to pay support to the other partner following termination of their relationship.

Imagine having lived with a man for ten years in a committed, monogamous relationship that you both intend to "last forever." Imagine going to pick him up at an airport and being greeted by airline personnel who advise you that he has experienced a heart attack midair and is being rushed to a hospital emergency room. You race to the hospital and the first question you are asked is "Are you a family member?" And that is only the beginning of a series of painful events with devastating consequences. You cannot be admitted to see him in intensive care. You cannot be advised of his condition due to federal privacy regulations, and you cannot consent to his medical treatment, although you know his wishes. You cannot write checks on his bank account to pay his obligations. If he dies, you have no say in the funeral and burial arrangements, and yet only you know what he would want. You cannot enter the home where you have lived together because when it was purchased by the two of you, it was put in his name only. You cannot access his safe deposit box, even though you have valuable personal property in it. You cannot inherit through him if he dies without a will, because you have no legally recognized interest in his estate. The two of you are, in effect, legal strangers.

What could you have done to protect each other in the event of such a tragedy? Cohabitants can use several devices to establish their respective rights and responsibilities and control the legal consequences of a disability or termination of their relationship by death or separation. They are commonly advised by counsel to do the following:

- **Execute health care proxies** in which each of you designates the other as the person entitled to obtain information regarding your condition and consent to the specifics of your care if you are unable to make medical decisions for yourself.
- **Execute durable powers of attorney** in which each of you designates your partner as the person authorized to act on your behalf with respect to a wide range of matters including, but by no means limited to, banking and business affairs in the event of disability or incapacitation.
- **Execute wills** in which you each designate the other as your personal representative and make appropriate provisions for him or her.
- **Purchase property as joint tenants with a right of survivorship** in case one of you dies while you still own the property.
- **Purchase life insurance policies** designating each other as primary beneficiaries.
- **Execute and fund trusts** that provide for each other under a variety of circumstances, such as the death or disability of a partner.
- **Designate your partner as a primary beneficiary on 401(k)s, IRAs, and/ or other retirement accounts** not otherwise restricted.
- **Execute a joint-partnership agreement** if you intend to invest in property jointly and/or operate a business together.
- **Execute a cohabitation/partnership agreement**.

COHABITATION AGREEMENTS

Historically, because of a strong public policy favoring marriage, the legal system has not provided cohabiting couples with a procedure for dissolving their relationships and resolving their disputes. Unlike marriage, absent a legally conferred status such as a domestic partnership or civil union, cohabiting partners do not automatically become entitled to particular rights and benefits when they decide to live together. If they want to establish rules and principles to govern particular aspects of their relationship and/or if they want to secure certain rights or assume specific responsibilities, then they need to do so by executing a contract—a cohabitation agreement (in addition to whatever other measures they may put in place).

A Cohabitation Agreement (sometimes called a Cohabitation Contract, a Living-Together Agreement, or a Nonmarital Agreement) is a private contract between two parties living together in a nonmarital relationship, which establishes mutually agreed-upon rights and responsibilities, many of which married persons obtain by statute, agreement, and custom. A cohabitation agreement is not a replacement for a will, a health care proxy, a durable power of attorney, or a deed to property protecting a surviving partner in the event the other dies. It also does not necessarily have the same force and effect after marriage as a premarital agreement. It does, however, provide the couple with an opportunity to identify, negotiate, and reach agreement with respect to their expectations, both financial

Cohabitation agreement
an agreement between two unmarried individuals who live or intend to live together, defining their intentions, rights, and obligations with respect to one another while living together and upon termination of their relationship

PARALEGAL PRACTICE TIP

If a same-sex couple previously executed a cohabitation agreement because they were unable to marry and now intend to do so, they should be advised to terminate the earlier agreement and execute a premarital agreement, which will be consistent with state and federal laws governing their relationship.

and personal. The parties to a **Cohabitation Agreement** may approach a single attorney to have their agreement drafted. However, because an attorney may not ethically represent parties with potentially adverse interests, each party should retain his or her own counsel in connection with negotiating, drafting, and/or reviewing the agreement. If only one party is represented, the agreement should indicate that both knew which party was represented and that the other party was aware of his or her right to representation and chose not to exercise it.

Cohabitation agreements reflect the general trend toward couples' private ordering of their legal rights and responsibilities. They are designed, in part, to avoid unanticipated and sometimes disastrous results when children are born, a party develops a long-term illness or dies, the relationship terminates, or a common law marriage is claimed by one of the parties. A majority of states now permit, and in many instances encourage, unmarried cohabiting couples to contract legally with each other, although sometimes the parties may need to seek the assistance of the courts to enforce those agreements. An individual provision of a cohabitation agreement may be held unenforceable because it violates a law, constitutional right, or strong public policy (such as an agreement to have children, to abort a pregnancy should one occur, or to pay a partner each time the parties engage in a particular sexual act). If the provision is so offensive that it taints the entire agreement, the whole agreement may be ruled unenforceable. However, even if not enforceable, the document may be presented in a legal proceeding as evidence of the parties' intentions with respect to certain issues, such as how they intended to treat property accumulated during the term of their cohabitation. Paralegal Application 2.1 identifies some of the provisions most commonly included in cohabitation agreements.

Paralegal **Application 2.1**

Cohabitation Agreements—Common Provisions

Models of cohabitation agreements may be located online, in form and practice books, and often in office files (paper and/or electronic). However, it is important to adapt the content of a particular agreement to the unique circumstances of the parties and to governing state law. The paralegal may be asked to gather information about the client's intentions, locate appropriate models, and draft for review a proposed agreement tailored to the client's needs based on the supervisor's instructions. Because there is little statutory or case law governing the contents of cohabitation agreements beyond the requirements of basic contract law, they tend to be more varied than premarital agreements although they contain many of the same kinds of provisions. Comprehensive cohabitation agreements typically include the following in a signed, witnessed, and notarized document:

- A number of standard **boilerplate** provisions that identify the parties and the purpose of the agreement.
- A statement identifying the state's law that will govern interpretation and enforcement of the agreement. The governing law chosen must be that of a state with which the parties have some connection (e.g., they must live, work, or plan to relocate there). Care also should be taken to select a state that recognizes and enforces cohabitation agreements and does not still have laws "on the books" criminalizing consensual sexual behavior (although such laws are rarely enforced and are likely to be held unconstitutional if challenged).[8]
- A description of the consideration for the agreement (usually the parties' mutual promises) making clear that the agreement is not based on a promise to provide sexual services.

- A statement regarding pertinent dates relevant to the agreement including when it will become effective; whether it will be affected by temporary separations (as when one party is away on business for extended periods); the timing of periodic reviews, if any; and the circumstances under which it will terminate and become null and void.
- A statement of the parties' agreement about how they will represent their relationship to the public and whether or not they intend it to potentially ripen into a common law marriage. If they do eventually marry, will the agreement become null and void or will it become their premarital agreement? If the latter, the agreement must expressly state that intention, satisfy any jurisdictional requirements for a valid premarital agreement, and be executed with all the appropriate formalities.
- A description of the parties' agreement with respect to the waiver of any rights such as the right to claim a common law marriage, the right to claim any form of maintenance or support if the relationship terminates, the right to share in the pension or retirement accounts of the other party, or the right to make any claim on the other's estate in the event of death (except as otherwise provided or to enforce a debt against the estate).
- A statement of the parties' understanding with respect to the division of household and other joint expenses during the period of cohabitation. This portion of the agreement may appear in the form of an itemized budget and may also address personal expenses including health insurance.
- The parties' agreement regarding the treatment of income and property acquired during the period of cohabitation. How will jointly purchased property be titled? Will one party have any claim to appreciation in the value of the other's separate property? Will contribution to increasing or decreasing the value of joint or separate property be of any effect?
- The parties' agreement with respect to treatment of debts and obligations acquired prior to and during the cohabitation period by either or both parties.
- A statement of intentions with respect to having and raising children. Although provisions concerning child-related matters such as custody and support remain under the jurisdiction of the court and are not necessarily enforceable, parties sometimes want to at least clarify their expectations in this area.

- A statement of the parties' intention, if any, to engage in business together.
- Acknowledgments that the parties have disclosed their respective assets and liabilities and that they have been represented by separate counsel during negotiation and execution of the agreement.
- A statement that the document represents the parties' entire agreement.
- A description of if, when, and how the agreement can be modified or amended and how related disputes will be resolved.
- A severability clause providing that if any provision of the agreement is held to be invalid, the remainder of the agreement will continue to be valid and enforceable.
- The agreement may contain additional provisions related to the parties' particular needs and circumstances. For example, will they have pets? Does either of them have a child from a prior relationship or a dependent adult for whom he or she is responsible? Who will do the shopping, cooking, and household chores? Are there any unique health needs? Are there any personal habits or idiosyncrasies the parties want to address such as smoking or personal hygiene? Counsel should advise the parties in writing that terms such as these may be helpful in establishing the contours of their personal relationship but that they may not be enforceable. If the parties have expectations with respect to their sexual relationship, particular caution should be exercised when including language on this topic. A court may not enforce an agreement if cohabitation is still prohibited in the jurisdiction or if it appears that financial support is being provided solely in exchange for sexual services, thereby constituting a contract for prostitution. The courts will not enforce an agreement to commit a crime. The phrase "**meretricious sex**" is commonly used in civil statutes and criminal codes to refer to unlawful or illicit sexual relations.

Boilerplate
standard language that is commonly used in a particular kind of document and that usually does not require negotiation

Meretricious sex
unlawful or illicit sexual relations, such as prostitution or sexual relations outside of marriage

Palimony

a term that originated in the media; palimony refers to a court-ordered allowance paid by one cohabitant to the other after their relationship terminates; recognized in some states by case law, but generally not by statute

FORMS OF RELIEF ABSENT A COHABITATION AGREEMENT

Prior to the 1970s, absent a valid business partnership or a non-relationship based contract, the courts typically denied any rights to unmarried cohabitants following a period of cohabitation. The contention was that granting financial and property rights to unmarried couples would demean the institution of marriage and condone "meretricious" or illicit sex. The landmark decision in this area is the high-profile case *Marvin v. Marvin*, decided by the California Supreme Court in 1976. (See Case 2.1.) Without abandoning the long-standing public policy favoring marriage, the *Marvin* court strongly endorsed the now widely held principle that when the facts warrant it, the courts should fashion appropriate equitable remedies for cohabitants to avoid hardship or injustice. Viewing the case as an alimony action between two unmarried cohabitants, the media coined the term **palimony** to describe it.

CASE **2.1** *Marvin v. Marvin*, 18 Cal.3d 660, 557 P.2d 106, 134 Cal. Rptr. 815 (1976)

FROM THE OPINION

During the past 15 years, there has been a substantial increase in the number of couples living together without marrying. Such nonmarital relationships lead to legal controversy when one partner dies or the couple separates. . . .

Plaintiff avers that in October of 1964 she and defendant "entered into an oral agreement" that while "the parties lived together they would combine their efforts and earnings and would share equally any and all property accumulated as a result of their efforts whether individual or combined." Furthermore, they agreed to "hold themselves out to the general public as husband and wife" and that "plaintiff would further render her services as a companion, homemaker, housekeeper and cook"; . . . in return defendant agreed to "provide for all of plaintiff's financial needs and support for the rest of her life."

Plaintiff alleges that she lived with defendant from October of 1964 through May of 1970 and fulfilled her obligations under the agreement. During this period the parties as a result of their efforts and earnings acquired in defendant's name substantial real and personal property, including motion picture rights worth over $1 million. In May of 1970, however, defendant compelled plaintiff to leave his household. He continued to support plaintiff until November of 1971, but thereafter refused to provide further support.

On the basis of these allegations plaintiff asserts two causes of action. The first, for declaratory relief, asks the court to determine her contract and property rights; the second seeks to impose a constructive trust upon one half of the property acquired during the course of the relationship.

In the case before us plaintiff, . . . maintains that the trial court erred in denying her a trial on the merits of her contention. Although the trial court did not specify the ground for its conclusion that plaintiff's contractual allegations stated no cause of action, defendant offers some . . . theories to support the ruling. . . .

Defendant first and principally relies on the contention that the alleged contract is so closely related to the supposed "immoral" character of the relationship between plaintiff and himself that the enforcement of the contract would violate public policy. He points to cases asserting that a contract between nonmarital partners is unenforceable if it is "involved in" an illicit relationship. . . .

Numerous other cases have upheld enforcement of agreements between nonmarital partners in factual settings essentially indistinguishable from the present case. . . .

. . . The fact that a man and a woman live together without marriage, and engage in a sexual relationship, does not in itself invalidate agreements between them relating to their earnings, property or expenses. . . . Agreements between nonmarital partners fail only to the extent that they rest upon consideration of meretricious sexual services. . . .

The principle that a contract between nonmarital partners will be enforced unless expressly and inseparably based upon an illicit consideration of sexual services not only represents the distillation of the decisional law, but also offers a far more precise and workable standard than that advocated by defendant. . . .

In summary, we base our opinion on the principle that adults who voluntarily live together and engage in sexual relations are nonetheless as competent as any other persons to contract regarding their earnings and property rights. Of course, they cannot lawfully contract to pay for the performance of sexual services, for such a contract is, in essence, an agreement for prostitution and unlawful for that reason. But they may agree to pool their earnings and to hold all property acquired during the relationship in accord with the law governing community property; conversely they may agree that each partner's earnings and property acquired from those earnings remains the separate property of the earning partner. So long as the agreement does not rest upon illicit meretricious consideration, the parties may order their economic affairs as they choose, and no policy precludes the courts from enforcing such agreements.

Both plaintiff and defendant stand in broad agreement that the law should be fashioned to carry out the reasonable expectations of the parties. . . .

. . . the cases denying relief do not rest their refusal upon any theory of "punishing" a "guilty" partner. Indeed, to the extent that denial of relief "punishes" one partner, it necessarily rewards the other by permitting him to retain a disproportionate amount of the property. Concepts of "guilt" thus cannot justify an unequal division of property between two equally "guilty" persons.

Other reasons advanced in the decisions fare no better. The principal argument seems to be that "[equitable] considerations arising from the reasonable expectation of . . . benefits attending the status of marriage . . . are not present [in a nonmarital relationship]" (*Vallera v. Vallera* . . .). But, although parties to a nonmarital relationship obviously cannot have based any expectations upon the belief that they were married, other expectations and equitable considerations remain. The parties may well expect that property will be divided in accord with the parties' own tacit understanding and that in the absence of such understanding the courts will freely apportion property accumulated through mutual effort. We need not treat nonmarital partners as putatively married persons in order to apply principles of implied contract, or extend equitable remedies; we need to treat them only as we do any other unmarried persons.

The argument that granting remedies to the nonmarital partners would discourage marriage must fail; . . . Although we recognize the well-established public policy to foster and promote the institution of marriage, . . . perpetuation of judicial rules which result in an inequitable distribution of property accumulated during a non-marital relationship is neither a just nor an effective way of carrying out that policy.

The mores of society have indeed changed so radically in regard to cohabitation that we cannot impose a standard based on alleged moral considerations that have apparently been so widely abandoned by so many. Lest we be misunderstood, however, we take this occasion to point out that the structure of society itself largely depends on the institution of marriage and nothing we have said in this opinion should be taken to derogate from that institution. The joining of the man and woman in marriage is at once the most socially productive and individually fulfilling relationship that one can enjoy in the course of a lifetime.

We conclude that the judicial barriers that may stand in the way of a policy based upon the fulfillment of the reasonable expectations of the parties to a nonmarital relationship should be removed. As we have explained, the courts now hold that express agreements will be enforced unless they rest on an unlawful meretricious consideration. We add that in the absence of an express agreement, the courts may look to a variety of other remedies in order to protect the parties' lawful expectations.

The courts may inquire into the conduct of the parties to determine whether that conduct demonstrates an implied contract or implied agreement of partnership or joint venture . . . or some other tacit understanding between the parties. The courts may, when appropriate, employ principles of constructive trust . . . or resulting trust. . . . Finally, a nonmarital partner may recover in quantum meruit for the reasonable value of household services rendered less the reasonable value of support received if he can show that he rendered services with the expectation of monetary reward.

Since we have determined that plaintiff's complaint states a cause of action for breach of an express contract, and, as we have explained, can be amended to state a cause of action independent of allegations of express contract, we must conclude that the trial court erred in granting defendant a judgment on the pleadings.

The judgment is reversed and the cause remanded for further proceedings consistent with the views expressed herein.

SIDEBAR

Do you agree with the court's holding and reasoning in this case? You can find the full opinion at *www.pearsonhighered.com/careersresources/* in the companion website material for Chapter 2 of this text under Cases. The decision initially appeared promising for Michelle Triola "Marvin," but on remand, the trial court held that, based on the facts, "no express contract was negotiated between the parties" and their conduct did not "give rise to an implied contract." On remand, the trial court nonetheless awarded her $104,000 so that she would have "the economic means to reeducate herself and to learn new, employable skills. . . ."[9] However, even that award was struck down on appeal and she eventually walked away with nothing.[10]

Despite all the media hype and academic commentary surrounding it, the impact of the 1976 *Marvin* decision has been surprisingly limited over the past forty years. Although legislatures have been compelled to assume a more active role in regulating nonmarital relationships, no state has yet enacted a comprehensive statutory scheme for addressing the rights and obligations of unmarried cohabitants who do not have a legally recognized status such as a domestic partnership or civil union.[11] The courts have continued to carry the primary responsibility for establishing rules governing the rights of cohabitants when their relationships dissolve in the absence of an agreement. Although it is impossible to estimate the number of cases that have settled, there is a limited amount of case law on the topic which tends to fall into a few basic categories:

- In general, a majority of the states continue to follow the *Marvin* doctrine approving valid contractual claims between cohabitants during and after their relationships terminate. The cases are heavily fact based, and the courts have applied strict evidentiary standards.

- A few states reject recovery based on an implied contract theory.[12] In Minnesota, for example, Minn. Stat. § 513.075 (2014) provides, "If sexual relations between the parties are contemplated, a contract between a man and a woman who are living together in this state out of wedlock, or who are about to commence living together in this state out of wedlock, is enforceable as to terms concerning the property and financial relations of the parties only if: (1) the contract is written and signed by the parties, and (2) enforcement is sought after termination of the relationship." Although the parties may live together "in contemplation of sexual relations," under Minn. Stat. § 513.076 (2014), sexual relations may not be the basis for a claim.

- In states such as Indiana and Ohio where both palimony suits and common law marriage are prohibited as contrary to public policy, courts have occasionally carved out exceptions and come up with legal theories to achieve equity for a cohabitant. For example, in *Putz v. Allie*, 785 N.E.2d 577, 579 (Ind. Ct. App. 2003), the parties had entered a settlement agreement upon termination of their 11 years of cohabitation, which provided that a former "boyfriend" would pay his "girlfriend" the sum of $40,000 in addition to paying off three charge accounts in her name and covering her health insurance and car payments for a year. The girlfriend had rendered services in the boyfriend's jewelry store for three to five days a week over four or five years while they cohabited, without receiving a paycheck. The parties had commingled funds, paid household expenses from store receipts, exerted joint efforts to make the business a success, and incurred various liabilities. The boyfriend contended that the agreement was unenforceable in its entirety because it was in essence a palimony agreement, contrary to the public policy of Indiana. The appellate court agreed with the trial court that the agreement was an enforceable contract. The court held that rather than palimony, the agreement could be construed as a means of fixing "liquidated damages" in lieu of an unjust enrichment claim.

- Multiple states (including among others California, New York, and Utah) have enforced support ("palimony") agreements between cohabitants, either oral or written. The state of New Jersey liberally enforced them for several years, but since 2010 generally has done so only if they are made in writing and with the guidance of an attorney. See N.J.S.A. 25: 1-5(h).

- A majority of states still will not provide relief to cohabitants based solely on their relationship. For example, in *Blanchard v. Houdek*, 810 N.W.2d 25 (Iowa Ct. App. 2011) an appellate court held that a trial court has no authority under state law to divide property accumulated by unmarried cohabitants absent a separate legal theory to support the decision. However, one high court (Washington State) has permitted recovery based on the fact of cohabitation alone, without any showing of unjust enrichment or an agreement. See, e.g., *Connell v. Francisco*, 898 P.2d 831 (Wash. 1995) and in 2003, New Mexico became the first state to allow a cohabiting party (who later married her partner) to sue for loss of consortium based on their close relationship and shared mutual dependence.[13]

As the previous examples suggest, unlike spouses, cohabitants generally lack established rights absent an enforceable agreement or a governing statute or case law. Without a guiding legal framework, when cohabitants seek relief, the courts must consider each petition on a fact-intensive case-by-case basis. Paralegal Application 2.2 describes the kinds of information a paralegal may be required to gather in a cohabitation case. A summary of the primary legal theories various courts have relied on to provide relief to cohabitants is provided in Exhibit 2.2.

Paralegal **Application 2.2**

Gathering Information in a Cohabitation Case

In a "palimony" case, the paralegal may be asked to gather information in an effort to shape and develop support for the client's case and anticipate opposing arguments and defenses that may be raised. Answers to questions such as the following may be obtained directly from the client and/or other individuals through interviews and also from documents:

- When, where, and why did the parties decide to live together?
- Did either party relocate, change employment, or make any other major changes in order to cohabit?
- What were the dates during which the parties lived together?
- What was the understanding with respect to the sexual relationship between the parties, if any? What specifically was said? To what extent, if at all, was sexual activity a consideration for the agreement? What was the nature of the parties' sexual relationship before and during the period of cohabitation? Was it exclusive?
- Did the parties discuss their intentions with respect to marriage, and, if so, to what did they agree?
- What, if any, commitments were made regarding:
  - housing: rental or purchase and payment of related costs?
  - payment of household expenses: food, utilities, etc.?
  - homemaking responsibilities: cooking, cleaning, etc.?
  - medical insurance and expenses?
- How did the parties describe their relationship to their families, employers, friends, and the general public? Did they call each other spouses, companions, partners, roommates, significant others, etc.?
- How did the parties manage their finances? Did they have joint and/or separate bank accounts?

- What was said and agreed to with respect to the parties' separate property and property accumulated during the period of cohabitation?
- Were there any discussions and/or agreements concerning: children, the making of wills or other legal documents (such as powers of attorney and health care proxies), or the giving of gifts to each other during the cohabitation period?
- Were any other commitments made and, if so, what were they?
- How, and to what extent, were the parties involved in each other's business activities, and what was the agreement, if any, with respect to that involvement?
- Did either party ever compensate the other for services rendered during the cohabitation period and, if so, for what and in what manner and amount?
- Were any of the parties' agreements written down or recorded? Were any notes taken?
- Were there witnesses to any of the agreements made?
- What are the names and addresses of witnesses who may be able to testify regarding the parties' relationship and express or implied agreements?
- What documents exist to support any of the above (e.g., lease agreements, deeds to property, checking and savings account statements, tax returns, and loan applications)?
- Are there any **defenses** available to either party, such as fraud, undue influence, **unclean hands**, lack of capacity, etc.?

Defense

a defendant's stated reason why a plaintiff has no valid claim or why the court should not grant the relief requested

Unclean hands

the principle that a party should not be granted relief if he or she has acted unfairly, wrongfully, or illegally

EXHIBIT 2.2 Legal Bases for Granting Relief to Cohabitants Upon Dissolution of Their Relationship

Legal Basis for Relief	Definition	Example	
Express contract	This is a contract that is created by an actual articulated agreement of the parties as to certain terms of their relationship. The parties negotiate and "express" the terms to each other. As with other contracts, an express contract requires an offer, acceptance, and consideration (other than sexual services). Absent a cohabitation agreement evidencing the parties' intentions, express contracts can be difficult to prove and often turn on the relative credibility of the parties.	Marlene and Walter decide to live together. They agree that during the period of their cohabitation (however long it may last), they will equally contribute to expenses, jointly perform household chores, and share equally in whatever assets they accumulate. Although they do not actually commit them to writing, they openly discuss these terms and agree that they are fair. Following the "Marvin Doctrine," many courts are likely to enforce this agreement.	**Express contract** a contract that is created by an actual articulated agreement of the parties as to certain terms of their relationship expressed orally or in writing
Implied-in-fact contract	This is a judicially created contract. The intentions of the parties are inferred from their conduct given the facts and surrounding circumstances. Even though its terms may not have been actually discussed or "expressed," a court may reasonably conclude there was an agreement based on the parties' actions.	Marlene and Walter agree to cohabit and they live together for seven years. They open joint checking and savings accounts into which they both make contributions. The couple shares most expenses equally, and household furnishings, etc., are purchased with commingled funds. Many of their friends assume that they are married. Based on these facts, a court could reasonably find an implied agreement to share assets accumulated during the relationship.	**Implied-in-fact contract** a judicially created contract, the existence of which is inferred from the conduct of the parties
Quasi-contract/ Implied-in-law contract	While express or implied-in-fact contracts are based on the actual language or conduct of the parties, in a quasi-contract, the court imposes contractual obligations on the parties to avoid unjust enrichment of one party at the expense of the other. It is a "legal fiction" created by the court in the absence of an express agreement.	Marlene gives up her job as an accountant in order to perform the couples' household chores and to take care of Walter's three-year-old son. She provides seven years of household and childcare services at a considerable benefit to Walter. A court may now treat her services as part of a bargained-for exchange rather than as a gift and require him to make some payment to her. Based on a *quantum meruit* (as much as is deserved) approach, the court may award Marlene the reasonable value of services she rendered less any payments actually received. An economist may testify as to the estimated economic value of the services in the open marketplace.	**Quasi-contract/implied-in-law contract** a contract imposed by a court to prevent unjust enrichment of one party at the expense of the other
			Quantum meruit [Latin: as much as he deserved] a basis for establishing damages or providing relief based on the reasonable value of services one person has provided to another

(Continued)

EXHIBIT 2.2 *(Continued)*

Resulting trust
a trust created by the court when one party contributes funds or services toward the acquisition of property and the title to that property is held in the name of the other party

Constructive trust
a trust imposed by the court on an asset of a party who improperly or wrongfully acquired the property

Implied partnership/joint venture
a judicially created partnership, the existence of which is inferred from the conduct of the parties

Resulting trust/ Purchase money resulting trust/ Implied trust	A **resulting trust** is created by the court when one party contributes funds or services toward the acquisition of property and the title to that property is in the name of the other party. It is imposed by the court on an asset for the benefit of a contributing party when it is demonstrated that he or she did not intend for the other party to have all or any ownership rights. The trustee (the one who "owns"/has title to the property) is deemed by the court to hold the property for the benefit of the beneficiary (the one who provided the funds).	Marlene and Walter purchase a small condo titled and mortgaged in Walter's name because of his better credit history, but Marlene pays the entire deposit of $25,000 and also pays the monthly mortgage payments out of her inheritance from her brother's estate. A court may reasonably find that Marlene did not intend for Walter to have ownership of the property, but rather that he holds title to the condo for her benefit.
Constructive trust	A **constructive trust** is imposed by the court on an asset of a party who improperly or wrongfully acquired the property. It is not based on the parties' intentions, but rather is designed to prevent unjust enrichment. The trustee (the holder of the property) is in effect ordered by the court to convey the property to the beneficiary (the wronged party)	Shortly before Marlene and Walter stopped living together, without Walter's knowledge or consent, Marlene took all of the funds out of the joint checking and savings accounts to which they each had contributed. The total amount taken was $24,000. A court may find that she holds at least 50% of that amount in a constructive trust for Walter's benefit and order her to pay him that amount.
Implied partnership/ Joint venture	Similar to an implied-in-fact contract, when the cohabiting partners work together in a business venture that is owned by one of the parties, the court creates an **implied partnership** or **joint venture** (more limited than a partnership) based on the conduct of the parties and then distributes the assets and liabilities of the business based on principles of fairness.	When Marlene and Walter began living together, Walter had a small sailboat chartering business. While she was at home, Marlene learned all she could about operating and marketing such a business. She spent about six hours a day for several years working to build the business. When the couple ceased living together, the business had grown to nearly forty times its value when they moved in together due primarily to her labors. Although she and Walter had no formal employment or partnership agreement, a court may hold that the chartering business represents a joint venture of the parties and that Marlene is entitled to a portion of its value.

EXHIBIT 2.2 *(Continued)*

Putative spouse doctrine	A **putative spouse** is a person who reasonably believes he or she entered a valid marriage, until some impediment to the marriage is discovered that renders the marriage invalid. Some courts will provide relief to an innocent "spouse" in such situations. This doctrine is sometimes extended to provide for other "innocent" unmarried partners.	Walter and Marlene initially met when he was forty years old and she was fifteen, and they began living together when Marlene was seventeen. To celebrate, they went on a vacation to an Indian Reservation in South Dakota. While there, they participated in a traditional celebration that Walter convinced Marlene was a wedding ceremony. Marlene, albeit naively, continued to believe they were married until they eventually ceased living together several years later. A court may apply the putative spouse doctrine to afford Marlene some degree of relief.

What Is a Premarital Agreement and What Is Its Purpose?

A **premarital agreement** (sometimes called a premarital contract, prenuptial agreement, or antenuptial agreement) is an agreement made by two persons about to be married. The agreement is an effort by the parties to define for themselves rights, duties, and responsibilities that flow from the marital relationship and that otherwise would be regulated and determined by state law upon death, separation, divorce, or annulment. What usually happens in a premarital agreement is that one or both of the parties agree to give up spousal support, an equal or equitable division of property, inheritance rights, or other rights they might be entitled to under state law.

Premarital Agreements in Perspective

One of the primary **public policies** that legislatures and courts in the United States historically have supported is one favoring the marital relationship as the fundamental structural unit of society. In support of that policy they have legislated and decreed regulations designed to protect the institution of marriage and family members in the event of death or divorce. These regulations have been influenced by prevailing societal views about sexual morality, the vulnerability of children, and the respective roles and relative power of men and women in society.

Although courts had, for many years, enforced premarital agreements that addressed property distribution upon death,[14] agreements made in contemplation of marriage that anticipated the possibility of divorce were viewed as *per se* **invalid** until the 1970s. The basic concern was that the party who would benefit most from the agreement (usually the male partner) would be motivated to terminate the marriage and the female partner would be left destitute. This perception has gradually changed over the past five decades along with views

Putative spouse
a person who believes in good faith that his or her invalid marriage is legally valid

Premarital agreement
an agreement made by two persons about to be married defining for themselves their respective rights, duties, and responsibilities in the event their marriage terminates by death, annulment, separation, or divorce

PARALEGAL PRACTICE TIP

The Uniform Premarital Agreement Act (UPAA) defines a premarital agreement as "an agreement between prospective spouses made in contemplation of marriage and to be effective upon marriage." The Uniform Premarital and Marital Agreements Act (UPMAA), approved by the National Conference of Commissioners on Uniform State Laws in 2012, provides the following definition: "A 'premarital agreement' means an agreement between individuals who intend to marry which affirms, modifies, or waives a marital right or obligation during the marriage or at separation, marital dissolution, death of one of the spouses, or the occurrence or nonoccurrence of any other event. The term includes an amendment, signed before the individuals marry, of a premarital agreement." Section 2 (5).

Public policy
an idea or principle that is considered right and fair and in the best interest of the general public

Per se invalid
invalid in and of itself, standing alone, without reference to any additional facts or circumstances

PARALEGAL PRACTICE TIP

If prospective spouses enter a marriage which is later determined to be void, their premarital agreement will typically be enforceable to the extent necessary to avoid an inequitable result. See, e.g., Cal. Fam. Code §1616.

PARALEGAL PRACTICE TIP

To learn about premarital (antenuptial) agreements in the state of Connecticut, visit *www.jud .ct.gov.*

Void
invalid and of no legal effect

about men and women, fault-based divorce, and the institution of marriage generally. We now live in a society in which the rate of divorce has risen, and few presume that marriage is a permanent union. As a result, we have an increasing number of individuals, both male and female, heterosexual and gay, taking steps to develop their own approaches to distribution of property upon divorce or death. A premarital agreement is one vehicle for accomplishing this end. Rather than encouraging divorce, such agreements may actually promote marriage as people may choose to marry who otherwise might not do so without the personalized "safety net" the premarital agreement provides. The opinion in the landmark *Posner* case (see Case 2.2) describes the shift in public policy from one that presumed and promoted the permanence of marriage to one that acknowledges and enforces, under certain conditions, agreements regulating rights upon the dissolution of marriage. In *Posner*, the wife appealed the portion of the divorce decree that awarded the divorce to her husband and limited alimony to her to $600 a month pursuant to the terms of a premarital agreement between the parties. The wife's position was that, consistent with prior case law, the agreement should not be enforced. The court held that such agreements should no longer be considered **void** as contrary to public policy when the divorce is pursued in good faith on proper grounds.

CASE **2.2** *Posner v. Posner*, 233 So. 2d 381 (Fla. 1970)

FROM THE OPINION

At the outset, we must recognize that there is a vast difference between a contract made in the market place and one relating to the institution of marriage.

It has long been the rule in a majority of the courts of this country and in this state that contracts intended to facilitate or promote the procurement of a divorce will be declared illegal as contrary to public policy. . . .

The state's interest in the preservation of the marriage is the basis of the rule that . . . an antenuptial agreement by which a prospective wife waives or limits her right to alimony or to the property of her husband in the event of a divorce or separation, regardless of who is at fault, has been in some states held to be invalid. . . .

There can be no doubt that the institution of marriage is the foundation of the familial and social structure of our nation and, as such, continues to be of vital interest to the State; but we cannot blind ourselves to the fact that the concept of the "sanctity" of a marriage—as being practically indissoluble, once entered into—held by our ancestors only a few generations ago, has been greatly eroded in the last several decades. . . .

With divorce such a commonplace fact of life, it is fair to assume that many prospective marriage partners whose property and familial situation is such as to generate a valid antenuptial agreement settling their property rights upon the death of either, might want to consider and discuss . . . —and agree upon, if possible—the disposition of their property and the alimony rights of the wife in the event their marriage, despite their best efforts, should fail. . . .

We know of no community or society in which the public policy that condemned a husband and wife to a lifetime of misery as an alternative to the opprobrium of divorce still exists. And a tendency to recognize this change in public policy and to give effect to the antenuptial agreements of the parties relating to divorce is clearly discernible. . . .

(Continued)

SIDEBAR

What are the major reasons for not recognizing premarital agreements? What are the major reasons for enforcing them? If you were presently contemplating getting married, would you want to have such an agreement? Why? The opinion in the *Posner* case is available at *www.pearsonhighered.com/careersresources/* in the companion website material for Chapter 2 of this text under Cases.

What Kinds of Individuals and Couples Might Want to Execute a Premarital Agreement?

Once thought of as appropriate only for the rich and famous, premarital agreements are becoming increasingly more common. This is not all that surprising when one considers that about half of first marriages end in divorce. Although statistics are scarce, according to one source, some 20% of remarried couples use premarital agreements, and they have quintupled in overall frequency over the past twenty years.[16]

Premarital agreements are particularly appropriate for parties in circumstances such as the following:

- There is a significant age difference between the parties.
- One or both of the parties have substantial property of their own including real estate, investments, businesses, and retirement accounts.
- A party has an interest in a family business that he or she wants to "keep in the family."
- A party is responsible for taking care of third parties, such as elderly parents or siblings with disabilities.
- One of the parties is pursuing a degree or license in a potentially lucrative field such as medicine, and the other party will be supporting the couple through an extended education program.
- Both of the parties have been out of high school for several years, remained single, and had an opportunity to accumulate significant property.
- One of the parties is giving up a successful career in order to be a "stay-at-home" parent.
- One or both of the parties have children or grandchildren from a previous marriage.
- One of the parties is involved in a speculative business venture that may result in a significant increase or loss in wealth.
- One or both of the parties want to ensure a new spouse's inheritance, especially if, upon marriage, the new spouse will lose his or her right to a Social Security benefit or alimony from a prior spouse.
- One or both of the parties suffered through a prior divorce that was emotionally and financially devastating, and they do not want to repeat the experience.

PARALEGAL PRACTICE TIP

According to a 2010 Harris Interactive Poll, approximately 3% of people with a spouse or fiancé in the United States have a prenuptial agreement up from the 1% recorded in a 2002 poll. Evidence of the growing trend is further supported by a recent poll of the members of the American Academy of Matrimonial Lawyers, in which 73% of divorce attorneys cited an increase in prenuptial agreements in the past five years.[15]

Mediation

an approach to resolving differences in which a neutral third person helps the parties identify their differences, consider their options, and structure a mutually acceptable agreement

Collaborative law

an approach to reaching agreements and resolving differences that stresses cooperation, joint problem solving, and the avoidance of litigation

PARALEGAL PRACTICE TIP

The more common premarital contracts become, the less sensitive a topic they are for couples approaching marriage. However, sometimes meetings with individuals negotiating premarital agreements can be tense. Although generally optimistic about the future, most individuals recognize that marriage can be a challenge and that many initially happy unions fail. A premarital agreement is about as close as the parties can come to obtaining an insurance policy in case things do not work out as they hope.

PARALEGAL PRACTICE TIP

Ordinary commercial contracts will customarily be enforced absent fraud, duress, misrepresentation, and the like. Premarital agreements differ from business contracts in several ways including the nature of the relationship between the parties, the subject matter, and the time between execution and enforcement (often decades). Because of these differences, courts in all states subject premarital agreements to greater scrutiny recognizing that the bargaining power of prospective spouses is often unequal.

Fiduciary

a person who owes another a duty of good faith, trust, loyalty, and candor

Procedural fairness

fairness in the negotiation and execution of an agreement

Substantive fairness

fairness in the specific terms of an agreement

How Are Premarital Agreements Developed?

The usual approach to creating a premarital agreement is that the parties first discuss the possibility of executing an agreement and their reasons for doing so. Then one of the parties (customarily the one with the greater incentive and the most to protect) selects an attorney to draft an agreement. The other party ideally retains a second attorney to review the agreement, recommend revisions, and advise him or her before signing. Occasionally the parties will utilize traditional **mediation** to resolve their differences concerning the proposed terms of their agreement.

An alternative approach to developing agreements tailored to the unique circumstances of the two people about to be married involves use of the relatively nonadversarial **collaborative law** process. When the collaborative law process is used, "the written agreement is prepared last and only after the partners have discussed the issues and concerns important to them and their shared life, and have reached shared agreements about those concerns. The collaborative agreement becomes a mutually developed blueprint for the marriage."[17] Although the parties still have to address challenging questions and require the assistance of specially trained counsel during the process, the "difference is that the collaborative process provides a safe and supportive setting . . . and . . . enhances the couple's togetherness rather than emphasizing their separateness."[18]

What Are the Legal Requirements for a Valid Premarital Agreement?

In this section of the chapter, the focus is on developing a premarital agreement in such a manner that it will be valid at the time of its creation because it satisfies basic threshold requirements. Later in the chapter we look at whether an agreement that may have been valid at the time of execution will actually be enforceable at the time of performance, i.e. divorce, separation, or death.

Unlike contracts negotiated in the business world involving strangers who deal at arm's length, a premarital agreement is a contract between two individuals presumably engaged in a relationship of mutual trust and confidence. Given the couple's special relationship, courts often impose additional requirements and a higher standard of care on the parties, whom they view as having a **fiduciary** duty to one another, a special duty of fairness in dealing. Although states vary with respect to specific requirements for validity, generally a premarital agreement must satisfy the following requirements which must be kept in mind during the negotiation, drafting, and execution of an agreement:

1. the basic requirements applicable to all contracts
2. the requirement of **procedural fairness**, meaning fairness in the negotiation and execution of the agreement
3. the requirement of **substantive fairness**, which means fairness in the actual terms of the agreement

THE BASIC REQUIREMENTS APPLICABLE TO ALL CONTRACTS

1. There must be an offer and acceptance (generally evidenced by the parties' voluntary signatures on a written agreement). Although not always the case, ideally there is a "**meeting of the minds**" with respect to the offer being made and accepted (i.e., a shared understanding of the terms and conditions of the contract).
2. The parties must have the legal capacity to contract in terms of age and mental competence.
3. The subject matter of the contract must not be illegal (i.e., the parties cannot agree to commit an illegal act).
4. Traditionally, the contract must be supported by **consideration**, a bargained-for exchange of something of value (usually the mutual promise to marry in the case of premarital agreements.) However, in some states (including those that have adopted the **Uniform Premarital and Marital Agreements Act (UPMAA)**, a premarital agreement is enforceable without consideration.

In addition to the above requirements, most contracts, including premarital agreements, must satisfy the applicable **statute of frauds**. The statute specifies the kinds of contracts that must be in writing and signed in order to be enforceable. Although oral premarital agreements have been enforced in a minority of states, a "contract in consideration of marriage" is one of the traditional statute of frauds exceptions to oral contract validity. Since the states differ on the requirements for a valid premarital agreement, it may be necessary to research whether an agreement at issue (e.g., an alleged oral agreement) falls within an exception in the particular statute of frauds governing the case.[19]

THE REQUIREMENT OF PROCEDURAL FAIRNESS[20]

The focus of procedural fairness is on fairness during the negotiation and execution of the agreement. In assessing procedural fairness, the courts usually will look at the surrounding circumstances to answer such questions as the following:

- Was each party represented by independent counsel?
- Was there adequate disclosure by each of the parties of the nature and value of their assets and liabilities?
- Was there sufficient time to discuss, negotiate, and reflect on the agreement prior to execution?
- Was there any fraud, duress, or undue influence in the negotiation or execution of the agreement?

Was each party represented by independent counsel? Even though the parties are generally not antagonistic as they look forward to their forthcoming marriage, they do have "adverse" interests. When they execute their agreement, each of them usually is being asked to waive or vary certain property, support, and inheritance rights to which they would otherwise be entitled upon divorce, separation, or death. Ideally both parties will have access to independent counsel to help them understand those rights and how the proposed agreement will alter them. This is an especially important consideration when the parties are of unequal bargaining power, such as when one party is much more highly educated and financially sophisticated than the other. (See Paralegal Application 2.3.)

Meeting of the minds
a shared understanding with respect to the terms and conditions of a contract

Consideration
a bargained-for exchange or mutual promises underlying the formation of a contract

Uniform Premarital and Marital Agreements Act (UPMAA)
The National Conference of Commissioners on Uniform State Laws approved the UPMAA in 2012 and has recommended it for adoption in all the states. It is designed to bring greater consistency to the enforcement of both premarital and postmarital ("marital") agreements across the country.

Statute of frauds
the requirement that certain types of contracts be in writing, such as a contract that by its terms cannot be completed within a year, a contract in consideration of marriage, or a contract for the sale of land

PARALEGAL PRACTICE TIP

The Focus on Technology activity at the end of this chapter identifies a selection of state statutes governing premarital agreements. Locate some additional statutes by navigating four of the state codes available online. MAINE: *www.legislature.maine.gov/legis/statutes*, INDIANA: *www.in.gov*, KANSAS: *www.kslegislature.org*, and NORTH DAKOTA: *www.legis.nd.gov*.

Paralegal **Application 2.3**

Representation by Independent Counsel

It is difficult, if not impossible, for one attorney to represent the interests of both parties to a premarital agreement. The conflict of interest inherent in such a multiple representation leaves the attorney open to allegations of ethical misconduct. In an effort to protect against such a result, the following steps may be taken:

1. If one party declines to seek counsel, it is wise for the attorney representing the other party to confirm in writing to both parties which of them he or she represents and to strongly advise and explain why it is important that the other party seek independent counsel. This should be done in the best interests of the client *and* the attorney. The paralegal may be asked to draft such a letter.

2. Many agreements now contain statements to be signed by counsel and/or by the parties under oath confirming that each has been instructed to seek legal counsel to advise them of their respective potential statutory rights in the property of the other and the effect that execution of the agreement will have on those rights. The paralegal should keep this option in mind when assisting in the drafting of an agreement, particularly one involving an unrepresented party.

3. In some states, prohibitions against multiple representation require that the nonrepresented individual provide a written statement acknowledging the fact that the sole attorney is not protecting his or her interests. This requirement affords additional protection against a later malpractice claim for the attorney representing the other party.

PARALEGAL PRACTICE TIP

Independent counsel twists:

- If a party declines to seek independent legal advice despite the opportunity to do so, a court may conclude their agreement was voluntarily entered. See, e.g., *Sailer v. Sailer*, 764 N.W.2d 445 (N.D. 2009).

- If a party signs an agreement against the advice of independent counsel, it is unlikely he or she will be able to successfully challenge enforcement of the agreement. See, e.g., *Tyler v. Tyler*, 990 So. 2d 423 (Ala. Civ. App. 2008).

- If a party's effort to seek independent advice is blocked or interfered with by the other party, it may be sufficient grounds for nonenforcement of the agreement. See, e.g., *Moore v. Moore*, 383 S.W.3d 190 (Tex. Ct. App. 2012).

- Although it may be a ground for a malpractice action, the fact a party received incompetent advice from counsel is not by itself a sufficient reason to set aside a premarital agreement. See, e.g., *Casto v. Casto*, 508 So. 2d 330 (Fla. 1987).

Most courts regard availability of independent counsel as one of several factors to consider when deciding whether or not to enforce an agreement assigning it varying degrees of weight depending on the circumstances. A limited number of states including California and Washington require independent representation. However, under the California statute, an agreement may still be enforceable if a party expressly waives representation "in a separate writing," and all of the following conditions are met: (1) the unrepresented party was fully informed of the terms and "basic effect" of the agreement, "as well as the rights and obligations he or she was giving up by signing"; (2) that party was proficient in the language in which the explanation was given and in which the agreement was written; (3) the written explanation was delivered to the party prior to execution; and (4) another separate writing was signed by that party declaring that the explanation was received and naming who provided the information.[21]

Was there adequate disclosure by each of the parties of the nature and value of their assets and liabilities? All states require some degree of financial disclosure but vary with respect to how much is necessary. Some states require full disclosure, while others provide that a general picture of one's financial worth is enough. Many states allow a party to waive his or her right to seek or receive disclosure sometimes subject to conditions. For example, under an Arkansas statute, a party can waive the right to financial disclosure only if represented by counsel.[22]

Ideally financial disclosure should accurately and adequately reveal a party's assets, liabilities, and net worth to protect against later claims of fraud or misrepresentation. However, inadvertent or unintentional errors or omissions are generally excused if they did not influence the other's decision to sign the agreement. The preferred form of disclosure is a separate schedule of income, assets, and liabilities for each of the parties that is referenced in the body of the agreement and appended as an exhibit. Completed financial affidavits, tax returns, and other documents such as deeds and appraisals may also be attached. The paralegal is often involved in the collection, review, and/or preparation of these materials.

In assessing adequacy of disclosure, a court is likely to ask: Given the surrounding circumstances, did both parties have, or should they have had, sufficient knowledge of the other's worth such that each of them could make an informed decision with respect to the terms of the agreement? Generally, there is no "meeting of the minds" with respect to the contract if one party was provided inadequate information regarding the other's assets and the value of the rights waived. Many states consider insufficient knowledge of the other party's financial information as an independent ground for not enforcing an agreement.

Was there sufficient time to discuss, negotiate, and reflect on the agreement prior to execution? Although the time period between execution of the agreement and the marriage ceremony is not necessarily determinative, it is a factor many courts will consider in evaluating the validity of an agreement. Some courts automatically invalidate any premarital agreement that is signed on the day of the wedding, others do not. Some states require by statute a minimum time period between execution or presentation of the agreement and the marriage, such as California (seven days) Ca. Fam. Code 1610–1617 and Minnesota (one day) Minn. Stat. Ann. § 519.11.

In general, the longer the time period (within limits) between when a party was presented with the agreement and when it was executed, the greater the likelihood the execution will be deemed voluntary based on an assumption that there was a reasonable time for negotiation and review. Timing usually will be considered in the context of the nature, scope, and complexity of the agreement. A simple agreement the parties discussed for months addressing one bank account of modest value may well be considered valid even if presented for review and signature on the wedding eve. On the other hand, a complex agreement covering millions of dollars of diverse assets between a party with significant bargaining power and an individual with little power, few assets, and much to lose warrants ample time for review and deliberation with the assistance of competent, independent counsel.

Although many courts will consider whether each of the parties had the background, experience, and time necessary to evaluate options and the consequences of choices to be made, there is not always a requirement that a party actually understand the legal effect of the terms of the agreement.[25] *Ignorantia legis non excusat*! (See Case 2.3, the *Simeone* case, later in this chapter.)

Was there any fraud, duress, or undue influence in the negotiation or execution of the agreement? Ideally, the parties should be equals in the process. However, because they are involved in a special relationship, they tend to be more vulnerable making agreements than strangers would be negotiating in the business world. They may be eager to please each other. One partner may dominate or even abuse the other emotionally or physically. One of the parties may have limited English skills[26] and/or may rely on the other, blindly trusting that individual's superior knowledge and skill. One of the ways in which some attorneys try to protect against a later claim that an agreement was executed under undue influence or duress is to have the parties and their respective attorneys all present at the execution and to videotape the event. A paralegal may be asked to schedule this taping and should be certain the necessary equipment is available

PARALEGAL PRACTICE TIP

Several states such as Minnesota, Virginia, and Connecticut require disclosure by statute. See Minn. Stat. Ann. § 519.11 (West 2013); Va. Code Ann. § 20-151 (West 2013); and Conn. Gen. Stat. § 46b-36g (West 2014).

PARALEGAL PRACTICE TIP

A party may be presumed to have independent knowledge of the other party's assets and liabilities if, for example, they lived with the other party and were exposed to their assets (real estate, collections, boats, etc.) or worked in a business owned by the other as a bookkeeper or in some other position in which they had access to financial information.

PARALEGAL PRACTICE TIP

Under the UPMAA, both parties must have "access" to independent counsel. If only one party was represented, the other party must have had the financial ability to retain a lawyer or the represented party must have agreed to pay the reasonable fees and expenses of the other's independent representation.

Ignorantia legis non excusat
[Latin: Ignorance of the law is not an excuse]

PARALEGAL PRACTICE TIP

Paralegals usually need to look to case law to learn about a specific jurisdiction's position on what constitutes adequate time for review. For example, in a New Hampshire case, that state's high court observed that New Hampshire had not adopted a rule holding last-minute premarital agreements are invalid *per se*.[23] An Ohio court took the opposite position and held "the presentation of an agreement a very short time before the wedding ceremony will create a presumption of overreaching or coercion ... the postponement of the wedding would cause significant hardship, embarrassment or emotional stress."[24]

PARALEGAL PRACTICE TIP

The courts are divided with respect to whether a threat to not marry a pregnant woman if she doesn't sign a premarital agreement constitutes duress. Consideration is usually given to the surrounding circumstances. For example, in *Hamilton v. Hamilton*, 404 Pa. Super. 533, 591 A.2d 720 (1991), the court found no duress when a man told his eighteen-year-old pregnant, unemployed fiancé that the wedding would not go forward if she did not sign the agreement based on the fact that she had signed it despite her attorney's advice not to do so. In *Ex Parte Williams*, 617 So. 2d 1033 (Ala.1992), the court found duress may be present when a prospective bride is pregnant, has strong moral objections to abortion, and lives in a small rural town where legitimacy of children is an important social consideration.

and in good working order. When the execution of the agreement is videotaped, a series of questions such as the following may be asked of each party:

1. Please identify yourself and the nature of the document you are about to sign.
2. When was a first draft of the document presented to you? Did you participate in negotiations and provide input into revisions of that draft? Have you had a sufficient amount of time to review the final version of the document and the attachments?
3. With whom have you consulted regarding the document and attachments including legal counsel, accountants, etc.? Did you select your own counsel?
4. Please describe your understanding of the basic rights you are waiving by signing this agreement. Do you have any questions regarding those rights?
5. Please describe your understanding of the basic terms of the agreement. Do you have any questions about those terms? Has anyone made any promises to you other than what is contained in the agreement? Are you satisfied with the terms?
6. Have you disclosed all of your assets and liabilities, and is a summary of them attached to the agreement? Please describe the financial disclosure provided to you by your prospective spouse. Are you satisfied with that disclosure, and do you believe it adequately reflects his/her assets and liabilities? Do you have any questions about the disclosure?
7. Are you presently under the influence of any drug or condition that might impair your ability to understand what you are signing? Are you prepared to sign the agreement at this time? Are you doing so of your own free will?

Paralegal **Application 2.4**

Elderly Clients

Premarital agreements provide an especially useful vehicle for addressing the challenges and fears the elderly face with respect to marriage and remarriage late in life. Among other goals, seniors want to protect and preserve wealth, benefits from previous marriages, relationships with their children, and interests of those children as well as "other objects of their bounty" such as siblings and grandchildren They also may want to avoid the partner's financial obligations related to health care and other debts.[27]

Agreements involving elderly clients or other clients whose competency may be questioned require special consideration. Many attorneys require elderly clients to obtain an **Affidavit of Competency** from a physician prior to execution of legal documents such as wills, powers of attorney, or premarital agreements to help protect against later claims that the documents were executed under undue influence. Paralegals may be asked to work with clients to facilitate this task.

Affidavit of Competency
an affidavit from a physician that an individual is competent to perform a particular act

THE REQUIREMENT OF SUBSTANTIVE FAIRNESS

Substantive fairness refers to fairness in the actual terms of the agreement. The states vary considerably with respect to the degree to which the courts will scrutinize the terms of an agreement for fairness. At one end of the spectrum are the states which require that an agreement be fair to both parties based on the circumstances existing at the time it is negotiated and executed (commonly labeled a "fairness" approach). Priority in this approach is placed on the nature of the confidential relationship between the parties and the tendency for them to be of unequal bargaining power. At the other end of the spectrum are the states that place priority on the parties' freedom to contract and their right to rely on the agreements they enter (sometimes termed a "freedom to contract" approach). An increasing number of states take the position that people are free to make "bad bargains."[28] Courts in these states hold that the terms of an agreement should not be reviewed for fairness unless they are "unconscionable."

States also vary with respect to whether the determination of substantive fairness or conscionability of premarital agreements is made only *as of the date of execution* or also at the time of performance. Fairness at the time of execution involves a review of the agreement as written under the parties' circumstances. A consideration of fairness *at the time of performance* (upon divorce or death) allows a court to take a "second look" or second glance and consider whether terms that were fair at the time of execution remain fair at the time of performance. Generally the focus is on whether, due to an unforeseen and substantial change in circumstances, an agreement that was once fair and reasonable has become so unfair that its enforcement would be **unconscionable**.

When drafting agreements, it is important to keep in mind the approach taken in the jurisdiction to assessment of substantive fairness. The two areas most often scrutinized are terms relating to division of property and waivers of spousal support.

- **Property Division:** Given that a primary purpose of a premarital agreement is to allow the parties to alter the usual division of property upon divorce and/or death, it is likely that an agreement will result in an unequal division of property. However, an agreement that calls for one party to receive everything while the other receives nothing and will end up on public assistance is unlikely to be enforced. Under a fairness analysis, the basic question is "does the agreement provide at least some level of self-sufficiency for both parties?" Under a conscionability or freedom to contract analysis, the question is whether an inequality is "so strong, gross, and manifest that it must be impossible to state it to one with common sense without producing an exclamation at the inequality of it. Conscionability means protection against onesidedness, oppression or unfair surprise. . . ." See, e.g. *Potts v. Potts*, 303 S.W.3d 177 (Mo. Ct. App. 2010).
- **Spousal support:** More than forty states permit waivers of spousal support,[29] provided they are entered into freely, with knowledge and understanding of the rights waived, and after adequate disclosure by both parties. Waivers made by parties with ample assets or waivers providing for the allowance of alimony under certain extreme and unforeseen circumstances (serious illness, disabling workplace accidents, natural disasters, etc.) or effective only if the marriage lasts less than a certain number of years are also likely to be enforceable. However, although a few states allow them (including Alaska, Missouri, New York, and Pennsylvania), the majority rule is that waivers of temporary spousal support are not permitted. As long as the parties are married, they generally are deemed to have a mutual duty of support as an incident of marriage, a duty that cannot be waived.

Unconscionable
so substantially unfair in terms or result as to shock the conscience

Preparation for Drafting a Premarital Agreement

Paralegal Application 2.5 identifies several of the tasks that should be performed prior to the actual drafting of a premarital agreement.

Paralegal Application 2.5

In Anticipation of an Agreement—Tasks for the Attorney and the Paralegal

- The attorney should learn what the client's motivations and goals are so that a decision can be made as to whether or not a premarital agreement is the most appropriate means for accomplishing the client's objectives. This may involve an assessment of any federal income tax, gift tax, and estate tax consequences of various options.
- The attorney should advise the client of the basic law governing rights and responsibilities upon separation, divorce, annulment, or death.
- The attorney should advise the client of the law regarding premarital agreements and their enforceability.
- The attorney should discuss the importance of independent representation for the prospective spouses.
- Necessary background information and copies of documents need to be gathered (often by or at least with the assistance of the paralegal) including the following:
  - the names, addresses, ages, and social security numbers of the parties
  - the date of the intended marriage and any flexibility with respect to that date
  - information regarding prior marriages and children/grandchildren of both parties and any related obligations (child support, spousal support, etc.)
  - information regarding all forms of income and assets of the parties (including expected assets such as inheritances or commissions). A threshold value may be set for assets that should be identified (e.g., any property valued at over $5,000 or $25,000 based on the size of the parties' estates). A paralegal or the attorney will often work with the client to be certain that all kinds of assets of value are included (collections, stock portfolios, antiques, etc.)
  - copies of potentially relevant documents, including, for example, trusts, deeds, retirement plans, court orders (e.g., for property division, support, or other judgments in addition to those flowing from prior marriages/relationships), insurance policies, and appraisals of real estate, artwork, jewelry, etc.
  - information regarding debts/liabilities of each of the parties
  - information about any unique and/or foreseeable circumstances (such as one party already having been diagnosed with a debilitating or terminal disease or special needs of any children of a party, such as severe physical or mental impairments)
- The paralegal should confirm current requirements for premarital agreements in the state of execution and, if different, the law of the state which will govern interpretation and enforcement of the agreement, such as whether any particular kinds of provisions are prohibited and whether the agreement must be witnessed, notarized, and/or recorded.

Clients often ask paralegals questions concerning the law as it applies to their cases. Even if the paralegal knows the answers, he or she must resist the temptation to engage in the unauthorized practice of law by responding with legal advice or analysis. The safest response is to indicate that he or she will bring their questions to the attention of the attorney and get back to the client with a response. Many firms prepare in-house publications covering "most frequently asked questions" on a variety of topics or obtain them from professional organizations, such as the American Bar Association. The availability of such publications allows the paralegal to avoid an ethical problem and yet meet clients' needs by giving them helpful handouts addressing their questions. An example of a Georgia firm's Prenuptial Agreement Frequently Asked Questions can be accessed at *www.georgiafamilylaw.com*.

What Kinds of Provisions Does a Premarital Agreement Contain?

Each premarital agreement is unique because it reflects the intentions of two specific people, each with his or her own goals and needs. However, agreements commonly include the following:

1. A preamble (introductory segment) that identifies the parties and describes their intentions
2. A definition of "separate property" and a description of how each party's "separate property" and its appreciation and proceeds, if sold, will be treated in the event of death or divorce
3. A definition of marital or "joint property" and a description of how marital property of various kinds (real estate, jewelry, investment accounts, etc.) and its appreciation will be treated and what role, if any, contribution will play
4. A statement of the rights each party will have to alimony or spousal support if the marriage ends in a legal separation or divorce, or a waiver of those rights
5. A provision relating to death benefits or waivers thereof
6. Attached schedules of each party's assets and liabilities, which may include anticipated gifts and inheritances that are reasonably certain and of known value

The UPAA (adopted in whole or part in half the states as of spring 2015) provides that the parties also are free to contract with respect to personal rights and obligations during their marriage, provided the terms do not violate public policy or existing statutes. For example, they may want to include provisions relating to several aspects of their life together. However, one or more of these terms may taint the entire agreement and render it void and unenforceable. When a client wants to include such a term, the attorney should advise the client in writing that there is no guarantee that the particular provision will be enforced by the courts. Paralegal Application 2.6 identifies some potentially problematic terms.

Paralegal **Application 2.6**

Potential Red Flags

- The parties cannot agree to engage in criminal activity.
- The parties may include provisions relating to child custody and support, but they cannot bargain away the rights of third persons (their children). Such provisions will be subject to approval by the court that retains jurisdiction over child-related issues. For example, an agreement that children from a party's prior marriage may not live with the parties may be held unenforceable as a violation of public policy and not in the best interests of the children.
- Terms that tread on constitutional rights may not be enforceable, such as:

- An agreement to raise children in a particular religion may be viewed as violating a party's (or a child's) right to freedom of religion,[30] although a court may enforce a provision that a party be required to participate cooperatively in obtaining a religious separation or annulment.[31]
- An agreement to work or render certain services may be deemed a form of involuntary servitude if enforced by the court.
- Terms that invade a party's "right to privacy" are unlikely to be enforced, such as:

(Continued)

- A promise to perform certain sexual acts or to engage in sexual relations according to a particular schedule.[32]
- A promise to use contraception or not to have an abortion.
- A promise not to have children.[33]
- Courts may not enforce a promise to prosecute or not prosecute a divorce action.

- Certain "spousal" waivers of retirement benefits may not be valid and enforceable if made prior to marriage under the requirements of the Employee Retirement Income Security Act (ERISA) and the Retirement Equity Act (REA). (See 29 U.S.C. Section 1055.)[34]

EXHIBIT 2.3 Sample Premarital Agreement

PREMARITAL AGREEMENT
PREAMBLE

THIS AGREEMENT is made this _____ day of _____, 2015, by and between _Name of prospective spouse A_ of _____ _address,_ _____,_ _____ _("first name")_ _____ and _Name of prospective spouse B_ of __address__, _("first name"),_ collectively referred to as "the parties."

DRAFTING TIP

- The preamble establishes the identity of the parties.

RECITALS

WHEREAS,

A. The parties plan to be married in _____ _city, state_ _____ on or about _____ _date_ _____, 2015. Neither of the parties has been married previously.

DRAFTING TIP

- Reference should be made in this part of the agreement to any prior marriages and existing children or grandchildren of either or both of the parties, if applicable. If there are such children, it is wise to insert language such as the following: "In no event will either party be responsible now or in the future for any parental or legal obligations with respect to the other party's children."

B. Each recognizes that the other is gainfully employed and possesses property and assets independently acquired prior to their intended marriage such that each is able to provide for his or her own individual needs. Each desires to enter this agreement realizing that either or both of the parties' financial, health, or other circumstances may change substantially in the future.

DRAFTING TIP

- Paragraph B lays the basis for a determination that the agreement is fair at the time of execution. It also makes clear that the parties intend their agreement to take effect with full knowledge of the uncertainties of life, such as early retirement, fluctuations in income, health problems, or pursuit of a new career. This helps defend against a later claim that a certain change was unforeseeable, such as poor health or a financial failure.

EXHIBIT 2.3 *(Continued)*

C. The parties intend by this Agreement to define and fix their respective rights and obligations to each other with regard to spousal support and to any property now owned or hereafter acquired before or after the date of their marriage, in the event of the termination of their marriage by death or legal process.

DRAFTING TIP

- Paragraph C addresses the basic purpose of the agreement.

D. A owns certain property, both real and personal, as listed on Exhibit 1 attached hereto and incorporated herein, the nature and approximate value of which has been fully disclosed to B prior to execution of this Agreement. Also listed on Exhibit 1 and previously disclosed to B is A's indebtedness exclusive of his personal expenses.

E. B owns certain property, both real and personal, as listed on Exhibit 2 attached hereto and incorporated herein, the nature and approximate value of which has been fully disclosed to A prior to execution of this Agreement. Also listed on Exhibit 2 and previously disclosed to A is B's indebtedness exclusive of her personal expenses.

DRAFTING TIPS

- Paragraphs D and E and the Schedules that will be attached to the agreement as Exhibits 1 and 2 address the requirement of disclosure of assets and liabilities. Some agreements provide that these schedules will be updated on a periodic basis without affecting the nature, validity, or effect of the underlying agreement.

- Sometimes the agreement will include a paragraph that provides the contents of the agreement, including the disclosures of property will be kept confidential absent consent or legal necessity. This is particularly appropriate when a party's business interests are listed and he or she would be disadvantaged if the document is made part of a public record and a competitor becomes aware of sensitive information.

- Other related exhibits may also be attached such as copies of trusts, tax returns, and appraisals.

F. The parties acknowledge that each has had an adequate opportunity to negotiate, review, and consider the terms of this Agreement prior to execution; that each has received satisfactory disclosure of the other's income, assets and liabilities; that each has been advised by independent counsel of his or her individual choice as to his or her rights as a spouse under the law with respect to alimony and the distribution of property and the legal effect of the Agreement on those rights; that each believes the provisions of the Agreement are fair, just, and reasonable; that each understands, assents to, and intends to be bound by its provisions; and that each enters the Agreement freely, voluntarily, and without any duress, undue influence, or illegal consideration.

EXHIBIT 2.3 *(Continued)*

DRAFTING TIP

- Paragraph F addresses procedural fairness in the negotiation and execution of the agreement, including the requirement that it be freely and voluntarily executed. The reference to counsel of individual choice makes clear that each party chose and retained his or her own independent attorney and not one chosen by the other party. The content presumes that counsel has described the applicable state's approach to allocation of property upon divorce and death, so both parties appreciate what they are gaining and/or giving up in the agreement. In some agreements the rights will actually be specified.

G. This Agreement shall become effective only upon the marriage of the parties within a period of one (1) year from the date hereof, and, if such marriage is not solemnized within said period, then this Agreement shall be null and void.

DRAFTING TIP

- The one-year time frame is intended to protect against such a long period passing that the nature of the assets and liabilities of the parties may have changed in some significant manner.

NOW THEREFORE, in consideration of the mutual promises and covenants set forth herein, the parties mutually agree as follows:

DRAFTING TIP

- This paragraph identifies the consideration that supports the agreement. Some agreements state that each party enters the marriage with the full intention that it will succeed and that the agreement is in no way intended as an inducement to divorce.

AGREEMENTS

1. **Definition of Separate Property**
   For purposes of this Agreement, "separate property" shall be defined as:
   a. all assets in which each presently has an interest exclusive of the other as shown on the Schedules contained in Exhibits 1 and 2;
   b. any inheritances, gifts, bequests, or devises received by either of them after the date of the parties' marriage;
   c. all appreciation, reinvestments, and proceeds of sale or redemption of any of the above property after the date of the parties' marriage;
   d. any property designated as separate property by both parties in writing after the date of their marriage; and
   e. any income earned by either party during the marriage including salaries and bonuses.

DRAFTING TIPS

- "Separate property" must be carefully defined because each party is giving up an interest he or she might otherwise have in the other party's separate property. The definition of separate property provided here is broad. For example, some agreements do not designate income earned by a party during the marriage as separate property.

EXHIBIT 2.3 *(Continued)*

- This definition does not include as separate property retirement benefits (pension, profit sharing, deferred compensation, etc.) because potential rights in certain retirement plans cannot be waived by a nonspouse under ERISA. However, the agreement could include a provision that the other party will agree to execute a waiver after an appropriate period post marriage.

- Sometimes the agreement will specify whether ownership of property will be exclusively determined by title or if one party's contributions (financial or nonfinancial) to appreciation in the value of the other party's property will be considered in some manner. For example, what happens if the parties purchase a boat together and each contributes to its purchase and maintenance but not equally? The agreement may also address the effect of commingling of assets and income or future increases in the value of separate property.

2. **Separate Property During Marriage**
   Each party agrees to keep and retain the sole ownership and control of any property held as his or her separate property as herein defined without interference from the other and in the same manner as if the marriage had not occurred.

3. **Separate Obligations of the Parties**
   Obligations of a party incurred prior to the marriage shall remain the separate obligations of that party. The other party shall not be liable for those obligations and shall be indemnified and held harmless from them by the responsible party. Such existing obligations shall be paid from the separate property of the responsible party.

DRAFTING TIP

- It is important to address liabilities as well as assets in premarital agreements. This provision could be expanded to address liabilities incurred during marriage by either or both of the parties. Occasionally a party agrees to contribute to payment of a debt of the other party, such as an educational loan with contributions ceasing in the event of a divorce. In some cases, the payments made will be deducted from the recipient's eventual share of the division of the marital property. The payor may agree to waive all claims to contribution to the other's degree or professional practice.

4. **Definition of Marital Property**
   For purposes of this Agreement, with the exception of either party's separate property as herein defined, marital property ("Marital Property") shall be defined as all property accumulated by the parties during the marriage until the date of the death of either party or the date on which any legal action for separation, annulment, or divorce is commenced. Marital property shall also include any property designated as marital property by both parties in writing after the date of the marriage.

DRAFTING TIPS

- This paragraph sets the date of the filing of an action as a key date. Other options might be the date of separation, the date of divorce, etc.

PARALEGAL PRACTICE TIP

Given the broad definition of "separate property" in this Agreement, each party may be in a position to transfer significant assets by will, trust, gift, or otherwise to children from a prior marriage, other parties, charities, or the spouse, if he or she chooses to do so.

EXHIBIT 2.3 *(Continued)*

- In the event of an annulment, if the marriage was *void ab initio* (invalid from the outset), no valid marriage will ever have occurred and the agreement will never have taken effect, absent a provision that addresses this circumstance. For example, the parties may provide that the agreement may be held enforceable to the extent that it avoids an inequitable result.

- Most often agreements address income and asset issues. At this point in the agreement, however, the parties may choose to include provisions regarding various aspects of their life together. Some agreements will address how various responsibilities will be managed during the marriage. How will bank accounts be set up? How will payment of bills be handled? Who will perform various household responsibilities? What are the parties' intentions with respect to childrearing roles and responsibilities? Provisions that pertain to medical, disability, life insurance, and long-term care expenses and insurance are especially appropriate in agreements involving elderly and/or disabled parties. Occasionally an agreement will address behavioral issues such as excess spending, gambling, drinking, smoking, drug abuse, or infidelity during the marriage. Although such provisions may clarify expectations of the parties, some of them may be unenforceable.

PARALEGAL PRACTICE TIP

Agreements containing provisions relating to misconduct during the marriage have been enforced in some circumstances. For example, in *MacFarlane v. Rich,* 132 N.H. 608, 567 A.2d 585 (1989), a provision provided that the entire agreement would be held invalid if the husband left the wife for another woman.

5. **Marital Property Upon Termination of the Marriage**
   a. In the event of termination of the marriage by legal proceedings, all assets then jointly owned by the parties as joint tenants, tenants by the entirety, or otherwise and not herein defined as separate property shall be divided equally between the parties.

DRAFTING TIPS

- This particular agreement provides for an equal rather than an equitable division of marital property regardless of the jurisdiction in which legal process is commenced and whether it is a community property or equitable distribution state. Parties to other agreements may elect different options. Sometimes specific provisions are included relating to the marital home such as who will be permitted to remain in it in the event of divorce or that each party's share of the equity in the home will be based on the parties' respective contributions to the home.

- This agreement adopts what some call a "three-pot" approach to property: "his," "hers," and "theirs." Some parties will set forth further provisions requiring the transfer of an asset of one party to the other (such as a vacation home or lump sum payment of a certain amount) or creation of an asset for the other party's benefit (for example, a health, disability, or life insurance policy). This is particularly likely if the agreement contains a waiver of a spousal support or an estate claim and/or a party is giving up employment or an alimony payment from a prior spouse as a result of the upcoming marriage. Such provisions are sometimes tied to the length of the marriage in "escalator clauses" providing that the amount of property or support a party receives will increase when certain marital milestones are attained, such as five-year anniversaries.

EXHIBIT 2.3 (*Continued*)

b. In the event of the termination of the marriage by the death of a party, all assets defined as marital property shall become the sole property of the surviving party and thus be excluded from the decedent's estate. The surviving party shall own said property subject to any liens, mortgages, or encumbrances secured by the property. However, if there is at the time of the death a pending complaint for divorce or separation, the decedent's share will pass to his or her estate. Liabilities will remain liabilities of the party who incurred them or of his or her estate.

DRAFTING TIP

- It is important to specify if the marital property will be transferred subject to encumbrances pursuant to the agreement (by contract rather than by inheritance). Otherwise, the decedent's estate would not receive the asset but would be liable for the decedent's share of the encumbrances.

6. **Mutual Waivers**
   a. Waiver of Rights to Property: In the event of termination of the marriage by divorce or annulment, each party agrees not to assert any claim of any kind to the separate property of the other as herein defined. This waiver shall not apply to marital property.
   b. Waiver of Rights to Maintenance and Support: In the event of a legal separation, divorce, or annulment, the parties agree to waive any rights to spousal support or maintenance of any kind to which either might otherwise be entitled. The parties agree that this provision may be entered as a complete defense by either party in response to an action for alimony. The parties further agree that nothing herein shall be deemed a waiver of either party's right to claim child support for support of any minor children born to or legally adopted during their marriage.

DRAFTING TIPS

- The parties cannot waive rights or obligations pertaining to child custody and support, which remain subject to the jurisdiction of the court. At least four states expressly prohibit alimony waivers: Iowa Code Ann. §596.5(2); CA Cal. Fam. Code § 1620; New Mexico N.M. Stat. Ann. §40-3A-4(B); and South Dakota *Sanford v. Sanford*, 694 N.W.2d 283, 287–291 (2005). Several states prohibit waivers of temporary alimony based on the existence of the marital duty of mutual support. When waivers of alimony are included there may be restrictive language such as "to the extent permitted by law," or that neither party will receive alimony unless one of the parties has an income at the time of divorce of a certain threshold amount, such as the national poverty level.

- This model sets forth a waiver of spousal support. If, in the alternative, it provided for support, the agreement could spell out a method for determining the appropriate amount to be paid. It could also identify the circumstances in which payment of alimony would commence, be modified, or terminate. For example, the amount could be tied to a certain event (e.g., disability, reduction in income) or the length of the marriage. Some agreements provide for reductions or elimination of support if there is proof of adultery by the recipient spouse during the marriage.

- The enforceability of spousal support waivers in premarital agreements varies from state to state, and they may not be effective if enforcement would bring about an "unconscionable" result.

PARALEGAL PRACTICE TIP

It is important to check the law governing agreements, both statutory and case law, that may impact the content of the agreement. Waivers of spousal support are especially subject to variations. In Louisiana, for example, by statute (LSA-C.C. art. 2329) spouses before or during marriage have the right to enter agreements "as to all matters that are not prohibited by public policy." By case law, parties may waive permanent spousal support but not temporary support in their prenuptial agreements based on public policy. See, e.g., *Barber v. Barber*, 38 So. 3d 1046 (La. 2010).

Waiver
the giving up of a right or privilege

EXHIBIT 2.3 (*Continued*)

c. Waiver of Estate Claims: In the event of the death of one of the parties, each party hereby relinquishes and waives all rights, claims, and interests that he or she may have or acquire as surviving spouse, heir at law, or otherwise in the estate of the other party.

DRAFTING TIP

- Paragraphs a and b are waivers of statutory rights upon divorce, and c is a waiver of rights upon death. It is common to specifically list the scope of the rights being waived upon death of a party (the right to inherit as a spouse under the state's laws of descent and distribution, the right to claim a distributive or forced share as a surviving spouse, the right to petition to serve as administrator of the deceased spouse's estate, etc.).

7. **Wills/Trusts**

Nothing contained herein shall preclude or prevent either party from freely executing a will or settling a trust that confers benefits on the other party, or from nominating the other party as a personal representative or trustee, or from exercising any power of appointment in favor of the other party.

DRAFTING TIP

- A premarital agreement is a contract and generally not a replacement for a will though its terms are customarily enforceable as claims against the estate of a party who dies. However, if the agreement is executed with all the formalities of a will, a party may assert that it serves as a will "substitute." Clients should consider their agreement and wills in tandem. Even though the parties may waive statutory rights in the agreement, they are still free to voluntarily make provisions for each other and to make gifts to each other during the marriage.

8. **General Provisions**
   a. Entire Agreement
   The parties agree that this Agreement contains their entire understanding and that there have been no additional promises, representations, or agreements made to either party by the other, oral or written, except as set forth herein.

DRAFTING TIP

- A paralegal should maintain a complete file including successive drafts, revisions suggested by either party, and written confirmations of telephone exchanges, etc. Even though an agreement may never be challenged, if it is, the contents of a complete file can be very valuable as forensic evidence for use in court.

   b. Modification
   This Agreement may be modified, amended, or rescinded at any time after the solemnization of the marriage, only by a subsequent written agreement between and signed by the parties.

PARALEGAL PRACTICE TIP

Under contract law, judges look to "the four corners" of the agreement (the "face" of the written instrument) to determine what the parties intended at the time the agreement was executed. Sometimes, however, if an agreement is ambiguous, the court will go outside the contract and hear testimony ("parol evidence") from witnesses, not to create terms but rather to clarify the parties' intentions with respect to specific existing terms.

EXHIBIT 2.3 *(Continued)*

DRAFTING TIP

- This paragraph leaves the door open for the parties to alter or rescind their agreement or cure deficiencies at a later date if their circumstances alter. However, modification provisions should not be included in a jurisdiction where postmarital agreements are prohibited. In such jurisdictions, inclusion of a modification provision may cause rescission of the entire agreement.
- Sometimes, agreements contain "sunset" provisions providing that the agreement will terminate at a certain point such as on a twenty-fifth anniversary, provided there is no pending complaint for divorce, legal separation, or annulment. Such clauses are used primarily by wealthier parties, concerned about the impact of a potential short-term marriage.

---

   c. Waiver of Breach or Default
     No waiver of breach or default with respect to a provision of this Agreement shall be deemed a waiver of any subsequent breach or default.

DRAFTING TIP

- This provision means that if a party allows the other party to default on a particular obligation under the agreement, he or she is not waiving the right to object to a subsequent default on that or any other provision.

---

   d. Binding Effect
     This Agreement shall be binding on the parties hereto and their respective legal representatives, heirs, successors, and assigns.

DRAFTING TIP

- The agreement binds the parties with respect to each other but is not necessarily binding on third parties such as creditors or bona fide purchasers of property without notice. To ensure that the agreement will be enforceable against a purchaser of a piece of real estate, for example, a copy of the agreement should be recorded in the appropriate Registry of Deeds. Some states have statutes that specifically address this issue.[35]

---

   e. Severability
     In the event any provision of this Agreement shall be held illegal, invalid, or otherwise unenforceable, such holding shall not invalidate or render unenforceable any other provisions hereof, and the offending provision shall be severed from this Agreement and be null and void and of no force and effect.

DRAFTING TIP

- Severability clauses are common in most contracts. They are especially important in premarital agreements when a client insists on including a provision that is likely to be unenforceable (such as a term that the parties will have no children or must practice a particular religion).

EXHIBIT 2.3 (*Continued*)

PARALEGAL PRACTICE TIP

The state designated to govern the agreement will affect the terminology used. For example, in a community property state "marital property" may be termed "community property."

f. Governing Law
This Agreement shall be governed, controlled, and interpreted under the laws of the state of _____.

DRAFTING TIPS

- The law of the state where the parties will reside is usually designated. If another state is chosen, the parties must have a significant connection with that state, presently or after marriage. Given that laws vary from state to state, this provision anticipates a possible "conflict of law" question. For example, the parties may agree that the law of Maryland will govern but they eventually divorce in California. According to basic choice of law principles, the California court will apply Maryland law in construing the agreement unless the result of doing so would violate strong public policy in California. This is a potentially important choice given the degree to which states vary in their approaches to dividing property upon divorce and to determining the validity of premarital agreements.[36]

- Some agreements include a provision that sets out the steps to be taken in the event of a dispute regarding any terms of the agreement in addition to judicial relief (a party seeking to enforce an agreement can sue for breach of contract and seek specific performance). It may include options such as mediation and arbitration. Some provide that if either party unsuccessfully contests the agreement, that party will pay all fees and costs of the prevailing party.

- The provisions in this last section of the sample premarital agreement are "boilerplate" to a considerable extent. Boilerplate is standard language commonly used in a particular kind of document that usually does not require negotiation. However, as with all documents, care must be taken to tailor even boilerplate to jurisdictional requirements and the facts of a case at hand.

IN WITNESS WHEREOF, the parties have signed, sealed, and acknowledged this Agreement on the day and year indicated below.

Witness _____   Prospective spouse A _____
                                      Date:_____

Witness _____   Prospective spouse B _____
                                      Date:_____

DRAFTING TIPS

- It is important to verify and comply with applicable jurisdictional procedural rules governing witnesses, signatures of counsel, notary certifications, and the like. Even if not required, each page of the agreement and any attached exhibits should be signed or initialed by the parties to protect against later claims that a particular provision was added at a later date or not included in the original agreement.

- Once executed, the agreement must be kept in a safe location as it may not be enforced for decades.

- Exhibits 1 and 2 referenced in paragraphs D and E under Recitals at the beginning of the agreement will be attached. They contain schedules or summaries of the parties' respective income, assets and liabilities.

What Are the Trends Regarding Enforceability of Premarital Agreements?

Since *Posner*, states have increasingly considered and enforced premarital agreements on a case-by-case basis. Each state sets forth by statute and/or case law its own requirements or standards for what constitutes a valid and enforceable agreement. Some states invest premarital agreements with a presumption of validity as long as certain threshold requirements (described earlier) are satisfied.[37] If there is never a controversy surrounding the agreement and the parties simply abide by its provisions, enforceability does not become an issue. However, if challenged, the burden of proof of invalidity is on the party challenging enforcement of the agreement under the approach applied in the jurisdiction.

Today, the law governing premarital agreements across the country continues to evolve. Some courts subject agreements to intense scrutiny for fairness being protective of the rights of vulnerable parties while others are highly pro-enforcement. Each state essentially applies one of the following four basic approaches to determining enforceability: The Uniform Premarital Agreement Act approach, the Uniform Premarital and Marital Agreements Act approach, the traditional fairness approach, or the contemporary conscionability approach. However, some states adopt a hybrid approach. For example, Massachusetts applies a traditional fair and reasonable approach to determine the validity of an agreement at the time of execution and a conscionability approach at the time of enforcement. See, e.g., *DeMatteo v. DeMatteo*, 436 Mass. 18, 762 N.E.2d 797 (2002).

THE UNIFORM PREMARITAL AGREEMENT ACT (UPAA) APPROACH

The thirteen states that have adopted the UPAA without making any significant changes apply its strong pro-enforcement approach. Under the UPAA, premarital agreements are enforceable unless the challenger proves either that the agreement was not entered voluntarily or that the agreement was unconscionable when executed AND before execution, the challenger was not provided with a fair and reasonable disclosure of the property or financial obligations of the other party and did not waive disclosure in writing or have an adequate knowledge of the other's property and obligations. An agreement cannot be challenged on the basis of unfairness or unreasonableness at the time of enforcement unless enforcing a spousal support provision would result in a party becoming eligible for public assistance upon divorce or separation. In that event, the act provides that a court may order the other party to provide support to the extent necessary to prevent that result.

THE UNIFORM PREMARITAL AND MARITAL AGREEMENTS ACT (UPMAA) APPROACH

The enforceability provisions contained in the 2012 UPMAA vary significantly from those in the UPAA. Like the UPAA, drafted and approved in 1983, it too was drafted and approved by the National Conference of Commissioners on Uniform State Laws and was approved in 2012. Now recommended for adoption in all the states, the UPMAA addresses both premarital and postmarital (termed "marital") agreements choosing to treat them according to the same legal standards. The

---

PARALEGAL PRACTICE TIP

Despite statutory requirements for validity of premarital agreements, the courts sometimes are moved to find ways of enforcing agreements where one or both of the parties have not strictly complied with the requirements. It is important to research both statutes and case law to discover potential "loopholes!" See, e.g., *Dove v. Dove*, 285 Ga. 647, 680 S.E.2d 839 (2009).

PARALEGAL PRACTICE TIP

Visit *www.uniformlaws.org* to see the full text of the Act and see which states have adopted the UPAA. The thirteen states that have adopted it without making significant changes are Arizona, Arkansas, Delaware, Hawaii, Idaho, Illinois, Kansas, Montana, Nebraska, North Carolina, Oregon, Texas, and Virginia. Several of the other states that have adopted the UPAA in part have adopted stronger procedural and substantive safeguards. For example, in Connecticut, unconscionability at the time of execution alone is a sufficient basis for denying enforcement. Even in jurisdictions where it has not been adopted, provisions of the UPAA have often been referenced and favorably considered by the courts.

PARALEGAL PRACTICE TIP

As of March 2015, the UPMAA has been adopted in Colorado and North Dakota and introduced in Mississippi and the District of Columbia.

general approach of the Act is that parties should be free, within broad limits, to choose the financial terms of their marriage. Compared with the UPAA, the UPMAA establishes more procedural safeguards in an effort to increase the probability that premarital agreements will be negotiated fairly. It adds the new requirement that the parties must "have access to independent legal representation," and Section 9 provides that an agreement will be unenforceable on any one of the following four grounds:

1. A party's consent to the agreement was involuntary or the result of duress.
2. A party lacked access to independent legal representation. The unrepresented party must have had reasonable time to retain and consult with counsel, and if they lacked sufficient financial means, the represented party must have agreed to pay the reasonable fees and expenses of independent legal representation, provided they had the financial ability to do so.
3. If a party was unrepresented, the agreement did not include a conspicuously displayed notice of waiver of rights or an explanation in plain language of the marital rights or obligations being modified or waived.
4. Adequate financial disclosure was not made. Each party must receive a "reasonably accurate description and good faith estimate" of the other's property, liabilities and income. The exchange of information may be excused if a party already had knowledge or a reasonable basis for knowledge of the other's information when the agreement was signed.

PARALEGAL PRACTICE TIP

Stemler v. Stemler, 36 So. 3d 54 (Ala. Civ. App. 2009) provides an example of a case in which a fairness test was applied at the time of performance. The parties agreement provided the wife would receive $50,000 plus any property titled in her name and a share of any property jointly titled with the husband. The court found the agreement was inequitable to the wife and disproportionate to the means of the husband. At the time of the divorce, no property was titled in the wife's name, only the marital home was titled in their joint names, and the husband's net worth had increased from approximately $2 million to between $5 and $10 million during the marriage.

The UPMAA further provides that a court may refuse to enforce a term of an agreement if, in the context of the agreement taken as a whole, the term was unconscionable at the time of signing or enforcement would result in substantial hardship for a party because of a material change in circumstances that arose after the agreement was signed. If the agreement modifies or eliminates spousal support making a party eligible for public assistance, a court, on request of that party, may order the other party to provide support to the extent necessary to avoid eligibility.

The UPMAA with its emphasis on due process in formation, on the one hand, and at least minimal standards of fairness, on the other,[38] makes an effort to "promote informed decision making and procedural fairness without undermining interests in contractual autonomy, predictability and reliance."[39] In its rejection of several provisions of the UPAA, it appears to represent the current trend in enforceability of premarital agreements.

THE TRADITIONAL FAIRNESS APPROACH

Second look doctrine
an approach to determining enforceability of premarital agreements adopted by some states that involves examining the terms of a premarital agreement for fairness at the time of performance as well as at the time of execution

Once the majority perspective, the traditional fairness approach still applied in some states treats premarital agreements as contractual agreements between people who bear a special "fiduciary" relationship to one another and holds them to a higher standard than that applied to contracts between strangers. In jurisdictions applying this approach, agreements typically must satisfy basic contractual requirements as well as the procedural and substantive fairness requirements described earlier in the chapter. In assessing fairness and enforceability, the court asks whether the terms of the agreement are fair and reasonable in light of the length of the parties' marriage; their standard of living; their respective assets, income, and liabilities; their ages, health, and support needs; and their intelligence, education, earning potential, and business acumen. Depending on the jurisdiction, fairness may be reviewed only at the time of execution or may be subject to the **second look doctrine** and be examined at the time of performance as well.

THE CONTEMPORARY CONSCIONABILITY APPROACH

The more contemporary conscionability approach reflects the trend in more recent years away from subjecting premarital agreements to a higher standard and toward a pro-enforcement approach that emphasizes the parties' "freedom to contract." Other than requiring adequate disclosure, this approach contends that premarital agreements should be treated like any other contracts and should be enforced absent fraud, misrepresentation, or duress. It is the approach that affords the most protection for the stronger party and the least protection for the more vulnerable one by providing that absent an unconscionable result, parties are free to make hasty, unfair bargains against their own self-interest. Applying a test of conscionability, the question is whether the terms are so unfair that they "shock the conscience of the court" by essentially stripping one of the parties of all marital interests and forcing them onto public assistance. There is no precise definition of "unconscionable" that binds all courts. The assessment is made on a case-by-case basis and is highly subjective with some courts applying stricter rules than others.

The opinion in the Pennsylvania case of *Simeone v. Simeone* describes how and why the trend has evolved towards a pro-enforcement rather than a traditional fairness approach in response to broad societal changes. (See Case 2.3.) In *Simeone*, the wife appealed a lower court's decision upholding the validity of the premarital agreement that she and her husband had executed on the eve of their wedding in 1975. At the time, the wife was an unemployed twenty-three-year-old nurse. Her spouse was a thirty-nine-year-old neurosurgeon earning $90,000 a year with an additional $300,000 in assets. She signed the agreement without the advice of an attorney or knowing which legal rights she was giving up. The terms of the agreement limited her to support payments of $200 per week in the event of separation or divorce, up to a maximum of $25,000. When the premarital agreement was upheld and her petition for further alimony was denied by the Superior Court, she appealed to the Pennsylvania Supreme Court.

PARALEGAL PRACTICE TIP

A New York court has defined an "unconscionable bargain" as one which "no person in his or her senses and not under delusion would make on the one hand, and no honest and fair person would accept on the other, the inequality being so strong and manifest as to shock the conscience and confound the judgment of any person of common sense." *Morad v. Morad*, 27 A.D.3d 626, 812 N.Y.S.2d 126 (2006).

PARALEGAL PRACTICE TIP

To learn more about the enforceability of premarital agreements grounded in religious beliefs (Jewish and Islamic), visit the companion website for this text in the material related to Chapter 2 under Resources. *www.pearsonhighered.com/careersrcsources/*

CASE **2.3** *Simeone v. Simeone*, 525 Pa. 392, 581 A.2d 162 (1990)

FROM THE OPINION

There is no longer validity in the implicit presumption that supplied the basis for . . . earlier decisions. Such decisions rested upon a belief that spouses are of unequal status and that women are not knowledgeable enough to understand the nature of contracts that they enter. Society has advanced, however, to the point where women are no longer regarded as the "weaker" party in marriage, or in society generally. Indeed, the stereotype that women serve as homemakers while men work as breadwinners is no longer viable. Quite often today both spouses are income earners. Nor is there validity in the presumption that women are uninformed, uneducated, and readily subjected to unfair advantage in marital agreements. Indeed, women nowadays often have substantial education, financial awareness, income, and assets.

Accordingly, the law has advanced to recognize the equal status of men and women in our society. . . . Paternalistic presumptions and protections that arose to shelter women from the inferiorities and incapacities that they were perceived as having in earlier times have, appropriately, been discarded. . . .

. . . Traditional principles of contract law provide perfectly adequate remedies where contracts are procured through fraud, misrepresentation, or duress. . . . Prenuptial agreements are contracts, and, as such, should be evaluated under the same criteria as are applicable to other types of contracts. . . . Absent fraud, misrepresentation, or duress, spouses should be bound by the terms of their agreements.

(Continued)

Contracting parties are normally bound by their agreements, without regard to whether the terms thereof were read and fully understood and irrespective of whether the agreements embodied reasonable or good bargains. . . . *Ignorant[i]a legis non excusat.*

Accordingly we find no merit in a contention raised by the appellant that the agreement should be declared void on the ground that she did not consult with independent legal counsel. To impose a *per se* requirement that parties entering a premarital agreement must obtain independent legal counsel would be contrary to traditional principles of contract law, and would constitute a paternalistic and unwarranted interference with the parties' freedom to enter contracts.

Further, the reasonableness of a prenuptial bargain is not a proper subject for judicial review. . . .

. . . If parties viewed an agreement as reasonable at the time of its inception, as evidenced by their having signed the agreement, they should be foreclosed from later trying to evade its terms by asserting that it was not in fact reasonable. . . .

Further, everyone who enters a long-term agreement knows that circumstances can change during its term, so that what initially appeared desirable might prove to be an unfavorable bargain. Such are the risks that contracting parties routinely assume. . . .

We are reluctant to interfere with the power of persons contemplating marriage to agree upon, and to act in reliance upon, what *they* regard as an acceptable distribution scheme for their property. A court should not ignore the parties' expressed intent by proceeding to determine whether a prenuptial agreement was, in the court's view, reasonable at the time of inception or at the time of divorce. . . .

. . . we do not depart from the longstanding principle that a full and fair disclosure of the financial positions of the parties is required. . . .

SIDEBAR

Read the full opinion in the *Simeone* case available at *www.pearsonhighered.com/careersresources/* in the companion website material for Chapter 2 of this text under Cases. After reading the opinion, do you agree with the outcome? Why? What do you think the requirements should be in order for a premarital agreement to be valid and enforceable?

Paralegal **Application 2.7**

Should Postmarital Agreements Be Enforced? What Do You Think?

A **postmarital** (postnuptial) **agreement** is an agreement made by two people already married to each other who want to continue their marriage and also define their respective rights upon separation, divorce, or death of one of the spouses. These agreements have been called "reconciliation agreements" in some states. They allow spouses to resolve financial issues and focus energy on other aspects of their marriage.[40] The enforceability of such agreements is inconsistent across the country. At least two states (Ohio and Oklahoma) ban them entirely. Some states have no case law or legislation addressing them and the remainder have adopted a variety of approaches. Some permit them but subject them to greater scrutiny and stricter procedural requirements than premarital agreements. For example, Minn. Stat. §519.11, subd. 1a(c) provides that a postmarital agreement is "presumed to be unenforceable if either party commences an action for legal separation or dissolution within two years . . . unless the spouse seeking to enforce the postnuptial contract . . . can establish that [it] is fair and reasonable." The UPAA does not cover them and the UPMAA recommends that pre- and postmarital ("marital") agreements be subject to the same legal standards and procedural requirements.

Consider this situation: Kenneth and Cheryl had been married for nineteen years when they began having serious marital problems. When marital counseling was not entirely successful, Kenneth told Cheryl that he needed her to sign a postmarital agreement because he was "uncertain" about her commitment to their marriage. Cheryl alleged that the request caused her a great deal of stress and made her physically ill. The parties separated for about six weeks until they resumed living together when she agreed to sign an agreement. Both parties retained counsel, engaged in extensive negotiations, and exchanged several drafts of an agreement. The final draft provided that Cheryl would disclaim any interest in property Kenneth owned in Florida valued at around $4–5 million. In return, Kenneth agreed to pay Cheryl $5 million and 30% of the appreciation in all marital property from the time of the agreement to the time of divorce. In addition to maintaining a life insurance policy for her benefit, the agreement further provided that he would pay for her health insurance until her death or remarriage and that if they divorced, she could remain in the marital home for a year and he would pay all reasonable expenses of the household. The agreement recited that the parties were fully satisfied that its terms would promote marital harmony.

At the time the agreement was executed, the couple's combined assets were valued at approximately $19 million. The couple subsequently went on a "second honeymoon" and bought and renovated a new home. But all did not go well and in about a year, Cheryl asked Kenneth to move out of the marital home. She began drinking heavily and became seriously involved with another man. To bring "closure" to their relationship, Kenneth eventually filed for divorce and sought enforcement of the postmarital agreement. Cheryl's position was that the agreement left her with a disproportionately small percentage of the couple's marital assets primarily because of the significant value of the Florida property. She argued that it should be declared void as against public policy because such agreements are "innately coercive" and that they are typically executed in the midst of threats of divorce and are induced by illusory promises of remaining in an already failing marriage.

Sidebar: Do you think Cheryl and Kenneth's postmarital agreement should be enforced? Explain your reasoning. Do you think it would be enforceable under the UPMAA? If such agreements are permitted, what kinds of procedural and substantive safeguards should be imposed, if any? The Massachusetts Supreme Judicial Court considered the validity of Kenneth and Cheryl's postmarital agreement in *Ansin v. Craven-Ansin*, 457 Mass. 283, 929 N.E.2d 955 (2010), a case of first impression in that state and a case often cited in other jurisdictions and in law review articles. Read the opinion to see whether the court agreed with your position.

Postmarital agreement
an agreement made by two people already married to each other who want both to continue their marriage and also to define their respective rights upon separation, divorce, or death of one of the spouses

The Role of the Paralegal in Cohabitation and Premarital Agreement Cases

The paralegal applications provided in this chapter address several aspects of the paralegal's role in matters involving cohabitation and premarital agreements. The nature of that role in a specific instance depends primarily on whether the case involves the negotiation and execution of an agreement, the enforceability of an already existing agreement, or the absence of an agreement.

When there is no agreement, the paralegal's role is driven by the facts and circumstances of the individual case and the types of relief sought. When an agreement is involved, the tasks to be performed will depend on whether the case is at the negotiation and execution stage or at the enforcement stage. In these contexts, an experienced paralegal may perform the following tasks:

Tasks Common to Both Stages

- Participate in meetings with the client as requested by the supervisor
- Research the jurisdictional requirements for valid and enforceable agreements
- Help the client and the attorney gather necessary information and documents
- Maintain communication with the client

- Schedule meetings with the client, the other party and his or her attorney, and any other essential individuals (e.g., mediators, tax accountants, appraisers, etc.)
- Prepare related forms and correspondence (including fee agreements and confirmation of meetings)
- Track/monitor progress on the case and ensure that required timelines are met

Negotiation and Execution of an Agreement

- Prepare exhibits for use in negotiations
- Draft successive versions of an agreement and related schedules and attachments based on instructions from the supervising attorney
- Review proposed agreements from the other party for consistency with the client's position and agreed-upon terms based on information provided by the supervisor
- Make arrangements for obtaining an affidavit of competency, if appropriate
- Arrange for execution of the agreement, including taping if desired

Enforcement of an Existing Agreement

- Obtain an original copy of the executed agreement along with the file, if available
- Locate the state statute(s) governing premarital agreements, if any, so it can be determined if its requirements were met
- Research circumstances surrounding the drafting and execution of the agreement such as:

    Who suggested the agreement?

    How was it developed? Who prepared the original draft? Were there revisions based on subsequent feedback and negotiation?

    Was each party represented? How was counsel obtained and who paid for the representation?

    What was the timing of the drafting, execution, and wedding?

    What financial disclosures were made and how complete and accurate were they?

    What were the parties' respective financial circumstances, education levels, and business backgrounds at the time of execution?

    Was there any history of threats or emotional or physical abuse prior to execution of the agreement?

    Was the execution taped? If so, obtain a copy of the tape.

- In a second look jurisdiction, find out how circumstances have changed since execution of the agreement. For example, what are the current financial circumstances of each of the parties? How great a disparity will there be between the parties' respective resources post divorce if the agreement is enforced? Will one of them be forced onto public assistance? Have children been born to the marriage? Has one of the parties developed a serious health problem? Is there a history of abuse during the marriage?
- Draft appropriate pleadings for review and be certain that the client's Complaint for Divorce (or Answer) puts the court on notice as to the existence of the agreement and the client's position with respect to its enforcement

- Prepare related memoranda based on research as requested
- Assist with discovery. Discovery methods for premarital agreement controversies are the same as for divorce: formal methods (interrogatories, depositions, requests for admissions, production of documents, or physical/mental examinations), and informal methods such as interviews, examination of public records, etc.
- Draft responses to discovery requests, working with the client and the supervising attorney
- Help identify potential witnesses with whom either party may have discussed the agreement, including attorneys, financial advisors, friends, and family members
- Assist with preparation for hearings or a trial on the merits, including drafting pretrial memoranda for review, preparing exhibits, arranging for service of subpoenas on potential witnesses, if needed, and helping prepare the client's witnesses, as directed

CHAPTER **SUMMARY**

When most people think of a family law practice, the image that usually comes to mind is of a couple engaged in a bitter divorce fueled by attorneys and an adversarial and impersonal legal system. The parties are struggling to divide the pieces of a failed relationship at a time when they can't even communicate with each other and their future may end up being decided by a stranger in a black robe according to laws they don't agree with or even understand. Fortunately, this scenario occurs less and less frequently as most courts today encourage parties to resolve their differences without costly litigation and attorneys make greater use of collaboration and alternative dispute resolution methods. Perhaps equally influential is the fact that couples choosing to marry or simply live together as unmarried partners increasingly recognize at the outset that relationships can fail and that more than half of all marriages end in divorce. At a time when they are looking forward to their life together, growing numbers of these couples elect to develop their own personalized blueprints for the future. They anticipate the problems that may arise, and they create agreements designed to minimize those problems and resolve them in advance at a point in time when they view each other as partners rather than adversaries. These cohabitation/living-together and premarital agreements are the primary focus of this chapter.

The early part of the chapter addressed cohabitation. The kinds of documents cohabitants can execute to create and protect their rights with respect to each other were identified, including, for example, cohabitation agreements, wills, trusts, health care proxies, beneficiary designations, and powers of attorney. Attention was also given to the theories used by courts to provide relief to cohabitants when their relationships terminate and they have no written agreement. The nature, purpose, and development of premarital agreements were then discussed, and a detailed model of a basic comprehensive agreement was provided, accompanied by extensive drafting tips. Many of the provisions in the agreement (particularly boilerplate language regarding disclosure, governing law, severability, and the like) may also appear in cohabitation agreements. Different approaches to determining whether or not a premarital agreement should be enforced were discussed, including the Uniform Premarital Agreement Act approach, the Uniform Premarital and Marital Agreements Act approach, a traditional fairness approach (at both the time of execution and the time of performance in the case of so-called second look jurisdictions), and a contemporary conscionability approach. Because cohabitation, premarital, and postmarital agreements are relatively recent developments, their origins and evolution were highlighted in pertinent case excerpts.

Throughout the chapter a number of tasks a supervisor might assign to a paralegal were identified with particular emphasis on gathering information, drafting agreements and other documents tailored to the client's specific needs, and researching enforceability issues. Several paralegal applications and tips were provided alerting the paralegal to ethical issues, jurisdictional variations, and special problems which might arise related to the drafting, execution, and enforcement of agreements. One of those problems has largely been resolved: Although same-sex couples have been able to execute premarital agreements in some states beginning in 2003, the viability of those agreements was threatened if the parties relocated to a state that did not recognize same-sex marriage. The controversial topic of gay marriage will no doubt continue to be debated for years to come by those who support a "traditional" definition of marriage, but marriage equality is now the law of the land. Today cohabitation, premarital, and postmarital agreements executed by same-sex couples should be enforceable in all states in the same manner and to the same extent as those executed by heterosexual couples with respect to matters governed by both state and federal law.

CONCEPT REVIEW AND REINFORCEMENT

KEY **TERMS**

Affidavit of Competency
Boilerplate
Cohabitation
Cohabitation agreement
Collaborative law
Constructive trust
Consideration
Defense
Durable power of attorney
Express contract
Fiduciary
Health care proxy
Ignorantia legis non excusat
Implied-in-fact contract

Implied partnership/Joint venture
Joint tenants with right of survivorship
Mediation
Meeting of the minds
Meretricious sex
Palimony
Per se invalid
Postmarital agreement (postmarital contract, postnuptial agreement)
Premarital agreement (premarital contract, antenuptial agreement)
Procedural fairness
Public policy
Putative spouse doctrine

Quantum meruit
Quasi-contract/implied-in-law contract
Resulting trust/Purchase money resulting trust/Implied trust
Second look doctrine
Statute of frauds
Substantive fairness
Unclean hands
Unconscionable
Uniform Premarital and Marital Agreement Act (UPMAA)
Void
Waiver

REVIEW **QUESTIONS**

1. Describe how the *Marvin* decision reflects a change in society's view of cohabitation over the past few decades.
2. Identify five documents cohabitants can execute in order to define their respective rights and responsibilities and protect and provide for each other.
3. Identify and give examples of three theories a court might rely on to justify relief to cohabitants when their relationship terminates and they have no enforceable agreement.
4. Describe the nature and purpose of a premarital agreement, and explain why such agreements are becoming more common.
5. Distinguish between substantive and procedural fairness and give an example of each.
6. List at least five of the provisions most commonly included in premarital agreements.

7. Identify three terms individuals may want to include in an agreement that may not be enforceable and explain why. In this context, explain the importance of a severability clause in an agreement.
8. Describe the historical trend from nonenforceability to enforceability of premarital agreements reflected in the *Posner* case. What is the significance of the *Simeone* case in this context?
9. Explain the difference between fairness and a conscionability approach to determining the enforceability of premarital agreements.
10. What is the second look doctrine?
11. Describe the differences between the UPAA and the UPMAA approaches to enforceability of premarital agreements.
12. Describe the role of the paralegal in cases involving cohabitation and premarital agreements.

DEVELOPING YOUR PARALEGAL SKILLS

FOCUS ON **THE JOB**

In this activity, the student has an opportunity to collaborate with other students in drafting a cohabitation agreement tailored to a detailed fact pattern.

The Facts

Tran Ng and Malia Barach have been going out for six months. Although they are very happy and plan to spend the rest of their lives together, for a number of reasons they have decided to live together and postpone marriage for a while.

Both parties are semiretired after long and successful careers, he as an engineer, she as a college dean. He is sixty-five years old, was married once before for twenty-two years, and has three adult children and four grandchildren.

She is sixty-three years old and a widow (receiving Social Security benefits through her deceased husband) and has no children or grandchildren.

His Primary Assets	Her Primary Assets
Vacation home on the New Jersey shore (assessed at $350,000)	Vacation cottage in Beverly Farms, Massachusetts (assessed at $200,000)
Artworks valued at about $40,000	State pension
Bell Laboratories pension	36-foot sailboat valued at $50,000
30-foot trawler valued at $125,000	Condominium in North Conway, New Hampshire (assessed at $250,000)
401(k) valued at $350,000	Jewelry valued at $27,000
Investment portfolio (current value $325,000)	Investment portfolio (current value $225,000)

Tran and Malia plan to purchase a new home in your state. Tran will pay a $200,000 down payment, and Malia will get a mortgage for $200,000 and make the associated payments. The deed and mortgage will be in Malia's name only, but they intend that the property will belong to them equally. They will share all home maintenance, utility, and daily living expenses equally and will pay those expenses from a joint account to which they will both contribute. Malia intends to do a significant amount of landscaping to improve and maintain their new home. Tran plans to add a music/art room to the house for his enjoyment and at his expense. Tran is concerned about Malia's housekeeping and has decided he wants to pay for daily maid services. The couple will share grocery shopping and cooking chores. Each party will maintain an individual bank account in addition to their joint account. Each party intends to work part time. Tran will work in a marine supply store two days a week, and both parties will teach one or two courses at a local college. Each will be entitled to his or her own earnings. Malia anticipates no inheritance through her family. Tran anticipates a substantial inheritance when his mother dies.

It does not bother them if other people think of or treat them as if they are married, but they have no intention of entering a marriage, common law or otherwise, for at least a year. They do share an intimate and sexual relationship and anticipate that will continue, but that is not the reason why they are moving in together. The couple expects to continue their current lifestyle and do considerable traveling together, particularly by boat. Malia has a beagle, "Spike," and, because Tran is allergic to dogs, she has agreed to not have Spike inside the house or on the boat and to be totally responsible for all expenses related to the dog.

The parties intend their agreement to take effect upon signing and to be unaffected by any periodic, temporary separations. It will terminate only when the parties sign a written declaration of termination or have lived separate and apart for a continuous six-month period. Neither party expects to benefit under the will of the other at this point, but each is free to make whatever provisions he or she wishes. Neither party intends to make a claim for any kind of support if their relationship should terminate even if permitted under current or future legislation. However, each does agree to do the following within thirty days of executing their agreement:

- Establish a $500,000 life insurance policy for the benefit of the other.
- Designate the other as his or her health care proxy.
- Execute a durable power of attorney naming the other as his or her attorney-in-fact in the event of incapacitating disability, serious illness, etc.

The agreement will be executed in your state, and the parties also intend that it be governed by the law of your state, if permitted. (If such agreements are contrary to law or public policy in your state, assume you live in a nearby state where they are permitted.) If either party breaches the agreement, attorney's costs will be paid by the nonprevailing party. Tran's attorney will draft the agreement for review and input from Malia. Malia will have her attorney, Nancy Riggs, review the document once it is drafted. She says she trusts Tran and whatever he wants is fine with her. Besides, she doesn't want to spend any more money on a lawyer than she has to.

The Assignment

Either individually or working in teams of three—one person playing the role of Tran, one the role of Malia, and the third the role of Tran's attorney, Juliana Dahl—draft a cohabitation agreement that is tailored to the above fact pattern. Assign local addresses within your state to each of the parties and counsel. Your draft should reflect what you have learned from reading this chapter, class discussion, and any additional research you may have done or are required by your instructor to do. You should begin by determining if there are any requirements for a valid cohabitation agreement in your jurisdiction and locating a variety of appropriate models in form books and/or online.

FOCUS ON **ETHICS**

In this activity, the students will draft a letter addressing the ethical issue of dual representation.

The Assignment

Assume that in the above fact pattern, Malia and Tran have decided to marry and they want to execute a premarital agreement. Tran's attorney will draft the agreement. Malia does not believe she needs to have another attorney advise her with respect to the negotiation and execution of the proposed agreement. She has told both Tran and his attorney, Juliana Dahl, how she feels and that she trusts both of them to be fair with her. Assume that you are the paralegal for Attorney Dahl. Draft a letter to Malia for your supervisor's review and signature in which you explain why it is strongly advised that she be represented by independent counsel and what the potential risks are of failing to do so. Indicate, if she insists on not obtaining counsel, what steps, if any, need to be taken in an effort to protect your client against a later allegation that the agreement was unfair in its terms or execution or that it was the product of fraud or duress, etc. The tone of the letter needs to be firm but also reflect sensitivity to the situation.

FOCUS ON **CASE LAW**

In this activity, the student is required to locate and brief a case involving the enforceability of a premarital agreement in his or her jurisdiction.

The Assignment

Locate the most recently decided case in the state where you live addressing the enforceability of a premarital agreement and the approach/standard to be applied in making that determination. Read the case and then brief it. If there is no case law on point in your state, select a case from a neighboring state. If needed, a format for briefing cases is available at *www.pearsonhighered.com/careersresources/* in the companion website material for Chapter 1 of this text under Resources.

FOCUS ON **STATE LAW AND PROCEDURE**

In this activity, the student is asked to research whether a premarital agreement is likely to be enforced in his or her state, given a hypothetical fact pattern. If there is no state law on point, the student should assume that the UPMAA has been adopted. A copy of the text of the UMPAA can be found at *www.uniformlaws.org*. Search for "Premarital and Marital Agreements Act."

Fact Pattern

Richard Marshall is a very wealthy seventy-two-year-old retired engineer who recently married a thirty-five-year-old model, Elaine. He has been married three times and is paying alimony to two of his three prior spouses. He also has five much loved adult children and twelve grandchildren whose futures he wants to secure when he dies. He told Elaine before they wed that he definitely wanted no more children and she agreed. Richard's assets total over $4 million and Elaine's add up to approximately $300,000, plus she is still working and earns about $250,000 a year. They generally disclosed their respective assets and liabilities prior to the marriage and executed a premarital agreement drafted by Richard's attorney, James Schornstein. Richard disclosed information about all of his real estate, retirement accounts, antique car collection, yacht, and investments. He "overlooked" disclosing several valuable paintings he inherited from his grandmother that are on display in a New York museum. He has never had them appraised but believes they are worth over a million dollars.

Richard's attorney delivered the agreement to Elaine the day before their lavish wedding. Elaine elected not to have an independent lawyer review the document, in part because there was no time to do so because she was busy with the wedding plans. She told Richard and his attorney that she trusted them and whatever "Rich" wanted was fine with her. Elaine failed to reveal that the week before the wedding she learned she was two months pregnant. She did not tell Richard about their "love child" until two months after their marriage. Richard was so upset by this turn of events that he promptly filed for divorce. He wants the court to enforce the parties' premarital agreement, which provides that, if the parties are married for less than two years, Elaine receives only what she brought into the marriage and no form of continuing support. Elaine does not want the agreement enforced and wants a substantial spousal support award for a six-year period, until the baby enters elementary school and she returns to work. She says that Richard should not be allowed to benefit from the agreement because he never told her about the paintings, and she only recently found out about them from her friend, Johnnie Rasmussen, at a museum fundraiser. She retains Attorney Olga Carroll to represent her in this matter. Assume that you are Attorney Carroll's paralegal and that she has asked you to research the enforceability of the agreement at issue in your state. Prepare a memorandum describing the results of your research and your conclusion with respect to Elaine's chances of prevailing. Your report should be in a basic internal memo format such as the following:

Memorandum

To: Olga Carroll, Esq.

From: *Your Name, Paralegal*

File Reference: *Name of client (followed by case caption with a docket number if provided by your instructor)*

Re: *Enforceability of the Client's Premarital Agreement*

Date: *The date your assignment is due*

Description of Issue/Assignment: *What is it that you have been asked to do?*

Results of Research: *What did you learn about the law governing enforceability of premarital agreements in your state?*

Application to the Case: *Apply the law (case and statutory) to the facts of the case at issue.*

Conclusion: *What is the likelihood that Elaine will prevail in an action to enforce the premarital agreement she and her husband executed?*

Remember: When considering the law governing enforceability of a premarital agreement, a series of questions must be answered:

1. The threshold question is are premarital agreements governing property and spousal support rights permitted in the jurisdiction and are there any restrictions on their content?

2. Does the agreement in question satisfy the requirements for a valid contract?

3. What are the minimum requirements for procedural fairness in the jurisdiction (e.g., full disclosure, independent representation, timing between presentation, execution, and the wedding, and absence of duress/undue influence)? Were they satisfied at the time of execution?

4. What test does the jurisdiction apply when measuring the substantive fairness of an agreement, if any: a fairness test or a conscionability test? Has the state adopted either the UPAA or the UPMAA? Did the agreement satisfy the applicable standard?

5. Will substantive fairness be measured only at the time of execution or also at the time of performance (divorce or death)? (Is the state a "second look" jurisdiction?)

FOCUS ON **TECHNOLOGY**

In addition to the websites mentioned throughout the chapter, this activity provides a series of useful sites for reference, along with technology-related assignments for completion.

Websites of Interest

www.deltabravo.net

This is the website for the Separated Parenting Access and Resource Center (SPARC). A "Sample Pre-Nuptial Agreement" can be located at this site. Be sure to remember that forms located online must be carefully reviewed to be sure that they comply with governing law and that they can be tailored to the specific needs of the parties.

www.divorcenet.com

This site contains information on a number of family law topics. Search by topic and/or by state.

www.divorcesource.com

Click on divorce laws and then search by topic and/or state. Links are provided to both articles and sites for cases. Cases reflecting the positions of several states regarding enforceability of cohabitation agreements can be found at *www.divorcesource.com*. Some materials on this site cannot be viewed without a subscription (available at a modest fee).

www.findlaw.com

This site contains a wide range of information about family law, marriage, living together, premarital agreements, and other topics related to the content of this chapter. A copy of a sample cohabitation agreement can be found at this site.

www.jlaw.com

The focus of this site is on Jewish law in a variety of topical areas. An example of a premarital agreement is provided (without any guarantee as to enforceability).

www.legalforms.com

This is an example of a site where individuals can purchase premarital agreement packages. There is no guarantee that the material provided satisfies particular states' current requirements, although the packages are promoted as state-by-state products.

www.palimony.com

The stated goal of this website is to provide a one-stop source of resources and information for unmarried couples (heterosexual or same-sex) who are living together as domestic partners or are considering doing so. The Resources section includes an extensive set of links to information and resources. The site also includes articles about cohabitation agreements. It focuses primarily on the state of California.

www.unmarried.org

This is the website for the Alternatives to Marriage Project. The site provides information and statistics on cohabitation, living single, domestic partner benefits, common law marriage, etc.

Assignments

1. Locate three models of formats for cohabitation agreements online. In your opinion, which of the three would be most useful as a model for developing a cohabitation agreement for the parties in the Focus on the Job assignment in this chapter?

2. Visit *www.divorcesource.com/tables/domesticagreements.shtml* and see what you can learn about your state's position with respect to the enforceability of premarital agreements. Remember to shepardize any cases referenced. Also keep in mind that there may be new cases that have been decided and/or statutes enacted relating to this issue in your state.

3. See what you can learn online about the "palimony" case of the late Johnnie Cochran, renowned attorney (89 Cal. App.4th 283, 106 Cal. Rptr.2d 899 (Cal. App. 2001)). Did he prevail?

4. Using online resources, determine whether or not your state has adopted the Uniform Premarital Agreement Act or the Uniform Premarital and Marital Agreements Act. Be sure to verify whatever you learn by checking your state's statutes governing premarital agreements, if any.

5. Assume that the firm where you are employed wants to develop a "common questions and answers" information/fact sheet regarding premarital agreements. Search the Web for ideas on what should be included in such a sheet. Start with *www.findlaw.com.*

6. To learn more about the law governing premarital agreements in various states, locate the following statutes through online resources:

Minn. Stat. § 519.11	Minnesota
ORC Ann. 3103.06	Ohio
N.C. Gen. Stat. § 52-10	North Carolina

PORTFOLIO PRODUCTS

1. Cohabitation agreement
2. Letter to a client's prospective spouse re the need for independent representation
3. Brief of a state case on premarital agreements
4. Internal memorandum re enforceability of a premarital agreement

chapter 3
MARRIAGE

© Jupiterimages/Getty Images

Mary, a fifteen-year-old girl who lives in Texas, has fallen madly in love with her first cousin, Marty, a twenty-three-year-old professional bull rider on the rodeo circuit who lives in Massachusetts. She has hatched a plan for them to wed and live happily ever after in Colorado. Marty is not so sure they can "get away with it."

LEARNING OBJECTIVES

After reading this chapter and completing related assignments, you should be able to:

- explain how and why the concept of "family" has evolved over the past fifty years

- distinguish among different types of marriage

- identify ways in which the states regulate and restrict the fundamental right to marry

- list common requirements for valid ceremonial and common law marriages

- describe the kinds of alternative relationships various states have recognized by statute or case law over the past two decades including civil unions and domestic partnerships

- distinguish among the rights, benefits, and obligations that flow from marriage, civil unions, and domestic partnerships under state and federal law

- identify key milestones in the road to marriage equality including the *Obergefell* decision

- describe the potential role of a paralegal in cases involving marriage and alternative relationships

Introduction

Once upon a time, there was a nation whose prime-time television shows included *I Remember Mama* and *Father Knows Best*. These programs featured storybook-perfect intact traditional families, characters playing highly gendered roles, and classic moral themes. Cohabitation was viewed as "living in sin" and constituted a crime in virtually all states. "Gay" meant cheerful and lighthearted, and "domestic agreements" referred to contracts with hired help to perform household chores.

The above description reflects the white, middle-class, "idealized" portrait of the nuclear family projected by the media of the day. Although a reality for some, it failed to capture the fact that throughout this country's history, the nature of the nuclear family has adapted to societal conditions such as war, racism, sexism, and economic depression, and it continues to do so today. Although the majority of adults in the United States still marry at least once in their lifetimes, significant changes in our society have resulted in expanded, publicly acknowledged, and legally recognized concepts of marriage and the family unit that encompass a wide range of lifestyles and diverse living arrangements. A number of forces have promoted this broader and more flexible view of both the family and intimate relationships: the women's rights, fathers' rights, and gay rights movements; a decreased emphasis on marriage as a defining event in life (particularly for women); an increased social acceptance of alternative lifestyles; and a greater protection of the right to privacy in sexual conduct between consenting adults.

In the last chapter we discussed cohabitation, the generic term for same-sex or different-sex couples living together without being married or having any other legally recognized status. This chapter addresses the topic of marriage. It would have been a very short and straightforward chapter years ago. However, since the 1990s, the nation, and particularly courts, legislatures, agencies, and family law practitioners, have been on a relationship-driven roller coaster. As a result, we must necessarily look at an expanded relationship menu including various kinds of marriage and marriage-like relationships heterosexual and same-sex couples have been able to enter over the past twenty-five years in an effort to access some or all of the benefits of "traditional marriage." Our initial emphasis will be on traditional and common law marriage and the ways in which they are defined and regulated by the states. The content will highlight the nature of marriage as a fundamental right and a source of rights, benefits, and obligations. Recognizing that we need to understand where we have been to appreciate where we are now, in the last half of the chapter we will review the expansion of the relationship menu and the evolution, or perhaps more accurately the revolution, in the recognition of the rights of same-sex couples culminating in the U.S. Supreme Court's monumental decision in *Obergefell v. Hodges* in the summer of 2015.

PARALEGAL PRACTICE TIP

The content of Exhibit 3.1 focuses on types of marriage common in the United States. However, throughout history, four fundamental forms of marriage have existed across the world: (1) monogamy; (2) polygyny (one man with several wives); (3) polyandry (one woman with several husbands); and (4) group marriage. The term "polygamy" encompasses both polygyny and polyandry. The various forms are rooted deeply in the cultures, religious beliefs, and social mores of the societies in which they appear.

EXHIBIT 3.1 Types of Monogamous Marriage in the United States

Ceremonial Marriage	Available in all fifty states, a ceremonial marriage customarily requires a license and solemnization in a ceremony performed by a person authorized by statute to perform weddings. The ceremony may be civil (performed by a government official/Justice of the Peace), religious (performed by a religious cleric), or, in the case of Native Americans, conducted according to tribal customs. Ceremonial marriages can be entered by heterosexual or same-sex couples.
Covenant Marriage	A covenant marriage is a form of ceremonial marriage available in a small number of states and under consideration in others. It developed in response to concerns about high divorce rates and the ease with which no-fault divorces are granted. It emphasizes the seriousness of the decision to marry and the goal of permanence in marital relationships. As a result, covenant marriages are more difficult to enter and exit than traditional ceremonial or common law marriages. See Exhibit 3.2.
Common Law Marriage	A common law marriage is created by the conduct of the parties rather than in a formal ceremony. As of June 2015, common law marriages still can be entered in a limited number of states. See Exhibits 3.4 and 3.5. The requirements for a common law marriage usually include capacity, simultaneous intent to marry, cohabitation, and a holding out to the public as husband and wife.[1] As of June 2015, common law marriage status may presumably be claimed by both heterosexual and same-sex spouses.

EXHIBIT 3.1 (*Continued*)

Putative Marriage	The putative marriage doctrine is recognized in a limited number of states. Section 209 of the Uniform Marriage and Divorce Act defines a putative spouse as follows: "Any person who has cohabited with another to whom he is not legally married in the good faith belief that he was married to that person is a putative spouse until knowledge of the fact that he is not legally married terminates his status and prevents acquisition of further rights. A **putative spouse** acquires the rights conferred upon a legal spouse, including the right to maintenance following termination of his status, whether or not the marriage is prohibited (Section 207) or declared invalid (Section 208)." The presumed marriage may be either common law or ceremonial in nature. The doctrine does not make the marriage valid, but it does allow the courts to treat it as a valid marriage for purposes of property division and spousal support.

EXHIBIT 3.2 Covenant Marriage

The **covenant marriage** movement began in the 1990s as an effort to reinforce the traditional model of marriage as a lifelong relationship. Its primary goals are (1) to strengthen marriage by encouraging premarital counseling that prepares couples to thoughtfully commit to marriage and (2) to reduce spiraling no-fault divorce rates by requiring professional guidance and proof of spousal fault before terminating a marriage.

The Louisiana legislature enacted the first covenant marriage legislation in the country in 1997, creating a two-tiered system of marriage in that state and defining covenant marriage as:

> . . . a marriage entered into by one male and one female who understand and agree that the marriage between them is a lifelong relationship. Parties to a covenant marriage have received counseling emphasizing the nature and purpose of marriage and the responsibilities thereto. Only when there has been a total and complete breach of the marital covenant commitment may the non-breaching party seek a declaration that the marriage is no longer legally recognized.

Divorce is granted on the following grounds only: adultery, sentence of death or imprisonment at hard labor for a felony, physical or sexual abuse, abandonment of the marital home for a year, or living separate and apart continuously without reconciliation for two years (La. Rev. Stat. Ann. § 9:272274).

Although covenant marriage legislation has been introduced in nearly half the states, it has passed in only three: Louisiana (1997), Arizona (1998), and Arkansas (2001). Opponents see it as a regression to the pre-no-fault era. In the states where it is in effect, approximately 1–3% of the population have chosen to enter this form of marriage.[2]

PARALEGAL PRACTICE TIP

The Illinois statute concerning putative spouses can be found at *www.ilga.gov* (Select Legislation and Laws, Illinois Compiled Statutes, Chapter 750 5/305).

Putative spouse
a person who believes in good faith that his or her invalid marriage is legally valid

PARALEGAL PRACTICE TIP

To learn more about the Uniform Marriage and Divorce Act visit *www.uniformlaws.org*. A primary objective of Uniform Acts in general is to promote legislative uniformity among the states. This particular Act is treated more as a "Model" than a "Uniform" Act. It suggests approaches to certain areas of family law and is cited frequently but does not call for uniform acceptance by the states. Also visit *www.law.cornell.edu* to find links to the text of the Act in the eight states where it has been adopted in whole or in part.

Covenant marriage
a type of marriage that emphasizes the permanence of marriage and limits the availability of divorce to fault grounds

PARALEGAL PRACTICE TIP

To learn about covenant marriage in Arizona visit *www.azcourts.gov*.

Marriage—Definitions and Historical Perspective

DEFINITIONS

In 1810, the Massachusetts Supreme Judicial Court described marriage as follows:

> Marriage is . . . a civil contract, founded in the social nature of man, and intended to regulate, chasten, and refine, the intercourse between the sexes; and to multiply, preserve, and improve the species. It is an

engagement, by which a single man and a single woman, of sufficient discretion, take each other as husband and wife. From the nature of the contract, it exists during the lives of the two parties, unless dissolved for causes which defeat the object of marriage. . . .[3]

In 2003 (193 years later), the same court, in a sharply divided decision, defined marriage as "the voluntary union of two persons as spouses, to the exclusion of all others."[4] The court held that "Limiting the protections, benefits and obligations of civil marriage to opposite sex couples violates the basic premises of individual liberty and equality under law protected by the Massachusetts Constitution."[5]

The above definitions reflect the fact that the way we define **marriage** depends to a considerable extent on prevailing social, cultural, and political environments. The first definition mirrors our early marriage laws, which, in a majority of the states, were based on English common law. It is moral in tone and emphasizes the union of a man and a woman and the procreative function of marriage. The second definition falls at the other end of the spectrum, where marriage simply involves two "persons" who voluntarily enter a "union" with each other without reference to gender or purpose.

HISTORICAL PERSPECTIVE

The history of marriage in the United States has its roots in ecclesiastical and English common law. In the common law states, upon marriage a husband and wife became one, and that one was embodied in the husband. The wife was entitled to support by her husband but essentially lost her independent legal status. Although she retained title to any real property she owned in her own name when she wed, her husband acquired an exclusive right to manage, control, and collect all income from that property. She lost her right to own personal property, and any she did own became her husband's. She could not execute a contract or a will, and any executed prior to marriage were automatically revoked. She could not sue or be sued in her own name. She could be employed, but any income she received belonged to her husband.

In the eight **civil law** or **community property states**, influenced primarily by Spanish civil law (Arizona, California, Idaho, Nevada, New Mexico, Texas, and Washington) or French civil law (Louisiana), the wife's independent legal identity technically did not merge with her husband's, and property acquired during marriage generally constituted "community property" belonging to both spouses. However, the spouses were not "equals." As under the common law tradition, the husband held complete control over his wife's property and earnings during the marriage.

By the mid to late nineteenth century, the situation of women began to improve somewhat as the states enacted **Married Women's Property Acts**. The acts were passed partly in response to pressure from reformers seeking equality for women in political, social, and domestic arenas. Generally, they eliminated several of the disabilities of married women. Despite this initial progress, it was not until the 1960s that a variety of forces converged and brought about fundamental change in both society and the law relating to marriage and the family: men and women both wanting to escape stereotypic roles; fathers wanting to parent their children and take care of their homes; women seeking economic independence; men wanting to be free of financial burdens upon divorce; gay and lesbian individuals wanting to have their identities and lifestyles acknowledged and respected; and both married and unmarried heterosexual couples wanting to shape the contours of their own relationships.

Marriage
a government regulated and approved legal status that two consenting adults attain by entering a contract with each other which confers rights, benefits, and obligations; a civil contract between a man and a woman or between two same-sex partners

Civil law
one of the two primary legal systems in the Western world, originating in the Roman Empire and influential in several parts of the world and a small number of states

Community property states
states in which a husband and wife hold property acquired during the marriage (exclusive of gifts and inheritances) in common, with each spouse entitled to a one-half interest in the property upon divorce

Married Women's Property Acts
state statutes that extended to women various property rights denied them under common law, including ownership and control of property

PARALEGAL PRACTICE TIP

The New York statute concerning the property of married women effective on February 17, 1909, can be found at *assembly.state.ny.us*. (Select New York State laws, DOM, Article 4.)

Paralegal Application 3.1

The Marriage Broker Business

Although "arranged" marriages are accepted in many cultures, under common law, marriage broker contracts, in which a person was paid to secure a spouse for another person, were considered void and unenforceable. Consider the extensive network of dating services doing business today in this country, many of which promise to locate lifetime partners for their customers and then feature the couples they introduced who subsequently married. Think also about the reality TV shows that involve contests in which the ultimate prize is a rose, a ring, and a spouse. Do you think such commercial ventures should be permitted? Should they be licensed or otherwise monitored and regulated? Read the opinion in *Ureneck v. Cui*, 59 Mass. App. Ct. 809, 798 N.E.2d 305 (2003). Do you agree with the decision in that case? Why? The opinion can be accessed at *www.pearsonhighered.com/careersresources/* in the companion website material related to Chapter 3 of this text under Cases.

Marriage—A Fundamental Right

In the landmark *Loving v. Virginia* decision rendered in 1967, the U.S. Supreme Court definitively established that marriage is a fundamental right under the due process clause of the Constitution:

> The freedom to marry has long been recognized as one of the vital personal rights essential to the orderly pursuit of happiness by free men. . . . Marriage is one of the "basic civil rights of man," fundamental to our very existence and survival.[6]

However, the right to marry is not absolute, and the states are permitted to regulate or restrict it to a reasonable extent to serve compelling governmental purposes. Examples of cases in which the courts have held that state law impermissibly restricted the right to marry include the *Loving* case referenced above in which the U.S. Supreme Court struck down Virginia's antimiscegenation law prohibiting marriage between white and "colored" persons. (See Case 3.1.) Examples of other statutes found to have impermissibly restricted the right to marry include the following:

- In *Zablocki v. Redhail*,[7] the U.S. Supreme Court struck down a Wisconsin statute requiring proof that child support payments due from a prior marriage were being met and prohibiting noncustodial parents behind in those payments from marrying. The Court reasoned that other collection methods were available to accomplish the intended purpose without encroaching on the fundamental right to marry.
- In *Salisbury v. List*,[8] a federal court struck down a blanket prohibition in Nevada against allowing prisoners with life sentences to marry except when certain conditions were met. Subsequently, in 1987, the U.S. Supreme Court held that a Missouri law denying confined persons the right to marry was unconstitutional. The Court observed that many important elements of marriage, such as expressions of emotional support, eligibility for receipt of government benefits, property rights, and the legitimation of children, remain after taking into account the limitations of prison life. The Court held that a prisoner should not be deprived of the right to marry unless exercise of the right would be inconsistent with the status of the prisoner or with legitimate penological objectives of the corrections system. The state's general interest in rehabilitation and security were deemed insufficient justifications for denial of the fundamental right to marry.[9]

- In *Obergefell v. Hodges*, 576 U.S. ____ (2015), the U.S. Supreme Court ruled 5-4 that gay couples have a fundamental right to marry and that the Fourteenth Amendment requires a state to license a marriage between two people of the same sex and to recognize such marriages when lawfully licensed and performed out-of-state. In a decision involving marriage bans in four states (Michigan, Kentucky, Ohio, and Tennessee), the majority opined that "[T]he marriage laws at issue are in essence unequal: Same-sex couples are denied benefits afforded opposite-sex couples and are barred from exercising a fundamental right. Especially against a long history of disapproval of their relationships, this denial works a grave and continuing harm, serving to disrespect and subordinate gays and lesbians." (J. Kennedy) The nature and implications of this decision are discussed at greater length later in this chapter.

CASE 3.1 *Loving v. Virginia*, 388 U.S. 1, 87 S. Ct. 1817, 18 L. Ed. 1010 (1967)

BACKGROUND

In this case, a couple, Mildred Jeter (an African-American) and Richard Loving (a white man), challenged Virginia's antimiscegenation law. Similar statutes were still in effect at the time in sixteen other states as well. In June 1958, the parties, residents of Virginia, traveled to the District of Columbia, where they married under the law of that jurisdiction. They subsequently returned to Virginia, where they were indicted and found guilty of violating the state's ban on interracial marriage. They were sentenced to one year in jail, a sentence that was suspended provided they left Virginia and did not return for twenty-five years. In his opinion, the trial judge stated:

> Almighty God created the races white, black, yellow, malay and red, and he placed them on separate continents. And but for the interference with his arrangement there would be no cause for such marriages. The fact that he separated the races shows that he did not intend for the races to mix.

The convictions were upheld on appeal. The couple relocated to the District of Columbia and filed a motion in the Virginia trial court to vacate their convictions on the ground that the statutes they violated were unconstitutional. The motion was denied and, on appeal, the Virginia Supreme Court of Appeals upheld the constitutionality of the statutes and the convictions. The appeal to the U.S. Supreme Court followed, and the statute was held to violate the Equal Protection Clause of the Fourteenth Amendment by restricting a person's choice of a spouse based on racial classifications. The Court also held that the right to marry is a fundamental right under the Due Process Clause.

FROM THE OPINION

This case presents a constitutional question never addressed by this Court: whether a statutory scheme adopted by the State of Virginia to prevent marriages between persons solely on the basis of racial classifications violates the Equal Protection and Due Process Clauses of the Fourteenth Amendment. . . .

The two statutes under which appellants were convicted and sentenced are. . . . § 2058 [and § 2059] of the Virginia Code:

> *"Leaving the state to evade law.* —If any white person and colored person shall go out of this State, for the purpose of being married, and with the

intention of returning, and be married out of it, and afterwards return to and reside in it, cohabiting as man and wife, they shall be punished as provided in sect. 2059. . . ."

"Punishment for marriage.—If any white person intermarry with a colored person, or any colored person intermarry with a white person, he shall be guilty of a felony and shall be punished by confinement in the penitentiary for not less than one nor more than five years."

. . . Penalties for miscegenation arose as an incident to slavery and have been common in Virginia since the colonial period. The present statutory scheme dates from the adoption of the Racial Integrity Act of 1924, passed during the period of extreme nativism which followed the end of the First World War. . . .

I. In upholding the constitutionality of these provisions . . . , the Supreme Court of Appeals of Virginia referred to its 1955 decision in *Naim v. Naim*, 197 Va. 80, 87 S. E. 2d 749. . . . In *Naim*, the state court concluded that the State's legitimate purposes were "to preserve the racial integrity of its citizens," and to prevent "the corruption of blood," "a mongrel breed of citizens," and "the obliteration of racial pride," obviously an endorsement of the doctrine of white supremacy. *Id.*, at 90, 87 S. E. 2d, at 756. The court also reasoned that marriage has traditionally been subject to state regulation without federal intervention, and, consequently, the regulation of marriage should be left to exclusive state control by the Tenth Amendment.

While the state court is no doubt correct in asserting that marriage is a social relation subject to the State's police power, . . . the State does not contend in its argument before this Court that its powers to regulate marriage are unlimited notwithstanding the commands of the Fourteenth Amendment. . . . [T]he State contends that, because its miscegenation statutes punish equally both the white and the Negro participants in an interracial marriage, these statutes, despite their reliance on racial classifications, do not constitute an invidious discrimination based on race. . . .

. . . the Equal Protection Clause requires the consideration of whether the classifications drawn by any statute constitute an arbitrary and invidious discrimination. The clear and central purpose of the Fourteenth Amendment was to eliminate all official state sources of invidious racial discrimination in the States. . . .

There can be no question but that Virginia's miscegenation statutes rest solely upon distinctions drawn according to race. . . . Over the years, this Court has consistently repudiated "distinctions between citizens solely because of their ancestry" as being "odious to a free people whose institutions are founded upon the doctrine of equality." *Hirabayashi v. United States*, 320 U.S. 81, 100 (1943). . . . [I]f they are ever to be upheld, they must be shown to be necessary to the accomplishment of some permissible state objective, independent of the racial discrimination which it was the object of the Fourteenth Amendment to eliminate. . . .

There is patently no legitimate overriding purpose independent of invidious racial discrimination which justifies this classification. The fact that Virginia prohibits only interracial marriages involving white persons demonstrates that the racial classifications must stand on their own justification, as measures designed to maintain White Supremacy. We have consistently denied the constitutionality of measures which restrict the rights of citizens on account of race. There can be no doubt that restricting the freedom to marry solely because of racial classifications violates the central meaning of the Equal Protection Clause.

PARALEGAL PRACTICE TIP

As of June 2015, Wisconsin had a statute which made it illegal for a same-sex couple residing in Wisconsin to travel out of state to marry and then return to continue living in Wisconsin. Couples who did so risked a fine of $10,000 and nine months in prison. (Wisc. Stats. Section 765(3)(1)(a)) If challenged today, it is unlikely such a statute would pass constitutional muster. In addition, post *Obergefell*, the couple would no longer need to leave Wisconsin in order to wed legally.

II. These statutes also deprive the Lovings of liberty without due process of law in violation of the Due Process Clause of the Fourteenth Amendment. The freedom to marry has long been recognized as one of the vital personal rights essential to orderly pursuit of happiness by free men.

Marriage is one of the "basic civil rights of man," fundamental to our very existence and survival. *Skinner v. Oklahoma*, 316 U.S. 535, 541 (1942). . . . To deny this fundamental freedom on so unsupportable a basis as the racial classifications embodied in these statutes, classifications so directly subversive of the principle of equality at the heart of the Fourteenth Amendment, is surely to deprive all the State's citizens of liberty without due process of law. The Fourteenth Amendment requires that the freedom of choice to marry not be restricted by invidious racial discriminations. Under our Constitution, the freedom to marry, or not marry, a person of another race resides with the individual and cannot be infringed by the State.

These convictions must be reversed.

SIDEBAR

Despite this ruling, the remnants of antimiscegenation statutes were still evident nearly twenty years later when the U.S. Supreme Court held in *Palmore v. Sidoti*[10] that a state cannot impose an indirect penalty on a person who marries another of a different race by depriving him or her of child custody based on race. The *Loving* case was referenced in many of the Constitutional challenges to state marriage laws alleging that they restricted access to marriage on the basis of sex as they formerly had done on the basis of race. The full opinion in *Loving* can be found at *http://www.law.cornell.edu*.

Paralegal **Application 3.2**

Is a Contract Enforceable if It Restricts an Individual's Right to Marry?

The facts

Rabbi Zaltman does not want his beloved daughter, Alexandra, to marry outside of the Jewish faith in which she has been raised. On the occasion of her graduation from college, he gives her a check for $500,000 on condition that, if she ever marries, she will marry only a Jewish man. She agrees, endorses the check, deposits the funds in her account, and spends the full amount over the next five years. At that time, she marries a Catholic man, Patrick Henry Purcell. Outraged, her father seeks to recover the $500,000.

Sidebar

Should the court enforce the terms of the agreement and require the return of the $500,000, or should it find the contract unenforceable because enforcement by the court would restrict the daughter's fundamental right to marry? Would it make any difference if the father had sought a promise that the daughter never marry? Not marry for a period of five years? Not marry until she completed law school? Should the courts as agents of the state become "entangled" in such disputes?

The law looks with disfavor on efforts to restrict the right to marry. A total prohibition against marriage is unlikely to be enforced by a court even if both parties initially agreed to the terms of the contract. However, a partial or limited restriction that serves a useful purpose may be enforceable. Is an interest in maintaining a particular cultural or religious tradition a sufficiently useful purpose? Explain your response.

Marriage Requirements

Although marriage is a contract between the parties, it is a contract regulated by the government. Having established that marriage is a fundamental right that cannot be restricted unreasonably by the states, what kinds of restrictions can and do the states legitimately impose? We cannot simply marry anyone wherever and whenever we please. Each of the states has established its own requirements that couples must satisfy in order to legally marry. Although there are variations, the requirements for a valid marriage are fairly standard state to state. There are basically two types: (1) requirements relating to legal capacity to marry and (2) technical requirements governing particular kinds of marriages. (See Exhibit 3.3 State Statutes—Marriage Requirements.) The choice-of-law rule traditionally applied with respect to interstate recognition of marriages provides that the validity of a marriage will be determined according to the law of the state in which it was entered.

REQUIREMENTS RELATING TO LEGAL CAPACITY TO MARRY

Historically, restrictions on legal capacity to marry have fallen into six main categories:

- Sex of the parties
- Age of the parties
- Marital status of the parties
- Degree of relationship between the parties by blood (consanguinity) and marriage (affinity)
- Mental capacity of each party
- Physical capacity of each party

A failure to comply with these restrictions may affect the validity of a marriage and is usually raised in the context of an annulment action.

Sex of the Parties

As of mid-June 2015, immediately prior to the U.S. Supreme Court's decision in *Obergefell* nationalizing the right of same-sex couples to marry, fourteen states still required that the parties to a marriage be of different sexes, male and female. This may appear to have been a reasonably straightforward requirement but in this era of advanced medical technology, it was not necessarily so. Several courts had to address (in annulment, custody, adoption, wrongful death, and probate cases) the issue of the sex of a transsexual individual who had successfully undergone sex reassignment surgery. In New Jersey, the state's highest court held that the "new" sex was the operative sex for determining marital status and legal rights.[11] Courts in other states (such as Texas) held that a person's sex at birth is controlling.[12]

Age of the Parties

At common law, the minimum age of consent for marriage was twelve for a female and fourteen for a male. Every state now establishes by statute an age of consent, the age at which parties may marry without parental consent, usually eighteen. Most all also identify an age of capacity under which a youth may not marry even

PARALEGAL PRACTICE TIP

At *www.law.cornell.edu* you can locate information about state marriage requirements and related links to state codes.

PARALEGAL PRACTICE TIP

American Indian tribes have the power to govern their members, and their marriage laws are not required to conform to the laws of the state where the tribe is located. For example, as of April 2015, at least ten tribes allowed same-sex marriages, some in states that had not yet enacted same-sex marriage laws.

PARALEGAL PRACTICE TIP

To see a form used by a minor to request the court's permission to marry (with parental consent), visit *www.vermontjudiciary.org.* Select Court Forms.

Emancipation
the point at which a child is considered an adult and granted adult rights; usually occurs at the age of majority or upon the occurrence of certain acts or events such as marriage or entering the armed services

Bigamy
the act of entering a subsequent marriage while a prior marriage of one or both of the parties is still in effect; in most states constitutes a criminal offense if committed knowingly; a ground for annulment and/or divorce in all states

Polygamy
the state of having more than one spouse at the same time

Void
invalid and of no legal effect

PARALEGAL PRACTICE TIP

It is estimated that there are at least 150,000 polygamists in the United States living on the margins of society. The Mormon Church repudiated the practice of polygamy in 1890, but periodic, high-profile news stories, such as the removal of more than 450 children from the Yearning for Zion compound in Texas in the spring of 2008, indicate it is still practiced by a number of Mormon fundamentalists. For more information on this topic, visit *www.religioustolerance.org.* See also Casey E. Faucon, *Marriage Outlaws: Regulating Polygamy in America,* 22 Duke J. Gender L. & Pol'y 1 (Fall 2014).

with parental consent. The basic rationale for this restriction is the assumption that individuals need to have attained at least some degree of maturity before they can appreciate the nature of marriage, understand the rights and responsibilities that flow from it, and be capable of bearing and raising children in a healthy and responsible family environment. There are, however, several common exceptions to the general rules:

- Youths within an age range such as between sixteen and eighteen may be permitted to marry if they have the consent of a parent or guardian and/or the court.
- Courts may waive the age requirement if the female is pregnant.
- If one or both of the parties is emancipated, the court may grant a request for waiver of the age requirement. **Emancipation** may be established in a number of ways and generally includes being self-supporting and no longer living with one's parents.

Even if a party marries while underage, he or she may ratify the marriage by remaining with the spouse in a marital relationship after attaining the statutory age of consent.

Marital Status of the Parties

Each of the parties must be "free" to marry in the sense that neither can be married to another individual still living at the time of the marriage. **Bigamy**, a crime in all states (usually a misdemeanor), is defined as entering a second marriage while a prior marriage is still valid. **Polygamy**, also a crime, refers to a situation in which one individual (usually a male) has multiple spouses at the same time.[13] Although still taboo under the law, prosecutions are rare. For example, after the television program *Sister Wives* debuted, police in Lehi, Utah threatened to prosecute Kody Brown and his four wives for bigamy, a third degree felony carrying a possible penalty of twenty years in prison for Brown and five years for each wife. Although no charges were eventually filed, in 2011 while living under a threat of prosecution, Brown filed a challenge to Utah's anti-bigamy law (Utah Code Ann. §76-7-101). In 2013, a U.S. District Court judge issued a ninety-one-page Memorandum Decision and Order (*Brown v. Buhman*, Case No. 2-11-cv-0652-CW) ruling that portions of the Utah law lumping together cohabitation and bigamy were unconstitutional under the First and Fourteenth Amendments. The court held that being "married" to one individual and cohabiting with additional persons does not constitute bigamy. Bigamy is limited to persons with multiple active marriage licenses. It should be noted, however, that only the legally married spouse is entitled to the rights and benefits of marriage.

Most states provide that bigamous and polygamous marriages are **void**, but if at least one party enters the marriage in good faith, the impediment is eventually removed (by death or divorce), and the parties continue to live together in a marital relationship, the marriage may be considered valid from the date the impediment was removed.

Degree of Relationship Between the Parties by Blood (Consanguinity) and Marriage (Affinity)

States establish, by statute, restrictions on the degrees of relationship that can exist by consanguinity and affinity in order for two persons to marry. Such regulations are based primarily on the state's interests in promoting family harmony, protecting children from sexual exploitation, and limiting the genetic transmission of negative recessive traits (such as hemophilia and congenital deafness). They are designed to be consistent with provisions of state criminal codes regarding crimes such as **incest**.

Consanguinity provisions specify impermissible blood relationships in marriage such as parent and child, sister and brother (of the whole or half-blood), and uncle and niece. Several states still prohibit the marriage of first cousins based on an assumption that such marriages result in genetic defects in children due to inbreeding. Rather than totally restricting the right of first cousins to marry, it has been suggested that this concern can be effectively addressed by providing genetic counseling for parties to such unions[14] or, as provided in some states, by permitting marriage only after the parties have passed their procreative years (e.g., both are over age sixty-five). The Uniform Marriage and Divorce Act permits first cousins, as well as individuals related to one another through adoption, to marry.

Affinity provisions establish impermissible unions based on relationships created by marriage rather than by blood, such as a wife and her father-in-law or a husband and his sister-in-law. Several states have eliminated restrictions based on affinity. Some states that have not eliminated them provide that the prohibitions are lifted when the person who created the prohibited relationship dies. There are also variations among the states with respect to the impact of relationships created by adoption or through stepparents.

Mental Capacity

Initially, the requirement that the parties have sufficient mental capacity to marry was based to some extent on a fear that mentally deficient individuals would marry, bear similarly limited children, and create financial and social burdens for society at large. Today, mental capacity most often becomes an issue in cases where a party is seriously ill, of advanced age, under guardianship, or under the influence of drugs or alcohol at the time of the marriage ceremony. It should be noted that even if a person lacks mental capacity a majority of the time, courts have held that he or she can contract a valid marriage in a "lucid interval."

Lack of sufficient mental capacity is described in the following excerpt from an opinion of a North Dakota court:

> While there has been a hesitancy on the part of the courts to judicially define the phrase "unsound mind," it is established that such [a] term has reference to the mental capacity of the parties at the very moment of inception of the marriage contract. Ordinarily, lack of mental capacity, which renders a party incapable of entering into a valid marriage contract, must be such that it deprives him of the ability to understand the objects of marriage, its ensuing duties and undertakings, its responsibilities and relationship. There is a general agreement of the authorities that the terms "unsound mind" and "lack of mental capacity" carry greater import than eccentricity or mere weakness of mind or dullness of intellect.[15]

Physical Capacity

Historically, the presence of "incurable diseases" acted as a bar to marriage in some states. In a small number of states (such as Nebraska[16]), applicants for a marriage license still must be free of syphilis, creating a particular dilemma for a clerk issuing licenses in a state (such as Ohio) where blood tests have been eliminated but the restriction remains in force.

Incest
sexual intercourse between two people who are too closely related for some purpose as defined by civil and criminal statutes; a term used in some states to describe prohibited degrees of consanguinity and affinity in the marriage context

Consanguinity
a blood relationship between individuals

PARALEGAL PRACTICE TIP

Visit *www.ncsl.org* to find a table (5/2010) on the status of state laws on the marriage of first cousins, which is banned in approximately half the states.

Affinity
relationship by marriage (i.e., the relationship a spouse has to the blood relatives of the other spouse)

PARALEGAL PRACTICE TIP

Some anti-incest taboos are based on broad cultural, political, and social rather than genetic concerns. For example, among the Navajo, incest has been based on membership in one of several major "clans," each potentially consisting of hundreds of people, resulting in a rule that a person must not be intimate with anyone in either the father's ("born for") clan or the mother's ("born to") clan.

PARALEGAL PRACTICE TIP

Consistent with their cultural traditions, Indian tribes often permit marriages to be validated in tribal ceremonies rather than through satisfaction of more formal state validation requirements. Such requirements can pose hardships for people living in remote areas who cannot easily comply with formalized procedural requirements or afford the expense of traditional weddings.

PARALEGAL PRACTICE TIP

To see the Massachusetts' provisions governing marriage requirements go to *https://malegislature.gov.* Chapter 207 Section 42 specifically addresses the effect of an irregularity in solemnization on the validity of a marriage.

PARALEGAL PRACTICE TIP

A copy of the Application for a Marriage License for the State of Hawaii can be found at *health.hawaii.gov* (online marriages, marriage license).

PARALEGAL PRACTICE TIP

Under common law, a wife automatically assumed her husband's surname upon marriage, a practice consistent with the doctrine of marital unity. This tradition has faded somewhat. States may address the topic by statute, case law, or procedural rules or practices. For example, in New York, the parties are given notice that their names will not automatically change upon marriage, and they are asked to indicate the names they intend to use after marriage on the application for a marriage license. Search for information about getting married in New York at *www.health.ny.gov.*

TECHNICAL REQUIREMENTS FOR A CEREMONIAL MARRIAGE

In addition to satisfying the legal requirements for capacity to marry, the states also establish fairly consistent technical requirements for ceremonial marriages. These requirements commonly include the following components:

- an application for a license
- a medical certificate or provision of information concerning certain diseases
- a license
- a waiting period
- a ceremony
- recording of the license/marriage certificate

When one or more of these "requirements" are not met, the marriage usually still will be upheld, given the strong public policy favoring the validity of marriages. Some states expressly provide by statute that if the marriage is lawful in all other respects and is consummated in the belief of either party that it is lawful, the marriage will be deemed valid notwithstanding any failure to satisfy a technical requirement. The penalty for noncompliance is usually in the form of a modest fine. However, falsifying public documents may carry a heavier penalty, including a period of incarceration.

Application for a License

The parties pay a fee and file a written application for a license to marry (sometimes called a notice of intention) usually in the county where they intend to marry. Both parties complete the application and sign it under pain and penalty of perjury. If one of the parties is seriously ill or in the armed services, a parent, guardian, or the other party may be permitted to provide the absent party's information. Customarily, the application requires the following:

- the parties' names and the names they intend to use once married
- their places of residence
- their birthplaces and ages (Documentation may be required, especially when there is reasonable doubt as to a party's stated age.)
- their parents' names
- the number of any prior marriages of each party and the means by which they were terminated or dissolved (Some states require documentation such as a death certificate or a divorce decree.)
- an affirmation by the parties that there are no legal impediments to the marriage such as a prohibited degree of blood relationship between the applicants

The parties may also be asked to provide any information required by the state's child support enforcement agency, including their respective Social Security numbers. Given the present-day emphasis on privacy rights and the potential for identity theft, the number is usually provided on a separate form for submission to the agency and does not become a part of the public record.

Medical Certificate

Historically, the requirement of physical examinations and/or blood tests was designed to determine whether either party had incurable tuberculosis or a sexually transmitted disease such as syphilis, or if the female had been vaccinated for rubella unless she was past her childbearing years. Today, many of the states have eliminated this requirement, largely because of advances in medical technology and an increased emphasis on privacy. However, some still require the filing of a medical certificate indicating that the parties have undergone certain laboratory tests within a specified period prior to filing their application. Others require that information regarding AIDS and other sexually transmitted diseases be provided to marriage applicants.

License

The license is issued by the statutorily designated authority, usually within a specified period after an application is filed.

Waiting Period

Some states establish a waiting period (commonly not more than three days) between application for and issuance of a license, although the period may be waived by statute under certain conditions or by the court on a Motion for a Marriage Without Delay. The general purpose of the waiting period is to promote deliberate consideration of the decision to marry.

Ceremony

A ceremony is performed, usually by a religious cleric, a Justice of the Peace, or another governmental official authorized by statute to perform such functions. During the ceremony, the parties express their intentions to marry usually in the presence of witnesses. Some states (such as Colorado and Texas) allow **proxy marriages**, in which the marriage ceremony takes place with one of the parties absent. A third-party agent is given authority to act on behalf of the missing person. Situations in which proxy marriages occur include those involving a party serving in the armed services and stationed overseas, a person who is incarcerated, or an American citizen who enters a proxy marriage with someone in another country, thereby qualifying that person for citizenship. Given the potential for abuse, proxy marriages generally are not favored.

Some states permit individuals who have been "ordained" online to perform ceremonies. Massachusetts has a procedure by which an individual may apply for a special one-day designation to perform/solemnize marriages. M.G.L. 207 § 39 provides that the governor may "designate any other person to solemnize a particular marriage on a particular date and in a particular city or town. . . ."

Recording of the License/Marriage Certificate

The individual who performs the ceremony records the license or certificate of marriage in the public office designated by statute within a certain time frame (usually from three to ten days). In some states, one document serves as the Notice of Intention to Marry and the Certificate of Marriage. See, for example, Vermont's Certificate of Marriage, which can be found at *www.vermontjudiciary.org*.

PARALEGAL PRACTICE TIP

To read the West Virginia statute on premarital testing, visit *www.legis.state.wv.us* (West Virginia Code 16-3C-2).

PARALEGAL PRACTICE TIP

To see a Motion for Marriage Without Delay, visit *www.mass.gov* and search for the form by title. On this site, you can also find a form used for requesting a one-day authorization to perform a marriage.

PARALEGAL PRACTICE TIP

Colorado's Solemnization Statute (Colo. Stat. 14-2-109) provides that, among other means, a marriage may be solemnized by the parties themselves, or in accordance with any mode recognized by any religious denomination or Indian tribe or nation.

Proxy marriage
a marriage ceremony in which a designated agent stands in for and acts on behalf of one of the absent parties (prohibited in most states)

PARALEGAL PRACTICE TIP

To read an excellent article on various kinds of marriage fraud, see Kerry Abrams, *Marriage Fraud*, 100 Calif. L. Rev. 1 (2012).

EXHIBIT 3.3 State Statutes—Marriage Requirements

Alabama	**Kentucky**	**North Dakota**
Ala. Code Tit. 30 Ch. 1	Ky. Rev. Stat. Tit. XXXV, Art. 402	N.D. Cent. Code Tit. 14, Ch. 14-03
Alaska	**Louisiana**	**Ohio**
Alaska Stat. Tit. 25, Ch. 5	La. Civil Code Bk. 1, Tit. 4, Ch. 1	Ohio Rev. Code Ann. Tit. 31, Ch. 3101
Arizona	**Maine**	**Oklahoma**
Ariz. Rev. Stat. Tit. 25 Ch. 1	Me. Rev. Stat. Ann. Tit. 19A, Pt. 2, Ch. 23	Okla. Stat. Tit. 43
Arkansas	**Maryland**	**Oregon**
Ark. Code: Tit. 9, Sub. 2, Ch. 11	Md. Fam. Law Code Tit. 2	Or. Stat. Tit. 11, Ch. 106
California	**Massachusetts**	**Pennsylvania**
Cal. Fam. Code, Div. 3	Mass. Gen. Laws Ch. 207	Pa. Cons. Stat. Tit. 23, Pt. II
Colorado	**Michigan**	**Rhode Island**
Colo. Rev. Stat. Tit. 14 Art. 2. Pt. 1	Mich. Comp. Laws Ch. 551	R.I. Gen. Laws Tit. 15, Ch. 1–3
Connecticut	**Minnesota**	**South Carolina**
Conn. Stat. Tit. 46b, Ch. 815e	Minn. Stat. Dom. Rel. Code, Ch. 517	S.C. Code Tit. 20, Ch. 1
Delaware	**Mississippi**	**South Dakota**
Del. Code Tit. 13, Ch. 1	Miss. Code Tit. 93, Ch. 1	S.D. Codified Laws Tit. 2 Ch. 25-1
District of Columbia	**Missouri**	**Tennessee**
D.C. Code Div. VIII, Tit. 46, Sub. 1, Ch. 4	Mo. Stat. Tit. 30, Ch. 451	Tenn. Code Tit. 36, Ch. 3
Florida	**Montana**	**Texas**
Fla. Stat. Ch. 741.01–741.212	Mont. Cod: Tit. 40, Ch. 1	Tex. Family Code Ann. Tit. 1 Ch. 1, 2
Georgia	**Nebraska**	**Utah**
Ga. Code Art. 19-3-1–19-3-68	Neb. Rev. Stat. Ch. 42, Art. 1	Utah Code Tit. 30, Ch. 1
Hawaii	**Nevada**	**Vermont**
Haw. Rev. Stat. Div. 3, Tit. 31, Ch. 572	Nev. Rev. Stat. Tit. 11, Ch. 122	Vt. Stat. Tit. 15 Ch. 1; Tit. 18, Part 6, Ch. 105
Idaho	**New Hampshire**	**Virginia**
Idaho Code Gen. Laws, Tit. 32, Ch. 2, 3, and 4	N.H. R.S.A. Tit. XLIII, Ch. 457	Va. Code Tit. 20 Ch. 2, 3
Illinois	**New Jersey**	**Washington**
Ill. Comp. Stat. Ch. 750 ILCS, 5, Parts II and III	N.J. Rev. Stat. Tit. 37, Ch. 1	Wash. Rev. Code Tit. 26, Ch. 26.04
Indiana	**New Mexico**	**West Virginia**
Ind. Code Tit. 31, Art. 11, Ch. 1–6	N.M. Stat. Ch. 40, Art. 1	W. Va. Code Ch. 48 Art. 2
Iowa	**New York**	**Wisconsin**
Iowa Code Tit. XV, Sub. 1, Ch. 595	N.Y. Cons. Laws Dom. Rel. Law Art. 2, and 3	Wis. Stat. The Family Ch. 765
Kansas	**North Carolina**	**Wyoming**
Kan. Stat. Ch. 23, Art. 25	N.C. Gen. Stat. Ch. 51	Wyo. Stat. Tit. 20, Ch. 1, Art. 1

Requirements for a Common Law Marriage

At the end of the nineteenth century, the U.S. Supreme Court ruled that **common law marriages** are valid unless prohibited by a state.[17] At that time, they were recognized in most states. However, because of the potential for abuse (especially when the existence of a common law marriage is claimed after the death of a party) and the argument that they promote immoral behavior, such marriages are not usually favored even in jurisdictions where they are authorized. However, abuse should not be presumed, given that people opt for common law marriage for a variety of legitimate reasons including, but not limited to, convenience, lack of expense, and a desire to minimize involvement with either the government or religious bodies. Common law marriages also provide a vehicle for protecting economically, socially, and educationally vulnerable women in particular, enabling them to legitimatize their children and gain access to both marital rights and vital social services.

In states where they are permitted, the requirements for a valid common law marriage are customarily set forth in statutes and/or case law. The requirements vary slightly from state to state but typically include the following:

- The parties must have the legal capacity to marry.
- They must intend and simultaneously agree to be married. (Some states require that the agreement be expressed; others will infer an agreement from the conduct of the parties.)
- They must cohabit (although consummation may not be required and cohabitation alone does not suffice). See, e.g., *Dyess v. Dyess*, 94 So. 3d 384 (Ala. Civ. App. 2012).
- They must hold themselves out to the public as husband and wife.

The popular belief that the parties to a common law marriage must cohabit for a specific length of time is largely a misconception. However, the New Hampshire statute does include a time requirement. (See Exhibit 3.4.) In all states where common law marriage is permitted, with the exception of New Hampshire, once a common law marriage is established, it carries with it the same rights, benefits, and duties as a traditional ceremonial marriage, and children born to the parties are legitimate. It also must be formally dissolved by divorce if the relationship terminates and either or both of the parties wish to marry another.

EXHIBIT 3.4 New Hampshire Statute Concerning Cohabitation: New Hampshire Revised Statutes Annotated 457:39

FROM THE STATUTE

457:39 Cohabitation, etc.—Persons cohabiting and acknowledging each other as husband and wife, and generally reputed to be such, for the period of three years, and until the decease of one of them, shall thereafter be deemed to have been legally married.

Note that the New Hampshire Cohabitation Statute is unusual in two respects:

1. It includes a requirement that the parties cohabit for at least three years.
2. It is applicable only in the context of inheritance or death benefit claims.

Common law marriage
a form of marriage created by the conduct of the parties rather than in a formal ceremony; usually requires capacity and intent to marry, cohabitation, and a holding out to the public as husband and wife; recognized in a limited number of states

PARALEGAL PRACTICE TIP

Although generally considered a dying doctrine, Utah enacted its common law marriage statute in 1987 (Utah Stat. § 30-1-4.5) in an effort to reduce welfare costs generated by women claiming to be single for welfare eligibility purposes but living in "polygamous marriages." The law provides that couples who cohabit but do not formally marry will be considered married if their relationships fulfill the requirements of a common law marriage.

PARALEGAL PRACTICE TIP

Visit *www.ncsl.org*, the site of the National Conference of State Legislatures, as a starting point for researching the status of common law marriage in the United States. The Iowa common law marriage statute can be found at *www.legis.iowa.gov*. To see a form used in Utah to seek judicial recognition of a common law marriage, visit *www.utcourts.gov*.

PARALEGAL PRACTICE TIP

Is it possible to enter a common law marriage by accident? Occasionally, a party will claim he or she entered a common law marriage because the couple annually vacationed in a state that permits common law marriage and in that state held themselves out as married. See, e.g., *Collier v. Milford*, 537 A.2d 474 (Conn. 1988).

Most states will recognize a common law marriage that is valid in the state where it was entered. When the existence of a common law marriage is asserted, it is important to check states that presently permit such marriages and under what circumstances. It is also important to check whether the alleged marriage was entered in a state that no longer recognizes common law marriage but formerly did and did so at a time when the parties resided in or spent a considerable period of time in that state. See Exhibit 3.5 and Paralegal Applications 3.3 and 3.4.

EXHIBIT 3.5 Common Law Marriage States

Alabama	Montana
Alaska until 1/1/64	Nebraska until 1923
California until 1895	Nevada until 3/29/43
Colorado (age restriction: must be over 18)	New Hampshire (for probate purposes only)
District of Columbia	New Jersey until 1/12/39
Florida until 1/1/68	New York until 4/29/33
Georgia until 1/1/97	Ohio until 10/10/91
Idaho until 1/1/96	Oklahoma until 1998 (law is unclear)
Illinois until 6/30/1905	Pennsylvania until 2005
Indiana until 1/1/58	Rhode Island
Iowa	South Carolina
Kansas (age restriction: must be over 18)	South Dakota until 7/1/59
Michigan until 1/1/57	Texas (called: informal marriages)
Minnesota until 4/26/41	Utah (enacted 1987; Condition: if validated by a court or administrative order in an action to recognize relationship as marriage)
Mississippi until 4/5/56	Wisconsin until 1913
Missouri until 3/3/21	

PARALEGAL PRACTICE TIP

There are those who argue that the common law marriage doctrine should be revived because it protects the interests of women, especially poor women and women of color. A greater percentage of these segments of the population do not marry but live with partners for extended periods and/or have children. When their relationships break up or their partners and breadwinners die, they are left without benefits and protections available to common law spouses. Courts increasingly try to find ways of providing relief in such cases.[18]

Paralegal Application 3.3

You Be the Judge

The parties in this case, Bob and Diane, had been ceremonially married and divorced from each other twice. The first marriage lasted from 1980 to 1989 when Bob began serving a prison sentence for "going armed with intent." After his release in 1990, the couple bought a home together in Norwalk, Iowa and began living together. They married again in 1995 and divorced again for the second time in 1999. Diane received a $70,000 property settlement in that action for her share of the Norwalk home. In 2001, when his then girlfriend was unable to go with him on a vacation to St. Lucia, Bob asked Diane to join him. She went and after the trip they continued seeing each other. Diane began spending significant time at the Norwalk property but kept most of her personal belongings at her parents' home.

In 2003, Bob was implicated in an illegal gambling and bookmaking ring. He pleaded guilty and forfeited $475,000 in cash and other assets as part of a plea agreement. Shortly thereafter, he suffered his first heart attack and Diane slowly began to move back into the Norwalk home with him. Diane alleges that her return in 2003 marked the beginning of a common law marriage. Bob claims she didn't move back in full-time until 2005 when he had a stent implanted in his heart. He testified: "My health was an issue. She was living in her mom's basement; that was an issue. She didn't have a job, and she didn't even have a checking account. So it kind of worked out for both of us that when I was traveling she could be at the house and I didn't have to worry about anyone breaking in."

The couple separated for a third time in 2010 and Diane filed a petition to dissolve a common law marriage. Bob was ordered to pay $1,300 a month in temporary alimony. The court granted his motion to bifurcate the issues of dissolution and common law marriage. The district court found the existence of a common law marriage reasoning that after 2003 the parties had returned to their usual married routine with Diane staying home gardening and canning and Bob gambling and bookmaking for a living. They maintained joint accounts but also conducted certain financial dealings independently of one another. They shared a cell phone plan and a car insurance policy. Diane testified that Bob's daughter introduced her as her stepmother and instructed her children to call her "Grandma." In Bob's mother's obituary, Diane was identified as a daughter-in-law. They agreed that Diane slept in the master bedroom and Bob on the couch but disagreed about whether or not they had sexual relations. She claimed they did. Bob said it was more of a friendship. He testified they never discussed reentering a marriage and that toward the end of their relationship he told her he never intended to get married again. She maintains she demonstrated her intent to be married again by returning her wedding ring to her left hand. He had not worn his ring since 1998.

Sidebar

To establish a common law marriage under Iowa law, Diane had the burden of proving three elements by a preponderance of the evidence: (1) a present intent and agreement by both parties to be married; (2) continuous cohabitation; and (3) public declaration that they were husband and wife. Do you think Diane met her burden? Why? To see whether the Iowa Court of Appeals agreed, locate and read the opinion in *Derryberry v. Derryberry*, 853 N.W.2d 301 (Iowa App. 2014). (Published in table format.)

Paralegal **Application 3.4**

Information Gathering in a Common Law Marriage Case

In a case in which a client is alleging the existence of a common law marriage, a paralegal may be asked to gather information from the client and other sources regarding the following:

- the date and circumstances under which the parties met
- any children born to or adopted by the parties
- the parties' decision to live together—when and how it was made
- details regarding when, where, and for how long the parties have lived together
- details regarding travel by the parties, if any, to other states that recognize common law marriage
- the nature of the parties' relationship, including whether or not they engaged in sexual relations
- details regarding the parties' financial arrangements, including payment of expenses, maintenance of bank and credit card accounts, etc.
- the parties' history with respect to payment of taxes—were joint returns filed?
- the existence and location of documents pertaining to any property, real or personal, owned by the parties, individually or jointly
- the existence and location of documents executed by the parties, such as wills, health care proxies, powers of attorney, trusts, insurance policies, etc.
- details regarding any oral or written agreement between the parties regarding marriage, including why they did not enter a traditional ceremonial marriage
- details regarding the parties' social life and how they have represented themselves to others
- names and contact information for individuals familiar with the parties as friends, relatives, and business associates who regard and treat them as husband and wife
- the existence and location of other evidence of the parties' intent, such as inscriptions on photographs, engraving on jewelry, inclusion of the parties' names and marital relationship in family trees and bibles, etc.

PARALEGAL PRACTICE TIP

For an authoritative but complex summary of 1,138 of the federal statutory provisions in the *United States Code* in which marital status is a factor in determining or receiving benefits, rights, and privileges, see a report entitled *Categories of Laws Involving Marital Status* (commonly referred to as "Rights and Responsibilities of Marriages in the United States") an enclosure in a letter found at *www.gao.gov*.

Intestate
dying without leaving a valid will

Laws of descent and distribution
the laws governing inheritance of property by heirs when a decedent dies without leaving a valid will. Usually, a surviving spouse will inherit the entire estate or will receive half of it, with the other half being distributed to any surviving children in equal shares. If the spouse dies testate (with a will) and the will largely disinherits or fails to make adequate provisions for the surviving spouse, some states allow him or her to "waive the will" and claim a "forced share" of the estate as set by statute.

PARALEGAL PRACTICE TIP

Attorneys often advise clients to protect their estates while a divorce is pending by executing wills that dispose of their property as they wish. If they fail to do so and die without a will before the divorce is final, their property will be distributed according to the applicable state's law of descent and distribution.

Tort
a civil wrong (other than breach of contract) for which a court provides a remedy, usually in the form of money damages; the wrong must involve harm resulting from breach of a duty owed to another

Marriage as a Source of Rights, Benefits, and Obligations

According to an audit report of the U.S. General Accounting Office, under federal and state law, there are more than 1,000 rights and duties that flow from a valid marriage, either ceremonial or common law. Some of the most important of these include the following:

- Each spouse is entitled to receive support from and has a duty to provide support to the other spouse.
- Absent a valid and enforceable premarital agreement to the contrary and subject to the statutory provisions of state law, parties to a valid marriage acquire an interest in all "marital property" acquired by the spouses during their marriage (generally exclusive of property received by a spouse through an inheritance or gift from a third party). A spouse may seek division of the marital property upon divorce.
- When the marital property is divided, one spouse may receive payment of a portion of the other spouse's pension. Given an exception to the general federal policy prohibiting assignment of retirement interests, a Qualified Domestic Relations Order (QDRO) issued by the court may make a spouse an alternate payee under an employee spouse's pension plan.
- In some states, spouses may hold title to real property as tenants by the entirety, a form of ownership available only to spouses, which grants each spouse a right in the whole property. Generally, if title to the marital residence is held in this form, the property will not be able to be seized by the creditors of a debtor spouse.
- Absent an enforceable premarital agreement, each spouse is entitled to inherit property from his or her spouse. If the spouse dies **intestate**, the surviving spouse will inherit property to the extent provided in the **laws of descent and distribution** in force in the state where the deceased spouse was domiciled at death. Essentially, these laws specify that the estate of the deceased will be distributed among his or her closest relatives (spouse, children, parents, siblings, etc.).
- Provided any necessary conditions are satisfied (such as age or a minimum length of marriage), spouses are entitled to receive certain governmental benefits, such as Social Security administration and veterans' benefits after the death of a wage earner or veteran.
- A divorced, separated, or surviving spouse may be entitled to continued employer-provided health insurance coverage for a specific period, generally up to thirty-six months under the Consolidated Omnibus Budget Reconciliation Act of 1985 (COBRA).
- In **tort** law, the existence of a valid marriage still is a threshold requirement in most states to recover for loss of consortium resulting from the negligent conduct of another. **Consortium** commonly includes a loss of services, companionship, support, guidance, comfort, affection, and, in the case of spouses, a loss of sexual relations. For example, if an individual is paralyzed as a result of the negligence of a drunk driver, then his or her spouse may seek to recover for loss of consortium.
- Surviving spouses are also eligible to file claims for the wrongful death of their marital partners. For example, if Carlos dies as a result of an explosion caused by the installation of a faulty furnace, his wife may file a wrongful

death action against the installer and the manufacturer of the furnace. As callous as it may sound, damages are measured by the monetary value of the decedent to the surviving spouse in terms of loss of reasonably expected income as well as loss of consortium.

- Marriage customarily confers the ability to make medical decisions on behalf of a spouse in times of crisis or incapacity.
- A nonresident alien who marries a U.S. citizen obtains permanent resident status (if no deportation proceeding is pending), although the marriage will be treated as conditional until two years after it takes place.[19]
- A spouse generally cannot be criminally charged as an accessory-after-the-fact for harboring or concealing his or her spouse after the latter has committed a felony.
- The law values the important functions served by confidential communications in a variety of contexts (attorney–client, priest–penitent, doctor–patient), and the relationship between husband and wife is one of those contexts. For example, the **marital communications privilege** prohibits compelled disclosure of statements made by spouses to each other within the privacy of the marital relationship. It does not apply to actions the spouse may have seen or to written communications. It also does not apply in civil actions for divorce, separation, custody, spousal or child support, or in criminal actions for nonsupport, incest, or abuse.

Consortium
companionship, affection, and, in the case of spouses, sexual relations, that one receives from another based on existence of a legal relationship (e.g., husband–wife, parent–child)

Marital communications privilege
the privilege that allows a spouse to refuse to testify about confidential communications between spouses during their marriage; does not apply in certain contexts, such as cases involving child custody and/or abuse

Expansion of the Relationship Menu

Every state has laws regarding the relationships formed by its people and particularly for relationships between intimate partners seeking to make long-term commitments. Over the past three decades, many states have broadened the scope of the relationships they recognize by adding new statuses to their "relationship menu." Each has its own rules for entry and exit, and each confers a variety of rights and benefits as well as obligations. Most were initially designed to meet the needs of same-sex couples formerly denied access to marriage. When debating enactment of its domestic partnership law in 2007, legislators in Oregon expressed the rationale for extending benefits to same-sex couples in these words:

> Many gay and lesbian Oregonians have formed lasting, committed, caring and faithful relationships with individuals of the same sex, despite long-standing social and economic discrimination. These couples live together, participate in their communities together and often raise children and care for family members together, just as do couples who are married under Oregon law. Without the ability to obtain some form of legal status for their relationships, same-sex couples face numerous obstacles and hardships in attempting to secure rights, benefits and responsibilities for themselves and their children. Many of the rights, benefits and responsibilities that the families of married couples take for granted cannot be obtained in any way other than through state recognition of committed same-sex relationships. This state has a strong interest in promoting stable and lasting families, including the families of same-sex couples and their children. All Oregon families should be provided with the opportunity to obtain necessary legal protections and status and the ability to achieve their fullest potential.[21]

PARALEGAL PRACTICE TIP

The U.S. Supreme Court has also recognized a husband-wife testimonial privilege permitting one spouse to refuse to testify against his or her spouse in criminal cases. However, the witness spouse may choose to waive the privilege.

PARALEGAL PRACTICE TIP

There are limitations on the extent to which a spouse may use private surveillance to "spy on" the other spouse while the parties are living separate and apart and getting a divorce. A client may need to be cautioned by counsel regarding any federal or state prohibition against electronically recording phone conversations with his or her spouse while a divorce action is pending.[20]

PARALEGAL PRACTICE TIP

Domestic partnerships and civil unions are important vehicles for recognition of nonmarital relationships on the international scene as well as in the United States, with the trend being most apparent in Europe. Beginning with Denmark in 1989, civil unions, under one name or another, were established in many countries, including, but not limited to, Israel, Norway, Sweden, France, Germany, Portugal, Finland, New Zealand, Switzerland, and the United Kingdom. By January 2007, Belgium, Canada, the Netherlands, Spain, and South Africa permitted same-sex marriage. Ireland began allowing same-sex marriages in 2015.

Although a comprehensive, current, and authoritative view of the status of same-sex marriage, civil union, and domestic partnership rights and debates around the world does not exist, the website of the International Lesbian and Gay Association, *www.ilga-europe. org*, publishes a country-by-country status report on the European countries. A useful reference for information on the various states is *www.ncsl.org*, the National Conference of State Legislatures website. The online encyclopedia *www.wikipedia.org* provides both historical and current information along with valuable links to many additional sources, including federal and state statutes. Keep in mind that online resources are useful starting points, but information should be verified before use.

PARALEGAL PRACTICE TIP

To view a Petition for Adult Adoption, go to *www.vermontjudiciary.org*.

Some of the "new" relationships serve the purposes of heterosexual couples as well—couples who want to make a commitment but not marry for a variety of reasons. The most common reasons include religious beliefs, a desire to keep their individual finances separate, and the need to retain economic benefits flowing from a prior relationship which would be forfeited upon marriage (spousal support, survivor benefits, etc.).

The nonmarital relationships recognized in the United States in the past twenty to thirty years have run along a continuum from cohabitation to marriage. Labels abound, definitions overlap, and each state's model has its own advantages and limitations. In Chapter 2 we discussed cohabitation, sometimes referred to as the umbrella under which all nonmarital relationships fall. But cohabitation, standing alone, is not a legally recognized status and affords little protection unless formalized in an enforceable cohabitation agreement. Four additional options that have emerged in what sometimes has seemed like a relationship laboratory experiment are: adult adoption, functional family status, domestic partnerships (sometimes called meretricious or reciprocal beneficiary relationships), and civil unions. Because there are no fixed definitions of these relationships that are consistent from state to state or country to country, the definitions provided in this chapter are generic. It is also impossible to provide a set list of benefits and obligations that flow from any status as they also vary from state to state and from time to time.

ADULT ADOPTION

Adult adoption can sometimes provide a means of achieving a recognizable family status. However, it is permitted in only a small number of states and is rarely used. With the recognition of same-sex marriage on a national scale, it is likely to be used even less often. From the parties' perspective, it is a desirable option in that it creates a relationship that brings with it a full array of family benefits. However, it is limited in that it generally cannot be dissolved if the parties' relationship later terminates. From the perspective of the courts, it is often viewed as distorting the intended purpose of adoption, the creation of a parent–child relationship.[22]

FUNCTIONAL FAMILY STATUS

Some courts extend at least limited rights to nonmarital partners in certain circumstances by applying a functional family approach that focuses on the "reality of family life"[23] and the nature of the partners' relationship rather than on definitions of family limited to persons related by blood, marriage, or adoption. Concentrating on the intimacy and strength of the bond between the parties, courts consider factors such as the following:

- how long the couple has lived together
- whether or not the relationship is exclusive
- the degree of the couple's emotional commitment
- the extent to which their finances are commingled
- how committed each of the partners is to supporting the other economically
- the manner in which the parties have conducted themselves in their daily lives (roles, sharing of household responsibilities, etc.)
- how they have represented themselves to the outside world (See Paralegal Application 3.5.)

Paralegal **Application 3.5**

Would You Evict?

Fact pattern

Miguel and Leslie were same-sex partners who lived together in a rent-controlled apartment for more than a decade until Leslie died. Leslie was the tenant of record, and after his death, the landlord tried to evict Miguel, claiming that he had no right to occupy the apartment, given the applicable rent-control statute. The statute provided that a landlord could not evict a "surviving spouse of the deceased tenant or some other member of the deceased tenant's family who has been living with the tenant of record." The landlord claimed Miguel was neither Leslie's spouse nor a member of his family. Miguel claimed that the interpretation and application of the statute should not be restricted by rigid legal distinctions based solely on a definition of family as individuals related by blood, marriage, or adoption. Rather, the definition of "family" should be extended to include two lifetime partners whose relationship is long term and characterized by an emotional and financial commitment and interdependence. Miguel and Leslie had lived together for more than ten years and were regarded by each other and their friends as spouses. They had attended family and other functions as a couple. Miguel considered the apartment his home, used the address on his driver's license and passport, and received his mail there. The couple had shared all household obligations and maintained joint bank and credit card accounts. Leslie had also granted Miguel power of attorney so that he could make necessary medical, financial, and personal decisions for him during his illness.

Sidebar

How do you think this case should be decided and why? What is the purpose of such laws? Spouses would automatically have qualified to remain in the apartment. Is it fair to require nonmarital partners to prove the nature and quality of their relationship in order to be protected by the rent-control law? To see how New York's highest court decided this case, read the opinion in *Braschi v. Stahl Associates Co.*, 74 N.Y.2d 201, 543 N.E.2d 49, 544 N.Y.S.2d 784 (1989). The *Braschi* opinion is available at *www.pearsonhighered.com/careersresources/* in the companion website for this text in the material related to Chapter 3 under Cases.

The paralegal should keep in mind that the same term may mean different things in different jurisdictions, at different times, and in different contexts. For example, traditionally the adjective "meretricious" has had a negative connotation and was associated primarily with illicit sexual conduct. However, in cases somewhat similar to *Braschi*, the state of Washington has on occasion looked beyond the traditional meaning of the word and used the phrase "meretricious relationship" in case law to refer to a "stable, marital-like relationship, where both parties cohabit with knowledge that a lawful marriage between them does not exist." Factors the courts have considered in determining whether or not a meretricious relationship exists have included, but not been limited to: ". . . continuous cohabitation, duration of the relationship, purpose of the relationship, pooling of resources and services for joint projects, and the intent of the parties." Once a meretricious relationship was established, a trial court could evaluate the interest each party had in the property acquired during the relationship and make an equitable distribution of that property. Although a meretricious relationship was not considered the same as a marriage, the courts focused on property that would have been community property had the parties been married. See, e.g., *In re Marriage of Lindsay*, 101 Wash.2d 299 at 304–5; 678 P.2d 328 (1984). See also *Connell v. Francisco*, 127 Wash.2d 339, 898 P.2d 831 (Wash. 1995).

DOMESTIC PARTNERSHIPS

The American Law Institute (ALI) has defined domestic partners as "two persons of the same or opposite sex, not married to one another, who for a significant

Domestic partnership
a status granted to an unmarried couple who live together and receive a variety of economic and noneconomic benefits customarily granted to spouses

PARALEGAL PRACTICE TIP

In some situations, the recognition of rights for same-sex partners led to challenges by heterosexual partners whose rights were less protected. For example, in *Irizarry v. Chicago Board of Education*, 251 F.3d 604 (U.S. App. 2001), a heterosexual woman who had been living with her opposite-sex partner for over twenty years raised an unsuccessful equal protection challenge to the Chicago Board of Education's policy of extending "spousal health benefits" to domestic partners, but only if the domestic partner was of the same sex as the employee.

PARALEGAL PRACTICE TIP

Extensive information about domestic partnerships in California, including forms for declaring and terminating a partnership, can be found at *www.sos.ca.gov*. To see the Nevada statute listing the rights and duties of domestic partners in that state visit *www.leg.state.nv.us/law1.cfm*. For information and forms related to declaring and terminating a domestic partnership in Wisconsin, visit *www.wilawlibrary.gov/topics/familylaw/domesticpartner.php*. The site also provides information about the benefits that flow from a domestic partnership in Wisconsin and a "Domestic Partnership Protections Reference Guide."

period of time share a primary residence and a life together. . . ."[24] According to the ALI, factors indicating the existence of a domestic partnership include, among others, oral statements, commingled finances, economic dependency, specialized roles, naming beneficiaries, emotional and sexual intimacy, community reputation, commitment or attempted marriage ceremony, common household, and joint procreation, childrearing, or adoption.

A **domestic partnership** is a status granted to an unmarried couple who live together and receive a variety of economic and noneconomic benefits customarily granted to spouses under state but not federal law. Some states have referred to domestic partnerships as reciprocal or designated beneficiary relationships. Whatever its title, the status is granted and regulated by the state. It may be available to heterosexual couples but in most instances has been limited to same-sex couples. Hawaii was the first state to offer a form of domestic partnership status to its employees in 1997 and was followed by California, Colorado, Maine, Maryland, Nevada, Oregon, Washington, and Wisconsin. Some, including Colorado, New Jersey, and Washington, still authorize domestic partnerships in limited circumstances. In addition to the states, several smaller governmental units, such as counties, cities, and municipalities, have also conferred limited domestic partnership benefits on employees but not a comprehensive legal status.[25] Many private companies and educational institutions also afford a variety of employee benefits to domestic partners under certain conditions.

The content of domestic partnership statutes, including the nature of benefits obtained, has not been uniform or constant. For example, Colorado's designated beneficiary agreement law covers more categories of relationships than other domestic partnership laws and allows the partners to select from among several options only those rights and benefits they choose to assign (Colorado Revised Statutes Section 1, Title 15, Article 22). Washington state's law has changed several times over the years. Since the enactment of its same-sex marriage law, domestic partnerships are only available to same- and different-sex couples over age sixty-two, the age at which many people choose to retire and become eligible to collect Social Security and pension benefits (Washington Revised Code §26.60.030). Although the benefits of domestic partnerships are generally less extensive than those of civil unions, California's law was expansive and afforded domestic partners the same rights, protections, benefits, and obligations as were granted to and imposed on spouses.

To become domestic partners, the couple usually must qualify for and register their relationship with the appropriate state agency. Typical requirements for qualification include the following:

- The parties are at least age eighteen.
- Each partner is unmarried and is not a party to another domestic partnership or a civil union.
- Their relationship is exclusive.
- They share a residence.
- They agree to be jointly responsible for each other's basic living expenses.
- They are not related in a way that would prevent them from legally marrying under applicable state law.
- They agree that if their relationship ends, they will file a certificate of dissolution.

Each state that authorizes the creation of domestic partnerships also establishes the means by which they can be terminated. Typically, termination is accomplished either by filing a form with the appropriate governmental office or by filing a termination action in the appropriate court. However, procedures vary. Washington state repealed its earlier simplified termination procedure in 2009 and now domestic partners must file for termination under the state's divorce statutes.

CIVIL UNIONS

In contrast to most domestic partnership laws, **civil unions** were essentially designed to afford same-sex partners the same benefits, protections, and responsibilities that married spouses had under state but not federal law. The dissolution of a civil union parallels dissolution of a marriage and the same forms generally are utilized. In order to be united in a civil union, the partners typically must meet the following requirements:

- Neither may be a party to another civil union, marriage, or domestic partnership/ reciprocal beneficiary relationship.
- Both parties must be of the same sex.
- The parties may not be close family members.
- Both must be at least eighteen years of age.
- Both must be mentally competent.
- Neither party may be under a guardianship unless the guardian consents in writing.

Vermont was the first state to enact civil unions in 2000. In 1999, the Vermont Supreme Court ruled in *Baker v. State*[26] that same-sex couples were entitled under Chapter 1, Article 7 of the Vermont State Constitution to the same benefits and protections afforded under Vermont law to heterosexual married couples. The ruling did not require the issuance of marriage licenses but rather ordered the legislature to create an "equivalent statutory alternative" that would afford essentially the same benefits to same-sex couples as those extended to married couples under Vermont law. After extensive and heated debate, the legislature finally passed H.B. 847, which went into effect on July 1, 2000.

Following Vermont's lead, civil unions were introduced in Connecticut, Delaware, Hawaii, Illinois, New Hampshire, New Jersey, and Rhode Island. Only Hawaii and Illinois still permit them. They are no longer authorized in the other states and existing civil unions generally have been converted to marriages by operation of law. See Paralegal Application 3.6.

Civil union
a formal legal status that provides a same-sex couple with the rights, benefits, protections, and responsibilities that a married heterosexual couple has under state law

PARALEGAL PRACTICE TIP

For information about entering a marriage or a civil union in Hawaii (as of 2013), go to *health.hawaii.gov.* Similar to legislation in Hawaii, Vermont's civil union law contained a "reciprocal beneficiaries" provision affording benefits to non-same-sex couples unable to marry.

PARALEGAL PRACTICE TIP

States that have recognized domestic partnerships and civil unions may afford state tax benefits to parties in such relationships. However, as of June 2015, federal tax law does not afford the same benefits to nonmarital families as it does to married persons. Parties in such relationships must be aware of how they will be treated under federal tax law. For example, under federal tax law, the amount an employer contributes for a domestic partner's health insurance coverage is includable in the employee's taxable income unless the partner qualifies as a dependent of the employee under the federal tax code.

Paralegal **Application 3.6**

Who Is Right?

When working with a client who has entered one or more kinds of relationships in the past, it is important to research what those relationships are, when and where they were entered, and whether or not they have been dissolved/terminated by the parties or by operation of law. Keep in mind that several states have granted different statuses to same-sex partners at different points in time. For example, New Jersey permitted domestic partnerships before enacting civil union and then same-sex marriage laws.

Consider the following fact pattern which illustrates the need to trace relationship histories and the laws that govern them:

In December 2008, Debbie and Donna entered a civil union in Sunapee, New Hampshire. They lived together in that community until Donna became involved with another woman in 2015 and moved out of the home the couple had purchased and lived in for six years. Donna now says she wants a divorce and Debbie says they don't need one because they were never married.

(Continued)

New Hampshire established civil unions in January 2008. In 2009, the governor of the state signed into law a same-sex marriage bill that took effect on January 1, 2010 (RSA 457). RSA 457:46 of that legislation provided that civil unions would be converted to marriages by operation of law on January 1, 2011 unless dissolved, annulled, or converted to marriage before that date. Debbie and Donna never took steps prior to January 1, 2011 to terminate their relationship or convert it to a marriage. Is Donna or Debbie correct about the need for a divorce?

The Road to Marriage Equality

THE CHALLENGE

The most significant addition to the relationship menu has been the gradual emergence of same-sex marriage and the demand among gays and lesbians for marriage equality throughout the United States. Reception has been mixed with powerful strongholds as well as deep pockets of resistance across the nation. As one commentator has phrased it, "A battle for the hearts and minds of the American people is being waged and the battleground is the institution of public marriage."[27] Even after the *Obergefell* decision the public debate wages on with some still calling for a Constitutional Amendment defining marriage as the union of a man and a woman.

More than any other family law issue, the reconceptualization of marriage to include same-sex spouses illustrates that changes in the law do not occur in a vacuum. They are influenced by social, religious, economic, and political forces. They encounter catalysts and roadblocks along the way. They are driven by public opinion, voter initiatives, legislation, and judicial decisions. They are seldom unanimously welcomed in a nation that thrives on diversity, debate, and individual freedom. Some readers of this text will have been aware of the march toward marriage equality from the outset, some only in more recent years. Some may be advocates, some opponents, and some indifferent. But whatever the reader's stance, it is important as a student of family law to understand how the nation came to the summer of 2015 and the monumental *Obergefell* decision. To that end, we will follow the march toward marriage equality using a timeline reflecting significant milestones.

HISTORY OF THE MOVEMENT TO EXTEND THE RIGHT TO MARRY TO SAME-SEX COUPLES—A TIMELINE

- **The 1950s Ground zero.** The 1950s were at the height of the era of traditional marriage. Gay Americans faced an anti-homosexual legal system and a hostile employment and social environment. Every state but one criminalized homosexual sex and the American Psychiatric Association classified homosexuality as a disease. The federal government would neither hire openly gay individuals nor permit them to serve in the military. Many other employers, both public and private, would not hire homosexuals. There were few gay rights groups, and same-sex marriage was nowhere on the horizon.
- **1969 The Stonewall Riots.** The Stonewall riots were a series of demonstrations by members of the gay community following a police raid on June 28, 1969, at the Stonewall Inn, a gay bar located in Greenwich Village. The "Riots" are widely considered to be the catalyst for the gay liberation

movement and the fight for LGBT rights in the United States. "This was the year we began to make ourselves real. For decades, homophiles had spoken in polite whispers. In 1969 a gay battle cry had been sounded at Stonewall. In 1970 we got organized and began to argue over our goals. Nineteen seventy-one was the year we grew loud enough to be heard, and like us or not, America could no longer deny that we were there." (Arnie Kantrowitz, in *Long Road to Freedom*, published in 1994 by *The Advocate* magazine)

- **Early 1970s The first suits.** In the early 1970s, a small number of gay couples filed suits in state courts after being denied marriage licenses. The first federal lawsuit seeking same-sex marriage rights was filed by the American Civil Liberties Union (ACLU). The suits were summarily dismissed. The U.S. Supreme Court upheld a Minnesota Supreme Court ruling in *Baker v. Nelson*, 291 Minn. 310, 191 N.W.2d 185 (1971) finding that the Constitution did not protect "a fundamental right" for same-sex couples to marry. It did so in a one-sentence order that read: "The claim of right to same sex marriage does not raise a substantial federal question." (*Baker v. Nelson*, October 10, 1972, docket 71-1027.) The Minnesota Supreme Court referenced the *Book of Genesis* as authority in its decision.

- **1973 A label removed.** The American Psychiatric Association removed homosexuality from its list of mental disorders.

- **1977 Harvey B. Milk and Anita Bryant in separate corners.** In 1977, Harvey Milk became the first openly gay person to be elected to public office when he won a seat on the San Francisco Board of Supervisors. He served almost eleven months and was responsible for passage of a gay rights ordinance for the city. On November 27, 1978, Milk and San Francisco Mayor George Moscone were assassinated. Despite his short career in politics, he became an icon and a martyr in the LGBT community. In the same year, former all-American Disney mouseketeer and politician, Anita Bryant, launched her campaign against expansion of gay rights called "Save our Children."

- **1980s Early Advocacy.** Gay activists began vigorously pursuing legal recognition of their relationships and their rights although public support generally remained low and not a single jurisdiction had yet recognized same-sex marriage. Advocacy focused on decriminalizing consensual homosexual sex, eliminating discrimination based on sexual orientation in employment and public accommodations, and electing openly gay public officials. The AIDS epidemic in particular energized advocacy.

- **1982 Anti-discrimination momentum builds.** In 1982, Wisconsin became the first state to outlaw discrimination on the basis of sexual orientation and by 2008 more than twenty states had slowly followed the lead.

- **1986 *Bowers v. Hardwick*, 478 U.S. 186, 106 S. Ct. 2841, 92 L. Ed.2d 140 (1986).** In a challenge to Georgia's anti-sodomy law, the U.S. Supreme Court ruled that the Constitution did not protect the right of gay adults to engage in consensual sodomy in private.

- **1993 Eyes close and eyes open.** In 1993, the Pentagon's "don't ask, don't tell" policy went into effect and Tom Hanks portrayed a gay man with AIDS in the film *Philadelphia*. He won an Academy Award for a brilliant performance that raised the consciousness of millions of Americans.

- **1993 *Baehr v. Lewin*, 74 Haw. 530, 852 P.2d 44 (1993).** Without the support of any national gay rights organization, three gay couples challenged the constitutionality of Hawaii's law limiting marriage to a man and a woman and the case reached the Hawaii Supreme Court. In its decision the

PARALEGAL PRACTICE TIP

In 1984, *The Times of Harvey Milk*, based on the life of the gay activist and the aftermath of his assassination, won an Academy Award for Best Documentary Feature, and in 2009, the biographical film, *Milk*, was nominated for eight Academy Awards and won five including Best Motion Picture of the Year.

court declined to find that same-sex couples had a right to marry, but it did hold that denial of the right *might* constitute a denial of equal protection under the Constitution of the State of Hawaii. On remand, the trial court ordered the state to stop denying marriage licenses to same-sex couples, holding that the marriage ban was not necessary for the protection of children as had been alleged by the state. The door that appeared to open while that decision was on appeal slammed shut when voters in Hawaii supported a Constitutional Amendment (69% to 31%) that gave the legislature the authority to limit marriage to opposite-sex couples. The legislature promptly passed a statute expressly stating that a valid marriage "shall be only between a man and a woman."[28] A vote in Alaska that same year produced a similar result. The political battle had truly begun and both sides were mobilizing.

- **1996 The Federal DOMA.** Fueled by events in Hawaii and amidst fears that the "homosexual agenda" threatened to destroy traditional marriage, Senator Robert Dole cosponsored the federal **Defense of Marriage Act (DOMA)** that was passed by both houses of Congress with large veto-proof majorities. It was swiftly signed by President Clinton. Positions taken regarding the legislation were decisive in several subsequent legislative campaigns including the 2004 presidential election when President George W. Bush advocated passage of a national Constitutional ban. Although DOMA did not technically declare same-sex marriage illegal, it did, through its language, deprive same-sex couples of more than a thousand federal benefits available to "traditional", i.e., heterosexual, spouses. It included two critically important provisions which would be successfully challenged within twenty years in cases before the U.S. Supreme Court:

Section 2. Powers reserved to the states: No State, territory, or possession of the United States, or Indian tribe, shall be required to give effect to any public act, record, or judicial proceeding of any other State, territory, possession, or tribe respecting a relationship between persons of the same sex that is treated as a marriage under the laws of such other State, territory, possession, or tribe, or a right or claim arising from such relationship.

Section 3. Definition of marriage: In determining the meaning of any Act of Congress, or of any ruling, regulation, or interpretation of the various administrative bureaus and agencies of the United States, the word 'marriage' means only a legal union between one man and one woman as husband and wife, and the word 'spouse' refers only to a person of the opposite sex who is a husband or a wife.

- **1996–2008 The mini-DOMAs era.** During this period, more than thirty states enacted statutes or constitutional provisions in defense of traditional marriage (so-called "mini-DOMAs"), most between 2004 and 2008. Some appeared to ban same-sex couples only from the institution of marriage. Others employed a variety of textual provisions designed to prevent both courts and legislators from creating any status similar to marriage such as prohibiting receipt of any "incidents," "benefits," or "rights" of marriage by same-sex couples (Nebraska). Some states (such as Wisconsin) established bans on marriage but left room for domestic partnerships.

- **1996 *Romer v. Evans*, 517 U.S. 620 (1996).** In *Romer*, the U.S. Supreme Court struck down a Colorado Constitutional Amendment that forbid laws banning discrimination against gays. The Amendment preventing

---

Defense of Marriage Act (DOMA)

a federal law restricting the definition of marriage to the union of one man and one woman for purposes of federal law and allowing the states to deny full faith and credit to same-sex marriages valid in a sister state

---

PARALEGAL PRACTICE TIP

For many years, some states have had **Marriage Evasion Statutes** under which a marriage may not be recognized if the parties leave their state of residence and go to another state with more lenient marriage rules for the sole purpose of marrying there and with the intention of returning to their home state following the marriage. These statutes essentially serve the same purpose as a mini-DOMA.

Marriage Evasion Statutes

laws designed to prevent a resident of State A from going to State B to get married if the marriage would have been illegal in State A. State A may elect to not recognize the marriage. Initially these laws were primarily designed to prevent underage couples from crossing state borders to enter into marriages that they couldn't legally enter into in their home states.

protected status based on homosexuality or bisexuality was held to violate equal protection.

- **Decade of the 1990s: Media momentum.** Dramatic changes were beginning to occur in the media. In 1990, only one network program had a regularly appearing gay character. By the mid-1990s, popular situation comedies such as *Golden Girls*, *Friends*, *Mad About You*, and *Will and Grace* were dealing with gay rights issues, including gay marriage. In 1997, Ellen DeGeneres "came out" in a one-hour special with forty-six million American viewers watching.

- **Decade of the 1990s: Employers and institutions respond.** The Village Voice Union had been the first in the nation to fight successfully for benefits for domestic partners back in 1982. In the 1990s shifts in public opinion were starting to translate into policy changes on a broader scale. Many businesses, colleges, and municipalities began extending a variety of benefits to employees with same-sex partners.

- **1995 A first.** In *Holtzman v. Knott*, (*In re H.S.H. -K*),193 Wis.2d 649, 533 N.W.2d 419 (1995) cert denied 516 U.S. 975 (1995), the Wisconsin Supreme Court rendered the first decision in U.S. history in which a court recognized a lesbian as the "*de facto* parent" of a child her partner had conceived and delivered during the course of their relationship.

- **1996 The pollsters pay attention.** Gallup began tracking public opinion regarding the legalization of same-sex marriage. The "issue" was clearly now on the horizon.

- **1997 First "domestic partnership" Act.** In 1997, Hawaii once again took a leadership role becoming the first state to legally recognize same-sex unions. It did so in the form of legislation creating reciprocal beneficiary partnerships.

- **1998 In the news: good and bad.** Tammy Baldwin became the first woman to represent Wisconsin in the U.S. Senate and the first openly gay senator in U.S. history. Gay teenager Matthew Shepard was brutally murdered in Wyoming. The murder eventually led to passage in 2009 of the Matthew Shepard and James Byrd, Jr. Hate Crimes Prevention Act extending the 1969 Act to include crimes motivated by a victim's actual or perceived gender, sexual orientation, gender identity, or disability.

- **1999–2000 First civil union act.** The Vermont Supreme Court ruled that the state's traditional definition of marriage discriminated against same-sex individuals under the Rights and Benefits Article of the Vermont Constitution. In the following year, Vermont became the first state to legalize same-sex civil unions. By December 2006, it had issued over 8,000 licenses for civil unions, and more than 80% of them involved couples from out of state.

- **2003 Massachusetts shatters the barrier.** The Massachusetts Supreme Judicial Court held in *Goodridge v. Department of Public Health*, 440 Mass. 309, 798 N.E.2d 941 (2003) that denying same-sex couples the right to marry constituted a denial of equal protection under the state's Constitution. The first same-sex couples in the nation were married in Massachusetts in May 2004. Some viewed the *Goodridge* decision as just the beginning and some as the beginning of the end of the institution of marriage. Few were without an opinion on the subject. The lengthy *Goodridge* opinion touches on the vast majority of questions raised in the cases and public debate surrounding same-sex marriage. See Case 3.2.

PARALEGAL PRACTICE TIP

In addition to having been the first state to enact same-sex marriage, Massachusetts was the first state to challenge the federal DOMA. In July 2010, a federal judge ruled in two separate lawsuits that the federal DOMA was unconstitutional. In one, *Commonwealth of Massachusetts v. Health and Human Services*, 698 F. Supp. 2d 234 (D. Mass 2010), the court ruled DOMA violated the Tenth Amendment of the Constitution by taking from the states powers that the Constitution gives to them. In the other case, *Gill v. Office of Personnel Management*, 699 F. Supp. 2d 374 (D. Mass. 2010), the court ruled that DOMA violated the equal protection principles embodied in the Due Process Clause of the Fifth Amendment, in an effort to "disadvantage a group of which it disapproves."

CASE **3.2** *Goodridge v. Department of Public Health*, 440 Mass. 309, 98 N.E.2d 941 (2003)

BACKGROUND

The plaintiffs in this case were fourteen individuals, seven couples, from five Massachusetts counties. They had been in committed same-sex relationships for periods ranging from four to thirty years. In March and April of 2001, each of the couples had applied for and been denied marriage licenses on the ground that Massachusetts did not recognize same-sex marriage. The couples then filed suit in Superior Court against the Department of Public Health (and the Commissioner), seeking a judgment that the exclusion of the couples, and other qualified same-sex couples, "from access to marriage licenses, and the legal and social status of civil marriage, as well as the protections, benefits, and obligations of marriage" violated state law, including the Massachusetts Constitution. The Superior Court judge dismissed the plaintiffs' claim. He concluded that the plain wording of the relevant Massachusetts marriage statutes precluded marriage between members of the same sex. With respect to the constitutional claims, the trial court judge held that . . . the Massachusetts Declaration of Rights did not guarantee a fundamental right to same-sex marriage. He concluded that the prohibition rationally furthered the state's legitimate interest in safeguarding the primary purpose of marriage—procreation—because opposite-sex couples are more likely to have children and to do so without relying on "inherently more cumbersome" noncoital means of reproduction. The ruling was successfully appealed to the Massachusetts Supreme Judicial Court, which found that the marriage ban violated both equal protection and due process clauses of the Massachusetts Constitution.

FROM THE OPINION

. . . Marriage is a vital social institution. The exclusive commitment of two individuals to each other nurtures love and mutual support; it brings stability to our society. For those who choose to marry, and for their children, marriage provides an abundance of legal, financial, and social benefits. The question before us is whether, consistent with the Massachusetts Constitution, the Commonwealth may deny the protections, benefits, and obligations conferred by civil marriage to two individuals of the same sex who wish to marry. We conclude that it may not. The Massachusetts Constitution affirms the dignity and equality of all individuals. It forbids the creation of second-class citizens. . . .

We are mindful that our decision marks a change in the history of our marriage law. Many people hold deep-seated religious, moral and ethical convictions that marriage should be limited to the union of one man and one woman, and that homosexual conduct is immoral. Many hold equally strong religious, moral, and ethical convictions that same-sex couples are entitled to be married. . . . Neither view answers the question before us. Our concern is with the Massachusetts Constitution. . . .

Barred access to the protections, benefits, and obligations of civil marriage, a person who enters into an intimate, exclusive union with another of the same sex is arbitrarily deprived of membership in one of our community's most rewarding and cherished institutions. That exclusion is incompatible with the constitutional principles of respect for individual autonomy and equality under law.

SIDEBAR

An expanded excerpt from the lengthy opinion in this case is available at *www .pearsonhighered.com/careersresources/* in the companion website for this text in the material related to Chapter 3 under Cases.

- **2003** *Lawrence v. Texas*, **539 U.S. 558 (2003) The judicial tide has begun to turn.** In another landmark decision in 2003, the U.S. Supreme Court in a 6–3 ruling struck down the sodomy law in Texas. *Lawrence* explicitly overruled *Bowers v. Hardwick*. In *Lawrence*, the Court held that intimate consensual sexual conduct was part of the liberty protected by substantive due process under the Fourteenth Amendment thereby invalidating similar laws throughout the United States that criminalized sodomy between consenting adults acting in private, whatever the sex of the participants.

- **1999–2012 The relationship menu expands.** During this period, the states began extending rights to same-sex partners through an expanding menu of legal statuses:

  <u>California</u>: Domestic Partnerships 1999, expanded in 2001, 2003, and 2011; Same-sex Marriage effective 6/16/2008–11/4/2008 (state court), 8/2010 effective 6/2013 (federal court)
  <u>Colorado</u>: Designated Beneficiaries 2009 (legislature)
  <u>Connecticut</u>: Civil Unions (no longer authorized post 10/2010, converted to marriages); Same-sex Marriage 2008 (state court)
  <u>Delaware</u>: Civil Unions 2012 (no longer authorized, converted to marriages) (legislature)
  <u>District of Columbia</u>: Domestic Partnerships (for health care benefits) 2009; Same-sex Marriage 2009 effective 2010 (District Council)
  <u>Hawaii</u>: Reciprocal Beneficiary Partnerships 1997; Civil Unions 2011 effective 2012 (still allowed as of 2015) (legislature)
  <u>Illinois</u>: Civil Unions 2011 (still allowed as of 2015) (legislature)
  <u>Iowa</u>: Same-sex Marriage 2009 (state court)
  <u>Maine</u>: Domestic Partnerships 2004; Same-sex Marriage 2012 (Voters)
  <u>Maryland</u>: Domestic Partnerships (limited and no registry) 2009; Same-sex Marriage 2012 effective 2013 (legislature and voters)
  <u>New Hampshire</u>: Civil Unions (no longer authorized, converted to marriages 1/2011); Same-sex Marriage 2009 effective 2010 (legislature)
  <u>Nevada</u>: Domestic Partnerships 2009 (legislature)
  <u>New Jersey</u>: Domestic Partnerships 2004 (still available to heterosexual partners over age sixty-two as of 2015); Civil Unions 2007 (legislature)
  <u>New York</u>: Same-sex Marriage 2011 (legislature)
  <u>Oregon</u>: Domestic Partnerships 2008 (still allowed as of 2015)
  <u>Rhode Island</u>: Civil Unions 2011 (no longer authorized, converted to marriages post 8/2013) (legislature)
  <u>Vermont</u>: Civil Unions (no longer authorized but those entered pre 9/1/2009 remain valid); Same-sex Marriage 2009 (legislature)
  <u>Washington</u>: Domestic Partnerships 2007 expanded in 2009 (as of 2015 still available to couples in which at least one of the parties is sixty-two years of age or older, for those under age sixty-two converted to marriages 6/2014); Same-sex Marriage 2012 (legislature and voters)
  <u>Wisconsin</u>: Domestic Partnerships 2007 expanded in 2009 (legislature)

- **2008 In the news: Good parenting is unrelated to sexual orientation.** In a 2008 decision, the California Supreme Court opined that "In contrast to earlier times, our state now recognizes that an individual's capacity to establish a loving and long-term committed relationship with another person and responsibly to care for and raise children does not depend upon the individual's sexual orientation." *In re Marriage Cases*, 43 Cal. 4th 757 at 782, 183 P.3d 384 at 400, 76 Cal. Rptr. 683 at 701 (2008). This position increasingly garnered support from well-respected medical and social science communities. Even the Sixth Circuit later opined: "[G]ay couples, no less than straight couples, are capable of raising children and providing stable families for them. The quality of [same-sex] relationships, and the capacity to raise children within them, turns not on sexual orientation but on individual choices and individual commitment." *DeBoer v. Snyder*, 772 F.3d 388 (6th Cir. 2014).

- **2010–2011 The Supreme Court, the President, and the Department of Justice step aside.** The U.S. Supreme Court decided not to stop enforcement of the same-sex marriage law that went into effect in the District of Columbia in May 2010 and President Obama directed the Department of Justice (DOJ) to stop defending DOMA in federal challenges, leaving any legal defense of the 1996 statute up to Congress. In July 2011, executive opposition to DOMA became more active and direct when the DOJ filed papers in a lawsuit in the U.S. Court of Appeals for the Ninth Circuit filed by an attorney whose partner was denied benefits based on DOMA. The DOJ argued in their brief that DOMA violated the U.S. Constitution's guarantees of equal protection.

- **2011 The Pentagon comes out of the closet.** In 2011, the Pentagon's "don't ask, don't tell" policy was repealed.

- **2012 Taking it to the people.** Maine, Maryland, and Washington became the first states where legalization of same-sex marriage was voter initiated.

- **2013 An inaugural address of note.** During his second inaugural address, President Obama made history by becoming the first president to ever mention gay rights in an inaugural address publicly affirming his shift from opposition to support of same-sex marriage.

- **2013** *United States v. Windsor***, 133 S. Ct. 2675_(2013).** In 2013, the Supreme Court rendered a pivotal decision in *Windsor* finding that Section 3 of DOMA violated the Fifth Amendment's guarantee of Equal Protection of the laws as applied to persons of the same sex who are legally married under the laws of their state. The basic issue in the case was whether Edith Windsor, whose same-sex marriage was legally recognized in New York, should be granted a federal tax exemption granted to spouses when her wife died and left Windsor her estate resulting in a federal tax liability of $363,053. The majority ruled that Section 3 of the Defense of Marriage Act was unconstitutional and that the federal government cannot discriminate against legally married lesbian and gay couples for the purposes of determining federal benefits and protections. Justice Kennedy writing for the majority stated that withholding federal recognition places same-sex spouses "in an unstable position of being in second-tier marriages" and "demeans the couple, whose moral and sexual choices the Constitution protects . . . and whose relationship the state has sought to dignify." However, the decision did not impact Section 2 of DOMA with respect to recognition of same-sex marriages by other states. Dissenting, Justice Scalia wrote prophetically: "No one should be fooled. . . . It is just a matter of listening and waiting for the other shoe."

- **2013–2015 The deluge.** *Windsor* was a major turning point in the march toward nationalizing same-sex marriage. The sweeping language of the opinion set off a wave of lower court rulings nullifying state bans one after another. When the Court decided *Windsor* in June 2013, same-sex couples could legally marry in nine states and the District of Columbia. Between the decision and April 2015, they gained that right in twenty-seven more states. The surge was largely the result of judicial decisions rather than legislation or voter initiatives.

- **January 2015 The other shoe starts to drop.** Forced by a split among federal appellate courts, the U.S. Supreme Court agreed to consolidate and hear Sixth Circuit cases from Kentucky, Michigan, Ohio, and Tennessee where recognition bans had been upheld raising anticipation that the national debate over same-sex marriage might be resolved. The consolidated cases included:

  Obergefell v. Hodges (Ohio) Case No. 14-556
  DeBoer v. Snyder (Michigan) Case No. 14-571
  Bourke v. Beshear (Kentucky) Case No. 14-574
  Tanco v. Haslam, (Tennessee) Case No. 14-562.

- **April 2015 The prelude.** By the time *Obergefell* was heard on April 28, marriage bans continued to exist in only fourteen states and all were under court challenge. In addition to Kentucky, Michigan, Ohio, and Tennessee, the other states still with bans were: Arkansas, Georgia, Kansas, Louisiana, Mississippi, Missouri, Nebraska, North Dakota, South Dakota, and Texas. Public opinion in support of same-sex marriage was at an all-time high. A 2015 CNN/Opinion Research Corporation Poll registered a 63% level of support for same-sex marriage with a 72% approval level among 18 to 34 year olds. 70% of Americans were living in states where same-sex marriages were authorized.

- **April 28, 2015 The case is heard.** An historically divided U.S. Supreme Court heard arguments in *Obergefell v. Hodges* (the combined case) on April 28, 2015. The thirty-two plaintiffs in the consolidated cases illustrated virtually every problem faced by gay and lesbian couples literally from the cradle to the grave.

The parties were to address two questions posed by the Court:

I. Does the Fourteenth Amendment require a state to license a marriage of two people of the same sex?

II. Does the Fourteenth Amendment require a state to recognize a marriage between two people of the same sex when their marriage was lawfully licensed and performed out-of-state?

The parties' arguments and the Justices' inquiries focused on challenging controversial questions such as the following:

- Should we change a definition of marriage that has been in place for hundreds of years or should we wait and see what effect, if any, same-sex marriage has on traditional marriage and the economic and social order in general?

- Does it make sense to shut down by judicial decision a fast moving national debate on the topic of same-sex marriage or should we rely on local discussion and consensus as the best methods for promoting social change?

- Should the definition of marriage be established by the courts or should it be determined by the people and their elected representatives?

- Is the purpose of marriage to promote and control procreation or is the right to marry separate from procreation?

- Is the traditional family the "optimal environment" for raising children or does limiting access to marriage disadvantage children of same-sex parents?

- Do marriage bans discriminate against gays and lesbians based on sexual orientation thereby creating a population of "second class" citizens or are they rationally related to legitimate governmental purposes?

- Does nationalizing the right to same-sex marriage threaten opponents' rights to hold and act on their religious, moral, and ethical beliefs or will those rights be protected?

- Does the Full Faith and Credit Clause of the Constitution require a state to recognize the validity of same-sex marriages entered in other states or can a state decline to recognize such marriages if they are in violation of strongly held public policies?
- Are same-sex couples seeking to create a new Constitutional right, the right to same-sex marriage, or are they seeking access to an existing fundamental right to marry as the plaintiffs did in *Loving v. Virginia*?

- **The other shoe drops. A landmark victory and new storms begin brewing.** On the morning of June 26, 2015, the anniversary of two other major gay rights cases (*Lawrence* and *Windsor*), a deeply divided U.S. Supreme Court released the *Obergefell* decision, the most significant family law decision in U.S. history transforming the core definition of marriage and extending the fundamental right to marry to same-sex couples across the nation.

  The 5–4 decision was greeted with wild jubilation in some quarters and harsh condemnation in others. President Obama hailed it as "an affirmation that all Americans are created equal" while Justice Scalia characterized it as a "threat to American democracy." In true partisan fashion, democratic presidential hopefuls welcomed the decision. Not a single republican candidate expressed support. Some described it as an "act of judicial tyranny" and vowed to fight on by seeking a "traditional marriage" Amendment to the Constitution. Others affirmed traditional marriage but somberly accepted the decision acknowledging a need to abide by "the rule of law." Most agreed that the battle will now likely shift to balancing freedom of religion and equal protection: protection of the First Amendment rights of religious institutions and the millions of Americans whose faiths hold a traditional view of marriage against the push for laws preventing discrimination by businesses, employers, agencies, landlords, organizations, educational institutions, etc. based on sexual orientation.

  Salient excerpts from the majority opinion crafted by Justice Kennedy and the four highly critical dissents (Justices Roberts, Scalia, Thomas, and Alito) are provided in Case 3.3.

CASE **3.3** *Obergefell v. Hodges*, 576 U.S. _____(2015)

MAJORITY OPINION, JUSTICE KENNEDY

- The lifelong union of a man and a woman always has promised nobility and dignity to all persons, without regard to their station in life. . . . Its dynamic allows two people to find a life that could not be found alone, for a marriage becomes greater than just the two persons. Rising from the most basic human needs, marriage is essential to our most profound hopes and aspirations.
- Far from seeking to devalue marriage, the petitioners seek it for themselves because of their respect—and need—for its privileges and responsibilities. And their immutable nature dictates that same-sex marriage is their only real path to this profound commitment.
- The history of marriage is one of both continuity and change. Changes, such as the decline of arranged marriages and the abandonment of the law of coverture, have worked deep transformations in the structure of marriage, affecting aspects of marriage once viewed as essential. These new insights have strengthened, not weakened, the institution. Changed understandings of

(Continued)

marriage are characteristic of a Nation where new dimensions of freedom become apparent to new generations. This dynamic can be seen in the Nation's experience with gay and lesbian rights.

- The nature of injustice is that we may not always see it in our own times. . . . When new insight reveals discord between the Constitution's central protections and a received legal stricture, a claim to liberty must be addressed.

- Four principles and traditions demonstrate that the reasons marriage is fundamental under the Constitution apply with equal force to same-sex couples. The first premise of this Court's relevant precedents is that the right to personal choice regarding marriage is inherent in the concept of individual autonomy. . . . A second principle in this Court's jurisprudence is that the right to marry is fundamental because it supports a two-person union unlike any other in its importance to the committed individuals.

- A third basis for protecting the right to marry is that it safeguards children and families and thus draws meaning from related rights of childrearing, procreation, and education. . . .Without the recognition, stability, and predictability marriage offers, children suffer the stigma of knowing their families are somehow lesser. They also suffer the significant material costs of being raised by unmarried parents, relegated to a more difficult and uncertain family life. The marriage laws at issue thus harm and humiliate the children of same-sex couples.

- As all parties agree, many same-sex couples provide loving and nurturing homes to their children, whether biological or adopted. And hundreds of thousands of children are presently being raised by such couples.

- Finally, this Court's cases and the Nation's traditions make clear that marriage is a keystone of the Nation's social order. . . . There is no difference between same- and opposite-sex couples with respect to this principle, yet same-sex couples are denied the constellation of benefits that the States have linked to marriage and are consigned to an instability many opposite-sex couples would find intolerable.

- The limitation of marriage to opposite-sex couples may long have seemed natural and just, but its inconsistency with the central meaning of the fundamental right to marry is now manifest.

- Many who deem same-sex marriage to be wrong reach that conclusion based on decent and honorable religious or philosophical premises, and neither they nor their beliefs are disparaged here. But when that sincere, personal opposition becomes enacted law and public policy, the necessary consequence is to put the imprimatur of the State itself on an exclusion that soon demeans or stigmatizes those whose own liberty is then denied.

- Indeed, in interpreting the Equal Protection Clause, the Court has recognized that new insights and societal understandings can reveal unjustified inequality within our most fundamental institutions that once passed unnoticed and unchallenged. . . . It is now clear that the challenged laws burden the liberty of same-sex couples, and it must be further acknowledged that they abridge central precepts of equality. . . . Especially against a long history of disapproval of their relationships, this denial to same-sex couples of the right to marry works a grave and continuing harm.

- The right to marry is a fundamental right inherent in the liberty of the person, and under the Due Process and Equal Protection Clauses of the Fourteenth Amendment couples of the same-sex may not be deprived of that right and that liberty.

- There may be an initial inclination in these cases to proceed with caution—to await further legislation, litigation, and debate. . . . Yet there has been far more deliberation than this argument acknowledges. There have been referenda,

(Continued)

legislative debates, and grassroots campaigns, as well as countless studies, papers, books, and other popular and scholarly writings. There has been extensive litigation in state and federal courts. . . . As more than 100 amici make clear in their filings, many of the central institutions in American life—state and local governments, the military, large and small businesses, labor unions, religious organizations, law enforcement, civic groups, professional organizations, and universities—have devoted substantial attention to the question. This has led to an enhanced understanding of the issue—an understanding reflected in the arguments now presented

- While the Constitution contemplates that democracy is the appropriate process for change, individuals who are harmed need not await action before asserting a fundamental right.

No union is more profound than marriage, for it embodies the highest ideals of love, fidelity, devotion, sacrifice, and family. In forming a marital union, two people become something greater than once they were. As some of the petitioners in these cases demonstrate, marriage embodies a love that may endure even past death. It would misunderstand these men and women to say they disrespect the idea of marriage. Their plea is that they do respect it, respect it so deeply that they seek to find its fulfillment for themselves. Their hope is not to be condemned to live in loneliness, excluded from one of civilization's oldest institutions. They ask for equal dignity in the eyes of the law. The Constitution grants them that right. The judgment of the Court of Appeals for the Sixth Circuit is reversed.

EXCERPTS FROM DISSENTS:

Chief Justice Roberts:

- The human race must procreate to survive. Procreation occurs through sexual relations between a man and a woman. . . . Therefore, for the good of children and society, sexual relations that can lead to procreation should occur only between a man and a woman committed to a lasting bond.
- Although the policy arguments for extending marriage to same-sex couples may be compelling, the legal arguments for requiring such an extension are not. The fundamental right to marry does not include a right to make a State change its definition of marriage. . . . In short, our Constitution does not enact any one theory of marriage. The people of a State are free to expand marriage to include same-sex couples, or to retain the historic definition. Today, however, the Court takes the extraordinary step of ordering every State to license and recognize same-sex marriage. Many people will rejoice at this decision, and I begrudge none their celebration. But for those who believe in a government of laws, not of men, the majority's approach is deeply disheartening.
- Supporters of same-sex marriage have achieved considerable success persuading their fellow citizens—through the democratic process—to adopt their view. That ends today. Five lawyers have closed the debate and enacted their own vision of marriage as a matter of constitutional law. Stealing this issue from the people will for many cast a cloud over same-sex marriage, making a dramatic social change that much more difficult to accept.
- Hard questions arise when people of faith exercise religion in ways that may be seen to conflict with the new right to same-sex marriage—when, for example, a religious college provides married student housing only to opposite-sex married couples, or a religious adoption agency declines to place children with same-sex married couples.

(Continued)

- If you are among the many Americans—of whatever sexual orientation—who favor expanding same-sex marriage, by all means celebrate today's decision. Celebrate the achievement of a desired goal. Celebrate the opportunity for a new expression of commitment to a partner. Celebrate the availability of new benefits. But do not celebrate the Constitution. It had nothing to do with it.

Justice Scalia:

- This practice of constitutional revision by an unelected committee of nine, . . . robs the People of the most important liberty they asserted in the Declaration of Independence and won in the Revolution of 1776: the freedom to govern themselves.
- Until the courts put a stop to it, public debate over same-sex marriage displayed American democracy at its best. . . .
- A system of government that makes the People subordinate to a committee of nine unelected lawyers does not deserve to be called a democracy. . . . to allow the policy question of same-sex marriage to be considered and resolved by a select, patrician, highly unrepresentative panel of nine is to violate a principle even more fundamental than no taxation without representation: no social transformation without representation.
- The five Justices who compose today's majority are entirely comfortable concluding that every State violated the Constitution for all of the 135 years between the Fourteenth Amendment's ratification and Massachusetts' permitting of same-sex marriages in 2003. . . .They have discovered in the Fourteenth Amendment a "fundamental right" overlooked by every person alive at the time of ratification, and almost everyone else in the time since.

Justice Thomas:

- Aside from undermining the political processes that protect our liberty, the majority's decision threatens the religious liberty our Nation has long sought to protect. . . . Numerous amici—even some not supporting the States—have cautioned the Court that its decision here will "have unavoidable and wide-ranging implications for religious liberty."

Justice Alito:

- Today's decision usurps the constitutional right of the people to decide whether to keep or alter the traditional understanding of marriage. The decision will also have other important consequences. It will be used to vilify Americans who are unwilling to assent to the new orthodoxy.
- The system of federalism established by our Constitution provides a way for people with different beliefs to live together in a single nation. If the issue of same-sex marriage had been left to the people of the States, it is likely that some States would recognize same-sex marriage and others would not. . . . The majority today makes that impossible. By imposing its own views on the entire country, the majority facilitates the marginalization of the many Americans who have traditional ideas.
- Even enthusiastic supporters of same-sex marriage should worry about the scope of the power that today's majority claims. Today's decision shows that decades of attempts to restrain this Court's abuse of its authority have failed.

Implications for the Future

The mix of approaches to family status and nonmarital relationships described in this chapter has sent shock waves into the social fabric of this country that reverberate into its legal system. No state has been entirely unaffected, and the federal government has been called upon to invade an area of law traditionally left to the states. Just when one may have been tempted to think the dust was settling, the entire legal landscape is being altered. Every area of substantive law is impacted by extension of the right to marry to same-sex couples: probate, tax, contract, business, immigration, health care, corporate, tort, criminal, conflict/choice of law, and constitutional among others.

The impact is perhaps greatest on family law. The recognition of same-sex marriage is just the beginning. Now family law practitioners are dealing with the fallout that accompanies extension of all the legal rights that go with it: parentage and adoption rights, estate planning options, and various provisions of the divorce code including custody, support, and property division. What if the client is a party to another legally recognized relationship? What is the effect of agreements entered in the past such as cohabitation and co-parenting agreements? Will same-sex couples who have been together for decades be able to challenge or satisfy eligibility tests for benefits such as veterans' death benefits and Social Security survivor benefits? What if the client's immigration status is challenged? What level of protection do state and federal anti-discrimination laws provide particularly in the employment context? Will businesses have the right to refuse to provide services to potential customers based on their sexual orientation? Dramatic changes in the law inevitably generate complex disputes, some involving multiple states and even nations. Perhaps more than ever before, lawmakers and the courts will be pressured to develop basic family law policies and procedures designed to address those disputes.

The Paralegal's Role

In 1965, this chapter would have been one-fifth as long and the content would have been cut-and-dried. It was a different era then. There really weren't what one would call "marriage" cases, and when there were, a paralegal's role would have been minimal. It might entail such tasks as obtaining certified copies of marriage certificates, preparing for an annulment action, or documenting the incidents of a traditional or common law marriage in a small number of cases. But we are in a new era. The past five decades have been a time of steady evolution in the structure of family life and intimate relationships in the United States, with reverberations likely to be felt for the foreseeable future. Going forward, the paralegal's role in this area will be determined at least in part by the degree to which the firm in which the paralegal is employed extends its expertise into areas of substantive law impacted by developments described in this chapter. For example, will the firm handle probate, contract, immigration, and tax law as well as family law? Will it take on constitutional challenges?

Issues related to intimate relationships between different- and same-sex partners are likely to remain on the legal landscape for years to come posing new cutting-edge challenges. Some paralegals will inevitably have an opportunity to work with attorneys, legislators, courts, and other interested parties engaged in addressing those challenges.

CHAPTER **SUMMARY**

In this chapter, we have reviewed:

- the evolution of marriage and other forms of family unions;
- the significance of the right to marry as a "fundamental" right and the ways in which it can be regulated by the states;
- the various types of marriage and alternative "family" relationships and the requirements for establishing each of them;
- the rights, benefits, and obligations that flow from marriage, domestic partnerships, and civil unions; and
- the history, trends, and controversy surrounding the rights of same-sex partners with particular attention to the right to marry culminating in the *Obergefell* decision in 2015.

We learn in this text that today fewer people are choosing to marry and increasing numbers of those who do marry eventually divorce. Marriage has become the focal point for a variety of causes including the gay, gender, religious, and states' rights agendas. It has become a political football at the national and local levels. It is now treated as an economic partnership between alleged equals who are increasingly privately structuring their "marital" rights. It is also decreasingly the environment in which children are born and raised.

Whatever view an individual espouses, we can be certain that the federal government and the states will continue to take a strong interest in marriage and the family as the fundamental social unit through which culture, values, and wealth are transmitted from one generation to the next. Cases like *Baehr*, *Goodridge*, *Lawrence*, and *Windsor* paved the way for *Obergefell*. Their impact is being felt across the nation and the changes that are taking place dislodge long-established family law principles and procedures. The years ahead promise to be challenging ones for family law practitioners and their paralegals!

CONCEPT REVIEW AND REINFORCEMENT

KEY **TERMS**

Affinity	Covenant marriage	Marriage
Bigamy	Defense of Marriage Act (DOMA)	Marriage Evasion Statute
Civil law	Domestic partnership	Married Women's Property Acts
Civil union	Emancipation	Polygamy
Common law marriage	Intestate	Proxy marriage
Community property states	Incest	Putative spouse
Consanguinity	Laws of descent and distribution	Tort
Consortium	Marital communications privilege	Void

REVIEW **QUESTIONS**

1. Describe how the definitions of "marriage" and "family" have evolved over the past 200 years.
2. Describe the significance of the Supreme Court's decision in *Loving v. Virginia*.
3. Identify the common requirements for a ceremonial marriage and indicate what the consequence usually is for failure to comply with a technical requirement.
4. Identify the usual requirements for a valid common law marriage.
5. Identify a minimum of six rights and benefits that flow from a valid ceremonial or common law marriage.
6. Identify the common requirements for establishing domestic partnerships and civil union and describe the kinds of benefits they confer. Name at least one state that provides for domestic partnerships and one that permits civil unions.
7. Distinguish the functional family approach from legally recognized "family" statuses.
8. Describe the significance of the *Obergefell* case decided by the U.S. Supreme Court in 2015. Identify three arguments in favor of same-sex marriage and three against it.

DEVELOPING YOUR PARALEGAL SKILLS

FOCUS ON **THE JOB**

This assignment requires the student to research requirements for a valid marriage in three different states and apply them to a hypothetical fact pattern.

The Facts

Mary W. is a fifteen-year-old girl who resides in Texas. She believes she has fallen madly in love with a man, Marty C., who rides bulls on the rodeo circuit. He is a resident of Massachusetts and is twenty-three years old. Mary says they were bound to find each other because, looking at their family histories, they have discovered they are actually first cousins. Mary says she has done her legal homework and that she and Marty have come up with a plan. Because her mother opposes the marriage, Mary is going to get her stepfather to consent to the marriage in writing. Then she will go to Massachusetts and she and Marty will get married there and then move to Colorado, where she is firmly convinced they will live happily ever after. Mary spoke with your supervisor, Attorney McGuigan, about this at a recent family party. He is not interested in becoming involved in the case, as he knows Mary's mother personally. However, he says that it would be a good exercise for

you, his paralegal, to research the legal issues relating to Mary's circumstances.

The Assignment

Research the law in Texas, Massachusetts, and Colorado to determine whether or not Mary and Marty can enter a valid marriage in any of those states under the circumstances described. You will need, at the least, to look at:

- the minimum age for marrying with and without parental consent in each state
- the circumstances under which a minimum age requirement may be waived in each state
- whether or not first cousins are permitted to marry in any of the states
- whether any of the states has a marriage evasion law that might affect the validity of a purported marriage
- whether any of the states permits common law marriages and, if so, under what circumstances

Summarize your research and conclusions in a memorandum to Attorney McGuigan. For help getting started, the following sites may be useful: *www.ncsl.org* and *www.findlaw.com*.

FOCUS ON **ETHICS**

In this activity, the student will prepare a short paper about ethical concerns related to the substance of an interview with a client.

The Assignment

Assume that you are Attorney McGuigan's paralegal and that he has been retained to advise Mary in the above fact pattern. He has asked you to interview her and prepare a brief report about what you learn and your general impressions of Mary. Assume that the fact pattern reflects the basic content of the interview with one exception: Mary tells you that she plans

to forge her mother's signature consenting to the marriage. She is confident she can do it because she "has been doing it for years on report cards and absence slips at school." She directs you not to tell Attorney McGuigan about this little scheme, because he knows her mom and would "tell on her." Write a one- to two-page paper in which you describe what you plan to do about what happened in the interview. Indicate how the ethical canons for paralegals promulgated by the National Association of Legal Assistants (contained in Appendix A) and ethics material discussed in Chapter 1 apply to this situation.

FOCUS ON **CASE LAW**

In this Focus, students have an opportunity to review, describe, and discuss the landmark decision in *Obergefell v. Hodges*, 576 U.S. ____ (2015).

The Assignment

The class should be divided into five groups. Group 1 will read the majority opinion authored by Justice Kennedy, Group 2 Chief Justice Robert's dissent, Group 3 Justice Scalia's dissent, Group 4 Justice Thomas' dissent, and Group 5 Justice Alito's dissent. Beginning with Group 1, students will describe the portion of the opinion they read, its main

points, and the extent to which they agree or disagree with the opinion and why. After all of the groups have reported, the class should vote on how they would have decided the case. As an alternative, students should do the following in a three- to five-page paper:

1. Identify the two primary questions the case addressed.
2. State the court's ruling with respect to each question.
3. Describe the court's basic reasoning with respect to its ruling.
4. Describe the essence of the dissent(s).

FOCUS ON **STATE LAW AND PROCEDURE**

In this exercise, students are required to research governing law in their respective jurisdictions with respect to marriage and alternative legally recognized statuses.

The Assignment

Research the law of your state (constitutional, statutory, and case law) to determine answers to the following questions, and present your findings in a written report:

1. What are the requirements for a valid marriage? Exhibit 3.2 might help you get started.
2. What is the minimum age for a person to marry and are there any exceptions to the rule?
3. Does your state allow common law marriages and, if so, what requirements must be satisfied?
4. Does any law in the state where you live make provisions for domestic partnerships or civil unions? If so, identify the applicable statute(s) and the related requirements and benefits.
5. Has your state enacted any legislation related to same-sex marriages in your state either prior to or following the Supreme Court's decision in *Obergefell*? This includes any so-called Religious Freedom Restoration legislation. The National Conference of State Legislatures website (*www.ncsl.org*), the Cornell University Law School's website (*www.law.cornell.edu*), and the online encyclopedia (*www.wikipedia.org*) may be useful resources as starting points. All information gleaned from these sites should be verified prior to use.

FOCUS ON **TECHNOLOGY**

In addition to the links provided throughout the chapter, this Focus provides a series of useful websites for reference, along with technology-related assignments for completion.

Websites of Interest

www.aclu.org

Information is available on this site regarding domestic partnerships, civil unions, and same-sex marriage. Search by key word.

www.findlaw.com

This site contains useful information on family law, marriage, domestic partnerships, civil unions, and other topics related to the content of this chapter. Search by key word. Accuracy and currency of information should be verified prior to use.

www.hrc.org

This is the website of the Human Rights Campaign. Search the site for information about domestic partnerships and civil unions.

www.infoplease.com

This site is an online encyclopedia that provides a wide range of information on a variety of topics. Of particular relevance to this chapter are *A Primer on Same-Sex Marriage, Civil Unions, Domestic Partnerships, and Defense of Marriage Acts* and a link to a comprehensive report on the status of related legislation in each state and countries around the world. References should be verified to be sure they are current.

www.lambdalegal.org

This site provides extensive information regarding states, municipalities, and other entities offering domestic partnership and civil union benefits. As with other sites, the information provided should be verified before use.

www.law.cornell.edu

This is an academically based site that is very informative. Among other resources, it provides a comprehensive table of state marriage requirements and provides related links to state codes.

www.legalout.com

This is a website established by a Georgia lawyer and gay rights activist. It is essentially an online document preparation service for the lesbian, gay, bisexual, and transgender community. In addition to document preparation, LegalOut offers document storage and sharing, news blogs, links to activist sites, and a referral network of lawyers sympathetic to LGBT causes.

www.lexisnexis.com

As of April 2015, statutory codes for the following could be accessed at this site: California, Colorado, Maryland, Mississippi, Tennessee, Vermont, Wyoming, Puerto Rico, and the U.S. Virgin Islands.

www.ncsl.org

This is the website for the National Conference of State Legislatures. It provides reports and summaries of state laws in several areas, such as common law marriage, covenant marriage, marriage between first cousins, domestic partnerships, and civil unions.

www.sos.ca.gov/

This site is maintained by the office of the California Secretary of State. Considerable information about domestic partnerships in California can be accessed with a "domestic partnership" search. Links are provided to information about registration, forms and fees, related legislation, and a "Frequently Asked Questions" resource with further links.

www.unmarried.org

This is the website for an organization called Unmarried Equality. It contains information and statistics on cohabitation, living single, domestic partner benefits, common law marriage, etc.

www.usmarriagelaws.com

This site provides a summary of marriage laws of the states and selected countries. Information should be verified prior to use.

Assignments

1. Use the Internet to determine whether your state permits domestic partnerships or civil unions. If so, what are the requirements for and benefits of establishing each type of relationship?
2. Identify two online resources that support the Supreme Court's decision in *Obergefell* and two that oppose it. In a two-page paper, briefly outline their respective arguments.
3. Use online resources to identify the requirements for each type of marriage recognized in your state. Exhibits 3.1, 3.3, and 3.5 may be helpful resources but be sure to verify the information you locate by accessing current statutes.

PORTFOLIO PRODUCTS

1. Memorandum regarding the validity of a potential marriage based on a fact pattern involving three states
2. Paper on ethical issues that arise in a client interview
3. Three- to five-page paper on the 2015 decision of the U.S. Supreme Court in *Obergefell v. Hodges*
4. Written report on governing law in the student's jurisdiction with respect to marriage and other legally recognized "family" statuses

chapter 4
ANNULMENT

© Getty Images

Audrey's husband, John, recently told her that he initially married her only because she was pregnant and that he hadn't intended to stay married once the baby was born. She is heartbroken and wants to have their marriage annulled. John insists that he no longer feels the way he did when they got married. He loves being a husband and father and there is no way he wants their marriage to end in an annulment or divorce.

LEARNING OBJECTIVES

After reading this chapter and completing related assignments, you should be able to:

- describe the nature, purpose, and effect of an annulment

- identify the differences between annulment and divorce

- distinguish between a void and a voidable marriage

- describe the procedure for obtaining an annulment

- list a minimum of four grounds for annulment

- identify potential defenses to an annulment action

- describe the potential role of a paralegal in an annulment case

Introduction

Chapter 3 focused on marriage as a civil contract and legal status that makes the spouses eligible for a wide range of state and federal benefits. As the chapter indicated, each state identifies the kinds of marriages it will recognize and the requirements each must satisfy. When the requirements are met, the courts generally presume that a valid marriage results. When they are not met, the alleged marriage may be either **void *ab initio*** (it never existed because of a legal impediment such as a still existing prior marriage of one of the parties) or **voidable** (able to be retroactively rescinded or revoked due to circumstances such as a party having been underage or incapable of consenting at the time of the marriage). If no action is taken to annul a voidable marriage, the marriage will continue to be considered valid. On the other hand, if a marriage is void *ab initio* because it is prohibited by law, the marriage is customarily deemed null and void, invalid from the outset.

The focus of this chapter is on **annulment**, the legal procedure for establishing that an alleged marriage is null and void even though the parties may have obtained a license, participated in a wedding ceremony, cohabited for an extended period, and even had children together. Although the content will emphasize similarities, it will also

Void *ab initio*
[Latin: from the beginning] of no legal effect from the outset; a contract is void *ab initio* if it violates a law or a strong public policy

Voidable marriage
a marriage capable of being nullified because of a circumstance existing at the time it was established; the marriage remains valid unless and until it is declared invalid by a court of competent jurisdiction

Annulment
the legal procedure for declaring that a marriage is null and void because of an impediment existing at its inception

109

PARALEGAL PRACTICE TIP

The Texas statutes governing annulment specifically distinguish between void and voidable marriages. They can be seen at *www.statutes.legis .state.tx.us*. Select Family Code Chapter 6 Subchapter B Grounds for Annulment and Subchapter C Declaring a Marriage Void.

PARALEGAL PRACTICE TIP

When addressing an annulment case, the courts sometimes refer to the influence of early **ecclesiastical (church) law.** For centuries, the Catholic Church, and subsequently the ecclesiastical courts of England, regarded marriage as a sacrament, and once entered, as indissoluble. Although technically there was no divorce under ecclesiastical law, certain "canonical disabilities" existing at the time of the marriage ceremony were viewed as entitling parties to an annulment, essentially a religious ruling that no marriage ever existed between them. These disabilities included, for example, consanguinity, affinity, and impotence.

Ecclesiastical law
[syn. Canon law] the law governing the doctrine and discipline of a particular church

PARALEGAL PRACTICE TIP

In Ohio, both divorce and annulment statutes provide relief from bigamous marriages. As a ground for divorce, R.C. 3105.01(A) only requires that either party had a husband or wife living at the time of the marriage from which the divorce is sought. The annulment statute (R.C. 3105.31(B)) requires that the prior marriage was in force at the time of the subsequent marriage and is still in force at the time the annulment is sought. See, e.g., *Kochaniec v. Kochaniec*, 2011 Ohio 5552 (Ohio App. 2011).

highlight the considerable differences that exist among the states with respect to the following:

- the circumstances in which a particular marriage will be considered void or voidable;
- the recognized grounds for annulment;
- the individuals who have standing to seek an annulment;
- the nature of an annulment action;
- the defenses that can be raised in response to a complaint for annulment; and
- the consequences for the parties, their children (if any), and third parties if an annulment is granted.

Divorce and Annulment

The state not only determines how valid marriages are created. It also determines when and how they may be dissolved or nullified. Depending on the circumstances, a party may ask a court to dissolve a marriage, annul it, or issue a declaratory judgment regarding the validity of the marriage.[1] Although rarely sought, annulments present a viable option for terminating a marriage when appropriate grounds exist and when it better meets a party's personal and strategic needs than a fault or no-fault divorce. For example, clients may prefer an annulment because divorce is contrary to their religious beliefs or because they want to avoid having to pay alimony. Exhibit 4.1 summarizes the major differences between an annulment and a divorce.

Occasionally the law of a state and the facts of a particular case are such that a party may seek either a divorce or an annulment based on the same ground. For example, in Tennessee, an annulment may be sought on the ground that a previous marriage was still in existence at the time of a subsequent marriage (unless the former spouse has been absent for five years or more and is not known to be living). Tennessee law also provides as a ground for divorce that "either party has knowingly entered into a second marriage, in violation of a previous marriage, still subsisting."[2]

EXHIBIT 4.1 Differences Between Divorce and Annulment

Annulment	Divorce
In an annulment action, one or both of the parties claim that a purported marriage is not valid and does not exist.	A divorce severs a marriage the parties acknowledge exists.
The ground for annulment existed at the time the alleged marriage was entered.	In the vast majority of cases, the cause for divorce arises during the marriage.
An annulment operates retroactively declaring an alleged marriage to be null and void *ab initio*.	A divorce terminates a legal marriage as of the date of divorce forward.
If a marriage is annulled, the parties generally regain the legal status they had before the marriage occurred.	Traditionally, after a divorce, the parties have a continuing legal status as former spouses with respect to division of property, custody of children, and child and spousal support.

EXHIBIT 4.1 *(Continued)*

Certain rights or entitlements, such as worker's compensation benefits or occasionally alimony from a previous marriage that terminated upon a recipient's remarriage, may be revived upon annulment of the later marriage.	Worker's compensation or alimony benefits flowing from a prior marriage will generally not be revived upon dissolution of the recipient's later marriage.
In some states, annulment will result in the extinguishing of interests in property acquired during the purported marriage. In other states, the interests may be preserved in whole or part through application of equitable remedies, such as the putative spouse doctrine (in effect, treating the property as **quasi-marital property**).	Upon divorce, property acquired during the marriage is divided between the parties based on equitable division or community property principles absent an enforceable agreement to the contrary.
An annulment establishes that no valid marriage ever existed. Because the right to potentially receive spousal support flows from a valid marriage, there customarily is no right to spousal support following an annulment.	Subject to limitations in some states, spousal support may be awarded based on one party's need and the other party's ability to pay.
If the parties obtain an annulment establishing that no valid marriage ever existed between them, they must each file amended returns (as unmarried persons) for all tax years within a three-year period of limitations.[3]	Divorced spouses may file a joint tax return for the year in which their divorce is granted provided they are married for some portion of that tax year.

Quasi-marital property
[Latin, quasi: as if] property treated as if it was acquired by the parties during the marriage even though the marriage was never valid

Procedure for Obtaining an Annulment

Under common law, in the absence of a controlling statute to the contrary, a void **marriage** was absolutely void from its inception (void *ab initio*) and continued to be so. Technically, no judicial pronouncement was necessary to annul the marriage and restore the parties to their original rights. Today the states vary with respect to whether or not a decree is necessary to invalidate a void marriage. However, even if not technically required to establish rights between the parties with respect to each other, it is often desirable to obtain a formal annulment when third parties may be impacted, such as lenders who act with respect to the parties under a belief that they are married. Sometimes the decision is made on a case-by-case basis. In Connecticut, for example, in the *Davis* case, the court determined that a marriage deemed void *ab initio* should be declared so by the court rather than by the parties simply asserting its invalidity. The case involved two nineteen-year-old residents of Connecticut who went on an automobile ride with some friends. In the context of the fun-filled occasion, the "wife" dared the "husband" to marry her. He accepted the dare, a license for the marriage was obtained in New York State, and the ceremony was performed there by a Justice of the Peace. Neither party intended at the time to assume a marital status and the parties never cohabited after the ceremony.[4]

When annulments are sought, procedures vary somewhat from state to state. The pleading that initiates a suit to annul a marriage may be called

Marriage
a government regulated and approved legal status that two consenting adults attain by entering a contract with each other which confers rights, benefits and obligations; a civil contract between a man and a woman or between two same-sex partners

PARALEGAL PRACTICE TIP

Visit *www.courts.delaware.gov*. Select Divorce Forms and scroll down to view Delaware's Petition for Divorce/Annulment (Form 442 revised 10/2013) and an Answer to Petition for Divorce/Annulment (Form 448). To view annulment forms used in the state of Colorado, visit *www.courts.state.co.us*. Select Self Help /Forms/Family Forms and scroll to Annulment.

Declaratory judgment
a binding adjudication that establishes the rights, status, or other legal relations between the parties

Preponderance of the evidence
a standard of proof requiring that the evidence show that it is more likely than not that an alleged fact is true or false as claimed

Clear and convincing evidence
a standard of proof requiring that the evidence show that it is highly probable or reasonably certain that an alleged fact is true or false as claimed; a greater burden than preponderance of the evidence, but less than evidence beyond a reasonable doubt, the standard for criminal trials

Burden of proof
the requirement that a party prove a disputed assertion or charge

Standing
an individual's right to bring a matter before the court and seek relief based on a claim that he or she has a stake in the outcome of the case

a Complaint or Petition for Annulment, a Libel for Annulment (or for a Judgment of Nullity), or a Petition for Declaration of Invalidity of Marriage, among other options. Several states require that the action be brought within limited time frames after the impediment is known, such as sixty or ninety days or one or two years. In Wisconsin, with the exception of cases involving bigamy, annulments of marriages prohibited by law must be sought within ten years (Wis. Stat. §767.313 (1)(d)). See Exhibit 4.3 for the time limits in North Dakota.

Sometimes a party who does not want, or is not able, to file for an annulment will seek clarification as to his or her marital status by filing a **declaratory judgment** action or an action to affirm the validity of a marriage. A Declaration of Annulment or a Declaration of Validity of Marriage may be essential when the rights of individuals are being determined in the probate context. For example, what are the rights of someone who claims to be a "surviving spouse" when the validity of their marriage is in question? Such issues may be especially problematic in states that recognize common law marriage.

When a Complaint for Annulment is filed, the process is essentially the same as in divorce actions. The defendant is served and files an Answer, and, if the case is contested, related motions may be filed, discovery sought, and negotiations conducted. Once the court conducts an evidentiary hearing/trial and establishes the legal status of the marriage, it may address any potentially related issues, such as child custody and support and, if allowed, "spousal" support and property division. As with other kinds of proceedings, the court will eventually issue a decree.

BURDEN OF PROOF

Because there is a presumption that a marriage is valid, the party challenging its validity has the burden of proving it is not. The general standard of proof in a civil action is **preponderance of the evidence**. However, the standard of proof in an annulment action is commonly the higher burden of **clear and convincing evidence**. For example, in 2006, the Nevada Supreme Court established this standard for that state in annulment cases involving allegations of fraud: "Nevada courts will now require a party seeking to annul a marriage on the grounds of fraud to prove the fraud with clear and convincing evidence. Nevada law favors this higher **burden of proof** because of a strong public policy in favor of marriage and against annulment."[5]

STANDING TO PETITION FOR ANNULMENT

Generally, either party to a purported marriage has **standing** to seek an annulment absent authority to the contrary. However, in some states, only an "innocent" party can seek relief in the form of annulment. In most states, a parent or guardian of a child may file a petition when parental consent was required for marriage and was not provided or the age of the child was misrepresented.

A conservator or guardian of an adult may be permitted to seek an annulment on behalf of a ward. In a Tennessee case, for example, a conservator filed a complaint alleging that his ward lacked the mental capacity to enter into a contract of marriage and that the defendant exerted undue influence on her.

A neurologist testified that the ward was unable "to understand and appreciate the benefits, obligations and responsibilities of marriage" well before the time of the marriage ceremony, that her condition was steadily deteriorating, and that she had no lucid intervals. Since she also had already been declared incompetent by a court, her ability to enter into contracts or other legally significant acts had been terminated. An appellate court affirmed a trial court's annulment of the marriage.[6]

Courts in several states have addressed the question of whether or not an administrator or executor of a decedent's estate may seek an annulment on behalf of a deceased "spouse" after he or she has died.[7] The prevailing rule is that a void marriage may be annulled after the death of one of the parties, absent a statute or case law to the contrary. The validity of void "marriages" may be challenged by someone who claims to be a surviving spouse as well as by third parties, such as children of the decedent whose legal rights depend on whether the marriage was valid or void. With a voidable marriage, third parties (including beneficiaries under the will of a decedent) are generally not permitted to seek an annulment of a decedent's marriage.[8] Even if permitted, there may be restrictions on such actions if, for example, the marriage was followed by cohabitation and the birth of children.[9]

Grounds for Annulment

In order to obtain an annulment, proper grounds must exist. Particularly with the advent of no-fault divorce, courts are more likely than ever to hold to strict standards for granting annulments and to apply the doctrine of *caveat emptor* (Latin: let the buyer beware) when it comes to marriages that fail to meet the parties' expectations. Generally, a party may not challenge the validity of a marriage based on the express or implied representations of the other party "with respect to such matters as character, habits, chastity, business or social standing, financial worth or prospects, or matters of similar nature. It is conclusively presumed that each of the parties made his or her own independent investigation and was satisfied with the result. . . ."[10] However, annulment still is an option for parties to an alleged "marriage" in some situations.

Each state establishes the grounds considered sufficient for annulment of a marriage. Some states, such as Delaware and North Dakota (see Exhibit 4.3), grant annulments only on grounds enumerated by statute. Other states (such as Kansas) have statutes setting forth some grounds but do not consider them to be the exclusive potential grounds. A small number of states (such as Florida) have no specific statutory provisions laying out grounds for annulment of voidable marriages. Although they vary considerably from state to state, grounds typically fall into four categories (see Exhibit 4.2)

1. Grounds related to technical procedural requirements for a valid marriage set by state statute/regulation;
2. Grounds related to legal capacity to marry based on state marital restriction laws;
3. Grounds related to consent/intent to marry; and
4. Grounds related to physical factors and sexual conduct established by statute and/or case law.

PARALEGAL PRACTICE TIP

Potential grounds for annulment in a given jurisdiction are usually reflected in the complaint form. For example, if you look at the state of Oregon's Petition for Annulment form, you will see several options: prior marriage still in effect; the parties are first cousins or more closely related by blood or adoption; fraud; force; and insufficient age or understanding.

PARALEGAL PRACTICE TIP

Several religions provide for annulment in one form or another. For example, although there are divergent views of Muslim family law, each provides for annulment—in effect, "cancellation" of a marriage—if a serious deficiency arises in either party, such as "chronic madness," serious disease, or an inability to fulfill "conjugal obligations" for an extended period. The civil laws that provide for such an annulment are solidly grounded in Islamic beliefs, principles set forth in the Qur'an, and the rulings of Imams (religious leaders). An annulment under the principles of Muslim family law thus represents both a secular (civil) and a religious event.

To learn about annulment in the Catholic faith, visit *www.catholicnewsagency.com*. A Declaration of Nullity issued by an Ecclesiastical Tribunal of the Roman Catholic Church is recognized by the Church but not by the state. Before marrying again, a marriage must also be dissolved under the civil law by divorce or annulment.

EXHIBIT 4.2 Grounds for Annulment

Category	Examples	Impact
1. Grounds related to technical procedural requirements for a valid marriage set by state statute/regulation	License Parental consent/judicial approval for marriage of some minors Ceremony performed by a person authorized by state law	Noncompliance usually does not defeat creation of a valid marriage. However, a marriage may be voidable in limited circumstances that are especially egregious.
2. Grounds related to the parties' legal capacity to marry based on state marital restriction laws	Nonage/underage Affinity (relationship by marriage) Consanguinity (relationship by blood) "Marital" status (currently married or in a legally recognized relationship such as a civil union or domestic partnership) Gender	The marriage may be void or voidable depending on the ground and jurisdiction, but in virtually all states bigamous and incestuous marriages will be void.
3. Grounds related to consent/intent to marry	Fraud Mental incapacity Duress Undue influence Sham/jest/dare	The marriage may be voidable depending on the circumstances.
4. Grounds related to physical factors and sexual conduct established by statute and/or case law	Pregnancy Disease Impotence Lack of consummation	The marriage may be voidable in some circumstances.

EXHIBIT 4.3 North Dakota Century Code Title 14 Chapter 14-04 Annulment of Marriage

Courtesy: State of North Dakota

14-04-01. Grounds for annulling marriage.

A marriage may be annulled by an action in the district court to obtain a decree of nullity for any of the following causes existing at the time of the marriage:

1. That the party in whose behalf it is sought to have the marriage annulled was under the age of legal consent, . . . or that such party was of such age as to require the consent of the party's parents or guardian and such marriage was contracted without such consent, unless, after attaining legal age, such party freely cohabited with the other as husband or wife.
2. That the former husband or wife of either party was living, and the marriage with such former husband or wife was then in force.
3. That either party was of unsound mind, unless such party, after coming to reason, freely cohabited with the other as husband or wife.
4. That the consent of either party was obtained by fraud, unless such party afterwards, with full knowledge of the facts constituting the fraud, freely cohabited with the other as husband or wife.

EXHIBIT 4.3 *(Continued)*

5. That the consent of either party was obtained by force, unless such party afterwards freely cohabited with the other as husband or wife.
6. That either party was at the time of the marriage physically incapable of entering into the marriage state, and such incapacity continues and appears to be incurable.
7. That the marriage was incestuous.

14-04-02. Action to annul - Limitations of time.

An action to obtain a decree of nullity of marriage for causes mentioned in section 14-04-01 must be commenced within the periods and by the parties as follows:

1. For causes mentioned in subsection 1, by the party to the marriage who was married under the age of legal consent, within four years after arriving at the age of consent, or by the party's parents or guardian at any time before such party has arrived at the age of legal consent.
2. For causes mentioned in subsection 2, by either party during the life of the other, or by such former husband or wife.
3. For causes mentioned in subsection 3, by the party injured, or a relative or guardian of the party of unsound mind, at any time before the death of either party.
4. For causes mentioned in subsection 4, by the party injured, within four years after the discovery of the facts constituting the fraud.
5. For causes mentioned in subsections 5 and 6, by the injured party, within four years after the marriage.
6. For causes mentioned in subsection 7, by either party at any time.

GROUNDS RELATED TO TECHNICAL PROCEDURAL REQUIREMENTS FOR A VALID MARRIAGE SET BY STATE STATUTE/REGULATION

As described in Chapter 3, each state lays out by statute or administrative regulation a series of technical "requirements" for a valid marriage. Those requirements generally include an application for and issuance of a license to marry signed under pain and penalty of perjury by persons eligible to marry (with parental consent or court approval if necessary), a marriage certificate, a ceremony performed by someone licensed in the state to perform marriages, and the return of an executed marriage certificate to the appropriate keeper of public records. Although a party may claim that failure to comply with such requirements should render a marriage void, states generally do not treat as void or voidable marriages contracted in violation of technical or procedural requirements especially when both parties intended to comply with them at the time of the marriage.[11] The California Family Code, for example, explicitly provides that noncompliance with procedural requirements does not invalidate a marriage (§306).

However, in some circumstances, egregious conduct related to a technical requirement may render a marriage voidable such as when both parties deliberately lie about their ages on an application for a marriage license. Although misstatements on applications for marriage licenses do not necessarily provide a sufficient basis for an annulment, a North Carolina Court of Appeals applying Georgia law

PARALEGAL PRACTICE TIP

Some states have unique variations on these basic prohibitions. For example, Rhode Island provides special exceptions to the prohibited marriages statute with respect to consanguinity and affinity for marriages allowed by Jewish religious law (R.I. General Laws §15–1–4). Wisconsin prohibits marriages between persons closer in kin than second cousins unless the parties are first cousins and the woman is fifty-five or one party is sterile (Wis. Stat. §765.03 (1)). Utah has a similar provision (Utah Code Ann. §30–1–1 (2)(b)).

PARALEGAL PRACTICE TIP

A marriage contracted by a party under the age of capacity is considered void in some states on the ground of nonage whereas a marriage under the age of consent is usually deemed voidable if not ratified.

held that an annulment was appropriate when a wife indicated under oath on a Georgia application for a marriage license that she had been married twice before, when in fact she had been married seven times.[12]

GROUNDS RELATED TO LEGAL CAPACITY TO MARRY BASED ON STATE MARITAL RESTRICTION LAWS

Based on prevailing public policies, all states enact "marital restriction laws" that establish when an individual lacks the legal capacity to marry. For example, virtually all states expressly prohibit marriage when a prior marriage of either or both parties is still in existence (**bigamy**/polygamy), when the parties are too closely related by blood (**consanguinity**), or when one or both of the parties are "too young" to marry even with parental consent according to state law (**nonage**). A decreasing number of states prohibit marriage when the parties are too closely related by marriage (**affinity**). When one or both of the parties lacked the legal capacity to marry based on such restrictions, the purported "marriage" is usually considered void from the outset.

Nonage/Underage

A marriage entered by an underage party in violation of state law may be deemed void or voidable if not ratified. Marriage laws in every state establish an age of capacity to marry, the age under which a party may not marry even with parental consent (usually termed nonage). With the exception of California, they also set an age of consent under which a party may not marry without the consent of a parent or guardian or the permission of the court (termed underage, i.e., above the age of capacity but below the age of consent). The age requirement may be waived if the female is pregnant or has given birth to a child out of wedlock. If an underage party goes to another state where he or she is of legal age, marries, and soon after returns to the state where he or she resides, some states will consider the marriage invalid (under so-called marriage evasion laws), while others will take the position that the marriage cannot be annulled, as it was valid where it was performed.

Bigamy/Polygamy

It is a requirement in every state that in order for a marriage to be valid, all prior marriages, if any, must have been terminated by death, annulment, or dissolution prior to entering the subsequent marriage. If terminated by divorce, the divorce must be final under the law of the jurisdiction where it was granted and any waiting period must have expired before a subsequent marriage takes place. Today this restriction is expanding in practice, if not yet by statute, to include any previously existing legal status conferred by a state such as a civil union or domestic partnership. Applications for marriage licenses customarily require that information regarding the termination of any prior marriages/legally recognized statuses be provided (for example, the date of death of the last prior spouse/partner or the date and jurisdiction in which the last decree of dissolution was entered).[13]

When a party is seeking to annul a marriage based on the contention that the other party was still married to another individual in another state or another country, proof will need to be presented to the court documenting the prior marriage and the fact that the earlier spouse is still alive.[14] If the other party claims the earlier marriage has been dissolved, proof of dissolution needs to be presented to the court as a defense.

Gender

For literally hundreds of years across the nation marriage was defined as, and restricted to, the union of a man and a woman under state and federal law. Beginning in 2003 in Massachusetts, this restriction began to erode as the right to marry gradually extended to same-sex couples. As of the U.S. Supreme Court's watershed *Obergefell* decision on June 26, 2015, all of the states must permit both heterosexual and same-sex couples to marry. In its sharply divided decision, the Court struck down marital access and recognition bans based on gender as unconstitutional violations of both Due Process and Equal Protection opening a new era of marriage equality and at least prospectively closing the door on violations of gender-based marital restriction laws as a ground for annulment.

GROUNDS RELATED TO CONSENT/INTENT TO MARRY

Even when parties to an alleged marriage had the legal capacity to marry, questions sometimes arise about whether one or both of them did so unintentionally, involuntarily, or under a misconception. Most states establish grounds for annulment of a marriage considered voidable based on a circumstance existing at the time it was entered such as a fraudulent representation by one of the parties, an absence of intent to assume the rights and responsibilities of marriage, or a lack of sufficient mental capacity to marry. For example, a small number of states identify "joke," "jest," or "dare" as a ground for annulment. (See, e.g., Colorado (CRS §14–10–111 (1)(f)) and Delaware (13 Del. C. §1506 (a)(6).) Being under the influence of alcohol or drugs at the time of the marriage is a ground for annulment in several states. (See, e.g., Texas Family Code §6.105 and Illinois 750 ILCS 5/301 (1).)

Fraud

The basic elements of fraud are illustrated in Paralegal Application 4.1. In addition to satisfying the elements, several states require that in order to obtain an annulment based on fraud, once the fraud is discovered, the petitioner must no longer voluntarily cohabit with the party who perpetrated it. To support a claim on this ground, the fraud must directly affect the marital relationship in some manner. It must go to "the essentials of marriage."

Courts are reluctant to annul a marriage for fraud unless the defrauded party would not have entered the marriage except for the fraud. Decisions are made on a case-by-case basis, because what is considered essential to a marriage by one party may be of considerably less significance to another. For example, annulments are sometimes sought based on the failure of one of the parties to live up to a premarital promise to practice a particular religion. Whether or not a court will grant an annulment in such circumstances tends to turn on the extent to which religion is central to the marriage and permeates multiple facets of marital life and culture (diet, dress, language, social life, etc.). See, e.g., *In re the Marriage of Linda A. and Robert S. Owen*, 2002 Cal. App. Unpub. LEXIS 1500.

PARALEGAL PRACTICE TIP

Before same-sex marriages were permitted, courts in Florida, Kansas, New Jersey, New York, Ohio, and Texas addressed issues related to marriages involving postoperative transsexual persons. A New Jersey court upheld the validity of a marriage involving a transsexual and denied an annulment to a husband sought on the ground that his wife was a male-to-female transsexual. Courts in other states tended to grant annulments applying a narrow traditional meaning of male and female, determining a party's gender based on chromosomal makeup rather than on the "gender identity" or "self-identity" test applied in New Jersey.[15]

PARALEGAL PRACTICE TIP

In *Desta v. Anyaoha*, 371 S.W.3d 596 (Tex. App. 2012), a husband sought an annulment from his wife, an Ethiopian citizen, whom he had met on an Internet dating site. She had induced him to marry her by claiming she loved and wanted to marry him and have several children. He subsequently learned that she had only married him so she could obtain a **green card** and that before she came to the United States she had a birth control injection so she could avoid becoming pregnant. Once learning of the fraud he ceased cohabiting with her thereby satisfying a requirement set forth in Tex. Fam. Code Ann. §6.107 for seeking an annulment.

Green card
a document (registration card) evidencing a resident alien's status as a permanent resident of the United States; a "green card marriage" is a sham marriage in which a U.S. citizen marries a foreign citizen for the sole purpose of allowing the foreign citizen to become a permanent U.S. resident

PARALEGAL PRACTICE TIP

The Minnesota Supreme Court declined to grant an annulment to a husband who discovered after marriage that his wife had been committed to a mental institution prior to their marriage. After the marriage, she had a relapse and was again committed. In denying the annulment, the court reasoned that there was no fraud because the wife had not actively concealed her prior commitment and her husband had never inquired about it.[16]

Fraud related to personal characteristics or habits is generally not considered sufficient to justify annulment of a marriage. Annulments are also rarely, if ever, granted solely based on fraud or misrepresentation of a purely financial nature (business interests, financial worth or prospects, etc.) even when a perpetrator of the fraud admits to misrepresenting financial circumstances or deceiving the other party with respect to allegedly joint-business ventures.[17]

Examples of fraud that some courts have held do go to the essentials of marriage include concealment of an inability or a lack of intention to have children, a woman's pregnancy by another man at the time of the marriage, or fraud related to sexual orientation, prior marital status, chastity, or matters of health or drug abuse.[18] The Superior Court of New Jersey granted an annulment to a wife because the husband told her after they had married that he wanted to have children despite the fact that he had signed a premarital agreement in which he stated that he did not want to. The court held that this situation constituted fraud relating to an essential element of the marriage contract.[19]

Paralegal Application 4.1

The Elements of Fraud

Fraud
a false statement of a material fact with intent that another rely on the statement to his or her detriment.

If a husband seeks an annulment on fraud grounds based on the fact that his wife lied to him about being pregnant so that he would marry her, he needs to plead and prove all of the elements of fraud:

a. a false representation by the wife—she told him she was pregnant when she was not
b. the wife's knowledge of the falsity—she knew she was not pregnant

c. the misrepresentation concerns an essential of the marital relationship—childbearing and rearing are essentials of the marital relationship
d. the wife's intention that the husband act on the representation—she told him she was pregnant so that he would marry her
e. his reliance on the truth of the representation—he believed her and married her as a result of the misrepresentation
f. he sustained injury as a result of the misrepresentation—he entered a marriage he would otherwise not have entered

Lack of Consent, Duress, and Undue Influence

Marriage is a contract and, like other contracts, may be voided by a lack of mental capacity of one or both of the parties. For a marriage to be valid there needs to be a shared intent to assume the rights and duties of marriage. Each party to a marriage must be capable of consenting at the time of the marriage and must be able to understand and appreciate the benefits, obligations, and responsibilities of marriage. A person who is mentally limited or incompetent for some purposes may still legally consent to marriage in a lucid moment. The standard is generally lower than it would be for a contract under the Uniform Commercial Code for a business transaction. Absent evidence to the contrary, it is generally assumed that an individual who is getting married basically understands what marriage is and wants to be married to his or her partner.

Several states set out by statute grounds for annulment that are related to lack of consent at the time the marriage was solemnized. For example, a party may be incapable of consenting due to a mental condition, duress, undue influence, or the effects of intoxicants of some kind. The lack of consent may also be expressed in statutes as a "lack of mutual assent" to the marriage relationship. If the marriage has been followed by cohabitation or otherwise ratified, consent grounds are usually unavailable.

Undue influence is generally said to occur where there has been a fraudulent influence over the mind and will of another to the extent that an action of that person is not freely done, but rather is the act of the one who procures the result. **Duress** is an extreme form of undue influence involving threats or force. Annulment actions on these grounds may be able to be brought by third parties as well as by a "spouse" and may, in some circumstances, be brought after the death of a party. (See Case 4.1.)

Undue influence
the improper use of power or trust in a way that deprives a person of his or her free will and substitutes another's purposes in its place

Duress
a threat of harm made to compel a person to do something contrary to his or her free will or judgment

CASE 4.1 *Estate of Goodwin v. Foust-Graham*, 171 N.C. App. 707, 615 S.E.2d 398 (2005)

BACKGROUND

Under North Carolina law, the marriage of a person who is incapable of contracting from want of will is voidable. It will remain valid until it is declared void in a legal action. Prior to this case, North Carolina courts had annulled marriages on the basis of duress, but neither the North Carolina Supreme Court nor an appellate court in the state had addressed "undue influence" as a ground for annulment.

FROM THE OPINION

In the instant case, there was evidence pertaining to each of the factors that our Supreme Court has identified as relevant in analyzing undue influence. . . . Specifically, Goodwin was elderly at the time of the marriage, and there was testimony tending to establish that he was suffering from dementia and/or Alzheimer's disease. It is not disputed that he was subject to constant association with, and supervision by, Foust-Graham and that he had little association with his family or friends in the months immediately preceding the marriage. The marriage left Goodwin's previously existing estate plan in doubt and placed Foust-Graham in a position to take action that would substantially reduce the amount that Goodwin's daughter would inherit. Further, there was evidence that Foust-Graham procured the marriage, including Goodwin's apparent confusion as to why he was at the magistrate's office, the fact that Foust-Graham had driven Goodwin to the magistrate's office, and the fact that the marriage was undertaken suddenly. Accordingly, the jury could find that Goodwin was subject to undue influence, that Foust-Graham had the opportunity and disposition to exert undue influence, and that the marriage occurred as a result of undue influence. . . . a finding of undue influence is tantamount to a finding that Goodwin was incapable of contracting from want of will, . . .

SIDEBAR

To what extent do you agree with the outcome in this case? Explain your response. The full opinion in the *Estate of Goodwin v. Foust-Graham* case is available at *www.pearsonhighered.com/careersresources/* in the website material for Chapter 4 of this text under Cases.

GROUNDS RELATED TO PHYSICAL FACTORS AND SEXUAL CONDUCT

Physical conditions and sexual conduct sometimes provide the basis for annulment actions either standing alone or in the context of a fraud allegation. Several states have recognized disease, impotence, and lack of consummation as grounds among others. In Mississippi, a cause for annulment is the "Pregnancy of the wife by another person, if the husband did not know of the pregnancy" (Miss. Code Ann. §93–7–3 (e)). Virginia will grant an annulment when, prior to the marriage, either party was, without the knowledge of the other, a prostitute (Va. Code Ann. §20–89.1(b)). Concealment of prior homosexuality may not be enough to support an annulment but concealment of one's sexual preference at the time of marriage may be sufficient.

Disease

Although such tests have largely been eliminated, historically parties planning to wed were required to undergo mandatory premarital physical exams or blood tests to detect the presence of diseases (such as syphilis, tuberculosis, and rubella) prior to being granted a marriage license. Although the tests may have been eliminated, some physical conditions still present a sufficient ground for annulment. When a party to a marriage conceals from his or her spouse the existence of an incurable sexually transmitted disease (e.g., syphilis or HIV/AIDS), an annulment may be granted in some circumstances. In Hawaii, a statute expressly provides as a ground for annulment that one of the parties was afflicted by a "loathsome disease" at the time of the marriage that was unknown to the party seeking an annulment. (HRS §580–21 (6).) In an unpublished California decision, an appellate court found that substantial evidence supported a trial court's finding that a wife's concealment of her incurable and highly transmittable syphilitic condition warranted granting a judgment of annulment to the husband. The court concluded that "a spouse's concealment of a medical condition or sexually transmittable disease that does not absolutely foreclose intercourse or child-bearing, but nevertheless endangers the life and health of the other spouse or their offspring, is so destructive of marital intimacy and the potential for procreation that it goes to 'the very essence of the marital relation.' . . ."[20]

Impotence

Impotence
lack of capacity to procreate due to inability to have sexual intercourse or to incompetent sperm or ova

In general, parties to a marriage reasonably anticipate having a sexual relationship with their spouse after marriage. **Impotence**, or lack of a party's capacity to have sexual intercourse or to procreate, may be a ground for annulment when the other party did not know of the condition at the time of the marriage. In some states, the impotence must be incurable. It may make the marriage voidable at the election of the unknowing party. However, after learning of the condition, the aggrieved party may ratify the marriage by continuing to live with the other party and claiming a marital status under the law and before the general public. Unlike grounds such as bigamy and consanguinity, impotence is usually viewed as a ground available only to a party to the marriage and not to third persons, given the nature of proof required.

Lack of consummation

Consummation is not usually considered a requirement for a marriage to be valid. However, a minority of states have identified as a ground for annulment the willful failure or refusal to consummate a marriage and/or cohabit without good cause. For example, Ohio Revised Code §3105.31(F) provides as a ground "That the marriage between the parties was never consummated although otherwise valid." See *Patel v. Patel*, 2014 Ohio 2150, 11 N.E.3d 800 (2014). If a party marries with an undisclosed "intent not to perform, followed by a refusal to perform, that party is guilty of fraud which goes to the essence of the marriage relationship." In *Janda v. Janda*, 984 So. 2d 434 (Ala. Civ. App. 2007), for example, a wife first thought her husband's refusal to engage in sexual relations stemmed from cultural differences between them or her weight problem. After losing 65 pounds in an unsuccessful effort to be more attractive to her husband, she finally realized he never had any intention of honoring his marital obligations and had only married her so he could obtain a green card and become a permanent citizen of the United States.

Consummation
making a marriage complete by engaging in sexual intercourse

Defenses to an Annulment Action

The most commonly raised defenses to an annulment action are:

- Compliance with state statutes governing marriage
- Ratification of the marriage by subsequent conduct
- Consummation of the marriage
- Laches
- Equitable estoppel
- Judicial estoppel
- Unclean hands

COMPLIANCE WITH STATE STATUTES GOVERNING MARRIAGE

When an annulment action is based on an allegation that a state law or regulation was violated at the time the marriage was entered, the defendant may produce proof that no violation of a marital restriction law occurred. For example, if the petition alleges that a party lacked legal capacity to marry due to a prior marriage still in force, official records may be searched and certified court documents produced showing that the earlier marriage was dissolved by a divorce or annulment in the same or another jurisdiction prior to the subsequent marriage. A petition may allege a procedural violation in that the person who performed the marriage ceremony was not authorized to do so due to a previously undiscovered lapse in his license resulting from a bureaucratic backup. The defendant may provide proof that the celebrant had been a pastor at her church for ten years and that she had a good faith belief that he was at all times authorized to perform marriages. A state statute on point may be introduced indicating that a lack of licensed authority does not warrant an annulment under state law.

PARALEGAL PRACTICE TIP

A Virginia statute provides as follows: VA Code § 20-31. Belief of parties in lawful marriage validates certain defects.

No marriage solemnized under a license issued in this Commonwealth by any person professing to be authorized to solemnize the same shall be deemed or adjudged to be void, nor shall the validity thereof be in any way affected on account of any want of authority in such person, or any defect, omission or imperfection in such license, if the marriage be in all other respects lawful, and be consummated with a full belief on the part of the persons so married, or either of them, that they have been lawfully joined in marriage.

RATIFICATION OF THE MARRIAGE BY SUBSEQUENT CONDUCT

Ratification

acceptance or confirmation of a previous act thereby making it valid from the moment it was done

A party usually may not ratify a void marriage, for example, a bigamous marriage. However, when a marriage is voidable, it may be ratified by the parties continuing to cohabit once an impediment is discovered (such as a fraud) or after the source of duress is removed. Several states provide by statute or case law that a marriage voidable due to lack of mental capacity may not be annulled if the parties freely cohabit after restoration of mental capacity. In the case of a minor who marries without parental consent, **ratification** is normally accomplished by the parties voluntarily continuing to live together as husband and wife after the minor attains the age of majority.

CONSUMMATION OF THE MARRIAGE

In annulment actions, courts may consider whether or not there has been cohabitation following a marriage. Cohabitation is evidence that the parties have been validly married, but it is not dispositive, nor is it essential to establish a marriage, particularly when there has been sexual intercourse prior to marriage. Generally, if a voidable marriage is consummated with knowledge of an impediment, it will be considered ratified. A Florida court, for example, has held that a marriage that has been consummated cannot be annulled on the basis of fraud alone.[21] There are also circumstances in which the parties may marry with full understanding that the marriage will never be consummated, as when one of the parties is incarcerated for life without possibility of parole or conjugal visitation.

LACHES

Laches

unreasonable delay in pursuing a right or claim that prejudices the other party's rights

The defense of **laches** is an equitable doctrine that precludes a litigant from asserting a claim if his or her unreasonable delay in raising the claim has prejudiced the opposing party. It is based on the notion that courts should not come to the aid of a party who has knowingly "slept on his rights" to the detriment of the other party.[22] This is a primary rationale for establishing time frames within which injured parties such as minors or victims of fraud must disaffirm their marriages. (See, e.g., the North Dakota statute in Exhibit 4.3.)

EQUITABLE ESTOPPEL

Equitable estoppel

preventing a party from asserting a claim or a defense because it would be unfair to an opposing party to do otherwise

A party may raise **equitable estoppel** as a defense when he or she was induced by another person to rely, to his or her detriment, on the statements or conduct of that other person. The person who asserts a claim of estoppel must have reasonably relied on the acts or representations of the other and have had no knowledge or means of knowing the facts. Assume, for example, that Dawn marries Gina not knowing that Gina is underage. Gina lies on the marriage application about her age and the couple marries and lives together for two years. Gina then decides she wants to move on and files a Complaint for Annulment on the ground that she was underage when they wed. Dawn is brokenhearted and asserts that, based on principles of fairness, the court should "estop" Gina from denying the validity of the marriage because she knew she was underage and lied on the marriage application.

In exceptional circumstances, some jurisdictions permit a marriage to be created by equitable estoppel to mitigate the effects of fraud and protect the rights of innocent persons who otherwise would be adversely affected. In marriage by estoppel, a marriage is presumed to be valid even though technically it is not. This remedy is generally available only with respect to voidable but not void marriages. For example, courts are highly unlikely to apply the doctrine when parties enter a bigamous marriage, even if neither party was aware of the impediment.[23]

JUDICIAL ESTOPPEL

A variation on equitable estoppel is **judicial estoppel**, a doctrine designed to protect the courts as well as good-faith litigants. Judicial estoppel is an equitable doctrine intended to prevent a party from gaining an unfair advantage over another party by making inconsistent statements on the same issue in different lawsuits. As a North Carolina court phrased it, ". . . our courts do not permit the submission of new theories, not previously argued, because the law does not permit parties to swap horses between courts in order to get a better mount. . . ."[24] In the *Pickard* case decided by a North Carolina Court of Appeals, the court applied this doctrine and upheld a district court's denial of an annulment to a petitioner. (See Case 4.2.)

Judicial estoppel
an equitable doctrine designed to prevent a party from gaining an unfair advantage over another party by making inconsistent statements on the same issue in different lawsuits

UNCLEAN HANDS

The doctrine of **unclean hands** provides that "he who comes into Equity must come with clean hands."[25] The rationale for the doctrine is that if a plaintiff has, through misconduct, injured or damaged the defendant, the court should not allow that plaintiff to benefit as a result of his or her own misdeeds. Although it may be raised as a defense in annulment actions involving voidable marriages, it cannot be used a defense to an action based on a prior existing marriage no matter how despicable a plaintiff's conduct may be. For example, in *Emmitt v. Emmitt et al.*, 174 S.W.3d 248 (Tenn. App. 2005), a trial court had allowed the defense and denied a claim for annulment brought by a woman who had married her second husband at a time when she had not confirmed that her first marriage had been dissolved. She later sought to annul her second marriage so she would be in a position to benefit financially from the death of the first husband. Despite her offensive motives, on appeal, the court reluctantly held that the trial court erred by not granting the annulment given that the second marriage was void because she was not legally capable of entering it when a prior marriage was still in force.

Unclean hands
the principle that a party should not be granted relief if he or she has acted unfairly, wrongfully, or illegally

CASE **4.2** *Pickard v. Pickard*, 625 S.E.2d 869 (N.C. App. 2006)

Carl Pickard and his wife, Jane, had been married by a Cherokee Indian in the Native American tradition in June of 1991. The parties had received a North Carolina license and certificate of marriage and filed it with the appropriate Register of Deeds. Both of the parties believed the ceremony was legally sufficient to bind them in marriage and they lived together and conducted themselves as husband and wife for the next eleven years. In 1998, the husband petitioned the court to adopt his wife's adult biological daughter. He provided the court with a sworn statement that he was "the stepfather of the adoptee, having married her natural mother." He also listed his marital status as "married." The clerk of the county superior court subsequently filed a decree of adoption based on his assertions. When the husband subsequently sought an annulment in 2002, he alleged that the marriage ceremony was not properly solemnized because the Cherokee Indian who performed it was not qualified to conduct a marriage ceremony. Because the husband had earlier represented himself to the court in the adoption proceeding as married, the court in

(Continued)

Res judicata
an issue that has been definitively settled by judicial decision; the three essential elements are: (1) an earlier decision on the issue, (2) a final judgment on the merits, and (3) the involvement of the original parties

effect held that the issue of his marital status was ***res judicata***, and he was judicially estopped from later claiming his marriage was not valid. The appellate court noted that it also would impose an unfair detriment on the wife if it were to undo an eleven-year marriage by allowing the husband to proceed with his inconsistent position.

SIDEBAR

Do you agree with the court's decision? The full opinion in the *Pickard* case can be accessed at *www.pearsonhighered.com/careersresources/* in the companion website material related to Chapter 4 of this text under Cases.

Paralegal **Application 4.2**

Which Law Will Apply?

When multiple states are involved in an annulment case, a conflict-of-law issue may arise. The general rule is that if a marriage would be valid in the state where it was entered, it will be valid in the state where a party is domiciled at the time of the annulment action unless it violates a strong public policy of that state. However, some states have marriage evasion statutes providing that if domiciliaries of that state go to another state solely to evade a marriage restriction, marry in the second state, and then return to their home state, the home state may refuse to recognize the "marriage."

Consider the following hypothetical:

John and Mary are first cousins. They have been lifelong residents of Louisiana but went to Georgia

in 2010 for a brief period where they were married. Their son was conceived in Georgia shortly before they returned to Louisiana where they have since resided. In approximately half the states, including Georgia, first cousins are permitted to marry. In Louisiana they are not. In 2015, John filed for an annulment in Louisiana on the grounds that as first cousins, they lacked the legal capacity to marry. The court in this case is faced with a conflict of law between the state where the parties wed and the state where they subsequently resided and the annulment is sought. The presiding court must choose which law to apply in the case. What issues might a paralegal be asked to research in this case? What defenses might Mary raise?

Consequences of An Annulment

FOR THE PARTIES

PARALEGAL PRACTICE TIP

Attorneys will advise clients in annulment cases to revise their respective wills particularly if they still want to provide for their "spouse." An annulment will revoke the designation of the "spouse" as personal representative and usually will also automatically revoke gifts and bequests made to that "spouse" as a "surviving spouse" unless the will expressly states otherwise. If no will exists, one should be prepared and executed.

The general rule is that if a marriage ends in an annulment, the parties are returned to the legal status they held prior to the marriage. Therefore, annulment of a second marriage may entitle a party to reinstatement of Social Security, insurance, retirement, and/or worker's compensation death benefits flowing from a prior marriage. The party may also again be able to inherit from the earlier (but not the later) "spouse" on the basis of marital status. On the other hand, alimony from a former spouse commonly terminates upon the recipient's remarriage. If the later "marriage" is subsequently annulled, the recipient may claim that the payor should have to resume paying alimony. Courts use a variety of approaches to address this question including the following:

- Alimony obligations revive after void but not voidable remarriages of alimony recipients.
- Alimony automatically terminates on the remarriage of the recipient regardless of subsequent events furthering interests of finality and certainty for the obligor when the obligee elects to look to another for support.

- The revival decision is made on a case-by-case basis.
- The decision is driven by the language of the parties' separation agreement if the issue is specifically addressed in an agreement incorporated in the court's decree dissolving the prior marriage.

(See the Focus on Case Law at the end of this chapter and read the *Fredo* case that addresses this issue.)

Property division and spousal support provisions that would be triggered upon divorce technically do not apply to the parties following an annulment because they are based on the existence of a valid marriage and are "incidents of divorce." If there is no marriage, there is no divorce, no "marital property" to divide, and no "former spouse" to pay or receive alimony.[26] However, a minority of states (including New York and Connecticut) specifically provide by statute that in some circumstances the court may grant alimony upon annulment as in the case of divorce.[27]

With respect to property division, most states provide for the parties by applying equitable principles on a case-by-case basis. For example, courts in some states (particularly community property states such as California, Texas, and Washington) may declare a marriage void and yet grant a putative spouse, who innocently believed the marriage was valid, a share of the couple's quasi-marital property. Such states use a good-faith analysis to determine whether either of the parties had reason to believe the marriage was invalid. In a 2004 case, the Nevada Supreme Court applied the **putative spouse** doctrine as a basis for dividing the parties' property. (See Case 4.3.) Even though the putative spouse may be deemed entitled to a share of the quasi-marital property, the marriage itself is considered void.

Putative spouse
a person who believes in good faith that his or her invalid marriage is legally valid

CASE **4.3** *Williams v. Williams*, 97 P.3d 1124 (Nev. 2004)

FROM THE OPINION

This is a case of first impression involving the application of the putative spouse doctrine in an annulment proceeding. Under the doctrine, an individual whose marriage is void due to a prior legal impediment is treated as a spouse so long as the party seeking equitable relief participated in the marriage ceremony with the good-faith belief that the ceremony was legally valid. A majority of the states recognize the doctrine when dividing property acquired during the marriage, applying equitable principles, based on community property law, to the division. However, absent fraud, the doctrine does not apply to awards of spousal support. While some states have extended the doctrine to permit spousal support awards, they have done so under the authority of state statutes.

We agree with the majority view. Consequently, we adopt the putative spouse doctrine in annulment proceedings for the purposes of property division and affirm the district court's division of property. However, we reject the doctrine as a basis for awarding equitable spousal support. Because Nevada's annulment statutes do not provide for an award of support upon annulment, we reverse the district court's award of spousal support.

On August 26, 1973, appellant Richard E. Williams underwent a marriage ceremony with respondent Marcie C. Williams. At that time, Marcie believed she was divorced from John Allmaras. However, neither Marcie nor Allmaras had obtained a divorce. Richard and Marcie believed they were legally married and lived together, as husband and wife, for 27 years. In March 2000, Richard discovered that Marcie was not divorced from Allmaras at the time of their marriage ceremony.

In August 2000, Richard and Marcie permanently separated. In February 2001, Richard filed a complaint for an annulment. Marcie answered and counterclaimed for one-half of the property and spousal support as a putative spouse. In April 2002, the parties engaged in a one-day bench trial to resolve the matter.

At trial, Richard testified that had he known Marcie was still married, he would not have married her. He claimed that Marcie knew she was not divorced when she married him or had knowledge that would put a reasonable person on notice to check if the prior marriage had been dissolved. . . .

The district court found that Marcie had limited ability to support herself. The district court also concluded that both parties believed they were legally married, acted as husband and wife, and conceived and raised two children. Marcie stayed at home to care for and raise their children. Based on these facts, the district court granted the annulment and awarded Marcie one-half of all the jointly-held property and spousal support. The district court did not indicate whether its award was based on the putative spouse doctrine or an implied contract and quantum meruit theory. . . .

A marriage is void if either of the parties to the marriage has a former husband or wife then living. Richard and Marcie's marriage was void because Marcie was still married to another man when she married Richard. Although their marriage was void, an annulment proceeding was necessary to legally sever their relationship. An annulment proceeding is the proper manner to dissolve a void marriage and resolve other issues arising from the dissolution of the relationship.

Under the putative spouse doctrine, when a marriage is legally void, the civil effects of a legal marriage flow to the parties who contracted to marry in good faith. That is, a putative spouse is entitled to many of the rights of an actual spouse. A majority of the states have recognized some form of the doctrine. . . .

The doctrine has two elements: (1) a proper marriage ceremony was performed, and (2) one or both of the parties had a good-faith belief that there was no impediment to the marriage and the marriage was valid and proper. "Good faith" has been defined as an "honest and reasonable belief that the marriage was valid at the time of the ceremony." Good faith is presumed. The party asserting lack of good faith has the burden of proving bad faith. Whether the party acted in good faith is a question of fact. Unconfirmed rumors or mere suspicions of a legal impediment do not vitiate good faith "so long as no certain or authoritative knowledge of some legal impediment comes to him or her." However, when a person receives reliable information that an impediment exists, the individual cannot ignore the information, but instead has a duty to investigate further. Persons cannot act "blindly or without reasonable precaution." Finally, once a spouse learns of the impediment, the putative marriage ends.

We have not previously considered the putative spouse doctrine, but we are persuaded by the rationale of our sister states that public policy supports adopting the doctrine in Nevada. Fairness and equity favor recognizing putative spouses when parties enter into a marriage ceremony in good faith and without knowledge there is a factual or legal impediment to their marriage. Nor does the doctrine conflict with Nevada's policy in refusing to recognize common-law marriages or palimony suits. . . . As a majority of our sister states have recognized, the sanctity of marriage is not undermined, but rather enhanced, by the recognition of the putative spouse doctrine. We therefore adopt the doctrine in Nevada.

We now apply the doctrine to the instant case. The district court found that the parties obtained a license and participated in a marriage ceremony on August 26, 1973, in Verdi, Nevada. The district court also found that Marcie erroneously believed that her prior husband, Allmaras, had terminated their marriage by divorce and that she was legally able to marry Richard. In so finding, the district court also necessarily rejected Richard's argument that Marcie acted unreasonably in relying on Allmaras' statements because she had never been served with divorce papers and that she had a duty to inquire about the validity of her former marriage before marrying Richard.

. . . The district court was free to disregard Richard's testimony, and substantial evidence supports the district court's finding that Marcie did not act unreasonably in relying on Allmaras' representations. The record reflects no reason for Marcie to have disbelieved him and, thus, no reason to have investigated the truth of his representations. . . .

Community property states that recognize the putative spouse doctrine apply community property principles to the division of property, including determinations of what constitutes community and separate property. Since putative spouses believe themselves to be married, they are already under the assumption that community property statutes would apply to a termination of their relationship. There is no point, therefore in devising a completely separate set of rules for dividing property in a putative spouse scenario. . . .

States are divided on whether spousal support is a benefit or civil effect that may be awarded under the putative spouse doctrine. Although some states permit the award of alimony, they do so because their annulment statutes permit an award of rehabilitative or permanent alimony. At least one state, however, has found alimony to be a civil effect under the putative spouse doctrine even in the absence of a specific statute permitting an award of alimony.

Nevada statutes do not provide for an award of alimony after annulment. . . .

. . . We adopt the putative spouse doctrine and conclude that common-law community property principles apply by analogy to the division of property acquired during a putative marriage. However, the putative spouse doctrine does not permit an award of spousal support in the absence of bad faith, fraud or statutory authority. Therefore, we affirm that portion of the district court's order equally dividing the parties' property and reverse that portion of the order awarding spousal support.

SIDEBAR

Do you agree with the outcome? How reasonable is it for a spouse to rely on the oral and undocumented representations of a former spouse that their marriage is dissolved? What would you do in the same circumstances? What do you think the result should be if one of the parties entered the marriage with knowledge of the impediment and does not qualify as a putative spouse? The full opinion in the Williams case is available at *www.pearsonhighered.com/careersresources/* in the website material for Chapter 4 of this text under Cases.

FOR THE CHILDREN

Although technically born "out of wedlock," in most states, children born to marriages that are subsequently annulled are deemed "legitimate" for legal purposes under state law. Some states, such as Nebraska and Iowa, specifically provide by statute that children born to annulled marriages are legitimate unless a court decrees otherwise. The courts generally will treat them as legitimate whenever possible within the law to achieve a desirable result. In some cases, the court in a state where a child of annulment is considered illegitimate may accomplish a positive result by applying the law of another state if the child in question was born in and would be considered legitimate under that state's law.

Regardless of the child's legal status, when an annulment is granted to his or her parents, the courts usually will make orders for the care, custody, and maintenance of the child. In addition, with the exception of inheritance rights, most other disabilities of "illegitimacy" have been eliminated by statute or constitutional interpretation. However, children of annulment may need to establish legal parentage to inherit from or through a parent or to claim benefits such as the right to file a wrongful death or workman's compensation claim for injury to a parent. They are also required to go through extra bureaucratic steps to establish their rights to a variety of federal dependent-based benefits or to establish citizenship.

Although alimony obligations of a prior spouse are usually not revived by annulment of a recipient's subsequent marriage, annulment of a child's marriage during his or her minority usually will revive the child's unemancipated status and also revive a parent's child support obligation. "Public policy directs that parents financially support their minor children, even if those children make unwise decisions. Moreover, assuming the parent with the support obligation might rely on the validity of the child's marriage in making financial plans, that period of reliance would not last indefinitely but only until the child would otherwise become emancipated."[28]

The Paralegal's Role in an Annulment Case

The tasks most commonly performed by a paralegal in an annulment case are:

- Researching the law governing annulment in the applicable jurisdiction and in other jurisdictions as well, if appropriate
- Preparing related memoranda based on research as requested
- Gathering information and documentation regarding topics including but not limited to the following:
  - The marriage: when, where, and how it was performed
  - Prior marriages/civil unions/domestic partnerships: when they were entered and when and how they were dissolved
  - Cohabitation and consummation of the marriage
  - Potential grounds for annulment
  - Any children conceived during the marriage
  - Property owned by each party prior to the marriage and acquired thereafter
- Drafting related correspondence
- Scheduling and participating in interviews as assigned
- Drafting complaints/petitions, motions, supporting affidavits, and proposed orders or responses to complaints/petitions

- Drafting discovery requests, if necessary, such as proposed interrogatories, deposition questions, requests for admissions, requests for production of documents and things, and requests for physical or mental examinations
- Assisting in preparation for hearings or trial, including drafting pretrial memoranda for review, organizing documents and exhibits, etc.
- Preparing subpoenas for witnesses, if necessary
- Helping to prepare the client as well as witnesses appearing for the client
- Tracking progress on the case and being certain that any timelines are met
- Making sure the client is kept informed of progress and upcoming deadlines, hearings, discovery matters, etc.
- Acting as a conduit for providing information such as brochures, charts, instructions, and frequently-asked-questions (FAQs) sheets

CHAPTER SUMMARY

Prior to the emergence of no-fault divorce in the 1970s, divorce actions were based on grounds such as cruel and abusive treatment, adultery, abandonment, imprisonment, and chronic alcohol abuse. The process was especially painful and antagonistic and often presented difficult problems of proof. Annulment actions sometimes provided an alternative but not necessarily an emotionally and financially less costly one. Today, annulment is still an appropriate option in some cases. However, no-fault divorce now may present most couples with a more desirable route to terminating their marriage.

This chapter first addressed the meaning of annulment and the distinction between an alleged marriage that is void *ab initio* (a marriage that never came into being because of a legal impediment that existed at the time of the marriage) and

a voidable marriage (one that remains valid until declared invalid by a court of competent jurisdiction). After clarifying the differences between annulment and divorce, the basic process for obtaining an annulment was briefly described. Various grounds for annulment were reviewed and illustrated including grounds related to procedural requirements for valid marriages, marital restriction laws, consent or intent to marry, and physical factors or sexual conduct. Also referenced were some of the more common defenses to an annulment action such as compliance with state law, laches, ratification, consummation, estoppel (equitable and judicial), and unclean hands. The paralegal's role in an annulment case was noted throughout the chapter, with emphasis on the particular importance of being aware of local law and procedure and jurisdictional variations.

CONCEPT REVIEW AND REINFORCEMENT

KEY TERMS

Affinity	Equitable estoppel	*Quasi*-marital property
Annulment	Fraud	Ratification
Bigamy	Green card	*Res judicata*
Burden of proof	Impotence	Standing
Clear and convincing evidence	Judicial estoppel	Unclean hands
Consanguinity	Laches	Undue influence
Consummation	Marriage	Void *ab initio*
Declaratory judgment	Nonage	Voidable marriage
Duress	Preponderance of the evidence	
Ecclesiastical law	Putative spouse	

REVIEW QUESTIONS

1. Define and distinguish between a marriage that is void *ab initio* and one that is voidable, and give an example of each.
2. Distinguish between annulment and divorce.
3. Describe the procedure for obtaining an annulment, and identify the kinds of individuals who have standing to bring annulment actions.
4. Identify four grounds for annulment and give an example of each.

5. Identify five potential defenses to an annulment action.
6. Identify consequences of an annulment for the parties and for their children.

7. Describe the role of a paralegal in an annulment action.

DEVELOPING YOUR PARALEGAL SKILLS

FOCUS ON **THE JOB**

In this activity, the student will draft a complaint for annulment based on a specific fact pattern.

The Facts

John and Audrey Morrison had a nonmarital relationship that began in 2010. John is an attorney and a partner in a law firm. Audrey is a certified public accountant. In the late spring of 2014, Audrey became pregnant. John claimed that the pregnancy was Audrey's fault and her responsibility and told her she should get an abortion as soon as possible. He said the pregnancy should be terminated because he was not prepared to be a father at that point in his life. A devout Catholic for her entire life, Audrey was determined not to have an abortion. She and John had a series of arguments on the subject, and Audrey became so upset by the situation that she went to a therapist and was put on strong medication that calmed her down but clouded her thinking. John believed she was suicidal and in an effort to prevent that outcome, agreed to marry her prior to the birth of their child. He felt very pressured and, although he didn't tell her at the time of the marriage, he did not plan to live together as husband and wife after the child was born, nor did he intend to remain married. He just wanted to stop her tirades and nagging and thought that if she felt their child was "legitimate," she would accept whatever happened between the two of them.

John was quite wrong on several fronts. After the baby was born, a healthy boy named John Morrison, Jr., John decided he wanted to remain married and raise the boy as a couple. He told Audrey that he was very happy as a family man and that he couldn't believe what he had initially intended to do. When she questioned him further and he told her about his earlier plan, she immediately went wild, took the baby, ran out of the house calling him all sorts of names, and went to live with her sister. The following week she went to meet with an attorney, your supervisor, in order to file for an annulment of their marriage based on her husband's conduct and intentions at the time the parties were married.

The Assignment

Assume that you are a paralegal in the firm representing Audrey in the above fact pattern. The firm is Wilson and Tauson, LLP, located at 390 Main Street, your city or town, state, and zip code, and the attorney handling the case is Juliana Wilson, Esq. Her office number is your area code-388-1555 and her Bar admission number is 554010. Attorney Wilson has asked you to research grounds for annulment in your state and then identify a potential ground given the facts in this case from the client's perspective (however weak you think the claim may be). Locate the proper form for bringing an annulment action in the state where you live and draft a complaint for review. Audrey is living with her sister at 2 Woodbine Road in your city or town, and John continues to reside at 3 River Road in your city or town (where the parties last resided together). They were married on October 28, 2014, in a Catholic church in your state (choose a location, if necessary) and were both residents of the state when they wed. The baby, John Morrison, was born on January 12, 2015. Audrey is filing the complaint and will seek custody and child support.

FOCUS ON **ETHICS**

In this activity, the student is asked to identify and address ethical issues that arise in the context of a client interview.

The Assignment

Assume the facts in the Focus on the Job hypothetical. Assume further that you have been asked to interview the client, Audrey Morrison, in order to gather background information about the facts of the case so that Attorney Wilson can determine whether or not an annulment is a viable option. During the interview with the client, she tells you, among other things, that she is heartbroken. She had believed that she and her husband were a happy couple, totally compatible, and committed to each other. She further reveals that they had been having sexual relations during the entire period of their relationship and relatively brief marriage. You recall something from your paralegal training about how an annulment cannot be obtained if the parties cohabit and engage in sexual relations after their marriage. You tell Audrey what you recall but reassure her that she doesn't have to worry, as she can still get out of her relationship with John by filing for a divorce instead of an annulment. Audrey tells you that you don't understand. She is a devout Catholic and divorce is simply not an option for her. She leaves the office sobbing hysterically. You try to go after her but the phone rings and you have to answer it, as you are the only one in the office at the time. When Attorney Wilson returns, she asks how the interview went and when you tell her what happened, she is not pleased to say the least. She asks you if you have any idea what you have done and tells you to leave the office and not return until you figure it out and identify in writing the

ethical errors you made. She also directs you to suggest an appropriate course of action. Do as she has requested, applying the material on ethics in Chapter 1 of this text as well as the ethical canons for paralegals promulgated by the National Association of Legal Assistants contained in Appendix A. Your response should be in the form of a memorandum to Attorney Wilson.

FOCUS ON **CASE LAW**

This activity provides the student with an opportunity to analyze an annulment case using an IRAC format.

The Assignment

Read the opinion *Fredo v. Fredo*, 49 Conn. Supp. 489, 894 A.2d 399 (Conn Super. 2005), and then analyze the case using an IRAC format:

Identify the ISSUE.

Identify the RULE of law.

ANALYZE the case in terms of how the rule of law applies to the facts of the case.

Draw a CONCLUSION.

The opinion in the *Fredo* case is available at *www.pearsonhighered.com/careersresources/* in the website material related to Chapter 4 of this text under Cases.

FOCUS ON **STATE LAW AND PROCEDURE**

In this activity, the student is asked to research the grounds for annulment in his or her jurisdiction.

The Assignment

Locate the grounds for annulment in the state where you are studying family law. You may need to check both statutes

and case law. A state practice manual or digest will be a good starting point. Remember to consider all of the categories of potential grounds for annulment.

FOCUS ON **TECHNOLOGY**

In addition to the links provided throughout the chapter, this focus provides some useful websites for reference along with technology-related assignments for completion.

Websites of Interest

www.divorcenet.com

This site offers links to state annulment laws. Search under alternatives to divorce.

www.findlaw.com

Choose "Family Law" under "Learn About the Law." This is a particularly well-organized site with access to resources for both public and professional inquirers. It provides general and state-specific information, including access to the laws of all fifty states on divorce and related family law topics. Search for annulment to locate a variety of materials on this topic.

www.usmarriagelaws.com

This site provides information about marriage and annulment laws in the fifty states.

Assignments

1. Learn more about annulment in the Catholic Church at *www.catholicnewsagency.com.*
2. Locate online the forms for bringing an action for annulment in three states other than your own. Links provided in the chapter and *www.forms.justia.com* may be of some assistance in completing this task.
3. Visit *www.findlaw.com* and see what you can locate in the way of information about annulment.

PORTFOLIO PRODUCTS

1. Complaint for Annulment
2. Memorandum on ethical issues in a hypothetical case
3. Analysis of an annulment case in an IRAC format

4. List of grounds for annulment in the student's jurisdiction

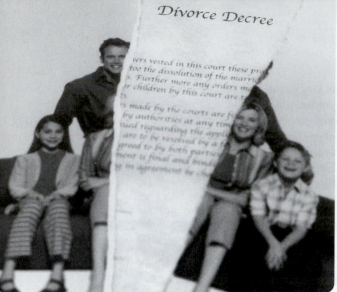

© Stockbyte/Getty Images

chapter 5

THE DIVORCE PROCESS

LEARNING OBJECTIVES

After reading this chapter and completing related assignments, you should be able to:

- describe how the "culture of divorce" has evolved over the past five decades

- list the four primary methods of altering the marital status

- identify the basic stages of the divorce process

- distinguish among the six major alternative dispute resolution methods used in the family law context

- provide examples of issues involving subject matter, personal, and *in rem* jurisdiction that may arise in divorce cases

- identify the most common fault and no-fault grounds for divorce

- list defenses available to defendants in divorce actions

- describe the role of the paralegal at each major stage of the divorce process

All is not well with David and Marie's fifteen-year marriage. He is convinced she has twice disrupted his educational goals by getting pregnant. Now, he says, she has begun drinking and not taking proper care of the children and the marital home. She claims he has abused her emotionally and physically, is obsessed with neatness, and is involved with another woman at work. Given the serious deterioration in their relationship, David has decided to move out of the house and file for divorce.

Introduction

Although the U.S. Supreme Court significantly altered the traditional definition of marriage in 2015, the states continue to exercise considerable control over regulation of the marital relationship whether the spouses are of the same or different sexes. Chapter 3 focused on its creation and Chapter 4 on its termination by annulment. This chapter addresses the termination of marriage by divorce, the "bread and butter" of most family law practices. A broad overview of the divorce process is provided along with descriptions of the paralegal's role at each stage. Because there are variations among the states, many references are made to individual state statutes, rules, forms, and cases. Although the vast majority of divorce cases do not go to trial, some do and many others settle on the proverbial "courthouse steps." Therefore, attention is given to both contested and uncontested divorces from the moment the client contacts the firm through postdivorce activities.

Historical Perspective

Until the early 1970s, family law practices focused primarily on divorce law and litigation. In order to get a divorce, one of the parties had to prove that there was serious wrongdoing by the other party. Even when both parties wanted to end the marriage, as was often the

132

case, the focus still was on fault and blame. Frequently, the system either trapped spouses in unhappy marriages or forced them to deceive the court about their true circumstances in order to fit into the fault mold.

The "culture of divorce" has changed dramatically since the 1970s. The emergence of **no-fault divorce** in all fifty states was the most dramatic catalyst in this evolution, and it has been buttressed by:

- an increased use of alternative approaches to dispute resolution and the collaborative efforts of attorneys to make the divorce process more civil;
- an emphasis on divorce as an economic event in which spouses are viewed as equal partners in the marriage;
- the institution of child support guidelines;
- the codification of criteria to guide decisions pertaining to custody, alimony, and property division;
- the introduction of parenting plans and programs;
- the creation of support systems and user-friendly court procedures for parties proceeding *pro se*; and
- a judicial and societal movement toward respect for autonomy and privacy in family relationships.

No-fault divorce
divorce based on an irremediable breakdown of the marital relationship rather than on the fault of one or both of the parties

Pro se
[Latin: for himself or on his or her own behalf] without legal representation

Methods of Altering a Marital Relationship

There are four primary methods used by parties seeking to separate and/or dissolve their marriage:

- Divorce
- Legal separation
- Separate maintenance
- Annulment

Each of these requires that there be grounds for altering the marital status. The grounds for the first three may be traditional **fault grounds** (such as adultery and cruel and abusive treatment) or **no-fault grounds** (irreconcilable differences, living separate and apart, etc.). The grounds for annulment differ because it is the validity of the marriage itself, rather than the relationship between the parties, that is faulty.

Fault grounds
grounds for divorce based on the fault of one of the parties

No-fault grounds
grounds for divorce based on an irremediable breakdown of the marital relationship rather than on the fault of one or both of the parties

Divorce *a vinculo matrimonii*
[Latin: from the chains or bonds of marriage] an absolute divorce that frees the parties to marry

Divorce
a judicial determination that a marriage is legally terminated

DIVORCE

Depending on the state, a divorce may be called an absolute divorce, a dissolution of marriage, or a **divorce *a vinculo matrimonii***. A **divorce** is a judicial determination that a marriage is legally terminated. Both ceremonial and common law marriages require judicial intervention to effect a termination and permit the parties to remarry. A divorce may be obtained on the basis of no-fault grounds in all fifty states and also on fault grounds in a majority of states. Termination of the marital status does not necessarily terminate duties arising upon marriage, such as spousal maintenance, nor does it eliminate responsibility for the custody and support of children of the marriage. It also does not automatically provide for the division of marital property. In a bifurcated or divisible divorce, the dissolution

PARALEGAL PRACTICE TIP

A list of terms used to describe or refer to divorce and a summary of selected statistics on divorce are provided at *www.pearsonhighered. com/careersresources/* in the resource website for this text in the material related to Chapter 5 under Resources.

of marriage is resolved in one proceeding, and all other issues such as property division and child custody are resolved in one or more later separate proceedings in the same or another state.

LEGAL SEPARATION

Legal separations are most often sought by parties who are not yet ready to divorce for a variety of personal reasons or who are opposed to divorce on religious grounds. A decree of **legal separation** establishes the rights and obligations of two spouses who wish to live separate and apart but remain married. The obligations can then be enforced by the court. Depending on the state it may be called a judicial or legal separation, a limited divorce, or a **divorce *a mensa et thoro***. Grounds must exist to support an action for a legal separation and are essentially the same as those used in the divorce context. The end result is not the same, however, because the marriage is not actually terminated and the parties are not free to remarry. The court can make alimony and child custody and support awards, grant a party freedom from interference by the other party, and incorporate in its decree a separation agreement executed by the parties that addresses these issues as well as division of property in some states. The agreement should state clearly whether any or all of its terms will continue to be binding on the parties if they eventually divorce or reconcile. Even if the parties do subsequently reconcile, the court's order of legal separation remains in force until it is vacated, one of the parties dies, or the marriage is formally terminated by annulment or a full divorce. Several states provide for the conversion of a legal separation into a divorce after a period of time set by statute. Usually the conversion is not automatic and the parties must petition the court to accomplish that purpose. In Wisconsin, as in many states, the form for seeking a legal separation is the same as the form for seeking a divorce. (See "Form 4110" at *www.wicourts.gov.*)

SEPARATE MAINTENANCE

An action for **separate maintenance** or separate support is usually an option in jurisdictions that do not grant legal separations. It, too, may require the existence of grounds that are essentially the same as the grounds for divorce. It serves the same purpose of allowing the parties to live apart under a court order that defines the terms of the separation, including provisions for spousal and child support, insurance coverage, occupancy and maintenance of the former marital home, etc. In some states, child custody is determined in a separate action. In order to bring an action for separate maintenance, the spouses can no longer be living together. See, e.g., *Theisen v. Theisen*, 716 S.E.2d 271 (S.C. 2011).

A decree granting separate maintenance does not terminate the marriage, permanently divide the parties' property, or permit either of the parties to remarry. Separate maintenance decrees can be enforced in the same manner as support awards in the context of a divorce or a legal separation. They also remain in effect, even if the parties reconcile, until such time as vacated by the court, one of the parties dies, or the marriage is terminated by divorce.

ANNULMENT

As indicated in Chapter 4, an **annulment** is a judicial determination that a valid marriage never existed between the parties. The purported marriage may have been either **void** *ab initio* or **voidable** because of a defect existing at the time it was allegedly entered. For example, one of the parties may still have been married to, or in a legally recognized relationship (such as a domestic partnership or civil union) with, someone else. One of them may have acted under duress or been unable to legally marry due to nonage or an inability to consent to marry because of a lack of mental capacity.

The Divorce Process—A Skeletal Road Map

For the client, the decision to seek a divorce is often a monumental, life-altering event that takes place after months, even years, of deliberation. When the client comes to the attorney's office, he or she often feels the hard part is over and a divorce is just around the corner. It can be a rude awakening to discover that getting a divorce, even on an uncontested basis, usually takes months, and hotly contested divorces may drag on for years. Although the vast majority of divorce actions are settled and do not proceed to trial, approximately 10% still do.

Every state establishes its own procedural rules for divorce/dissolution actions. In some states, they are the same as for civil actions in general. In others they are specific to domestic relations cases, and still others use a combination of the two. The basic steps in the process in a contested case are outlined in skeletal form in Exhibit 5.1. Although the attorneys are responsible for making the legal decisions during a divorce action, other members of the family law team are actively involved in the process and all major decisions are made with the client's consent. The role played by a paralegal in the process depends on the specific paralegal's level of expertise and on the policies and procedures of individual law firms and supervisors. Whenever actions are taken by a paralegal, such as filing a document or communicating with a client, it is presumed that the actions are taken only with a supervisor's approval.

Void *ab initio*

[Latin: from the beginning] of no legal effect from the outset; a contract may be void *ab initio* if it seriously offends law or public policy

Voidable marriage

a marriage capable of being nullified because of a circumstance existing at the time it was established

PARALEGAL PRACTICE TIP

Sometimes courts provide helpful guidance to parties seeking a divorce. To see some of the ways in which courts in Alaska have done this, visit *www.courts.alaska .gov.* (Self Help Center: Family Law/ Divorce and Dissolution: Ending Your Marriage)

EXHIBIT 5.1 A Skeletal Outline of the Basic Process in a Contested Divorce Case

1. The Plaintiff's attorney conducts an initial interview with the client.
2. The attorney identifies the primary issues in the case (grounds for divorce, custody, child and spousal support, property division, need for emergency orders, etc.).
3. The attorney explores the potential for mediation, counseling, etc. (This may occur at any point during the process and may occur more than once.)
4. The attorney identifies and resolves any jurisdictional questions and determines the proper forum and court in which to file the action for divorce.
5. The Plaintiff's attorney drafts and files a Complaint for Divorce on the client's behalf and also files an **Appearance.**
6. The Summons and Complaint are served on the Defendant and the Return of Service is filed with the court.
7. The Defendant usually files an Answer (which may include a Counterclaim for Divorce) or files a Motion to Dismiss and Defendant's attorney files an Appearance (General or Limited if for the sole purpose of contesting jurisdiction).

(Continued)

Appearance

a document filed with the court by an attorney, indicating that he or she will be representing a specific party in a matter before the court

EXHIBIT 5.1 (*Continued*)

8. The Plaintiff and Defendant file and serve Motions for Temporary Orders and motions for other purposes, if appropriate (e.g., to protect assets, compel a party to vacate the marital home, or appoint an appraiser or guardian *ad litem* (GAL)).
9. The Parties conduct discovery if warranted and feasible given their assets and liabilities.
10. Counsel for one or both parties draft Separation/Marital Agreement(s) for discussion.
11. The Parties/counsel engage in negotiations. (Negotiations may occur throughout the process.)
12. The Parties' counsel prepare a Separation Agreement addressing uncontested issues.
13. The Parties prepare for and attend a Pretrial Conference.
14. The Parties prepare for Trial.
15. If the case does not settle, the Trial takes place.
16. The Court issues a Decree/Judgment.
17. Follow-up matters are addressed (transfers of property, execution of QDROs, etc.).
18. The Parties file post-trial Motions and/or an Appeal, if warranted.
19. The Parties seek to enforce the Judgment, if necessary (contempt actions, etc.).
20. The Parties seek modifications of the Judgment, if appropriate, based on substantial changes in circumstances or other appropriate bases.

It should be noted that, for some clients, religious recognition of the termination of a marriage may be more important than a civil divorce even though it has no legal effect. See, e.g., *Age v. Age*, 340 S.W.3d 88 (Ky. Ct. App. 2011). When a Jewish couple wants to divorce, they go to a Jewish court called a Beth Din, presided over by a rabbi, and the husband delivers to his wife a *get*, a written "bill of divorce." If the wife refuses to accept the *get*, and she subsequently remarries in a civil ceremony, she is considered an adulteress, as she is still married under Jewish law. If a Jewish wife wants a divorce, the husband may refuse to give her a *get* and may use her desire for one as a bargaining tool in the context of a civil divorce. If he deserts his wife or refuses to give her a *get* under any circumstances, she is called an *agunah* and cannot be married again by a rabbi even if she obtains a civil divorce. An Islamic divorce generally is performed by a husband by pronouncing the word "talak," an Arabic word meaning to release or divorce. Additional requirements may exist nation to nation and sect to sect, such as how many times "talak" must be said and in whose presence.

The Initial Interview in a Divorce Case

An initial interview sets the tone for the working relationship between the client and the family law team. Some law firms and legal resources provide client questionnaires and interview checklists for suggested use in initial interviews. However, many practitioners find it more practical, productive, and economical to have the client complete a detailed questionnaire at home. The interview can then be used to establish a relationship with the client, obtain answers to important threshold questions, and address fundamental preliminary matters. (See Paralegal Application 5.1.) Subsequent interviews can focus in more detail on particular issues, such as the potential grounds for divorce, the nature and extent of the marital estate, completion of the financial statement, and child-related issues.

PARALEGAL PRACTICE TIP

Occasionally, potential clients interview a series of attorneys before retaining specific counsel. In such situations, some attorneys will conduct brief, exploratory interviews at no charge. Others will charge a flat fee or full hourly rate. Even if not retained, once such an interview takes place, a conflict of interest may exist should the attorney subsequently be contacted by the opposing party in the matter, a situation not uncommon in smaller communities.

PARALEGAL PRACTICE TIP

If the defendant knows that the spouse intends to file for divorce, he or she may meet with an attorney before the case is filed or may wait to do so until after being formally served.

Paralegal **Application 5.1**

The Client's Initial Interview With the Family Law Team

An initial interview is customarily conducted by the attorney with or without the presence and assistance of the paralegal. If the paralegal does participate, he or she is usually asked to take notes and prepare an intake memorandum confirming information gathered, agreements reached, and follow-up needed. If the paralegal is asked to assist with part of the interview, the following list can be used to guide the process, but it must be customized to avoid any unauthorized practice of law. Whatever role the paralegal plays, communications within the interview are confidential.

1. Get acquainted with the client. Establish a comfortable rapport, being sensitive to the emotionally charged nature of the topics discussed, the cultural background of the client, and any unique communication issues and/or barriers. Invite the client to ask questions at any point during the interview.

2. Obtain sufficient background information about each party and any children of the marriage (including ages and current addresses) so that basic jurisdictional questions can be assessed and a thorough conflicts check can be completed.

3. Learn more about why the client has contacted the firm and what his or her short- and long-term goals are. If the client appears to have unrealistic expectations, it is useful for the attorney to establish at the outset that there are no winners in divorce and no guarantees about the outcome, no matter how hard the team works or how much the client pays. Discuss alternatives to divorce, including legal separation and annulment (if appropriate). Ask if the parties have engaged in counseling or mediation and/or are willing to do so. The attorney may suggest such options, especially if the client appears to be uncertain about whether or not the marriage really is irretrievably broken or if mediation eventually may be required by the court.

4. If the client is intent on seeking a divorce, identify the primary reasons for doing so (e.g., Have the parties simply "grown apart"? Is one or both of them involved in a new relationship? Are there financial problems?).

5. Inquire about the spouse's knowledge of the pending action and likely response. Will the action be joint or contested? Have any prior actions been filed? Is the spouse presently represented by counsel? If so, obtain contact information. If not, is he or she likely to be?

6. Obtain a preliminary client history covering basic financial information (major assets, employment of both spouses, dependence on public assistance), prior marriages or legally recognized relationships such as domestic partnerships, and additional information about any children of the marriage, such as the existence of special needs, problems, or talents. Is either party responsible for additional children from other relationships or conceived through the use of assisted reproductive technology? With whom are the children residing and what arrangements exist for visitation, if any? If participation in a parent education program is recommended or required by the court, provide information about approved programs in the area.

7. Did the parties execute a pre- or postmarital agreement?

8. Identify any potential emergency issues. Are there any immediate financial or housing needs? If there is a history of abuse of either or both of the spouses and/or the children, have the police or social services been contacted? With what result(s)? Explain that copies of relevant documents will need to be obtained from appropriate agencies. Suggest that the client prepare a personal safety plan if abuse of either the client or the children is known or suspected.

9. Determine whether or not there are or will be any immigration issues as a result of the divorce.

10. Determine if there are any religious considerations involved.

11. Describe the firm's approach to cases, the roles played by various members of the family law team, fees, and billing policies and procedures. Some attorneys address these topics at the outset of the interview but that approach has a tendency to distract a client, who then may spend the balance of the interview quietly obsessing about cost rather than paying attention to the substance of the interview.

12. Does the client have any questions or concerns?

If the decision is made to accept the case and the client agrees to the terms of engagement, the attorney should outline the process of getting a divorce and identify the next steps to be taken by the client and members of the family law team. A contact person at

(Continued)

the firm should be designated (customarily the paralegal rather than the attorney, partially in an effort to control costs).

Some firms give the client "homework" assignments to complete at this point, including, but not necessarily limited to, the following:

- Complete a client questionnaire.
- Complete a preliminary financial statement for review.
- Photograph the contents of the marital home.
- Keep a daily journal highlighting matters related to the case, such as abuse, parenting, and financial issues (e.g., the dissipation of marital funds).
- Gather and/or make copies of important documents such as deeds, tax returns, passports, Social Security cards, and bank account statements.
- Remove valuable separate property (e.g., jewelry, family heirlooms) from the marital home for safekeeping lest it mysteriously disappear!

Some firms provide (or recommend that the client create) a notebook to organize documents related to the divorce, such as pleadings, financial affidavits, court orders, and discovery requests. If desired, the paralegal may be assigned to help the client organize his or her "notebook." If nothing else, assignments and a notebook may help to create in the client a sense of some control over the process.

PARALEGAL PRACTICE TIP

An example of a basic client questionnaire for use in a divorce case is available at *www.pearsonhighered.com/careersresources/* in the website material related to Chapter 5 of this text under Resources.

PARALEGAL PRACTICE TIP

Firms frequently have informational materials available in office reception areas, including, for example, "Ten Most Commonly Asked Questions About Divorce" sheets; flowcharts outlining the steps involved in the divorce process comparing contested and uncontested options; blank copies of personal safety plans for victims of abuse; lists of community resources for spouses and children; descriptions of alternative dispute resolution options; information regarding times and locations of state-approved parenting programs; blank financial statements; lists and descriptions of services available through the state's Title IV-D agency; and blank child support guidelines worksheets. The paralegal may be responsible for ensuring that such material is up to date and in good supply. To see an example of a "Ten Most Commonly Asked Questions About Divorce" sheet developed by an attorney, visit *www.anthonypiazza.com* (Under Divorce).

PARALEGAL PRACTICE TIP

A sample fee agreement is provided at *www.pearsonhighered.com/careersresources/* in the website material for this text related to Chapter 1 under Forms.

Fee agreement
a contract between an attorney and a client regarding payment for the attorney's professional services

Letter of engagement
a letter from an attorney to a client confirming that the attorney agrees to represent the client in a particular legal matter

Letter of nonengagement
a letter from an attorney to an individual confirming that the attorney will *not* be representing that individual with respect to a particular legal matter

After the initial interview, members of the family law team will perform a number of important follow-up tasks:

- **Complete and execute a fee agreement and a letter of engagement.** The attorney must define the scope of work to be performed and establish the fees to be charged for services performed by various members of the family law team. The paralegal may draft the agreement or "fill in the blanks" on a boilerplate fee agreement used by the firm and ensure that two originals are signed by both the client and the attorney before placing one in the office file. The second original goes to the client. If the prospective client decides not to retain the attorney or the attorney elects not to accept the case, a **letter of nonengagement**/declination should be drafted to confirm that decision in order to avoid any misunderstanding or a later malpractice action for failure to perform legal services. No reason needs to be given for declining the case. The person should be advised of any upcoming deadlines or matters requiring immediate attention with or without the assistance of another attorney. The paralegal may be assigned the task of drafting this letter.
- **Establish a file and a tracking system.** The paralegal usually sets up "the file" (both paper and electronic) and performs several related activities throughout the case:
  - marks all appropriate calendars with deadlines, appointment and hearing dates, etc.
  - develops a personal "tickler" (reminder) system

- monitors follow-up activities and deadlines
- tracks the case maintaining a chronology of activity

- **Gather preliminary information and documents necessary to shape the nature and theory of the case.** The paralegal usually assists in gathering information, working with both the client and the supervising attorney, and then collects, organizes, and maintains a comprehensive filing system with appropriate subheadings (pleadings, witnesses, discovery, financial statements, research, etc.). The attorney uses this material to develop a theory of the case: What relief will the client seek? Why is the client entitled to that relief? What law and evidence support the client's position? What is the nature of the opposing party's case and how can it be countered? What discovery efforts are warranted?

- **Determine if there is a need to seek emergency relief.** It may be determined during conversations with the client that circumstances warrant the filing of *ex parte* motions (motions without advance notice to the defendant). Some, such as a restraining order to protect the client and/or the children, to protect marital assets, or to prevent removal of the children from the jurisdiction, may need to be filed immediately. Others, such as motions for temporary custody and child support, may be filed with the complaint for divorce or shortly thereafter according to local rules. The paralegal may:

  - suggest warranted forms of relief to the attorney
  - draft *ex parte* motions for review and signature (along with affidavits and proposed orders, if required)
  - help the client prepare an application/complaint for a restraining/protective order

> **PARALEGAL PRACTICE TIP**
>
> Visit *www.courts.wa.gov/forms* to see an example of a Motion for an Ex Parte Restraining Order (Washington). (Search by name of form.) To see another sample Petition for a Restraining Order, visit *www.wicourts.gov* (Wisconsin).

Dispute Resolution Options in Family Law Cases

When a divorce case proceeds to trial, the parties essentially lose control over the making of decisions affecting not only their lives but also the lives of their children, if any. Given the cost of litigation in time, money, and emotional stress, nonjudicial means of resolving differences offer the parties potentially more productive alternatives that allow them to exercise more control over both the process and the end result. Although the alternatives to litigation also carry a price tag, they are usually considerably less costly than a trial. They are also more likely to lead to a mutually agreed-upon resolution of the parties' differences in a fraction of the time a fully litigated case would take. In addition, the rules governing most **alternative dispute resolution (ADR)** proceedings require, with limited exceptions, that information shared in that context remains confidential. On the other hand, court proceedings are open to the public, and most documents filed become part of a public record.

The courts strongly encourage the use of ADR, sometimes explicitly in court rules or standing orders (as in Texas). Some states require participation in court-affiliated mediation services with respect to disputed issues, particularly child-related issues. In Massachusetts, attorneys are required to sign a statement that they have advised their clients of the availability of court-facilitated mediation.

> **Alternative Dispute Resolution (ADR)** a procedure for settling a dispute by means other than litigation, such as mediation or arbitration

> **PARALEGAL PRACTICE TIP**
>
> New Jersey is a state in which attorneys are required to certify to the court that they have advised their clients about the availability of divorce resolution alternatives to conventional litigation. To find the certification form used in New Jersey that must be signed by both attorney and client, visit *www.judiciary.state.nj.us* (Form 10890).

On occasion, a party may ask the court to order mediation. To see a form used in Wisconsin to request this form of relief, visit *www.wicourts.gov* (Form FA 4134).

ADR options can be used at any stage of the process. More than one option may be used and on more than one occasion, if desired. However, the earlier they are used, the more effective they are likely to be. Research also shows higher levels of satisfaction and compliance with mediated agreements than with litigated decrees. In the short run, the parties each play a greater role in shaping the outcome of their case and, in the long run, in shaping their futures. There are several dispute resolution alternatives to litigation in the family law context. The most common methods are identified and described in Exhibit 5.2.

EXHIBIT 5.2 Common Methods of Alternative Dispute Resolution (ADR) in Family Law Cases

> - **Direct negotiation between the parties.** The parties negotiate directly with each other in person, by telephone, and by mail (including e-mail). They initially operate without the assistance of any professional, legal or otherwise, in an effort to reach as many terms of their agreement as possible. In direct negotiation, attorneys are usually not involved, if at all, until contacted by the parties after they have essentially already reached their own agreement. Because of the potential for a power imbalance to exist in the parties' relationship, direct negotiation usually is not recommended in high-conflict cases or cases in which there is a history of abuse between the parties.
> - **Mediation.** The parties may participate in **mediation** voluntarily or be ordered to do so by the court. In this process, a neutral third person, called a mediator, facilitates identification, discussion, and resolution of issues in negotiations between the parties and occasionally their attorneys. Typically, the mediation takes place in one or a series of face-to-face meetings, as needed. Occasionally the mediator will meet with each client individually within a session. The primary role of the mediator is to overcome barriers that prevent the parties from reaching agreement. Mediators focus on resolving issues rather than on winning and losing. The mediator is impartial, does not advocate the position of either side, and is committed to reaching a "fair deal," one that will serve both parties and the family as a whole in the long run. The role of the parties' attorneys in mediation varies from case to case. Generally speaking, the attorney's role is different from the mediator's in the sense that an attorney has an ethical duty to advocate zealously for the client and obtain the most favorable settlement possible. Whether they actually attend and participate in the sessions or not, attorneys commonly brief their clients about the process, help define issues and goals for the mediation, and act as consultants before and after the sessions. They also review any draft agreements from the mediation before they are executed. Most attorneys and mediators do not consider mediation an appropriate option when there is a continuing history of concealing or destroying assets and/or abuse between the parties.
> - **Collaborative law.** Collaborative law "combines the positive problem-solving focus of mediation with the built-in lawyer advocacy and counsel of traditional settlement-oriented representation. . . . In collaborative practice, specially trained lawyers agree to represent clients in negotiating a divorce with both parties and their lawyers committing to settle the case without litigation. While the clients cannot be prohibited from later switching to litigation, the lawyers are disqualified from representation should that happen."[1]
> - **Negotiation through counsel.** This is the traditional and most common method of negotiating divorce settlements. Proposals (written and/or oral) are exchanged between the attorneys until an agreement is reached or the parties come to an impasse with respect to unresolved issues. The parties participate in the process mostly through counsel and occasionally in four-way conferences (sometimes mandated by the court). Initial proposals rarely reflect the parties' bottom lines, and the negotiation process frequently involves considerable give-and-take and a series of compromises before a settlement is reached. Each topic

Mediation
an approach to resolving differences in which a neutral third person helps the parties identify their differences, consider their options, and structure a mutually acceptable agreement

Collaborative law
an approach to reaching agreements and resolving differences that stresses cooperation, joint problem solving, and the avoidance of litigation

PARALEGAL PRACTICE TIP

Four-way meetings can be productive, but clients should be prepared for them in advance. Which issues will be discussed at the meeting? What are the client's goals with respect to those issues? Where is there room for compromise? What is the other side likely to propose? What kind of response will be called for? How should the client conduct himself or herself?

EXHIBIT 5.2 *(Continued)*

may be addressed separately, but usually no agreement is finalized on a major issue until a comprehensive agreement is reached.

- **Neutral case evaluation.** This option is customarily used later in the process, after discovery has been completed, the parties' positions have crystallized, and other ADR options, if tried, have failed. At this point, there Is a strong incentive for the parties to settle, given the stress and expense associated with an imminent trial. In a **neutral case evaluation,** an experienced trial attorney or judge provides the parties with a reality check. The evaluator listens to a summary of the conflict by each side and offers an opinion about settlement potential and a prediction about the likely outcome if the matter proceeds to trial. The evaluator then makes an attempt to resolve the case. The attorneys will provide various documents to the evaluator in advance of the actual case evaluation session(s), including the complaint and the answer, the parties' financial statements, pretrial memoranda, and the like. The attorneys may or may not attend the actual meeting(s) but will customarily brief their clients regarding the nature of the process, its goals, and the potential alternative outcomes.

- **Arbitration.** In **arbitration**, one or more neutral third parties who are trained arbitrators hear arguments, review evidence, and render a decision with respect to the issues identified by the parties for arbitration. The arbitrator is often an attorney and is usually affiliated with a professional organization such as the American Arbitration Association. Prior to divorce, arbitration is used less frequently than mediation. It is used more commonly post divorce pursuant to a dispute resolution provision in the parties' separation agreement in which they agree to submit certain kinds of disputes to arbitration if they cannot resolve them themselves or with the assistance of counsel. The parties' attorneys describe the process to their clients and assist them in shaping the arbitration in advance to some extent by recommending the arbitrator, identifying the issues to be addressed, and limiting the range of remedies the arbitrator can consider. The parties can also decide whether the arbitration will be binding or nonbinding. In **binding arbitration**, the parties agree to abide by the arbitrator's decision. In **nonbinding arbitration**, the parties can accept or reject the decision. The actual arbitration proceeds somewhat like a mini trial. The attorneys present their clients' positions along with supporting evidence. The parties may testify and respond to questions from both counsel and the arbitrator. Witnesses may be called. Any decision reached by the arbitrator remains subject to review by the court, which may be unwilling to relinquish its decision-making authority, particularly with respect to child-related issues.[2] However, with respect to other kinds of issues, courts usually will not disturb an award that results from binding arbitration unless the arbitration process itself was flawed in some manner, such as by fraud or corruption.

Neutral case evaluation
a process in which a neutral third party, usually an experienced trial attorney or judge, listens to the parties' positions and offers an opinion about settlement potential and the likely outcome if the matter proceeds to trial

Arbitration
a process in which one or more neutral third persons who are trained arbitrators hear arguments, review evidence, and render a decision with respect to the issues selected for arbitration by the parties involved in a dispute

Binding arbitration
arbitration in which the parties agree to abide by the arbitrator's decision as final and unappealable

Nonbinding arbitration
arbitration in which the parties are free to accept or reject the arbitrator's decision

An additional emerging option for ADR in family law cases is parenting coordination. **Parenting coordinators** have a limited scope of responsibility. They are most commonly appointed by a court to deal with design and implementation of parenting agreements in high-conflict cases and cases in which children may be at risk. Parenting coordinators mediate disputes and, in some instances, are granted limited decision-making authority in an effort to reduce the number of return trips to court. To see a sample Motion to Appoint a Parenting Coordinator, visit *http://www.utcourts.gov* (search by title of form).

Parenting coordinators
individuals, usually appointed by the court, who assist with design and implementation of parenting agreements and enforcement of decrees in high-conflict cases involving minor children

The paralegal's role in the ADR context generally includes the following:

- being familiar with the various forms of dispute resolution utilized in the jurisdiction
- maintaining lists of local ADR specialists, with pertinent information on each

- preparing any required forms
- scheduling ADR sessions/meetings
- helping the attorney prepare for conferences/meetings
- attending settlement meetings to listen and take notes on the parties' respective positions and any agreements reached
- communicating with ADR resources and arranging for payment
- drafting agreements based on understandings reached by the parties in various forms of ADR
- drafting provisions relating to dispute resolution for inclusion in separation agreements

Jurisdictional Issues in Divorce Actions— What Is the Proper Forum?

Jurisdictional questions must be addressed at the outset of every case. In many instances, the answers are straightforward: The parties and their children live in the same county within a single state, own no real estate, and possess minimal personal property. In others, the answers are far more complex and eventually may have to be resolved by the court. For example, the whereabouts of a party may be unknown or the parties may live in different states and have three children, two living with one parent and one with the other; and each spouse may own personal property, real estate, and business interests in multiple states. The paralegal's role with respect to jurisdictional issues usually involves researching governing law and gathering the facts needed by the attorney to determine where a given action should be filed. In complex situations, the law of multiple states will need to be researched along with potential **conflict-of-law** issues.

Jurisdiction in a family law case is primarily a matter of state law and procedure subject to overriding federal constitutional limitations as interpreted by the U.S. Supreme Court. From a jurisdictional perspective, there are basically two facets of divorce actions: (1) dissolution of the marital status and (2) resolution of corollary matters, such as division of the marital estate (property division), custody, and support issues. Most divorce actions involve both, and the court hearing the case needs to have subject matter jurisdiction over family law matters, personal jurisdiction over both of the parties, and *in rem* jurisdiction over the property in dispute. (See Exhibit 5.3.)

Conflict of law

a conflict arising out of a difference between the laws of two jurisdictions, such as two states or two nations

Subject matter jurisdiction

the authority of a court to hear and decide a particular kind of claim or controversy

EXHIBIT 5.3 Jurisdiction in Divorce Actions

Type of Jurisdiction	How It Is Acquired	What the Court Can Do
Subject matter jurisdiction is the authority of a court to hear and decide a particular type of claim or controversy.	Subject matter jurisdiction is conferred by a state statute authorizing the court to hear and decide divorce actions. It cannot be created by agreement of the parties.	A court can hear divorce actions, if authorized to do so by state statute, provided (a) the plaintiff satisfies the state's applicable residency requirements, if any, and (b) the defendant is given proper notice of the action and an opportunity to be heard.

EXHIBIT 5.3 *(Continued)*

Personal jurisdiction is the authority of the court to issue and enforce orders binding a particular individual.	In order for the court to exercise personal jurisdiction over a defendant, he or she must have notice of the action and an opportunity to be heard. Personal jurisdiction is acquired over a defendant by personal service of process, consent, or substituted service (e.g., by mail or publication in a newspaper) or under a state's long-arm statute if the defendant is a nonresident who has sufficient minimum contacts with the state.	The court can issue enforceable orders binding a defendant in a divorce action regarding alimony, child support, and property division.
***In rem* jurisdiction** is the authority a court has over a property (mine, real estate, etc.) or thing (including the marital status of the plaintiff in some states) rather than over a person.	A state court can exercise its powers over property located inside of that state's boundaries. In order to acquire *in rem* jurisdiction over a marital status, the plaintiff must be domiciled in the state and reasonable notice of the action must be given to the defendant by a means authorized by state statute.	The court can issue orders affecting the parties' property located within the state's boundaries. However, even if the court has personal jurisdiction over a defendant, the court's power to distribute marital property located outside of the state may be limited.

Personal jurisdiction
the authority of a court to issue and enforce orders binding a particular individual; sometimes called *in personam* jurisdiction

***In rem* jurisdiction**
the authority a court has over a property or thing rather than over persons located within its jurisdictional borders

When the plaintiff satisfies applicable residency requirements, the appropriate court will be able to exercise subject matter jurisdiction over dissolution of the marriage, even if the defendant is beyond the reach of the court, provided he or she is given proper notice. The subject matter is the marital status of the plaintiff. It is the basic "thing" being addressed in the action. It is possessed by each of the spouses and exists, for jurisdictional purposes, in any state where either of the spouses resides. Other related matters may also be addressed only if additional jurisdictional requirements are met.

Although it is not favored, occasionally a court may be willing to divide or bifurcate a divorce proceeding under unusual circumstances (such as advanced age or illness of a party). In a **bifurcated divorce**, the court dissolves the marriage but does not adjudicate other issues, such as support, custody, and property division. It may reserve jurisdiction over those issues until a later date or leave them to be determined by courts in one or more other states with jurisdiction over the defendant, the marital property, and/or the parties' children. (See, e.g., *In re Marriage of Wade*, 946 N.E.2d 485 (Ill. App. Ct. 2011). The court allowed bifurcation in this case because the particularly contentious nature of the divorce was having a detrimental impact on the parties' children.)

Bifurcated divorce
a divorce in which the dissolution of marriage is resolved in one proceeding, and all other issues, such as property division and child custody, are resolved in one or more later, separate proceedings in the same or another state

In Chapters 9, 10, 11, and 12, we review jurisdictional issues related to child custody, support and property division. In this chapter, we consider jurisdiction as it relates to actions for divorce. We are particularly concerned with obtaining answers to the following five questions as they apply in an individual case:

1. Does the plaintiff satisfy the state's residency requirements?
2. Which type of court has subject matter jurisdiction over divorce and related matters?

3. Does the court have personal (*in personam*) jurisdiction over the defendant?
4. Does the court have *in rem* jurisdiction over the property involved in the action?
5. In which specific court should the complaint for divorce be filed—that is, where is venue proper?

DOES THE PLAINTIFF SATISFY THE STATE'S RESIDENCY REQUIREMENTS?

> Each state as a sovereign has a rightful and legitimate concern in the marital status of persons domiciled within its borders. . . . it is plain that each state can alter within its own borders the marriage status of the spouse domiciled there, even though the other spouse is absent.[3]

In order to file for divorce in a particular state, the general rule is that one of the parties must satisfy its domicile or residency requirement for bringing such actions. There is considerable variation in these requirements, ranging from six weeks in states such as Idaho and Nevada to six months in Pennsylvania, and one year in approximately one-fifth of the states, including, for example, Rhode Island and Iowa. Even when there is a basic residency requirement, however, there are frequently exceptions that may or may not work to the client's advantage. For example, in Maryland, there is no residency requirement unless the cause of the marital breakdown occurred outside of the state (one year) or if the ground for the action is insanity (two years). Tennessee and Massachusetts have residency requirements of six months and one year, respectively, unless the party bringing the action is domiciled in the state and the cause of the marital breakdown arose within the state, in which case there is no requirement. Some states, such as Texas and California, also have county residency requirements.

The U.S. Supreme Court speaks of **domicile** when addressing the issue of a state's power to dissolve a marriage. The states speak in terms of residency (or, in some instances, both domicile and residency). The distinctions can be confusing and have occasionally led to challenges with respect to the validity of a divorce. Your domicile is the place you consider your permanent home and to which you intend to return when away. Your residence may, in fact, be your domicile. However, you may have several residences where you reside on occasion, but only one domicile. Where one is domiciled is a question of law and fact. The court will look at several factors when determining an individual's domicile, such as:

- how long the person has resided in a particular state
- if renting, whether the person has a short or long-term lease
- whether the party owns property in the state
- where the party votes
- which state issued the party's driver's license
- where his or her car is registered
- where he or she pays income taxes
- what the party's mailing address is for billing purposes
- where the person is employed
- whether the party is an employee-at-will or has a long-term employment contract
- where the person's extended family lives

Domicile
a person's legal residence; the place one considers his or her permanent home and to which he or she intends to return when away

WHICH COURT HAS SUBJECT MATTER JURISDICTION OVER DIVORCE AND RELATED MATTERS?

"Subject matter jurisdiction" refers to a court's authority to hear and render a decision with respect to a particular type of case. All divorce matters are brought in state rather than federal courts. Subject matter jurisdiction is conferred by state statutes and the parties cannot confer it on a court by agreement. Each state determines the type of court authorized to grant divorces within its jurisdiction. In many states, there are specialized family courts, and in others, divorce actions are heard in courts of general jurisdiction, such as superior courts, chancery courts, circuit courts, or courts of common pleas that hear other kinds of matters as well. A court can have subject matter jurisdiction sufficient to dissolve a marriage, even if it lacks personal jurisdiction over a defendant, as long as the plaintiff satisfies the state's residency requirement. It is the plaintiff's relationship with the state where the action is filed that matters. However, if a plaintiff travels to another state solely for the purpose of obtaining a divorce and plans to return afterwards to his or her "true" domicile, the defendant-spouse, particularly one who did not receive actual notice of the action, may be able to attack the validity of the divorce decree for lack of proper subject matter jurisdiction.

> **PARALEGAL PRACTICE TIP**
>
> Before the right to marry was recognized nationwide, states that had not yet enacted same-sex marriage laws were divided on whether parties who had entered valid same-sex marriages in other jurisdictions were allowed to file for divorce in their states. In 2010, a Texas court held no. (See *In re Marriage of J.B. v. H.B.*, 326 S.W.3d 654 (Tex. App. 2010).) In 2011, a Wyoming court held yes. (See *Christiansen v. Christiansen*, 253 P.3d 153 (Wyo. 2011).)

DOES THE COURT HAVE PERSONAL (*IN PERSONAM*) JURISDICTION OVER THE DEFENDANT?

> It has long been the rule that a valid judgment imposing a personal obligation or duty in favor of the plaintiff may be entered only by a court having jurisdiction over the person of the defendant. The existence of personal jurisdiction, in turn, depends upon the presence of reasonable notice to the defendant that an action has been brought and a sufficient connection between the defendant and the forum State as to make it fair to require defense of the action in the forum. (Citations omitted.)[4]

In order for a court to issue an order that will be enforceable against a particular defendant (such as an order for property division or spousal support), it must have personal jurisdiction over that defendant. Given the Fourteenth Amendment's requirements of due process and procedural fairness, a defendant is entitled to reasonable notice and an opportunity to be heard in the matter at issue and is also protected from being hailed into court in a state with which he or she has no connection. There are four primary means of acquiring personal jurisdiction over a defendant in a domestic relations proceeding that are consistent with due process requirements:

- **Presence.** Personal service of process on a resident defendant or on a nonresident defendant while physically present in the state as a temporary resident, visitor, or otherwise. The U.S. Supreme Court has held that a nonresident of a state is subject to the jurisdiction of that state if he or she is properly served while physically present in the state.[5]
- **Domicile.** Actual service of process or substituted (or constructive) service over a defendant who is domiciled in the state by publication in the paper

and mailing the summons and complaint to the defendant's last known address.

- **Consent.** The defendant, including a nonresident defendant, may voluntarily consent to the court's jurisdiction by accepting service or by appearing and defending the action.
- **Minimum contacts.** Each state has a **long-arm statute** that identifies the kinds of minimum contacts a nonresident defendant may have with the state that are considered sufficient to give rise to personal jurisdiction over that defendant provided he or she has notice of the action. The focus is usually on more recent contacts. The basic premise is that it is fair and reasonable to exercise personal jurisdiction in certain circumstances. State statutes vary but generally include provisions such as the following (some of which are tailored to domestic relations cases):

  - The defendant conducts business in the state.
  - The defendant contracts to provide services in the state.
  - The defendant has caused tortious injury by an act or omission in the state.
  - The defendant has an interest in real property located within the state.
  - The defendant has maintained a residence in the state (most often a marital residence).
  - The defendant is subject to an order of alimony, property division, parentage of a child, child custody, or child support issued by a court in the state.
  - The litigation relates to some action of the nonresident defendant within the state.
  - The defendant had sexual relations in the state that may have resulted in the birth of a child to the parties.

DOES THE COURT HAVE *IN REM* JURISDICTION OVER THE PROPERTY INVOLVED IN THE ACTION?

A state court with subject matter jurisdiction has authority over real property located within the state's boundaries and can issue orders with respect to that property. A court can distribute property within its jurisdiction pursuant to a divorce decree, but if the property in dispute is immovable (such as a piece of real estate or mining rights) and is located in another state, the court's powers may be limited.

The *Russo* case[6] provides an illustration of what can be subtle differences in interpreting and applying personal and *in rem* jurisdiction. In *Russo*, a Pennsylvania trial court ordered the parties to sell real property located in the state of Ohio and divide the proceeds. The defendant husband appealed that portion of the divorce judgment, alleging that the court lacked jurisdiction to distribute property located outside of Pennsylvania. The husband argued that jurisdiction extended only to property located in Pennsylvania and that a Pennsylvania court could not exercise *in rem* jurisdiction over real or personal property located outside the state. The appellate court held that when the trial court ordered the parties to sell the Ohio property, it was not exercising *in rem* jurisdiction over the property. Rather, it was ordering the parties, over whom it had personal jurisdiction, to sell the property and distribute the proceeds.

Long-arm statute
a statute setting forth the circumstances in which a state may exercise personal jurisdiction over a nonresident defendant; identifies the minimum contacts a defendant must have with the state where the statute is in effect

PARALEGAL PRACTICE TIP

To see a survey of long-arm statutes in all fifty states, Google "Long-Arm Statutes: A Fifty-State Survey."

PARALEGAL PRACTICE TIP

Phrasing can be critically important not only in court orders but also in requests for relief. The client wants to ask the court to order actions which are within its power to order. The *Russo* case provides an example of how important phrasing can be when requesting relief involving the disposition of out-of-state property in a divorce. The opinion in the *Russo* case can be accessed at *www.pearsonhighered.com/careersresources/* in the resource website for this text in the material related to Chapter 5 under Cases.

Paralegal **Application 5.2**

A Jurisdictional Issue—What Do You Think?

Fact pattern

In 1987, a wife who was domiciled in Virginia went to Hawaii to marry a man who was a U.S. Marine stationed there. The parties subsequently lived at duty stations in Virginia Beach, Virginia, from 1996 to 1999 and in Guantanamo Bay for a year, at which time the husband was reassigned to Camp Pendleton in California. The wife, initially without the husband's knowledge, decided to return to live in Virginia because of the husband's admitted infidelity and a generally deteriorating marital relationship. She filed for divorce in Virginia and the husband was served with the summons and complaint while he was in Virginia visiting the parties' children. The husband claimed that the Virginia court lacked both subject matter and personal jurisdiction. He alleged that neither party qualified as a bona fide resident or domiciliary of Virginia and that the court lacked personal jurisdiction over him because he was fraudulently induced to come to Virginia by the actions of the wife and would not have been there otherwise. The wife asserted that for purposes of subject matter jurisdiction, both parties were bona fide residents of Virginia based on the following evidence:

- One of the family's vehicles was still registered, licensed, and titled in Virginia.
- Each of them possessed a Virginia driver's license while they lived in Cuba.

- They held accounts in Virginia banks.
- The wife had a brother, sister, and brother-in-law living in Virginia.
- Prior to her marriage, the wife filed taxes in Virginia.
- The parties lived in Virginia for three years prior to moving to Cuba, and the wife returned to Virginia to reestablish her residency.
- When she left Virginia to go to Cuba, the wife left solely because of her husband's military orders.

Under Virginia law, the issue of subject matter jurisdiction requires a determination of the plaintiff's domicile and bona fide residency in the state of Virginia for at least six months prior to the filing of the action for divorce.

Sidebar

In your opinion, did the Virginia court have subject matter jurisdiction sufficient to dissolve the marriage? Why? Do you think the court properly exercised personal jurisdiction over the defendant? Explain your response. Read the opinion in *Blackson v. Blackson*, 579 S.E.2d 704 (Va. Ct. App. 2003) to see if you agree with the court's decision. You can access the *Blackson* opinion at *www.pearsonhighered.com/careersresources/* in the website material for this text related to Chapter 5 under Cases.

IN WHICH SPECIFIC COURT SHOULD THE COMPLAINT FOR DIVORCE BE FILED?

This question asks where venue will be proper. **Venue** refers to the particular geographical location within the state where the action should be filed—in which city, town, or county. As with subject matter and personal jurisdiction, the states establish rules governing venue. Typically, in a divorce action, venue will be proper in the county where the defendant resides, where the plaintiff resides, or where the parties last resided together as husband and wife.

Venue
refers to the geographical location within which a particular action should be filed

Grounds for Divorce

Divorce is a creature of statute, and each state establishes its own **grounds for divorce**, the reasons it considers sufficient to warrant the termination of a marriage. Paralegals need to be familiar with the applicable statutes in their respective jurisdictions so they are aware of the specific requirements to establish each ground. In several of the states, some of the statutory grounds for divorce are also potential grounds for

Ground for divorce
the reason for filing the action, the basis on which relief is sought in a divorce action; may be a fault or no-fault ground

annulment, such as impotency (e.g., in Massachusetts), bigamy (e.g., in Ohio), and fraud (e.g., in Connecticut). The statutory scheme in Tennessee (see Exhibit 5.4) is one of the most comprehensive. Similar to divorce statutes in just over 60% of the states, it includes both no-fault grounds (e.g., irreconcilable differences or living separate and apart) and fault grounds (e.g., adultery or cruel and abusive treatment).

A single divorce action may involve assertion of multiple alternative grounds by one or both parties. In a Virginia case, for example, the husband alleged four fault grounds (desertion, adultery, sodomy, and cruelty) and the wife cross-complained, alleging no-fault grounds. (See *Jones v. Jones*, 2004 Va. App, LEXIS 455.) The trial court's decree awarded the divorce to the wife, finding that the parties had lived separate and apart for more than the required one-year period. Most divorces are granted on a no-fault basis. Although no-fault divorce is generally less costly, both emotionally and financially, some clients insist on pursuing fault grounds for personal reasons such as anger, revenge, and a desire to publicly establish themselves as "blameless" for the failure of the marriage.

EXHIBIT 5.4 Tenn. Code Ann. § 36–4–101. Grounds for Divorce from Bonds of Matrimony

---

FROM THE STATUTE

The following are causes of divorce from the bonds of matrimony:

1. Either party, at the time of the contract, was and still is naturally impotent and incapable of procreation;
2. Either party has knowingly entered into a second marriage, in violation of a previous marriage, still subsisting;
3. Either party has committed adultery;
4. Willful or malicious desertion or absence of either party, without a reasonable cause, for one (1) whole year;
5. Being convicted of any crime that, by the laws of the state, renders the party infamous;
6. Being convicted of a crime that, by the laws of the state, is declared to be a felony, and sentenced to confinement in the penitentiary;
7. Either party has attempted the life of the other by poison or any other means showing malice;
8. Refusal, on the part of a spouse, to remove with that person's spouse to this state, without a reasonable cause, and being willfully absent from the spouse residing in Tennessee for two (2) years;
9. The woman was pregnant at the time of the marriage, by another person, without the knowledge of the husband;
10. Habitual drunkenness or abuse of narcotic drugs of either party, when the spouse has contracted either such habit after marriage;
11. The husband or wife is guilty of such cruel and inhuman treatment or conduct towards the spouse as renders cohabitation unsafe and improper, which may also be referred to in pleadings as inappropriate marital conduct;
12. The husband or wife has offered such indignities to the spouse's person as to render the spouse's position intolerable, and thereby forced the spouse to withdraw;
13. The husband or wife has abandoned the spouse or turned the spouse out of doors for no just cause, and has refused or neglected to provide for the spouse while having the ability to so provide;
14. Irreconcilable differences between the parties; and
15. For a continuous period of two (2) or more years that commenced prior to or after April 18, 1985, both parties have lived in separate residences, have not cohabited as man and wife during such period, and there are no minor children of the parties.

NO-FAULT GROUNDS

No-fault grounds for divorce are grounds that do not require a party to prove that the other party is to "blame" for the breakdown of the marriage. Marital misconduct is largely irrelevant. Each state establishes its own no-fault grounds or standards, and approximately 40% of the states have eliminated fault grounds entirely and have only a single no-fault standard. The two most common no-fault grounds are:

- irreconcilable differences
- living separate and apart

Irreconcilable Differences (Also Called Irretrievable or Irremediable Breakdown of the Marriage or Incompatibility)

Whatever it may be called, the core of **irreconcilable differences** as a ground for divorce is that the marriage has broken down and is beyond repair, and one or both of the parties want to terminate it. Some jurisdictions require that the parties actually live separate and apart for a period of time prior to filing. Others recognize the economic challenges faced by many divorcing spouses and allow the parties to continue living under the same roof, provided they do not engage in "marital relations" during the period of "separation." When this ground is alleged on an uncontested or joint basis, the court's inquiry is generally limited. The parties may be asked to briefly describe the nature of the differences that have caused the breakdown, approximately how long they have persisted, whether the parties have sought counseling or participated in some form of alternative dispute resolution in an effort to resolve their differences and save the marriage, and whether they believe the marriage has irretrievably broken down.

If a divorce action alleging this no-fault ground is contested, proof must be presented regarding the nature and extent of the parties' differences that have resulted in the alleged breakdown of the marriage. The breakdown may be due to an inability to communicate, or to serious disagreements between the parties about finances, childrearing issues, value systems, or marital priorities, or the parties may simply have grown apart and developed such divergent interests and incompatible lifestyles that they can no longer live together in a "normal" marital relationship. Whatever the explanation, the court's task is to determine that the marriage is beyond repair without examining the individual conduct of the parties in fault terms.

Irreconcilable differences
a no-fault ground for divorce, the essence of which is that the marriage has irreparably broken down due to serious differences between the parties

PARALEGAL PRACTICE TIP

From a practical perspective, if one of the parties is intent on obtaining a divorce and the other is adamantly opposed, the breakdown is self-evident. However, that alone may not be seen by the court as enough.

PARALEGAL PRACTICE TIP

To see a statute in a state that has no fault grounds and grants divorces solely when there is "an irretrievable breakdown of the marriage relationship," see the Minnesota statute at *www.revisor.leg.state.mn.us* (518.06).

Living Separate and Apart for a Specified Period of Time

The essence of this no-fault ground is that the marriage has broken down and, as a result, the parties are **living separate and apart**. Marital fault is essentially irrelevant as long as the parties have lived apart for the requisite period of time. There is considerable variation in state statutes with respect to the length of time the parties must have lived separate and apart (commonly from one to three years), whether the period of separation must be uninterrupted by attempts at reconciliation, whether the parties are living apart pursuant to a court order, whether the decision to separate is mutual, whether the separation is voluntary (e.g., not due to incarceration, hospitalization, or military service), and whether or not the parties must actually have lived under separate roofs. The applicable Utah statute, for

Living separate and apart
a no-fault ground for divorce based on the fact that, due to a breakdown of the marriage, the parties have lived apart from each other for a requisite period of time

PARALEGAL PRACTICE TIP
Although usually described as a no-fault state, Arizona has a statute addressing grounds for dissolution of a covenant marriage that includes fault grounds. To see that statute, visit *www.azleg.gov* (Arizona Revised Statutes 25.903 and 25.312).

example, provides for a divorce on this ground "when the husband and wife have lived separately under a decree of separate maintenance of any state for three consecutive years without cohabitation."[7]

When this ground is alleged and contested, evidence should be produced to establish the nature and length of the separation. This is accomplished through the testimony of witnesses familiar with the parties' living arrangements and documents such as leases, rent receipts, and telephone bills.

FAULT GROUNDS

The most common fault grounds include:

- adultery
- desertion/abandonment
- cruelty
- habitual drunkenness or drug abuse
- criminal conviction and incarceration

Adultery

Adultery
voluntary sexual intercourse between a married person and a person other than his or her spouse; a fault ground for divorce recognized in some states

Adultery as a ground for divorce commonly means voluntary sexual intercourse between a married person and a person other than his or her spouse, usually called the co-respondent. The specific language in state statutes varies. However, with the extension of marriage rights to same-sex partners on a national basis, it is likely that divorce statutes generally will be construed in a gender neutral fashion and that definitions of adultery will not be limited to heterosexual intercourse. This was the position already taken by a majority of the states that addressed the issue prior to June 2015. The minority view was reflected in a New Hampshire case, *In the Matter of Blanchflower and Blanchflower*, 150 N.H. 226, 834 A.2d 1010 (2003), decided before that state implemented its civil union legislation in 2008 and same-sex marriage in 2010. In the *Blanchflower* case, a husband sued for divorce on the ground of adultery, alleging that his wife had engaged in a "continuing adulterous affair" with the co-respondent, a woman, resulting in the irremediable breakdown of the parties' marriage. The co-respondent successfully sought to dismiss the petition, contending that a homosexual relationship between two people, one of whom is married, did not constitute adultery under the state statute.

Because of its nature, adultery usually may be proved by circumstantial evidence. Mere suspicions or the opportunity to commit adultery is not enough. Evidence of an "adulterous disposition" is typically established by evidence such as public displays of intimacy observed by others, e-mails and other forms of correspondence referencing sexual activity, unexplained absences and travel, and contracting of a venereal disease. In some states, the circumstantial evidence must be substantial, such as when a wife gives birth to a child genetically unrelated to her husband.

Marital communications privilege
the privilege that allows a spouse to refuse to testify, and to prevent others from testifying, about confidential communications between the spouses during their marriage

The **marital communications privilege**, which prevents a spouse from testifying in court about confidential communications with the other spouse during their marriage, usually does not apply in divorce actions or cases in which the defendant is alleged to have committed a crime against the spouse and/or their children. However, if adultery is alleged and is still a crime in the jurisdiction, the defendant may claim a Fifth Amendment right against self-incrimination if questioned about the existence of an adulterous relationship that falls within the applicable statute of limitations period.

Some states require that in order to claim adultery, both the petitioner and the respondent must be residents of the state where the divorce action is brought. In some jurisdictions, if adultery is alleged, the name of the alleged co-respondent must be provided in the complaint for divorce and the individual must be served. In others, the adultery may be alleged, but in order to name the third party, the petitioner must file a motion with the court for permission to disclose the name. The latter approach helps to reduce the number of baseless and malicious allegations. To see the New Hampshire statute regarding service on the co-respondent, go to *www.gencourt.state.nh.us* (RSA 458.11). On rare occasions, a wronged spouse may bring a tort action for **criminal conversation** against a third party who has committed adultery with the plaintiff's spouse.

> **Criminal conversation**
> a tort action for adultery brought against a third party who has sexual intercourse with another's spouse; abolished as a cause of action in most jurisdictions

Paralegal **Application 5.3**

Adultery Postseparation—A Ground for Divorce?

Clients who have already separated from their spouses often ask if it is okay for them to "date" while the divorce action is pending. The paralegal should refer the question to the attorney and avoid providing a response that might constitute the giving of legal advice to the client. For a case in which a New York court granted a divorce to a wife based on her husband's postseparation adultery, see *Golub v. Ganz*, 22 A.D.3d 919, 802 N.Y.S.2d 526 (2005). Although many courts would not view a "new" relationship in terms of a potential fault ground for divorce, they may look for dissipation of the marital estate that occurs in conjunction with the new relationship. Do you think postseparation relationships should be considered in the divorce context? Why?

Desertion/Abandonment

To obtain a divorce on the ground of **desertion/abandonment**, the petitioner usually must show that the defendant deliberately and without consent left the marital relationship with no intention to return, and that the absence has continued for a specified continuous period of time (customarily a year or more). The desertion must be unnecessary and without sufficient cause. Since it also must be voluntary, an absence due to military service, incarceration, or institutionalization in a mental or other facility such as a rehabilitation center will not constitute desertion.

When abandonment is alleged, it involves abandonment of the relation between the husband and wife and not necessarily the house in which they live. The desertion may be **constructive desertion** if a spouse's objectionable conduct is so abusive or otherwise intolerable that it renders continuation of the marital relationship impossible and forces the "innocent spouse" either to move out or to move into a separate area within the marital residence in order to maintain his or her health, safety, or self-respect. The spouse who leaves has a defense to a claim by the other party of desertion and also has his or her own ground for divorce.

> **Desertion/abandonment**
> a fault ground for divorce in some states; the plaintiff must show that the defendant deliberately and without consent left the marital relationship with no intention to return, and that the absence has continued for a specified continuous period of time (customarily a year or more)

> **Constructive desertion**
> a situation in which a spouse's objectionable conduct is so abusive or otherwise intolerable that it renders continuation of the marital relationship impossible and forces the "innocent spouse" either to move out or move into a separate area within the marital residence in order to maintain his or her health, safety, or self-respect

A refusal of sexual relations and/or moving to a separate bedroom may form the basis of a ground for divorce (such as desertion or cruelty), depending on the facts of the case.[8] An unjustifiable refusal for an extended period (a year or more) may be sufficient unless the refusal is based on sexually abusive conduct of the defendant or a reasonable suspicion of his or her infidelity. For example, in a Virginia case, an appellate court held that a wife's refusal of sexual relations did not constitute desertion when the husband engaged in recurring extramarital sexual relations without using protection. His conduct was also deemed to constitute cruelty.[9]

Cruelty

Cruel and abusive treatment
a fault ground for divorce available in some states; conduct that is so physically or mentally damaging that it endangers the spouse's health, safety, or reason

Cruelty may be termed **cruel and abusive treatment**, cruel and inhumane treatment, indignities, physical and mental cruelty, or treatment that endangers health and reason. Although a single act may be sufficient if it is atrocious or severe, cruelty usually involves a course of conduct. In some states (such as Illinois), the cruelty must constitute "extreme and repeated physical or mental cruelty."[10] Particularly in states with a limited number of specific fault grounds, cruelty is often used as a catchall ground. For example, excessive drinking, drug addiction, or failure to provide for the needs of the family when there is an ability to do so may cause such severe emotional stress that a court may deem the conduct cruel and abusive.

Cruelty generally encompasses both acts of physical violence and the reasonable apprehension thereof and also "acts and conduct the effect of which is calculated to permanently destroy the peace of mind and happiness of one of the parties to the marriage and thereby render the marital relationship intolerable."[11] Nagging, temper tantrums, name-calling, rudeness, cursing, and criticism usually are not sufficient to constitute cruelty, although they may be, depending on the known vulnerabilities of a specific plaintiff and an intention to cause pain and anguish.[12] Some states require that the plaintiff demonstrate proof of the harm suffered as a result of the defendant's conduct, such as medical records, medications prescribed for stress, counseling sought, significant weight loss or gain, and sleep disturbances. (See Case 5.1.)

CASE **5.1** *Pfoltzer v. Morris-Pfoltzer*, 9 A.D.3d 615, 779 N.Y.S.2d 668 (N.Y. App. Div. 2004)

FROM THE OPINION

Supreme Court granted plaintiff a divorce following the parties' 15-year marriage on the ground of cruel and inhuman treatment. Defendant appeals, arguing that there was insufficient evidence upon which to grant plaintiff a divorce on this ground. Noting that Supreme Court's determination as the factfinder on this issue will not be lightly disturbed by this Court . . . , we disagree with the defendant's contention and accordingly affirm.

Domestic Relations Law § 170 (1) provides that a divorce will be granted on a theory of cruel and inhuman treatment after a showing "that the conduct of the defendant so endangers the physical or mental well being of the plaintiff as renders it unsafe or improper for the plaintiff to cohabit with the defendant." "[I]n order to make out a prima facie case of cruel and inhuman treatment, a party must show something more than 'mere incompatibility' and 'serious misconduct [must] be distinguished from trivial'" (citations omitted). While a high degree of proof of serious or substantial misconduct was required in this case owing to the long duration of the parties' marriage . . . , we are satisfied that plaintiff made such a showing. . . .

The evidence revealed that defendant has engaged in a constant barrage of harassing and controlling behavior toward plaintiff, often underscored by harsh religious accusations. According to plaintiff, defendant has alienated him from certain members of his family and he was forced to obtain a temporary order of protection to remove his personal items from the marital residence following his departure therefrom. He also obtained an order of protection preventing defendant from continuing to make harassing telephone calls. The record further reveals that defendant has engaged in a course of verbal and mental abuse by harassing and embarrassing plaintiff with public accusations that he has loathsome personal hygiene, has engaged in sexual-related criminal conduct and that he suffers from a particular venereal disease, as well as Acquired Immune Deficiency Syndrome.

The evidence also sufficiently established that the anguish and embarrassment suffered by plaintiff has had an effect on his physical and mental health thus providing a basis for finding that cohabitation with defendant would be either unsafe or improper. . . . Plaintiff was receiving medical treatment for a stress-related ulcer at the time of the trial and had been receiving mental health counseling for some time to address his depression and to help him understand and overcome the abusive relationship between himself and defendant. Indeed for a one-year period in the latter part of the parties' marriage, plaintiff had been prescribed medication to treat his depression caused by the turmoil in the marriage.

Mercure, J.P., Crew III, Lahtinen and Kane, JJ., concur.

Ordered that the amended judgment is affirmed, without costs.

SIDEBAR

Read the opinion in this case. Do you agree that the defendant's conduct was sufficient to warrant a divorce? Explain your response. The *Pfoltzer* opinion can be accessed at *www.pearsonhighered.com/careersresources/* in the resource website for this text in the material related to Chapter 5 under Cases.

Habitual Drunkenness or Drug Abuse

This ground is most commonly called habitual drunkenness, but the precise terminology may vary. In Massachusetts, it is called "gross and confirmed habits of intoxication."[13] The Georgia statute includes both "habitual intoxication" and "habitual drug addiction" as independent grounds for divorce.[14] Some states require that the abuse have continued for a certain period. The Illinois statute, for example, reads, "the respondent has been guilty of habitual drunkenness for the space of 2 years" and "the respondent has been guilty of gross and confirmed habits caused by the excessive use of addictive drugs for the space of 2 years."[15]

Criminal Conviction and Incarceration

The state statutes that include criminal conviction and incarceration as a ground for divorce vary with respect to the type of crime committed, the jurisdiction in which the crime was committed, the length of the sentence, and whether or not the respondent is/was actually confined. The pertinent Maryland statute lists as a ground "conviction of a felony or misdemeanor in any state or in any court of the United States if before the filing of the application for divorce the defendant has: (i) been sentenced to serve at least 3 years or an indeterminate sentence in a penal institution; and (ii) served 12 months of the sentence."[16] The Georgia statute specifies that the offense be one that involves "moral turpitude."[17] In Ohio, the respondent must be incarcerated at the time the complaint is filed.[18] The Virginia statute addresses the potential impact of a subsequent pardon.[19]

Examples of some of the less common statutory fault grounds for divorce include the following:

- The respondent has infected the spouse with a sexually transmitted disease.[20]
- Either party has joined any religious sect or society that professes to believe the relation of husband and wife is unlawful and has refused to cohabit for a six-month period.[21]
- Insanity under certain conditions. For example, a ground in Connecticut is the legal confinement of a spouse "in a hospital or hospitals or other similar institution or institutions because of mental illness, for at least an accumulated period totaling five years within the period of six years next preceding the date of the complaint."[22]
- "Excessively vicious conduct toward the complaining party or a minor child of the complaining party, if there is no reasonable expectation of reconciliation."[23]
- "Willful neglect of the respondent to provide for the petitioner the common necessaries of life."[24]
- "Any gross neglect of duty."[25]

Defenses to a Divorce Action

Defense
a defendant's stated reason why a plaintiff has no valid claim or why the court should not grant the relief requested

Defenses to a divorce action commonly include:

- Lack of subject matter jurisdiction.
- Lack of personal jurisdiction.
- Lack of proper venue.
- Forum *non conveniens*.
- Lack of proper service of process.
- Failure of the complaint to state a claim upon which relief can be based. The plaintiff has alleged a ground for divorce that is not available in the jurisdiction.
- The matter is *res judicata*. The marriage was previously dissolved in an action for divorce or annulment in another state or country.
- Invalidity of the marriage.

When the divorce action is based on one or more fault grounds, additional defenses may be available. These "traditional" defenses have their origins in common law and include the following:

- **Condonation**. This defense is used when the defendant asserts that the petitioner has, in effect, condoned the alleged blameworthy conduct, such as an adulterous affair, by forgiving it to the extent that he or she has resumed "normal" marital relations with the defendant spouse, who, with forgiveness, regains innocence. As an Illinois court described it in a 2005 decision, "Condonation in the law of divorce is the forgiveness of an antecedent matrimonial offense on condition that it shall not be repeated and that the offender shall thereafter treat the forgiving party with conjugal kindness."[26]

- **Provocation**. When this defense is raised, the defendant is claiming that the plaintiff provoked the conduct alleged in the complaint. For example, if the alleged ground for divorce is desertion/abandonment, the defendant may defend by saying that the plaintiff's excessive drinking and abuse forced a departure from the marital home for the defendant's safety and protection.

- **Recrimination**. Eliminated in several states, this defense is raised when the defendant claims that the plaintiff has also committed a marital wrong such as adultery and thus should not be granted a divorce. Some states have adopted the **doctrine of comparative rectitude** to deal with situations in which both parties are at fault. Under the doctrine, a court grants the divorce to the party whose wrongdoing is least serious. Other courts occasionally award **dual divorces**, in which each party is granted the divorce.

- **Connivance**. Connivance is an appropriate defense when the plaintiff allegedly consented to or created the opportunity for the defendant to commit the act complained of in the complaint. For instance, if the petitioner alleges habitual drunkenness as a ground for divorce, the defendant may defend stating that the plaintiff both participated in and promoted ("enabled") the defendant's drinking and actively sabotaged his or her efforts to seek treatment.

- **Collusion**. Collusion is less a defense than it is a legal bar to a divorce. Collusion is a determination by the court that the parties should not be granted a divorce because they had an agreement to, in effect, deceive the court as to the nature and true purpose of the action. Essentially, they conspired to fabricate a reason for the divorce when no legally recognized ground existed. Although far more common in the fault era, collusion is not unheard-of today. For example, in an Oklahoma case in 2005, a court vacated a divorce decree based on the fact that the husband and wife sought a divorce with no intention of separating and solely for the purpose of increasing the wife's public benefits in support of her chronic illness.[27]

Before raising a common law defense, the paralegal needs to research whether or not "traditional" defenses are still available to defendants in the jurisdiction. For example, Minnesota provides by statute that the defenses of condonation, connivance, collusion, recrimination, insanity, and lapse of time are abolished (Minn. Stat. §518.06). Florida law provides in Title VI Chapter 61 (61.044) that the defenses of condonation, collusion, recrimination, and laches are abolished.

Condonation
the forgiveness of a matrimonial offense

Provocation
a traditional defense claiming that the plaintiff provoked the conduct alleged in the complaint and therefore should be denied relief

Recrimination
a defense raised when the defendant alleges the plaintiff has also committed a marital wrong and therefore should not be granted a divorce

Doctrine of comparative rectitude
in the divorce context, the granting of a divorce to the party who is least at fault when both parties have committed marital wrongdoing

Dual divorce
a divorce granted to both parties

Connivance
a traditional defense in which the defendant alleges the plaintiff consented to, or participated in, the act complained of in the complaint

Collusion
a determination by the court that the parties should not be granted a divorce because they jointly deceived the court as to the true nature and purpose of the action

Drafting and Filing of the Complaint

A divorce action technically begins when a complaint/petition is filed with the court and the defendant is served. The **complaint** (or petition for dissolution) is the main pleading in a divorce case. It sets forth the nature of the action, the requested relief, and the basis of the court's jurisdiction over the action. It usually calls for the following information:

- names and addresses of the parties
- date and place of the parties' marriage
- date when the parties separated/last resided together as husband and wife
- names and dates of birth of any minor children
- alleged ground(s) for the divorce
- declaration regarding property in a community property state
- request (or "prayer") for relief (e.g., division of property, custody, child and/or spousal support, maintenance of health insurance, sale of the marital home, resumption of maiden name). It often includes a final open-ended request for any further relief the court deems fair and equitable. In some states, the court may not be authorized to grant more relief in the judgment than has been requested in the complaint and a party may not be able to request additional forms of relief (such as alimony) at a later date. If there is a premarital agreement between the parties, it is important that the complaint put the court on notice of its existence—for example, by attaching a copy and asking that the court enforce (or not enforce) the premarital agreement executed by the parties on a certain date.

The complaint should be prepared in a manner that complies with applicable state statutes and procedural rules re grounds, format, jurisdiction, venue, etc. Careful attention must be given to using jurisdictionally appropriate terminology. For example, some states use the terms "divorce" and "dissolution" interchangeably. Others, such as Ohio, use "dissolution" strictly to refer to uncontested actions. In a complaint, the parties are commonly referred to as the plaintiff and the defendant. In a petition, they are typically called the petitioner and the respondent. If the petition for divorce is a joint petition, the parties are usually labeled petitioner and co-petitioner or as spouse a and spouse b.

The paralegal is often asked to draft the complaint/petition. Before doing so, the grounds, proper jurisdiction, and venue should be confirmed with the supervising attorney based on the facts of the case (where each of the parties resides, where the parties last lived together as husband and wife, where the children are located, etc.). The next step is to determine the form to be used. Many states mandate the use of uniform preprinted forms or formats for divorce actions that are available online and on disks that accompany practice manuals. The states may have special rules governing the use of computer-generated forms in particular. For example, there may be a requirement that the form be printed on a particular color or weight of paper or that the origin of the form be noted (e.g., cgf—computer-generated form—marked on a bottom corner of the form). A copy of a Complaint for Absolute Divorce used in the state of Maryland is provided in Exhibit 5.5.

Complaint

the main pleading in a case that sets forth the nature of the action and the request for relief

---

PARALEGAL PRACTICE TIP

Even in an uncontested or joint petition for a no-fault divorce, a ground must be indicated (e.g., the parties are seeking a divorce due to irreconcilable differences that have caused the irremediable breakdown of the marriage). Typically, one party's attorney will complete the necessary documents for review by the other party's attorney and the clients prior to signing and filing.

PARALEGAL PRACTICE TIP

A majority of the states now make Complaints/Petitions for Divorce available online. Take a look at the forms in these states:

NEW HAMPSHIRE: *www.courts. state.nh.us*

INDIANA: *www.in.gov/judiciary/ forms*

MONTANA: *courts.mt.gov*

WYOMING: *www.courts.state .wy.us*

To see a Joint Petition for Simplified Dissolution of Marriage in an Illinois county, visit *www.cookcountyclerk ofcourt.org* (Court forms/domestic relations/Form 346.004).

EXHIBIT 5.5 Complaint for Absolute Divorce

Courtesy of the State of Maryland

Circuit Court for_____ **Case No.** _____
City or County

VS.
Name _____   Name _____

Street Address _____ Apt #   Street Address _____ Apt #
( )   ( )
City _____ State _ Zip Code _ Area _ Telephone   City _____ State _ Zip Code _ Area _ Telephone
Code   Code
Plaintiff   *Defendant*

COMPLAINT FOR ABSOLUTE DIVORCE
(CC-DR 20)

I, _____ , representing myself, state that:
Name

1.   The Defendant and I were married on _____
                                         Month   Day   Year
     in _____ in a ☐ civil ☐ religious ceremony.
        City/County/State where Married

2.   *Check all that apply:*
     ☐ I have lived in Maryland since:_____
                                       Month/Year
     ☐ My spouse has lived in Maryland since:_____
                                             Month/Year

3.   *Check all that apply: (See paragraph 13)*
     ☐ The grounds for divorce occurred in the State of Maryland.
     ☐ The grounds for divorce occurred outside the State of Maryland and I or my spouse have been a
        resident for at least six (6) months prior to the date of the filing of this Complaint.

4.   *Check one:*
     ☐ We have no children together (skip paragraphs 6 through 10) or
     ☐ My spouse and I are the parents of the following child(ren):

     _____ _____   _____ _____
          Name   Date of Birth   Name   Date of Birth

     _____ _____   _____ _____
          Name   Date of Birth   Name   Date of Birth

     _____ _____   _____ _____
          Name   Date of Birth   Name   Date of Birth

5.   I know of the following related cases concerning the child(ren) or parties (such as domestic
     violence, paternity, divorce, custody, visitation, termination of parental rights, adoption or other
     cases):

     Court   **Case No.**   **Kind of Case**   **Year Filed**   **Results or Status (if you know)**

     _____   _____   _____   _____   _____
     _____   _____   _____   _____   _____
     _____   _____   _____   _____   _____

CC-DR 20 (Rev. 10/2015)   Page 1 of 4

(Continued)

EXHIBIT 5.5 *(Continued)*

6. I have been a party, witness, or otherwise involved in the following cases about custody or visitation of the child(ren):

State	Court	Case No.	Date of Child Custody Determination
_____	_____	_____	_____
_____	_____	_____	_____
_____	_____	_____	_____

Attach the most recent court order for the above-referenced court cases.

7. I know of the following people, not parties to this case, who have physical custody of, or claim rights of legal custody or physical custody of, or visitation with the child(ren):

Name _____ Current Address _____

Name _____ Current Address _____

Name _____ Current Address _____

8. The child(ren) are currently living with: _____
                                                          Name

9. The child(ren) have lived in the following places, with the persons indicated during the last five years:

Time Period	Place	Name(s)/Current Address of Person(s) with whom Child Lived
_____	_____	_____
_____	_____	_____
_____	_____	_____

10. It is in the best interests of the child(ren) that I have (*check all that apply*):

☐ joint ☐ sole physical custody of _____.
                                                     Name of Children

☐ joint ☐ sole legal custody of _____.
                                                  Name of Children

☐ visitation with _____.
                                 Name of Children

11. I ☐ am ☐ am not seeking alimony because _____.

12. (*You do not have to complete paragraph 12 if you are not asking the court to make decisions about your property*). My spouse and/or I have the following property and debts (*check all that apply*):

☐ House(s)   ☐ Furniture
☐ Pension(s)   ☐ Bank account(s) and investment(s)
☐ Motor Vehicle(s)   ☐ Family Use Personal Property
☐ Debts (attach list)   ☐ Other: _____

13. My grounds for an absolute divorce are (*check all that apply*):

☐ **Twelve (12) Month Separation** - From on or about _____, my spouse and I
                                                                          Month/Day/Year
have lived separate and apart from each other in separate residences, without interruption, without sexual intercourse, for more than 12 months.

CC-DR 20 (Rev. 10/2015)   Page 2 of 4

EXHIBIT 5.5 *(Continued)*

☐ **Adultery** - My spouse committed adultery.

☐ **Actual Desertion** - On or about _____, my spouse, without just cause or reason,
  _{Month/Day/Year} abandoned and deserted me, with the intention of ending our marriage. This abandonment has
  continued without interruption for more than 12 months and there is no reasonable expectation
  we will reconcile.

☐ **Constructive Desertion** - I left my spouse because his/her cruel and vicious conduct made the
  continuation of our marriage impossible, if I were to preserve my health, safety, and self-respect.
  This conduct was the final and deliberate act of my spouse and our separation has continued
  without interruption for more than 12 months and there is no reasonable expectation that we will
  reconcile.

☐ **Criminal Conviction of a Felony or Misdemeanor** - On or about _____, my
  spouse was sentenced to serve at least three years or an indeterminate sentence in a penal
  institution and has served 12 or more months of the sentence.

☐ **Cruelty/Excessively Vicious Conduct Against Me or my Minor Child** - My spouse has
  persistently treated me or my minor child cruelly and has engaged in excessively vicious
  conduct rendering continuation of the marital relationship impossible and there is no reasonable
  expectation that we will reconcile.

☐ **Insanity** - On or about _____, my spouse was confined to a mental institution,
  _{Month/Day/Year} hospital, or other similar institution and has been confined for 3 or more years. Two doctors
  competent in psychiatry will testify that the insanity is incurable and there is no hope of
  recovery. My spouse or I have been a resident of Maryland for at least two years before the
  filing of this complaint.

☐ **Mutual Consent** - My spouse and I do not have any minor children in common. My spouse
  and I have a written settlement agreement resolving all issues relating to alimony and property.

FOR THESE REASONS, I request *(check all that apply)*:

☒ An Absolute Divorce.

☐ A change back to my former name: _____
  _{Full Former Name}

☐ Joint ☐ Sole physical custody of the minor child(ren) and reasonable child support.

☐ Joint ☐ Sole legal custody of the minor child(ren) and reasonable child support.

☐ Visitation with the minor child(ren).

☐ Use and possession of the family home for up to three years from the date of the divorce.

☐ Use and possession of the family use personal property for up to three years from the date of the
  divorce.

☐ Child support (attach Form DR 30 or DR 31).

☐ Health insurance for the child(ren).

☐ Health insurance for me.

☐ My share of the property or its value.

☐ Transfer of family use personal property.

☐ Transfer of the real property jointly owned by the parties located at

  _____

  from _____ to _____

CC-DR 20 (Rev. 10/2015)   Page 3 of 4

(Continued)

EXHIBIT 5.5 *(Continued)*

☐ Authorize _____ to purchase from _____
        Name of Party   Name of Party
_____ an interest in real property located at _____
_____

☐ A monetary award (money) based on marital property.
☐ Alimony (attach Form DR 31).
☒ Any other appropriate relief.

I, _____ solemnly affirm under the penalties of perjury,
      Name
that the contents of this document are true to the best of my knowledge, information, and belief.

_____   _____
      Date   Signature

CC-DR 20 (Rev. 10/2015)   Page 4 of 4   **Reset**

PARALEGAL PRACTICE TIP

To view examples of some of the documents referenced in this section, check out the following:

South Dakota Affidavit of Indigency *www.ujs.sd.gov* Form UJS 305

West Virginia Bureau of Vital Statistics Form *www.state.wv.us*

New Hampshire Appearance form *www.courts.state.nh.us*

California Forms re electronic service and filing *www. courtinfo.ca.gov*

Once completed, reviewed, and signed, the Complaint is filed, accompanied by the filing fee and any other required documents. The client may be able to seek a waiver of the filing fee by filing a motion and affidavit of indigency, if required. If granted, the person usually is said to proceed *in forma pauperis* (Latin: as a poor person). Although the states vary with respect to the additional documents that must be filed, most require the following:

- A certified copy of the Marriage Certificate (with a certified translation if in a foreign language)
- A Disclosure Affidavit concerning any orders in force or pending regarding care, custody, and support of the parties' minor children, if any

- A Financial Statement (must be updated at trial and every time a motion with financial implications is heard)
- A Military Affidavit if the defendant/respondent is unlikely to appear or is in the service and will not be able to appear
- A Bureau of Vital Statistics Form used to collect data on divorcing couples

The paralegal often gathers the necessary forms and files the complaint along with the accompanying documents and a transmittal letter to the court when directed to do so by the supervisor. Copies of all documents filed with the court should also be placed in the client's file and sent to the client. The paralegal needs to be familiar with filing requirements and practices in the jurisdiction (in person, by mail, electronically, etc.).

The attorney customarily also files an Appearance at this point, indicating that he or she will be representing the plaintiff in the divorce action. The paralegal may draft the Appearance (or complete the court's appearance form) and file it after it is reviewed and signed. A party may also want to file and record (where property records are recorded) a **memorandum of *lis pendens*** (Latin: pending matter) if real estate owned by one or both of the parties may be affected by the eventual divorce judgment, to put third parties, such as potential buyers, on notice of the divorce action and the existence of a pending claim to ownership of the property.

When the complaint is filed, the court clerk assigns a docket number and issues a **summons**. The docket number should appear on all subsequent documents and correspondence related to the action. Sometimes the summons is completed by court staff, but in some counties necessary information is filled in by a member of the family law team, usually the paralegal.

Occasionally, a party may request, or the court may require, that third parties be joined in a divorce action at some point. For example, if one of the spouses creates a sham trust, allegedly for someone else's benefit; makes a substantial "loan" to a sibling; holds property in the names of other persons; or otherwise transfers property in a scheme designed to deprive the other spouse of a fair share of the marital assets, the third party may be drawn into the divorce, usually by use of an "equity" complaint for a **declaratory judgment** and/or injunctive relief. See, e.g., *Howard v. Howard*, 2 A.3d 318 (Me. 2010). Some states add financial institutions, putting them on notice that the assets they hold are subject to a court order, thereby facilitating discovery with respect to those assets.

Service of the Complaint and Return of Service

Service of the Summons and Complaint must comply with all applicable local rules and customarily must be made within a specified period after the filing date (usually sixty to ninety days). The summons informs the defendant that he or she has been sued and needs to answer within a certain period (usually twenty to thirty days) or risk the possibility of a default judgment in some jurisdictions. **Service of process** is usually accomplished by:

- **Acceptance of service**. If a defendant is aware (by whatever means) of the summons, he or she may voluntarily go to a courthouse, receive the summons, and sign a form acknowledging service.

Memorandum of *lis pendens*
a notice that ownership and disposition of certain real property is subject to a pending legal action, and that any interest acquired during the pendency of that action is subject to its outcome; usually filed in a Registry of Deeds where the property is located

Summons
a formal notice from a court informing a defendant of an action filed against him or her and ordering the defendant to respond and answer the allegations of the plaintiff within a certain period or risk entry of a default judgment

Declaratory judgment
a binding adjudication that establishes the rights, status, or other legal relations between the parties

Service of process
delivery of a summons and complaint to a defendant in a manner consistent with state and federal law; usually accomplished by personal "in-hand" service by an authorized individual such as a sheriff or by publication in a newspaper and mailing to the defendant's last known address

PARALEGAL PRACTICE TIP
To see an example of a Summons for Divorce used in South Carolina, visit *www.judicial.state.sc.us* (South Carolina) (Search by name of form). You can find an example of a Wisconsin Affidavit of Service at *www.wicourts.gov* (Forms/Circuit Court/ Family Forms Form FA-4120).

PARALEGAL PRACTICE TIP

When a defendant accepts service or is personally served, it is called "actual service" and the defendant is thereafter considered to be subject to the personal jurisdiction of the court hearing the matter.

PARALEGAL PRACTICE TIP

To see an example of a form requesting the court's permission to serve a defendant by publication, visit *http://www.courts.state.co.us.* (Search Form JDF 1301.)

PARALEGAL PRACTICE TIP

To see some interesting "tips on locating people" to effect service, visit *www.courts.alaska.gov.* (Search by title.)

Answer
a pleading filed by a defendant in response to a plaintiff's complaint, setting forth the defendant's defenses and counterclaims

PARALEGAL PRACTICE TIP

To see an example of a standard Answer form in West Virginia, visit *www.wv.gov* (Form FC 108).

- **Personal service**. An approved process server delivers the summons into the hand of the defendant. The server then completes the "return of service" information indicating the summons has been served (or that service was attempted on multiple occasions but not accomplished). The proof of service information on the summons must be completed by the process server, who certifies when, where, and how service was made. The completed summons is returned by the server to either the court or the attorney's office, depending on local rules. The original is kept in the court's file, and a copy should be placed in the client's file.
- **Publication in a local newspaper and mailing to the defendant's last known address**. Service may be made by this means if the defendant is evading service or his or her whereabouts are unknown (requires permission of the court). The plaintiff is usually required to show that a good faith effort has been made to locate and serve the defendant.

The paralegal must be familiar with the rules and procedures governing service of process and will usually perform the following related tasks:

- Complete the summons, if required.
- Maintain a list of approved process servers and fees. Process servers usually include sheriffs, constables, marshals, etc. Some jurisdictions permit service by a disinterested adult.
- Make arrangements for proper service and alert the client as to where and when it is likely to be made in case there are safety issues to address.
- If service is by publication, draft a Motion for Permission to Serve by Publication, if required. If approved, mail a copy of the order of notice of the action, the complaint, and the summons by certified mail to the defendant's last known address, and arrange for publication in the appropriate newspaper(s).
- If the defendant is located in another state or nation, arrange to have him or her properly served in that location.
- Track and ensure that service is properly completed and documented and advise the supervisor and client to that effect.
- Return proof of service to the court, if necessary, keeping copies for the client and the file.
- Arrange for payment of the process server's fee.

Occasionally, a party may want or need to amend a Complaint, for example, to correct an error in an address in the original filing, provide the name of a co-respondent, or add an additional fault or no-fault ground for divorce. Local rules dictate whether the Complaint can be amended with or without the permission of the court, and it may depend on whether or not the Complaint has already been served. The paralegal may be asked to draft a Motion to Amend the Complaint, along with a supporting Affidavit and Proposed Order, if required.

Defendant's Response to the Complaint

The defendant's initial pleading is customarily an **Answer** to the complaint/petition for divorce, which must be filed within the period set by statute or procedural rule (usually twenty to thirty days after being served). In the answer, the defendant admits, denies, or indicates lack of information sufficient to respond to each of the paragraphs/allegations in the complaint. The defendant may also:

- Raise any defenses he or she has to the allegations in the Complaint (condonation, existence of a binding premarital agreement, lack of jurisdiction, etc.).

- Include a **counterclaim** for divorce and his or her own request for relief. If the defendant also wants a divorce, it is good practice to file a counterclaim (even if the grounds are the same as in the Complaint, e.g., irreconcilable differences). In the event the other party subsequently withdraws his or her Complaint, the date the counterclaim is filed will be preserved and there is no need to start the process all over again. If the parties are able to reach an agreement, the contested claims may be converted to a joint uncontested action, and the parties can proceed on that basis.

When responding to a complaint for divorce on behalf of a nonresident defendant, careful consideration must be given to the nature of the response. In appropriate circumstances, in lieu of an answer, the defendant may file a **Motion to Dismiss** (for lack of subject matter or personal jurisdiction, improper venue, or deficiencies in service, etc.) and *not* an Answer. If a nonresident defendant files an Answer, he or she will trigger personal jurisdiction. If the defendant is represented, his or her attorney should file a limited appearance for the sole purpose of contesting jurisdiction. Any personal appearance by a nonresident defendant will confer full personal jurisdiction on the court even if the defendant appears solely to seek dismissal of the action. The paralegal may be asked to draft whichever response will be filed.

If a defendant receives notice and fails to respond to a Complaint, he or she may not be permitted to seek relief at a later date. However, courts are reluctant to issue default judgments in divorce cases and customarily will not do so without a hearing. Even in states that permit them, a default judgment is unlikely absent a party intentionally or recklessly impeding the judicial process. (See, e.g., *In re Marriage of Lewis*, 375 S.W.3d 870 (Mo. Ct. App. 2012).) Once the plaintiff's attorney has notice that counsel for the opposing party has filed an appearance, all communication from the firm should be with that attorney and not directly with the party he or she represents. Direct communication between the parties themselves is virtually impossible to avoid, even when restraining orders have been issued. Such communication is a double-edged sword. Voluntary resolution of differences and maintenance of a civil, even positive, relationship between the parties is encouraged, particularly when children are involved and /or resources are limited. However, in high-conflict cases or when there is a considerable power differential between the parties, communication is best left to counsel. In either situation, a client should always consult counsel before signing or otherwise finalizing any agreements with the other party.

Motions for Temporary Orders and Other Purposes

After the defendant is served and jurisdiction is established, one or both of the parties may file a request for **temporary orders**, most often addressing custody and support issues. Usually, the request is made in the form of a **motion** (a request to the court for an order) accompanied by an **affidavit** in support of the motion. States vary with respect to whether requests for temporary relief may or must be made in one motion or in separate motions or may be contained in the initial complaint or the answer. Some jurisdictions mandate that uniform forms be used for particular motions and/or make samples available online. If not, firms should

Counterclaim
a defendant's claim against the plaintiff

Motion to Dismiss
a request that the court dismiss the case because of some procedural or other defect, such as lack of jurisdiction or failure to state a claim on which relief can be based

PARALEGAL PRACTICE TIP
To see an example of a Limited Appearance form, visit *www. courts.state.nh.us*. Search Form NHJB-2294-DFPS.

Temporary orders
orders designed to protect the parties and maintain the status quo while a matter is pending before the court

Motion
an oral or written request that the court issue a particular ruling or order

Affidavit
a first-person statement signed under oath laying out facts in support of the motion

Pendente lite
Latin: while the action is pending

Ex parte motion
a motion made without advance notice to the opposing party; a motion considered and initially ruled on by the court without hearing from both parties, based on the urgency of the matter or the harm that might otherwise result

have available templates, forms on disk, models in form and practice books, and motions in files from past cases that involved similar fact patterns that may readily be tailored to the case at hand. A sample of a Motion for Temporary Orders is provided at *www.pearsonhighered.com/careersresources/* in the resource website for this text in the material related to Chapter 5 under Forms. It is only a sample and uses terminology regarding child custody and support that is appropriate for some, but not all, jurisdictions.

Requests for temporary orders are primarily designed to maintain the status quo *pendente lite*, (while the action is pending). Because of their potential to subtly impact "permanent" orders, absent an emergency, some attorneys prefer to postpone filing for temporary orders seeking custody and support until after sufficient discovery is conducted. However, motions serving other purposes may need to be filed as the action progresses, seeking, for example:

- protection of marital assets held by third parties, such as banks or investment firms
- preservation of marital assets, requesting that the other party be enjoined from disposing of or encumbering a specific asset
- allowance of attorney's fees and costs *pendente lite* enabling a party to maintain the action (usually requires an affidavit of the attorney, a schedule of anticipated expenses, a financial statement, etc.)
- use and occupancy of the marital home and responsibility for related expenses including an order that one of the parties vacate the marital home, if necessary (see Exhibit 5.6 for a sample of a Motion to Vacate the Marital Home)
- appointment of an investigator, custody evaluator, and/or guardian *ad litem* (GAL)
- protection from abuse by means of a restraining, stay-away, or no-contact order (may be based on a complaint rather than a motion, depending on the jurisdiction and circumstances)
- prevention of removal of the parties' children from the state while the litigation is pending
- appointment of an appraiser to assess the value of a major asset such as the marital home
- consolidation with the divorce action of a prior order from another court that is still in force relating to protection from abuse, child custody, and/or occupancy of the marital home

Because of their nature, some motions may be filed ex parte (without advance notice to the opposing party). For example, the purpose of a motion for an order restraining transfer or dissipation of marital assets, or to prevent removal of the minor children from the jurisdiction, may be totally defeated if advance notice is provided. *Ex parte* **motions** usually must be accompanied by an affidavit setting forth the nature of the emergency and explaining how the giving of notice would pose a substantial risk of harm.

Many states issue "automatic restraining orders" that are effective with regard to the plaintiff upon filing of the Complaint and to the defendant when served with the Summons and Complaint. The orders generally remain in effect while the matter is pending unless modified by agreement of the parties or by order of the court. These orders usually restrain transfer or disposal of any of the parties' property (except to cover reasonable living or ordinary business expenses), incurring of debt, and changing of any insurance or pension beneficiaries. The client may need to be alerted to and reminded about the existence of these orders.

The court may choose to appoint a **guardian *ad litem*** in cases where custody is contested, even if not requested by the parties. The guardian is likely to request from each party a variety of documents, such as pleadings, reports in the parents' possession, and medical records. Releases will need to be provided where necessary. The guardian usually interviews the parents, the children, school personnel, day care providers, pediatricians, and others to gather information about the children's history and current home and school environment. The guardian then makes a custody recommendation to the court, which it may accept or reject. Counsel is customarily permitted to question the GAL at trial regarding the report and the basis for any findings and recommendations. The report is usually impounded and not part of the public record to protect the privacy of the children and the parties. The role of a GAL is discussed more fully in Chapter 9.

Guardian *ad litem*
a person, often a lawyer, appointed by the court to conduct an investigation and/or represent a party who is a minor or otherwise unable to represent himself or herself in a legal proceeding; the guardian's role may be limited to a particular matter, such as custody

EXHIBIT 5.6 Sample of a Motion to Vacate the Marital Home

STATE OF NEW HAMPSHIRE

HILLSBORO COUNTY

SUPERIOR COURT   DOCKET NO. XXXXXXX

JANE TURNER,   )

Plaintiff   )

)   PLAINTIFF JANE TURNER'S

v.   )   MOTION TO VACATE THE

)   MARITAL HOME

JAMES TURNER,   )

Defendant   )

)

NOW COMES JANE TURNER, plaintiff in the above-captioned matter, and respectfully requests this Honorable Court order the defendant, JAMES TURNER, to vacate the marital home forthwith.

In support of her motion, the plaintiff states as follows:

1. The parties were married at Fort Myers, Florida, on November 16, 1998, and are presently residing in the marital residence at 306 North Dunstable Road, Nashua, New Hampshire, together with the parties' two minor children, Calvin Turner, age 10 (DOB April 16, 2004), and Elizabeth Turner, age 7 (DOB June 11, 2007).

2. The plaintiff has filed a Complaint for Divorce (Docket No. XXXXXXX) on the grounds of irreconcilable differences that have caused the irretrievable breakdown of the marriage.

3. The defendant's abusive behavior in the home has caused the plaintiff severe emotional stress and physical side effects. Moreover, tension caused by the defendant's actions and disagreements pertaining to the pending action for divorce are causing the parties' minor children emotional trauma and distress.

4. The relationship between the parties has significantly deteriorated in the five months since the Divorce Complaint was filed and conflict between the parties has escalated to a level that requires that the parties live apart.

5. It is in the best interests of the children that they remain in the marital home with the plaintiff, who has been their primary caretaker since birth.

EXHIBIT 5.6 (*Continued*)

In further support of this Motion, the plaintiff submits the accompanying Affidavit, which is herein incorporated by reference.

WHEREFORE, for the reasons set forth above and in the plaintiff's Affidavit, the plaintiff requests that this honorable Court order the defendant to vacate the marital home forthwith.

Respectfully submitted,
Jane Turner
By her attorney,

Date:_____

_____

Attorney's name
Attorney's address
Attorney's telephone number
Attorney's Bar number

CERTIFICATE OF SERVICE

I, (*Plaintiff's Attorney*), hereby certify that I have today served the above Motion and accompanying Affidavit, and Proposed Order on the Defendant, James Turner, by first-class mail to the office of his attorney, (*name and address of defendant's attorney*), together with notice that the Motion has been marked for hearing before the presiding Justice sitting in the _____ Court at 8:30 a.m. on Monday, May 16, 2014.

Date: _____

_____

Name of Plaintiff's Attorney

HEARINGS ON MOTIONS

Motions are usually heard in what commonly are called motion sessions, in which the court hears several motions in a sequence essentially controlled by the clerk. Sometimes, the sequence will be determined in advance and specific time blocks will be allocated for each case. Usually, the docket is posted in the courthouse on the date of the hearing. Many courts require that all parties and attorneys expecting to be heard report at the same time (e.g., 8:30 a.m.). The clerk will "call the list" to confirm that all necessary individuals are present and determine whether there are any special needs, such as for an interpreter or a referral for mediation or a meeting with a family service worker.

In many states, if the parties have not already reached agreement with respect to a child-related motion prior to coming to court, they will be required to meet with a family service worker or court-based mediator to see if the matter can be resolved prior to the hearing. If an agreement is reached by the parties, it is reduced to a written **stipulation** and submitted to the court for consideration. If the matter is not resolved, the family service worker may submit a recommendation, and the motion will be argued before the court.

Motion hearings are usually quite brief, and rules of evidence are rarely strictly followed, unlike in a trial. In some states, the parties are required to be present for hearings unless their absence is excused by the court. When a party

Stipulation
an agreement between the parties concerning some matter; may be filed with the court to be entered as an order

fails to appear without explanation or excuse, the moving party must file a **military affidavit** in accordance with the Soldiers and Sailors Relief Act,[28] stating under pain and penalties of perjury that the absent party is not currently serving in the armed services.

The paralegal may perform the following tasks related to temporary orders and other motions:

- Gather information necessary to draft, support, and file the motion (or oppose it).
- Draft motions, supporting affidavits, and proposed orders, if required, for review.
- File and send copies of the documents to the client and opposing counsel with transmittal cover letters when approved and signed.
- Assist with preparation of accompanying financial statement and child support guidelines worksheet, if necessary.
- Check all appropriate calendars (including those of opposing counsel) if the court permits scheduling in advance, and arrange to mark motions for hearing or diversion to court conciliation or mediation services, if appropriate (often the procedure with child-related motions). If the hearing date is known at the time of service, include it in the certification along with the time and place for the hearing.
- Mark hearing dates on all appropriate calendars and on the firm's "docket control system" if applicable. The client should also be notified of the date. The attorney will usually describe the nature of the proceeding to the client and will review the roles of each party, counsel, and the court.
- Assist with preparation for motion hearings.

In order to carry out these responsibilities, the paralegal must keep current with respect to the rules governing various aspects of motion practice, including special rules of civil procedure for domestic relations courts, local court rules, and practices of various courts and judges. For example:

- Are uniform forms for motions, affidavits, and proposed orders required?
- How far in advance of a hearing must a motion be served? In an emergency, may a party request and be granted a "short order of notice" reducing the required notice period?
- Can motions be filed and/or served electronically?
- What are the procedures for scheduling motion hearings in the court where the motion is filed? Does the court permit counsel to schedule dates in advance and serve notice of the hearing date along with the motion if there has been prior consultation with opposing counsel? Or does the court strictly control scheduling and mark motions only after they are filed and without any opportunity for input from counsel?
- When a party opposes a motion for temporary orders, does the court require submission of a memorandum or affidavit in opposition to the motion, or does it simply rely on testimony presented at the hearing on the motion?
- Is the motion being filed governed by rules over and above those regulating domestic relations matters? For example, motions to protect marital assets may need to comply with procedural rules governing motions for **trustee process**, a process that in effect freezes assets of the other party, directing a third-party holder of the assets, such as a bank, to hold them in trust, pending resolution of the action.

Military affidavit
an affidavit submitted by a party stating under pain and penalties of perjury that an absent party is not currently serving in the armed services

PARALEGAL PRACTICE TIP

To see an example of a Military Affidavit, visit *www.vermontjudiciary .org* (Vermont) (Form 231). You can find an example of a Stipulation for Temporary Orders at *www. wicourts.gov.* (Wisconsin) Search by title of the form.

PARALEGAL PRACTICE TIP

Throughout the process, consideration should be given to the availability of alternative dispute resolution options. In some states litigants are required to mediate. When a court orders that a case be diverted for conciliation or mediation services at any point, it places a subtle but especially strong pressure on the parties and counsel to settle the matter at issue.

PARALEGAL PRACTICE TIP

The paralegal should maintain a file of clerks/contacts in each court and agency with which the office has frequent contact. It is always helpful to establish a network and be able to refer to personnel by name. It also is a good idea to maintain a record of any of the "idiosyncrasies" of particular courts and special instructions and "pet peeves" of particular judges.

Trustee process
a legal process by which a third party holds the property of a party in trust at the direction of a court

Discovery

Discovery is a pretrial process for obtaining information relevant to the divorce proceeding. Although it is sometimes used as a "fishing expedition," its proper focus is on relevant, unprivileged information pertaining to all issues involved in a case, such as custody, support, and property division. Its primary purposes are:

- to learn about the claims and defenses of the other side
- to understand the strengths and weaknesses of the case from the perspective of each of the parties
- to avoid surprises at hearings and at trial
- to promote settlement

Discovery is governed by procedural rules, limitations, and timelines that must be carefully followed. The paralegal must master these rules and any related amendments or variations county to county. The state may require specific basic kinds of mandatory discovery/production within a certain time period following service of the complaint (e.g., forty-five days). In addition, informal discovery may be completed by the entire family law team with the assistance of the client. Formal discovery methods available in every state include:

- Interrogatories
- Depositions
- Requests for Production of Documents or Things or Entry Upon Land
- Requests for Admissions
- Requests for Medical or Physical Examinations

There are several discovery-related motions that may be filed. The most common include the following:

- Motion for a Protective Order to limit discovery
- Motion to Compel Discovery (and impose sanctions, if appropriate)
- Request for Status Conference regarding discovery to clarify issues, resolve disputes, and outline a plan, methods, and timeline (such conferences may be required by the court)
- Motion for Fees to cover the costs of various discovery initiatives, such as accountants, appraisers, and the like

Discovery is discussed at considerable length in Chapter 6 on Discovery and Financial Statements and the paralegal's role with respect to both formal and informal discovery as well as financial statements is highlighted.

Negotiation and Drafting of the Separation Agreement

If the parties reach agreement on all unresolved issues following discovery, a **separation agreement** can be drafted, reviewed, and executed, and the case can move forward on an uncontested basis. If the parties have resolved some, but not all, issues, a partial separation agreement can be prepared that addresses all issues not in dispute. Whether the agreement is full or partial, the parties customarily request that the court incorporate it into the divorce judgment. Depending on its terms, the agreement either will "merge" into the judgment and lose its separate identity, or it will "survive" (with the exception of child-related provisions) as an independent contract with legal significance apart from the judgment. The concepts of "merger" and "survival" are discussed more fully in Chapter 13, which addresses the topic of separation agreements. It provides drafting advice, a comprehensive model of a complete agreement, and a description of the related tasks commonly performed by paralegals.

Pretrial Activities

States vary with respect to the specific nature and sequencing of activities that take place between the time the parties decide to proceed to trial because they have reached an impasse regarding one or more issues and the date of the actual trial. Typically, the following activities occur, although they may be labeled differently in various jurisdictions.

- The moving party files a *Request for Pretrial Conference/Hearing*, if required (may be in the form of a request for a trial that automatically triggers a court-ordered pretrial conference/hearing). The paralegal for the moving party may draft the request (or prepare the required form for signature and filing).
- The court issues a *Pretrial Conference Notice and Order* indicating what is required at the pretrial conference/hearing. When the notice is received, the paralegal will mark the assigned pretrial conference date, place, and presiding judge on all appropriate calendars and advise the client of the date and location in writing.
- Many states require that a *four-way conference* be held at this point prior to the formal pretrial conference.
- Each side prepares a *Pretrial Memorandum*, which customarily must address the following:

    - procedural history of the case
    - uncontested issues
    - contested issues, including contested issues of fact (concerning finances, parenting skills, etc.) and contested issues of law (governing custody, alimony, attorney's fees, etc.), including the status of agreement with respect to each issue
    - status of discovery and time frame for completion (usually must be completed prior to filing a request for trial)
    - list of exhibits (including written objections, if any)
    - list of proposed witnesses (including experts)
    - property values (agreed on and disputed)
    - estimated length of trial

An experienced paralegal may be asked to prepare the first draft of the Pretrial Memorandum.

- The *Pretrial Conference* is held and the court reviews the topics covered in the parties' memoranda. The judge/marital master who conducts the hearing usually strongly urges the parties to settle their differences and avoid the necessity of a trial. Many judges even suggest how they are likely to rule on particular issues.
- Following the pretrial conference, if there is a need to complete further discovery and/or there is any potential for settlement, the court may, at the request of counsel or on its own initiative, schedule one or more status conferences.

- If and when the parties arrive at a clear impasse, one or both of them will file a *Request for Trial*. The paralegal may draft the Request or prepare the required form for signature and filing.
- The court then issues a *Pretrial Order* and assigns a trial date. The paralegal should mark the trial date on all appropriate calendars and notify the client in writing.

The Trial

PREPARATION FOR TRIAL

The opposing sides prepare for trial, although negotiations often continue in hopes the case can be settled thereby avoiding further litigation expense and emotional trauma. The nature, extent, and cost of trial preparation depend on the type, number, and complexity of disputed issues to be addressed at trial. For example, some couples may be able to resolve all issues with the exception of the disposition of the marital home, an issue they can argue in a half-day trial with only the parties as witnesses and an agreed-upon appraisal of the property. Others may be unable to agree on any issues and maintain fixed positions with respect to the grounds for divorce, alimony, property division, and child custody and support. In such cases, the trial may take a matter of weeks and involve extensive testimony of witnesses (including experts, private investigators, employers, and GALs, among others), complex exhibits, sophisticated audiovisuals and computer graphics, business and property valuations, etc.

Whatever the scope of the trial, an experienced paralegal may play a major supportive role in all aspects of trial preparation. Some tasks are common to virtually all trials, no matter what their scope. The members of the family law team need to:

- **Verify that all required documents have been filed or are ready for filing**, including a current Financial Statement, Child Support Guidelines Worksheet, and Parenting Plan, if necessary.
- **Request and confirm a stenographer**, if necessary, to preserve the record for possible appeal. Most court proceedings are audio taped, and court stenographic services now frequently offer an option of obtaining a simultaneous transcription during the trial at a cost.
- **Prepare witnesses** for questions likely to be asked in both direct and cross-examination. Witnesses cannot be told what to say or to not tell the truth, but they can be given advice with respect to how to most effectively answer questions and handle themselves in the face of various styles of questioning by opposing counsel. Preparation may include a trip to the courthouse to orient them to the environment and nature of the proceedings. Witnesses, including the client, also need to be familiar with and understand the significance of exhibits to be presented and about which they may be questioned.
- **Prepare/assemble a Trial Notebook**. (See Paralegal Application 5.4.)
- **Draft a Trial Memorandum of Law, and Proposed Findings of Fact, Conclusions of Law, and Judgment, if required**. Counsel for each party is customarily required to prepare these documents in anticipation of trial

Trial notebook
a term used loosely to describe the organizational system used by an attorney to assemble all of the materials needed for a trial

with a focus on contested issues and the factors the court will consider when making decisions regarding those issues:

- **Trial Memorandum of Law:** The Trial Memorandum essentially lays out the basic facts of the case along with the client's arguments regarding contested issues supported by appropriate authority (statutes, case law, secondary sources, etc.). This document provides the court with references to potential authoritative support for its findings.

- **Proposed Findings of Fact:** In Proposed Findings of Fact, the attorney (on behalf of the client) asks that the court accept certain facts as true, such as the date and length of the marriage, the parties' ages and health status, their education and employability, and their respective contributions to the marriage. In most cases, the parties will stipulate, or agree to, a number of basic facts in advance of trial so that proof will not need to be presented with respect to those matters.

- **Conclusions of Law:** Conclusions of Law are statements for the court's potential adoption as to how governing law should apply to the case from the client's perspective. For example, the attorney may propose conclusions such as the following based on the facts in a contested no-fault divorce case:

  - That the court has jurisdiction over the case and the parties (based on the particular statutes authorizing jurisdiction)
  - That a judgment of divorce should be entered when the court is satisfied that the parties' marriage is so irretrievably broken that it cannot be remedied and the parties can no longer live together (referencing the state's no-fault statute and possibly case law or other authority)
  - That, in dividing the parties' property, the court may consider the source of assets, particularly if acquired through inheritance or a party's family of origin (based on the applicable state statute and case law or other authority)
  - That custody decisions are to be guided by the best-interests-of-the-child standard (depending on the jurisdiction) and there is a presumption against awarding custody to a parent who has a documented history of abuse (based on statute and case law)

- **Proposed Judgment:** A Proposed Judgment is a judgment written from the client's perspective that the court is urged to adopt as its own. An example of a Proposed Judgment appears in Exhibit 5.7.

Proposed Findings of Fact
facts that a party asks a court to accept as true

PARALEGAL PRACTICE TIP

To see an example of a form for a court's Findings of Fact, Conclusions of Law, and Judgment, visit *www.wicourts.gov.* (FA-4160).

Conclusions of Law
statements as to how governing law applies to a case

PARALEGAL PRACTICE TIP

Increasingly, courts are requesting that certain documents, such as Trial Memoranda, Proposed Findings of Fact, Conclusions of Law, and Proposed Orders, be submitted in both hard copy and electronic formats, partially in anticipation that the court may adopt in its decision all or a significant portion of a party's submission. The chances of this happening are significantly increased when the proposals are realistic and consistent with governing authority.

Paralegal **Application 5.4**

Trial and Exhibit Notebooks

In all cases to be tried, no matter how uncomplicated, *organization* is critical. Thorough preparation is extremely important to the success of a case and leaves a favorable impression on the court (and the client). The term "trial notebook" is used loosely to describe the organizational system used by an individual attorney to assemble all of the materials needed for trial. The physical form of the trial notebook may vary—it may truly take the form of an indexed loose-leaf binder or it may be in the shape of a series of well-labeled files

(Continued)

organized in boxes, if necessary. It often is comprised of multiple "notebooks":

- **The Trial Notebook.** This notebook essentially contains a script for the attorney that organizes materials according to each stage of the trial: an overall trial outline, an opening statement, outlines of witness examinations (and potential questions for cross-examination), identification and description of all exhibits, excerpts of deposition transcripts and interrogatories to be used, and a closing argument.
- **Supplemental "trial" notebooks.** These notebooks organize all of the materials related to the case that may or may not be needed at trial, including, but not necessarily limited to:
  - a notebook containing all pleadings and rulings with those that are central to the case, clearly tabbed, and accessible, if needed
  - a notebook containing tabbed discovery materials with accompanying summaries
  - a notebook containing clearly indexed financial information, including financial statements of each party, tax returns, bank records, credit card statements, mortgage applications, pay stubs, pension data, etc.
  - a witness notebook containing subfiles for each witness in alphabetical order, including curriculum vitae, deposition summaries/transcripts, correspondence, etc. This notebook may include appraisals of various assets (real estate, collections, businesses, etc.), medical reports, and reports of investigators, including court-ordered evaluations
  - a notebook containing indexed research files by issue (for example, when a party can be granted a greater than 50% share of the marital assets,

child support awards outside of the guidelines, or designation of certain assets as marital property). If any seminal cases may be referenced at trial, four copies of relevant opinions should be available "just in case" (one for the court, one for the stenographer, and the other two for counsel)
- an indexed notebook containing correspondence with the court, opposing counsel, the client, and others, organized separately and usually by date with the most recent appearing first

- **The Exhibit Notebook.** Many courts, particularly in complex cases, require counsel to prepare indexed Exhibit Notebooks for the convenience of the court and to save considerable trial time sorting through and marking exhibits during the trial. Four copies usually are prepared: one for each attorney, one for the court, and one for use with witnesses who are testifying. The Exhibit Notebook generally contains:
  - The plaintiff's exhibits (disputed and undisputed)
  - The defendant's exhibits (disputed and undisputed)
  - Copies of current financial statements for each party
  - The GAL's report if the guardian will be called as a witness by either party
  - Stipulations of the parties with respect to such issues as tax matters, property values, and business valuations (depending on the court, these may be read into the record)

Exhibit notebook

a notebook, prepared for the convenience of the court and counsel, containing all exhibits to be introduced at trial by either or both parties

---

In more complex trials, there are additional tasks that the family law team may need to complete prior to trial, including the following:

- Prepare **subpoenas** for witnesses (including the GAL, if warranted) and subpoenas *duces tecum*. A subpoena is a document ordering a witness to appear and provide testimony in a court hearing or trial. A **subpoena *duces tecum*** requires the witness to bring to court certain documents such as bank, pension, or employment records.
- Obtain certified copies of public documents as appropriate, for example, certified copies of necessary documents (pleadings, orders etc,) from related legal proceedings conducted in other jurisdictions.
- Gather documentation regarding any expert witnesses so that the court will be positioned to qualify them as "experts" able to render expert opinions.

Subpoena

a document ordering a witness to appear and provide testimony in a legal proceeding, such as a deposition, court hearing, or trial

Subpoena *duces tecum*

a subpoena ordering a witness to appear in a legal proceeding such as a deposition, court hearing, or trial and to bring with him or her specified documents, records, or things

- Prepare **Motions** *in limine* and memoranda in support of or in opposition to admissibility of particular evidence.
- Prepare a Motion to Assess Counsel Fees, if warranted.
- Prepare a Complaint for any arrearages in payments due under temporary orders.
- Create PowerPoint presentations, illustrative graphics, etc., that will clearly illustrate major points and complex topics in a "simplified" form for the court.

THE TRIAL

The trial in a contested case is a full trial involving opening and closing statements, presentation of each party's case through direct and cross-examination of witnesses, and introduction of evidentiary exhibits. The usual standard of proof in divorce cases is **preponderance of the evidence** (i.e., it is more likely than not that the facts alleged are true). The trial is intended to resolve all disputed issues. Divorce trials are open to the public although rarely attended except in higher-profile cases. Some states, such as New York and Texas, permit jury trials in divorce cases. See, e.g., *Strack v. Strack*, 916 N.Y.S.2d 759 (Misc. 2011).

Although the attorney presents the client's case, the paralegal may perform several functions during the trial:

- With the court's permission, the paralegal may attend the trial and be seated at the counsel table with the client and the attorney. Counsel will introduce the paralegal by name and will indicate his or her paralegal status. The paralegal may then assist counsel by quickly locating needed documents, pointing out relevant materials, and providing support and encouragement to the client.
- Both the paralegal and the client may make notes during the trial regarding important issues, documents needed, ideas for additional questions, portions of exhibits to counter the defendant's testimony, etc.
- The paralegal is available to make needed copies and phone calls and confirm the arrival of a scheduled witness (or track down an absent witness).

THE JUDGMENT

After the case is presented, the judge reviews the evidence, testimony, etc., and makes a decision on the merits of the case. Some judges render decisions promptly, and others take a matter of weeks, even months, depending in part on the complexity of the case. The judge may first enter an **Interlocutory Decree** (or a **Decree** *Nisi*) along with accompanying findings of fact and conclusions of law. An interlocutory decree is not final, and the parties are technically still married until a final decree issues. If they reconcile in the interim period, a **Motion to Vacate the Judgment** may be filed. The **Final Judgment** (sometimes called the **Judgment Absolute**) usually enters automatically in most jurisdictions after a specified period of time (commonly thirty to ninety days). The paralegal should obtain certified copies of the decree and send them to the client, who will need them for a variety of postdivorce matters, such as changing accounts and insurance policies.

PARALEGAL PRACTICE TIP

To see an example of a Stipulation and Order Vacating a Judgment of Divorce or Legal Separation, visit *www.wicourts.gov.* (Wisconsin) (Form 4164).

EXHIBIT 5.7 Example of a Proposed Judgment

STATE OF_____

_____COUNTY   FAMILY COURT

                                                      DOCKET NO:_____

TIFFANY HEALEY,   )

Plaintiff   )

)   PLAINTIFF'S

v.   )   PROPOSED JUDGMENT

)

NOEL HEALEY,   )

Defendant   )

All interested persons having been notified in accordance with law and after hearing, it is adjudged *nisi* that a divorce be granted to the Plaintiff for the cause of irretrievable breakdown of the marriage (*cite statute*) and that upon the expiration of ninety (90) days from entry of this judgment it shall become absolute unless, upon application of any person within such period, the court shall otherwise order. It is further ordered that:

1. The Agreement of the parties dated April 1, 2015, is incorporated and merged in this judgment and hereafter shall have no independent legal significance.
2. The property located at 1125 Marlboro St., _____, shall be conveyed to the wife by the husband within one hundred and twenty (120) days of this date.
3. The parties shall have joint legal custody of the minor child, Bethany Healey, and physical custody shall be with the mother with reasonable rights of visitation to the father consistent with the parenting plan filed with this court and dated April 1, 2015.
4. The husband shall pay child support in the amount of $465.00 per month, payable on the first day of each month commencing on June 1, 2015, said amount being consistent with this state's guidelines for child support.
5. Each party shall be responsible for his or her own health insurance and uninsured medical, dental, and/or psychiatric expenses, and the father shall maintain health insurance for the benefit of the minor child and pay for the child's uninsured medical expenses.
6. Each party shall pay his or her own legal fees and costs.

_____
Presiding Justice

Dated:_____

Postdivorce Proceedings

Depending on the circumstances of each case, a variety of postdivorce proceedings may be necessary.

POST-TRIAL MOTIONS

Post-trial motions may include the following:

PARALEGAL PRACTICE TIP

To see an example of a motion for a new trial, Google "Sample Form 40 Motion for New Trial." (Alabama)

- **Motion to Alter and Amend the Judgment:** This motion is brought in an effort to correct factual and substantive errors in the Judgment.
- **Motion for a New Trial:** In this motion, a party seeks a new trial alleging that prejudicial errors were made during the trial that affected the outcome. This motion usually must be brought promptly (e.g., within ten days).

- **Motion for Relief From Judgment:** In this kind of motion, a party seeks to have the initial judgment modified based on fraud, mistake, or newly discovered evidence, etc. The motion usually must be brought within a reasonable period (e.g., within a year after entry of judgment). When the motion is allowed, the court may modify its initial judgment or vacate it and order a new trial.

The paralegal may be asked to draft these motions with careful attention to governing rules and strict timelines. Prior to doing so, he or she will need to obtain a copy of the transcript of the trial or portions of it, as necessary.

APPEAL OF A FINAL JUDGMENT

Occasionally, a client will elect to appeal a final judgment or the portion of it that is adverse. The party filing the appeal is called the **appellant** and the opposing party is the **appellee**. The appeal is usually heard by an intermediate appellate court unless the state does not have one, in which case it goes directly to the state's highest court. A decision of an intermediate appellate court usually can be appealed to the state's highest court.

The appeals process is governed by procedural rules and strict time standards/statutes of limitations that must be honored throughout the process, and an appeal can be dismissed for failure to meet applicable deadlines. For example, in a 2006 Texas case, following the death of her former husband, a woman unsuccessfully sought relief when she learned that, shortly before he died, he had changed his will in favor of his current wife. The change violated a provision of the parties' divorce decree that required all finances and insurance policies through the time of divorce be granted to the ex-wife. A Texas appellate court held that her claim was subject to a two-year statute of limitations governing family law actions rather than the longer six-year statute of limitations governing contracts.[29]

An appellate court does not retry the case. The appeal is based on the record of what took place at the trial court level. New evidence is not introduced. The focus is on whether the trial court made any errors in applying the law to the facts of the case or abused its discretion and made findings of fact unsupported by the evidence. Great deference is shown to the trial court's findings, because that court was in the best position to hear and assess the credibility of the witnesses.

The basic steps in the appeals process are the following:

- The appellant files a notice of appeal in the appropriate court within the required period after the final judgment (or the date of the decree *nisi* depending on the state).
- The appellant designates the portion of the trial court materials he or she wants in the record on appeal (including any relevant portions of the transcript), and the appellee may cross-designate materials.
- The court clerk assembles the record and then dockets the case with the appeals court.
- The parties submit briefs (first the appellant, then the appellee), and, after the submissions, the appellant has an opportunity to respond to the appellee's brief.
- The appellate court may decide the appeal based on the briefs and the record or may hear oral argument.
- The appellate court affirms, reverses (in whole or in part), and/or remands for a new trial/further action consistent with its opinion. In some cases, the appeal

Appellant
the party bringing an appeal of a lower court's judgment

Appellee
the party against whom an appeal is brought

PARALEGAL PRACTICE TIP

To review a variety of appellate forms used in the state of Washington, visit *www.courts.wa.gov/forms.* The state of Alaska has an extensive self-help appeals process that guides the litigant through the process and provides necessary forms. You can find this material at *http://www.courts.alaska.gov.*

may be dismissed as a sanction as in a 2011 Connecticut case in which the husband had continually and deliberately defied a trial court's financial and discovery orders. See *Bubrosky v. Bubrosky*, 20 A.3d 79 (Conn. App. Ct. 2011).

The paralegal may:

- Draft the notice of appeal for review, signature, and filing.
- Monitor the appeals process (deadlines, notice of appeal, submission of materials, etc.).
- Contact a stenographer and make arrangements to have the relevant portions of the transcript prepared and filed.
- Research and draft the appellate brief, although such assignments are generally given only to highly skilled and experienced paralegals.

COMPLAINT FOR MODIFICATION

At some point after a judgment has entered, either party may want to file a Complaint (or Motion, depending on the jurisdiction) for modification of one of its terms. The standards for whether and under what circumstances modifications of child custody, child support, or spousal support can be brought and granted are established in state statutes and case law. The usual basis for a modification is that there has been a substantial change in circumstances (such as a change in employment status, income, marital status, residence, and/or health). If the parties executed a separation agreement that survived the divorce judgment as an independent contract, the agreement may serve as a bar to modification of non-child-related provisions or may set forth the conditions under which modifications can occur. Although a family court may still elect to modify an order in the face of a restrictive surviving agreement, it will customarily require that there have been a "more than substantial change of circumstances." If sought and warranted, the court may issue temporary orders while a modification action is pending, discovery is conducted, and the parties try to negotiate a resolution.

The paralegal may be asked to research and draft the Complaint for Modification (or the Answer to a Complaint if representing the defendant) as well as a request for temporary orders for review, signature, and filing. Absent an agreement between the parties, the court will issue its order after a hearing on the merits.

COMPLAINT FOR CONTEMPT

An existing order of the court remains valid until the court declares otherwise. Although it sometimes happens, the parties are not free to simply decide they should not have to comply with an order because of changed circumstances, such as the loss of a job or development of a serious medical condition, or because the other party is not abiding by the terms of the decree in some manner. For example, if the noncustodial parent fails to pay child support, the custodial parent may unilaterally decide to deny court-ordered visitation without the court's authorization.

The appropriate course of action when one party fails to comply with the terms of the judgment is for the other party to file a Complaint for Contempt (sometimes called a Petition for Contempt or a Motion to Enforce Litigant's Rights). The paralegal may be asked to research and draft the Complaint for Contempt (or the Answer to a Complaint if representing the defendant) for

---

PARALEGAL PRACTICE TIP

Modifications of custody, child support, and spousal support orders are discussed more fully in Chapters 9, 10, and 11. Property division orders are customarily not modifiable absent fraud or the discovery of assets that were previously intentionally not disclosed, etc.

PARALEGAL PRACTICE TIP

If the parties' separation agreement survives as an independent contract, relief may also be sought in a **court of equity** (for **specific performance** of the contract).

Court of equity
a court that has authority to decide controversies in accordance with rules and principles of equity (principles of fairness)

Specific performance
a remedy for breach of contract in which the court orders the breaching party to complete the contract as promised

review, signature, and filing. In addition to holding a defendant in contempt, several other remedies may be requested to enforce the decree, such as garnishment of wages or a declaration of a **constructive trust** over property, depending on the nature of the defendant's noncompliance with the court's order. There may be a statutory presumption that attorney's fees will be awarded to the prevailing party in a contempt action but, if not, they should be requested. After a hearing, the court will issue its order. The paralegal should ensure that a copy is promptly sent to the client.

Follow-up Matters

After the divorce is final, a number of follow-up tasks may need to be completed by one, the other, or both of the parties with or without the assistance of the attorneys who handled the divorce. These actions may include, for example:

- Preparation of deeds transferring real property interests
- Preparation and processing of one or more **Qualified Domestic Relations Orders (QDROs)**
- Transfer of stock ownership, certificates of deposits, vehicles, memberships, etc.
- Closing of joint accounts
- Payment of joint debts
- Drafting of a petition for name change if desired and not addressed as part of the divorce action
- Preparation of a new estate plan (may include a will, trust, health care proxy, etc.)

If any of these tasks fall within the attorney's scope of employment, the paralegal may monitor their completion to ensure they are carried out in a timely manner.

The initial fee agreement/letter of engagement should specify the point at which the attorney's responsibility to the client with respect to the case will end and, specifically, whether or not it includes postdivorce activity. Even with an agreement, it is wise to send the client a letter of termination of services when the agreed-upon scope of representation concludes, noting any need for follow-up in various areas. Some attorneys conduct closing interviews with the client in which they review the representation from start to finish, discuss the results obtained, identify matters requiring the client's attention, and answer any questions the client may have.[30]

The Uncontested Scenario

This chapter has focused in large part on the divorce process in a contested case. Although generally less costly in terms of time and dollars, an uncontested divorce can still be very costly emotionally. The two primary ways in which a divorce may be uncontested are (1) when the divorce is sought jointly by the parties and (2) when the defendant does not oppose the divorce and either participates without opposition or fails to participate at all.

The following material briefly outlines the process when the divorce is jointly sought by the parties, who may proceed *pro se* or with the assistance of counsel at each stage.

Constructive trust
a trust imposed by the court on an asset of a party who improperly or wrongfully acquired the property

PARALEGAL PRACTICE TIP

To see an example of a Petition for Contempt, visit *http://www.courts.state.nh.us.* (New Hampshire) (Form NHJB-2199-FS).

Qualified Domestic Relations Order (QDRO)
a court order directing the administrator of a pension plan to pay a specified portion of a current or former employee's pension to an alternate payee to satisfy a support or other marital obligation

- The parties make the decision to dissolve their marriage on an uncontested (usually no-fault) basis with or without having participated in counseling and/or contacting attorneys.
- The parties (with or without the assistance of dispute resolution options) negotiate the terms of an agreement resolving all of their marital rights and obligations and dividing their personal property and realty.
- The parties identify the proper forum in which to file their action for divorce.
- The parties draft and file their Joint Petition for Divorce, usually accompanied by the following:

  - Filing fee (or request for waiver, if eligible)
  - Certified copy of the parties' marriage certificate
  - Joint affidavit of irretrievable breakdown of the marriage
  - Financial statements
  - Fully executed separation agreement
  - Affidavit disclosing any care and custody proceedings, if the parties have minor children
  - Certificates of Completion of Parent Education Program, if required
  - Parenting Plan, if required
  - Child Support Guidelines Worksheet, if there are minor children
  - Income Assignment Worksheet, if applicable

- The parties request a final hearing (sometimes called a Request for Trial).
- The final hearing takes place and the court renders a Judgment.

PARALEGAL PRACTICE TIP

Even if the case is uncontested, if the court reviews the agreement and considers it grossly one-sided, the judge may continue the matter until a seemingly disadvantaged party proceeding *pro se* consults with an attorney and provides documentation to the court that he or she has done so.

Some courts require that both parties (and/or their respective attorneys) be present at the final hearing unless an absence is excused by the court. However, the trend is toward minimizing court appearances, and some jurisdictions no longer require either party to be present in a joint action. Hearings on joint petitions are customarily quite brief (five to fifteen minutes). However, a limited number of questions are usually asked so that it is apparent the court has made some inquiry and not simply rubber-stamped the parties' agreement. If the parties are represented, the court may have counsel question their clients. If a party is unrepresented, the court will conduct the questioning. The questions are very basic and usually address the following:

- the parties' names and addresses
- facts about the marriage: when and where the parties married and when and where they last lived together as husband and wife
- the names and ages of minor children, if any
- the parties' shared belief that the marriage is irretrievably broken
- the separation agreement: whether the parties have read it, discussed it with counsel, understood its terms, and signed it voluntarily

The court may then ask specific questions on key issues, such as insurance coverage, custodial arrangements, wage assignment, and waivers of spousal support. It is important that the parties understand the terms of the agreement so they can respond intelligently to questions if asked.

Even in an uncontested divorce, postdecree activity is sometimes warranted, including:

- Post-trial motions
- Actions to enforce the judgment (contempt actions, etc.)
- Modification of the judgment (based on substantial change in circumstances)

CHAPTER **SUMMARY**

This chapter opened with a description of how family law has changed dramatically over the past five decades from a fault-based system that made litigation inevitable to one that emphasizes the parties' capacity to resolve their differences without blame and courtroom battles. The no-fault model recognizes the complexity of human relationships and that in any given marriage both parties make contributions and neither bears full responsibility for its success or failure.

Couples who want to separate or dissolve their relationship have four potential legal options, depending on the facts of their case: divorce, legal separation, separate support, or annulment. For some individuals, it is also important to seek a religious termination of the marital relationship that will allow them to remarry within their faith.

Although the content of this chapter focuses primarily on the sequence of events in a contested case from the initial interview through post-trial activities, approximately 90% of divorces are obtained without the necessity of a trial.

To some extent, this is the result of an increasing emphasis by the legal profession, including the courts, on the use of alternative methods of resolving disputes, such as direct negotiation between the parties, mediation, collaborative law, negotiation through counsel, neutral case evaluation, and arbitration.

This chapter has provided an overview of the basic stages in the divorce process. Tasks needing to be performed and selected issues that arise at each stage were identified. Major topics considered included: interviews, jurisdictional determinations, fault and no-fault grounds for divorce, defenses, drafting and service of the complaint, the defendant's response, motions including motions for temporary orders, discovery, separation agreements, and pretrial, trial, and postdivorce activities. Depending on his or her skills and experience, the paralegal may play a key role at virtually every stage in both uncontested and contested cases. Various aspects of that role are described.

CONCEPT REVIEW AND REINFORCEMENT

KEY **TERMS**

Adultery
Affidavit
Alternative dispute resolution (ADR)
Annulment
Answer
Appearance
Appellant
Appellee
Arbitration
Binding arbitration
Bifurcated divorce
Collaborative law
Collusion
Complaint
Conclusions of Law
Condonation
Conflict of law
Connivance
Constructive desertion
Constructive trust
Counterclaim
Court of equity
Criminal conversation
Cruel and abusive treatment

Declaratory judgment
Defense
Desertion/abandonment
Discovery
Divorce
Divorce *a mensa et thoro*
Divorce *a vinculo matrimonii*
Doctrine of comparative rectitude
Domicile
Dual divorce
Exhibit notebook
Ex parte motion
Fault grounds
Fee agreement
Final Judgment/Judgment Absolute
Grounds for divorce
Guardian *ad litem* (GAL)
In rem jurisdiction
Interlocutory Decree/Decree *Nisi*
Irreconcilable differences
Legal separation
Letter of engagement
Letter of nonengagement/declination
Living separate and apart

Long-arm statute
Marital communications privilege
Mediation
Memorandum of *lis pendens*
Military affidavit
Motion
Motions *in limine*
Motion to Dismiss
Motion to Vacate the Judgment
Neutral case evaluation
No-fault divorce
No-fault grounds
Nonbinding arbitration
Parenting coordinator
Pendente lite
Personal jurisdiction
Preponderance of the evidence
Proposed Findings of Fact
Pro se
Provocation
Qualified Domestic Relations Order (QDRO)
Recrimination
Separate maintenance

Separation agreement	Subpoena	Trustee process
Service of process	Subpoena *duces tecum*	Venue
Specific performance	Summons	Void *ab initio*
Stipulation	Temporary orders	Voidable marriage
Subject matter jurisdiction	Trial notebook	

REVIEW **QUESTIONS**

1. Describe how the "culture of divorce" has changed over the past fifty years.
2. Identify the four legal methods parties use to alter their marital status, and give an example of the circumstances in which each of them might be appropriate.
3. Define "bifurcated divorce" and identify a circumstance in which one might occur.
4. Identify the six most common dispute resolution options used in divorce cases. What are the primary differences among them?
5. Define subject matter, personal (*in personam*), and *in rem* jurisdiction in the divorce context, and indicate how each is acquired by a court.
6. Identify the primary difference between fault and no-fault grounds for divorce, and give a common example of each.
7. Identify a minimum of five potential defenses to a divorce action.
8. Describe the nature and purpose of a complaint.
9. Identify the primary ways of serving process, and describe the nature and purpose of a long-arm statute.
10. Identify the two most common responses of a defendant to an action for divorce, and indicate the differences between them.
11. Describe the nature and purpose of temporary orders.
12. Identify a minimum of five kinds of motions sometimes filed in divorce actions while the litigation is pending.
13. Explain why a party might choose to file a motion on an *ex parte* basis. Give an example.
14. Identify the primary purposes of discovery.
15. Describe the nature and purpose of a separation agreement.
16. Identify and describe a minimum of four major "documents" prepared in anticipation of trial.
17. Identify the most common kinds of divorce-related legal proceedings brought post divorce.
18. Describe the role of the paralegal in the various stages of the divorce process.

DEVELOPING YOUR PARALEGAL SKILLS

FOCUS ON **THE JOB**

In this Focus on the Job, the student has an opportunity to participate in an interview and draft a variety of documents tailored to the needs of the parties in a hypothetical divorce action.

The Facts

David and Marie Rogers were married on July 17, 2001, in your city and state at St. Patrick's Church. Marie was born on September 7, 1981, and David was born on October 3, 1980. Both parties were born in your city and state and were raised as devout Catholics. David no longer practices his religion, but Marie has remained very active in her local church. The children often attend Mass with her, and religion is a source of considerable tension between the parties.

David and Marie were high school sweethearts. After graduation from high school, Marie remained at home with her parents. She worked as a cashier in a local Starbucks and attended "beauty school" in the evenings at the regional vocational school. She was unable to complete her course of study because her mother became very ill and Marie had to stay home and take care of her. David went off to your state's university to study mathematics.

David and Marie initially planned to get married following David's graduation from college, and in the interim, they continued to see each other during his school vacations. During his senior year, David wrote to Marie and said he wanted to go out with other women. Marie was devastated. During spring break, they went to Florida and, while there, had sexual relations for the first and only time prior to marriage. Marie became pregnant and, as a result of the pregnancy, the couple decided to get married.

Because of David's concerns that they were rushing into marriage prematurely, they executed a premarital agreement essentially providing that any assets or liabilities a party had entering the marriage would remain that party's and any assets and liabilities accruing during the marriage would be divided equally. Despite his reservations about the timing, David thought getting married was what he wanted and should do. Now, in retrospect, he feels he had no choice. The wedding was held shortly after his graduation, and their son, Jon, was born on December 12, 2001. A second son, Charles, was born on May 12, 2004, and a daughter, Megan, was born on June 16, 2011.

Since their marriage, David has been employed as a math teacher at the local community college. Initially, he had hoped to begin working on his master's degree in math following graduation while Marie continued her cashier's job, but the parties jointly decided it was important for Marie to stay home with Jon. Accordingly, to his great disappointment, David was unable to pursue his educational plans.

David earns $68,000 a year at his teaching job, and his family is covered on his insurance plan. He has paid into the state employees' pension fund since starting at the college in 2001 and became vested after ten years of service. He earns an additional $8,000 a year "under the table" doing odd jobs for people during the summer months and on weekends. The couple has never paid taxes on this extra income. They have filed a joint return every year since they married.

David has been a good provider and a devoted father to his two sons but has had trouble relating to his daughter. Since the birth of Jon, Marie has not been employed outside of the home. She maintains the household and is the primary caretaker of the children. At the time Marie became pregnant with Megan, David had been accepted into a master's degree program and Marie was going to return to work to help support the family. The plan was that when David completed his degree, he would then support Marie so she could complete beauty school and possibly a four-year-degree program if she wanted to go to college.

David believes that Marie got pregnant deliberately by failing to use birth control. He thinks that she was trying to sabotage his plans to return to school as she had done years before. He asked her to have an abortion, but she refused, given her strong religious beliefs. This was a major crisis in their relationship, and, during the pregnancy, the marriage began to fall apart. David's frustration kept building and he became increasingly resentful that, once again, he would have to defer his educational plans because of Marie's pregnancy.

David remained bitter and, according to Marie, has never bonded with Megan. His interaction with her has been minimal, although he continues to engage in weekend activities with the boys. He acknowledges that he has difficulties with his daughter but says he was initially the same way with his boys until they got a little older and could talk and "do things."

Since Megan's birth, Marie has experienced several bouts of severe depression. She has been briefly hospitalized twice and is seeing a therapist regularly. She gained fifty pounds during her pregnancy with Megan and has put on an additional thirty pounds since giving birth. According to David, she also has begun to drink heavily and has neglected the household and the children. On several occasions, a neighbor has found her wandering around the neighborhood so inebriated that she was unable to find her way home.

Marie claims that David has become verbally abusive and has hit her on a few occasions. He denies hitting her but acknowledges that he sometimes may have sounded "gruff" when he was particularly upset by her conduct. He says that she has closed herself off to any emotional support from him and has refused to engage in sexual relations since she became pregnant with Megan. He admits feeling trapped and overwhelmed by Marie's problems. This is particularly painful for him because he saw his own parents weighed down by the responsibilities of several children and vowed the same thing would never happen to him.

As for the children, Megan appears to be developmentally delayed. No one is quite sure why, but her pediatrician speculates that it may be due to the problems at home. A specialized play group has been recommended, but David and Marie have not followed through on the recommendation. The pediatrician has struggled with whether or not to file an abuse and neglect complaint but so far has opted against doing this.

A few months ago, Jon was caught shoplifting CDs from a local store, but the store let him "work off" the offense without calling the police. David and Marie also learned recently that he and several other boys have been gathering at a friend's house after school to watch pornographic videos that an older neighbor rents for them. There is some concern that they may also have involved some younger neighborhood children in this activity at the man's request. Each parent blames the other for Jon's behavior. Marie is at a loss as to how to deal with him, and David tends to be quite strict and restricts the teenager's activities when Jon is with him.

Charles is doing extremely well in school academically but has limited social skills and no friends. He largely keeps to himself and Marie says he is a real computer "geek," spending hours at a time in front of the computer screen just like his father. He says he likes being with his dad because they are interested in a lot of the same things.

Things finally reached the breaking point on February 1, 2015, and David moved out of the house at 903 Hale

Street, your city and town (your area code-555–2712). He has refused to go to any kind of counseling despite Marie's request, unless the whole family is involved. He has moved to a small apartment at 412 High Street, your city and town (your area code-555–3010). David sees the boys on a regular basis each weekend and has spent a little time with Megan, although Marie seems very nervous about him doing so. David claims that since he has moved out, the house has become a "pigsty," and on several occasions when he went to pick up the boys, the children were filthy, there were no clean clothes to pack for the weekend, and there was virtually no food in the refrigerator. On one Sunday, it was ten in the morning and the children asked him if they could go get some breakfast before going to his apartment. Marie was at home, asleep on the couch in the living room, and David claims he smelled alcohol all around her. Marie alleges that he woke her up, shook her, and threatened to choke her if she did not get her act together. David doesn't deny shaking her but does deny threatening her. He said he shook her in a desperate effort to try and get through to her. Marie acknowledges that she has a problem dealing with caring for the home and the children on her own, but says that she is not neglectful and that David is just a compulsive "neatnik," a regular "Mr. Monk" who can't stand it when everything isn't just so.

Since he left the marital home, David has been dating a co-worker, Trisha Cronin. Marie suspects that he began dating her after she got pregnant with Megan, but David denies this. Trish is also a teacher and is working on a Ph.D. in comparative literature. She loves children and is unable to have any of her own because of a chronic medical condition. She and David are planning on moving in together at the end of the spring semester.

With respect to assets, the parties own the small condominium in which Marie presently resides with the children. They paid $180,000 for it shortly after their marriage with a $20,000 down payment. It is now assessed at about $280,000, but David claims the real estate market is greatly overinflated. They still owe about $77,000 on the mortgage. The money for the down payment came half from wedding presents and half from the proceeds of an insurance settlement from an automobile accident that Marie had been in. They have about $1,800 in a savings account and owe about $3,500 in credit card debt. David has about $19,000 in his retirement account and a government bond (with a present value of $15,000) that his father gave him before the parties married and that he has kept for a rainy day or an emergency. He also has a collection of seascape paintings by local artists that he began collecting as a small boy. Marie has a collection of quilts valued at about $3,500 and also a collection of Hummel figures she inherited from her grandmother as a young child. They own basic household furnishings valued at not more than $10,000, along with two cars, a Honda and a Toyota of relatively equivalent value, both of which are paid for.

David filed for divorce on March 15, 2015. The docket number assigned to the case is 15D-1351-DI1 (or another docket number provided by your professor). David's attorney is Juliana Wilson, Esq.

> 390 Main Street
>
> Your city, town, and zip code
>
> Your area code-555-2354
>
> Bar Number: 0283412

David's Social Security number is 022–34–1919.

Marie will eventually retain Attorney James Sims. His address is 30 Washington Street in your city and town. His phone number is your area code-555-2424. His Bar Number is 346271. Marie's Social Security number is 044–43–6704.

The Assignment

If possible, the class should be divided into an even number of groups with up to six students in each group. Half of the groups will work as a family law team representing David and the other half representing Marie. The students on each team should develop a method for assigning the following tasks (e.g., by choice or drawing assignments), unless otherwise assigned by the course instructor.

David's Team	**Marie's Team**
1. Two students role-play David's initial interview, one as David and one as the paralegal.	1. Two students role-play Marie's initial interview, one as Marie and one as the paralegal.
2. Draft a Complaint for Divorce.	2. Draft an Answer (and a possible counterclaim for divorce) in response to David's Complaint.
3. Draft a Motion for Temporary Orders with a Supporting Affidavit and Proposed Order.	3. Draft a Motion for Temporary Orders with a supporting Affidavit and Proposed Order.
4. Draft a Motion for Appointment of a Guardian *ad litem*, with a supporting Affidavit and Proposed Order.	4. Draft a Motion for Attorney's Fees with appropriate affidavits and a Proposed Order.
5. Draft a Motion for Appointment of an Appraiser with a supporting Affidavit and a Proposed Order (to appraise the value of the marital home).	5. Draft a Motion for Appointment of an Appraiser with a supporting Affidavit and a Proposed Order (to appraise the value of David's art collection).

FOCUS ON **ETHICS**

In this activity, the student is required to draft a memo to his or her supervisor summarizing the results of an interview in which a client expressed an intention to falsely accuse her husband of sexual abuse in an effort to gain custody of their children. The student is asked to make a recommendation regarding a future course of action in light of ethical canons governing the conduct of paralegals and attorneys.

The Assignment

Assume that you are the paralegal working for the attorney representing Marie in the above comprehensive fact pattern. You were present at the initial interview with her conducted by your supervisor, Attorney Sims. It was clear during that interview that although she is angered by the fact her husband is having an affair and knows their marriage is over, Marie's top priority is to gain custody of all three children at all costs. She is afraid David is going to try to take them away from her because of her psychological problems, alleged drinking, and poor housekeeping. Since the initial interview, you have been asked to conduct a follow-up meeting with her to gather information in anticipation of a potential counterclaim for divorce and a motion for temporary orders including custody. In that interview, Marie tells you that she is prepared to falsely claim that the reason David is having trouble developing a relationship with Megan is that he has been sexually abusing her. She says in this day and age, no judge is going to take a chance awarding custody to a father who may be sexually abusing his daughter. Marie says she has heard from her divorced friends that if she can get temporary custody, she is a "shoo-in" for permanent custody. Attorney Sims does little family law work in his practice but is a respected attorney known for his diligent and zealous advocacy on behalf of his clients. He has asked you to report to him regarding the

interview and to make recommendations regarding the appropriate actions to be taken with respect to the counterclaim, the motion for temporary orders, and Marie personally.

Review the ethics material in Chapter 1 as well as the ethical canons for paralegals promulgated by the National Association of Legal Assistants contained in Appendix A of this text. Also obtain a copy of the ethical standards governing attorneys in your state. You should prepare a memorandum to your supervisor reporting the results of the interview and your recommendations with the ethics material as a backdrop or frame of reference. Use the following basic format:

Interoffice Memorandum

TO: *Your supervisor*

FROM: *Your name*

RE: *Follow-up Interview with Marie Rogers*

DATE:

CASE: David Rogers v. Marie Rogers

OFFICE FILE NUMBER/ DOCKET NUMBER:

Brief description of assignment: *What is it that you have been asked to do?*

Summary of interview: *Summarize the highlights of the interview.*

Ethical issues implicated: *Identify the ethical duties the paralegal and attorney have that are related to this situation and a future course of action.*

Analysis of the issues: *Discuss the applicability of the identified ethical duties to the facts of the case.*

Recommendations: *What actions do you recommend be taken? Suggestion: You may want to consider more than one scenario.*

FOCUS ON **CASE LAW**

In this Focus, the student will brief an appeal of a case involving bifurcation of a divorce action and jurisdiction over a defendant serving overseas in the military.

The Assignment

Read the opinion in *In re Marriage of Anthony J. Harris and Teasha J. Harris*, 922 N.E.2d 626 (Indiana 2010), and then

brief the case using the format on the companion website for this text or one provided by your instructor. The opinion in the *Harris* case is available at *www.pearsonhighered.com/careersresources/* in the website material related to Chapter 5 under Cases. The format for briefing a case is provided in the material related to Chapter 1 under Resources.

FOCUS ON **STATE LAW AND PROCEDURE**

In this activity, students are asked to locate and prepare a list of basic laws and procedures related to divorce proceedings in their respective jurisdictions.

The Assignment

Prepare a list of the responses to the following questions:

1. Which chapters/sections of your state code govern divorce and related matters (custody, child and spousal support, and property division)?

2. Which rules of procedure govern domestic relations matters in your jurisdiction (including service of process).

3. What are the grounds for divorce in your state and where are they set forth?

4. What residency requirement, if any, must a plaintiff satisfy in your state in order to be able to file a complaint for divorce?

5. What defenses to divorce are available in your jurisdiction?

FOCUS ON **TECHNOLOGY**

In addition to the links provided throughout the chapter, this focus provides a series of useful websites for reference along with technology-related assignments for completion.

Websites of Interest

http://www.americanbar.org

This is the website of the American Bar Association. Go to the website and search for divorce charts containing state-by-state information, particularly Chart 4 Grounds for Divorce and Residency Requirements. Search for "Family Law in the Fifty States."

www.divorcelawinfo.com

This is the website for the Divorce Law Information Center. It offers "do-it-yourself divorce kits" and state-by-state divorce and family law information, including child support calculators. Caution should always be exercised prior to actually using unofficial forms from commercial sites.

www.divorcelinks.com

This site offers links to state and federal divorce laws by topic.

www.divorcenet.com

This site offers links to state divorce laws, indicating statutory references and brief narratives on topics such as residence, grounds for divorce, "military divorce," approaches to division of property, alimony, and child custody, visitation, and support.

www.divorcesource.com

This site provides information on divorce laws by state. It also offers an online, for-fee QDRO preparation

service. Caution should be exercised as QDRO formats vary employer to employer and must satisfy the requirements of plan administrators (as well as the courts).

www.findlaw.com

(Choose "Family Law" under "Learn About the Law.")

This is a particularly well-organized site with access to resources for both public and professional inquirers. It provides general and state-specific information, including access to the laws of all fifty states on divorce and related family law topics.

Assignments

1. Determine which, if any, divorce-related forms are available online in the state in which you are studying family law. Most states have state-sponsored sites (through courts or law libraries) that provide basic family law forms that can be printed or completed online. (See Appendix C and sites referenced in this chapter.)

2. Locate and visit a website that contains information about divorce laws in all fifty states, and describe the range of information provided with respect to your state.

3. Many people believe that the institution and traditional significance of marriage are seriously threatened by no-fault divorce. A number of national organizations and initiatives such as the Alliance for Marriage, the National Marriage Project, and the covenant marriage initiative have emerged, seeking to "save" traditional marriage. Locate online four websites, two supporting no-fault divorce and two opposing it. What are the arguments on each side?

PORTFOLIO PRODUCTS

1. Complaint for Divorce or Answer/Motion to Dismiss
2. Motion for Temporary Orders with Supporting Affidavit
3. Motion for Appointment of Guardian *ad Litem* (with Supporting Affidavit and Proposed Order) or Motion for Attorneys Fees (with Affidavit(s) and Proposed Order)
4. Motion for Appointment of Appraiser (with Supporting Affidavit and Proposed Order)

5. Memorandum re ethical issues in a hypothetical situation
6. Brief of Case: *In re Marriage of Anthony J. Harris and Teasha J. Harris*, 922 N.E.2d 626 (Indiana 2010)
7. List of basic laws and procedures related to divorce proceedings in the student's jurisdiction

chapter 6
DISCOVERY AND FINANCIAL STATEMENTS

Walter and Renee have been married for more than three decades. Throughout the marriage he has totally controlled their finances and, it would appear, not always to his wife's benefit. Now that she has filed for divorce, he has no desire to share information with her or her attorney about whatever modest assets he may have accumulated.

LEARNING OBJECTIVES

After reading this chapter and completing related assignments, you should be able to:

- define discovery and describe its nature, purpose, and scope in the domestic relations context

- define informal discovery and list examples of how it may be used in family law cases

- identify and describe the five formal discovery methods

- describe strengths and weaknesses of the various formal discovery methods

- list objections that can be made to discovery requests, and identify the kinds of sanctions that can be imposed for failing to comply with discovery requests, rules, and orders

- explain how to locate and complete financial affidavits

- list ways of identifying and uncovering hidden assets

- define e-discovery and identify ways of accessing electronically stored information

- describe the use of evidence from social networking sites in family law cases

- describe the roles of the client, the paralegal, and the court in the discovery process

Introduction

In this chapter you will learn about the topic of discovery, an essential working tool of the legal profession. Although often neglected in family law texts, it is an extremely important topic. Broadly construed, discovery refers to the process of gathering factual information and materials relevant in a particular legal action. This chapter includes a review of the three primary means of conducting discovery in the family law context: informal discovery initiatives, formal discovery methods, and financial affidavits. It also highlights the court's potential role in assisting with discovery-related issues. Particular attention is given to two areas of heightened importance in contemporary family law cases: (1) the search for hidden assets and (2) electronic discovery (e-discovery), the accessing of electronically stored information (ESI) including material available on social networking sites. The nature of the paralegal's role in all aspects of discovery is featured.

The Nature, Purpose, and Scope of Discovery in Family Law Cases

In the family law context, the primary purpose of **discovery** is to gather as much information about a case as possible so that attorneys can make appropriate recommendations and clients can make informed

Discovery
the process of gathering information and materials relevant to a matter at issue; includes both formal and informal methods

decisions regarding their options, including whether they should settle a case or proceed to trial. In uncontested cases or cases involving few assets and no dispute with respect to custody or support, little or no discovery may be sought. In more complex or hotly contested cases in which it is appropriate, extensive discovery may be pursued. The results of discovery efforts usually facilitate settlement negotiations but, if no agreement is reached, they can be used to help shape trial preparation.

The scope of **informal discovery** is broad and essentially includes the gathering of any information that will be helpful in resolving a case regardless of whether or not it will eventually be admissible at trial. The scope of **formal discovery** methods such as interrogatories and depositions is more limited and is governed by established procedural rules in every jurisdiction. Formal discovery methods can only be used to seek information on a matter when the information sought is: relevant to the subject matter of the case, reasonably calculated to lead to admissible evidence, and not protected by a **privilege** such as the attorney-client privilege. Although the information sought need not necessarily be admissible as evidence in its present form, it should be designed to lead to evidence that may be admissible at the time of trial.

In conducting comprehensive discovery, family law teams seek information pertaining to the parties and their claims, defenses, and requests for relief. Today discovery is most commonly sought regarding:

- financial assets and liabilities
- current income and expenses
- financial and nonfinancial contributions to the marriage
- dissipation of marital assets
- employment history, including efforts to find employment
- parenting history, skills, and weaknesses
- marital misconduct, such as substance abuse, infidelity, or treatment that has endangered a party's health and safety if fault grounds for divorce continue to exist in the jurisdiction or if conduct during the marriage is a factor the court considers when making property division decisions
- history of the parties' relationship prior to the marriage such as its length and nature, whether they cohabited and were economically interdependent for an extended period or entered a domestic partnership or civil union

THE DISCOVERY PLAN

Early in a case, a discovery strategy will be established. It will identify the kinds of information needed, the techniques to be utilized (both formal and informal), the sequencing of efforts, the assignment of tasks, and the projected cost. The plan may need to be modified after discussion with the client—particularly if there are financial constraints or if new informational needs develop. As difficult as it is to explain to clients, consideration needs to be given to identifying both the strengths and the weaknesses of each of the parties and their respective positions. Thorough research and preparation are essential.

In a well-orchestrated discovery plan, the various methods of gathering information work together in a case. For example, informal discovery initiatives (use of a private investigator, client conversations with friends, and a review of

Informal discovery
information gathering not governed by specific procedural rules, such as researching public records and locating *Bluebook* values

Formal discovery
discovery methods that are subject to procedural and court rules

Privilege
a legal right or exemption granted to a person or a class of persons not to testify in a legal proceeding; generally based on the existence of a special relationship

material stored on the "family computer" and on social networking sites) may reveal that a husband who claims he cannot pay child or spousal support due to an injury is in fact leading a very active and social lifestyle. A Financial Affidavit may indicate that he is paying for a fitness club membership and has no medical expenses. Interrogatories may be served requesting information about his credit cards, the online sites he visits, and memberships he holds in clubs. Requests for production may yield credit card statements that document substantial "entertainment" expenses, or hiking and other vacations he has taken. Depositions may then be used to question the party about all of the above and expose contradictions and outright deception.

Depending on its nature and extent, discovery can be very expensive, but a failure to conduct adequate discovery when it is warranted can be disastrous. In some instances, the family law team may fail to achieve the best possible result for the client. In the most egregious cases, a failure to conduct or produce discovery may result in a malpractice action against an attorney. (See Paralegal Application 6.1.) In many cases, one of the parties has significantly more resources than the other and is better positioned to conduct discovery. In such situations, the court may entertain a motion for attorneys' fees to allow the disadvantaged party to pursue or defend the action in order to avoid being forced to accept a settlement based on insufficient information.

> **PARALEGAL PRACTICE TIP**
>
> Although students commonly learn about discovery in civil litigation courses, it is important to understand that, in many jurisdictions, governing rules may vary in the domestic relations context. It is also useful to learn how various formal and informal information-gathering methods are utilized in family law cases to facilitate settlement and provide a framework for trial preparation, if necessary.

Paralegal Application 6.1

What if the Client Will Not Authorize Discovery?

In some circumstances, after examining various documents, the attorney may tell the client that it appears the other party has removed funds from certain accounts and is "hiding" them. Further discovery could be conducted to trace and locate those funds, but not without expense. Even though discovery might well result in a significantly more favorable property settlement in the long run, the client may say that he or she simply cannot afford additional legal costs and will insist that no further discovery be conducted.

In such situations, it is wise for the attorney to have the paralegal draft a letter to the client reiterating the advice given and its potential benefits and costs. The letter should confirm that, notwithstanding that advice, the client has explicitly directed the attorney not to conduct further discovery. To avoid any misunderstanding, the client should be advised that the letter is forthcoming and that he or she will be asked to provide a written acknowledgment of receipt. Such a letter, promptly sent by certified mail, documenting that the advice was given and specifically declined, helps defeat a potential later claim by the client that he or she received inadequate representation to his or her financial detriment.

THE PARALEGAL'S ROLE

Paralegals are often charged with considerable responsibility in the information-gathering effort. The nature and extent of an individual paralegal's role is largely a function of his or her level of expertise. For example, an experienced paralegal may be asked to help develop a discovery plan and draft complex, sophisticated discovery requests. An entry-level paralegal is more likely to be asked to check "Blue Book" values, draft motions to compel, and prepare relatively standard discovery requests, such as requests for production of employment contracts, insurance policies, or bank account statements.

One of the most important tasks performed by paralegals is the marking of discovery deadlines on all appropriate calendars. This task includes critical deadlines prescribed by rules governing the various forms of discovery, dates of scheduled court appearances, meetings, and depositions, etc., and self-imposed deadlines for completion of discovery-related tasks, allowing sufficient time for review and revision.

Informal Discovery

Informal discovery refers to lawful information-gathering efforts not governed by the procedural rules restricting formal discovery methods. Clients frequently engage in it in anticipation of a divorce or other legal actions. For members of the family law team, informal discovery begins with the first client contact and may continue throughout a case. Initial investigative efforts often shape the theory of a case and the action to be filed—for instance, whether a fault or no-fault Complaint for Divorce should be filed in states where both options are available.

Even if it is not all admissible as evidence at trial, information gathered through informal discovery efforts such as the following often provides leverage in negotiations:

- A paralegal consults online resources to establish the value of various marital assets such as boats and motor vehicles.
- A client inventories content stored on the "family" computer and makes copies of relevant documents.
- A private investigator is retained and documents that a party is performing work "under the table" or is carrying on an extramarital affair.
- Potential witnesses, such as coaches, counselors, school nurses, and teachers, are interviewed informally (if possible) about the impact of a parent's behavior on a child.
- A forensic accountant is retained and prepares a "lifestyle analysis" to illustrate that a party's expenses far exceed his or her reported income.
- For a modest fee, a national firm provided with a party's Social Security number produces a report on topics such as ownership of real estate, vehicles, and interests in business entities.
- The client or a member of the family law team browses sites such as Facebook and Match.com to search for legally accessible documentation of a party's conduct and false representations regarding marital status.
- The client completes a comprehensive questionnaire providing information about a wide range of topics such as the history of the parties' relationship; the nature and value of assets owned by either or both of the parties; any children of the marriage or of either party; and medical, employment, and educational histories of the parties. (See Paralegal Application 6.2.)
- To avoid the costs of formal discovery, the parties agree to voluntarily work cooperatively to exchange information and make joint requests to mortgage companies, banks, pension plan administrators, and other third parties for records not available online. This approach obviously works best in a collaborative environment in which the parties basically trust each other and there is a shared commitment to reaching a mutually agreed-upon settlement without litigation.

PARALEGAL PRACTICE TIP

A member of the family law team should check the publicly accessible content of the client's online activity to protect against potential damage to the case down the road.

PARALEGAL PRACTICE TIP

An example of a Comprehensive Client Questionnaire is available at *www.pearsonhighered.com/careersresources/* in the website material related to Chapter 5 of this text under Resources.

Paralegal **Application 6.2**

The Client as a Resource

When a client first seeks representation in a divorce action, he or she customarily is asked to respond to a Comprehensive Client Questionnaire. In addition, even before an action is filed, many attorneys ask clients to perform some initial informal discovery. The client may be asked to:

- Photograph the contents of the marital residence (house or apartment) with particular attention to any potentially valuable items such as jewelry, antiques, art work, and gun collections.
- Keep a journal concerning such topics as parenting situations reflecting the particular strengths or weaknesses of each parent, unexplained phone calls and absences from the home, incidents of abuse of any kind and work being performed "under the table."
- Locate and make copies of important documents such as deeds, titles, registrations, bank account statements, credit card statements, travel materials (e.g., airline tickets and hotel invoices), employment records, brokerage account statements, state and federal tax returns, and mortgage applications.
- Make copies of relevant electronic documents such as e-mails and financial records if legally accessible.
- Make a list of the names, addresses, and telephone numbers of potential **lay witnesses** for the client and for the other party, and identify the matters about which they might testify.
- Make a list of the names, addresses, and contact numbers of any professionals, such as physicians, therapists, accountants, financial advisors, and appraisers, consulted by either or both of the parties for their benefit or the benefit of their children.

Lay witness

a witness who is not an expert on a matter at issue in a legal proceeding, who testifies as to opinions based on firsthand knowledge

---

In some jurisdictions, once a Complaint is filed and served and before formal discovery methods may be utilized, the parties are required to make **mandatory self-disclosure** of certain information within a specified period. (See Paralegal Application 6.3.) In most instances, these requirements help reduce discovery costs. If a party fails to make the required disclosure within the mandatory period, the other party's attorney will usually contact the party (or the attorney, if she or he is represented) and reach an agreement with respect to what is needed and by when. If informal efforts are unsuccessful, a motion to compel compliance may be filed, and related costs may be charged to the noncompliant party by the court.

Mandatory self-disclosure

material specified by statute or court rule that each party in a particular legal action must provide to the other party within a certain period after filing and service of a summons and complaint

Paralegal **Application 6.3**

Mandatory Self-Disclosure

Mandatory self-disclosure requirements typically provide that absent agreement of the parties or order of the court, each party is required to deliver to the other documents such as the following within a certain period after service of the summons in an action for divorce or separate support (e.g., forty-five days):[1]

- federal and state tax returns and supporting documentation for the past three years (individual, limited-partnership, and privately held corporate returns)
- bank statements for the prior three years for any bank accounts held in the name of the party or jointly with another party for the benefit of either party or the parties' minor children

- the four most recent pay stubs from each employer for whom the party works
- documentation of the cost and nature of available health insurance coverage
- statements for the past three years for any securities, stocks, bonds, notes or obligations, certificates of deposit (for the benefit of either party or the minor children), 401(k), IRA, and pension plans (for all accounts listed on the party's financial statement)
- copies of any loan or mortgage applications filed within the past three years
- copies of any financial statements or statements of assets and liabilities prepared within the last three years

Formal Discovery

After a Complaint has been filed and served, formal discovery can be initiated. The five basic formal discovery methods are:

1. Interrogatories
2. Depositions
3. Requests for Admissions
4. Requests for Production of Documents or Things or Entry Upon Land
5. Requests for Physical or Mental Examinations

Each of these methods is described in the following narrative, paralegal applications, and exhibits. The role of the paralegal is emphasized, given its potential importance in the discovery process.

Although the basic principles remain the same, the exact names for each of the discovery methods and the applicable procedural requirements vary from state to state. Some jurisdictions have special discovery rules and procedures tailored to family law/domestic relations matters. Others apply the same rules as are used in civil matters generally. Still others require reference to multiple sets of rules. For example, a Request for Production of Documents may be called a Demand for Documents or a Request for Production of Documents and Entry Upon Land, or it may be folded into a set of Interrogatories. In some states formal discovery may only be conducted by stipulation or court order. In others, it may not be necessary to file any discovery documents with the court or to file only a certain type such as a **Request for Admissions** (in New Hampshire, for example) or a **Request for a Physical or Mental Examination**. In some states, such as Tennessee, the rules may vary from county to county. Because of these variations, it is critically important for the paralegal to be familiar with applicable terminology and rules governing discovery in general and domestic relations matters in particular.

In any given case, all, none, or some formal discovery methods will be utilized, depending on the nature and complexity of the case, how hotly it is contested, and the financial resources of the parties. Information obtained through methods such as interrogatories, depositions, and requests for admissions is provided by the respondent under oath and is potentially very helpful to the requesting party. Customarily, states impose a duty to supplement responses if circumstances change, new information comes to light, or errors are discovered. The sequence in which formal discovery methods are used may vary, but interrogatories are most commonly propounded first.

INTERROGATORIES

Interrogatories are written requests for information sent by a party to an opposing party in a lawsuit. Although states frequently provide standardized forms online, particularly for parties proceeding *pro se*, use of those forms is customarily not mandatory. Caution needs to be exercised when using generic sets of interrogatories found in form books or online or versions designed to meet the objectives in other cases handled by the office. Although they may provide a reference or starting point, they must be tailored to the client's case. Failure to do so may give rise to accusations of harassment or to incurring of unnecessary costs.

Interrogatories must be responded to in writing under oath within a prescribed period, usually thirty days. The period for responding may be extended

---

Request for Admissions
a discovery method in which a party makes written requests to an opposing party, calling for an admission or denial of specific facts at issue or verification or denial of the genuineness of documents relevant to the case

Request for Physical or Mental Examination
a method of discovery in which one party requests that the court order the other party (or, in some instances, a third party) to submit to a physical or mental examination

Interrogatories
a method of discovery in which one party submits a series of written questions to an opposing party to be responded to in writing within a certain period of time under pain and penalty of perjury

under the applicable rules of procedure if the interrogatories are served by mail. Jurisdictional rules of procedure typically provide when they may be served and limit the total number allowed (commonly fifty or fewer, not including subparts) absent permission of the court or agreement of the parties. They can usually be served all at once or in several sets, provided the total allowable limit is not exceeded. Many attorneys prefer to serve an initial set of fewer than the maximum number and hold the balance in reserve in case information is obtained warranting additional questions that could not have been anticipated. The primary strengths and weaknesses of interrogatories along with those of other formal discovery methods are described later in this chapter in Exhibit 6.3.

In order to produce useful information, interrogatories need to be clear, concise, and appropriate to the facts of the specific case. For example, a question such as "Do you have any retirement income" asked of a thirty-year-old working party will yield little useful information. The question should request detailed information with respect to any and all forms of retirement programs in which the respondent is participating. If the respondent is unaware of specifics, he or she is obligated to ascertain them prior to responding and to supplement responses later, if warranted.

Interrogatories commonly request information from the opposing party with respect to the following:

- current and former address(es), age, prior marriages, and children
- educational background, training, and job skills
- past and present employment as well as future plans including efforts to seek employment
- real property owned individually or jointly with others before and during the marriage
- the nature and value of personal property, such as automobiles, jewelry, and collections (guns, artwork, collectibles, etc.), owned before and during the marriage
- how a party spends his or her leisure time (personal and social life and membership in any clubs, civic organizations, etc.)
- the other party's spending habits (what he or she spends money on; where he or she shops/dines; whether he or she pays by cash or credit, etc.)
- income from all sources
- the responding party's investments, business interests, retirement accounts, interests in any trusts, anticipated inheritances, etc.
- bank accounts, safe deposit boxes, etc.
- financial liabilities
- the parties' respective strengths and weaknesses as parents, if applicable
- the opposing party's physical and mental health, treatment programs, physicians, medications, etc.
- the history of the marriage, such as prior separations, counseling sought and obtained, conduct of the parties during the marriage, and nature of changes in the parties' relationship during the marriage
- the history of the spouses' relationship prior to the marriage, such as periods of cohabitation, entry into a domestic partnership or civil union, economic interdependence, and agreements with respect to children

In this age of technology, interrogatories are also likely to seek information about topics such as the following:

- the location(s) where the respondent stores business and financial records, including hard drives and/or other electronic storage devices
- any and all social and professional networking sites utilized during the past two years
- any and all electronic mail accounts through which the party has sent or received mail during a certain period
- any and all instant messaging services subscribed to during a specified period
- any and all online dating services subscribed to during the past two years
- whether the party has formatted or destroyed any physical media storage device on any computer he or she has used during a specific period

Paralegal **Application 6.4**

Interrogatories—The Potential Role of the Paralegal

The paralegal must be familiar with the procedural rules in the jurisdiction governing each form of discovery in the family law context and with the established role of the paralegal in the firm where he or she is employed. *All discovery-related tasks are carried out under the direction and supervision of an attorney.* The following reflects a common, but not necessarily universal, approach with respect to interrogatories.

If serving interrogatories

- Identify information to be gathered via interrogatories.
- Draft proposed interrogatories for review by the client and the supervising attorney.
- Finalize interrogatories for review, approval, and signature(s) as required and then, if directed to do so, serve on the opposing party in the manner provided in local rules, with a copy to the client. A limited number of jurisdictions require that interrogatories also be filed with the court or that the parties file a notice of filing interrogatories and a notice of responding to and/or objecting to interrogatories.
- When answers are received, review them for completeness and, if incomplete, draft a letter for the supervising attorney's signature requesting that the responses be supplemented.
- If the responding party fails to respond or to supplement his or her answers on request, draft a motion to compel responses for review and possible filing.
- Summarize the responses and recommend follow-up measures, if warranted, such as questions for a second set of interrogatories or deposition questions.

If responding to interrogatories

- Mark receipt and return dates on all appropriate calendars and also schedule draft and review dates for responses.

- Give a copy to the supervising attorney, who will make the legal determination as to whether any of the interrogatories call for privileged information and, thus, an objection rather than an answer. If appropriate, draft a motion for a **protective order**.
- Draft a letter to the client for the supervisor's signature explaining the process and enclose a copy of the interrogatories for review and preparation of initial responses within an appropriate time frame. The letter should also remind the client that all answers must be true and accurate to the best of his or her knowledge, as they are provided under oath.
- Schedule a meeting for the client with the paralegal and/or the attorney, as appropriate, to review draft responses the client provides.
- Delete nonresponsive answers, correct errors, complete incomplete responses, and note objections identified by the supervising attorney.
- If needed, draft a letter to opposing counsel requesting additional time to respond. If the request is denied, draft a motion asking the court to grant the requested extension in response time.
- Prepare final responses expressed in the light most favorable to the client, as long as the factual content is accurate and based on information provided by the client.
- Schedule a meeting in which the supervisor and the client review final responses and affix signatures in the required form.
- Serve the responses on the opposing party (and with the court, if required in the jurisdiction) along with a notice of responding to and/or objecting to interrogatories, if necessary.

Protective order
a court order restricting or prohibiting a party from unduly burdening an opposing party or third-party witness during the discovery process

DEPOSITIONS

In a **deposition**, one party asks the other party, or a third person who has or may have information and/or documents pertaining to the case, a series of questions to be answered under oath. The person being questioned is called the **deponent**. The responses given are recorded verbatim by a court reporter or another individual licensed to record testimony. In some jurisdictions, depositions may be audio- or videotaped according to procedural rules.

If the deponent is a party, a **Notice of Deposition** is sent to the deponent or his or her attorney, if represented, specifying the date, time, and location of the deposition. As a courtesy and convenience, counsel will usually agree on a date, time, and place for the deposition in advance of notice to ensure the availability of counsel and the parties. A party deponent is not required to bring any documents to a deposition unless specifically requested to do so. Such a request usually is accomplished by combining a Notice of Deposition with a Request for Production of Documents. Even if deponents fail to bring requested documents to a deposition, their memories can be "refreshed" by showing them a particular document and asking if the document refreshes their memory about the topic of a question.

If the deponent is a third-party witness, such as an employer, the third party must be served with notice of the deposition by **subpoena**. A subpoena is a document signed by an officer of the court that requires the person who receives it to appear at the date, time, and place indicated, under penalty of law. Blank subpoenas can generally be obtained from the court and can be filled in with appropriate information as the need arises. They are then returned to the court to be issued. If it is requested that the deponent bring certain documents to the deposition, the subpoena is called a **subpoena** *duces tecum*. Sometimes the subpoena will specify that it can be satisfied by delivery of the requested document(s) to the requesting attorney's office within a certain period of time, and then the actual deposition need not take place. In most, if not all, jurisdictions, third-party witnesses must be reimbursed for their related travel expenses.

Depositions usually take place in an attorney's office but may be scheduled at other mutually convenient sites, particularly if the deponent is located in another state. The paralegal should be alert to the rules governing a situation in which a subpoena is to be served in another state. A letter of request (usually called **letters rogatory**) is a document a court in one state issues to a court in another state requesting that the "foreign" court serve process on an individual or corporation within the foreign jurisdiction and return the proof of service for use in the pending case.

At the beginning of a deposition, the deponent is sworn in and promises to answer truthfully and to the best of his or her ability. Questions are usually asked orally (a deposition upon oral examination) but may be presented in written form. Counsel for the deponent has a limited role in the deposition and, depending on the jurisdiction, is usually restricted to clarifying information, registering objections, and indicating omissions to the deponent. The deponent customarily cannot consult with counsel prior to answering questions.

Because of the costs associated with a deposition, once noticed, counsel for the parties may discuss the nature of the information sought, and the deponent may agree to voluntarily provide it without the need for the actual deposition. Although this happens occasionally, depositions are often designed to serve multiple purposes, such as observing the demeanor of the deponent when

Deposition
a method of pretrial discovery in which one party questions the other party or a third person under oath; responses to oral or written questions are reduced to writing for possible later use in a court proceeding

Deponent
the individual who is asked to respond under oath to questions asked in a deposition

Notice of Deposition
the notification sent to an opponent (or his or her attorney, if represented) of an intention to depose him or her at a certain date, place, and time

PARALEGAL PRACTICE TIP

In cases involving complex, large, and diverse marital assets or thorny custody and visitation issues, it may be necessary to schedule one or more "deposition days," during which a series of potential witnesses are deposed. This approach to scheduling is more efficient, convenient, and cost-effective for both parties and counsel than consuming several days over a more extended period.

Subpoena
a document ordering a witness to appear and provide testimony in a legal proceeding, such as a deposition, court hearing, or trial

Subpoena *duces tecum*
a subpoena ordering a witness to appear in a legal proceeding such as a deposition, court hearing, or trial and to bring with him or her specified documents, records, or things

Letters rogatory
documents issued by a court in one state to a court in another state requesting that the "foreign" court serve process on an individual within the foreign jurisdiction

PARALEGAL PRACTICE TIP

Attorneys conducting depositions need to maintain a delicate balance between unethical questioning designed to serve an improper purpose (such as harassing or intimidating the deponent) and strategic questioning conducted in the good-faith belief it will lead to admissible evidence. (See Exhibit 6.1.)

questioned under oath, assessing his or her credibility, creating a record that can be used at trial to impeach the deponent's testimony, and "fishing" for additional useful information. In such cases, depositions are unlikely to be canceled.

EXHIBIT 6.1 Sample Deposition Questions

The following questions are presented as a sampling of the kinds of questions that may be asked at depositions. One of the strengths of depositions as a discovery technique is that questions may be modified or expanded as responses lead to new areas worthy of pursuit.

1. Where are you presently employed?
2. What is your current salary?
3. Do you receive any additional compensation such as bonuses, tips, or stock incentives?
4. Does your employer reimburse any of your expenses, such as parking, meals, or travel?
5. With respect to the marital residence, what do you estimate to be its present value?
6. Are there any mortgages or other liens on the property?
7. What was the purchase price for this property?
8. What was the amount of the down payment?
9. What was the source of funds for the down payment?
10. From what source of funds has the mortgage been paid during the marriage?
11. Do you presently have any credit card debt?
12. Is there a name on any of your credit card accounts other than your own?
13. I want to show you Exhibit 2. Do you recognize this credit card statement? Would you please identify the Exhibit for the record?
14. Let's look at some of the individual items on this statement, starting with the $3,567 charge at the Casino Royale. . . .
15. Page 2 of the statement indicates a charge of $715 for a "bracelet" purchased at Shreve, Crump, and High. For whom was this bracelet purchased?
16. Let's shift gears for a moment and look at your individual tax return for the 2014 tax year. Would you please identify this return for the record?
17. Calling your attention to Schedule B, do you see any interest or dividend income listed there?
18. I have here a Financial Statement dated April 1, 2014, signed by you and filed with the court. Would you please identify this Statement for the record and verify that it was signed by you?
19. Looking at the statement, can you tell us where your interest- and dividend-producing assets appear?
20. What computers do you use at home and work, including desktops and laptops?
21. With whom do you share use of any of those devices?
22. Do you know of any other computers besides those you have already identified that contain information about any of the issues in this case?
23. Do you have access to the Internet?
24. What sites have you visited in the last six months relating to issues in this case?
25. What devices do you use to electronically store information?

Paralegal **Application 6.5**

Depositions—The Potential Role of the Paralegal

If taking the deposition

- Make recommendations to the supervisor regarding witnesses who should be deposed.
- Prepare a notice of intent to take deposition if the person to be deposed is a party or a subpoena or subpoena *duces tecum* if the deponent is a nonparty.

- Arrange for service of the subpoena, if directed to do so, and later confirm that service has, in fact, been made. If the deponent is a party, serve notice on opposing counsel or the party directly if he or she is not represented.
- Draft recommended deposition questions.

- Organize information and documents, such as responses to interrogatories, witness statements, bank records, and credit card statements, which will be useful and/or referenced at the deposition. To the extent possible, the material should be organized in the order in which it will be addressed in the deposition.
- If the deponent previously was required to produce documents, review them for compliance with the request.
- If items are to be presented as exhibits at the deposition, they should ideally be marked by the reporter in advance of the start of the deposition. The supervising attorney will most likely want to have at least four parallel sets of documents available: one clean copy to show to the deponent, one for the opponent's attorney, one marked up for personal use, and a fourth to give to the reporter and have admitted as an exhibit.
- If directed by your supervisor, attend the deposition, listen carefully, take notes, and be prepared to assist the attorney with locating any needed documents or suggesting additional follow-up questions.
- Following the deposition, review the transcript (audiotape or videotape), prepare a summary (usually called a deposition digest), and make recommendations for follow-up.
- Arrange for any required payment to the reporter and to third-party deponents for travel expenses.

If defending the deposition

- If the client is responding to a subpoena *duces tecum* and there is an objection to the requested production, draft a motion for a protective order and, if there is no objection, organize the document(s) he or she is asked to produce for review by the attorney.
- If the client being deposed is a party, describe the process and assist the attorney in anticipating likely questions and preparing the client for questioning. Some attorneys choose to conduct mock depositions with their clients to familiarize them with the process and the types of questions likely to be asked. The sessions can also be used to identify and address potential weaknesses in the deponent's performance. It may become apparent that some clients will need help developing strategies for dealing with various styles of questioning.
- Attend the deposition, listen carefully, take notes, and be prepared to assist the attorney with locating any documents as appropriate or suggesting clarifications, gaps, or errors in responses.
- Following the deposition, request a copy of the transcript, review it for accuracy, and correct mistakes as directed by the attorney in a manner consistent with applicable rules.
- Prepare a summary and recommendations for any necessary follow-up including the supplementing of responses if appropriate.

REQUESTS FOR ADMISSIONS

A Request for Admission is a written request to an opposing party calling for an admission or denial of a specific fact at issue or verification or denial of the genuineness of a document relevant to the case. Unlike interrogatories, which are presented in the form of questions, requests for admission (or requests to admit, as they are called in some jurisdictions) are presented as statements of fact. They are used to confirm rather than collect information. (See Exhibit 6.2.)

Responses to requests are customarily short and include the following potential options:

- Admit the matter.
- Deny the matter.
- Indicate lack of sufficient knowledge to admit or deny the matter.
- State a specific objection to the request.
- Respond with a combination of the above (e.g., admit in part and deny in part).

A party who intends to allege lack of sufficient knowledge has a duty to look into the matter (examine his or her records, files, etc.) before responding. If a respondent denies a fact that is subsequently proven at trial, he or she may be assessed fees and costs incurred by the requesting party in proving the truth of the matter. If a party does not object to a request for admission and fails to respond within the period prescribed by the applicable rules of procedure (usually thirty days), the content of the admission is deemed admitted without further action, and the facts or authenticity of

PARALEGAL PRACTICE TIP

An example of a standardized Request for Admission form can be found at *www.courtinfo.ca.gov* (Forms and Rules/Category-Discovery/Disc 020).

PARALEGAL PRACTICE TIP

Attorneys are occasionally somewhat cavalier about responding in a timely manner to discovery requests. They may delay responding until a deadline passes and opposing counsel calls or files a motion to compel. This is not good practice in general, but with requests for admissions, it can have serious and costly consequences.

documents need not be proved at a subsequent hearing or trial. The seriousness of a failure to respond to a request for admissions was evident in a 2010 Missouri case in which a wife's omission resulted in several matters being deemed admitted including:

- that she failed to participate in counseling;
- that she failed to cooperate with the court-appointed guardian ad litem;
- that the father was fit to have custody of the minor children;
- that she had shoplifted items from a store;
- that she had "shared a bed" with other men while married to her husband; and
- that she had physically abused her husband and called him derogatory names.

See *In re the Marriage of Claire Noland Vance and Brent Vance*, 321 S.W.3d 398 (Mo. App. 2010).

Requests for admissions are not often utilized. This is surprising, given their potential to help parties avoid significant time and expense and narrow the issues needing to be proved at trial. They may cover facts or documents about which no dispute is anticipated, clarify disputed issues, and confirm suspicions. Requests can cover a wide range of topics, but each individual request should address only one fact, document, or signature to avoid confusion and minimize denials.

When a request calls for authentication of a document or signature (as on a Voluntary Acknowledgment of Parentage or a Certificate of Civil Union), a copy of the document at issue is attached to the request. If the responder admits that a document—a mortgage application, for example—is genuine, the application may be entered as evidence at trial without having to be introduced through foundation testimony of the mortgage broker. The party can then be questioned about the contents of the application, which may conflict with information on a financial statement or responses in depositions.

EXHIBIT 6.2 Sample Request for Admissions

STATE OF NEW HAMPSHIRE

HILLSBOROUGH, SS   SUPERIOR COURT
SOUTHERN DISTRICT   DOCKET NO. 14-M-0000
IN THE MATTER OF JOHN B. SMITH
AND JANE SMITH

REQUEST FOR ADMISSIONS

John B. Smith, by his attorney, submits the following requests for admissions to Jane Smith:

1. I admit that my husband and I separated on four occasions during the five years of our marriage, immediately preceding the filing of my pending action for divorce.
2. I admit that the attached deed to a property in Boring, Oregon, held in trust and bearing my name and signature, is authentic, genuine, and accurate.
3. I admit that the Bank North loan my husband and I obtained in 2007 was used to cover my tax liability (including interest and penalties) for previously undeclared income I earned as a waitress.
4. I admit that I have a joint bank account at First Third Bank with my friend, Alberto Bonilla.
5. I admit that I take medication for depression on a daily basis and have been doing so for the past five (5) years.
6. I admit that my husband provided the initial down payment of $40,000 on the marital residence out of his own personal funds in 1995.
7. I admit that my husband performed all of the carpentry, plumbing, and electrical work completed over ten (10) full months when the marital home was fully renovated in 2010.
8. I admit that during our marriage, my husband was the primary caretaker of the children and the marital home.
9. I admit that the present value of the marital home is $550,000, based on the attached appraisal performed by a mutually agreed-upon appraiser in December 2014.

EXHIBIT 6.2 *(Continued)*

10. I admit that I have contributed less than 30% of my income to the payment of joint expenses during the course of our marriage.

11. I admit that two weeks before filing for divorce, I withdrew $14,000 from the savings account at Bank of America held jointly with and funded solely by my husband.

12. I admit that I have filed a wrongful termination suit against my former employer.

13. I admit that I have been arrested for operating under the influence of drugs or alcohol on three occasions in the two years immediately preceding my filing for divorce.

14. I admit that the attached e-mail, addressed to abonilla@comcast.net dated December 10, 2013, is a true and accurate copy of an e-mail I authored and transmitted on that date.

15. I admit that the signature on the attached application for a $15,000 loan from Citizen's Bank dated December 15, 2014, is my signature.

16. I admit that since I filed my complaint for divorce I have deleted files from my computer that were relevant to this action.

If any of the foregoing requests for admission is denied because of lack of information or knowledge, identify the request and give a detailed account of every effort made by you or your attorney to inquire into the subject matter of the request, including the date of each effort, the person making such effort, the substance of such effort, and the information obtained by such effort.

ANY PARTY, WHO WITHOUT GOOD REASON OR IN BAD FAITH, DENIES UNDER RULE 54 ANY SIGNATURE OR FACT, WHICH HAS BEEN REQUESTED AND WHICH IS THEREAFTER PROVED, MAY, ON MOTION OF THE OTHER PARTY, BE ORDERED TO PAY THE REASONABLE EXPENSE, INCLUDING COUNSEL FEES, INCURRED BY SUCH OTHER PARTY.

> Respectfully submitted,
> John B. Smith
> By his attorney,
>
> _____
> Juliana Wilson, Esq.
> Address
> Telephone No.: xxx-xxx-xxxx

Dated: _____

Paralegal **Application 6.6**

Requests for Admissions—The Potential Role of the Paralegal

If requesting admissions

- Draft a proposed Request for Admissions based on facts, events, and documents involved in the case that may be suited to this technique.
- Review the draft with the client and the supervising attorney.
- Prepare a final draft that incorporates any corrections, additions, deletions, or edits.
- Serve the reviewed, approved, and signed request on opposing counsel, if directed to do so, and, if required, also file it with the court in compliance with applicable procedural rules in the jurisdiction.
- Mark on all appropriate calendars the date when a response is due to be returned.
- If the response is incomplete or objections are raised, draft documents to implement the course

of action determined by the supervising attorney. These may include a letter to and negotiation with opposing counsel and/or a motion to compel compliance with an accompanying proposed order.

- If responses are not received and no objections are filed within the prescribed response period (usually thirty days), notify the supervising attorney, and the facts contained in the request will be deemed admitted in accordance with local governing rules.

If responding to a request

- When a request is received, bring it to the attention of the supervising attorney and (if so directed) send a copy to the client, with a cover letter describing the nature, purpose, and effect of this form of discovery and asking that the client promptly review

(Continued)

the requests and determine whether the statements are true and accurate.

- At the attorney's direction, schedule a meeting with the client in which the attorney will review the requests and potential responses and determine whether there are grounds for objecting to any of the requests. If some or all of the requests are objected to, counsel may agree on a mutually acceptable revised request that can then be filed with the court, if required. If a compromise cannot be reached, the court may consider the objections in a hearing at which both parties and their counsel are present.
- Draft a proposed final response for review by the client and the attorney.
- Serve the reviewed, approved, and signed response on the opposing party, if directed to do so, and file it with the court if required

REQUESTS FOR PRODUCTION OF DOCUMENTS OR THINGS

Request for Production of Documents or Things
a method of pretrial discovery in which a party makes a written request that the other party, or a third person, produce specified documents or other tangible things for inspection and/or copying

A **Request for Production of Documents or Things** is a written request for documents or things in the possession, custody, or control of the opposing party or a nonparty third person (such as an employer) for inspection and copying, if necessary. As with all discovery requests, requests for production of documents and things should be tailored to the facts of each case. The request should state the time, place, and manner of production and be sufficiently specific that the responding party will be able to comply. For example, if requesting bank records, a request might read as follows: "Copies of all records of any accounts of any kind including, but not limited to, checking accounts, savings accounts, NOW accounts, Certificates of Deposit, and equity lines of credit with any bank, credit union, or other financial institution for the three years preceding the date of this request."

Requests for production of documents most commonly seek financial records and information such as bank statements, tax returns, and employment records. They can encompass other things as well, such as diaries, collections, photographs, stock certificates, corporate by-laws, partnership agreements, trusts, deeds, wills, credit card records, airline tickets, and titles to motor vehicles, boats, recreational vehicles, etc. Occasionally requests for production will ask that large items (vehicles, artworks, antique furniture, etc.) be made available for inspection, appraisal, and/or photographing.

PARALEGAL PRACTICE TIP

A sample Request for Production of Documents or Things can be found at *www.pearsonhighered.com/ careersresources/* in the website material related to Chapter 6 of this text under Forms. An example of a standardized request for production from a third party can be found at *www.flcourts.org* (Forms/ Form12931).

As discussed more fully later in this chapter, electronic communications and electronically stored information have become prime discovery targets over the past decade. Consistent with this trend, requests for production might seek, for example:

- any and all printouts or computer files evidencing electronic communications between the opposing party and a named third party, whether sent or received during a certain time period.
- any and all documentation of any cell phone or other mobile communications device, including an itemization of incoming and outgoing calls, text messages, e-mails or picture files, as well as an indication of the sender and/ or recipient during the year preceding the filing of the complaint for divorce.
- any and all computer files from any personal financial management computer program used over the two years immediately preceding the date of the request such as Quicken, Microsoft Money, or Turbo Tax.
- any and all computer files that contain electronic copies of monthly statements for any credit cards or installment accounts in the opposing party's name or his or her name with another from a certain date to the present.

Requests for production of electronically stored information in particular must be carefully drafted and targeted to secure specific information directly relevant to the case. Courts are unlikely to compel production if requests are overbroad. For example, in 2010, a New York court held that where a request was made supposedly for the purpose of discovering information pertinent to the value of the husband's law practice, a wife's general and unlimited-in-time request seeking access to the entirety of her husband's business and personal data stored on his office computer was deemed overbroad. See *Schreiber v. Schreiber*, 904 N.Y.S.2d 886 (2010).

A party responding to a request for production must produce all documents or things requested unless there is a valid objection. For example, the items requested may be subject to a privilege or may not be in the possession or control of the responding party. Unreasonable and irrelevant requests may constitute harassment of the opposing party or a third party. On occasion, the materials requested may contain trade secrets or material about to be but not yet copyrighted or patented. In such situations, the responding party may file a motion for a protective order, or the parties may execute a confidentiality agreement (with or without the assistance of the court) warranting that confidentiality of certain information will be protected under penalty of law for failure to do so.

Paralegal **Application 6.7**

Requests for Production of Documents and Things—The Potential Role of the Paralegal

If serving a request

- Review the file to identify and compile a list of documents or things needed that are in the possession or control of the opposing party or of third parties such as the IRS, a banking institution, or an employer.
- Discuss the list with the supervising attorney, who will determine a discovery strategy, including which documents and things to request and from whom.
- Draft a proposed Request for Production for review by the supervising attorney and the client.
- Finalize the request for review and signature(s) as required and then, at the supervising attorney's direction, serve it on the opposing party and/or named third party in the manner provided in local rules.
- When production is received, compile a log and review production to confirm that it fully complies with the request and, if it does not, draft a letter for the supervising attorney's review requesting that the production be supplemented.
- If the responding party continues to fail to comply, draft a motion and proposed order to compel production for review and possible filing.
- Organize the materials produced, make copies/take photographs as directed, summarize the response, and recommend follow-up measures, if warranted, such as questions for a first or follow-up set of interrogatories or deposition questions raised as a result of a review of the documents produced.

If responding to a request

- Mark receipt and return dates on all appropriate calendars and also schedule response draft and review dates.
- Give a copy to the supervising attorney, who will make a legal determination as to whether any of the requests call for confidential or privileged information and thus a confidentiality agreement or an objection rather than production.
- Draft a letter to the client, enclosing a copy of the request for review, and ask that he or she assemble as many of the requested materials as possible within an appropriate time frame.
- Schedule a meeting for the client with the paralegal and/or attorney as appropriate to review materials, filter out any not specifically requested, and remove any privileged documents or things based on the supervising attorney's instructions.
- If an extension is needed, notify the supervising attorney and draft a motion for extension of time for production (unless the supervising attorney negotiates a revised timeline with opposing counsel).

(Continued)

- Mark all appropriate calendars with revised draft, review, and return dates.
- Compile the production for delivery to the opposing party, being certain to limit it to material specifically requested and not privileged.

- Serve the materials on the opposing party in an appropriate manner after receiving authorization from the supervising attorney.

REQUESTS FOR PHYSICAL OR MENTAL EXAMINATION

Unlike other discovery techniques, because of its intrusiveness, a request to have a physical or mental examination conducted usually must be sought by motion. Generally, courts will grant such requests and compel attendance of a party or third person at an examination only after a hearing in which good cause is shown. There are sometimes circumstances in which a request may be appropriate, such as when

- a party raises his or her own or the other party's mental or physical health as an issue.
- the parentage of one or more of the parties' children is challenged.
- the mental instability or physical disability of a party is raised as a reason why he or she should be denied custody.
- one of the parties seeks alimony or a disproportionate division of marital assets based on the existence of an alleged disability that makes it impossible for that party to be self-supporting.
- one of the parties seeks a divorce from the other on a fault ground that alleges the other party is a chronic alcoholic or abuser of other drugs.
- a party claims on his or her financial affidavit to have significant and continuing monthly costs for uninsured medical expenses or treatments of some kind.

In rare instances, requests may also be made for examination of a third person in the custody of a party. For example, if a deviation from the child support guidelines is requested because of expenses associated with a child's medical condition, an examination and assessment of the child's treatment needs may be appropriate. An examination may also be appropriate in cases in which custody is at issue and a credible allegation of physical or sexual abuse of a child is raised.

Paralegal **Application 6.8**

Requests for Physical or Mental Examination—The Potential Role of the Paralegal

If requesting an examination

- Review the case file and consider whether a physical or mental examination may be appropriate given the facts of the case and, if so, make a recommendation to the supervising attorney to that effect.
- Develop a list of proposed examiners (such lists often already exist in the resource files of a family law practice and may be maintained by a paralegal).
- If directed to do so, draft a Motion/Request for a Mental or Physical Examination and a proposed

order as appropriate with an accompanying affidavit to be signed by the client in support of the motion.
- When approved and signed by the attorney, if directed to do so, file the original request, affidavit, and proposed order with the court, serve copies on the opposing party, and mark on the calendar the date of service, the time and date of the court hearing on the request (if necessary), and the date by which any objection to the request must be filed.

- If the opposing party does not file an objection within the period prescribed by the applicable rules of procedure and/or the court allows the request, notify the supervising attorney for authorization to contact the office of the opposing counsel and make arrangements for scheduling the requested examination.
- If the opposing party does not submit to an examination within a reasonable period of time, notify the supervising attorney for authorization to prepare, file, and serve a motion to compel examination and a proposed order, with a copy to the client. Before or after filing of a motion to compel, counsel for the parties may be able to negotiate an agreement covering the purpose and scope of the examination; the selection process for choosing the examiner; the date, time, and place of the examination; and the use to which the information obtained will be put. If the parties are unable to reach an agreement, the open hearing will proceed.
- When a hearing date is set, notify the attorney, mark the date on the calendar, and notify the client (by phone and in writing) that he or she should plan to be present for the hearing. The attorney and the paralegal will usually prepare the client for the hearing and the kinds of questions that may be asked.
- If the examination subsequently occurs, be sure that the office receives a copy of the examiner's report and copies of the results of any tests for review and analysis, and suggest needed follow-up such as questions for the examiner in case the report is introduced at trial.

If responding to a request for an examination

- When a request is received, the paralegal will customarily arrange a meeting for the attorney to discuss the request with the client and determine how to proceed.
- If there is no objection, the attorney will usually negotiate terms, which are confirmed in writing, limiting the nature, scope, and use of the examination.
- If there is an objection, draft the objection and supporting affidavit or memorandum for review.
- After review, finalize the objection, obtain the supervising attorney's signature and approval, and file the objection with the court within the period provided by local rules (usually thirty days).
- When a hearing date is set on the objection, notify the attorney, mark it on the calendar, and notify the client (by phone and in writing) that he or she should plan to be present.
- If the examination is to take place, the paralegal may be asked to schedule it and ensure that the client (or other person to be examined) keeps the appointment. On occasion, a paralegal may accompany the client to a medical examination. If questions arise (usually concerning the scope of the examination), the paralegal can contact the attorney for clarification and/or instructions.
- After the examination, a copy of the examiner's report and the results of any tests may be sought for review and analysis, but the client then is usually required to produce any similar medical reports in his or her custody or control. Under both state and federal law, the person examined may be required to execute releases waiving privacy rights with respect to medical records.

EXHIBIT 6.3 Summary Table Re Formal Discovery Methods

Method	Strengths	Weaknesses
INTERROGATORIES	• Interrogatories are cost-effective. • They can be designed to obtain information that can then be used as a basis for formulating other discovery requests. • They may be used to identify potential witnesses, including **experts**, physicians, and co-respondents when adultery is alleged. • Responses to interrogatories may be more complete than answers at depositions because the respondent has a duty to locate necessary information and provide complete responses.	• Interrogatories can usually be served only on parties and not on third persons. • A responding party's responses are reviewed with counsel and carefully drafted to reveal as little potentially damaging information as possible. • Responses to interrogatories are written. As a result, the requesting party does not have an opportunity to assess the respondent's credibility and potential weaknesses as a witness.

Expert

a person who, through education or experience, has developed special skill or knowledge in a particular subject

(Continued)

EXHIBIT 6.3 (*Continued*)

DEPOSITIONS	• Depositions can be used with both parties and nonparty witnesses, including expert witnesses. • Necessary information usually can be obtained more quickly than with other methods. • The credibility and performance of the deponent under oath can be assessed. • Follow-up and clarifying questions can be asked if further information is needed or if an answer is incomplete, evasive, or opens up a new area for inquiry.	• Depositions are expensive. The costs are in the preparation, follow-up, and analysis time as well as in the conducting of the actual deposition, court reporter time, transcript preparation, and copying, each of which varies based on the length and complexity of the deposition. • Deposition questions may reveal the deposing party's theory of the case and give the deponent a better chance to prepare for negotiation and/or trial.
REQUESTS FOR ADMISSIONS	• Requests for Admissions are cost-effective. • They can be used to narrow the issues needing to be addressed at trial. • They can be used to clarify disputed issues and to confirm suspicions. • They can reduce the number of facts (or the validity of signatures or documents) needing to be proved at trial.	• Requests may reveal the theory of the client's case and/or available defenses.
REQUESTS FOR PRODUCTION OF DOCUMENTS OR THINGS OR ENTRY UPON LAND	• These requests can be used with both parties and nonparty witnesses. • They allow a party to obtain critical information from entities such as employers and the IRS. • They often yield a wealth of information that leads to further productive discovery.	• They can be expensive, depending on the nature and extent of production. • Responses to requests for electronically stored information from third parties/providers are difficult to obtain given current federal and state laws.
REQUESTS FOR PHYSICAL OR MENTAL EXAMINATION	• Requests may lead to discovery of otherwise privileged information.	• These requests can usually only be served on parties although the court may allow examinations of children in appropriate circumstances, such as when there is an allegation of abuse. • Requests are highly intrusive and may exacerbate an already acrimonious dispute. • Usually, a request must be sought by motion, and such motions are granted only upon a showing of good cause.

PARALEGAL PRACTICE TIP

A Request for Entry Upon Land would be appropriate if a party needed to inspect the condition of a property in dispute or access an object on the property that cannot readily be moved or otherwise presented for inspection.

PARALEGAL PRACTICE TIP

If a party is ordered to comply with discovery orders, that party's attorney also has a legal and ethical duty to comply if the attorney has the requested documents and/or information in his or her possession. A failure to do so constitutes a deliberate disregard for the court's authority. See, for example, *Meier v. Meier*, 835 So. 2d 379 (Fla. Dist. App. 2003).

Objections to Formal Discovery Requests

A party who receives a request for discovery has a duty to respond to the request. In general, a party must respond to all questions and/or requests for which there is no legally accepted objection. Objections are commonly governed by procedural rules and common practice. If there is an appropriate objection, it is usually specifically stated in lieu of an answer. However, local rules may structure the nature and registering of objections. For example, in some jurisdictions, deposition questions should be answered and objections raised for consideration at trial unless the questions call for privileged or constitutionally protected information.

The most common objections to discovery requests are the following:

1. **The request creates an undue burden or expense.** For example, in a no-fault case involving few assets, the opposing party requests ten years of bank statements for an account that rarely held more than $2,000, and the parties have already essentially agreed on the division of their minimal property. Compliance with the request would be costly to the respondent and yield nothing productive for the party making the request.

2. **The request seeks discovery of material that is not relevant to the issues in the case.** For example, in a no-fault divorce action in a jurisdiction that does not consider marital fault as a factor in property division or spousal support decisions, requests for information pertaining to marital infidelity are not relevant.

3. **The document or information requested is not within the party's possession or control.** In some marriages, one party has maintained control over the parties' finances, paying the bills, completing the tax returns, and maintaining records—often on a personal computer to which the other party has no access. In such circumstances, the other party may simply be incapable of complying with a discovery request calling for financial records.

4. **The document, thing, or information requested is protected by a privilege that is legally recognized within the jurisdiction.** The most obvious privilege is the attorney-client privilege, which protects communications between the attorney and the client as well as the attorney's "work product." **Work product** customarily includes material prepared in anticipation of litigation, such as comprehensive financial reports prepared by accountants. Most jurisdictions recognize additional privileges, such as priest-penitent and doctor-patient privileges. A minority of jurisdictions recognize a social worker-client privilege and/or a parent-child privilege. A party may waive a privilege under certain circumstances. For example, if a spouse is seeking spousal support and/or a more favorable property settlement based on an alleged health problem, medical information pertaining to that condition which otherwise might be protected by a doctor-patient privilege will likely be discoverable by the other party.

5. **The information being sought is cumulative.** This objection is based on the argument that the party seeking the information previously has requested it in another request or format or already has the information in his or her possession or control.

6. **The form of the question is improper.** For example, the question is redundant or overbroad. It would warrant an objection on this ground if information is sought about a party's entire medical and psychiatric history rather than about the sole medical condition at issue in the case.

7. **The request is made in bad faith solely for the purpose of harassment.** For example, the request seeks information unrelated to any matter at issue and is designed solely to embarrass or cause emotional distress. Questions relating to an abortion obtained as a teenager or the fact that the party was in the

Work product
written or oral material prepared for or by an attorney in preparation for litigation, either planned or in progress

PARALEGAL PRACTICE TIP

Because the paralegal is an agent of the client's attorney, acting under the attorney's direction and supervision, the paralegal's presence in client interviews or contributions to "work product" do not destroy the privileged character of those communications or materials.

PARALEGAL PRACTICE TIP

In a 2009 case, a California appellate court held that a father's medical records were discoverable in a custody battle, at least with respect to a neurological condition the wife claimed exposed the parties' minor son to risk. The court found the father had waived the doctor-patient privilege and that his constitutional right to privacy was outweighed by the state's compelling interest in protecting the child's best interest. See *Manela v. Superior Court of Los Angeles County, David Y. Manela, Real Party in Interest,* 177 Cal. App. 4th 1139, 99 Cal. Rptr. 3d 736 (2009).

country illegally at one point before becoming a citizen could be objected to on this ground.

8. **The request calls for production of material that constitutes a trade secret.** Production should be excused because it would result in serious economic loss to a business. Sometimes such objections can be dealt with through privacy agreements setting agreed-upon limits on what will be produced and how it will be used.

9. **A respondent may raise a Fifth Amendment right against self-incrimination if appropriate.** For example, in a state where adultery still constitutes a criminal offense, a person may refuse to answer questions relating to an adulterous affair during the time falling within the applicable statute-of-limitations period.

Financial Statements

Every state requires each party to an action for divorce, separate support/legal separation, or child support to exchange with the other party and file with the court a document containing basic financial information about his or her respective needs, resources, and liabilities. (See Exhibit 6.4.) The document is commonly called a Financial Statement, a Financial Affidavit, or an Inventory of Assets and Liabilities, and it must be filed with the Complaint or within a certain period after the action is commenced. It is designed to provide the parties with data needed to inform their decisions, especially with respect to matters of support and property division. It also provides the court with a frame of reference for assessing the fairness of a proposed settlement or for making decisions in a contested case. The client is required to sign it under pain and penalty of perjury. Several states require that counsel also sign the document affirming that it does not contain information known by the attorney to be false. Clearly, a financial affidavit can be the single most important document presented to the court, as it not only provides essential information, but also reflects both the client's credibility and the attorney's level of preparedness.

The specific format of financial statements varies from state to state, but the basic information called for is essentially the same. All forms cover income, assets, expenses, and liabilities. Assets include both real property (real estate) and personal property (such as bank accounts, stocks and bonds, cash, collections, household furnishings/antiques, and notes payable to the party). Liabilities include such items as mortgages, equity loans, car loans, credit card debt, court judgments, and debts owed. Some states, such as Massachusetts, have more than one form—one for parties of more modest means and a second, more detailed form for parties with more substantial income and assets. Many states now make divorce forms, including financial statements, available online. In addition, there are several software packages that allow family law practitioners to create and print financial affidavits in approved formats, although it may be necessary to indicate that the form is computer-generated and/or to print it on a particular color paper. Such programs are helpful because they automatically calculate the figures and store them for future use. However, considerable care must still be taken to ensure that the data input is accurate in initial and updated editions. (See Paralegal Application 6.9.)

PARALEGAL PRACTICE TIP

For readers wanting to work their way though some financial statements available online, check out the following:

ARIZONA *www.azcourts.gov* (Petition for Dissolution without Children)

FLORIDA *www.flcourts.org* (Forms/12.902 long and short forms)

GEORGIA *www.georgiacourts .org* (Court Forms/Statewide Domestic Relations/ Domestic Relations Financial Affidavit)

MASSACHUSETTS *www.mass .gov* (Forms/Divorce/ Financial Statements-long and short forms)

Forms for many other states are also available online at state sponsored sites. (See Appendix C.)

The paralegal often is asked to coordinate preparation of financial statements. At first blush, completing an affidavit may appear to be a simple fill-in-the-blanks and tally-the-figures task, and in cases involving an unemployed client and few if any assets, it may be reasonably straightforward. Nonetheless, each affidavit requires careful attention given its potential importance. Initially the client gathers the financial information for inclusion on the form provided by counsel or the court and completes a preliminary draft for review.

EXHIBIT 6.4 Example of a Financial Affidavit—State of Connecticut

Courtesy of the State Of Connecticut

FINANCIAL AFFIDAVIT
JD-FM-6-SHORT New 1-14
P.B. §§ 25-30, 25a-15

STATE OF CONNECTICUT
SUPERIOR COURT
www.jud.ct.gov

Court Use Only
FINAFFS

ADA NOTICE
The Judicial Branch of the State of Connecticut complies with the Americans with Disabilities Act (ADA). If you need a reasonable accommodation in accordance with the ADA, contact a court clerk or an ADA contact person listed at *www.jud.ct.gov/ADA*.

Instructions

*Use this short version if your **gross annual income is less than $75,000** (see Section I. Income) and your **total net assets are less than $75,000** (see Section IV. Assets). Otherwise, use the long version, form JD-FM-6-LONG.*

Docket number
- FA -   - S

For the Judicial District of _____   At (Address of Court) _____

Name of case _____

Name of affiant (Person submitting this form) _____

☐ Plaintiff   ☐ Defendant

Certification

I understand that the information stated on this Financial Statement and the attached Schedules, if any, is complete, true, and accurate. **I understand that willful misrepresentation of any of the information provided will subject me to sanctions and may result in criminal charges being filed against me.**

I. Income

1) Gross Weekly Income/Monies and Benefits From All Sources

Computed based on year-to-date, but no less than the last 13 weeks. If computation is based on less than 13 weeks or if your computations are not reflective of current wages, explain:

_____

Paid: ☐ Weekly   ☐ Bi-weekly   ☐ Monthly   ☐ Semi-monthly   ☐ Annually

If income is not paid weekly, adjust the rate of pay to weekly as follows:

Bi-weekly → divide by 2	Semi-monthly → multiply by 2, multiply by 12, divide by 52
Monthly → multiply by 12, divide by 52	Annually → divide by 52

(a)   Employer(s)   Address(es)   Base Pay:

Job 1 _____ _____ ☐ Salary ☐ Wages $_____
Job 2 _____ _____ ☐ Salary ☐ Wages $_____
Job 3 _____ _____ ☐ Salary ☐ Wages $_____

Total of base pay from salary and wages of all jobs .... $_____

(b) Overtime .... $_____
(c) Self-employment .... $_____
(d) Tips .... $_____
(e) Social Security .... $_____
(f) Disability .... $_____
(g) Unemployment .... $_____
(h) Worker's compensation .... $_____
(i) Public Assistance (Welfare, TFA payments) .... $_____

(j) Child Support (Actually received) .... $_____
(k) Alimony (Actually received) .... $_____
(l) Rental and income producing property.... $_____
(m) Contributions from household member(s) $_____
(n) Cash income .... $_____
(o) Veterans Benefits .... $_____
(p) Other: _____ $_____

(q) Total Gross Weekly Income/Monies and Benefits From All Sources (Add items a through p) $_____

Hours worked per week _____

Gross yearly income from prior tax year. Provide amount of income, not copies of forms .... $_____

List here and explain any other income including but not limited to: non-reported income; and support provided by relatives, friends, and others:

_____
_____

(Continued)

PARALEGAL PRACTICE TIP

Financial Statement: An attorney cannot condone or assist a client who is providing false, inaccurate, or incomplete information on a financial statement. The attorney should advise the client of the potential consequences of such conduct, correct the record if already filed, or withdraw from the case to avoid an ethical violation. See New York State Bar Association Committee on Professional Ethics Opinion 781-12/8/04.

EXHIBIT 6.4 *(Continued)*

2) Mandatory Deductions *(If consistent deductions don't occur every pay check **provide average amounts**.)*

	Job 1	Job 2	Job 3	Totals
(1) Federal income tax deductions (claiming ___ exemptions)	$	$	$	$
(2) Social Security or Mandatory Retirement	$	$	$	$
(3) State income tax deductions (claiming ___ exemptions)	$	$	$	$
(4) Medicare	$	$	$	$
(5) Health insurance	$	$	$	$
(6) Union dues	$	$	$	$
(7) Prior court order — child support or alimony	$	$	$	$
(8) Total Mandatory Deductions (add items 1 through 7)	$	$	$	$

3) Net Weekly Income... $ _____

Subtract the Total Mandatory Deductions [see item I., 2), (8)] from the Total Gross Weekly Income/Monies and Benefits From All Sources [see item I., 1), q)]

II. Weekly Expenses Not Deducted From Pay

If expenses are not paid weekly, adjust the rate of payment to weekly as follows:

Bi-weekly → divide by 2	Semi-monthly → multiply by 2, multiply by 12, divide by 52
Monthly → multiply by 12, divide by 52	Annually → divide by 52

Insert an ("x") in the box if you are **not** currently paying the expense, or if someone else is paying the expense.

Home:

Rent or Mortgage *(Principal, Interest — Real Estate Taxes and Insurance if escrowed)* ☐ $ _____   Property taxes and assessments .... ☐ $ _____

Utilities:

Oil .... ☐ $ _____   Telephone/Cell/Internet........................... ☐ $ _____

Electricity .... ☐ $ _____   Trash Collection .... ☐ $ _____

Gas .... ☐ $ _____   T.V./Internet .... ☐ $ _____

Water and Sewer............................. ☐ $ _____

Groceries *(after food stamps):* Including household supplies, formula, diapers .... ☐ $ _____

Transportation:

Gas/Oil .... ☐ $ _____   Auto Loan or Lease .... ☐ $ _____

Repairs/Maintenance .... ☐ $ _____   Public Transportation............................ ☐ $ _____

Automobile Insurance/Tax/Registration ... ☐ $ _____

Insurance Premiums:

Medical/Dental *(Out-of-pocket expense after Health Savings Account/Plan)*....... ☐ $ _____   Life .... ☐ $ _____

Uninsured Medical/Dental not paid by insurance .... ☐ $ _____

Clothing .... ☐ $ _____

Child(ren):

Child Support of this case .... ☐ $ _____   Child Care Expense *(after deductions, credits and subsidies)*........................ ☐ $ _____

Child Support of other children other than this case *(attach a copy of the order)* ☐ $ _____   Child(ren)'s activities *(e.g., lessons, sports, etc.)* .... ☐ $ _____

Alimony: Payable to this spouse .... ☐ $ _____   Alimony: Payable to another spouse .... ☐ $ _____

Extraordinary travel expenses for visitation with child(ren) .... ☐ $ _____

Other *(Specify):* _____ ☐ $ _____

Total Weekly Expenses Not Deducted From Pay .... $ _____

III. Liabilities *(Debts)*

Do not include expenses listed above. Do not include mortgage current principal balance or loan balances that are listed under "Assets."

Creditor Name /Type of Debt		Balance Due	Date Debt Incurred/ Revolving	Weekly Payment
Credit Card, Consumer, Tax, Health Care, Other Debt				
	☐ Sole ☐ Joint	$		$
	☐ Sole ☐ Joint	$		$

EXHIBIT 6.4 *(Continued)*

	☐ Sole ☐ Joint	$	$
	☐ Sole ☐ Joint	$	$
	☐ Sole ☐ Joint	$	$

(A). Total Liabilities *(Total Balance Due on Debts)* .... $

(B). Total Weekly Liabilities Expense .... $

IV. Assets

Note: Under "Ownership" indicate S for sole, JTS for joint with spouse, and JTO for joint with other.
You must complete the last column to the right "Value of Your Interest" in each applicable section.

A. Real Estate *(including time share)*

Address	Ownership S / JTS / JTO	a. Fair Market Value *(Estimate)*	b. Mortgage Current Principal Balance	c. Equity Line of Credit and Other Liens	d. Equity (d = a minus (b + c))	e. Value of Your Interest
Home						
	☐ ☐ ☐ $		$	$	$	$
Other						
	☐ ☐ ☐ $		$	$	$	$
	☐ ☐ ☐ $		$	$	$	$

Total Net Value of Real Estate: $

B. Motor Vehicles

Year	Make	Model	Ownership S / JTS / JTO	a. Value	b. Loan Balance	c. Equity (c = a minus b)	d. Value of Your Interest
1:			☐ ☐ ☐ $		$	$	$
2:			☐ ☐ ☐ $		$	$	$

Total Net Value of Motor Vehicles: $

C. Bank Accounts

Do not include custodial accounts or child(ren)'s assets — complete Section V. below.

Institution	Account Number *(last 4 numbers only)*	Ownership S / JTS / JTO	Current Balance/ Value	Value of Your Interest
Checking			☐ ☐ ☐ $	$
Savings			☐ ☐ ☐ $	$
Other			☐ ☐ ☐ $	$

Total Net Value of Bank Accounts: $

D. Stocks, Bonds, Mutual Funds

Company	Account Number *(last 4 numbers only)*	Listed Beneficiary	Current Balance/ Value
			$
			$

Total Net Value of Stocks, Bonds, Mutual Funds: $

E. Insurance *(exclude children) D = Disability   L = Life*

Name of Insured	D	L	Company	Account Number *(last 4 numbers only)*	Listed Beneficiary	Current Balance/ Value
						$
						$

Total Net Value of Insurance: $

F. Retirement Plans *(Pensions on Interest, Individual IRA, 401K, Keogh, etc.)*

Type of Plan	Name of Plan/Bank/Company	Account Number *(last 4 numbers only)*	Listed Beneficiary	Receiving Payments	Current Balance/ Value
				☐ Yes ☐ No	$
				☐ Yes ☐ No	$

Total Net Value of Retirement Plans: $

G. Business Interest/Self-Employment

If you own an interest in a business, or are self-employed, complete this section.

Name of Business	Percent Owned	Value
	%	$

Total Net Value of Business Interest/Self-Employment: $

(Continued)

EXHIBIT 6.4 (Continued)

H. Other Assets

Name of Asset	Current Balance/Value	Name of Asset	Current Balance/Value
	$		$
	$		$
	$		$
	$		$
		Total Net Value of Other Assets:	$

I. Total Net Value All Assets (add items A through H).. $

V. Child(ren)'s Assets

Include Uniform Gift to Minor Account, Uniform Trust to Minor Account, College Accounts/529 Account, Custodial Account, etc.

Institution	Account Number (last 4 numbers only)	Listed Beneficiary	Person Who Controls the Account (Fiduciary)	Current Balance/Value
				$
				$
			Total Net Value of Child(ren)'s Assets:	$

VI. Health (Medical and/or Dental Insurance)

Company	Name of Insured Person(s) Covered by the Policy

Do you or any member of your family have HUSKY Health Insurance Coverage? ☐ Yes ☐ No ☐ I Don't Know
If Yes, whom?

_____

_____

Important:
If you have other financial information that has not yet been disclosed, you have an affirmative duty to disclose that information. List additional information below:

_____

_____

_____

Summary (Use the amounts shown in Sections I. through IV.)

Total Net Weekly Income (See Section I. 3) .... $_____

Total Weekly Expenses and Liabilities (Total From Section II. + III.(B)) .... $_____

Total Cash Value of Assets (See Section IV. I.) .... $_____

Total Liabilities (Total Balance Due on Debts) (See Section III. (A)) .... $_____

Certification

I certify under the penalties of perjury that the information stated on this Financial Statement and the attached Schedules, if any, is complete, true, and accurate. **I understand that willful misrepresentation of any of the information provided will subject me to sanctions and may result in criminal charges being filed against me.**
I, _____ the ☐ Plaintiff ☐ Defendant herein, residing at
_____ , telephone number _____ , being duly sworn, depose and say that the following is an accurate statement of my income from all sources, my liabilities, my assets and my net worth, from whatever sources, and whatever kind and nature, and wherever situated.

Signed (Affiant)		Date signed
Signed (Notary, Commissioner of Superior Court, Assistant Clerk, Other Proper Officer under Section 1-24 of the Connecticut General Statutes)	Print name and title of person signing at left	Date signed

Depending on the client's financial, organizational, literacy, and record-keeping skills as well as the size and complexity of the marital estate, the paralegal may be assigned to work with the client on this task. The paralegal should verify that the figures provided are current, accurate, and able to be documented to the greatest extent possible. The client needs to understand the contents of the affidavit and be able to respond to questions which may be posed by the court or by the other party. For example, in the context of a deposition, it is not uncommon for a party to be questioned about:

- each and every expense item
- how each figure was calculated
- what documentary evidence exists to corroborate the figures
- how any discrepancies between income and expenses can be explained

Paralegal Application 6.9

Pointers on Completion of Financial Affidavits

1. Instructions for completing financial affidavits should be followed carefully.
2. The affidavit should be complete, with every space filled in with a figure, a "0," "none," or "NA" ("not applicable"), as appropriate.
3. If allowed, footnotes or attachments should be used

   a. when necessary to supplement or more fully explain figures that might otherwise be confusing or misleading out of context

   b. if the form doesn't permit the party to adequately represent his or her specific circumstances

4. Most attorneys believe the affidavit should provide a complete picture of the client's financial situation in an organized, coherent, and consistent manner. A failure to do so opens the door for attack by opposing counsel or questioning by a judge about figures that are inaccurate, double-counted, confusing, or not included.
5. The affidavit should reflect a party's current financial circumstances. However, if a party's income varies seasonally, with market fluctuations, or for some other reason, averages may usually be used.
6. If weekly or monthly income and expenses do not balance, the party must be able to explain how a shortfall is covered or where the excess income is placed. For example, if the party claims to be spending more than is earned, is he or she borrowing money, withdrawing from savings, selling assets, and/or receiving funds, gifts, or other subsidies from third parties?
7. Contested cases frequently drag on for months and involve multiple court appearances for temporary orders, motion hearings, discovery conferences, and the like. Whenever a hearing is for the purpose of addressing an issue with financial implications, such as child or spousal support or occupancy of the marital residence, a current financial affidavit is customarily required. A party must be able to explain any discrepancies between prior and current affidavits.
8. In cases involving complex assets and liabilities, it may be necessary to consult with accountants, financial advisors, appraisers, and other experts to establish values and appropriate figures to be included on financial affidavits.
9. Care should be taken that figures appearing on affidavits can be documented wherever possible and that they are consistent with other documents that may be provided to the court or available to the other party.[2]

Hidden Assets

One of the greatest challenges, particularly in cases involving substantial assets, is to determine whether or not an opposing party (or a client for that matter!) is disclosing all of his or her assets and income. There are many kinds of assets that can be hidden (cash, bonds, insurance policies with cash value, etc.) and an unlimited number of ways of hiding them. It requires skill, persistence, funds, and creativity to locate them, especially when a party with significant assets has been planning to file for divorce for an extended period. However, if it appears likely, or the client suspects, that assets are being hidden, the attorney has a duty to reasonably investigate the possibility.

The biggest challenges in locating hidden assets are that the searcher often does not know exactly what he or she is looking for or if it even exists, and the burden of looking usually falls on the party with the most limited resources. The search can involve both formal and informal discovery methods. Many resources for locating hidden assets are already in the client's possession or can be accessed legally and informally, such as credit card statements and public records. Others will need to be obtained through formal discovery methods. Interrogatories may seek information about retirement assets, employee benefits,

PARALEGAL PRACTICE TIP

If a safe deposit box exists, an *ex parte* request for a restraining order may be filed asking the court to freeze the box for a limited period so an inventory of its contents may be prepared in the presence of both parties and counsel.

PARALEGAL PRACTICE TIP

Loan applications are valuable in two respects: the applicant is likely to list all assets in order to present the most positive picture possible and it is a federal crime to knowingly provide false information to a federally insured banking institution.

deferred compensation plans, safe deposit boxes, or loan applications filed by a party in the past year. The actual loan applications may then be obtained via requests for production. See Paralegal Application 6.10.

Although clients are often able to detect errors, omissions, and outright deceit in the financial information provided by their spouses, five of the best resources for detecting hidden assets are tax returns, bank statements, credit card statements, financial statements, and public records, all of which can be accessed legally and frequently informally. Discrepancies among these various documents can be especially enlightening. For example, when reviewed in combination with a financial statement, the opposing party's tax returns can provide a virtual roadmap for the client and the family law team to follow:

- **W-2 Wage and Income Statements:** W-2 Wage and Income Statements reflect deferred compensation and executive "extras" as well as basic wages.
- **Dividend income:** On Schedule B, the taxpayer lists payors and amounts of dividend income received, but what about the underlying asset? Is it disclosed on the financial statement? The value of that asset can be determined with online resources to establish the dividend per share rate.
- **Royalty income:** Royalty income may be listed on Schedule E for a patent or a published book or film. Has the taxpayer disclosed the value of the underlying asset?
- **Interest income:** If the taxpayer reports $1,500 of interest income and the prevailing interest rate is 3%, that means there is an underlying asset worth $50,000. Has it been disclosed?
- **Rental income:** If rental income is declared on Schedule E, have all real estate holdings been disclosed and appraised for current market value?
- **Retirement fund contributions:** Has there been a change in the amount the taxpayer is contributing toward IRAs and other retirement funds? Is there evidence of a recent distribution from a retirement fund?
- **Mortgage interest:** Did the amount of mortgage interest being claimed go up in the most recent tax year? Was the underlying property refinanced and, if so, where are the proceeds from the refinancing?
- **Trusts:** The tax return will reveal the existence of a trust, but what is its underlying value to the taxpayer in terms of principal and annual distributions?
- **Excise tax:** If excise tax is being paid, what are the values of the cars, trucks, and/or boats being taxed, and are those vehicles disclosed as assets?
- **Medical expenses:** When medical expenses are claimed, were they reimbursed?
- **Quarterly tax payments:** If quarterly tax payments have been made, is there a surplus that will be credited toward future tax liabilities? Has a tax refund been applied toward the next year's taxes?

Forensic accountant
an accountant who applies accounting principles and analysis to gather and present evidence in a lawsuit

PARALEGAL PRACTICE TIP

There are many resources for locating computer forensic experts including other practitioners and professional associations such as the International Society of Forensic Computer Examiners.

Counsel and skilled paralegals are often able to uncover hidden assets, and **forensic accountants** are sometimes able to unravel complex schemes used to conceal assets. However, in many cases, the funds are simply not available to support the search and even if they are, some hidden assets simply cannot be located despite best efforts. In such a situation, language should be built into the parties' separation agreement providing for the possibility that previously undisclosed assets will be revealed at a later date. The agreement may provide, for example, that if the later-discovered asset was accidentally undisclosed, it will be divided equally; if it was negligently undisclosed, it will be divided with a greater percentage going to the spouse who was not negligent; and if it was intentionally not disclosed, the asset will vest solely in the "innocent" party.

Paralegal **Application 6.10**

The Search for Hidden Assets

In searching for hidden assets, the family law team might explore the following:

1. Does a party report a modest income and yet live a lavish lifestyle with frequent vacations, an expensive residence with no mortgage, high-end motor vehicles, pricey clothing, and jewelry? From what source has the discrepancy between income and expenses been paid?

2. Has a party experienced a sudden or recent decrease in salary? Has he or she deferred receipt of any income, raises, bonuses, or other forms of compensation to a date subsequent to the divorce? A review of past income history is often helpful in detecting such activity.

3. If the other party is self-employed and claiming a reduction in business and income since initiation of divorce proceedings, is the decline in marked contrast to past history or market trends?

4. Does the other party receive unacknowledged "perks" over and above direct salary at his or her job, such as a company car for business and personal use; subsidized housing or relocation costs; an allowance for uniforms or parking; an expense account for travel, dining, and entertainment; or club memberships?

5. Has the other party made sham or allegedly "bad" loans to a family member or friend?

6. Does the other party hold any as yet potentially valuable unexercised stock options in a company where he or she is or was employed?

7. Has the other party accumulated substantial sick, personal, or vacation time at work for which he or she may be compensated at some point after the divorce?

8. Has the other party accumulated a high number of frequent flier miles?

9. Has the other party recently made large withdrawals from various accounts for unknown or unexplained purposes, funds that do not appear in another form on an affidavit? Look especially for round-numbered amounts in multiples of $10,000.

10. What is the spouse's travel history? Does he or she receive calls or mail from another country? Does a credit card statement or Passport reflect an overnight trip to the Cayman Islands the day of or after substantial bank withdrawals? Does he or she have business interests in another country or associations with people who do?

11. Is cash being kept in a safe deposit box or in some other location?

12. What kind of business(es) is the other party engaged in? How is the income received? For example, does the party own or work at a gas station where receipts are tied to gas pump readings, or in a restaurant where large sums of cash and tips are received and may or may not be declared or deposited in the business's accounts? Does the other party have a history of working "under the table"? Has the person postponed executing lucrative business contracts until after the divorce?

13. If the other party owns a business, are funds being paid to nonexistent employees or close relatives or friends for work that was never performed or services that were never received?

14. Is cash being kept in the form of traveler's checks?

15. Has the other party set up a custodial account in the name of a child, using the child's Social Security number?

16. Have investments been made in certificate "bearer" municipal bonds or Series EE Savings Bonds, which are not registered with the IRS and do not appear on account statements?

17. Has the other party recently paid off (from marital funds) mortgages or credit card balances in his or her name? Are intentional overpayments being made to other creditors?

18. During the marriage, and especially recently, has the opposing party transferred assets to a relative, friend, or paramour?

19. Did the other party cease having bank and other statements sent to the marital residence?

20. Does a credit report check reveal any irregular or otherwise suspicious activity?

E-Discovery: The Discovery of Electronically Stored Information (ESI)

Over the past two decades, technological innovation has dramatically altered the ways in which we learn, conduct business, communicate, entertain ourselves, and store information about every aspect of our lives. The primary focus of **electronic discovery** (e-discovery) is on finding this electronically stored information. Electronically stored information (ESI) has been defined as "information created, manipulated, communicated, stored and best utilized in digital form, requiring the use of computer hardware and software."[3] It includes, for example, documents and spreadsheets, e-mails, voicemails, text messages, metadata, digital images, and video. ESI may be stored in many kinds of devices, including laptops, desktops, cell phones, digital cameras, business networks, company e-mail servers, and loose media devices (e.g., DVDs and thumb drives). It includes data stored online from free Internet mail servers like Juno and Hotmail, **social network** services such as Facebook and Twitter, and Personals sites including Match.com and Adult Friend Finder.[4] It can also be found in less common places such as iPhones, MP3 players, video game consoles, GPS devices, and in the "**cloud**" in online sources of data and backup storage such as Mozy or Carbonite.

The impact of technological advances has inevitably been felt throughout the legal system as legislatures, courts, and lawyers try to weave discovery of electronically stored information into legal practice and decision making. The challenge of doing so is an evolving one, which is unlikely to end anytime soon. In a 2008 survey, 88% of the members of the American Academy of Matrimonial Lawyers (AAML) reported that they had seen an increase in the use of electronic evidence in family law cases over the previous five years. Most commonly used or encountered were e-mails, text messages, and browsing histories in addition to evidence from Facebook, MySpace, Twitter, and other social networking sites including YouTube and LinkedIn. Used to a lesser extent are electronically stored documents such as word files, contact lists, and financial programs and spreadsheets.[5]

Thus far the trend among the states appears to be to treat discovery of ESI in essentially the same manner as discovery of other kinds of materials and adapt existing rules to accommodate its unique nature when necessary. This approach is consistent with the amended Federal Rules of Civil Procedure and Evidence, the Guidelines for State Courts promulgated by the Conference of Chief Justices in 2006, and the Uniform Rules Relating to Electronically Stored Information (adopted in Wisconsin and Connecticut and introduced in Rhode Island as of January 2015). The Uniform Rules impose upon litigants the obligation to discuss electronic discovery at the outset of litigation. Parties must confer regarding the forms of production and the extent to which data is to be preserved. Once a party receives a request for production of electronically stored information, the party must permit discovery of information that is relevant, not privileged, and reasonably accessible.

Although they are likely to increase in future years as new technologies emerge and precedents are set, fewer electronic discovery cases have reached the appellate level than one might expect. (See Paralegal Application 6.11.) Thus far, cases have largely been decided on a fact-driven case by case basis with the courts trying to balance the parties' rights to privacy with their need for information relevant to their cases. When addressing objections to production of ESI, especially social media evidence, the courts typically do one or more of the following:

- refuse to grant a motion to compel production of ESI because the request is overbroad, calls for privileged information, or is otherwise objectionable on some common ground
- grant the motion and compel production in some instances, going so far as to order the parties to exchange passwords directly or through counsel[6]
- elect to conduct an in-camera review of the requested material
- order a party to exercise a consent to allow the other party access to the information
- allocate costs between the parties or assign them to the requesting party
- order that a party's computer and storage media be seized and searched if it is demonstrated there is a strong likelihood the opponent is likely to destroy electronic evidence prior to production

PARALEGAL PRACTICE TIP

A request for production/seizure of the other party's computer equipment, storage devices, etc., may be made by means of an *ex parte* motion to the court when there is a strong fear that the other party will destroy or alter the data stored on the computer equipment. Care must be taken to make such requests in a form the client and/or attorney can read, understand, analyze, and afford.

Paralegal **Application 6.11**

Electronic Discovery Case: You Be the Judge

Read the full opinion in the following case and see if you agree with the court's reasoning.

1. *Byrne v. Byrne*, 650 N.Y.S.2d 499 (1996). In this case, the court considered a dispute over who should be permitted access to the husband's notebook computer. The husband's employer provided him with the computer for use in his employment. The husband routinely brought the device home with him and allowed his children to use it to complete their homework. The wife, believing it contained personal and financial records relevant to the pending divorce, took it to her attorney to access relevant documents. At the time of the hearing on this issue, the computer was under the control of the court. The husband claimed it was personal property, albeit not owned by him (although the employer did not restrict its use), and that it was not subject to discovery. The wife claimed she should have access because it contained relevant financial records that are normally subject to discovery. The court reasoned that the real issue was not who possessed the computer but rather who had access to its memory. Because of the way it was used, the court found that the computer could be characterized as a "family computer" and further held that "… computer memory is akin to a file cabinet. Clearly the plaintiff could have access to the contents of a file cabinet left in the marital residence. In the same fashion, she should have access to the contents of the computer." The court held that the only way to determine if the wife was correct was to have the contents of the computer memory opened up or "dumped" and analyzed and in its order the court outlined the process by which this would take place (an inventory of contents to counsel, a period of review and raising of any claims of privilege, a release of the contents to the wife's counsel, and return of the computer to the employer).

E-discovery provides both challenges and opportunities for attorneys. ESI provides a rich source that can be mined for information which can be used to support (or refute) a client's case. But it also triggers ethical duties such as the duty to provide competent representation and to avoid revealing client confidences. (See Paralegal Application 6.12.) Family law attorneys must develop their technical skills, stay current with respect to technological advances, and know how to economically and effectively locate, preserve, collect, review, and utilize reasonably necessary electronically stored information. They must review information sent to opposing counsel and screen material produced in response to discovery requests to avoid inadvertent disclosure of confidential or privileged information. They also must make a reasonable effort to ensure that their paralegals' conduct is consistent with these same ethical obligations. In addition, attorneys need to provide appropriate guidance to clients with respect to their online activities and security measures.

Paralegal **Application 6.12**

Hypothetical Dilemmas: What Do You Think?

Revisit Chapter 1 to review the distinction between an evidentiary privilege and an ethical duty and then consider the following dilemmas that involve storage and transmission of electronically stored information.

Is the attorney-client privilege waived?[7]

Suppose Attorney Wasik accidentally sends the wrong attachment in an e-mail to opposing counsel in a hotly contested custody case. Instead of a proposed Stipulation regarding Temporary Custody, he inadvertently attaches a recent e-mail to him from his client, Pat S., in which she admits that in the past, she has physically abused the parties' son, especially when under the influence of illegal drugs. The e-mail was initially protected by attorney-client privilege. Has the privilege now been waived? Can the e-mail now be admitted as evidence against the mother in the custody litigation? Check to see if it would be waived if the situation were governed by the revised Federal Rules of Evidence, specifically 502(b). Would it be waived under your state's rules of evidence?

Has the attorney violated the ethical duty to maintain client confidences?[8]

Suppose Attorney Cheff directs his paralegal, Lucy, to send a proposed separation agreement (a Word Document) to opposing counsel in a divorce case for review and consideration. The agreement has previously undergone several revisions as Attorney Cheff's settlement strategy has evolved. When she sent the document, the paralegal was unaware that it contained metadata—invisible data that is generated during creation and editing of the document. Among other things, it provides information about when and by whom the document was created. It also tracks edits and reveals prior versions of the document. Metadata is automatically linked with an electronically stored document and travels with it when it is transmitted if steps to remove it are not taken, such as using metadata scrubbing software. Has the sending attorney violated the ethical duty to maintain client confidences? Has he violated other ethical duties? Can the receiving attorney (whose paralegal knows how to access it) use the metadata or would that constitute an intrusion into the attorney–client relationship to gain an unfair advantage? Look at Rule 4.4(b) of the *ABA Model Rules of Professional Conduct* as well as Formal Op. 06-442 of the ABA Standing Committee on Ethics addressing this topic. Both can be found at *www.americanbar.org*. The states are divided in their positions. What approach has your state taken, if any? What do you think is the right course of action?

DISCOVERY OF ELECTRONICALLY STORED INFORMATION

Earlier in this chapter, examples have been provided of how both traditional informal and formal discovery methods can be used to discover ESI. The approach taken depends in part on the nature of the documents sought, the reason for seeking them, the use to be made of them, and the relative likelihood of the other party altering or destroying them. If all that is needed is a copy of a document from a trusted source, then a simple (and inexpensive) informal request for the document may suffice. At the other end of the spectrum, if what is needed are complex records concerning the values of multiple business interests of an uncooperative and deceptive opposing party, an e-discovery request in the form of a request for production may seek seizure of one or more computers and ancillary equipment for detailed inspection by forensic computing experts using sophisticated tools.

Properly obtained, ESI may be admitted as evidence to prove facts in a case or to impeach the credibility of a party or witness. For example, if access to ESI storage devices themselves is obtained, a computer forensic expert can uncover a wealth of information such as the following:

- Elaborate user profiles on Facebook, LinkedIn, and Google Profile etc. may reveal a wide range of personal data, which may or may not accurately reflect the user's identity and circumstances. Paralegal Application 6.13 provides some suggestions about obtaining information from social networking sites in particular.
- Installed programs will include file sharing applications that allow a user to search for and collect digital images that may be analyzed in terms of the types of images sought (e.g., pornographic).
- Analyses of unallocated file space may reveal "deleted" data that hasn't yet been overwritten by new data.
- Because Internet web browsers keep files (called cache files) that automatically index a user's browser history in detail, an expert can create a timeline of computer activity reflecting when and with what frequency users visited certain sites, such as the thousands that offer online legal and illegal purchases of prescription drugs.[9]

PARALEGAL PRACTICE TIP

In *Stafford v. Stafford*, 641 A.2d 348 (Vt. 1993), a wife in a divorce action put informal discovery to good use. She had previously found a notebook in the marital home, containing a list and description of her husband's sexual encounters, but the notebook disappeared. She subsequently found a document on the family computer called "My List" saved by the husband and sought to admit it as evidence at trial. The court concluded there was no error in admitting the electronically stored document and inferring from it the husband's infidelity.

PARALEGAL PRACTICE TIP

In *Lewton v. DiVingnzzo*, 772 F. Supp.2d 1046 (2012) (U.S. Dist. Ct. D. Nebraska), a man sued his wife under the Electronic Communications Privacy Act for civil damages after she hid a digital recording device in their child's teddy bear and recorded conversations between the child and her father for several months. The wife had resorted to "self help" measures after her husband was awarded unsupervised visitation with the child.

Paralegal **Application 6.13**

Social Media Sites as Discovery Targets

Characterized less than ten years ago by a court as "one large catalyst for rumor, innuendo and misinformation,"[10] and more recently as "electronic exhibitionism,"[11] social media have transformed the way people communicate. Social networking sites are incredibly seductive for millions of users who choose to upload highly personal information, post pictures and videos depicting themselves in a variety of settings and engaging in diverse activities, airing their concerns, interests, opinions as well as their relationship status and preferences. With more than half of all Americans using them, social networking sources provide a rich opportunity to seek and find incriminating information about parties and witnesses. Facebook claims to be the most popular site with Twitter being the second most popular, as of 2014. LinkedIn, the world's largest professional network, has well over 120 million users.

The evidence obtained from such sources can support alleged grounds for divorce, influence custody and visitation orders, and impact support and property division awards.

- A profile may represent a party seeking a divorce and custody as being single, childless, and interested in dating.

(Continued)

- A post promoting a party's professional services might reveal an "under-the-table" source of income not listed in a financial statement.
- Photographs and their captions posted on a network page or "wall" can reveal compromising relationships, possessions, activities, etc.
- A list of interests, group affiliations, and activities might yield names of potential witnesses and dates and places of meetings at which parties or other key people can be found.
- Social plans or experiences shared with friends might lead directly to compromising revelations.

There are several ways of accessing information from these sites. Consider the following examples.

Informal discovery

Some informal discovery appears to be acceptable, subject to ethical considerations. It is often the easiest and least expensive tool. Search for and view as much publically available information as possible. For example:

- Conduct a search on a name on Google, Bing, or other search engines for any social networking profiles that are publicly viewable
- Go to search engines of social networking sites directly
- Go to a site like Spokeo.com, which aggregates information on any person from multiple sites

When engaging in informal discovery, caution must be exercised to avoid running afoul of federal and state laws. No matter how relevant the material may be to a case, the Electronic Communications Privacy Act 18 U.S.C. § 2510 et seq. makes it unlawful for a person to intentionally intercept (while it is being sent from the sender to the recipient) any oral, wire, or electronic communication or to use or disclose any such communication. Reading a copy of a document already sent will not violate this Act but may violate some other Act such as the Stored Communications Act 18 U.S.C. §2701 et seq. (SCA), which imposes liability on individuals for accessing ESI without authorization and third party providers such as Facebook for revealing ESI created by or about their customers and subscribers. In effect, this Act creates Fourth Amendment-like protection for e-mail and digital communications stored on the Internet. See *O'Brien v. O'Brien*, 899 So. 2d 1133 (Fla. Dist. App. 2005). Even if ESI is not discoverable through informal means, it may be through formal discovery methods.

Formal discovery

If a party wants and needs information from social networking sites, it is worth trying and letting the courts address objections. Consider the following examples of how formal discovery might be used.

Interrogatories: Interrogatories open the door. Early in the case, they can be used to seek information about the opposing party's use of social media sites, screen names, passwords, and other account information.

Requests for Admissions: A party may be asked to admit that they: (1) terminated all of their social networking services immediately after being served with the complaint for divorce; and (2) authored and transmitted on a specific date a particular post to a particular **social network** and that the copy of the post attached to the request is a true and accurate copy of the transmitted message. Given how easy it is to manipulate posts and make them look as if they were made by someone else, it can be hard to establish the authenticity of such material at trial. A properly crafted admission can accomplish this in advance.

Depositions: The deponent may be asked questions about their online social networking activities including personal profiles that misrepresent their marital status. Paper printouts of screen shots of a website may be produced or their Facebook page may be opened in the context of the deposition and questions can be asked about various photos, status updates, and posts.

Requests for Production:

From third parties: A subpoena may be served on a service provider/social media site but it is unlikely to yield any more than basic subscriber account information given federal regulations.

From the opposing party directly: The best method is a well-tailored request to the other party who is already in possession of the desired information or has ready access to it. The request should not seek unrestricted access to all social media content. It should be time-limited, narrowly tailored to produce relevant information and reasonably calculated to lead to admissible evidence related to a fact at issue. For example, if the opposing party alleges he has a disability that prevents him from working and paying support, the spouse should be entitled to discover evidence that he is not injured as claimed. The request might seek "all online profiles, postings, messages (including but not limited to tweets, direct messages, status updates, wall comments, and blog entries), photographs, videos, and online communication relating to his physical condition and employment over the past six months." Facebook can actually facilitate production because it has a feature that allows a user to download a copy of material he or she has shared on the site. As an alternative to production, the opponent may be asked or ordered by the court to execute a notarized consent/authorization permitting the holder to obtain private social media content directly from the site (an option permitted by the SCA). Once requested, there is a duty to preserve the requested material or risk sanctions for spoliation. If a party refuses to respond to a request for production, a motion to compel may be filed at which point the court will likely hear an objection that the request violates a right to privacy. (See Paralegal Application 6.14.)

Paralegal **Application 6.14**

Is There a Social Networking Privilege?[12] Do Privacy Concerns Trump a Party's Right to Discovery of Social Networking Evidence?

Many social networking sites provide some measures of privacy protection to users although surprisingly many users post freely. The sites also typically refuse to respond to direct subpoenas, claiming that their data is protected under the federal Electronic Communications Privacy and Electronic Communications Acts. But that is not the end of the matter. Several courts have held that Facebook information, even if "protected" by privacy settings, is discoverable if relevant and material to the claims of a party. Do you think users of social networking sites should have a right to privacy in their online activity? Should information on sites such as Facebook be discoverable even if allegedly protected by privacy settings? When people create Facebook accounts and the like, do you think they may have impliedly consented to the possibility that personal information might be shared with others notwithstanding their privacy settings?

Court Involvement in the Discovery Process

Courts generally affirm a party's right to conduct comprehensive and liberal discovery and prefer not to become involved in the process unless mandated by procedural rules (as in the case of Requests for Mental or Physical Examinations) or by the unique circumstances of individual cases or the conduct of counsel or the parties. The most common ways in which the courts become involved are:

1. **Discovery Conferences.** A court may, on its own initiative, pursuant to court rule, or at the request of a party, order that a discovery conference be convened, at which time a discovery plan is reviewed or developed and agreed upon. The plan typically sets out the appropriate topics for discovery, the discovery methods to be used by each of the parties, and the timeline within which discovery must be completed. Most states have in place procedures for managing discovery under the court's supervision (through a "discovery master") to ensure that the parties make reasonable and timely requests and responses.

2. **Protective Orders.** A court will entertain a motion for a protective order brought by a party who contends, for example, that a discovery request seeks privileged information, is excessive and would lead to undue burden or

PARALEGAL PRACTICE TIP

An example of a case management agreement can be accessed at *www.jud.ct.gov* (Connecticut) (Attorneys/Forms/Family/JD-FM-163).

expense, or is made in bad faith solely for the purpose of harassment. If the motion is granted, the court will establish limitations on discovery.

3. **Orders to Compel and Impose Sanctions for Noncompliance.** When a party fails to comply with a discovery request, the party making the request may file a motion to compel. If granted, the discovery request then becomes, in effect, an order of the court, and a failure to comply may result in sanctions. For example, the noncomplying party may be held in contempt of court and be ordered to pay the fees the other party incurred in pursuing the matter. In especially egregious cases, if he or she is the moving party in the underlying action, the matter may be stayed or dismissed or the party may be prevented from introducing related evidence at trial. In some jurisdictions, prior to filing a motion to compel, the parties are required to exhaust efforts to settle the discovery dispute without the assistance of the court.

CHAPTER **SUMMARY**

This chapter provides a comprehensive survey of the discovery process—its nature, scope, purposes, and methods, both formal and informal. Attention is given to the ways in which the client can contribute to information-gathering efforts. The five major formal discovery methods are described and examples are provided from family law cases: interrogatories, depositions, requests for admissions, requests for production of documents and things, and requests for physical and mental examinations. The nature, role, and importance of financial affidavits are also addressed.

Throughout the chapter, the paralegal's role in the discovery process is heavily emphasized. Several reminders are provided regarding related ethical duties and the importance of being aware of the substantive laws and procedural rules governing discovery. Additional topics relevant to discovery are also considered, including objections to discovery requests, the challenge of uncovering hidden assets, and the court's involvement in the process. Given the extent to which technology has greatly altered the manner in which businesses and individuals create, store, and retrieve information, particular attention is given to electronic discovery—the accessing of electronically stored information—and the Internet and social networking sites in particular as fertile sources of information.

CONCEPT REVIEW AND REINFORCEMENT

KEY **TERMS**

Cloud
Deponent
Deposition
Discovery
Electronic discovery
Expert
Forensic accountant
Formal discovery
Informal discovery

Interrogatories
Lay witness
Letters rogatory
Mandatory self-disclosure
Notice of deposition
Privilege
Protective order
Request for Admissions

Request for Physical or Mental
   Examination
Request for Production of Documents
   or Things
Social network
Subpoena
Subpoena *duces tecum*
Work product

REVIEW **QUESTIONS**

1. Distinguish between "formal" and "informal discovery", and give an example of each.
2. Describe how the client can assist in the information-gathering process.

3. Identify each of the five formal discovery methods, and give an example of when and how each might be used in a family law case.
4. Identify the strengths and weaknesses of each of the five formal discovery methods.

5. Identify the kinds of objections that can be made to discovery requests.
6. Describe the nature and purpose of financial statements/affidavits.
7. Identify a minimum of five ways of concealing assets and how they might be detected.
8. Describe e-discovery and give three examples of when and how it might be used.
9. Describe the significance of social networking sites in the family law context.
10. Describe the role of the paralegal in the discovery process.
11. Describe the role the court plays in the discovery process.

DEVELOPING YOUR PARALEGAL SKILLS

FOCUS ON THE JOB

In this activity, the student will develop a discovery strategy tailored to the facts of a specific case.

The Facts

Walter and Renee Albertson have been married thirty-seven years and have three adult children: Eleanor, Edward, and Walter, Jr. The marriage has been rocky and each party believes that the other has been "unfaithful" on several occasions. The only confirmed affair occurred in 1996, when Renee became involved with a next-door neighbor and at one point moved in with him after Walter "threw her out" of the marital home because of the ongoing and open affair. After a month, he begged her to come home. She did, and they went to counseling, reconciled, and resumed their marital relationship. However, Walter never really trusted Renee after that. As a result, he kept all of his assets as separate as possible from hers, with the exception of a joint bank account, out of which he paid all of the expenses related to the marital home as well as the food bills and car-related costs. Renee has been depositing her entire paycheck into this account, but Walter only matches what she puts in. He earns funds from four sources: Social Security, a modest salary as a school bus driver, an investment portfolio he established in 1985 and has maintained ever since, and money he earns doing electrical work "under the table," for which he is paid cash or "in-kind" (e.g., he does some wiring for his mechanic, and the mechanic repairs Walter's vehicle without charging him). He deposits his Social Security into the joint account along with about 20% of his check from the bus company. Throughout the marriage, he has maintained the couple's finances and largely kept Renee "in the dark," although he does give her a modest weekly "allowance." He has always kept extensive financial and business records on his computer. He pays his bills online and uses Turbo Tax to prepare the parties' joint tax returns.

The marital home (jointly held) is assessed at $350,000 for property tax purposes, but Walter claims it is worth closer to $500,000, based on work he has done building an addition that includes a den, bedroom, and bath with a hot tub in it. He spent the better part of a year doing the work in his free time. There is a $112,000 mortgage and a $20,000 equity loan secured by the property. The parties had to obtain the loan to cover income taxes (plus interest and penalties) due on previously undeclared income Walter had collected doing electrical work for friends and acquaintances. He asserts that he is not still doing this work, but Renee is certain he continues to do it and not pay taxes on the funds collected or on in-kind services received. He claims to never have any money but went to Aruba for a week in January 2015, allegedly alone, and has a new Toyota convertible, for which Renee believes he paid cash. She also saw a credit card statement that listed expenditures at two local jewelry stores and several local restaurants that she has not been to with him.

In December 2014, Renee became suspicious that Walter was having an affair with his old high school sweetheart, Valentina Ferrara, with whom he "reconnected" at his fiftieth high school reunion. Valentina had recently been widowed. Walter admits that he is "in touch" with her (particularly by telephone and e-mail) but that she would never consider having an intimate relationship with him as long as he is still married. Besides, he claims that at the age of seventy, he is no longer able to function sexually. Renee believes he is seeing a doctor and has a prescription for "that little blue pill." Renee's heart is broken, and she has filed for divorce on the ground of adultery in a jurisdiction that retains fault grounds.

The Assignment

Assume that you are a paralegal working for Attorney Juliana Dahl Johnson who represents Renee in the above hypothetical. You have been asked to suggest an appropriate discovery plan to guide the information-gathering effort in this case. The plan you propose should identify the kinds of information needed, the techniques to be utilized (both formal and informal), the sequencing of efforts, and the assignment of tasks. After she reviews and approves the plan, the attorney will eventually estimate the projected cost and discuss the plan with Renee. The fact pattern indicates Renee is filing for divorce on the grounds of adultery. Assume that in the jurisdiction where you reside and/or are employed, when making property division decisions, the court considers both conduct during the marriage and financial and nonfinancial contribution to the marital enterprise. Your plan should include at a minimum five examples of informal discovery.

It should also include use of at least three methods of formal discovery with examples of the kinds of information to be sought using each method. You should consider weaving electronic discovery into various aspects of your plan.

FOCUS ON **ETHICS**

In this assignment, the student has an opportunity to consider the ethical issues raised when a client appears to be providing inaccurate and deceptive information on a financial affidavit.

The Assignment

Assume that Walter is your supervising attorney's client. He has given you a completed draft of his financial affidavit/statement and claims that it accurately reflects all of his assets and liabilities. You are aware of all of the information presented in the above Focus on the Job fact pattern and are concerned that Walter's affidavit is very likely not accurate, and yet he must sign it under oath. In addition, you are employed in a jurisdiction where his attorney must also sign the affidavit, indicating that to the best of his or her knowledge, the document contains no false information. Some of the things you are concerned about are that Walter has listed no credit card debt but does reflect a loan from his brother for $8,000, which he tells you should help him in the property settlement even though he doesn't really have to pay his brother back.

He indicates his Social Security and bus driving income but reflects no income from investments or his work as an electrician, income you are reasonably certain he receives. He lists the joint account but no other accounts or cash assets. He has listed the value of the marital home as $500,000 less the mortgage and claims he doesn't have to list the equity loan because it was incurred to buy a car for Renee and he should not have to be liable for any of it. He also indicates that he pays 100% of the household expenses because, after all, he writes all the checks. None of this surprises you as you have disliked this client from the outset and find his conduct during the marriage reprehensible. As a paralegal, what course of action should you take, and how would you recommend the situation be addressed? Which of the ethical canons for paralegals promulgated by the National Association of Legal Assistants, contained in Appendix A, are applicable in this context? Also consider the material on ethics provided in Chapter 1 of this text as well as the code governing the professional conduct of attorneys in your state. Present your recommendations in a one- to two-page report.

FOCUS ON **CASE LAW**

In this activity, the student is asked to brief a case in which a wife in a divorce proceeding sought attorneys fees for legal costs she incurred when her husband hid assets and failed to comply with the court's discovery orders.

The Assignment

Brief the case, *Ramin v. Ramin*, 281 Conn. 324, 915 A.2d 790 (2007), using the format available at *www.pearsonhighered*

.com/careersresources/ on the website for this text in the material related to Chapter 1 under Resources, unless an alternative format is provided by your instructor. You can find the opinion at the same site in the material related to Chapter 6 under Cases.

FOCUS ON **STATE LAW AND PROCEDURE**

In this focus, the student is asked to research discovery-related rules, procedures, and forms in his or her jurisdiction.

The Assignment

1. Locate the rules governing the five formal discovery methods in family law cases in your jurisdiction.

   Does the state mandate any particular discovery forms/formats?
2. Does your jurisdiction have any rules governing electronic discovery in family law cases?
3. What forms of mandatory self-disclosure, if any, does the state in which you reside (or are employed) require of parties to a divorce action?

4. Obtain and review a copy of your state's financial affidavit form. Assume that Walter is the client in the case you are working on and the facts are the same as in the Focus on the Job hypothetical in this chapter. Make a list of the kinds of documents and information you need to gather in order to help him complete his financial affidavit/statement.

FOCUS ON **TECHNOLOGY**

In addition to the links contained in the chapter, this activity provides a series of useful websites for reference, along with technology-related assignments for completion.

Websites of Interest

www.findlaw.com

Findlaw's Legal Technology Center has instituted an Electronic Discovery Rule Wizard, an online interactive tool to help legal professionals understand the amended Federal Rules of Civil Procedure and improve their use of e-discovery methods and procedures.

www.lectlaw.com

At this site, you can locate a set of interrogatories approved by the Florida State Supreme Court for use in family law cases. Go to "General Law Practice Forms" and select Interrogatories to Client (FL Domestic Relations).

www.courts.ca.gov

At this California courts site, you can locate a number of forms, including family law interrogatories, financial affidavits, a subpoena, and a subpoena duces tecum (Forms and Rules/ Discovery).

Assignments

1. Locate online the financial statements for five states including your own. A good place to start your search is with the websites for courts in various states. The list of websites provided in Appendix C may be helpful.
2. Assume that you are currently married and a party to a divorce action. Complete (online, if possible) the appropriate financial affidavit/statement you would need to submit in the jurisdiction where you reside. This assignment is designed to be a private individual exercise.

There is no requirement that it be shared with fellow students or the instructor, absent consent.

3. Assuming the facts in the above Focus on the Job hypothetical, draft an *ex parte* motion on Renee's behalf, seeking to stop Walter from using his laptop and storage devices (such as CD-ROMs, flash memory devices, or any other similar type of storage device). You might want to request that he immediately produce and deposit the laptop and storage devices with the court in which the divorce action has been filed (your local family court) for examination by a recognized computer expert, who may later present testimony under oath regarding relevant contents. You should consider building in provisions addressing how and by whom the contents will be examined, how privileged contents will be protected, what arrangements will be made for temporarily replacing the laptop, and who will bear related costs.

4. Using *www.findlaw.com*,
   a. locate the federal rules of civil procedure regarding electronic discovery.
   b. locate electronic discovery rules in effect in your state, if any.

5. Assume that the client, Renee, has tried to access her husband's Facebook account and her access is blocked. Your supervisor suggests that one of her friends gain access without revealing any connection to her attorney. Would this course of action be ethical? Begin your research by reviewing two conflicting bar association opinions available online: Philadelphia Bar Association Guidance Committee Op. 843 (2010) and NYC Bar Association Committee on Professional Ethics Op. 843 (2010).

PORTFOLIO PRODUCTS

1. Discovery Plan in a hypothetical case
2. Recommendations regarding ethical issues pertaining to completion of a financial statement
3. Brief of a case involving an electronic discovery issue
4. List of rules governing discovery matters in the student's jurisdiction
5. List of documents/information needed to complete a client's financial statement

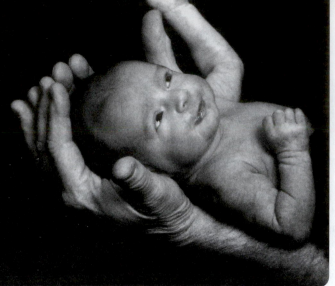

© Richard Tauson

chapter 7

PARENTHOOD

Stephen and Mary are in their early thirties. They have been married for four years and want to spend the rest of their lives together. The only thing needed to complete the picture is a child, but Stephen carries a rare genetic disease, and Mary had a hysterectomy a few years ago due to uterine cancer. They have decided to search for egg and sperm donors who carry the traits they consider desirable and then have Mary's best friend, Carol, serve as a surrogate mother. Carol and her husband, Chip, are all for the idea.

LEARNING OBJECTIVES

After reading this chapter and completing related assignments, you should be able to:

- identify the three parties most interested in parentage determinations

- identify the most common ways in which legal parenthood is established

- list examples of presumptions sometimes used to determine parenthood

- describe the nature and effect of a voluntary acknowledgment of parentage

- provide examples of claims to parenthood that may be addressed through adjudication

- describe the basic process for adjudicating paternity

- explain how parenthood may be disestablished

- define paternity fraud

- identify various applications of assisted reproductive technology

- give examples of ways in which gays and lesbians, married and unmarried, can become parents

- discuss some of the ways in which courts and legislatures are addressing surrogacy agreements, cryopreserved embryos, and posthumous reproduction

- describe the role of the paralegal in cases involving determination of parentage

Introduction

The content of this chapter and the next three on adoption, child custody, and child support further extend a basic theme of this text: Society and the law are confronting changes in the way people define parenthood, create families, and assign responsibility for children. Although preference for the "traditional family" model is still strong, doors have opened to innovative means of conceiving and giving birth and to new bases for establishing legal parenthood, especially for same-sex spouses. These developments and the primary reasons for them are highlighted in the following excerpts from opinions of the Maine Supreme Court and the U.S. Supreme Court.

> For some time now, we and other courts have been considering the law of parentage in light of advancements in technology, changes in social norms and family structures, and the resulting ever-expanding list of legal issues relating to children and families. . . .[c]hanges in family structure have been identified and attributed to "at least three areas in our society which have undergone significant change," namely, (1) "considerable scientific and technological advances," (2) "the acknowledgement by

many states of the rights of persons of the same sex to be considered parents of the same child," and (3) "the change from what we once knew as the traditional American family" consisting of two married parents and their children. *Pitts v. Moore,* 2014 ME 59, 90 A.3d 1169 (2014) quoting *Bancroft v. Jameson,* 19 A.3d 730, 738-39 (Del. Fam. Ct. 2010).

> [T]he demographic changes of the past century make it difficult to speak of an average American family. The composition of families varies greatly from household to household. While many children may have two married parents and grandparents who visit regularly, many other children are raised in single-parent households. . . . Understandably, in these single-parent households, persons outside the nuclear family are called upon with increasing frequency to assist in the everyday tasks of child rearing. *Troxel v. Granville,* 530 U.S. 57, 63-64, 120 S. Ct. 2054, 147 L. Ed. 2d 49 (2000) (plurality opinion)

In this chapter and the next, we explore some of the ways in which families are formed. The upcoming chapter on adoption discusses the creation of parent–child relationships solely by legal process. In this chapter, the primary focus is on situations in which biology and "acting like a parent" play the key roles as determinants of a child's legal **parentage**. We will examine some of the most common ways of establishing **parenthood** in cases involving both heterosexual and gay individuals with an emphasis on how paternity is established and may be "disestablished." A discussion of the contemporary concept of parenthood in a family law text would be incomplete without some consideration of the fascinating, complex and, for some, disturbing topic of assisted reproductive technology (ART): its use to create children and related questions and problems it raises.

"Who's your mother?" was once a reasonably simple question to answer. Even "Who's your father?" was not that complicated, depending on the mother's marital status. However, with the emergence of reproductive technologies and recognition of the right of same-sex couples to marry, even the answer to "Who's your mother?" is not so simple anymore. (See Exhibit 7.1.) Consider the following questions:

- Should parenthood flow on a strict liability basis, solely from the performance of a sexual act regardless of the circumstances or intent of the parties to create a child? If so, how do we deal with cases involving nonconsensual sexual relations, statutory rape,[1] or partners who lie about the use of birth control measures?
- Should children be permitted to have more than two "legal" parents?
- Should parents have to act like parents in order to be considered parents?
- Should the mother's marital status be the sole criterion for determining parentage?
- Should individuals be able to assign parental status by contract?
- Should parenthood be a fixed status—once a parent, always a parent?
- Should children have a voice in parentage determinations?
- Should same-sex couples, who cannot procreate without the assistance of reproductive technology, be permitted by law to become parents (by marriage, contract, adoption or otherwise)?

Parentage
the identity and origins of one's parents

Parenthood
the position, function or standing of being a parent; the state of being or acting as a co-parent with all of the associated responsibilities

PARALEGAL PRACTICE TIP

One of the arguments often raised in opposition to legal recognition of gay co-parents is that a child needs both a mother and a father, as opposed to simply two parents including the option of two mothers or two fathers. The claim is that "A child needs both a mother-figure and a father-figure in order to develop to his (or her) maximum potential. Implicit in this argument . . . is the assertion that fathers have certain traits that mothers cannot utilize or model as well as fathers can, and that mothers have certain traits that fathers cannot utilize or model as well as mothers can."[2] Do you agree?

Biological parent
a blood-related parent who contributes half of a child's genetic material by means of a reproductive cell (egg or sperm); sometimes called a genetic or natural parent

Co-parent
a person who is engaged in a non-marital relationship with the legal parent of a child and who regards himself or herself as a parent rather than as a legal stranger to the child; a person who shares childrearing responsibilities with a partner with or without benefit of a legally recognized relationship

De facto parent
[Latin: in point of fact] an individual who performs a caretaking role without compensation for an extended period knowing he or she is not a child's legal parent; often with the consent of the legal parent(s)

Gestational mother
a woman who carries and gives birth to a child; the woman may or may not be biologically related to the child

Legal parent
a person who is recognized as a child's parent under state and/or federal law

Parent by estoppel
essentially provides that a person may be designated the legal parent of a child if he or she has held himself or herself out as the child's parent and has supported the child emotionally and financially; a theory used to establish parenting rights that asserts a legal parent should not be permitted to deny a co-parent's parental status based on a prior agreement with the legal parent, on which the co-parent relied, to raise a child together; parenthood based on the fact an individual has functioned as a parent with the approval of a child's legal parents

Psychological parent
the individual who has the strongest "parental" bond with the child, who has provided the most significant care in quality and quantity, and whom the child often regards as the "parent"

EXHIBIT 7.1 When Is a Parent a Parent?

- **Acknowledged parent:** a parent who has executed an affidavit acknowledging parentage
- **Adoptive parent:** a person who, by means of legal process, becomes a parent of a child to whom he or she is usually biologically unrelated
- **Biological parent:** a blood-related parent who contributes half of the child's genetic material by means of a reproductive cell (egg or sperm); sometimes called a genetic or "natural" parent
- **Co-parent:** a person who shares childrearing responsibilities with a partner with or without benefit of a legally recognized parent–child relationship
- **De facto parent:** a person who has been a primary caregiver and financial supporter of a child, usually with consent of the legal parent and for a requisite period of time
- **Egg or sperm donor:** a person who donates genetic material (sometimes for a fee) to help others have a child; donors often remain anonymous and usually give up any parental rights they would otherwise have to a child they may help to create
- **Equitable parent:** a parent based on principles of fairness rather than on biological connection; a person who is willing and able to assume parental rights and responsibilities and has done so in the past
- **Foster parent:** a person who takes care of a child for a temporary period of time, usually for a modest payment through a child welfare agency
- **Gestational mother:** a woman who carries and delivers a child
- **Intended parent(s):** a person or couple who intend to take custody of and assume all parental rights and responsibilities for a child as a result of an adoption, a surrogacy arrangement, or some other technique of assisted reproduction; an intended parent may or may not be genetically related to the child
- **Legal parent:** a person who is recognized as a child's parent under state and/or federal law
- **Natural parent:** a mother or father who is a biological (genetic) parent of a child
- **Parent by estoppel:** an individual who, although not a legal parent, lives with and accepts parental responsibilities for a child and on whose emotional and financial support the child and the other parent have relied
- **Presumed father:** a man who is presumed to be the father of a child who is conceived/born during the course of his marriage to the mother (or within a certain period thereafter)
- **Psychological parent:** the individual who has the strongest "parental" bond with the child, who has provided the most significant care for the child in quality and quantity, and whom the child often regards as a "parent"
- **Putative father:** a man who may be the father of a child but who was not married to the child's mother at the time of birth and whose paternity has not yet been established through legal process
- **Stepparent:** a person who marries the legal mother or father of a child to whom he or she is biologically unrelated
- **Surrogate mother:** a woman who agrees to carry and deliver a baby with an understanding that she will surrender the child to the intended parents at birth or shortly thereafter; a surrogate mother may or may not be genetically related to the child and may or may not be compensated for her services.

Who Are the Interested Parties?

In an era in which several individuals may have legitimate claims to parenthood in a given case, the fundamental question at issue in disputes usually is who are the child's "legal" parents? There are three constituencies most interested in the answer to this question: children, parents, and the government.

THE CHILD

Under early common law, the child's legal status essentially depended on the marital status of his or her parents. Children were regarded as legitimate if born to married parents and illegitimate if born to unmarried parents. If the mother was married and the child was the product of an illicit affair, then legal parentage was established based on a **marital presumption** of legitimacy rather than on biological parenthood. The child of unwed parents was deemed a *filius nullius*, a "child of no one," a bastard with a legal bond to neither parent—essentially a public ward. By the nineteenth century, the states began to move away from penalizing children for their parents' sexual misconduct and toward treating them as innocents warranting protection, support, and nurturance rather than punishment and the stigma of illegitimacy.

Although the law has evolved to some extent, society also has evolved and not always to the benefit of children. According to the U.S. Census Bureau's 2014 Current Population Survey Annual Supplement, the number of children who live with one parent has more than tripled since 1960 from about 9% to 27% of all children under age eighteen. "[M]ore than 13 million children in the U.S. live alone with their single mothers."[3] The precise number of these and other children who may not even know the identities of their biological fathers is virtually impossible to establish, but the numbers are significant. The impact of not knowing the identity of a parent can be monumental for a child as he or she grows into adulthood. The answer to the question "Who am I?" inevitably rests, at least in part, on the answer to the question "Where did I come from?" Even if the answer is not entirely satisfactory, it has many potential emotional, social, economic, medical, and legal advantages for a child. It helps build the child's identity and grants him or her membership in an extended family. It provides the basis for support and inheritance rights. It establishes eligibility for a host of dependent-based governmental benefits. It gives the child standing to sue for wrongful death or other harm to the parent. It opens access to potentially critical medical histories. However, despite its importance, children often confront legal obstacles when they attempt to discover their true parentage. (See Paralegal Application 7.1.)

Marital presumption
the presumption that when a woman gives birth to a child while married or within 300 days of termination of the marriage, her husband is presumed to be the child's legal father

Filius nullius
[Latin: the son (child) of no one]

Paralegal **Application 7.1**

Obstacles to Discovering Parentage

- **The Marital Presumption:** Under the marital presumption, a man married to a child's mother at the time of birth (or within 300 days of termination of the marriage) is presumed to be the child's father even though he may be biologically unrelated to the child. The presumption still carries considerable weight in many jurisdictions.
- **The Doctrine of Estoppel:** The doctrine of estoppel holds a mother and/or a man accountable for their conduct regarding paternity in some circumstances. If either or both of them acts as if the man is a child's father, and the child believes the man to be his or her father, a court may declare the man to be the father by law, and neither the mother nor the "father" may be permitted to request genetic testing to deny paternity at a later date.

- **Issue Preclusion/*res judicata*:** Issue preclusion and *res judicata* principles prevent parties from relitigating in a subsequent suit an issue that was fully litigated and decided in an earlier action. For example, if the issue of paternity of a particular child is raised and decided in the context of a divorce proceeding, in most states neither party is permitted to file a later paternity action seeking to have someone else designated the father of the child.
- **Reproductive Technology Statutes:** Depending on the method of assisted reproductive technology used

(Continued)

to produce a child, states may dictate by statute who will or will not be deemed a legal parent. For example, the Uniform Parentage Act of 2000 (as amended in 2002), adopted in some states, provides that the donor of semen for use in artificial insemination (of a woman other than the donor's wife) will be treated as if he were not the father of a child thereby conceived.

- **Sealed Records/Confidentiality Statutes:** After an adoption is finalized, many states still require that all records of the adoption be sealed, including the child's original birth certificate and any other documents that identify the child's birth parents. In most states, absent an agreement to the contrary, no one can have access to identifying information about the biological parents without a showing of good cause, such as a medical emergency.

Sidebar

Do you believe all children are entitled to know who their "real" parents are, no matter how complex or disturbing their origins may be?

Res judicata

[Latin: a thing adjudicated] an issue that has been definitively settled by judicial decision; requires three essential elements: (1) an earlier decision on the issue, (2) a final judgment on the merits, and (3) the involvement of the original parties

THE PARENTS

The constitutionally protected interest of parents in the care, custody, and control of their children is one of the oldest fundamental liberty interests recognized in American law. But the "right" to be a parent, to establish a home, to raise children and enjoy their companionship and, in many cases, to direct their destinies, technically only attaches to individuals who are legally recognized as parents.

Given the relative ease of establishing maternity based on the biological realities of pregnancy and birth, the legal bond between a mother and her child was the first to be recognized, rendering children "legitimate" at least with respect to their birth mothers. Traditionally, motherhood and a mother's constitutionally protected rights to parent her child flow from the critical role she plays in nourishing the child in her womb and enduring the pain and risks of childbirth. The Supreme Court has described the relationship as "verifiable from the birth itself."[4]

In cases involving establishment of the father–child relationship, particularly those involving men outside of the marital unit, the law has been slower to evolve. However, recognizing the negative impact of illegitimacy on unwed fathers and their children, states began enacting legislation in the early 1800s providing for acknowledgment of paternity and legitimization of children whose parents subsequently married. Further progress was slow but was energized in the 1960s by that era's focus on equal rights and elimination of discrimination in many areas. In a piecemeal fashion and with mixed results, scrutiny has gradually extended to laws that treat unwed mothers and fathers differently and unwed parents and their children differently from married parents and their children based solely on marital status. Consider the following examples:

- In the 1968 *Levy* case, the U.S. Supreme Court held that Louisiana's wrongful death statute violated the Equal Protection Clause of the Constitution by denying children the right to recover for the death of their mother because they were "illegitimate."[5]
- Beginning with *Lehr v. Robertson*[6] in 1983, the U.S. Supreme Court at least began extending rights to unwed fathers in the adoption context, where they previously had none. The Court held that unlike an unwed mother whose legal parenthood is established at birth, an unwed father's rights should be determined using a **"biology-plus" rule**. Under this approach, a biological

PARALEGAL PRACTICE TIP

Laws that discriminate against children based on their parents' marital status continue to exist in some areas. However, to pass constitutional muster, they must serve legitimate governmental purposes such as preventing fraudulent claims for state and federal benefits. For example, it is considered reasonable to condition receipt of dependent-based benefits (such as Social Security Disability Income (SSDI) benefits) on an adjudication or acknowledgment of paternity.

Biology-plus rule

the rule that an unwed father's parental rights are worthy of constitutional protection if the father grasps the opportunity to develop a relationship with and accept responsibility for his child connection alone is not enough. In order to be recognized as a parent under the law, the man must also act as a father and accept some measure of responsibility for his child.

- Differential treatment of unwed mothers and fathers also has implications for children in the immigration context. In *Nguyen v. Immigration and Naturalization Services*,[7] for example, the U.S. Supreme Court upheld a provision of the Immigration and Naturalization Act[8] applicable to children born outside of the country when only one parent is a citizen. The statute imposed different requirements for a nonmarital child's acquisition of citizenship based on whether the citizen parent was the unwed mother or the unwed father. According to the Act, the child of an unwed mother acquires citizenship if the mother, prior to the birth, was a citizen and met a one year residency requirement.[9] If the father was the citizen parent, he must have been a citizen when the child was born, have established a blood relationship to the child by clear and convincing evidence, have agreed to support the child until age eighteen, and have acknowledged paternity or been adjudicated the father before the child turned eighteen.[10]

Despite some progress, the bottom line is still that when a child is born to unmarried parents, no legal bond exists between the biological father and his child until "legal fatherhood" is established.

Once established, a parent's status as a mother or a father automatically brings with it a variety of rights and obligations that, for the most part, attach whether or not one exercises them. Much of the legislation and litigation on parenthood focuses primarily on the economic obligations of being a parent. However, in addition to rights such as the rights to potentially inherit from their children or to sue for the wrongful death of a child, parenthood also brings with it the commonly acknowledged satisfactions of raising children. Parental rights for married parents and unmarried birth mothers include, for example, the rights to discipline and educate their children; to make decisions regarding their medical treatment, religion, place of residence, and social contacts; to receive and release information about them; and to speak for and raise or waive their rights. For unmarried fathers or divorced parents, these rights may be more limited, because they are shaped to a great extent by law and established by the courts.

THE GOVERNMENT

The government's interest in establishing parentage is essentially economic.[11] It is motivated less by a desire to provide for the needs of an individual child than by an interest in controlling the costs of public assistance. This interest is well founded, given that under the federal definition of poverty, approximately one in five to six children in the United States lives in poverty. This statistic is at least in part due to a lack of economic support from unknown and absent fathers.[12]

The child's entitlement to support exists without regard to the legal parents' marital status or the nature and extent of their relationship with the child. When parents are unknown, unavailable or otherwise unable to adequately provide for their children, help is often sought in a variety of forms funded by the federal government and distributed through **IV-D agencies** in the states. However, in order to continue to receive federal funds for this purpose, the states must take mandatory steps to contain the costs of financial support, food stamps, health insurance benefits, etc. For example, since 1975, the states have required mothers receiving

IV-D agency
the state agency charged with responsibility for enforcing child support obligations

PARALEGAL PRACTICE TIP

Go to *domestic.cuyahogacounty.us* to see an Application for IV-D Services used in an Ohio County. Select Forms/IV-D Application. Note that a party trying to find a missing parent can select "locator services only."

public assistance or applying for IV-D services to cooperate with the state in an effort to identify and locate the child's father, who may then become a defendant in an action to recoup child support. In its eagerness to hold someone other than the public accountable, however, the government sometimes may prevent identification of a child's "real" father by pressuring the mother into providing information which may or may not be accurate.

How Is Parentage Established?

Disputes regarding parenthood arise in a number of contexts, including among others, divorce, custody, child support, adoption, assisted reproductive technology, immigration, inheritance, and health care. As mentioned earlier, determination of a child's parentage was once reasonably straightforward. A child had two parents, and they were presumed to be a biological mother and her husband. Given medical advances and diversity in family structures, determining a child's parents can be a far more complicated task today than it once was. That said, we will now look at the most common ways of establishing legal parenthood incident to which the law confers and imposes rights, privileges, duties, and obligations. We will first identify some of the relevant provisions of the Uniform Parentage Act concerning establishment of legal parenthood and then examine more fully the three primary methods of establishing parentage:

- Presumptions including the marital presumption
- Acknowledgment of parentage
- Adjudication of parentage

PARALEGAL PRACTICE TIP

The full texts of the Uniform Acts referenced in this paragraph can be found at *www.uniformlaws.org*.

UNIFORM PARENTAGE ACT

The Uniform Parentage Act (UPA) was first introduced by the National Conference of Commissioners on Uniform State Laws in 1973 and was subsequently adopted in nineteen states. It was designed primarily to set standards for relationships between biological fathers and children that were independent of the parents' marital status. It was subsequently revised in 2000 to reflect updates in assisted reproductive technology and was amended again in 2002 to ensure a more equitable approach to parentage for children of unmarried parents. The Act forms the basis of parentage acts in several states and is often referred to favorably by judges. As of May 2015, the 2002 revision of the UPA had been enacted in whole or in part in nine states and was under consideration in others. The current version creates a single, coherent act regarding parentage by integrating the 1973 UPA with the Uniform Putative and Unknown Fathers Act (UPUFA) and the Uniform Status of Children of Assisted Conception Act (USCACA). Its provisions are also consistent with the principles and requirements of two other key uniform acts, the Uniform Child Custody Jurisdiction and Enforcement Act (UCCJEA) and the Uniform Interstate Family Support Act (UIFSA).

PARALEGAL PRACTICE TIP

Alabama, Delaware, New Mexico, North Dakota, Oklahoma, Texas, Utah, Washington, and Wyoming are the nine states that had adopted the revised 2002 UPA as of May 2015.

Article 2 of the 2002 Act addresses both paternity and maternity determinations and treats marital and nonmarital children equally with respect to their legal status and rights. Although the Act acknowledges the availability of genetic testing as a means of determining parentage, it makes clear that a biological father is not the only man who can be legally recognized as a child's father. Section 201 of the Uniform Parentage Act (2002) provides the following bases for establishing parent–child relationships:[13]

(a) The mother–child relationship is established by:

    (1) the woman having given birth (except as otherwise provided in Article 8 governing gestational surrogacy);

    (2) an adjudication of maternity;

    (3) an adoption; or

    (4) an adjudication confirming the woman as a parent of a child born to a gestational mother if the agreement was validated under Article 8 or is enforceable under other law.

(b) The father–child relationship is established between a man and a child by:

    (1) an unrebuttted presumption of paternity under Section 204 (governing presumptions of paternity);

    (2) an effective acknowledgment of paternity (Article 3) unless the acknowledgment has been rescinded or successfully challenged;

    (3) an adjudication of paternity;

    (4) an adoption;

    (5) the man having consented to assisted reproduction by a woman which resulted in the birth of a child (Article 7 Child of Assisted Reproduction); or

    (6) an adjudication confirming the man as a parent of a child born to a gestational mother if the agreement was validated or enforceable under other law.

PRESUMPTIONS

The earliest and most common presumption used to establish a child's parentage continues to be the marital presumption. As mentioned earlier in Paralegal Application 7.1, under common law, parentage was based on the marital presumption (sometimes called the legitimacy presumption) that when a married woman gave birth to a child while the parties were married or within 300 days of termination of the marriage, the woman's husband was presumed to be the child's legal father. In the interest of preserving marriages, the general rule was that all of the potentially interested parties (the husband, the mother, the child, and the biological father) were precluded from bringing a paternity action. "Lord Mansfield's Rule" of evidence prohibited either spouse from giving testimony that the husband was not the father, even in the face of strong biological evidence to the contrary. When challenges were allowed, the presumption could be rebutted only with evidence of the husband's sterility, impotency, or nonaccess to the wife at the time of conception. The interests served by the presumption were described as follows by a Michigan Supreme Court justice in a 2006 case:

> The presumption that children born or conceived during a marriage are the issue of that marriage is deeply rooted in our statutes and has been consistently recognized throughout our jurisprudence. . . . This presumption vindicates a number of interests, not the least of which include the interest of the child in not having his or her legitimacy called into question, the interest of the state in ensuring that children are properly supported, and the interest of both in assuring the effective operation of intestate succession. The presumption also reflects the

PARALEGAL PRACTICE TIP

Arizona's Marital Presumption Statute can be seen at *www.azcourts .gov.* The statute identifies multiple "presumptions" and describes the circumstances under which the marital presumption specifically can be overcome.

recognition that "[t]here is no area of law more requiring finality and stability than family law."[14]

The states now generally set forth by statute or case law the rules for if, when, and by whom the marital presumption can be rebutted. Courts in several states still uphold it, even when conclusive scientific proof of biological paternity is available, at least as long as the marital unit is intact. However, in most states, a putative biological father or a husband who has reason to believe he is not the child's biological father may attempt to rebut the presumption, but usually must do so within a limited period of time.

In addition to the marital presumption, several states have legislated additional presumptions (some of which are included in Section 204 of the 2002 UPA) identifying circumstances in which a person will be presumed to be the parent of a child. Presumptions essentially are effective by **operation of law** unless rebutted. Section 23-2208 of the Kansas Parentage Act includes a number of presumptions as well as provisions specifying how a presumption can be rebutted and how to address situations in which two or more presumptions conflict. See Exhibit 7.2. States also establish limitations on when proceedings challenging presumptions can be brought. Under the UPA (2002), a proceeding brought by a presumed father, the mother, or another individual to adjudicate the parentage of a child having a presumed father must be commenced not later than two years after the birth of the child, but may be maintained at any time if the court determines that: (1) the presumed father and the mother of the child neither cohabited nor engaged in sexual intercourse with each other during the probable time of conception; and (2) the presumed father never openly held out the child as his own.

Operation of law
a process by which a result occurs automatically because the law mandates it regardless of whether or not a party agrees or intends that result; a party does not need to take any further action to bring about the result

EXHIBIT 7.2 Kansas Parentage Act Section 23-2208 (2014) Presumption of Paternity

Courtesy: Kansas Legislature

(a) A man is presumed to be the father of a child if:

  (1) The man and the child's mother are, or have been, married to each other and the child is born during the marriage or within 300 days after the marriage is terminated by death or by the filing of a journal entry of a decree of annulment or divorce.

  (2) Before the child's birth, the man and the child's mother have attempted to marry each other by a marriage solemnized in apparent compliance with law, although the attempted marriage is void or voidable and:

    (A) If the attempted marriage is voidable, the child is born during the attempted marriage or within 300 days after its termination by death or by the filing of a journal entry of a decree of annulment or divorce; or

    (B) If the attempted marriage is void, the child is born within 300 days after the termination of cohabitation.

  (3) After the child's birth, the man and the child's mother have married, or attempted to marry, each other by a marriage solemnized in apparent compliance with law, although the attempted marriage is void or voidable and:

    (A) The man has acknowledged paternity of the child in writing;

    (B) with the man's consent, the man is named as the child's father on the child's birth certificate; or

    (C) the man is obligated to support the child under a written voluntary promise or by a court order.

EXHIBIT 7.2 (*Continued*)

> (4) The man notoriously or in writing recognizes paternity of the child, including but not limited to a voluntary acknowledgment made in accordance with K.S.A. 2014 Supp. 23-2223 or K.S.A. 65-2409a, and amendments thereto.
>
> (5) Genetic test results indicate a probability of 97% or greater that the man is the father of the child.
>
> (6) The man has a duty to support the child under an order of support regardless of whether the man has ever been married to the child's mother.
>
> (b) A presumption under this section may be rebutted only by clear and convincing evidence, by a court decree establishing paternity of the child by another man or as provided in subsection (c). If a presumption is rebutted, the party alleging the existence of a father and child relationship shall have the burden of going forward with the evidence.
>
> (c) If two or more presumptions under this section arise which conflict with each other, the presumption which on the facts is founded on the weightier considerations of policy and logic, including the best interests of the child, shall control.
>
> (d) Full faith and credit shall be given to a determination of paternity made by any other state or jurisdiction, whether the determination is established by judicial or administrative process or by voluntary acknowledgment. As used in this section, "full faith and credit" means that the determination of paternity shall have the same conclusive effect and obligatory force in this state as it has in the state or jurisdiction where made.
>
> (e) If a presumption arises under this section, the presumption shall be sufficient basis for entry of an order requiring the man to support the child without further paternity proceedings.
>
> (f) The donor of semen provided to a licensed physician for use in artificial insemination of a woman other than the donor's wife is treated in law as if he were not the birth father of a child thereby conceived, unless agreed to in writing by the donor and the woman.

Historically most presumptions have been applicable to men but with the expansion of marriage equality and gay rights many marriage-based rules and presumptions now are being applied to both men and women and heterosexual and same-sex couples where feasible. (See Paralegal Application 7.2.) This shift in the legal landscape is being implemented by both statutes and judicial decisions. Several states have amended their rules of statutory construction. For example, section 517.201, subdivision 2 of the Minnesota Statutes provides: "When necessary to implement the rights and responsibilities of spouses or parents in a civil marriage between persons of the same sex under the laws of this state, including those that establish parentage presumptions based on a civil marriage, gender-specific terminology, such as "husband," "wife," "mother," "father," "widow," "widower," or similar terms, must be construed in the neutral manner to refer to a person of either gender."

Several states are accomplishing the same result through judicial decisions. For example, although the presumptions in the Kansas Parentage Act (Exhibit 7.2) read as though they are applicable only to men, the Kansas Supreme Court has held that provisions of the Act applicable to the father–child relationship are applicable to the mother–child relationship as well in so far as practicable. See *Frazier v. Goudschaal*, 296 Kan. 730, 295 P.3d 542 (2013). In *Della Corte v. Ramirez*, 81 Mass. App. Ct. 906 (2012), the Massachusetts Court of Appeals held that following the principles of *Goodridge*, statutes related to marriage and parentage are to be read as gender neutral. The case involved a custody dispute following a same-sex divorce in which a biological mother alleged that her former spouse was not a legal parent in part because she did not fit the definition of parent in the state's artificial insemination statute. M.G.L. c. 46, § 4b provides: "any child born to a married woman as a result of artificial insemination with the consent of her husband, shall be considered the legitimate child of the mother and such husband." Finding that the child was conceived with the explicit support and consent of the nonbiological parent and was born during the parties' marriage, the court held that "husband" in the statute must be read to be gender neutral as "spouse" thereby establishing the nonbiological mother as a legal parent without the necessity of her having to adopt the child. The court held that Massachusetts must consider a child born in a same-sex marriage to automatically be a child of both spouses, the same as in a heterosexual marriage.

Paralegal **Application 7.2**

Applications of the Marital Presumption—Then and Now

***Michael H. v. Gerald D.*, 491 U.S. 110, 109 S. Ct. 2333, 105 L. Ed. 2d 91 (1989)**

In this case, the U.S. Supreme Court dealt with two fathers and a situation in which genetics and the marital presumption collided. In 1981, a woman named Carol gave birth to a daughter named Victoria. Carol's husband, Gerald, was identified on the birth certificate as the child's father, and he lived with the mother and child on and off during the years following the birth. However, the child actually was the product of Carol's extramarital affair with a man named Michael, who shortly after the child's birth went for testing with the mother and was genetically determined (within a 98.7 degree of probability) to be the child's father. He, too, lived with Carol and Victoria on and off during which time he established a relationship with his daughter. However, Gerald and Victoria subsequently reconciled. When Michael filed a paternity action seeking to be declared the child's legal father and to establish a right to visitation based on the fact he was her biological father, Gerald opposed, claiming that, under California law, he was the child's father based on the marital presumption. Each man had a *bona fide* basis for claiming paternity and the child asserted that she should be entitled to maintain her relationship with both "fathers."

The governing California statute provided that (1) a child of a married woman cohabiting with her husband is presumed to be a child of the marriage where the husband is not impotent or sterile, and (2) the presumption may be rebutted by blood tests, but only if a motion for such tests is made within two years from the date of the child's birth, by (a) the wife, if the natural father has filed an affidavit acknowledging paternity, or (b) the husband. Since the husband met the requirements of the marital presumption and the rebuttal requirements were not met, the Superior Court granted the husband's motion for summary judgment and rejected challenges by the putative father and the child as to the constitutionality of the statute. The California Court of Appeals affirmed holding that (1) the conclusive presumption statute did not violate the rights of the putative father or the child under the Due Process Clause of the federal Constitution's Fourteenth Amendment, (2) the statute did not violate the child's rights under the Fourteenth Amendment's Equal Protection Clause, and (3) the Superior Court had impliedly determined not only that the husband was the child's presumed father, but that the putative father was not entitled to any visitation rights under the pertinent California statute.

In the appeal to the U.S. Supreme Court, five members of the Court agreed (in a sharply divided decision) that the conclusive presumption statute did not infringe on the due process rights of the putative father or the child, or on the child's equal protection rights. The Court concluded that California was not required to recognize a claim of paternity asserted by a man other than the husband when the mother of the child was married to and cohabiting with the husband (who was neither impotent nor sterile) at the times of conception and birth and both the mother and the husband wished to raise the child as their own. The plurality further opined that it was not unconstitutional to prefer the husband over the natural father as the exclusive legal father of the child in this situation concluding that the "adulterous natural father" had no fundamental liberty interest in a relationship with the child.

Sidebar

Faced with the forced choice between the two fathers in this case, do you think the Court reached the right decision? Explain your response. Should it matter that the child is the product of an extramarital affair? Should the biological father be permitted to rebut the marital presumption? Must one father be rejected in favor of the other father, or do you think the courts should recognize both fathers as the child requested? The full opinion in *Michael H. v. Gerald D.* can be accessed at *www. pearsonhighered.com/careersresources/* in the website material related to Chapter 7 of this text under Cases.

Gartner and Gartner individually and as Next Friends of Mackenzie Jean Gartner v. Iowa Department of Public Health, 830 N.W.2d 335 (Iowa 2013)

In this case, the plaintiffs were married female spouses who were the parents of a child conceived by means of artificial insemination using an anonymous donor. Only the birth mother's name appeared on the child's birth certificate and the parties requested that the Iowa Department of Public Health add the name of the nonbirthing spouse. The Department refused interpreting the presumption of parentage statute containing the terms "husband," "father," and "paternity," to apply only to a male spouse in an opposite-sex marriage. The parties sought a court order to compel them to amend the birth certificate. The trial court granted their request based on its interpretation of Iowa Code section 144.13(2) known as the Iowa Presumption of Parentage Statute. The Department requested review by the Iowa Supreme Court. The state's high court affirmed the lower court's judgment finding that the presumption of parentage statute violated equal protection and due process clauses of the Iowa Constitution as applied to married lesbian couples. In its decision, the court opined: "It is important for our laws to recognize that married lesbian couples who have children enjoy the same benefits and burdens as married opposite-sex couples who have children. By naming the nonbirthing spouse on the birth certificate of a married lesbian couple's child, the child is ensured support from that parent and the parent establishes fundamental legal rights at the moment of birth. Therefore, the only explanation for not listing the nonbirthing lesbian spouse on the birth certificate is stereotype or prejudice. The exclusion of the nonbirthing spouse on the birth certificate of a child born to a married lesbian couple is not substantially related to the objective of establishing parentage."

Sidebar

Instead of striking the statute, the Court preserved it as to married opposite-sex couples but required the Department to apply the statute to lesbian couples as well when one of the spouses conceives a child during their marriage using an anonymous sperm donor.

ACKNOWLEDGMENT OF PARENTAGE

Since 1993 under federal law, all states must have in place simple procedures enabling parents to voluntarily acknowledge parentage by completing an appropriate notarized acknowledgment, stipulation, or affidavit. The document is most often called a voluntary acknowledgment or affidavit of parentage. Under federal law, the document must contain the names, addresses, birth dates, Social Security numbers, and signatures of both parents in addition to the name, birth date, and birthplace of the child. Depending on the state, it may also include the phone numbers of both parents, the mother's maiden name, the father's place of employment, the child's gender and custody status, and the ethnicity of the parents.

The acknowledgment may be executed (completed, signed, and witnessed) at a hospital at the time of birth usually for free or at any time thereafter prior to entry of a judicial order of parentage provided the parties' signatures are notarized. Witnesses and notaries will usually ask for a photo ID and Social Security number for identification purposes. In addition to hospitals, acknowledgment forms are also commonly available online, at IV-D agencies, social service agencies, and other locations where children and their parents receive services. The form contains, or is accompanied by, a description of the legal consequences of executing the document with respect to child support, custody, visitation rights, and obligations along with notice that the acknowledgment may be rescinded within a limited period after signing by complying

PARALEGAL PRACTICE TIP

The form for voluntarily acknowledging paternity in New York can be located at *www.childsupport.ny.gov* (Form LDSS 4418 (Rev. 1/14)). The content required on such forms facilitates establishment and enforcement of child support orders as well as the maintenance of public records.

PARALEGAL PRACTICE TIP

Congress has provided that an unmarried father's name may appear on a birth certificate only if the mother and father have executed an acknowledgment of parentage or there has been an adjudication of paternity.[16] Unlike a fully executed acknowledgment, a man's name on a birth certificate is not conclusive proof of paternity. Steps may need to be taken to change/amend the child's birth certificate following execution of an acknowledgment.

PARALEGAL PRACTICE TIP

To see an example of a form rescinding a voluntary acknowledgment of paternity form, visit *www.childsup .ca.gov*. (California).

PARALEGAL PRACTICE TIP

In 2010 alone, there were an estimated 13,062 cases of false paternity in Texas and over 85% of them resulted when paternity was initially established by marital presumption or voluntary acknowledgment. Elan Renee-Guerin Longstreet, *Who's My Real Daddy? Reducing the Prevalence of False Paternity in Texas,* 1 Tex. A&M Law Review 183 (2013).

with specific procedures. Once fully executed, a voluntary acknowledgment constitutes an admission and becomes the equivalent of a judicial finding of paternity subject to a sixty-day rescission period.[15] The acknowledgment then is entitled to full faith and credit in all states. It usually must be filed with the court or sent to the vital statistics/public records office that maintains birth records in the jurisdiction.

Some states have a relatively simple rescission procedure but others require a formal judicial action. The client may have to file a Complaint to Rescind Voluntary Acknowledgment or a Petition to Determine Parentage. Genetic tests will be ordered by the court, and if they exclude the petitioner as the child's father, the applicable vital statistics agency will be authorized to delete his name from the birth certificate. Because of the strong public policy favoring the finality of parentage determinations, after the sixty-day rescission period has elapsed, the acknowledgment usually can be challenged only on the grounds of fraud, duress, or mistake of fact (e.g., the alleged father honestly believed he was the child's father but has since learned that he is, and always has been, incapable of producing sperm). Such challenges usually can only be brought within a limited period, such as a year from the date of signing or filing.

Unfortunately, unmarried fathers often voluntarily acknowledge paternity without legal counsel and without benefit of genetic (DNA) testing. The attorney representing a client in this situation is sometimes present with both parties when an acknowledgment is going to be signed. The attorney must be absolutely clear which of the parties he or she represents and should recommend that the other party seek legal advice before signing the document. In addition, given the potentially devastating consequences of false assumptions about paternity and the ability to establish paternity to a near certainty through DNA testing, counsel should strongly advise clients to confirm paternity through testing.

It is as yet unclear how voluntary acknowledgments will be treated in the evolving legal environment surrounding marriage and reproduction. They were initially intended for use by unmarried couples who believed they were the biological parents of a child. However, there is concern among some attorneys that they "are being used in situations for which they were never intended to be used, primarily by same-sex couples or intended parents involved in assisted reproduction situations where donated genetic material was used for conception and where the intended parent is not necessarily the genetic or biological parent of the child."[17]

ADJUDICATION OF PARENTAGE

Adjudications of parentage typically involve traditional paternity actions. However, they may also occur in other contexts as well, such as adoption contests, claims involving parenting contracts/agreements, or assertions of parentage of a child based on equitable theories.

Adjudications involving adoptions

All adoptions require judicial approval which is customarily granted in or following a formal hearing closed to the public. They are not usually adversarial proceedings but can be if the adoption is contested typically by a person (such as a putative father or a minor) who argues their consent to the pending adoption is required or was given involuntarily or that their parental rights have been wrongfully terminated.

Stepparent adoptions are generally an option for both heterosexual and same-sex married parents to become "legal parents" if the parental rights of a living parent not in the new family unit are surrendered or terminated. They are strongly recommended for nonbiological parents who want to secure parental rights that may otherwise be lost upon dissolution of marriage. In addition, over the past three decades, courts in several states began granting so-called co-parent or second-parent adoptions to unmarried heterosexual, gay, and lesbian couples jointly parenting a child when one of the partners was already a "legal" parent of the child. They remain an option in several states but are still not permitted in a minority of jurisdictions. In both step- and second-parent adoptions, the adoptive parent becomes a legal parent in all respects and the initial "legal" parent in the couple is not required to give up any legal rights. Both second-parent and stepparent adoptions are discussed more fully in Chapter 8.

Adjudications involving parenting contracts/agreements

Parents have a fundamental right to the care, custody, and control of their children. In addition, they have a right to choose who associates with those children and, in some circumstances, who will perform parent-like responsibilities. Occasionally parents execute written agreements, typically called co-parenting agreements, in which they share and/or delegate their parental responsibilities to others. Courts have sometimes found that when a legal parent relinquishes a significant amount of parenting to another in an agreement, the other individual will acquire status as a parent under the law. See, e.g., *Frazier, Appellee v. Goudschaal, Appellant*, 296 Kan, 730, 295 P.3d 542 (2013) (Kansas), discussed more fully in Chapter 9. "Very detailed agreements have long been entered into by same-sex couples, including (1) cohabitation provisions and other written contracts spelling out how the parents will conceive, bear, and support a child; (2) what their respective parenting roles will be; and (3) what steps each partner must take in order to obtain some form of legal recognition of the parent-child relationship . . . same-sex couples who choose not to get married will still face significant challenges in establishing sound legal parentage and should continue to memorialize agreements and obligations in written agreements and contracts, . . ."[18] Such agreements are consistent with Section 2.03 of the *ALI Principles*, often cited by the courts, which provides that a person who is not an adoptive or biological parent may be deemed a parent by estoppel with all the rights and responsibilities of a legal parent if he or she: ". . .lived with the child since the child's birth, holding out and accepting full and permanent responsibilities as a parent, as part of a prior coparenting agreement with the child's legal parent . . . to raise a child together each with full parental rights and responsibilities, when the court finds that recognition of the individual as a parent is in the child's best interests."[19]

Enforceable parenting agreements may be entered by heterosexual as well as same-sex couples. For example, in *L. F. v. Breit*, 285 Va. 163; 736 S. E. 2d 711 (2013), an unmarried biological father, William Breit, sought to have his paternity established and to obtain custody and visitation rights with a child conceived via *in vitro* fertilization using his sperm. Prior to the child's birth, Virginia Beach Attorney Breit and his long time, live-in girlfriend entered into a written custody and visitation agreement that gave him reasonable visitation rights. After the child was born, they both signed a sworn affidavit of paternity stating that Breit was the legal and biological father, and his name was put on the birth certificate. Four months after the child's birth, the couple separated, but Breit continued to visit and provide for the child. Nine months after the separation, the mother ended all contact between Breit and the child. He sued to establish parentage and a circuit judge dismissed the case treating the parties' agreement as a surrogacy agreement. The lower court relied in part on language in Virginia Code §§ 20-158(A)(3) that a "sperm donor is not the father of a child unless he is the husband of the gestational mother." But the Court of Appeals reversed and the Virginia Supreme Court upheld the Appeals Court. The basic issue before the court was whether Virginia statutes prevented an unmarried, biological father from establishing legal parentage of a child born as a result of assisted conception pursuant to a voluntary written agreement. After a thorough analysis of the parties' arguments and the applicable state and federal laws, the Court concluded that Mr. Breit was entitled to establish paternity with a written acknowledgement of paternity despite the statutory presumption. The Court found that because Mr. Breit had demonstrated a commitment to his parental responsibilities in the written agreement and acknowledgment, the Due Process Clause of the U.S. Constitution's Fourteenth Amendment protected his fundamental right to make decisions concerning the care and custody of his child.

Adjudications based on equitable theories

Cases based on equitable theories are not necessarily brought in family courts but rather in courts with general equity jurisdiction. They involve the application of a variety of equitable doctrines to justify decisions establishing legal parenthood after finding that a person is, for example, a *de facto* parent, a psychological parent, a co-parent, or a parent based on equitable estoppel. Equitable theories provide a flexible remedy for establishing parenthood that complements existing legislative provisions when parent–child relationships arise in ways that are not addressed by any existing legislative scheme.

In Chapter 9, we discuss the acquisition of some degree of parental rights (such as rights to custody and visitation) by establishing one's status as a *de facto* parent. See *In re Custody of H.S.H.-K*, 533 N.W.2d 419 (Wis. 1995), the *Holtzman* case, in which the Wisconsin Supreme Court became the first to hold that a same-sex, nonlegal parent had a right to maintain a relationship with a child she jointly planned and cared for. Since *Holtzman*, an increasing number of states have concluded that once a person establishes status as a "functional" parent, he or she stands on an equal footing with "legal" parents. For example, in *Parentage of L.B.*, 122 P.3d 161 (Wash. 2005), a same-sex couple had decided to have a child together through ART. After the child was born the couple parented the child together for almost six years. When their relationship ended, the biological mother cut off all contact between the nonbiological parent and the child. The Washington Supreme Court found that the nonbiological parent was an equitable parent entitled to seek custody and visitation and also, as a *de facto* parent, stood "in parity" with the other parent and was entitled to the same rights and responsibilities which attach to other parents in the state. Some states codify *de facto* or functional parenting in their parentage presumptions. For example, in New Hampshire, RSA 168-B:2,V(d) presumes parentage when a person receives a child into his or her home and holds the child out as their own. The statute applies equally to men and women. (See *In re Guardianship of Madelyn B.*, 166 N.H. 453, 98 A.3d 494 (2014).) This topic is discussed further in Chapter 9 on child custody.

PARALEGAL PRACTICE TIP

www.familyequality.org is a starting point for researching the existence of laws across the country regarding legal recognition of *de facto* parents, recognition of parents using donor insemination, stepparent adoption, and second-parent adoption.

PARALEGAL PRACTICE TIP

In *In the Matter of the Custody of B.M.H. (Holt v. Holt)*, 179 Wn.2d 224, 315 P.3d 470 (2013), the Washington Supreme Court held that a man's status as a former stepfather did not preclude him from seeking status as a *de facto* parent after he unsuccessfully sought custody of his former wife's child in his capacity as a stepparent.

Equitable theories are used "as a shield" when the courts apply them to recognize and protect the rights of individuals who have functioned as parents and want to maintain their relationships with the children they have helped to raise. For example, in Case 7.1, the Wisconsin Supreme Court applied the **equitable parent doctrine** against a biological father in favor of a nonbiological father in a custody case. Parenthood by estoppel, on the other hand, is most often used "as a sword." It essentially provides that a man may be designated the legal father of a child if he has held himself out as the child's father and has supported the child emotionally and financially. It is assumed that both the child and the mother have come to rely on that support and that it would be inequitable to deprive them of its continuation. A paralegal may be called on to gather information to support a claim that a father has held a child out as his own. Some of the kinds of conduct to be considered include the following:

> A man is deemed to have held out a child as his biological offspring when he engages in parental conduct such as: changing the child's diapers; feeding him; taking him to the doctor; bathing him; taking the child on visits away from the mother's home; allowing the child to call him daddy; giving the child gifts or cards; attending parent-teacher conferences or school events; giving the child his surname; voluntarily providing financial support for the child; and providing or building a loving relationship with the child. He can also put the child on his insurance, claim governmental benefits for the child under his name, or claim to be the child's father to the public at large, such as the child's school, daycare or even to friends, relatives and neighbors.[20]

Equitable parent doctrine
a doctrine used to extend parenthood to an individual who is willing and able to assume parental rights and responsibilities and/or who has done so in the past

CASE 7.1 *A.J. v. I.J.,* 2002 WI App 307, 259 Wis. 2d 120, 655 N.W.2d 195 (2002)

BACKGROUND

In this case, a mother, Norma, gave birth to a child in January 1998 while she was married to her husband, Randy. Randy did not learn until he filed for divorce in October 1999 that the child's biological father was actually the mother's boyfriend, Brendan. The child knew only Randy as her father, although before being sentenced to prison for eight years, the mother did take her to Brendan's for weekly visits. After the mother's incarceration, the child lived with Randy. In December 1999, Norma filed a counterclaim in the divorce action and alleged Brendan was the child's father. Brendan filed a motion to intervene and sought to be adjudicated the child's natural father and requested legal custody and primary physical placement of the child. The trial court denied the motion to intervene and declared Randy the child's equitable parent and awarded him custody. Norma and Brendan appealed.

FROM THE OPINION

This divorce case presents an unusual factual scenario. Randy A.J. is willing to continue supporting and providing care for a child that is not biologically his own. He seeks to maintain the parent-child relationship he established with a child born during his marriage to the natural mother, Norma I.J., despite the fact that genetic tests have established to a 99.99% degree of certainty that Brendan B. is the child's father. Norma and Brendan argue that because the genetic tests showed that Brendan is the biological father of the child, the trial court had no authority to determine that establishing Randy as the legal father and awarding him custody were in the best interests of the child. We conclude that Randy is the equitable parent of the minor child and affirm the trial court's decision that otherwise awarded Randy custody of the child.

. . .

On appeal, Brendan and Norma assert that once the parties submitted to genetic testing and the tests showed Brendan to be the biological father, the trial court erred in concluding that Wis. Stat. §§ 767.463 and 767.458 (1m) granted it the authority to conduct a best interests of the child hearing and dismiss the paternity action. Brendan and Norma further contend that once the genetic tests demonstrated that Brendan was the biological father . . . , he overcame the marital presumption.

. . .

The statute explicitly permits the court to dismiss an action to establish the paternity of a child based upon the best interests of the child only if genetic tests have not yet been taken.

. . .

The trial court next concluded that despite the fact that the genetic tests had established Brendan's parentage to a 99.99% degree of certainty, Brendan had not rebutted the marital presumption. . . . The presumption is rebutted by the results of a genetic test establishing by a statistical probability of 99.0% or higher the parentage of a man other than the man presumed to be the father under subsec. (1). Sec. 891.41(2).

. . .

While the trial court may have used the incorrect vehicle in the law, the court clearly felt compelled by the evidence to declare that Randy, not Brendan, should be the child's father. The trial court made unmistakable, but implicit, findings that Brendan should not be entitled to whatever foothold he had gained by reason of the genetic tests. . . . the trial court was wrong on the law, but its factual findings supported the correct result, had the proper standard been applied.

. . .

We first reiterate what we have already written—that the marital father is presumed to be the natural father unless rebutted. A genetic test showing another man to be the natural father rebuts that presumption. But that does not end the matter. Under Wis. Stat. § 767.48(1m), the natural father then only gains a *rebuttable presumption* that he is the child's parent. Thus, it is evident from the law that even if a test shows a man to be the natural father, his legal fatherhood is only presumed. Next, we must consider "how" such a presumption may be overcome. In our view, the presumption may be overcome by evidence that the marital father has so bonded with the child as to be considered the "equitable parent." . . .

Wisconsin has recognized the equitable parent doctrine. See *J.J. v. R.J.*, 162 Wis. 2d 420, 429–30, 469 N.W.2d 877 (Ct. App. 1991). The equitable parent doctrine extends the rights and responsibilities of a natural parent to a nonbiological parent seeking custody or visitation. . . . Once a court determines that a party is an equitable parent, there is no distinction between the equitable parent and any other parent; each is endowed with the same rights and responsibilities of parenthood. . . . We have permitted a mother in a divorce action to estop a nonbiological father from denying paternity in order to avoid child support obligations. . . . Here we face the unusual situation where the mother is in prison, the child does not recognize the biological father as being her parent, and the nonbiological father not only wants to continue the parent-child relationship, but also wishes to support the child emotionally and financially by maintaining custody of the child.

. . .

While we acknowledge that the equitable parent doctrine has not been invoked in Wisconsin against a natural parent for the purpose of awarding custody to a nonparent, we have invoked the doctrine. . . against a natural parent for the purpose of awarding visitation to a nonparent in a situation that bears some factual similarity to this case. . . .

. . . In this case, the trial court held several days of hearings concerning the best interests of the child in which all parties participated. . . . we acknowledge that in exercising its equitable powers, the trial court did not expressly use the equitable parent doctrine to declare Randy the legal father and otherwise award him custody. However, . . . the trial court made substantial and careful findings of fact regarding the relationship each party had established with the child and the conduct of the parties concerning the child's paternity and we use these findings in our analysis of the equitable parent doctrine as applied to this case. Whether the facts as found permit the application of equitable estoppel is a question of law that we review independently of the trial court's determination. . . .

During the pregnancy and up until Norma's incarceration, Randy, Norma and the child lived together. After Norma's incarceration, Randy became the sole custodian of the minor child and has continued to assume responsibility for her. The child considers Randy to be her only father and, up until the divorce proceedings, Randy believed her to be his biological daughter. The trial court found that "there clearly is a-what would otherwise be viewed as a normal parent-child relationship and bond between [Randy] and [the child], and, in fact, he has been her only parent from the standpoint of regular and daily contact and custodial care since May of 1999." . . .

Prior to the divorce proceeding, and with Norma's cooperation, Randy believed he held the status of a natural parent and assumed the rights and responsibilities of fatherhood. Norma and Brendan never took any steps to change Randy's belief despite the fact that they had suspected Brendan was the father of the child. The trial court found that it was in both Norma's and Brendan's best interests not to take any action concerning the child's paternity. Norma was involved in significant criminal legal difficulties at the time and needed Randy's financial backing. During legal proceedings, Randy supported Norma and funded the costs of her legal representation, using all of the family's cash and equity in their home. It was not until Norma was incarcerated and Randy filed for divorce that Norma raised the paternity issue.

The trial court also found that Brendan had the opportunity and ability to assume parental responsibility for the child and chose not to do so. The court determined that while Brendan saw the child on a weekly basis prior to Norma's incarceration, the relationship established between the two was not that of father and daughter. The relationship arose simply upon the event of Norma's relationship with Brendan. The trial court further determined that Brendan, having to purchase such things as diapers, formula, and some clothing for the child during her extended weekend stays prior to Norma's incarceration, in no way constituted support of the child either emotionally or financially. Finally the court noted that Brendan did not raise the issue of his paternity in this state until the child was well over three years old. . . .

The trial court also relied upon the testimony and recommendations of the psychologist. . . . She recommended that Randy remain the father of the child. . . . Finally, the court also gave due consideration to the substance abuse problems of the parties.

We have . . . determined that Brendan may not assert his parentage based on the facts as found by the trial court and the applicable law. . . . We affirm the trial court's determination that it was in the child's best interests that the court estop Norma from asserting the child's parentage. We hold that Randy is the legal father and affirm the trial court in that regard. We also hold that Randy is entitled to custody and affirm the trial court's determination on that issue.

SIDEBAR

How would you define the equitable parent doctrine? Do you agree that it properly applied to the facts of this case? Explain your response. The opinion in *A.J. v. I.J.* is available at *www.pearsonhighered.com/careersresources* in the website material for Chapter 7 of this text under Cases.

Adjudications based on claims of biological parenthood, i.e., "traditional" paternity actions

PARALEGAL PRACTICE TIP

An example of an Affidavit in Support of Establishing Paternity (initiating a IV-D case) is accessible at *www.acf.hhs.gov*. Search for the form by its title.

Putative father

a man who is reputed or believed to be the father of a child but who was not married to the mother when the child was born and whose paternity has not yet been established by legal process

PARALEGAL PRACTICE TIP

To see examples of Complaint forms that may be filed by a mother and a IV-D Agency in Vermont, visit *www.vermontjudiciary.org*.

Historically, paternity actions were primarily criminal in nature and were designed to punish sexual misconduct. Today, they are largely civil proceedings that commence with the filing of a Complaint to Establish Paternity (see Exhibit 7.4) or a Petition for Declaration of Parentage. They are most often brought by mothers seeking child support, IV-D agencies on behalf of recipients of public assistance, or men seeking to establish or disestablish paternity. Under federal law, when paternity is contested, states must require genetic testing of the parties and the child, if requested. If the tests indicate paternity to a high degree of probability, a rebuttable presumption of paternity is established, and the burden shifts to the **putative father** to prove nonpaternity if he chooses and is able to do so.

The procedure for establishing paternity is governed by both state and federal law and varies somewhat from state to state. A basic outline of the process is provided in Exhibit 7.3. Prior to filing a paternity case in a particular jurisdiction, there are several threshold questions that should be addressed.

- **Standing:** Mothers, fathers (established, alleged, and others with legitimate claims), and IV-D child support enforcement agencies are the common claimants with standing. Article 6 of the Uniform Parentage Act and some states that have not adopted the Act, further extend standing to children and additional parties, including adoption agencies, intended parents under a surrogacy agreement, and representatives of deceased, incapacitated, or minor persons.
- **Personal jurisdiction:** Because establishment of paternity will result in associated obligations including child support, the court must have personal jurisdiction over the defendant. In interstate cases, personal jurisdiction over a nonresident defendant often can be established under the long-arm statutes of the state or the Uniform Interstate Family Support Act. When personal jurisdiction cannot be obtained, IV-D agencies can initiate a case in the petitioner's state and send it to "the responding state" where the defendant resides. The responding state then will be responsible for obtaining jurisdiction and establishing paternity.
- **Subject matter jurisdiction:** Subject matter jurisdiction may reside in more than one court. Most paternity actions are brought in family courts. However, as discussed above, if a father's claim to paternity is based on his having raised, supported, and held the child out as his own without being the biological father, the action may have to be brought in a court with general

equity jurisdiction. As a threshold requirement, the man usually will have to show that he has already established a substantial relationship with the child.

- **Venue:** Venue is usually proper in the judicial district where the child resides.
- **Statutes of limitations:** Statutes vary by jurisdiction and need to be determined based on the facts of each case. Under the Uniform Parentage Act, there is no statute of limitations on paternity actions if there is no legally established father. If there is an established father, challenges must be brought within two years of the child's birth. Federal law establishes an eighteen-year statute of limitations for bringing paternity actions for the purpose of establishing child support obligations.
- **Binding effect of judgments:** A judgment of paternity is binding with respect to the parties as in an action for divorce but is not necessarily binding on a child who is not a party to that action.
- **Potential defendant(s):** If the mother was married to a man other than the named defendant at the time she became pregnant, gave birth, or within 300 days thereafter, the husband may need to be added as a second defendant unless he has previously been determined not to be the father in another judicial proceeding. As an alternative in some states, the husband may sign a notarized affidavit denying paternity.
- **Burden of proof:** The burden of proving paternity is on the petitioner, who must prove his or her case by a preponderance of the evidence in most jurisdictions. In a small minority, clear and convincing evidence is required.
- **Legal advice:** Although not required, it is wise for anyone seeking to establish paternity to obtain legal advice to ensure that he or she fully understands the implications of a judgment of parentage. For example, if an unmarried mother wants to establish paternity solely as a stepping-stone to receiving child support, she needs to understand that if she is successful, the "father" will then have a legally enforceable right to seek custody and/or visitation. She must also accept the fact that she may be required to provide and respond to testimony and evidence regarding sexual intercourse she engaged in during the probable period of conception. An unmarried father hoping to establish a relationship with his child needs to understand that if he prevails, he will also become obligated to support the child.

EXHIBIT 7.3 Adjudication of Paternity—The Basic Process

This outline assumes that the client rather than the state's child support enforcement (IV-D) agency is pursuing the paternity claim. Terminology and procedures will vary based on the jurisdiction, but the following provides a basic description of the process.

1. The Complaint/Petition is drafted by the party seeking to establish parentage (the Plaintiff or Petitioner). State-specific forms are widely available online, in courts, in form books, and in law office files (paper and electronic). (See an example of a Complaint in Exhibit 7.4.) A separate Complaint must be drafted for each minor child whose parentage is at issue. In some states, the mother, but not the father, may file an action during the pregnancy, although paternity will not be established until after the child's birth. If the petitioner is receiving public assistance, the state's IV-D agency is joined as a party and must receive notice of all filings, notices, hearings, etc.
2. The Plaintiff completes a care and custody disclosure form regarding the child's custody and whereabouts. If not addressed in the form, an affidavit will need to be filed indicating any proceedings or orders pertaining to the child that are pending or that have already been entered. This includes custody, support, and restraining orders.

(Continued)

PARALEGAL PRACTICE TIP

A child may discover that despite a determination of paternity in a legal proceeding involving his/her mother and alleged father (such as a divorce), his/her true biological father is another man. If the child was not a party to the prior action and the "true" father acknowledges him or her prior to death, the child may be able to bring an action to establish paternity and claim inheritance and other rights.

PARALEGAL PRACTICE TIP

To see the equivalent of an affidavit denying paternity used in Oklahoma, visit www.okdhs.org. Search for Denial of Paternity (Form number 03PA210E).

PARALEGAL PRACTICE TIP

Although not addressed in this Exhibit, it should be noted that many Native American Tribal Codes include provisions regarding establishment of paternity that should be considered when applicable. Visit www.wa.gov to see several Indian Child Welfare Act (ICWA) notice forms for various kinds of actions.

PARALEGAL PRACTICE TIP

To see examples of a Petition for Adjudication of Paternity and an Answer, visit www.courts.delaware.gov.

EXHIBIT 7.3 (Continued)

PARALEGAL PRACTICE TIP

To see an example of an Affidavit Disclosing Care and Custody Proceedings, visit *http://www .mass.gov* Probate and Family Court-Scroll down to Miscellaneous Forms to locate the Affidavit (Massachusetts).

PARALEGAL PRACTICE TIP

You can see examples of Answers admitting and denying paternity at *www.mass.gov.* Search Massachusetts Law About Paternity–Best Bet–Paternity Issues (Chapter 7) Family Law Advocacy for Low and Moderate Income Clients.

To see an example of a Motion for a Default Order used in the state of Washington, visit *www.courts .wa.gov/forms*.

PARALEGAL PRACTICE TIP

Once paternity is established and the court can issue enforceable child support orders, it sometimes chooses to order support back to the date of the child's birth.

3. If receiving public assistance or otherwise unable to pay, the Plaintiff completes an Affidavit of Indigency requesting that the state cover the costs of serving the Defendant.
4. The Plaintiff files the Complaint, the Affidavit Disclosing Care and Custody Proceedings (and the Indigency Affidavit, if appropriate), in the proper court. The Clerk will assign a docket number to be used on all future documents pertaining to the case.
5. The Plaintiff obtains a Summons and completes it if it has not been completed by the clerk's office.
6. The Plaintiff arranges service of the Summons, Complaint, and Affidavit on the Defendant(s) in a manner authorized in the jurisdiction.
7. The Plaintiff files the original Summons with the court when service has been made and the server has completed the relevant section of the Summons.
8. The Defendant answers the Complaint within the required period (usually twenty to thirty days). In the Answer, the Defendant may admit or deny paternity. If paternity is admitted, the case may settle. Under federal law, if the Defendant has been properly served and fails to respond or appear, the state is required to provide for entry of a default order that serves as a legally binding determination of paternity and the basis for a child support order.
9. The parties may be required to file Financial Statements at this point.
10. Motions for Temporary Orders related to the child may be filed by one or both parties, and hearing dates will be assigned. Some states require that proposed orders be filed with the motions. The court can issue temporary child support, custody, and health insurance orders if the Defendant has previously acknowledged paternity or if genetic marker testing has been done and the state's threshold of probability of paternity is met (usually over 95%). If emergency circumstances exist, a motion (accompanied by a supporting affidavit) may be filed on an *ex parte* basis.
11. When paternity is disputed and a party is unwilling to voluntarily submit to testing, a Motion for Genetic Marker Testing (with a supporting Affidavit) may be filed. (See Exhibits 7.5 and 7.6.) The courts will usually grant such motions when there is probable cause to believe that the parties engaged in sexual intercourse during the "probable period of conception." When the alleged father has died or is otherwise unavailable, the court can order testing of his close relatives. Although they are more intrusive than genetic tests, blood-typing tests are also still sometimes used. However, their use is essentially limited to excluding a man as the father of a specific child or including him as a "possible" father of the child.
12. Hearings on Motions take place. The parties may be required to meet with family service officers prior to hearings in an effort to reach agreement on the matter in dispute.
13. Discovery is conducted.
14. Pretrial steps are followed that track the steps outlined in Chapter 5 with respect to the divorce process. Absent a history of abuse, the court may require that the parties have a face-to-face four-way (clients and counsel) meeting in an effort to settle the case without further litigation. If the parties marry while the paternity action is pending, the court can still issue an order of paternity.
15. The trial takes place. The nature of evidence offered and testimony of witnesses will vary depending on the nature of the case. For example, an unmarried plaintiff mother may present the following:
    - A certified copy of the child's birth certificate identifying the defendant as the child's father
    - A certified copy of a Genetic marker testing report. Although DNA test results provide compelling evidence of biological paternity, they are not necessarily determinative of "legal" paternity. They usually can be admitted without foundation unless there is an objection (e.g., they were not performed at an accredited laboratory, they were tainted or tampered with, etc.).
    - Evidence and testimony regarding sexual intercourse with the defendant during the probable period of conception, such as motel registration records or joint leases on an apartment where the parties lived together
    - Certified copies of medical records or testimony of physicians/experts, especially if the child was born prematurely raising a question as to the time of conception
    - Documents evidencing the defendant's apparent acknowledgment of paternity, such as a letter urging the plaintiff to get an abortion and offering to pay for it, an earlier voluntary acknowledgment of paternity signed by the defendant but never filed by the mother,

EXHIBIT 7.3 (Continued)

and bank records indicating checks received from the defendant on a regular basis allegedly for support of the child

- Testimony from witnesses who have firsthand knowledge that the Defendant has raised and supported the child and held him or her out as his own natural child

The defendant father may allege and present evidence that another man, possibly one of his relatives, had sexual access to the mother during the probable period of conception. He may challenge the validity of the genetic marker tests, claiming they were tainted or fraudulent. He may need to counter several legal "presumptions" if, for example, his name is on the child's birth certificate, he signed a voluntary acknowledgment, he was married to the mother at any relevant time, or he has held himself out as the child's father.

16. The case is dismissed or a Judgment is entered declaring that the Defendant is the child's father and ordering that his name be added to the child's birth certificate. If the Defendant is excluded as the father, he should request that the court officially rule that he is not the child's father.

PARALEGAL PRACTICE TIP

Visit *www.vermontjudiciary.org* to see a parentage affidavit for a mother and for a father. Reading through these forms will give you an idea of some of the kinds of evidence that may be presented in a paternity case.

PARALEGAL PRACTICE TIP

To see an example of a Judgment in a paternity action, visit *www.courts.wa.gov/forms* (Washington).

EXHIBIT 7.4 Complaint to Establish Paternity

Courtesy of Commonwealth of Massachusetts

Commonwealth of Massachusetts
The Trial Court
Probate and Family Court Department

Division _____   Docket No. _____

COMPLAINT TO ESTABLISH PATERNITY

_____, Plaintiff   v.   _____, Defendant

1. Plaintiff, who resides at _____ (Street Address) _____ (City/Town) _____ (County) _____ (State) _____ (Zip), is
   - ☐ the ○ mother ○ father of a child born out of wedlock.
   - ☐ a child born out of wedlock.
   - ☐ the ○ guardian ○ custodian of a child born out of wedlock.
   - ☐ the ○ parent ○ personal representative of the ○ mother ○ father of a child born out of wedlock.
   - ☐ the ○ Department of Social Services ○ agency licensed under G.L. c. 28A.
   - ☐ the Department of Revenue.

2. The child who is the subject of this complaint is.
   Name _____   Date of Birth _____
   _____ (Street address) _____ (City/Town) _____ (State) _____ (Zip)

3. Defendant, who resides at _____ (Street Address) _____ (City/Town) _____ (County) _____ (State) _____ (Zip), is the ○ mother ○ father of the above-named child who was born out of wedlock.

4. The plaintiff and defendant are not married.

5. The mother of the child was not married at the time of the child's birth and was not married within three hundred days before the birth of the child.

6. Wherefore, the plaintiff requests that the Court:
   - ☐ adjudicate the ○ plaintiff ○ defendant to be the father of the child.
   - ☐ order a suitable amount of support for the child.
   - ☐ order the ○ plaintiff ○ defendant to ○ maintain ○ provide health insurance for the benefit of the child.
   - ☐ prohibit the defendant from imposing any restraint on the personal liberty of the ○ plaintiff and/or ○ the child.
   - ☐ grant the ○ plaintiff ○ defendant custody of the child.
   - ☐ grant the ○ plaintiff ○ defendant visitation rights with the child.

Date _____

_____ (Signature of attorney or plaintiff, if pro se)
_____ (Print name)
_____ (Street address)
_____ (City/Town) _____ (State) _____ (Zip)
Tel. No. _____
B.B.O. # _____

CJ-D 106 (4/07)   C.G.F

PARALEGAL PRACTICE TIP

In Massachusetts, the appropriate form is called a Complaint for Paternity and it is available online. It may be called other things in other states such as a Petition to Establish Parental Relationship (California) or a Filiation Petition (Oregon).

PARALEGAL PRACTICE TIP

The docket number is assigned by the clerk's office when the Complaint is filed.

PARALEGAL PRACTICE TIP

If disclosing the plaintiff/petitioner's address on the Complaint will place him or her at risk, a request can be made to have it impounded. You can see an example of a "Motion for Confidential Address" at *www.courts.delaware.gov*.

PARALEGAL PRACTICE TIP

If the state's child support enforcement agency is involved in the case, it may arrange for the testing. The agency can also order testing administratively if no other man is presumed to be the child's father and the mother or the alleged father submits an affidavit that the parties had sexual relations during the probable period of conception. Although the agency can order the testing without court involvement, the court must issue the actual judgment of paternity if the tests are conclusive and uncontested.

PARALEGAL PRACTICE TIP

The parties also may voluntarily submit to testing. The test itself is painless and noninvasive and involves a simple "buccal swab" to obtain a saliva sample from inside the mouth.

PARALEGAL PRACTICE TIP

If a defendant father fails to comply with an order for testing, the court can draw an adverse inference, hold him in contempt, and issue a paternity order.

PARALEGAL PRACTICE TIP

If a party objects to the results of the genetic marker test, the objection usually must be made in writing within a specified period, commonly thirty days.

PARALEGAL PRACTICE TIP

To see an example of a court order for paternity testing, visit *www .judicial.state.sc.us* (South Carolina).

EXHIBIT 7.5 Motion for Genetic Marker Testing

Courtesy of Commonwealth of Massachusetts

Commonwealth of Massachusetts

The Trial Court

Probate And Family Court Department

Essex County   Docket No. XXXXXXX

Susan Westcott,

Plaintiff   Motion for

v   Genetic Marker Testing

Peter Cann,

Defendant

NOW comes Susan Westcott, the plaintiff in this action who moves this honorable court as follows:

1. To order the plaintiff, defendant, and minor child to submit to genetic marker testing, with results expressed as a probability of paternity.
2. To order that the testing of the parties and the minor child be performed within thirty (30) days at a designated laboratory certified to perform such testing.

Respectfully submitted,

Susan Westcott

By her attorney

_____

Juliana Wilson, Esq

390 Main Street

Newburyport, MA 01950

978-465-1500

BBO# 55342

CERTIFICATE OF SERVICE

I certify that I have served a copy of this Motion, the accompanying Affidavit in Support of the Motion, and the Notice of Hearing upon Peter Cann, 22 Surfer Lane, Newburyport, MA 01950, by first-class mail postage prepaid on September 2, 2014 together with notice that the Motion will be heard in the Essex County Probate and Family Court by the presiding justice sitting in Newburyport, Massachusetts on September 15, 2014, at 8:30 am.

_____

Juliana Wilson, Esq.

EXHIBIT 7.6 Affidavit in Support of Motion for Genetic Marker Testing

Courtesy of Commonwealth of Massachusetts

Commonwealth of Massachusetts

The Trial Court

Probate and Family Court Department

Essex County   Docket No. XXXXXXX

Susan Westcott,

Plaintiff   Plaintiff's Affidavit in Support of Motion for

v   Genetic Marker Testing

Peter Cann,

Defendant

I, Susan Westcott, the Plaintiff in the above captioned matter do hereby swear that:

1. I am the biological mother of the minor child, Christopher Westcott, born on May 28, 2013, in Newburyport, Massachusetts.

EXHIBIT 7.6 *(Continued)*

2. I know the defendant, Peter Cann, and he is the only man I had sexual intercourse with during the probable period of conception of Christopher Westcott.

3. I had sexual intercourse with the defendant, Peter Cann, every weekend between June 21, 2012, and September 30, 2012, while we were registered at the Merromar Inn in Newburyport, MA.

4. After I became pregnant, Peter Cann wrote me a letter saying he wanted me to have an abortion and that he would pay for it.

5. Peter Cann has acknowledged to members of his family that he is Christopher's father.

Signed under pain and penalties of perjury.   _____

                                                                                        Susan Westcott

Date: September 1, 2014

Paralegal **Application 7.3**

Know Your Paternity Basics

Given the considerable variation among the states with respect to paternity actions and the rules that govern them, paralegals need to know the answers to the following questions when working on paternity cases:

- What are the various ways in which parentage can be established in your state? Acknowledgments? Paternity actions? Legitimation actions?
- Which court(s) have subject matter jurisdiction over paternity proceedings?
- How can a court establish personal jurisdiction over resident and nonresident defendants?
- Which statutes of limitations govern the bringing of various kinds of paternity actions (domestic relations, probate, tort, etc.)?

- Are there mandatory forms to be used when filing paternity actions?
- Who has standing to bring a paternity action: mother, husband, putative father, child, IV-D agency, third parties (such as co-parents, grandparents, and personal representatives)?
- What is the standard of proof in paternity actions? Preponderance of the evidence? Clear and convincing evidence?
- When and how can genetic testing be used?
- Does the state recognize any presumptions of paternity (including the marital presumption) and, if so, when and how can they be rebutted?
- Has the state adopted the equitable parent doctrine?

How Is Paternity Disestablished?

A natural consequence of the availability of DNA testing is that some putative fathers learn with scientific certainty that they are not the biological fathers of children they have been raising and supporting in good faith as their own. In many instances, they have mistakenly formally acknowledged paternity or been adjudicated fathers by the court. Although paternity judgments are binding and not easily challenged, an increasing number of states have determined by statute or case law that, in the interest of fairness, a father faced with such circumstances should be permitted to seek an order vacating an earlier paternity judgment, in effect disestablishing an existing father–child relationship. (See Paralegal Application 7.4.)

Several states, such as Alaska,[21] Georgia,[22] Maryland,[23] and Ohio,[24] have established statutory procedures by which an otherwise legally recognized father can disestablish paternity. However, based on the potentially devastating effect of disestablishment on the child, legislatures and courts in a number

PARALEGAL PRACTICE TIP

The state has a statutory right to, in effect, "disestablish" parentage in some contexts. For example, the state may terminate a parent's rights if it proves parental unfitness by clear and convincing evidence. However, parental rights may not be terminated merely to advance the parents' convenience and interests, either emotional or financial.

Disestablishment of paternity
a court order vacating an earlier
paternity judgment or acknowledgment based on evidence the man
is not the child's father, in effect
disestablishing a previously existing
father–child relationship

PARALEGAL PRACTICE TIP

A copy of the Alaska Disestablishment of Paternity statute can be
found at *www.legis.state.ak.us*
(Alaska Statute 25.27.166).

PARALEGAL PRACTICE TIP

Visit *www.clasp.org* (the Center
for Law and Social Policy) to
find state-by-state material on
disestablishment.

of other states have taken a more cautious approach and have expressly not permitted petitions to disestablish paternity. The child, rather than the nonbiological father, is viewed as the victim. Courts in still other states approach **disestablishment of paternity** actions on a case by case basis weighing the relative benefits of knowledge of the truth against disruption in the child's life. Factors these courts consider include:

- the nature and stability of the present home environment
- whether or not there is an existing relationship with a nonbiological father figure
- the desire and willingness of the biological father to assume parenting responsibilities
- whether the child already has established a bond with the biological parent
- the motive of the party bringing the paternity or disestablishment action
- the age of the child
- whether or not the child is uncertain of his or her parentage
- the child's physical and emotional needs
- whether or not there exists a compelling medical need to establish the father's identity

The law with respect to disestablishment actions continues to evolve. When they are permitted, there is considerable variation state to state in terms of when they may be brought and by whom, whether genetic testing must be conducted prior to or as part of the petition to set aside paternity, and whether or not restitution of past child support payments will be granted.[25] (See Cases 7.2 and 7.3 involving efforts to disestablish paternity and maternity respectively.)

Paralegal **Application 7.4**

To Disestablish or Not to Disestablish—That Is the Question

In your opinion, which of the following three approaches to disestablishment should legislatures and courts adopt and why? Should they:

1. act in the interests of the nonbiological father seeking to be relieved of parental responsibility for a child he did not procreate by allowing disestablishment without consideration of the best interests of the child?

   Under Maryland law, for example, in proceedings to modify or set aside paternity declarations, a "determination of the best interests of the child in ordering . . . testing, or in the consideration of paternity, whether original or revised, is inappropriate."[26] "Simply stated, the fact of who the father of a child is cannot be changed by what might be the best interests of the child."[27] Finality of paternity determinations is outweighed by fairness to a man who is not a child's biological father. The "law will not compel one who has stood in the place of a parent

   to support the child after the relationship has ceased."[28]

2. act in the best interests of the child by maintaining an existing parent–child relationship and not allowing disestablishment?

   The Vermont Supreme Court has described this position as follows:

   . . . [T]he financial and emotional welfare of the child, and the preservation of an established parent-child relationship, must remain paramount. Where the presumptive father has held himself out as the child's parent, and engaged in an ongoing parent-child relationship for a period of years, he may not disavow that relationship and destroy a child's long-held assumptions, solely for his own self-interest. . . . Whatever the interests of the presumed father in ascertaining the genetic "truth" of a child's origins, they remain subsidiary to the interests of the state, the family, and the child in maintaining the continuity, financial support, and psychological security of an established parent-child relationship.[29]

3. act in the best interests of the child by allowing disestablishment on the ground that the child should have the opportunity to know his or her biological father?

. . . [C]hildren have a profound right to know their father. They have an interest in their father's care and companionship. . . . In certain cases, it will be in the child's best interest to know the father's identity. Moreover, it is in the child's best interest to have the opportunity to establish a relationship with him.[30]

CASE 7.2 *Paternity of Cheryl*, 434 Mass. 23, 746 N.E.2d 488 (2001)

BACKGROUND

The mother in this often cited case gave birth to a child, Cheryl, in August 1993. In November of that year, the Department of Revenue filed a complaint in the family court against the father to establish paternity on behalf of the mother. The following month, the mother and father executed an acknowledgment of parentage in which both stated that the man was Cheryl's father. The father further acknowledged that he understood the document would have the effect of a judgment against him and that he would be obligated to support the child. That same day a judge entered a judgment of paternity. The father was not represented by counsel and did not submit to a genetic marker test.

The parties never married but for the next seven years, the father sought and expanded visitation rights and behaved as though he was the child's father. He and his family visited with her and he supported her. According to the mother, he was the only man the child had ever known as her father. She called him "daddy," and was bonded to him.

In 1999, the Department sought to increase the father's child support and for the first time, he filed a motion for genetic marker testing and an amendment of the paternity judgment should the results warrant it. In a number of unsworn statements he indicated that he had reason to believe he was not Cheryl's father and that his suspicions to that effect dated back to her birth. The court denied his motion for testing. He subsequently took the child for genetic testing without the knowledge of the mother. The test report indicated conclusively that he was not the father and he once again moved to amend or vacate the paternity judgment and sought reimbursement of all the child support he had paid.

The trial court ordered testing and stated that if the results established he was not the biological father, he would be entitled to prospective relief from the 1993 paternity judgment because to do otherwise would prolong an apparent fraud and falsehood. His interests in not being obligated to support a child not his own outweighed the child's interest in maintaining a relationship with someone she believed to be her father.

However, the mother appealed and the Massachusetts' Supreme Judicial Court granted direct appellate review. The high court subsequently denied the "father's" request for relief.

FROM THE OPINION

There is a compelling public interest in the finality of paternity judgments . . . .Where a father attacks a paternity judgment, courts have pointed to the special needs of children that must be protected, noting that consideration of what is in the child's best interests will often weigh more heavily than the genetic link between parent and child. . . . Like those courts we have recognized that stability and continuity of support, both emotional and financial, are essential to a child's welfare. . . .

Social science data and literature overwhelmingly establish that children benefit psychologically, socially, educationally and in other ways from stable and predictable parental relationships. . . .

Where a father and child have a substantial parent-child relationship, . . . and the father has provided the child with consistent emotional and financial support, an attempt to undo a determination of paternity "is potentially devastating to a child who has considered the man to be the father." Hackley v. Hackley, 426 Mich. 582, 598 n. 11, 395 N.W.2d 906 (1986)

We assess the reasonableness of the five and one-half year interval between the entry of the paternity judgment in 1993, and the father's first motion for relief filed in 1999. . . . in 1993, the father had an opportunity to, but did not seek genetic testing. . . . He never claimed, . . . that his decision to acknowledge paternity voluntarily . . . was conditioned solely on his understanding that he was Cheryl's biological father. A man may acknowledge paternity for a variety of reasons. . . .

Moreover, the father failed to challenge the paternity judgment at the earliest reasonable opportunity. He took no action in 1995 after he was informed, he says, by friends of the mother that he was not Cheryl's biological father. He took no action after the mother "unequivocally" confirmed, he says, that he was not Cheryl's biological father. He took no action after he observed that Cheryl did not share his, his parents', the mother's, or the mother's parents' physical attributes. He took no action in 1996 when he discovered that his low sperm count could explain his and his wife's fertility problems. During all those years, Cheryl knew and relied on him as her father, and he enjoyed her love and companionship. . . .

[We] conclude that, as a consequence of the father's long delay before he challenged the paternity judgment, Cheryl's interests now outweigh any interest of his. . . .

. . . We harbor no illusion that our decision will protect Cheryl from the consequences of her father's decision to seek genetic testing and to challenge his paternity. We cannot protect Cheryl from learning about her genetic heritage. . . . No judgment can force him to continue to nurture his relationship with Cheryl, . . . But we can protect her financial security and other legal rights. . . .

SIDEBAR

Do you think the court reached the right decision in this case? Why?

CASE **7.3** *In the Matter of the Paternity and Maternity of Infant T*, 991 N.E.2d 596 (Ind. Ct. App. 2013)

In this case, a biological father and his wife elected to have a child through a gestational surrogate. The surrogate mother was implanted with embryos created with the biological father's sperm and eggs from an anonymous donor. While the surrogate mother was pregnant, a non-adversarial petition with relevant affidavits was filed by the biological father, the surrogate mother, and the surrogate mother's husband seeking to: (a) establish the biological father's

(Continued)

paternity of the child; and (b) "disestablish" the surrogate mother's maternity of the child. The trial court denied both requests for relief and certified its order for interlocutory appeal by the Indiana Court of Appeals. While the case was pending, the surrogate mother gave birth to the child and the results of genetic testing conducted were consistent with the affidavits filed with the parties' original petition.

I. Decisions regarding the biological father's paternity

The trial court determined that, under Indiana law, the husband of a woman who gives birth is presumed to be the child's legal father, absent clear and convincing evidence otherwise. While the Court of Appeals acknowledged this presumption, it found that case law provided that the presumption could be overcome with a stipulation by the birth mother and putative father. The parties all stipulated that the alleged biological father was, in fact, the biological father of the child, and this stipulation, without more, was sufficient to establish the biological father's paternity. The trial court erred when it denied the biological father's petition to establish paternity.

II. Surrogate mother's maternity

After commenting on the lack of statutory authority and relevant case law on the topic, the Court of Appeals held that the surrogate mother's unopposed petition to "disestablish" maternity, by virtue of her not being the child's biological mother, was not a cognizable legal claim and was properly dismissed by the trial court. The court opined that it would not be in the best interest of the child, and would be contrary to public policy, to allow the birth mother to have the child declared a child without a mother. And it would be inconsistent to allow for petitions to disestablish maternity when petitions to disestablish paternity were prohibited in the jurisdiction. The Court of Appeals noted, however, that in a maternity case, maternity could theoretically be "indirectly disestablished" by establishing the maternity of another woman much the same as Indiana law allows one to "indirectly disestablish" the paternity of one man by establishing the paternity of another. But, maternity can be established only with clear and convincing evidence that a putative mother is the biological mother of the child, meaning that, at least in this case, the biological father's wife (who was not a party) could not petition for maternity, since it was uncontroverted that the eggs were provided by a third party donor.

PATERNITY FRAUD

In some cases, a misunderstanding with respect to biological parenthood may be innocent. A mother truly may not know the identity of the father, or a man may choose to perpetuate a falsehood about the identity of a child's biological father out of love for a spouse and/or a child. However, in other cases, for a variety of reasons, the mother may have deliberately withheld information and/or fraudulently misled both the child and a man believing himself to be the child's father.

- She may not want contact with the biological father because of the circumstances of conception (e.g., rape).
- There may be a history of abuse by the father and she fears for her safety and/or the safety of the child.

- If she is married, she may not want to jeopardize marital harmony or financial security by revealing that the child is the product of an adulterous affair.
- She may want to place the child for adoption and fears that if the father has notice, he will delay or block the adoption.
- In an effort to receive needed public assistance, she may have responded to pressure to designate someone else as the child's father by naming a man she knew was not the real father.

Paternity fraud

fraud in which a mother has intentionally misled a man into believing he is the father of a child to whom he is genetically unrelated

Although **paternity fraud** is old news, paternity fraud actions are a relatively new phenomenon made possible by advances in genetic testing. "In 1999 alone, almost one-third of 280,000 paternity cases evaluated by the American Association of Blood Banks excluded the individual tested as the biological father of the child. In a period of only one year, that is almost 100,000 men who were falsely accused of being the father of a child which, they simply did not father."[31] Paternity fraud actions may involve husbands, ex-husbands, or unmarried fathers, but they all essentially have one thing in common: A man has discovered that he has no genetic relationship to a child he formerly believed was his offspring, and he no longer wants to be legally obligated for support. Much like wrongly convicted felons, some fathers greet DNA testing as a route to freedom. The U.S. Citizens Against Paternity Fraud website goes so far as to display the motto, "If the genes don't fit, you must acquit."[32] But is the cure worse than the disease? "Unlike Pinocchio, a fairy tale ending is neither guaranteed nor likely. . . . Marriages, relationships, and families end. Children are abandoned by the only fathers they ever knew. Fathers are bitter and fight to disown the nonbiological child. Children lose their sense of identity. And the damage cannot be undone."[33]

There are basically two primary remedies for paternity fraud: an action to disestablish paternity as just discussed and a common law action for fraud. Unlike a disestablishment action, which may be prohibited in the victim's jurisdiction, a fraud action affords an opportunity for obtaining relief but does not seek to disrupt a parent–child relationship, at least not intentionally or as a matter of law. Case 7.4 provides an example of a case in which a defrauded father successfully sought relief in an action for fraud.

CASE **7.4** *Hodge v. Craig*, 382 S.W.3d 330 (Tenn. 2012)

In this case, a father, Craig Chadwick, discovered seven years after his divorce from his former wife, Tina Hodge, that Kyle Chadwick was not his biological son. When Tina first informed Craig that she was pregnant, he asked her if she was sure that he was the child's father and she responded that the child could not have been fathered by anyone else. Relying on what she told him, he married her. They later decided that they did not want to have any more children, and as a result Craig underwent a vasectomy. After nine years of marriage, Tina filed for divorce due to irreconcilable differences. The divorce decree incorporated the couple's marital dissolution agreement and adjudicated Craig as Kyle's father.

Seven years later, Craig discovered that he was not Kyle's biological father. He sued Tina for $150,000 in compensatory damages and $150,000 in punitive damages. The trial court held that Tina had "purposefully defrauded" Craig into believing Kyle was his child and that her conduct amounted to "fraud" and "intentional misrepresentation." The court awarded him $134,877.90. Tina appealed and

(Continued)

the Supreme Court of Tennessee eventually held that a former spouse of a child's mother should not be prevented from pursuing common law claims against the child's mother if she intentionally misrepresents the identity of the child's biological father. The Court also explained that its decision did not result in an impermissible retroactive modification of a child support obligation because (1) Craig did not have a legally enforceable obligation to pay child support at the time of the judgment, (2) he did not have any child-support arrearages, and (3) he was never delinquent in paying child support during the time when he was obligated to do so. The Court explained that rather than a retroactive modification of child support, the relief granted constituted an award for damages in an intentional misrepresentation action, and the court merely considered the amount of child support paid in calculating damages. The case was remanded to the trial court with directions to award damages to Craig based on child support, medical expenses, and insurance premiums.

SIDEBAR

The Iowa Supreme Court reached a similar result in *Dier v. Peters*, 815 N.W.2d 1 (Iowa 2012). In that case, an unmarried "disestablished" father brought a common law fraud action against a mother based on her misrepresentation that he was the father of her child. The District Court dismissed the action for failure to state a claim and the petitioner successfully sought review. The facts demonstrated that the mother, Peters, knew that Dier was not the father but had told him he was. Based on that misrepresentation, he provided financial support for both her and the child although he was never under a court order to do so. After he filed an action for custody of the child, she requested a paternity test to exclude him as the biological father and defeat his custody claim. The Iowa Supreme Court reversed and remanded the case after finding that the facts appeared to satisfy all of the elements of a common law fraud action: (1) the mother made a material misrepresentation; (2) she knew it was false; (3) based on the misrepresentation, he provided for the child; and (4) he incurred damages as a result of the misrepresentation.

A Closer Look at Assisted Reproductive Technology

The focus of this chapter now shifts from an emphasis on the painful collapse of family bonds to the joyful promise of **assisted reproductive technology (ART)** as a means of building families. One commentator has described the evolution of the use of this technology as follows:

> The technology of assisted reproduction, developed primarily to aid married couples with infertility, has been made available to people who are physically unable to engage in coitus, or who have an aversion to coitus. . . . It has been made available to people for whom gestation and childbirth pose unacceptable risks, and extended further toward the more controversial use of gestational mothers so that the genetic and/or intended mothers can avoid the inconvenience of going through a pregnancy. It has been made available to people who wish to avoid the risks of having children with genetically determined diseases, and extended further to sex selection and perceived enhancement of

Assisted reproductive technology (ART)
treatment or procedures designed to make parenthood possible for persons with fertility problems or individuals who are otherwise unable or personally unwilling to reproduce

the genome of the intended child, in a word to eugenic practices. . . . ART has been utilized to enable procreation by dead people, by the use of gametes obtained with their knowledge and consent, and sometimes without, and sometimes obtained only after their death. It can potentially be used to enable procreation by fetuses who will never be born.[34]

Exhibit 7.7 provides definitions of some basic ART terms reflecting the breadth and complexity of this topic. In the remainder of this chapter we will focus on some of the issues that arise in the ART context specifically with respect to surrogacy, cryopreservation (freezing) of embryos and gametes, and posthumous reproduction. A concerted effort is made to reference cases and statutes from many states to illustrate the tremendous variation that exists in this rapidly evolving area.

PARALEGAL PRACTICE TIP

As a general rule, when parties enter into assisted reproduction arrangements, they should execute written agreements and consent forms documenting their intentions and expectations. To learn more about such documents, go to the companion website for this text *www.pearsonhigh-ered.com/careers resources/* and look in the material for Chapter 7 under Resources. Select the document called Assisted Reproduction Documents.

Artificial insemination
the process of inseminating a woman by means other than sexual intercourse

Cryopreservation
freezing and storage of genetic material for later use in procreation or research

Donor
the one who gives a gift; in ART, a person who donates genetic material

In vitro fertilization
a technology that involves retrieval of eggs from a female to be fertilized in a laboratory by sperm from a male

Posthumous reproduction
reproduction that occurs after the death of one or both of the gamete donors

EXHIBIT 7.7 Assisted Reproductive Technology—Basic Terminology

Artificial insemination/intrauterine donor insemination	This procedure involves insertion of the sperm of a donor into a female's reproductive system (fallopian tube) by a means other than sexual intercourse, with the intent to bring about a pregnancy.
Cloning	Cloning is the genetic replication of a living organism.
Cryopreservation	This process involves the freezing of gametes (eggs and sperm) or embryos to preserve them for use at a later date.
Cytoplasmic egg donation	In this procedure, genetic material is extracted from the eggs of a donor and injected into the eggs of another woman. In effect, the process technically results in the potential for a child to have two genetic mothers.
Donor	A donor is an individual who produces eggs or sperm (gametes) for use in assisted conception. The donor may or may not receive compensation.
Embryo adoption	Embryo adoption occurs when one or more embryo donors give an embryo to a recipient with the intention that the recipient become pregnant. The recipient (and her spouse, if any) may subsequently adopt the resulting child post birth.
In vitro fertilization (IVF)	An egg is fertilized by sperm outside the womb with the intention that the resulting zygote be transplanted into the reproductive system (uterus) of the genetic mother or a surrogate or that it be available for cryopreservation, donation, or research.
Posthumous reproduction	Posthumous reproduction occurs after the death of one or both of the gamete contributors.
Preimplantation genetic diagnosis (PGD)	This technique involves the biopsy of a single cell or embryo prior to implantation, usually to determine sex, detect genetic disorders, or custom-create or select embryos with desirable traits.
Surrogacy Agreement/Contract	In a surrogacy agreement, a woman agrees to conceive a child through natural or artificial insemination or to implantation of an embryo, to serve as the birth mother, and to relinquish her parental rights to the resulting child whom she agrees to surrender post birth to the intended parent(s).

Paralegal **Application 7.5**

Should ART Be Available to Everyone?

Procreation is a right that enjoys constitutional protection, but does that right extend only to reproduction through traditional means (sexual relations) or also to assisted methods as well? ART provides a valuable resource for a variety of individuals and couples seeking to have children: infertile couples, couples engaged in same-sex relationships, and parties seeking to avoid transmission of disease (such as sickle cell anemia, Tay Sachs, or sexually transmitted diseases). Do you believe everyone should be able to make use of the technology available, or should access be restricted? Consider the following:

> William Gerber is a forty-one-year-old inmate at Mule Creek State Prison in California serving a sentence of 100 years to life plus eleven years. Given the length of his sentence it is unlikely

that he will ever be paroled. He and his wife want to have a child. To that end, Mr. Gerber has requested that he be allowed to provide his wife with a sperm specimen she can use to be artificially inseminated. He argues that a refusal to permit him to do so would constitute cruel and unusual punishment and violate his fundamental right to procreate.

How do you think the warden should respond to this request? Why? A sharply divided opinion dealing with this fact pattern was rendered in *Gerber v. Hickman*, 291 F.3d 617 (9th Circ. Ct. of Appeals 2002). The full opinion can be accessed at *www.pearsonhighered.com/careersresources* in the website material related to Chapter 7 of this text under Cases.

Since the 1970s, hundreds of thousands of children have been conceived through ART rather than "naturally" through coitus. Many state legislatures have been reluctant to tackle this development but several have begun to do so, particularly since marriage equality and recognition of the rights of same-sex partners have become the law of the land. Where laws and procedures regulating the technology and its use do exist they tend to be fragmented and far from uniform. For example, Illinois has a comprehensive set of statutes regulating surrogacy;[35] New Hampshire has passed legislation regarding evaluation of gestational carriers;[36] Massachusetts criminalizes experimentation on embryos before or after implantation;[37] Pennsylvania requires "all persons conducting or experimenting with *in vitro* fertilization" to file quarterly reports with the state;[38] Arkansas requires facilities that provide *in vitro* fertilization services to be certified and achieve a "reasonable success rate with both fertilization and births";[39] several states, including Maryland,[40] have laws addressing insurance coverage for persons undergoing assisted reproductive technology procedures; and an increasing number of states (including Delaware,[41] Nevada,[42], New Mexico,[43] and Washington[44]) have passed statutes treating any person, regardless of marital status, who consents to bring a child into the world through ART as a legal parent of the resulting child.

SURROGACY

In general, surrogacy refers to a situation in which a woman agrees to serve as the birth mother of a child conceived through assisted conception for the benefit of another individual or couple. She may or may not be biologically related to the child and may or may not receive compensation for her services. Typically she agrees to surrender the child she carries to the **intended parent**(s) post birth and to relinquish all of her parental rights. There are two kinds of surrogacy agreements: traditional and gestational.

Traditional surrogacy, a technique developed prior to gestational surrogacy, occurs when a woman is artificially inseminated with the sperm of a man other than her husband for the purpose of carrying a child to term for another woman, a man, or a couple who intend to raise the child as

---

PARALEGAL PRACTICE TIP

The two most commonly cited model acts dealing with surrogacy agreements are the American Bar Association Model Act Governing Assisted Reproductive Technology (2008) and Article 8 of the Uniform Parentage Act (2002), drafted by the National Conference of Commissioners on Uniform State Laws. Both allow traditional and gestational surrogacy contracts subject to extensive regulation that includes judicial preapproval, limits on compensation, and provisions concerning the revocation rights of the parties to the agreement.

Intended parent
a person or couple who intend to take custody of and assume all parental rights and responsibilities for a child as a result of an adoption, a surrogacy arrangement, or some other technique of assisted reproduction; an intended parent may or may not be genetically related to the child.

Traditional surrogacy
occurs when a woman is artificially inseminated with the sperm of a man other than her husband for the purpose of carrying a child to term for another woman, a man, or a couple who intend to raise the child as their own.

their own. In the case of a heterosexual couple entering a traditional surrogacy agreement, the semen used in the artificial insemination process is often that of the intended mother's husband (the intended father). Because traditional surrogacy uses the surrogate's own egg to conceive the child, the traditional surrogate is both a birth mother and a genetic mother. Given this biological relationship, many states decline to enforce traditional surrogacy agreements. Several that do enforce them will not treat an intended mother as a legal mother until the birth mother surrenders her parental rights and the intended mother formally adopts the child.

Gestational surrogacy differs medically from traditional surrogacy in that it involves harvesting eggs from either an intended mother or a third party donor and then fertilizing them outside of the gestational carrier's womb with sperm of the intended father or a third party donor (*in vitro* fertilization). After fertilization, an embryo (or often multiple embryos), is implanted in the gestational surrogate's uterus for her to carry to term and deliver. The resulting child is then transferred to the intended parents to raise as their own. Although the gestational surrogate is the birth mother, she is otherwise biologically unrelated to the child because the genetic parents are the intended parents, gamete donors, or a combination of the two. Because gestational surrogacy often involves a genetic connection between an intended mother and the child, a majority of states will enforce gestational surrogacy agreements, provided the birth mother's rights are terminated or maintained in a manner consistent with governing law in the jurisdiction.

The law governing traditional and gestational surrogacies in the United States is at best unsettled. Many states have no controlling statutory or case law. A small minority have enacted comprehensive statutes. The Tennessee Supreme Court provided an excellent overall review of laws addressing surrogacy across the nation in 2014 in *In re Baby et al.*, 447 S.W.3d 807 (Tennessee 2014).

In approximately one-third of the states, legislatures have enacted statutes addressing surrogacy, the majority of which fall into one of three categories. First, some states have legislatively prohibited all surrogacy contracts, declaring their terms unenforceable and, in some instances, imposing criminal penalties for those who attempt to enter into or assist in creating such a contract. See, e.g., D.C. Code §§ 16-401(4)(A)-(B), -402(a) (prohibiting all "[s]urrogate parenting contracts" as defined by statute); Mich. Comp. Laws Ann. §§ 722.851-.863 (declaring surrogate parentage contracts, as defined by statute, to be "void and unenforceable" and imposing criminal penalties for participation in a "surrogate parentage contract for compensation" or a surrogacy contract involving a surrogate who is an unemancipated minor or who has "a mental illness or developmental disability"). A second category of states prohibit only certain types of surrogacy contracts—typically those involving a traditional surrogacy. See, e.g., Ky. Rev. Stat. Ann. § 199.590(4) (prohibiting traditional surrogacy contracts, as defined by statute, without addressing gestational surrogacies); N.D. Cent. Code §§ 14-18-05, -08 (declaring traditional surrogacy agreements void but allowing gestational surrogacies by providing that "[a] child born to a gestational carrier is a child of the intended parents for all purposes and is not a child of the gestational carrier and the gestational carrier's husband, if any"). Finally, states in the third category authorize both traditional and gestational surrogacy contracts, subject to regulation and specified limitations. See, e.g., N.H.

Gestational surrogacy
involves harvesting eggs from either an intended mother or a third party donor and then fertilizing them outside of the gestational carrier's womb with sperm of the intended father or a third party donor (*in vitro* fertilization) for implantation in the surrogate mother's uterus

PARALEGAL PRACTICE TIP

Florida's statute governing gestational surrogacy contracts can be accessed at *www.leg.state.fl.us* (742.15).

PARALEGAL PRACTICE TIP

The Arkansas Code provides for recognition of surrogacy agreements and discusses scenarios in which the surrogate mother is married and unmarried, and where the intended parent or parents are either married or unmarried (Ark. Code Ann. § 9-10-201).

PARALEGAL PRACTICE TIP

Under Utah law, the intended mother cannot be receiving Medicaid or other state assistance, and she must be married to the intended father.[45]

PARALEGAL PRACTICE TIP

In New Hampshire, parties to a surrogacy agreement must have their agreement judicially approved prior to impregnation.[46]

Rev. Stat. Ann. §§ 168-B:1 to -B:32 (generally permitting traditional and gestational surrogacy agreements subject to certain conditions, including a traditional surrogate's right to revoke the agreement within seventy-two hours of birth); Va. Code Ann. §§ 20-156 to 20-165 (generally permitting surrogacy contracts, as defined by statute, and providing a multi-step process for judicial pre-approval of such contracts); Wash. Rev. Code Ann. §§ 26.26.210-.260 (generally permitting traditional and gestational surrogacy agreements but prohibiting compensation beyond reasonable expenses and agreements involving a surrogate who is "an unemancipated minor female or a female diagnosed as having an intellectual disability, a mental illness, or developmental disability").

Although **forum shopping** is generally discouraged and, in some instances, not permitted by the courts, parties from one state may be permitted to execute an agreement in a more surrogacy-friendly state, provided that state has at least some connection with the matter and the result is not contrary to a strong public policy. For example, in one case, the Massachusetts Supreme Judicial Court allowed a pre-birth judgment of parentage when the intended parents resided in Connecticut, the surrogate and her husband lived in New York, and the baby was scheduled to be born in Massachusetts.[49]

EXHIBIT 7.8 Nevada Statute NRS 126.045 Governing Surrogacy Contracts

1. Two persons whose marriage is valid under chapter 122 of NRS may enter into a contract with a surrogate for assisted conception. Any such contract must contain provisions which specify the respective rights of each party, including:
   a. Parentage of the child;
   b. Custody of the child in the event of a change in circumstances; and
   c. The respective responsibilities and liabilities of the contracting parties.
2. A person identified as an intended parent in a contract described in subsection 1 must be treated in law as a natural parent under all circumstances.
3. It is unlawful to pay money or anything of value to the surrogate except for the medical and necessary living expenses related to the birth of the child as specified in the contract.
4. As used in this section, unless the context otherwise requires:
   a. "Assisted conception" means a pregnancy resulting when an egg and sperm from the intended parents are placed in a surrogate through the intervention of medical technology.
   b. "Intended parents" means a man and woman, married to each other, who enter into an agreement providing that they will be the parents of a child born to a surrogate through assisted conception.
   c. "Surrogate" means an adult woman who enters into an agreement to bear a child conceived through assisted conception for the intended parents.

Despite the unsettled status of surrogacy law across the country, for several years, surrogacy agreements have been an option for establishing parenthood, particularly for opposite-sex married couples and for lesbian couples who each have an opportunity to be related to a child, one by genetics, the other by gestation. A gay man who wants to have a biologically related child without vaginal intercourse has no choice but to use a surrogate/embryo carrier.

Many courts have been receptive to agreements involving lesbians who contract with a donor for artificial insemination, but there is little case law involving gay couples who do not fit the traditional mold as well as females. For example, problems sometimes arise with respect to the distinction between a man who wants solely to be a donor and a man who wants not only to donate sperm but also to assume responsibilities of fatherhood. In some states, a sperm donor is a legal

PARALEGAL PRACTICE TIP

Although generally a surrogacy-friendly state, Virginia prohibits surrogacy "brokers."[47]

PARALEGAL PRACTICE TIP

Illinois provides considerable protection for parties to surrogacy agreements and permits pre-birth establishment of the legal parentage of children of assisted conception, effective immediately upon birth.[48]

Forum shopping

seeking a court in a jurisdiction that will provide the most favorable ruling in a case nonentity as a parent, but in others a donor is allowed to retain parental rights under certain conditions. For example, in New Jersey, there is a statutory exception to the paternity presumption in the context of artificial insemination (N.J.S.A. 9:17-44(b)): *Unless the donor of semen and the woman have entered into a written agreement to the contrary* [emphasis added], the donor of semen provided to a licensed physician for use in artificial insemination of a woman other than the donor's wife is treated in law as if he were not the father of a child thereby conceived and shall have no rights or duties stemming from conception of the child.

As the law evolves, the light on the horizon for gay couples is getting brighter. In the groundbreaking case *Raftopol v. Ramey*, 299 Conn. 681 (2011), for example, the Connecticut Supreme Court held that a presumption of legitimacy should extend to the domestic partner of the father of twins born through surrogacy. The case involved two men, Anthony Raftopol and Shawn Hargon, who entered a written agreement with a gestational carrier, Karma Ramey. Under the agreement: a third party donated eggs which were fertilized with Raftopol's sperm, Hargon was an intended nonbiological parent, and Ramey agreed to terminate her parental rights and consent to the adoption of any children born pursuant to the agreement. Prior to the birth of twin boys, Raftopol and Hargon sought a declaratory judgment (essentially a pre-birth parentage order) that their gestational agreement was valid and that they were the children's legal parents. The trial court ruled (1) the gestational agreement was valid; (2) Raftopol was the children's genetic and legal father; (3) Hargon was the children's legal father; and (4) Ramey was not the children's genetic or legal mother. The court ordered the state Department of Public Health (DPH) to issue a replacement birth certificate under CGS § 7-48a. DPH appealed. On appeal, the Connecticut Supreme Court concluded: 1. Under Connecticut law, "a gestational carrier who bears no biological relationship to the child she has carried does not have parental rights with respect to that child." 2. Under CGS § 7-48a, an intended parent who is a party to a valid gestational agreement may become a parent without first adopting the children, regardless of their biological relationship to the children. 3. The trial court properly ordered DPH to issue a replacement birth certificate listing Hargon as the children's parent. The court, based on the statute's plain language, rejected DPH's argument that the legislature intended that only biological intended parents may acquire legal status as parents. The court found that DPH's interpretation would lead to "an absurd result" because it could lead to a parentless child. The court limited its holding to valid gestational agreements.

To increase the likelihood that a surrogacy agreement will be enforceable, the family law team must research surrogacy, parentage, adoption, and marriage laws in the jurisdiction where each party to the agreement resides and, if in a different jurisdiction, the state where it will be executed. A failure to do so can have serious consequences. The scope of liability for attorneys who handle ART cases is unknown. Potential conflicts of interest are many; legal risks and obligations for clients are unlimited; "agreements" are not necessarily enforceable; and the legal landscape provides no clear road maps for counsel to follow. Ethical, liability, and enforcement issues can easily explode in the surrogacy minefield. Consider the following:

- If an intended mother fails to obtain a pre-birth parentage order[50] and doesn't officially adopt the child in a manner consistent with state law, she may end up being treated as a third party, in effect a legal stranger to the child, rather than as a parent in a later custody dispute in the context of an action for divorce from the biological father.[51]

- A court may determine that a provision in a traditional surrogacy agreement does not independently act to terminate the surrogate mother's parental rights despite the fact that the parties, each with advice of counsel, negotiated and executed a detailed agreement. See, e.g., *In re the Paternity of F.T.R.: David J. Rosecky, Petitioner-Appellant v. Monica M. Schissel, Respondent-Respondent*, 2013 WI 66, 349 Wis.2d 84, 833 N.W.2d 634 (2013), holding that those rights can only be terminated in a manner which complies with existing statutory procedures: involuntary termination based on unfitness or voluntary termination by surrender or consent to adoption.

- Clinics providing ART donor services may falsely advertise or fail to properly screen donors for medical issues, including the presence of sexually transmitted diseases resulting in significant health risks to both surrogate mothers and the children they bear. See, e.g., a Michigan case, *Stiver v. Parker*, 975 F.2d 261 (5th Cir. 1992), involving transmission of a serious condition characterized by mental retardation and other defects.

- Fertilization centers may negligently implant embryos in the wrong recipients or redirect them for use by other clients or in research.[52] See, e.g., *Perry-Rogers v. Obasaju*, 282 A.D.2d 231 (N.Y. App. Div. 2001), involving accidental implantation in a Caucasian woman of an African American embryo.

- In one of the worst case scenarios, a court may determine that surrogacy agreements are simply unenforceable. In the high-profile *Baby M.* case,[53] the New Jersey Supreme Court held that a traditional surrogacy "contract" between a biological father, his wife, and a genetically related surrogate mother was against public policy and unenforceable as a matter of law. The court created a new "family" configuration for the child by awarding physical custody to the intended/biological father and visitation to the surrogate mother, who was also the child's genetic mother. In describing its reasoning for not enforcing such agreements, the court commented:

> The long-term effects of surrogacy contracts are not known, but feared—the impact on the child who learns her life was bought, that she is the offspring of someone who gave birth to her only to obtain money; the impact on the natural mother as the full weight of her isolation is felt along with the full reality of the sale of her body and her child; the impact on the natural father and the adoptive mother once they realize the consequences of their conduct. . . . The surrogacy contract is based on principles that are directly contrary to the objectives of our laws. It guarantees the separation of a child from its mother; it looks to adoption regardless of suitability; it totally ignores the child; it takes the child from the mother regardless of her wishes and her maternal fitness; and it does all of this, it accomplishes all of its goals, through the use of money.[54]

Generally, when disputes about parentage stemming from surrogacy agreements reach the courts, the parties include some combination of the surrogate mother and her husband, gamete donors, and the intended parents, who may or may not be married and who may be of the same or different sexes. The courts basically apply one of the following four tests to determine parentage, each of which may produce a significantly different result.

PARALEGAL PRACTICE TIP

Agreements that a donor will remain anonymous may not always be enforceable against a physician, clinic, or hospital. For example, it may be necessary to reveal the identity (or at least the characteristics) of the donor in the event of a medical emergency involving the child. It is also not outside the realm of possibility that even a posthumously conceived child of a deceased donor could discover the donor's identity and make a claim to his or her estate.

PARALEGAL PRACTICE TIP

The opinion in the Baby M. case is available at *www.pearsonhighered .com/careersresources/* in the website material related to Chapter 7 of this text under Cases. New Jersey now allows gestational surrogacy agreements in some circumstances.

Genetic test
the position taken in parentage determinations in surrogacy cases that the individuals who contribute a child's genetic material should be considered his or her legal parents

Gestational test
the position taken in maternity determinations in the surrogacy context that the woman who carries and gives birth to a child should be deemed the child's legal mother

Best interests of the child test
the position that determinations of legal parentage in surrogacy cases should be based upon who is best able to fulfill the social and legal responsibilities of parenthood

Intent test
the position taken in parentage determinations in surrogacy cases that the individual(s) who set the procreative process in motion with the intent of raising any resulting children should be deemed the legal parent(s) of those children

PARALEGAL PRACTICE TIP

The full opinion in *Johnson v. Calvert* can be found at *www.pearsonhighered.com/careersresources* in the website material for Chapter 7 of this text under Cases.

- **A genetic test**: Courts that apply a genetic test in parentage determinations in surrogacy cases give priority to genetic heritage, based on the premise that genes contribute to the greatest extent in shaping the child's nature and future life. A genetic parent will be deemed a legal parent under this test. In cases in which the surrogate mother is also the genetic mother, courts are especially reluctant to terminate her parental rights. Under this test, absent an enforceable agreement to the contrary, the individuals (potentially including third party donors) who contribute the genetic material to produce the embryo are considered the child's legal parents.

- **A gestational test**: This test places the greatest emphasis in surrogacy disputes on the significance of the fact that the birth mother is responsible for the health and safety of the fetus for the nine months of pregnancy. Her lifestyle, habits, and physical and psychological condition potentially have a permanent effect on the child. This test is consistent with the traditional common law approach to the establishment of maternity.

- **A best interest of the child test**: This is the standard traditionally applied in the family law context with respect to matters pertaining to the custody of children. It serves to ensure that in resolving disputes affecting minor children, protection of the child will be the primary consideration. The court looks to who is best able to fulfill the social and legal responsibilities of parenthood, including not only financial support but also physical and psychological nurturing of the child, intellectual and moral guidance, and stability and continuity of care.

- **An intent test**: Under this test, the individual or individuals who want to become parents and put the birth process in motion will be considered the legal parents of the resulting child. The California Supreme Court was the first to adopt the intent test in the landmark *Johnson v. Calvert* case[55] involving a "contest" between an intended biological mother and a gestational mother. Mark and Crispina Calvert had executed a gestational surrogacy agreement with Anna Johnson in 1990 providing that an embryo created by the sperm of Mark and the egg of Crispina would be implanted in Anna, and post birth, Mark and Crispina would have and raise the resulting child "as their child." Anna agreed to relinquish "all parental rights" to the child. In return, Mark and Crispina agreed to pay Anna $10,000 in a series of installments. They also agreed to pay for a $200,000 life insurance policy on Anna's life.

After disputes arose between the parties during the pregnancy, Anna sent a letter demanding the balance of the payments due to her or else she would refuse to give up the child. The following month, Mark and Crispina filed a lawsuit, seeking a declaration that they were the legal parents of the unborn child. Anna filed her own action to be declared the mother of the child, and the two cases were consolidated. The trial court ruled that Mark and Crispina were the child's "genetic, biological and natural" father and mother, that Anna had no "parental" rights to the child, and that the surrogacy contract was legal and enforceable against Anna's claims. The court also terminated the order allowing visitation. Anna appealed, the Court of Appeals affirmed, and the California Supreme Court granted review. The Court rejected Anna's arguments that surrogacy contracts violated the law and public policy prohibiting the payment for consent to adoption of a child and pre-birth waivers of parental rights. In reaching its decision, the California high court was guided by the Uniform Parentage Act adopted in that state in 1975. The Court held that although the Act recognized both genetic consanguinity and giving birth as means of establishing a mother-and-child relationship, California law recognized only one natural mother. When the two means do not coincide in one woman, the mother who intends to bring about a child to raise as her own will be considered the natural mother. The Court described the importance of intent in this context as follows:

> Because two women have each presented acceptable proof of maternity, we do not believe this case can be decided without enquiring into the parties' intentions as manifested in the surrogacy agreement. Mark and Crispina are a couple who desired to have a child of their own genes but are physically unable to do so without the help of reproductive technology. They affirmatively intended the birth of the child and took the steps necessary to effect in vitro fertilization. But for their acted-on intention, the child would not exist. Anna agreed to facilitate the procreation of Mark's and Crispina's child. The parties' aim was to bring Mark's and Crispina's child into the world, not for Mark and Crispina to donate a zygote to Anna. Crispina from the outset intended to be the child's mother. Although the gestative function Anna performed was necessary to bring about the child's birth, it is safe to say that Anna would not have been given the opportunity to gestate or deliver the child had she, prior to implantation of the zygote, manifested her own intent to be the child's mother. No reason appears why Anna's later change of heart should vitiate the determination that Crispina is the child's natural mother.[56]

CRYOPRESERVED EMBRYOS AND GAMETES

As more and more couples utilize ART to create and freeze embryos for use at a later date, it is inevitable that the courts will increasingly be called upon to resolve controversies involving the parties' rights and responsibilities with respect to those embryos. It is estimated that there are already hundreds of thousands of unused embryos in cryopreservation.[57] Two of the contexts in which the courts have begun to address this development are when frozen embryos need to be disposed of upon divorce and when they are used posthumously (after the death of of a party).

Disposition of Frozen Embryos Upon Divorce

After four decades of experience applying this technology, it has become apparent that, in addition to planning for use of *in vitro* fertilization and freezing of surplus embryos, couples also must anticipate and provide for the disposition of those embryos in the event of separation, death, divorce, or changes in plans or circumstances. Options for disposition include storing them for use at a later date, donating them for "embryo adoption"[58] or research, preserving them for an indefinite period, or thawing and discarding them.

A limited number of states have enacted legislation addressing issues specifically relating to use, storage, and disposition of preserved embryos.

New Hampshire and Louisiana, for example, have provisions addressing some aspects of maintenance and duration periods for storing prezygotes outside of the body.[59] Under Louisiana law, the embryos are considered legal persons,[60] and embryo donations are essentially regulated by adoption statutes. Florida requires by statute that couples and their treating physicians execute written agreements addressing disposition of preembryos in the event of death, divorce, or other unforeseen circumstances.[61] Oklahoma law refers to embryo donation as "human embryo transfer and donation." Only biological parents may donate embryos; both the donor and the donee couples must be married; and the donee couple, the physician, and a judge in a court with jurisdiction over adoption must execute a written consent form.[62]

In the absence of legislation, courts in some states have been forced to judicially address disposition upon divorce with and without written agreements between the parties. Some courts refuse to enforce agreements based on state law, public policy, or other considerations. Courts that do enforce them generally apply one of three approaches described in Case 7.5, *Szafranski v. Dunston*, 993 N.E.2d 502 (Ill. App. 2013): a balancing approach, a contractual approach, or a contemporaneous mutual consent approach.

Related case law reflects a fact-based approach and a general trend toward enforcing modifiable agreements but not compelling unwanted parenthood. In the landmark *Davis* case,[63] the Tennessee Supreme Court considered disposition of seven frozen embryos belonging to an already divorced couple, each of whom had remarried. The wife sought to donate the embryos to another childless couple, but the husband wanted them destroyed. The Tennessee Supreme Court determined that the lower court had erroneously applied a best-interests-of-the-child test (appropriate for a custody determination) and ruled that "pre-embryos are not, strictly speaking, either 'persons' or 'property,' but occupy an interim category that entitles them to special respect because of their potential for human life."[64] In reaching its decision, the Court recognized that "the right to procreational autonomy is composed of two rights of equal significance—the right to procreate and the right to avoid procreation."[65] The wife's interest in donating the embryos was viewed as less significant than the husband's interest in avoiding parenthood. Although the parties in this case had not executed a written agreement, the court indicated in *dicta* that such agreements should be upheld in the event of separation or divorce, stating, "the state's interest in the potential life of these pre-embryos is not sufficient to justify any infringement upon the freedom of these individuals to make their own decisions as to whether to allow a process to continue that may result in such a dramatic change in their lives as becoming parents."[66]

In the *Kass* case,[67] New York's highest court emphasized the importance of agreements stating:

> . . . [P]arties should be encouraged in advance, before embarking on IVF and cryopreservation, to think through possible contingencies and carefully specify their wishes in writing. Explicit agreements avoid costly litigation. . . . Advance directives, subject to mutual change of mind that must be jointly expressed, both minimize misunderstandings and maximize procreative liberty by reserving to the progenitors the authority to make what is in the first instance a quintessentially personal, private decision. Written agreements also provide the certainty needed for effective operation of IVF programs.[68]

CASE 7.5 *Szafranski v. Dunston*, 993 N.E.2d 502 (Ill. App. 2013)

In this case of first impression in Illinois, the appellate court considered the proper approach to resolving disputes over the disposition of frozen embryos. The case involved an unmarried couple who produced several preembryos using the boyfriend's sperm and a donor's eggs because the girlfriend was unable to produce her own eggs as a result of ovarian cancer. The parties executed an Informed Consent for Assisted Reproduction with a clinic. The document provided that no use could be made of the embryos "without the consent of both partners." They also met with an attorney and considered (but never actually signed) a "co-parenting agreement." Eight embryos were produced and shortly thereafter the couple broke up. The boyfriend, Szafranski, subsequently sought to enjoin Dunston from using the preembryos and forcing him to become a father against his will. She then sought sole custody and control and the right to use them to bear children. She alleged both breach of contract and promissory estoppel as bases for her claim. The trial court granted her request and Szafranski appealed. The appellate court thoroughly reviewed case law in other jurisdictions and then identified and assessed the three approaches taken in other jurisdictions that enforce agreements:

The Contractual Approach: The courts should enforce contracts governing the disposition of cryopreserved preembryos as long as they do not violate public policy (New York, Oregon, Tennessee, Texas, and Washington).

The Contemporaneous Mutual Consent Approach: No embryo should be used or destroyed without the contemporaneous mutual consent of the couple that created the embryo thereby preserving the status quo and making it possible for the partners to reach an agreement at a later time (Ohio).

The Balancing Approach: Under this approach, the courts enforce agreements to a point allowing for the parties to change their minds and, in the absence of an agreement, apply a balancing test (balancing the right to create v. the right not to procreate). They consider the positions of the parties, the significance of their interests, and the relative burdens that will be imposed in different scenarios (New Jersey and Pennsylvania).

After weighing the alternatives, the appellate court adopted the contractual approach honoring the parties' own mutually expressed intent as expressed in their prior agreements. The court held that such agreements should generally be presumed valid and binding. In the absence of an agreement, the relative interests of the parties in using or not using the preembryos should be weighed and generally the party wishing to avoid procreation should prevail. The court vacated the circuit court's decision so the parties could reconsider their positions in light of its adoption of the contractual approach. The Illinois Supreme Court denied a petition for appeal (996 N.E.2d 24 (2013)).

SIDEBAR

In *Reber v. Reiss*, 2012 PA Super 86, 42 A.3d 1131 (2012), the Pennsylvania appellate court affirmed a trial court's decision in a case of first impression in that state on this issue. The case involved disposition of frozen embryos in the context of a divorce. The embryos were deemed property subject to equitable division. The court applied a balancing approach and awarded the embryos to the wife. On appeal, the court held the trial court did not abuse its discretion when it found that the wife's inability to achieve parenthood without use of the preembryos (due to cancer treatment) outweighed the husband's desire to avoid procreation. In Massachusetts, in *A.Z. v. B.Z.*, 431 Mass. 150, 725 N.E.2d 1051 (2000), that state's high court found that an alleged agreement was ambiguous and unenforceable.

(Continued)

> In *dicta*, the court opined that even if there had been an unambiguous agreement regarding disposition of frozen preembryos, the court would not enforce an agreement that would compel a donor to become a parent against his or her will.
>
> ### SIDEBAR
>
> Which approach do you think is most appropriate in such cases?

Posthumous Reproduction

Given advances in assisted reproductive technology, it is now possible for children to be conceived after the death of one or both of their genetic parents through the use of cryopreserved gametes or embryos. (See Paralegal Application 7.6.) Posthumous conception customarily occurs in one of two ways: (1) a survivor harvests genetic material after an individual's death for use in producing an embryo or (2) more commonly a survivor uses cryopreserved embryos created during a decedent's lifetime using their genetic material. There are several legal questions that may arise in this context including but not limited to the following:

> Is there a constitutionally protected fundamental right to procreate posthumously? No such right has been recognized to date.
>
> Will a deceased gamete-provider be considered a parent of a posthumously conceived child?
>
> Will posthumously conceived children be treated differently than children born to parents who are both alive (as they are technically nonmarital children)?

Most disputes regarding posthumously conceived children arise in connection with claims for Social Security Benefits and probate matters. The issue regarding eligibility for Social Security Survivor Benefits was addressed by the U.S. Supreme Court in *Astrue v. Capato* in 2012. (See Case 7.6.) Several states identify the intestate inheritance rights of posthumously conceived children by statute. For example, the applicable Florida statute referenced in the *Capato* case requires that the intended parents and treating physician must have signed a written agreement regarding disposition of cryopreserved eggs, sperm, and preembryos in the event of the death of one of the spouses. The decedent also must have provided for the child in his or her will.[69] In Louisiana, a posthumously conceived child has inheritance rights, provided the child is born to the surviving spouse within three years of the death of the decedent.[70]

PARALEGAL PRACTICE TIP

Clients contemplating cryopreservation should be encouraged to anticipate the possibility of posthumously conceived children and prepare wills that spell out their intentions with respect to children born as a result of assisted reproductive technology.

CASE 7.6 *Astrue v. Capato*, 132 S. Ct. 2021 (2012)

In 1999, Karen Capato's husband, Robert Capato, was diagnosed with esophageal cancer. Out of fear that he would become sterile due to chemotherapy, he and his wife, Karen, decided to have some of his sperm frozen and banked. Before Robert died, they were able to have a son through natural means. After he died in 2002, Karen used some of the banked sperm and conceived via *in vitro* fertilization. She gave birth to twin sons eighteen months after her husband's death. Although they had told their lawyer that they wanted more children, Robert's will only provided

(Continued)

for the parties' son and two of his children from a prior marriage. It made no provision for future children born after his death.

When she applied for Social Security Survivors Benefits based on her husband's earnings during his lifetime, her claim was rejected. The Administrative Judge for the Social Security Administration (SSA) ruled that Robert had died in Florida and that under Florida law children cannot inherit from a parent if they were conceived after that parent's death absent a written agreement and a provision for the child in the decedent's will. Since the 1940s, the SSA has used state inheritance laws as the deciding factor in determining whether a person is a "child" under the Social Security Act and therefore eligible for survivors benefits. Capato appealed and the U.S. Court of Appeals for the Third Circuit reversed the SSA's decision. The SSA appealed and the U.S. Supreme Court granted certiorari because of a split in approaches taken in four circuits: Courts of Appeal in the Third and Ninth Circuit had allowed for the granting of Social Security benefits when biological parentage was undisputed. Courts in the Fourth and Eighth Circuits denied benefits to children who could not inherit under state intestacy laws.

In a unanimous decision, the Supreme Court reversed the Appeals Court holding that a child conceived and born after a parent's death cannot rely solely on a genetic connection to the deceased parent in order to qualify for Social Security Survivors Benefits. Siding with the SSA's interpretation of the law, the Court held that all children, including those born via assisted reproduction technology, must either demonstrate that they would be eligible to inherit from their late parent under state law or satisfy one of the statutory alternatives to that requirement (which they did not). The Court found that the SSA position was a reasonable interpretation of the Social Security Act and was rationally related to two legitimate state interests: (1) conserving benefits for children who have actually lost a parent's support and (2) avoiding the need for individualized inquiries into dependency. In its opinion, the Court noted that it was unlikely the technology that made the twins' conception and birth possible was contemplated by Congress when the relevant provisions of the Social Security Act (Act) originated (1939) or were amended to read as they now do (1965).[71]

Paralegal **Application 7.6**

Life After Death—What Do You Think?

Do you think that people who are terminally ill, going off to combat, or participating in other inherently dangerous activities should be permitted to freeze gametes for use postdeath? What are the arguments for each side of the question? Would it make a difference in your opinion if the eggs or sperm are harvested post death? Without prior consent of the decedent? For use by parties other than the donors?

The Role of the Paralegal

The paralegal's role in this area will be determined largely by the prevailing law in the jurisdiction where the paralegal is employed and the degree to which the firm handles cases involving parentage determinations and assisted reproductive technology. Tasks performed are likely to include the following:

- locating controlling statutes and case law governing parentage determinations and/or techniques of assisted reproduction

- researching related jurisdictional issues, including the potential existence of multiple forums in which to execute an ART agreement or seek to establish or disestablish paternity
- gathering information in preparation for drafting pleadings and/or documents related to parentage issues
- maintaining a list of reputable test banks and arranging for DNA testing, if required
- drafting pleadings and/or agreements
- drafting discovery materials, such as proposed interrogatories, deposition questions, and requests for admission and production of documents and things
- drafting responses to discovery requests received from the opposition
- maintaining a file of experts on related topics
- coordinating communication with experts and other witnesses, if necessary
- preparing affidavits, exhibits, memoranda, correspondence, etc., as assigned
- assisting with preparation for hearings and/or a trial on the merits
- organizing materials for appeals, if necessary
- making sure the client is kept informed of progress and upcoming deadlines, hearings, discovery matters, etc.

CHAPTER **SUMMARY**

Perhaps more than any other in the text, this chapter gives us cause to reflect on the fascinating times in which we live. Scientific technology and the structure of the American family are undergoing dramatic change. We have multiple paths to parenthood unconstrained by marital or biological ties. Children may have any combination of parents in terms of gender and potentially any number of parents. Technology has "advanced" to such a point that anyone can go online and order a "home insemination kit." Parents can establish and "disestablish" parenthood. It is no wonder that the courts are struggling to adapt traditional legal principles to contemporary realities. The many references in the chapter to a variety of state statutes along with case examples involving heterosexual and gay couples, married and unmarried, illustrate some of the complex issues courts are facing on a daily basis.

This chapter began by identifying some of the many kinds of "parents" recognized in contemporary society.

We reviewed various methods of establishing parenthood, including the marital and other presumptions, voluntary acknowledgment of parentage, and adjudication of parentage based on adoption, contractual agreements, equitable principles and biology in the context of "traditional" paternity actions. Particularly in the latter part of the chapter, we looked briefly at some developments in the field of assisted reproductive technology, especially with respect to surrogacy, cryopreservation of embryos, and posthumous reproduction.

The nationalization of marriage equality and the increased use of ART are compelling changes in the legal framework governing the various topics we have discussed. No matter what the reader's personal opinions may be with respect to these developments, courts continue to be called upon to determine the lawful parentage of children in increasingly diverse scenarios. Family law teams inevitably are going to continue to play an active and important part in that process.

CONCEPT REVIEW AND REINFORCEMENT

KEY **TERMS**

Artificial insemination	*De facto* parent	Gestational mother
Assisted reproductive technology (ART)	Disestablishment of paternity	Gestational surrogacy
Best interests of the child test	Donor	Gestational test
Biological parent	Equitable parent doctrine	Intended parent
Biology-plus rule	*Filius nullius*	Intent test
Co-parent	Forum shopping	*In vitro fertilization*
Cryopreservation	Genetic test	IV-D agency

Legal parent

Marital presumption

Operation of law

Parent by estoppel

Parentage

Parenthood

Paternity fraud

Posthumous reproduction

Psychological parent

Putative father

Res Judicata

Traditional surrogacy

REVIEW **QUESTIONS**

1. Identify the three parties with the strongest interests in parentage determinations and describe the basic nature of those interests.

2. Identify and describe the three primary ways of establishing legal parentage.

3. Identify four examples of contexts in which parenthood is established through adjudication.

4. Describe the basic process for adjudicating paternity.

5. Describe the equitable parent doctrine and explain how it was applied by the Wisconsin Supreme Court in *A.J. v. I.J.*

6. Define paternity fraud. Explain what it means to "disestablish" paternity. Identify some of the common arguments in favor of and against disestablishment.

7. Identify and describe the four tests most often applied by the courts to resolve disputes arising out of surrogacy arrangements.

8. Describe the trend with respect to resolution of disputes regarding disposition of cryopreserved embryos upon divorce.

9. Define posthumous reproduction and give an example of circumstances in which it might be utilized.

10. Identify at least three ways in which gays and lesbians can become legal parents.

DEVELOPING YOUR PARALEGAL SKILLS

FOCUS ON **THE JOB**

In this activity, students have an opportunity to consider with their classmates the relative merits of seven parties' claims to legal parenthood of a baby boy.

The Facts

Stephen and Mary recently married after dating each other for four years. They want to share a life together and have a child, but Stephen carries a rare genetic disease, and Mary has had a hysterectomy due to uterine cancer. They have decided to execute a surrogate parenting agreement with their friends Carol and Chip. Chip feels he and Carol could use the money they would receive. Carol really doesn't care about the money and just loves having babies. She and Chip are raising their three daughters in their small five-room home, which they are hoping to remodel.

Carol signs a contract with Stephen and Mary in which Carol agrees to have an embryo implanted in her womb, to carry it full term (absent severe medical complications), and to release the child and execute a consent to adoption one week after the child's birth. Chip also signs a consent to the agreement in his capacity as Carol's husband.

The embryo will result from *in vitro* fertilization using egg and sperm from two unmarried donors identified by Stephen and Mary following exhaustive research concerning

their backgrounds and characteristics. The donors, Bill and Barbara, each take great pride in their genetic heritage and are very honored to be selected as donors. Each is professionally successful and independently wealthy. Neither will accept payment for services as a donor. No formal, written contract is executed with the donors.

Over the course of the gestation period, several events occur:

1. Stephen and Mary develop marital problems when Stephen becomes intimately involved with his best friend, David. Mary and Stephen agree to separate and consider their respective options for the future. Each of them wants custody of the baby about to be born. David is looking forward to marrying Stephen and raising the child together.

2. Bill and Barbara meet at the fertility clinic, begin dating, and decide they should get married and seek custody of the baby about to be born. They want to protect the product of their genes and ensure that the child has the best opportunity to develop his or her potential. They claim separate and joint rights to be declared the child's parents.

3. Chip gets a promotion at work and decides he can afford to move his family to a much nicer and more spacious home, spacious enough to accommodate a fourth child.

He decides that if the baby his wife is carrying is a boy, he wants to keep it. Carol also has had a change of heart. She has bonded with the fetus she is carrying and wants to keep it post-birth with or without her husband's consent.

One week after Carol gives birth to a seven-pound, eight-ounce healthy baby boy (Baby B), each of the seven parties seeks a declaration of legal parentage, and the cases are consolidated.

The Assignment

The members of the class should be divided into seven groups, with each group working for an attorney representing the interests of one of the parties in this case: Stephen, David, Mary, Carol, Chip, Bill, and Barbara. Each group should research governing law (both statutory and case law) in their jurisdiction and develop an argument in support of their client's claim to legal parentage of Baby B. If completing this assignment in a group format is not feasible, each student should select one of the parties and research the merits of that party's claim in light of the law governing the case. Each argument should be submitted either orally in class or in a paper with the heading: "Argument in Support of the Claim of *client's name* to Parentage of Baby B."

FOCUS ON **ETHICS**

In this exercise, the student addresses ethical issues that arise regarding "confidential" information, conflicts of interest, and dishonesty of a party in a hypothetical case.

The Assignment

Assume that you are a paralegal in the large firm where Attorney Jane Newton is a partner. Attorney Newton represents Carol in the above fact pattern. You work for Attorney Judie Woodford, an associate at the same firm. Attorney Woodford has represented Chip and Carol in the past on a variety of matters. An ethical wall presently insulates both Attorney Woodford and you from the present case. However, as you are riding down in the elevator to go to lunch, you realize that Carol and a friend of hers are also in the elevator. You say "hi" but Carol does not recognize you and continues to carry on a conversation with her friend. She "confides" to the friend that, even though there was a celibacy clause in her surrogacy agreement, she engaged in a "one-night stand" with a stranger she met at a bar around the time when she conceived. She says there is a slight chance that Baby B is the product of that incident, but she doesn't intend to risk Chip's and her chances for legal parenthood by admitting it. How should you address this situation? In preparing your response, refer to the canons of the National Association of Legal Assistants contained in Appendix A and ethics material provided in Chapter 1 of this text for guidance. Your response should be in the form of an internal memorandum to your supervisor.

FOCUS ON **CASE LAW**

In this activity, the student is asked to brief a case involving establishment of parentage.

The Assignment

Select one of the following cases to read and brief using the format provided at *www.pearsonhighered.com/careersresources/* in the material related to Chapter 1 of this text under Resources (unless your instructor directs you to use an alternative form):

1. *Kevin Q. v. Lauren W.*, 174 Cal. App. 4th 1557 (2009). This case involves a paternity contest between two men whose claims are based on conflicting presumptions: a presumption based on a voluntary declaration of paternity and a presumption of paternity based on a man's having received a child into his home and openly holding him out as his natural child.

2. *In the Matter of the Parentage of the Child of Kimberly Robinson*, 383 N.J. Super. 165, 890 A.2d 103 (2005). In this case, a same-sex partner of the biological mother of a child seeks to be designated as the child's other legal parent under New Jersey's Artificial Insemination Statute.

3. *Pitts v. Moore*, 2014 ME 59, 90 A,D,3d 1169 (2014). In this case, the Supreme Judicial Court of Maine leaves the door open to the possibility of a child having three parents by applying the doctrine of *de facto* parenthood.

All three cases are available at *www.pearsonhighered.com/careersresources/* in the website material for Chapter 7 of this text under Cases.

FOCUS ON **STATE LAW AND PROCEDURE**

In this Focus exercise, the student is asked to draft a Complaint for Paternity based on a specific fact pattern using a jurisdictionally appropriate format.

The Facts

Susan Westcott, your firm's client, wants to file an action to establish paternity of her one-year-old son,

Christopher Westcott, born on May 28, 2014. She is certain the child's father is Peter Cann, who lives at 22 Surfer Lane in your city or town. He was born on May 5, 1991, in the capital city of your state and his Social Security number is 016-23-1947. Susan resides at 2 Woodbine Road in your city or town. She was born in that city or town on January 30, 1992, and her Social Security number is 106-23-1904. She and Peter had sexual relations every weekend between June 21, 2013, and September 30, 2013, at the Merromar Inn in your city or town, where they were registered guests. She got pregnant during that period and Christopher was born approximately nine months later. She was not intimately involved with any other man during that time frame and she has never been married. On his birth certificate, the child is identified as Christopher Westcott although the father is listed as unknown. The child's Social Security number is 092-23-9437. Susan intends to seek full custody and child support in an amount consistent with your state's child support guidelines.

Assignment

Locate the statute(s) governing paternity in your state, along with the form used in actions to establish paternity in contested cases. Complete the form tailoring it to the above fact pattern.

FOCUS ON **TECHNOLOGY**

In addition to the links provided throughout the chapter, this Focus on Technology provides a series of websites for reference along with technology-related assignments for completion.

Websites of Interest

bioethics.gov

Sponsored by the President's Council on Bioethics, this user-friendly site offers a rich variety of resources, including transcripts, reports, background materials, and books on ethical issues related to ART. The reports may either be downloaded or ordered in print form.

cdc.gov/art

This is the Center for Disease Control's site on assisted reproductive technology. It provides a wealth of information about ART, including reports on success rates.

family.findlaw.com

This site has links to state paternity laws. Many of the links provide access to forms related to establishment of parentage, including Voluntary Acknowledgments, Complaints, and Affidavits.

www.paternityfraud.com

This is the website of the New Jersey Citizens Against Paternity Fraud, an organization founded by Patrick McCarthy, a man who unsuccessfully sought to disestablish paternity after learning postdivorce that he was not the biological father of his fourteen-year-old daughter.

Assignments

1. Locate three sites on the Internet that market eggs and/or sperm for ART purposes. Describe each of the sites.

What quality control measures are in place, if any? How does one donate? How does one make a purchase? What costs are indicated?

2. Locate the website for the Title IV-D child support enforcement agency in your state. Describe the information and forms you find there regarding establishment of paternity. A directory of IV-D agencies in all states is available at *www.ocse.acf.hhs.gov*.

3. Several states provide online user-friendly resources for individuals seeking to establish paternity. Check out:

   - Connecticut's site, which includes a booklet called "Establishing Paternity for Your Child. . . and For You." *www.ct.gov*. Select "Publications." Under "Publications and Brochures," select "Brochures." Then scroll down to the title of the booklet.
   - The California Courts Self Help Center, which provides information, forms, and instructions for parentage cases. *www.courtinfo.ca.gov*. Select "Self Help," then "Families and Children" and "Parentage" as your topic.
   - New York's site, which provides a narrative that walks a person through a paternity case and includes a twenty-minute video with Spanish subtitles that illustrates the process in the child support context. *www.courts.state.ny.us*. In the FAQs box in the top right-hand corner of the screen, insert "paternity" and you can then explore the various materials that are available. The link for the video is at the bottom of the page.

PORTFOLIO PRODUCTS

1. Paper on merits of a client's claim to parentage
2. Internal memorandum concerning ethical issues in a hypothetical case
3. Brief of a case on establishment of parentage
4. Complaint for Paternity

chapter 8
ADOPTION

LEARNING OBJECTIVES

After reading this chapter and completing related assignments, you should be able to:

- explain what adoption is and the purposes it serves

- identify various types of adoption

- distinguish between an open and a closed adoption

- list the major steps in the adoption process

- discuss the rights of wed and unwed parents in the adoption context

- explain what a putative father registry is

- describe the nature and purpose of safe haven laws

- identify who must consent to an adoption

- identify circumstances in which parental rights may be terminated

- explain when an adoption may be challenged and by whom

- describe the role of the paralegal in an adoption case

De facto **adoption**

[Latin: in point of fact] an adoption that does not meet formal statutory requirements but is considered an adoption based on the conduct of the parties and the surrounding circumstances; sometimes called equitable adoption or adoption by estoppel

---

Scott and Hayley Martinelli want Scott's son, Mike, to be a part of their family, and so they plan to have Hayley adopt him. . . . Mike's mother, Jessica Olivio, doesn't feel that she can handle the responsibility of raising Mike and sees adoption as a good solution, as long as she can maintain enough contact to watch him grow up. . . .

Introduction

In Chapter 7, the primary focus was on establishment of legal parentage of children by biology, marriage, and assisted reproductive technology (ART). In this chapter the focus shifts to establishment of parentage and the creation of family relationships through the legal process of adoption, a process largely driven by state and, to some extent, federal statutes. The emphasis is on types of adoption, the common steps in the adoption process, and the rights of various individuals in the termination of "old" families and the formation of "new" families. Attention is also given to variations in adoption laws across the nation as well as the role played by paralegals in the overall process.

HISTORICAL PERSPECTIVE

Adoption has existed in one form or another for centuries and has served a variety of purposes. In other times and cultures, it primarily served the needs of adults seeking to maintain political power, ensure heirs, and transfer wealth. Historically, the primary purpose of adoption in this country has been to protect children and ensure their futures within the context of a family unit. Although Mississippi and Texas recognized informal adoptions prior to the 1850s, Massachusetts passed the nation's first comprehensive adoption statute in 1851, and other states promptly followed suit. These early acts essentially formalized the parent–child relationship for children already living in *de facto* family relationships.

They also advanced welfare reforms targeted at abandoned and orphaned children living in institutions and providing a source of cheap labor as apprentices.

DEFINITION OF ADOPTION

Adoption is the judicial process by which a new parent–child relationship is created. It constitutes, in effect, a birth by legal process in which an adoptive parent assumes the legal rights and duties of a biological parent. Adoption is essentially a two-step process in which an existing parent–child relationship (usually between the child and one or both of his or her birth parents) is terminated and a new parent–child relationship is judicially created. The birth parents may voluntarily surrender their rights and consent to an adoption, or their parental rights may be involuntarily terminated by a court. An adoptive parent may be a stranger to the child, a relative, a stepparent, or a known but unrelated adult, as is usually the case in an adult adoption. The adoption may and in some states must be coordinated by a state-approved public or private agency and, in the assisted reproductive technology context, may be facilitated by a contractual agreement enforceable in the courts.

Adoption
the judicial process by which a new parent–child relationship is created and an adoptive parent assumes the legal rights and duties of a biological parent

LEGAL EFFECT OF ADOPTION

According to U.S. Census Bureau estimates, there are more than two million adopted children in the United States.[1] Once an adoption is finalized, the relationship between the **adoptee** and his or her adoptive parents is as permanent as the relationship between a child and a biological parent in the sense that it does not end with divorce or the death of a parent. Only the court can end the relationship by invalidating or revoking the adoption or by terminating the parental rights and responsibilities of the adoptive parent for cause. Adoption brings to the child the wide range of benefits that flow from the parent–child relationship, including, for example, the right to be supported by the adoptive parent(s) while a minor, to inherit by and through the adoptive parent(s), to receive adoptive parents' worker's compensation benefits for dependents, and to have **standing** to bring a wrongful death action on the death of an adoptive parent.

Adoptee
the individual who is adopted

PARALEGAL PRACTICE TIP
Throughout this chapter, we generally refer to the adoptee as "the child." Although the adoption process establishes a parent–child relationship, an adoptee may be an adult.

Standing
an individual's right to bring a matter before the court and seek relief based on a claim that he or she has a stake in the outcome of the case

Types of Adoption

Adoptions commonly fall into three categories based on:

- how they are created (through an agency or privately etc.);
- whether they are open or closed; and
- according to who can adopt (e.g., married couples, single persons, stepparents, and co-parents).

TYPES OF ADOPTION BASED ON HOW THE ADOPTION IS CREATED

The five major types of adoption based on how the adoption is created are:

Agency adoption

Independent adoption

International adoption

Equitable adoption/adoption by estoppel

Illegal/black market adoption

Agency adoption
an adoption facilitated by an agency licensed by the state

Termination of parental rights
the judicial severing of the legal relationship between a parent and child and of the associated rights and responsibilities; may be voluntary or involuntary based on clear and convincing evidence of unfitness

PARALEGAL PRACTICE TIP

Massachusetts is an example of an "agency" state. Exceptions are made when the petitioner is a stepparent or blood relative of the child to be adopted or is a guardian or prospective adoptive parent named in a biological parent's will.

Independent adoption
an adoption usually facilitated by a third party such as a physician or attorney, rather than by a licensed state agency; sometimes called private, designated, or identified adoption

PARALEGAL PRACTICE TIP

To learn more about advertising and payment of facilitators in adoption, visit www.childwelfare.gov. Select Adoption and then search for Use of Advertising and Facilitators in Adoptive Placements. Google Alabama Code 26-10A-36 Advertisement as to adoption by persons, organizations, etc., not licensed by Department of Human Resources to see that state's statute prohibiting payments for facilitating adoption.

PARALEGAL PRACTICE TIP

Careful records must be kept by attorneys and other facilitators to document that fees collected are paid for services actually provided and NOT as incentives for a parent to release a child for adoption.

International adoption
an adoption in which a child residing in one country is adopted by a resident of another country

Agency Adoption

Each state has a designated state agency responsible for regulating adoptions within its borders. In an **agency adoption**, a public or private agency licensed by the state takes temporary custody of a child for subsequent placement in a permanent adoptive home. Children come into the custody of an agency through two primary routes: (1) The parent(s) voluntarily transfer custody of the child to the agency by executing a written surrender relinquishing their parental rights or (2) a court terminates their parental rights for cause, based on clear and convincing evidence of parental unfitness, and places the child in the temporary custody of an agency pending an adoption.

All states permit agency adoptions, and in some states, all adoptions must be facilitated by an agency except in limited circumstances, e.g., when the adoption is by a stepparent or close family member. The agency is essentially responsible for all phases of the adoption process, including, among other tasks, recruiting foster care and adoptive homes, screening prospective parents, conducting comprehensive home studies, locating potential adoptees, and securing proper consents / **terminations of parental rights**.

Independent Adoption

In an **independent** (or private) **adoption**, the biological parent(s) transfer custody of the child directly to the adoptive parents. The process is usually facilitated by a third party—such as a physician, a member of the clergy, and/or an attorney specializing in adoption law—who performs most of the tasks usually handled by an agency. This type of adoption generally allows biological parents to designate adoptive parents or to prescribe more fully the characteristics they would like prospective adoptive parents to possess. Adoption is marketed especially to financially and emotionally challenged pregnant women as a morally acceptable means of achieving a positive result for children who are "unwanted" for any of a variety of reasons. Sometimes the parents are brought together as a result of ads or by adoption exchange organizations listed in the yellow pages. However, adoption has become a big (nearly $2-billion-a-year) business.[2] Competition is stiffening for traditional facilitators of adoptions, as newly emerging profit-making entrepreneurs increasingly make extensive use of the Internet to find and match birth parents and prospective adoptive parents.

Although privately arranged, independent adoptions still must be approved by a court. A majority of the states permit them, but some do not, due to concerns that they are not regulated and screened as carefully as agency adoptions. Birth parents usually do not receive counseling regarding their options, and preplacement home studies are not necessarily required. As a result, even in states where they are permitted, independent adoptions may be subject to regulations regarding the fees that may be charged by intermediaries, and adoptive parents may need to be approved or certified by the state.

International Adoption

An **international adoption** (sometimes called intercountry or transnational adoption) takes place when a child residing in one country is adopted by a resident of another country. Each year thousands of U.S. citizens adopt children from abroad and many families in other countries adopt children from the

United States.[3] The United States is the largest receiving country for intercountry adoptions followed by Spain, France, Italy, Canada, and the Netherlands.[4] It is estimated that approximately 25% of adopted children in the United States come to their families through international adoptions.[5] Although the figures vary from year to year, U.S. parents most often adopted children from the following countries in fiscal year 2013: China (2,301), Ethiopia (993), Haiti (388), Russia (250), Ghana (170), and Colombia (159).[6] Based on government data, there were 7,094 intercountry adoptions in 2013 down from a high in 2004 of 22,991.

International adoption is a highly specialized and complex area of family law. It is governed by the adoption and immigration laws of both the country in which the child to be adopted lives and the country in which the prospective adoptive parents reside. The costly and protracted process for a U.S. resident to adopt a child from another country has undergone significant changes in recent years following ratification by the United States of the Hague Convention on Protection of Children and Co-operation in Respect of Intercountry Adoption (the Convention), which went into effect in the United States in 2008. "The Convention is designed to prevent the abduction, sale, and trafficking of children and to promote their best interests. In this country, the U.S. Department of State has overall responsibility for implementing the Hague Convention, although the U.S. Citizenship and Immigration Services (USCIS) within the Department of Homeland Security also plays a significant role."[7] As of June 2015, more than ninety nations were parties to the Convention. A list of these nations is available at *www.hcch.net* Select Welcome, the Intercountry Adoption Section, and then Contracting States (Status Table).

Since 2008, under U.S. law, there are two distinct intercountry adoption processes for potential use by U.S. citizens: the Hague Convention process and the non-Hague Convention process. The process followed depends on whether the other country involved is also a party to the Hague Convention. The basics of each process and distinctions between the two are outlined in a "Comparison of Adoptions from Convention vs Non-Convention Countries" (part of the Factsheets for Families Series), which can be found at *www.childwelfare.gov*. (See Paralegal Application 8.1.)

Equitable Adoption/Adoption by Estoppel

An **equitable adoption**, sometimes called an **adoption by estoppel**, is not technically an adoption. Rather it involves the application of equitable principles to avoid the unfair consequences of a literal application of the law. It refers to a situation in which prospective adoptive parents accept a child into their home and raise the child as their own without ever formally finalizing an adoption. Some states allow a child in such circumstances to inherit from the "adoptive" parents should they die intestate (without a will), even though the adoption process was never completed. The adoption is treated by the court as if it took place, and the "adoptive" parents' estates are estopped (prevented) from denying the child's claim. In *James R.D. v. Maria Z (In re Scarlett Z.D.)*, 2015 IL. 117904, 28 N.E.2d 776 (2015), the Illinois Supreme Court addressed the doctrine and held that although Illinois recognizes the doctrine of equitable adoption, it only recognizes the concept in the probate context for inheritance purposes and does not apply it to proceedings for parentage, custody, and visitation. It is not intended to create a legal adoption.

Illegal/Black Market Adoption

Illegal/black market adoption

an adoption brokered by an individual who collects a substantial fee for locating a child who is transferred from one person or couple to another without proper legal process

Illegal or black market adoptions are often referred to as baby selling. They are brokered by individuals who collect a substantial fee for locating a child who is transferred from one person or couple to another without proper legal process. Historically, black market adoptions have been pursued by individuals who do not qualify as adoptive parents under agency standards or who seek to adopt children in high demand (commonly infants). Such "arrangements" are high risk and likely to be deemed void if challenged at a later date.

Paralegal **Application 8.1**

Do You Want to Learn More About International Adoption?

One of the best ways to learn more about the complexities of international adoption is to visit the website of the U.S. Department of State's Bureau of Consular Affairs on Intercountry Adoption *www.adoption.state .gov*. This site literally addresses this topic from A to Z. It provides a wealth of information, including, for example:

- an excellent description of the international adoption process (along with several forms)
- responses to frequently asked questions (FAQs) and information on who can adopt

- background information about various countries and variations in the adoption process in Hague and non-Hague Convention member countries
- state links for approved/accredited U.S.-based adoption service providers for Hague Convention adoption cases
- information about all members of the international adoption community, including adopters and adoptees, judges, social workers, and agencies
- a description of the Child Citizenship Act of 2000 and its requirements and instructions for obtaining a visa for a child adopted from another country
- a Glossary of related terms

OPEN AND CLOSED ADOPTIONS

Closed adoption

an adoption in which biological and adoptive parents essentially know nothing about each other, and adoptees have no access to their original birth certificates or identifying information about their biological parents

Adoptions in the United States fall along a continuum from closed to open. In a **closed adoption**, the biological and adoptive parents essentially know nothing about each other, and adoptees have no access to their original birth certificates or any identifying or nonidentifying information about their biological parents. In an **open adoption**, the biological parents, the adoptive parents, and the adoptee have varying degrees of contact with each other.

Closed Adoption

Open adoption

an adoption in which biological parents, adoptive parents, and the adoptee have varying degrees of contact with each other

Many adoptions are still initially closed adoptions in which the biological and adoptive parents do not know each other's identities. The general rule is that once an adoption is finalized, the court orders the record sealed, and a new birth certificate is issued in an effort to protect the privacy of the birth parents and the security of the adoptive parents from interference with the new family bond. However, these interests have not stopped adoptees from challenging the constitutionality of confidentiality laws. (See Paralegal Application 8.2.)

Paralegal **Application 8.2**

Adoptee Challenges to Sealed Records

Adoptees occasionally challenge the confidentiality of adoption records through the courts. In one early landmark case, *Alma Society Inc. v. Mellon*, 601 F.2d 1225 (2d Cir. 1979), the appellants were an association of individual adult adoptees who claimed the New York statutes that required the sealing of adoption records violated their Fourteenth Amendment Equal Protection and Due Process rights. They also raised the novel argument that the statutes violated the Thirteenth Amendment prohibiting slavery because much like slavery they in effect abolish the parental relationship likening adoptees to slave children "sold off" and separated from their parents while too young to consent to, or even know, what was happening.

The adoptees claimed that upon reaching adulthood they should be entitled, without a showing of cause, to obtain their sealed adoption records, including the names of their natural parents. Some appellants argued that lack of access caused serious psychological trauma, pain, and suffering; potential medical problems and misdiagnoses due to a lack of medical history; the danger of unwitting incest; and an impairment of religious freedom due to not being reared in the religion of their natural parents.

The District Court dismissed their Complaint, and the second circuit appellate court affirmed that decision. The courts emphasized that the statutes serve important interests such as erasing the stigma of illegitimacy from the adopted child's life by sealing his or her original birth certificate and issuing a new one under a new surname; encouraging natural parents unwilling or unable to care for their offspring to use the adoption process and protecting their privacy when they do; and promoting the security of the newly formed family unit. The courts took this position even though they acknowledged that once an adopted child reaches adulthood, some of the considerations that apply at the time of adoption and throughout the child's tender years may no longer apply. Today, many biological mothers are willing to have their adult adopted children contact them, and many adoptive parents would not object to, or would even encourage, the adopted child to seek out the identity of or a relationship with a natural parent.

Sidebar

The full opinion in the *Alma Society* case can be accessed at *www.pearsonhighered.com/careersresources/* in the companion website material for Chapter 8 of this text under Cases. It was decided in 1979 and since then a growing number of states have elected to allow adult adoptees access to their original birth or adoption records. Several challenges to laws that do not allow access have been successful. In *Does 1-7 v. State*, 993 P. 2d 822 (Or. Ct. App. 1999), for example, an Oregon appellate court opined that birth is a matter of public record and the state does not extend to birth mothers a constitutionally protected right to conceal their identities from their children. The policy of closed adoption continues to be a source of controversy among adoption professionals. What are the primary arguments on each side of this issue? What is your position? Many believe that the Internet has sounded the death knell for closed adoption. What do you think? (See Paralegal Application 8.7 later in this chapter.)

Despite a trend toward increased openness, in some states, the adoptee's desire to establish his or her roots and personal identity still is not deemed sufficient for the records to be opened by court order, although over the years some exceptions to the rule of secrecy have developed particularly in unusual or emergency circumstances.

- A number of states have established an exception for medical reasons when the adoptee or a child of the adoptee requires information about inherited diseases and medical conditions or is in need of a bone marrow or organ transplant. Even in the absence of an emergency, it may be argued that individuals need information about their genetic and medical family histories in order to make informed decisions about preventive measures and lifestyle adjustments that may be appropriate.

PARALEGAL PRACTICE TIP

To see examples of Applications for Adoption Registry forms for parents, adoptees, and relatives for the Nevada Registry, visit *www.dcfs .state.nv.us.* Forms/Adoption Registry.

PARALEGAL PRACTICE TIP

To learn more about search and reunion and accessing adoption information, visit *www.childwelfare .gov.* Select Adoption/Search and Reunion.

PARALEGAL PRACTICE TIP

To see the statute governing open adoption in Oregon, go to *www .oregonlaws.org* Search for statute 109.305.

PARALEGAL PRACTICE TIP

Some commentators urge that adoption law should expand further than it has by eliminating requirements for petitioners to be in marriage or marriage-like relationships and even allowing petitions by more than two individuals within reasonable limitations. See, e.g., Cynthia Mabry, *Joint and Shared Parenting: Valuing All Families and All Children in the Adoption Process with an Expanded Notion of Family,* 17 Am. U. J. Gender Social Pol'y & L. 659 (2009).

Joint petition for adoption
a petition to adopt a child that is brought by both parties to a marriage (or by co-parents)

- Several states (including Colorado)[8] maintain **adoption reunion registries** that allow adoptees after a certain age (usually eighteen) to try to contact their biological parents and siblings. Once contacted by the adoptee, the registry attempts to contact the birth parents, and if they consent, arrangements are made to put the child and the birth parents in touch with each other. If a birth parent refuses, no further contact is made.
- Some states have statutes providing for the release to adoptees of nonidentifying information about their biological parents. Such information usually includes medical, ethnic, socioeconomic, and educational information and, in some cases, information about the circumstances under which the adopted person became available for adoption.[9]
- A small number of states, including Alabama, Alaska, Kansas, and Oregon[10] have legislated that an adoptee, upon reaching the age of majority (usually eighteen), may request a copy of his or her original birth certificate.

Open Adoption

An open adoption is a form of adoption in which the birth parents, the adoptive parents, the adoptee, and sometimes the adoptee's biological siblings maintain a degree of postadoption contact with each other. The contact may assume a variety of forms, including, for example, the sending of annual or seasonal photographs, written or electronic correspondence with or about the child, and visits. In states where open adoptions are permitted, the terms of the agreement are customarily expressed in a contract submitted for approval by the court. If the adoptee is over age twelve, his or her consent to the agreement may be required. More than half the states now have statutes allowing written and enforceable postadoption agreements. (See *www.laws.adoption.com,* Postadoption Contact Agreements.) Most states that allow them do not permit them in cases where a parent's rights were terminated involuntarily unless the agreement would be in the best interest of the child.

TYPES OF ADOPTION BASED WHO CAN ADOPT

The third primary way of categorizing adoptions is based on who can adopt. Some states have broad eligibility statutes that will be given effect if the language is clear and unambiguous. For example, the applicable Idaho statute (I.C. § 16-1501) allows "any adult person residing in and having residence in Idaho to adopt 'any minor child' without restrictions on marital status." Generally, children may be adopted by qualified family members, stepparents, married couples, single persons, or co-parents, depending on the jurisdiction.

Married Couple Adoption

The most common form of adoption is one in which a married couple seeks to adopt a child who is biologically unrelated. The couple is usually required to file a **joint petition for adoption**. Several states expressly prefer married couples as adoptive parents and some biological parents condition placement of their child with an agency on eventual adoption by a married heterosexual couple.

Single Parent Adoption

Today, single persons are eligible to adopt in almost all states. However, historically, some states have prohibited single persons (regardless of sexual orientation) from adopting and others have not considered them desirable candidates. Old attitudes die hard, and some agencies still have biases, expressed or masked, in favor of placing children with traditional married couples.

Family Member Adoption

Several states establish by statute or administrative regulation a preference for adoption by family members such as aunts, uncles, and grandparents, ostensibly to minimize disruption and maintain some degree of family connectedness for children. However, states also may place restrictions on adoptions of family members. For example, the Massachusetts adoption statute provides, "A person of full age may petition the probate court . . . for leave to adopt as his child another person younger than himself, unless such other person is his or her wife or husband, or brother, sister, uncle or aunt, of the whole or half blood."[11]

Stepparent Adoption

Even though stepparents may live with and care for their spouse's children on a daily basis, they have fewer rights with respect to those children than a **foster parent**, guardian, or noncustodial biological parent. They cannot consent to medical treatment or make educational or other decisions relating to the children. In addition to formalizing an emotional bond, stepparent adoption addresses this situation. A stepparent adoption occurs when the spouse of a divorced or widowed and remarried biological parent or the spouse of a parent of a nonmarital child seeks to adopt the child. The child retains a legal relationship with one parent, but his or her other parent (if living and known) generally must voluntarily consent to the adoption or have his or her parental rights involuntarily terminated. Unlike a typical adoption, in which both biological parents' rights are extinguished, the **cut-off rule** does not apply to the custodial biological parent who remains in the new family unit. Although the adoption still must be approved by the court, most states have in place simplified procedures designed to expedite stepparent adoptions. Depending on the circumstances and extent of the relationship between the child and the parent whose rights are being terminated, the court may grant some degree of postadoption contact similar to that provided in an open adoption agreement.

Foster parent
a person or persons who provide a temporary home for a child when his or her parents are temporarily unwilling or unable to do so, usually through a child welfare agency for a modest payment

Cut-off rule
the rule requiring that a biological parent's rights to his or her child be terminated prior to adoption of the child by a third party; does not apply to the custodial biological/legal parent who remains in the new family unit

Co-parent Adoption

Co-parent or second-parent adoptions as they are often called are basically hybrid adoptions combining aspects of direct placement adoptions and stepparent adoptions. In the usual co-parent adoption, one partner in an unmarried couple has or adopts a child and the other partner who is co-parenting the child seeks full parental status through an adoption. That status affords the second partner legally protected parental rights, including the right to make decisions regarding the child's health, education, and welfare, along with the responsibility of providing financial support. Should the parties' relationship terminate, both parties have equal custodial and visitation rights.

Courts in a number of states have granted co- or second-parent adoptions when they find them to be in the best interest of the children involved. However some states have been slow to accord rights to nontraditional family units. For example, in the *Matter of the Adoption of Garrett*, 17 Misc. 3d 414, 841

Co-parent
a person engaged in a nonmarital relationship with the legal parent of a child who regards himself or herself as a parent rather than as a legal stranger to the child; a person who shares childrearing responsibilities with a partner with or without benefit of a legally recognized relationship

N.Y.S.2d 731 (N.Y. Misc. 2007), a mother and her brother (the child's uncle) who lived together sought to adopt her child as co-parents. The court denied the petition acknowledging that although adoption law has undergone significant revision in recent years, it was unwilling to further expand it "to virtually unlimited boundaries, namely, to authorize the adoption of a child by a natural parent and another member of that parent's family, namely, the brother of the natural mother."

Historically, the obstacles have been particularly high in some states for same-sex partners seeking second-parent adoptions. For example, a Utah statute provides that "A child may not be adopted by a person who is cohabiting in a relationship that is not a legally valid and binding marriage under the laws of this state."[12] Even when co-parent adoptions are permitted gay co-parents sometimes face resistance. In an Idaho case, *In re Doe*, 156 Idaho 345, 326 P.3d 347 (2014), the prospective adoptive parent had to pursue her case to the state's highest court. The Idaho Supreme Court reversed a lower court's judgment finding that it had violated the petitioner's right to due process when it dismissed her petition to adopt her long-time same-sex partner's two biological children without affording her the opportunity to be heard in a meaningful manner. The lower court had stated that it could find no "provision that allows for the adoption of a person's adopted and/or biological children by that person's cohabiting, committed partner." The petitioner had been the children's primary caregiver for more than a decade and her petition to adopt the child as a second parent was unopposed, strongly supported by the home study, and desired by the children and their other parent. The couple had entered a civil union in Canada and a same-sex marriage in California but neither was recognized at the time under Idaho law (although Idaho became a same-sex marriage state less than a year later). In reversing the lower court, the Idaho Supreme Court noted that this was not a case dealing with same-sex marriage but rather a case dealing strictly with Idaho's adoption laws and that Idaho's adoption statutes unambiguously allow a second, prospective parent to adopt, regardless of marital status.

Now that marriage equality is the law of the land, it is likely that a number of same-sex couples raising children together who could not previously marry now will do so resulting in a decrease in co-parent adoptions and an increase in step-parent adoptions. As with heterosexual married couples, it may be necessary for non-parent same-sex spouses to pursue stepparent adoptions if they want to establish and secure parental rights with respect to the children they are co-parenting. However, even as spouses, they may still face roadblocks. A new obstacle to adoptions by gays is coming from the so-called religious freedom bills that critics say use religious freedom to legalize LGBT discrimination. For example, in June 2015, the Governor of Michigan signed into law a hurriedly passed bill allowing faith-based agencies that contract with the Michigan Department of Health and Human Services (including those that are publicly funded) to refuse to serve prospective adoptive parents like same-sex or unmarried couples if doing so would violate the agencies' sincerely held religious beliefs embodied in a written agency policy. Although the agencies are required to provide prospective parents with a list of alternative placement agencies, at the very least the law will limit resources and delay adoptions by same-sex spouses and unmarried partners in Michigan. The future of such laws is unclear in light of the *Obergefell* decision but it is fair to say that they will be challenged.

The Adoption Process

An adoption is the creation of a parent–child relationship by law. Subject to applicable state and federal laws, each state has enacted its own adoption procedures and practices, which vary considerably from one jurisdiction to another. However, the basic steps in the adoption process in virtually all states include the following:

1. Identify and locate the legal/biological parents of a potential adoptee and determine their rights
2. Free the child for adoption by parental consent or termination of parental rights
3. Identify potential adoptive parents
4. Conduct home study(ies) (depending on the jurisdiction and type of adoption)
5. Determine proper jurisdiction and venue
6. File a Petition for Adoption
7. Serve Notice on all interested parties
8. Conduct a Preliminary Hearing
9. Issue an Interlocutory Decree granting temporary custody to the adoptive parents
10. Arrange Preadoption Placement of the child with the adoptive parents
11. Issue a Final Decree
12. Consider challenges to the Adoption Decree, if any

These steps are carried out by several actors, whose precise roles and relationships depend on governing law and the facts of the case: biological parents, adoptive parents, agency personnel, third-party facilitators, judges, and attorneys. The states vary with respect to whether dual representation of biological parents and adoptive parents is permitted. Very few states expressly permit it, and some states, including Kentucky, Maine, Minnesota, and Wisconsin, expressly prohibit it by statute.

The Rights of Biological / Legal Parents in the Adoption Context

The legal parents of a potential adoptee are most often the child's biological parents, married or unmarried, but may also include individuals whose legal status as parents is uncertain or has been established by presumption, adjudication, or a prior adoption. They usually fall into one of three primary categories and each is likely to have some degree of rights in the adoption context: the legal mother, the married father, and the unmarried father, known or unknown.

THE LEGAL MOTHER

As discussed in Chapter 7, a biological mother's parental rights are essentially established at birth. However, a woman may become a legal mother by other means as well such as by adoption or adjudication as a result of litigation stemming from a co-parenting or surrogacy agreement. Whatever the basis of a legal mother's parental status, she has the right to choose to place her child for adoption by voluntarily surrendering her parental rights to an agency and/or consenting to an adoption. If the state seeks to terminate her parental rights involuntarily, it can do so only based upon clear and convincing evidence of parental unfitness.

THE MARRIED "FATHER"

If the biological mother is married, under a marital presumption her husband commonly is deemed to be the father of any child born during their marriage or within 300 days of its termination. If no other man has been ruled the legal father of her child, an adoption cannot take place unless the married father's rights are terminated or he surrenders his parental rights and/or consents to the adoption.

THE NONMARITAL BIOLOGICAL FATHER

Under common law, the father of an illegitimate child had no standing to intervene in an action to adopt his biological child, and prior to 1972, there was little case law specifically addressing the rights of unwed fathers with respect to their children in the adoption context.

Four landmark decisions of the U.S. Supreme Court between 1972 and 1983 have since largely defined those rights.

- *Stanley v. Illinois*, 405 U.S. 645 (1972)
- *Quilloin v. Walcott*, 434 U.S. 246 (1978)
- *Caban v. Mohammed*, 441 U.S. 380 (1979)
- *Lehr v. Robertson*, 463 U.S. 248 (1983)

Beginning with the *Stanley* case in 1972, the Court established that fathers of nonmarital children have constitutionally protected legal rights as parents under the Equal Protection Clause of the Fourteenth Amendment and a privacy interest in children they have sired and raised, such that the state cannot terminate their parental rights without affording them notice and an opportunity to be heard. However, the unmarried father's rights are neither automatic nor unlimited.

> The significance of the biological connection [between father and child] is that it offers the natural father an opportunity that no other male possesses to develop a relationship with his offspring. If he grasps that opportunity and accepts some measure of responsibility for the child's future, he may enjoy the blessings of the parent-child relationship and make uniquely valuable contributions to the child's development. If he fails to do so, the Federal Constitution will not automatically compel a State to listen to his opinion of where the child's best interests lie.[13]

Biology-plus rule
the rule that an unwed father's rights are worthy of constitutional protection if the father grasps the opportunity to develop a relationship with and accept responsibility for his child

Under what has come to be known as the **biology-plus rule**, an unmarried father must take affirmative steps to demonstrate his parental commitment. However, the U.S. Supreme Court has provided no clear guidance with respect to what he must do to preserve his parental rights. Sometimes they may be lost based on a simple technicality. For example, in some states, an unwed father may lose his rights based on a finding that he failed to establish a relationship with his newborn child because he did not support the mother emotionally and financially during the pregnancy, was not present at the birth, and did not visit the mother and child in the hospital.[14] Simply not being registered in a state's putative father registry may be deemed sufficient cause to deprive an unmarried biological father of his parental rights. Consider for example an Arkansas case, in which an unwed father was not notified of a petition for adoption of his two children. The mother and stepfather, who adopted one of the children, swore that the father was "unknown." The Arkansas Supreme Court upheld the adoption despite the mother's and stepfather's deceit and the fact that the father had alleged he was the child's natural father, had established a substantial *de facto* relationship with the child, and had received no notice of an earlier paternity proceeding. The adoption was upheld because the father was not registered in the state's putative father registry.[15]

The Uniform Adoption Act (UAA):

> . . . distinguishes between fathers who willfully abandon their children and those whose attempts at fatherhood have been thwarted. The thwarted father has somehow been prevented from meeting his parental responsibilities, because the mother either never informed him of her pregnancy or the child's birth, lied to him about her plans for the child, disappeared with the child, named another man as the birth father, or was married to another man in a state that presumes the legitimacy of a child born to a married woman. According to the UAA, the unmarried father in these circumstances has not willfully abandoned his child but has instead been externally prevented from carrying out his parental responsibilities. Thwarted fathers can assert parental rights during the pendency of adoption proceedings, but they must prove a compelling reason for not having performed their parental duties. The thwarted father must also defend against other parties who try to prove that termination of his rights is necessary to avoid "detriment or a risk of substantial harm to the child."[16]

Depending on the jurisdiction and the extent of his demonstrated commitment, the rights of an unmarried father may include the following:

- He may be entitled to notice of an adoption proceeding as an interested party who may not be able to block the adoption but who can speak to whether it will be in the best interests of the child.
- He may be entitled to an opportunity to prove to the court that his consent should be required because he has taken sufficient steps to establish a relationship with his child, because his efforts to do so have been actively thwarted, or because his failure to do so should be excused for some other legitimate reason.
- Once his right to consent is established, he may have the capacity to block the adoption unless he is determined to be unfit and his parental rights are involuntarily terminated.

THE PARENT WHOSE IDENTITY OR WHEREABOUTS ARE UNKNOWN

On occasion, the identity of both parents may be unknown at the time of the adoption as when the child has been left anonymously at a **safe haven** location. (See Paralegal Application 8.3.) More commonly, the mother does not know the identity of the father. In that event, she (or the agency to which she has relinquished custody) usually must file an affidavit attesting to that fact before the adoption can proceed. If the identity of the father is known but his whereabouts are unknown, a diligent search must be made to locate him, and proof of the effort may be required by the court. The effort typically involves a search of telephone, military, and post office records; driver and voter registration rolls; and publication of notice in newspapers published in areas where the father has been known to reside. A number of locater services are now available online. A failure to conduct a proper search may result in a later challenge to the adoption on the grounds that the father did not receive proper notice to which he was constitutionally entitled.

Paralegal Application 8.3

Safe Haven Laws: State-Sponsored Abandonment of Newborns?

Beginning in 1999, when Texas passed its "Baby Moses" law, a majority of the states enacted safe haven laws allowing a parent, or an agent of a parent, of an unwanted newborn to anonymously leave the baby at a "safe haven" center without fear of legal charges of abandonment or child endangerment, etc., as long as there is no evidence of abuse. The applicable Florida statute provides: "Except where there is actual or suspected child abuse or neglect, any parent who leaves a newborn infant . . . has the absolute right to remain anonymous and to leave at any time and may not be pursued or followed unless the parent seeks to reclaim the newborn infant."[17]

Safe haven centers are usually located at medical facilities and police and fire stations. When a child is left at a center, it is subsequently delivered to the appropriate child-protective agency. Although the parent is not required to provide any information, some states require the safe haven provider to whom the newborn is relinquished to ask the parent for medical and family information and to give the parent information regarding adoption resources. No two states' safe haven laws are exactly the same, but all set maximum age limits for babies that can be left, with most ranging from three to thirty days of age (although Missouri R.S.Mo. §210.950 allows up to forty-five days and North Dakota N.D. Cent. Code §27-20-02 up to a year). In some states, the parent may be able to reclaim the child within a certain period of time by following prescribed procedures. As mentioned above, in the case of abandoned babies, the identity and whereabouts of both biological parents are unknown, and the burden of making a good-faith effort to identify and notify them of a petition for adoption eventually rests with the state's primary social services agency.

Sidebar

Safe haven laws help protect newborns from infanticide and abandonment in dumpsters, high school lavatories, and other sites where they are at considerable risk. They provide an incentive to mothers to bring their babies to locations where they will receive appropriate care and medical attention and be placed in nurturing homes pending adoption. This serves mothers and babies well, but what about the fathers of these children? Do safe haven laws violate their rights to notice and an opportunity to be heard and consent before their children are effectively abandoned and placed for adoption? To learn about the safe haven laws of various states, visit *www.childwelfare.gov*. Search for Infant Safe Haven Laws.

Putative father

a man who is reputed or believed to be the father of a child but who was not married to the mother when the child was born and whose paternity has not yet been established by legal process

Putative father registry

a vehicle available in several states that is designed to protect a putative father's parental rights by giving him notice of a pending adoption proceeding without his having to rely on the birth mother or prospective adoptive parents for such information

STATE INITIATIVES ON BEHALF OF NONMARITAL FATHERS

There is a lack of uniformity among the states with respect to the level of support available to nonmarital fathers in the adoption context beyond the limited protection afforded by federal law. Many states have taken steps to protect their interests in assuming a role in the future of their children. The two primary methods used to do so are putative father registries and publication notice requirements.

Putative Father Registries

A **putative father** is a man who may be a child's father but whose paternity has not yet been established legally by voluntary acknowledgment, in a court proceeding, or by virtue of the child having been born during his marriage to the child's mother or within 300 days of its termination. When a putative father registers with a **putative father registry**, he is registering his intent to assert his rights and responsibilities as a parent. If he registers within a specified time frame, he will be given notice of a proposed adoption of his child and/or a petition for termination of his parental rights. The notice advises the putative father that the action has been filed and includes the date, place, and time of any scheduled hearing.

Putative father registries of one form or another have been established by law in a majority of states. They are sometimes called parental claim, paternity, or responsible father registries among other options. Although the states differ with respect to the information maintained in their registries, they typically include the following:

- Registration date
- Name, address, Social Security number, and date of birth of both the putative father and the birth mother
- Child's name and date of birth, if known, or anticipated month and year of birth

The features of putative father registries vary from state to state with respect to:

- the time frame within which a putative father must register (ranging from prior to the child's birth to any time prior to the filing of an adoption petition)
- the consequences of a failure to register (usually an irrevocable implied consent to adoption and/or loss of the right to notice)
- the permissible exceptions to the registration requirement, if any (such as a failure to register due to the mother's concealment of the pregnancy)
- whether or not a putative father who registers can subsequently revoke or rescind a notice of intent to claim paternity

The information contained in the registry is essentially confidential and usually is available only to "interested parties," such as birth mothers, adoption agencies, state departments of social services and child support enforcement, adoptive parents, courts, attorneys for parties in a case, and others for good cause shown.

Registries are ostensibly designed to protect the parental rights of a putative father who has registered by giving him notice of a pending adoption proceeding without his having to rely on the birth mother or prospective adoptive parents for such information. By default or design, they serve a number of additional purposes:

- They help reassure the birth mother and prospective adoptive parents that an adoption will not be disrupted at a later date when the father, whose whereabouts or identity was previously unknown, appears and challenges the validity of the adoption.
- Consistent with Supreme Court decisions, they satisfy in part the requirement for an assumption of responsibility by a putative father who wants to establish a relationship with his child.
- They allow the birth mother to protect her privacy by not having to publish details of her personal life, and they relieve the pressure on her to perjure herself if she is unwilling or unable to identify the putative father and wants to receive public assistance.
- They generate revenue for the states through modest filing fees and potential establishment of paternal responsibility for child support and the expenses of the mother's prenatal and birth expenses.

Although touted as a protection for the rights of unknown fathers, the long-term impact and effectiveness of registries are yet to be measured. Critics argue that registries unreasonably restrict realization of the rights of putative fathers and serve instead to facilitate adoption and promote early bonding with adoptive parents. One commentator phrased her concerns in these terms:

The draconian nature of most registry acts protects neither the interests of responsible fathers nor the long-term emotional interests of the child. In actuality, the function of most registries is usually to cut off the birth father's rights, often before he knows of the child's birth or whereabouts. In an astonishing number of instances, the unwed father has been actively deceived by the birth mother into believing that the baby died. In other cases, the birth mother leads the father to believe

PARALEGAL PRACTICE TIP

You can find information about state registries at *www.childwelfare .gov* Search for Rights of Unmarried Fathers and then select Paternity Registries.

PARALEGAL PRACTICE TIP

To learn about the Ohio Putative Father Registry and see an Application for Search of Putative Father Registry and a Registration Form for Fathers, visit *www.jfs.ohio.gov* (Ohio Department of Job and Family Services) and under P select Putative Father Registry.

the baby is not his, or she never allows him to know that she is pregnant. Such statutes' interest in identifying the father is suspect and borders upon the pretextual, considering the absurdly short periods of time in which the father's rights are terminated for failure to file with the correct registry. The result is catastrophic for the child. . . . [18]

Additional criticisms and concerns include the following:

- In Alabama the Putative Father Registry has been designated by the legislature as the exclusive vehicle entitling a putative father to notice of and an opportunity to contest an adoption proceeding.[19] In addition, under the Alabama prebirth abandonment statute, a father can be deemed to have abandoned his child and by implication have consented both to termination of his parental rights and to an adoption by failing, with reasonable knowledge of the pregnancy, to offer financial and/or emotional support to the mother for a period of six months prior to the birth, OR by failing to file with the putative father registry within thirty days of the birth.[20]

- No registry presently requires the mother to inform a putative father of her pregnancy, although some state registries have a provision recognizing that some mothers may intentionally conceal their pregnancy to deceive the father. Such registries allow him to register when he discovers the existence of the baby. For example, the applicable Minnesota statute provides that a putative father will be considered to have timely filed if he proves by clear and convincing evidence that (1) it was not possible for him to register timely; (2) his failure to register was through no fault of his own; and (3) he registered within ten days after it became possible for him to do so.[21]

- Some states such as Arizona, Missouri,[22] and Utah do not accept a putative father's ignorance of a pregnancy or birth as an excuse for not registering. For example, a Utah statute provides that "[a]n unmarried biological father, by virtue of the fact he has engaged in a sexual relationship with a woman: (i) is considered to be on notice that a pregnancy and an adoption proceeding regarding the child may occur; and (ii) has a duty to protect his own rights and interests."[23] In effect, it would appear under the statute that a putative father needs to register every time he has sexual relations with a woman in order to protect his potential parental rights.

- The burden is placed on the unmarried biological father to establish his claim of paternity by registering, and yet many putative fathers are unaware of the existence of putative father registries and may lose their parental rights by default, as most states provide that failure to register in a timely manner constitutes a waiver and surrender of any parental rights to notice. A small number of states make a special effort to publicize the existence of their putative father registries. Missouri does so through public service announcements and by requiring the Department of Health and Senior Services to provide, on request, pamphlets describing the registry to hospitals, libraries, medical clinics, schools, universities, and other providers of child-related services.[24]

Publication Notice Requirements

Publication requirements are not in place in all states, and in states that do have them, they vary widely. At one extreme is a Utah adoption statute that provides: "… an unmarried mother has a right of privacy with regard to her pregnancy and adoption plan, and therefore has no legal obligation to disclose the identity of an unmarried biological father prior to or during an adoption proceeding, and has no obligation to volunteer information to the court with respect to the father."[25]

At the other extreme is Florida's "Scarlet Letter law," enacted in 2001 and subsequently held unconstitutional on privacy grounds in 2003[26] and replaced with that state's Putative Father Registry. A Florida District Court essentially held that the Florida Constitution protects the privacy rights of individuals to avoid disclosure of personal matters and to make certain decisions independently. In effect, the prior law had required a genetic mother who could not identify or locate the father of the child she wanted to place for adoption to publish detailed information about dates and places where she had engaged in sexual relations and descriptions of partners who might be the child's father.[27] Some states, such as Kansas,[28] require the court in which the adoption petition is pending to provide publication notice to unknown putative fathers, while other states leave it to the court's discretion. Still other states, such as North Carolina,[29] place the burden of publication on the individual petitioning for adoption.

Permanency Planning and Termination of Parental Rights

PERMANENCY PLANNING

Prior to the 1960s, public policy in the United States favored preservation of the biological family as a priority. When a child was removed from a home, voluntarily or involuntarily, the move was considered temporary whenever possible. The priority articulated by state legislatures and social service agencies was reunification of the biological family after effective completion of a service plan for the parents and children. For better or worse, today the focus is on permanency planning for the thousands of children in state care who have lost their parents to death, abandonment, incarceration, and/or abuse and neglect. **Permanency planning** is designed to move children as soon as possible into healthy, stable, and "permanent" homes.

The Adoption and Safe Families Act of 1997 (ASFA)[30] requires state agencies to petition for termination of parental rights when a child has been in state care for fifteen of the prior twenty-two months. Although the Act appears to serve the best interests of children by not leaving them in limbo indefinitely, some commentators contend that this requirement does a disservice to poor families in particular. "Formerly, poor parents encountering housing, marital, economic, or health crises had foster care as a 'safety net' to provide temporary substitute care at public expense while they got back on their feet. Now, even voluntary placements by good parents in difficult times can rapidly lead to disintegration of a family and permanent loss of family ties."[31]

FREEING THE CHILD FOR ADOPTION: VOLUNTARY AND INVOLUNTARY TERMINATION OF PARENTAL RIGHTS

In order for an adoption to proceed, the groundwork usually is laid for extinguishing the biological/legal parents' rights, through voluntary surrender and consent or involuntary termination, in one of four ways:

- The parents voluntarily surrender their parental rights, and the court transfers custody of the child to an agency, which then places the child in foster care or some other residential setting, depending on the circumstances. If and when the child is subsequently adopted, it is the state agency that consents to the adoption. In some states, the voluntary surrender effectively

Permanency planning
planning for the return home of a child following removal or for termination of parental rights within a legally specified period of time in an effort to promote stability for the child

PARALEGAL PRACTICE TIP

To see an example of a Petition for Permanency Planning Hearing used in Virginia, go to *www.courts.state. va.us*Forms/Juvenile and Domestic Relations District Court, Juvenile Forms and Instructions Petition for Permanency Planning Hearing DC-556.

PARALEGAL PRACTICE TIP

To see the Termination of Parental Rights Forms used in Delaware, go to *www.courts.delaware.gov*Family Matters/Termination of Parental Rights, Forms.

PARALEGAL PRACTICE TIP

To see examples of a number of adoption forms used in Michigan, visit www.courts.michigan.gov (Court Forms under Quick Links, Search box-Adoption Forms). Note in particular: the various consent forms (by adoptee, agency, guardian, and parent); Order Placing Child after Consent; Order Placing Child (Step-parent Adoption); Release of Child by Parent; Order Terminating Parental Rights after Release or Consent; Petition for Direct Placement Adoption; Order of Adoption; Petition for Rescission of Adoption and Order.

At-risk adoption

an adoption that is at risk of being challenged at a later date because the rights of one or both biological parents have not been terminated; an alternative to permanent foster care

PARALEGAL PRACTICE TIP

To learn about consent laws in each state, visit www.childwelfare.gov. Select Adoption and then search Consent to Adoption.

PARALEGAL PRACTICE TIP

The petitioners in *Adoption of a Minor*, J.S. and V.K., were a married same-sex couple seeking to adopt their son Nicholas. Nicholas was born to J.S. in 2014, during the petitioners' marriage. He was conceived through *in vitro* fertilization (IVF), using a known sperm donor they selected. They initially sought to adopt their son as a means of ensuring recognition of their parentage when they traveled to an area where same-sex marriage was not yet recognized.

terminates the parents' rights. In other states, the surrender allows the agency to petition the court for a termination.

- The biological parents consent to the adoption directly, and their consents are filed with the petition for adoption.
- The biological parents' rights are terminated by the court for cause, and the state is granted custody of the child pending adoption.
- One of the biological parents, a third party, or a prospective adoptive parent asks the court to dispense with parental consent given the circumstances of the case. For instance, the mother of a child who has been in long-term foster care may be willing to consent to adoption, but the father who is serving an extended sentence in prison for battery on the child unreasonably refuses to consent.

Ideally, the rights of both biological parents are extinguished by consent or court-ordered termination, in order to minimize the risk that the validity of the adoption may be challenged at a later date. However, this is not always possible, particularly in cases involving abandoned newborns, unknown fathers, or children left at safe havens. Virtually all states permit **at-risk adoptions** of children in such circumstances as an alternative to having them remain in permanent foster care placements. Parents who adopt at-risk children knowingly assume the risk that a biological parent may later appear and attempt to challenge the adoption.

CONSENT

Each state establishes by statute or administrative regulation the requirements governing consent to the kind(s) of adoption permitted in the jurisdiction: who must consent, the form of the consent, when the consent can be given, and under what circumstances it can be revoked. The rules are designed to respect and balance the constitutionally protected rights of birth parents and the rights of the adoptive parents who are seeking to establish a new family unit with confidence in its permanence.

Who Must Consent?

Absent involuntary termination, the mother's consent (or surrender of parental rights) is required, and the father's consent may be required depending on the circumstances (whether he is married to the mother, is the child's legal father as a result of an earlier adoption, has an established relationship with the child, etc.). Depending on the jurisdiction, the consent may be solely to a termination or surrendering of parental rights or both to termination of parental rights and to a specific adoption, as in an independent adoption. In the case of a step- or second-parent adoption, the consent of the custodial spouse/parent is solely to the adoption and not to a termination of his or her parental rights. If the adoptee has attained the age of majority, parental consent is not required. In most states, courts will consider the wishes of the child, and in some states, the adoptee's consent may be required if he or she has reached a certain age (usually twelve to fourteen).[32] If the parental rights of the biological parents have been terminated, parental consent to the adoption is not required, and the parent(s) cannot block an adoption of their child.

In cases involving children conceived as a result of artificial insemination, absent an agreement to the contrary, sperm donors generally are not treated as legal parents, even though they are technically genetic parents and putative fathers. As the Massachusetts Supreme Judicial Court opined in *Adoption of a Minor*, 471 Mass. 373 (2015): "As to a child who is conceived via artificial insemination, Mass. Gen. Laws 46 § 4B, by its nature contemplates that a third party must provide genetic material for the child's conception. Nonetheless, as is consistent with the paternity statutes and longstanding presumption of the legitimacy of children, § 4B confers legal parentage only upon a mother's consenting spouse, not a sperm donor." Given that he has no status as a legal parent, a sperm donor is not entitled to notice of a pending adoption nor is his consent required. However, the consent of the biological mother's spouse (regardless of gender) is required.

In What Form Is the Consent Given?

If the birth/legal parents are willing to relinquish their parental rights, this is usually accomplished by their executing a formal document commonly called a **surrender** of parental rights or a consent to adoption and termination of parental rights. The consent must be in an impartially witnessed and notarized writing that clearly identifies the child and the parental rights being terminated. To be valid, it must be fully informed and free from duress, fraud, and undue influence. In some states, a voluntary surrender must be followed by a court order confirming the termination of parental rights.

> **PARALEGAL PRACTICE TIP**
>
> If the biological mother is a minor, the court will often appoint a GAL to investigate whether the minor's consent is being given freely and voluntarily.

> **Surrender (of parental rights)**
>
> a formal document in which a legal (usually biological) parent gives up his or her parental rights to a specific child

---

Paralegal **Application 8.4**

Making Consent Count

The Child Welfare League of America and other advocates and practitioners recommend that, in order for a mother's consent to adoption to be meaningful and binding, certain precautions be taken even if not mandated by state law or administrative regulation. Such steps protect both the biological mother, by informing her decision, and the prospective adoptive parents, by promoting finality in adoptive placements. They also help to balance the power relationship between mothers with few resources who are experiencing maximum stress and adoptive parents, who are more likely to be economically secure, emotionally stable, and eager for the adoption to proceed. Suggested measures include:

- **Counseling:** More than half the states require that the mother participate in some degree of counseling before placing her child for adoption. "Counseling for parents, . . . can help parents to 'own' their decisions. . . . Counseling for mothers should include providing information about alternatives to adoption, options within adoption, legal steps and consequences involved in adoption, and possible effects of adoption on themselves and their children. Ideally, counseling will also help mothers resolve issues that arise with the fathers and family

members."[33] The counselor should be a neutral third person who has no interest in the mother's ultimate decision.

- **Legal advice:** Mothers should be given copies of all documents they will be asked to sign and have an opportunity to review them and raise questions with an attorney. They should be advised about "whether they may give binding consent before the birth, after the birth, or only after the passage of a certain number of days or hours after the birth. They should be informed about whether they have any right to revoke their consent and, if so, when and how to do so and whether revocation means automatic return of the child or a judicial best-interests determination. If any agreements are contemplated between the mother and the prospective adoptive parents, such as agreements concerning providing information about the child's development, they should be informed about whether and under what circumstances the agreements are enforceable."[34]

- **Sufficient time:** Mothers relinquishing their parental rights and consenting to adoption should not be rushed into the decision, a luxury most state laws do not afford them.

When Can the Consent Be Given?

Ideally, if the consent is voluntary, it should (and in some states must) be given prior to or simultaneously with filing of the adoption petition. If the adoption is of a newborn, some states permit consent to be given prior to the birth of the child, but the majority of states specify that it can be given only after a certain period following the birth (generally three days). The rationale for such restrictions is to minimize the situations in which a birth mother experiencing the emotional impact of delivering the child changes her mind and claims that an earlier consent was given under duress. The Indian Child Welfare Act prevents a mother from consenting to an adoption until ten days after the child's birth and allows her to revoke her consent until the adoption is final.

Under What Circumstances Can Consent Be Revoked?

Most states provide that a consumer has seventy-two hours to rescind an ordinary business contract and yet, in many states, a mother's consent to adoption may be given and become irrevocable in fewer than four days after a child's birth. The general rule is that a consent to adoption that is given voluntarily, knowingly, and intelligently cannot be revoked absent proof that the consent was obtained by means of fraud, duress, or undue influence. Absent such circumstances, many states do not permit revocations. When revocation is permitted, it usually must be written, witnessed, and notarized and given within a limited period of time. Generally, the revocation must be submitted to the court and may or may not be approved based on the court's discretion and standards which vary from state to state. Simple changes of heart are usually insufficient. but a minor's claim that she received no counseling, was provided with no information about other options, and was coerced into consenting by her parents may well prevail. See, e.g., *In re Adoption of A.L.O.*, 2006 MT 59, 331 Mont. 334, 132 P.3d 543 (2006). When the matter is considered by the court, the adoptive parents may contest the revocation and ask that the court dispense with the parental consent requirement in the best interests of the child.

Paralegal **Application 8.5**

You Be the Judge

1. *In re Adoption of Baby Boy B.*, **2012 Ark. 92, 394 S.W.3d 837 (2012):** In a case of first impression in Arkansas, the state Supreme Court considered the rights of a "thwarted putative father" in the adoption context. In this case, the adoptive parents filed a petition for adoption. The Circuit Court granted the petition and held that the putative father's consent to the adoption was not required. The father appealed. Under Arkansas law, a putative father's consent is required if he satisfies one of several conditions. One of those conditions is that he prove the existence of a significant custodial, personal, or financial relationship with the child before the adoption petition is filed (Ark. Code Ann. § 9-9-206). In his appeal, the father alleged that he had satisfied this condition. He had filed with putative-father registries in four states and also filed paternity actions in both Texas and Arkansas. He had refused to consent to an adoption in an action brought in Texas. He had attempted to provide the mother with emotional and financial support during the pregnancy and had established an account for the support of the baby. He would have provided financial support to the mother after she left the state, but she refused to communicate with him or tell him specifically where she lived.

Sidebar

Do you think the father satisfied the state's condition? Should the Arkansas Supreme Court reverse the Circuit Court decision? Read the opinion to see if the state Supreme Court agreed with your position.

2. *F.R. v. Adoption of Baby Boy Born Nov. 2, 2010,* **135 So. 3d 310 (Fla. Dist. Ct. App. 2012):** In this case, a district court dismissed a mother's motion to vacate and set aside her consent to adoption. The mother was born in the Democratic Republic of the Congo and lived most of her life in Tanzania before immigrating to the United States with her sister in 2010 with the assistance of the World Relief organization. Shortly before relocating, she was raped in a transition camp in Tanzania and, after coming to the United States, at the age of sixteen, delivered a son on November 2, 2010. While in the hospital, she was approached about giving her child up for adoption but did not consent. After leaving the hospital, she was taken to an attorney's office on November 4 and 5 in repeated unsuccessful attempts to secure her consent. On November 15, she and her sister were taken to the office of another lawyer, the executive director of

Angelic Adoptions, Inc., in a further effort to obtain her consent. A representative from World Relief was present as well. The mother's sister, who had very limited English skills based on reading and listening tests, was designated the translator. The mother finally signed a consent during this meeting and her parental rights were subsequently terminated without notice. In this action, the mother alleged her consent was not given knowingly and voluntarily and had been obtained through fraud, duress, coercion, and misrepresentation. The mother spoke and understood only Swahili and her sister's assistance with translating was inadequate. The consent she signed was not written in a language she could understand and the agency failed to provide her with a translation sufficient for her to understand the nature, effect, and consequences of a consent to adoption. The mother appealed the decision of the lower court.

Sidebar

What do you think the appellate court should do in this case? Do you think the mother should be permitted to revoke her consent? Why? Read the opinion to see whether the court agreed with you.

INVOLUNTARY TERMINATION OF PARENTAL RIGHTS

A termination of parental rights is a judicial declaration that ends the legal relationship between a parent and a child. Because parents have a constitutionally protected right in the parent–child relationship, their rights as parents generally cannot be involuntarily terminated without notice and an opportunity to be heard in a termination proceeding. However, there is no parallel constitutional requirement that they be provided with counsel if they cannot afford an attorney. The U.S. Supreme Court held in *Lassiter v. Department of Social Services*, 452 U.S. 18 (1981), that while courts may appoint counsel on a "case by case" basis, there is no categorical right to counsel under the federal constitution when parents are in danger of having their parental rights terminated. Nonetheless, many states do provide a statutory right to counsel in termination proceedings and parents of Indian children have a right to counsel under the Indian Child Welfare Act (ICWA 25 U.S.C. § 1912). Even when parents have counsel however, problems and challenges arise.

> The ethical duty to provide competent and zealous representation extends to all clients, including those faced with potential termination of their parental rights. Personal biases cannot compromise advocacy on behalf of the client. The vast majority of parents in termination proceedings are indigent, which often means that their counsel is appointed by the court or provided through a public defender or contract system. The representation of parents by overworked and underpaid attorneys results in claims by parents that their counsel was ineffective.[35]

GROUNDS FOR TERMINATION

The states establish by statute, administrative regulation, and case law the circumstances in which termination may occur, given clear and convincing evidence of parental unfitness and the best interests of a child. Paralegals are often surprised and troubled about the substantial degree of current "unfitness" that must be present in order for a parent's rights to be terminated. Given that parental rights are afforded a high degree of constitutional protection, before they can be terminated there must be clear and convincing evidence of severe inadequacies in parenting that place the child at risk. It is not necessarily enough that parents are poor; that they are overly strict or lax in discipline; that they fail to supervise their children

PARALEGAL PRACTICE TIP

Adoptive parents, like biological parents, may have their parental rights terminated if they prove to be unfit to care for their adopted children.

PARALEGAL PRACTICE TIP

To review examples of a Petition for Termination of Parental Rights and an Answer to a Petition for Termination of Parental Rights, visit *www.courts.delaware.gov/forms*. Select Family Court and then scroll to forms by title (Forms 112 and 113).

PARALEGAL PRACTICE TIP

Competent representation includes paying attention to deadlines. A failure to do so can have serious consequences. For example, in *In re C.M.M.*, 273 P.3d 313 (Or. Ct. App. 2012), a father failed to timely appeal termination of his parental rights due to his attorney's error and therefore his appeal was barred and the court had no procedure available to provide him with a remedy.

and "let them run wild"; that the home is messy; that "negative" influences are present; or that the parents drink excessively, use "recreational" drugs, or have criminal records. On the other hand, circumstances that may result in a termination include but are not limited to the following:

- Although nonsupport alone may not be enough, sustained failure to financially support a child's basic needs when able to do so may be: Wyo. Stat. Ann. § 1-22-110(a) allows the adoption of a child without the consent of a parent if a putative father or nonconsenting parent has "(ix) willfully failed to pay a dollar amount of at least 70% of the court ordered support for a period of two (2) years or more and has failed to bring the support obligation one hundred percent (100%) current within sixty days after service of the petition to adopt." See *In re Adoption of S.D.L.*, 278 P.3d 242 (Wyo. 2012).

- Failure to see or contact the child for a specified period of time: The failure must be willful in the sense that the parent must have the ability to act and fails to do so. See *In re Doe*, 281 P.3d 95 (Idaho 2012), in which the Idaho Supreme Court held a magistrate's order terminating a father's parental rights based on abandonment was in error. The father was a Mexican citizen whose child was born and resided in the United States. His failure to establish a relationship with the child was deemed not to be willful because he was barred from entering the United States.

- Failure to provide a safe environment for the child: See, e.g., *In re H.S.*, 805 N.W.2d 737 (Iowa 2011), in which the Iowa Supreme Court upheld a juvenile court's decision to terminate a mother's parental rights because she had mental health conditions for which she refused treatment and as a result continually put her chronically ill son in danger.

- Incarceration of a parent for serious crimes particularly crimes against the child and/or the other parent of the child(ren): Although incarceration alone may not be sufficient grounds, N.H. statute RSA 170-C:5,VI authorizes termination of parental rights when a parent, as a result of incarceration for a felony offense, is unable to discharge his responsibilities to and for the child and has been found to have abused or neglected his child.

- Failure to participate in a court-ordered rehabilitation or family-reunification plan: In *In re H.T.*, 276 P.3d 1054 (Okla. Civ. App. 2011), one of the parties' children was found to be "deprived" due to the parents failure to correct conditions which had led to an earlier termination of the parents' rights to the child's four older siblings. The appellate court affirmed the trial court's order which found H.T. deprived and terminated the parents' rights. The appellate court reasoned that the parents were on notice that their conduct had been and remained insufficient. They had been provided with the programs and tools necessary to achieve a level of adequacy but did not pursue them with any level of conviction.

- Legal determination of incompetence of the parent: See *In re Termination of Parental Rights to R.W.B.*, 73 Pa. D. & C.2d 369 (Phila. 1975), in which a mother had a history of mental illness (paranoid schizophrenia) and her prognosis for recovery was very poor. The child had never actually lived with her, but the mother maintained a constant interest in and concern for her daughter. Notwithstanding that fact, the court concluded there was sufficient evidence of incapacity which could not be remedied. The court terminated the mother's parental rights, although it found that the incapacity was not her fault.

Even if these factors all are present, before rights can be terminated, the parent must be given an opportunity to address his or her parental deficiencies with or without the child being present in the home. The state must show that it made a "reasonable effort" to keep the parent and child together through the provision of appropriate supportive services. The Americans with Disabilities Act (ADA) provides: ". . . no qualified individual with a disability shall, by reason of such disability, be excluded from participation in or denied the benefits of the services, programs, or activities of a public entity, or be subjected to discrimination by any such entity."[36] Under the Act, a disability includes a physical or mental impairment that substantially limits one or more of a person's major life activities. The states are divided with respect to the question of whether or not the ADA applies to termination proceedings. Courts in states such as Iowa, Maine, and Washington have held that it does apply, whereas courts in Connecticut, Vermont, and Wisconsin have concluded that it does not. If it does apply, the state may be required to accommodate the special needs of parents with recognized disabilities that impact their parenting skills when those individuals are threatened with termination of their parental rights.

In the final analysis, the best interests of the child standard is the paramount consideration when the courts weigh the impact of parental inadequacies on the child's physical, emotional, and mental welfare and need for a stable home and continuity in care. To the extent feasible, many courts also will consider "the child's opinion of his or her own best interests in the matter."[37]

Paralegal **Application 8.6**

Would You Give Mom Another Chance?

The facts

A mother of five children had an extensive history of substance abuse and dysfunctional relationships with a series of men, three of whom had abused both her and some of the children. Her problem with drugs over the years impaired her ability to parent and exposed the children to drugs, drug paraphernalia, and other drug users. She had come to the attention of the Department of Social Services on multiple occasions, based on complaints that she was neglecting the children, and the children were removed from the home. For two years, she failed to cooperate in the service plan designed to reunify the family. The department eventually changed the goal of the plan from reunification to adoption. Six weeks before the initially scheduled trial on termination of her parental rights, the mother entered a four- to six-month residential treatment program from which she eventually successfully graduated. The mother presented evidence that she was responding well to therapy and had submitted to required drug screens, all of which were negative. She was actively involved in outpatient services including substance abuse programming that encompassed five AA meetings a week, early-recovery and relapse-prevention counseling, and domestic violence therapy. She was living with her mother, working two jobs, and visiting her five children once a month.

Sidebar

When deciding whether to terminate the rights of a parent, what factors do you think the court should consider? What if the parent's lack of fitness is "temporary" rather than chronic? What if the parent is taking steps and making significant progress toward addressing his or her inadequacies as a parent? How much leeway should be given to parents when an indeterminate period of time will be required for their recovery? Would you terminate the mother's parental rights in this particular case? To see what the Massachusetts Supreme Judicial Court decided to do and why, read the opinion in the case *Adoption of Elena*, 446 Mass. 24, 841 N.E.2d 252 (2006). It can be accessed at *www.pearsonhighered.com/ careersresources/*in the website material for Chapter 8 of this text under Cases.

PARALEGAL PRACTICE TIP

Can a person ever be too old to become an adoptive parent? See *In re A.C.G.*, 894 A.2d 436 (D.C. App. Ct. 2006), a case in which a seventy-seven-year-old paternal great-aunt petitioned to adopt a four-year-old child who had lived with her since the age of two months. Although the child had supervised visits with her mother every two weeks, the great-aunt had provided a stable and loving home for the child for virtually all her life and had done so with little support from either of the child's parents. In the event of her death or disability, she had arranged for two backup caretakers, aged forty-one and sixty-seven, who were family members well known to the child. She had also made financial arrangements to provide for the child. The mother opposed termination of her parental rights and granting of the petition.

PARALEGAL PRACTICE TIP

You can find an overview of the major provisions of the Multiethnic Placement Act at *www.childwelfare.gov*. Use the search box to access the overview by searching for Multi-ethnic Placement Act of 1994. An additional resource, *Ensuring the Best Interests of Children through Compliance with the Multiethnic Placement Act, as amended, and Title VI of the Civil Rights Act of 1964* can be found at *www.hhs.gov* Search for the document by its full title.

Identification of Potential Adoptive Parents

As indicated earlier in the chapter, children may be adopted by family members, stepparents, married couples, single persons, and co-parents, depending on the jurisdiction. The characteristics and qualifications of prospective adoptive parents are considered by social service agencies and the courts to assess their suitability as parents and their capacity to act in the best interests of the children they seek to adopt. Basic threshold requirements for potential adoptive parents vary but customarily relate to age, race, religion, health, and historically, sexual orientation. Additional factors relating to parenting skills, emotional stability, financial resources, and nature of the home environment are also scrutinized, generally in the context of home studies conducted prior to placement and finalization of an adoption.

Age

Adoption statutes usually require that the petitioner be an adult under state law (typically at least eighteen to twenty-one years of age). Although there is customarily no maximum age set, given the basic purpose of adoption, adoptive parents usually must be older than the adoptee and of such an age that they are able to provide continuity of care to adoptees until they reach the age of majority.

Race

The pendulum has swung back and forth with respect to the role of race in adoption decisions. Prior to the 1950s, many states banned transracial adoptions by statute until such laws were struck down as unconstitutional. In the 1950s and 1960s, transracial adoptions became more common, given a decline in white infants available for adoption. However, by the 1970s, black advocacy groups took a strong stand against the adoption of black children by white families, even if it delayed placement, claiming that only black families could appropriately address the unique developmental needs of black children. Racial matching once again became the norm, motivated not by racial discrimination but rather by a concern for the best interests of minority children. The roller coaster finally stopped in 1994 when Congress passed the Multiethnic Placement Act (MEPA), which provides:

> A person or government that is involved in adoption or foster care placements may not (A) deny to any individual the opportunity to become an adoptive or a foster parent, on the basis of race, color, or national origin of the individual, or of the child involved; or (B) delay or deny the placement of a child for adoption or into foster care, on the basis of the race, color or national origin of the adoptive or foster parent, or the child, involved.[38]

As with custody decisions, race should not be used as the sole basis for adoption decisions, subject to limited exceptions. However, the court can consider race as a factor when determining if a particular placement will be in the best interests of the child. As a practical matter, courts and agencies often prefer to place a child with parents of the same race and ethnic background if possible. In the case of American Indian children, under federal law race MUST be considered, in an effort to address a congressional finding that a high percentage of Indian families are broken up by the removal of their children by nontribal public and private agencies and placement in non-Indian foster and adoptive homes and institutions.[39] The Indian Child Welfare Act provides: "In any adoptive placement of an Indian child under state law, a preference shall be given, in the absence of good cause to the contrary, to a placement with (1) a member of the child's extended family; (2) other members of the Indian child's tribe; or (3) other Indian families."[40] The Act is intended to protect the best interests of Indian children and to promote the stability and security of Indian tribes and families. To that end, it established heightened standards that must be applied in child custody actions involving Indian children (including adoptions and actions to terminate parental rights). The Act defines an "Indian child" as "an unmarried person who is under eighteen and . . . (b) is eligible for membership in an Indian tribe and is the biological child of a member of an Indian tribe."[41]

Religion

As a matter of practice, agencies customarily place children in homes practicing the same religion as their biological parents, especially when the child is older and has already begun practicing a particular religion. However, interfaith adoptions are not constitutionally prohibited.

Health

An individual with a disability should not be discriminated against as a potential adoptive parent, provided the disability does not unduly interfere with the capacity to parent such that an adoption would not be in the best interests of the child.

Sexual Orientation

As mentioned earlier, historically, gay individuals and same-sex co-parents were not considered suitable adoptive parents but that position has gradually eroded. Over the past three decades, gays and lesbians seeking to adopt began to encounter distinctly different results depending on where they resided. Some states, such as California, Connecticut, and Vermont, enacted legislation allowing adoption by same-sex partners when deemed to be in a child's best interests.[42] Appellate courts in several states, such as Illinois, New Jersey, New York, Ohio, and Tennessee, interpreted their respective general adoption laws to allow same-sex partners to adopt. In 2010, after an appellate court upheld a lower court's decision that Florida's three-decade-old ban on gay adoption was unconstitutional, that state began permitting adoption by gays. With the decriminalization of sexual activity between consenting adult homosexuals by the U.S. Supreme Court in 2003,[43] federal recognition of same-sex marriages in 2014, and the nationalization of marriage equality across the nation in June 2015, gay spouses now should be able to adopt children regardless of where

PARALEGAL PRACTICE TIP

To learn more about lesbian, gay, bisexual, and transgender families, visit *www.childwelfare.gov*. Also check *www.adoptionchildwelfarelaw .org*. In addition to same-sex adoption, you can also search by other topics such as "Who can adopt," "Stepparent adoption," and "Form and Filing of Petition," among many other options.

they live. However, as of 2014 Arkansas and Utah still banned any unmarried gay or heterosexual couples from adopting, and Mississippi continues to ban gay couples but not single gays from adopting. When the decisions in such cases are not prescribed by statute or regulation, they are left to the court's discretion and are generally decided according to a best-interests-of-the-child standard. In most states, much like race, sexual activity, homosexual or heterosexual, should not factor into the decision unless, given the facts, it can be shown to have a detrimental impact on the child to be adopted. It is unlikely that discrimination in the adoption context on the basis of sexual orientation would withstand judicial scrutiny. That said, lingering biases may still subtly persist in some courts.

PARALEGAL PRACTICE TIP

To view an example of a Petition for Adult Adoption, Google Petition for Adult Adoption and you will find forms used in several states including California, Colorado, Delaware, North Carolina, Vermont, and Wisconsin.

Who May Be Adopted?

Although in the vast majority of cases the individual adopted (the adoptee) is a child, in several states both children and adults may be adopted, provided that all of the requirements for a valid adoption are satisfied. However, adoptions of one partner by the other in a same-sex couple have not been permitted in some states. In *In the Matter of the Adoption of Robert Paul P.*, 63 N.Y.2d 233 (N.Y. 1984), the New York Court of Appeals held that adoption "is plainly not a quasi-matrimonial vehicle to provide nonmarried partners with a legal imprimatur for their sexual relationship, be it heterosexual or homosexual. . . . Moreover, any such sexual intimacy is utterly repugnant to the relationship between child and parent in our society, and only a patently incongruous application of our adoption laws – wholly inconsistent with the underlying public policy of providing a parent-child relationship for the welfare of the child."

Home Studies

Home studies

assessments of prospective adoptive parents and home environments, customarily conducted by social workers licensed by the state

Home studies commonly occur at two points during the adoption process: before and after temporary placement with the adoptive family. Although not usually required in independent adoptions, in agency adoptions all states require that a home study be conducted to ensure the suitability of the adoptive home prior to placement. Virtually all states require postplacement studies, with limited exceptions such as in stepparent adoptions. An example of the nature and focus of home studies is provided in Exhibit 8.1, which contains an excerpt from provisions of the Iowa Administrative Code for the Human Services Department governing adoption services.

Home studies customarily involve multiple visits. The first home study is designed to screen the adoptive parents and usually involves extensive interviews with the parents themselves regarding their goals and expectations with respect to the adoption as well as their attitudes and beliefs about childrearing. It may also include interviews with the parents' neighbors, school personnel, employers, extended-family members, and other references in an effort to assess the adoptive parents' emotional and financial stability, character, work history, and relationships with others. The second home study is designed to assess the child's adjustment to the adoptive home before the adoption is finalized.

EXHIBIT 8.1 Iowa Administrative Code/Human Services Department [441]/Chapter 108 Licensing and Regulation of Child-Placing Agencies/441-108.9(238)(4) Services to Adoptive Applicants (c) Adoptive Home Study and (d) Record checks

Courtesy of State of Iowa

c. Adoptive home study. The home study consists of a family assessment which shall include at least two face-to-face interviews with the applicant and at least one face-to-face interview with each member of the household. At least one interview shall take place in the applicant's home. The assessment shall include, but need not be limited to, the following:

1. Motivation for adoption and whether the family has biological, adopted or foster children.
2. Family and extended family's attitude toward accepting an adopted child, and plans for discussing adoption with the child.
3. The attitude toward adoption of the significant other people involved with the family.
4. Emotional stability; marital history, including verification of marriages and divorces; assessment of marital relationship; and compatibility of the adoptive parents.
5. Ability to cope with problems, stress, frustrations, crises, separation and loss.
6. Medical, mental, or emotional conditions which may affect the applicant's ability to parent a child.
7. Ability to provide for the child's physical and emotional needs and respect the child's cultural and religious identity.
8. Adjustment of biological and previously adopted children, if any, including their attitudes toward adoption, relationship with others, and school performance.
9. Capacity to give and receive affection.
10. Statements from at least three references provided by the family and other unsolicited references that the agency may wish to contact.
11. Attitudes of the adoptive applicants toward the birth parents and the reasons the child is available for adoption.
12. Income information, ability to provide for a child, and a statement as to the need for adoption subsidy for a special needs child, or children.
13. Disciplinary practices that will be used.
14. History of abuse by family members and treatment.
15. Assessment of, commitment to, and capacity to maintain other significant relationships.
16. Substance use or abuse by members of the family and treatment.
17. Recommendations for type of child, number, age, sex, characteristics, and special needs of children best parented by this family.

d. Record checks. The licensed child-placing agency shall submit record checks for each applicant and for anyone who is 14 years of age or older living in the home of the applicant to determine whether they have any founded child abuse reports or criminal convictions or have been placed on the sex offender registry. . . .

Home visits are usually conducted by state-licensed social workers who prepare reports and make recommendations to the court, much as GALs appointed by the courts do in contested custody cases. Although sometimes criticized by prospective adoptive parents as unwarranted, overly intrusive, and biased toward the middle-class concept of the ideal family, most social workers would agree that home visits serve to protect the safety and well-being of adopted children. Agencies and courts will not knowingly place adoptees in homes in which the parents have a documented history of substance abuse, violence, or criminal activity.

Courts recognize that there is no such thing as a perfect parent, but prospective adoptive parents need to be able to effectively care for children in a manner that supports and promotes the children's best interests. The prospective adoptive parents do not need to be wealthy, but they should at least be financially responsible and have sufficient resources to adequately provide for each individual child's unique needs. In some cases, those needs may be substantial. For example, a child may have a serious medical condition requiring around-the-clock care and major modifications to the physical structure of the adoptive home.

Jurisdiction and Venue

In order for a court to grant an adoption, the court must have subject matter jurisdiction over adoption. Subject matter jurisdiction is established by statute and may reside in a court of general jurisdiction such as a Superior Court or in courts of limited jurisdiction such as a Probate, Family, or Juvenile Court. Venue is commonly proper in the county where the child or the biological or the adoptive parent(s) reside.

Any adoption, other than one involving a stepparent, relative, or guardian, that involves adoption of a child who is born or lives in one state (the "sending state") by someone who resides in another state (the "receiving state") must comply with the requirements of the Interstate Compact on the Placement of Children (ICPC), adopted in all fifty states. Each state has a designated ICPC office charged with responsibility for coordinating interstate adoptions. When an adoption is proposed by a court in a sending state, the ICPC office in that state provides written notice of the proposed adoption to the ICPC office in the receiving state. The notice includes basic identifying information about the child, the child's parents or guardian, and the proposed placement, along with the reason for the placement. The receiving state then conducts a home study and, if approved, notifies the sending state that approval for the child's entry to the receiving state to be placed has been granted. A failure to comply with ICPC requirements can result in a voiding of the adoption.

PARALEGAL PRACTICE TIP

To locate Interstate Compact on the Placement of Children (ICPC) Forms and information in Utah, visit *www.hsdcfs.utah.gov* Enter ICPC in the search box and you will be able to find both forms and other useful resources, particularly documents titled "The Seven Steps to ICPC" and "ICPC Basics Handbook."

Petition For Adoption

An adoption action is usually commenced when a Petition for Adoption is filed in the name of the child by the prospective adoptive parents or the agency (see the detailed Colorado Petition provided in Exhibit 8.2). In most jurisdictions, the Petition must be accompanied by the affidavits or consent forms from the biological parents surrendering their rights. The form and content of the petition varies from state to state but usually includes the following at a minimum:

- The name(s) and address of the petitioners
- The nature of their relationship to each other (married, unmarried, partners)
- Data about the petitioners, such as their ages and occupations
- The name, sex, age (date of birth), and religion of the child, if any
- The name by which the adoptive child will be known once adopted
- Documentation of any prior custodial actions involving the child
- Consents to the adoption attached or an indication of why there is no consent
- Type of adoption (agency, independent, etc.)
- Certification that there are no additional persons interested in the proceeding

EXHIBIT 8.2 Petition for Adoption Courtesy of the State of Colorado

☐ District Court ☐ Denver Juvenile Court	
_____County, Colorado	
Court Address:	
IN THE MATTER OF THE PETITION OF:	
_____ (name of person (s) seeking to adopt)	
FOR THE ADOPTION OF A CHILD	▲ **COURT USE ONLY** ▲
Attorney or Party Without Attorney (Name and Address):	Case Number:
Phone Number: E-mail:	
FAX Number: Atty. Reg. #:	Division Courtroom

PETITION FOR ADOPTION

The Petitioner(s) being desirous of adopting a child so as to make said child for all intents and purposes the legal child of Petitioner(s) and to render him/her capable of inheriting their estate, state(s) the following facts:

Information about the Petitioner(s):

Petitioner #1: _____ **(Full Name)**

   Date of Birth: _____ Race: _____ Place of Birth: _____

   Current Mailing Address: _____

   City & Zip: _____

   Home Phone #: _____ Work Phone #: _____ Cell #: _____

   Email:_____ Length of Residence in Colorado:_____

   Occupation: _____

   Place of residence at the time of birth of the child.

   _____
   Street Address   City   State   Zip Code

Petitioner #2: _____ **(Full Name)**

   Date of Birth: _____ Race: _____ Place of Birth: _____

   Current Mailing Address: _____

   City & Zip: _____

   Home Phone #: _____ Work Phone #: _____ Cell #: _____

   Email:_____ Length of Residence in Colorado: _____

   Occupation: _____

   Place of residence at the time of birth of the child.

   _____
   Street Address   City   State   Zip Code

JDF 501 R7-12 PETITION FOR ADOPTION   Page 1 of 3
© 2012 Colorado Judicial Department for use in the Courts of Colorado

(Continued)

EXHIBIT 8.2 *(Continued)*

❑ If applicable, maiden name of adopting mother:_____ Date of Marriage: _____

❑ The Petitioner(s) has/have attached as "Attachment A" a current fingerprint-based criminal history records check as required by §19-5-207(2.5)(a)(I)-(IV), C.R.S.

❑ The Petitioner (s) has/have attached as "Attachment B" the TRAILS background check as required by §19-5-207, C.R.S.

If the Petitioner(s) has/have been convicted of a felony or misdemeanor in any of the following areas, please check the appropriate box and identify for the Court the date of the conviction and if it was a felony or misdemeanor.

❑ child abuse or neglect on_____ (date). ❑ Felony ❑ Misdemeanor

❑ spousal abuse on _____ (date). ❑ Felony ❑ Misdemeanor

❑ any crime against a child on _____ (date). ❑ Felony ❑ Misdemeanor

❑ any crime, the underlying factual basis of which has been found by the Court to include an act of domestic violence on _____ (date). ❑ Felony ❑ Misdemeanor

❑ violation of a Protection/Restraining Order on _____ (date). ❑ Felony ❑ Misdemeanor

❑ any crime involving violence, rape, sexual assault, or homicide on _____ (date).
❑ Felony ❑ Misdemeanor

❑ any felony involving physical assault or battery on _____ (date).
❑ Felony ❑ Misdemeanor

❑ any felony drug-related conviction within the past five years, at a minimum on _____ (date).
❑ Felony ❑ Misdemeanor

Identify all children of the Petitioner(s) (both natural and adopted and both living and deceased).

Full Name of Child	Full Name of Child

Facts concerning the child to be adopted. (Do not fill in if placement is by an agency or Department of Social Services.)

Full Name: _____Date of Birth: _____

Place of Birth: _____ Relationship of child to Petitioner(s), if any _____

Place of Residence: _____

The child ❑ is ❑ is not a member or eligible to be a member of an Indian tribe as defined by the Indian Welfare Act. If applicable, name of tribe _____

❑ Notice of this Petition has been provided to the parent or Indian custodian of the child and to the tribal agent of the tribe, as required by §19-1-126(1)(c), C.R.S.

❑ Reasonable efforts have been made to send notice to the identified persons as follows:

_____

_____

Attach the postal receipts to this petition, indicating that notice was properly sent. If the postal receipts have not been returned at the time of filing, the postal receipts or copies shall be filed with the Court within 10 days of the filing of this petition. (§19-1-126(1)(c), C.R.S.)

JDF 501   R7-12   PETITION FOR ADOPTION

© 2012 Colorado Judicial Department for use in the Courts of Colorado

Page 2 of 3

(Continued)

EXHIBIT 8.2 *(Continued)*

☐ If applicable, inquiries have been made by the County Department of Social Services or child placement agency to determine whether the child is an Indian child as follows:

_____

_____

The child has been in the care and custody of Petitioner(s) since _____ (date).

The legal custody of the child is with _____ (name).

Full description of the property of the child, if any: _____

_____

Name and address of the Guardian(s) of the child and estate of the child, if any, have been appointed:

_____

Name of agency, if any, to which custody of the child has been given by proper order of the Court:

_____

Information about the Birth Parents of the Child:

Full Name of Birth Father: _____

_____

Street Address   City   State   Zip Code

Full Name of Birth Mother: _____

_____

Street Address   City   State   Zip Code

The written consent(s) of the birth parent(s) ☐ is/are attached **or** ☐ is/are not attached.

The child will not be the subject of a pending dependency and neglect action when the adoption is heard.

If parental rights are relinquished, are terminated, or are being terminated in this action pursuant to §§19-5-101-108, C.R.S., as amended, or parent is deceased, state details:

_____

_____

Wherefore, the Petitioner(s) pray(s) that a Decree of Adoption be entered herein declaring said child to be the child of Petitioner(s) and that the name of said child be changed to: _____
_____ (full name) and that said child shall be entitled to all of the rights and privileges and be subject to all of the obligations now conferred and imposed by law.

VERIFICATION AND ACKNOWLEDGEMENT

I swear/affirm under oath that I have read the foregoing Petition and that the statements set forth herein are true and correct to the best of my knowledge and belief.

_____		_____	
Petitioner Signature	Date	Petitioner Signature	Date
_____		_____	
Petitioner's Attorney Signature, if any		Petitioner's Attorney Signature, if any	

Subscribed and affirmed, or sworn to before me in the County of _____, State of _____, this _____ day of _____, 20____.

My Commission Expires: _____

_____
Notary Public/Deputy Clerk

Subscribed and affirmed, or sworn to before me in the County of _____, State of _____, this _____ day of _____, 20____.

My Commission Expires: _____

_____
Notary Public/Deputy Clerk

JDF 501   R7-12   PETITION FOR ADOPTION   Page 3 of 3
© 2012 Colorado Judicial Department for use in the Courts of Colorado

Notice, Preliminary Hearing, Interlocutory Decree, Preadoption Placement, and Final Decree

Once the Petition is filed, it must be served on all interested parties. If the child is a nonmarital child and the biological father has neither consented to the adoption nor had his parental rights terminated, he should be served with notice of the petition for adoption by personal service or by publication if necessary. Other interested parties who may be given notice include foster parents, relatives who may have been caring for the child, and preadoptive parents if an agency is filing the petition. The court then holds a preliminary hearing in which the pending adoption may or may not be contested. If it is uncontested or not successfully contested, the court customarily then issues an interlocutory decree granting temporary custody of the child to the adoptive parents. The adoption is generally not finalized until the final hearing is held six months to a year later. During that period, a follow-up home study is usually conducted.

Whatever their type, all adoptions must be approved by the court. The court makes a determination as to whether or not all statutory requirements have been met and the adoption will be in the best interests of the child. Most adoption final hearings are joyful events and may be conducted in the judge's chambers, depending on the circumstances. Even if held in the courtroom, the proceedings are closed to the public and the related records are sealed. Once the adoption is finalized, a Final Decree of Adoption is issued by the court, and a new birth certificate designating the adoptive parents as the child's legal parents is issued for the public record.

Challenges to the Adoption

Adoption abrogation
an annulment, repeal, or undoing of an adoption

In general, adoptions are considered final, but challenges do arise. The three most common sources of challenges are unwed biological fathers who never received notice of their child's adoption (see Case 8.1), biological parents who seek to revoke their consents, and adoptive parents who seek to **abrogate** an adoption they believe was wrongfully procured by an agency or individual.

CASE **8.1** *In re Doe*, 159 Ill. 2d 347, 638 N.E.2d 181 (1994)

THE FACTS

Similar to the infamous "Baby Jessica" case[44] in 1993, this high-profile case, popularly known as the "Baby Richard" case, caused a national media frenzy. Baby Richard was the biological child of Daniella Janikova and Otakar Kirchner. When he was born, his parents were not married. At the time of the birth, the father was out of the country taking care of his dying grandmother in Czechoslovakia. Four days after the child was born, Daniella consented to have the child adopted by John and Jane Doe after being told by a relative of the father that Otakar was involved with another woman. She subsequently told Otakar that the baby had died at birth. He was suspicious of her story and promptly began checking birth and death records and even checked the garbage at the mother's home to look for evidence that a baby was living there. Approximately two months after the birth, he learned the truth. Daniella and Otakar subsequently reconciled and were married about six months after the child's birth and sought the return of the child. They challenged the legality of the adoption and alleged that the father's consent was required, because he had not abandoned the child and there was no evidence

(Continued)

that he was an unfit parent. He further argued that his lack of contact with the baby immediately after birth was solely due to the mother's fraudulent conduct.

The trial court held that the father was unfit because he had failed to demonstrate a reasonable degree of interest, concern, or responsibility for his son during the first thirty days of his life as required by statute, and thus his consent was not required. The court determined it was in Richard's best interests to remain with his adoptive parents, with whom he had lived since he was four days old. The trial court's decision was upheld by the appeals court, basing its decision on the best interests of the child. The appeals court stated:

> Fortunately, the time has long past when children in our society were considered the property of their parents. Slowly, but finally, when it comes to children even the law has rid itself of the Dred Scott mentality that a human being can be considered a piece of property "belonging" to another human being. To hold that a child is the property of his parents is to deny the humanity of the child. Thus, in the present case we start with the premise that Richard is not a piece of property with property rights belonging to either his biological or adoptive parents. Richard "belongs" to no one but himself.
>
> . . .
>
> A child's best interest is not part of an equation. It is not to be balanced against any other interest.[45]

The Illinois Supreme Court disagreed, finding that the father had been wrongfully deprived of the opportunity to express his interest in the child. It focused in its analysis of the situation on the preemptive rights of a natural parent in his own children apart from the best interest of the child.

Multiple appeals by the adoptive parents eventually failed despite a national public outcry and efforts by both the governor and state legislature of Illinois to influence the outcome by enacting a bill that provided for a hearing to consider a child's best interests when an adoption is denied or revoked on appeal as it was in this case. At the age of four, the crying child was taken from his adoptive mother's arms and handed over to his biological father in the bright media glare.

SIDEBAR

This case basically involved the weighing of the best interests of the child against the biological father's right to consent to the adoption of his child. What relative weight do you think should be given in such situations to the best interests of the child? The interests of the adoptive parents? The conduct of the mother? The interests of the nonmarital father? Should it matter whether the nonmarital father learns about the adoption before or after it is finalized? Do you agree with the outcome in this case? Explain your response. The opinion in the *In re Doe* case can be accessed at *www.pearsonhighered.com/careersresources/* in the companion website material for Chapter 8 of this text under Cases.

Adoptive parents are no different from biological parents in the sense that their adopted children do not always turn out as they might hope. However, neither biological nor adoptive parents get to trade in their children for models they like better! Much as the courts are resistant to allowing biological parents to revoke their consents to adoption, they are likewise reluctant to permit adoptive parents to abrogate (undo) an adoption. The majority view is that adoptions cannot be abrogated by an adoptive parent.

However, a few states, by statute or case law, permit adoptive parents to abrogate an adoption in exceptional circumstances. In isolated cases, adoptive parents do not get what they believe they bargained for because an adoption

PARALEGAL PRACTICE TIP

For more information about wrongful adoption, visit *www.childwelfare.gov.* Use the search box and search for wrongful adoption.

Wrongful adoption
a tort action that an adoptive parent can bring against an adoption agency for failure to provide accurate and sufficient information regarding an adoptive child prior to adoption

PARALEGAL PRACTICE TIP

Many argue that rather than criminalizing "rehoming," what is needed is the provision of additional resources to adoptive parents to help them address the stresses and challenges of coping with adoptees who present serious problems, particularly problems that threaten other family members. Adoptive parents, like other parents, must be held accountable for "abandoning" their children to strangers. However they and their children also need to be afforded a wide range of support services and treatment options, including placement of their children in residential facilities if necessary.

agency or biological parent failed to inform (or actively deceived) them with respect to a major issue relating to the adoptee. For example, an agency may have failed to disclose the existence of a serious or costly medical condition or a history of psychiatric and behavioral problems, including fire setting, animal abuse, or violent conduct. Adoption agencies cannot warranty the children they place, but they do have a duty to provide accurate information known to them, on the basis of which adoptive parents can make informed decisions. When they fail to do so, the adoptive parents may seek to revoke the adoption and/or if that fails bring an action against the agency for the tort of **wrongful adoption**. The adoptive parents may, for example, seek to recover the costs of the lifelong institutionalization of a child.

Because it is very difficult to "undo" an adoption, for years some adoptive parents have "rehomed" their adopted children. In effect, an adoptive parent unable to manage a particular adoptee privately transfers "possession" of the child to another "parent." Sometimes the transfer is accomplished via the Internet and is executed by a simple power of attorney letter or notarized statement without the involvement of the court or any vetting of the new parent(s). It is essentially an unregulated, underground activity. However, it is increasingly receiving attention from family law attorneys, the ABA, and state legislatures. In April 2014, Wisconsin became the first state to make it illegal for anyone not licensed by the state to advertise a child older than age one for adoption or any other custody transfer both in print or online. Violators face up to nine months in jail or as much as $10,000 in fines.

Paralegal Application 8.7

The Internet Explosion and the Adoption Revolution

Over the past decade, the Internet has transformed the landscape of every aspect of adoption. No longer is adoption controlled solely by "adoption professionals." No longer is it a "buyers' market" with adoption agencies and prospective adoptive parents driving the "matching" of families. No longer are birth parents without options. No longer are adoptees isolated. And no longer can there truly be a "closed" adoption. These are just some dimensions of the adoption revolution. Self-help through social media is the rallying cry. Make connections, find information, stay in touch, eliminate intermediaries, and save time and money. Consider the following:

Matching Resources

Expectant parents and prospective adoptive families now have a wide range of online resources to help them connect with each other.

Adoption matching websites are plentiful such as *www.adoptionhelp.org, www.parentprofiles.com, www. childconnect.com,* and *www.myadoptionportal.com*

Public and private agencies now have websites on which they post photo profiles and information

about "waiting" or "looking to adopt" families. *www.adoptuskids.org* is a national child welfare site with extensive resources and photolistings of children in U.S. foster care available for adoption and families who are home studied and approved to adopt.

Support groups

There are online support groups (websites, social networking sites, blogs, etc.) for a wide range of target populations such as adoptees (*www.landofagazillionadoptees .com*), birth families, adoptive families, adoptees from specific nations, adoptive parents of children with special needs, peer-to-peer groups, single adoptive parents, same-sex parents, transracial adoptees (*www .transracialadoptees.org*), and children who are aging out of foster care (*www.camellianetwork.org*).

Resources for professionals

Adoption attorneys increasingly make use of the Internet in their practices. Attorneys and their investigators often have access to Internet databases not available to the general public. The Internet is especially helpful with locating missing parties who need to be served and/or given notice of a pending matter.

Education

Informal sites: Information from many perspectives is provided on these sites about topics such as advertising and connecting, conducting searches and related issues, and navigating adoption subsidies and tax credits.

Formal sites: Sites such as *www.adoptededucation .com* and *www.adoptionmosaic.org* offer pre- and postadoption training, seminars, webinars, etc. Adoptive Families (accessible at *www.adoptivefamilies. com*) is a leading adoption information and educational resource for families before, during, and after adoption.

Open adoption options

The Internet affords many vehicles that can be used to implement open adoption agreements such as Facebook pages where updates, photo albums, and messages can be posted spontaneously or according to a specific schedule.

Postadoption search and reunion resources

The Internet has not replaced Registries but it does provide additional resources to support search and reunion efforts that may be used at any point in the process by any party, parent, adoptee, siblings, and other relatives. Searchers often begin with free social networking sites open to the public such as Facebook, YouTube, Google, and LinkedIn. When adoptees learn their birth names, they may create a page using their respective birth names. *www.classmates.com* can be used for searching on a birth mother's maiden name. It has a "double-blind" e-mail system for member-to-member communications while allowing other communications to be public. There are several private mutual consent run registries, some with an international reach: International Soundex Reunion Registry *www.isrr.org* Metro Reunion Registry *www.metroreunionregistry.org* and The Alma Society *www.almasociety.org* The U.S. Department of Health and Human Services Administration for Children and Families provides information and advice about search and reunion initiatives at *www .childwelfare.gov*.

Red flags

It is difficult if not impossible to regulate the Internet and its reach cannot be confined to a particular state. As a result, it presents a virtual minefield for both private parties and professionals. Consider the following examples of potential problems:

The Internet provides a fertile ground for criminals eager to make money through defrauding prospective adoptive parents.

There are imposters who try to exploit and benefit from search efforts creating fictitious profiles and posing as long lost relatives making use of detailed information revealed online.

Predators use revealing data and personal contact information for identity theft purposes.

Online resources may contain inaccurate or misleading information often posted by well-intentioned but misinformed sources.

Because state laws vary with respect to who and where advertising for adoption of children can occur (if at all), caution must be exercised. For example, ads should include disclaimers ("This ad is not intended for states that prohibit such ads.").

Overzealous reunion seekers need to be cautious about potential charges of cyberstalking, cyberharrassing, or invasion of privacy. They also need to recognize the potential negative consequences of unguided contact: not all stories have fairytale endings, some people don't want to be found, and others need time and emotional preparation.

Service providers and others need to avoid running afoul of the Children's Online Privacy Protection Act of 1998 (provides protections for children under age thirteen).

Resources for this Paralegal Application include *Use of Social Media in Post-Adoption Search and Reunion*, Ann M. Haralambic (41 CAP. U. L. REV. 177 (2013)) (includes an appendix with a state-by-state summary about statutory access to birth records); *Meeting the Challenge of Adoption in an Internet Age*, Mary Kate Kearney and Arrielle Millstein (41 CAP. U. L. REV. 237 (2013)); and *Internet Promises, Scares, and Surprises: New Realities of Adoption*, Michelle M. Hughes (41 CAP. U. L. REV. 279 (2013)).

The Paralegal's Role in Adoption Cases

The paralegal's role in adoption cases depends primarily on four factors:

1. the extent to which the firm where the paralegal is employed specializes in adoption
2. the type of adoption involved
3. the client's role in the litigation: Is he or she the petitioner? Is he or she seeking to block the adoption? Is the client an agency?
4. the nature and level of the paralegal's skills

Primary tasks performed may include the following:

- researching state and federal statutes, case law, and procedural rules and regulations governing adoption in the applicable jurisdiction(s)
- creating websites and marketing strategies to recruit prospective adoptive parents and locate potential adoptees
- interviewing prospective adoptive parents, parents considering relinquishing their rights, and parents facing involuntary termination of their rights, to gather information relevant to the client's case
- researching issues such as the rights of nonmarital fathers to object to an adoption, the right of a child to consent to his or her adoption, involuntary termination of parental rights, and adoption by single persons or same-sex partners/spouses
- conducting a thorough search for a biological father whose whereabouts are unknown
- locating, drafting, and filing necessary paperwork, including petitions, consents, surrenders, ICPC paperwork, etc.
- drafting open adoption agreements
- scheduling and calendaring events such as home studies, hearings, and client meetings
- providing support to clients as they progress through the often emotionally draining adoption process
- monitoring payments for medical expenses to a birth mother intending to give up her child for adoption

PARALEGAL PRACTICE TIP

Visit *www.adoptionhelp.org*, the website of the Independent Adoption Center, to see a good example of a forward looking resource that addresses needs of singles, LGBT couples, and parties interested in open adoption.

CHAPTER **SUMMARY**

This chapter opened with a description of the nature and purposes of adoption. Various types of adoptions were introduced classified on the basis of how they are created (agency, independent, international, equitable, and black market); whether the adoption is open or closed; and who can adopt. The major steps in the adoption process were described. Several topics related to adoption were discussed and illustrated including the nature and role of putative father registries, the contrast between the rights of married and unmarried parents, safe haven laws, the importance of effective consents, termination of parental rights, characteristics of prospective adoptive parents, home studies, and challenges to adoptions. Multistate variations in adoption law and procedure were highlighted.

The chapter closed with a description of the roles a paralegal might be called upon to play in the context of adoption cases.

The primary emphasis of this chapter is on what might be called "traditional adoption law." However, the material on the challenges faced by nontraditional families and the final paralegal application addressing the multifaceted impact of the Internet illustrate that the traditional adoption model is increasingly ill-suited to the reality of the modern "family" and contemporary culture. Inevitably, adoption codes and customs are going to be compelled to undergo an evolution. They will also need to accommodate the impact of marriage equality across the nation. Some dimensions of that challenge are raised in this chapter.

CONCEPT REVIEW AND REINFORCEMENT

KEY TERMS

Adoptee
Adoption
Adoption abrogation
Adoption reunion registry
Agency adoption
At-risk adoption
Biology-plus rule
Closed adoption
Co-parent
Cut-off rule

De facto adoption
Equitable adoption/adoption by
     estoppel
Foster parent
Home studies
Illegal/black market adoption
Independent adoption
International adoption
Joint petition for adoption
Open adoption

Permanency planning
Putative father
Putative father registry
Safe haven law
Standing
Surrender (of parental rights)
Termination of parental rights
Wrongful adoption

REVIEW QUESTIONS

1. Identify and distinguish among various types of adoption based on how adoptions are created and who can adopt.
2. Distinguish between an open and a closed adoption and identify the merits of each approach.
3. Identify the basic steps in the adoption process.
4. Describe the nature and significance of the "biology-plus rule."
5. Describe the nature and purpose of putative father registries.
6. Identify the kinds of circumstances in which a parent's rights may be terminated.
7. Identify who must consent to an adoption and under what circumstances a consent can be revoked.
8. Describe the role each of the following plays in adoption determinations: race, age, marital status, and sexual orientation.
9. Describe the nature and purpose of a home study.
10. Identify three circumstances in which an adoption may be challenged.

DEVELOPING YOUR PARALEGAL SKILLS

FOCUS ON THE JOB

In this Focus, the student will draft documents tailored to a specific fact pattern: a Petition for Adoption, appropriate Surrender and Consent forms, and a Proposed Open Adoption Agreement.

The Facts

Jessica and Scott met in 2013 at a local tavern, where Jessica was tending bar and dealing drugs on a small scale, essentially to support her own habit. They quickly became involved. Scott did not join Jessica in using drugs until after he was involved in an automobile accident and was initially prescribed Oxycontin for pain. A year after they met, Jessica became pregnant. Although she did not entirely stop using drugs while pregnant, she did cut back and eventually gave birth on June 23, 2015, to a healthy baby boy they named Michael ("Mike") after Jessica's father. Scott formally acknowledged paternity, and his name appears on the child's birth certificate. The couple (along with the baby) lived with Jessica's parents until Scott lost his job and the parents found out about the couple's drug use. The parents blamed all of Jessica's problems on Scott and threw him out of the house but allowed her to continue living there with the baby.

Scott was unemployed and homeless for about two months before he entered detox for a week, a secure rehabilitation facility for a month, and then a halfway house for six months. He regularly visited Mike and sent whatever financial support he could to Jessica, although he feared it simply went toward her cocaine addiction. He eventually got a job in construction (earning approximately $68,000 a year with overtime) and met and married Hayley, a high school English teacher (earning $45,000 a year) who is a caring and supportive partner eager to make a good life with him and raise Mike. Jessica is relieved at the prospect of not being responsible for the boy and is willing to consent to a stepparent adoption by Hayley as long as they will allow her to visit with the child twice a year for an afternoon and send her pictures and letters on a monthly basis.

Jessica's last name is Olivio and Scott's is Martinelli. The baby was given the father's last name at birth. Jessica's date of birth is February 9, 1990, and her current address is 33 Main Street in your city and state. Scott is living with Hayley in her home at 903 Hale Street in your city and state. Scott was born on October 21, 1989, and Hayley was born on November 17, 1991. They are members of a Unitarian church. Jessica was formerly a practicing Catholic but has left the church. She is presently unemployed. She was receiving public assistance for the benefit of Mike, but now Scott pays monthly child support through the state's IV-D agency.

The Assignment

Assume that you are employed by Attorney Juliana Dimitry, whose office is located at 390 Main Street in your city and state, and that she represents Scott and Hayley in this matter. Research the appropriate forms used in your state and draft the following:

1. A Petition for Adoption
2. Appropriate Surrender and Consent Forms
3. A proposed Open Adoption Agreement, assuming that such agreements are permitted in your jurisdiction.

FOCUS ON **ETHICS**

In this Focus, the student will discuss ethical issues raised in a client meeting, particularly with respect to privilege, confidentiality, and candor.

The Assignment

Assume that you are employed by Attorney Kelly Brantley, whose office is located at 220 High Street in your city and state. She has an established general practice and is well respected by her colleagues. The office has been retained to represent Jessica in the adoption action described in the above comprehensive fact pattern. In the initial interview you were assigned to conduct with Jessica, she asks if everything she tells you is "private," and you assure her that yes, all of her communications with the family law team working on her case are protected by the attorney–client privilege. She then tells you that Scott is not actually Mike's father, but that she convinced him he was so that he

would acknowledge paternity and she would have no problem applying for public assistance. It all worked out, she says, because Scott has gotten his life back together and has turned out to be a great father. She says everything is going well now and she doesn't want to upset the applecart by telling the truth. She just wants to give up her legal rights and get the adoption finalized as soon as possible. In a one- to two-page report describe what you are going to do in response to this conversation. Personally, you would really like to see the adoption take place because it is clearly in the best interests of the child. Relate your response to the ethical canons for paralegals promulgated by the National Association of Legal Assistants, which are contained in Appendix A, the material on ethics in Chapter 1 of this text, and the code of ethics applicable to attorneys in your state. Although he is not your client, would any other options potentially be available to Scott if and when the truth comes out?

FOCUS ON **CASE LAW**

In this activity, the student has an opportunity to brief a case on a topic relating to adoption.

The Assignment

Locate and brief a case decided in your state within the past three years on one of the following topics:

1. Termination of parental rights
2. Revocation of parental consent to an adoption

3. Co-parent adoption
4. The state's putative father registry, if any
5. Access to adoption records

A format for briefing a case can be found at *www.pearsonhighered.com/careersresources/* in the companion website material for this text related to Chapter 1 under Resources.

FOCUS ON **STATE LAW AND PROCEDURE**

This Focus requires students to research laws and procedures governing adoptions in their respective jurisdictions.

The Assignment

Locate and review the laws and procedures governing adoption in your state of residence and then prepare written responses to the following questions:

1. Under what circumstances, if any, may a parent have his or her parental rights terminated?
2. Who is required to consent to an adoption?
3. Is a parent permitted to revoke a consent to adoption and, if so, under what circumstances?
4. What kinds of adoptions are permitted?
5. Does your state have a safe haven law? If yes, describe its provisions.

6. Who may adopt and who may be adopted?
7. Does your state have a putative father registry? If yes, describe its basic provisions.

8. Are adult adoptees permitted to contact their biological parents? If yes, how do they go about doing so?

FOCUS ON **TECHNOLOGY**

In addition to the links throughout the chapter, this activity provides a series of useful websites for reference along with technology-related assignments for completion.

Websites of Interest

www.abcadoptions.com

This site contains information about the adoption process and includes adoption postings. It serves as a support for both birth parents seeking adoptive parents and adoptive parents seeking children. It provides information for both populations and appears to act as a "meeting ground."

www.adoptionchildwelfarelaw.org

This is the Adoption and Child Welfare Lawsite, a service of the National Center for Adoption Law and Policy at Capital University Law School. It allows the visitor to search cases, statutes, and articles about adoption on a state-by-state basis.

www.adoptioninstitute.org

This is the website for the Evan P. Donaldson Adoption Institute. It contains links to putative father registries, open records information, state registries, and confidentiality statutes. It states as its mission, "To provide leadership that improves adoption laws, policies, and practices—through sound research, education, and advocacy—in order to better the lives of everyone touched by adoption."

www.chask.org

"CHASK" is an acronym for Christian Homes and Special Kids. It is a Christian service organization that serves as a meeting place for adoptive parents and birth mothers seeking adoptive homes for their children with special needs.

www.childwelfare.gov

This is the website for the Child Welfare Information Gateway, an organization of the U.S. Department of Health and Human Services. It contains links to a number of sites addressing topics such as open adoption, access to adoption records, single-parent adoption, and gay and lesbian adoptive parents. It also provides links to federal and state laws, fact sheets, statistics, and publications.

www.law.cornell.edu

This site provides links to the adoption laws of all fifty states.

Assignments

1. Locate websites for three adoption reunion registries and describe their contents. Begin with the Georgia Adoption Reunion Registry, located at *www.ga-adoptionreunion.com*

2. Locate and describe websites for putative father registries in three states. Begin with the Illinois Registry at *www.putativefather.org*

3. Locate three websites that offer information and support to gays and lesbians seeking to adopt.

PORTFOLIO PRODUCTS

1. Surrender and Consent to Adoption
2. Petition for Adoption
3. Proposed Open Adoption Agreement
4. One- to two-page report concerning ethical issues in a hypothetical case
5. Brief of an adoption case
6. List of selected laws and procedures governing adoption in the student's jurisdiction

© Estelle Tomson

chapter 9
CHILD CUSTODY

Diana and Ramon Acevedo are the grandparents of Melody and Paco, the children of their unmarried daughter, Christina, and her former boyfriend, Miguel Rodriguez. They believe they should be awarded visitation with their grandchildren so they can at least temporarily rescue them from the harmful influence of their parents. Although Christina and Miguel are no longer a couple, they both say, "No way...."

LEARNING OBJECTIVES

After reading this chapter and completing related assignments, you should be able to:

- identify various types of child custody

- identify at least three jurisdictional issues that sometimes arise in child custody cases

- describe the primary standards the courts apply when making custody decisions, including the "best interests of the child"

- list some of the major factors courts may look at when assessing competing claims for custody and visitation

- describe the nature and purpose of parenting plans

- explain why parent education programs are important

- describe when and how custody and visitation orders may be modified

- explain how custody and visitation orders can be enforced

- identify rights of third parties (including grandparents, stepparents, and *de facto* parents) in the custody context

- explain when and how a guardian *ad litem* may be involved in a child custody case

- discuss the paralegal's role in cases involving custody issues

Introduction

Many married parents whose marriages fail get divorced, and unmarried parents whose relationships break down leave each other without ceremony. But married or divorced, together or apart, parents cannot change the fact they are parents. Custody issues do not simply involve parents battling over inanimate pieces of property. Custody is about live children who have interests in the outcome of the battle. They are what the battle is supposed to be about.

Issues related to the care, custody, and maintenance of children are highlighted throughout this text particularly in the material addressing parentage determinations, custody disputes, adoption, child support, and family violence. The focus of this chapter is on custody in the context of divorce and third-party actions, actions involving nonparents who are technically legal strangers to children they have cared for but with whom they have formed "parent-like" relationships. Chapter content includes a review of topics such as where and when custody and visitation are sought, standards and factors considered by the courts when making custody determinations, the nature and purpose of parenting plans, when and how awards can be modified and enforced, and the purposes served by guardians *ad litem*. The role played by paralegals in custody cases is also described. In the majority of divorces, there is no dispute with respect to which parent should have custody of the children or if custody should be shared. The parties establish an agreed-upon schedule and related provisions and present their agreement to the court for approval and incorporation in the decree dissolving their marriage. In some cases, however, before an agreement is reached, a considerable amount of negotiating may occur. One parent may even threaten the other parent with the loss of custody in an effort to obtain some unrelated advantage, such as a more favorable property division.[1]

In a small minority of cases, there is such hostility and disagreement between the parties that they are unable to reach an agreement even with the assistance of mediation. At considerable emotional and financial cost, these high-conflict cases will go to trial to be decided by a judge. Each party will present evidence and testimony and will have an opportunity to cross-examine the other party and his or her witnesses. Customarily, the parties will testify about their relationship with the child relating anecdotes about involvement in as many aspects of the child's life as possible–health, education, recreation, daily routines, medical care, religious training, discipline, and the like. **Lay witnesses**, such as friends, neighbors, teachers, and counselors, may be called to buttress a parent's testimony, and occasionally a battle of experts may ensue–especially if the child or either or both of the parents have health, psychiatric, or behavioral problems impacting on their fitness as a parent or if there is evidence that either parent is abusing the child in some manner. The court may also appoint its own resources, including a **guardian *ad litem***, to provide a neutral assessment of the situation and may interview the child **in camera** as to his or her feelings and parental preference. The court then has to make a decision about the course of action that will best serve the child's interests after objectively assessing the evidence and weighing the credibility of the various witnesses. States afford judges broad discretion, and a trial court's decision will customarily not be disturbed on appeal absent a showing of an abuse of discretion, insufficient evidence to support the court's conclusion, or an error in declaring or applying the law.

Types of Custody

In general, **physical custody** (called residential custody or physical placement in some states) refers to where the child will live, and **legal custody** refers to decision-making authority. A **sole award** is vested primarily in one parent. A **joint award** involves shared responsibility. The various types of custody described in traditional terms are as follows:

Sole legal custody One parent has the right and responsibility to make the major decisions regarding the child's welfare, including matters of education, medical care, and emotional, moral, and religious development.

Joint legal custody Both parents have continued mutual responsibility and involvement in the making of major decisions regarding the child's welfare. Absent an emergency, when legal custody is joint, neither parent should make a major decision related to the child without first consulting the other parent. Although this arrangement sounds fine in principle, conflicts frequently arise, especially with respect to what constitutes a "major" decision. For instance, is getting a tattoo or dyeing one's hair purple a major or a day-to-day decision? It is often the case that parents with shared legal custody cannot reach a decision on an issue. To avoid continual and costly trips back to court, judges may appoint a parenting coordinator or may

Lay witness
a witness who is not an expert on a matter at issue in a legal proceeding who testifies as to opinions based on firsthand knowledge

Guardian *ad litem*
[Latin: for the suit] a person, usually a lawyer, appointed by the court to conduct an investigation and/or to represent a party who is a minor or otherwise unable to represent himself or herself in a legal proceeding; the guardian's role may be limited to a particular matter, such as custody

In camera
in the judge's chambers

Physical custody
custody relating to where and with whom the child resides; can be either sole or joint

Legal custody
custody relating to decision-making authority with respect to major issues affecting a child; may be sole or joint

Sole award
an award made to one parent only; may apply to legal or physical custody

Joint award
an award made to both parents; may apply to legal or physical custody

Custodial parent

the parent with whom the child primarily resides; the parent who has the right to have the child live with him or her

Noncustodial parent

a parent who does not have sole or primary physical custody of a child but who is still a legal parent with enforceable rights and responsibilities

Split custody

a custody arrangement in which each parent has legal and/or physical custody of one or more of the parties' children

designate one of the parents as the "final decision-making authority." See, for example, *Rembert v. Rembert*, 285 Ga. 260, 674 S.E.2d 892 (2009).

Sole physical custody The child resides with and is under the day-to-day supervision of one parent, subject to reasonable visitation with the other parent unless a court determines that visitation would not be in the best interests of the child. The parent with whom the child primarily resides is commonly called the **custodial parent** and the parent with visitation rights is referred to as the **noncustodial parent.**

Joint or shared physical custody The child has periods of residing with and being under the day-to-day supervision of each parent. The custody is shared in such a way that the child has frequent and continuing contact with each parent.

Split custody Each parent has sole legal and/or physical custody of one or more of the parties' children. Strong public policy supports keeping siblings together. Absent an extraordinary emotional, medical, or educational need or some other compelling circumstance, split custody is not favored by the courts. (See, e.g., *Ardizoni v. Raymond*, 40 Mass. App. Ct. 734 (1996), involving identical twins.) In affirming a modification order splitting custody of two sisters, the Iowa Court of Appeals identified several competing factors to be considered in split custody cases, including (1) the difference in the siblings' ages; (2) the extent to which they would be together if split care was not ordered (same schools, friends, activities, etc.); (3) the nature of the relationship between the siblings and any half-siblings; (4) the likelihood that one of the parents would turn the children against the other parent; (5) the children's relationship with stepparents; (6) the capability of the parents to care for the children and the nature of their past involvement. (See *In re the Marriage of Pamela J. Walters and Chad J. Walters*, 820 N.W.2d 160 (Iowa App. 2012).) The potential for the siblings to visit with each other and maintain regular contact is another factor to be considered. (See, e.g., In the Interest of K.B.K, M.A.K., and J.C.K., Children, 2014 Tex. App. LEXIS 3433 (2014), a case in which an appellate court upheld a trial court's decision that two older daughters should live with their father in Texas due to family relationships there and a younger son should live with his mother and her new husband in Colorado where he was settled and had bonded with his stepfather. The order provided for the siblings to visit every other weekend.)

Although many still use traditional terms to refer to custody, several states have abandoned the old terms that tend to increase conflict such as "sole" custody and "visitation" in favor of new terminology that emphasizes allocation of parental responsibilities for the benefit of the child.[2] One of the "new" approaches to custody-related terminology is reflected in the New Hampshire Parental Rights and Responsibilities Act, which replaces the term "custody" with the phrase "parental rights and responsibilities" and refers to legal custody as "decision-making responsibility" and physical custody as "residential responsibility."[3] The emphasis is on custody as a shared effort to meet the needs of children rather than as a battle between parents for possession and control.

Whatever terminology is used, there is no fixed formula for child custody determinations. Under the guidance of state statutes and case law, courts are free to create multiple forms of custody arrangements tailored to meet the unique needs and challenges of each family. This flexibility is especially useful in complex, interstate, or high-conflict cases.

The two most common forms of custodial awards are:

1. Joint legal custody and sole physical custody in one parent with reasonable rights of visitation in the other parent
2. Joint legal and physical custody

Prior to the 1970s, the first option was predominant and it continues to be common today. However, with the coming of no-fault divorce, gender-neutral custody laws, and equal rights movements in their many forms, joint physical and legal custody awards have become more common. Most states now provide by statute or case law that, absent a history of domestic violence, joint awards are in the best interest of children. However, joint awards have met with mixed results. Their prospects for success are greatest when implemented by parties who are able to communicate effectively or when parents want to become or remain actively involved in their children's lives. They are less likely to be successful when imposed on disinterested parents, parties who cannot each afford to maintain a residence for the children, or parents who are unable to rise above hostility toward each other in order to commit to a shared role for the benefit of their children. Joint custody can also be difficult for children, particularly if they are forced to live in two different homes in two totally different communities.

Jurisdictional Issues in Child Custody Cases

A court's authority to issue a child custody order is based on statute. Personal jurisdiction over a parent or a child is not sufficient. Subject matter jurisdiction is required. The parties cannot confer subject matter jurisdiction by agreement, and therefore, a party must establish it by complying with governing statutes.

Jurisdictional problems are minimal in child custody cases when the parents' identities are known and both parties and the child reside in the same state. However, problems can arise when multiple states are involved, particularly in domestic violence cases or when variations in jurisdictional requirements exist. Interstate conflicts were especially prevalent prior to 1968, when courts based jurisdiction for custody decisions on the child's physical presence in a state at the time an action was filed. This sometimes led to **forum shopping** by parents, some of whom would abduct their children and go to another state or nation where they might secure a more favorable custody award.

Four Acts have made a particular effort to address custody cases involving multiple jurisdictions:

1. The Uniform Child Custody Jurisdiction Act (UCCJA)[4]
2. The Uniform Child Custody Jurisdiction and Enforcement Act (UCCJEA)[5]
3. The Federal Parental Kidnapping Prevention Act (PKPA)[6]
4. The Hague Convention on the Civil Aspects of International Child Abduction[7]

UCCJA

The National Conference of Commissioners on Uniform State Laws (NCCUSL) promulgated the Uniform Child Custody Jurisdiction Act in 1968, and by 1981 it was adopted in all fifty states, the District of Colombia, and

PARALEGAL PRACTICE TIP

In *Jackson v. Jackson*, 82 So. 3d 644 (Miss. Ct. App. 2011), a joint physical custody award was upheld because the court was persuaded the parents were committed to communicating and able to make the arrangement work. In *Shinall v. Shinall*, 964 N.E.2d 619 (Ill. App. Ct. 2012), a denial of joint custody was upheld on appeal because the court found the parents lacked the capacity to cooperate in raising their daughter. There was so much disrespect and friction between them that they needed third-party witnesses at exchanges. Their animosity sometimes was expressed in front of the child and even led to resignation of a day care provider "caught in the middle."

Forum shopping
seeking a court that will grant the most favorable ruling in a case

PARALEGAL PRACTICE TIP

You can find a copy of the UCCJEA and information about its adoption at *www.uniformlaws.org.* View All Acts/Child Custody Jurisdiction and Enforcement Act. To learn more about the Act go to *www.ncjrs.gov.* OJP Publications/find the Act under U.

PARALEGAL PRACTICE TIP

To see a variety of UCCJEA related forms, visit *www.nycourts.gov.* Search for Forms/UCCJEA.

PARALEGAL PRACTICE TIP

In *Friedman v. Eighth Jud. Ct. of Nev.,* 264 P.3d 1161 (Nev. 2011), the parties' divorce decree incorporated their agreement that Nevada would have exclusive continuing jurisdiction over any future child custody disputes. The parents and children subsequently moved to California and had resided there for more than two years when the father initiated custody proceedings in that state. With everyone gone from Nevada, the father maintained that, despite the parties' agreement, Nevada lacked subject matter jurisdiction. The Nevada Supreme Court held that Nevada had jurisdiction to make the initial child custody determination but two years later California had become the children's "home state" as defined by the Nevada UCCJEA. Under the Act, the Nevada court was required to stay its proceeding, communicate with the California court, and if the California court did not determine that Nevada was a more appropriate forum, stand down and not assert custody jurisdiction.

Home state jurisdiction
jurisdiction in custody matters based on where the child has lived for a specified period of time

Significant connection jurisdiction
jurisdiction based on the existence of substantial evidence in a state concerning a child

the Virgin Islands. The Act authorized four independent bases of jurisdiction for initial custody determinations: home state, significant connection, emergency, and last resort/vacuum. None of these required the presence of the child in the state at the time of filing, thus reducing the incentive to temporarily take a child to another state solely to file a custody action there. The Act also required states to enforce and not modify sister states' valid child custody and visitation orders.

The UCCJA was an improvement over pre-1968 law governing jurisdiction in child custody cases and helped to reduce the filing of competing custody actions in multiple states. However, some problems remained. For example, because priority was not given to home state jurisdiction, multiple orders from different states could still potentially exist, with one based on home state and the other on significant connection jurisdiction.

UCCJEA

Drafted by the National Conference of Commissioners on Uniform State Laws in 1997, the Uniform Child Custody Jurisdiction and Enforcement Act has been adopted by 49 states, the District of Columbia, Guam, and the U.S. Virgin Islands. As of the spring of 2015, only Massachusetts and Puerto Rico had not yet adopted it. Like the UCCJA, the UCCJEA is a uniform law designed to reduce jurisdictional conflicts between states, deter child abductions for the purpose of obtaining jurisdiction in another state, avoid relitigation of decisions from other states, and ensure that custody matters are heard in the state that has the closest connection with the child and the family. The UCCJEA addresses weaknesses in the UCCJA that had continued to result in costly litigation and inconsistent decisions in interstate custody cases. It accomplishes this in part by tightening the four bases for initial jurisdiction under the UCCJA and preserving exclusive, continuing jurisdiction in the decree state as long as that state has a basis for keeping jurisdiction. The primary bases for initial jurisdiction under the UCCJEA are as follows:

a. **Home state** Home state jurisdiction exists when a child has lived with a parent or a person acting as a parent for at least six consecutive months immediately before the commencement of a child custody proceeding. In the case of a child less than six months of age, the term means the state in which the child has lived from birth. Periods of temporary absence from the state are included in the six-month period. Once the home state is established, if the child is removed from the state, a parent (or person acting as a parent) who remains there may bring a custody action within a six-month period. Consistent with federal law (the PKPA), the UCCJEA makes the child's home state the priority ground for original jurisdiction in interstate child custody cases. If the minor child has a home state, jurisdiction will be proper only in the home state unless that state declines jurisdiction.

b. **Significant connection** Sections 201(a)(2)(A) and (B) of the UCCJEA provide that **significant connection jurisdiction** exists when "(A) the child and the child's parents, or the child and at least one parent or a person acting as a parent, have a significant connection with a State other than mere physical presence; and (B) substantial evidence is available in that State concerning the child's care, protection, training, and personal relationships; . . ."

Under the UCCJEA, a state can exercise "significant connection" jurisdiction only if the "home state" declines jurisdiction, there are **forum *non conveniens*** or parental misconduct grounds, or there is no home state. The potential exists for more than one state to have jurisdiction on this basis but only one may exercise it. The Act resolves the conflict in favor of the first-filed proceeding unless the courts agree otherwise after mandatory communication.

c. **More appropriate forum** This type of jurisdiction exists when both the home state and the significant connection state(s) decline jurisdiction in favor of a third more appropriate state based on inconvenient forum or parental misconduct grounds. Under Section 207 of the UCCJEA, a court may consider factors, including whether domestic violence has occurred and, if so, which state can best protect the parties and the child; how long the child has lived outside of the state; where the evidence is located; and which court is most familiar with the case.

d. **Vacuum/last resort jurisdiction** If no state has jurisdiction under options a, b, or c above, vacuum jurisdiction provides an alternative that allows a state to exercise jurisdiction over an initial custody proceeding in certain limited circumstances. For example, it is an appropriate option in cases involving migrant or homeless children or children of military personnel who do not remain in any state for a period of time sufficient to establish any other type of jurisdiction.

e. **Temporary emergency jurisdiction** Under Section 204 of the UCCJEA, courts can exercise temporary emergency jurisdiction when a child in the state has been abandoned or when emergency protection is necessary because a child, or a sibling or parent of the child, has been subjected to or is threatened with mistreatment or abuse. Courts may exercise emergency jurisdiction even if a custody proceeding has been initiated in another state but may only issue temporary orders. If there is no prior order and no proceeding has been initiated in a state with jurisdiction, the temporary order may become final once the issuing state becomes the child's home state.

Under the UCCJEA, exclusive, continuing jurisdiction will remain in the initial decree state until one of two events occurs: (a) a court in the decree state or another state determines that the child, the child's parents, and any person acting as a parent no longer resides in the decree state; or (b) the decree state determines that neither the child, the child's parents, nor any person acting as a parent still has a significant connection with the decree state and there is no longer substantial evidence in the state concerning the child.

Establishing jurisdiction in interstate modification cases can be very fact-intensive. For example, the family law team may need to gather evidence to show that even though one of the parties in a custody case still resides in the decree state, his or her relationship with a child now in a new home state is so attenuated that the court that issued the initial custody order will no longer be able to find a significant connection or substantial evidence in that state. In such circumstances, the decree state may determine that continuing jurisdiction no longer exists.

Other major improvements in the UCCJEA as compared with the UCCJA include the following:

- The UCCJEA brought the UCCJA into compliance with more recent federal statutes, such as the Parental Kidnapping Prevention Act (PKPA) and the Violence Against Women Act (VAWA).

Forum *non conveniens*
[Latin: an unsuitable court] the forum in which an action is filed is not convenient for one or both of the parties, and the court, in its discretion, may find that justice would be better served if the matter is heard in another court

Vacuum/Last resort jurisdiction
jurisdiction based on the fact no other state is willing or able to exercise jurisdiction, and it is in the child's best interest for a state to do so

Temporary emergency jurisdiction
jurisdiction based on a child's physical presence in a state and need for emergency protection

---

PARALEGAL PRACTICE TIP

In determining jurisdiction, the courts will look at the totality of the circumstances. For example, in *Brandt v. Brandt*, 268 P.3d 406 (Colo. 2012), the parties divorced in Maryland before the Army transferred the father to Colorado. The couple's son was in the mother's physical custody in Maryland as well as after the Army transferred her to Texas. Later when she was deployed to Iraq, the son went to live with his father. When the mother came back to Texas after her tour, the son returned to her care. After she received orders to move back to Maryland, the father petitioned a Colorado court to assume jurisdiction and award him custody. The district court concluded it could do so under Colorado's UCCJEA because no party presently resided in Maryland. On review, the Colorado Supreme Court held the district court erred in finding that no party presently resided in Maryland. The mother had continuously maintained a home, driver's license, nursing license, and voting registration in Maryland and had paid Maryland state taxes. She also received her orders to transfer back to Maryland 10 days before the father filed his petition.

- It creates mechanisms for courts in different states to "communicate and cooperate" with one another.
- It provides procedures for interstate registration and enforcement of a child custody and visitation order, provided the order was issued in substantial conformity with the UCCJEA.
- It authorizes the issuing of warrants authorizing law enforcement officers to protect children at risk of being unlawfully removed from a state.
- Unlike the UCCJA, the UCCJEA is not applicable in adoption cases, but it does apply to tribal court proceedings.

PKPA

The major federal child custody jurisdiction act is the Parental Kidnapping Prevention Act (PKPA) enacted in 1980 to address interstate custody problems that continued to exist after the adoption of the UCCJA and before the UCCJEA was created. Its scope is not limited to "kidnapping" cases; rather, its primary purpose is to maintain jurisdiction in one court over custody orders pertaining to a given child in interstate cases. The PKPA has essentially the same primary jurisdictional bases as the UCCJEA and it, too, fills a major gap in the UCCJA by giving priority in initial child custody determinations to home state jurisdiction. By doing so, it prevents a "significant connection" state from exercising jurisdiction over a custody matter as long as the child involved has a "home state." If it does exercise jurisdiction, its order will not be entitled to recognition by other states.

To avoid the issuing of conflicting custody orders, the PKPA mandates that states give full faith and credit to other states' custody determinations as long as they are made in conformity with the provisions of the PKPA. Subject to the emergency jurisdiction provision, it also provides for exclusive continuing jurisdiction over modification of custody actions involving the child as long as the original decree state continues to have jurisdiction. Jurisdiction continues in the decree state until such time as (1) the initial state has lost jurisdiction because it is no longer the home state and it no longer has a significant connection to the case because substantial evidence is not present there or (2) neither the child nor either parent continues to reside in the decree state.

Although the UCCJEA is designed for adoption by the states and the PKPA is a federal act, the goals and procedures of the two Acts largely mirror each other. When there is a conflict, the jurisdictional provisions of the PKPA will prevail, given the supremacy of federal law over state law under the Constitution.

THE HAGUE CONVENTION ON THE CIVIL ASPECTS OF INTERNATIONAL CHILD ABDUCTION

International child custody disputes present highly complex, specialized, and challenging issues. The major challenge is that laws and court orders issued in the United States are not always recognized and enforceable internationally, and not all orders issued in foreign countries are necessarily enforceable in the United States.

There are a number of federal laws in place concerning custody, parental child abduction, and missing children, such as the National Child Search Assistance Act,[8] the International Parental Kidnapping Crime Act (IPKCA),[9] and the Fugitive Felon Act.[10] One of the most effective resources in the area of international child abduction is the Hague Convention on the Civil Aspects of International Child Abduction (Hague Convention) endorsed by more than ninety nations and implemented as federal law in the United States in 1988 by the International Child Abduction Remedies Act (ICARA).[11] The Hague Convention establishes administrative and judicial procedures to expedite the return (usually to their "habitual residence") of children who have been abducted or wrongfully retained and to facilitate the exercise of visitation rights across international borders. Each member nation designates a central governmental authority to carry out duties related to the Convention. In the United States, the designated body is the Department of State's Office of Children's Issues (OCI).

The court hearing a Hague Convention case in the abducted-to country has jurisdiction to adjudicate the merits of the abduction claim but not the merits of the underlying custody claim. Even if a petitioner establishes that a child has been wrongfully removed or retained, the court may deny the petition if the respondent establishes by clear and convincing evidence that one or more of the following exceptions applies:

1. *The well-settled exception*: A year or more has elapsed between the removal and the petition and the child is now well settled in his or her new environment.
2. *The wishes of the child exception*: The child objects to being returned and has attained an age and degree of maturity at which it is appropriate to take account of his or her views.
3. *The grave risk of harm exception*: Return to his or her habitual residence would expose the child to physical or psychological harm or otherwise place the child in an intolerable situation.

(See Focus on Case Law at the end of this chapter.)

Paralegal Application 9.1

Which State Has Jurisdiction?

Fact pattern

Assume that the parties in this custody case are the unmarried parents of one son who was born in 2005 when they were living together in Hawaii. While there, the mother, Samantha, was the primary caretaker for the child. The relationship between Samantha and the father, Timothy, was abusive. On several occasions he threatened and assaulted her, sometimes in front of their son, who was traumatized and potentially endangered by the abuse. As a result of the domestic violence, Samantha (along with the parties' son) moved to Maine where several of her relatives, including her mother, resided. After the move, Timothy continued to threaten Samantha by telephone and she sought and was granted a protection-from-abuse order.

Sidebar

Assume that within a month after Samantha moved to Maine, Timothy filed a complaint for determination of paternal rights and responsibilities in Hawaii, and shortly thereafter, Samantha filed a complaint for determination of parental rights and responsibilities in Maine. Under the UCCJEA, on what basis might Hawaii have jurisdiction? On what basis might the state of Maine have jurisdiction? In which state do you think jurisdiction is most appropriate? Read the opinion to see what the courts decided in *Rainbow v. Ransom*, 2010 ME 22, 990 A.2d 535 (2010). It can be accessed at *www.pearsonhighered .com/careersresources/* in the resource material for Chapter 9 of this text under Cases.

PARALEGAL PRACTICE TIP

To see an example of a Complaint for Determination of Parental Rights and Responsibilities, visit *www.courts.state.me.us.* (Maine) Forms and Fees/ Court forms/ Family Matters/ Form FM-006.

Evolving Legal Standards For Making Custody Decisions

Once the appropriate jurisdiction for bringing a custody action is identified, the standard used for making custody decisions in that state can be ascertained. Over the years, a variety of approaches have existed, depending on social trends, economic forces, gender stereotypes, and prevailing public policies with respect to children. Some approaches have been fairly cut-and-dried; others are more flexible and open-ended. The most prominent approaches have included the following:

- Paternal Preference
- Maternal Preference
- Tender Years Doctrine
- Best Interests of the Child
- Primary Caretaker Presumption
- American Law Institute's Approximation Rule

PATERNAL PREFERENCE

Paternal preference
the common law doctrine that fathers had an absolute right to the care and custody of their children

In the early history of child custody awards, a **paternal preference** was predominant. When the identity of the father was known, custody virtually always was granted to the father. Under the doctrine of *pater familias* (Latin: father of the family), he had an absolute legal right to custody (in effect, physical possession) of his offspring regardless of their welfare. In essence, custody was a matter of property law. The father had complete authority over his children and controlled all aspects of their lives, their education, their training, and their labor. This "paternal preference," under which mothers had no legal authority with respect to their children, persisted in the United States until the late eighteenth century and is still evident in present-day patriarchal families and societies elsewhere in the world.

MATERNAL PREFERENCE

By the early nineteenth century, the Industrial Revolution, urbanization, and the decline of an agrarian way of life had brought about major societal changes and a redefining of roles within the family. Although the father remained the head of the family and the ultimate maker of major decisions, his primary role was that of breadwinner, and the mother's role was that of homemaker. She was viewed as the "heart" of the home and tended to all of the children's physical, emotional, and spiritual needs. Upon divorce, consistent with his role, the father was customarily ordered to pay spousal and child support for his dependent wife and children. However, given a **maternal preference** for the mother as caretaker, the mother was most often granted physical custody, even over the father's objection.

Maternal preference
the concept that custody should be awarded to a mother over a father, provided she is fit

TENDER YEARS DOCTRINE

Tender years doctrine
the doctrine holding that custody of very young children should be awarded to the mother rather than the father unless she is found to be unfit

By the end of the nineteenth century, the common law doctrine of paternal rights had been firmly replaced by the **tender years doctrine**. Based on tradition and biological dependence, it was assumed that young children should be placed in the care of their mother as the natural custodian of the young and immature, provided she was fit to have custody. Occasionally, custody of older children, especially teenage boys, was awarded to fathers, particularly if the parties agreed and the children expressed a preference to that effect. The desire for "young men" to have "male role models" was commonly a factor in the decision.

The preference for awarding custody to mothers remained strong until the 1960s and the onset of the various "rights" movements. It was inevitable that the effects of the "civil rights," "women's rights," "children's rights," "gay rights," and "equal rights" movements would spill over into the custody context. "Fathers' rights" came to the fore at the same time as many women were choosing the world of work over homemaking as their primary focus (sometimes out of necessity). The father was no longer necessarily the primary breadwinner, and the mother was no longer the undisputed choice for physical custody. Custody laws in most states became gender-neutral. Without a rule of gender preference to drive decision-making, parents and the courts necessarily sought a more flexible standard that could accommodate diverse family models. Enter the **best interests of the child** which is now the dominant standard across the country.

BEST INTERESTS OF THE CHILD

Applying the best interests of the child standard, the custody determination ideally involves an analysis of the child's needs and an assessment of which parent can most effectively meet those needs. Whether the arrangement is established by the parties or by the court, it must serve the best interests of the child. States identify by statute and/or case law a series of "best interest" factors that courts should consider, among others, in making custody determinations. The factors are not prioritized and the court is free to assign weight to them based on the facts of each case. The New Jersey statute in Exhibit 9.1 contains an extensive, representative list of these factors. Others appearing in various state statutes include but are not limited to the following:

- the ability of each parent to provide the child with nurture, love, affection, and guidance; the emotional ties existing between the parties and the child; whether one parent, both parents, or neither parent has provided primary care of the child; the relationship of the child with any other person who may significantly affect the child
- the mental and physical health of all individuals involved
- the child's adjustment to his or her home, school, and community; the length of time the child has lived in a stable, satisfactory environment and the desirability of maintaining continuity; the intention of either party to relocate the principal residence of the child
- the ability of each parent to ensure that the child receives adequate food, clothing, shelter, medical care, and a safe environment
- the child's developmental needs and the ability of each parent to meet them, both in the present and in the future
- the capacity and disposition of the parties to continue the education and raising of the child in his or her religion or creed, if any
- the wishes of the child's parents as to his or her custody; the nature and extent of coercion or duress used by a parent in obtaining an agreement regarding custody and which parent is more likely to allow the child frequent and meaningful continuing contact with the other parent
- the moral fitness of the parties involved; if a parent is incarcerated, the reason for and length of the incarceration and any unique issues that arise as a result of the incarceration

Customarily, there is a final catchall provision allowing the court to consider any other factors it deems necessary and relevant.

PARALEGAL PRACTICE TIP

Although weakened in theory, the tender years doctrine still plays a role in practice. For example, in *Clair v. Clair*, 281 P.3d 115 (Idaho 2012), the Idaho high court affirmed a custody award to a father but opined that the preference for the mother as custodian of a child of "tender years" is a factor that can be considered in custody decisions but only where all other considerations are found to be equal. In a Mississippi case, *Davis v. Davis*, 85 So. 3d 943 (Miss. Ct. App. 2012), the court opined that Mississippi appellate courts have held a child's age is "one factor out of many to be considered in a child custody case," generally favoring the mother when the child is of "tender years." However, the court noted that the rule has been "whittled down in recent years and is no longer absolute."

Best interests of the child
the legal standard for resolving custody disputes that focuses on the needs of the child over the rights or wishes of the parents

PARALEGAL PRACTICE TIP

Take a look at some best interest statutes in addition to New Jersey's in Exhibit 9.1:

Michigan *http://www.legislature.mi.gov* Section 722.23 "Best interests of the child" defined; Section 712B.5 relates specifically to Indian children

Tennessee *http://www.michie.com* Select Tennessee Code/ Section 36-6-106

Utah *http://le.utah.gov* Title 30 Chapter 3 Section 34 (30-3-34)

EXHIBIT 9.1 New Jersey Statute Re: Custody of Child, Rights of Both Parents Considered N.J. Stat. § 9:2–4

Courtesy of State of New Jersey

FROM THE STATUTE

The Legislature finds and declares that it is in the public policy of this State to assure minor children of frequent and continuing contact with both parents after the parents have separated or dissolved their marriage and that it is in the public interest to encourage parents to share the rights and responsibilities of child rearing in order to effect this policy.

In any proceeding involving the custody of the minor child, the rights of both parents shall be equal and the court shall enter an order which may include:

a. Joint custody of a minor child to both parents, which is comprised of legal custody or physical custody which shall include: (1) provisions for residential arrangements so that a child shall reside either solely with one parent or alternatively with each parent in accordance with the needs of the parents and the child; and (2) provisions for consultation between the parents in making major decisions regarding the child's health, education and general welfare;

b. Sole custody to one parent with appropriate parenting time for the noncustodial parent; or

c. Any other custody arrangement as the court may determine to be in the best interests of the child.

  In making an award of custody, the court shall consider but not be limited to the following factors:

- the parents' ability to agree, communicate and cooperate in matters relating to the child;
- the parents' willingness to accept custody and any history of unwillingness to allow parenting time not based on substantiated abuse;
- the interaction and relationship of the child with its parents and siblings;
- the history of domestic violence, if any;
- the safety of the child and the safety of either parent from physical abuse by the other parent;
- the preference of the child when of sufficient age and capacity to reason so as to form an intelligent decision;
- the needs of the child;
- the stability of the home environment offered;
- the quality and continuity of the child's education;
- the fitness of the parents;
- the geographical proximity of the parents' homes;
- the extent and quality of the time spent with the child prior to or subsequent to the separation;
- the parents' employment responsibilities; and
- the age and number of the children.

  A parent shall not be deemed unfit unless the parent's conduct has a substantial adverse effect on the child.

  The court, for good cause and upon its own motion, may appoint a guardian *ad litem* or an attorney or both to represent the minor child's interests. The court shall have the authority to award a counsel fee to the guardian *ad litem* and the attorney and to assess that cost between the parties to the litigation.

d. The court shall order any custody arrangement which is agreed to by both parents unless it is contrary to the best interests of the child.

e. In any case in which the parents cannot agree to a custody arrangement, the court may require each parent to submit a custody plan which the court shall consider in awarding custody.

f. The court shall specifically place on the record the factors which justify any custody arrangement not agreed to by both parents.

The best interest test is child-centered and individualized. It affords courts maximum discretion in making custody decisions and parents minimal predictability with respect to likely outcomes. The child's best interests are supposed to be paramount.[12] However, the test clearly is subjective and inevitably forces judges to make qualitative judgments into which they may subtly project personal views of what constitutes a "good" or a "bad" parent. What is "best" varies by child, and what a court considers "best" is not always what a parent may consider "best." A judge sitting in one family court may emphasize and reward parenting that is firm and regimented and emphasizes rules, discipline, and control. Another family court judge sitting in an adjacent courtroom may look more favorably on parents who promote individuality, creativity, and self-actualization of their children.

THE PRIMARY CARETAKER PRESUMPTION

In an effort to refine the best interests standard into a manageable test capable of producing predictable results, in the 1980s some courts began applying a "primary caretaker presumption" in making custody determinations.[13] A child's **primary caretaker** is the individual who has performed most of the significant parenting tasks for the child since birth or in the years preceding the divorce. The presumption builds on a wealth of child development research that suggests a child is likely to form the closest bond with the individual who is most involved in meeting his or her daily needs and who is his or her secure base in times of stress. Child psychologists generally agree that maintenance of this relationship is essential to healthy development, supporting the presumption that custody should be awarded to the primary caretaker.

Rather than "custodial" and "noncustodial" parents, states applying this approach often refer to the parents as "the primary caretaker" and "the secondary caretaker."[14] Although both roles can be filled by either a father or a mother, many claim that the primary caretaker presumption is simply the maternal preference in disguise, as the determination focuses on activities traditionally performed by "moms." Paralegal Application 9.2 describes a sampling of the kinds of caretaking activities that are considered in attempts to identify a "primary caretaker."

THE AMERICAN LAW INSTITUTE'S APPROXIMATION RULE

The **ALI Approximation Rule** with respect to custody is that the custodial responsibilities of the parents at dissolution should be allocated in a manner that approximates the proportion of time each parent spent caring for the child when the family was intact.[15] The Rule assumes that after the divorce, each parent will be granted some level of access to the child, a level that will be comparable to his or her daily involvement with the child prior to the divorce. The Rule is not absolute, however. It allows for variation under certain circumstances, for example, to keep siblings together, to accommodate reasonable child preferences, or to protect a child from abuse or a parent who has abandoned their parental responsibilities as a result of drug or alcohol problems.

Similar to the primary caretaker presumption, the focus of the ALI Rule is on concrete acts of parenting rather than on subjective judgments. It removes considerations of race, gender, religion, sexual orientation, marital misconduct, and economic circumstances from the custody decision. As a result, to some extent it relieves judges of having to make subjective, relative judgments about parental fitness. The Rule is still essentially focused on the best interests of the

Approximation Rule
the rule that the custodial responsibilities of the parents at dissolution should be allocated in a manner that approximates the proportion of time each parent spent caring for the child when the family was intact

PARALEGAL PRACTICE TIP

Relevant excerpts from the West Virginia child custody statutes can be found at *www.legis.state.wv.us*. West Virginia Code/ 48-9-101 and 48-9-206 (Allocation of Custodial Responsibilities).

child, but it provides parents the greater predictability and children the greater continuity in care afforded by the primary caretaker presumption. Although only adopted in West Virginia, the ALI standard has been cited favorably by courts in several states. For example, the Supreme Court of Iowa has opined: "While no post-divorce physical care arrangement will be identical to predissolution experience, preservation of the greatest amount of stability possible is a desirable goal . . . we believe that the approximation principle is a factor to be considered by courts in determining whether to grant joint physical care. By focusing on historic patterns of caregiving, the approximation rule provides a relatively objective factor for the court to consider. The principle of approximation also rejects a 'one-size-fits-all' approach and recognizes the diversity of family life. Finally, it tends to ensure that any decision to grant joint physical care is firmly rooted in the past practices of the individual family." See *In re the Marriage of Lyle Martin Hansen and Dolores Lorene Hansen*, 733 N.W.2d 683 (Iowa 2007).

Paralegal **Application 9.2**

Caretaking Activities

Whether the standard applied is best interests, primary caretaker, or the ALI Approximation Rule, courts will consider the nature of each parent's relationship with the child in making custody determinations. Therefore, paralegals are often assigned to work with clients to gather information about the activities performed by each parent and the extent of their involvement with the child. Careful interviewing and preparation are critically important in anticipation of direct testimony and cross-examination at trial. For example, cross-examination can be very effective when a parent falsely claims to be the primary caretaker of a child. The party might be asked when the child last went to the doctor, who took him or her, what the doctor's name was, how the child behaved, what the diagnosis was, what treatment was prescribed, who administered the treatment, etc. In relation to school, the party may be asked about the names of the child's teachers, the grades the child receives, the child's most and least favorite subjects, when the last parent–teacher conference was, who attended it, who the child's best friend at school is, etc. An uninvolved parent is often unlikely to be able to answer these questions.

Courts commonly consider the extent to which each parent performs the following kinds of caretaking activities. The importance of any single activity varies according to the age and developmental needs of the child. The list is drawn in large part from Section 2.03 of the ALI Principles of Marital Dissolution.

- Managing wake-up and bedtime routines
- Taking care of the child's personal hygiene needs, such as bathing, washing, and brushing teeth
- Attending to dressing and grooming

- Facilitating toilet training
- Attending to the child's needs when sick or injured and arranging for medical care
- Playing with the child
- Arranging for recreational activities
- Providing transportation to and from recreational and educational activities
- Protecting the child's physical safety
- Meeting the child's motor, cognitive, and socioemotional development needs
- Providing discipline and promoting moral and ethical development and self-discipline
- Arranging for the child's education, including remedial or other special services, communicating with school personnel, and working on homework
- Building the child's self-confidence
- Maintaining appropriate relationships with peers, siblings, and extended family members
- Arranging for and monitoring alternative care arrangements, including day care, babysitters, or other childcare providers
- Attending to the basic nutritional needs of the child

PARALEGAL PRACTICE TIP

Nutrition can be a particularly important topic when a child has special dietary problems or needs such as chronic deficiencies, allergies, or diabetes. Caretakers should document that they are alert to dietary concerns both at home and when the child is at school and visiting family and friends. In the way of evidence, a monthly menu can be prepared and copies of advisory letters sent to schools, etc., may be submitted to the court.

A Closer Look at Some of the Factors Courts Consider When Making Decisions About Custody and Visitation

Some of the factors courts may consider that warrant further discussion include the following:

- the relative availability of the parents to provide basic caretaking activities
- the maintenance of stability for the child
- the rights of parents to custody regardless of their gender, race, or religion
- the effect of a parental disability absent demonstrated harm to the child
- the impact of a parent's sexual conduct and individual lifestyle on the child
- the consequences of a history of abuse against or in the presence of the child
- the child's preference for a particular custodial arrangement
- the parents' relative willingness and ability to implement a shared custody plan

PARALEGAL PRACTICE TIP

A useful resource on custody criteria in the various states can be found at *www.americanbar.org*. Search for Family Law in the Fifty States and select Chart 2 Custody Criteria. The Chart is updated on an annual basis.

AVAILABILITY

Although not usually articulated as a discrete factor in statutory codes, availability is a consideration in custody decisions by implication. As indicated earlier in Paralegal Application 9.2, courts look at the nature and scope of activities parents participate in with their children such as routines they perform (e.g., getting up and going to bed, making meals and eating together), attendance at school, sports and other recreational events, attending to medical and dental appointments, doing homework, and providing religious training. To do these things, a parent has to be available, and therefore custody determinations often favor the parent who has more time to devote to the children. Availability may be reduced or enhanced by work schedule, and a flexible work schedule or an ability to work at or near home may be especially attractive.

In today's busy world, however, most parents need to arrange with third parties for varying degrees of periodic child care. Courts often consider the nature and extent of such arrangements when making custody decisions. An Idaho appellate court held that "consideration of a parent's work schedule and need for third-party child care is appropriate in a custody determination to the extent that these circumstances are shown to affect the well-being of the children."[16] In a Connecticut case, for example, a Superior Court was persuaded by a guardian *ad litem* that the children should reside primarily with the defendant mother because "although the plaintiff spends considerable periods of time at home as part of his employment schedule, he also is away from home for extended periods of time. It was an important consideration to the GAL that one of the parents be available in the immediate area to deal with the inevitable emergencies that young children experience. The defendant's current employment, as well as her potential full-time employment with the West Hartford school system, would result in a very short drive from the children's school and give her the ability to respond as necessary. While the plaintiff could do the same for those periods of time he is at home, when he is away that role would have to be filled by the paternal grandparents. Although they are certainly capable and loving grandparents, they are the grandparents and not the parents." (See *Bornn v. Bornn*, 2014 Conn. Super. LEXIS 1984.)

PARALEGAL PRACTICE TIP

The opinion in the Idaho case (*Silva v. Silva*, 136 P.3d 371 (Idaho App. 2006)) is available at *www.pearsonhighered.com/careersresources/* in the website material related to Chapter 9 of this text under Cases.

When working on a case in which child care is an issue, the paralegal may be asked to research case law in the jurisdiction to learn when the courts are likely to decide that a child's "well-being" is affected by the need for third-party care and why. For example, does it matter who provides the child care or how regular, frequent, or costly it is? The paralegal also may be asked to develop exhibits that illustrate why the client is the better custodial choice based in part on availability. The paralegal can prepare one or more maps showing the geographical proximity of each parent's residence to the child's school, church, recreational centers/parks, homes of relatives and friends, daycare providers, etc. Another potential exhibit is a schedule indicating where the children will be, who they will be with, and what they will be doing 24/7 if the client is designated primary caretaker.

STABILITY

Stability is an important factor in custody deliberations. Recognizing that children's lives are seriously disrupted by divorce, courts often strive to maintain as much stability and continuity for them as possible. When fashioning custody agreements, the model that is likely to provide the greatest degree of stability for the child is one based on caretaking patterns during the marriage. Essentially, this amounts to the ALI or primary caretaker approach. If a child is doing well in his or her current setting, courts are generally reluctant to disturb the status quo. A parent who has temporary custody while a divorce action is pending often has a subtle advantage in a contested custody case. In relocation cases, the parent with primary physical custody is likely to have an advantage, and, in some states, there is a presumption to that effect. The basic assumption is that imposing a new physical care arrangement on children that significantly differs from their past experience can be unsettling and emotionally harmful, and thus not in the child's best interest.

GENDER

Gender-based presumptions have largely been abolished or declared unconstitutional as a violation of equal protection. The public policy of virtually all states is that fit heterosexual parents have equal custody rights regardless of gender. Sometimes the policy is expressly referenced in court decisions, as in the following excerpt from a South Carolina case: "When analyzing the right to custody as between a father and a mother, equanimity is mandated. . . . The parents stand in perfect equipoise as the custody analysis begins."[17]

Many states have codified a gender-neutral position as Missouri has in its child custody statute: "As between the parents of a child, no preference may be given to either parent in the awarding of custody because of that parent's age, sex, or financial status, nor because of the age or sex of the child."[18]

Whatever the stated policy may be, the reality is that gender stereotypes persist in practice. The functions considered as evidence of caretaking of children involve activities still performed predominantly by mothers and over 80% of custody awards are made to women. As of the spring of 2012, only 2.2 million men in the United States had primary custody of their children,[19] representing approximately one-sixth of the total number of custodial parents, a very modest increase over the one-ninth proportion in 1970.[20]

RACE

The U.S. Supreme Court made clear in the landmark case of *Palmore v. Sidoti* that the Equal Protection Clause of the Constitution prohibits the making of custody decisions based upon racial bias and a fear of potential harm to a child as a result of racial prejudice. (See Case 9.1.) Although special rules apply with Native American children, the race of the parents or the child may not be used as the sole factor in determining what will be in the child's best interests. However, if two parents are equally qualified to parent a child, race may tip the balance in favor of one of them. For example, in an Illinois case, an appellate court held the fact that the mother was African-American made her more qualified than the Caucasian father to parent their biracial child, as she was better prepared to help the child deal with hostility toward biracial individuals *In re Marriage of Gambla*, 367 Ill. App. 3d 441, 853 N.E.2d 847 (2006). You can find the opinion in this case at *www.pearsonhighered.com/careersresources/* in the resource website material related to Chapter 9 of this text under Cases.

CASE **9.1** *Palmore v. Sidoti*, 466 U.S. 429, 104 S. Ct. 1879,
80 L. Ed. 2d 421 (1984)

BACKGROUND

In this case, custody of the parties' minor daughter initially was granted to the Caucasian mother. The father (who also was Caucasian) subsequently petitioned for and was granted a modification of custody based on allegations of several instances of the mother's failure to properly care for the child and the fact that she was planning to marry an African-American man with whom she had been living. A lower court and the Florida District Court of Appeals affirmed that the change in custody would serve the best interests of the child. The mother appealed the decision to the U.S. Supreme Court.

The Supreme Court reversed and stated the following:

FROM THE OPINION

. . . The goal of granting custody based on the best interests of the child is indisputably a substantial governmental interest for purposes of the Equal Protection Clause.

. . . It would ignore reality to suggest that racial and ethnic prejudices do not exist, or that all manifestations of those prejudices have been eliminated. There is a risk that a child living with a stepparent of a different race may be subject to a variety of pressures and stresses not present if the child were living with parents of the same racial or ethnic origin.

. . . The question, however, is whether the reality of private biases and the possible injury they might inflict are permissible considerations for removal of an infant child from the custody of its natural mother. We have little difficulty concluding that they are not. The Constitution cannot control such prejudices, but neither can it tolerate them. Private biases may be outside the reach of the law, but the law cannot directly or indirectly give them effect.

SIDEBAR

Do you agree with the Court's reasoning? Do you think that race should be considered in custody determinations? The opinion in *Palmore v. Sidoti* is available at *www.pearsonhighered.com/careersresources/* in the companion website material related to Chapter 9 of this text under Cases.

RELIGION

Although the courts must respect religious freedom and, under the Establishment Clause of the U.S. Constitution, cannot favor one religion over another, they can properly consider which parent can best meet the religious needs of a child. Some states address this factor in their statutes governing custody decisions. For example, Michigan includes as a statutory best interest factor "the capacity and disposition of the parties involved to give the child love, affection, and guidance and to continue the education and raising of the child in his or her religion or creed, if any."[21]

The majority of courts that have addressed custody conflicts between parents arising from religious differences have affirmed each parent's right to freedom of religion and to parent a child by providing religious exposure and instruction as he or she sees fit. Conflicts involving religious differences most frequently arise in situations in which there is a dispute regarding medical care or disciplinary measures (particularly excessive corporal punishment), when a religion promotes illegal activities (polygamy, animal sacrifice, use of illegal drugs, etc.), or when one parent has no religious affiliation. By way of example, in 2011, the Kansas Supreme Court considered a custody battle involving an unwed Jehovah's Witness mother and a Muslim father. The father was especially concerned about the fact that the mother "forced" the child to proselytize with her door-to-door and prohibited him from celebrating birthdays and holidays, participating in extracurricular activities and having relationships with non-Witnesses. He was also concerned that her religious beliefs would prevent her from allowing the boy to receive a blood transfusion if one were necessary. In upholding an award of joint legal custody and physical custody to the mother, the court stated "Custody cases implicating questions of religious belief and practice require a delicate balancing of the rights of each parent and the welfare of the child whose custody is in question." "Disapproval of mere belief or nonbelief cannot be a consideration in a custody determination—judges are not trained to mediate theological disputes." While the court opined that consideration of religiously motivated behavior with an impact on a child's welfare cannot be ignored, it warned that "courts must be vigilant to avoid invidious discrimination against religious beliefs or practices merely because they seem unconventional." *Harrison v. Tauheed*, 292 Kan. 663, 256 P.3d 851 (2011).

Although courts generally are reluctant to intervene in cases involving disputes over religion, if the conduct of a parent or a challenged religious belief or practice presents a substantial threat of present or future physical or emotional harm to the child, they have been willing to restrict parental custody or behavior in the least intrusive manner possible. However, the harm in such situations must be actual or highly likely and not simply speculative.[22] Stress on children caused by parental disputes over religion may not be enough. In a Pennsylvania case, the Superior Court opined that "For children of divorce in general, exposure to parents' conflicting values, lifestyles and religious beliefs may indeed cause doubts and stress. However, stress is not always harmful, nor is it always to be avoided and protected against. The key is not whether the child experiences stress, but whether the stress experienced is unproductively severe."[23] (See Paralegal Application 9.3.)

Paralegal Application 9.3

You Be the Judge . . .

Fact Pattern

Although such agreements are generally held to be unenforceable, a Jewish mother and a Catholic father agreed prior to marriage that their children would be raised in the Jewish faith. They subsequently had three children: Ari, ten, Moriah, six, and Rebekah, four, at the time of this action. Three years after the parents married, the father joined a Fundamentalist Christian church. The mother adopted Orthodox Judaism, the strictest of the Jewish movements. Ari was circumcised and was described as having a "Jewish identity," which is akin to having an ethnic identity as well as a religious faith. The two girls had traditional naming ceremonies, and all three children attended a Jewish school. The father testified at trial that he would never stop trying to save his children. His behavior toward them projected a negative image of the Jewish faith and culture, and he opposed their being taught about the Holocaust. The father told the children that all individuals who do not accept his faith are sinners and will burn in hell. In addition, he cut off his son's payes (sideburns with religious significance) and threatened to cut off his tzitzitz (clothing fringe). The guardian *ad litem* reported that Ari's motivation and academic performance were declining and that he was uncomfortable and unhappy when visiting his father when he had "to do stuff he's not supposed to do on [S]habbas." The elder of the two daughters was experiencing stress relating to the ongoing conflict between the two parents. The mother sought to limit the children's exposure to their father's religion and the father responded that any limitation would constitute a restriction of his right to freedom of religion under the state and U.S. Constitutions.

Sidebar

What do you think the court should do given the facts of this case? Why? Read the opinion in *Kendall v. Kendall*, 426 Mass. 238, 687 N.E.2d 1228 (1997), and see if you agree with the result. The opinion can be accessed at *www.pearsonhighered.com/careersresources/*in the resource website material for Chapter 9 of this text under Cases.

PARENTAL HEALTH OR DISABILITY

Families in which at least one parent is disabled constitute approximately 6.5% of all families in the United States. The percent is higher in minority and nontraditional family settings. Although nearly 15% of disabled parents involved in custody litigation report discriminatory treatment,[24] poor physical or mental health does not necessarily mean an individual will be deemed unfit as a custodial parent. The disability must be of a sufficient nature or duration as to render the parent unable, even with assistance, to care for the physical, mental, and emotional needs of his or her child. Simply taking medication for depression or being "disabled" and receiving Social Security disability checks is not enough. (See *Webb v. Webb*, 78 So. 3d 933 (Miss. Ct. App. 2011).) The court will examine the "nexus" or connection between the condition and the parent's capacity to provide proper child care.

Cases tend to be fact intensive and may go either way, for example:

- In an Illinois case, an appellate court upheld the decision of a trial court to grant custody of a child to a mother with an IQ of sixty-seven against the advice of a custody evaluator. The court found that the mother had been the child's primary caregiver, was capable of protecting the child from harm, and, with assistance, was able to foster the child's intellectual development.[26] However, the outcome might have been different if the child had a serious medical condition that required administering oxygen, balancing medications, and maintaining complicated dietary restrictions.

PARALEGAL PRACTICE TIP

Some courts also consider a disability of a parent's partner. A Kentucky court found, for example, that cohabitation of a custodial parent with an HIV-infected partner is, taken alone, a sufficient ground for modifying custody in favor of the noncustodial parent.[25]

- In a Massachusetts case, the appeals court upheld a lower court's award of custody to a mother suffering from debilitating multiple sclerosis, contrary to the recommendation of the guardian *ad litem*. The court found that the lower court had properly considered the best interests of the child and noted that the mother had a full-time personal care assistant.[27] In this case, the result may well have been different if the mother did not have the personal care assistant.

Because courts sometimes assume a client's parenting skills will be deficient based on a disability, the family law team may need to "educate" the court and personalize the client's condition and capacity to be an effective parent. This may be accomplished by showing videos of the parent caring for the child. Copies of professional articles about the disability and lists of available support services can be provided. Testimony of expert witnesses and demonstrations of sophisticated adaptive equipment can also be used to help dispel myths and stereotypes.

SEXUAL CONDUCT

The majority view is that a parent's sexual conduct or cohabitation with a heterosexual or same-sex partner may be considered by a court in some circumstances when making a custody determination. However, it should not play a role in the decision unless there is a demonstrated negative impact on the health and welfare of the child. The states vary with respect to treatment of various kinds of sexual activity, and cases are heavily fact-based. For example, the Georgia Supreme Court upheld a lower court's decision naming a husband/father primary physical custodian and "final decision-maker" based at least in part on the fact that the wife/mother had been romantically involved with a married man before filing for divorce from her husband. See *Rembert v. Rembert*, 285 Ga. 260, 674 S.E.2d 892 (2009). Reflecting a contrary outcome, the South Carolina Court of Appeals held that a family court erred in awarding custody of the parties' children to the father because the court placed an improper emphasis on the mother's extramarital affair when there was no evidence the relationship had any detrimental effect on the children. (See *Moeller v. Moeller*, 394 S.C. 365; 714 S.E.2d 898 (S.C. App. 2011).)

Some courts have held that extramarital cohabitation is contrary to a public policy of maintaining a stable environment for children and that "a parent's unmarried cohabitation with a romantic partner, or a parent's promiscuous conduct or lifestyle, in the presence of a child cannot be abided."[28] Courts have also enforced agreements between parties prohibiting either party from having "overnight guests" in front of the children even if no adverse impact is shown.[29] For example, the Georgia Court of Appeals upheld a contempt finding against a mother who violated a provision in her divorce agreement by repeatedly allowing her boyfriend to stay overnight in her home while the parties' children were in her physical custody. Although she later claimed it was overly broad and unduly burdensome, both parties had initially agreed to the following provision and did so acting with advice of counsel:

> When the minor children of the parties hereto are in either of the party's physical custody, neither party shall allow a nonrelative adult person of the opposite gender to remain overnight in the same house, apartment, or other place being occupied by that party and the minor children, provided, however, this restriction shall not apply to an

overnight guest of the minor children. (See *Norman v. Norman*, 329 Ga. App. 502 (2014).)

Today the courts consider the potential harm to children resulting from directly observing the sexual activity of a parent without regard to sexual orientation. In the past, however, in custody disputes involving a gay parent they looked beyond conduct to orientation as well. Many states applied a ***per se* rule** that harm was assumed to occur if a child were being raised by a gay or lesbian parent. That perspective was buttressed by statutes restricting marriage to heterosexual couples statutes viewed as protecting the traditional family, promoting procreation within the family unit, and discouraging illegal sexual activity between unmarried and specifically same-sex partners. The start of the legal shift away from that position in the custody context was explicitly captured in a 2004 opinion of the Idaho Supreme Court:

> . . . It is important to observe that last year's landmark United States Supreme Court decision in *Lawrence v. Texas*, 539 U.S. 558, 156 L. Ed. 2d 508, 123 S. Ct. 2472 (2003) legalized the practice of homosexuality and in essence made it a protected practice under the Due Process clause of the United States Constitution.
>
> . . . This decision also has at least some bearing on the degree to which homosexuality may play a part in child custody proceedings. . . .
>
> . . . Sexual orientation, in and of itself, cannot be the basis for awarding or removing custody; only when the parent's sexual orientation is shown to cause harm to the child, such that the child's best interests are not served, should sexual orientation be a factor in determining custody.[30]

Although heterosexual and same-sex spouses across the country are now entitled to be treated according to the same rules and criteria in the custody context, unmarried gay and lesbian parents (especially those who had children while parties to heterosexual marriages) are sometimes subtly subjected to different treatment. Depending on the facts of the case and the "sympathies" of the presiding justice, it may be necessary to counter lingering stereotypes particularly in conservative, rural communities where homosexual behavior may still be viewed by some as immoral and children may be subject to bullying because of their parent's sexual orientation. When the issue arises, consideration should be given to introducing legal research and/or expert testimony regarding the effects on children of being raised by gay and lesbian parents. Legal and psychological journal searches and sites for organizations such as the American Psychological Association (*www.apa.org*) are good starting points for researching this topic.

PARENTAL LIFESTYLE

Judges are expected to rise above their own prejudices and to base their decisions on an objective analysis of the needs of children and the course of action best suited to meet those needs. However, judges are human. They have their own views of the world, and their own biases, moral codes, and levels of tolerance for what might be called "nonmainstream" behaviors or unusual beliefs. Some behaviors clearly are simply lifestyle choices, such as the decision to have pets or to engage in social drinking. Others are sufficiently extreme or potentially harmful that they may be viewed by the courts as lifestyle choices that cross an invisible dividing line between moral conduct and immoral conduct that may be harmful to children.

Per se **rule**
[Latin: by itself] without reference to any additional facts or circumstances

PARALEGAL PRACTICE TIP
In reaching their decisions, judges must rely on evidence properly introduced in court and not on independent personal research. In *Rutanhira v. Rutanhira*, 35 A.3d 143 (Vt. 2011), the Vermont Supreme Court reversed an award of primary custody to a mother finding an abuse of discretion on the part of the trial court. In reaching its decision, the court had relied on its own online research rather than on the evidence presented in court to tip the balance between two fit parents toward the mother. In particular, the court questioned the father's judgment with respect to his plan to take his daughter to Zimbabwe for a planned visit, a trip the judge considered unsafe based on his independent research.

It is apparent from judicial decisions and state statutes that moral character and conduct count under some circumstances. The Michigan "best interest statute," for example, lists as a factor for consideration: the "moral fitness of the parties involved."[31] A Georgia court has held that a parent may be denied custody of a child by putting "her own desires and perceived needs ahead of and to the detriment of her children" and lacking "the moral fiber" to be a role model for her children.[32] On the other hand, an Illinois statute reflects the general rule regarding the relationship between conduct and custody decisions that the "court shall not consider the conduct of a present or proposed custodian that does not affect his relationship to the child."[33] The critical question is, "Does the behavior harm the child?" Even common lifestyle choices may be deemed harmful under certain circumstances. For example, a Florida court conditioned a father's right to visitation on his agreement to remove his cats from his home before his allergic sons would be allowed to stay overnight with him.[34]

Courts in several states have either denied or conditioned custody on a smoking parent's agreement to not smoke in the presence or environment of a child suffering from respiratory problems. Although smoking used to be considered a relatively harmless lifestyle choice, it is increasingly viewed as a behavior that puts both the smoker and others at risk. In the custody context, it is usually raised by a nonsmoking parent as a risk to the child. However, in a highly unusual action, an Ohio court raised the issue of the danger of secondhand smoke on behalf of a healthy child under the **parens patriae doctrine**. The court took **judicial notice** of the dangers of secondhand smoke, citing overwhelming authoritative scientific evidence. It then issued an order restraining a custodial mother and her significant other from smoking in the presence of the mother's healthy eight-year-old daughter to protect her from having her health compromised by being forced to breathe secondhand smoke. The court held that the parent's right to privacy did not include the right to inflict secondhand smoke on the child.[35]

Often the parents both have problems, and some states reflect this possibility in the statutory factors to be considered in custody determinations. For example, the applicable Wyoming statute calls for the court to consider the "relative competency and fitness of each parent."[36] However, the courts are often willing to grant considerable benefit of the doubt to parents who have had conduct issues such as drug or alcohol abuse, particularly if a parent is seeking treatment and making progress.

HISTORY OF ABUSE

Every state provides by statute or case law that a history of domestic abuse will be considered in custody determinations.[37] Although it has not always been the case, some courts now also will take judicial notice of the research documenting the effect of being a victim of and witnessing domestic violence. Most especially, the courts have begun to recognize that children who have witnessed domestic abuse are at significantly greater risk of both becoming abusers and being abused in their intimate relationships as adults. Many states include a history of domestic violence as a statutory "best interests" factor to be considered by the court when making custody determinations, as in the New Jersey Statute in Exhibit 9.1. Other states go further and have established a rebuttable presumption against granting custody to a parent who is a documented perpetrator of domestic violence. Alabama has addressed this topic in detail in its state code by providing a definition of what constitutes an act of domestic violence, a description of the kinds of evidence that can be used to determine if someone has committed an act of domestic violence; a rebuttable presumption against awarding custody to an abuser; a list of ways in which the presumption can be rebutted; and suggested

---

PARALEGAL PRACTICE TIP

In a 2002 New York case, a thirteen-year-old child successfully sought a ruling that he not be exposed to environmental tobacco smoke while visiting his mother during court-ordered visitation. See *Johnita M. D. v. David D.D.*, 191 Misc.2d 301, 740 N.Y.S.2d 811 (2002).

Parens patriae doctrine

[Latin: parent of the country] the doctrine holding that the government, as parent of the country, has standing to act on behalf of a citizen, particularly one who is a minor or under a disability

Judicial notice

a court's acceptance of a well-known fact without requiring proof

PARALEGAL PRACTICE TIP

In *Nichols v. Nichols*, 74 So. 3d 919 (Miss. Ct. App. 2011), a father was awarded custody of the parties' three children based on the mother's prior conviction for domestic violence and her failure to overcome the presumption that it would be detrimental for the children to be placed in the care of a parent with a history of perpetuating domestic violence. In *Nemec v. Goeman*, 810 N.W.2d 443 (S.D. 2012), however, a father with a prior conviction of domestic abuse was able to rebut the presumption that he should not be awarded custody based on evidence that he was no longer drinking alcohol or using illegal drugs.

conditions that may be placed on parenting time, if granted, to best protect the child and the other parent from further harm (25-403.03. Domestic violence and child abuse). See Chapter 14 for a more extensive treatment of this topic.

CHILD PREFERENCE

Historically, children's custodial preferences carried no weight, given their lack of legal status and the existence of strong paternal and maternal preferences. This situation has changed dramatically over the years, and today children's wishes may be considered to some extent in all states. Many states include consideration of a child's preference as a "best interest" factor in their statutes governing allocation of residential responsibility. The South Carolina Code reflects the majority view with respect to parental preferences of minor children: "In determining the best interests of the child, the court must consider the child's reasonable preference for custody. The court shall place weight upon the preference based upon the child's age, experience, maturity, judgment, and ability to express a preference."[38] Usually, minimal weight is given to the preferences of children under the age of seven. However, once children reach the teenage years, most courts have taken the position that their preferences should be given serious consideration. In some states, the child's preference will be determinative under certain circumstances. (See Exhibit 9.2.) Although a child's preference will not necessarily be dispositive, sometimes it appears to be, especially in cases involving teenagers. North Dakota statute Section 14-09-06.2, N.D.C.C., provides: "If the court finds by clear and convincing evidence that a child is of sufficient maturity to make a sound judgment, the court may give substantial weight to the preference of the mature child." Consistent with the statute, in *Schlieve v. Schlieve,* 2014 ND 107, 846 N.W.2d 733 (2014), the North Dakota Supreme Court affirmed a trial court's award of custody of two teenage girls to their mother in a close modification case. The court found that the preferences of the children, ages fourteen and seventeen, played a "substantial" role in the decision. The younger girl's preference was communicated in direct testimony at trial and the older girl's by deposition. The essence of their testimony was that although both parents were capable of parenting them, they were closer to their mother, could communicate better with her, and enjoyed doing "girl things" with her. They did not like the prior one week on and one week off arrangement and believed it was especially confusing for their little brother who they felt should be with them and their mother.

> **PARALEGAL PRACTICE TIP**
>
> In *Mulkey v. Mulkey,* 118 So. 3d 357 (La. 2013), the Louisiana Supreme Court reinstated a trial court's ruling in a modification proceeding that custody of a fourteen-year-old boy should be with his father. The court found that the boy was mature and grounded and able to clearly communicate his sincere desire to live with his father. Although he loved his mother and had a good relationship with his stepfather, he spent a considerable amount of time alone when in her care. He preferred the routine, structure, and family interaction in his father's household.

EXHIBIT 9.2 Statutory Provisions Re Child Preference in Custody Context—Ga. Code Ann. §19–9–3

Courtesy of State of Georgia

> **FROM THE STATUTE**
>
> (a)(5) In all custody cases in which the child has reached the age of 14 years, the child shall have the right to select the parent with whom he or she desires to live. The child's selection for purposes of custody shall be presumptive unless the parent so selected is determined not to be in the best interests of the child.
>
> (a)(6) In all custody cases in which the child has reached the age of 11 but not 14, the judge shall consider the desires and educational needs of the child in determining which parent shall have custody . . . the child's desires shall not be controlling. . . . The best interests of the child standard shall be controlling.

> **PARALEGAL PRACTICE TIP**
>
> In *Harbin v. Harbin,* 238 Ga. 109, 230 S.E.2d 889 (Ga. 1976), the Georgia Supreme Court held that when a child has a right of election, the child's choice will be controlling absent a showing of present unfitness even if there have been prior showings of unfitness.

Children's true feelings in custody conflicts are often difficult to discern and not infrequently change over time. Their expressed preferences may be suspect, as they are often consciously or unconsciously influenced by a variety of factors and circumstances. Children may believe they are to blame for the breakup of the marriage and the ensuing conflict. They may be the pawns of one of the parents or subject to manipulation by both parents. They may be overtly angry in general or at one of the parties in particular. One of the parents may be viewed as more likely to "spoil" them with material benefits. One may be viewed as the more lax in setting and enforcing rules and administering discipline. The courts are especially cautious about expressed preferences in situations where there is a history of abuse, as a child may fear or identify with an aggressor who will not necessarily be the parent best suited to meet the child's needs. Given these variables, how can children's preferences be determined in a sensitive and age-appropriate manner?

When determining which custodial arrangement will be in a child's best interests, judges consider evidence from several sources.[39] If resources permit, evidence about a child's needs, feelings, and preferences is usually presented to the court by means of evaluations and recommendations prepared by a guardian *ad litem* or a mental health professional appointed by the court, or through representations of the child's attorney or some other advocate such as a CASA volunteer (Court Appointed Special Advocate) designated by the court. Although there is no uniform agreement about methods or means of directly soliciting children's preferences, sometimes courts allow either party to call a child as a witness or the judge is asked, requested, or required to interview the child. (See Exhibit 9.3.)

A few jurisdictions have statutory presumptions that judges will meet with children at the request of a parent and/or the request of a child. In states where such meetings are mandatory in some circumstances including Ohio and Michigan, the court's failure to meet with a child may be reversible error.[41] A small number of states have developed guidelines or protocols for judges' meetings with children (see, e.g., California Rules of Court 5.250 (2012) and Ohio Revised Code §3109.04), but most have none. It is generally up to the court's discretion as to where the interview will be conducted; who, if anyone can be present; what questions will be asked; how long it will last, whether or not it will be electronically recorded; whether there will be a written record and whether that record will be sealed or shared with counsel and/or the parties, etc. Because parents are typically not present at or provided transcripts of in camera meetings, some critics believe it constitutes a violation of parents' rights to due process when judges, especially those who are untrained, interview children out of court about the sensitive and complicated topic of custodial preference.

EXHIBIT 9.3 Statutory Provisions Re Testimony in Custody Cases—Utah Code Ann. §30–3–10(1)(d), (e) and (f)

Courtesy of State of Utah

FROM THE STATUTE

d. The children may not be required by either party to testify unless the trier of fact determines that extenuating circumstances exist that would necessitate the testimony of the children be heard and there is no other reasonable method to present their testimony.

e. The court may inquire of the children and take into consideration the children's desires regarding future custody or parent-time schedules, but the expressed desires are not controlling. . . . The desires of a child 14 years of age or older shall be given added weight, but is not the single controlling factor.

f. If interviews with the children are conducted by the court . . . , they shall be conducted by the judge in camera. The prior consent of the parties may be obtained but is not necessary if the court finds that an interview with the children is the only method to ascertain the child's desires regarding custody.

THE "FRIENDLY PARENT" AND PARENTAL ALIENATION SYNDROME

In assessing which parent would be the preferred custodial parent, the court will look at the extent to which each parent has the capacity to rise above his or her own desires and hostility to focus on the child's need to maintain a warm and positive relationship with both parents. Sometimes referred to as the "friendly parent doctrine," a parent's willingness to promote contact with the other parent often influences custody decisions. For instance, in *In re Marriage of Chamberlain*, 262 P.3d 1097 (Mont. 2011), primary residential custody was awarded to the mother because the evidence suggested she would be more likely to promote and support a relationship with the husband than he would with her.

For some parents, however, this is an impossible challenge. In the extreme, such a parent may do everything within his or her power to disrupt visitation, denigrate the other parent in front of the child, and alienate the child from the other parent. Some experts believe that a child who was close to both parents before the divorce may come to idealize one parent and demonize the other as a result of the former's pressure and manipulation. Some psychologists label this condition the **parental alienation syndrome**. Critics claim there is no scientific basis for the syndrome and that it is often difficult to discern whether the children really have been manipulated by a spiteful parent or in fact have legitimate grounds for rejecting the alienated parent.

Parenting Postdivorce

Although it is generally acknowledged that children benefit most when they have the sustained physical and emotional support of both parents, divorce often makes this ideal an impossible one to realize.

> Like Humpty Dumpty, a family, once broken by divorce, cannot be put together in precisely the same way. The relationship between the parents and the children is necessarily different after a divorce and, accordingly, it may be unrealistic in some cases to try to preserve the noncustodial parent's accustomed close involvement in the children's everyday life. . . .[42]

Plans for parenting postdivorce are typically laid out in an exhibit/article in a **Separation Agreement** (see Exhibit B in the Sample Separation Agreement in Chapter 13) or in a **Parenting Plan**. (See Paralegal Application 9.4.) They vary considerably depending in large part on the degree to which parents are able to communicate with one another regarding their children's needs and schedules and the extent to which they share a common vision as to appropriate parenting behaviors and goals for the children's welfare. The overriding goal is to provide a sufficient amount of time to enable both parents to remain a significant part of each child's life at the time of divorce and going forward into the future. They must be tailored to a number of variables, most especially the relative availability of the parents, the proximity of the parents' residences to one another, and the ages, activities, and developmental needs of the children. If custody is a contested issue, each parent must submit a proposed custody implementation plan at trial. The court may issue an order that tracks the proposal of one or the other of the parties' plans in whole or part or may reject both and create its own order. For example, in *Holmes v. Holmes* (2014 Tenn. App. LEXIS 48), a Tennessee Appeals

---

Parental alienation syndrome
a condition in which a child involved in a custody dispute comes to idealize one parent and demonize the other parent as a result of the former parent's pressure and manipulation

PARALEGAL PRACTICE TIP

In *Jeannemarie O. v. Richard P.*, 943 N.Y.S.2d 246 (App. Div. 2012), a father was granted custody despite the fact that the mother had been a fit parent and primary caretaker of the children. The court found that her positive attributes were outweighed by her "cumulative efforts" to interfere with the father's relationship with the children and prevent him from having a meaningful role in their lives by cancelling visitation, moving away, and making unsubstantiated allegations about him regarding substance abuse, violence, and sexual abuse.

Separation agreement
an agreement made between spouses in anticipation of a divorce or legal separation, concerning the terms of the divorce or separation and any continuing obligations of the parties to each other

Parenting plan
a written agreement in which parents lay out plans for taking care of their children postseparation or postdivorce

PARALEGAL PRACTICE TIP

Two publications of the ABA which are potentially useful for clients are the following:
 Family Advocate Summer 2010, Vol. 33, No. 1, Your Parenting Plan: A Client Manual; and
 Family Advocate Summer 2007, Vol. 30, No. 1, Coparenting During and After Divorce: A Handbook for Parents—How to Help Your Child Thrive

Court upheld a trial court's rejection of a an alternate week schedule proposed by parents based on a belief they would not be successful implementing the plan given the differences between them and a history of conflict. In lieu of the parties' plan, the court awarded the father primary custody and decision-making authority during the school year and the mother primary custody and decision-making authority during the summer.

Paralegal **Application 9.4**

Parenting Plans

In some states, parents are encouraged to develop parenting plans covering their children's remaining childhood years. In an increasing number, they are required to do so. The court may waive the requirement in a limited number of cases, such as those involving a history of domestic violence.

A primary goal of a parenting plan is to promote cooperative parenting and minimize disputes and continued hostility around parenting issues after dissolution of the marriage. By statute, the state of Washington has identified the following objectives of a parenting plan:

a. Provide for the child's physical care;

b. Maintain the child's emotional stability;

c. Provide for the child's changing needs as the child grows and matures, in a way that minimizes the need for future modifications to the permanent parenting plan;

d. Set forth the authority and responsibilities of each parent with respect to the child. . . ;

e. Minimize the child's exposure to harmful parental conflict;

f. Encourage the parents . . . to meet their responsibilities to their minor children through agreements in the permanent parenting plan, rather than by relying on judicial intervention; and

g. To otherwise protect the best interests of the child.[43]

The range of topics covered in plans is reflected in the Wisconsin Proposed Parenting Plan, which can be accessed at *www.wicourts.gov/forms* (Form FA-4147). The topics are similar to those contained in detailed child-related provisions of separation agreements such as when and where the child will live, the visitation schedule, responsibility for decision-making, special needs of the child, and methods of communicating and resolving disputes. The essential differences are in process and focus rather than specific terms. The focus in a separation agreement is on contractual terms binding the adversarial parents with respect to each other. At least in spirit, a parenting plan is focused more on the children and on the importance of shared involvement and cooperation in meeting their ongoing needs.

Several states now make parenting plan formats available online, generally through court-sponsored websites (see, e.g., **ALASKA** *www.courts.alaska.gov* DR-475 Model Parenting Agreement; **FLORIDA** *www.flcourts.org* Parenting Plan Form 12.995; **HAWAII** *www.courts.state.hi.us* 1 F-P-796 Proposed Parenting Plan; and **TENNESSEE** *www.tncourts.gov* Forms and Publications/Court Forms/Parenting Plan forms).

PARENTING SCHEDULES

Parenting plans typically include a "parenting schedule." Ideally, schedules for parenting postdivorce will be agreed on by the parties and may reflect the results of consultation with the children, depending on their ages and levels of maturity. A number of computer programs are available to help parties and counsel establish parenting schedules and courts to more easily and quickly review their nature and scope. Some programs generate color-coded calendar graphics to help courts, parties and children visualize the schedule and plan ahead. These programs are especially useful in complex cases involving multiple children and frequent visitation. Some attorneys and courts rely heavily on models prepared by legal and mental health professionals that take developmental needs and milestones into account. For example:

- In Minnesota, a court-appointed task force has promulgated parenting schedules for reference by parties and use by the courts when parents are unable to agree on their own terms. They are provided in a document called "A Parental Guide to Making Child-Focused Parenting Time Decisions," which can be found at *www.mncourts.gov.*
- A manual has been produced in Massachusetts called "Planning for Shared Parenting: A Guide for Parents Living Apart." It combines research about children and the impact of divorce with strategies for addressing the practical needs of parents and children postdivorce. Sponsored by the Association of Family and Conciliation Courts and the Chief Justice of the Probate and Family Court, it can be accessed at *www.mass.gov.*
- The New Jersey Judiciary has produced a publication about parenting time issues called "Parenting Time: A Child's Right" available at *www.judiciary. state.nj.us.*
- The Arizona Court site provides a publication called "Planning for Parenting Time: Arizona's Guide for Parents Living Apart." It offers ideas for various scheduling options based on children's needs. Color-coded options are available. To see the Guide, visit *www.azcourts.gov.*

VISITATION

When joint physical custody is neither desirable nor feasible, the parenting schedule will provide for visitation when appropriate. Visitation will customarily be awarded to a fit noncustodial parent, unless it would pose a threat to the child's health and welfare. There are no fixed formulas for visitation provisions. Assuming the parents live near each other and the children are in elementary school, a common schedule is to have visitation Wednesdays after school, one to two weekends a month (or one day each weekend with an occasional overnight), alternating holidays, shared school vacation weeks, and an extended period during the summer months (at least one month). This schedule amounts to the child being with the noncustodial parent approximately 20% of the time.

Defined Versus Flexible Visitation Schedules

Visitation schedules range from those described in flexible, open-ended terms, such as "visitation as the parties may reasonably agree," to highly detailed provisions, such as the one contained in Exhibit B in the Sample Separation Agreement in Chapter 13. Open-ended schedules tend to work best when parents have been separated for an extended period and already have worked out a mutually satisfactory plan. Defined schedules usually address weekly/monthly visitation, holidays and vacations, pickup and delivery times and places, out-of-state travel with the children, illness and medical treatment of a child, transportation arrangements and costs (if incurred), contact by phone or other electronic means, guidelines for handling cancellations and other deviations from the schedule, provision of clothing and other supplies for the children during visitation, any conditions with respect to third parties being present during visitation, dispute resolution measures, etc.

Most visitation provisions fall somewhere between the two extremes. Some degree of structure is preferred by a majority of family law practitioners

Visitation
a noncustodial parent's period of access to a child; may be supervised or unsupervised

PARALEGAL PRACTICE TIP

In a Florida case, an ex-wife claimed that her right to free speech was violated when the court ordered her to do everything in her power to create in her children a loving feeling toward their father and to encourage meaningful contact with him. The Florida Supreme Court found that the order did not violate her rights. The order promoted an important governmental interest—the well-being of minor children—and a parent has an obligation to encourage a positive relationship between the minor child and the other parent. *Schutz v. Schutz*, 581 So. 2d 1290 (Fla. 1991).

PARALEGAL PRACTICE TIP

To see an example of an Agreement to Enter Parent Coordination, visit *www.vermontjudiciary.org.* Family Court/Agreement to enter PC.

PARALEGAL PRACTICE TIP

To see an example of a "Supervised Order of Visitation," visit *www.cookcountyclerkofcourt.org.* (Illinois) Court Forms/Domestic Relations Division/ CCDR 0036.

PARALEGAL PRACTICE TIP

In *Shady v. Shady*, 858 N.E.2d 128 (Ind. Ct. App. 2006), the Indiana court of appeals affirmed an order of supervised visitation to a father after finding a risk that he might abduct his daughter and take her to Egypt. Although he had become a naturalized U.S. citizen, he was born in Egypt and had dual citizenship. The court based its decision on expert testimony regarding international child abduction. It should be noted that Egypt was not then (and still was not as of March 2015) a contracting member of the Hague Convention on the Civil Aspects of International Child Abduction.

to minimize potential misunderstandings and disputes between the parties. The basic parameters are provided and provision is made for alterations as mutually agreed upon. This approach offers each parent a desirable degree of flexibility, while guaranteeing a basic level of involvement of the noncustodial parent that each parent and the children can plan on.

Although detailed visitation plans often are useful, they may also give rise to or be unable to prevent disagreements in high-conflict cases. Disputes may focus on technical violations (such as arriving late, failing to return the children exactly on time, or making disparaging remarks about the other parent) or major issues (concealing a child's whereabouts or engaging in inappropriate sexual behavior with a new partner in front of the children). These cases are costly and burdensome to everyone involved—parents, attorneys, and the court—and they can be very stressful for children. Courts make every effort to provide for traditional and innovative dispute resolution strategies to avoid repeated return trips to court.[44] A visitation monitor or parenting coordinator may be appointed to oversee visitation on an ongoing basis, with the cost to be divided between the parties. In the extreme, if the actions of one of the parents deprive the child of having any kind of relationship with the other parent, the court may remove the child from the custody of the uncooperative parent as a last resort, even if such an action is contrary to the preference of the child.[45]

Supervised and Unsupervised Visitation

Unsupervised visitation occurs when a parent is free to spend visitation time with children as he or she wishes without additional persons being present or being subject to conditions imposed by the court or the other parent. Most visitation is unsupervised.

Supervised visitation may be ordered in a variety of circumstances in which a question exists as to the fitness or competency of the noncustodial parent to appropriately or adequately care for his or her child. In extreme cases, there are situations in which a parent may be deemed unfit to parent, and his or her parental rights may be terminated. Even without a termination of rights, courts may deny not only custody but also visitation if such an action is in the best interest of the child.

The most common circumstances in which a court might order supervised visitation are (1) when a parent has a history of substance abuse problems, mental illness, and/or domestic violence; (2) the parent has failed to properly supervise and care for a child while in his or her custody; or (3) when there is a reasonable fear that the noncustodial parent may try to abduct the child. The visitation may take place in an informal setting with supervision by a friend or family member, or it may be in a facility equipped to monitor visitation in a controlled environment that charges a fee for services, such as a YMCA or Domestic Violence Center. A parent who has been denied unsupervised visitation may eventually ask the court to consider elimination of restrictions, a request that may or may not be granted, depending on the circumstances.

In some problematic situations, a court will not necessarily order that visitation be supervised, but rather will condition the right to visitation on a parent's agreeing to abstain from or engage in a particular behavior or activity. A parent may be ordered to attend parenting classes or participate in family counseling or a treatment program for anger management. A parent with a substance abuse problem may be required to agree to abstain from the use of drugs or alcohol as a condition of having visitation with his or her child.[46]

Restrictions may also be placed on the kinds of activities the children can participate in while in the noncustodial parent's care, on the third parties who may be present during visitation, or on activities the parent may participate in with his or her child present.

Virtual Visitation

The potential of technology for promoting communication between parents and children during periods of absence seems boundless. Technology offers benefits for parents who are separated from their children by blocks, counties, states, or national boundaries. Video- or text-based e-mails, instant messaging, facetime, and interactive online games are just the beginning. A host of social networking sites, such as Facebook, My Space, and blogs, provide virtual journals and scrapbooks. Whether across town or separated by thousands of miles, many parents and children can now have real-time auditory, vocal, and visual interaction on a daily basis, if desired. The technology needed to support this form of virtual visitation is currently widely available and increasingly affordable. Many households already have the basics: phones or computers with built-in webcams and microphones and video software programs such as Skype, which can be downloaded for free.

When drafting documents relating to custody, consideration should be given to including **virtual visitation** provisions in parenting agreements for incorporation in court orders. A variety of techniques can be proposed that will allow parents and children who are physically separated to share information daily about what is happening in their respective lives, discuss problems, and work on projects or plans together. Provisions may be complex or very basic, such as the following order of the court in a Connecticut relocation case (See *Marshall v. Marshall*, 2014 Conn. Super. LEXIS 1610.):

> Both parties shall be entitled to reasonable contact on a daily basis with the minor child when in the custody of the other via telephone, Skype, Face Time or other means of virtual visitation. Each shall keep the other parent informed of all telephone numbers and e-mail addresses.

Recognizing its potential, some states, including Utah, Florida, Illinois, North Carolina, Texas, and Wisconsin, have passed legislation authorizing judges to include virtual visitation provisions in their decrees. Judges in other states have begun to do so on their own initiative. The trend is most apparent in the context of cases involving parents residing in different nations and in relocation cases. For example, in the *McCoy* case, a New Jersey appellate court granted a mother permission to relocate from New Jersey to California with her nine-year-old disabled daughter over the objection of the child's father. The court praised the mother's "virtual visitation" proposal to develop an interactive website to facilitate the child's communication with her father as "creative and innovative." Through the use of camera–computer technology, the site would give the father and others the ability to communicate face to face with the daughter daily and to review her schoolwork and records on an ongoing basis.[47]

Although virtual visitation has the potential to enhance the quantity and quality of contact between parents and children while they are apart, it is neither appropriate nor available in all cases. An argument can be made for or against it depending on the client's circumstances. Even when it is available, it

Virtual visitation
communication between parents and children through the use of technology

PARALEGAL PRACTICE TIP

To see the North Carolina Statute, visit *www.ncga.state.nc.us*. General Statutes/§50-13.2(e).

should be designed to supplement rather than replace actual visitation. As an Illinois Appellate Court cautioned in a relocation case: ". . . while a trial court may consider the availability of electronic communication in a removal case, it may not rely on the use of electronic communication in granting a petition for removal. One cannot hug, kiss, tickle, soothe, etc. a virtual image." (See *In re A. E. B.-K., a Minor (Tania L. B. v. Keith T. K.)* 2012 Ill. App. Unpub. LEXIS 1665.)

Parent Education Programs

Parents struggling with their own needs, conflicts, and stress during divorce proceedings often forget that it is not all about them. Parenting programs are designed to sensitize parents to the needs and feelings of their children who are frequently victims of their parents' anger, frustration, and bitterness.

Many states require parents who are getting divorced to complete a parent education program, and virtually all of the rest recommend it. Some states also recommend that the parties' children in a certain age range also participate. The programs for children are designed to help them cope with divorce and share their feelings with others in their age group. Courts make available information about approved program providers in pamphlets or Q&A sheets, and many do so online, including the names and locations of various programs by city and town. Some states grant waivers of participation in a limited number of circumstances, such as when a party is institutionalized or has a language barrier, or when there is chronic and severe abuse that negates safe parental communication.

The primary purposes of parent education programs are to

- encourage parents to work cooperatively for the benefit of their children
- help children through the difficult period of divorce and separation
- reduce postdivorce litigation and court appearances

The curriculum of parent education programs varies from state to state and program to program, but commonly includes topics such as the following:

- the emotional effects of divorce or separation on parents and children
- what parents can do to help their children adjust
- harmful effects of parental conflict on children and how to avoid them
- communication and co-parenting skills
- developmental stages and needs of children
- factors that contribute to a child's healthy adjustment
- the function and value of parenting plans
- techniques of problem solving and conflict resolution
- warning signs that children are having problems
- community resources

In jurisdictions where participation in parent education programs is mandatory, failure to complete a program may have serious consequences. Among other options, the court may:

- refuse to move the case forward
- dismiss the case
- hold one or both parties in contempt

PARALEGAL PRACTICE TIP

An example of a state statute requiring participation in a parenting education program of a minimum of eight hours in duration is the Minnesota statute located at *www.revisor.mn.gov.* Statutes/Section 518.157.

PARALEGAL PRACTICE TIP

"Earthquake in Zipland" is the first computer therapy game designed to help school-aged children manage the stress of their parents' divorce and separation. It provides a nonthreatening platform for asking questions and expressing feelings that are likely to arise in children in the wake of a divorce.

PARALEGAL PRACTICE TIP

To see an example of a motion to waive attendance at a parent education program, visit *www.mass.gov/courts.* Search for the form by title or number CJD 444. To see an example of a "Parenting Education Program Order, Certificate and Results," go to *www.jud.ct.gov.* Attorneys/Forms/JD-FM-149 Parenting Education Program under Individual Family Forms (Connecticut).

Modification of Custody Orders

At some time after the court issues its initial order, either parent may come to believe that a change in custody and/or visitation is warranted. Customarily, courts will not allow the parents to agree in advance to self-executing grounds for modification, as custody decisions are supposed to be based on a determination of the best interests of the child at the time of the modification. Occasionally, parties try to accomplish changes informally and this may work as long as the parties are in agreement. However, an informal approach can be a problem if child support is an issue or if one of the parties later files for contempt, claiming he or she never agreed to a change.

The usual process for obtaining a modification involves filing a Motion (Petition/Complaint) for Modification of Custody (commonly accompanied by an affidavit in support of the Motion) in the court that has continuing jurisdiction. The filing is followed by service of notice on the other party who may file an affidavit or memorandum in opposition to the Motion. The court then holds a hearing at which time the parties each have an opportunity to testify, call witnesses, and present documentation in support of their respective positions.

A party seeking to modify a custody order generally must show that:

- there has been a substantial and material change of circumstances that affects the child's welfare,
- the change has occurred since entry of the decree and was not foreseeable,
- the change warrants a modification in custody, and
- the change will be in the child's best interests (any harm to the child from a modification must be outweighed by its benefits).

Although theoretically a Motion for Modification can be brought whenever a substantial change occurs that impacts the child's best interests, in states that have adopted the Uniform Marriage and Divorce Act (UMDA),[48] absent an emergency, a modification cannot be sought for at least two years from the date the decree or prior order was issued. The rationale for the rule is that children need stability in their lives, and changes in primary custody should be discouraged because they disrupt the child's life. Although it has not adopted the UMDA, in North Dakota under N.D. Cent. Code, § 14-09-06.6 (2014), a court may not modify primary residential responsibility within two years of entry of the order or judgment establishing primary residential responsibility unless the court finds (1) modification is necessary to serve the best interests of the child and (2) one of the following three factors is present:

a. The persistent and willful denial or interference with parenting time;
b. The child's present environment may endanger the child's physical or emotional health or impair the child's emotional development; or
c. The residential responsibility for the child has changed to the other parent for longer than six months.

Motions will usually be granted if the parties agree to the modification; if it is apparent that an initial allocation of parental rights and responsibilities is not working; if there is clear and convincing evidence that the child's present environment is harming his or her physical, mental, or emotional health; or if the court finds that there is repeated, intentional, and unwarranted interference by one parent with the rights and responsibilities of the other parent.

PARALEGAL PRACTICE TIP

To see an example of a Motion for Modification that can be used to request modifications in both custody and support in Connecticut, visit *www.jud.ct.gov.* Attorneys/ Forms/Family Forms/Individual Family Forms/JD-FM-174.

PARALEGAL PRACTICE TIP

A federal law called the Service Members Civil Relief Act[49] is designed to protect military personnel on active duty by staying civil court actions or administrative proceedings during periods of military activation. Although child custody proceedings are civil in nature, some family court judges have held that in custody actions, state law must trump federal law. They argue that custody disputes are not comparable to civil property disputes, and such cases must proceed in the best interests of children. In effect, this means that parents may be forced to decide between custody and service to the country, unless they can regain custody once they are no longer deployed.

PARALEGAL PRACTICE TIP

To learn more about the Uniform Marriage and Divorce Act, visit *www .uniformlaws.org.* Under Find an Act, search for Marriage and Divorce Act.

PARALEGAL PRACTICE TIP

To read an opinion applying the North Dakota rule, see *Kartes v. Kartes,* 2013 ND 106, 831 N.W.2d 731 (2013), in which the North Dakota Supreme Court affirmed denial of a mother's modification request primarily because it was part of a willful and persistent effort to interfere with the father's relationship with the children.

Commonly, the request for modification relates to a change in the circumstances of the custodial parent, but occasionally it results from a change in the noncustodial parent's circumstances that significantly alters his or her relative fitness and/or availability as a parent. (See Paralegal Application 9.5.) For example, modification actions frequently involve military personnel about to be transferred or deployed overseas. In most cases, there is no automatic presumption that modification is warranted solely because of the deployment. The child's best interests drive the court's deliberations. See, e.g., *Faucett v. Vasquesz*, 411 N.J. Super. 108, 984 A.2d 460 (2009).

Paralegal Application 9.5

When Does a Change Warrant a Modification in Custody?

Do you agree with the decisions in the following cases?

***In re Marriage of Kirkpatrick*, 248 Ore. App. 539, 273 P.3d 361 (2012)**

In this case, the parties were divorced in 2008 and although both parents were deemed fit, the mother was granted custody of their three sons based on the undisputed fact she had been their primary caretaker throughout their lives. From day one, the mother made efforts to interfere with the father's parenting time and after trying to have her held in contempt, he finally sought a modification. The trial court found the mother's actions were significant enough to qualify as a change of circumstances warranting modification. The court focused on the quality rather than the quantity of the mother's interference stating that the number of missed parenting days alone would not have been sufficient to warrant a change in custody. What was sufficient was that she "intentionally, repeatedly and substantially" interfered with the father's visitation in a particularly manipulative and hurtful manner clearly calculated to undermine the father's relationship with the children. Among other actions, she made baseless allegations about the children being sexually abused while in the father's care (resulting in them being needlessly interviewed about the allegations), denied the father parenting time around the children's birthdays and Christmas holiday, attempted to keep them away from the father's wedding, and threatened to move the children farther away from where he resided. After interviewing the children in chambers, the court ruled that changing custody from the mother to the father with designated parenting time for the mother under the state's model parenting plan would be in the children's best interests. The mother appealed and the trial court order was affirmed.

***Brown v. Brown*, 2012 Ark. 89, 387 S.W.3d 159 (2012)**

At the time of their divorce, the parties in this case agreed on an initial limited visitation schedule to accommodate the wife's nursing of their infant child. They further agreed that once their daughter reached 18 months of age, they would implement a standard visitation schedule. The trial court approved the agreement and incorporated its terms in the divorce decree. The mother subsequently moved to modify the visitation agreement on the ground that she was still breast-feeding when the child reached 18 months and wanted to continue to do so until the age of two and possibly beyond as the child was an "aggressive" nurser. She alleged that her desire to continue nursing was consistent with the suggestions of the World Health Organization and the American Academy of Pediatricians as well as her lactation consultant. The trial court dismissed her motion to modify visitation. The mother appealed and the Arkansas Supreme Court affirmed the trial court's ruling that she had failed to prove that a material change in circumstances had occurred. The court reasoned that the length of time the mother would breast-feed was certainly within the contemplation of the parties at the time the divorce decree was entered and she could have weaned the child based on the agreed upon schedule. Although she had ample time to do so before the decree entered, she had failed to follow-up in a timely manner with her lactation consultant about the weaning process. The court held that she was not permitted to allege a material change in circumstances which she herself had created.

***Jackson v. Jackson*, 2004 WY 99, 96 P.3d 21 (Wyo. 2004)**

In this case, the mother had been awarded primary physical custody of the parties' two children at the time of divorce. From September to December 2002, the mother changed jobs five times. In February 2003, after being unemployed for over two months, she enrolled in cosmetology school. She subsequently dropped out of that program and enrolled in a different school a few months later. While she was at school the children attended day care. During essentially the same time period, the father remained in the town where he had been living and continued working for a cable company. He made significant improvements in his lifestyle, including quitting drinking and smoking, and ended his association with "bad influences." He received a promotion at work and was able to provide health insurance for the children. He also developed a stable relationship with a woman whom he married shortly before the hearing on his request for modification of custody. The father's petition for modification alleged a material change of circumstances (that he had substantially improved his life and had become more stable, whereas the mother had not). The trial court found that although both parents had issues, the balance had shifted in favor of the father and awarded him primary physical custody of the children. The Wyoming Supreme Court affirmed the change.

RELOCATIONS

Inevitably following divorce, at least one of the parents establishes a new place of residence. In today's mobile world, this initial relocation is often the first of several moves due to job changes, remarriages, economic conditions, extended family needs, and other life changes. Although courts have held that a parent has a constitutional right to travel and cannot be required to live in a particular place,[50] a problem often arises when a custodial parent wants to relocate with a minor child against the wishes of the other parent.

Relocation cases present a particular challenge for the courts as they involve seemingly irreconcilable conflicts between custodial and noncustodial parents. They typically implicate "two legitimate interests—the custodial parent's interest in making unfettered decisions for the benefit of the new nuclear family and the noncustodial parent's interest in maintaining a close bond with the children."[51] The balancing act the court must perform tries to satisfy three primary goals under the umbrella of the best interests of the child: stability and continuity in the child's life; maximum involvement and participation of both parents in a joint custodial arrangement; and minimum disruption as a result of the transportation of the child between the parents.[52]

States usually identify by statute and/or case law the factors to be considered in relocation cases. Although the child's best interests are paramount, courts commonly also will assess the following:

- Each party's reasons for seeking or opposing the move;
- The nature, extent, duration, and quality of the relationship of each parent and other significant persons (siblings, etc.) with the child;
- The age, developmental stage, and needs of the child and the likely impact the relocation will have on the child's physical, emotional, and educational development;
- The child's preference taking into consideration his or her age and degree of maturity;
- The current employment and economic circumstances of each parent;
- The extent to which the objecting parent has fulfilled his or her financial obligations to the other parent and the child (child support, spousal support, marital property, and debt obligations);
- Any history of substance abuse or domestic violence by either parent including seriousness and any rehabilitative success;
- The feasibility of preserving the relationship between the noncustodial parent and the child through suitable visitation arrangements;

PARALEGAL PRACTICE TIP

Although the constitutional right to travel is customarily raised in interstate cases, the Montana Supreme Court addressed a situation in which a trial court had amended a parenting plan to make a father primary custodial parent on the grounds that the mother should be the one to pay the price for reduced parental contact due to her moving a substantial distance within the state of Montana. The state's high court reversed. "It is difficult to conceive that the right to travel protected by the United States Constitution does not include a right to freely travel within each of the states. The right to travel between states would mean little if a person did not also have the right to travel within a state after crossing its borders. We hold, therefore, that the right to travel guaranteed by the United States Constitution includes the right to travel within Montana." *Griffen v. Plaisted-Harmon*, 2009 MT 169, 350 Mont. 489 (2009).

PARALEGAL PRACTICE TIP

Examples of reasons held sufficient to support a relocation have included, among others, the desire to enhance one's professional career (see, e.g., *Schrag v. Spear*, 22 Neb. App. 139, 849 N.W.2d 551 (2014)) and the desire to move to another country (Mexico) in order to live with one's deported husband. See *Daniels v. Maldonado-Morin*, 288 Neb. 240, 847 N.W.2d 79 (2014).

PARALEGAL PRACTICE TIP

To see an example of a "Notice of Intent to Move," visit http://courts. mt.gov. Legal Community/Forms/ Child Custody Notice of Intent to Move. The Form is under Generic Forms.

PARALEGAL PRACTICE TIP

The Colorado relocation statute can be found at *www.leg.state.co.us*, US and Colorado Constitutions, Statutes, and Session Laws/Colorado Revised Statutes/14-10-129.

PARALEGAL PRACTICE TIP

In *Tania L. B. v. Keith T. K.*, an Illinois Appellate Court reversed a trial court's order granting a mother's petition to move with the parties' minor daughter from Illinois to California. The reversal was based in large part on the impact the move would have on the father who had custodial time with the minor child on multiple days of the week. The court was unpersuaded by the argument that reasonable visitation could be achieved through virtual visitation (2012 Ill. App. Unpub. LEXIS 1665).

PARALEGAL PRACTICE TIP

If removal is to another country, the court will consider whether the destination country is a Hague Convention signatory because if not, enforcement of visitation orders may be very difficult.

- The likelihood of compliance with the new parenting schedule once the relocating parent is beyond the jurisdiction of the court; and
- The degree to which the custodial parent's and the child's life may be enhanced economically, socially, emotionally, educationally, and professionally by the move.

The parent wishing to relocate usually has the burden of proving by a preponderance of the evidence that relocation is in the best interest of the child. If that burden of proof is met, the burden then shifts to the nonrelocating parent to show by a preponderance of the evidence that the proposed relocation is not in the best interest of the child.

The trend is "generally to allow the residential parent to move away with the child so long as satisfactory alternative parenting time arrangements with the nonresidential parent can be achieved and there are no bad faith motives for the geographical move."[53] However, there is no uniform position among the states. Approaches run the gamut. In Washington, there is a statutory presumption favoring a primary residential parent's relocation decision. (See, e.g., *In re Marriage of Weir*, 267 P.3d 1045 (Wash. Ct. App. 2011).) In California, the custodial parent has a presumptive right to relocate with a minor child, subject to a court restraining a change on the ground that it would prejudice the rights or welfare of the child. In Minnesota, if a custodial parent seeks to move permanently to another state with the minor children over the noncustodial parent's objection, an evidentiary hearing is not required absent a prima facie case of endangerment to the child or a showing that the move was intended to deprive the noncustodial parent of visitation. The relevant Missouri statute provides that a person entitled to custody of a child shall not relocate the residence of the child for a period of more than ninety days except upon order of the court or with the written consent of the parties with custody or visitation rights.[54] The applicable Colorado statute reflects a compromise approach in which the geographical extent of the relocation is critical.

In some states, the test applied by the courts depends in part on whether the party seeking to relocate is the primary custodial parent or has shared physical custody. For example, in Massachusetts, if the party seeking to relocate is the primary custodial parent, the burden is lighter and the court looks at whether the relocation is sought in good faith, there is a "real advantage" to the move for the child and the custodial parent, and the relocation will not terminate the child's relationship with the other parent because of logistical, financial, or developmental realities. (See *Yannis v. Frondistou-Yannis*, 395 Mass. 704 (1985).) If custody is shared, the burden is higher. The court will consider the best interests of the child and will also weigh more heavily the impact of a relocation on the degree of contact between the child and the nonrelocating parent. (See *Mason v. Coleman*, 477 Mass. 177 (2006).) In some cases, a parent may effectively be forced to choose between custody and relocation.

Enforcement of Custody and Visitation Orders

When a parent fails to comply with court-ordered custody and visitation provisions, the other parent may be forced to return to court to enforce the order. The parent in violation may be found to be in criminal or civil contempt and be ordered to pay a fine, go to jail, or both. Depending on the circumstances, a court may issue a writ *ne exeat* prohibiting a party from removing the child from the state (see, e.g., *Faris v. Jernigan*, 939 So. 2d 835 (Miss. App. 2006)) or it may require that a bond be posted by a party that can be reached in the event of a violation. In especially egregious cases, the court may deny custodial rights, impose a plan for supervised visitation, or in the extreme, terminate a parent's rights. Several states recognize a tort action for interference with parental rights and in many, custodial interference is a crime.

Two especially difficult situations in this context occur when:

1. A parent who is failing to pay court-ordered child support insists on exercising his or her visitation rights. It is difficult for an attorney to explain to a client who is not receiving child support payments that he or she cannot refuse visitation and must comply with the court's order regarding custody and visitation. However unfair it may seem, the two orders are independent of one another, and each party's remedy is to pursue enforcement relief through the court.

2. A parent harbors a strong belief that the other parent is sexually abusing the child and refuses visitation or, in the extreme, flees with the child or conceals the minor's whereabouts, as in the high-profile case of Dr. Elizabeth Morgan, who at one point was incarcerated for more than two years for contempt of court because she refused to produce her daughter based on her fears of further abuse.[55]

Third Parties in the Custody Context

Thus far in this chapter it may have seemed as if custody and visitation disputes only arise in traditional families in the context of divorces between married biological or adoptive parents. However, a basic theme of this text is that the "traditional American family" is becoming the exception rather than the rule. Approximately one-third of families in this country have no father living in the home (in some urban areas, the figure is considerably higher). Persons outside of the nuclear family such as kinship caregivers and day-care workers are increasingly providing everyday child rearing. Nearly 14 million children live with parties other than their "legal" parents, and that number continues to grow.[56] We have more stepparents than ever before. We have "thwarted" nonmarital biological fathers who for a variety of reasons have been unable to establish their legal status as parents. We have same-sex and heterosexual marriages, civil unions, and domestic partnerships. We have grandparents, surrogate parents, foster parents, co-parents, *de facto* parents, and **psychological parents**, among other "parental" variations.

> Family law's acknowledgment of the importance of adults who are not parents, historically referred to as "third parties" or "legal strangers" to the child, has extended to the point that today functioning in a parent-like role can lead to becoming a parent. . . . Adults who formerly might have been considered a legal stranger to a child may now be recognized by the law as having rights and obligations towards a child with whom they have no biological or formal legal connection. . . . Modern family law's "functional turn" has exploded the notion that children have only two "natural" parents who must be their sole caregivers, with the state as the only alternative in the absence of parents. This functional

PARALEGAL PRACTICE TIP

A minority of states impose financial child support obligations on stepparents upon divorce in limited circumstances, such as when the stepparent voluntarily assumed a parental obligation to the child while married to the child's mother.[58]

PARALEGAL PRACTICE TIP

See *In re Scarlett Z.-D.*, 2015 IL 117904, 28 N.E.3d 776 (2015), in which the former fiancé of the mother of an adopted child was denied standing to file a claim for custody of the child, a claim he had based on several forms of functional parent–child relationships asserting he was "the *de facto*, equitable and psychological parent" of, and stood *in loco parentis* to the child. The Supreme Court of Illinois reaffirmed that functional parent theories are not recognized in that state.

PARALEGAL PRACTICE TIP

New Jersey has established that when there is a conflict between a legal parent and a psychological parent, the case will be decided as if it involved two legal parents and the standard to be applied is the best interest of the child.[59]

approach to the family exemplifies family law's ongoing efforts to reflect more accurately 'the reality of family life.' . . .[57]

Some legislatures and courts have basically begun to establish parenthood gradations recognizing parental responsibilities and parenting time for "functional parents" of children who often are unrelated by biology or adoption. However, the effort to adapt the law to the evolution in family structure is not without controversy and, as of 2015, some states such as Illinois still do not recognize functional parent theories as a basis for extending rights to third parties.

There are two primary and competing views regarding the custodial and visitation rights of third parties:

1. One school of thought holds that a legal parent has a presumptive and constitutionally protected right to custody of his or her child. This approach focuses on the fundamental right of fit parents to care for, nurture, and control their children, to direct their upbringing and education, and to determine the individuals with whom their children will associate.

2. The other school of thought asserts it is in the best interests of a child to be placed in the custody of whichever adult(s) will provide the healthiest and most stable environment. This approach focuses on the needs of the child and the nature and strength of the emotional bond between the child and the third party.

Historically, the focus has been on the "rights" of parents rather than on the providers of actual caregiving and the needs of children. As between an unrelated nonparent and a biological parent, the parent has usually been held to have the superior right to custody unless the nonparent is able to establish that the legal parent has relinquished that right due to surrender, abandonment, neglect, unfitness, or some other "extraordinary circumstance," which may include an involuntary disruption of custody over an extended period of time. See, e.g., *Holmes v. Glover*, 2009 NY Slip Op 9228, 68 A.D.3d 868, 890 N.Y.S.2d 629 (2009). Still today, in cases involving disputes between legal parents and third parties, the parties usually do not start out on an equal footing. The right of legal parents to in effect possess and control access to their children remains a powerful public policy.

Despite sometimes strong opposition, however, rights are gradually being extended to nonparent third parties as legislatures and courts increasingly recognize the important bond that can develop between children and the "legal strangers" who have played meaningful positive roles in their lives. As the Pennsylvania Superior Court has put it:

> . . . the need to guard the family from intrusions by third parties and to protect the rights of the natural parent must be tempered by the paramount need to protect the child's best interest. Thus, while it is presumed that a child's best interest is served by maintaining the family's privacy and autonomy, that presumption must give way where the child has established strong psychological bonds with a person who, although not a biological parent, has lived with the child and provided care, nurture, and affection, assuming in the child's eye a stature like that of a parent. Where such a relationship is shown, our courts recognize that the child's best interest requires that the third party be granted standing so as to have the opportunity to litigate fully the issue

of whether that relationship should be maintained even over a natural parent's objections.[60]

When a third party seeks custody or visitation rights, the court must engage in a two-part inquiry:

1. Does the third party have standing to seek custody or visitation? **Standing** is a jurisdictional concept that refers to an individual's right to bring a matter before a court and seek relief based on a claim that he or she has a stake in the outcome of the case. Standing is usually based on statute (see Exhibits 9.4 and 9.5) but may be grounded in case law. Nearly all states have statutes specifying which third parties have standing and under what circumstances. Some are broad and extend it to "any person with a legitimate interest," including but not limited to grandparents, stepparents, blood relatives, and family members. See, e.g., Code of Virginia §§20-124.1-2.B. Some only extend standing to certain categories of third parties related to the child by blood or marriage such as stepparents and grandparents. Still others are very restrictive requiring that the third party have been the child's primary caretaker for a period of six months or more without the participation of the parent or that the parent has abandoned, neglected, or otherwise exhibited disregard for the child's well-being. (See, e.g., Minnesota Statutes Chapter 257C De Facto Custodian and Interested Third Party.) Some states' visitation statutes permit a third party to have standing even if both of the child's parents are alive and fit. However, most, especially if custody is sought, require that the child's family not be intact due to a circumstance such as a parent's death or because the parents never married or are separated or divorced.

   The ALI principles give the legal parents priority if they are able to care for their children but state that custody ought to be available to individuals in addition to biological parents whose continued caregiving is presumed beneficial to a child. Specifically included are adults who have functioned in good faith as parents, believing they were legal parents, **parents by estoppel**, and/or *de facto* **parents**. Legislatures and the courts have relied on a variety of such theories of **equitable parenthood** to enable third parties to be granted rights to custody, visitation, and guardianship. Some jurisdictions recognize the concept of the "psychological parent," the individual who has the strongest "parental" bond with the child, who has provided the most significant care for the child in quality and quantity, and whom the child often regards as the "parent." Some states extend standing to third parties when the child has been in their custody for a certain minimum period. In extreme cases involving abuse and neglect, the state has third-party standing to seek custody of a child.[61]

2. If the third party has standing, what test or standard will be used to determine whether or not the third party should be granted custody or visitation? The tests applied vary from state to state and are also to some extent based on whether the third party is seeking custody or visitation. The tests typically begin with recognition of the established presumption that fit parents act in the best interests of their children, including when they oppose third-party petitions for visitation or custody. Petitioners must rebut that presumption. When seeking visitation, they usually will need to establish more than simply that visitation will be in the child's best interest. For example, to succeed in Massachusetts, the petitioner must show that either (1) there is an important and significant

PARALEGAL PRACTICE TIP

To see an example of a Petition for Third Party Visitation, visit *www.courts.delaware.gov.* Family Matters/Third Party/Grandparent Visitation Form #172 Petition for 3rd Party/Grandparent Visitation.

Standing
an individual's right to bring a matter before the court and seek relief based on a claim that he or she has a stake in the outcome of the case

PARALEGAL PRACTICE TIP

As of 2014, thirteen states specifically provide for sibling visitation: California, Hawaii, Illinois, Louisiana, Nevada, New Jersey, Ohio, Oklahoma, Oregon, Rhode island, South Carolina, Texas, and Virginia. A sibling could also petition in any state that allows "any person" to seek visitation.

Parent by estoppel
a theory used to establish parenting rights; essentially provides that a person may be designated the legal parent of a child if he or she has held himself or herself out as the child's parent and has supported the child emotionally and financially; parenthood based on the fact an individual has functioned as a rent with the approval of a child's legal parents

***De facto* parent**
an individual who performs a caretaking role without compensation for an extended period, knowing he or she is not a child's legal parent, often with the consent of the legal parents

Equitable parenthood
parenthood established on the basis of equitable principles of fairness rather than on biological connection

PARALEGAL PRACTICE TIP

Having a thorough understanding of the rules governing third-party standing as well as the interplay with other areas of law in the client's jurisdiction can be very important. For example, the Virginia rules extend third-party standing to, among others, grandparents and persons related to a child by blood. When a grandchild has been surrendered and adopted, the grandparent's legal bond with the child is extinguished under adoption law. However, the blood relationship survives providing a second basis for standing in the custody context. See *Thrift v. Baldwin,* 23 Va. App. 18, 473 S.E.2d 715 (1996).

PARALEGAL PRACTICE TIP

The same rules should apply to stepparents in both heterosexual and same-sex marriages. Unmarried same- or heterosexual nonparents seeking to establish or enforce their parental rights typically must do so through second parent adoptions, as co-parents or *de facto* parents, functional or psychological parents or under some other equitable theory (see discussion below and related material in Chapter 7).

relationship in existence between the child and the nonparent and that the court's refusal to grant visitation will be harmful to the child's health, safety, or welfare or (2) there was no preexisting relationship but visitation rights are required to protect the child from significant harm. See *Blixt v. Blixt*, 437 Mass. 649 (2002). The burden is usually even higher when custody is sought because it constitutes a significantly greater intrusion on parental rights than does visitation. For example, the petitioner may be required to show that the parent is unfit, has harmed or abandoned the child, or that the child has some extraordinary need that cannot be met by the parent. See Minnesota Statutes Chapter 257C.

Some third-party statutes list the kinds of factors courts should consider when assessing the best interests of children in this context. They may include, for example, the quality of the child's relationship with the parent(s), the preferences of the child, the mental and physical health of all the parties involved, the history or threat of domestic violence, the extent and quality of the relationship between the child and the third party, the impact of the presence or absence of the third party on the child, and the level of antagonism between the parents and the third party.

Most third-party case law has involved four categories of "parents": stepparents, grandparents, *de facto* parents, and co-parents, people other than legal parents who often function like parents and play such an important role in a child's life that they achieve a parent-like status. They are quite literally parents in fact though not at law.

Stepparents

It is estimated that one in every four children will live with a stepparent before reaching the age of majority.[62] Although stepparents have become part of American family life and are often at least as important in children's lives as biological or legal parents, the law is unclear and inconsistent with respect to their rights and obligations. The majority view is that a stepparent's rights flow from marriage to the child's parent and do not survive dissolution of that marriage. Stepparents who want to continue relationships with their stepchildren often face considerable obstacles, especially when the children have two living and fit parents. Most states do not specifically afford them standing to petition for custody and visitation, although some do in limited circumstances, including California, Illinois, Kansas, New Hampshire, Oregon, Tennessee, Virginia, and Wisconsin. (See Exhibit 9.4.)

EXHIBIT 9.4 Illinois Statute 750 ILCS 5/601(b)(3) Jurisdiction; Commencement of Proceeding

Courtesy of State of Illinois

FROM THE STATUTE

(b) A child custody proceeding is commenced in the court: . . .

(3) by a stepparent, by filing a petition, if all of the following circumstances are met:

    A. the child is at least 12 years old;

    B. the custodial parent and stepparent were married for at least 5 years during which the child resided with the parent and stepparent;

    C. the custodial parent is deceased or is disabled and cannot perform the duties of a parent to the child;

    D. the stepparent provided for the care, control, and welfare of the child prior to the initiation of custody proceedings;

    E. the child wishes to live with the stepparent; and

    F. it is alleged to be in the best interests and welfare of the child to live with the stepparent as provided in Section 602 of this Act [750 ILCS 5/602].(58).

In the absence of statutory authority courts often struggle to find legal theories to support the good-faith desires of stepparents to continue to play a meaningful role in the lives of children they have lived with and cared for. Equitable estoppel, *de facto* parenthood, the concept of the psychological parent, and the doctrine of *in loco parentis* have each been utilized on a limited basis along with other rationales to recognize a stepparent's history of parenting a child who is "not their own."[63] See the following examples of cases involving a variety of stepparent scenarios:

- In *In re the marriage of Vanderheiden v. Vanderheiden*, **2013 WI App 128, 351 Wis. 2d 223, 838 N.W.2d 865 (2013)**, a Wisconsin Court of Appeals upheld a trial court decision awarding a stepfather visitation with the mother's son because the award would maximize the amount of time the stepchild spent with the parties' son and would be in the best interests of both boys. The award was strongly supported by both a custody study and the recommendation of the stepchild's guardian *ad litem*.

- In *C.P. v. R.S.*, **961 N.E.2d 592 (Mass. App. Ct. 2012)**, the Massachusetts Court of Appeals affirmed a trial court award of sole legal and physical custody to the stepfather of the child of his deceased wife since the biological father had had virtually no contact with the child since the mother's death. The court opined that the stepparent was the child's sole caregiver and the child would suffer harm if the relationship was severed.

- In *Daniel v. Spivey*, **386 S.W.3d 424 (Ark. 2012)**, the Arkansas Supreme Court reversed a circuit court's grant of custody to a stepfather who had characterized his relationship to the child as being *in loco parentis*. The father testified that he had disciplined and praised the child as appropriate, occasionally tended to her needs and provided necessaries, babysat, and attended school programs. The Arkansas high court held that these facts demonstrated that he fulfilled the role of a caring stepfather but fell short of establishing that he embraced the rights, duties, and responsibilities of a parent.

- In *In re Marriage of Rayman*, **273 Kan. 996, 47 P.3d 413 (2002)**, the Kansas Supreme Court affirmed a lower court's denial of a noncustodial mother's motion for a change in custody for a one-year period, during which time the custodial father would be overseas on a tour of duty in Korea. The children had been living with the father and his new wife, the children's stepmother, for four years and were securely bonded and thriving in their care. In finding it was in the children's best interests to remain in the primary residential custody of the father, the court essentially reasoned that even though the children would be living with the stepmother during the father's absence, the custody contest was between the mother and father, not the mother and stepmother, and that cases involving military families must be decided on a case-by-case basis.

- In *McAllister v. McAllister*, **2010 ND 40, 779 N.W.2d 652 (2010)**, a stepfather, Mark, was granted "stepfather visitation" with a child he had raised for six years believing the boy, E.M., was his biological son. When his wife left him she took the boy with her and told him Mark was not his real father. Mark sought to maintain his relationship with the child testifying that he loved E.M. as he did his two biological children, had been there for the child essentially since birth, and functioned as a parent to the child, who called him "dad" or "daddy." In its findings, the court described Mark's role in E.M.'s life as that of a "psychological parent" who provides a child's daily care, develops a close bond to the child, and is the one a child looks to for love, guidance, and security.

In loco parentis
[Latin: in the place of the parent] taking on some or all of the responsibilities of a parent

PARALEGAL PRACTICE TIP

In some states, a parent who is on active military duty can designate a person (such as a new spouse) to exercise their visitation rights in their absence. The designation is viewed as an exercise of the absent parent's right to visitation rather than as the new spouse's independent right as a third party. See, e.g., *In re Marriage of DePalma*, 176 P.3d 829 (Colo. Ct. App. 2007).

PARALEGAL PRACTICE TIP

To see an example of a Petition for Grandparent Visitation used in New Hampshire, visit *www.courts.state .nh.us*. Superior Court/Forms, Domestic Forms/NHJB-2228-FS Petition for Grandparent Visitation.

PARALEGAL PRACTICE TIP

When drafting a petition and affidavit in support of a petition for grandparent visitation, it is important to address relevant statutory requirements. For example, the Grandparent Visitation Provision of the Alabama Code (Section 30-3-4.1) provides that in determining best interests in such cases, the court shall consider (1) The willingness of the grandparent(s) to encourage a close relationship between the child and the parent(s); (2) The preference of the child if of sufficient maturity; (3) The mental and physical health of the child; (4) The mental and physical health of the grandparents; (5) Evidence of domestic violence inflicted by one parent on the mother or the child; and (6) Other relevant factors, including the wishes of any parent who is living.

Grandparents

In 2013, more than 16.7% of all children in the country were living in households with at least one grandparent present and 15.7% of those grandparents were responsible for the basic needs of one or more of the grandchildren under age 18 who were living with them.[64] Although under common law grandparents had no right of access to their grandchildren, legislatures in every state now have provided standing for grandparents to petition for custody and/or visitation rights under certain circumstances.[65]

In most states grandparents will have standing only under certain limited conditions, such as when the child's parents never married, the parents are divorced or separated, one or both of the parents have died, the parental rights of one or both of the parents have been terminated, the child has lived with the grandparent for an extended period, or the child is in the custody of someone other than a parent. Most states also provide that in order to have standing, there must have been a significant preexisting relationship between the child and the grandparents. Once a grandparent establishes standing to seek visitation over the objection of a parent, he or she must satisfy the test for resolving visitation disputes between legal parents and grandparents in the state where the action is brought (customarily the state in which the child resides). Tests necessarily reflect the decision of the U.S. Supreme Court in *Troxel v. Granville*. (See Case 9.2 and Paralegal Application 9.6.) A number of states interpreting *Troxel* have held that the courts must give presumptive validity to a fit parent's decision, and in order to rebut that presumption, the grandparents must show by a preponderance of the evidence that failure to grant visitation to the grandparents will cause the child significant harm by adversely affecting his or her health, safety, and welfare. For example, in *Rideout v. Riendeau*, 761 A.2d 291, (Me. 2000), the maternal grandparents had helped raise the grandchildren, had been their primary caretakers for extended periods, and the mother and children lived with them when the mother was having marital problems. After they reconciled, the child's parents opposed grandparent visitation. In affirming the grandparents were entitled to obtain visitation, the Maine Supreme Court held "The cessation of contact with a grandparent whom the child views as a parent may have a dramatic, and even traumatic, effect on the child's well-being. The state, therefore, has an urgent, or compelling, interest in providing a forum for those grandparents having such a 'sufficient existing relationship' with their grandchildren."

CASE **9.2** *Troxel v. Granville,* 530 U.S. 57, 120 S. Ct. 2054, 147 L. Ed. 2d 49 (2000)

DISCUSSION OF THE CASE

This decision represents one of the rare instances in which the federal government has intervened in a family law matter traditionally left to regulation by the states. "The opinion marks an evolution in parental autonomy protection. . . . By balancing the State's interest in protecting the child with the parent's interest in making child-rearing decisions free from unnecessary State interference, the Court no longer accords blind unquestioning deference to the decisions of presumptively fit parents."[66] At issue in the case was the state of Washington's third-party visitation statute that provided "Any person may petition the court for visitation rights at any time including but not limited to, custody proceedings." The U.S. Supreme Court

(Continued)

described this language as being "breathtakingly broad." The case involved the two minor daughters of an unmarried couple, Tommie Granville and Brad Troxel, whose relationship ended in 1991. Brad committed suicide in 1993, but before doing so had established a relationship between his daughters and his parents. After the father's death, the mother had not entirely denied the grandparents visitation but wanted to limit it and not permit any overnight visits. The grandparents petitioned to continue their relationship with the children on a more extensive basis than the mother was willing to allow. On the mother's second appeal of a lower court's ruling allowing the visitation, the appeals court reversed the lower court's order on the grounds that the grandparents lacked standing to petition for visitation absent a pending custody action. The Washington Supreme Court reviewed the case at the request of the grandparents. It held that the Troxels did have standing but that visitation should not be ordered over the mother's objection, as such an action would infringe on the mother's fundamental right to parent her children as she sees fit. The grandparents then sought certiorari and the U.S. Supreme Court agreed to hear the case. The Court subsequently held that the statute was unconstitutional as applied to the facts of the case.

In a decision that many say raises as many questions as it answers, the Court at the least held the following:

- Parents have a fundamental liberty interest in the care, custody, and control of their children, which previously has been deemed by the Court to be protected by the Due Process Clause of the Fourteenth Amendment. The Washington statute was held to deprive the mother of this liberty interest without due process of law.
- Given this liberty interest, any decision made by a fit parent should be given "special weight." There was no allegation that the mother in this case was unfit, yet the Washington statute contained no requirement that her decision be given any weight whatsoever.
- Courts should presume that a fit parent will act in his or her child's best interest. The Court did not indicate what kind of evidence is required to overcome this presumption.
- The courts are not free to simply substitute their view of what is in a child's best interest for that of the parent. The Washington statute had placed the best interest determination solely in the hands of the judge rather than the parents.

The lengthy and convoluted opinion in this case can be accessed in its entirety at *www.pearsonhighered/careersresources/* in the companion website material for Chapter 9 of this text under Cases. Note that the nine-justice court was divided four/two/three as to the specifics of the case.

SIDEBAR

Do you think grandparents should be granted visitation when it is against the wishes of the children's parent(s)? Explain your response.

Paralegal **Application 9.6**

Rebutting the Presumption in Grandparent Visitation Cases

The *Troxel* decision is clear about at least two principles: (1) a fit parent's decision denying or limiting visitation to a grandparent is entitled to special weight and (2) there is a rebuttable presumption that their decision is made in the best interests of the child. What remains unclear is what is necessary to rebut the presumption. Lacking further guidance from the U.S. Supreme Court, the states have tended to fall into two camps:

1. ***The permissive camp:*** Grandparents can rebut the presumption by proving that visitation is in the

(Continued)

child's best interests. Title 30 Chapter 5 Section 2 of the Utah code reflects this position. It provides that the court may override the parent's decision and grant the petitioner reasonable rights of visitation if it finds that the petitioner has rebutted the presumption based upon factors such as whether:

(a) the petitioner is a fit and proper person to have visitation with the grandchild;

(b) visitation with the grandchild has been denied or unreasonably limited;

(c) the parent is unfit or incompetent;

(d) the petitioner has acted as the grandchild's custodian or caregiver, or otherwise has had a substantial relationship with the grandchild, and the loss or cessation of that relationship is likely to cause harm to the grandchild;

(e) the petitioner's child, who is a parent of the grandchild, has died, or has become a noncustodial parent through divorce or legal separation;

(f) the petitioner's child, who is a parent of the grandchild, has been missing for an extended period of time; **or**

(g) **visitation is in the best interest of the grandchild.** (Emphasis added.)

New York also falls into this camp. In *Gort v. Kull*, 949 N.Y.S.2d 62 (App. Div. 2012), the appellate court affirmed a Family Court order granting a grandmother visitation to the extent of allowing her to have the visitation time her son, the child's father, did not use. In New York, when a grandparent seeks visitation, the court must make a two-part inquiry: First, it must find standing, based on the death of a parent or equitable circumstances, which permit the court to entertain the petition. If the grandparent establishes the right to be heard, then it must determine if visitation is in the best interests of the child. The appellate court found visitation was in the child's best interests based on the fact the grandmother and the child had an existing meaningful and loving relationship. Animosity between the mother and grandmother was not a sufficient reason to deny visitation.

2. ***The restrictive camp:*** In order to overcome the presumption, the grandparents essentially must show that denial of visitation would cause harm to the child or that, in the extreme, the parent is unfit to make the decision. The detailed Arkansas statute governing visitation rights of grandparents when the child is in the custody of a parent reflects this position (Arkansas Code 9-13-103). To have standing, the grandparent must prove the prior existence of a substantial relationship with the child (such as having lived with or been the child's caretaker for six consecutive months). To rebut the presumption, the grandparent must establish (1) he or she has the capacity to give the child love, affection, and guidance; (2) the loss of the relationship is likely to harm the child; and (3) the grandparent is willing to cooperate with the "custodian" if visitation is allowed. See, e.g., *Bowen v. Bowen*, 2012 Ark. App. 403 (2012), reversing a circuit court's extension of visitation rights to the children's paternal grandparents. The appellate court opined that to overcome a parent's right to uninterrupted custody, a grandparent must show a substantial relationship with the grandchildren without which the children will likely be harmed. Having lunch with the children once a week was insufficient to establish the substantial relationship needed to overcome the father's wishes regarding his children. See also *Blixt v. Blixt*, 437 Mass. 649, 774 N.E.2d 1052 (Mass. 2002).

Sidebar

Which camp are you in and why?

De Facto Parents

The Washington Supreme Court has described *de facto* parentage as "a flexible remedy that compliments legislative enactments when parent-child relationships arise in ways that are not contemplated by any statutory scheme." See *In the Matter of the Custody of B.M.H.: Holt v. Holt*, 179 Wn.2d 224, 2315 P.3d 470 (2013), a case in which the court held that a former stepfather could seek status as a *de facto* parent of his former wife's child based on having undertaken an unequivocal and permanent parental role with the consent of the mother.

In an often quoted passage, the Massachusetts Supreme Judicial Court defined a *de facto* parent in *E.N.O. v. L.M.M.*, 429 Mass. 824 (1999), as "one who has no biological relation to the child, but has participated in the child's life as a member of the child's family. The de facto parent resides with the child and, with the consent and encouragement of the legal parent, performs a share of caretaking functions at least as great as the legal parent. . . . The de facto parent shapes the child's daily routine, addresses his developmental needs, disciplines the child, provides for his education and medical care, and serves as a moral guide."

EXHIBIT 9.5 Kentucky Statute KRS § 403.270 (2006) Pertaining to Custody Issues—Best Interests of Child Shall Determine—Joint Custody Permitted—De Facto Custodian

Courtesy of State of Kentucky

FROM THE STATUTE

(1) (a) As used in this chapter and KRS 405.020, unless the context requires otherwise, "de facto custodian" means a person who has been shown by clear and convincing evidence to have been the primary caregiver for, and financial supporter of, a child who has resided with the person for a period of six (6) months or more if the child is under three (3) years of age and for a period of one (1) year or more if the child is three (3) years or older or has been placed by the Department for Community Based Services. . . .

   (b) A person shall not be a de facto custodian until a court determines by clear and convincing evidence that the person meets the definition of de facto custodian established in paragraph (a) of this subsection. Once a court determines that a person meets the definition of de facto custodian, the court shall give the person the same standing in custody matters that is given to each parent under this section. . . .

When courts address cases involving petitioning parties who lack a legal connection to the children they seek to "parent," many have been heavily influenced by the *de facto* parent test articulated in the landmark Wisconsin decision, *Holtzman v. Knott (In re H.S.H.–K)* 193 Wis.2d 649, 533 N.W.2d 419 (1995), cert. denied, 516 U.S. 976 (1995), the first decision in the history of the United States in which a court recognized a lesbian as the "*de facto* parent" of a child her partner had conceived and delivered during the course of their relationship. The *Holtzman* Court identified four elements a petitioner must prove in order to demonstrate a "parent-like relationship" with a child to establish standing to petition for visitation:

(1) that the biological or adoptive parent consented to, and fostered, the petitioner's formation and establishment of a parent-like relationship with the child;

(2) that the petitioner and the child lived together in the same household;

(3) that the petitioner assumed obligations of parenthood by taking significant responsibility for the child's care, education, and development, including contributing toward the child's support, without expectation of financial compensation; and

(4) that the petitioner has been in a parental role for a length of time sufficient to have established with the child a bonded, dependent relationship parental in nature.

Although a number of states now recognize the doctrine, the effect of being declared a *de facto* parent varies from state to state. For example, in Massachusetts once a party is found to be a *de facto* parent they can seek visitation but

PARALEGAL PRACTICE TIP

Prior to the nationalization of marriage equality in June 2015, same-sex spouses often encountered problematic conflicts in law. For example, when the partners married in a same-sex marriage jurisdiction, they would have whatever rights were afforded to spouses under that state's laws based on their circumstances (as legal parents, stepparents, adoptive parents, etc.). However, that was not the case if the parties later relocated to another jurisdiction that did not recognize same-sex marriage for any purpose. See, for example, *Damon v. York*, 54 Va. App. 544, 680 S.E.2d 354 (2009), in which the parties were legally married in Canada but later moved to Virginia. The Virginia Court of Appeals held that the Canadian marriage was void under the Virginia Marriage Affirmation Act and the "girlfriend" was simply "another presence in the child's life" and not a person with a legitimate custody interest under current Virginia law.

Co-parent

a person who is engaged in a non-marital relationship with the legal parent of a child and who regards himself or herself as a parent rather than as a legal stranger to the child

PARALEGAL PRACTICE TIP

Although it did not find such an agreement actually existed in the case at bar, the Ohio Supreme Court opined in *In re Mullen*, 953 N.E.2d 302 (Ohio 2011), that a co-parent can acquire parenting rights by virtue of an enforceable shared parenting agreement if the agreement constitutes a purposeful relinquishment of some portion of the biological parent's exclusive right to custody, the co-parent is a "proper person" to assume caretaking responsibilities, and the agreement is in the child's best interest.

must convince the court that such visitation will be in the child's best interests and that the child will suffer psychological harm if visitation is not granted. Although no longer a legal stranger to the child, they do not possess the same rights as the parent with legal custody such as the rights to consent to medical treatment or make other important life decisions for the child. In Maine, however, that state's high court has held that "A determination that a person is a de facto parent means that he or she is a parent on equal footing with a biological or adoptive parent, that is to say, with the same opportunity for parental rights and responsibilities. . . . In short, once the court finds that a party is a de facto parent, that party is a parent for all purposes, . . ." *Pitts v. Moore*, 2014 ME 59, 90 A.D.3d 1169 (2014). See also *Carvin v. Britian (In re Parentage of L.B.)*, 155 Wn.2d 679, 122 P.3d 151 (2005), cert. denied 12 S. Ct. 2021 (2006) in which the Washington Supreme Court held that once a party has established standing as a *de facto* parent, both parents have a fundamental liberty interest in the care, custody, and control of their child.

Co-parents

A number of custody and visitation cases brought in the past two decades have involved gay co-parents. A **co-parent** is a person who is engaged in a nonmarital relationship with the legal parent of a child and who regards himself or herself as a parent who should be entitled to full parental rights rather than as a legal stranger to the child. The perception is usually based on a mutual intent to parent a child together, the performance of a variety of caretaking functions, and the provision of some degree of financial support for the child for an extended period of time. As with *de facto* and stepparents, co-parents have relied on a variety of legal constructs in an effort to maintain a relationship with a child they have helped to raise after the relationship with the child's legal parent has terminated.

In a minority of states, including Kansas, Minnesota and Ohio, co-parents are able to establish parenting rights by virtue of shared parenting agreements. See, e.g., *Chapelle v. Mitten*, 607 N.W.2d 151 (Minn. Ct. App. 2000). In *Frazier v. Goudschaal*, 296 Kan. 730, 295 P.3d 542 (2013), two women executed a coparenting agreement providing that one of them would give birth to two children (through the use of assisted reproductive technology) and the other would be deemed a *de facto* parent. The agreement expressly provided that they would equally share parental rights and responsibilities. When their relationship ended, the nonbiological co-parent sought rights under the agreement and the biological mother claimed the agreement was unenforceable. The Kansas Supreme Court held that a parent who has a constitutional right to make the decisions regarding the care, custody, and control of his or her children, free of government interference, has the right to enter into an enforceable coparenting agreement to share custody with another as long as the agreement is in the best interests of the children. "[P]arental preference can be waived and the courts should not be required to assign to a mother any more rights than that mother has claimed for herself. . . . Denying the children of a same-sex couple an opportunity to have two parents, the same as children of a traditional marriage, impinges upon the children's constitutional rights. The Equal Protection Clause of the Fourteenth Amendment to the United States Constitution requires that all children—both legitimate and illegitimate—be afforded equal treatment under the law."

Decisions involving *de facto* parents and co-parents continue to be mixed particularly those involving unmarried same-sex co-parents. Some states deny petitioners "parental" status but afford them third-party standing similar to grandparents and stepparents who bear a significant relationship to the child. Other courts claim that recognizing co-parents' rights in the absence of statute, precedent, or well-established legal principle constitutes judicial lawmaking that denigrates fundamental parental rights and infringes on the province of the legislature. This area of the law clearly will continue to evolve as the full impact of marriage equality and increased recognition of the rights of same-sex partners is realized.

Who Speaks for The Child in Custody Matters?

THE GUARDIAN *AD LITEM*

When minor children are involved in a legal matter, the law generally presumes that their interests will be represented by their parents, guardians, or others acting *in loco parentis* (Latin: in the place of a parent) on their behalf. Until children have the knowledge and maturity to act on their own, parents act and speak for them in virtually all contexts.[67] In custody cases, however, parents are often so wrapped up in their own concerns that they lose sight of their children's interests. Historically, those interests have most often been communicated to the courts through guardians *ad litem* (GALs). However, there is little agreement or uniformity among the states regarding GALs particularly with respect to when they should be appointed and what functions they should serve.[68]

- Some states mandate if and when GALs are to be appointed and others leave the matter to the court's discretion. Some states such as Wisconsin mandate that GALs be appointed in all custody disputes (Wisconsin Statute 767.045). Under federal law, GALs must be appointed in abuse and neglect cases.
- Some states, such as Minnesota, have codified basic guidelines for GALs and others provide guidelines on a case-by-case basis (*www.revisor.mn.gov*, Retrieve by number Minn. Stat. § 518.165).
- Some states require that GALs be attorneys and others permit individuals such as licensed social workers, psychologists, or, in some instances, trained volunteers to serve depending on the nature of the case.
- Some states specify by statute or rule the nature of the GAL's role and others do not. Depending on the state, a GAL may function, for example, as an expert witness, investigator, advocate, court advisor, or mediator.
- Although it triggers potential ethical and other issues, some states permit GALs to perform hybrid roles. For example, driven in part by practical concerns about costs, Wyoming endorses a blend of responsibilities as GAL and attorney for the child. Pennsylvania requires courts to appoint attorneys as GALs to present the best interests of the child in child welfare cases. If the GAL believes the child has sufficient capacity, the guardian must advocate the child's position as well as his or her own position as guardian

PARALEGAL PRACTICE TIP

To see an example of an Order Appointing Guardian Ad Litem on Behalf of Minor in the state of Washington, visit *www.courts. wa.gov/forms*. Browse Forms by Category/Parenting Plan/Residential Schedule/Guardian *ad litem* Form WPF PS 10B.0850.

(42 PA. CONS. STAT. §6311). The state of Maine also specifically requires the GAL to report the child's wishes to the court. (ME. REV. STAT. ANN. Tit. 22 §4005 (1)) Montana on the other hand rejects the hybrid role.[69] Notwithstanding variations among the states, it is generally agreed that a guardian *ad litem* (GAL) serves as a neutral evaluator appointed by a judge (often at the request of one or both of the parents) to investigate, report, and make recommendations to the court regarding the interests of a child. (See Exhibit 9.6.) GALs are appointed in a variety of kinds of cases involving children in which the courts consider among other issues:

- a child's best interests in a custody and visitation dispute
- the advantages and disadvantages of removing/relocating a child from one state or geographical location to another
- the changes in circumstances that might warrant modification of an existing custodial arrangement
- the existence of a *de facto* parent–child relationship
- parental fitness as related to termination of parental rights or guardianship
- the paternity of a minor child
- whether or not a social worker or psychotherapist privilege should be waived in cases where the child is incompetent to exercise or waive the privilege
- voluntariness of a minor parent's surrender of parental rights/consent to an adoption
- abuse and neglect
- delinquency
- judicial consents for abortion

PARALEGAL PRACTICE TIP

To see an example of an Order for Appointment of a Best Interest Attorney, go to *www.md.courts.gov*. Search for Order (Best Interest Attorney) (Maryland).

EXHIBIT 9.6 Motion to Appoint a Guardian *ad litem* to Investigate and Report

---

COMMONWEALTH OF MASSACHUSETTS

PROBATE AND FAMILY COURT

ESSEX, SS.   DOCKET NO. ES14D1137DR

KENDRA RIDEMOORE,)

Plaintiff)

)

) MOTION TO APPOINT A

v.) GUARDIAN *AD LITEM*

) TO INVESTIGATE AND

DONALD RIDEMOORE,) REPORT UNDER

Defendant) M.G.L. C. 215 § 56a

)

Now comes the plaintiff, Kendra Ridemoore, and hereby moves that the court appoint a Guardian *ad litem* to investigate and report pursuant to M.G.L. c. 215 § 56A and gives as reasons the following:

1. There is pending before this Court a Complaint for Divorce filed by the plaintiff on April 1, 2014.

EXHIBIT 9.6 *(Continued)*

2. The parties have two minor children: George Ridemoore, born 2/27/2009 and Clancy Ridemoore, born 1/12/2011.
3. On July 5, 2014, the plaintiff filed a report with the Department of Children and Families.
4. On or about July 15, 2014, the Department of Children and Families supported a finding of neglect of the minor children while in the care of the defendant.
5. The plaintiff filed a motion for temporary orders on July 15, 2014, seeking custody and supervised visitation of the parties' two minor children.
6. The parties are unable to agree as to the care, custody and maintenance of the minor children, and the issues related thereto are likely to be submitted to the court for final resolution as provided for under M.G.L. c. 208 § 28.
7. It is in the best interests of the minor children that a guardian *ad litem* be appointed to investigate and report to the court on the issues relating to custody, care and maintenance of the minor children, and specifically on the respective home environments of the parties, schooling, primary care, custody, visitation, medical care, and emotional and moral development of the children.

WHEREFORE, the plaintiff moves that this court appoint a guardian *ad litem* to investigate and report pursuant to M.G.L. c. 215 §56a.

RESPECTFULLY SUBMITTED
FOR KENDRA RIDEMOORE
BY HER ATTORNEY
Robert G. Wilson, III
10 Barristers Hall
Amesbury, MA 01913

978-388-0147
BBO No. 554127

Date: _____

Except as otherwise ordered or provided by statute, when investigating facts affecting a child in a custody case in order to report to the court, the GAL is acting to "assist the court in carrying out its duty" and usually is not functioning in the traditional manner of an attorney advocating the wishes of a client with a single-minded duty solely to that client.[70] The primary role of the GAL is to objectively examine the child's situation as fully as possible, with special attention to the nature and quality of the child's relationship with each parent. At a minimum, the GAL usually will visit the parties' homes and interview each of the parents, the children, and any other individuals who may be able to contribute helpful information, such as schoolteachers, counselors, neighbors, or members of the clergy. The court may assign or approve additional responsibilities for a GAL as well. For example, a Wisconsin court approved a provision in a marital settlement agreement (later rejected by the mother) that a GAL and a family counselor would have the right to break any impasse between the parties regarding decisions pertaining to their son's schooling.[71] In a Massachusetts case, a trial court judge provided in the parties' judgment of divorce that, in the event of a dispute concerning whether or not a particular religious belief or practice is harmful to the children, a GAL named by the court would be retained at the expense of the parties to investigate and evaluate the dispute.[72]

EXHIBIT 9.7 Scope and Content of a Guardian *ad litem*'s Investigation and Report

Based on the Massachusetts Standards for GAL/Investigators

Some states provide little guidance to GALs. Others provide specific standards with respect to how they are appointed and paid, the nature of their investigation and report, their ethical obligations, and their role in discovery and at trial. Typically, the GAL's investigation and report will address the following:

A. The Parents
- parenting tasks performed by each parent and who has been the primary caretaker
- history with respect to any third party caretakers
- any history of physical, sexual or emotional abuse of the child
- any history of parental substance abuse, mental or physical illness
- each parent's past and present parenting skills and deficits including parenting techniques and disciplinary practices
- nature, strength and quality of each parent's relationship with the child
- ability of each parent to promote and support appropriate social, emotional and educational development and provide a stable home environment for the child
- past history of joint decision-making and each parent's ability to support the child's relationship with the other parent and to communicate and cooperate with the other parent regarding the children
- presence of new relationships, partners, or their children
- relationships with significant caretakers, grandparents, relatives, child care providers
- education and employment history of each parent
- any relevant, ethnic, cultural, religion, and lifestyle issues

B. The Child
- the child's basic developmental history
- the child's functioning in school
- the child's activities and any scheduling issues
- special needs of the child: medical, learning, or developmental problems
- assessment of child's relationships with siblings/stepsiblings, peers, community, and extended family
- child's temperament and response to transitions
- child's concerns about a parent's needs, wishes, safety or problems
- Relevant concerns raised in the case by each parent including facts related to how each parent's proposed parenting plan serves or conflicts with the child's best interests

The GAL will present the court with a written report as to the needs of the child, the strengths and weaknesses of each party as a parent, and, if requested by the court, a recommendation with respect to the course of action most likely to serve the best interests of the child as well as any supportive services that may be warranted. The court considers, but is not necessarily bound by, the GAL's report, and the parties may cross-examine the GAL on issues related to the report and the basis for the recommendations made. The cost of the GAL is usually fully paid or heavily subsidized by one or both of the parties. However, the GAL is not intended to represent the interests of either of the parties, nor (in most cases) is the GAL technically an advocate for the child unless so designated by the state and/or the court. Some regard this as a flaw in the process and believe that in especially complex cases, involving parental manipulation, concealing of information, or allegations of abuse or parental unfitness, an attorney should be appointed to represent the child. The "child ought to be a player and not the football."[73]

ADDITIONAL RESOURCES

Because of the complexity of custody decisions, the courts may look to multiple resources for guidance over and above the GAL. Customarily, when custody is at issue on a contested or uncontested basis, the parties will be required to meet with a representative of a family services division located at the courthouse. Family service personnel are usually not attorneys, but they generally are individuals with strong backgrounds in social work and developmental psychology who are trained in working through the maze created by disputing adults to come up with custody recommendations for the court. Although their recommendations are not binding, they are usually accorded considerable respect by judges.

Another important resource for children and the courts in every state is the **CASA Program**. CASA (Court Appointed Special Advocates) is an organization that trains court-appointed volunteer advocates to work one on one with abused and endangered children. Much like GALs, CASA volunteers gather information in child abuse and neglect cases, assess each child's situation, and make objective recommendations to the court concerning the environment that will best ensure a particular child's safety and well-being.

The judge may also hear testimony from expert witnesses called by the parties on a variety of topics. In some states, the court may designate a neutral court-appointed psychologist essentially a clinical GAL (sometimes called a "custody evaluator" or "custody investigator"). The court will order that the parties and children cooperate with that individual by participating in interviews, producing relevant documents and records, and potentially submitting to psychological testing if deemed warranted. The parties must each waive their confidentiality rights in this context, thereby allowing the psychologist to reveal and discuss information that might otherwise be privileged.

CASA Program
a national program that trains court-appointed volunteer advocates to work one on one with abused and endangered children; CASA volunteers provide objective recommendations to the court concerning the environment that will best ensure a particular child's safety and well-being. Although CASA has nearly 1,000 programs across the country and a presence in every state, it is not an available resource in every county.

PARALEGAL PRACTICE TIP

For information on CASA Programs across the country, visit *www .casaforchildren.org*.

What is The Paralegal's Role in a Custody Case?

The tasks a paralegal may perform in a child custody case typically include the following:

- researching the law governing custody actions in the jurisdiction
- preparing related memoranda based on research as requested
- gathering information and documentation essential to successful negotiation and resolution of custody cases (See Paralegal Application 9.7.)
- scheduling and participating in interviews as assigned
- drafting correspondence, complaints/petitions, supporting affidavits, and proposed orders or responsive pleadings to complaints/petitions involving custody matters
- drafting discovery materials such as interrogatories, requests for admissions, and questions for depositions
- drafting parenting plans/child custody provisions for inclusion in agreements (See Exhibit B in the Sample Separation Agreement in Chapter 13.)

- assisting with preparation for temporary hearings or trials on the merits, including drafting pretrial memoranda for review and preparing subpoenas for potential witnesses if needed
- helping to prepare witnesses under the supervision of the attorney
- tracking progress on the case to be certain timelines are met
- coordinating communication with the GAL, CASA volunteer, etc.
- making sure the client is kept informed of progress and upcoming deadlines, hearings, discovery matters, etc.

Paralegal **Application 9.7**

Information Gathering in a Contested Custody Case

Contested custody cases are fact-intensive, and considerable information needs to be obtained about the relationship of the child or children with *each* of the parents. While the court may be gathering information through the use of a court-appointed psychologist, GAL, or other resources, the members of the family law team conduct their own information gathering effort on behalf of the client. This is accomplished through client interviews and questionnaires; traditional discovery vehicles such as interrogatories, depositions, and examination of documents and audiovisual materials; and interviews with individuals familiar with the child and the parents. The paralegal often plays a key role in this process exploring topics and issues such as the following:

- The various caretaking functions performed by each parent need to be identified. Which parent has been primarily responsible for meeting the child's daily needs?
- Although clients are not always cooperative with the effort, the parenting strengths and weaknesses of each party need to be identified.
- Does either of the parents have any special problems or limitations that may interfere with his or her capacity to parent effectively? For example, does either parent have a mental health or substance abuse problem?
- The client's motivation for seeking custody needs to be assessed. Is it realistic? Is it based on revenge, a need to prove oneself, or some other unhealthy motive?
- Descriptions of the children need to be provided. What are they like? What are their favorite and least favorite activities? How are they doing in

school? What are their parental preferences, if known?

- Any special needs, medical issues, or behavior problems of a child need to be identified, along with an explanation of how they are being handled and by whom.
- It is useful to know if there are any major areas of disagreement between the parents with respect to the raising of the children, such as disciplinary measures, religious practices, or activities the children should be allowed to engage in.
- If there are siblings, step- or otherwise, the relationships between the child and those individuals should be explored.
- The nature of the relationship each parent has with the child needs to be described.
- In addition to basic parenting activities, what kinds of activities does each parent participate in with the child?
- Questions should be asked about the child's friendships, role models, and involvement in community activities and organizations.
- It is important to know whether either parent has intentions to remarry or reside with another romantic partner (of either gender) and whether there will be any additional children in that parent's home.
- If the parties have not already established new "permanent" residences, does either parent plan to relocate in the near future and, if so, how far away? The potential impact of any relocation on proposed custody plans needs to be considered.
- The work schedules and relative availability of the parents need to be determined. Does either party's job require him or her to travel or be called out on

emergencies at irregular hours? Will child care need to be provided by a third party when the child is with either parent? Does either party have a support system, such as parents, grandparents, friends, or neighbors?

- Potential witnesses should be identified, including friends and relatives but more importantly, teachers, neighbors, childcare providers, coaches, medical professionals, clergy, probation officers, mental health professionals, etc. Issues of privileged

communications may be raised, depending on the type of professional.

- Available documents should be identified and copies gathered, such as photos, videos, written reports of professionals, correspondence relevant to parental fitness and cooperation (attempts to visit, etc.), and materials produced by the child (with the child's knowledge and consent), such as e-mails, letters, creative work, and journals.

CHAPTER **SUMMARY**

Although children are no longer deemed the "property" of either parent, this is not always apparent in contested custody battles in which parents duel with each other over their respective rights to physical custody and decision-making authority. In most cases, the parents themselves are able, with or without the assistance of counsel or mediators, to arrive at agreed-upon custodial arrangements and parenting plans. When they cannot, the courts are left to deal with the agonizing task of allocating responsibility between two parents each of whom likely has parental strengths and weaknesses. The relative fitness of parents usually turns on the extent to which either parent has been the primary caretaker and whether or not either parent has engaged in conduct that would negatively affect the welfare of the child.

The controlling consideration in a child custody case, be it an initial award or a modification, is the child's best interests. How will living with one parent and/or the other impact all aspects of the child's life: physical, psychological, cognitive, emotional, spiritual, familial, educational, and recreational? In order to make that decision, the court must examine and assess each parent's "fitness," character, parenting skills, and bond with the child. The assessment is guided by state statutes and case law identifying factors to be considered and the overall measuring stick to be used (best interests, primary caretaker, etc.). The court considers the weight of the evidence, the credibility of witnesses, and the recommendations of experts, GALs, and other resources. Each case must be decided on its own facts and the totality of the circumstances as perceived and interpreted by individual judges.

The consideration and weighing of the factors in a custody dispute is essentially factual. . . .

Cases with very similar facts may be decided in divergent ways by courts of different states, and even by courts within the same state. The differing results often come from the hearts and emotions of judges, rather than from the facts of the case.[74]

In this chapter, the focus has primarily been on custody decisions in the context of divorce. However, attention has also been given to the rights of the increasing numbers of third parties who have undertaken committed and responsible roles in children's lives with particular attention to stepparents, grandparents, *de facto* parents, and co-parents. It is reasonable to anticipate that in our rapidly evolving society with its multiplicity of "family" models, state courts and legislatures will continue to explore creative ways of extending custodial and visitation rights to these "third parties." There is a fear among advocates of family autonomy that in doing so, they will "open the door to virtually unfathomable exercises of judicial discretion, all in derogation of the constitutionally protected interests of natural parents with respect to their children."[75]

We have treated child custody in this chapter as if it were a discrete topic, but it is important to keep in mind the extent to which it is intertwined with other areas, such as support and tax issues; property division and who remains in the marital home, if anyone; conflict of law when multiple states are involved; paternity questions; gay rights issues; adoption; reproductive technology; domestic violence, abuse, and neglect; and constitutional rights of children and parents.

CONCEPT REVIEW AND REINFORCEMENT

KEY TERMS

ALI Approximation Rule	Joint award	Primary caretaker
Best interests of the child	Judicial notice	Psychological parent
CASA Program	Lay witness	Separation agreement
Co-parent	Legal custody	Significant connection jurisdiction
Custodial parent	Maternal preference	Sole award
De facto parent	Noncustodial parent	Split custody
Equitable parenthood	*Parens patriae* doctrine	Standing
Forum *non conveniens*	Parental alienation syndrome	Temporary/emergency
Forum shopping	Parent by estoppel	jurisdiction
Guardian *ad litem*	Parenting plan	Tender years doctrine
Home state jurisdiction	Paternal preference	Vacuum/last resort jurisdiction
In camera	*Per se* rule	Virtual visitation
In loco parentis	Physical custody	Visitation

REVIEW QUESTIONS

1. Identify the various types of custody and describe the two most common kinds of custodial awards.
2. Identify the primary purposes of the UCCJEA and the PKPA and describe their bases for jurisdiction.
3. Identify the major purpose of the Hague Convention in custody cases.
4. Describe how standards for making custody awards have evolved.
5. Describe the best interest standard and give examples of factors considered by the courts in applying it.
6. Explain what a "gender-neutral standard" is in the context of custody decisions. Do you believe that custody decisions are, in fact, gender-neutral? Why or why not?
7. Describe the primary caretaker presumption and explain how the courts determine the identity of a child's primary caretaker.
8. Identify the majority position with respect to each of the following in the making of custodial decisions: availability, stability, gender, race, religion, parental health/disability, sexual orientation and conduct, parental lifestyle, child preference, and a history of abuse.

9. Define visitation (supervised and unsupervised) and describe a common schedule, including a suggested virtual visitation component.
10. Describe the nature and purpose of a parenting plan.
11. Describe the nature and purposes of a parent education program.
12. Describe the circumstances under which a modification in custody is likely to be sought and granted.
13. Identify the important interests that must be balanced in relocation disputes.
14. Describe the two-part inquiry the court engages in when third parties such as stepparents, grandparents, *de facto* parents, and co-parents seek custody or visitation rights.
15. Explain what a guardian *ad litem* (GAL) is. What role do GALs play in custody cases? What other kinds of individuals may advocate for the child in a custody dispute?
16. Describe the potential role of the paralegal in a custody case.

DEVELOPING YOUR PARALEGAL SKILLS

FOCUS ON THE JOB

This activity requires the student to assess the relative strengths and weaknesses of the custody claims of two unmarried parents and to draft a recommended parenting plan.

The Facts

Miguel Rodriguez and Christina Acevedo are the unmarried parents of a daughter, named Melody, who was born on

September 4, 2010, and a son, Paco, born on November 26, 2013. Miguel voluntarily acknowledged paternity of each child at birth. The parties lived together for a four-year period from 2010 to 2014, at which time they separated, largely due to arguments over Christina's drug use and Miguel's suspicion that she was abusing their daughter. The daughter had experienced a series of unexplained broken bones and bruises, and on one occasion, the emergency room physician filed a report with the state's Social Services Agency responsible for investigating complaints of suspected abuse. An investigation was conducted, but no conclusive finding was issued. The case has remained open, but no complaints have been filed for eighteen months since Christina completed a recommended parenting-skills course.

Christina has lived with her parents, Diana and Ramon Acevedo, on and off since she and Miguel separated. She recently moved out of their home because she had grown tired of their constant preaching to her about what an evil person they think she is. They are deeply religious and have been trying to "heal" and "save" their daughter from the life she has been living. They also want to "save" the children who they believe are the fruit of immoral unions. They are quite wealthy and have a large farmhouse in the country with animals, including horses and rabbits. There is also a swimming pool, a pond for skating in the winter, and an extensive exercise/play gym on the property. Christina has taken the children to visit her parents on several occasions (accompanied by Miguel as a "supervisor"), and the children have enjoyed participating in all the activities available at the farm. They like going there as long as their grandparents do not lecture them about "sin and all that stuff." Neither Miguel nor Christina wants to allow the grandparents to visit with the children without one of them being present.

Christina has had a series of jobs over the past few years but until recently has rarely managed to keep one for more than three months at a time. She has been waitressing at a local restaurant and playing the organ in a nearby church, where she has become a regular member. She is also volunteering at a shelter for abused women and children. Although she had participated in a number of treatment programs, she was still drinking heavily and using cocaine and heroin on a regular basis until about a year ago, when she seemed to get her act together. Shortly thereafter she was diagnosed HIV-positive but she shows no signs of full-blown AIDS. She continues to smoke cigarettes but is trying to give them up.

Miguel works full time as a conductor on a commuter train. His regular shift is Wednesday through Sunday each week, ten hours a day. He recently married a woman who is a native of Uruguay. He met her when he began taking courses at a local community college where she was enrolled in an English-as-a-second-language program. She hopes eventually to master English and become a nurse. In the meantime, she is working as an aide in a local nursing home Monday through Friday 11 pm to 7 am.

When Miguel and Christina split up, Miguel took the children with him and refused to let Christina visit them for the first two years. She went to court and, over Miguel's objection, obtained an order granting her supervised visitation at the local shelter where she is now volunteering. Her lawyer has told her that he is reasonably confident she will be able to successfully pursue primary custody of the children, now that her life has changed dramatically. The staff at the shelter say she is a very attentive and sensitive parent.

The children have been doing well living with Miguel and his wife, Remigia. They have no health problems, with the exception of Melody's asthma, which is reasonably well controlled with medication and inhalers. Melody says that she would like to live with her mother because she can talk with her, as she understands English. She also feels sorry for her because "everyone has been so mean to her." Paco does not seem to have bonded with his mother and appears largely indifferent toward her. He adores his dad and follows him around like a shadow. Miguel is close to and very involved with both children. He enjoys taking care of and playing with them. He especially likes teaching them new games and skills.

The Assignment

Assume that Miguel and Christina are in agreement that they should share the responsibility of making major decisions affecting the children. However, they cannot agree on which parent the children should live with and each is seeking physical/residential custody of both Melody and Paco. Miguel does not want Christina to have anything more than supervised visitation, given her history. Christina doesn't want Miguel to have visitation because she believes he will take the children away from her, as he did when they split up. You are working for the judge who is hearing this case, Judge Solomon Stevens.

a. Assuming evidence has been presented at trial on all of the above topics, outline in a memorandum to the judge the relative strengths and weaknesses of each of the parties' positions based on prevailing governing law in your state.

b. Draft a recommended parenting plan tailored to this case in a format used in your state.

Courts in many states provide parenting-plan forms online. As a default, you may use the Permanent Parenting Plan Order form available online for use in the state of Tennessee or the Wisconsin Proposed Parenting Plan format.

FOCUS ON ETHICS

In this activity, the student is required to consider the ethical issues raised when a client tells a paralegal that she intends to remove her child from the country and the paralegal shares this information with her parents.

The Assignment

Assume that you are a paralegal in the law office of Attorney Sofia Hidalgo, who is representing Christina Acevedo in the above comprehensive fact pattern. While you were interviewing Christina recently about her parenting skills at your supervisor's request, she shared with you that she is quite certain that the court will not grant her custody of her two children. She says the only way she will ever be able to be with them is to take them to Canada, where her older sister and her husband live. They would welcome them and be able to provide for both Christina and the children. She believes she could do this at the time of one of her visits with the children, as supervision has become very informal. This conversation is troubling you, and over dinner, you tell your parents about what she said. Your father says he doesn't blame you for being concerned and that you should go to the police about this woman, who must be mentally unstable and a danger to the children if she would even think of doing such a thing. Your mother says she thinks you should keep your reservations to yourself and just do your job. Analyze this situation, applying the ethical canons for paralegals promulgated by the National Association of Legal Assistants contained in Appendix A and the ethics material in Chapter 1 of this text. Include in your analysis a description of what, if anything, you plan to do about this situation.

FOCUS ON CASE LAW

In this activity the student reviews two cases to learn more about international custody disputes and the role played by the Hague Convention.

The Assignment

Read the opinions in the two cases below and then respond to the questions that follow. Both opinions can be accessed at *www.pearsonhighered.com/careersresources/* on the companion website for this text in the material related to Chapter 9 under Cases. Your instructor may ask you to answer the questions orally in class or in a one- to three-page paper.

- *Blanc v. Morgan*, 721 F. Supp. 2d 749 (2010)
- *Castillo v. Castillo*, 597 F. Supp. 2d 432 (2009)

1. Briefly summarize the facts and the holding in *Blanc v. Morgan*.
2. Briefly describe the facts and the holding in *Castillo v. Castillo*.
3. The courts reached opposite results in these two cases. Describe those results and the courts' reasoning in each case.

FOCUS ON STATE LAW AND PROCEDURE

In this activity, the student assesses the claim of maternal grandparents seeking visitation with their grandchildren against the wishes of both of the children's parents.

The Assignment

Assume that you are a paralegal working in the law firm of Wilson and Tauson, LLP, and your supervisor is Attorney Tauson. Your firm represents Ramon and Diana Acevedo in the comprehensive Focus on the Job fact pattern above. They are seeking visitation with their grandchildren, Melody and Paco, against the wishes of the children's parents, Miguel and Christina. Your supervisor has asked you to research the law governing grandparent visitation in your jurisdiction and assess the likelihood of the Acevedos' prevailing given the facts of their case. Present your findings in an internal memorandum and include your conclusion with respect to the clients' prospects, given the facts and the governing law. Use the following format unless directed otherwise by your instructor.

Memorandum

TO: *Your supervisor*

FROM: *Your name and title*

RE: *Assessment of Diana and Ramon Acevedo's Petition for Grandparent Visitation*

DATE: *The date your assignment is due*

Brief description of the assignment: *What is it that you have been asked to do?*

Brief description of the facts: *Describe the basic facts of the case.*

Basic description of the governing law: *Describe the applicable governing law in your state (statute(s)/case law) based on your research.*

Discussion: *Apply the governing law to the facts of this case.*

Conclusion: *What is your opinion (expressed in a one- or two-sentence conclusion) about the prospects of the grandparents being granted visitation?*

FOCUS ON **TECHNOLOGY**

In addition to the links provided throughout the chapter, this activity provides a series of useful websites for reference, along with technology-related assignments for completion.

Websites of Interest

www.americanbar.org

This is the website for the American Bar Association. Of particular relevance to this chapter are "Family Law in the Fifty States Tables" Chart 2 on custody criteria and Chart 6 on third-party visitation.

www.childcustody.org

This site contains information about child custody organizations nationwide with links to state codes, topic- or state-specific discussion forums, and "friendly" websites.

www.courts.state.nh.us

Family-law-related forms for New Hampshire are available at this website, including a parenting plan.

www.dadsdivorce.com

This site has the flavor of a support system and contains a variety of tools and guides useful to those involved in custody disputes, including a newsletter and links to divorce laws by state.

www.deltabravo.net

This is the site of the Separated Parenting Access and Resource Center (SPARC). The stated goal of this site is to ensure that children of divorce have access to both parents—regardless of marital status. It offers links to a rich variety of resources, including an online parenting plan generator.

www.divorceinfo.com

This site is offered by a rather upbeat divorce attorney/mediator who limits his work to people who want a divorce and are prepared to interact reasonably. The site offers guidance and tools to minimize difficulty and stress. It also includes links to state-specific information.

www.divorcenet.com

This site is similar to *dadsdivorce.com* but is broader in scope. It contains information on all aspects of divorce. It also provides a guide to finding resources and professional support by geographical area. Specific attention is given to the impact on divorce procedures of being in the military.

www.findlaw.com

This site provides links to the child custody laws of all states and the District of Columbia. Some of the links include forms. Findlaw also provides some judicial opinions, particularly U.S. Supreme Court decisions and a selection of opinions from courts in California, Texas, New York, and Florida.

www.internetvisitation.org

The purpose of this site is to educate and provide information on virtual visitation and to promote and track related legislation. It provides access to helpful articles and other resources on this topic.

www.custodyxchange.com

This is the site of the Custody X Change, a resource for joint custody software.

Assignments

1. Assume that the mother in this chapter's Focus on the Job fact pattern is willing to agree at this point to virtual visitation between the grandparents and the children. Draft a provision for inclusion in an agreement between the parties that addresses this topic. *www.internetvisitation.org* may be a useful resource when completing this assignment.

2. Locate three websites providing support to fathers seeking custody of their minor children. In a brief report, describe the kinds of information available at each site.

3. Go to the following website for the Oregon Judicial Department: *www.ojd.state.or.us*. Select the Parenting Plan Information link. Access and review the Basic Parenting Plan Packet for Parents containing

information about parenting plans and the Oregon Parenting Plan Form and Instructions. Complete the form as if your client is Christina in the Focus on the Job fact pattern.

4. Working with another student in your class, locate the Permanent Parenting Plan Order Form for the State of Tennessee (available online). Each student should independently complete the form, with one student representing Miguel and the other representing Christina in the comprehensive fact pattern above. After completing the form, each student should meet with his or her partner and identify any differences between the two proposed plans. The students should then negotiate a resolution to the differences. If the differences cannot be resolved, solicit the assistance of another classmate to function as a "mediator" (albeit untrained!).

5. Locate the CASA Program contact in your jurisdiction.

6. Locate the most current information in your state regarding parent education programs. Is participation required? Do minor children have to attend a program? Where is the nearest/most accessible program for divorcing parents in the town where you live? Is there an online program option?

7. Locate the statutes addressing virtual visitation in the states of Utah and Wisconsin.

PORTFOLIO PRODUCTS

1. Parenting Plan
2. Analysis involving application of ethical canons to a hypothetical situation
3. Memorandum on the merits of a custody claim
4. Paper on two Hague Convention custody cases
5. Memorandum assessing a petition for grandparents' visitation

chapter 10
CHILD SUPPORT

© Jupiterimages/Getty Images

> William and Betty married three years ago after having had three daughters together. An accountant for ten years, William now has "found himself," quit his job, and decided to head to Africa to be a missionary. He says God will provide for Betty and the girls, since he will not be able to, and, besides, if he won't be seeing them, why should he have to pay child support?

LEARNING OBJECTIVES

After reading this chapter and completing related assignments, you should be able to:

- explain what child support is and when, how, and to whom it is awarded

- distinguish between child support and spousal support

- list primary initiatives the federal government has undertaken in the area of child support

- identify major jurisdictional issues that arise in child support cases

- explain what child support guidelines are and how they are applied

- list factors courts consider when establishing child support orders

- explain when and how a child support order can be modified

- list ways of enforcing child support orders

- identify the primary tax implications of child support

- identify the kinds of tasks paralegals perform in child support cases

Introduction

This chapter begins by looking at the duty of child support: when it arises, who has it, how long it lasts, and how it differs from the duty of spousal support. The basics of establishing, modifying and enforcing child support awards are reviewed with particular attention to the nature and role of child support guidelines. Related jurisdictional issues and variations among the states are highlighted. Attention is also given to the prominent role played by the federal government in shaping contemporary child support policies and practices.

Child support refers to a parent's legal obligation to contribute to the economic maintenance of his or her child. It is usually in the form of a payment made by a **noncustodial parent** to a **custodial parent** for the benefit of a minor child for whom the parent is deemed legally responsible, including, for example, biological and adopted children. Historically, mothers were awarded custody of children, and child support was deemed to be the father's moral obligation— sometimes enforced under the **doctrine of "necessaries."** The duty of support was eventually codified as a legal duty, and willful nonsupport was made a crime in all states. Today, the duty is imposed on all legal parents regardless of their gender.

Child support
a parent's legal obligation to contribute to the economic maintenance of a child; the payments made by a parent to meet his or her obligation to contribute to the economic maintenance of a child until the age of majority or emancipation or some other time or circumstance set by a court

Noncustodial parent
a parent who does not have sole or primary physical custody of a child but who is still a legal parent with enforceable rights and responsibilities

Custodial parent
the parent with whom the child primarily resides; the parent who has the right to have the child live with him or her

Doctrine of necessaries
under common law, a husband's duty to pay debts incurred by his wife or children for "necessaries" indispensable to living, such as food, shelter, and clothing

PARALEGAL PRACTICE TIP

To see an example of a Complaint for Support used in Massachusetts, go to *www.mass.gov*. Search under Forms by title.

PARALEGAL PRACTICE TIP

Although the noncustodial parent is customarily the payor of child support, in some circumstances the argument is made that the custodial parent should be the payor when the other parent has custody of the child a significant portion of the time and is on the short end of a major disparity in income and assets. See, e.g., *Colonna v. Colonna*, 581 Pa. 1, 855 A.2d 648 (2004).

PARALEGAL PRACTICE TIP

For examples of cases in which sperm donors have been held liable for child support see, e.g., *Mintz v. Zoernig*, 145 N.M. 362, 198 P.3d 861 (N.M. App. 2008) and the highly publicized Kansas case of *State v. W.M.*, Shawnee District Court Case, No. 12D 2686 (2014).

IN WHAT CONTEXTS DO CHILD SUPPORT ISSUES ARISE?

Child support issues arise in several contexts. Temporary and permanent child support are commonly sought in divorce or separate support actions. Support is also frequently an issue in care and protection proceedings, in cases in which a child is institutionalized or under guardianship, and in paternity and other actions to establish legal parentage of a child. When child support is ordered, subsequent modifications may be sought. Single or multiple states, even nations, and state, federal and tribal law may be involved.

Temporary Child Support

Temporary child support is designed to provide for children while an underlying action is pending. Temporary orders are usually issued after brief hearings with limited testimony. The court will customarily review the parties' financial affidavits, their child support guidelines worksheets (which may differ from each other), the pleadings, and any supporting affidavits. In some jurisdictions, courts will issue temporary orders without a hearing based on the documents submitted. Requests for temporary child support orders must be taken seriously, as they often lay the groundwork and set a precedent for permanent orders.

"Permanent" Child Support

In a contested case, a trial on the merits of a support issue is considerably more in-depth than a hearing on temporary orders. Counsel usually will address issues such as the reasons for any proposed deviation from the guidelines, unique needs of the children, and potential tax consequences related to the child support order. The case will be decided on the basis of the sworn testimony of the parties and witnesses (sometimes including experts), along with exhibits such as financial affidavits and documentation of expenses, work history, needs of the children, and standard of living. Although often called "permanent" orders, the characterization really is not accurate as child support orders remain subject to the continuing jurisdiction of the court and may be modified or terminated in a variety of circumstances.

WHO HAS A DUTY TO PAY CHILD SUPPORT AND WHO HAS A RIGHT TO RECEIVE IT?

In an era in which the concept of "family" is evolving and scientific technology is expanding, the answer to the question of who has a duty of child support is becoming increasingly complex. For example, in *Okoli v. Okoli*, 81 Mass. App. Ct. 381, 963 N.E.2d 730 (Mass. App. Ct. 2012), the appellate court affirmed a divorce judgment in which a man was held to be the father of twins conceived through artificial insemination and was ordered to pay child support. The court found that he had voluntarily consented to the procedure even though he claimed not to have read the consent form and his former wife pressured him to sign it by threatening to withdraw support for his visa application. Donors who have provided sperm to lesbian couples seeking to have a child have been held liable for child support in some circumstances. A stepparent may perform the role of a parent even if he or she has not formally adopted a child. However, the majority rule is that the stepparent will not have a legal duty to support the child absent an agreement or court order. In some instances, a support duty may be imposed on a man who has voluntarily acknowledged paternity but who is later proven by DNA evidence not to be a parent.[1]

Although typically paid to a custodial parent, some states impose a duty on a parent to pay support to a third party who is not the child's biological or adoptive parent, but who acts *in loco parentis*. For example, support may be paid to a grandparent acting as a custodian or guardian of a child, or to a psychological parent with whom a child has been living with the consent of one or both of the parents.[2] The parents' duty to support their child may continue even if the child is in the custody of a government agency (a residential treatment program, a juvenile justice department, a department of social services, etc.) rather than in the custody of one of the parents. The agency that has custody may initiate an action for support.[3] In a 2012 case, however, the Utah Supreme Court affirmed a district court's order denying a father's request to redirect support from the "custodial" mother to a shelter where the child was staying. The court reasoned that the shelter did not qualify as a physical custodian and at most provided the child with food and a bed. The mother had not relinquished her right and responsibility to control and supervise the child. She continued to care for the daughter by buying her clothes, paying school registration fees, and transporting her to and from dental, medical, and therapy appointments and paying associated fees. Finding that she would remain the child's physical custodian until someone else is assigned that role under the law or until the child reaches the age of majority, the court opined: "If physical custody changed every time a child took shelter somewhere other than her custodian's home, the child's best interests would be jeopardized. Those interests include stability and continuity, and protection from the prospect of ping-pong custody awards. A child's development depends upon the continuity and character of the relationship with the adult he perceives as his parent, and that relationship would be threatened if child support payments were in jeopardy of being redirected whenever a child is cared for by a third party for any extensive period of time." *Hansen v. Hansen*, 2012 Ut. 9, 270 P.3d 531 (Utah 2012).

WHEN DOES THE CHILD SUPPORT DUTY END?

The duty to support a child most often continues until the child's emancipation. **Emancipation** usually means that the child has reached the **age of majority** (age eighteen in most states). However, it can also refer to some other statutory, judicial, or agreed-upon indicator that the child should no longer be considered a minor subject to parental control, such as entering military service, getting married, moving out of the custodial parent's home, or becoming self-supporting. The award will also end if the obligor's parental rights are terminated or upon the death of the obligor, absent agreement or court order to the contrary. For example, the court may order, or the parties may agree, that the **obligor** will maintain a life insurance policy for the benefit of the child or establish a trust or some other vehicle to help ensure the child continues to receive an appropriate level of support during his or her minority in the event the obligor dies.

In some circumstances, the court has the discretion to order continuation of support beyond the age of majority, such as when a child would otherwise become a **public charge**. For example, variations exist among the states with respect to how long parents remain responsible for the support of their disabled children. A Kansas Appellate Court held that Kansas common law no longer required a parent to support a disabled son with cerebral palsy beyond the end of the school year in which the child turned nineteen. Under Arizona law, however, the family court can order either or both parents to provide support for mentally or physically disabled

In loco parentis
Latin: in the place of the parent; taking on some or all of the responsibilities of a parent

Emancipation
the age, act, or occasion that frees a child from the control of a parent and usually the parent from a child support obligation unless otherwise ordered or agreed

Age of majority
the age, usually eighteen, at which a person attains adulthood and associated legal rights. The age varies from state to state. As of March 2015, for example, the age of majority was twenty-one in Mississippi and nineteen in Alabama and Nebraska.

Obligor
a person who owes a legal duty; in the child support context, the parent who owes the duty of support

Public charge
a person dependent on public assistance programs for necessaries

adult children after they reach the age of majority.[4] Several states also provide by statute that the duty of support may continue provided the youth remains in a qualifying program of higher education, a topic discussed more fully later in the chapter.

Sometimes language in the parties' separation agreement will control when the support duty terminates. For example, in *Moss v. Moss*, 91 A.D. 783, 937 N.Y.S.2d 270 (App. Div. 2012), a father sought to modify his support obligation with regard to the parties' younger daughter who had developmental disabilities and had been placed in a facility that provided both educational and therapeutic services. The father contended that this was a permanent placement and constituted a "termination event" with respect to his support obligation for that child. The parties' agreement provided that the father's child support obligation would terminate if "[a] child ceases to permanently reside with the . . . 'custodial parent,'" but stated that "[r]esidence away from the Mother's home, . . . at boarding school . . . shall not terminate the child support obligations. . . ." The Support Magistrate concluded that the facility was, in essence, a boarding school with a therapeutic component and, as such, fell within one of the exceptions listed in the agreement.

In some circumstances, a child may forfeit a right to be supported by a parent. For example, in *Jacobi v. Lewis*, 92 A.D.3d 1100, 938 N.Y.S.2d 379 (App. Div. 2012), the appellate court reversed a Family Court's determination that a child was not emancipated when she moved out of her father's residence and began living with her boyfriend. The court held that under the doctrine of "constructive emancipation," a parent's obligation to support a child until he or she reaches age twenty-one may be suspended when the child abandons that parent's home without sufficient cause and withdraws from the parent's control, refusing to comply with reasonable parental demands. Although she was still financially dependent, she forfeited any right to support because she chose to disregard her father's reasonable mandates and voluntarily abandoned his home to avoid his parental discipline and control.

Paralegals should be alert to applicable jurisdictional variations in procedural as well as substantive law governing termination of child support. For example, in 2006 and again in 2011, Pennsylvania amended its rule regarding termination of a child support award upon emancipation and established a requirement that the court conduct an "emancipation inquiry" within six months of the date a child who is the subject of a support order reaches age eighteen. If there is an order in place that applies to more than one child, the obligor may need to file a petition for modification or a petition to terminate child support for a specific child upon emancipation if there would be a reduction in the current support amount as a result. The obligor should not just start paying a reduced child support amount absent a court order authorizing the reduction.

EXHIBIT 10.1 Child Support and Spousal Support (Alimony)—A Comparison

Child Support	Spousal Support (Alimony)
Child support is a right of the child.	Alimony involves a spousal duty at the time of divorce or legal separation. It is based on a showing of need by one spouse and an ability to pay on the part of the other spouse.

(Continued)

EXHIBIT 10.1 (Continued)

Child support obligations cannot be permanently waived in premarital or separation agreements between the parties.	In most states, rights to spousal support can be waived in valid premarital and separation agreements between the parties.
Child support is calculated using federally mandated child support guidelines developed in each state.	In the majority of jurisdictions, there are no guidelines for courts to use when establishing amounts and duration of alimony awards.
Child support awards remain under the continuing jurisdiction of the court and can be modified upon a substantial change in circumstances or based on periodic reviews.	Alimony awards may be modified upon a material change in the parties' circumstances unless otherwise provided by statute, court decree, or a surviving agreement of the parties.
Child support obligations are not terminated as a result of the remarriage of either spouse.	In most jurisdictions, remarriage of the recipient spouse customarily will terminate an alimony award.
Child support is neither deductible by the obligor nor includable in the income of the recipient.	Alimony is usually tax-deductible to the obligor and taxable income to the recipient.
Child support obligations are not discharged in bankruptcy and are entitled to priority in payment.[5]	Spousal support obligations usually are not dischargeable in bankruptcy.

Initiatives the Federal Government Has Undertaken in the Area of Child Support

In order to understand the operation of child support procedures in the individual states, it helps to be aware of how they are in many respects shaped by federal law. Although the federal government leaves regulation of most family law matters to the states, since the 1970s, it has assumed a powerful leadership role in an effort to accomplish several important objectives related to the establishment and enforcement of child support obligations:

- In order to contain the costs of **public assistance programs**, the federal government now holds both mothers and fathers accountable for support of their children.
- In an effort to address historical inadequacies and inconsistencies in child support awards from state to state, county to county, and judge to judge, it has taken dramatic steps to promote uniformity in procedures used by the states to determine child support awards.
- Given the high rate of noncompliance with child support orders, particular emphasis is placed on strengthening and streamlining enforcement of child support obligations, especially when multiple jurisdictions are involved.

It is impossible to cover the many initiatives undertaken by Congress over the past four decades, but reference to some of them is appropriate to convey a

Public assistance programs government programs providing financial and other forms of assistance to poor and low-income families

PARALEGAL PRACTICE TIP

According to U.S. Census Bureau data on custodial parents, in 2011:

- 14.4 million parents had custody of children under 21;
- 82% were mothers;
- 33% were divorced and 35% never married;
- 50% worked full-time;
- 29% had income below poverty level and 39% received some form of public assistance;
- 62.3% of 37.9 billion owed was paid and 43.4% of recipients received the full amount they were due.

Carmen Solomon-Fears, *Child Support: An Overview of Census Bureau Data on Recipients, Congressional Research Service,* December 2013.

IV-D agency
the state agency charged with responsibility for enforcing child support obligations

Putative father
a man who is reputed or believed to be the father of a child but who was not married to the mother when the child was born and whose paternity has not yet been established by legal process

Child support guidelines
guidelines developed by states in response to federal mandate that are presumed to generate an appropriate amount of child support, given a particular set of assumptions and circumstances

Uniform Interstate Family Support Act (UIFSA)
a model act designed to facilitate establishment and enforcement of interstate child support orders

Long-arm jurisdiction
jurisdiction over a nonresident defendant on the basis of his or her contacts with the state that is seeking to exercise personal jurisdiction

sense of the nature and scope of federal involvement in the child support arena. Although these efforts have had a significant impact, support generally still remains inadequate to meet the daily needs of many American children, predominantly those in female-headed households.

- **The Child Support Enforcement and Establishment of Paternity Act of 1974**[6] (added Title IV-D to the Social Security Act).
    - a. This Act established the Office of Child Support Enforcement (OCSE), the federal agency now responsible for monitoring and helping states develop and manage their child support programs in accordance with federal law.
    - b. It required each state to develop a comprehensive child support program to be run by a single state agency (designated the state's **IV-D agency**) charged with facilitating parents' efforts to obtain and enforce child support awards. Currently, the primary tasks of a IV-D agency are to:
        1. when necessary, assist in establishing paternity through testing of **putative fathers**
        2. assist with location of noncustodial parents through state and federal parent locator services empowered by statute to search records of state and federal agencies
        3. facilitate entry of support orders after paternity is established and noncustodial fathers are located
        4. periodically review child support awards
        5. enforce existing orders through an arsenal of resources
- **The Child Support Enforcement Amendments of 1984 (CSEA)**[7]
    - a. This Act required states to establish advisory numeric, formula-based **child support guidelines** for reference by judges and other officials who set child support amounts in separation, divorce, and paternity cases.
    - b. It required each state to have a law addressing procedures for establishing paternity of a child at any time before the child attains eighteen years of age.[8]
    - c. It required state child support agencies to seek medical support as part of any petition to establish or modify support whenever health care coverage is available at a reasonable cost.
    - d. It strengthened Title IV-D enforcement efforts by requiring the states to implement income withholding, state and federal tax intercepts, and liens against the property of obligors in default.
    - e. It mandated that states receiving public assistance funds make the full range of parent locator and child support services available to all custodial parents and not solely to those receiving public assistance.
- **The Family Support Act of 1988** This Act mandated that by 1994, the states implement presumptive rather than advisory guidelines to be used in establishing initial child support awards and any subsequent modifications.[9] The Act called for the National Conference of Commissioners on Uniform State Laws (NCCUSL) to create a new Uniform Act designed to improve the interstate collection of child support by replacing and addressing problem areas in the prior Uniform Reciprocal Enforcement of Support Act (URESA) drafted in the 1950s and revised several times. The "new" Act, eventually called the **Uniform Interstate Family Support Act (UIFSA)**,[10] was designed to promote uniformity in the processing of interstate cases; eliminate the potential for multiple, conflicting support orders; and expand **long-arm jurisdiction** to make it easier for a custodial parent to prosecute a child support case in his or her own state.[11]

- **The Personal Responsibility and Work Opportunity Reconciliation Act of 1996 (PRWORA)**[12]
  a. This Act abolished the former Aid to Families with Dependent Children program (AFDC) and replaced it with the **Transitional Assistance to Needy Families program (TANF)**.
  b. The Act called for creation and maintenance of a **State Case Registry** containing basic information regarding all child support orders within the state and the creation and maintenance of state and national **Directories of New Hires**.
  c. It required all states to adopt the 1996 version of UIFSA by 1998 in order to remain eligible to receive federal child support funds, thereby creating a powerful incentive for states to comply with federal mandates.
  d. The Act provided a mechanism for dealing with international child support cases.
  e. For the first time, PRWORA provided authority under title IV-D (Section 455(f)) for direct funding to qualifying tribes and tribal organizations for operation of comprehensive child support enforcement (CSE) programs. Prior to the enactment of PRWORA, title IV-D placed authority to administer the delivery of IV-D services solely with the states. Cooperative agreements between tribes and states had helped bring child support services to some reservations. However, because federal law reserves to Indian tribes important powers of self-government, including the authority to make and enforce laws and to adjudicate civil and criminal disputes including domestic relations cases, on most Indian reservations, the authority of state and local governments is limited or nonexistent. Consequently, states that attempted to provide IV-D services on tribal lands were constrained in their abilities to establish paternity and to establish and enforce child support orders.

The Major Jurisdictional Issues in Child Support Cases

SUBJECT MATTER JURISDICTION

The processes by which child support awards are established, modified, and enforced all involve jurisdictional issues. The court issuing, modifying, or enforcing an order must have **subject matter jurisdiction** over child support actions and also **personal jurisdiction** over the obligor. Based on state statutes governing subject matter jurisdiction, child support actions are usually filed in family courts, particularly if child support is an issue in a pending divorce action. However, they may also be heard in juvenile courts or the equivalent of district or county courts dealing with protective orders and other matters pertaining to children and their parents.

OBTAINING PERSONAL JURISDICTION OVER A RESIDENT DEFENDANT

Each state has its own statutes and procedural rules governing the ways in which personal jurisdiction can be obtained over a defendant. If the defendant in a child support action resides in the state where the action is brought, most often a copy of the complaint/petition and court summons will be personally served on the defendant.

Transitional Assistance to Needy Families Program (TANF)
a federal block grant program that provides support to poor families subject to certain conditions; replaced the former Aid to Families with Dependent Children Program

State Case Registry (SCR)
a federally mandated statewide database containing basic information on all child support orders entered by courts within the state

Directories of New Hires
federally mandated databases maintained by both the state and federal governments containing basic information from employers regarding all newly hired employees and applicants for unemployment compensation

PARALEGAL PRACTICE TIP
To learn more about tribal courts, go to *www.ncsc.org*, the site of the National Center for State Courts. Select Information and Resources and then Browse Topics A-Z to find Tribal Courts.

Subject matter jurisdiction
the authority of a court to hear and decide a particular type of claim or controversy

Personal jurisdiction
the authority of the court to issue and enforce orders binding a particular individual; sometimes called *in personam* jurisdiction

PARALEGAL PRACTICE TIP
Subject matter jurisdiction over a child support action depends on the particular kind of case involved. See, for example, *In the Interest of J.L., Jr.*, 763 S.E.2d 654 (W.Va. 2014) involving a care and protection action and a question whether child support should be addressed by a circuit court with exclusive jurisdiction over care and protection matters or by a family court.

Actual service of process
actual delivery of notice to the person for whom it is intended

This is called **actual service of process**. If the defendant is believed to be in the state, but his or her precise whereabouts are unknown, the court may authorize an alternative mode of service, such as mailing the complaint to the defendant's last known address or service by publication in area newspapers. A defendant may also consent to the court's jurisdiction by voluntarily accepting service at the courthouse, or by filing a general appearance or a responsive pleading to a complaint.

OBTAINING PERSONAL JURISDICTION OVER A NONRESIDENT DEFENDANT IN THE PETITIONER'S OWN STATE

PARALEGAL PRACTICE TIP

For examples of long-arm statutes in the states of Florida and Ohio, visit *www.leg.state.fl.us,* Fla. Stat. § 48.193, and *www.codes.ohio.gov.* Ohio Revised Code 2307.382.

Approximately one-third of child support orders involve parents living in different states. Obtaining jurisdiction over a nonresident defendant and enforcing support orders across state lines can be challenging. If the defendant is a nonresident, a court may be able to obtain personal jurisdiction over the defendant in the petitioner's own state under its long-arm statute or under one of UIFSA's long-arm provisions. Under UIFSA, which now has been adopted in every state, if a defendant has one or more of the following eight kinds of "purposeful minimal contacts" with another state, it is considered fair and reasonable for a court in that other state to exercise personal jurisdiction over the individual and to adjudicate a child or spousal support dispute:

1. The nonresident is personally served in the state.
2. The nonresident submits to the jurisdiction of the state by consent, by entering a general appearance, or by filing a responsive document having the effect of waiving any contest to personal jurisdiction.
3. The nonresident once resided with the child in the state.
4. The nonresident once resided in the state and provided prenatal expenses or support for the child.
5. The child resides in the state as a result of the acts or directives of the nonresident.
6. The nonresident engaged in sexual intercourse in the state and the child may have been conceived by that act of intercourse.
7. The nonresident asserted parentage in the state such as through a **putative father registry**.
8. Any other basis consistent with the constitutions of the state and the United States for the exercise of personal jurisdiction.

(See Paralegal Application 10.1.)

Putative father registry
a vehicle available in several states that is designed to protect a putative father's parental rights by giving him notice of a pending adoption proceeding without his having to rely on the birth mother or prospective adoptive parents for information

Paralegal **Application 10.1**

Jurisdiction Under UIFSA

Fact Pattern

Susan and her husband were married in Texas, by operation of common law, in 1997. Throughout their marriage, her husband (a known gang member) abused her both physically and psychologically. Susan also believed her husband was sexually abusing her daughter from a previous relationship. He threatened to kill her if she turned him in. Despite his threats, she contacted the police and reported both the death threats and the abuse, but the police did not investigate because she had not personally witnessed the abuse. She eventually left her husband and moved into a friend's trailer, but her husband continued to stalk her and slashed the tires on her car at work.

She again reported the incidents to the police, and they told her she should move to a women's shelter. After that, her husband and a friend were seen armed with guns breaking into the trailer where she used to live. Her husband also made threatening phone calls to her father, who lived in Colorado. Early in January of 1999, pregnant by her husband and fearing for her life, she fled to her father's home in Colorado, where she gave birth to a son. In April 2000, she filed for divorce in Colorado and sought child support, maintenance, and division of property and debt. After being personally served in Texas, her husband filed a motion to dismiss for lack of personal jurisdiction.

Sidebar

Should the Colorado court be able to exercise personal jurisdiction over Susan's husband under UIFSA? On what basis? To learn how the Colorado Supreme Court resolved this question, read the opinion in the case, *In re Marriage of Malwitz*, 99 P.3d 56 (Colo. 2004). The opinion can be accessed at *www.pearsonhighered.com/ careersresources/* in the website material for Chapter 10 of this text under Cases.

OBTAINING PERSONAL JURISDICTION OVER A NONRESIDENT DEFENDANT IN HIS OR HER STATE

If the court cannot obtain personal jurisdiction in the petitioner's state, the matter cannot be adjudicated in that state. However, another avenue remains open to the petitioner working through the state's IV-D agency with the agency acting on the petitioner's behalf with or without the assistance of counsel.

- The petitioner files a petition for child support in his or her own state.
- The IV-D agency in that state forwards the petition to the IV-D agency in the nonresident defendant's state.
- The appropriate court in the nonresident defendant's state obtains personal jurisdiction over the defendant and conducts an administrative or judicial hearing on the child support issue.
- The IV-D agency in the nonresident defendant's state then uses its enforcement powers to collect the child support amount from the defendant.

PARALEGAL PRACTICE TIP

Forms relating to interstate cases can be viewed at *www.acf.hhs.gov.* Select Forms.

CONTINUING EXCLUSIVE JURISDICTION UNDER UIFSA

Under UIFSA, there should be only one valid support order between the parties that is enforceable in all states, and the states are required, under the Full Faith and Credit for Child Support Orders Act (FFCCSOA),[13] to respect properly issued support orders from other states (including orders issued by tribal courts). Once a court issues a valid child support order, under UIFSA that court will have continuing exclusive jurisdiction over the case for purposes of modification, and no court in any other state can modify the order as long as either parent or the child continues to reside in that state or the parties file written consents that another state assume jurisdiction. If either of these conditions is satisfied the state that issued the initial order loses its continuing exclusive jurisdiction and a court in another state can acquire it. It is conceivable that the parties may then simultaneously seek orders in different states, resulting in multiple and potentially conflicting orders. Under UIFSA, preference will be given to the child's **home state**. If neither state is the child's home state, the more recent order will control.

To further complicate such situations, it is possible for jurisdiction over child custody and child support to be in two different states. For example, under the

PARALEGAL PRACTICE TIP

To read the full text of UIFSA visit *www.uniformlaws.org.* In Find an Act, search for Interstate Family Support Act Amendments.

Home state
under UIFSA, the state where the child has lived for six consecutive months prior to the filing or since birth if the child is less than six months old

UCCJEA, a state that has issued custody and support orders may cede custody jurisdiction to another state when one parent and the child relocate to that other state for an extended period. However, under UIFSA, jurisdiction over child support will continue to be in the initial state as long as the other parent resides there (unless the parties execute written consents that another state assume jurisdiction). See, e.g., *In the Matter of Jeffrey M. Gray and Janette L. Gray*, 160 N.H. 62, 993 A.2d 203 (2010).

PARALEGAL PRACTICE TIP

To see examples of child support guidelines and instructions in Massachusetts, Utah, and Virginia, visit the following: *www.mass .gov.* Search for Child Support Guidelines effective August 1, 2013 (Massachusetts); *www.utcourts .gov.* Child Support. You will find worksheets tailored to various custodial arrangements. (Utah); and *www.courts.state.va.us.* Forms /Juvenile and Domestic Relations District Court/Forms and Instructions. Scroll to Child Support Guidelines Worksheets. (Virginia). You can also check out the current Indiana child support calculator at *www.in.gov* or the Tennessee Guidelines calculator at *www.tn.gov.* Search for Child Support Calculator.

Rebuttable presumption

an inference drawn from certain facts that can be overcome by the introduction of additional or contradictory evidence

PARALEGAL PRACTICE TIP

See e.g., *Cash v. Cash*, 122 So. 3d 430 (2013 Fla. App.). Under Florida law, a child support deviation in excess of 5% over the Guidelines amount must be supported by a written finding explaining why ordering payment of the Guidelines amount would be unjust or inappropriate. The court's failure to do so in this case resulted in reversal of its child support judgment. The court had ordered a deviation of 10% over the guidelines amount.

Child Support Guidelines: What Are They and How Are They Applied?

Once the proper jurisdiction for a child support action is determined, the paralegal can locate the appropriate child support guidelines and forms to utilize.

THE ORIGIN AND PURPOSE OF THE GUIDELINES

In response to federal mandate, every state has put in place a system of child support guidelines designed to help parents and judges determine how much child support should be ordered in a given case. The basic requirements for each state's child support guidelines under federal law are as follows:[14]

- Application of the guidelines will produce a **rebuttable presumption** of the appropriate amount of support to be ordered.
- The guidelines must consider all earnings and income of the noncustodial parent.
- The guidelines must incorporate specific descriptive and numeric criteria.
- They must provide for children's health care needs.
- They must apply to all child support orders, whether at establishment or modification.
- Any order that deviates from the guidelines must include written findings of what the order would have been under the guidelines and why a deviation is warranted.
- Every four years each state's guidelines must be reviewed and revised, if necessary, to ensure that their application results in appropriate child support awards. The review must consider economic data on the cost of raising children and must analyze the application of the guidelines to ensure that awards are consistent and deviations limited.

THE NATURE OF STATE GUIDELINES

Although the federal government mandated their creation, it left the design of child support guidelines up to the individual states. As a result, no two states' guidelines are identical.

State guidelines vary with respect to the income basis for the determination of support; the estimate of spending on children upon which the guidelines are based; the treatment of child care costs; the treatment of medical insurance and out-of-pocket expenditures for medical care; provisions for other children to whom the parent owes a duty of support; adjustments for parenting time; and provisions for adjusting support when the obligor is low-income.[15]

The states essentially use one of the following three approaches to designing their child support guideline formulas:

- Percentage of income: The support amount is a fixed percentage of the non-custodial parent's income.
- Income shares: The incomes of both parents are combined and a basic child support obligation is computed. The amount is then allocated between the parents in proportion to their respective incomes.
- Melson Formula: The noncustodial parent is permitted to retain a self-support reserve for personal basic needs and then the children's basic needs are provided for. A percentage of any remaining parental income is then applied to increase the basic support amount.

As of 2013, thirty-eight states and the District of Columbia based their guidelines on the Income Shares Model, nine on the Percentage Model, and three on the Melson Formula. Even if based on the same model, however, guidelines rarely produce identical amounts because the states factor in different assumptions about the cost of raising children and adjust for a range of variables such as shared parenting, age and number of children.

PARALEGAL PRACTICE TIP

As of 2013, California, Massachusetts and New Jersey generally produced the highest awards in a variety of scenarios and Mississippi, Virginia and West Virginia the lowest. See Jane Venohr, *Child Support Guidelines and Guidelines Reviews: State Differences and Common Issues*, 47 Fam. L. Q., #3 Fall 2013.

Paralegal **Application 10.2**

Child Support Guidelines Worksheets

Paralegals in a family law practice are frequently asked to draft child support guidelines worksheets. Depending on the guidelines formula, a Worksheet may need to be completed for each child for whom support is an issue. Many firms have purchased software packages that can be used to calculate the amount of child support due under a given state's guidelines. The guidelines for virtually all states are available online, and most states post worksheets on the Web pages of their courts or IV-D agencies. A copy of the worksheet for the state of Missouri (effective in 2015) is contained in Exhibit 10.2. Instructions for completing the worksheet, along with a "calculator" for determining the appropriate amount of child support in a specific case, are available at *www.courts.mo.gov.*

When preparing child support guidelines worksheets, it is important to know what kinds of income are considered includable for purposes of calculating child support in a given state. Because of the potential value of child support awards, the family law team needs not only to identify and document sources of the client's income but also to conduct sufficient discovery to establish the nature and extent of the other party's income. When a particular source of income is likely to be challenged, or when income may be imputed, appropriate research needs to be done with respect to the issue in an effort to support the client's position.

If a deviation from the guidelines amount will be sought, the paralegal may be asked to gather the information necessary to support or oppose that deviation, based on governing law and the facts of the case.

PARALEGAL PRACTICE TIP

There is nothing like being organized and prepared. Many attorneys will prepare alternative versions of various documents in anticipation of the court's potential actions. For example, if there is a question with respect to whether or not a certain type of income will be includable in an obligor's income for purposes of calculating child support, alternative versions of the child support guidelines worksheet should be prepared. The one that best supports the client's case is offered first, but the second is available as backup.

EXHIBIT 10.2 Child Support Amount Calculation Worksheet for the State of Missouri
Courtesy of the State of Missouri

IN THE CIRCUIT COURT OF _____ COUNTY, MISSOURI

In re the Matter of _____ v _____

DIV/CT ROOM _____   CASE NO. _____

FORM NO. 14 CHILD SUPPORT AMOUNT CALCULATION WORKSHEET

☐ FATHER / ☐ MOTHER is the "Parent Paying Support"

Total Number of Children: _____

	PARENT RECEIVING SUPPORT	PARENT PAYING SUPPORT	COMBINED
1. MONTHLY GROSS INCOME			
1a. Monthly court-ordered maintenance being received			
2. ADJUSTMENTS			
2a. Other monthly child support being paid under court or administrative order			
2b. Monthly court-ordered maintenance being paid			
2c. Monthly support obligation for other children.			
(1) Number of other children primarily residing in each parent's custody			
(2) Each parent's support obligation from support schedule using the parent's Line 1 monthly gross income			
(3) Monthly child support received under court or administrative order for children included in line 2c(1)			
2c. TOTAL adjustment [Line 2c(2) minus Line 2c(3)]			
3. ADJUSTED MONTHLY GROSS INCOME (sum of lines 1 and 1a, minus lines 2a, 2b and 2c).			
4. PROPORTIONATE SHARE OF COMBINED ADJUSTED MONTHLY GROSS INCOME (Each parent's line 3 income divided by combined line 3 income).			
5. BASIC CHILD SUPPORT AMOUNT (From support chart using combined line 3 income).			
6. ADDITIONAL CHILD-REARING COSTS OF PARENTS			
6a. Child Care Costs of Parent Receiving Support			
(1) Reasonable work-related child care costs of the parent receiving support.			
(2) Child Care Tax Credit (**See Form 14 Directions**)			
6a. TOTAL adjusted Child Care Costs [Line 6a(1) minus Line 6a(2)]			
6b. Reasonable work-related child care costs of the parent paying support			
6c. Health insurance costs for the children who are subjects of this proceeding			
6d. Uninsured agreed-upon or court-ordered extraordinary medical costs			
6e. Other agreed-upon or court-ordered extraordinary child-rearing costs			
7. TOTAL ADDITIONAL CHILD-REARING COSTS (Enter sum of lines 6a, 6b, 6c, 6d and 6e).			
8. TOTAL COMBINED CHILD SUPPORT COSTS (Sum of line 5 and line 7).			
9. EACH PARENT'S SUPPORT OBLIGATION (Multiply line 8 by each parent's line 4)			
10. CREDIT FOR ADDITIONAL CHILD-REARING COSTS (Line 7 of parent paying support).			
11. ADJUSTMENT FOR A PORTION OF AMOUNTS EXPENDED BY THE PARENT OBLIGATED TO PAY SUPPORT DURING PERIODS OF OVERNIGHT VISITATION OR CUSTODY. (**See Form 14 Directions**) (Multiply line 5 by _____ %).			
12. PRESUMED CHILD SUPPORT AMOUNT (Line 9 minus lines 10 and 11).			

DEFINITION AND PROOF OF INCOME

Guidelines are generally designed to calculate child support obligations when the parties' total combined income (**net**, **adjusted**, or **gross**, depending on the state) is under a certain maximum. For example, the maximum in March 2015 was $141,000 in New York and $250,000 in Massachusetts. States vary with respect to treatment of parental income above the maximum. Some, such as Wisconsin, have guidelines for high income and low income payors. Some, including Nevada, establish maximum presumptive amounts. Many states leave the matter to the discretion of the court and some consider a percentage approach.[16]

If not controlled by federal law, the question of what should be included in income for purposes of calculating child support obligations will be determined by state statutes, administrative regulations, and case law. Most states define income broadly as "income from whatever source." All states include income from employment, including commissions, and virtually all include income from investment earnings, unemployment compensation, pensions, social security, and veterans' benefits. In determining whether income from investments will be included in income for the purpose of calculating child support, courts usually consider whether the income is realized (actually received by the party) or unrealized (a paper-only increase in the value of an investment to which a party may not have access). Courts will also consider whether a party's interest in a corporation's earnings is undistributed in an effort to serve a legitimate business purpose or to shield income.

Proof of income is often a central issue in a child support case. There are few types of income that continue totally unchanged from year to year. People lose or change their jobs, bonuses may be variable, interest rates rise and fall, and business conditions can result in inconsistent profits and losses, especially in cases where one or both of the parties are self-employed. The more something resembles a steady source of annual income that one can reasonably expect to receive in the future, the more likely it will be considered income for purposes of calculating a child support obligation. However, treatment of occasional or irregular income (e.g., from odd jobs, overtime, tips, bonuses) varies. Questions also occasionally arise with respect to sources of income such as the following:

- **Spousal or child support from a person not a party to the order** Spousal support is usually considered income. Child support received by either party for children other than the child for whom support is being determined typically is not.
- **Cash and gifts from family members** Gifts are not usually considered income for federal tax purposes, but the states are divided on whether they should be included as income in child support calculations. Those that decline to do so refer to federal tax law and also to the fact that the donor of a gift has no legal obligation to continue giving. Other states include gifts when they are recurring cash gifts of predictable amounts from dependable persons. So an occasional modest gift may not be included, but if every year a party receives substantial gifts from his or her parents directly or from a family trust and does not have to repay or pay taxes on those sums, the amounts are likely to be included in income.[17] Loans from friends, family, employers, and others that are forgiven are usually considered income. See, e.g., *In the Matter of Timothy and Dorothy Sullivan*, 159 N.H. 251, 982 A.2d 959 (2009).
- **Lump-sum severance pay** Payments associated with compensation for employment are generally included in income. The same reasoning applies to severance pay and settlement amounts in suits for wrongful termination of employment that include compensation for lost pay.

Net income
total income from all sources minus voluntary and nonvoluntary deductions

Adjusted gross income
income after nonvoluntary deductions are taken out, such as federal and state tax obligations, social security withholding, union dues, and wage assignments related to prior support orders

Gross income
total income from all sources before any deductions are made

PARALEGAL PRACTICE TIP

Colonna v. Colonna, 581 Pa. 1, 855 A.2d 648 (2004) provides a good example of some of the issues that arise in high income cases.

PARALEGAL PRACTICE TIP

Appendix IX B of the New Jersey Court Rules governing that state's Child Support Guidelines is accessible at *www.judiciary.state.nj.us*. It includes a detailed description of the kinds of income included for purposes of calculating child support in New Jersey.

PARALEGAL PRACTICE TIP

In *Herrera v. Herrera, now Espinosa,* 2013 OK CIV APP 25, 298 P.3d 1209 (2013), considering personal injury settlement proceeds as income in modifying a child support order was deemed proper because it furthered a legislative intent to consider ALL funds. Moreover, the settlement proceeds in this case were payable in three installments with specified dates and amounts and thus were neither speculative nor dependent upon future events.

PARALEGAL PRACTICE TIP

See, e.g., *Childs v Childs,* 310 P.3d 955 (Alaska 2013), a case in which a father's military basic housing allowance was deemed includable in income when calculating child support under governing law in Alaska. (Alaska R. Civ. P. 90.3.)

- **Bonuses** When bonuses are reasonably certain in the sense that they are awarded each year, even if in varying amounts, they are likely to be included in income. If a bonus is an occasional and uncertain event, a court may be reluctant to include it, depending on the circumstances. Some states, such as California, expressly include bonuses as part of a parent's annual gross income. In states that do not address the matter by statute, courts tend to hold that if a bonus is speculative, completely discretionary, or dependent on performance or the success of an industry (such as residential housing in a sluggish economy), it may not be included as income in the child support calculation. But if it is predictable, such as annual bonuses from a Tribe, it may be included. See, e.g., *M.S. v. O.S.,* 176 Cal. App. 4th 548, 97 Cal. Rptr. 3d 812 (2009).

- **Lump-sum personal injury settlements** Although lump-sum personal injury settlements are often not treated as assets subject to property division between the parties, they usually are considered income in the child support context. The court may choose to prorate an award over a number of years.[18]

- **Lottery or gambling winnings, prizes, and awards** Even though these are not customarily "continuing" sources of income, they are usually included but may be apportioned over a period of time if significant in amount.

- **Social Security Disability Benefits (SSD/SSDI)** A person becomes eligible to receive SSD/SSDI benefits if he or she meets certain disability requirements and an employer has paid into the social security retirement system for his or her benefit. SSD is essentially an insurance policy intended to replace lost income when the employee is disabled and unable to work. Because SSD benefits derive from prior employment, they are usually deemed includable in income.[19] Although the benefit will be included in his or her income, a disabled parent is ordinarily entitled to have Social Security Disability Benefits paid to a child (because of that parent's disability) credited against his or her child support obligation for that child.[20]

- **Means-tested sources of benefits, such as Pell grants, TANF benefits, food stamps, and Supplemental Social Security Income (SSI)** These usually are not considered income. Means-tested benefits are essentially social welfare programs designed to meet the basic needs of low-income persons. Congress has expressly exempted SSI from child support payments.[21]

- **Military allowances for housing (BAH) and subsistence (BAS)** A BAH is a monthly sum paid to members of the military who do not reside in government-supplied housing. It is intended to offset the cost of civilian housing and varies according to the member's pay grade, geographic location, and dependency status. A BAS is an additional monthly sum paid to active-duty members to subsidize the cost of meals purchased for the benefit of the member on or off base. It is based on average food costs as determined by the federal government. Although these subsidies are not included in income for income tax purposes, several states (including New York,[22] Pennsylvania, Ohio, and Minnesota) have held them includable in gross income for purposes of calculating child support.

- **Military retirement benefits** These benefits are includable as income, although under federal law there are limitations on the maximum percentage of the benefit that can be distributed pursuant to orders for property distribution, alimony, or child support.[23]

- **Reimbursements received in the course of employment** When the reimbursements are significant and reduce personal living expenses, such as free housing, use of a company car, and allowances for meals, they may be included. Louisiana, for example, specifically includes such "reimbursements" in income by statute.[24]

IMPUTED INCOME

Imputed income is income that is attributed to a party based upon his or her earning capacity rather than on actual earnings. Most states will impute income to one or both of the parties if appropriate. (See Paralegal Application 10.3.) This practice is designed to prevent a party from avoiding a child or spousal support obligation by manipulating his or her income, for example, by voluntarily retiring early or remaining unemployed or underemployed. Many states will impute income when a party's wrongdoing results in the loss of gainful employment. Most states will not impute income if there is a good-faith reason for unemployment, such as physical disability or remaining at home for child-related reasons (e.g., to care for an infant or a disabled child). However there are variations among the states. For example, in *Carr-MacArthur v. Carr*, 296 Ga. 30, 764 S.E.2d 840 (2014), the Georgia Supreme Court held that a trial court did not err by imputing income to a mother when there was evidence that she and her new husband had determined it was to the advantage of their children that she not work outside the home.

Several states will impute income to affluent parents who have sufficient income-producing assets to support themselves and their child support obligations without working. They may also factor in the value of non-income-producing assets such as boats, cars, and collections of such items as jewelry or artwork. If not considered by the formula, such assets may be used to justify a deviation from the guidelines if it appears a parent is deliberately trying to tie up funds that would otherwise be available to meet family obligations.[25]

Some states establish by statute a formula for imputation of income. For example, in New Hampshire, RSA 458-C:2, IV(a) provides that, in cases in which a parent is determined to be voluntarily unemployed or underemployed, a trial court "in its discretion, may consider as gross income the difference between the amount a parent is earning and the amount a parent has earned unless the parent is physically or mentally incapacitated." The court is also free to impute a lesser amount.[26] The amount set may depend in part on the noncustodial parent's educational background and job skills, as well as work history and job opportunities in the area. Guidelines in some states, such as North Carolina, provide that if a parent has no recent work history or vocational training, potential income should be estimated at not less than the minimum hourly wage for a forty-hour week. When imputing income, courts also sometimes look to economic indicators and industry reports to establish a salary to be imputed. For example, a New York court imputed an annual income of $45,000 to an underemployed plumber suspected of underreporting income. The amount was based largely on average salaries of plumbers according to a New York State Department of Labor history of earnings report. See *Sharlow v. Sharlow*, 77 A.D.3d 1430, 908 N.Y.S.2d 287 (2010). Absent governing statutory or case law, if the individual is unemployed and has no recent work history, the amount will be left to the court's discretion.

Most courts will consider averaging the income of a parent over a period of months or years, especially if the individual is self-employed in a seasonal or highly volatile profession that is subject to market trends or when he or she has a windfall year that is totally inconsistent with an overall employment history. Income averaging imputes consistency in income rather than the income itself. In some jurisdictions, income averaging is specifically authorized by statute or court rule (for example, in Alaska, Ohio, and Nebraska). New Hampshire expressly prohibits income averaging based on case law rather than statute.

Imputed income
income that is attributed to a party based upon his or her earning capacity rather than on actual earnings

PARALEGAL PRACTICE TIP

In Wyoming when income is imputed in a child support case, the court shall consider:

(A) Prior employment experience and history;

(B) Educational level and whether additional education would make the parent more self-sufficient or significantly increase the parent's income;

(C) The presence of children of the marriage in the parent's home and its impact on the earnings of that parent;

(D) Availability of employment for which the parent is qualified;

(E) Prevailing wage rates in the local area;

(F) Special skills or training; and

(G) Whether the parent is realistically able to earn imputed income.

See *Levine v. Levine*, 2014 WY 161 (Wyo. 2014) in which the Wyoming Supreme Court applied the statute. (Wyo. Stat. Ann. § 20-2-07(b).)

Paralegal Application 10.3

An Imputed Income Case—What Do You Think?

***J.M. v. D.A.*, 935 N.E.2d 1235 (Ind. Ct. App. 2010)**

In this case, a father of four children unsuccessfully sought a modification of child support. He had lost his job "either by being fired for absenteeism or by not appearing" and at the time of the hearing was enrolled as a full-time student. An Indiana Circuit Court concluded that he was voluntarily unemployed and that he should be attributed a weekly gross income of $480, his last gross weekly wage. He claimed that even if he previously was voluntarily unemployed, that status ended when he became a full-time student. On appeal, in support of his argument that he should not be considered unemployed or underemployed, he relied on another Indiana Court of Appeals decision that characterized pursuit of higher education in a child support case as follows:

> . . . we believe that it is a parent's responsibility to continually try to better herself and to create more and better opportunities for the child and

the family unit. We are hard-pressed to come up with a better example of a way to do just that than by pursuing education. . . . A parent who finds within herself the diligence and ambition to obtain a degree will be rewarded not only with better job prospects and increased earning potential, but also with a child who has learned by example that education is essential and valuable. *Thomas v. Orlando*, 834 N.E.2d 1055 (Ind. Ct. App. 2005)

J.M.'s appeal was denied. The courts in these two cases reached different conclusions based on the fact patterns presented. Do you think they may have been influenced by gender bias? In your opinion does enrolling in a program of higher education constitute voluntary unemployment? Both opinions can be accessed at *www.pearsonhighered.com/careersresources/* in the resource website material for Chapter 10 of this text under Cases.

PARALEGAL PRACTICE TIP

A copy of a Massachusetts form for documenting a deviation from the guidelines is available at *www.pearsonhighered.com/careersresources/* in the website material for Chapter 10 under Forms. The form provides a record of the trial court's reasoning for reference if the deviation is appealed.

DEVIATIONS FROM THE GUIDELINES

Child Support Guidelines set a base from which a judge can then exercise discretion in a manner consistent with governing statutes, regulations, and case law. In addition, federal regulations specifically require that any deviation from the guidelines' amount be in the best interests of the child.[27] The presumption that application of the guidelines will result in an appropriate amount of child support is rebuttable. A court may deviate from the guidelines' amount if it is unjust, unreasonable, or inappropriate under the circumstances or not in the best interests of the child, provided the court issues findings regarding the reason(s) for the deviation. Some of the factors or circumstances that may justify a deviation include the following:

Extraordinary Expenses

Extraordinary expense
an unusual, unanticipated childrearing expense that is substantial in cost and/or duration

In general, it is assumed that the custodial parent is responsible for payment of a child's ordinary day-to-day living expenses. These are costs that are reasonably predictable and consistent from child to child. On occasion, an unusual, unanticipated childrearing expense may arise that is substantial in cost and/or duration. Such **extraordinary expenses** are often medical in nature. For example, a child may require either physical or psychological therapy on an ongoing basis or have a chronic medical condition, such as diabetes or cystic fibrosis. Such situations can involve costly medical care and medications, some of which may not be fully covered by insurance. Some conditions may require a custodial parent to make physical accommodations in the child's residence. Extraordinary expenses may be of other kinds as well such as legal fees for a child charged with a serious criminal offense or the cost of training for a prospective Olympic athlete or a piano child prodigy.

States vary with respect to how responsibility for extraordinary costs will be apportioned between the parents. Most commonly, they are handled as a deviation from the guidelines for a temporary or extended period. A prorated amount may be added onto the child support obligation based on the respective incomes of the parties.

Multiple Families

According to the U.S. Department of Health and Human Services, almost 75% of people who divorce remarry.[28] A new marriage often results in a his, hers, and ours situation when it comes to children, frequently resulting in both emotional and financial stress. Although a new partner generally has no legal obligation to support his or her spouse's children from prior marriages or relationships, states may give consideration to such circumstances within their guidelines. Some states address this situation by statute. For example, in New Hampshire, RSA 458-C:4 provides, "When considering a request for an original support order or modification of a support order, . . . the court shall take into account any stepchildren for which either parent may be responsible."

The contemporary view is that there is no precise, mathematical formula for calculating child support when multiple families are involved. The determination is left to the discretion of the court. Many still follow the traditional rule that "first families come first" and an obligor usually is not able to obtain a downward modification in support due a first family based upon his or her new obligations to a second family. However, some states will deduct the amount of support due to "first" or prior families from the income available to support potential obligations flowing from the more recent relationship. The obligor also may be able to use obligations to a new family as a defense to a claim by a former spouse for an upward modification in child support to a prior family. For example, in 2002, the rules for the Nebraska Guidelines were amended to include the following provision:

> Limitation on Decrease: An obligor shall not be allowed a reduction in an existing support order solely because of the birth, adoption, or acknowledgement of subsequent children of the obligor; however, a duty to provide regular support for subsequent children may be raised as a defense to an action for an upward modification of such existing support order.[29]

> **PARALEGAL PRACTICE TIP**
>
> Even if support obligations to a prior family can be deducted from income, a deviation from the guidelines amount will generally not be permitted on the sole basis that the noncustodial parent has a child from a prior relationship living with him or her. See, e.g., *Beck v. Beck*, 165 Md. App. 445, 885 A.2d 887 (Md. Spec. App. 2005).

Educational Needs of the Children

In the preschool, elementary, middle, and high school years, educational needs of the minor children may include enrollment in a private or alternative school, participation in extracurricular activities, tutoring and other forms of compensatory education for a child with disabilities, or special lessons for a gifted child who demonstrates unusual potential in a particular field such as technology, art or mathematics.

Several states that set the age of emancipation and termination of child support at eighteen years provide that if the child continues his or her high school education past age eighteen, the court, in its discretion, may order the continuation of support until the child finishes high school or reaches the age of nineteen. This is the approach taken in Idaho, for example. The Idaho Supreme Court has described the rationale behind the policy as follows:

> There is a strong public policy in favor of providing support to students.
> A large population of educated persons greatly benefits society.

All students should be encouraged to finish high school, regardless of whether they have reached the age of eighteen, and the absence of child support should not influence the decision to stay in school.[30]

The current trend with respect to higher education is away from requiring parents to pay for college expenses absent an agreement, but there is a range among the states that address the issue by statute. At one end is New Hampshire, which revised its statute in 2004 to provide that absent an agreement of the parties, "No child support order shall require a parent to contribute to an adult child's college expenses or other educational expenses beyond the completion of high school. . ."[31] Neighboring Massachusetts is at the other end of the spectrum. By statute, it provides that a court may order support "for any child who has attained age twenty-one but who has not attained age twenty-three, if such child is domiciled in the home of a parent, and is principally dependent on said parent for maintenance due to the enrollment of such child in an educational program, excluding educational costs beyond an undergraduate degree."[32]

Iowa is an example of a state that falls in the middle. Iowa Code section 598.21(F) authorizes courts to order a postsecondary education subsidy under certain conditions for good cause shown. However, the amount to be paid by each parent cannot exceed one-third of the total cost of postsecondary education. The court determines "the cost of postsecondary education based on the cost of attending an in-state public institution for a course of instruction leading to an undergraduate degree and shall include the reasonable costs for only necessary postsecondary education expenses." By case law, the Iowa courts have expanded the nature of what will be considered necessary educational expenses: "We recognized the reasonable and necessary costs of attending college surpass the costs of tuition, books, room, board, and supplies. A college education is not limited to what is learned in the classroom; it includes social, cultural, and educational experiences outside the classroom."[33]

Custodial and Visitation Arrangements

Most early versions of state child support guidelines were based on a traditional custody model, with one parent having primary physical custody and the other parent having "reasonable visitation rights" approximately 20% of the time. Deviations were sometimes allowed to accommodate infrequent **joint** or **split custody** arrangements. As the concept of family has evolved, and parents have adopted new custodial models, legislatures and courts have gradually recognized the need to calculate child support awards tailored to those models.

Child support amounts now may be adjusted based on variations in visitation patterns or degrees of shared custody, etc. In more than half the states, the deviation is left to the discretion of the court, but several states (such as Wisconsin,[34] Arizona,[35] Colorado,[36] Maine,[37] and New Jersey[38]) apply a different formula once visitation or shared custody reaches a certain level. (See Exhibit 10.3.) The relevant Oklahoma statute provides for an adjustment in the base amount of child support when "shared parenting" time has been ordered by the court or agreed to by the parents. Shared parenting time means that each parent has physical custody of the child or children overnight for more than one hundred twenty (120) nights each year.[39] In determining what constitutes parenting, the courts may look beyond the quantitative number of days a child is technically in the custody of each parent, to qualitative factors such as participating in school activities and arranging for and attending extracurricular activities in which the child is involved.

Joint physical custody
a custody arrangement in which a child spends a more-or-less equal amount of time living with each parent

Split custody
a custody arrangement in which each parent has legal and/or physical custody of one or more of the parties' children

PARALEGAL PRACTICE TIP

Visit *www.alaska.gov* to see examples of forms and calculators of child support tailored to a variety of custodial arrangements. Search for "Child Support Guidelines."

PARALEGAL PRACTICE TIP

Occasionally, a custodial parent relinquishes possession and control of a child to a noncustodial parent without a formal change in custody. In doing so, the custodial parent may well lose a right to child support previously ordered by the court. In such situations, the most appropriate course of action is to seek an order of the court formally modifying both child custody and support based on the change in circumstances. Texas addresses this situation by statute and provides that an obligor may plead the obligee's actions as an affirmative defense (in whole or in part) to a motion for enforcement of child support.[40]

Given the considerable variety of approaches among the states, paralegals need to be familiar with the current formula applicable to the child support cases they work on. If unique custodial models are not addressed in the applicable guidelines formula, arguments may need to be made for a deviation. For example, what if a parent spends only the summer months with the child or has to travel across the country monthly at considerable expense to exercise visitation rights? Supporting case law should be researched. For example, in *Black v. Black*, 292 Ga. 691, 740 S.E.2d 613 (2013), the Georgia Supreme Court upheld a deviation in child support due to visitation-related travel expenses to be incurred by the father as a result of the mother's actions. Although she had the option to remain with the children in the marital home in Georgia for which the father was financially responsible, she chose instead to move to New York thereby incurring unnecessary expenses.

EXHIBIT 10.3 North Dakota Formula for Child Support with Equal Physical Custody

---

FROM THE ADMINISTRATIVE CODE

Equal physical custody—Determination of child support obligation. A child support obligation must be determined as described in this section in all cases in which a court orders each parent to have equal physical custody of their child or children. Equal physical custody means each parent has physical custody of the child, or if there are multiple children, all of the children, exactly 50% of the time. A child support obligation for each parent must be calculated under this chapter, assuming the other parent is the custodial parent of the child or children subject to the equal physical custody order. The lesser obligation is then subtracted from the greater. The difference is the child support amount owed by the parent with the greater obligation.[41]

Cost of Living in a Geographical Area

The states vary with respect to whether or not cost of living will warrant a deviation from the guidelines when the parents live in different geographical localities. For example, an individual living in New York City is likely to have a considerably higher cost of living than one living in Littleton, New Hampshire. The Maryland Court of Appeals has held that "a lower cost of living in the child's locality is not a proper basis for deviating from the guidelines."[42] However, other courts have held that a noncustodial parent's higher cost of living may be an acceptable reason for deviating from the guidelines if substantiated by concrete evidence.

Standard of Living

The primary purpose of child support is to provide for a child's basic survival "needs." However, when substantial resources are available, an effort is made to provide the child with the standard of living he or she would have had if the family had remained intact. The higher the parents' income, the more likely a court will consider standard of living—the country club life, overseas travel, pedigree pets, private school, summer camp, etc. In effect, a child's needs are viewed as relative and directly related to the parents' incomes, and therefore, support awards may vary accordingly. "To be sure, many people, adults and children alike, have far more than they truly 'need' to survive, or even to live comfortably. . . . Even among middle class populations, there is a range of tastes with varying costs. . . . Simply put, given a choice between rhinestones and rubies, many people opt for the latter if they can afford to do so."[43]

PARALEGAL PRACTICE TIP

The Connecticut Supreme Court took the position that an affluent non-custodial parent should not have to contribute more than 15.89% of his income over the maximum guideline amount as additional child support (the maximum percentage at the upper limit of the state's guidelines). See *Maturo v. Maturo*, 296 Conn. 80, 995 A.2d 1 (2010).

Additional examples of circumstances that may justify a deviation include, but are not limited to, the following:

- **Number and ages of the children** This information may be considered if not already factored into the guidelines formula.
- **The financial resources of the child(ren)** A child may receive governmental benefits (such as social security disability income), be a beneficiary of a trust established by a grandparent, or be employed and earning limited or substantial income.
- **Needs, liabilities, and resources of the custodial and the noncustodial parents** Income from a new partner may be considered if it frees up parental income and makes it available for child support purposes. For example, the new partner may be covering the rent or mortgage payment and other household expenses. The child support amount may also include adjustments for substantial liabilities such as student loans.
- **Financial misconduct of either parent** The court may consider whether either parent has failed to comply with discovery requests, made excessive expenditures, or fraudulently concealed or disposed of property in an effort to reduce a child support obligation. Under such circumstances a court may order child support in an amount that deviates from the guidelines and at a level substantially disproportionate to the guidelines amount or to the obligor's alleged ability to pay. (See Case 10.1.)
- **Existence of an agreement between the parties** Based on the strong public policy in favor of protecting the rights and needs of children, the courts retain jurisdiction over child-related issues, including child support. Parents cannot totally waive or relinquish support obligations by agreement, because the right to support is the child's right. However, an agreement of the parties containing provisions relating to child support may be given considerable weight by the court if the terms are reasonable and beneficial to the child, and do not provide for a level of child support below the minimum called for by the child support guidelines as applied to the parties. Courts in many states have enforced provisions in agreements in which noncustodial parents agree to pay child support amounts far in excess of the guidelines amount. For example, in the *Pursley* case, the Kentucky Supreme Court observed that parties to divorce frequently have valid motives for making what may appear to others to be "bad bargains." (See Case 10.2.)

PARALEGAL PRACTICE TIP

The parties need to be sure that the language in their agreement accurately reflects their intentions. For example, in *Cummings v. Lamoureax*, 81 Mass. App. Ct. 506, 964 N.E.2d 993 (2012), the parties' agreement provided that in addition to regular child support, the father would pay the mother 25% of his annual "bonus." She later sought to have all additional income such as commissions included as bonus no matter how it was labeled by the employer. The father disagreed and the court concurred with his position.

CASE 10.1 *Farish v. Farish*, 279 Ga. 551, 615 S.E.2d 510 (2005)

DISCUSSION OF THE CASE

In this case, the Georgia Supreme Court affirmed a district court's order that a noncustodial parent of five children with a gross monthly income of $10,374 be required to pay $3,000 per month for support of the parties' three minor children and $2,000 per month in alimony to his wife of twenty-six years. The court stated that, in determining the obligor's ability to pay, the district court had:

> . . . properly considered appellant's income, property in his possession, the fact that he appropriated for his own use $55,000 of joint or marital assets after the parties' separation for which he had not accounted at the time of trial, and the fact that the appellant accumulated substantial debt after the separation by providing monetary support for his paramour and her family to the detriment of his own children and wife.

(Continued)

CASE 10.2 *Pursley v. Pursley*, 144 S.W.3d 820 (Ky. 2004)

BACKGROUND

Under the parties' agreement in this case, the wife was awarded custody of the parties' two minor children. The husband agreed to pay 30% of all of his income from salaries and bonuses as child support until such time as the children turned eighteen or graduated from college or graduate school, whichever was latest. He also agreed to pay the cost of undergraduate and graduate educations for the children at any school that they chose in the United States. Additionally, he agreed to maintain the children's medical and health insurance and to pay any medical and dental expenses not covered by insurance.

In finding the agreement was not "unconscionable," the court noted the husband was "an educated and sophisticated businessman" with a strong moral desire to meet his obligations and that he was advised by counsel during extensive negotiations.

FROM THE OPINION

. . . One of the primary goals in enacting child support guidelines was to "increase the adequacy of child support awards." Unquestionably, Kentucky took a giant step towards this goal when it enacted the Guidelines. And the purpose of the Guidelines is not offended, but rather is aided by allowing divorcing parents to agree to provide greater support for their children. The Guidelines do not constitute the maximum support that a parent may agree to provide for his or her children. Although, as a rule, it is not in the best interests of the children when their parents agree to an amount of child support below the Guidelines, no one can convincingly argue that the best interests of children are not served when their parents agree to support in excess of the amount established by the Guidelines. Although a court is not bound by such agreements, . . . the Guidelines should not act as a barrier.

SIDEBAR

Do you agree with the court's reasoning? The full opinion in the *Pursley* case is available at *www.pearsonhighered.com/careersresources/* in the website material related to Chapter 10 under Cases.

> **PARALEGAL PRACTICE TIP**
>
> Courts have broad discretion when calculating child support in high-income cases but may exercise restraint when an award appears to serve more as disguised alimony or property division award than as child support.

> **PARALEGAL PRACTICE TIP**
>
> Visit *www.vermontjudiciary.org* to view a child support order form that contains information about parentage, parental responsibilities, medical support, child support (current and arrearages), duration of payment, and method of payment (including a wage-withholding option). Search The List: Master Forms Library for Child Support Order Form.

When and How Can a Child Support Award Be Modified?

Modification of child support awards is governed by federal and state statutes, case law, and specific court rules. There are three primary bases for modification of a child support award:

1. modification triggered by a self-executing provision in an agreement of the parties that has been incorporated into a court's decree

2. modification based on proof of a substantial change in circumstances
3. modification based on a periodic review and adjustment of orders by the state's IV-D agency

MODIFICATION BY AGREEMENT

Although the courts generally encourage settlements, parental agreements that prohibit or limit the power of a court to establish or modify future child support are usually held invalid based on public policy. (See Case 10.3.) However modifications by agreement sometimes are accepted by the courts when they do not waive the child's right to a reasonable level of support consistent with the guidelines and they are in the best interests of the child. Modification provisions in agreements should be tied to actual financial circumstances such as a greater than 20% increase or decrease in the income of one of the parties. Courts have rejected provisions that call for a simple pro rata adjustment in the child support amount as each child reaches age eighteen.[44]

CASE **10.3** *Lee v. Lee*, 2005 ND 129, 699 N.W.2d 842 (2005)

BACKGROUND

In this case, the Supreme Court of North Dakota awarded a custodial father child support despite a provision in his divorce agreement that he would receive primary physical custody of the child and pay a reduced amount of spousal support to his spouse in exchange for her not having to pay child support.

FROM THE OPINION

"The best interests of the children require child support obligors to provide adequate support and maintenance for their minor children." *Smith v. Smith*, 538 N.W.2d 222 (N.D. 1995). . . . For this reason, the court has said, . . . Trial courts should not accept parental stipulations regarding child support if the court determines the stipulation is not in the child's best interests.

SIDEBAR

Do you think parents rather than courts should be able to determine their child support responsibilities? Explain your response. The full opinion in the *Lee* case is available at *www.pearsonhighered.com/careersresources/* in the companion website material related to Chapter 10 under Cases.

MODIFICATION BASED ON PROOF OF A SUBSTANTIAL CHANGE IN CIRCUMSTANCES

Because children's needs and parents' resources can change unpredictably over the life of a support order, states provide for periodic review and modification—up or down as changed circumstances dictate. Either parent can bring a modification action based on a substantial change in circumstances. The moving parent has the burden of proving by a preponderance of the evidence that the requested modification is warranted. State IV-D agencies also can initiate requests for modification on a client's behalf. Although there is no guarantee that a complaint/motion for modification will be granted, it is likely to be if the court is persuaded that the change is substantial enough to make the prior award inequitable and the change is in the best interests of the child. In most states, the burden of showing a substantial change in circumstances will be satisfied if there is a given level of difference between the current presumptive guideline amount and the amount of the order then in force. The difference is sometimes expressed in a percentage. As of January 2015, for example, the percent in Tennessee was 15% (if the current support is $100 or greater per month) and in Indiana, 20%.

Many states require the change to have been "unforeseeable" at the time the initial order was entered. The claims raised most often relate to unanticipated changes in the employment or financial resources of one or both of the parties, a serious injury or illness of a parent or child, the impact of a subsequent family on either party's resources, a change in custody, a major change in the law governing some aspect of child support, or a change in a child's level of need. Generally, a parent may not rely on a claim of decreased income to obtain a modification of support if the parent's reduced earning capacity and inability to pay child support is voluntary. (See Paralegal Application 10.4.) Parents who intentionally try to avoid payment of support or who do not consider their children's needs when changing employment, etc., may not be entitled to a change in child support.

PARALEGAL PRACTICE TIP

To see a Massachusetts "Complaint for Modification of Child Support," and a "Joint Petition for Modification of Child Support" Form, visit *www.mass.gov*. Search under Forms by title. Visit *www.vermontjudiciary.org* to find an example of a form that can be used by a party proceeding *pro se* to request modification of child support or spousal support in Vermont.

Paralegal **Application 10.4**

Does Incarceration Constitute a Substantial Change of Circumstances in the Child Support Context? Yes? No?

The courts have applied three primary approaches when assessing the impact of incarceration on child support obligations:

1. **A no justification rule:** Incarceration does not justify a modification of child support.

    Courts that have adopted the "no justification" rule generally base their decisions on three underlying considerations:

    - It is not in the child's best interest to modify, suspend, or terminate an award because even if not paid during the period of incarceration, the door to reimbursement in the future remains open through collection of arrearages.

    - It is unfair to allow the obligor to benefit from criminal conduct by allowing him or her to use incarceration as a means of escaping child support obligations.

    - It is not appropriate to treat incarceration in the same manner as other forms of voluntary unemployment.

    Pennsylvania's high court took this position in a case of first impression in that state, *Yerkes v. Yerkes*, 573 Pa. 294, 824 A.2d 1169 in 2003. However, the

Pennsylvania legislature subsequently modified that rule when it promulgated 23 Pa. C.S.A. §4352(A.2) which provides: "Incarceration, except incarceration for nonpayment of support, shall constitute a material and substantial change in circumstance that may warrant modification or termination of an order of support where the obligor lacks verifiable income or assets sufficient to enforce and collect amounts due."

2. **A complete justification rule:** Incarceration alone is sufficient to warrant a modification in child support.

    Indiana essentially adopted this approach in *Clark v. Clark*, 902 N.E.2d 813 (Ind. 2009). In that case, the father had been ordered to pay child support of $53 per week, based on the minimum wage. The father claimed that he was unable to fulfill this obligation because he made less than $21 per month at his prison job assignment. The Indiana Supreme Court affirmed the appellate court's ruling vacating the trial court's denial of the father's petition for modification. The court held that it was error in determining support orders to impute potential income to an imprisoned parent based on

(Continued)

pre-incarceration wages or other employment-related income. In petitions to modify support, incarceration may constitute a changed circumstance so substantial and continuing as to make the terms of the existing support order unreasonable. Support orders should be based on the actual income and assets available to the parent while incarcerated. See also *In the Matter of the State of New Hampshire and Cory R. Lounder*, 166 N.H. 353, 96 A.3d 970 (2014) (Respondent's incarceration caused a substantial change of circumstances because respondent lost his employment due to his incarceration, had no ability to obtain employment while incarcerated, and had no other income.)

3. **A one factor rule:** Incarceration should be considered along with other relevant factors when making decisions regarding modification of child support.

    Massachusetts essentially adopts this rule in its child support guidelines providing that incarceration is a sufficient justification for a deviation from the presumptive guidelines amount if "the Payor is incarcerated, is likely to remain incarcerated for an additional 3 years and has insufficient financial resources to pay support." Courts adopting this rule may also consider the nature of the offense resulting in incarceration among other factors.

The second and third rules described above are based primarily on the following assumptions:

- Child support orders should reflect current earning capacity even if earnings are below minimum wage. It is error to set support based on income that is not there during incarceration.
- Imposing high child support payments on incarcerated parents is a punitive measure that can potentially damage the parent-child relationship.
- Incarceration should be distinguished from voluntary unemployment and underemployment when there is an ability to earn more income as well as a deliberate effort to reduce or avoid child support obligations.
- Studies show that unsustainable support orders make it statistically more likely the child will not receive adequate support over the long term.
- When prisoners are released and face the twin barriers of substantial child support arrearages and problems finding employment, they are more likely to face jail time for nonpayment and to enter the "underground economy."

Sidebar

Which of the three rules do you think is most likely to serve the best interests of children? Why? Would you select a different rule if it is not the obligor who is incarcerated but rather the child for whom support is being paid? See *Baumgartner v. Baumgartner*, 237 Ill.2d 468, 930 N.E.2d 1024 (2010).

MODIFICATION BASED ON A PERIODIC REVIEW AND ADJUSTMENT OF ORDERS BY THE STATE'S IV-D AGENCY

Under federal law,[45] without having to show a change in circumstances, the parties to a child support order may request a review every three years to determine whether the child support order in force continues to comply with the state's child support guidelines. States are free to institute shorter review cycles but cannot extend the period beyond three years.

How and by Whom Are Child Support Orders Enforced?

An action to enforce a support order may be brought by a custodial parent, a custodian or guardian of a child, a IV-D agency on behalf of a client, or an agency substantially contributing to the support of the child. There are three primary approaches to enforcement of child support orders:

- The custodial parent may proceed on his or her own with or without counsel, using the resources available through the court system.
- The custodial parent may retain the services of a private child support agency that charges a fee for helping the parent recover the amount of child support owed.
- The custodial parent may use the services of the state's IV-D agency, which has a broad array of available resources and enforcement tools.

THE BASIC TITLE IV-D PROCESS

Under federal law, all child support orders must include an income-withholding provision that allows child support payments to be deducted from an employment related source of income such as the obligor's pay check or a pension, social security or government benefit. Although all orders include such provisions, only IV-D cases (cases involving recipients applying for or receiving public assistance) are subject to an immediate withholding requirement absent good cause shown or an alternative agreement.

When a custodial parent applies for public assistance, he or she is automatically referred to the state's designated IV-D agency for child support services. As a condition of receiving assistance, the parent must assign his or her rights to support to the state and must agree to cooperate with the state in identifying and locating the other parent unless a good cause for noncooperation can be established, such as a prior history of abuse that continues to pose a threat of serious violence. Once a support order is issued, the support obligation runs directly from the noncustodial parent to the state. Any support collected is then used to reimburse the state and federal governments for public assistance payments made to the custodial parent. Under federal law, states may elect to "pass through" to the custodial parent a modest portion of the amount collected, usually not more than fifty dollars.

Many recipients not applying for or receiving public assistance choose, but are not required, to receive assistance from the state's IV-D agency. If the parent does not initially apply for IV-D services, he or she can still elect to do so later by completing the appropriate application. Although the parties may not initially favor income withholding, it does have practical advantages. For example, it ensures payments will be made regularly and that there will be a written record of payments made. If the recipient (usually the custodial parent) elects to use IV-D services, when the support order is obtained, he or she (with or without the assistance of counsel), can ask the court to order that the payments be made through the state's designated IV-D child support enforcement agency. When the agency accepts the recipient's application, it assumes responsibility for collecting and disbursing payments, for monitoring compliance, and for initiating appropriate enforcement measures if a delinquency occurs. The underlying rationale for providing this service is that, if parents receive their child support payments, their need for public assistance will be reduced.

PARALEGAL PRACTICE TIP

Applications for IV-D services are fairly consistent state to state. The form for New Jersey can be viewed at *www.njchildsupport.org*. The "Application for Services of Child Support Services Division" used in the state of Alaska can be seen at *www.courts.alaska.gov*.

PARALEGAL PRACTICE TIP

Although the employer may be inconvenienced, it is illegal to fire someone because of an income assignment order and a failure to comply can subject the employer to sanctions, including fines. The employer also may be held responsible for the amount of any support not withheld due to the employer's omission.

Paralegal **Application 10.5**

An Ethical Issue

Regardless of whether or not a parent with a child support issue is receiving public assistance, the services of a state's IV-D agency are available at little or potentially no cost and without the need to have legal counsel. An attorney has an ethical duty to advise clients of the availability of free IV-D services before undertaking a child support enforcement matter on behalf of a client so that the client can make an informed decision with respect to the need for representation. The IV-D agency is not intended to eliminate the need for counsel but rather to complement it. If a client chooses to retain counsel, the family law team may explain IV-D procedures and assist the client in locating necessary information and completing required paperwork. It is not the paralegal's role to provide legal advice, but the paralegal should be aware of the policy in this area at the firm where he or she works. Some firms have information sheets that can be provided to clients, describing various enforcement and representation options available.[46]

WHEREABOUTS OF THE NONCUSTODIAL PARENT

Often, the first major obstacle to enforcing a child support order is locating the noncustodial parent whose whereabouts may be concealed or unknown. When an **arrearage** arises, the custodial parent typically will be asked to provide counsel with the following kinds of information about the obligor in order to facilitate collection efforts:

Arrearage
a payment that is due but has not been made

- Social Security number
- place of birth
- last known residential address
- current marital status
- responsibility for additional children
- current and past employers' names and addresses
- nature, sources, and location of assets and income
- names and addresses of relatives and friends
- clubs and organizations the obligor has joined
- licenses held (driver's, professional, etc.)
- local banks, public utilities, and other creditors of the obligor

State Parent Locator Service (SPLS)
a federally mandated service provided by each state for the purpose of helping to locate parents who are delinquent in meeting their child support obligations

In enforcement cases, counsel and the custodial parent can also potentially benefit from the availability of a wide range of centralized databases that can be accessed through the state-sponsored IV-D agency or through a private company engaged in the business of collecting delinquent child support payments. As one of its mandated services, each state's IV-D agency provides a **State Parent Locator Service (SPLS)** that connects a variety of data sources at the federal, state, and local levels. The sources include vital statistics, state and local tax records, real and personal property records, records of occupational and professional licenses, employment security, and public assistance records. SPLS also has access to records of other state agencies, such as the Division of Motor Vehicles, Unemployment Commission, Department of Revenue, and Bureau of Prisons. It also maintains the federally mandated State Case Registry (containing information about all support cases within the state's jurisdiction) and the State Directory of New Hires.

If unsuccessful in locating addresses and information about income and assets at the state level, the state's IV-D agency can seek assistance from the **Federal Parent Locator Service (FPLS)** operated by the OCSE. The FPLS, in turn, can draw on the records of other federal agencies such as the Internal Revenue Service, Social Security Administration, Selective Service System, and the Departments of Defense and Labor, as well as the Federal Case Registry of Child Support Orders (FCR) and the National Directory of New Hires.

Federal Parent Locator Service (FPLS)
a service operated by the Office of Child Support Enforcement (OCSE) for the purpose of locating parents delinquent in meeting their child support obligations when multiple states are involved

Paralegal Application 10.6

Alert Re Victims of Domestic Violence

Sometimes the resources of state and federal locator services are misused by individuals who have abused a former partner who has fled in order to protect himself or herself from further abuse. When a client is initiating a search, it is sometimes difficult to assess whether or not the search is being made in good faith. If the client is a victim and IV-D services will be used, it is important that the IV-D agency be advised of the history of abuse so that appropriate protective steps can be initiated at both the state and federal levels. In order to protect victims of domestic violence, a family violence indicator (FVI) is placed on the at-risk individual's name and the names of the children, indicating a restriction on disclosure of data. States are prohibited from releasing information on the whereabouts of "flagged" parents and children to anyone who has committed or threatened domestic violence. The address of the victim(s) will be blocked out in paperwork pertaining to both initial and enforcement actions.

ENFORCEMENT OF AN ORDER AGAINST A NONRESIDENT DEFENDANT

Once a child support order is properly issued, it can be enforced in any state where the obligor or his or her assets are located. However, traveling to the nonresident defendant's state, retaining counsel, and asking the court in that state to enforce the child support order can be time-consuming, costly, and inconvenient. In the alternative, under UIFSA, the petitioner can use the services of the IV-D agency in his or her state to send the court order to an appropriate court in the state where the obligor resides. This is called "registering" the order with the second state, which can then enforce (but not modify) it as if it were an order of that state's court. The petitioner's state is called the "initiating state" and the defendant's state is called the "responding state." Once the order is registered, it is important to keep track of when the nonregistering party receives notice of the order. Generally, if the nonregistering party fails to contest the validity, enforcement, or modification of the registered order, or to seek to vacate the registration within twenty days after notice of registration, the order will be conformed (considered a legal copy) by **operation of law**.[47] If the responding state determines that the order was not properly issued, it may choose not to enforce it.

PARALEGAL PRACTICE TIP

To see an example of an "Inter-state Registration of Support Form," visit *www.courts.delaware.gov.*

Operation of law
a result that occurs automatically because the law mandates it regardless of whether or not a party agrees or intends that result; a party does not need to take any further action to bring about the result

ENFORCEMENT METHODS

There are several mechanisms available to help the **obligee** enforce a child support order. Some flow from federal law and some from state law. Most can be initiated by a state's IV-D agency on behalf of a client, and some can be pursued privately without agency assistance and with or without the assistance of an attorney.

Obligee
a person to whom a debt is owed

The strongest and most comprehensive arsenal is available to the state's IV-D agency. The IV-D process is especially helpful in dealing with nonpayment of support by obligors whose identity or whereabouts are unknown or who have moved to another state or are traveling from state to state to avoid paying support.

A brief description of various enforcement methods is provided below. The success of many of these measures is possible because of the extensive linkages between various state and federal agencies that allow for sharing of data at an unprecedented level.

Criminal Prosecution

In virtually all states, intentional failure to pay child support is a crime that can be prosecuted and punished by probation, fine, and/or incarceration. An intentional failure to pay is distinguished from an involuntary inability to pay. Before a delinquent obligor can be prosecuted at either the state or federal level, the obligor must be financially able to pay the overdue child support. In several states, failure to pay child support is viewed as a "continuing" offense. However, actions to enforce child support orders usually are subject to **statutes of limitations** to protect defendants from having to defend stale claims long after witnesses and evidence may have been lost. Under the federal Deadbeat Parents Punishment Act,[48] criminal nonsupport is a federal felony offense that can result in imposition of a prison sentence of from six months to two years. The nonsupport must have persisted for at least a year and be in an amount greater than $5,000. To trigger federal involvement, multiple states must be involved.[49] For example, the obligor and the child may reside in different states or the obligor may have left the child's home state to avoid paying his or her support obligations. Sometimes criticized as an unwarranted intrusion into matters best left to the states, this option is usually pursued only in the most egregious cases and, generally, when other federal offenses are involved, such as use of a false Social Security number. An action can be initiated by the state, the IV-D agency, or the individual obligee.

Contempt Action

An action may be brought against the delinquent obligor for civil or criminal contempt or both, depending on the circumstances. Although both civil and criminal contempt for nonsupport potentially can result in fines, probation, or jail sentences, the purposes they serve are distinctly different. The purpose of **civil contempt** is remedial in nature. It is designed to encourage the obligor to comply with the child support order and catch up on payment of child support arrearages and thereby purge the contempt and avoid jail. The purpose of **criminal contempt** is punitive. It is designed to punish an individual for willfully disobeying an order of the court. The former serves the needs of the recipient of child support. The latter serves the dignity of the criminal justice system.

In a criminal contempt case, the defendant has a Sixth Amendment right to counsel and contempt must be proven beyond a reasonable doubt. The rights of a respondent in a civil contempt action are less clear. The U.S. Supreme Court has held that the Due Process Clause does not automatically require provision of counsel to indigents in civil contempt proceedings even if they face incarceration. The right to counsel in such cases depends on several factors such as ability to pay and sufficiency of procedural safeguards afforded by the state such as adequate notice and a fair opportunity to present and defend the case. *Turner v. Rogers et al*, 131 S. Ct. 2507, 180 L. Ed. 2d 452 (2011). When researching a case involving right to counsel in this context, paralegals need to also review state laws and cases.

Statute of limitations
a statute that bars a certain type of claim after a specified period of time

PARALEGAL PRACTICE TIP

In Michigan, in a civil context the statute of limitations for bringing an enforcement action for failure to pay support "is ten (10) years from the date that the last support payment is due under the support order regardless of whether or not the last payment is made."[50] The crime of felony nonsupport is subject to a six-year period of limitations.[51]

Civil contempt
a sanction for failure to obey a court order issued for another's benefit; a civil contempt proceeding is remedial in nature and its purpose is to promote compliance with the order

Criminal contempt
a punishment for failure to comply with a court order; a criminal contempt proceeding is punitive in nature and designed to punish an attack on the integrity of the court

PARALEGAL PRACTICE TIP

Although some courts have linked child support and custody/visitation orders, the majority view is that they are independent. If the custodial parent denies visitation in retaliation for a failure to pay child support, he or she also may be subject to a contempt action for custodial interference. The better course of action for the obligee is to seek enforcement of the support order by filing a complaint for contempt.

For example, Ohio courts have held counsel is required in contempt proceedings on child support arrearages and visitation issues unless it is shown the respondent had an ability to pay or waived or otherwise forfeited the right to counsel. See, e.g., *Crain v. Crain, nka Protsman*, 2012 Ohio 6180 (Ohio App. 2012). In family law proceedings in Texas, if incarceration may result, the court is obligated to inform respondents of the right to counsel, and, if indigent, the right to an appointed attorney, Tex. Fam. Code Ann. §157.163 (a), (b).

Income Withholding

The most effective enforcement tool is **income (wage) withholding**, an automatic deduction from the paycheck of an obligor. As indicated earlier in the chapter, all child support orders must include a wage-withholding provision, and an income-withholding order can be sent to an employer in any state. If it is a Title IV-D public assistance case, the wage withholding will take effect immediately absent good cause to suspend it or an alternative arrangement agreed to by the parties. If there is an arrearage, the income-withholding order may be increased on a percentage basis until the arrearage is paid off. If income withholding initially is suspended, it will go into effect when a month of support arrearages has accrued. Prior to this happening, the obligor is entitled to notice and a hearing.

More than half of all child support orders are enforced through this method. There are few defenses to income withholding other than a mistake in the amount of the support or arrearage due or a claim that the amount will exceed the maximum amount that can be withheld from the obligor's disposable earnings under the Federal Consumer Protection Act.

Seizure of Assets

Under federal law, states are required to create administrative procedures designed to automatically create a **lien** on the real or personal property of an obligor located within the state in the amount of unpaid child support. The lien arises by "operation of law" without any action having to be taken by the custodial parent. Under federal law, states must give full faith and credit to liens arising in another state.[52] The lien on the property restricts the ability of the obligor to sell, transfer, or borrow against the property until the arrearage is paid. The custodial parent may need to "perfect" the lien under some circumstances. For example, a lien against real estate should be recorded in the appropriate registry for public records of deeds in order for it to be effective against third parties. This measure is especially effective in cases in which the obligor lacks any income subject to withholding but does own property.

Title IV-D agencies can also attach and seize accounts of a delinquent obligor in financial institutions that operate in more than one state. The seizure can cover several kinds of accounts, such as checking and savings accounts, certificates of deposit, and mutual funds. The obligor will have a limited ability to sell or otherwise transfer those funds until the child support arrearage is satisfied.

Tax Refund Intercepts

Both state and federal tax refunds due to obligors can be intercepted and offset up to the amount of an obligor's child support arrearage. State IV-D agencies submit to the Internal Revenue Service and state Departments of Revenue the names, social security numbers, and amounts of past-due child support arrearages. The Tax Refund Offset Program can collect past-due child support payments from the refund after the obligor

Income (wage) withholding
an automatic deduction of child support from an obligor's paycheck

PARALEGAL PRACTICE TIP

To see an example of an income-withholding form, visit *www.acf .hhs.gov.* Note that the form includes information with respect to limitations on the total amount that may be withheld under federal law.

PARALEGAL PRACTICE TIP

The income-withholding notice can also include a requirement that the employer enroll the obligor's children in the group health insurance program available to the obligor, without the necessity of formally petitioning the court for a **Qualified Medical Child Support Order (QMCSO)**. Prior to federal legislation in this area, many insurance companies denied coverage unless the employee was the custodial parent or claimed the child as a dependent.

Qualified Medical Child Support Order (QMCSO)
a court order requiring provision of medical support or health benefits for the child of a parent covered by a group insurance plan

Lien
an encumbrance on the property of another that operates as a cloud against clear title to the property

PARALEGAL PRACTICE TIP

To see a Notice of Lien Form, visit *www.acf.hhs.gov/programs/cse.*

has received notice of the pending action and been given an opportunity to correct possible errors in a hearing. Only the IV-D agency has access to the federal intercept.

Unemployment Compensation Intercepts

A state's IV-D agency can arrange to intercept social security or unemployment compensation benefits to meet both past-due and continuing child support obligations. Needs-based benefits, such as Social Security Supplemental Income (SSI), are not subject to interception or withholding.

License Denials or Revocations

Under federal law, IV-D agencies can arrange to have a delinquent obligor's vehicle registration and/or driver's license suspended. They may be reinstated once the child support arrearage is paid. The agency can also seek denial or revocation of professional, recreational, or occupational licenses required by states to practice in a variety of professions, such as real estate, plumbing, and teaching. Virtually every state's Bar Association provides that the licenses to practice law of attorneys in contempt for failure to pay child support may be suspended. In particularly egregious cases, an attorney may be disbarred.

Passport Denial

Under federal law, an individual owing over $5,000 in child support may be denied a passport or have an existing passport restricted or revoked.

Credit Reporting

Under federal law, IV-D agencies must periodically report to credit bureaus such as Experian and Equifax the names of delinquent obligors whose support arrearages have reached a specific dollar amount.[53] Prior to the report being made, the obligor must receive notice and have an opportunity for an administrative review. The reporting of child support debts creates a "cloud" on the obligor's credit and alerts potential creditors that an obligor may be a poor risk.

Other Measures

To encourage compliance with support orders, Title IV-D agencies use a variety of additional, less onerous preliminary techniques, such as frequent delinquency notices and telephone reminders. Occasionally, states also implement creative measures such as "Denver"/wheel boots and intercepts of lottery winnings. Many states publish "wanted" posters in public buildings, such as town halls and courthouses, containing photographs of the state's most serious offenders for whom arrest warrants have been issued. Some states have had "amnesty days" when an obligor can settle arrearages and avoid penalties. The threat of prosecution and public humiliation sometimes provides a sufficient incentive to a delinquent obligor to pay off overdue child support.

Tax Implications of Child Support

TAX TREATMENT OF CHILD SUPPORT PAYMENTS

Unlike spousal support payments, child support is a tax-neutral event. Child support payments are not deductible by the payor and are not includable as income to the recipient for income tax purposes. However, when spousal and

---

PARALEGAL PRACTICE TIP

To view an example of an "Order Suspending License (Child Support or Parenting Time)," visit *www.courts .Michigan.gov*.

PARALEGAL PRACTICE TIP

Some enforcement measures raise issues of constitutional dimension. For instance, according to the U.S. Supreme Court, a state cannot deny a marriage license to a delinquent obligor.[54] However, in 2001, the Wisconsin Court of Appeals held, as a condition of probation, that a father who intentionally failed to pay child support for the nine children he'd fathered by four different women could be prevented from having additional children until he made sufficient efforts to support his current children. The dissent expressed deep concern that a dangerous precedent had been set in the area of reproductive rights as the decision in effect established a state-sponsored court-enforced financial test for future parenthood.[55]

child support payments are lumped together in a single payment without any designation as to what portion, if any, constitutes child support, the entire unallocated support amount will be treated as alimony by the Internal Revenue Service (IRS). The full amount paid will then be deductible from the payor's gross income and will be includable in the recipient's income. As tempting as it may be to use this approach (assuming the recipient is in a lower tax bracket and unallocated payments result in a net tax gain for the parties), there may be costly consequences in the long run. As of 2015, the federal tax code retained specific provisions governing unallocated support payments. If, for example, any portion of the unallocated amount is associated in the parties' agreement with a child-related contingency such as a child's reaching the age of majority, getting married, or enlisting in the armed services, there is a rebuttable presumption that a portion of the amount is child support. The IRS may then disallow a previously claimed deduction for that portion and require the obligor to pay taxes, interest, and penalties on it. The obligee, in turn, should be entitled to a refund of the tax paid on that amount.

THE DEPENDENCY EXEMPTION

The general rule is that the custodial parent is entitled to claim the children as dependents for tax purposes, resulting in an adjustment to that party's gross income.[56] The amount of the exemption is subtracted from gross income before the tax is calculated. Because of the potential value of the exemption, parties to a divorce frequently negotiate other arrangements. The parties may agree, for example, to alternate years for claiming the exemption(s), or to divide the exemptions if there is more than one child. In any tax year in which the custodial parent agrees that the other parent may claim one or more of the minor children as dependents, the custodial parent is required to sign a written release, which must be submitted with the tax return of the parent claiming the deduction (IRS Form 8332).

THE CHILD TAX CREDIT

Since 1997, the parent claiming the exemption is also entitled to a child tax credit. This benefit provides the parent with a credit against his or her tax liability rather than an adjustment to gross income.[57] The amount of the credit in 2014 was $1,000. The basic rules and a worksheet for calculating eligibility to claim the credit are explained in IRS publication 972.

The Role of the Paralegal in Child Support Cases

GENERAL RESPONSIBILITIES

The most common tasks a paralegal performs with respect to child support cases are the following:

- Identifying and gathering information concerning any related jurisdictional questions
- Researching the law governing child support actions in the applicable jurisdiction(s)

PARALEGAL PRACTICE TIP

As of spring 2015, problems may arise when the parent mandated to provide health insurance under the Affordable Care Act (the parent who claims the tax exemption) is not the parent ordered to provide insurance for the children under the child support order.

PARALEGAL PRACTICE TIP

One of the most fundamental tasks a paralegal performs in a child support case is to organize and monitor workflow and timelines in the office. An attorney has an ethical duty to carry out contracts to provide legal services and not to neglect or cause damage or prejudice to clients. A failure to file the documents necessary to secure child support for a client that results in a loss of payments to which that client would otherwise be entitled may result in a suspension from the practice of law.[58]

- Collecting, documenting and organizing financial data and other kinds of information necessary to complete appropriate forms and prepare necessary documents and pleadings
- Drafting complaints/petitions, supporting affidavits and proposed orders for child support, or responsive pleadings to complaints/petitions
- Assisting with completion of child support guideline worksheets and drafting related memoranda if a deviation is at issue
- Assisting with preparation of the client's financial affidavit
- Recommending and drafting discovery materials such as interrogatories and deposition questions, and drafting responses to discovery requests received from the opposition
- Drafting child support provisions for inclusion in separation agreements or parenting plans (See Paralegal Application 10.7)
- Assisting with preparation for temporary hearings or trials on the merits
- Tracking the progress of the case to be certain timelines are met
- Drafting Title IV-D correspondence and forms
- Making sure the client is kept informed of progress and upcoming deadlines, hearings, discovery matters, etc.

PARALEGAL PRACTICE TIP

On occasion the paralegal will attend the trial and assist counsel with locating documents when needed, checking numerical calculations, etc.

PARALEGAL PRACTICE TIP

Increasingly states are providing standardized agreement forms that address all issues related to dissolution of a marriage including child support. The parties fill in the blanks on the form to reflect their facts, circumstances, and mutual agreements. To see one such form used in Minnesota, visit *www.mncourts.gov.*

SPECIFIC TASKS PERTAINING TO SEPARATION AGREEMENTS

Child support is frequently a hotly debated issue in a divorce case. Even though the guidelines provide some direction and are intended to be fair to both parents, the issue is not always simple enough to be distilled into a set formula. If the divorcing parties are able—either on their own or with the assistance of counsel and/or a mediator—to negotiate child support terms, they may develop a child support component for inclusion in their separation or parenting agreement. (See Paralegal Application 10.7 and the child support provision in the sample separation agreement in Chapter 13.)

Prior to drafting a child support provision or a proposal to be submitted to the court, information needs to be gathered regarding several preliminary questions:

- What are the financial resources of each of the parties? What is the presumptive figure when child support is calculated according to the guidelines? How long will support last? Is a deviation warranted?
- Do the children have any special needs? Will child support cover expenses like orthodontia, summer camp, clothing for when the child is with the noncustodial parent, dance lessons, private school or college expenses, and uninsured therapy for psychological problems?
- Does either of the parents have any limitations with respect to being able to provide for the children?
- What was the family's standard of living before the parties' separation? Will each of the parties be able to maintain that standard following the divorce, or will the child's standard of living be negatively impacted by living with one parent or the other?
- What is the anticipated parenting plan? Will physical custody be shared or split? Will the children be with the noncustodial parent for significant portions of time? Do the parties live at a considerable distance from each other?
- What are the expectations and motivations of the parties? Is there any chance that a client feels threatened and is agreeing to a low amount of child support because of a fear that if he or she does not comply, custody will not be awarded in the manner desired?

Paralegal Application 10.7

Drafting Pointers for a Child Support Provision in a Separation Agreement or Parenting Plan

A child support provision should address the following:

Amount of child support. The agreement may state that "child support will be in an amount consistent with the child support guidelines," or it may set an amount. If the parties want to deviate from the guidelines in their agreement, the child support amount must first be calculated according to the guidelines. Counsel must be prepared to provide evidence to show that application of the guidelines amount would be unjust, inappropriate, or not in the best interests of the child. If lower than the guidelines amount, it should be shown that the deviation was bargained for in exchange for some other benefit for the child under the agreement.

Timing of support payments. Will there be one or more payments per month, and when are they due?

Method of payments. If neither the child nor the custodial parent is receiving public assistance, will payments be made directly to the recipient? In person? By mail? By direct deposit? If none of these, will payments be made through the state's IV-D agency?

Termination of child support. The agreement should specify the circumstances that will constitute emancipation and be sufficient to trigger termination of child support, such as a child moving away from home or getting a job and covering his or her own living expenses.

Escalation clause. Sometimes the parties build in an automatic-increase clause by tying increases in the child support amount to an official indicator, such as the Consumer Price Index. Some courts do not favor or permit this approach, because it is not sufficiently related to the parties' specific financial circumstances or to the best interests of the child. Another option is to provide that the parties will exchange basic financial information annually and recalculate the child support amount based on the guidelines. This approach takes into account fluctuations in the income of the respective parties but requires continuing contact and may be difficult to implement if the parties' relationship is especially strained.

Income of the child. Will payments be influenced by resources that may become available to the child as a result of employment, trust income, inheritances, etc.?

Visitation/time with the noncustodial parent. Will any adjustment be made in child support payments during periods when the child is with the noncustodial parent? This is an especially important consideration if physical custody is shared or if a child will be spending extended periods (such as the entire summer) with the noncustodial parent.

Extended absences from the custodial parent's home. Will any adjustments be made in the child support amount if, for example, a child will be away at a private school for much of the year or at a summer camp for two months in the summer?

Costs of higher education. In a number of states, the parties may agree on coverage of the costs of higher education. The child support exhibit in the sample separation agreement provided in Chapter 13 contains a detailed provision addressing this issue. Consideration needs to be given to the resources of the parties, where the children will go to college, their special needs or abilities, the resources that may be available to them through scholarships and financial aid, and the costs associated with a basic program of study. For instance, will "college expenses" cover tuition, room, board, books, computers, uniforms, fees, etc.? Will expenses be capped at a particular level? Will payments go to the custodial parent or directly to the educational institution?

Extracurricular activities. There are a host of activities available to children today, such as music, dance, art or drama lessons, computer camps, and athletic activities, including sports clinics, but not without cost. The parties need to spell out how decisions will be made with respect to participation in these activities as well as how associated costs will be covered.

Medical insurance. Which party will pay for coverage for the children and how will uninsured medical expenses be handled? "Medical" should be broadly defined to include dental and eye care (glasses, etc.).

Income tax treatment of the child support payments. Assuming there will not be an unallocated support amount, the parties should indicate that child support payments will be nondeductible to the payor and nonincludable in the income of the recipient.

Dependency exemption. The parties should set forth their understanding regarding who will claim the exemption. If the noncustodial parent is going

(Continued)

to claim the exemption for one or more of the children, the agreement should provide that the custodial parent agrees to cooperate by executing IRS Form 8332 in a timely manner so that it can be filed with the obligor's return.

Security for child support payments. The parties may agree on some form of security for child support, such as a trust or insurance policy with the child as the named beneficiary.

Dispute resolution. The general provisions of the parties' separation agreement usually include a dispute resolution provision, but if not, it is useful to indicate how the parties intend to resolve disputes pertaining to child support.

CHAPTER **SUMMARY**

As much as the concept of family has evolved over the past five decades, one feature has remained constant: the belief that parents have a duty to provide for the children they adopt or bring into the world until such time as those children reach the age of majority or are otherwise emancipated. The economic impact of a parental failure to do so is sufficiently costly to society at large that the federal government has assumed a dramatic leadership role in an area historically left to regulation by the states. It has taken giant steps in a national effort to hold parents accountable by mandating the designation of Title IV-D agencies in each state and facilitating interstate cooperation through UIFSA.

In order to establish and enforce child support awards, the courts must have subject matter jurisdiction over matters relating to the financial needs of children and personal jurisdiction over potential obligors. These requirements are not always easily satisfied. The child may have been moved from state to state. The identity of a child's father or the whereabouts of a noncustodial parent may be unknown. To help address this challenge, the federal government has required the states to have expedited procedures for establishing legal paternity, mandated the adoption of the Uniform Interstate Family Support Act, and created massive interrelated databases such as parent locator services, child support case registries, and new hire directories.

At the heart of a child support case is the establishment of a child support award through application of guidelines mandated by the federal government and designed by the states to promote efficiency and fairness. Each state chooses its own underlying model and identifies the kinds of factors the courts can consider when establishing and modifying child support awards, taking into account special circumstances such as the existence of multiple families, shared parenting arrangements, and educational needs. However, whether dealing with an initial order or a modification, an order is essentially worthless if it cannot be enforced. Once again, the federal government has stepped into the arena, creating the federal crime of criminal nonsupport and mandating that the states put in place a variety of other enforcement strategies, such as income withholding, tax intercepts, and denial of professional and driver's licenses, in addition to the more traditional methods of civil and criminal contempt. Statistics suggest that progress is being made, but that there is still much to be done to ensure that parents meet their legal obligations and adequately provide for their children.

Although historically much of the legislation at the state and federal level has focused on "paternity" and holding fathers accountable, child support laws apply equally to mothers and fathers. The gradual and now nationwide extension of the right to marry to same-sex couples many of whom choose to have families has not altered the basic principle that legal parents have a duty to support their children. The changes that have occurred relate more to adjusting and gender neutralizing long existing rules, forms and procedures to accommodate an increasing diversity in family structures.

Because of the complexity and fact-intensive nature of child support cases and the considerable variation in approaches from one state to another, the content of this chapter includes many illustrative examples. When working with a specific child support issue, it is important for paralegals to be aware of, and to research as necessary, the governing law in the jurisdiction where the case arises to help ensure that all clients are well represented.

CONCEPT REVIEW AND REINFORCEMENT

KEY **TERMS**

IV-D agency
Actual service of process
Age of majority
Arrearage

Case registry (federal and state)
Child support
Child support guidelines
Civil contempt

Criminal contempt
Custodial parent
Directory of New Hires (state and national)

Doctrine of necessaries
Emancipation
Extraordinary expense
Home state
Imputed income
Income withholding
In loco parentis
Joint physical custody
Lien
Long-arm jurisdiction

Noncustodial parent
Obligee
Obligor
Operation of law
Parent Locator Service (state and federal)
Personal jurisdiction
Public assistance programs
Public charge
Putative father
Putative father registry

Qualified Medical Child Support Order
    (QMCSO)
Rebuttable presumption
Split custody
Statute of limitations
Subject matter jurisdiction
Transitional Assistance to Needy
    Families Program (TANF)
Uniform Interstate Family Support Act
    (UIFSA)

REVIEW **QUESTIONS**

1. Define "child support" and explain the public policy behind requiring parents to pay child support.
2. Identify conditions under which the duty to pay child support commonly terminates. Under what kinds of circumstances might the duty of support continue?
3. Distinguish between child support and spousal support.
4. Describe the origin and purposes of Title IV-D agencies.
5. Describe the origin and primary purposes of the Uniform Interstate Family Support Act, and identify three bases on which a court might obtain personal jurisdiction over a nonresident defendant under UIFSA's long-arm provisions.
6. Identify the primary purposes child support guidelines serve.
7. Define income. Identify three types of "income" that are usually not considered income in the child support context.
8. Define the term "imputed income." Give two examples of circumstances in which income might be imputed to a party.
9. Identify three circumstances in which a court might consider deviating from a child support amount that is presumptively appropriate under the guidelines.
10. Identify three ways in which a parent may obtain a modification of child support.
11. Define and give two examples of "extraordinary expenses." How do the courts generally deal with such expenses?
12. Describe how the majority of courts treat the existence of multiple families when making decisions about child support.
13. Identify some of the ways in which courts address parental responsibility for the cost of their children's higher education.
14. Identify at least five methods of enforcing child support obligations.
15. Identify and describe the major tax implications of child support.
16. Identify at least five terms paralegals may include when drafting child support provisions for separation agreements.

DEVELOPING YOUR PARALEGAL SKILLS

FOCUS ON **THE JOB**

In this activity, the student is asked to draft a Motion for Temporary Child Support, a supporting affidavit, and a proposed order tailored to a comprehensive fact pattern.

The Facts

William Pelletier and Betty Kelley began living together in the month of September nine years ago and got married three years ago on Valentine's Day. They have three daughters, Jennifer, Judie, and Jessica. Jennifer was born on June 26, 2005; Judie was born on June 24, 2007; and Jessica was born on July 4, 2010. William voluntarily acknowledged paternity at the time of each child's birth and has been a consistently adequate provider for Betty and the children. The three children are presently living with their mother in the home she inherited outright from her mother.

The home is assessed at $375,000. Betty's father also has been very generous to her throughout her life. Over the past nine years, he has given her gifts of furniture, clothing, an automobile, several vacations with William and the children, and occasional cash gifts of up to $10,000 a year to help out with expenses, including special activities for the children. Betty hopes that he will continue to help her out when William is gone. She is aware that when her father dies, he plans to leave his fortune to a cancer research facility.

William has been working as an accountant for the entire period the parties have been together. His income has varied from a low of $24,000 in 2009 to a high of $97,000 in 2006. His income for last year was $62,000. Betty was a nurse before the children were born, and in her last year of full-time work, 2004, she earned about $42,000. She has occasionally worked night shifts since then but last year earned only $2,000. William and Betty agreed when Jennifer was born that Betty should stay home and care for the baby, and they have maintained that arrangement until the present time. Recently William decided to leave his job as an accountant working for wealthy people whose values and business ethics he found offensive. He has developed a fervent desire to become a missionary in Africa, where he will be receiving a token stipend of $5,000 a year. He will not have to pay for his food or housing, and his primary means of transportation will be a bicycle. He has not left the state yet but plans to leave before next Christmas. For now, he is living with a friend at 120 Bay Road in your town and state. Betty's address is around the corner at 250 Harrison Avenue, your town and state.

Betty is not certain what William has in the way of assets, as he has managed all the finances and paid all the bills during their relationship, saying it was "the least I can do, given that you take care of the kids all day." She knows at the very least that he has an investment portfolio valued at about $500,000, which generates interest and dividends of a minimum of $25,000 a year. They had a joint bank account with $17,000 in it, but William closed it out without notice to Betty. About $10,000 of that amount was a gift to Betty from her dad. Neither of the parties has any debts.

Betty says she doesn't care about herself but anticipates that she will continue to require the basic necessities for the children's benefit, such as food, clothing, and housing costs (taxes, insurance, utilities, etc.), medical expenses, and education-related expenses. In addition, Jennifer shows considerable promise as a figure skater, and Betty hopes she can continue to keep up with her lessons and practice time,

which cost about $250 a month. All three children are likely to require orthodontia work at some point down the road. Although he plans to stay in Africa for an indefinite period of time, William intends to retain his citizenship and residency in the state by using his sister's address. Although he realizes there are some negatives to this arrangement, such as having to pay taxes, he is a patriotic American citizen and wants to be able to complete absentee ballots and vote in each election.

William has filed a Complaint for Divorce in your local jurisdiction. He says that, since he will be in Africa and unable to visit the children, he doesn't think he should have to pay child support. Betty says the two of them brought the children into the world and each of them has a duty to support them.

The Assignment

Betty has contacted your supervisor, Attorney Howell, and wants to seek child support. She feels she should at least get the amount she would receive under the state's child support guidelines but isn't sure she can do that given the circumstances. At this point, Attorney Howell has asked you to draft the appropriate documents for your jurisdiction to seek temporary child support including a Motion for Temporary Child Support, a supporting affidavit for Betty's review and signature, and a proposed order. You should locate the statute in your jurisdiction that allows the court to order William to pay temporary child support. Locate models of all three documents, but be sure to tailor your documents to the facts of this particular case, applying the material covered in this chapter as appropriate.

FOCUS ON **ETHICS**

In this activity the student is asked to prepare an internal memorandum regarding the conduct of a paralegal in the context of a meeting with a client.

The Assignment

Assume that you are a paralegal in the law office of Christopher Riggs, Esquire, a solo family law practitioner who represents William Pelletier in the above fact pattern. You are impressed with William and the personal sacrifice and commitment he intends to make as a missionary. While sitting with you in your lovely private office, William tells you that he expects Attorney Riggs to represent him on a *pro bono* basis. In response, you tell him that Attorney Riggs never accepts *pro bono* cases. William also tells you that he realizes that, because he has some substantial assets, he probably will be ordered to pay child support, but doesn't think he should have to under the circumstances. You sympathize with him and suggest that if he can get Betty to agree to let him satisfy

his child support obligation in the form of "alimony" rather than "child support," he will be able to deduct it from his income and at least receive that advantage. You also suggest that he should try to get the dependency exemptions for the three children. You later tell Attorney Riggs about this conversation and he is very concerned. He gives you a copy of the ethical canons for paralegals promulgated by the National Association of Legal Assistants (contained in Appendix A) along with a copy of the material on ethics included in Chapter 1 of this text. He then directs you to review that material and prepare a memorandum to him in which you (a) describe the issues the incident with Mr. Pelletier raises, (b) explain how you have violated basic ethical principles including the canons and (c) recommend an appropriate course of action given your conduct. For example, should you be fired or reprimanded? Should you be required to enroll in an ethics course for paralegals? Should you be required to draft a letter to the client, and if so, what should it say?

FOCUS ON **CASE LAW**

In this Focus on Case Law, the student is asked to respond to a series of questions regarding a case that involves several of the issues addressed in this chapter.

The Assignment

Read the New Hampshire case *Donovan v. Donovan, Jr.,* 152 N.H. 55, 871 A.2d 30 (2005) and then respond to the following questions:

1. What is the legal history of the case: Where was it brought prior to reaching the New Hampshire Supreme Court and with what result?

2. What were the issues being appealed and by whom?

3. On what authority did the trial court impute income to the mother? How was the figure for imputed income determined and by whom? What did the New Hampshire Supreme Court decide with respect to this issue and why? Do you agree with the trial court's or the state supreme court's decision? Explain your reasoning.

4. Describe the respective positions of the parties regarding whether or not the basic support award covered the cost of extracurricular activities. What did the New Hampshire Supreme Court decide with respect to this issue, and do you agree with that position?

5. What did the parties' agreement provide with respect to an annual increase in child support? Did the New Hampshire Supreme Court agree with this position? Why?

6. What was the state of the law in New Hampshire regarding the court's ability to order parents to pay for the college education of their children at the time the case was tried? What was the parties' agreement with respect to coverage of college expenses? Did the New Hampshire Supreme Court modify the parties' agreement? Why? What was the position of the dissent? Do you agree with the majority or the dissent? On what grounds?

The opinion in the *Donovan* case can be accessed at *www.pearsonhighered.com/careersresources/* in the resource material related to Chapter 10 under Cases.

FOCUS ON **STATE LAW AND PROCEDURE**

This activity requires the student to complete a jurisdictionally appropriate child-support-guidelines worksheet based on a specific set of facts.

The Assignment

Assume that the firm where you are employed represents William in the above Focus on the Job exercise. On his behalf, locate and complete the child support guidelines form/worksheet used in your state. Two websites may be of assistance with this task: *www.findlaw.com* and *www. supportguidelines.com*. For purposes of the guidelines calculation, assume that the parties have agreed on the following:

- The three children will live with their mother and the father will have no visitation for the foreseeable future, given his unique circumstances.

- Betty is caring for the children a majority of the time, and childcare expenses should amount to no more than $250 per month.

- Betty's annual gross income is $2,000 and her adjusted gross income is $1,850.

- William's annual gross income is $59,000 and his adjusted gross income is $49,000 (Federal taxes $7,500, social security tax $2,500).

- William has agreed to maintain health insurance coverage for Betty and the children at a cost of $320 per month. He will not carry insurance for himself, as he will be in a remote African village where medical services although minimal, are available at no cost to missionaries.

- Betty's dad has agreed to make arrangements to cover Jennifer's ice skating program for as long as she remains actively involved.

FOCUS ON **TECHNOLOGY**

In addition to the many links included throughout the chapter, this activity provides a series of useful websites for reference, along with technology-related assignments for completion.

Websites of Interest

www.abanet.org

This is the website for the American Bar Association. The Home page provides a search option where you can search for child support, child support guidelines, etc. You should be able to locate a number of excellent resources, including a chart that indicates the type of child support model used in each state (and the District of Columbia) and whether each state's guidelines address extraordinary medical expenses, child care expenses, college support, and shared parenting. See "Chart #3 Child Support Guidelines" at *www.americanbar.org*.

www.acf.hhs.gov

This is the site for the Administration for Children and Families (ACF), the federal agency that assists the states, territories, and tribal organizations through programs in support of children and families. It contains links to a number of topics related to family law, including child support. A useful *Handbook of Child Support Enforcement* is available at this site.

www.acf.hhs.gov

This is the website for the federal Office of Child Support Enforcement. There is a wealth of material available on this website, including the publication "Essentials for Attorneys in Child Support Enforcement" (3rd edition, 2002) and a listing of and links to child support (IV-D) agencies in each state.

www.alllaw.com

This site offers a feature called child support calculators for all states. Care must be taken to verify that appropriate and current guidelines are used.

www.ancpr.org

This is the website of the Alliance for Noncustodial Parents' Rights. It is both an informational and advocacy site, particularly for noncustodial fathers. Cases relating to various child support issues are identified.

www.census.gov

This site provides a number of statistical reports related to the topic of child support. Visit *www.census.gov*. One of the most informative reports available at this site is by T. Grail, "Custodial Mothers and Fathers and Their Child Support."

www.divorcenet.com

This site provides advice on family-law-related issues, including child support.

www.findlaw.com

Select "Legal Professionals" and then "Family Law" under "Practice Areas," and then search for child support guidelines. Relevant links are provided to information about child support in all states and the District of Columbia.

www.supportguidelines.com

This is a comprehensive resource on child support guidelines in the United States. It provides a number of useful resources and links. Child support guideline worksheets for most states can be accessed via links on this site.

Assignments

1. Visit the following three websites, which are designed to help custodial parents receive the child support to which they are entitled. Explore the sites, summarize the kinds of information available, and indicate which site you think is most helpful.
   www.jfs.ohio.gov This is the site for the Office of Child Support in the Ohio Department of Jobs and Family Services.
   www.judiciary.state.nj.us This is the Home Page of the New Jersey Judiciary. Scroll to the bottom of the page to the "Quick Site Index." Open the dropdown menu in the box and select "Child Support." Click on "Go." Check out the resources "Guide to Applying for Child Support and Application," "Guide to Court Enforcement of Child Support," etc.
   www.dss.virginia.gov This is the site for the Virginia Department of Social Services. Select "Child Support" on the top banner of the Home Page.

2. Go to *www.supportguidelines.com*. Click on "Resources and Links" and then on "Child Support Guidelines on the Web." Find your state and see what information and forms you are able to find.

3. Locate online information about your local IV-D agency and the services it provides. In particular, search for an Application to receive services.

PORTFOLIO PRODUCTS

1. Motion for temporary child support with an affidavit and a proposed order
2. Memorandum on ethics issues in a hypothetical case
3. Responses to questions on a New Hampshire child support case
4. Completed Child Support Guidelines Worksheet

chapter 11
SPOUSAL SUPPORT

© vovan/Shutterstock

LEARNING OBJECTIVES

After reading this chapter and completing related assignments, you should be able to:

- define spousal support and describe how it has evolved

- distinguish between spousal support and property division

- identify various types of spousal support

- identify the kinds of factors courts consider when making spousal support determinations

- list at least five terms a spousal support provision in a separation agreement should contain

- explain when and how spousal support awards can be modified, terminated, and enforced

- identify the primary tax and bankruptcy implications of spousal support

- describe the role of the paralegal in a spousal support case

Introduction

In Chapter 10 we examined the duty of parents to provide for their children. In this chapter we look at the evolution of the common law duty of spouses to support each other during their marriage and upon divorce if warranted by the circumstances. The distinctions between spousal support, child support, and property division are highlighted. While recognizing that variations exist among the states, the content initially focuses on the most common types of alimony and the kinds of factors considered by the courts when making decisions about spousal support. It then identifies key features of alimony provisions in separation agreements and discusses the modification, termination and enforcement of spousal support awards.

What Is Spousal Support?

Spousal support is an allowance for support and maintenance that one spouse may be ordered by a court to pay to the other spouse while they are divorced or living apart. If the parties are divorced, it is usually called **alimony**, maintenance, or spousal support. If they are legally separated, it is customarily called separate support or separate maintenance.

Spousal support/alimony
an allowance for support and maintenance that one spouse may be ordered by a court to pay to the other spouse while they are divorced or living apart; also called separate maintenance, or separate support depending on the circumstances and the jurisdiction

399

Each state has developed its own approach to if and when spousal support will be awarded, what it will be called, what its purpose is, who will receive it, how much will be received, and for how long.

Spousal support is distinct from child support. (See Exhibit 10.1 in Chapter 10.) Parents have a legal duty to support their children that cannot be waived or bargained away. Spousal support, on the other hand, is a duty that flows from one spouse to the other. However, marriage does not create an "entitlement" to spousal support upon divorce or separation. It generally can be waived or bargained away, and it may not be awarded absent one spouse's demonstrated need and the other spouse's ability to pay. It may also be subject to other restrictions based on state law.

How Has Spousal Support Evolved?

AN HISTORICAL PERSPECTIVE

The origins of alimony in the United States can be traced to the English legal system. In England, ecclesiastical or church courts initially had exclusive jurisdiction over family-related legal matters. The church courts applied **canon law**, the church's body of law. Ecclesiastical courts granted two kinds of "divorces": **divorce *a mensa et thoro***, a divorce from bed and board that allowed the parties to live separate and apart but not remarry (as in a present-day **legal separation**), and in rare instances **divorce *a vinculo matrimonii***, essentially an **annulment** of an invalid marriage based on a canonical disability existing before the marriage (e.g., bigamy). Upon a divorce *a mensa et thoro*, an ecclesiastical court could require a husband to pay support to his wife (provided she was an innocent spouse) based on the belief that he had a lifelong duty to provide for her, even if they ceased living together.

The Divorce Act of 1857[1] (the Matrimonial Causes Act) relieved the ecclesiastical courts of their divorce jurisdiction and established **absolute divorce** by judicial decree under English common law, allowing the courts to terminate valid marriages. The Act also granted judges jurisdiction to order a husband to provide for an innocent wife after their marriage ended. The amount he was required to provide was based on her wealth, his means, and their respective conduct during the marriage. The assumption was that innocent women who were abandoned by or separated from their husbands should be awarded alimony because they lacked the ability to provide for themselves. That assumption was reasonable, given that, upon marriage, women in most states gave up their rights to enter into contracts, own property in their own names, and possess and control their earnings. The English common law system eventually adopted by a majority of the states brought with it this dual emphasis on fault and the economic dependence of wives on their husbands. Up until the 1970s, men still tended to hold title to the majority of assets obtained during the marriage. Upon divorce, they kept their assets, and "innocent" wives often received substantial long-term alimony awards with which to support themselves. The courts continued to retain the remnants of a husband's duty of support into the early no-fault era, although **Married Women's Property Acts**, eventually passed in all fifty states, eliminated many of the economic legal disabilities that had made it impossible for women to earn money or own property in their own names while married.

Canon law
church law; the body of law developed within a particular religious tradition

Divorce *a mensa et thoro*
[Latin: from board and hearth] a divorce from bed and board only; a legal separation

Legal separation
a judicial decree that allows the parties to live separate and apart without dissolving their legal relationship as husband and wife; sometimes called a limited divorce

Divorce *a vinculo matrimonii*
[Latin: from the chains or bonds of marriage] literally, a divorce from the chains or bonds of matrimony; a divorce that frees the parties to remarry

Annulment
the legal procedure for declaring that a marriage is null and void because of an impediment existing at its inception

Absolute divorce
a total divorce of husband and wife that dissolves the marital bond; frees the parties to remarry

Married Women's Property Acts
state statutes that extended to women various property rights that were denied to them under common law, including ownership and control of property. The majority of states passed such acts in the 1850s.[2]

A CONTEMPORARY PERSPECTIVE

Since the onset of no-fault divorce in the 1970s and the revision of property division laws allowing women to be awarded a "fair" or equal share of the marital assets, alimony awards have decreased in number and generally become limited in duration. Today, a reasonable estimate of the frequency of alimony awards granted upon divorce is 10% to 15%, and the vast majority of these are to women. They are primarily designed to enable a dependent spouse to develop skills, enter or reenter the workforce, and become self-sufficient. The ultimate goal is, in a relatively short time, to cut permanently the economic cord between the husband and wife.

The general rule is that, even if marital fault is sometimes factored into alimony determinations, the purpose of alimony is no longer to punish an obligor for some alleged misconduct or to reward an "innocent" spouse. The *Mani* case in New Jersey reflects the challenge faced by a court in a heavily "no-fault" state struggling with the question of what role, if any, fault should play in alimony determinations. (See Case 11.1.)

CASE 11.1 *Mani v. Mani,* 183 N.J. 70, 869 A.2d 904 (2005)

DISCUSSION OF THE CASE

Unusual for several reasons, this case involved an alimony award to a husband. After a twenty-seven-year marriage, the wife was ordered to pay her spouse $610 per week in spousal support. She had well over $2 million in assets, and her spouse had assets totaling a few hundred thousand dollars and a minimum earning capacity of about $25,000 per year. The trial court based its award on the husband's "economic dependency." Both parties appealed. The husband sought more alimony, claiming he would otherwise be unable to meet his monthly expenses and maintain his standard of living. The wife argued he should receive no alimony whatsoever based on his "indolence" in meeting his own needs and his lack of noneconomic contribution to the marriage as well as his marital infidelity and extreme cruelty. The appeals court refused to eliminate the alimony award but also refused to raise it, based on the husband's alleged adulterous and abusive conduct during the marriage (which was not taken into account by the trial court). Both parties appealed to the New Jersey Supreme Court.

The New Jersey Supreme Court's opinion includes a thoughtful review of the history of alimony in general and specifically in New Jersey. It describes alimony as an economic right arising out of marriage that is designed to provide a dependent spouse with a standard of living generally commensurate with the quality of economic life that existed during the marriage. While noting that New Jersey can be characterized as a "no-fault" state in most respects, the court addressed the issue of what consideration, if any, should be given to marital misconduct in alimony determinations. The court ruled that marital fault is irrelevant except in two narrow instances:

1. when the fault affects the couple's economic life, as when one spouse gambles away the parties' assets
2. when the fault "so violates societal norms that continuing the economic bonds between the parties would confound notions of simple justice." Hiring someone to murder a spouse would constitute such a fault

PARALEGAL PRACTICE TIP

The South Carolina alimony statute can be found at *www.judicial.state.sc.us.* Note that under the statute marital fault can be considered in alimony determinations if it affected the economic circumstances of the parties or contributed to the breakup of the marriage, and that no alimony will be awarded to a spouse who commits adultery prior to execution of a separation agreement or entry of an order of separate maintenance.

The dependent husband's marital infidelity standing alone was not viewed as a sufficiently shocking violation of social norms to deny him alimony in the context of a divorce.

SIDEBAR

The New Jersey Supreme Court reversed and remanded the case to the appellate division for reconsideration of the alimony award without regard to fault. Do you agree with that decision? To what extent, if at all, do you believe marital fault should factor into the alimony equation? The full opinion in the *Mani* case is available at *www.pearsonhighered.com/careersresources/* in the website material related to Chapter 11 of this text under Cases.

In the current no-fault environment, the primary focus is on spousal support as an economic event flowing from the marital partnership, and either the husband or the wife may be ordered to pay alimony. Most states gender-neutralized their alimony statutes on their own initiative in the 1970s. The issue was settled for the remainder of the states by the U.S. Supreme Court's 1979 decision in *Orr v. Orr*. In *Orr*, the Court declared an Alabama statute that imposed alimony obligations only on husbands unconstitutional as a violation of the Fourteenth Amendment's Equal Protection Clause.[3]

What Are the Differences Between Alimony and Property Division?

In states where it is allowed, decisions about alimony are generally not made until after the court has determined a suitable division of marital property. If each party is allocated sufficient property to maintain the standard of living that characterized their marriage, alimony may not be even become an issue. It is also unlikely to become an issue in many divorces because the parties have more liabilities than assets, and there is insufficient income for an alimony award to even be considered.

Although an order for alimony cannot realistically be viewed apart from a division of marital assets, the considerations involved in each decision are different. The primary distinctions between alimony and property division are briefly summarized in Exhibit 11.1.

EXHIBIT 11.1 Alimony and Property Division—A Comparison

Alimony	Property Division
Alimony originated in the common law duty of a husband to support his wife, a duty now deemed gender-neutral.	Property division evolved with no-fault divorce and its emphasis on marriage as a partnership.
At the time of divorce, alimony focuses on what each party will need going forward into the future.	At the time of divorce, property division looks back to identify assets accumulated by the parties during the marriage that should be divided upon divorce.

(Continued)

EXHIBIT 11.1 (Continued)

Alimony awards are based on need and ability to pay, along with other factors considered relevant by statute and/or case law.	Division of property is based on the concept that both parties contribute to the marital enterprise, and thus each party is entitled to a share of the partnership upon divorce according to community property or equitable distribution principles.
The court must have personal jurisdiction over the defendant, who must be provided with notice in order for an alimony order to be issued and enforceable.	The court must have jurisdiction over the parties and the property to be divided.
Alimony is usually in the form of cash payments payable on a periodic basis (e.g., monthly).	Property division usually involves transfers of property at the time of the divorce, such as an interest in a marital residence or a bank account.
Although lump-sum alimony is occasionally awarded, alimony is usually payable over a period of time. Payments **vest** as they fall due.	A property division order is effective as of the date of divorce, at which time the rights to property are vested and enforceable against the other party's estate as a debt.
Absent an agreement to the contrary, alimony is usually modifiable upon a material change of circumstances that significantly affects the payee's need or the payor's ability to pay, although some jurisdictions consider alimony awards final absent a specific reservation of jurisdiction.	Absent fraud, etc., property division is rarely modifiable.
Alimony is tax-deductible to the payor and income to the payee.	Payments or transfers made pursuant to a property division are not taxable events.
Alimony is generally not dischargeable in bankruptcy.	Property division settlements in the nature of "support" are generally not dischargeable.
Death usually terminates alimony obligations (with the exception of arrearages) absent a judgment or agreement to the contrary.	Property division is not affected by the death of a party after the court has rendered a judgment. A property division is enforceable against the estate of a decedent.
Alimony obligations usually terminate on the recipient's remarriage, absent a statute, court order, or agreement to the contrary.	Property division is not affected by the remarriage of either party.
Alimony is no longer primarily punitive in nature, although in some states, the courts consider misconduct during the marriage, particularly economic misconduct, as a factor in calculating an alimony award.	In a divorce granted on fault grounds (still available in many states), a court may award a larger portion of the marital assets to the aggrieved party. Even in states where fault grounds are unavailable, serious misconduct during the marriage (particularly misconduct with economic consequences) may influence the division of property in both community property and equitable division jurisdictions.

Vest
to give a person an immediate, fixed right of ownership and present or future enjoyment; this right usually cannot be taken away by subsequent events or circumstances

How Does a Party Obtain an Alimony Award?

PROCEDURE

PARALEGAL PRACTICE TIP

To see an example of a Motion and Declaration for Temporary Order (including alimony), visit *www.courts .wa.gov/forms.* (Washington)

Customarily, the procedure for obtaining spousal support is for the parties to exchange proposals, negotiate, and agree to an alimony provision in a separation agreement, or for one or both of the parties to petition the court for a suitable award given the facts of the case. In rare instances, however, a court will make an alimony award on its own initiative.[4] Requests for temporary alimony may be made while a divorce action is pending.

PARALEGAL PRACTICE TIP

The 2005 *Thornley* case (*In re Marriage of Thornley*, 361 Ill. App. 3d 1067, 838 N.E. 2d 981 (2005)), provides an example of a case in which a court ordered alimony on its own initiative. It can be found at *www.pearsonhighered.com /careersresources/* in the material related to Chapter 11 under Cases.

INITIAL STEPS TOWARD AN ALIMONY AWARD

Initial efforts of the family law team on behalf of a client in an alimony case usually focus on answering the following five questions:

1. What is the governing law in the jurisdiction with respect to alimony awards?
2. Have the parties executed a premarital agreement, and if so, what does it provide with regard to alimony?
3. Does one party have a need for alimony that the other party has the ability to pay?
4. What factors will the court consider when making an alimony decision?
5. Is one or both of the parties likely to file for bankruptcy at some point in the future?

What is the governing law in the jurisdiction with respect to alimony awards?

PARALEGAL PRACTICE TIP

Paralegals need to be familiar with the approach to alimony/spousal support in their jurisdiction. For example, absent exceptional circumstances, Utah does not permit an alimony award to last longer than the length of the parties' marriage, and a minority of states, including Louisiana, only allow alimony to be awarded to a party who is "free of fault" prior to the filing of a divorce action.

This is the threshold question in an alimony case as the response may be dispositive. The current statutes, rules, and case law that govern alimony in the jurisdiction where the action may be brought must be identified given the wide variations that exist among the states and even among counties and individual judges within states. The kinds of questions about controlling law that need to be answered include the following:

- Are alimony awards allowed in the jurisdiction?
- If alimony is allowed, what kinds of alimony awards are made? (See Exhibit 11.2.)
- Are waivers of alimony permitted?
- Are awards of limited duration?
- Are there guidelines in place that need to be considered with respect to setting the amount of alimony to be paid?
- Is marital fault a bar to receiving alimony or a factor to be considered in the amount of the award?
- What factors do the courts consider most important in the alimony context?

Based on the answers to these initial questions, counsel will have a preliminary opinion about the merits of a potential alimony claim and the form or forms of alimony that may be available, an opinion which may or may not be altered after questions about property division and child support are answered.

Have the parties executed a premarital agreement and, if so, what does it provide with regard to alimony?

If the parties have executed a **premarital agreement**, a copy needs to be obtained for review by the attorney. If the agreement contains a full or limited **waiver** of alimony, research may need to be done on the enforceability of the particular waiver in the jurisdiction. A majority of the states that have considered premarital agreements waiving spousal support have upheld them.[5] although a limited number (such as South Dakota) exclude alimony waivers from premarital agreements by statute or case law. (See Case 11.2.)

The Uniform Premarital Agreement Act, (UPAA) adopted in whole or in part in about half of the states, as well as the more recent Uniform Premarital and Marital Agreements Act (UPMAA) allow provisions in otherwise valid premarital agreements that establish or eliminate spousal support unless enforcement would bring about an unconscionable result, such as causing a spouse to become eligible for public assistance at the time of separation or divorce. Most states that have not adopted the UPAA or the UPMAA apply a similar standard. See, for example, *O'Daniel v. O'Daniel,* 419 S.W.3d 280 (Tenn. App. 2013), in which a Tennessee appeals court upheld a trial court's order voiding a provision in the parties' premarital agreement waiving or limiting alimony because it would probably result in the former wife becoming a **public charge**. Absent such an outcome however, the general rule appears to be that "No public policy is violated by permitting enforcement of a waiver of spousal support executed by intelligent, well-educated persons, each of whom appears to be self-sufficient in property and earning ability, and both of whom had the advice of counsel regarding their rights and obligations as marital partners at the time they executed the agreement."[6]

Premarital agreement
an agreement made by two persons about to be married defining for themselves their respective rights, duties, and responsibilities in the event their marriage terminates by death, annulment, separation, or divorce

Waiver
the giving up of a right or privilege

PARALEGAL PRACTICE TIP

The full texts of the UPAA and the UPMAA can be accessed at *www .uniformlaws.org.*

Public charge
a person dependent on public assistance programs for necessaries

PARALEGAL PRACTICE TIP

If the parties did waive their alimony rights in a premarital agreement but later wish to agree to an award, there is case law (in New York, for example) to the effect that they may be able to do so.[7]

CASE **11.2** *Sanford v. Sanford,* 2005 SD 34, 694 N.W.2d 283 (2005)

DISCUSSION OF THE CASE

The premarital agreement executed by the parties in this case included a single unallocated payment structure for alimony, support, and property division. The husband claimed that this provision not only protected his $55-million net worth, but also constituted a waiver of alimony by his wife.

Although the state of South Dakota had adopted the Uniform Premarital Agreement Act, it did not include the provisions allowing parties to contract regarding elimination or modification of spousal support. The legislature chose instead to exclude alimony waivers from prenuptial agreements by statute (SDCL 25–2–18), thereby protecting the rights of both men and women asked to sign away these rights.

The court noted that the agreement in question did not include a specific reference to alimony and support, but that even if it had, a waiver would be of no effect. The Court held that provisions in a premarital agreement purporting to waive spousal support are void and unenforceable as they are contrary to public policy and they may be severed from valid portions of an agreement without invalidating the agreement in its entirety.

SIDEBAR

Do you think spouses should be able to waive alimony in premarital agreements? The full opinion in the *Sanford* case is available at *www.pearsonhighered .com/careersresources/* in the website material related to Chapter 11 of this text under Cases.

Separation agreement
an agreement made between spouses in anticipation of divorce or a legal separation concerning the terms of the divorce or separation and any continuing obligations of the parties to each other

Quid pro quo
[Latin: this for that] an action or thing exchanged for another action or thing of relatively equal value

Even if there is no premarital agreement, the parties may choose to waive their respective rights to alimony in their **separation agreement**. However, notwithstanding the parties' freedom to contract to this effect, many judges will not incorporate such a waiver in a divorce decree if one of the spouses will be forced onto public assistance or, in the case of a long-term marriage, unless there has been a sufficient *quid pro quo*. For example, a spouse waiving alimony might be awarded a greater share of the marital assets in lieu of alimony.

Does one party have a need for alimony that the other party has the ability to pay?

Whether or not alimony will be sought depends in large part on the respective needs of the parties and their relative abilities to pay. Before making the decision to pursue an alimony claim, the client must prepare a complete and realistic budget of his or her needs, and a thorough review of the financial assets and liabilities of each of the parties should take place. An assessment can then be made as to whether after the marital property is divided, one of the parties will have a need for alimony that the other party will be able to satisfy. In short-term marriages involving few, if any, assets, alimony awards are rarely made. There simply are not enough resources "to go around," or the resources are limited in terms of how they can reasonably be divided. In marriages involving substantial assets, need will be determined relative to the standard of living the parties maintained during the marriage.

What factors will the court consider when making the alimony decision?

If it appears that alimony is needed and should be sought, information needs to be gathered regarding all of the factors potentially considered by the court in the jurisdiction to assess the strengths and weaknesses of the client's case. Although need and ability to pay are threshold factors, courts usually consider a number of additional factors as well, such as the ages and health of the parties, the education and employment history of each spouse, their reasonably anticipated future income and earning potential, and the duration of the marriage. It is likely that courts addressing alimony questions involving divorcing same-sex spouses will increasingly be asked to consider the length of time the parties have cohabited or been in legally recognized alternative relationships (such as civil unions) prior to marrying.

Is one or both of the parties likely to file for bankruptcy at some point in the future?

If bankruptcy looms in the future of either or both of the parties, counsel will discuss with the client its potential impact. Particularly relevant is the fact that property division settlements in a divorce that are not in the nature of "support" may possibly be discharged in bankruptcy, whereas spousal and child support generally are not. In such circumstances, a client needing financial security may choose to settle for less in the way of an unprotected property award and seek a higher and potentially more secure award of alimony.

After these questions are addressed, counsel will consult with the client about the nature and merits of a potential alimony claim and recommend a course of action. If alimony will be sought, negotiations with the opposing party/counsel then will begin or continue if already begun. If negotiation does not lead to an agreement, the parties may attempt to mediate their dispute. If that fails, a proposed alimony provision will be drafted by each party for the court's consideration. Later in this chapter, Paralegal Application 11.2 provides basic drafting suggestions for alimony provisions.

What Are the Various Types of Alimony?

Although alimony is legally recognized to some degree in virtually every jurisdiction, there is no consensus regarding its purpose, amount, or duration. Some states are reluctant to make any awards at all and allow only short-term, limited-purpose maintenance except in certain circumstances. Others, like South Carolina, are flexible and define a number of alimony options by statute. A brief summary of the most common types of alimony is provided in Exhibit 11.2.

PARALEGAL PRACTICE TIP

The cases and statutes referenced in this chapter reflect the considerable variation that exists across the states in terms of the types of alimony awards permitted in different jurisdictions and favored by particular judges. An understanding of the legal environment in which the client's case is filed will help guide interviewing, discovery, and drafting efforts.

EXHIBIT 11.2 Types of Alimony/Spousal Support[8]

Temporary Alimony/Alimony *Pendente Lite*	Interim alimony ordered by the court pending an action for divorce or separation in which a party has made a claim for alimony
Permanent/Traditional Alimony	Alimony usually payable in weekly or monthly payments, either indefinitely or until a time or circumstance specified in a court order
Term Alimony	Alimony payable in weekly or monthly payments for a specified period of time or until a condition specified in a court order or agreement
Rehabilitative Alimony (sometimes called limited or transitional alimony)	Alimony found necessary to assist a divorced person in acquiring the education or training required to find employment outside the home or to reenter the labor force
Restitution/Reimbursement Alimony	Alimony designed to repay a spouse who during the marriage made financial contributions that directly enhanced the earning capacity of the other spouse
Transitional Alimony	The periodic or one-time payment of support for the purpose of transitioning the recipient to an adjusted lifestyle or a new location as a result of the divorce
Separate Maintenance	Money paid by one married person to the other for support if they are not divorced but are no longer living together as husband and wife
Lump-Sum Alimony/Alimony in Gross	Alimony in the form of a single and definite sum usually not subject to modification

PARALEGAL PRACTICE TIP

A copy of the relevant section of the Texas Family Code is accessible at *www.statutes.legis.state.tx.us* (Family Code Title 1 The Marriage Relationship Chapter 8).

PARALEGAL PRACTICE TIP

A copy of the act reforming Alimony in Massachusetts effective March 2012 can be found at *www.lawlib.state.ma.us*. The act largely eliminates permanent alimony.

TEMPORARY ALIMONY/ALIMONY *PENDENTE LITE*

Temporary alimony or **alimony *pendente lite*** is support awarded to a dependent spouse in order to maintain the status quo as to financial circumstances while a marital action is pending. The action could be one seeking an annulment, a legal separation, or a divorce. The timing and procedure governing a filing for temporary support are established by statute or court rules. A request is usually made in

Temporary alimony/alimony *pendente lite*
[Latin: while the action is pending] support awarded to a dependent spouse in order to maintain the status quo as to financial circumstances while a marital action is pending.

PARALEGAL PRACTICE TIP

A sample Motion for Temporary Orders with a Supporting Affidavit can be accessed at www.pearsonhighered.com/careersresources/ in the website material related to Chapter 5 of this text under Forms.

the initial complaint or by separate motion. Notice will be given to the other party, and a hearing will customarily be held. The burden is on the requesting party to establish that the parties are married; that a petition has been filed for divorce, legal separation, or annulment; and that facts exist justifying an award. The appropriate facts often are laid out in a supporting affidavit addressing the factors considered by the court in making alimony determinations. The respondent has the right to submit an affidavit in opposition to the motion for temporary alimony, and sometimes courts will make their decisions based on the parties' affidavits without holding a hearing. In a limited number of jurisdictions, the amount of a temporary alimony award is based on a formula similar to the guidelines used to calculate child support awards.

Motions for temporary alimony are not always granted. For example, if the petitioning spouse has sufficient means to support himself or herself according to the parties' accustomed lifestyle and to prosecute or defend the pending action, that party's motion for temporary alimony will not likely be granted. There are also some specific circumstances that may bar alimony *pendente lite*, such as the petitioner's voluntary departure from the household and abandonment of the other spouse, unless it can be shown that the other spouse's conduct justified the departure (abuse, threats, etc.). Although some states, such as Louisiana, do not permit waivers of temporary alimony in premarital agreements (see, e.g., *Barber v. Barber*, 38 So. 3d 1046 (2010)), in others a defendant spouse may raise as a defense a provision in a premarital agreement in which the parties both waived their respective rights to any form of alimony upon the filing of an action for divorce or legal separation. The agreement may specifically bar a claim for temporary alimony unless the petitioning party has no other source or reasonable means of support.

If granted, temporary alimony generally continues until the matter is settled on the merits (i.e., an annulment, legal separation, or divorce is granted). The general rule is that temporary alimony will not continue beyond the voluntary dismissal or abandonment of the underlying action or entry of the judgment and exhaustion of all appeals. In some jurisdictions, resumption of sexual relations between the parties will constitute a reconciliation warranting termination of the divorce action and the temporary alimony order.

Motions for temporary alimony need to be taken seriously as they often set the stage for permanent orders. If there is an urgent need, the request may have to be made early in the proceedings. However, if there are substantial assets, counsel may want to wait at least until initial discovery is conducted and a clearer picture emerges regarding alimony prospects.

PERMANENT ALIMONY

Permanent alimony
alimony usually payable in weekly or monthly payments either indefinitely or until a time or circumstance specified in a court order

Surviving agreement
an agreement of the parties incorporated in a court's divorce decree that also retains its existence as an independent contract enforceable under basic principles of contract law

Permanent alimony is somewhat of a misnomer, given that in most jurisdictions, a court-ordered award is not truly permanent, but rather customarily remains modifiable given a change in circumstances, unless the order incorporates a **surviving agreement** of the parties that specifically addresses duration. For example, the parties may agree that alimony payments will continue until either party dies or the recipient spouse remarries, cohabits with another, or attains a certain age. Absent an agreement to the contrary, permanent alimony usually terminates upon remarriage of the recipient or the death of either party.

The primary purpose of permanent alimony is to provide financial assistance to the spouse who is in an economically weaker position. No duty is imposed on the dependent party to obtain employment and achieve economic self-sufficiency. When a permanent alimony award is granted, it is most likely to occur in a case involving a long-term marriage and a spouse who was a homemaker and primary caretaker of the parties' children for the bulk, if not all, of the marriage. The underlying premise is that, absent some extenuating circumstance, it would be unfair for one party's standard of living to remain high following divorce, while the other party's quality of life markedly declines as a result of mutual choices made during the marriage.

Although substantial permanent alimony awards were once common, they are relatively rare today. They are viewed as inconsistent with current assumptions about female economic independence. In addition, obligors, understandably, do not welcome permanent awards by which they will remain economically tied to a former spouse, and courts usually prefer to facilitate a clean break.

TERM ALIMONY

Term alimony continues for a set period of time or until a condition specified in a court order or agreement. It is customarily payable in weekly or monthly payments and usually remains modifiable upon a change in circumstances. In some states, the duration of term alimony will be limited by statute to no more than the length or some percentage of the length of the marriage.

LUMP-SUM ALIMONY/ALIMONY IN GROSS

Lump-sum alimony, sometimes called **alimony in gross**, is alimony ordered payable in the form of a definite sum, usually in a single or limited number of installments. It has distinct advantages to each party. It may appear to be more in the nature of a component of a comprehensive property division settlement. However, because it is characterized as alimony, if structured properly, it usually will be deductible by the payor for income tax purposes. From the recipient's perspective, although it will be taxable as income, it vests in the recipient when awarded and thus may be recovered from the obligor's estate if necessary. It is also generally not subject to modification, to elimination upon remarriage or cohabitation, or to discharge should the obligor declare bankruptcy. It also has the added advantage of "cutting the cord" and not dragging out the financial connection between the parties.

Lump-sum alimony may be particularly appropriate in some situations. For example, assume that a wife, fifty-five years old, has a demonstrated need for alimony and that her eighty-year-old spouse has an ability to pay it. Assume also that the husband is suffering from a terminal illness and is near death. A spousal support award of $5,000 a month for seven years is illusory, given that it is unlikely the husband will live more than a matter of months. Assuming the resources exist, an equivalent lump-sum award of $420,000 (adjusted for interest) may be more appropriate. See, e.g., *Schwartz v. Schwartz*, 225 P. 3d 1273 (Nev. 2010).

TRANSITIONAL ALIMONY

Transitional alimony is the periodic or one-time payment of support to a spouse for the purpose of transitioning the recipient to an adjusted lifestyle or a new location as a result of the divorce. In some states, such as Florida, courts have awarded what they term "bridge the gap" alimony. It is generally short term in length

---

PARALEGAL PRACTICE TIP

It is important that terms be clearly defined in agreements. For example, what exactly does "cohabitation" mean to the parties? Cohabiting with either a man or a woman? Living with an adult or a child? Sharing a residence and its expenses? Living together with someone in a relationship that has a romantic or sexual component? For a case that explicitly addresses this issue, see *Remillard v. Remillard*, 297 Conn. 345, 999 A.2d 713 (2010).

Term alimony
alimony payable in weekly or monthly payments that continue for a set period of time or until a condition specified in a court order or agreement

Lump-sum alimony/alimony in gross
alimony ordered payable in the form of a definite sum, usually in a single or limited number of installments; usually not subject to modification

Transitional alimony
the periodic or one-time payment of support to a spouse for the purpose of transitioning the recipient to an adjusted lifestyle or a new location as a result of the divorce.

and designed to help a party make the shift from married life to single life. For instance, the recipient may need to find a job and a new place to live, triggering one-time related costs (job search, moving, new furniture, etc.).

REHABILITATIVE ALIMONY

Rehabilitative alimony is sometimes awarded in situations in which one spouse has delayed or given up education or a career in order to remain at home and care for the parties' children and the household. It is customarily awarded for a period sufficient in length to allow the dependent spouse to obtain education and training that will enable him or her to acquire greater earning power, reenter the workforce, and become self-sufficient with the exercise of reasonable effort. It is usually awarded for a fixed period and is generally not modifiable. Ideally, the recipient spouse proposes a plan for rehabilitation along with a timeline and an estimate of related costs. Some states, such as Florida, specifically require by statute that a detailed plan be provided to the court.

In some states, a limit on the length of rehabilitative alimony is established by statute. More often, the court will set a time period within which the recipient is expected to make a realistic good-faith effort to complete a rehabilitative program and attain self-sufficiency. If either of the parties wants the award to be reviewable, their agreement or the court order should include language to that effect. Circumstances in which a review might be warranted are, for example, when an educational program is interrupted due to a chronic illness or when the recipient fails to pursue an agreed-upon "rehabilitation" plan.

Consistent with no-fault reform, rehabilitative alimony represents a departure from the historical view of alimony as being fault-based and unlimited in duration. The preferred approach in several jurisdictions, it accomplishes the dual purposes of (1) affording an economically dependent spouse an opportunity to build his or her job skills, obtain employment, and become economically self-sufficient and (2) setting a predictable end to the ongoing obligations of the parties to each other. Despite these advantages, some courts are reluctant to make rehabilitative alimony awards, particularly in cases of long-term marriages in which one party has a dramatically reduced earning capacity due to the allocation of responsibilities during the marriage. It may also be denied if the planned rehabilitation is unrealistic or if the petitioner is already employed or employable and does not plan to change jobs.

In the *Anliker* case, the Iowa Supreme Court considered that state's alimony statute and weighed the relative merits of permanent "traditional" alimony awarded by the trial court against the appeals court position that rehabilitative alimony was more appropriate. (See Case 11.3.)

CASE **11.3** *In re Marriage of Anliker,* 694 N.W.2d 535 (Iowa 2005)

FROM THE OPINION

The factors in section 598.21(3) pertinent to this case include (1) the length of the marriage; (2) the age and physical and emotional health of the parties; (3) the property distribution; (4) the educational level of each party at the time of the marriage and at the time the action is commenced;

(5) the earning capacity of the party seeking alimony, including educational background, training, employment skills, work experience, length of absence from the job market; (6) the feasibility of the party seeking alimony becoming self-supporting at a standard of living reasonably comparable to that enjoyed during the marriage, and the length of time necessary to achieve this goal; and (7) other factors the court may determine to be relevant in an individual case. Iowa Code § 598.21(3)(a)-(f), (j) (Supp. 2001). . . .

The district court considered these factors in deciding to award Donna traditional alimony as an appropriate form of spousal support. In applying these factors, we think the district court had it exactly right when it made the following findings:

> In this case, neither party is receiving a substantial amount of property. The property being divided relates to minimal household goods and furnishings as well as Donna's basic transportation. The debts being assigned to Scott are no more onerous to him than the debts being assigned to Donna pursuant to this decree. . . .
>
> While Donna is only 51 years of age, the record supports a finding that her health has deteriorated since 1996 and is not likely to improve. She suffers ongoing pain and incapacity, and even Scott does not believe that she has exaggerated her testimony regarding her physical health. She is currently on several medications and is limited in her ability to alleviate her pain due to her loss of a kidney several years ago. Donna has been determined to be disabled by the Social Security Administration and her sole source of income at this point is her disability benefits, which net her $309 per month. Although Scott feels that any alimony award should be for rehabilitative purposes only, the record does not support such a conclusion. Due to her physical infirmities, Donna is an unlikely candidate for further education or training. She has never been able to put what training and experience she has accrued in 51 years to practical use in the job market. The Court does not find it to be realistic to think that Donna is employable in her current condition. . . .
>
> This is a long-term marriage of nearly 20 years. Scott has a substantially better earning capacity than Donna, who is permanently disabled. Donna's earning capacity appears limited to her social security disability benefits. Scott continues to have an earning capacity of $50,000 annually or more. Scott will have far greater social security retirement benefits than Donna. Additionally, Scott receives use of a vehicle as an employment benefit and does not currently have the expense of car payments. . . . the Court takes note that the settlements she received for her injuries and future disabilities were invested in the marriage and are no longer available to Donna at the very time she needs the money.

In view of these findings, which are fully supported in the record and which we adopt, we think the spousal support award of $1,250 per month in traditional alimony until Donna attains the age of sixty-five or either party dies was equitable and should not be disturbed.

SIDEBAR

Do you agree with the court's decision? Why would the court have the award terminate at age sixty-five? Would any other form of alimony have been more appropriate? The opinion in the *Anliker* case is available at *www.pearsonhighered.com/careersresources/* in the website material for this text related to Chapter 11 under Cases.

Restitution/reimbursement alimony
alimony designed to repay a spouse
who made financial contributions
during the marriage that directly
enhanced the future earning
capacity of the other spouse

PARALEGAL PRACTICE TIP

The Utah alimony statute can be
found at *www.utah.gov.* Note that
in determining alimony, the courts
in Utah may consider fault and
also whether a spouse paid for
or "allowed" his or her spouse to
attend school during the marriage.
Although alimony cannot be ordered
for longer than the duration of
the marriage (absent extenuating
circumstances), the court may use
it in an attempt to equalize the parties' standards of living. By statute,
the court also may factor into the
alimony calculation a subsequent
spouse's ability to share living
expenses.

RESTITUTION ALIMONY

Restitution or reimbursement alimony is designed to repay a spouse who made financial contributions during the marriage that directly increased the future earning capacity of the other spouse. It is not based on need but rather on equitable considerations—considerations of fairness. The recipient spouse may have interrupted his or her education and earned and expended resources for the other party's benefit in the belief that the marital enterprise and the parties' future lifestyle would be enhanced in the long term. If the marriage is terminated, it is considered fair that the contributing spouse be paid or reimbursed for the investment he or she made in the marriage. When permitted, it is most likely to be awarded when there is a short-term marriage, no children, limited assets, and one spouse has delayed or interrupted his or her education or career and worked to allow the other spouse to pursue graduate studies. Some courts may choose to use restitution alimony for the purposes served by rehabilitation alimony. Such an approach avoids the stigma that there is some-how something deficient or unhealthy in the recipient spouse that needs to be "rehabilitated."

Because it runs counter to traditional alimony principles, which base alimony on need, ability to pay, and standard of living of the parties during the marriage, restitution or reimbursement alimony is viewed with disfavor in some states and by some individual judges. It may be denied if the petitioner is self-sufficient, even if only as a result of receiving disability benefits. It also may be deemed unwarranted if the requesting party already has a degree, does not require additional training, or is already employed in a good job and his or her earning capacity did not suffer as a result of contributions to the marriage.

The concept of restitution/reimbursement alimony was introduced in 1982 by the New Jersey Supreme Court in the landmark *Mahoney* decision. (See Case 11.4.) In *Mahoney*, the husband left the marriage shortly after attaining an advanced degree that he had earned with the wife's support. The court held that she was entitled to reimbursement for household expenses, educational costs, school travel expenses, and any other contribution she made enabling her husband to attain his degree.

CASE **11.4** *Mahoney v. Mahoney,* 91 N.J. 488, 453 A.2d 527 (1982)

FROM THE OPINION

In this case, the supporting spouse made financial contributions towards her husband's professional education with the expectation that both parties would enjoy material benefits flowing from the professional license or degree. It is there-fore patently unfair that the supporting spouse be denied the mutually anticipated benefit while the supported spouse keeps not only the degree, but also all of the material benefits and rewards flowing from it.

. . . Also the wife has presumably made personal financial sacrifices, resulting in a reduced or lowered standard of living. Additionally, her husband, by pursuing preparations for a future career, has foregone gainful employment and financial contributions to the marriage. . . . She has postponed, as it were, present consumption and a higher standard of living, for the future prospect of greater support and material benefits. . . . The unredressed sacrifices . . . coupled with the unfairness attendant upon the defeat of the supporting spouse's shared expectation of future advantages, further justify a remedial reward. . . .

SIDEBAR

Do you agree with the court's decision? Which form(s) of alimony do you think are appropriate in such cases? The opinion in the *Mahoney* case can be accessed at *www.pearsonhighered.com/careersresources/* in the website material for this text related to Chapter 11 under Cases.

What Factors will a Court Consider When Making an Alimony Determination?

The power to award spousal support is statutory, but unlike child support awards, which are essentially formula-based, alimony decisions usually are left to the discretion of judges. The threshold question asked is "Does one of the parties have a need for financial support that the other party has the ability to meet?" Virtually all states, whether by statute or judicial decision, have identified additional economic and noneconomic factors to be considered by the courts. These factors afford judges considerable flexibility in tailoring their decisions to the unique facts of each case. They also help guide the information-gathering efforts of the family law team on behalf of the client. The Uniform Marriage and Divorce Act (UMDA)[9] lists the following factors as appropriate for consideration in the making of alimony determinations:

- the financial resources of the party seeking alimony, including marital property apportioned to him or her; the party's ability to meet his or her needs independently; and the extent to which a provision for support of a child living with that party includes a sum for that party as custodian
- the time necessary to acquire sufficient education or training to enable the party seeking alimony to find appropriate employment
- the standard of living during the marriage
- the duration of the marriage
- the age and physical and emotional condition of the spouse seeking alimony
- the ability of the spouse from whom alimony is sought to meet his or her needs while meeting those of the spouse seeking alimony

Additional kinds of factors that may appear in a given state's spousal support statute include the following:

- the earned and unearned income of each party, including, but not limited to, earnings, dividends, and benefits such as medical, disability, retirement, or Social Security
- the relative current and future earning capacities of the spouses
- the respective liabilities of the parties
- the backgrounds of the parties in terms of education and training and the prospects of the spouse seeking alimony to become self-supporting within a reasonable period of time

PARALEGAL PRACTICE TIP

The California alimony statute can be found at *www.leginfo. ca.gov* (California Family Code Sections 4320-4326) and the New Hampshire statute at *www.gencourt .state.nh.us* (RSA 458:19).

PARALEGAL PRACTICE TIP

The full text of the Uniform Marriage and Divorce Act can be found at *www.uniformlaws.org*.

- contribution of each of the parties to appreciation of the marital estate or to the education, training, career, and increased earning power of the other party
- contribution as a homemaker
- the misconduct/fault of either or both of the parties up to the time of the separation—most particularly fault with financial consequences
- the property brought to the marriage by the parties (or their families)
- the federal, state, and local tax ramifications of the alimony award
- a final catchall provision allowing the court to consider any additional factors it may consider relevant

A judge usually is required to consider and make findings with respect to each of the statutorily defined factors in the jurisdiction but customarily may assign whatever weight he or she believes is appropriate to any particular factor in light of the facts of each case. Absent an abuse of discretion or an error of law, an alimony decision will generally not be disturbed on appeal. Although this approach maximizes flexibility for the courts, it provides little predictability for clients and often escalates the cost of a divorce.

In a contested alimony case, the family law team may be presented with a monumental information-gathering challenge. Meeting that challenge usually begins with a review of controlling law in the jurisdiction. An effort then is made through interviews, formal discovery, and other methods to identify and assess the strengths and weaknesses of the client's case. It is not enough simply to identify the relevant factors. Each must be addressed and supported by provable facts backed by admissible evidence. It is also important to identify the merits of the opposing party's case. For example, if one party is seeking alimony, can the proposed obligor raise any defenses to the claim?

Alimony cases are fact-intensive. THERE ARE NO SUBSTITUTES FOR CAREFUL LISTENING AND THOROUGH PREPARATION! The decision of the Supreme Court of Oklahoma in the *Ray* case illustrates the potential consequences of failing to provide sufficient facts on the client's behalf for the court's consideration. (See Case 11.5.)

CASE 11.5 *Ray v. Ray,* 2006 OK 30, 136 P.3d 634 (Okla. 2006)

FROM THE OPINION

The trial court's "quasi summary" dissolution hearing produced a paucity of facts serving as a basis for the alimony award. . . . There is here no evidence of (a) the amount of money wife reasonably needs for readjustment of her lifestyle to a new economic situation, (b) her income-producing capacity, such as the number of hours she works per week and her monthly income; (c) her monthly expenses and future living plans and expenses, (d) her physical condition, (e) the cost of her desired education, (f) whether her station in life or standard of living has changed since the separation; (g) how much her cohabiting partner contributes to her monthly needs. Neither is there any evidence of (a) the husband's ability to pay support alimony, (b) the value of his home, (c) his net worth, (d) his physical condition, (e) his living standard based on monthly income and expenses. . . .

PARALEGAL PRACTICE TIP

Attorneys have an ethical duty to provide competent representation and to advocate zealously on the client's behalf. A well-trained paralegal who is aware of inadequate preparation may discuss the case with the supervisor or even send an unsolicited internal memorandum courteously bringing facts and documentation in support of the client's case to the attention of the supervisor "in case it might be helpful."

. . . Because the wife has failed to meet, before the trial court, her burden of affirmatively demonstrating the amount of needed support, if any, during the period of her economic readjustment, the trial court's alimony award is reversed and the cause remanded for further proceedings to be consistent with today's pronouncement.

SIDEBAR

Do you agree with the court's decision? Why? Do you think the wife may have a malpractice claim against her attorney? Explain your response. The opinion in the *Ray* case is available at *www.pearsonhighered.com/careersresources/* in the website material for this text related to Chapter 11 under Cases.

Paralegal Application 11.1

The Fact-Finding Mission in an Alimony Case

Length of marriage

How long have the parties been married? This is the customary starting point when assessing the potential of an alimony claim. There is consensus among the majority of states that marriages of different lengths should have different consequences with respect to alimony. For example, absent unusual circumstances, in some states alimony is generally not an option in a short-term marriage of less than five years and may not last longer than the length of the marriage. The premise is that the parties have not as yet made a significant investment in their marriage, built up substantial economic reliance on one another, or changed their premarital work patterns for a sufficiently extended period. In a marriage of more than fifteen years, many courts agree that long-term support may be warranted if necessary to enable both spouses to maintain as closely as possible the standard of living that characterized their married life. Most litigation and inconsistencies in outcome occur with intermediate-length marriages of between five and fifteen years in duration.

The answer to the question "How long have the parties been married?" is not always as simple as it might seem. Look behind the answer. Although it technically may not count, how long were the parties together prior to marriage? Had they entered a "domestic partnership" or "civil union?" Were they simply dating or living together? Were there periods during the marriage when the parties were separated due to problems in the marriage or factors such as military deployment or other substantial work-related travel (as an entertainer, merchant mariner, etc.)?

Don't let "general rules" restrict thinking given the facts of a specific case. If it is a short-term marriage and the client is seeking alimony, what unusual factors are present that argue for an award when it normally would not be granted? Illness? Abuse? Does the case involve same-sex spouses who lived together for several years prior to being able to legally marry? If it is a long-term marriage and the client is fighting alimony, what distinguishes the case at hand from others in which permanent alimony would likely be awarded based on precedent?

Examples of Proof: Certificates of Marriage, Domestic Partnership or Civil Union; leases in either party's name; employment records; military service, counseling or court records documenting periods of separation; records evidencing premarital cohabitation; and medical records.

Income

A complete employment history should be compiled for each of the parties, including job titles, hours worked, salaries, job skills, and responsibilities. With respect to current employment, if any, is each party bringing in income to his or her full capacity, or is he or she intentionally decreasing income to an artificially low figure; refusing to seek gainful employment; quitting second jobs and part-time work performed while married; falsely claiming to be disabled; not reporting "under the table" income; postponing taking raises, bonuses, or commissions; or otherwise manipulating income? Under such circumstances, income may be imputed to the party who is deliberately reducing his or her earnings. On the other hand, is one party's income inflated in a given year by, for example, receipt of a substantial

(Continued)

contingent fee, making it appropriate to average that party's income over a period of years? Is either party holding an unreasonable number of assets in a low or non-income-bearing form to the detriment of the potential recipient? If either spouse is cohabiting with another person, does that other person contribute to support of the household, so that more funds are available to the spouse to meet an alimony obligation or fewer funds are needed by the recipient?

Examples of Proof: Resumes, tax returns, employment records, pay stubs, mortgage applications; documentation that the payor spouse will receive or has received appreciating assets in the property division; evidence of transfers made to third parties; evidence of purchases of luxury/non-income-producing items; and logs of efforts to find work.

Needs

What are the *reasonable* needs of the parties as reflected in food, clothing, housing, and other basic living expenses as well as debts? Is either party living beyond his or her needs? The client should prepare a realistic budget of his or her living expenses for careful review. Keep in mind that "need" is a relative concept and cannot be considered apart from the parties' standard of living. What Lady Gaga, the CEO of Starbucks, or your U.S. senator "needs" is likely very different from what a laborer, teacher, or unemployed person needs.

Examples of Proof: Financial statements, copies of trusts, individual and corporate tax returns, credit card statements, bank statements, mortgage statements, utility bills, and car payments.

Standard of living during the marriage

In most cases, the level of assets in a marriage is such that it is simply not possible for both parties to maintain the marital standard of living post divorce. The issue is more one of how the negative impact of divorce on lifestyle can be equally or equitably shared. However, in cases involving substantial assets, it is important to establish the nature of the parties' lifestyle during the marriage. What was the marital home like? Did it have a pool, tennis courts, or game room? What kind of neighborhood was it in? How did the parties spend their free time? Did they belong to golf, tennis, or yacht clubs? Did they take vacations and, if so, where? Did they own or have access to vacation homes? How often and in what manner did they entertain company? Did they make many charitable donations and attend prestigious fundraising events? What kind of a clothing budget did they have? Where did they shop? How did they pay their bills (cash, credit, loans, employment bonuses, gifts from parents,

etc.)? How sustained was their lifestyle (were there a couple of good years and a decade of poor ones, or the reverse)? Was there a considerable amount of readily available cash that was put into savings for a later date rather than spent? Did they spend their funds on property, on tangible assets, or on events like lavish celebrations of birthdays and anniversaries? Were the parties unusually frugal?[10]

Examples of Proof: Photographs, receipts, credit card statements, bank statements, newspaper articles (society columns), membership records, invitations, employment records, deeds, titles to boats and RVs, and expense accounts.

Contribution

Identify and document to the fullest extent possible the financial and nonfinancial contributions of each of the parties to the marriage, including homemaking, home maintenance and improvement, childrearing, entertaining in support of one of the parties' careers, and/or vacations at retreats owned by the family of one of the spouses. Financial contributions should be broadly defined and may include trust income, inheritances, accident settlements, and gifts from family members that were spent on marital expenses, etc.

Examples of Proof: Bank statements, credit card statements, appraisals, receipts, copies of trust instruments, photographs, deeds, and titles.

Fault

Much to the consternation of wronged clients, approximately half the states do not consider fault when making alimony determinations. With those that do, the fault generally must have resulted in some form of economic loss. For example, the mere existence of an adulterous relationship usually is not enough. The family law team should research how the adultery impacted the marital relationship and estate. Were significant funds spent on gifts, travel, lodging, etc., that would otherwise have been available to support the marriage? Was the aggrieved spouse's emotional and physical health injured by the conduct?

Other types of fault also should be explored: criminal conduct; abusive behavior (physical and/or psychological); reckless spending, dissipation (such as through gambling), or diversion/concealment of assets; excessive use of alcohol or drugs; willful failure to provide essential support to the spouse and children. An isolated incident normally is not enough (unless especially egregious), so search for patterns in misconduct.

Examples of Proof: The type of supporting documentation needed will depend on the specific type of misconduct but is likely to include admissions, statements of the co-respondent or witnesses; photographs/videos; bank and credit card statements; reports of private investigators; police and court records; phone records, e-mails and other forms of correspondence; hotel/motel records; and medical and rehabilitation facility records.

Education

Compile histories for each of the spouses, covering all kinds of education and training received along with information about each party's career goals.

Examples of Proof: Resumes, college transcripts, job applications, certificates of completion, on-the-job training records, and college applications.

Employability

A party may have an impressive educational history and yet have obsolete job skills and be unemployable. What are the employment prospects for each party? Are there any factors that limit employment options, such as age, physical capacities, or chronic health problems? Has the party been terminated for cause at prior places of employment due to poor performance or misconduct in the workplace? Is the party's level of employability the result of his or her own efforts, or of market forces?

Examples of Proof: Labor market forecasts produced by reputable sources, medical records, job descriptions listing required skills, testimony from employment counselors.

Age

The age factor seems to be straightforward, but its importance stems less from the number of years a person has lived than it does from how age influences employment prospects, health issues, capacity to acquire additional assets to improve living standard, etc. For example, a seventy-year-old attorney or stockbroker may be at the height of his or her career, whereas a professional football player may be barely hanging onto employment at age thirty-five.

Examples of Proof: Medical records, employment records, and tax returns.

Health

Does either party suffer or allegedly suffer from any illnesses or injuries that impede earning potential and result in additional uninsured medical costs? An illness doesn't have to be manifest at the time of dissolution. It can be enough that a party has a condition that goes through periods of active symptoms and periods of remission. See *Moore v. Moore*, 858 So. 2d 1168 (Fla. 2003), a case in which the alimony recipient suffered from Crohn's disease.

Examples of Proof: Work absence records and medical records.

Paralegal Application 11.2

Drafting Pointers for an Alimony Provision in a Separation Agreement

This Application highlights the major topics that need to be addressed in an alimony provision of a separation agreement. The precise content needs to be tailored to specific client needs, given the facts of each case.

- **Goal** The goal of the alimony award should be stated. For example, if the award is in the nature of rehabilitative alimony, a plan should be provided that includes a description of the program, a timeline for completion, and the associated costs. If the award will be in the form of restitution/reimbursement alimony, the expenses being reimbursed should be specified.
- **Designation of the payment as alimony** For income tax purposes, the designation of the payment to be made as "alimony" should be clearly spelled out, along with a statement of the parties'

intentions as to whether or not it will be includable in the taxable income of the recipient and deductible to the obligor.

- **Amount** The amount should be established. Usually a fixed dollar amount is stated, which facilitates wage assignments, if warranted. However, if the payor's income fluctuates seasonally or otherwise, the amount may be set in the form of a percentage of that income. This approach has the disadvantages of uncertainty for the recipient and the need for periodic documentation and review of the payor's financial status.
- **Duration** The duration of the alimony should be established. Under what conditions will the obligation terminate? Some jurisdictions have specific limitations regarding the duration of alimony awarded by the court. The parties may

(Continued)

agree on events that will terminate the alimony obligation, such as remarriage, cohabitation with another person for longer than a specified period, completion of an educational program, or obtaining full-time employment at a particular wage or higher.

- **Frequency and timing of payments** The frequency and timing of payments should be laid out. Will there be a lump sum or periodic payments? Will payments be made weekly or monthly?

- **Form of payments** The form of payments may be agreed on. For example, alimony may be paid by check payable to the recipient spouse and sent by mail or by direct deposit. Each party should be required to notify the other of any change in address or applicable accounts. The parties may agree that payment will be made to a third party for the recipient's benefit to meet an obligation such as a mortgage on the marital residence, which is in the recipient's name. Another option is to have a court-ordered payroll deduction by the payor's employer (wage assignment or income withholding). Some states require payment through a state IV-D agency in a variety of circumstances. Whatever the method of payment, a party with an obligation to pay alimony should be advised by his or her attorney to keep detailed records and corroborative evidence of all payments to protect against a potential claim of contempt for nonpayment.

- **Modification of alimony** The modifiability of the alimony award should be addressed in the agreement if modification is permitted in the jurisdiction. The courts generally link changes to actual financial circumstances. However, the parties may agree on self-executing provisions that will result in an automatic modification based on an annual cost-of-living increase, a certain percentage increase or decrease in the payor's income, or receipt of an anticipated inheritance by either party. The triggering events should not be child-related, in order to protect deductibility of the alimony payment for income tax purposes.

- **Health care costs** The topic of health insurance needs to be addressed in the agreement at some point. It is important for the client to be aware of any potential health insurance coverage issues prior to or upon divorce. If the client is insured through his or her employer, the state, or a private policy, there should be no interruption in coverage. However, if the client is covered through the spouse's employer, proactive steps may need to be taken. It should be expressly indicated in the agreement if alimony is at least partly designed to cover medical, dental, and/or mental health expenses. Several states provide that when making an alimony order, the court "shall" as in "must" determine if the obligor has health insurance available at a reasonable cost that can be extended to cover the spouse. The obligor can exercise the option, obtain comparable coverage, or reimburse the spouse for health insurance (without any adjustment in the alimony award amount).

The Consolidated Omnibus Budget Reconciliation Act (COBRA) codified as 26 U.S.C. section 4980B(f) enables a nonemployee spouse to continue health insurance coverage provided by the spouse's employer for as long as three years post divorce at his or her own expense unless otherwise ordered. If the employee spouse is required by the divorce decree to pay COBRA premiums for his or her spouse, the employer should be promptly notified and provided with a certified copy of the order.[11] Although a spouse may be eligible for COBRA extension coverage, some plans allow employees to remove someone from their health plan, including a spouse. As a result, there may be a gap in coverage between the date of removal and the date of divorce, when COBRA eligibility commences.

- **Security for alimony payments** The recipient spouse will want to include security for the payment of alimony. Most states authorize courts to order the obligor spouse to maintain life insurance or some other form of security such as a trust for the recipient's benefit. Life insurance policies for the benefit of the recipient are the most common form of security for alimony payments.

- **Survival or merger of the alimony provision** If alimony will be waived or paid pursuant to the terms of the parties' separation agreement, the attorney will consider with the client the issue of survival or merger of the alimony provision. If the agreement is incorporated in the divorce decree but also survives as an independent contract, the provision will generally not be able to be modified by the family court, absent a showing of something more than a substantial change in circumstances (such as the likelihood the recipient will become a public charge absent modification). Even then the obligor may pursue contractual remedies to recover the difference between the agreement amount and the amount in the new court order. This is a difficult choice, but given the uncertainties in life, many practitioners believe it wisest to have alimony provisions merge in the decree. Then, in the event of a later economic downturn or windfall or the serious illness of either party, the option to modify the alimony award upon a material change in circumstances usually remains open to both parties. The concepts of survival and merger are discussed more fully in Chapter 13. Exhibit A in the Sample Separation Agreement in that chapter provides an example of a provision in which the parties to a divorce both waived alimony.

When and How Can Alimony Awards Be Modified or Terminated?

The decision as to whether or not alimony can be modified or terminated is made on a case-by-case basis and is driven by statute, court order, case law, and/or the language of the agreement executed by the parties. Many of the cases addressing this issue demonstrate the importance of careful drafting.

MODIFICATION

If permanent or term alimony was awarded in the parties' divorce decree after trial or based on the terms of a separation agreement that merged in the decree, states generally allow a party to later file a Complaint or Petition for Modification based on a **material change in circumstances**. However, in most jurisdictions, absent agreement, extraordinary circumstances, or extreme hardship, a lump-sum, rehabilitative, or restitution alimony award will not be modifiable. In some states, if alimony was not addressed in the divorce judgment, an alimony claim may not be pursued at a later date unless the right to pursue alimony was preserved by a nominal award (e.g., $1.00 per year) at the time of the divorce.

Not infrequently the parties' separation agreement provides that they will initially attempt to resolve modification issues through mediation prior to resorting to litigation. If mediation fails or is not an option, a complaint for modification is usually filed in the court that issued the original order if it retains continuing jurisdiction over the matter. The burden of proving the change of circumstances rests with the party seeking the modification. The kinds of changes in circumstances that might justify an up or down adjustment in alimony include forced unemployment or early retirement, a windfall increase in income or assets, the onset of a serious medical condition resulting in permanent disability triggering increased uninsured medical expenses, a third-party mortgagee's exercising its option to accelerate payment of a mortgage loan on the marital home, and cohabitation with a person who assumes responsibility for many of the dependent spouse's living expenses. The court will examine the nature of the change and assess whether or not the request is made in good faith. For example, if it is based on a reduction in the payor's income, is the reduction the fault of that individual? Has he or she engineered circumstances so that it appears there is a reduction in income or an increase in liabilities when there is not? Or is the increase in liabilities the result of spendthrift spending or an extravagant lifestyle? There are no fixed rules for determining what meets the threshold, and each case is decided in the context of the surrounding circumstances.

Material change in circumstances a change in the physical, emotional, or financial condition of one or both of the parties sufficient to warrant a change in a support order; a change that, if known at the time of the divorce decree, would have resulted in a different outcome

PARALEGAL PRACTICE TIP

Florida is one of the states that permit a party to preserve a right to alimony by making an award of $1.00 in permanent periodic alimony. See, e.g., *Blanchard v. Blanchard*, 793 So. 2d 989 (Fla. App. 2001). Some states (including Alaska and Massachusetts) allow a Complaint for Alimony to be filed subsequent to the divorce, given an unanticipated change in the parties' circumstances since the time of divorce.

PARALEGAL PRACTICE TIP

To see an example of a Motion to Modify or Terminate Maintenance/Alimony, visit *www.courts.state.co.us* (Colorado).

In about half of the states, misconduct on the part of the recipient may constitute a sufficient change in circumstances to support a modification. For example, an alimony obligation may be reduced or even terminated if the recipient persistently, openly and intentionally embarrasses the obligor, adversely affecting his or her reputation and business. However, the courts are reluctant to modify payments when the change in circumstances underlying the request is the consequence of the petitioner's own wrongful acts. For example, if the obligor claims incarceration as a change in circumstances warranting modification, most courts have adopted a "no justification rule" in the alimony context. Being in prison standing alone is not sufficient to justify modification. The reasoning behind the rule is that criminal activity that could lead to incarceration is seen as being within the control of the individual, as distinguished from other involuntary obstacles to payment such as injury, illness, or job loss. Even if the alimony payments are suspended during the period of incarceration, the obligor is unlikely to be relieved of his duty to pay the accrued arrearages upon release. See, e.g., *Willoughby v. Willoughby*, 2004 PA. Super. 439, 862 A.2d 654 (2004). See also Paralegal Application 10.4 in Chapter 10 addressing the effect of incarceration on child support orders.

When the parties' separation agreement is incorporated but does not merge in the judgment of divorce, the surviving agreement may constrain the family court's options if the agreement provides that alimony shall be unmodifiable or modifiable only under certain limited circumstances Some family courts honor "no modification" clauses. Others refuse to do so on public policy grounds. Most hold the parties to their agreement absent an extraordinary or a "more than substantial" change in circumstances such that enforcement would, for example, force a spouse onto public assistance.

PARALEGAL PRACTICE TIP

The *Willoughby* opinion is available in its entirety at *www.pearsonhighered.com/careersresources/* in the website material for this text related to Chapter 11 under Cases.

Paralegal Application 11.3

Did the Court Get It Right?

1. *Elbaum v. Elbaum,* **141 So. 3d 658 (Fla. App. 2014):** The former husband sought a modification of alimony based on the fact his ex-wife was living in a "supportive relationship." §61.14(1)(b)(1) Even though the husband's assertion may have been accurate, his request was denied because the parties' marital settlement agreement unambiguously limited modifications to situations involving deteriorations in the husband's health or business.

2. *Owens v. Owens,* **2013 Tenn. App. LEXIS 499 (2013):** A former wife successfully sought a modification of alimony converting a rehabilitative award to alimony *in futuro* (term alimony). She was in her mid-60s and had been unable to become self-sufficient as a real estate agent as originally planned. She had a continuing need for support and her former husband's income

had increased and his needs had decreased since the initial award.

3. *Albu v. Albu,* **150 So. 3d 1226 (Fla. App. 2014):** The former husband sought termination of alimony based on the fact that he had a heart attack and as a result his former business was involuntarily closed causing a significant drop in his income. At the time of his petition to terminate or reduce alimony, he was receiving a total of $1,949 a month in Social Security disability benefits from which he was paying $900 in alimony. His 60-year-old ex-wife's sole source of income was alimony and she was totally dependent on it as she was unable to work, had significant medical problems, and was not yet eligible to receive Social Security benefits. To warrant a modification, the husband needed to prove a substantial change in circumstances

that was not contemplated at the time of dissolution of the marriage and that the change was sufficient, material, involuntary, and permanent in nature. Although he met his burden, the court held that the need of one spouse and the ability to pay of the other remained the most important factors to consider. The trial court's ruling continuing the alimony payment but eliminating the husband's responsibility for medical insurance and $80 a month towards prescriptions was affirmed. The court noted neither party could cover their expenses and that they were in equally miserable circumstances. It reasoned their incomes should basically be equalized because there was no reason the former wife should be left completely destitute and the husband have all the resources available to both parties.

4. *Richardson v. Richardson*, **218 S.W.3d 426 (Mo. Supreme Court 2007):** The parties in this case were divorced in December 1997. They executed a separation agreement containing the terms of the divorce which they agreed would be incorporated into the decree of dissolution. The Agreement provided that the husband, Joseph, would pay maintenance in the amount of $2,425.00 per month. The obligation was to terminate upon the ex-wife's remarriage or the death of either party. The Agreement stated that "[t]he terms of this Agreement shall not be subject to modification or change, regardless of the relative circumstances of the parties . . . ." In 2007, the ex-husband filed a motion to terminate his maintenance obligation alleging his ex-wife "sought out a person(s) for the purpose of burglarizing the husband's home," and "for the purposes of murdering the husband." The trial court dismissed the motion with prejudice for failure to state a claim upon which relief could be granted. The husband appealed. The Missouri Supreme Court affirmed reasoning that the parties were free to execute a separation agreement that provided its terms would not be subject to change or modification. It opined that a non-modification provision can cut both ways. No one can know which party will need more or deserve less as time passes. As with all contract terms, a non-modification provision is a bargained-for allocation of future risk. A non-modifiable agreement that the court found conscionable at the time of its execution does not suddenly become unenforceable due to changed circumstances. Neither the agreement, nor the decree, nor the applicable statute authorized a court to modify the terms of the agreement or the decree on account of subsequent circumstances.

TERMINATION

Unless otherwise provided in a final divorce decree, or by its nature as in alimony in gross, an alimony obligation will usually terminate upon the earliest to occur of the following events:

- death of the recipient
- death of the payor
- expiration of a stated period of time
- remarriage of the recipient
- cohabitation of the recipient with another

The court frequently sets a termination date in the decree or incorporates one or more self-executing termination dates that the parties set forth in their agreement. For example, they may agree that cohabitation with another adult in an intimate relationship for greater than one month, recovery from a serious illness, retirement on or before a certain age, completion of a specific educational program, or obtaining full-time employment will trigger a cessation of alimony. Regardless of how the alimony obligation terminates, the payor (or his or her estate in the case of death) generally remains liable for arrearages (i.e., unpaid back payments) unless otherwise ordered by the court.

Prima facie showing

[Latin: first face] a legally rebuttable showing

Termination Upon Remarriage

The general rule is that "permanent" alimony will terminate upon remarriage of the recipient or on whatever date or condition the parties agree to in their agreement. Some states, such as New Jersey and North Carolina, have automatic-termination-on-remarriage rules. Some, such as Illinois, Maryland and Washington, recognize an exception to automatic termination when the parties have expressly agreed to continue alimony after the recipient's remarriage. Provisions to that effect must expressly state that alimony survives the statutory presumption. Parties who know they want to remarry sometimes elect to choose this route and provide for a reduction in the amount of alimony to be paid upon remarriage. In this essentially win-win situation, the former spouse who wants to remarry can do so without a total loss of alimony and the paying spouse is relieved of a portion of the full alimony obligation.

In states such as South Dakota, remarriage establishes a ***prima facie*** **showing** supporting termination of alimony on remarriage unless the recipient is able to show the existence of extraordinary circumstances that require its continuation. If the obligor remarries, his or her alimony obligation will continue, absent a court order to the contrary. For example, a court may entertain a complaint for downward modification if children are born to the obligor's subsequent marriage or for an upward modification if the recipient can show that the paying spouse has more of his or her income available as a result of a new spouse's contributions to his or her customary living expenses.

Termination Upon Death

If either of the parties dies, alimony payments customarily cease unless the parties' separation agreement or the court expressly provides otherwise. For example, the parties may agree that payments will continue to be paid from the decedent's estate or from a trust. The American Law Institute's Principles of the Law of Family Dissolution provide that the alimony obligation may survive the obligor's death if the court makes written findings establishing that the termination of the award would work a substantial injustice because of facts not present in most cases. The most common approach is for the divorce decree to include an order requiring the obligor to maintain a life insurance policy for the recipient's benefit.

Termination Upon Cohabitation

When drafting agreements about the impact of cohabitation on alimony awards, the language used needs to accurately reflect the parties' intentions especially if they vary from state law. It is important to understand at the outset that the states have varying definitions of "cohabitation." For example, under Florida law, it is referred to as a "supportive relationship" and in Massachusetts as maintaining "a common household . . . with another person for a continuous period of at least three months" and sharing "a primary residence together with or without others."

Several states have statutes that explicitly address the effect of cohabitation on alimony. Some, such as North Carolina, provide alimony will terminate automatically upon cohabitation without regard to need (GS 50-16.9). In California, cohabitation of a recipient with a nonmarital partner raises a rebuttable presumption there is a decreased need for alimony (Cal. Fam. Code Section 4323). In Connecticut, cohabitation may result in termination of alimony if it results in a diminished financial need (Conn. Gen. Statutes Section 46b-86(b)). In some states. the governing rule is established in case law. For example, in Mississippi, cohabitation creates a presumption that a material change in circumstances has occurred. The alimony recipient has to rebut a presumption of "mutual support." See, e.g., *Rester v. Rester*, 5 So. 3d 1132 (Miss. 2008). Absent a specific statute or governing case law, most states apply general alimony statutes and treat cohabitation as a "substantial change in circumstances." See Case 11.6 for an illustration of the kinds of evidence courts will consider when determining if there has been a substantial change in circumstances.

CASE 11.6 *Reese v. Weis F/K/A Reese,* 430 N.J. Super. 552, 66 A.3d 157 (2013)

BACKGROUND

In this case, the parties were divorced after a 13 year marriage and the husband, Ronald Reese, was ordered to pay the wife, Rebecca Weis, "permanent alimony of $100,000 per year." He also paid her an additional $137,872 in support for their three children. He met his obligations but eventually filed a motion to terminate alimony based on the wife's cohabitation with her long-time boyfriend, Mr. Stein ("Stein"). The trial court held that the economic benefit derived by the former wife from the cohabitation relationship warranted termination. She appealed.

FROM THE OPINION

Here the defendant readily admits she and Stein have cohabited since 1998. . . . We start by restating why alimony is awarded.

Alimony is . . . rooted in the prior interdependence occurring during the parties' marital relationship. "[A]limony is neither a punishment for the payor nor a reward for the payee.". . .

The cohabitation of a dependent spouse constitutes an event of changed circumstances, which requires further review of the economic consequences of the new relationship and its impact on the previously imposed support obligation. . . .

Cohabitation involves an "intimate[,] "close and enduring" relationship, requiring "more than a common residence" or mere sexual liaison. . . . Cohabitation involves conduct whereby "the couple has undertaken duties and privileges that are commonly associated with marriage.". . .

Modification of alimony is warranted when either the cohabitant contributes to the dependent spouse's support or lives with the dependent spouse without contributing. . . . When a dependent spouse economically benefits from cohabitation, his or her support payments may be reduced or terminated. . . .

We reject the notion that permanent alimony yields only to the death of the supporting spouse or remarriage of the dependent spouse. The legislature's use of the term permanent alimony is a misnomer in the sense that the award is not everlasting. That changed circumstances dictate modification is well-established, as is the possibility that modification may include termination. . . .

Unquestionably, quantifying whether a dependent spouse receives a benefit from cohabitation is a fact-sensitive determination. . . .

When examining the cohabiting household, a trial judge starts with a review of the parties financial arrangements, to discern whether the cohabitant actually pays

PARALEGAL PRACTICE TIP

Poor drafting and a failure to clearly express the parties' intentions about what constitutes cohabitation and what effect it has on alimony obligations can result in litigation and sometimes absurd results. For example, in *Fecteau v. Fecteau,* 97 A.D.3d 999, 949 N.Y.S. 2d 511 (2012), the parties' agreement provided spousal support would terminate if the recipient "lived habitually with another person in a spousal type relationship." The defendant/ex-husband understood that language to include any situation "where two adults were living under the same roof." The ex-wife thought it meant "being married in every way other than having a legal piece of paper." In *Craissati v. Craissati,* 997 So. 2d 458 (Fla. Dist. Ct. App. 2008), cohabitation was defined as "the Wife living with another person (not including the parties' child) for a period of 3 (three) consecutive months or more." The husband's petition for modification was granted on appeal based on the fact the wife was deemed to be living with a cell-mate while incarcerated for 9 years on a driving under the influence charge.

or contributes toward the dependent spouse's necessary expenses, such as housing, food, clothing, transportation, or insurance. If so, the cohabitant provides the dependent spouse with a direct economic benefit.

Further, indirect economic benefits, . . . must be considered, including . . . when a dependent spouse moves into the home of the cohabitant. . . .

More subtle economic benefits also may result from the parties' intertwined finances. . . .

. . . it is fair and equitable for the trial judge to consider lifestyle enhancements realized from the new relationship, which raise the dependent spouse's standard of living above that enjoyed during the marriage.

In addition to Stein's disproportionate payment of joint expenses and complete satisfaction of the American Express credit card bills, . . . he also provided car, health, and possibly homeowner's insurance; purchased automobiles for use by the defendant and her children; paid the costs of vacations . . .; and shouldered the bulk of restaurant and entertainment expenses. . . .

. . . The facts unequivocally establish defendant's direct and indirect receipt of economic benefits resulting from cohabitation.

. . . Further, defendant and Stein commenced cohabitation in 1998. At this point, their relationship has surpassed the length of the marriage. Throughout this time, Stein paid defendant's expenses and augmented her standard of living. The facts showed the combined families operated as a single household, with defendant and Stein committed to each other economically, devoted to each other emotionally, and faithful to their monogamous union. Considering the totality of the evidence, we find no error in the order terminating alimony.

PARALEGAL PRACTICE TIP

Visit *www.acf.hhs.gov* to see an example of a "Uniform Support Order" under UIFSA. The order addresses all forms of support.

Civil contempt

a sanction for failure to obey a court order issued for another's benefit; a civil contempt proceeding is remedial in nature and is designed to promote compliance with the order

Criminal contempt

a punishment for failure to comply with a court order; a criminal contempt proceeding is punitive in nature and is designed to punish an attack on the integrity of the court

Order to Show Cause

an order directing a party to appear in court and explain why he or she took, or failed to take, some action and why relief should not be granted

How Are Alimony Awards Enforced?

In most jurisdictions, the primary enforcement vehicle for nonpayment of alimony is a **contempt** action, **civil** or **criminal**, depending on the circumstances. When court-ordered alimony is not paid, the aggrieved recipient is entitled to file appropriate papers in the applicable court (usually a Motion or Complaint for Contempt or a Citation with an **Order to Show Cause**) to enforce the order. If the obligor is found to be in civil contempt of an alimony order, the court will usually order payment of the overdue amount according to a schedule tailored to the obligor's ability to pay. Although the court has the authority to impose a jail sentence for an indefinite period to compel payment, customarily the defendant in a civil contempt case will be given the opportunity to pay the arrearages and thereby purge the contempt and avoid jail. Usually the obligor will not be found in contempt if there was an inability to pay at the time the delinquent payments were due or if the recipient contributed to the nonpayment, for example, by failing to provide the obligor with notice of a change of address. In a criminal contempt case, a sentence may be imposed for a fixed period, and the contempt cannot be purged by payment.

If the alimony recipient is or has been receiving court-ordered child support, he or she may also seek assistance from the state's Title IV-D agency and its arsenal of enforcement measures, such as income withholding and tax refund intercepts. If the obligor presently resides in another state, the recipient can seek enforcement across state lines under the Uniform Interstate Family Support Act. In addition, under federal law, the state IV-D child support agency can enforce a spousal support order for an individual not a party to a child support order at the request of the government of a foreign country.

In some circumstances, the recipient may seek to place a lien on property owned by a defendant found in contempt. In many states, statutes that protect property from legal process for collection of debts (attachment, etc.) do not apply to alimony or support claims. Another, more extreme measure, abolished in many states, is for the aggrieved party to file for a **writ** *ne exeat*, a court order restraining a person from leaving the jurisdiction until the petitioner's claim has been satisfied.

When the parties have a surviving separation agreement, contract remedies may also provide an enforcement option. The general rule is that when the alimony obligation is based on an agreement of the parties not merged in the divorce judgment, the agreement continues to exist and is enforceable by either party as an independent contract. For example, if, given an unusual or more than substantial change in circumstances, the family court modifies the initial alimony obligation notwithstanding the surviving independent contractual agreement, the aggrieved party can pursue traditional breach-of-contract remedies, such as a suit for damages in a court with equity jurisdiction (to recover the difference between the alimony to be paid under the modified family court order and the amount, if any, provided for in the parties' agreement).

If the obligor dies while there are outstanding alimony payments due, the recipient can seek to recover the accrued amount of arrearages from the decedent's estate as a creditor if payment has not otherwise been secured by agreement of the parties or by order of the court.

What Are the Tax and Bankruptcy Implications of Alimony?

The material that follows provides a very basic description of the relationship between alimony or spousal support obligations and tax and bankruptcy law. Each of these areas is a complex and specialized area of law, and determinations made by the Internal Revenue Service and Bankruptcy Courts will depend on the facts of each individual case.

TAX IMPLICATIONS

It is important for clients and the family law team to understand and factor tax implications into alimony and property division provisions. Several states require by statute that they do so. When negotiating an alimony case, attorneys are essentially engaging in a form of tax planning. By sharing the tax benefits of the alimony deduction, in many cases the financial burden of divorce can be reduced. Potential alimony obligors in higher tax brackets who are resistant to the prospect of paying alimony, are sometimes persuaded that they can avoid a costly trial and obtain a long term benefit as a result of being able to deduct alimony payments from their income and have them included in the income of a recipient in a lower tax bracket.[12] However, to secure this benefit, agreements must be carefully drafted. In general, the parties cannot come up with their own private agreement dictating the deductibility and includability of alimony payments unless the agreement satisfies applicable tax regulations. Under federal and state tax law, alimony is deductible from gross income by the payor and is income to the payee provided the following criteria are satisfied:[13]

1. The payments are made to a spouse or former spouse incident to a divorce decree or separation agreement. (An order for temporary alimony *pendente lite* will also qualify.)
2. The parties do not file a joint tax return for the period during which alimony payments are made.
3. The parties are not living in the same household when the payment is made.
4. The payments are made in cash (bank check, money order, etc.) and not in-kind (services rendered).
5. The payor has no liability for payments after death.
6. The payment is not improperly disguised child support (as when there are children but no child support is agreed to, and reductions in alimony amounts are tied to child-related events such as a child reaching the age of eighteen, graduating from high school, moving out of the custodial parent's home, or entering the military service).
7. The parties have not designated the payments as nonincludable in the recipient's income.

When alimony payments are made to a third party for the recipient's benefit (typically for payment of a mortgage), to be deductible the payment to the third party must be at the written request of the recipient to the payor and the payor must not be independently liable for the debt. The writing must specify that the payments are in lieu of alimony payments directly to the recipient and that both spouses intend the payments to be treated as alimony.

The IRS requires the payor deducting alimony to provide on his or her tax return the Social Security number of the recipient spouse. This information allows the IRS to verify that the recipient is including alimony received as income. Failure to provide the number can result in a disallowance of the deduction and/or a penalty.

Alimony recapture rule
the IRS rule that the government can recover a tax benefit (such as the prior claiming of a deduction for payment of alimony) by taxing the income that no longer qualifies for the benefit

The **alimony recapture rule** found in Section 71(f) of the Internal Revenue Service Code is designed to prevent parties to divorce from disguising what is actually part of a property division settlement as alimony in order to obtain the benefit of a tax deduction. It applies when there appears to be a front-loading of alimony payments that decrease substantially or end during the first three calendar years following the divorce. The determination of whether or not the rule will apply is based on a formula. If the Internal Revenue Service determines that the alleged support payments are actually in the nature of a property settlement, the negative consequences can be especially dramatic for the payor. Any claimed deduction on previously filed tax returns in the applicable period is disallowed, and the amount of "alimony" previously deducted is "recaptured" and subject to taxes, interest, and penalties. The recipient spouse becomes entitled to a corresponding refund for taxes previously paid on "alimony" declared as income.

BANKRUPTCY

Discharge
to extinguish a legal obligation; a discharge relieves an obligor of the legal obligation to pay a debt

In general, individuals who are deeply in debt have the right to file for bankruptcy in federal bankruptcy court in an effort to be relieved of full or partial payment of as many of their debts as possible. In the event that a bankruptcy petition is successfully filed, the Bankruptcy Court has the authority to **discharge** some debts, but other debts cannot be discharged, based largely on public policy grounds. For example, the Bankruptcy Abuse Prevention and Consumer Protection Act (BAPCPA) has made it more difficult to avoid domestic support obligations (DSOs) to former spouses. In the bankruptcy context, a DSO is a debt incurred before or after a bankruptcy filing that is owed to or recoverable by a spouse, former spouse, child, or governmental unit in the nature of alimony, maintenance, or support established in a court decree, a separation agreement, a property settlement agreement, or an administrative determination. The extent to which DSOs will be dischargeable depends to some degree on whether the obligor files a Chapter 7 (liquidation) or Chapter 13 (reorganization) bankruptcy. In general, "support payments" pursuant to a divorce cannot be discharged under either Chapter 7 or 13. Under Chapter 7, domestic relations obligations are not dischargeable whether they are in the nature of "support," or property or hold harmless provisions if they are incurred as a result of a divorce. The potential discharge is broader under Chapter 13 because it can include debts arising from a property division settlement unless the debt constitutes "support." Every provision in a judgment of divorce or separation made solely for the purpose of "support" will be considered support whether it is expressly labeled as such or not, and irrespective of whether it is paid in a lump sum or in intervals. The Bankruptcy Court looks at a number of factors in determining whether or not an award is in the nature of support. The bottom line is ". . . if it looks like a duck, walks like a duck, and quacks like a duck, then it probably is a duck,"[14] and a party cannot avoid paying alimony simply by filing bankruptcy.

Although a family court can enter a divorce decree, it has no authority to determine whether or not a debt addressed in that decree is dischargeable in bankruptcy. However, if a debt is discharged in a bankruptcy proceeding (such as the responsibility to pay joint credit card bills), the injured spouse can go to family court and seek an increase in alimony or child support based on changed circumstances.

Trends

As the content of this chapter indicates, approaches to spousal support vary considerably from state to state and court to court. While some believe alimony has lost its rationale in a no-fault era, others believe it still has a role to play in helping ensure that the choices made by spouses during marriage (often jointly) do not financially benefit one party to the other's detriment upon divorce. Although data is sparse, Bureau of Labor and Census Bureau statistics on source of income indicate that a significant number of individuals still receive alimony payments 97% of whom are women and nearly 75% of whom are over age 45.[15] Efforts to develop a national uniform alimony law (including the UMDA and recommendations of the ALI) have not been particularly successful to date. However, several states, including Texas, have implemented significant changes in their alimony laws in recent years and a few states, such as New Jersey in 2014 and Massachusetts in 2011 (effective March 2012), have enacted comprehensive and progressive alimony models. These developments suggest we are entering a new era in alimony practice that will better balance predictability, flexibility and judicial discretion. Several trends can be identified:

1. **Establishment of durational limits on alimony awards:** The trend toward imposing durational limits is apparent in: (1) the elimination in some states of so-called "permanent alimony" and establishment of the

obligor's full retirement age as presumptively controlling termination of alimony except for "good cause shown," or evidence of a material change in circumstances warranting continuation of the order; and (2) the establishment of durational limits on other kinds of alimony based on the length of the parties' marriage and the extent of their economic interdependence.

2. **Identification of specific forms of short term alimony:** Particularly in recognition of the large number of couples divorcing after short-term marriages, an increasing number of states are identifying by statute specific forms of short term alimony designed to: (1) enhance economic self-sufficiency rather than long term economic dependence (such as rehabilitation alimony); (2) facilitate the transition from married life to life postdivorce (such as transitional/bridge the gap alimony); and (3) repay a spouse for having financially contributed to advancement of the other spouse's education and career development during the marriage (such as restitution and reimbursement alimony).

3. **Recognition of "lost economic opportunity" as a result of marriage:** Even though women have made great strides, on average they still earn less than men and are disproportionately represented on welfare rolls. They continue to be more likely than men in the context of marriage and the family to make sacrifices that reduce their earning potential and standard of living if and when they exit the marriage. "Overall, divorced women suffer, on average, a twenty-seven percent decrease in their marital standard of living in contrast to men whose standard of living increases, on average, ten percent."[16] As one court has put it, recognition of lost opportunity has "nothing to do with feminism, sexism, male chauvinism or any other trendy social ideology. It is ordinary common sense, basic decency and simple justice."[17] The view of alimony as compensation for lost opportunity is reflected in the Illinois maintenance statute that requires a court to consider, among other factors, "any impairment of the present and future earning capacity of the party seeking maintenance due to that party devoting time to domestic duties or having forgone or delayed education, training, employment, or career opportunities due to the marriage."[18] See the *Sutphin* case (Case 11.7) in which an Ohio trial court specifically labeled an award to the wife "compensatory spousal support."

4. **Decreased emphasis on fault in alimony determinations:** Section 308 of the Uniform Marriage and Divorce Act (1973) provides that maintenance awards should be set "without regard to marital misconduct." Although adopted in only a minority of states to date,[19] the Act has been cited as persuasive authority in many jurisdictions, and the trend continues to be away from a consideration of "moral fault" of either partner when making alimony determinations. If fault is considered, it usually appears in a state statute listing factors to be weighed by the court. For example, Virginia and Utah are among the minority of states that still specifically include adultery as a factor to be considered.[20] Several states regard physical or mental abuse as a factor and still others consider economic fault.

5. **Increased acknowledgment of premarital and postdivorce cohabitation:** Statistics released by the Department of Health and Human Resources indicate that half of all women and nearly half of all men report having cohabited at some point in their lives.[21] The increased frequency and social

PARALEGAL PRACTICE TIP

In North Carolina, a party can request a jury trial on the issue of marital misconduct. The North Carolina statute can be found at *www.ncga.state.nc.us* (50-16-3A(c)).

PARALEGAL PRACTICE TIP

In 1995, the Utah Legislature amended the Utah Code to include a subsection allowing trial courts to consider fault in determining alimony awards.

acceptance of cohabitation and the fact that it has been decriminalized in a majority of the states, along with the extension of the right to marry to same-sex couples are leading to significant changes in alimony law. For example, under the Massachusetts Alimony Reform Act, in establishing the length of a marriage, the courts can now can consider "significant premarital cohabitation that included economic partnership." With respect to postdivorce cohabitation, we noted earlier in this chapter that an increasing number of states are addressing the impact of cohabitation on the modification, suspension and termination of alimony by statute.

6. **Movement towards the development of guidelines for calculating alimony:** Unlike child support awards, there is no federal requirement that states adopt guidelines and numeric, income-based criteria for the calculation of spousal support. To address the resulting lack of consistency and predictability in awards, the American Law Institute (ALI) recommends the adoption of computational guidelines, and an increasing number of states, counties within states, and individual judges[22] have experimented with and implemented guidelines in an effort to improve efficiency, decrease litigation, and provide predictability in this area.[23] Commentators in particular emphasize the need for formulas for calculating alimony to help increase predictability of awards and balance judicial discretion.[24]

CASE 11.7 *Sutphin v. Sutphin,* 2004 Ohio 6844 (Ohio App. 2004)

DISCUSSION OF THE CASE

Prior to the parties' marriage in 1987, they had signed a premarital agreement in which the wife, Susan, agreed to be a stay-at-home parent. Per the agreement, the wife quit her job and did not work outside the home until their one minor child graduated from high school. Based on evidence presented, the trial court found that the parties had maintained an "opulent" lifestyle during their marriage with income and expenditures of nearly $500,000 a year. After they separated in 1998, the husband, Stuart, continued to support Susan in a comfortable lifestyle.

At trial, the court heard testimony from Ann Crittenden, author of the book *The Price of Motherhood* (which was admitted into evidence), regarding lost income opportunities of stay-at-home mothers. Crittenden had received a master's degree in economics and had worked as a financial writer for *Fortune* magazine, *Newsweek*, and the *New York Times*. She was also an economics commentator for CBS News and had authored three books. Based in part on her testimony and that of Dr. Louis Noyd, an economist, about the value of the wife's total projected earnings, the trial court ordered Stuart to pay Susan spousal support in the amount of $1,415,620 in monthly installments of $9,000 and to contribute $100,000 toward her legal fees. In determining the amount of spousal support (which it referred to as "compensatory spousal support"), the trial court took the total projected earnings of the wife, subtracted the projected earnings for the period after the minor child graduated from high school, and subtracted an amount attributable to the duration of the parties' marriage.

The husband appealed, claiming that his substantial rights were affected by Crittenden's testimony and that her book should not have been admitted

(Continued)

in evidence. The Ohio intermediate appellate court affirmed the lower court's decision. The appellate court held that Stuart was not prejudiced by Crittenden's testimony as the trial court was required by statute to consider "the lost income capacity of either party that resulted from that party's marital responsibilities," and he was also not prejudiced by admission of the book because the author testified and was available for cross-examination.

The appellate court did express reservations about the characterization of the award but that reservation was based on the fact that the phrase "compensatory spousal support" was not found anywhere in the state's maintenance statute.

SIDEBAR

Do you agree with the court's decision? Explain your response. The opinion in the *Sutphin* case can be found at *www.pearsonhighered.com/careersresources/* in the website material for this text related to Chapter 11 under Cases.

The Role of the Paralegal in a Spousal Support Case

The tasks most commonly performed by a paralegal in a spousal support case are:

- researching current governing law (statutes, court rules, and case law) regarding spousal support in the applicable jurisdiction(s)
- scheduling and participating in interviews as assigned
- making discovery-related recommendations and drafting discovery requests as instructed, with particular attention to the factors the court will consider when making the spousal support decision
- drafting complaints, motions, supporting affidavits, and proposed orders (including motions for temporary support)
- drafting spousal support provisions for inclusion in separation agreements
- assisting in identification and preparation of prospective witnesses
- drafting a pretrial memorandum, if required, advising the court of the merits of the client's request for or opposition to alimony
- assisting with gathering and preparation of exhibits related to spousal support requests for use in negotiations and at hearings and trial
- drafting proposed findings of fact and conclusions of law addressing each of the factors to be considered by the court
- tracking progress on the case to be sure all deadlines are met
- making sure the client is kept informed about progress on the case, upcoming deadlines, hearings, etc.

PARALEGAL PRACTICE TIP

It is important to remember that when a marriage dissolves, the courts have multiple tools to work with in effecting a fair termination that will allow the parties to move forward. Alimony, child support, and property division are the three primary tools. Clients should not make agreements about one in a vacuum, without consideration of the other two.

CHAPTER **SUMMARY**

In this chapter we have explored the topic of spousal support beginning with a brief description of its origins under ecclesiastical and common law and concluding with projections for the future. The focus has been on general principles as well as on variations among the states as illustrated by cases, statutory references, paralegal applications and tips. The primary dimensions of the topic addressed in the chapter are highlighted below.

Since the onset of the no-fault era in the 1970s, the primary vehicle for allocating marital resources upon divorce has been property division. As a result, most parties now waive their respective rights to alimony although it is still awarded in a small percentage of cases. Some awards are granted following contested trials but most are based on agreements between the parties submitted to the court for approval. Alimony awards are allowances ordered by a court for support and maintenance of one spouse payable by the other spouse upon separation or divorce. Although by law, alimony has been gender-neutral since 1979 following the U.S. Supreme Court's decision in *Orr*, the vast majority of alimony recipients continue to be women.

There is considerable variation across the country with respect to the alimony options available to meet the diverse needs of spouses postdivorce. The most common types include temporary, permanent, term, lump-sum, rehabilitative, restitution, and transitional alimony. The types vary primarily with respect to purpose, duration, and conditions governing termination and modification.

Unlike child support awards, which are based on guidelines established in each state, there are few guidelines for determining when alimony will be awarded, in what amount, and for what purpose or duration. Alimony decisions are largely left to the discretion of individual judges, and awards are seldom overturned absent an abuse of discretion or an error in applying the law. In making alimony determinations, courts consider a variety of factors established by statute and case law. Given the limited assets in most marriages, the initial focus is usually on relative need and ability to pay. Other commonly considered factors include the length of the marriage, the age of the parties, the employability and earning capacity of each spouse, the standard of living that characterized the marriage, and in some states marital fault, particularly misconduct with economic consequences.

Alimony cases are fact-intensive at all stages from negotiation and trial to enforcement, modification and termination. As members of the family law team, paralegals often play key roles researching governing law and procedure, gathering and organizing information, and drafting documents to support the client's position.

CONCEPT REVIEW AND REINFORCEMENT

KEY TERMS

Absolute divorce
Alimony recapture rule
Annulment
Canon law
Civil contempt
Criminal contempt
Discharge
Divorce *a mensa et thoro*
Divorce *a vinculo matrimonii*
Legal separation
Lump-sum alimony/alimony in gross

Married Women's Property Acts
Material change in circumstances
Order to show cause
Permanent alimony
Premarital agreement
Prima facie showing
Public charge
Quid pro quo
Rehabilitative alimony
Restitution/reimbursement alimony
Separation agreement

Spousal support/alimony
Surviving agreement
Temporary alimony/alimony
    pendente lite
Term alimony
Transitional alimony
Vest
Waiver
Writ *ne exeat*

REVIEW QUESTIONS

1. Define spousal support/alimony and identify its purpose.
2. Describe how a premarital agreement might influence whether or not a spouse obtains alimony.
3. Describe the significance of the *Orr* decision.
4. Distinguish between alimony and property division.
5. Describe the nature and purpose of each of the following types of alimony: temporary, "permanent," lump-sum, rehabilitative, transitional, and restitution.
6. Identify the type or types of alimony that might be granted to a spouse who supported his or her spouse while the latter pursued a graduate degree during the marriage.

7. Identify the kinds of factors courts will consider when making alimony determinations.
8. Describe the kinds of evidence that need to be gathered to document the parties' standard of living during the marriage when significant assets are involved.
9. Identify the general rule governing modification of alimony awards.
10. Identify a minimum of three events that commonly result in the termination of an alimony obligation.
11. Describe the basic tax rule applicable to alimony awards with respect to includability and deductibility.
12. Describe how bankruptcy law treats property division and spousal support awards.

DEVELOPING YOUR PARALEGAL SKILLS

FOCUS ON **THE JOB**

This activity provides students with an opportunity to apply the content of this chapter by drafting a proposed alimony provision for inclusion in a separation agreement based on a comprehensive fact pattern.

The Facts

Jim Jones, thirty, has been married to Julie Jones, twenty-nine, for seven years. They have two children, Morgan, age four, and Logan, age six. When they got married, Jim was in his senior year of college and planning to graduate the following June and go on to get his master's degree in education. His lifelong dream has been to be a teacher. However, Julie got pregnant right after they were married and stopped working for a year. As a result, Jim dropped out of college and went to work in a local steak house. He continues to work part-time waiting tables and earns about $500 per week. He gets no employment benefits.

Morgan was born on September 15 six years ago and Logan was born on January 12 four years ago. Right after Morgan was born, Julie enrolled in law school. She received some financial aid and took out substantial student loans to support the cost of most of her tuition and books. Jim paid the remainder of her educational expenses as well as the household expenses for the three years she was in law school. Julie did not work at all during those years because she wanted to put all her energy into her studies. She graduated with high honors and was promptly hired at a major urban law firm where she had interned for a semester. Her supervisor was Marcus Tye, a senior partner in the firm. She and Mr. Tye became very close and Jim has reason to believe that he and Julie are having an affair, given that Attorney Tye's wife recently filed for divorce. Although he doesn't know for sure, Jim believes Tye's wife is claiming that her husband is having an affair with "some new employee at the office."

While Julie was going to school and for the couple of years she has been working, the parties agreed that Jim would only work part-time and would primarily stay home and manage the household and be primary caretaker for the children. He really didn't mind, because he loves the children and always figured that his turn would come once Julie got settled in her $170,000-a-year job, where she receives bonuses of varying amounts each year and benefits including medical insurance and a pension plan. Jim and the children are presently covered by her insurance.

The parties' only asset is the marital home, which is valued at $350,000, and they are carrying a $150,000 mortgage. Jim's parents gave them the $50,000 for the down payment when Jim and Julie bought it. They have been very generous to the couple and have frequently picked up the slack when debts piled up and upset Jim. They figured he had enough stress. The way Jim dealt with his stress (to no one's knowledge) was to gamble online, and his gambling often ate up his paychecks. He also ran up substantial credit card debt taking cash advances. He did have a few big hits, though, and has hidden away about $70,000, which no one knows about as yet.

Jim recently told Julie that he feels the time has come for him to go back to school and resume his career goals. He said she is making plenty of money now and could support their expenses along with day care for the kids when needed. In response, Julie said she had been meaning to talk with him about her desire to get a divorce and move on. It was nothing personal, she said, just that their individual lives have evolved in different directions. The life they are living is too "low-end" for her. She said she wants to start living "the good life." He can plod along playing video games and going to amusement parks with the kids for vacations, but she wants more. Jim is very hurt and angry but said he will make the best of a bad deal, and she can pay him support so that he can get his life back on track. She told him that he had to be kidding and then left the house and hasn't come home since. He is not sure where she is.

The Assignment

Jim, the client, has decided to file for divorce and is hoping to negotiate an agreement with Julie, who will be representing herself in the divorce. Anticipating the likely outcome of the negotiations, your supervisor, Attorney Moore, has asked you to draft a reasonable alimony provision for inclusion in a potential separation agreement. The provision should be tailored to the facts of the case and be sufficiently defensible that a court in your state would approve it. You should research some models and be sure to reflect what you have learned reading this chapter about the nature of alimony provisions and the various types of alimony that may be available.

FOCUS ON **ETHICS**

This focus on ethics asks the student to consider some of the ethical issues that arise when the client in the Focus on the Job fact pattern asks a paralegal to engage in a potentially illegal act.

The Assignment

The family law firm where you are employed represents Jim in the above fact pattern. You have been interviewing Jim and gathering information from him regarding his divorce and claim for alimony. You and Jim have become quite friendly, and he apparently trusts you. Today, when the two of you met regarding the case, Jim asked if you could "grab a bite to eat" with him at the local delicatessen. It was lunchtime and you needed to eat, so you decided to go but insisted on paying for your own lunch so that Jim would not get the wrong impression. While eating lunch, Jim shared with you the fact that as a result of his gambling, he has accumulated nearly $70,000 in cash, which he has kept at home in a bureau drawer. He told you that Julie doesn't know about the cash and he doesn't plan to tell her about it or declare it on his financial statement, because he doesn't want her to get any of it. He is going to move to a small apartment in a tough neighborhood and doesn't want to take the money with him. He asked if you would be willing to hold it in safekeeping for him and said that he will give you 10% of it if you do. He told you not to answer right away and to think about it. You told him that if you do not agree to hold the cash, your supervisor probably will. In a one- to two-page paper respond to the following questions. What are you going to do? Why? What do you think will happen if and when you report the details of this incident to your supervisor? Relate your response to the ethical canons for paralegals promulgated by the National Association of Legal Assistants contained in Appendix A as well as the ethics material in Chapter 1 of this text and the rules governing the professional conduct of attorneys in your state.

FOCUS ON **CASE LAW**

This activity requires the student to respond to a series of questions about an alimony case that addresses several topics covered in this chapter.

The Assignment

Read the Iowa Supreme Court case *In re the Marriage of Olson*, 705 N.W.2d 312 (Iowa 2005), and then respond to the following questions. The opinion can be found at *www.pearsonhighered.com/careersresources/* in the website material related to Chapter 11 of this text under Cases.

1. Describe the legal history of the case.
2. What issue is addressed in the appeal to the Iowa Supreme Court?
3. Briefly describe the facts of the case.
4. How did the district court treat the husband's overtime income? Was it included in his income for purposes of calculating alimony? Did the state's high court agree with this approach?
5. What factors do the Iowa courts consider when determining whether or not an award of alimony is appropriate? Where are those factors set forth?
6. Describe the types of alimony considered by the court in this case.
7. Which type of alimony did the court conclude was appropriate and why?
8. Explain how the court factored the wife's gambling into the alimony decision, if at all.
9. What was the decision of the Iowa Supreme Court in this case?
10. What was the essence of Justice Carter's concurring opinion?

FOCUS ON **STATE LAW AND PROCEDURE**

This activity requires the student to locate the rules governing spousal support in his or her state and apply them to the Focus on the Job fact pattern by assessing the potential of the client's claim for alimony.

The Assignment

Locate the statute(s) and/or case law in your jurisdiction governing initial alimony awards. Identify the factors considered by the courts when making those awards. Assume that in your capacity as a paralegal, you have been asked by your supervisor, Attorney Moore, to assess Jim Jones's prospects for receiving an alimony award in your state based on those factors. Be sure to include a list of the factors in your assessment. Is marital fault relevant and, if so, under what circumstances? Do any of the sources you located specify the kinds of support that can be awarded? If yes, which kind would be appropriate in this case, if any? Present your findings in an internal memorandum using the format below.

Memorandum

To: *Your Supervisor*

From: *Your name, paralegal*

Re: *Assessment of James Jones's Claim for Alimony*

Date:

Description of assignment: *What is it that you have been asked to do?*

Results of research: *Describe the applicable statute(s)/case law.*

Discussion: *Apply the governing law to the specific facts of Jim's case.*

Conclusion: *What is your opinion about the client's likelihood of success with respect to his claim for alimony?*

FOCUS ON **TECHNOLOGY**

In addition to the links provided throughout the chapter, this activity provides a series of useful websites for reference along with technology-related assignments for completion.

Websites of Interest

www.divorceonline.com

This site provides a wide range of articles and information on various aspects of divorce. It includes links to state divorce laws. Select "Professional Resources" and then "State Divorce Laws."

www.divorcehelp.com

This site is operated by a lawyer. One of the resources it provides is a copy of "A Short Divorce Course" for people considering and/or going through a divorce.

www.divorcelinks.com

This site provides direct links to state and federal divorce laws by topic.

www.divorcenet.com

This site offers family law advice on divorce. It provides links to state resource pages that contain a wealth of articles and links on a variety of topics, including alimony.

www.findlaw.com

A search on "spousal support" will prove fruitful. The site offers alimony information by state along with articles on types of alimony and criteria for awards. Primary sources should be checked to verify information when appropriate.

www.irs.gov

This is the website for the Internal Revenue Service. In addition to provisions of the federal tax code, many useful publications are available at this site, including Publication 504 containing tax information for Divorced and Separated Individuals.

www.totalbankruptcy.com

This site provides a wealth of information about bankruptcy, including links to state laws. The information provided should be verified to be sure it reflects current law.

Assignments

1. Using online resources, locate the factors considered by the court when making alimony determinations in your state.
2. Go to the website for the U.S. Department of Labor (*www.dol.gov*) and locate information about COBRA health insurance coverage post divorce.
3. Go to *www.americanbar.org*, the website for the American Bar Association. Search for the table on alimony/ spousal support factors (Table 1), which contains a state-by-state summary indicating:

   * which states have a statutory list of factors for courts to consider when making alimony decisions
   * which states consider marital fault
   * which states consider standard of living
   * which states consider a party's status as a custodial parent

   To locate the table at the site, search for "Family Law in the 50 States Tables" in resources available to the public. This table also appears annually in the *Family Law Quarterly* (Winter Volume) published by the ABA. What did you learn about your state from this resource? Is the information you found current?

PORTFOLIO PRODUCTS

1. Alimony provision for a separation agreement
2. One- to two-page paper on ethical issues in a hypothetical fact pattern
3. Responses to questions regarding an alimony case
4. Memorandum: Assessment of a client's claim for alimony

chapter 12
PROPERTY DIVISION

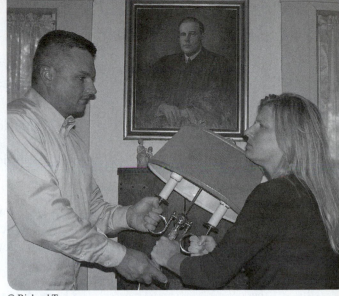

© Richard Tauson

> Jimmy and Alice had been married for ten years and lived a comfortable life with their three children—that was until Alice had an affair with her boss and Jimmy found out about it. He says he will make her pay for hurting the family like that. He tells his lawyer he wants to file for divorce on the grounds of adultery and that he intends to win at all costs. She will walk away with nothing.

Introduction

Jimmy makes a naïve assumption in the opening scenario in the sense that no one really "wins" in a divorce. Each party ends up materially with less than he or she had during the marriage. The old idea that a wronged spouse can punish his or her former partner and "get everything" largely passed from the legal scene nearly five decades ago with the coming of no-fault divorce. Today, marriages essentially are dissolved as if they were business partnerships. The **marital estate** is divided between the spouses based on an assumption that, since marriage is a partnership, when it terminates both parties have an interest in the assets accumulated during the marriage and are accountable for the liabilities incurred. Generally, courts first divide the marital estate and then, if allowed in the jurisdiction, make a determination with respect to whether or not an alimony award is appropriate. A comprehensive comparison of property division and alimony was provided in Chapter 11 in Exhibit 11.1.

Our focus in this chapter is specifically on the complex topic of property division, the primary economic event in a divorce. Property division addresses the allocation of assets and liabilities the parties have accumulated both prior to and during their marriage. The chapter will examine the following five phases of the overall property

LEARNING OBJECTIVES

After reading this chapter and completing related assignments, you should be able to:

- identify the five phases of the property division process

- distinguish between separate and marital property

- identify kinds of property subject to division when a marriage dissolves

- distinguish between the community property and equitable distribution approaches to property division

- list factors the courts consider when dividing property and liabilities upon divorce

- describe the paralegal's role in the property division process

Marital estate
the property acquired during the marriage other than by gift or inheritance that is subject to division at the time of marital dissolution

435

division process with references to variations in state law and procedure as well as the role of the paralegal in each phase:

1. Definition of property: What is "property" and what property do the parties have?
2. Classification of property: Is the property "separate" or "marital?"
3. Identification of property subject to division upon divorce: Which property can the courts reach to effectuate a division?
4. Valuation of property: What is the property worth—how and when is it valued?
5. Division of property: How is property divided—what factors do the courts consider? Is the state an equitable distribution or a community property jurisdiction?

The Five Phases of the Property Division Process

DEFINITION OF PROPERTY

The threshold question in a property division case is: Does a particular asset fall within a definition of property? In most cases, this question does not even arise because the parties' only assets are clearly property, such as automobiles, household furnishings, bank accounts, or a marital home, but some cases involve assets that are less clearly property. Assets that are mere expectancies (such as a possible inheritance or future earning capacity) or that have no presently determinable value (such as a patent on an obscure and not particularly useful boat engine part) will generally not be considered property subject to division.

It is important that all actual and potential assets and liabilities be identified. Before filing for divorce, counsel will usually ask the client to identify (and document where possible) the **tangible** and **intangible** property the parties may have. Clients often initially fail to recognize the nature and extent of property they and/or their spouses may own that has value. They need to be encouraged to think in broad terms. This process can be facilitated by the completion of a client questionnaire, such as the sample provided at *www.pearsonhighered .com/careersresources/* in the website material related to Chapter 5 under Resources. Exhibit 12.1 lists some examples of property that may be subject to division upon divorce. Case 12.1 and Paralegal Applications 12.1 and 12.2 provide illustrations of items listed in Exhibit 12.1 which may or may not be treated as property depending on the jurisdiction.

EXHIBIT 12.1 Property Potentially Subject to Division

- annuity contracts
- antiques, heirlooms
- appreciation in the value of property during the marriage, depending on whether it relates to separate or marital property and active or passive appreciation
- artwork
- bank accounts (checking, savings, credit union, etc.)
- boats
- bonuses

(Continued)

PARALEGAL PRACTICE TIP

Given state variations, it may help readers to identify at this point the basic terminology applied in their respective jurisdictions. For example, in a community property state, marital property will be referred to as "community property."

PARALEGAL PRACTICE TIP

A failure to identify, value, and seek distribution of property for the client may amount to malpractice if significant assets or liabilities are overlooked. See *Briggs, F.K.A. Moelich v. Darlene Wilcox. D.B.A. Darlene A. Wilcox, L.L.C.*, 2013 Ohio, 1541, 991 N.E.2d 262 (Ohio App. 2013).

Tangible property
property that has a physical form, capable of being touched and seen

Intangible property
property that has no physical presence or form such as legal claims, patents, and trademarks

PARALEGAL PRACTICE TIP

For readers seeking an introduction to or a review of basic property concepts, a list of definitions relating to types of property (real and personal, tangible and intangible, etc.) and forms of ownership is available at *www.pearsonhighered.com/ careersresources/* in the website material related to Chapter 12 under Resources.

EXHIBIT 12.1 (*Continued*)

- business interests (sole proprietorships, corporations, partnerships, etc.)
- cash
- certificates of deposit
- clothing (including furs, etc.)
- club memberships (social, golf, tennis, yacht, etc.)[1]
- collectibles (guns, china, figurines, stamps, coins, baseball cards, etc.)[2]
- contingent fee agreements[3] and accounts receivable
- contracts (such as a professional athlete's contract)[4]
- copyrights, patents, and trademarks
- deferred compensation
- disability awards
- employment "perks" (housing, car, parking space, etc.)
- frequent-flier miles
- furniture and appliances
- gifts
- goodwill of a business
- governmental benefits
- inheritances
- insurance policies with cash-surrender values
- jewelry
- licenses (e.g., pilot's license or a taxi medallion)
- lottery winnings[5]
- motor vehicles, including cars, trucks, recreational vehicles, motorcycles, and trailers
- mutual funds
- pending lawsuits and judgments
- pension plans (IRAs, 401(k)s, etc.)
- personal injury awards
- pets/companion animals[6]
- professional degrees
- profit-sharing plans
- real estate (residence, vacation homes, rental property, time-shares, cemetery lots, deeded rights to parking spaces, etc.)
- season tickets to athletic events, theaters, concerts, and other cultural events
- silverware
- Social Security benefits[7]
- stocks and bonds
- stock options (vested and unvested)[8]
- tax refunds and overpayment of state and federal taxes
- trusts (beneficial interests)
- accrued vacation or sick leave time
- worker's compensation benefits[9]
- frozen embryos

PARALEGAL PRACTICE TIP

Sometimes it may be necessary to determine if a gift being claimed as separate property is truly a gift. For example, during the marriage, an elderly aunt gives a "gift" of $50,000 to a niece who has been her primary caretaker for a year. It might be argued that the cash is not in fact a gift but rather compensation paid for the niece's services and that it is therefore marital property.

PARALEGAL PRACTICE TIP

Occasionally, despite the best efforts of a client and the family law team, an asset concealed by the other party will not be discovered until after entry of the judgment dissolving the parties' marriage and dividing their assets. Although property distributions are generally held to be final and not subject to modification, courts will sometimes reopen a case based on discovery of additional assets concealed at the time of the divorce[10] (usually subject to statutes of limitation). See, e.g., *Olio v. Olio*, 54 A.3d 510 (Vt. 2012).

Paralegal Application 12.1

To Be or Not To Be Property #1

The goodwill of a business

Goodwill has been defined as "the favor which the management of a business has won from the public and probability that old customers will continue their patronage."[11] The financial value of goodwill sometimes can be determined by an expert. When goodwill is based on personal characteristics of a party or is intrinsically tied to the attributes and skills of a particular individual such as an attorney, physician, actor, or athlete (i.e., personal goodwill), most states do not consider it to be property subject to division. That kind of goodwill cannot be sold—it does not survive the disassociation of the individual from a business. However, goodwill that is wholly attributable to a commercial business, such as an automobile dealership or a hardware store, the business itself, its location, and customer lists (i.e., enterprise goodwill), may be considered property subject to valuation and division upon divorce.[12] Illustrations of the minority and majority approaches taken by the courts with respect to goodwill are provided below. In addition to these two approaches, there are rare circumstances in which neither personal nor enterprise goodwill may be considered divisible property as in the case of a solo practitioner whose business cannot continue without him or her. See, e.g., *Hartline v. Hartline*, 2014 Tenn. App. LEXIS 7 (2014).

The Minority View: Both personal and enterprise goodwill constitute marital assets subject to division— Walsh v. Walsh, 230 Ariz. 486, 286 P.3d 1095 (Ariz. App. 2012)

This case involved a dispute over the value of a husband's goodwill in his law practice. The husband's position was that "personal goodwill" is distinct from "enterprise goodwill" and is not divisible marital property. His expert testified that any goodwill he had in his legal practice was limited to a $140,000 stock redemption agreement with his firm. The wife's expert applied a "capitalization-of-earnings approach" and examined the husband's tax returns, historical income performance, earning sustainability, reputation, and client loyalty arriving at a value for the professional practice of $1,269,000. The family court found that the husband's interest in the firm and the value of his law practice were limited to the $140,000 stock redemption value.

The appellate court rejected the husband's position and reversed and remanded the case holding that "[T]he family court should have considered the Husband's personal goodwill in valuing Husband's law practice" and should not limit its value to "realizable" goodwill, "something that can be bought or sold on the open market." It observed that "[A]lthough some states hold that personal goodwill may not constitute marital property, . . . Arizona does in fact consider qualities that are attributable to the individual in determining community property." The court acknowledged that value must be determined based on the facts and circumstances of each case and that "[I]t is a difficult task at best to arrive at a value for the intangible component of a professional practice attributable to goodwill." It suggested that in determining a value for professional goodwill in a law practice, the court may look at factors such as age, health, past earning power, length of time in practice, skill and knowledge, reputation and comparative professional success. See also *Poore v. Poore*, 75 N.C. App. 414, 331 S.E.2d 266 (N.C. App. 1985).

The Majority View: Enterprise but not personal goodwill constitutes a marital asset subject to division—May v. May, 214 W. Va. 394, 589 S.E.2d 536 (W. Va. 2003)

This case involved a dispute over the value of the husband's solo dental practice. During the family court proceeding, the husband's expert valued the dental practice at $55,000.00, and the wife's expert placed a fair market value on it of $120,000 including a value of $80,568 for personal goodwill. The family court judge adopted the wife's valuation and ordered an equitable distribution payment for her interest in the dental practice in the amount of $ 889.00 per month from June 1, 2004, to May 31, 2012. The husband appealed.

In its opinion, the West Virginia Supreme Court of Appeals acknowledged the split of authority among the states on whether enterprise and/or personal goodwill in a professional practice may be characterized as divisible marital property. The West Virginia high court adopted the majority position. The court held that "personal goodwill, which is intrinsically tied to the attributes and/ or skills of an individual, is not subject to equitable distribution. It is not a divisible asset. It is more properly considered as the individual's earning capacity that may affect property division and alimony. On the other hand, enterprise goodwill, which is wholly attributable to the business itself, is subject to equitable distribution." Because the trial court judge adopted the wife's valuation, which included a personal goodwill component, the case was reversed and remanded for a reassessment of the value of the dental practice. See also *Yoon v. Yoon*, 711 N.E.2d 1265 (Ind. 1999).

Paralegal **Application 12.2**

To Be or Not To Be Property #2

Professional degrees and licenses

Sofia and Adam married right after graduation from college. Although they had few resources, they agreed that Adam should continue on to medical school and become a licensed physician. The plan was that while Adam earned his medical degree, Sofia would find employment so she could support their living expenses as well as the portion of Adam's education expenses not covered by grants. She would then pursue her MBA and further her career. In the long term they expected to enjoy a comfortable lifestyle together. What they did not anticipate was that after seven years of her working three jobs, Adam would earn his degree and license to practice medicine and decide he wanted a divorce. How should the court address this situation? Should Adam's medical degree be considered marital property divisible upon divorce? Does Sofia have any recourse or did she assume the risk that their marriage would fail? The courts are divided in their responses as they strive to treat both parties fairly in light if the facts of each case. They have typically adopted one of five positions:

1. **The degree should be treated as marital property subject to division upon divorce.** A minority of courts have been willing to recognize in theory the existence of a property interest in an educational degree. For example, in *Farrell v. Cleary-Farrell*, 306 A.D.2d 597, 761 N.Y.S.2d 357 (N.Y. App. Div. 2003), a husband was considered entitled to a distributive award of 7½% of the value of his wife's dental hygienist license. Although he had sought more, the court found that the wife had "exerted extraordinary efforts to complete her degree and obtain her license." She had worked, taken care of the parties' children, and been responsible for the household chores while her husband contributed little and focused on advancing his own career. The degree and license were largely the result of the wife's own ability, perseverance and hard work. (See also the landmark decision in *O'Brien v. O'Brien*, 66 N.Y.2d 576, 498 N.Y.S.2d 743, 489 N.E.2d 712 (1985) in which the court awarded a wife $189,000 for her share of her husband's medical degree; *Inman v. Inman*, 578 S.W.2d 266 (Ky. 1979) affirming in principle allowance of a professional degree (or the increased earning capacity that it represents) as marital property; *In re the Marriage of Horstmann*, 263 N.W.2d 885 (Iowa 1978); and *Woodworth v. Woodworth*, 126 Mich. App. 258,

337 N.W.2d 332 (1983) finding that the husband's law degree was the end product of a concerted family effort and the result of mutual sacrifice and effort by both the husband and the wife.

2. **The degree should not be treated as marital property subject to division upon divorce.** A majority of the courts have rejected the characterization of a degree as divisible property. In a case in which the wife, a flight attendant, had provided 70% of the couple's financial support while her husband successfully pursued B.S. and M.B.A. degrees, the Colorado Supreme Court reasoned:

   An educational degree, such as an M.B.A., . . . does not have an exchange value or any objective transferable value on an open market. It is personal to the holder. It terminates on the death of the holder and is not inheritable. It cannot be assigned, sold, transferred, conveyed, or pledged, . . . It may not be acquired by the mere expenditure of money. . . . In our view, it has none of the attributes of property in the usual sense of that term.[13]

3. **An appropriate amount of restitution should be made to the contributing spouse.** This approach calls for restitution to an individual who directly or indirectly contributed to acquisition of a spouse's degree by, for example, paying for living expenses, tuition, books, and fees. The Minnesota Supreme court espoused this position when it awarded a wife "restitutionary relief" in the amount of $11,400 for having worked full-time to support her husband through part of his undergraduate education and two and one-half years of medical school. See *DeLa Rosa v. DeLa Rosa*, 309 N.W.2d 755 (Minn. 1981).

4. **The contributing spouse should be compensated by means of an alimony award.** In *Drapek v. Drapek*, 399 Mass. 240 (1987), the Massachusetts Supreme Judicial Court rejected a trial court's classification of a husband's medical degree as "part of his estate subject to equitable assignment" but stated that on remand "the judge may amend the alimony in order to reflect the value of his degree and enhanced earnings." The Wisconsin Supreme Court pursued the same course when it reversed a lower court decision that awarded $14,316 to a wife which it viewed as an attempt to "place a dollar value on something

(Continued)

so intangible as a professional education, degree, or license. . . ." In choosing alimony over property division as an option, the court reasoned:

> A person qualified by education for a given profession may choose not to practice it, may fail at it, or may practice in a specialty, location or manner which generates less than the average income enjoyed by fellow professionals. The potential worth of the education may never be realized for these or many other reasons. . . . Unlike an award of alimony, which can be adjusted after divorce to reflect unanticipated changes in the parties' circumstances, a property division may not.[14]

5. **The marital estate should be equitably divided between the parties taking contribution into consideration.** This approach is most suited to equitable distribution jurisdictions where the courts have the authority to distribute the parties' property in accordance with factors usually laid out by statute. Those factors typically include vocational skills, employability, occupation, opportunity for future acquisition of income and assets, and economic and noneconomic contributions to the marriage. However, community property jurisdictions may also achieve equity either by treating a degree earned during the marriage as community property or by giving consideration to contribution. For example, a California appellate court acknowledged that education acquired with community funds is of such a character that a monetary value cannot be placed on it. However, the court then awarded the wife who had supported her husband's pursuit of undergraduate and law degrees $111,500 in community assets and her husband a total of $89,116. The wife thus realized her investment through a more favorable division of property.

PARALEGAL PRACTICE TIP

Creative arguments can be made to support a client's case. When one argument doesn't work, another might. For example, in a 2010 case, the Utah Supreme Court took an unusual approach and held that alimony is not necessarily an adequate remedy nor is it intended to be the sole remedy in cases in which one spouse has supported the family unit while the other spouse pursued a medical degree. Provided it is brought in the context of the divorce action, a spouse who provided support can bring an action for breach of student support claim seeking damages to "make her whole" and place her in the position she would have been in had her husband "tendered performance according to the contract's terms." Had he done so, she would have been supported and enjoyed a standard of living commensurate with the income normally obtained by a holder of a medical degree. The court viewed the contract as analogous to a postnuptial agreement that would be enforceable if negotiated in good faith. See *Ashby v. Ashby*, 2010 Utah 7, 227 P.3d 246 (2010).

PARALEGAL PRACTICE TIP

When researching this issue, paralegals should look at journal articles as well as case law. Consider, for example, Heidi Stroh, *Puppy Love: Providing for the Legal Protection of Animals When Their Owners Get Divorced*, 2 J. ANIMAL L. & ETHICS 231 (2007), arguing for a best interests standard, and *Juelfs v. Gough*, 41 P.3d 593 (Alaska 2002), in which the court considered the parties' dog, Coho, in the context of a property settlement but ultimately granted sole "custody" to the husband believing it to be in the dog's "best interests."

CASE 12.1 *Hament v. Baker*, 2014 VT 39, 97 A.3d 461 (2000)

BACKGROUND

It is estimated that pets or "companion animals" are present as treasured additions in more than 50% of American households. So it is not surprising that what happens to Spike and Mittens, can present a challenging issue for divorcing spouses and the courts. Some couples provide for "custody and visitation" with cherished pets by formal agreement, and others do so by informal cooperative arrangements. When disputed, the courts grapple with whether they should treat them like children and consider the animal's best interests (the position advocated by the Animal League Defense Fund and Lawyers in Defense of Animals) and make custody awards or deem them personal property and distribute them along with the dishes, ipods, cars, and bank accounts. Most of the courts that have considered this issue have determined that they are personal property subject to division[15] but increasingly accord them "special" treatment as in this case.

FROM THE OPINION

The only issue in this contested divorce was which spouse should receive the family dog. Belle is an eleven-year-old wirehaired pointer who is greatly loved by husband and wife. . . .

Prior to the hearing, counsel for the parties met with the family court to discuss the criteria the court would apply in assigning the dog to one party or the other. The court stated that the primary factor for its decision would be which spouse was most active in caring for the dog during the marriage. The court also stated that the family division would not enforce a shared visitation schedule even if the parties agreed to it.

During the hearing, both parties testified about their strong emotional ties to the dog and to the care that each spouse provides. Husband is a veterinarian and takes the dog to work with him. Wife spends time walking the dog in the woods near her home and is very involved in daily care of the dog.

At the conclusion of the hearing, the court awarded the dog to husband. It found that either party would provide the dog with a good life. It gave a slight edge to the husband because the dog is accustomed to the routine of going to the clinic every day. The court balanced that factor against the dog's familiarity with the marital home, which the parties agreed wife would receive as part of the property settlement. . . . The court concluded that the dog would do better with husband's balanced attitude towards the animal.

I. ALLOCATION OF THE DOG

This Court has consistently ruled that pet animals are property. . . . But pets are different from other property. They are alive and form emotional attachments with their owners that run in both directions. Their long and intimate association with people gives rise to special concerns for their well-being and humane treatment. See, e.g., 13 V.S.A. §§ 351-400 (prohibiting cruelty to animals); 15 V.S.A. § 1103(c)(2)(G) (permitting court to include provisions concerning the possession, care and control of family pet in fashioning domestic relief-from-abuse order); 20 V.S.A. §§ 3901-3915 (regulating sale and euthanasia of animals). In most cases, they have little or no market value, but we spend generously to feed and care for them. See *Morgan v. Kroupa*, 167 Vt. 99, 103, 702 A.2d 630, 633 (1997) (noting that the value of most pets is primarily emotional rather than financial). As this case illustrates, they frequently become close companions and an important part of daily life for countless owners.

. . .

. . . We hold first that the allocation of a pet in a divorce is subject to 15 V.S.A. § 751. In contrast to a child, a pet is not subject to a custody award following a determination of its best interests. Because a pet is property, the family division must assign it to one party or the other. Like other aspects of the property division, the assignment is final and generally not subject to modification.

Few of the statutory factors which appear in § 751(b) apply to the equitable distribution of a pet. These factors relate primarily to property as a source of income and material advantage. 15 V.S.A. § 751(b). The tenth statutory factor—"the party through whom the property was acquired"—could apply in the case of a pet obtained by one spouse alone, but the evidence in this case is that Belle was placed with both husband and wife through a pet adoption process. 15 V.S.A. § 751(b)(10).

The family division is not limited to considering the factors enumerated in § 751(b). See 15 V.S.A. § 751(b) ("In making a property settlement the court may consider all relevant factors, including [the statutory criteria]."). . . .

In the case of pets, we hold that the family division may consider other factors not set out in the statute: the welfare of the animal and the emotional connection between the animal and each spouse. These factors underlie our animal welfare laws and our case law, which recognizes the value of the bond between the animal and its owner. . . . Evidence concerning welfare of the animal includes evidence about its daily routine, comfort, and care. Evidence concerning the emotional connection may include testimony about the role of the animal in the lives of the spouses.

In this case, the parties were afforded an opportunity to put on evidence regarding both factors without restriction. . . . Facts concerning Belle's welfare and her emotional connection with husband and wife were fully developed through the testimony of the parties and others. The testimony included a detailed description of Belle's typical day and of her veterinary needs, now and in the future. Husband and wife were both candid in their description of the dog's role in assuaging the loneliness and dislocation each has experienced during the divorce. . . .

The court's oral decision primarily reflected its concern for the welfare of the animal. The court found in favor of husband on the basis of evidence that Belle's long-standing routine includes spending most days of the week at the veterinarian clinic where she has the run of the place. The court considered the emotional connection between the dog and its owners and concluded that husband showed the right "balance" while wife treated the dog like a child.

. . .

The family court recognized how much the dog means to both parties. It is clear that her primary concern was the treatment of the dog. This was an appropriate factor upon which to base the decision. The court's specific findings about Belle and her owners are supported by the evidence. The factors the court considered—the dog's welfare and its emotional relationship with the parties—are the same factors that we recognize today as appropriate for the resolution of similar questions in the future. Accordingly, we affirm the court's decision to assign ownership of the dog to husband.

SIDEBAR

In the family law context, do you believe pets should be treated as personal property and distributed like other assets or treated more like children for whom custody and visitation determinations need to be made? Explain your answer.

PARALEGAL PRACTICE TIP

A trial court's failure to distinguish between separate and marital property can cause problems on appeal. For example in *Farlee v. Farlee*, 812 N.W.2d 501 (S.D. 2012), the South Dakota Supreme Court held that it was unable to review whether the circuit court had equitably divided the parties' property because it failed to classify all of the disputed property. The judgment was reversed and remanded for reconsideration of the property division after the trial court resolves valuation and marital property issues on the record.

Marital property
property that is acquired by either or both parties during the marriage, other than by gift or inheritance, that is subject to division at the time of dissolution

Separate property
property that a spouse owned before marriage or acquired during the marriage by inheritance or gift from a third party; may include property acquired during marriage in exchange for separate property

CLASSIFICATION OF PROPERTY AS SEPARATE OR MARITAL

Classifying property as separate or marital is a critical step in the property division process because it essentially establishes the pool of assets which will be subject to division by the court when the marriage terminates. The paralegal may be involved in gathering the information necessary to support the classification and distribution most favorable to the client.

Generally, in both community property and equitable distribution jurisdictions, the parties begin acquiring **marital property** at the commencement of the marriage and cease to do so at the time of separation, the filing of the complaint for divorce, or as of the date of the divorce decree. Many states have legislatively established statutory definitions of marital and separate property. For example, the South Carolina legislature has defined marital property as "all real and personal property which has been acquired by the parties during the marriage and which is owned as of the date of filing or commencement of marital litigation. . . ."[16] It usually includes property classified as marital regardless of how title to that property is held. For example, the deed to the marital home may be in the name of both parties as tenants by the entirety, joint tenants with rights of survivorship, or solely in the name of one spouse. Marital property excludes **separate property**, property owned by a party prior to marriage although in some states it may include appreciation in the value of separate property during the course of the marriage. (See Paralegal Application 12.3.) Most states also exempt from marital property gifts and inheritances received by either of the parties from third parties during the marriage, but some consider interspousal gifts purchased with joint funds to be marital property. Some states distinguish between segregated separate property and separate property supported, maintained, and improved with marital funds, time and effort.

Sometimes classification of property as separate or marital is especially challenging. For example, when the parties are common law spouses, they usually do not have to prove precisely when their marriage began. Therefore, an argument for a "start" date for accumulation of marital assets and liabilities will need to be made that best meets the client's objectives for purposes of property division. See, e.g., *Kelly v. Thompson,* 2009 MT 392, 353 Mont. 361, 220 P.3d 627 (2009). A somewhat similar issue arises with same-sex spouses who may have been accumulating property together for decades but who have only been able to legally marry in the past few years. Should property acquired before they formally wed be deemed "marital" or "separate?"

When a division of property action involves immovable property such as real estate or mineral rights in another state, the basic choice of law rule is that the law of the situs (the place where the property is situated) will govern all rights, title, and interests in and to the property. Depending on the location of the property, it may be necessary for the paralegal to research the governing law of another jurisdiction to determine whether a particular asset is likely to be treated as separate or marital.[17] See Paralegal Applications 12.3 and 12.4 for additional examples of classification issues that arise with particular kinds of assets.

PARALEGAL PRACTICE TIP

The section of the West Virginia Code defining marital and separate property can be found at *www.legis .state.wv.us.* West Virginia Code § 48-1-233, 237.

PARALEGAL PRACTICE TIP

Not infrequently courts will deviate from general rules to achieve a fair result. For example, in *In re Marriage of Adams,* 805 N.W.2d 397 (Iowa Ct. App. 2011), the appellate court held that a trial court can divide gifts received by a party before or during a marriage when a failure to do so would be inequitable to the other party or to the parties' children.

Paralegal **Application 12.3**

Separate or Marital Property?

Disability awards

The majority of courts that have considered the proper classification of disability benefits have adopted an approach which focuses on the underlying purpose of the specific disability benefits at issue, separating awards into retirement and true disability components when appropriate. Where justified by the particular facts of a case, the retirement component is considered marital property and the disability component separate property because it is personal to the spouse who receives it.[18] In determining the character of disability benefits in a specific case, courts usually will look at several factors:

- Does a state or federal statute specifically exclude disability benefits from marital property?
- Are the benefits the result of a private disability policy paid for with marital funds?
- Are the benefits compensation for past services rendered during the marriage?

- Did the right to receive benefits result from employment during the marriage?
- Do the benefits replace future income?
- Does the benefit compensate for lost earning capacity?
- Does the benefit represent retirement pay earned during the marriage?
- Did the parties discuss the benefit and view it as a joint investment to secure their future?

Personal Injury Awards

Some courts classify personal injury awards based on whether or not the injury occurred during the marriage and some have classified them as solely the separate property of the injured party. Most jurisdictions have adopted an analytical approach. As with disability payments, the courts will customarily look at the purpose(s) served by the award. The West Virginia Supreme Court of Appeals expressed it this way: ". . . to the

(Continued)

extent that its purpose is to compensate an individual for pain, suffering, disability, disfigurement, or other debilitation of the mind or body, a personal injury award constitutes the separate nonmarital property of an injured spouse. However, . . . economic losses, such as past wages and medical expenses, which diminish the marital estate are distributable as marital property when recovered in a personal injury award or settlement."[19]

Accrued vacation or sick leave time

The courts that have considered these assets are divided. If an employee has an enforceable right to be paid the value of accrued vacation or sick leave time at some point, courts may construe time credits that accrued during the marriage as a marital asset divisible upon divorce or at a later date when actually received by the employee spouse such as on retirement. However, if accrued sick time cannot be cashed in or can only be applied toward the employee's postretirement health insurance premiums, it may not be deemed marital property because it is personal, intangible, difficult to value, and impossible to transfer.[20] See, e.g., *Cardona v. Castro*, 2014 CO 3, 316 P.3d 626 (2014), in which the Colorado Supreme Court reviews alternative approaches to this issue.

Appreciation in the value of separate property

Property owned by one of the parties prior to marriage often appreciates in value during the marriage, even during a short term marriage. Consider, for example, the *Calhoun* case (*Calhoun v. Calhoun*, 844 N.W.2d 469 (Iowa App. 2014). In this case, the parties, Joseph and Theresa, were married on 9/8/2011 and the wife filed for divorce less than three months later on 11/29/2011. Shortly before the marriage, the wife's father gifted to her two parcels of farmland both of which significantly increased in value over a brief period of time:

Property	Value when gifted	Value on date of marriage	Value at time of trial
Packwood	$200,000	$278,500	$354,112
Henry County	$212,000	$262,000	$397,500

The uncontested testimony of a professional auctioneer established that the increases were partly attributable to market trends in farmland and would have occurred had the parties taken no action whatsoever (**passive appreciation**) and partly to improvements made by the husband (**active appreciation**). It was undisputed that the husband expended considerable time and funds (about $22,000) to make the land potentially more profitable. For example, he repaired fences and waterways, hauled away trash and debris, helped construct a pole barn, repaired a house on one of the properties (which the parties lived in during the marriage), and converted pasture land to fields suitable for row crops.

At trial, Joseph did not claim that the properties had converted from separate to marital property but he did seek 50% of the appreciation in value during the marriage. Theresa claimed it would be inequitable to grant her husband any of the increase in the value of her inherited, separate property. The trial court awarded Joseph 25% of the appreciation. Both parties appealed.

On appeal, the court held that under Iowa law (Iowa Code § 598.21(6)), property may be marital or premarital but it is all subject to division upon dissolution of a marriage except for property inherited or received as a gift by either party prior to or during the marriage unless a refusal to divide it would be inequitable. Factors relevant to whether or not inherited property is subject to division include: the length of the marriage; contributions made by either party toward the property's care, preservation or improvement; and the impact of the property on the parties' standard of living. In affirming the decision of the trial court, the appeals court reasoned: "Although the marriage was very short in duration, it would be inequitable to award Joseph none of the appreciation of the property as proposed by Theresa given the improvements he made to the farmland which increased its value. Furthermore although the marriage was not lengthy, the parties used the Packwood farm as the marital home and Joseph managed the farms as part of the parties' livelihood, even after the couple separated."

This case provides a particularly good example of how important it is to establish the nature of property as separate or marital, to determine whether it is property that may be subject to division upon divorce, and to research changes in value even in short term marriages.

Passive appreciation
increase in the value of an asset that results without effort and as a result of market forces and the passage of time

Active appreciation
increase in the value of an asset that results from effort rather than simply market forces or the passage of time

Can Property Change From Separate to Marital or Marital to Separate?

An argument is sometimes made that separate property has lost its identity as separate and has become marital property during the course of a marriage i.e. that a **transmutation** or change has taken place in the character of the property due to certain circumstances such as the following:

- After ten years of "a wonderful marriage," in a state that permits them to do so, the parties may decide to execute a **postmarital agreement** in which they mutually designate their separate property as marital.
- For estate-planning purposes, they may decide to jointly title the marital home or certain other property.
- The parties may use or treat a separate asset as a marital asset by spending both marital time and funds on the asset. For example, the husband may own a home in his name prior to marriage. After marriage, he and his wife live in the home for twenty years. During the marriage they both participate in remodeling, redecorating, and landscaping initiatives paid for with marital funds, and they warmly refer to the residence as "our home."
- The transmutation may result from a **commingling** of separate resources with marital resources. For example, the wife sells a condominium she owned prior to the marriage for $250,000, and the parties then buy a new marital residence with that amount plus $10,000 from the husband's savings account that he held prior to the marriage, $100,000 in marital funds, and a mortgage in both their names.
- One spouse may add the other spouse's name to a deed to separate property for a variety of reasons. In determining whether that property should be considered separate or marital at the time of divorce, in most states, courts will look to the intent of the spouse who added the name. Did he or she intend to convey a half interest in the property or was he or she merely trying to accomplish some other purpose such as obtaining a mortgage on the property? See, e.g., *Barrett v. Barrett*, 232 P.3d 799 (Idaho 2010).

Courts sometimes characterize ownership of property based on either an **inception of title** or a **source of funds/*pro rata*** theory. Under an inception of title approach, the character of property as separate or marital is fixed at the time of its acquisition and subsequent events/contributions are of no effect. The majority approach to establishing ownership, source of funds theory, bases ownership on contribution toward acquisition of the property. The two theories can lead to opposite results in the same situation. For example, suppose the marital home cost $150,000 and was initially titled in the wife's name but the husband paid 60% of the deposit, taxes, and mortgage payments. Under inception of title theory, the property is viewed as owned by the wife despite the husband's substantial financial contribution. Under source of funds theory, it belongs to both of them according to their respective contributions. If the wife contributed 40% of the deposit, taxes, and mortgage payments, the property would be considered 40% hers and 60% her husband's. Courts may even consider the contributions of third parties when relevant to determining each party's interest in the marital property. For instance, if in the above fact pattern the entire down payment came from the wife's parents, then the wife's share may be greater.[21]

If either party seeks to establish that he or she did not intend for his or her separate property to lose its identity as separate, that party must be able to **trace** his or her contribution to what appears to be marital property back to separate property. The property may retain its separate identity even if it is refinanced and the proceeds of the refinancing become marital property.[22] If all or part of the transmuted property can be retraced to separate property, the burden usually shifts to the other party to establish that there was an intention to make a gift of the separate property to the marital estate.

Transmutation
a change in the classification of an asset from separate to marital or marital to separate

Postmarital agreement
an agreement made by two people already married to each other who want both to continue their marriage and also to define their respective rights upon separation, divorce, or death of one of them

Commingling
mixing together a spouse's separate property with marital property, or mixing together the separate property of both spouses

Inception of title theory
a theory that fixes ownership of property at the time it is acquired and holds that subsequent contributions are of no effect

Source of funds/*pro rata* theory
a theory that bases ownership of property on contribution; an asset may be characterized as both separate and marital in proportion to the respective contributions of the parties

Tracing
the process of tracking ownership of a property from the time of inception to the present

Paralegal Application 12.4

Separate or Marital? What Do You Think?

In each of the following situations do you think the property should be considered separate or marital? Explain the reasoning behind your response.

1. During their thirteen-year marriage, the parties lived in a home given to the husband by his mother one week before the wedding. The taxes, insurance, and maintenance expenses were paid from marital funds. The wife cleaned and maintained the house throughout the marriage. At the time of the divorce, the husband claimed that the house was his separate property. What do you think? In *Miller v. Miller*, 105 P.3d 1136 (Alaska 2005), the Alaska Supreme Court held that it was marital property.

2. A husband is a beneficiary under his parents' wills and the spouses have meager assets and considerable debt at the time of the divorce. The wife claims his inheritance should be considered marital property. What do you think? In a case of first impression in that state, the Vermont Supreme Court held in *Billings v. Billings*, 35 A.3d 1030 (Vt. 2011), that any interest the husband has as beneficiary under a will is not marital property if the testator is still alive. However, such a beneficial interest can be considered in allocating marital property between the parties if it creates an "opportunity . . . for future acquisition of capital assets and income" under 15 V.S.A. § 751(b)(8).

3. A husband, a veteran who served in the Vietnam War, received federal veterans disability benefits since his discharge in 1969, including during the parties' marriage. Under federal law such benefits are considered nonmarital/separate property. During his first marriage, he deposited the benefits in an investment account which increased in value during that marriage as well as during his second marriage. Is any or all of the investment account marital property subject to division upon divorce from his second wife? What do you think? In *Goodmote v. Goodmote*, 44 A.3d 74 (Pa. Super. Ct. 2012), the Pennsylvania Superior Court held that the husband had converted the disability benefits into a permanent investment account and that the increased value of that account during the marriage was marital property subject to equitable division.

Dual property states
states that distinguish between marital and separate property for distribution purposes and permit only marital property to be divided and distributed at divorce

All property states
states in which divorce courts may reach all property however acquired without distinguishing between separate and marital property if necessary to achieve an equitable distribution.

PARALEGAL PRACTICE TIP

A copy of the Connecticut "all property" statute is available at *law.justia .com*. Connecticut General Statutes, Connecticut Code Section 46(b)-81.

IDENTIFICATION OF THE PROPERTY SUBJECT TO DIVISION

When parties to a marriage sever their relationship, they (or the courts) necessarily must divide their property. The general rule is that only the property acquired during the marriage is subject to division by the court. Property belonging to a spouse prior to marriage usually remains the property of that spouse unless the parties otherwise agree (as in a premarital agreement or separation agreement) or the property has undergone a transmutation from separate to marital property as described above. Jurisdictions that classify property as separate or marital and allow only marital property to be distributed at divorce are called **dual property** jurisdictions. The limited number of states, such as Massachusetts and Connecticut, in which the court may assign any of a spouse's property to the other spouse are called **all property states**. If necessary to accomplish an equitable division, the courts in these states are permitted to disregard the distinction between separate and marital property and to reach (or "dip into") all of the parties' assets (including separate property) regardless of when, how, and by whom they were acquired. It has been argued that this approach deprives an individual of property without due process of law, but such statutes have been upheld as constitutional.[23]

VALUATION OF PROPERTY

When dividing marital property, courts seek to allocate the parties' property, with each spouse receiving a portion of an equal and/or equitable value depending on the jurisdiction and the facts of the case. In order for the court to do so, ideally the value of each major piece of property to be divided needs to be determined. **Valuation** is the process of assessing the financial worth of property, **real** or **personal**. If contested, the value of a particular piece of property is a question of fact to be determined by the judge based on testimony and evidence presented by the parties. Technically, it may constitute reversible error for a trial court to order a division of property without first establishing values. See, e.g., *Farlee v. Farlee*, 812 N.W.2d 501 (S.D. 2012), but see *In re Marriage of Hluska*, 961 N.E.2d 1247 (Ill. App. Ct. 2011).

Few states specify how particular assets are to be valued, and a wide variety of approaches are used. If opposing parties use different methods or propose conflicting values using the same method, the court has the discretion to accept the valuation of either of the parties or to establish its own. Usually there is no "right" answer to a valuation question, but rather a range of possible answers, each supported by a rationale and documentation whenever possible. Thorough preparation is essential. Attorneys will often generate multiple valuations and first present the one most favorable to the client in negotiations or to the court. If that one is rejected, the alternatives are ready for backup. If a party fails to present evidence as to the value of a contested asset at trial, he or she may waive a right of appeal on the issue.

There are three basic issues in valuation cases:

1. Which property of the parties should be valued?
2. What is the appropriate date for valuation?
3. Who will conduct the valuation and how?

Which Property of the Parties Should Be Valued?

In some cases, the parties have few if any assets, and valuation is not an issue. In other cases, the parties may be able to agree on a division of property without engaging in valuation. If so, they can avoid a costly and time-consuming process, but they will have no way of knowing whether their agreed-upon settlement really is fair. Absent agreement on a fair allocation of assets and liabilities that a court will be willing to approve, property subject to division may need to be valued. This includes, but is not necessarily limited to, all of the property identified at the beginning of this chapter in Exhibit 12.1. Sometimes the parties will agree that only property above a certain threshold amount will be valued. That amount may be $500, $5,000, or even $50,000 or more, depending on the nature and extent of the marital estate.

The kinds of property most commonly warranting valuation are retirement plans (**vested** or unvested), business interests, and the marital home (and any other real estate such as a rental or vacation property). If there is a mortgage and/or a loan secured by the real estate, the amount of **equity** in the property needs to be determined. Equity is the **fair market value** of the property less any encumbrances (mortgages, loans, tax liens, etc.).

Valuation
the process of assessing the financial worth of property, real or personal

Real property
land and anything growing on, attached to, or erected on it, excluding anything that may be severed without injury to the property

Personal property
any movable or intangible thing that is subject to ownership and is not classified as real property

Vest
to give a person an immediate, fixed right of ownership and present or future enjoyment; a vested interest is fixed or accrued and is usually unable to be taken away by subsequent events or circumstances

Equity
in real estate law, the fair market value of a property less any encumbrances (mortgages, loans, tax liens, etc.)

Fair market value
the price a willing buyer would pay a willing seller in an arm's-length transaction (e.g., not between friends or family members) when neither party is under any compulsion to buy or sell

What Is the Appropriate Date of Valuation?

Some states establish by statute or case law the date as of which marital assets are to be valued, but most prefer a flexible approach. Common options include the date when the parties separate, the date on which the divorce complaint (or action for division of property) is filed, the date when discovery is completed, the date of the trial or final hearing, or the date when the decree of dissolution is entered. This issue can be critical, for example, when:

- there is a long period between the date of separation and the filing for divorce;
- the marriage is terminated in one proceeding and other issues (such as custody, support, and division of property) are decided at a later date in the same or a different state;
- the value of an asset is highly volatile and likely to change during the pendency of the divorce litigation due to rapid shifts in the market or broader economic climate; and/or
- one of the parties dissipates or increases the value of assets while the case is pending.

If no date is set by statute and there is flexibility regarding the date for valuation, multiple alternative dates should be explored so that the attorney can determine which will work to the client's best advantage.

Paralegal **Application 12.5**

Does Cohabitation Count—What Do You Think?

The paralegal should be alert to the fact that contribution to property owned during a period of premarital cohabitation is increasingly being considered by courts when valuing the marital estate and fashioning a division of assets, particularly if the contribution was made in contemplation of marriage.

Fact Pattern: *McLaren v. McLaren*, 268 P.3d 323 (Alaska 2012)

In this case decided by the Alaska Supreme Court, a husband, Darren, sued his wife, Theresa, for divorce. The couple had begun living together in 1988 shortly before the wife's divorce from her second husband became final. They continued living together and eventually married in 1999. During their ten-year cohabitation period, they raised and supported Theresa's two children from a prior marriage without the benefit of child support. They commingled their finances in a joint bank account out of which they paid their expenses. Together they purchased a residence in Anchorage as well as a lot on Lake Louise. It was essentially undisputed that the parties formed an "economic unit" from at least 1989 until their divorce. They separated in 2005 and Darren filed for divorce in 2006. Theresa was initially represented by counsel but

her attorney withdrew in 2007 due to "a breakdown in the attorney-client relationship." Although Darren was at all times represented by counsel, Theresa appeared pro se for the remainder of the proceedings. Despite several requests concerning the value of her retirement benefit, she failed to provide discovery even after the superior court issued an order to compel discovery. At trial, lacking the documentation he had requested, Darren presented an expert who estimated the value of the "marital portion" of Theresa's retirement to be $139,532. Theresa questioned the figure but did not offer an alternative estimate and the court adopted the expert's valuation. The trial court valued the entire marital estate, including property acquired by the parties during their premarital cohabitation, at $277,868.44 and awarded approximately 52% to Theresa and the remainder to Darren. It characterized the portion of Theresa's civil service retirement benefit earned in the ten years the couple cohabited prior to their marriage as part of the marital estate. Theresa appealed multiple aspects of the property division but the Alaska Supreme Court affirmed the lower court's decision in all respects. It specifically held that the general rule is that courts divide property "acquired only during marriage," but that under Alaska Statute 25.24.160(a)(4) "the court, in making the division, may invade the property, including retirement benefits, of either spouse acquired before marriage when the balancing of the equities between the parties requires it."

Sidebar

Do you think that premarital contributions to marital assets should be considered marital property upon dissolution and, if so, under what circumstances? Should it make a difference if a prospective spouse purchases property during a period of cohabitation in anticipation of marriage such as a home for the couple to eventually live in post marriage? What if a same-sex couple lived together in Alabama for fifteen years but were not officially married until after the 2015 *Obergefell* decision made it possible for them to do so in their home state? If they divorce in 2020, should property accumulated during the fifteen years they cohabited be valued and distributed between them or only property acquired during the years since they formally married?

Who Will Conduct the Valuation and How?

Valuation of assets such as bank accounts is reasonably straightforward and can usually be accomplished by the client, who often is in a position to obtain account statements directly. Paralegals can research the value of several kinds of property such as automobiles, recreational vehicles, stock values, and the like, by checking "blue book" values and stock listings online or in the business section of the newspaper. Some family law practitioners and paralegals are skilled at other kinds of valuation, but because valuation issues are sometimes beyond their expertise, most maintain inventories of **experts**, including their respective areas of expertise, fee schedules, and current resumes. The task of maintaining these inventories may be assigned to the paralegal. Experts may include, among others, appraisers, accountants, **actuaries**, financial planners, and investment counselors able to assess the values of such things as real estate, jewelry, pensions, degrees, a party's interest in a professional practice or ongoing business, a pending lawsuit, a copyright, or a spouse's contribution as homemaker and caretaker for the children.

Expert
a person who, through education or experience, has developed special skill or knowledge in a particular subject

Actuary
a statistician who determines the present value of a future event; one who calculates insurance and pension values on the basis of empirically based tables

Paralegal **Application 12.6**

Protecting the Firm

The standard approach to a property division case is to identify assets and liabilities, value them, factor in the client's goals, and then propose an appropriate allocation. Throughout the process, the family law team works in consultation with the client, always mindful of an ethical obligation to provide competent and zealous representation. In turn, the client needs to understand the strengths and weaknesses of his or her case in order to make informed decisions after reviewing with counsel the risks and benefits of various courses of action.

Sometimes a client will not agree to follow the legal advice provided. He or she may direct that the firm not search for concealed property or value a significant asset. Occasionally in order to avoid a trial or as a trade-off for some other objective, the client may insist on settling for less than he or she would otherwise reasonably be entitled. Under such circumstances, the client should be sent a letter reiterating the recommendations made and noting that, notwithstanding that advice, the attorney has been explicitly directed by the client not to pursue the recommended course of action. The attorney may choose to send the letter by certified mail.

DIVISION OF PROPERTY

In cases involving few if any assets or liabilities, property division is a relatively straightforward matter often settled by the parties without advice of counsel. Agreements are usually based on the parties' relative needs, personal preferences, and emotional attachments to particular possessions. The primary task of attorneys in such cases is to advise clients with respect to whether or not they have settled for the shares to which they may be legally entitled. Sometimes this is a challenge, as clients often exaggerate or deflate the values of property based on their own subjective appraisals. For example, in exchange for getting to keep the family pet, a client may "give away" all of the household appliances and furnishings.

If the parties are unable to agree on how their property and liabilities should be divided, it falls on the courts to determine the distribution. In the current no-fault era, an equal division of the marital estate is implicit in the community property approach and strongly favored in equitable distribution jurisdictions. This is particularly the case given a long-term, traditional marriage in which the husband contributed primarily as the "breadwinner" and the wife as the homemaker, and there is a reasonably conventional mix of assets. However, the courts may deviate based on the facts of an individual case and one can never predict a certain outcome. Whatever the division may be, for a court to issue an enforceable order dividing the marital estate, it must have personal jurisdiction over the parties and *in rem* jurisdiction over the property to be divided. As indicated in Chapters 1 and 5, the paralegal often gathers the information the attorney needs to address the relevant jurisdictional issues.

There are three primary ways in which the property of parties to a divorce may be divided:

1. The parties may have executed a **premarital agreement**, a contract in which they mutually agreed as to how their property should be divided in the event of divorce, annulment, or death. The court hearing the divorce case will first determine the validity of the agreement, which should be brought to its attention at the outset of the divorce proceeding. If an agreement is held to be valid, property usually will be distributed according to its terms. See, e.g., *Yarbrough v. Yarbrough*, 144 So. 3d 386 (Ala. Civ. App. 2014).

2. If there is no premarital (or postmarital) agreement or it is held to be invalid, the parties may negotiate a mutually agreeable property division, include its terms in a settlement or **separation agreement** and submit it to the court for approval. (See Chapter 13.) A court will usually accept the parties' agreement, provided its terms are consistent with governing law, do not violate public policy, and are not unconscionable.

3. Judges strongly urge attorneys and counsel to settle cases in order to save costs and conserve judicial resources. However, when the parties are unable to reach an agreement with respect to the distribution of their assets and liabilities, the matter will be tried before the court. Guided by case law and either **community property** or **equitable distribution** statutes, trial courts have considerable discretion in resolving property division disputes on a case-by-case basis, given the evidence and testimony presented by the parties. A trial court's decision regarding property distribution generally will not be reversed on appeal absent an **error of law** or an **abuse of discretion**. See Exhibit 12.2.

Premarital agreement

an agreement made by two persons about to be married defining for themselves their respective rights, duties, and responsibilities in the event their marriage terminates by death, annulment, separation, or divorce

Separation agreement

an agreement made between spouses in anticipation of divorce or a legal separation concerning the terms of the divorce or separation and any continuing obligations of the parties to each other

Community property

assets owned in common by a husband and wife as a result of having been acquired during the marriage by a means other than an inheritance or a gift to one spouse, each spouse generally holding a one-half interest in the property no matter in whose name it is held; usually divided equally between the parties upon dissolution of the marriage absent an agreement to the contrary

Equitable distribution

the legal concept that upon divorce property accumulated during a marriage should be divided between the parties equitably, but not necessarily equally, based upon principles of fairness

Error of law

a mistake made by a court in applying the law to the facts of a case

Abuse of discretion

the failure of a court to exercise sound, reasonable, and legal decision making

EXHIBIT 12.2 Overview: Equitable Distribution and Community Property Approaches

Equitable Distribution Approach	When this approach is used, property accumulated during a marriage is divided between the parties based upon principles of fairness.
	• The majority of states apply this approach to property division upon dissolution of a marriage.
	• Each state adopts by statute and/or case law a series of factors to be considered by the court when making a property distribution.
Community Property Approach	The premise of the community property approach is that property acquired during the marriage, with the exception of gifts and inheritances, belongs equally to the spouses and therefore should be divided equally upon divorce. Community property generally includes all earnings, assets, and liabilities accumulated during the marriage by either or both of the parties.
	• This approach is applied by a minority of the states: Arizona, California, Idaho, Louisiana, New Mexico, Nevada, Texas, and Washington. Wisconsin[24] and Alaska[25] are also sometimes characterized as community property states.
	• Community property statutes may allow for unequal divisions under some circumstances such as when the parties otherwise agree, when there has been "economic misconduct," or when basic fairness requires.

EXHIBIT 12.3 Community Property and Equitable Distribution States

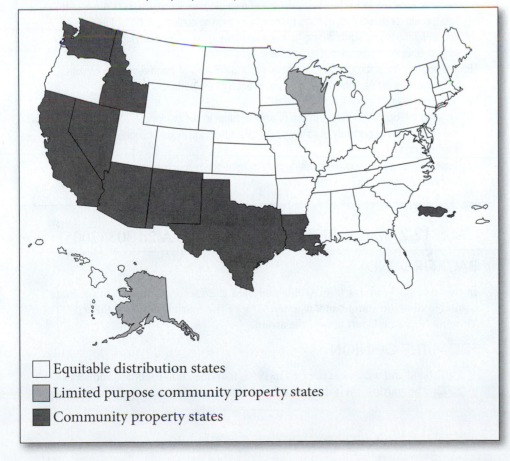

☐ Equitable distribution states

▨ Limited purpose community property states

■ Community property states

PARALEGAL PRACTICE TIP

The territory of Puerto Rico is also considered a community property jurisdiction.

Mississippi is one of the few states that have not codified the factors which guide decisions regarding property division in that state. The factors are referred to as the "Ferguson Factors" and they were established by the Mississippi Supreme Court in 1994 in *Ferguson v. Ferguson*, 639 So. 2d 921 (Mississippi 1994).

The Equitable Distribution Approach

A majority of the states are equitable distribution jurisdictions, in which the courts apportion marital property between the parties in a manner that is fair and "equitable" (albeit not necessarily equal) based on a consideration of factors laid out in case law and/or statutes. (See the Illinois statute in Exhibit 12.4.) The courts are not required to give equal weight to each factor but rather to consider them in light of the facts of each case, recognizing that both parties contributed to the marriage in a variety of ways (financially, maintaining and improving the home, raising the children, etc.). In some equitable distribution states there is a presumption that the division will be equal; but the presumption is rebuttable. See Case 12.2.

EXHIBIT 12.4 Illinois—An Equitable Division Jurisdiction—750 ILCS 5/503 (8)(d)

Courtesy of State of Illinois

FROM THE STATUTE

(d) In a proceeding for dissolution of marriage or declaration of invalidity of marriage, or in a proceeding for disposition of property following dissolution of marriage by a court which lacked personal jurisdiction over the absent spouse or lacked jurisdiction to dispose of the property, the court shall assign each spouse's non-marital property to that spouse. It shall also divide the marital property without regard to marital misconduct in just proportions considering all the relevant factors, including:

1. the contribution of each party to the acquisition, preservation, or increase or decrease in value of the marital or non-marital property, including (i) any such decrease attributable to a payment deemed to have been an advance from the parties' marital estate . . . and (ii) the contribution of a spouse as a homemaker or to the family unit;
2. the dissipation by each party of the marital or non-marital property;
3. the value of the property assigned to each spouse;
4. the duration of the marriage;
5. the relevant economic circumstances of each spouse when the division of property is to become effective, including the desirability of awarding the family home, or the right to live therein for reasonable periods, to the spouse having custody of the children;
6. any obligations and rights arising from a prior marriage of either party;
7. any antenuptial agreement of the parties;
8. the age, health, station, occupation, amounts and sources of income, vocational skills, employability, estate, liabilities, and needs of each of the parties;
9. the custodial provisions for any children;
10. whether the apportionment is in lieu of or in addition to maintenance;
11. the reasonable opportunity of each spouse for future acquisition of capital assets and income; and
12. the tax consequences of the property division upon the respective economic circumstances of the parties.

CASE **12.2** *Wade v. Wade*, 178 Vt. 189, 878 A.2d 303 (2005)

BACKGROUND

In this case, a Vermont family court applied the factors set forth in the state's equitable division statute and awarded 90% of the marital estate to the wife. The Vermont Supreme Court upheld the award.

FROM THE OPINION

Husband and wife were married in 1991, had one child together, and separated in 2002. The parties, their daughter and husband's son from a prior relationship lived in the town of Waitsfield in a home that wife purchased before the parties married. Since 1985, wife used part of the home to run the Sunshine Montessori School, Inc., a nursery school she founded and continues to operate. Husband has a landscaping business. During the marriage, the husband took on seasonal work in the restaurant, construction and ski industries. Over the last four years, husband earned between $13,000 and $23,000 annually. Wife's income from the Sunshine School averaged $21,824 in 2000–2002.

In 1996, wife received a series of gifts from her mother. She was given title to her mother's home, which wife rented out until 2002 when she sold the property. Wife also received $22,000 in cash and put $40,000 from her mother into a VUGMA account for the parties' minor daughter. The $22,000 went into an account in her name only. Wife subsequently exhausted the money in the account by using it to pay for various family expenses. . . .

After wife sold the home her mother gave her in 2002, the parties each received $10,000 from the proceeds. The remaining proceeds of $59,000 were placed into escrow pending distribution in the divorce proceeding. After her mother died, wife used some of her inheritance to purchase a twenty-nine foot sailboat and a catamaran for the family. Husband spent time repairing and maintaining the boats for the family, and used his carpentry and other handyman skills to maintain and improve the parties' residence. The family also owned a camper, and husband held a half interest in a seasonal camp in Rochester, Vermont.

Throughout the marriage, wife paid the mortgage on the marital residence and most of the household expenses. Husband paid half of the utilities and charged many of his own expenses, and those of his landscaping business to credit cards. At the time the parties separated, husband had over $23,000 in personal and business credit card debt. Wife's credit card debt was a fraction of the husband's. After separating, wife remained in the marital home, and husband moved into a friend's home where he acts as a caretaker.

Wife filed for divorce in October 2002. She sought primary custody of the parties' daughter and most of the parties' property. . . . Husband . . . asked the court to split their property roughly fifty-fifty. Both parties hired expert witnesses to testify about the value of the Sunshine School. It was undisputed that the husband's business had no value.

The court issued a written order following a hearing in December 2003. Wife received approximately ninety percent of the marital property, including the parties' home and all of its equity, the catamaran, the camper, and the escrowed proceeds from the sale of her mother's home. The court awarded husband the sailboat, $10,000 from the sale proceeds that he had already received, his interest in the Rochester camp, and his tools. Crediting wife's expert witness, the court found that the Sunshine School, while valuable to the wife personally, had no market value. . . .

In support of the property award, the court explained that wife had lived in the parties' home since 1985, six years before the parties married. Wife paid the mortgage and property taxes. She also paid for the parties' two boats and contributed all of her income to other household expenses. The court acknowledged that what money husband earned was spent primarily on the household, but it noted that husband "never earned much in any year." The court found that the husband had not "followed a conventional career; instead he has enjoyed the freedom of working on a seasonal basis and taking time when he wishes to work on his own business." The court found that husband could earn more money working a full-time job in construction or some other business if he chose.

Husband . . . argues that the court awarded a disproportionate share of the marital property to wife by ignoring some of the statutory factors in 15 V.S.A. §751 and giving too much weight to others. Section 751 of Title 15 directs the family court to divide the marital estate in an equitable manner after considering several factors:

1. the length of the marriage
2. the age and health of the parties
3. the occupation, source and amount of income of each of the parties
4. vocational skills and employability
5. the contribution by one spouse to the education, training, or increased earning power of the other
6. the value of all property interests, liabilities and needs of each party
7. whether the property settlement is in lieu of or in addition to maintenance
8. the opportunity of each for future acquisition of capital assets and income
9. the desirability of awarding the family home or the right to live there for reasonable periods to the spouse having custody of the children
10. the party through whom the property was acquired
11. the contribution of each spouse in the acquisition, preservation, and depreciation or appreciation in value of the respective estates, including the nonmonetary contribution of a spouse as a homemaker
12. the respective merits of the parties

. . . The family court has broad discretion when analyzing and weighing the statutory factors in light of the record evidence. . . . When fashioning an equitable award, the court must explain the underlying rationale for its decision . . . , which we will not disturb absent a showing that the court abused its discretion. . . .

Husband asserts that the property division lacks equity because the court did not consider the length of the marriage; husband's lack of a college education and his contribution to wife's business; husband's inability to acquire capital assets or additional income; husband's sweat equity in maintaining and improving the marital home and the rental property acquired from wife's mother; and the lack of a proper home for their daughter when she spends time with husband. We find no merit to husband's contention because the text of the court's decision reflects that it considered all of those factors.

The court found that the parties were married for twelve years. It determined that in light of all the factors the length of marriage did not weigh in favor of either party. The court acknowledged husband's lack of a college degree, but it found that husband could increase his annual income by taking a full-time position in the construction industry or in another industry in the Mad River Valley. Husband is healthy and his age—forty-eight-years old—at the time of the divorce did not preclude him from acquiring his own home or other assets in the future. On the issue of maintenance, husband did not request maintenance in lieu of property, and cannot now fault the family court for not considering this factor.

As for husband's suggestion that the property award left him without an ability to obtain a suitable residence where his daughter can stay when she is in his care, there is no factor in §751 that directly addresses this issue. . . . the court must consider the "desirability of awarding the family home . . . to the spouse having custody of the children." . . . The court considered that factor when it determined the child's best interests were served by allowing her to remain in the marital residence—the only home the child has ever known—under wife's primary care.

According to the family court, the statutory factors that weighed most heavily in its decision were numbers (10) and (11): through whom the assets were acquired, and which party contributed more to their preservation. . . . All of the assets in this case came through wife, either because she acquired them before marriage or purchased them after marriage with money wife's mother provided. All of wife's income, as well as her inheritance, went to support the family and the family's recreational interests. She paid the mortgage and property taxes on the marital home. Husband's financial contribution was recognized through the $10,000 he received from the sale of the wife's mother's home and the sailboat court awarded husband. The court declined to allocate the parties' debt because it found that husband's larger share of credit card debt was due to the relatively low income he earned by choice. In light of the wife's substantial monetary contribution to the family's expenses, the court determined that it would be unfair to saddle her with a portion of husband's personal and business debt. . . .

We recognize that wife received ninety percent of the parties' assets. Had the family court failed to explain in detail the reasons for the facially, disproportionate property distribution, the outcome of this case would likely be different. But the family court carefully explained why it weighed factors (10) and (11) more heavily in reaching its decision. As trier of fact, the family court was in the best position to assess the merits of the parties' contentions, and its decision addresses the relevant statutory factors. Therefore we cannot say that the court abused its discretion in fashioning the property award in this case. . . .

SIDEBAR

Do you agree with the Vermont Supreme Court's holding? Read the entire opinion including the strong dissent by Justice Skoglund, in which he states his belief that the "lopsided award" in this case would not have been affirmed "if it had been the wife and not the husband who received the paltry ten percent share of the parties' marital estate." Do you agree with the majority or with the dissenting justice? How would you have decided the case? Explain your response. The full opinion in the *Wade* case is available at *www.pearsonhighered.com/careersresources/* in the website material related to Chapter 12 under Cases. For an example of a case in which the husband received a greater proportion of the marital estate than the wife, see *Peiffer v. Peiffer*, 840 N.W.2d 726 (Iowa App. 2013).

The Community Property Approach

A minority of the states are community property jurisdictions in which property acquired during the marriage is viewed as belonging equally to the spouses and, therefore, as rightfully divided equally between them upon divorce. Predominantly located in the American Southwest, most community property states were originally settled by Spanish colonists and adopted a system of law rooted in Spanish (or French, in the case of Louisiana) civil law rather than English common law. Although only about one-fifth of the states are community property states, approximately one-quarter to one-third of the population of the United States lives in those states (which include both Texas and California).

The contemporary community property approach is based on a view of marriage as a partnership and an assumption that both the husband and the wife contribute to the acquisition and accumulation of marital assets and liabilities. It assumes that each spouse acts for the benefit of the marital unit and is, therefore, entitled to an interest in half of the property acquired during the marriage through the expenditure of marital funds or the efforts of either or both spouses. Separate property remains separate property in community property jurisdictions, and it generally includes assets brought into the marriage, property acquired in exchange for separate property, and gifts and inheritances received by a spouse during the marriage.

PARALEGAL PRACTICE TIP

A copy of the Nevada community property statute can be found at *www.leg.state.nv.us* Nevada Revised Statutes 123.220-123.259. To find the Alaska Community Property Act, visit *www.legis.state.ak.us*. To see a California Property Declaration Form, visit *www.courts.ca.gov*.

PARALEGAL PRACTICE TIP

Whether the client resides in an equitable distribution or community property jurisdiction at the time of divorce, the family law team needs to be aware of any community property states in which the parties have resided and purchased property that may be treated as community property, upon divorce and at death.

EXHIBIT 12.5 Community Property—Ten Commonly Asked Questions

QUESTION 1: What are the community property states?

ANSWER: The traditional community property states are Arizona, California, Idaho, Louisiana, Nevada, New Mexico, Texas, and Washington. Wisconsin is also sometimes classified as a community property state and is recognized by the federal government for tax purposes as such. Alaska is technically not a community property state; however, under Alaska's Community Property Act, ". . . property of the spouses is community property . . . to the extent provided in a community property agreement or a community property trust."[26]

QUESTION 2: Is the law governing community property the same in all the community property states?

ANSWER: No. The marital property laws of the community property states differ significantly, not only from the marital property laws in **common law property states**, but also from one another's laws. Although the federal government recognizes community property for tax purposes, it has established no mandatory definition of community property for use by all of the states. There are variations among the community property states, for example, in terms of how they define community property, how they treat income from separate property, and when they hold that the "marital community" terminates for purposes of accumulation of community property. To fully appreciate the impact of these differences, compare the Texas and Arizona community property laws. Texas is conservative in the sense that its rules lead to a smaller community estate and greater protection for separate assets. For example, Texas does not consider personal goodwill to be community property while Arizona does.[27]

QUESTION 3: How is community property treated upon divorce?

ANSWER: Under community property theory, when the parties marry, they form a "marital community." Absent an agreement of the parties to the contrary, upon dissolution, the courts start with a presumption that all property acquired (and liabilities incurred) during the marriage and still existing at the time of divorce is community property and subject to a fifty-fifty division regardless of the relative contributions made by each of the parties. With respect to liabilities, in Wisconsin, for example, by statute, "An obligation incurred by a spouse during marriage, including one attributable to an act or omission during the marriage, is presumed to be incurred in the interest of the marriage or the family."[28] The time period in which the debt was incurred is more relevant than the name on the account under which the debt was created.

QUESTION 4: How is community property treated at death?

ANSWER: The primary advantage of the community property system is evident upon the death of one of the spouses in the form of a "double step-up" in **basis** for the surviving spouse. Basis is defined as the value assigned to a taxpayer's investment in property. It is the reference point used for calculating a gain or a loss when the property is transferred to another. Assuming assets increase in value while they are owned, there is a tax incentive to hold property as community property because when one spouse dies, the shares of both spouses receive a "step-up" in basis, and not solely the share of the decedent. A higher basis translates to a smaller capital gain (or greater loss) if the surviving spouse sells the property. If the asset is depreciable, larger depreciation reductions will be available. These advantages are lost if the property has decreased in value between the date it was acquired and the date of death of the first spouse to die.[29]

QUESTION 5: Does conduct have any impact on the division of community property?

ANSWER: The general rule is that conduct will not play a role in a no-fault divorce. However, in most community property states, the courts may consider conduct when dividing the marital estate, particularly economic misconduct. For example, if a party has committed "community waste" by concealing assets or disposing of them in a fraudulent or irresponsible manner (such as through excessive gambling), that party's share of the community property upon divorce may be reduced.

(Continued)

Common law property state
a state in which property is generally owned by the party who acquired it during the marriage; with limited exceptions, property acquired during the marriage is divided equitably upon divorce in common law property states

Basis
the value assigned by the IRS to a taxpayer's investment in property

EXHIBIT 12.5 *(Continued)*

QUESTION 6: **What are the primary disadvantages of holding property as community property?**

ANSWER: The two primary disadvantages are:

- The former/surviving spouse may receive a larger share of the assets upon divorce or death than desired or intended by the other spouse.
- A spouse does not have complete management or control over the community property. Some of the kinds of restraints that may be imposed include prohibitions against:
  - Devising or bequeathing by will more than one-half of the community property
  - Gifting community property without the express or implied consent of the other spouse
  - Selling, conveying, or encumbering community real property without the other spouse's participation and acknowledgment
  - Purchasing or contracting to purchase community real property without the other spouse joining.[30]

QUESTION 7: **What happens if spouses move from a common law property state to a community property state and later divorce?**

ANSWER: In some community property states (such as Arizona and California), if the parties are both residents of the community property state at the time of the divorce, the court will treat property acquired during the marriage in a common law property state as if it were acquired in the community property state and apply the concept of quasi-community property.

QUESTION 8: **What happens to community property if spouses move from a community property state to a common law property state?**

ANSWER: The general rule is that property acquired with, or traceable to, community funds will continue to maintain its character as community property in most states. However, if an asset (such as a vacation home) is actually located in the common law property state, the common law state may decline to treat that particular asset as community property, based on public policy.[31] The Restatement (Second) of Conflicts of Laws rule[32] is that, absent an effective choice of law by the parties, the law of the spouses' domicile at the time of acquisition will usually determine the rights of each spouse in tangible and intangible personal property.

QUESTION 9: **Can the parties change the nature of property from separate to community or community to separate during their marriage?**

ANSWER: Yes, in most states. Spouses often choose to change the characterization of property by means of agreements (e.g., a pre- or postmarital agreement where permitted) or by gifting an interest in property to the community or to the other spouse in his or her sole name. The spouses may also, intentionally or unintentionally, convert a separate asset to community property by commingling separate property with community assets such that the separate property loses its identity. The burden of tracing the asset is on the spouse who claims a separate interest.

QUESTION 10: **Can the parties influence the division of community property upon divorce?**

ANSWER: Yes, by executing a separation agreement or a premarital agreement, or by proposing a division to the court in contested cases.

PARALEGAL PRACTICE TIP

An illustration may help to clarify what may happen when spouses move from a community property state to a common law property state. In an Iowa case in which the parties had made no agreement regarding governing law, an appellate court held that Texas community property law should govern disposition of a brokerage account created and funded when the spouses lived in Texas, a community property state. The court held that greater weight should be given to the law of the state where the spouses were domiciled when the movable property was acquired.[33]

The Role of Conduct in the Context of Property Division

A majority of the states have adopted the position advocated in section 307 of the Uniform Marriage and Divorce Act, which provides that decisions about property division should be made "without regard to marital misconduct." In general, the courts

PARALEGAL PRACTICE TIP

To learn more about the Uniform (Model) Marriage and Divorce Law, visit *www.uniformlaws.org*.

PARALEGAL PRACTICE TIP

Upon filing and serving of a divorce complaint, many states automatically restrain the parties from disposing of assets subject to division during the pendency of a divorce action unless otherwise agreed by the parties or ordered by the court.

PARALEGAL PRACTICE TIP

Cashing out accounts may be especially tempting when one of the spouses is in the military overseas and is unable to monitor property and income deposits at home. See, e.g., *Leininger v. Leininger*, 766 N.W.2d 649 (Iowa 2009).

Dissipation

the use of an asset for an illegal or inequitable purpose, such as when a spouse uses or expends marital property for personal benefit when a divorce is pending

have little patience with a party rambling on about how his or her spouse "cheated and lied." However, many states still consider misconduct—particularly extreme instances of abuse or economic misconduct, which can come in many forms (See Case 12.3):

- Incurring excessive credit card debt for unnecessary expenses that do not support the family unit
- Failing to make a contribution of any kind (financial or otherwise) to the marital partnership over an extended period
- Using marital funds or assets to entertain or support an adulterous relationship
- Gambling excessively during the course of the marriage
- Making sham loans and transfers of property for less than fair market value to friends and family members, etc., in anticipation of divorce[34]
- Transferring or concealing assets after being served with notice of an impending divorce and while under a court order not to do so
- Intentionally destroying marital or the other spouse's separate property
- Making high-risk or speculative investments during the marriage
- Cashing out joint accounts without the consent of the other party
- Engaging in criminal conduct that results in the imposition of fines that must be paid during the course of the marriage[35]
- Refusing to cooperate in the discovery process

When **dissipation** of assets is demonstrated at trial based on evidence and testimony, the court in its discretion may choose, among other options, to award a greater percentage of the assets to the innocent spouse and/or assign the bulk of the liabilities to the offending spouse. In some situations, the court may require that it be shown only that assets disappeared and not necessarily how they were spent. A Kentucky appeals court took this position when it held that a wife "did not have any information as to how the dissipated funds were spent, or the means to discover such information. It would be inequitable to require the party claiming dissipation to show exactly what use was made of the marital assets, because this information is not as readily available to the complaining party as it is to the dissipating party."[36]

CASE 12.3 *Lesko v. Stanislaw*, 2014 ME. 3, 86 A.3d 14 (2014)

BACKGROUND

The parties in this case, Lisa Lesko and Theodore Stanislaw, were married in 1992 and had one son born in 2002. The wife (Lesko) was a family physician. The husband (Stanislaw) was primarily a homemaker and part-time piano and voice teacher. In 2008, Stanislaw was arrested and indicted for multiple counts of sexual abuse of girls who had been his piano students. He was convicted and began serving his sentence in early 2010. Lesko filed for divorce in November of 2010. The case was heard in 2012 and the court primarily heard evidence related to division of the marital estate. During the trial, and over her husband's objections, Lesko presented evidence intended to demonstrate the effect of her husband's criminal behavior on the parties' finances.

The trial court subsequently issued a divorce judgment and awarded 73% of the marital property to the wife and 27% to the husband. Based on its findings, the trial court concluded that the husband's conduct constituted "financial misconduct" and even if it didn't, the consequences of his actions were relevant factors to consider in the division of property given the "enormous economic impact" it had on the parties. The husband appealed and the Maine Supreme Court affirmed.

(Continued)

The state's high court drew a distinction between moral and financial misconduct and noted the court's desire to prevent "evidence of marital misconduct from being used to subvert the legislative objective of fault-free divorce and to 'minimize the use of the courtroom and, in particular, the process of dividing marital property, as a forum for the parties to vent their hostilities.'"

FROM THE OPINION

. . . Because the court was required to consider the economic circumstances of each spouse at the time of the property division, and because this analysis necessarily involves consideration of a party's criminal conduct if that conduct affects the household finances, we conclude that the court acted within the bounds of its discretion in ordering a division of marital property that reflected the financial impact of Stanislaw's criminal conduct on the marital estate. We affirm the judgment.

. . .

B. Criminal Conduct as a Relevant Factor in Marital Property Division
Stanislaw's main contention on appeal is that the court erred when it expressly considered his criminal conduct as a relevant factor in dividing the marital property. . . .

[Me. Rev. Stat. Ann.] Title 19-A §953(1) (2013) states:

1. Disposition: In a proceeding for a divorce, . . . the court shall set apart to each spouse the spouse's property and shall divide the marital property in proportions the court considers just after considering all relevant factors including:

   A. The contribution of each spouse to the acquisition of the marital property, including the contribution of a spouse as homemaker;
   B. The value of the property set apart to each spouse; and
   C. The economic circumstances of each spouse at the time the division of property is to become effective, including the desirability of awarding the family home or the right to live in the home for reasonable periods to the spouse having custody of the children. . . .

Here, the court methodically evaluated how Stanislaw's criminal conduct, convictions, and incarceration had and would continue to financially affect the household. Specifically, the court found that (1) Stanislaw's criminal conduct resulted in the expenditure, from the marital estate, of "tens of thousands of dollars in legal fees"; (2) his conduct, particularly his victimization of some of Lesko's patients, caused Lesko to lose income through the loss of patients in her practice; (3) his lengthy incarceration, which will likely extend into their son's adulthood, would cause Lesko to suffer the loss of a financially contributing co-parent; (4) his incarceration would adversely affect his current and future earning potential; and (5) the specific nature of his criminal conduct would preclude him from doing many of the jobs for which he was qualified. Importantly, the court did not consider evidence of Stanislaw's criminal conduct for purposes of discerning moral fault and expressly excluded the introduction of sentencing transcripts, witness statements, and other materials bearing on the specific offenses for which Stanislaw was convicted, stating that this evidence "would be at best cumulative and at worst inflammatory."

. . . We have never declared, and we decline to do so here, that courts are prohibited from considering the fiscal impact of a party's use of marital funds to pay legal expenses in determining a just division of marital property pursuant to section 953(1). Whether those fiscal impacts are characterized by the court as a form of "financial misconduct" is not material to the analysis.

Division of Major Assets

It is virtually impossible to divide each piece of marital property equally, and it is seldom practical to liquidate all of the parties' assets so that the proceeds can be equally divided. Rather, the courts try to assign property of an appropriate amount and type to each party. If there are sufficient assets, the court will assign to each party a variety of different properties up to a determined value. For example, one party may be awarded the marital home and the other a vacation property; each party may retain his or her pension; a stock portfolio may be divided; joint bank accounts might be split; etc.

THE MARITAL RESIDENCE

Given the fact that it is often the parties' only major asset, many emotionally charged property disputes focus on the marital residence. Disposition is especially complicated when minor children are involved. Some states specifically require that the courts consider custodial issues when dividing this asset. The most common options for treatment of the marital residence are the following:

- If neither spouse wishes to keep it, the residence may be sold and the proceeds divided equally or in some other agreed-upon or court-ordered proportion.
- When the marital home is the only asset the parties have, the court may be forced to order the sale of the residence and division of the proceeds so that the parties can receive cash awards and move forward with their respective lives.
- One spouse may buy out the other spouse's interest (often refinancing the property) and keep the home.
- One spouse may be awarded the marital home, while the other spouse is awarded offsetting assets such as a bank account or pension.
- The house may continue to be held jointly, with one party having the right to exclusive use and occupancy until a future date (usually connected with a child-related contingency), at which time the property will be sold and the proceeds divided. The precise terms of such an arrangement need to be laid out carefully in the parties' agreement or the court's order (i.e., who is responsible for payment of the mortgage, taxes, insurance, maintenance, and repairs; what will be deducted from the proceeds prior to distribution; how will appreciation and depreciation be treated; and how will the proceeds eventually be divided?).

PENSIONS, RETIREMENT BENEFITS, AND QUALIFIED DOMESTIC RELATIONS ORDERS (QDROs)

PARALEGAL PRACTICE TIP

Visit *www.courts.alaska.gov* to learn more about a variety of pensions including federal and military. Notice in the information provided that a QDRO must be approved both by the Plan Administrator and the court.

Individuals in a position to do so usually anticipate and plan for eventual retirement from the world of work. Acquired either individually or through an employer, retirement plans come in a variety of forms such as pensions, individual retirement accounts (IRAs), 401(k) plans, deferred compensation, profit sharing, and stock option plans. Retirement plans are generally tax-deferred, which means that the income produced will not be taxed until the income is paid during retirement. Along with the marital home, retirement plans are commonly one of the few large assets available for division upon divorce.

A **pension** is a job-related retirement benefit acquired by an employee and funded through contributions by the employer, the employee, or a combination of both. It is a form of deferred compensation. There are two primary types of pension plans:

- In a **defined-benefit plan**, the amount of the benefit is usually determined according to a formula based on the participant's earnings, length of service, or a target monthly benefit. The value of a defined-benefit plan (a "traditional" pension) is usually established by an actuary, who determines the total benefits the employee is likely to receive based on his or her life expectancy and then calculates the present cash value of the right to receive that amount in the future. Upon retirement, the employee is entitled to receive the defined benefit in a lump sum or in periodic payments.
- In a **defined-contribution plan**, each employee has his or her own separate account, such as a 401(k) plan. Such plans may involve purchase money arrangements, profit sharing, stock bonuses, etc. The eventual benefit is based on the amount of contributions and investment earnings in the years during which the employee is covered by the plan. The value of a defined contribution plan is based on its current value without any adjustment for income taxes and/or penalties if the balance were withdrawn early. Upon retirement, the employee is entitled to withdraw the pension funds as he or she sees fit (subject to certain constraints imposed by the government such as mandatory minimum withdrawals). Because a defined-contribution plan has an account value in the participant's name, its value can be determined without actuarial assistance in property division deliberations.

In either type of plan, the employee is entitled to receive the pension funds that he or she contributed. In addition, the employee is entitled to receive those funds contributed by the employer, provided the pension is vested. A pension vests when an employee has met certain threshold requirements—for example, being employed for a certain period of time such as ten years. If an employee has not satisfied the minimal threshold requirements, the pension is unvested. When employees leave employment prior to vesting of their pensions, they generally are entitled to receive only the funds contributed personally and none of the funds contributed by the employer.

A vested pension is customarily considered marital property although the general rule is that only that portion of the pension attributable to the period of the marriage (coverture) is subject to division upon divorce. For example, if the husband's pension is based on twenty-five years of employment and he was married to his wife for ten of those years, 10/25 or 2/5 (40%) of his pension constitutes marital property. His spouse may be awarded half of that amount (20% of the total pension [$2/5 \times 1/2 = 1/5 = 20\%$]), especially if the pension is the parties' only major asset. If there are other assets, the pension may be left intact and the wife may be awarded other property equivalent in value to 20% of the pension. Courts vary in their treatment of unvested pensions. Some consider them future expectancy interests not subject to division. Others consider the amount of the contribution made by a party to the pension fund during the marriage to be marital property.[37]

State law generally establishes how property will be divided upon divorce, but federal law largely controls retirement benefits. Most employers must comply with the Employee Retirement Income Security Act (ERISA), a federal statute passed in 1974 and amended by the Retirement Equity Act (REA) of 1984.

Pension
a job-related retirement benefit acquired by an employee and funded through contributions by the employer, the employee, or a combination of both

Defined-benefit plan
a retirement plan in which the amount of the benefit is usually determined according to a formula based on the participant's earnings, length of service, or a target monthly benefit

Defined-contribution plan
a retirement plan funded by the employee's contributions and the employer's contributions (usually in a preset amount) in which the eventual benefit is based on the amount of contributions and investment earnings in the years during which the employee is covered by the plan

The Act is designed to protect employee pensions in the event an employer goes out of business or declares bankruptcy. Under ERISA, a qualified retirement plan is one that does not discriminate in favor of highly compensated employees. Although most are, not all retirement plans are subject to ERISA. For example, some governmental and church-offered plans are not. Military pensions are also subject to their own rules and regulations at the state and federal levels. Generally, the federal government will honor domestic relations orders dividing military pensions if the parties have been married for at least ten years and the award to the alternate payee does not exceed 50% of the net pension.

When one or both of the parties are participants in pension plans, it is necessary to obtain from each plan administrator (through the client or during the discovery process) copies of the plan and a record of contributions. The plan should then be valued. As indicated above, depending on the nature of the plan, valuation may require the assistance of a pension valuation expert/service. If a client waives valuation, the waiver should be in writing and preferably expressly stated in the parties' separation agreement to avoid a later malpractice claim against the attorney advising the client.

Pension plans can pose complex challenges for the family law team including, but not limited to, the following:

- As noted above, the value of a participant's interest in a retirement plan may not be ascertainable without expert advice. For example, it is hard to predict a specific retirement date, the life expectancy of the participant, the amount of the contributions that eventually will be made by the employer and the participant, or the ultimate value of the account at some future date.
- The participant may choose not to retire at his or her earliest retirement age unless required to do so. If not otherwise agreed, continued employment beyond the age projected at the time an agreement is negotiated may result in the other party receiving less of a benefit than he or she bargained for![38]
- Problems may arise when calculating the interests of same-sex spouses who were unable to legally marry until several years into their relationship. Historically, periods of cohabitation have not been factored into computations of "marital" shares.
- Pensions of various kinds (e.g., the military and public and private employers) are governed by an array of federal, state, and employer rules and regulations. The rules governing distribution of pensions are complex and must be followed scrupulously.
- As indicated earlier in this chapter, questions may be raised as to whether disability retirement pensions constitute property divisible as marital property.[39]

Pensions may be divided in a variety of ways depending on the parties' preferences, assets, needs, and circumstances. Commonly employed options include the following:

- Assume that a wife has a pension presently valued at $120,000, which she does not wish to have divided. She has other assets totaling $60,000 that she is willing to liquidate and use to "buy out" her husband's share of her pension and thereby leave it intact.
- Assume the husband has a pension presently valued at $300,000. He and his spouse own a marital home as tenants by the entirety. The home is valued at $300,000 and is owned outright. He does not wish to divide his pension

and is willing to offset the pension by transferring his interest in the marital home to his wife. She, in turn, is pleased with this arrangement, as she wants to remain in the home and sell it at a later date after the children have graduated from high school.

- Assume the parties met when they began teaching at a Midwestern, state-funded community college, where they have continued to teach for the last twenty years. Each has been contributing to the state retirement system for the full period. Although their contributions have not been exactly equal, the parties are willing to waive valuation and their respective potential rights in each other's pensions.

- Applying an "if, as, and when" approach, a nonemployee spouse may be awarded a share of an employee spouse's pension funds if, as, and when the employee spouse receives them. The share is most often determined according to a "marital fraction" formula based on the ratio of the years of marriage to the number of years of employment at the time of distribution. The present value of the pension does not need to be determined and no offsetting award is required at the time of the divorce.

- If the parties have been married for an extended period and one spouse's pension is the sole marital asset, a fair share of that pension may be allocated to the other spouse.

If one spouse is awarded a portion of the other's pension funds based on an agreement or after trial, to directly reach those funds the nonemployee spouse needs to obtain a **Qualified Domestic Relations Order (QDRO)**. A QDRO is a court order directing the administrator of a pension plan to pay a specified portion of the pension to an alternate payee, the nonemployee spouse.[40] It may be drafted by one of the attorneys on the case, if qualified, or by an expert/pension appraisal service. Considerable care must be taken to specify whether the QDRO includes only the retirement benefit or also the death benefit as well.[41] The QDRO must be approved by counsel for each party, the Plan Administrator, and the court in order to be effective. A certified copy of the divorce judgment reflecting the nature and extent of the award should be filed with the motion to approve the QDRO along with any additional paperwork required by the plan.

Qualified Domestic Relations Order (QDRO)
a court order directing the administrator of a pension plan to pay a specified portion of the pension to an alternate payee

PARALEGAL PRACTICE TIP

If there is no QDRO and the parties' agreement does not provide otherwise, the employee should be advised to designate a new permitted survivor beneficiary post dissolution assuming he or she wishes to do so.

Division of Liabilities

Although we have primarily focused in this chapter on the division of assets when a marriage terminates, it is equally (and sometimes more) important to consider personal and business debts. Often substantial debt has contributed to the breakdown of the relationship between the parties, and they have come to view divorce as the only way to bring an end to an escalating debt that is spiraling out of control. The parties' debts should be classified as separate and marital. **Marital debt**, like marital property, is usually specifically identified, valued, and apportioned between the parties. The general rule is that debt incurred prior to marriage is a separate debt, as it was presumably not incurred for the benefit of the marriage, although that assumption may be rebutted by the facts and circumstances. Debts for **necessaries** for the family unit (such as shelter, food, clothing, and medical care, for example) are considered marital debts. For purposes of equitable distribution, the South Carolina courts have defined a marital debt as a debt incurred for the joint benefit of the parties regardless of who incurred the obligation.[42]

Marital debt
debt incurred during the marriage for the benefit of the marital enterprise regardless of which party incurred the obligation

Necessaries
things that are indispensable to living, such as food, clothing, and shelter

Paralegal Application 12.7

Identification of Debts

The paralegal may be asked to work with the client in an effort to compile a summary of the parties' debts, both individual and joint. For each debt, the summary should indicate:

- the amount of the debt
- the identity of the party who incurred it
- when the debt was incurred (before the marriage, during the marriage, post separation, or after commencement of the divorce proceeding)

- why the debt was incurred (i.e., for what purpose)
- the amount and frequency of payments
- who is making the payments and out of what source of funds
- the duration of the obligation
- whether or not the debt is secured (for example, a mortgage secured by the marital home, a car loan secured by the vehicle)

As with marital assets, there are three primary ways in which separate and marital debts are divided.

1. The parties may have executed a pre- or postmarital agreement that addresses responsibility for separate and marital debt.
2. The parties may allocate responsibility for debt in their separation agreement.
3. Absent an agreement of the parties, the issue may be presented to the court for resolution.

The courts use a variety of approaches to allocating responsibility for debt, including but not limited to the following:

- The court may require payment of the parties' debt out of existing assets and then allocate the remaining assets, if any.
- The debt may be factored into the overall property division. For example, rather than awarding a wife $15,000 of property, the court may order the husband to pay $15,000 of her outstanding student loans.
- The court may make an equal allocation of debt.
- The court may decide to assign all or a disproportionate amount of the debt to one of the parties. (See Case 12.2.)

Hold harmless provision
a provision specifying that a particular spouse will be solely responsible for payment of certain debts and that the other spouse shall be free and clear of any obligation regarding those debts and will be indemnified by the debtor spouse if forced to pay them

Although a divorce decree may allocate responsibility for marital debt between the parties, the family court does not have the power to limit the rights of third-party creditors. For example, if both parties took out a car loan and the divorce decree provides that the wife will pay the balance of the loan and she fails to do so, the lender is free to try to collect from either spouse individually or both spouses jointly. To help protect against such situations, it is important to include a **hold harmless provision** in the parties' separation agreement. A hold harmless provision specifies that a particular spouse will be solely responsible for payment of certain debts and that the other spouse shall be free and clear of any obligation regarding those debts and will be indemnified by the debtor spouse if forced to pay them.

Sometimes the debt burden is so extensive and overwhelming that, subsequent to divorce, one of the parties declares personal bankruptcy. Bankruptcy involves complex issues and procedures usually handled by attorneys who specialize in this area of the law, but there are two basic points of particular relevance to the topic of property division:

- With the exception of debts in the nature of child support and spousal maintenance, bankruptcy law may provide for discharge of the bulk of a petitioner's debts. If a jointly held debt is discharged in this context, the creditor is still free to pursue the other spouse to collect on the remainder of the debt.
- Although child support and alimony generally are not dischargeable in bankruptcy, payments due to a former spouse under a court-ordered division of property may be dischargeable under limited circumstances.

Tax Consequences of Property Division

Under current federal tax law, transfers of real or personal property between spouses during a marriage or at dissolution as incidents of divorce are not taxable events.[43] A transfer is "incident to a divorce" if it occurs within one year after the date on which the marriage ends or if it is related to the ending of the marriage. However, this does not mean that there are no tax issues to be considered. In fact, several jurisdictions require that the court consider the tax implications of a property division for each of the parties.[44] Attorneys have an ethical duty to advise clients of the tax consequences of divorce and an attorney's failure to advise a client regarding related tax issues may give rise to a malpractice claim in some circumstances. For example, assume that a wife is awarded a substantial number of shares of Starbucks stock worth $150,000 at the time of the divorce. If and when she elects to sell the stock, she may receive a rude awakening when she learns that she is liable for payment of a significant **capital gains tax** because the stock was initially purchased at a mere fraction of its current worth. She will actually realize much less than the $150,000 she thought she'd bargained for and would receive. Of course, if the stock sells for less than its purchase price, a loss may be claimed.

Examples of other tax-related issues that may arise include:

- If the property division is such that a party must withdraw funds from a retirement plan before he or she is entitled to in order to "pay off" the other spouse, the value of the retirement plan is reduced, and the participant also is likely to face an early-withdrawal tax penalty.
- The parties may attempt to disguise as alimony a portion of the property division in order for one party to receive a tax deduction for the transfer. This is usually accomplished by "front-loading" the first two or three years of "alimony" payments, i.e., making them significantly larger than in subsequent years. Under its **alimony recapture rule**, the IRS will determine whether the transfer is alimony or property division based on its own criteria, not on others' labels or titles. If the IRS determines that the "alimony" paid was in fact property division, it will recapture the tax deduction claimed by the payor, who will then have to pay taxes, interest, and penalties on the improperly deducted amount. The recipient, on the other hand, will be able to recover the amount he or she previously paid in taxes purportedly on alimony income.
- Sometimes, part or all of a division of property is paid to a third party. For example, a husband may pay off his wife's mortgage on her condominium. The Internal Revenue Service will still allow the transfer between the spouses to be a nontaxable event between them if:

1. the transfer is made pursuant to a divorce or separation agreement,
2. the transfer is made pursuant to a written request of the beneficiary spouse, and
3. the transferring spouse receives a written acceptance of the property after it has been transferred.

PARALEGAL PRACTICE TIP

Although the parties may not appreciate the distinction between alimony and property division, it is especially significant in the tax or bankruptcy context. In most circumstances it is best to label payments or transfers as either alimony or property division to avoid confusion and postdivorce litigation. However, language in the parties' agreements or labels in family court orders are not necessarily determinative in every context. The IRS and bankruptcy courts make their own determinations as to the character of each transaction.

Capital gains tax
a tax on income derived from the sale of a capital asset as defined by the Internal Revenue Code

PARALEGAL PRACTICE TIP

In complex cases, accountants may be retained to calculate costs and benefits for the client. Although attorneys' fees in general are not tax-deductible for income tax purposes, the portion of fees attributable to services pertaining to tax matters is tax-deductible, and the client should be advised in writing as to that amount.

Alimony recapture rule
the IRS rule that the government can recover a tax benefit (such as the prior taking of a deduction for payment of alimony) by taxing the income that no longer qualifies for the benefit

Paralegal **Application 12.8**

Additional Property-Related Tax Issues

There are several additional tax issues related to division of property, debt, and spousal support. Of particular importance is the designation of who will be obligated to pay any taxes due and who will be eligible to claim tax benefits. For example, the following issues should be addressed in the parties' separation agreement:

- Have the parties failed to file any required state or federal tax returns for any year(s) during their marriage?
- Who will be responsible for paying any tax deficiencies, interest, and penalties should the Internal Revenue Service or a state department of revenue impose them for any prior years during which the parties filed joint tax returns?
- In some cases, both parties signed joint tax returns during the marriage but only one prepared the forms, controlled the information that went into them, and is responsible for errors, omissions, and/or fraudulent claims made which may result in significant penalties. Congress provides some relief for an **innocent spouse** under certain circumstances. The "innocent" spouse must be able to prove that at the time the return was signed, he or she did not know and had no reason to know that the other spouse understated taxes that were due. Otherwise,

the parties will be jointly and individually liable for the deficiency, meaning that the IRS can collect from one or both of them. An "innocent spouse" will want to include language in the agreement that the spouse who prepared the returns will indemnify the innocent spouse against any taxes and penalties arising out of any joint returns filed during the marriage.

- Will the parties file joint or separate tax returns for the year in which they separate and sign their agreement, and who will pay the taxes due, if any? Who will be entitled to any tax refund that may be due to the parties?
- If the parties are going to continue to jointly own the marital home post divorce, who will be responsible for paying property taxes, and who will be entitled to claim any related mortgage interest and taxes as deductions?
- If the marital home is subsequently sold, how will the capital gains tax be handled should any be due?

Innocent spouse

a spouse who may be relieved of liability incurred if the other spouse prepared the tax forms, controlled the information that went into them, and is solely responsible for errors, omissions, and/or fraud that resulted in imposition of significant taxes, interest, and penalties

A Property Division Illustration

Hugh and Nancy are divorcing after fifteen years of marriage. It is an "amicable" divorce and they have worked out what they believe is a fair division of their major assets. They will now "run it by" their respective attorneys. In the way of basic background: Hugh has owned (individually) and operated a sub shop for the past thirteen years (which he is about to sell for $125,000) and Nancy has been a probation officer for ten years. Hugh inherited $175,000 from his mother fourteen years ago. He used $75,000 of the inheritance to buy the sub shop outright. He used another, $50,000 to open his IRA (now valued at $100,000 based on an additional $25,000 in contributions from his inheritance and $25,000 in appreciation due to market forces). He put the balance of the inheritance in a checking account in his name only (remaining balance = $14,000). He used $30,000 of his earnings from the sub shop (along with $30,000 from Nancy's earnings) to purchase a boat (present value $62,000). The two of them have shared the expenses for the boat and worked on it in free time. Nancy has contributed $50,000 of her earnings during the parties' marriage to her state pension (now vested). They jointly own a condo which they bought for $175,000. Although Nancy paid the $40,000 down payment with her earnings during the marriage, they have shared all other related expenses over the years. There is a balance on the mortgage of $50,000. They purchased a time-share together five years ago for $11,000 that is in both their names. They have a joint bank account to which they have both contributed (current balance = $24,000) although they have no record of their respective contributions. They own two cars (of approximately equal value), household furnishings, and two pets. They have agreed to divide their $2,500 credit card debt equally and to sell the condo. They have negotiated the following division of their assets and liabilities. Can you explain why they reached these specific terms based on what you have learned in this chapter about property division upon divorce? Do you agree that the division is fair and reasonable?

ASSET/LIABILITY	VALUE	SEPARATE AND/OR MARITAL	HUGH	NANCY
MARITAL HOME (CONDO)	To be listed at $240,000 and sold at fair market value	M Titled in their joint names	50% of net proceeds after deduction of mortgage and costs and Nancy's $40,000 downpayment	$40,000 plus 50% of remaining net proceeds after deduction of downpayment, mortgage and costs
SUB SHOP	Under agreement for sale at $125,000.	S/M	$100,000	$25,000
HUGH'S CHECKING AC-COUNT AT PILOT'S NA-TIONAL BANK	BALANCE = $14,000	S	$14,000	0
JOINT CHECKING ACCOUNT AT COMPASS ROSE SAV-INGS AND LOAN	BALANCE = $24,000	M	$12,000	$12,000
IRA	$100,000	S/M	$87,500	$12,500
STATE PENSION (Nancy's)	Not available	M	$25,000 Nancy will pay Hugh $5,000 per year for five years.	Nancy will keep her pension. She will retain Hugh as survivor beneficiary on pension for five years until he is paid $25,000.
VEHICLES	Approximately equal resale value	M	Toyota Avalon	Toyota Solara convertible
30' MARINE TRADER POWER BOAT	Present value = $62,000	M	50% Owner; Will pay 50% of basic maintenance expenses and have use of boat February to July	50% Owner; Will pay 50% of basic maintenance expenses and have use of boat August to January
TIME SHARE—ARUBA	$11,000	M	Week 12 use; expenses divided equally	Week 13 use; expenses divided equally
HOUSEHOLD FURNISHINGS	Not valued	M	@ 50% (items agreed upon)	@ 50% (items agreed upon)
DEBTS (CREDIT CARD)	Approximately $2,500.	M/S	Liable for 50% marital credit card debt as of date of separation; liable for own debt incurred since separation.	Liable for 50% marital credit card debt as of date of separation; liable for own debt incurred since separation.

The Paralegal's Role in A Property Division Case

The tasks most commonly performed by a paralegal in a property division case are:

- compiling a list of the parties' assets indicating when and by whom the property was obtained, how it is titled, its value at key points in time, and how the value was calculated
- compiling a summary of liabilities (See Paralegal Application 12.7)
- scheduling and participating in interviews as assigned
- drafting complaints/petitions, motions, supporting affidavits, and proposed orders, as well as correspondence related to the case
- making discovery-related recommendations and drafting interrogatories, depositions, requests for admissions and requests for production of documents, as directed, to assist in identifying and valuing assets and the parties' respective contributions to those assets. In equitable distribution jurisdictions, discovery efforts may also be designed to gather information relating to factors to be considered by the court when making property distributions.
- researching current law (statutes, case law, and secondary sources) to support the client's position with respect to contested assets so that the court will have a rationale on which to base a decision.[45] In some cases, this may mean both state and federal law need to be considered.[46]
- suggesting issues on which expert testimony may be necessary, such as valuation of pensions, and maintaining lists of experts qualified to assist with and potentially testify as to specific issues, such as valuation of a business interest or the marital home
- drafting a pretrial memorandum, if required, informing the court of the nature and extent of the marital estate and the merits of the client's claim as to property distribution
- assisting in preparation for motion hearings
- drafting a property article/paragraph/exhibit for inclusion in a separation agreement if the parties negotiate a mutually agreed-upon division (Examples of property division provisions addressing real property, personal property, taxes, and debts and liabilities in a separation agreement are contained in the sample agreement provided in Chapter 13.)
- assisting with gathering and preparing evidentiary exhibits related to each of the property-related issues for trial, including, where applicable, statutory factors to be considered by the court
- helping to identify prospective witnesses
- drafting proposed conclusions of law and findings of fact, which, in an equitable distribution jurisdiction, should address each of the factors to be considered by the court
- making sure the client is kept informed of progress and upcoming deadlines, hearings, discovery matters, etc.
- tracking progress on the case to be certain timelines are met
- if within scope of expertise, preparing a preliminary draft of a QDRO

CHAPTER **SUMMARY**

The division of marital property upon divorce is one of the most hotly contested and emotionally charged issues addressed in a family law practice. The discussion in this chapter reflects the contemporary view of marriage as a partnership to which each party is presumed to make both economic and noneconomic contributions. When that partnership dissolves, both assets and liabilities need to be allocated between the parties. This may be accomplished via an enforceable pre- or postmarital agreement, a separation agreement negotiated by the parties and approved by the court, or a court order following a trial on the merits of the parties' respective proposals.

In this chapter, we have reviewed the five basic phases of the property division process:

1. Definition and identification of the parties' "property"
2. Classification of the property as separate, marital, or both
3. Identification of the property subject to division upon divorce
4. Valuation of major assets and liabilities
5. Division of the parties' property according to the appropriate jurisdictional standard: community property or equitable distribution

Particular attention was given to some of the more challenging issues confronted in the property division context. For instance, are assets such as a professional degree or the goodwill of a business actually property on which a dollar value can be placed, and, if so, do they constitute separate or marital property? Does separate property lose its identity as separate when it becomes commingled with marital property? Should the conduct of the parties (such as dissipation of assets) be considered when allocating marital property? Should one party be permitted to access the other party's pension? What are some of the potential tax issues related to property division?

This is an area in which the role played by a paralegal will vary considerably based on training, skills, and experience. A property division case provides an opportunity for the paralegal to do some creative thinking about assets, conduct in-depth research, develop arguments and theories to support a proposed division, and organize materials (exhibits, charts, PowerPoint presentations, etc.) to persuade a court to adopt the client's position at trial.

The chapter provides a broad array of statutes and case references illustrating the diversity in how various jurisdictions treat major topics covered. The paralegal needs to be attentive to the current governing law in his or her state and in other states as well, when appropriate. There simply are no guidelines a family law attorney can use with a client to predict the precise outcome of a property distribution upon divorce. Particularly in equitable distribution jurisdictions, even though judges may be required to consider certain factors in reaching a decision, no specific formula applies, and they are free to exercise broad discretion and weigh the various factors as they see fit in each individual case. Their decisions are rarely overturned absent an abuse of discretion or an error in application of the law. Effective and well-prepared representation can make a critical difference in the overall result for a client.

CONCEPT REVIEW AND REINFORCEMENT

KEY **TERMS**

Abuse of discretion	Equitable distribution	Postmarital agreement
Active appreciation	Equity	Premarital agreement
Actuary	Expert	Real property
Alimony recapture rule	Fair market value	Qualified Domestic Relations Order
All property state	Hold harmless provision	(QDRO)
Basis	Inception of title theory	Separate property
Capital gains tax	Innocent spouse	Separation agreement
Commingling	Intangible property	Source of funds/*pro rata* theory
Common law property state	Marital debt	Tangible property
Community property	Marital estate	Tracing
Defined-benefit plan	Marital property	Transmutation
Defined-contribution plan	Necessaries	Valuation
Dissipation	Passive appreciation	Vest
Dual property state	Pension	
Error of law	Personal property	

REVIEW **QUESTIONS**

1. Identify the five phases of the property division process.
2. Distinguish between separate and marital property. Give an example of each.
3. Describe three ways in which an asset may change from separate to marital (or marital to separate) property.
4. Identify the majority view regarding treatment of each of the following in the property division context: professional degrees; disability and personal injury awards; and pets.
5. Define valuation and indicate why it is important and when it occurs.
6. Distinguish between active and passive appreciation.

7. Identify the three most common ways in which property will be divided upon dissolution of a marriage.
8. Distinguish between a community property approach and an equitable division approach to property division.
9. Identify a minimum of six factors generally considered by courts dividing property in equitable distribution jurisdictions.
10. Describe the nature and purpose of a QDRO.
11. Describe how the courts generally treat debt in a property distribution.
12. Identify three tax issues related to property division cases.
13. Describe the paralegal's role in a property division case.

DEVELOPING YOUR PARALEGAL SKILLS

FOCUS ON **THE JOB**

In this activity, the student will have an opportunity to propose a division of property appropriate to a specific fact pattern.

The Facts

Jimmy and Alice have been married for ten years and have three children. They appeared to have a good life and a decent marriage until recently, when Alice had an affair with her boss and Jimmy found out about it. He is filing for divorce and says he wants to "take Alice to the cleaners so she walks away with nothing." His lawyer appreciates his feelings, but has told him that that's just not the way it works anymore.

The assets involved in this case include the following:

- When the parties married, the wife had a jewelry collection valued at approximately $10,000. During the marriage she received as gifts from her relatives an additional $15,000 worth of jewelry. The collection is now valued at $35,000, $10,000 of which is attributable to appreciation in the value of the rings, watches, and necklaces included in the collection.
- Before marriage, the husband had a baseball card collection valued at $7,300 that is now worth approximately $29,100. Half of the increase is the result of the purchase of new cards with marital funds and the balance is due to appreciation in the value of the cards owned prior to the marriage.
- The parties have resided in the marital home since their marriage ten years ago. The property has been appraised at $225,000. The down payment of $40,000 came from the wife's mother and father, who insisted that the home be titled solely in their daughter's name. The purchase price was $170,000 and there is a mortgage on the property with a remaining balance

of $72,000. The husband added a den to the property through his own labor over a six-month period. It is estimated that this increased the value of the home by approximately $15,000. The remainder of the increase in value is attributable to market forces. The parties have contributed equally throughout the marriage to payment of the mortgage, insurance, property taxes, and household expenses. The wife wants to remain in the marital home for the next five years until the parties' youngest child graduates from high school, and she doesn't figure this is any problem because the house is in her name.

- The wife is a nurse and the husband is a physical therapist. They have each worked throughout the marriage and contributed to their respective pension plans. Both plans are vested but neither has been valued. The parties believe they are approximately equal and they do not want to go to the expense of having them valued. They each want to keep their own pension intact and have advised their respective attorneys to this effect.
- The parties bought two pets during their marriage: a now seven-year-old beagle named "Spike" and a five-year-old cat named "Stanley." They both adore the pets and have contributed to their care throughout their marriage. Both pets were obtained from a local pet shelter at no cost other than the cost of an initial medical examination and shots.
- The parties have an investment portfolio that they opened together and have funded equally in the total amount of $60,000. The account is presently worth $92,000; $12,000 of this amount is due to market forces, and the balance appears to be the result of the husband's sound management of the asset.

- The parties have a joint bank account used for necessaries. The balance in the account is presently $2,632.18. They have contributed equally to the account.
- The parties have a joint savings account to which they have both contributed, but neither has maintained any records regarding their respective contributions to the account over the years. They each acknowledge that it was established to support the marital enterprise in the event of an emergency or a special opportunity. The account presently contains $16,234.
- The wife has credit card debt in the amount of $1,368, and the husband has credit card debt in the amount of $4,786.
- Although they each had their educational degrees prior to marriage, the wife has been paying back student loans throughout the marriage. The balance on the loans is now only $924. She has paid off approximately $7,000 during the marriage out of joint marital funds.

The Assignment

Working with another student in your class, negotiate an appropriate division of the property given the above fact pattern. You will need to:

1. Determine whether you are in an equitable distribution or community property jurisdiction.
2. Identify on a chart (similar to the one provided above in the Property Division Illustration) what you believe to be the parties' marital and separate assets and liabilities. The chart should reflect the value of each asset and liability (and the amount attributable to each spouse). Note that some assets may be part separate and part marital/community property.
3. Indicate on the chart the results of your negotiation with respect to how the assets and liabilities should be divided between the parties, given the standard in your state and the facts of this case.

FOCUS ON **ETHICS**

In this activity, students address a situation in which a supervisor basically directs a paralegal to engage in negotiation of a property settlement with opposing counsel.

The Assignment

Assume that you are a paralegal in the law office of Attorney Karen Goldberg. Attorney Goldberg represents Alice in the above hypothetical but is presently away on her honeymoon with her fourth husband. She has told you that the client just wants what is fair. Alice feels bad about the affair but does not think it should be held against her. Attorney Goldberg has directed you to negotiate a property settlement with representatives of the law firm representing Jimmy. As a paralegal, what course of action should you take, and how should this situation be addressed? Which of the ethical canons for paralegals promulgated by the National Association of Legal Assistants, contained in Appendix A, are applicable in this context? Which provisions of the code governing attorney conduct in your state? Present your responses to these questions in a one- to two-page paper.

FOCUS ON **CASE LAW**

In this Focus on Case Law, the student will brief a case decided in his or her jurisdiction which addresses some aspect of the property division process.

The Assignment

Locate a case decided within the past three years in your jurisdiction concerning some aspect of the property division process. For example, you might select a case that addresses an unequal distribution of property or a court's treatment of a professional license or degree. Then brief the case using a format required by your instructor or, if none, the format available at *www.pearsonhighered.com/careersresources/* in the material for Chapter 1 of this text under Resources.

FOCUS ON **STATE LAW AND PROCEDURE**

In this activity, the student is asked to research basic property division topics in a single jurisdiction.

The Assignment

Locate the primary property distribution statute(s) in your jurisdiction and then respond to the following questions:

1. Is your state an equitable distribution or a community property jurisdiction?

2. How is marital/community property defined? How is separate property defined?
3. If you are in an equitable distribution state, do the courts apply a dual or all property approach?
4. What factors does a court consider when dividing marital property?
5. Are the nonfinancial contributions of spouses considered?

FOCUS ON **TECHNOLOGY**

In addition to the links provided throughout the chapter, this Focus segment provides a series of useful websites for reference along with related assignments for completion.

Websites of Interest

www.abanet.org

This is the site of the family law section of the American Bar Association. At this site you can find a Chart (Chart 5) which provides a state-by-state survey of approaches to property division. To locate the Table, search for "Family Law in the Fifty States Tables" in "Resources Available to the Public." This chart also appears on an annual basis in the *Family Law Quarterly (Winter Volume)* published by the ABA.

www.dol.gov

The U.S. Department of Labor provides a wealth of information at this site about insurance and retirement benefits including informative publications regarding QDROs.

www.findlaw.com

This site provides links to articles and state laws concerning a variety of divorce-related topics including property division. It also includes links to a checklist for dividing property and a settlement agreement form.

Assignments

1. Locate online an example of a property division provision/exhibit for a separation agreement.
2. Locate online an example of a QDRO.
3. Locate online information about a firm/company that values pensions and prepares QDROs.
4. Of what use, if any, are the following websites with respect to the topic of property division in your jurisdiction?

   a. *www.divorceinfo.com*
   b. *divorcelinks.com*
   c. *www.divorcenet.com*
   d. *divorcesource.com*

PORTFOLIO PRODUCTS

1. Property division proposal
2. One- to two-page paper concerning ethical issues in a hypothetical case
3. Brief of a property division case
4. Responses to questions about property division statute(s) in the student's jurisdiction

chapter 13

SEPARATION AGREEMENTS

© Pixland/Getty Images

> Herman, an elderly multimillionaire, and Anna, a relatively young model, have been married for twelve years and have a minor son, Theodore. The couple has decided to seek a no-fault divorce because they no longer seem to have anything in common. Anna believes she is getting a pretty good settlement, given that she came into the marriage with little more than good looks. She figures she recognizes a good deal when she sees it and doesn't need some high-priced attorney telling her what she already knows.

Introduction

Separation agreements are relative newcomers to the family law legal scene. For centuries, and even after the passage of married women's property acts, a husband and wife could not execute a valid contract with each other. Separation agreements, in particular, were considered contrary to public policy favoring the preservation of marriage, because they appeared to promote divorce by providing financial incentives for terminating the marital relationship. As late as the 1960s, state legislatures and courts were still in the process of lifting such restrictions.

Today, separation agreements have become important centerpieces in most divorce actions. A comprehensive, well-drafted agreement tailored to the specific needs of a divorcing couple brings closure to their past relationship as spouses and establishes a roadmap for their futures as independent individuals. Because of the significance of these agreements, we devote a full chapter to studying them. Our primary focus is on what they are, the purposes they serve, how they are developed, the customary nature of their contents, and how they are approved, modified, and enforced by the courts. The role potentially played by a paralegal from initial client contact through enforcement of an agreement is highlighted.

LEARNING OBJECTIVES

After reading this chapter and completing related assignments, you should be able to:

- explain the nature and purpose of a separation agreement

- identify the characteristics of an effective separation agreement

- describe how a separation agreement is developed

- describe the role of a paralegal in preparing a separation agreement

- list the basic components of a separation agreement

- describe the role the courts play in approving, modifying, and enforcing separation agreements

- explain the difference between a merged and a surviving agreement

Separation agreement
an agreement made between spouses in anticipation of divorce or legal separation concerning the terms of the divorce or separation and any continuing obligations of the parties to each other

Legal separation
a judicial determination that allows the parties to live separate and apart without dissolving their legal relationship as husband and wife; sometimes called a limited divorce

PARALEGAL PRACTICE TIP

In some cases, a court will find that a postnuptial agreement constitutes a separation agreement. The Kansas Supreme Court did so under the state statute governing marital agreements entered after marriage regardless of whether the parties intended to remain married at the time of execution. See *Traster v. Traster*, 339 P.3d 778 (Kan. 2014).

Meeting of the minds
a shared understanding with respect to the terms and conditions of a contract

Consideration
a bargained-for exchange or mutual promises underlying the formation of a contract

PARALEGAL PRACTICE TIP

In *Hament v. Baker*, 2014 VT. 39, 97 A.3d 461 (2014), the parties reached an agreement on all issues except which party was entitled to have the family dog. They battled over this single issue all the way to the Vermont Supreme Court!

What Is a Separation Agreement?

A **separation agreement** is a contract that sets forth the understanding reached by parties to a divorce or **legal separation** regarding their individual rights and obligations with respect to matters relating primarily to finances, property, and minor children, if any. The name given to the document varies by jurisdiction. For example, it may be called, among other options, a marital agreement, marital dissolution agreement, marital property settlement, or a permanent stipulation of the parties. In theory, a separation agreement addresses any and all rights and obligations arising out of the marital status. In an increasing number of states, the agreement is divided into two parts: a parenting plan that addresses child-related provisions and a stipulation/property settlement agreement that covers all other issues.

Since the agreement is a contract, it must meet all the requirements of a valid contract:

- The parties must have the legal capacity to contract—they must be able to understand the nature and effect of the agreement.
- The parties must enter the contract of their own free will—they must not be acting under duress.
- There must be an offer and an acceptance—there must be a **meeting of the minds** with respect to the terms of the agreement.
- There must be **consideration** for the agreement—a separation agreement is a bilateral contract in which the parties have reciprocal obligations, and the consideration is the mutual promises of the parties contained within the agreement.

In an uncontested divorce, the parties' agreement must customarily be filed with the divorce petition or shortly thereafter. Timing of the submission is based on procedural rules or local practice in each state. In a contested case, the parties may file no agreement or may file a partial agreement that addresses the issues they agree on and separate proposed agreements with respect to the remaining issues. The contested issues are left for the court to determine following a trial. For example, the parties may agree on custody, visitation, and child support but be at loggerheads when it comes to division of their property.

What Are the Characteristics of an Effective Separation Agreement?

An effective agreement is comprehensive and written in language the parties can understand. The attorneys must carefully review the agreement with their respective clients before execution to be certain that it reflects what has actually been agreed to, that there are no misunderstandings or extraneous oral or written agreements between the parties, and that each party knows what is expected of them. A well-drafted agreement will help minimize postdivorce litigation such as claims for breach and contempt. The primary characteristics of effective separation agreements are described below along with illustrations of some of the consequences of poor drafting.

The agreement is comprehensive. The agreement should address and resolve all of the rights and obligations that arise out of the marital status, including but not necessarily limited to property division, spousal support, insurance, taxes, and matters pertaining to minor children, if any. For example, to avoid potentially serious consequences for both the parties and counsel, if a party has a pension, it should be specifically identified, described, and assigned to one or both of the parties. In *Reville v. Reville*, 312 Conn. 428, 93 A.3d 1076 (2014), the Connecticut Supreme Court held a dissolution judgment should be reopened because the former husband had failed to disclose the existence of a pension. In *Brennenstuhl v. Brennenstuhl,* 169 N.C. App. 433, 610 S.E.2d 301 (2005), the parties' property settlement agreement simply stated "Retirement Benefits: Issues of retirement will be addressed at a later date." When the former husband subsequently retired from the military, his former wife successfully sought a share of the pension over his objection. Had he anticipated this result, he might not initially have agreed to other terms in the property settlement. It is important for the parties to have a clear picture of the whole pie before they settle for any piece of it!

The terms used in the agreement are clearly defined. Terms used in agreements need to be clearly defined in order to accurately capture the parties' intentions at the time they execute the agreement. A lack of clarity can lead to unnecessary and costly litigation at a later date. For example, if a provision of an agreement will vary with a party's income, does "income" include both earned and **unearned income**? See, e.g., *Larson v. Larson*, 37 Mass. App. Ct. 106, 636 N.E.2d 1365 (1994). In *Isham v. Isham*, 292 Conn. 170, 972 A.2d 228 (2009), the husband's alimony obligations were described as being based on both "salary" and "income" and neither term was defined. In *Matheny v. Matheny*, 2013 Ohio 2946 (2013), the parties' agreement provided that the wife would receive "half of profit if home is ever sold" but nowhere in the agreement was the term "profit" defined. The magistrate in the court of common pleas determined "profit" meant "the difference between the sale price and the cost of construction" resulting in the wife receiving nothing from the sale. When it reversed and remanded the case, the appellate court found the term "profit" was ambiguous and could just as reasonably be construed as "the excess of the sales price (return) over the mortgage balance and/or costs (expenditure) at closing." If alimony will terminate upon "cohabitation," does "cohabitation" mean for a certain period of time, with an intimate partner, or with anyone who subsidizes the recipient's living expenses, including roommates or adult children? The New Hampshire Supreme Court considered a case in which the parties' agreement provided that the husband's alimony payments would cease if the wife "cohabitates with an unrelated adult male." See *In the Matter of Raybeck and Raybeck*, 163 N.H. 570, 44 A.3d 351 (2012). Lacking any definition in the agreement of the meaning of "cohabitates," the state's high court basically defined cohabitation as "a relationship between persons resembling that of a marriage." It considered several indicators that such a relationship exists, including, but not limited to, continuity in the relationship, financial arrangements between the individuals, the ages of the cohabitants, etc. See also *Fecteau v. Fecteau*, 97 A.D.3d 999, 949 N.Y.S.2d 511 (2012).

The provisions in the agreement are fully described. An effective agreement will put each party on notice of their respective rights and obligations and what they need to do to comply with its provisions. For example, if one of the parties agrees to maintain a life insurance policy, several questions should be addressed. The policy or policies should be identified. Do they currently exist or must they be obtained? Can the obligation be satisfied by more than one policy?

Can substitutions of the policies be made during the period of obligation? Can they be borrowed against? What if the obligor changes a beneficiary? What if the required insurance coverage does not still exist when the obligor dies and the obligation is still in effect? See, e.g., *Foster v. Hurley & Another*, 444 Mass. 157, 826 N.E.2d 719 (2005). If the agreement is ambiguous with respect to how long a party is required to maintain a life insurance policy, the court may construe the ambiguity against the drafter of the agreement. See *DeAngelis v. DeAngelis et al*, 104 A.D.3d 901, 962 N.Y.S.2d 328 (N.Y. App. Div. 2013). Frequently, agreements provide that the parties agree they will "contribute to their children's higher education to the extent each party is financially able." What does this mean? Who gets to decide which college a child will attend? What expenses will be covered (tuition, fees, room, board, travel, supplies, extracurricular activities, etc.)? Will grants and student loans be used to offset parental obligations? Will a parent be required to obtain a loan or sell assets to cover costs? See, e.g., *Dykes v. Scopetti*, 2015 VT 53 (2015), and *In the Matter of Poulin and Wall*, 164 N.H. 41, 53 A.3d 522 (2012). If one of the parties will continue to reside in the jointly owned marital home, the agreement should specify who will be responsible for payment of a mortgage and/or equity loan (if any), property taxes, insurance, utilities (including water and sewer, Internet and cable services), an alarm system, and maintenance expenses such as repairs, landscaping, painting, or snow removal, if warranted. What if the party remaining in the home allows it to fall into disrepair?

In some instances when the provisions of an agreement are unclear, resolution by the court may come down to a matter of grammar. In *Salter v. Salter nka Elijah*, 2013 Ohio 559 (Ohio App. 2013), the parties' agreement provided that the husband would indemnify and hold the wife harmless "on his Chase, both his Fifth Third, and his Capital One credit cards." The husband argued that he was not obligated under the agreement to pay both his and his wife's Fifth Third credit card bills. The appellate court affirmed the trial court's finding that he was required to pay both concluding that "both" was a subsequent modifier meaning that "his" would not apply to the Fifth Third portion of the clause.

The agreement is fair and reasonable and free from fraud and coercion. Agreements should be both **procedurally and substantively fair**. Although the parties are free to voluntarily settle for less than they might be entitled to under the law, agreements must not be so lopsided that one of the parties is forced to seek public assistance or is otherwise seriously disadvantaged. Sometimes it is difficult to assess fairness and other times it is not. For example, the North Dakota Supreme Court granted "relief from judgment" in the *Eberle* case (2010 ND 107 (2010)) finding that the parties' settlement agreement was "so one-sided no rational, undeluded person" would make the agreement and "no honest and fair person would accept it." The court found that the facts suggested there was some duress or undue influence in the negotiation and execution of the agreement. The wife was not represented by counsel, the agreement was rushed, and there was little discussion of its terms. The wife said she had a chance to read the agreement and knew what she was signing but that she was on medication that "affected her ability to think" and resist her husband's demands. The Virginia Court of Appeals had little hesitation when it affirmed a trial court's judgment rejecting a proposed agreement in a 2009 case. In *Bailey v. Bailey*, 54 Va. App. 209, 677 S.E.2d 56 (2009), a wife presented her husband a marital property agreement to sign while he was

Procedural fairness
fairness in the negotiation and execution of the agreement

Substantive fairness
fairness in the specific terms of an agreement

on a weekend furlough from a psychiatric hospital. She told him that he would not be able to come home unless he signed. Under the "agreement," he transferred all marital property to his wife and all debts incurred during the marriage were assigned to him. The husband had suffered from serious psychiatric problems for more than a decade.

The agreement must be consistent with governing law. Agreements must be consistent with federal, state, and local law. The parties cannot agree to engage in any form of illegal conduct such as agreeing not to pay federal, state, or local taxes. Although agreements cannot promote criminal behaviors such as drug use, they can include provisions acknowledging a history of such conduct by, for example, making visitation rights contingent on a parent participating in a treatment program and having clean drug tests. Generally, the parties cannot legally bargain away the rights of their children. Contractual provisions will be ineffective to eliminate a party's duty to pay child support or prohibit a modification of child support when warranted by the circumstances. See, e.g., *Guidash v. Guidash et al*, 211 Md. App. 725, 66 A.3d 122 (Md. App. 2013), *Thomlinson v. Thomlinson*, 305 Conn. 539, 46 A.3d 112 (Conn. 2012), and *In the Matter of Asch v. Asch*, 30 A.D.3d 513 (N.Y. 2006).

How Is a Separation Agreement Developed?

In the majority of cases, the parties to a divorce or separation reach an agreement with or without the assistance of counsel and/or mediation. This may be accomplished in a variety of ways including the following:

- The parties may reach an agreement on their own and proceed ***pro se*** or present it to their respective attorneys for review and submission to the court.
- The parties may retain counsel and discuss with their respective attorneys what each considers his or her goals and **bottom line** terms. Financial information will be exchanged, and necessary documents, such as bank statements, deeds, and mortgages, will be gathered. If there is no need for formal discovery, counsel may negotiate an agreement via telephone, e-mail, formal correspondence, and four-way conferences. In relatively uncomplicated cases, one attorney will prepare a draft reducing the agreement to writing for the other's review and input. Successive drafts will be exchanged until an agreement is reached that reflects a "meeting of the minds." Many family law attorneys prefer to prepare the first draft, as it may provide them with an opportunity to subtly shape the negotiations in a particular direction.
- In more complex cases, drafts will not be prepared until discovery is completed, the value of major assets is established, and each party has an opportunity to consider his or her options after carefully examining the full nature and extent of the **marital estate**. In high-conflict cases, the attorneys often draft and exchange initial proposals outlining their clients' respective positions on issues such as child custody, visitation, support, alimony, health insurance, property division, distribution of debts, and attorneys' fees. Areas of agreement, if any, will be identified, and negotiation will proceed with respect to the remaining issues. Once the agreed-upon terms are framed, a partial or full agreement is prepared. If the agreement does not address all

PARALEGAL PRACTICE TIP

To see a Connecticut *pro se* agreement, visit *www.jud.state.ct.gov*. You can review sample *pro se* parenting plan and separation agreement forms provided by the Colorado courts at *www.courts.state.co.us*.

Pro se
[Latin: for self] the condition under which a person represents himself or herself in a legal proceeding without the assistance of an attorney

Bottom line
the limit beyond which a party will not go in a negotiation

PARALEGAL PRACTICE TIP

Successive editions of the agreement, including copies of those marked up by counsel for the other party, should be retained in the client file. Occasionally, questions arise later as to whether the opposing party knew about or had input into a particular provision. **Forensic** material can help establish that he or she clearly was aware of the challenged provision and may even have proposed it.

Forensic
gathered as potential evidence in a lawsuit

Marital estate
the property acquired during the marriage other than by gift or inheritance that is subject to division at the time of marital dissolution

of the issues, the remaining topics may be referred for mediation. The issues that remain unresolved after exhaustive efforts will be presented to the court for resolution. More often than not, even those issues may be settled "on the courthouse steps" by parties not wishing to incur the risk or expense of a trial.

The client ultimately controls the case in the sense that he or she has the final word on terms, on the scope of discovery, and on whether or not a case will proceed to trial. With respect to agreements, the client must have input and approve all proposals communicated to the other party and also must have an opportunity to review and consider all counterproposals.

Paralegal **Application 13.1**

Information Gathering for Separation Agreements

Except in cases involving few if any assets, before an agreement is actually drafted, a considerable amount of information should be gathered from the client, the other party, and third parties as well, if appropriate. The parties should have a comprehensive picture of their circumstances before negotiating an agreement or agreeing to a single term in isolation. For example, a party initially opposed to paying spousal support may eventually prefer to pay tax-deductible alimony over time if it means his or her pension will remain intact.

What follows is a summary of the kinds of documents and information that should be collected and compiled in summary form for easy reference when drafting an agreement. The paralegal generally plays an active role in gathering this information through informal and formal discovery, if necessary.

- Personal data:
  - Names
  - Addresses (home and business)
  - Parties' dates of birth
  - Social Security numbers
  - Home, business, and cell phone numbers
  - E-mail address (for communication purposes)
  - Details regarding the date and location of the marriage
  - Names and birthdates of children born to both and/or either of the parties
- Contact information for all attorneys involved in the divorce and any other potentially related matters, such as abuse complaints and pending claims
- Summary of all property owned by the parties indicating how it is held (by husband, wife, jointly, with third parties, in trust, etc.), where and when

it was acquired (before or during the marriage, before or after the date of separation), the value of the property, and the means by which the value was established
- Income from all sources of both parties
- Liabilities of both parties: identity (and relationship) of each creditor, amount of debt, who incurred the debt, when and for what purpose, whose name the debt is in, etc.
- Documents to collect (not intended as an exhaustive list):
  - Pre- or postmarital agreements
  - Deeds
  - Leases
  - Titles
  - Contracts for purchase or sale of property
  - Mortgage/loan applications
  - Insurance policies
  - Wills and trusts
  - Tax documents
  - Financial statements (current and past)
  - Business and professional licenses
  - Pension/retirement account plans, statements, etc.
  - Bank account statements
  - Appraisals
  - Medical reports
  - Pending claims (personal injury, etc.)
  - Court orders or judgments affecting the rights and liabilities of either or both of the parties (including decrees from previous divorces, if any)
  - Credit card statements
  - Royalty statements
  - Articles of Incorporation, corporate by-laws, etc.

The Form of the Separation Agreement

The actual document is usually in one of four formats:

1. **A two-part format consisting of a main body and a series of Exhibits on relevant topics:**

   Main body: The main body typically contains:
   - a recital of pertinent facts (names and addresses of the parties; names and ages of the parties' children, if any; date and place where the parties were married; and when and where they last lived together)
   - several general provisions/articles common to most agreements (clauses relating to waivers, disclosure, interpretation, implementation, modification, severability, nonmolestation, and enforcement of the agreement)

   Exhibits: A series of individual "exhibits" are **incorporated by reference** into the overall agreement. Each addresses a specific topic (such as spousal support, child custody and visitation, or property division) (See Exhibit 13.2.)

2. **A two-part document consisting of a Parenting Agreement and a Marital or Property Settlement Agreement covering all other relevant topics.**

3. **An integrated document.** Integrated documents usually have numbered sections (Articles I, II, III, etc.) following the introductory "recitals" of pertinent facts. Each Article is customarily labeled, for example, General Provisions, Custody and Visitation, Personal Property, etc.

4. **A format recommended or prescribed in the jurisdiction.** Several states provide forms online on state/court-sponsored websites. For example, the New Hampshire courts provide standard forms online for parenting plans and permanent stipulations, which contain numbered paragraphs on all major topics. Several options are provided under each main topic with boxes for the parties to check indicating their choices. This approach vastly simplifies the process for parties proceeding *pro se* who lack knowledge about the nature and scope of issues that need to be resolved when their marriage dissolves. If the parties are represented by counsel who choose to develop their own agreements, those agreements must use the same topical numbering system as is used in the court's format. This requirement facilitates review by judges who do not have to struggle with the organization of each individual agreement to locate the terms (such as custody, spousal support, or health insurance) that most concern them.

Whatever the basic format, there is considerable similarity agreement to agreement. However, each separation or divorce involves two parties, each with his or her own unique goals, needs, and circumstances. Therefore, considerable care must be taken to ensure that the agreement is tailored to those circumstances and meets the client's specific goals and needs to the greatest extent possible (understanding that there are rarely any fully satisfied customers in the divorce context).

Incorporation by reference
adoption by reference; made a part of the agreement by including a statement in the agreement that the Exhibits are to be treated as if they are part of the agreement

PARALEGAL PRACTICE TIP

To see the New Hampshire forms, visit *www.courts.state.nh.us.*

PARALEGAL PRACTICE TIP

It is unusual, but some jurisdictions permit agreements to be made by oral stipulation of the parties in court rather than by written agreement. If the agreement is read into the record under oath and determined by the court to be fair, reasonable, and freely entered, it may be approved, made a part of the judgment, and be just as binding on the parties as a written agreement.

The Paralegal's Role in Drafting the Separation Agreement

Paralegals are often asked to draft separation agreements based on the specific terms provided by the supervising attorney after consultation with the client. A basic approach generally includes the following steps:

- The supervising attorney will first review the client's priorities and expectations as well as his or her rights and responsibilities under governing law. In order to establish the basis for an agreement, the attorney must identify the client's position on fundamental issues, such as child custody, pensions, and the division of any real property, including the marital residence. After discovery is completed, if the basic terms are negotiated and agreed upon (or formulated as proposals), an outline of the agreement is prepared. The paralegal is sometimes present for these initial discussions and may be asked to take notes and develop an outline for review.

- The paralegal should review (or already have knowledge of) the law (case and statutory), rules, and procedures governing the content and format of agreements. For example, do courts in the applicable jurisdiction mandate specific numbered paragraphs and topics? Are child-related provisions addressed in the agreement or in a separate parenting plan?

- The paralegal will examine available "model agreements" in firm files, both paper and electronic. Form books, state practice manuals, and other resources may also be consulted. Previously drafted agreements in closed divorce files may be especially useful when cases present similar fact patterns (for example, high-conflict child custody and visitation situations or cases in which bankruptcy or tax audit issues are looming in the immediate future). There are many online resources for agreements—some are helpful, but all need to be carefully assessed, tailored to the facts of the specific case, and adapted to reflect jurisdictionally appropriate terminology and formats.

- The paralegal carefully drafts an agreement for review based on the outline provided/approved by the supervising attorney. Drafting generally involves considerably more than filling in the blanks or simple cut-and-paste activity. Although there is no need to reinvent the wheel, the content must reflect the facts and intentions of the parties in the particular case and comply with current governing law and procedure. For example, there may be a recent change in the state's treatment of some issue in an agreement, such as whether or not the court will approve a provision pertaining to responsibility for college expenses. Particular caution must be exercised when duplicating or using **boilerplate** provisions.

- The paralegal may be asked to review a proposed agreement or feedback received from the opposing party. Generally the paralegal will check to be sure all of the appropriate terms are included, identify any differences from the client's position, and, if necessary, recommend potential additions, deletions, and/or alternative language for review by the supervising attorney.

- The complete Final Draft must be carefully reviewed prior to signature and submission to the court for incorporation into the judgment. Before signing, counsel should walk through the entire document with the client and address any questions that may arise.

Boilerplate
standard language that is commonly used in a particular kind of agreement and that usually does not require negotiation

EXHIBIT 13.1 Checklist of Basic Topics Covered in Separation Agreements

Identification Clause/Opening Paragraph

    Date of execution

    Names and addresses of the parties and names used to refer to the parties in the agreement

Recitals/Statement of Facts

    Date and place of marriage and the number of the marriage for each party

    Names and birthdates of all children born to or adopted by the parties

    Date of separation and location where the parties last resided together

    Reason for separation (e.g., irreconcilable differences)

    Current living status (usually separate and apart)

    Identification of any pending action for divorce or legal separation (separate maintenance) with name of court and docket number

    Purpose of the agreement and parties' intent with respect to its effect

    Confirmation of participation in negotiation of agreement and knowledge of rights and liabilities

    Confirmation agreement is signed freely and voluntarily

    Consideration for agreement (mutual promises)

General Provisions

    Separation

        Intention to live separate and apart

        Nonmolestation provision (an agreement not to restrain or interfere with each other)

    Mutual/General Release (acceptance of the agreement in full satisfaction of all claims against each other except those arising from the agreement and subsequent divorce)

    Waiver of Estate claim (a waiver of any rights in the other's estate upon death)

    Execution of Documents necessary to implement agreement (deeds, QDROs, etc.)

    Acknowledgments

        Independent representation of choice (or opportunity for it or an acknowledgment that one or both of the parties chose to proceed *pro se*)

        Full disclosure made or opportunity to do so

        Parties have read and understood terms of the agreement

        Agreement is free from fraud or coercion

        Agreement is fair and reasonable

    Situs/Governing Law (designation of the state's law that will govern interpretation and enforceability of the agreement)

    Validity/Severability/Savings Clause (a clause stating that if any provision of the agreement is declared void, the remaining provisions will continue to be valid)

    Entire Agreement (statement that the agreement embodies the parties' complete understanding with respect to resolution of the rights and responsibilities flowing from their marital relationship)

    Effective Date

    Binding Effect on heirs, assigns, etc.

    Intention with respect to merger or survival of agreement (whether the agreement will merge in the divorce decree or survive as an independent contract)

    Modification (under what circumstances, if any, the agreement can be modified)

    Strict Performance (whether a party can waive an occasional "breach" by the other party without waiving other breaches or whether strict performance of the terms of the agreement will be required)

(Continued)

EXHIBIT 13.1 *(Continued)*

Dispute Resolution (method; process for selection of mediator, arbitrator, etc.; coverage of costs; binding effect)

Breach of Agreement

Attorneys' Fees

Number of counterparts executed, each constituting an original

Signature and Acknowledgment/Certification

Specific Exhibits

Alimony

Waiver(s) OR

Payment of alimony

Type (permanent, lump sum, restitution, etc.)

Amount and form of payment

Payment schedule and duration

Termination contingencies—cohabitation, death, remarriage, etc.

Modifications/cost-of-living adjustments

Intended income tax consequences (intention that payments will be tax-deductible to the payor and includable in the income of the recipient)

Security (insurance policy, trust, etc.)

Interest on unpaid balance (arrearages)

Child Custody and Visitation ("parenting time") (may be covered in a parenting plan)

Physical and legal custody—joint/sole

Allocation of decision-making responsibility (major and day-to-day)

Identification of topics considered "major" and requiring consultation (e.g., religious upbringing, education, major surgery, and participation in hazardous activities)

Parental cooperation

Access to school, medical, and dental records, etc.

Visitation/parenting time schedule

Reasonable rights based on mutual agreement

Structured

Days, weekends, weeks

Holidays

Birthdays, Mother's Day, and Father's Day

Transportation arrangements and cost

Illness—emergency medical treatment

Removal/absence from the state—temporary, long term

Contact by phone, e-mail—virtual visitation

Visitation with extended family

Adjustments to schedule—cancellation provisions

Supervised visitation, if warranted

Agreement with respect to children's surname(s)

Child Support (may be covered in a parenting plan)

Amount—relationship to guidelines

Payment schedule

Form of payment—wage assignment, if appropriate

(Continued)

EXHIBIT 13.1 *(Continued)*

Duration—definition of emancipation

Child care (built into child support formula in several states)

Modification

Expenses related to special activities

Education—elementary, secondary, postsecondary, if permitted

    Public, private

    Costs covered

    Allocation of responsibility

    Use of children's assets, scholarships, etc.

    Decision-making process and cooperation in seeking financial assistance

    Access to records

    Security for obligation (trust fund, etc.)

    Extracurricular activities (sports, music, etc.)

Dependency exemption

Treatment for tax purposes, execution of necessary tax forms

Effect of bankruptcy (not dischargeable)

Security for child support (insurance, trust for benefit of children, etc.)

Property Division

    Personal property

        Waiver of any rights to each other's property

        Delivery of documents evidencing ownership

        Vehicles

        Schedule of property already divided, if appropriate

        Property remaining to be divided—time frame and process for division

        Retirement funds—Qualified Domestic Relations Order(s)

    Real property

        Identification/description of all real property

        Disposition of each parcel—timing of conveyances, treatment of proceeds, closing costs, commissions, fees, encumbrances, shares to parties, etc.

        Assumption and/or payment of mortgages and operating expenses

        Marital home—exclusive right to occupy, responsibility for related expenses, mortgage, right of inspection, etc.

        Rights to purchase/agreements to sell

        Execution of deeds

        Tax treatment and capital gains distribution

Liabilities

    Allocation of joint debt

    Hold harmless provisions for past and future debts

    Responsibility for individual debt

Insurance

    Medical insurance

        Medical insurance for parties

        Medical insurance for children

        Name of insurer—policy number(s)

        Notice of changes

(Continued)

EXHIBIT 13.1 (*Continued*)

Payment obligations

Duration of coverage

Release from obligation (remarriage, change of employment, emancipation, etc.)

Responsibility for uninsured medical costs of spouses

Responsibility for uninsured medical costs of children

Scope of expenses included (dental, orthodontic, psychological, optical, prescriptions, etc.)

Agreement regarding elective and cosmetic surgery

Claim and reimbursement procedures

Rights under state/federal law (COBRA, etc.)

Other kinds of insurance

Life

Identify policy(ies) and ownership

Amount

Beneficiaries

Responsibility for payment

Proof of policy

Changes

Right to provide alternative coverage

Property

Liability

Automobile

Other

Taxes

Status of all prior returns (state and federal)

Allocation of refunds

Liability for past-due taxes, interest, and penalties

Notification of audits or assessments, etc.

Innocent spouse language, if appropriate

Cooperation in preparation, etc.

Bankruptcy Filing (if appropriate)

Notice of intention to file

Support obligations not dischargeable

Sample Separation Agreement

Exhibit 13.1 provides a summary of the basic elements that should be considered for inclusion in a separation agreement. The following sample agreement is based almost entirely on an agreement executed and filed in a divorce case in the Commonwealth of Massachusetts. The names of the parties have been changed and other identifying information is omitted. Some brief additions have been made to the actual text for instructional purposes. Specific terms of the agreement are tailored to the needs of a middle-income couple married for twelve years who have two minor children. They have been separated for approximately eighteen months. The parties have filed a joint petition for divorce on the grounds that irreconcilable differences have caused an irremediable breakdown of their marriage. They have reached agreement on all issues after an extended period of negotiation, initially in the context of mediation without counsel present and then with counsel. The most challenging issues for these parties involved the specific provisions concerning custody and visitation, disposition of the marital home, payment of substantial joint debt, and the parties' respective retirement funds.

The content of the sample agreement is written in "plain English" and avoids excessive use of "legalese" wherever possible. Some of the language is common boilerplate. Note that after the initial statement of facts/recitals, headings are used for each major topic. Each Article is designated with a Roman numeral and each Exhibit with a letter. Whatever system is used, it should satisfy any jurisdictional requirements and afford easy reference for the parties, counsel, and the court. Drafting and Paralegal Practice Tips appear throughout the agreement to indicate some possible variations, explanations, cautions, etc. Places in the agreement where specifics (name of the court, county, state, etc.) need to be filled in are indicated by blanks and italicized lettering.

EXHIBIT 13.2 Sample Separation Agreement

NAME OF STATE
NAME OF COURT

NAME OF COUNTY   Docket No. *14D-xxxx-DVI*

SEPARATION AGREEMENT

DRAFTING TIP

- The title of the agreement will vary according to local custom, practice, and procedure.

This Agreement ("Agreement") is made this *date* day of January 2015 by and between **Stephen Morgan** (hereinafter referred to as "**Stephen**") of *address* and **Juliana W. Morgan** (hereinafter referred to as "**Julie**"), of *address*. The term "parties," as used in this Agreement, refers to Stephen and Julie.

DRAFTING TIPS

- This is the "Identification Clause" of the Agreement. The date is often filled in by hand on the specific date of signing. The parties' names and current addresses are included, along with the names that will be used to refer to each of the parties throughout the agreement. The two most common approaches are to use the first names by which the parties are commonly known or to use "husband" and "wife." In the case of same-sex marriages, the parties may be referred to as "spouse A" and "spouse B." The use of "plaintiff" and "defendant" has fallen into disfavor with the institution of no-fault divorce, and given the potential for confusion when multiple actions are filed involving the parties.

EXHIBIT 13.2 *(Continued)*

Impounded

kept in the custody of the court and not available to the public, and, in some instances, to other parties

- If there is a history of serious abuse and/or a restraining order in force against one of the parties, the address of the other party may not appear in the agreement and also may be **impounded**.

- Some attorneys include the parties' Social Security numbers in the agreement. Most no longer do so, however, because of the potential for identity theft, given that agreements filed in divorce actions are part of a public record.

PARALEGAL PRACTICE TIP

Remember the "marital presumption" discussed in Chapter 7? Under the presumption, a husband is presumed to be the father of any children born to a woman while she is married to him or within a certain period thereafter.

STATEMENT OF FACTS

The parties were married on May 16, 2002, in Fort Lauderdale, Florida. This was the first marriage for both parties.

Two children have been born of this marriage, both minors: Robert G. Morgan, born 1/14/2005, and Jennifer Ruth Morgan, born 04/10/2008. Julie has borne no other children during the marriage.

Due to serious and irreconcilable differences that have arisen between the parties, causing the irretrievable breakdown of their marriage, Stephen and Julie separated on January 16, 2013. They continue to live separate and apart, and it is their wish and intent to remain living apart from each other.

The parties have filed a Joint Petition for Divorce (Docket No. # *number*), which is currently pending in the *name of court*.

The parties have decided to confirm their separation and effect this Agreement to settle between themselves all of the issues relating to their respective property and estate rights, spousal support, care and custody of their minor children, and all other claims and demands each might have against the other by reason of their marital relationship.

Each of them fully understands the facts, each has been fully informed of his or her legal rights and liabilities, and each signs this Agreement freely and voluntarily.

NOW, THEREFORE, in consideration of the mutual promises and covenants contained herein, the parties agree as follows:

DRAFTING TIPS

- The above section is often referred to as the "Recitals." It includes the basic facts of the case. In some models, the section begins with the heading "Witnesseth," and each paragraph begins with "Whereas. . . ."

- One of the recitals confirms that the parties have separated. Historically the courts looked with disfavor on agreements negotiated while the parties were still living together, particularly when the agreement provided that if one party subsequently filed a complaint for divorce, the other party would not appear or defend against that action (even if he or she had a valid defense). Such promises constituted a form of **collusion** or fraud on the court in order to obtain a divorce. Courts have been less concerned about such provisions since the arrival of no-fault divorce.

- If no complaint for divorce has yet been filed, the agreement should indicate what effect, if any, a subsequent filing will have on the validity of the agreement. If the complaint has been filed, the agreement may indicate the effect of a reconciliation between the parties.

Collusion

an agreement by the parties to a divorce action to jointly deceive the court as to the true nature and purpose of the action

EXHIBIT 13.2 (*Continued*)

- The fact that one of the recitals states that the agreement was signed freely and voluntarily is evidence that it was so signed, but is not necessarily dispositive. Abused spouses frequently sign agreements out of fear and a desire to escape a threatening situation, but may later challenge them once in a safe environment.

ARTICLE I SEPARATION

From this date forward, Stephen and Julie will continue to live separate and apart from each other, as if sole and unmarried, and free from the authority of or interference by the other. Each agrees to respect the other's privacy. However, the parties do not intend to create a restraining order or intend that either of them be entered on the computer tracking system for restraining orders on account of this provision or any other provision hereof.

DRAFTING TIP

- This provision is sometimes called a "Nonmolestation Clause." It does not constitute a restraining order and is not designed to prevent all contact between the parties. Rather, it serves as a confirmation that each party is free to live his or her individual life as if never married, without interference from or unwanted contact with the other party. If there is a restraining order in place, the language in this paragraph would be modified to reflect that fact.

ARTICLE II MUTUAL RELEASES

Subject to other provisions of this Agreement, each party, individually, and for his or her heirs, legal representatives, executors, administrators, and assigns, releases, and discharges the other of and from all causes of action, all claims, rights, or demands in either law or in equity, which either of the parties ever had or now has against the other or which may hereafter arise by reason of their marriage. This does not apply to any or all causes of action for this divorce, and such liabilities as may accrue or any payments due under the terms of this agreement.

DRAFTING TIP

- This general mutual release is designed to prevent postdecree litigation between the spouses for any cause of action arising out of or occurring during the marriage. For example, this provision could foreclose a wife who was physically abused during the marriage and never raised the abuse as an issue during the divorce proceeding from filing a postdivorce civil complaint seeking damages for assault and battery and intentional infliction of emotional distress. Although this may serve the interests of judicial economy and bring some closure to the parties, it does not take into consideration the dynamics of an abusive relationship. Until free and clear of the marriage, an abused spouse may not dare risk raising such an issue, and may later claim that he or she signed the agreement under duress.

ARTICLE III WAIVER OF ESTATE CLAIM

Except as otherwise provided in this Agreement, each party hereby waives and releases any and all rights that she or he may now have or hereafter acquire as spouse under the present or future laws of any jurisdiction:

  a. To elect to take against any will or codicil of the other party now or hereafter in force;
  b. To share in the other party's estate in case of intestacy; and
  c. To act as executor, personal representative or administrator of the other party's estate.

PARALEGAL PRACTICE TIP

In *In re Marriage of Grossman*, 338 Ore. 99, 106 P.3d 618 (2005), the parties executed a marital settlement agreement, separated briefly, and then reconciled and lived together for another ten years before seeking to dissolve their marriage. The husband then sought to enforce their earlier agreement. The wife successfully argued that the court should divide their property in a "just and proper" manner under the applicable state statute without enforcing their initial agreement, given the long period of time since it was signed. The opinion in this case can be found at *www.pearsonhighered .com/careersresources/* in the website material related to Chapter 13 under Cases.

PARALEGAL PRACTICE TIP

This release extends to a variety of kinds of actions. For example, in *Watkins v. Watkins*, 152 Conn. App. 99, 96 A.3d 1264 (2014), a former wife was precluded by a "mutual releases" provision in a separation agreement from bringing a negligence action against her husband based on an incident that occurred during the marriage which caused her personal injuries.

EXHIBIT 13.2 *(Continued)*

Both parties intend that their respective estates shall be administered as though no marriage between them ever existed. However, each is specifically not waiving any rights he or she may have in: (1) claims against the other's estate by reason of a breach of this Agreement; (2) any testamentary provisions that are voluntarily made for his or her benefit by the other; and/or (3) any rights either may have to Social Security benefits by virtue of their marriage to the other.

DRAFTING TIPS

- Generally, a divorce automatically revokes bequests to a former spouse unless otherwise provided in a will. However, the revocation is not effective until the divorce is granted and the parties are no longer "spouses." It is therefore wise for the parties to cover the time period between the date of separation and the date of divorce in their agreement, especially if there will be an extended period of separation.
- The personal representative of a decedent (executor, administrator, etc.) may be required to satisfy remaining alimony, child support, and property division obligations under the agreement from the assets of the decedent's estate.

ARTICLE IV EXECUTION OF IMPLEMENTING DOCUMENTS

Within a reasonable time after this Agreement has been signed, each party will execute, seal, deliver, file, or record such bills of sale, deeds, leases, waivers, or other instruments or documents as the other party requests and may reasonably require to effectuate the terms of this Agreement.

DRAFTING TIP

- Some agreements expressly provide that if either party fails to comply with the provisions of this paragraph, the agreement itself will constitute a satisfactory substitute for the unexecuted document. However, third parties may not be satisfied with this alternative to an executed deed or transfer of title of a vehicle or boat, etc. A party's failure to comply with this Article that results in damages to the other party also may constitute a breach of the agreement.

ARTICLE V ACKNOWLEDGMENT OF THE PARTIES

Each party to this Agreement acknowledges and agrees:

a. that each is represented by a competent attorney of her or his own choosing or has freely chosen not to be represented;

b. that each of the parties has made full disclosure of his or her respective assets and liabilities, that each is satisfied with the disclosure provided by the other and foregoes further discovery, and that this Agreement is entered into with sufficient knowledge of the financial circumstances and needs of the other party;

c. that each has carefully read this Agreement, has discussed it with his or her respective counsel, understands the provisions contained within it, and considers the Agreement to be fair and reasonable;

d. that this Agreement is not the product of fraud or coercion; and

e. that this Agreement is fair and reasonable at the time it is being signed and at the time it is being submitted to the court as part of the parties' divorce proceedings.

DRAFTING TIPS

- The "acknowledgments" in this Article are sometimes called "representations" and may appear in separate Articles to highlight their importance.

PARALEGAL PRACTICE TIP

Some states, such as Ohio, have case law and statutes providing that a final decree of legal separation terminates the rights of a surviving spouse unless the parties' separation agreement provides otherwise. See, e.g., *Dragovich v. Dragovich*, 2012 Ohio 4114, 976 N.E.2d 920 (Ohio App. 2012).

PARALEGAL PRACTICE TIP

Sometimes the parties' counsel are specifically identified especially in jurisdictions where they are required to co-sign the agreement.

EXHIBIT 13.2 *(Continued)*

- When only one party is represented by counsel, courts may be reluctant to approve or enforce an agreement if it appears that the unrepresented party did not understand the effect of the agreement or was pressured to sign it under duress. In such circumstances, it is wise to include language such as the following: "Husband acknowledges that this agreement was drafted by wife's attorney, that he has been advised to seek independent counsel, and that he has declined to do so of his own volition."

- Occasionally, when one party is represented by counsel and the other is not, the agreement is lopsided in favor of the represented party. Before issuing a decree, the court may require the unrepresented party to seek counsel for the limited purpose of reviewing the agreement and ensuring that he or she understands its terms and the impact of any rights that may be waived, etc.

- (Article V b) provides an example of when boilerplate might be dangerous. In this case, the parties believed there was full disclosure. However, if a party has been concealing assets that have not been located despite due diligence or if a client has refused to pursue adequate discovery despite counsel's recommendation, this language may be modified to provide for later discovered assets presently "unknown" to either party. For example, "The parties further agree that any intentional material misrepresentation by either of them in his or her financial statement shall be grounds to seek **rescission** of the agreement or other equitable relief. In the alternative, it will constitute grounds for seeking modification of any court order or judgment incorporating the terms of this agreement or for objecting to consideration of the agreement in any subsequent legal proceeding between the parties or their personal representatives, heirs, or assigns."

- Either here or elsewhere in the agreement, there usually is a reference to attorneys' fees, for example, "Except as herein otherwise provided, each party agrees to pay his or her own attorney's fees incurred in negotiation, preparation, and execution of this agreement." (See Article XIV.)

Rescission
the cancellation or unmaking of a contract for a legally sufficient reason

ARTICLE VI SITUS

This Agreement shall be construed, governed, and enforced in accordance with the applicable laws of the state of *name of state*.

ARTICLE VII VALIDITY/SEVERABILITY

In the event that any provision of this Agreement is held to be invalid and unenforceable, such invalidity shall not invalidate the whole agreement, but the remaining provisions of this Agreement shall continue to be valid and binding to the extent that such provisions reflect fairly the intent and understanding of the parties at the time of execution.

DRAFTING TIP

- This clause is a "severability" or "savings" provision. It provides, for example, that if the Exhibit pertaining to alimony is held to be invalid as violating public policy, the rest of the Agreement will still be valid and enforceable.

ARTICLE VIII ENTIRE AGREEMENT

There are no representations, warrantees, conditions, promises, or undertakings other than those set forth in this Agreement, which contains the entire agreement of the parties.

PARALEGAL PRACTICE TIP

Illustrative case: In *Filstein v. Bromberg*, 944 N.Y.S.2d 692 (App. Div. 2012), the parties' agreement contained a "no-divorce" provision requiring them to sell the marital residence as a condition precedent to either party filing for divorce. The clause was determined to be void as against public policy but because it was severable, the agreement was otherwise enforceable.

PARALEGAL PRACTICE TIP

"Side agreements" can cause problems for both clients and attorneys. In *Reaser v. Reaser*, 2004 SD 116, 688 N.W.2d 429 (2004), for example, the husband initiated divorce proceedings against his wife in January 1999. He was represented by counsel, but she was not. The parties entered a stipulation prepared by the husband's attorney that addressed child custody, child support, alimony, and property division. Under the agreement, he was to have custody of the children and she waived any claim to alimony. He relieved her of any claim for child support. The judge refused to grant the divorce because the stipulation did not provide for child support. The parties then modified the stipulation to establish a child support obligation for the wife, but prior to submitting it to the court, the husband's attorney drafted a "document of private agreement" in which the wife "was to have no duty to pay ongoing [child] support despite the language of the Divorce Decree." This "private agreement" was kept in the lawyer's office and was not disclosed to the judge, who subsequently approved the second stipulation. In 2002, the wife sought a change in custody and child support. During the course of the hearing, the "private agreement" came to light! The South Dakota Supreme Court affirmed a trial court's decision to set aside the divorce decree by reason of fraud upon the court. The Court described the conduct of the parties and the attorney as "egregious conduct involving corruption of the judicial process itself." It also opined that it may have violated a criminal statute and clearly constituted a violation of the attorney's professional duty of candor before the court. The opinion in this case can be found at *www.pearsonhighered.com/careersresources/* in the website material related to Chapter 13 under Cases.

EXHIBIT 13.2 *(Continued)*

DRAFTING TIP

- Any "side" agreements between the parties are unenforceable and in the extreme may invalidate the entire agreement if they appear to constitute a fraud upon the court.

ARTICLE IX EFFECTIVE DATE

This Agreement shall be effective upon execution by the parties.

ARTICLE X BINDING EFFECT

Except as otherwise stated herein, all the provisions of this Agreement shall be binding upon the respective heirs, next of kin, trustees in bankruptcy, personal representatives, executors, administrators, and assigns of the parties.

ARTICLE XI INDEPENDENT CONTRACT

This Agreement may be submitted to any court before which any Complaint or proceeding for divorce or dissolution of marriage shall be tried, and in the event that a Judgment of Divorce shall be entered, the same shall incorporate in full or in substance the provisions of this Agreement and the Agreement shall be incorporated and not merged but shall survive as a document having independent legal significance, and the property settlement and any alimony provisions herein shall forever be binding upon the parties. Notwithstanding the foregoing, any provisions of this Agreement relating to children who are not emancipated shall remain modifiable by the court upon a change in governing law, a material change in circumstances of a party or a child, or if a modification is consistent with the best interests of the child.

DRAFTING TIPS

- If the agreement merges in the decree, this Article will reflect that distinction. For example, "After approval of this agreement it shall be incorporated and merge in the final judgment of divorce and may not be altered or modified except pursuant to the court's order."
- The parents cannot bargain away the rights of their children, and all child-related provisions remain subject to the continuing jurisdiction of the court.

ARTICLE XII MODIFICATION

A modification or waiver of any of the provisions of this Agreement shall be effective only if made in writing and executed with the same formality as this Agreement or by order of a court of competent jurisdiction.

ARTICLE XIII STRICT PERFORMANCE

The failure of either party to insist upon strict performance of any of the provisions of this Agreement shall not be construed as a waiver of any subsequent default of the same or a similar nature.

DRAFTING TIP

- This paragraph provides that if, for example, Julie chooses to excuse Stephen's failure to pay child support for the month of December because he is experiencing a temporary financial crisis, she is not agreeing to excuse his failure to pay support in any other past or future months. Rather, she can insist that the agreement be enforced with respect to those other periods. Such "informal" waivers of breach do not deprive the court of its ultimate jurisdiction over child-related issues and may occur at the risk of either or both parties.

EXHIBIT 13.2 *(Continued)*

ARTICLE XIV RESOLUTION OF DISPUTES, BREACH OF AGREEMENT, AND ATTORNEYS' FEES

Except as herein otherwise provided, Stephen and Julie will each pay their own attorneys' fees incurred in connection with negotiation of this Agreement and the pending Joint Petition for Divorce.

In the event that a dispute arises between the parties regarding any of the provisions of this Agreement that Stephen and Julie are unable to resolve on their own or with the assistance of counsel, they agree that prior to filing any legal action in court, they will make an effort to resolve the dispute through mediation at Thomas Kelley and Associates or another similar agency mutually agreed upon. The fees and costs of the mediation shall be borne equally by the parties unless the court later determines that the actions of one party were so unreasonable as to require such mediation, in which case, the party responsible for the unreasonable action shall be liable for that portion of the fees and costs that the court deems equitable. Nothing in this paragraph shall prevent either party from proceeding directly to court or pursuing any other legal remedy if either party defaults on a financial obligation under this Agreement.

If either party commits a breach of any provisions of this Agreement and legal action is reasonably required to enforce such provisions and is instituted by the nonbreaching party, the party in breach shall be liable to the party who prevails in the court action for all statutory interest from the date of breach and for all court costs and reasonable attorneys' fees incurred in instituting and prosecuting such action. If either party brings legal action against the other on frivolous, insubstantial grounds or in bad faith, and does not prevail in that action, then the prevailing party shall be awarded reasonable attorneys' fees and other costs and expenses incurred in defending against such action.

DRAFTING TIP

- If one of the parties promises in the agreement to pay the fees of the other party, the attorney for that other party becomes a creditor of, and can seek to recover fees directly from, the promisor as a **third-party beneficiary** of the contract between the parties.

Third-party beneficiary
a person who, though not a party to a contract, benefits from performance of the contract

ARTICLE XV ARTICLE HEADINGS OF NO EFFECT

The headings at the beginning of each Article and Exhibit of this Agreement are included for convenience and reference purposes only and do not constitute terms or conditions of the Agreement.

ARTICLE XVI EXHIBITS

There are annexed hereto and incorporated by reference Exhibits A through K. Stephen and Julie agree to be bound by and to perform and carry out all of the terms contained in said Exhibits to the same extent as if each Exhibit was fully set forth in the text of this Agreement.

Exhibits A through K are enforceable and may not be discharged in any bankruptcy action brought by or against either of the parties, as they are necessary provisions for the support and maintenance of the other as a consequence of disparities in income, the special needs of the parties, and the allocation of resources.

IN WITNESS WHEREOF the parties have signed, sealed, and acknowledged this Agreement in three (3) counterparts, each of which shall constitute an original.

Witnesses to Husband's Signature

_____

_____   _____
                                 Stephen Morgan
                                 Date:_____

Witnesses to Wife's Signature

_____

_____   _____
                                 Juliana W. Morgan
                                 Date:_____

PARALEGAL PRACTICE TIP

Attention must be paid to execution formalities. An unsigned agreement will not be valid and binding on a party who did not sign it and who denies agreeing to the document. See, e.g., *Ballinger v. Ballinger*, 2015 Ohio 590 (Ohio App. 2015).

EXHIBIT 13.2 *(Continued)*

DRAFTING TIPS

- The signature section should comply with any governing procedural requirements. For example, some states require each signature to be witnessed by two disinterested parties. Others require counsel to sign the agreement as well as the client.

- The names used by the parties should conform to the names used in the underlying action for divorce or legal separation.

CERTIFICATION

STATE
COUNTY_____

On this _____ day of January 2015, personally appeared JULIANA W. MORGAN, known to me to be the person whose name is subscribed to the within instrument and acknowledged that she executed the same for the purposes therein set forth, as her own free act and deed, before me.

　　IN WITNESS WHEREOF, I hereunto set my hand and official seal.

　　　　　　　　　　　　　　　　　　　　　　_____

　　　　　　　　　　　　　　　　　　　　　　Notary/Justice of the Peace
　　　　　　　　　　　　　　　　　　　　　　(Seal)

STATE
COUNTY_____

On this _____ day of January 2015, personally appeared STEPHEN MORGAN, known to me to be the person whose name is subscribed to the within instrument and acknowledged that he executed the same for the purposes therein set forth, as his own free act and deed, before me.

　　IN WITNESS WHEREOF, I hereunto set my hand and official seal.

　　　　　　　　　　　　　　　　　　　　　　_____

　　　　　　　　　　　　　　　　　　　　　　Notary/Justice of the Peace
　　　　　　　　　　　　　　　　　　　　　　(Seal)

EXHIBIT A

ALIMONY

A.1　Each party currently receives income and incurs expenses at a level consistent with the financial statements filed at the time of the final hearing on this matter, which statements are incorporated herein.

A.2　Each party is able to provide for his or her own needs without any support or contribution from the other party.

A.3　Julie waives any and all right to alimony, past, present, and future from Stephen to the extent permitted by law.

A.4　Stephen waives any and all right to alimony, past, present, and future from Julie to the extent permitted by law.

A.5　Each party understands that this waiver of alimony can be forever binding and intends that his/her waiver be so binding on him/her even if the circumstances of either party change with the passage of time.

DRAFTING TIPS

- Depending on the jurisdiction and circumstances, alimony may be referred to as spousal support, separate maintenance, or by some other designation.

EXHIBIT 13.2 (*Continued*)

- Because of the parties' limited resources and the fact that each of them is presently employed and able to be self-supporting if necessary, Stephen and Julie have chosen to permanently waive alimony. Assuming they remain healthy and employed, this may not present a problem, but what if one of them should hit the lottery and the other become indigent? Some courts do not look favorably on permanent alimony waivers even if they are "voluntary, knowing, and intelligent." Counsel must make every effort to ensure that the parties understand the potential consequences of such waivers and, in the alternative, that ultimately they may be unenforceable under certain conditions (extreme hardship, debilitating illness, the likelihood of one of the parties becoming a public charge, etc.).

- For a discussion of terms commonly included in alimony provisions in separation agreements when a party will be granted alimony, see Chapter 11.

- In some situations, the parties may agree to a flexible approach to alimony payments. For example, if the obligor's sole income is from an ice cream stand he owns and operates twelve hours a day from April 1 through October 1 each year, the parties may agree that alimony will be paid only during that six-month period when there is a steady flow of income. If the obligor's employment is steady, the alimony amount may be a fixed amount or be based on his or her adjusted gross income for tax purposes. Sometimes agreements will provide that alimony will be adjusted based on changes in the income level of the recipient.

- Some jurisdictions hold that if alimony is not awarded in the final decree, it cannot be sought at a later date. In such circumstances, the parties may agree to a nominal alimony award of $1.00 simply to preserve their options.

- Largely depending on the jurisdiction, an alimony provision may designate the type of alimony to be paid (rehabilitative, permanent, restitution, etc.).

EXHIBIT B

CHILD CUSTODY AND VISITATION

B.1 Stephen and Julie shall have joint legal custody and Julie shall have physical custody of the two minor children. The parents agree that it is of paramount importance for each of them to remain involved in the major parental decisions and guidance of the children, for the children to feel deep affection for each parent, and for each parent to foster and nurture in the children respect and affection for the other parent, to the end that each parent's relationship with the children will remain as close as possible. Accordingly, each parent agrees to keep the other well and promptly informed of the academic, physical, emotional, and social status and activities of each child. Each parent may, without further permission of the other, review all school, medical, dental, and other reports or written communications concerning the welfare of the children, and consult with individuals providing medical, psychological, dental, educational, or other services for either or both children. Each may give authorization for provision of emergency services for the children. Each also may exercise sole authority and responsibility for decisions concerning the daily living needs and activities of a child while in his or her physical custody.

B.2 The parties shall consult on significant issues concerning the welfare of each child, including, but not limited to, medical, mental health, and dental treatment; religious education; educational choices and alternatives; social and recreational activities, including participation in any inherently dangerous or unusual activities; and the time spent with each of the parties.

PARALEGAL PRACTICE TIP

When there is more than one minor child, the agreement may include a parenting/custody provision for each child. This is especially likely if custody is split or there are significant differences in the ages of the children and/or the nature of their relationships with each parent.

PARALEGAL PRACTICE TIP

If there are serious communication problems between the parents regarding the children, a parent coordinator may be appointed by the court. In such cases, the agreement will usually include a detailed provision regarding the selection, appointment, funding, and role of the coordinator.

EXHIBIT 13.2 *(Continued)*

PARALEGAL PRACTICE TIP

If a child already has problems, the agreement should include a detailed provision regarding counseling/treatment.

    a. If either parent learns that a child is engaged in activities involving alcohol, tobacco, a controlled substance, pornography, body piercings/tattoos, weapons, or bullying, he or she will promptly notify the other parent so the parties can attempt to reach consensus as to how the matter will be addressed.

    b. Each parent has the right to manage communication devices, media access, and Internet-based accounts used by the children when with that parent and may impose controls or limitations deemed appropriate with the goal of promoting safe and appropriate use of such devices.

B.3   Stephen's visitation rights shall remain open and liberal at all reasonable times and places as agreed between the parties, subject to timely advance notice to Julie and the school schedule and activities of the children. However, in the event that the parties are unable to agree as to reasonable visitation rights, the following schedule will define minimum visitation rights.

    a. Stephen will pick up the children at Julie's residence at 6:00 p.m. on the second and fourth Fridays of each month for the weekend, and will return them on Sunday afternoon at 4:00 p.m.

    b. On each Wednesday evening, Stephen will pick up the children at Julie's residence at 5:30 p.m. and return them at 8:30 p.m. (unless otherwise agreed).

    c. The parties agree to alternate the major holidays such that if the children spend Christmas Day of 2015 with one parent, they will spend Christmas Day of 2016 with the other parent and so on. This provision will affect the following holidays:

Christmas Eve

Christmas Day

Thanksgiving

Easter

Independence Day

Halloween

    d. In 2015, the children will be with Julie on Easter, Thanksgiving Day and Christmas Eve 5 p.m. to 9 a.m. Christmas morning and with Stephen on Independence Day, Halloween and Christmas Day from 9:00 a.m. to 9:00 p.m. In 2016, they will be with Julie on Independence Day, Halloween, and Christmas Day and with Stephen on Easter, Thanksgiving, and Christmas Eve from 5:00 p.m. to 9:00 a.m. Christmas morning.

    e. The children will spend Father's Day with Stephen and Mother's Day with Julie (from 10:00 a.m. to 8:00 p.m. if there is a conflict with another visitation provision). Stephen and Julie will make arrangements such that the children are able to spend some portion of each parent's birthday with that parent.

    f. Stephen and Julie agree that they each should be able to spend time with them on the children's birthdays. They agree that each child should have a single birthday party at which both parents will be present. The parent who has physical custody of the child on the day of the birthday will be responsible for planning and paying for the costs of the party.

    g. The children shall spend a total of four weeks with Stephen during the summer months (July and August) in two uninterrupted two-week periods in addition to the full week of the February school vacation.

    h. Unless otherwise agreed, Stephen will be responsible for any transportation of the children necessary to implement the visitation provisions of this Agreement.

B.4   During any period when a child is in the physical custody of the other parent, the absent parent shall have the right to communicate with the child by phone and/or electronic means at all reasonable times. The parties agree that they will not use the children as the means of communicating with each other and that they will communicate directly.

B.5   Stephen and Julie acknowledge that at some future time, either or both of them may marry again. Until that time, when the children are present, neither parent will entertain an overnight guest with whom he or she has an intimate sexual relationship. Each parent will notify the

EXHIBIT 13.2 (*Continued*)

other if a new significant relationship develops and will limit the children's involvement with that person until a committed relationship is established.

B.6 In the event of any serious illness of a child, the parent with whom the child is then staying shall immediately notify the other parent and, under such circumstances, shall permit the other party to visit the sick child upon reasonable notice and request.

B.7 Neither party shall permanently remove the children from the state or change the children's principal residence more than twenty-five miles from their current residence in *location* without obtaining prior written consent of the other party, or, if said consent is denied, the permission of the *name of court* pursuant to applicable state law.

B.8 Both parties shall have the right to take trips with the children, including the right to take the children out-of-state for trips and vacations that are temporary in nature, but shall notify the other parent in advance of such trips and vacations. This provision shall include the making of a "safe call" after arrival at the destination, advising the other parent of the arrival, where the children will be staying, and how the other parent may reach the children by telephone or other means.

B.9 The parties agree that it is important for the children to maintain an ongoing relationship with each of their extended families, including, among others, grandparents, aunts, uncles, and cousins, and each will seek to foster and support those relationships.

B.10 The parties acknowledge that there will be occasions when something occurs that may require an adjustment in the visitation schedule, such as an illness, a school trip, or a major work-related commitment. When such situations arise, Stephen and Julie agree to make every effort to accommodate them and ensure that Stephen does not experience any loss in overall visitation time.

PARALEGAL PRACTICE TIP

Some agreements contain provisions regarding international travel particularly to non-Hague Convention countries.

DRAFTING TIPS

- The agreement should use the appropriate terminology pertaining to custody in the jurisdiction, for example, primary/secondary parent, custodial/noncustodial parent, or residential/nonresidential parent. Many states require that a primary caretaker be designated.

- Any agreement made by the parties concerning child custody remains subject to the continuing jurisdiction of the court and is modifiable based upon a change in circumstances and what will serve the best interests of the child.

- Although the courts cannot realistically enforce parental cooperation clauses, they may penalize a parent who actively seeks to alienate a child from the other parent or who obstructs the other parent's custodial or visitation privileges. Some states, such as Tennessee, require that Marital Dissolution Agreements and Parenting Plans include a list of the statutorily guaranteed rights of noncustodial parents.

- The nature of a custody and visitation provision depends heavily on the extent to which the parties are able to communicate with each other. The provisions in this particular agreement are quite specific, in an effort to minimize questions and misunderstandings between parties who have a history of conflict about child-related issues.

- When the parties have been separated for an extended period and communicate effectively with each other, they may already have in place an acceptable custody and visitation plan. In such situations, the Custody and Visitation Exhibit may simply state that the noncustodial parent shall have reasonable visitation with the child at all times mutually agreed upon by the parties.

EXHIBIT 13.2 (*Continued*)

- The right to access medical and school records in B.1, etc., may be restricted if an abuse order is in effect or if necessary to otherwise protect a parent or the children.

- This sample agreement involves a situation in which the parties reside within ten miles of each other. Significant variations necessarily occur when parents reside at a considerable geographical distance. Although the noncustodial parent may have as much visitation in real time as he or she would have if the parents lived in close proximity, it is likely to occur in large blocks of time. In such situations, provisions may also address telephone access, virtual visitation, and transportation costs, if not already factored into child support.

EXHIBIT C

CHILD SUPPORT

C.1   Commencing the first month after execution of this Agreement and continuing each month thereafter until the children are emancipated, as hereinafter defined, Stephen will pay $_____ per week to Julie as child support, said amount being consistent with the state's child support guidelines. The payment shall be sent or delivered so that it is received by Julie no later than the first day of each month.

C.2   Currently, the child support obligation is based on the parties having two children who are not emancipated. The parties agree that, when either child becomes emancipated, as defined below, the amount of child support Stephen pays will be adjusted accordingly without need for intervention from the *name of court*. The adjusted Child Support obligation shall be consistent with the amount for the remaining one minor child under the state's Child Support Guidelines in effect at the time of the first child's emancipation.

C.3   Emancipation with respect to each minor child shall occur on the earliest to happen of the following:

   a. At age eighteen (18) or graduation from high school, but not later than at age 20, which-ever occurs later, unless the child is pursuing postsecondary schooling as a full-time student as defined in b) below.

   b. At age twenty-three (23), if a child is attending an accredited postsecondary educational training school or a two-year or four-year college program as a full-time student, such schooling has not been completed, and the child is still a dependent of the parents;

   c. At the completion of schooling as it is defined in b) above;

   d. Death or marriage of the child;

   e. Permanent residency away from the custodial parent's home. Residency at boarding school, camp, or college (if the child is engaged in activities pursuant to a) and b) above) is not to be deemed a permanent residence away from the custodial parent's home.

   f. Engaging in full-time employment, including the military, after the age of eighteen (18), except that full-time employment during vacation and summer periods shall not be deemed emancipation. Such emancipation shall be deemed to terminate upon cessation by the child for any reason of full-time employment, including the military, provided the child thereafter becomes engaged in activities pursuant to a) or b) above, or other applicable provisions of this paragraph.

C.4   Any payment of support as required by this Agreement may be made in cash or by check or money order payable to Julie. Child support shall not be paid by wage assignment, except as may hereafter be required by a court of competent jurisdiction or any applicable federal or state statute, rule, or regulation, or in the event that Stephen breaches this provision of the Agreement. If Stephen falls behind in child support payments by three or more months, Julie will utilize the services of the state's IV-D agency to secure payment of past-due and future payments.

C.5   Upon request of either party, before February 15 in any year in which Stephen is obligated to pay child support, the parties agree to exchange W-2 forms. Either party may seek a change in the amount of the child support obligation upon a material change in circumstances.

EXHIBIT 13.2 *(Continued)*

C.6   The parties agree that they will consult with each other regarding extracurricular activities and agree to share equally the mutually agreed-upon expenses of said activities for the children, which shall include but not be limited to driving, music and dance lessons, sports and sports-related equipment and clothing, and summer camp.

C.7   The parties agree that their children should receive the best education available to them, including education at the college level. They further agree that choices of educational institutions for the children shall be made on the basis of joint consultation with due regard for the parties' financial circumstances and the children's aptitudes and interests. It shall be the children's and the custodial parent's obligation to consult with the other parent and come to an agreement regarding reasonable and affordable postsecondary schooling for the children. To the extent that they are then financially able to do so, the parties shall contribute equally to the net expenses of postsecondary education for their children who are not emancipated to the extent that educational expenses are not otherwise covered by scholarships, grants, loans, and the children's savings and earnings. For purposes of this Exhibit, the term "expenses" shall include application fees and related before-college expenses, tuition, board, room, books, uniforms (if required), basic computer equipment, usual and normal student activity fees and other expenses normally charged on college or university bills, and a reasonable allowance for transportation to and from such institution. The parties agree to cooperate with each other in applying for financial aid. However, it shall be the children's obligation to pursue scholarships, grants, loans, and other financial aid, as well as to contribute earnings from summer jobs and other part-time employment. The parents' obligation shall extend only to those costs not covered by the foregoing and shall be capped at the tuition level of the highest-cost in-state public university. The obligation to contribute to schooling shall terminate upon a child's emancipation.

C.8   The parties hereby agree that all payments designated for the support and maintenance of the minor children under the terms of this Agreement are exclusively for child support and maintenance, and further agree that such payments shall be excludable from Julie's gross income and nondeductible by Stephen subject to the law governing such deductions on any future federal or state income tax returns.

C.9   The parties agree that for the tax year beginning on January 1, 2015, and as to any tax year thereafter, Julie shall be entitled to claim the dependency exemption for Robert, and Stephen shall be entitled to claim the exemption for Jennifer, subject to applicable federal and state laws. When Robert becomes emancipated, the parties will claim the exemption for Jennifer in alternate years with Julie taking the exemption in the first tax year. Julie agrees to execute any tax forms necessary to enable Stephen to claim an exemption under the terms of this Agreement. In the event that the dependency exemption results in no tax benefit for the party entitled to take it in a given year, then he or she shall notify the other party no later than March 1 of that year to allow the other party to claim the unutilized exemption.

C.10 Stephen's obligation to make payments for the support and maintenance of the minor children under this section of the Agreement is an obligation in the nature of support as defined under the relevant provisions of the United States Bankruptcy Code, as amended, and the said obligation shall not be dischargeable in bankruptcy. In the event that any arrearages for support due to Julie under this Exhibit, or any obligation to make future payments due under the Agreement, shall be discharged in bankruptcy, Julie shall have the unrestricted right to seek appropriate relief in any court of competent jurisdiction to obtain further orders of support.

PARALEGAL PRACTICE TIP

In *Milark v. Meigher*, 17 A.D.3d 844, 793 N.Y.S.2d 581 (2005), the parties' agreement provided that "the parties shall equally divide all primary and secondary school tuition, the cost of all school supplies, all mutually acceptable extracurricular activities,. . ." At the time the agreement was executed, the children were enrolled in private school. After two years, the wife failed to pay her share of the private school tuition, claiming unsuccessfully, among other things, that she should not be compelled to pay private school tuition when the community makes available a public school. The court reasoned that if private school were not contemplated, the agreement would not have referred to "tuition." This case can be accessed at *www .pearsonhighered.com/careersresources/* in the website material related to Chapter 13 under Cases.

DRAFTING TIPS

- Because of the circumstances and conflict between the parties in this case, this is an extensive and detailed child support provision.
- Although it is not necessarily stated in an agreement, clients paying child or spousal support are usually advised to make all payments by direct deposit, check or money order (NOT in cash) so that their payments are documented.

EXHIBIT 13.2 *(Continued)*

- Child support provisions remain subject to the continuing jurisdiction of the court. Modifications are governed by state law. If permitted in the jurisdiction, some parties build an annual review process into the agreement. Even if the parties agree to a change, child support is an order of the court, and any changes should be approved by the court to avoid a later contempt claim.

- Although the terms of the agreement provide that the obligor's child support obligations will not be dischargeable, that determination is ultimately made by the bankruptcy court.

- Occasionally, child support and alimony/spousal support payments are lumped together ("unallocated"). To minimize potential tax problems, it is often better to differentiate between them. For tax purposes, alimony is deductible to the payor and income to the recipient, and child support is neither.

- Many agreements provide that the obligor will maintain a life insurance policy in a set amount for the benefit of the minor children. It is designed to guarantee an income source for the children in case the parent with the child support obligation should die prematurely. Another option is to establish a trust fund as in Exhibit H of this agreement.

- Courts in several states will no longer order a parent to pay a child's college expenses. This particular agreement reflects the law in Massachusetts (as of 2015), a state that still strongly supports a parental duty to provide the costs of a child's basic college expenses, up to the age of twenty-three under some circumstances. Although the agreement references educational contributions by the children, it does not bind them to those obligations because they are not parties to the agreement.

- If the minor children are enrolled in private school, related decisions and expenses should be addressed in the agreement.

- In some states, child care costs are factored into the child support formula. If not, they should be addressed in the agreement.

EXHIBIT D

DIVISION OF PERSONAL PROPERTY

D.1   Except as otherwise specifically provided in this Agreement, Stephen and Julie have already divided their personal property. Each agrees that from now on each shall continue to possess, own, have, and enjoy independently of any claim of right of the other, all of his or her personal property of every kind, nature, and description with full power to dispose of the same as fully and with such effect in all respects and for all purposes as though he or she were unmarried.

D.2   Julie specifically waives any right, title, interest, or claim she may have to the proceeds, if any, of a settlement or judgment obtained by Stephen in connection with a pending personal injury action filed by him relating to a motorcycle accident on January 1, 2012, in which he received extensive injuries.

D.3   The parties agree that all of the personal property (books, records, tools, etc.) currently stored in the shed in the yard at the marital home located at *location* presently belongs to Stephen. With reasonable notice to Julie, he will remove the property within thirty (30) days of the execution of this Agreement. If not removed within thirty (30) days, the property will belong to Julie, who will be free to keep, sell, or destroy it as she sees fit.

D.4   Each party shall deliver to the other all property or documents evidencing ownership of property that, by the terms of the Agreement, is to remain or become the property of the other. All property acquired from now on by either Stephen or Julie and all income and earnings of each party shall constitute and be the sole and separate property of the person by whom the said property is acquired or earned.

EXHIBIT 13.2 *(Continued)*

D.5   Each party shall retain as his or her sole property free of any claim of right of the other the vehicle in his (the Dodge truck) or her (the Toyota Camry) possession and shall be solely obligated for payment of any expenses incurred for use, operation, maintenance, and financing thereof. Each shall indemnify and hold the other harmless from any liens or debts in connection with the vehicle he or she is retaining.

D.6   If permitted by club rules, the parties will continue to hold a family membership in the American Yacht Club with each party paying half of the annual dues and assessments. In the event that, as a result of the divorce, they are not permitted to continue their "family" membership, Stephen will relinquish his membership card to Julie and thereafter she will be responsible for all expenses in connection with the membership.

DRAFTING TIPS

- Depending on the nature and extent of the parties' personal property, the various items assigned to each party may be listed to avoid confusion (e.g., "Husband receives his Roth IRA account *identifying information*; the joint savings account at First Third Bank, account # *number*; his General Electric pension *identifying information*; and his baseball card collection. Wife receives her 401(k) account *identifying information*; her pension *identifying information*, her china collection, her jewelry, bank CD *identifying information*, and three checking accounts: bank account # *number*, bank account # *number*, and bank account # *number*."). When the assets are specified in such a manner, it makes it more difficult for a party to claim later that a particular asset on the list was not disclosed and distributed at the time of divorce. However, the account numbers and values may be provided on separate schedules for each party and a request may be made to impound the schedules with other financial information to reduce the potential for identity theft.

- Ideally, the parties should divide their personal property prior to executing the agreement in order to avoid problems post divorce. Paragraph D.3 gives the husband the opportunity to collect his possessions that are still stored on the marital property where the wife now resides. However, by establishing a reasonable time frame, it does not grant him an unlimited opportunity to do so. If the property remaining to change hands is not all conveniently located in one place (the shed, in this instance), the items should be specifically listed, if possible, to avoid disputes and misunderstandings. In extremely high-conflict cases in which a restraining order is in force, the agreement may set a particular time for the pickup and require that a police officer be present.

- The personal property of most divorcing couples is of modest value. However, parties in some divorce actions own substantial assets such as business interests; valuable antiques and artworks; stock portfolios; and rights to receive funds in the future, such as contingent fees for services performed during the marriage. To avoid confusion and subsequent litigation, these assets should be specifically addressed in the agreement. A schedule reflecting the division of this property also may be appended to the agreement.

EXHIBIT E

REAL ESTATE

E.1   Stephen and Julie own real property, the marital home, located at *location*, as tenants by the entirety, having taken title by deed dated May 18, 2002, recorded in the *name of county* Registry of Deeds in Book 7539, page 031. The property is encumbered by two mortgages on which Stephen and Julie are co-signors and co-mortgagors, dated May 18, 2002, and June 13, 2009, both to Berger Mortgage, Inc., and each secured by the marital home. The first is a purchase

EXHIBIT 13.2 (*Continued*)

money mortgage with a remaining principal balance of $124,000. It is recorded at the above-referenced Registry in Book 7539, page 045. The second mortgage recorded in Book 9887, page 331, was obtained in order to pay off jointly incurred marital debt of the parties. The remaining principal balance on this account is $21,900.

E.2 The parties agree that Julie shall have exclusive possession, use, and control of the marital home effective upon the execution of this Agreement.

E.3 Within ninety (90) days of execution of this Agreement, Stephen shall convey his interest in the above property to Julie by quitclaim deed.

E.4 Julie agrees that within ninety (90) days of execution of this Agreement, she shall obtain financing sufficient to:

a. pay off both of the outstanding mortgages referenced in E.1 above; and

b. pay Stephen the sum of fifty thousand dollars ($50,000) for his equity interest in the marital home, which the parties agree is currently valued at $270,000 based on the appraisal completed by Marjorie Anderson, a mutually agreed-upon licensed appraiser.

E.5 Julie further agrees that from the time of her receipt of the deed from Stephen, she shall indemnify and hold him harmless from any responsibility for all sums due, and that may become due in the future, on the two outstanding mortgages.

E.6 Both Stephen and Julie understand that Sections 1041(a) and (b) of the U.S. Internal Revenue Code of 1980, as amended, are applicable to the conveyance and transfer described in E.3 above; that no gain or loss will be recognized by Stephen upon his conveyance or transfer of any property interest to Julie; and that Julie will have a carryover basis in said property and receive Stephen's interest at his adjusted cost basis. Each party will provide the other with any and all documentation in his or her possession and control establishing the cost basis of the property.

DRAFTING TIPS

- In this case, the wife was able (with assistance from a "friend") to buy out the other party's interest in the property. If resources had been more limited and the marital home was the only major asset, the agreement may have provided that the custodial parent continue to remain in the home with the parties' children until the youngest reached the age of emancipation. At that time, the house would be sold, with the parent in residence having a "right of first refusal" to buy the home at fair market value. The net proceeds then would be divided between the parties in agreed-upon percentages.

- All kinds of "real property" should be covered in the agreement, including, for example, residences, vacation homes, business properties, leases, time-shares, and contracts to purchase or sell property that may impact the nature and extent of the marital estate.

- Part of this provision spells out the tax consequences of the transfer so that the party receiving the property cannot later claim she was unaware of a related capital gains tax possibly being due.

EXHIBIT F

JOINT AND SEVERAL DEBTS

F.1 Stephen and Julie have four (4) jointly held credit card accounts on which they are co-signors with balances that remain outstanding. Each party acknowledges that they are equally responsible for incurring this debt and that the balances owed constitute joint marital debt. The following is a complete list of the joint credit card accounts that remain outstanding, in the amounts owed at the time of execution of this Agreement:

EXHIBIT 13.2 (*Continued*)

Creditor	Indebtedness
a) MBNA America	$21,000.
b) Citizens	$22,300.
c) AT&T Universal	$ 7,500.
d) Discover Card	$ 2,350.
	$53,150.

F.2   Julie agrees that from the date of this Agreement forward, she will indemnify and hold Stephen harmless for all sums remaining to be paid on these four unsecured debts.

F.3   Julie agrees that she shall assume the indebtedness for all four of the above jointly held credit cards and that, as soon as practicable after the execution of this Agreement, she will obtain sufficient financing to pay off the remaining balances on all four cards and close the accounts. Julie has agreed to these terms because in January 2011, Stephen liquidated his entire retirement annuity from his employer in order to pay off part of the joint marital debt the parties had incurred. At that time, Julie had a retirement account through her employer that was approximately equal in value to Stephen's. Julie did not then, and has not since, withdrawn any of her retirement funds—her account remains entirely intact and has since grown in value and become vested due to her years of service. The parties acknowledge that they jointly agreed that Stephen's retirement annuity should be used to pay down the joint marital debt and that Julie could have contributed one-half of that amount from her own funds but did not do so per their agreement. Julie's assumption of the remaining credit card debt will fairly compensate Stephen for liquidating his retirement savings in 2011. Assumption of the debt by Julie will allow Stephen to make a fresh start and continue to prepare for his future retirement needs.

F.4   Neither Stephen nor Julie may hereafter incur any debts or obligations on the credit of the other, and shall indemnify and hold the other harmless from any such debt or obligation incurred.

F.5   Except as otherwise provided herein, and as set forth on each party's Financial Statement filed at the time of the final hearing on this matter, each of the parties represents to the other that he or she knows of no other debts for which the other may be liable, and each shall be responsible for and hold the other harmless for any liability incurred as a result of his or her nondisclosure. If either party violates this Agreement and the other party becomes obligated to make payment to any third party as a result of such breach, then the nonbreaching party shall have the right to be indemnified by the breaching party and the breaching party shall pay all of the nonbreaching party's costs and attorneys' fees in connection therewith.

F.6   Except as provided in paragraph F.1 of this Exhibit and as may be otherwise provided herein, Stephen shall be solely responsible for and indemnify Julie for all of the debts set forth on his financial statement filed with the Court at the time of the final hearing on this matter.

F.7   Except as provided in paragraph F.1 of this Exhibit and as may be otherwise provided herein, Julie shall be solely responsible for and indemnify Stephen for all of the debts set forth on her financial statement filed with the Court at the time of the final hearing on this matter.

DRAFTING TIPS

- The heading of this section may vary, but whatever it is called, it addresses liabilities of the parties.
- It is important to include **"hold harmless" provisions** in this Exhibit. (See F.4, F.5, F.6, and F.7.)
- Paragraph F.3 is somewhat unusual. However, in this case, the judge specifically required that the agreement address the rationale for why the wife was assuming a seemingly disproportionate percentage of the marital debt.

Hold harmless provision

a provision specifying that a particular spouse will be solely responsible for payment of certain debts and that the other spouse shall be free and clear of any obligation regarding those debts and will be indemnified by the debtor spouse if forced to pay the debt

EXHIBIT 13.2 *(Continued)*

EXHIBIT G

MEDICAL INSURANCE AND UNINSURED MEDICAL EXPENSE

G.1 For the benefit of the children, Julie shall maintain in full force and effect her current health insurance coverage, or its equivalent, as long as it is available through her employer, and as long as each child is not emancipated as that term is defined herein.

G.2 For the benefit of Stephen, Julie shall maintain in full force and effect her current health insurance coverage, or its equivalent, as long as it is available through her employer, and as long as the cost or premium is not in excess of that which Julie is required to pay to maintain such coverage for herself and the children who are not emancipated.

G.3 Stephen agrees that maintaining health insurance coverage for the children is a duty that he bears equally with Julie. Therefore, as long as Julie maintains family health insurance coverage through her own employer for the benefit of the children, or for the benefit of both Stephen and the children, Stephen agrees that if not otherwise addressed in the governing Child Support Guidelines, he shall pay Julie a sum equal to one-half the difference between what Julie would pay for individual health insurance coverage and what she must pay for family health insurance coverage. Upon Stephen's request, Julie shall provide him with evidence of the cost of the premiums for coverage.

G.4 In the event that Julie remarries and thereby affects Stephen's eligibility for continued coverage, or in the event that Stephen can no longer be covered by Julie on her plan without additional cost to her, Stephen shall have the right, pursuant to state and other applicable law, to continue to receive benefits as are available to Julie by any means then existing, including by rider to the existing policy or conversion to an individual policy. If Stephen elects to continue such coverage, Julie shall cooperate with him in making the necessary arrangements for, and shall execute any documents necessary to effectuate, the continuation of said coverage. If such coverage results in an additional cost or premium to Julie and Stephen elects to continue such coverage, then Stephen shall pay to Julie the additional cost or premium incurred as a result of his election as such payment comes due. In addition to any obligation imposed by applicable law upon the insurer to notify Stephen of cancellation of coverage, Julie shall forthwith notify Stephen as soon as she becomes aware of any circumstance that would affect his eligibility for, the availability of, or the nature of, his continued health insurance coverage.

G.5 Each party shall be responsible for payment of his or her own uninsured medical, dental, psychiatric, prescription, hospital, and other expenses of a medical nature.

G.6 Julie shall pay the first $500 of uninsured medical expenses of each minor child per year, including, among other costs, insurance deductibles, co-payments, and over-the-counter medications. The parties shall share equally the payment of reasonable and necessary uninsured medical and dental expenses of each minor child over $500 per year. Each party shall obtain the other party's prior consent before incurring any nonemergency uninsured medical expense for a minor child costing more than $250, which consent shall not be unreasonably withheld.

G.7 In the event that individual or family insurance coverage is no longer available through Julie's current employer or that she is no longer eligible, insurance coverage for the children will be secured through Stephen's employer or Julie's subsequent employer as mutually agreed upon by the parties. If said insurance incurs a cost, the cost will be borne equally by the parties.

DRAFTING TIPS

- This Exhibit should cover medical insurance for both the parties and the children and should address insured and uninsured expenses. If a parent and/or child has any extraordinary medical needs, these should be considered (e.g., physical therapy, counseling, home care). In circumstances in which the parties are unemployed and have few assets, consistent with governing federal and state law, the parties may go without medical insurance or apply for government benefits.

EXHIBIT 13.2 *(Continued)*

- The courts tend to be especially interested in this provision, particularly as applied to any minor children. In some states, including Massachusetts, the cost of medical insurance for the children now is factored into the child support formula.

EXHIBIT H

LIFE INSURANCE

H.1 Stephen shall maintain a total of $250,000 of term insurance on his life ($125,000 for the benefit of each of the minor children). Stephen shall maintain said insurance for the benefit of each child until such time as that child becomes emancipated and Stephen is no longer obligated to pay child support for the benefit of that child.

H.2 At Stephen's option, the life insurance provided for the benefit of the minor children in paragraph H.1 above shall be held in trust by a trustee of his choosing selected by him in a form of trust to be approved by Julie, whose approval shall not be unreasonably withheld.

H.3 Stephen will, from time to time, and as requested by Julie, furnish her with satisfactory evidence that said insurance policies are in full force and effect.

H.4 Except as otherwise provided in H.1 and H.2 above, after execution of the Agreement, Julie and Stephen shall each have the right to make any changes in his or her respective insurance policies, including, but not limited to, changing his or her beneficiaries, increasing or decreasing coverage, or canceling such policies.

DRAFTING TIPS

- This provision is designed to guarantee an income stream for the benefit of the minor children and often appears in the Exhibit pertaining to child support. The designation of the children as beneficiaries should be irrevocable as long as the child support obligation continues.
- The parties often have several kinds of insurance in addition to life insurance, such as health, homeowners', automobile, and liability in connection with a business or professional practice, that may be covered in one Exhibit or separately.

EXHIBIT I

RETIREMENT ACCOUNTS

Except as otherwise herein provided, from the date of this Agreement forward, all 401(k), IRA, and other retirement-type accounts and state and federal retirement plans standing individually in a party's own name shall be retained by that party as his or her sole property free of any claim of any right of the other, with full power in that party to dispose of the same as fully and with such effect in all respects and for all purposes as though he or she were unmarried. However, either party may voluntarily name or retain the other as a beneficiary, or as trustee of said funds for the benefit of the parties' children.

EXHIBIT J

BANKRUPTCY FILING

J.1 In the event that either party to this Agreement decides to petition for bankruptcy under the provisions of the United States Code, that party must notify the other of his or her intention to file such a petition. Such notice shall be in writing and shall be given to the other party at least

EXHIBIT 13.2 (*Continued*)

ninety (90) days prior to the filing of such petition. The notice shall be given by certified first-class mail, return receipt requested. The notice must include, but is not limited to, the name, address, and telephone number of the attorney, if any, who has been retained to represent the petitioning party in the bankruptcy action and must identify the court in which the petition will be filed. The receipt of such notice shall not in any way limit, restrict, or prevent the right of the party receiving notice from seeking any appropriate remedy or relief available to him or her under existing law or this Agreement prior to the filing of the petition in bankruptcy, nor shall the receipt of such notice limit, restrict, or prevent the party receiving the notice from asserting any claim available to him or her under law after such petition has been filed.

J.2 In the event that a party to this Agreement petitions for bankruptcy under the United States Code, that party shall be liable for attorneys' fees incurred by the other party in protecting his or her rights under this Agreement to the extent that they are incurred as a consequence of the filing.

DRAFTING TIPS

- This provision is not included in some agreements, but in this case, one of the spouses was seriously considering filing for bankruptcy.

- Although bankruptcy court rulings will ultimately control in the event that a bankruptcy action is subsequently filed, an effort should be made to protect as many of the obligations created under this agreement as possible by designating them as being in the nature of "support" and thus generally not dischargeable in bankruptcy.

EXHIBIT K

TAXES

K.1 Stephen and Julie agree that they will file a joint tax return for the 2014 tax year.

K.2 Stephen and Julie hereby warrant to each other that all income taxes, local, state, and federal, on all joint returns filed by the parties have been paid, and that to their knowledge, no interest or penalties are due and owing, and no tax deficiency proceeding or audit is pending or threatened.

K.3 If there is a deficiency assessment in connection with any of the joint returns, the party receiving notice of such deficiency shall notify the other party immediately in writing. The party responsible for the act or omission that caused the deficiency assessment shall be solely liable for any deficiency assessment, penalty, and interest and shall hold the other harmless against any loss or liability in connection therewith. In the event that neither party is responsible for the act or omission that caused the deficiency assessment, the parties shall pay the assessment in proportion to their income in the tax year for which the assessment is due.

K.4 In the event that there is a refund, the parties shall divide the amount of the refund equally.

The Court's Role

The courts encourage the parties to resolve their differences and negotiate agreements whenever possible. However, this does not mean that the courts play no role. In fact, they play a variety of roles with respect to separation agreements. The most common are the following:

- Reviewing the agreement at the time of the final hearing or trial for possible incorporation in the decree

- Modifying the agreement
- Enforcing the agreement
- Vacating/setting aside the agreement

REVIEW OF THE AGREEMENT AT THE TIME OF TRIAL OR FINAL HEARING

Before approving an agreement, the court will assess whether or not it is fair and reasonable. It will determine if the agreement is procedurally and substantively fair after examining several factors such as the following:[1]

- Was there full disclosure? Are the financial provisions fair and reasonable when the agreement is viewed as a whole? For example, is one party left nearly destitute while the other receives substantial assets?
- Is the agreement consistent with the statutory or case law factors governing alimony, property division, and custody issues in the jurisdiction? Does it appear to attempt to relieve one parent of his or her statutory duty to support a child?
- Under what circumstances did negotiations take place? Was one party under considerable duress, such as a threat of abuse or loss of custody of the children?
- How complex are the issues? Were experts consulted to assist with complicated valuation problems?
- How legally sophisticated are the parties? What kinds of education and professional background do they each have?
- Was each party represented by separate counsel competent in family law matters? Was one party not represented? Did both parties believe themselves to be represented by the same attorney?
- Did each party understand their respective rights? Did each party believe the agreement was fair and reasonable?

When a complete or partial separation agreement is presented for approval, the court generally exercises one of three options (the first two at the request of the parties):

- It may incorporate and **merge** the terms of the agreement into the decree. In a technical sense, if an agreement merges, it loses its identity and retains no independent legal significance apart from the judgment.
- It may incorporate the terms of the agreement into the decree but provide that it will not merge but rather will survive as a separate contract with **independent legal significance** (thereby constituting a "**surviving agreement**").
- It may reject the agreement in whole or in part because it violates the law or a strong public policy. In contrast to negotiation of a commercial contract, the parties' freedom to contract the terms of the dissolution of their marriage is not unlimited.

In an uncontested case, neither spouse objects to the granting of the divorce, and the parties execute a mutually agreed-upon separation agreement. However, even in an uncontested case, the court customarily holds a brief hearing with one or both of the parties present. The judge/magistrate does not simply rubber-stamp the agreement (even if it resulted from arbitration) but rather reviews and occasionally asks questions about it. Particular attention is usually given to the conditions for payment of child support (e.g., will there be a wage assignment?); the arrangements made for continuing health insurance; the presence of waivers of

---

PARALEGAL PRACTICE TIP

The courts have the discretion to adopt a negotiated separation agreement but are not required to do so. See, e.g., *Rainer v. Rainer,* 2012 Ohio 6268 (2012 Ohio App.).

Merge
the process by which a separation agreement is incorporated in a divorce judgment and does not survive but rather loses its identity as a separate and independent contract

Independent legal significance
legally binding in its own right

Surviving agreement
an agreement of the parties incorporated in a court's divorce decree that also retains its existence as an independent contract enforceable under basic principles of contract law

PARALEGAL PRACTICE TIP

Some states have a strong policy favoring survival even if the parties' intent is merely implied or ambiguous unless the terms clearly express otherwise. See *Parrish v. Parrish,* 30 Mass. App. Ct. 78, 566 N.E.2d 103 (1991).

alimony, if any; and whether the agreement will merge with the divorce or separation decree or survive as an independent contract. (See Exhibit 13.3.) Usually each of the parties is asked whether he or she has read, understood, and freely signed the agreement; whether each has exchanged and reviewed relevant financial information and agrees that there has been full disclosure of assets and liabilities; and whether each believes the agreement is fair.

In a contested case, if a partial agreement is submitted, the court may approve it and incorporate its terms into the divorce decree along with determinations regarding the contested issues following a trial. As in an uncontested case, the partial agreement may be incorporated and merged into the decree or survive as an independent contract.

EXHIBIT 13.3 Distinction Between Merger and Survival as an Independent Contract

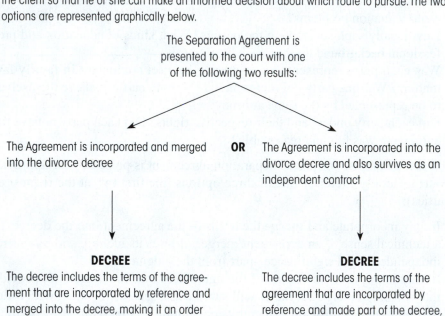

A separation agreement is a contract that is effective upon signing unless otherwise provided. If a judge eventually approves the agreement at the request of the parties, it is either incorporated and merged into the court's decree OR it is incorporated by reference in the decree but does not merge. Rather, it continues to survive and retain its independent legal significance as a contract separate and apart from the divorce decree. Often, the distinction between merger and survival is confusing for clients, but its consequences can be dramatic. Counsel needs to explain the options clearly to the client so that he or she can make an informed decision about which route to pursue. The two options are represented graphically below.

The Separation Agreement is presented to the court with one of the following two results:

The Agreement is incorporated and merged into the divorce decree   **OR**   The Agreement is incorporated into the divorce decree and also survives as an independent contract

DECREE

The decree includes the terms of the agreement that are incorporated by reference and merged into the decree, making it an order of the court. The terms are enforceable only by the family court.

NO INDEPENDENT CONTRACT/AGREEMENT

The agreement has merged into the decree and no longer exists as an independent contract.

DECREE

The decree includes the terms of the agreement that are incorporated by reference and made part of the decree, making it an order of the court. The decree is enforceable by the family court according to its terms and applicable law.

AND

INDEPENDENT CONTRACT/AGREEMENT

The agreement continues to exist as a contract with independent legal significance separate from the decree and is enforceable as a contract in a court of equity.

It is important that the parties understand what the terms of the agreement mean and what they have agreed to. Occasionally, a judge will address a question directly to a party in a hearing. It is a poor reflection on counsel if the client is able only to stare blankly at the court or look helplessly to the attorney in response! Given that no one "wins" in a divorce and that agreements invariably reflect compromises between what a party wants and what she or he can reasonably expect to have, clients are rarely 100 percent satisfied with agreements. Given a chance to speak, inadequately prepared clients occasionally vent such dissatisfaction, to the end that a court may send the parties back to the drawing board. When helping to prepare a client for court, the paralegal must be careful to leave explanations of the legal effect of various provisions to the attorney, but the paralegal can be a source of moral support to the client.

MODIFICATION OF THE AGREEMENT

If the agreement is incorporated and merged into the divorce decree, the court issuing the decree retains the authority to modify it based on a substantial change in circumstances.

If the agreement is incorporated but survives as an independent contract, the general rule is that it can be modified in only a limited number of circumstances:

- The agreement itself may provide for modification of a provision under certain conditions, such as allowing the termination of alimony upon cohabitation or remarriage of the recipient or permitting an adjustment based on a substantial increase or reduction in the payor's income. The parties may agree to review child support on an annual basis to insure it remains consistent with the guidelines and to jointly file for a modification if warranted.
- Since the court retains jurisdiction over child-related matters, provisions relating to the parties' children remain modifiable, given a substantial change in circumstances that affects the welfare of the children. For example, in *McIntosh v. Landrum*, 377 S.W.3d 574 (Ky. App. 2012), the parties' son was autistic and required child care and constant supervision. At the time of the divorce, the mother was not working and the parties' detailed agreement included no provision for work-related childcare expenses. When the mother's spousal maintenance ended, she began working and a year later successfully sought a modification to help cover new childcare costs.
- If there has been a more-than-substantial change in circumstances such that one of the parties will become a public charge if a modification is not granted, many courts will order a modification rather than have the indigent person be supported by the taxpayers.

ENFORCEMENT OF THE AGREEMENT

If the agreement is incorporated and merged into the divorce decree, then enforcement is pursued in the family court because the "breach" is a violation of an order of that court. The aggrieved party generally files a contempt action or a motion to enforce the judgment. In order to establish contempt, there must be a clear and unequivocal command and a clear and undoubted disobedience. If the agreement language is ambiguous or unclear, contempt will not provide a viable remedy. See, e.g., *Hetterick v. Hetterick n.k.a. Clonch, et al*, 2013 Ohio 15 (Ohio App. 2013), and *Milona v. Tatakis*, 81 Mass. App. Ct. 1127, 965 N.E.2d 224 (2012).

PARALEGAL PRACTICE TIP

There has to actually be a change to support a modification. For example, in *Moffet v. Sickles*, 2012 Ohio 1928 (2012 Ohio App.), a father sought a modification of custody because the mother was continuing to use marijuana and was failing mandated drug tests. The court held there had been no change of circumstances because the father was aware of the mother's drug use at the time their agreement was executed.

PARALEGAL PRACTICE TIP

In *Monahan v. Monahan*, 85 Mass. App. Ct. 1101, 3 N.E.3d 615 (Mass. App. 2014), the parties' surviving agreement provided the wife would receive a portion of the husband's military pension. The husband subsequently waived his military pension in order to receive Veterans' disability benefits thereby depriving the wife of "the benefit of her bargain." The court found that this bad faith change in circumstances was sufficient to warrant a modification requiring the husband to pay out of his resources the equivalent of what the wife would have received.

PARALEGAL PRACTICE TIP

More than one kind of relief may be sought. For example, in a 2009 South Dakota case, the husband filed three alternative motions: a motion for a new trial, a motion to vacate the judgment, and a motion to enforce a personal property provision of the property settlement agreement. See *Vann v. Vann*, 2009 ND 118, 767 N.W.2d 855 (2009).

If the agreement is incorporated into the decree and also survives as an independent contract, the courts generally make every effort to enforce the terms of the agreement, unless doing so would violate the law or contravene a strong public policy. With a surviving agreement, the aggrieved party has two routes to use to enforce the agreement. As with a merged agreement, he or she may file a contempt action in the court that issued the decree. In addition, however, because the agreement retains its existence as an independent contract, contract remedies are also available. For example, the aggrieved party may sue for breach of contract, seeking damages or specific enforcement of a term of the agreement.

A confusing situation can develop when a family court modifies an agreement that was not only incorporated into its decree but also survived as an independent contract. For example, assume the parties' agreement provides that wife will pay husband $500 per month in spousal support. She does so for the first two years following the divorce but then stops paying after losing her job. She seeks and is granted a modification by the family court based on a more-than-substantial change of circumstances. The court reduces her payment to $100 a month and she resumes making payments. Since the original agreement survives, technically the husband can sue in contract to recover the $400 difference between the new amount of court-ordered alimony ($100) and the contractually agreed-on amount ($500).

The agreement may also be enforced in the context of other kinds of actions. For example, a party to a divorce who has been ordered to transfer property to a former spouse and to pay child support and alimony may try to avoid these obligations by filing for bankruptcy. The bankruptcy court will determine which of the obligations are in the nature of "support" and not **dischargeable** in bankruptcy. Agreements may also be considered in probate proceedings. For example, a spouse who has remarried may have been ordered to maintain an insurance policy for the benefit of his children but changes the beneficiary to his new wife. Upon his death, the children may seek to recover from the estate the amount they should have received from the policy.[2]

Discharge
to relieve an obligor of the legal obligation to pay a debt

ACTION TO VACATE THE AGREEMENT

A post-trial motion to reconsider and vacate "is not a time machine in which to travel back to a recently concluded trial in order to try the case better with hindsight." See *Shih Ping Li v. Tzu Lee*, 210 Md. App. 73, 62 A.3d 212 (2013). These actions are taken very seriously. After the divorce is "final," a party may seek (in an appeal, new trial, or other action) to have the court vacate or set aside the judgment incorporating the agreement. For example, six months after the decree has issued, one of the parties may discover that, despite his or her best efforts to obtain full disclosure before negotiating their agreement, the other party successfully concealed a substantial asset. Had the asset been brought to light in a timely manner, the property settlement would have been significantly different. Another scenario involves the situation in which an agreement was executed under duress. For example, an abusive husband may have threatened physical harm to both his wife and their children if she did not sign an agreement granting him custody of the children and a disproportionate share of the marital assets. Several months after the divorce, when the wife feels more confident and safe from harm, she may seek to set aside the earlier agreement in order to obtain a settlement that is truly fair and reasonable, including custody of the children and a greater portion of the marital assets.

Decrees issued by trial courts appealed to higher courts within the state may be affirmed, remanded, or set aside. In a 2009 case, for example, the Virginia Court of

Appeals set aside a property settlement agreement which awarded all the marital assets with the exception of an automobile and a few personal possessions to the husband. The assets included the marital residence valued at $300,000. Although the wife acknowledged reading the agreement, she had a third-grade education and numerous health problems and claimed she didn't really understand its legal effect. She just knew if she signed it she would "be able to get a divorce." The initial decree left her on public assistance after thirty-eight years of marriage. The court found the agreement unconscionable and observed how divorce creates a situation which is "particularly susceptible to overreaching and oppression." See also *Geier v. Geier*, 2013 SD 24, 828 N.W.2d 804 (2013).

PARALEGAL PRACTICE TIP

See, e.g., *Re the Marriage of Sertz and Sertz*, 2012 Ohio 2120 (Ohio App. 2012), in which the husband secured a separation agreement which was overwhelmingly favorable to his own financial interests in part by failing to disclose information about the value of his pension and other assets.

CHAPTER **SUMMARY**

In this chapter we have examined the nature and purpose of agreements in the context of divorce and separation. The primary focus has been on the structure and components of separation agreements and the importance of tailoring them to the facts of each individual case. Attention has been given to the role paralegals play in developing effective agreements and to the consequences of poor drafting. We have also reviewed the court's role in approving, modifying, and enforcing agreements and in vacating them when warranted by the facts and circumstances of a particular case. In a sense, this chapter brings together many of the other chapters in the text given the topics covered in separation agreements such as marital rights and responsibilities, child custody, child support, spousal support, and division of property both real and personal.

In today's legal climate, separation agreements are welcome. From the court's perspective, they conserve judicial resources by eliminating the need for lengthy, costly, and bitter trials. From the clients' perspective, they allow the parties to privately negotiate the terms of their separation or divorce without governmental interference. The separation agreement provides a blueprint for them to follow as their marriage terminates. A carefully drafted agreement, which the parties negotiate, review, and understand, not only allows the case to proceed on an uncontested basis but also helps minimize postdivorce confusion, aggravation, disagreements, and litigation. It is a win-win for the parties and the judicial system.

CONCEPT REVIEW AND REINFORCEMENT

KEY **TERMS**

Boilerplate	Independent legal significance	Rescission
Bottom line	Legal separation	Separation agreement
Consideration	Marital estate	Substantive fairness
Discharge	Meeting of the minds	Surviving agreement
Forensic	Merge	Third-party beneficiary
Hold harmless provision	Parol evidence rule	Unearned income
Impounded	Procedural fairness	
Incorporation by reference	*Pro se*	

REVIEW **QUESTIONS**

1. Describe what a separation agreement is and identify the purposes it serves.
2. Identify five characteristics of an effective separation agreement.
3. Describe how most separation agreements are developed and identify the role potentially played by the paralegal.
4. Define "boilerplate." Identify at least five sections of a separation agreement that generally consist of boilerplate.
5. Identify the major topics commonly addressed in separation agreements.
6. Describe the nature and purpose of a severability clause.
7. Distinguish between a separation agreement that is incorporated and merges into a divorce decree and one that is incorporated and survives as an independent contract. Explain the significance of the distinction.
8. Identify the various ways in which the courts become involved with separation agreements.

DEVELOPING YOUR PARALEGAL SKILLS

FOCUS ON **THE JOB**

In this activity, the student drafts a separation agreement tailored to a specific fact pattern involving a divorcing couple and their minor son.

The Facts

Anna and Herman Nicole were married on August 16, 2001, in San Diego, California. It was the first marriage for Anna and the fourth for Herman. At the time of their marriage, Anna was twenty-seven years old and Herman was eighty-two. The parties have one minor child, Theodore Carleton Nicole, born on November 16, 2002. Anna presently lives at 23 Chandler Street in Chicago, Illinois, and Herman lives at 1102 Country Club Drive in your city and state. They separated on Christmas Day 2014 after opening gifts at the Country Club Drive residence and intend to continue to live separately for the rest of their lives. On January 2 of this year, they filed jointly for a no-fault divorce because of the irreconcilable differences that have arisen between them. The action has been filed in your county in the appropriate court.

Both parties want to remain actively involved in their son's life but agree that Anna will be his primary caretaker, particularly during the school year so that there will at least be continuity in that aspect of his life. He is presently enrolled in a private school and is very active in a variety of sports. He is taking trumpet lessons and shows considerable musical talent. Herman will pay reasonable child support in an amount consistent with the state's child support guidelines (to the extent they apply) based on an unearned income of $400,000 a year. It will be payable monthly.

The parties have exchanged financial statements but have engaged in no additional discovery. Anna earns approximately $125,000 a year as a model, and intends to continue her career. She has no retirement fund. Herman has been retired for some time but is independently wealthy. His assets are valued at approximately $5.5 million. Herman has managed all of the couple's financial affairs, and his accountant has prepared all of the joint tax returns submitted during the marriage based on the information Herman provided.

Herman was both physically and emotionally abusive to Anna during their twelve-year marriage, but she is willing to forget all that if he pays her alimony of $10,000 per month for the rest of his life and lets her have their apartment in New York City, their summer home in Newport, Rhode Island, and the condo where she is presently residing. All of the properties are owned outright by Herman. (Anna owns no real estate in her own name.) He has also agreed to split his General Electric pension with her (requiring preparation of a QDRO) and to make her the sole beneficiary of a $500,000 Prudential life insurance policy. She will receive the Rolls-Royce and he will keep his collection of vintage automobiles. For understandable reasons, Herman is willing to waive any rights to ever claim alimony and wants the alimony provisions of the agreement to be nonmodifiable by any court under any circumstances. He has no objection to paying his own debts but refuses to pay Anna's credit card debts, which have been a constant source of tension between them. (Anna is somewhat of a shopaholic.) Anna figures he will end up paying some of the debt anyway, because two of her three cards are in their joint names. The accounts are a Bank of America account in Anna's name only numbered 1772-2356-7631-8976 (balance $7,980), a Jet Green Master charge account numbered 028-3456-93 (balance $13,569), and an American Express account numbered 1357-2468-0864 (balance $22,567).

The parties have already divided their personal property, except that Herman needs to remove from the New York and Newport properties all the works of art he has collected over the years.

Herman says he feels sort of bad about the divorce and that he may decide to provide for Anna in his will, but she is not counting on that. However, she is happy that he will pay for comprehensive medical insurance for her until his death and for Theodore until his emancipation. That is important to her because she has heavy bills for psychiatric treatment and medications. Anna figures that she is "making out like a bandit" and has chosen not to obtain legal advice because she doesn't want to waste any of the funds she is receiving on an attorney.

The Assignment

Assume that you are a paralegal in the family law firm representing Herman in the above hypothetical. Draft a proposed separation agreement tailored to his wishes and benefit. Use a format that is appropriate in the jurisdiction where you are studying family law. This may mean that, instead of an integrated separation agreement, you will be preparing a parenting plan and a marital property settlement/stipulation. You should also be sure to use the appropriate terminology in your jurisdiction for child-related, property division and spousal support matters.

FOCUS ON **ETHICS**

In this activity, the student explores ethical issues involving billing, conflict of interest, and the unauthorized practice of law among others in the context of a specific case.

The Assignment

Edward E. Edwards III is the attorney who represents Herman in the above fact pattern. His office is located at 20 Beacon Street in your city and state. You are his paralegal. Edward is thrilled to be handling this case and has told you to prepare monthly invoices for as long as the case continues; he figures he will be able to "drag it out for a while." He tells you to keep track of your hours as well as his and to bill them all at his regular hourly rate of $250. He says he is

happy to split the fee with you because you are such a good employee. You are uneasy about this—it just doesn't feel right but you really need the money. Besides, you are aware that Herman has abused all of his wives and you figure he deserves to pay. As a matter of fact, when you saw Anna at a local club recently, you told her she really ought to get a lawyer because she could probably "do better."

Discuss this situation from an ethical perspective in a one- to two-page paper. Relate your response to the ethical canons for paralegals promulgated by the National Association of Legal Assistants, which are contained in Appendix A of this text, the ethics material in Chapter 1 of this text, and the code governing the conduct of attorneys in your jurisdiction.

FOCUS ON **CASE LAW**

This activity allows the student to respond to questions about a case involving the enforceability of a separation agreement.

The Assignment

Read the opinion of the North Dakota Supreme Court in *Vann v. Vann*, 2009 ND 118, 767 N.W.2d 855 (2009), and then respond to the following questions in a two- to three-page paper. The full opinion is available at *www.pearsonhighered.com/careersresources/* in the material related to Chapter 13 of this text under Cases.

1. Where, when, and by whom was the case first brought? What was the result?

2. What issues are raised on appeal and by whom?

3. What did the parties' property settlement basically provide?

4. Do the North Dakota courts favor such agreements in divorce actions? What do they consider when deciding whether a property settlement agreement should be enforced?

5. Did the North Dakota Supreme Court determine the Vanns' agreement was procedurally fair or unconscionable? Why?

6. Did the North Dakota Supreme Court find the agreement substantively fair or unfair? Why?

7. What concern did Justice Sandstrom raise in the concurring opinion?

FOCUS ON **STATE LAW AND PROCEDURE**

This activity requires students to locate and brief a case involving a separation agreement in the jurisdiction where they are studying family law.

The Assignment

Locate and brief a recent case in the state where you are studying family law regarding the enforceability of

separation agreements. If your instructor does not require a specific format, you can find a suitable model at *www.pearsonhighered.com/careersresources/* in the material related to Chapter 1 under Resources.

FOCUS ON **TECHNOLOGY**

In addition to the links in the chapter, this activity provides a series of useful websites for reference along with a technology-related assignment for completion.

Websites of Interest

www.divorcelawinfo.com

This is the website for a commercial service that provides, for sale, online interactive preparation of a variety of

forms having to do with divorce. The service comes in two forms, a do-it-yourself format and a paralegal-assisted format. Forms and services are purportedly state-specific. The site also has a frequently asked questions feature.

www.divorcesupport.com

This site provides material related to a broad range of divorce-related topics. For separation agreements, there are generic informational features such as Frequently Asked

Questions (FAQ), online discussion forums, and state-specific separation agreement preparation services. The site also provides links to state divorce law information.

www.findlaw.com

This site provides a sample separation agreement (which is not state-specific) for a short-term marriage with no children. It also provides links to divorce forms by state. Several of the state links contain sample separation agreements and parenting plans.

www.uslegalforms.com

This is the website for a service that provides, for sale, either downloadable or hard-copy forms for a variety of legal situations that are purportedly state-specific. For each state, it offers a number of different separation agreement forms that are tailored to the requirements of various general separation situations. Remember, caution must be exercised when considering using commercial/online packages. Always confirm that they comply with individual state rules and practices and tailor them to the client's case.

Assignments

Locate three online resources that provide information about separation agreements in your state.

PORTFOLIO PRODUCTS

1. Separation agreement tailored to a hypothetical fact pattern
2. One- to two-page discussion of ethical issues in the context of a specific case
3. Responses to questions regarding a case involving the enforceability of a separation agreement
4. Brief of a case on the enforceability of a separation agreement in a specific state

chapter 14
FAMILY VIOLENCE

© Richard Tauson

Joe has been served with a Complaint for Divorce, and he is furious. His rage is apparent to the paralegal in his attorney's office, who has suspected for some time that Joe abuses his wife. Fearful for the wife's safety, the paralegal speaks with the supervising attorney, and they both struggle with the question of what they should do.

LEARNING OBJECTIVES

After reading this chapter and completing related assignments, you should be able to:

- explain what family violence is, and who the victims and perpetrators are

- identify remedies available to adult victims of family violence, including criminal actions, civil actions, protective orders, and guardianships

- explain how to recognize and respond when a client is a victim or perpetrator of abuse

- identify various kinds of child abuse and neglect

- describe who is required to report abuse and to whom, and how the state responds

- explain how abuse and neglect influence custody decisions

- discuss the ethical duty of members of the family law team in the family violence context

After years of studying family and intimate violence, . . . Richard Gelles wondered aloud how we had ever come to characterize the family as "warm, intimate, stress reducing, and the place that people flee for safety."[1] His research had shown that the family was one of society's most violent institutions, in that people were "more likely to be killed, physically assaulted, hit, beat up, slapped, or spanked in their own homes by other family members than anywhere else, or by anyone else."[2]

Introduction

The history of family violence in this country has long been colored by the old common law right of a husband to treat both his wife and his children as property and to maintain domestic order through the use of physical force. **Interspousal immunity** and the law of **coverture**, which gave men control over their wives' bodies and property, created a climate that essentially fostered and condoned violence in the home environment. Although there were isolated efforts to address this problem prior to the 1900s, it was not until the 1960s and 1970s that advocates for the rights of women and children galvanized public and legislative support for victims of family violence. Initially, the focus was on abuse as a problem to be dealt with privately through treatment aimed primarily at maintenance of the family unit. In more recent years, the shift has been toward a focus on protection of victims and the treatment of abuse as a crime.

Interspousal immunity
a doctrine preventing spouses from suing each other in civil actions

Coverture
the legal doctrine that upon marriage, a husband and wife become one person (the husband), and the wife loses many of the legal rights she possessed prior to marriage

513

This chapter focuses on the topic of family violence, first with respect to adult intimate partners and then in the context of parent–child relationships. In each instance, we examine the nature and extent of the abuse, the federal government's recognition of the problem, and some of the remedies available to victims. We also consider how intimate partner violence and child abuse and neglect impact custody determinations. Finally, we explore the duty of members of the family law team in cases involving family violence and the ethical challenges it presents. For organizational convenience, family violence against adults and child abuse are treated separately. However, the reader should be aware that there is a significant overlap between the two. A majority of studies find that both forms of abuse occur in 30% to 60% of violent families.[3] The correlation is so strong that Lenore Walker concluded in her classic work, *The Battered Woman Syndrome*, that wife abuse is the single strongest identifiable risk for child abuse.

Defining Family Violence

Family violence
a pattern of coercive behavior designed to exert power and control over a person in a familial relationship

Family violence goes by many names, most commonly domestic violence, domestic abuse, intimate partner violence, and spousal and child abuse. Generally, it involves a pattern of coercive behavior designed to exert power and control over a person in a familial relationship. It comes in no single form, but rather may involve any combination of behaviors such as threatening, intimidating, belittling, harassing, and outright physical attacks sometimes resulting in death. Legal definitions of various kinds of abuse differ from state to state. Most focus on the infliction of physical abuse that causes bodily injury, compelled sexual activity, and fear of physical assault. Some definitions encompass abuse inflicted through neglect, stalking (including cyberstalking), and other psychological tactics and behaviors.

PARALEGAL PRACTICE TIP

The Missouri statute defining "abuse" can be found at *www.moga.mo.gov* (Missouri Revised Statutes Chapter 568 Offenses Against the Family Section 568.060.1). The Georgia statute defining "stalking" is located at *www.legis.ga.gov* (O.C.G.A. §16-5-90 to 94). To find the state of Washington's cyberstalking statute Google Revised Code of Washington § 9.61.260.

PARALEGAL PRACTICE TIP

Because the victims of intimate partner violence are predominantly female, in this chapter we generally refer to adult victim as females.

Family Violence Against Adult Victims
THE SCOPE OF THE PROBLEM

"Domestic violence crosses all geographic, socioeconomic, racial, cultural, religious, educational, and occupational boundaries. The overwhelming majority of domestic violence is committed by men against women, although some women are abusive to their male or female partners. It occurs with about the same statistical frequency in heterosexual and homosexual relationships, . . ."[4] Although domestic violence appears disproportionately to impact minorities, immigrants, and individuals on welfare, the reader should not be misled by popular statistics into thinking that domestic violence is a problem solely in low-income families.

EXHIBIT 14.1 Family Violence—A Statistical Profile

- In April 2014, the Bureau of Justice Statistics (BJS) reported that domestic violence accounted for 21% of all violent victimizations reported between 2003 and 2012 based on National Crime Victimization Survey (NCVS) figures.
- National Intimate Partner and Sexual Violence Survey data suggest that a significant percentage of both women and men experience rape, physical violence, psychological aggression, and/or stalking by an intimate partner at some point during their lifetime. However, Bureau of

(Continued)

EXHIBIT 14.1 (*Continued*)

Justice Statistics indicate that the burden of intimate partner violence is considerably greater on women who comprise about 85% of domestic violence victims.[5]

- Domestic violence occurs in same-sex as well as in heterosexual relationships. Based on a National Violence Against Women Survey, 11% of lesbians and 15% of gay men who had lived with a same-sex partner reported being victimized.[6]
- In a study of adolescent mothers, approximately one of every eight pregnant adolescents reported having been physically assaulted by the father of her baby during the preceding twelve months.[7]
- Although rates of domestic violence are highest for persons between eighteen and twenty-four years of age, elders are also victims of abuse. The National Center on Elder Abuse (NCEA) defines elder abuse as "any knowing, intentional, or negligent act by a caregiver or any other person that causes harm or a serious risk of harm to a vulnerable adult." Estimates of the frequency of elder abuse range from 2% to 10%. An NCEA Survey of Adult Protective Services (APS) indicated that 89.3% of incidents of alleged elder abuse occurred in a domestic setting.[8] Research has uncovered several key perpetrator characteristics associated with abuse of elders: (1) drug and/or alcohol abuse, (2) impairments such as mental illness and developmental disabilities, (3) financial dependence on the elder, and (4) a bad past relationship with the elder.[9]
- Incidence of domestic violence varies considerably by race and ethnicity.[10] For example, Center for Disease Control (CDC) statistics indicate that approximately four out of every ten women of non-Hispanic Black, American Indian, or Native Alaskan race/ethnicity and one in two multiracial non-Hispanic women have experienced rape, physical violence, and/or stalking by an intimate partner in their lifetime.[11] A survey of immigrant Korean women found that 60% had been battered by their husbands.[12]
- Approximately 60% of the incidents of nonfatal intimate partner violence are unreported, and the primary reasons given for nonreporting include a preference for treating the incident as a private or family matter, a desire to protect the offender, a fear of reprisal, a belief that the crime was minor, and an assumption that, if contacted, the police would be biased, ineffective, or unresponsive.[13]
- Intimate partner violence is by no means unique to the United States. It is especially prevalent in patriarchal societies such as Egypt, India, Jordan, Pakistan, and Uganda, in which women have few, if any, rights. In the extreme, "honor killings" of women are still perpetrated for a wide range of alleged "offenses," such as marital infidelity, engaging in premarital sex, flirting, being a rape victim, or participating in any behavior that is perceived as impugning family honor. Such killings often occur with the full support of both male and female family members and are usually punished, if at all, with lenient sentences.[14]

Federal Recognition of the Problem: The Violence Against Women Act

At the federal level the most dramatic illustration of the legislative attention brought to bear on the problem of family violence is the Violence Against Women Act (VAWA), a comprehensive, landmark piece of legislation designed to improve criminal justice and community-based responses to domestic violence, dating violence, sexual assault, stalking, and trafficking. It was initially passed in 1994 (VAWA I) and then reauthorized three times, most recently in 2013.[15] It is administered by the Department of Health and Human Services and the Department of Justice.

Since VAWA was signed into law, the following (among others) have become federal crimes: cyberstalking; crossing state or tribal boundary lines in order to injure, intimidate, or stalk an intimate partner or to violate a protective order; and stalking on Indian Reservations or military bases. VAWA has provided crucial services by funding twenty-four-hour emergency hotlines, emergency shelters, rape crisis centers, and child advocacy centers, among other initiatives. Culturally and linguistically diverse programs are designed to meet the needs of all victims and not just those of one race, cultural background, or income level. Special efforts are made to address the needs of particularly vulnerable target populations: victims with disabilities, the elderly, youth under the age of eighteen, those who live in rural communities, Native Americans, immigrants, and the homeless. For example, VAWA includes provisions expanding transitional housing options for the homeless and ensures victims' confidentiality within the homeless services system. It also forbids discrimination in public housing to prevent landlords from denying housing or evicting tenants based on their status of being victims of domestic violence.

Successive versions of the Act have provided increased protections for immigrant victims of domestic violence. Immigrant spouses and children have access to alternative procedures for obtaining visas without the cooperation of the abusive spouse by permitting them to self-petition for legal permanent resident status. Additional protections are afforded immigrants who divorce their abusers or whose marriages are invalid because the citizen spouse was already married. In recognition of the fact that immigrants often lack access to shelters, professionals, court interpreters, hotlines, and 911 services due to language barriers, VAWA legislation has required the Secretary of Homeland Security to develop a pamphlet (translated into at least fourteen languages) containing information on the illegality of domestic violence and the rights of an abused immigrant.

Of particular significance in VAWA 2013 (Public Law 113-4) are the following:

1. It recognized the rights of lesbian, gay, bisexual, and transgender people to access VAWA protections and services without discrimination; and
2. It granted tribal authorities "special domestic violence criminal jurisdiction" over non-Indians who have committed intimate partner violence or who have violated an order of protection in Indian country. It afforded federally recognized tribes the option of prosecuting such offenders as of March 2015.

Remedies Available to Adult Victims

In addition to the kinds of social services and assistance supported by VAWA, other remedies available to victims of abuse include criminal prosecution, civil actions, protective orders, and guardianships.

CRIMINAL PROSECUTION

Involvement of the criminal justice system most often begins when the police receive and respond to a 911 call reporting a "domestic incident." In general, when responding to such calls, an officer must use all reasonable means to prevent further abuse whenever there is reason to believe that a "family member" has been abused or is in danger of being abused. The officer usually is required by statute and/or department policy to do the following:

- provide protection for the victim at the scene
- assist the victim in obtaining medical treatment, if appropriate

---

PARALEGAL PRACTICE TIP

You can find an Application for Cancellation of Removal and Adjustment of Status for Certain Nonpermanent Residents (including victims of abuse) at *www.justice.gov.*

PARALEGAL PRACTICE TIP

The second of these was the most controversial aspect of VAWA 2013. It was opposed as potentially unconstitutional by several legislators. It has also been opposed by some tribes concerned about losing features of their own justice traditions. One such tradition is the use of restorative justice programs, including peacemaking circles which involve community participation.

- assist the victim in relocating to a safe location, if warranted
- provide oral and written instructions (preferably in the victim's native language) about how to apply for a protective order. Many states print applications for restraining orders in several languages
- assist the victim in accessing emergency judicial help if the courts are closed. States have in place procedures allowing plaintiffs to obtain emergency orders on weekends, holidays, and any other nonbusiness days. This is generally accomplished by having local judges/magistrates serve twenty-four-hour on-call shifts on a rotating basis. Any orders issued on an emergency basis are usually effective only until the next business day when a hearing can be held
- arrest the perpetrator if the officer witnesses an incident of abuse or has probable cause to believe that the person has committed a felony assault and battery, or has violated a temporary or permanent restraining, vacate, or no-contact order. In some states or localities, arrest is mandatory regardless of the victim's wishes. In others, it is discretionary
- advise the victim that if the abuser is arrested, he or she will likely be eligible for bail or release

Research suggests arrest is most effective with batterers who have community ties and who want to avoid further embarrassment and stigmatization. It is less effective with offenders who lack such ties and are more prone to future violence. Supporters of mandatory arrest and "no-drop" policies assert that victims often are too helpless and/or too fearful to make appropriate decisions about arrest and prosecution. Opponents supportive of victims' rights argue that such policies disempower victims by depriving them of the opportunity to realize strength and power by making decisions about how the abuser should be treated.[16]

The role of the police in investigation and documentation of abuse incidents is critically important because not infrequently, the victim will refuse to participate as a complaining witness for a variety of reasons, thereby potentially exposing themselves to a risk of further abuse. However, today many prosecutors have adopted "no-drop" policies and will proceed with **evidence-based prosecutions** using photographs, medical records, incident reports, and the testimony of police officers and other witnesses to establish a case. In many states, police officers are required to complete supplemental incident reports in domestic violence cases.

PARALEGAL PRACTICE TIP

Applications for restraining orders and civil stalking protective orders are available online in Korean, Russian, Spanish, and Vietnamese in Oregon. See *www.ojd.state.or.us.*

PARALEGAL PRACTICE TIP

To learn about domestic violence arrest policies in each of the states, visit *www.americanbar.org.*

Evidence-based prosecution prosecution of a defendant that relies on physical evidence and testimony of persons other than the victim, such as police officers; formerly called "victimless" prosecutions

PARALEGAL PRACTICE TIP

To see the supplementary incident report form used in New Jersey, visit *www.njsp.org.* Search for UCR Domestic Violence Form.

Paralegal **Application 14.1**

"Why Do They Stay? If Anyone Ever Hit Me, I Would Be Out the Door in a Minute."

It is often difficult for people who have never been in such a situation to comprehend why a person would remain in an abusive relationship and/or not prosecute or testify against his or her abuser. As an unfortunate result, courts, juries, and members of the legal profession often do not find claims of abuse to be credible. Research indicates that victims (primarily women) protect their abuser and stay in such relationships for several reasons:

- Fear of retaliation against themselves and/or their children
- Isolation from friends and extended family, resulting in the lack of a social and emotional support system

(Continued)

- Fear of loss of social status and professional associations
- Economic dependence, lack of marketable skills, or lack of adequate public assistance
- Desire to keep the family together and fear of losing custody of children
- Cultural and religious beliefs about the permanence of marriage
- Sense of responsibility for or loyalty to the abuser
- Belief that they love their abuser and that he or she will change
- Fear that the abuser will reveal information pertaining to sexual preference, immigration, HIV status, etc.[17]
- Chronic depression and exhaustion to the point of being unable to make decisions or major life changes
- Guilt and self-blame when the abuser convinces the victim the abuse is his or her fault
- Low self-esteem and feelings of failure as a spouse, partner, and/or person

- Conviction that no one other than the abuser would ever want or love them and that a bad relationship is better than no relationship at all
- Learned helplessness, a condition in which the victim comes to believe that all avenues of escape are closed and that she or he is powerless to leave
- Traumatic bonding, a psychological adaptive response in which the victim actually becomes attached to or bonded with his or her abuser (as in the "Stockholm syndrome" when kidnapped victims bond with their kidnappers)
- Lack of information about options for escape and resources available such as shelters and hotlines
- Inability to make use of support services due to language or cultural barriers, disabilities, lifestyle issues, or substance abuse problems
- Lack of effective responses to prior efforts to seek assistance

PARALEGAL PRACTICE TIP

Not infrequently, a divorce action will involve allegations of abuse during the marriage. If a related criminal action is pending at the same time, the defendant may successfully claim that participation in the civil trial on the divorce action will violate his 5th Amendment privilege against self-incrimination in the criminal trial. See, e.g., *Ex parte Rawls (In re Theresa Lynn Rawls v. Bryan C. Rawls)*, 953 So. 2d 374 (Ala. 2006), in which the civil divorce trial was ordered stayed until the criminal trial was adjudicated at the trial level. The husband's Constitutional right trumped the wife's desire for a speedy divorce trial.

Stalking
a knowing and willful course of conduct intended to cause another substantial emotional distress or fear for his or her safety; includes behaviors such as following, telephoning, or watching a person's place of residence or employment

Abusive conduct may be prosecuted under a variety of criminal statutes, ranging from murder and manslaughter in cases involving deaths to assault, battery, aggravated assault, rape/sexual assault, stalking, and cyberstalking, among others. Many states have criminalized domestic battery specifically and provide for heightened penalties when other crimes are committed against family members.

Stalking

Stalking statistics paint a chilling picture. According to the Stalking Resource Center of the National Center for Victims of Crime, approximately 6.6 million people are stalked each year in the United States. 1 out of 6 women and 1 out of 19 men will be stalked during their lifetime to the extent they will be very fearful that they or someone close to them will be harmed or killed. Between 80% and 90% of stalking victims report being stalked by either a current or former intimate partner or acquaintance.[18] 40% of stalking victims experience at least one unwanted contact per week and 11% have been stalked for 5 years or more.[19] The average length of stalking of intimate partners is 2.2 years.[20] 76% of women deliberately killed by an intimate partner were stalked by that partner prior to being murdered.[21] Overall, 87% of stalkers are men. 55% of female victims and 48% of male victims reported the stalking to the police and 28% of the females and 10% of the males were granted orders of protection. More than 65% of those orders were violated.[22]

Stalking consists of a continuing sequence of undesired, harassing, and/or threatening activities which often escalate in frequency and severity. Although a wide range of methods are used, the most common include the following:

- unwanted telephone calls (both completed and hang up), texts, letters, e-mails and other communications
- verbal or physical threats directed at the victim, their children, relatives, friends, and pets

- following or conducting surveillance of the victim
- repeated, unsolicited, and uninvited visits at home, work, or other locations
- damage to the victim's property, including their vehicle(s)
- physical assaults ranging from minor to severe

Stalkers are frequently obsessed with their victims. They are not embarrassed by their behavior and often do not regard it as inappropriate or criminal. They are usually good at playing "mind games" and frequently try to pass their behavior off as innocent jokes not intended to cause their victims distress. They generally refuse to believe that their victim does not want a relationship with them.

Every state, the District of Columbia, the U.S. Territories, and the federal government all have enacted one or more antistalking measures designed to provide protection for victims of this specific form of abuse with or without the existence of a "special relationship." Most stalking statutes provide for enhanced penalties for aggravated stalking, such as when the stalking occurs in violation of a protective order or involves a repeated offense or the use of a weapon. However, among stalking cases, only between a fifth and a quarter of cases reported to the police are prosecuted.[23]

Cyberstalking and **cyberharassment** are especially troubling forms of stalking. Cyberstalking involves repeated use of the Internet, e-mail, or other electronic communications designed to cause a particular person emotional distress and/or fear of physical harm. It is customarily prosecuted as a felony or misdemeanor depending on the circumstances. Cyberharassment differs in that it generally does not involve a credible threat of violence. Rather it involves repeated harassing e-mail messages, instant messages, blog entries, or website postings dedicated solely to tormenting the victim. Some states have standalone cyberharassment statutes and others include it in general harassment statutes.

Technology provides a wealth of tools cyberstalkers can use (often anonymously) to psychologically terrorize their victims. GPS, cell phones, and other electronic devices can be used to track targets. If stalkers can access their victims' computers, they can use spyware software, sometimes sent through e-mail, to track keystrokes (including passwords), e-mails sent, and websites visited. They can verbally attack by posts (including incriminating photos) on message boards or in discussion forums and on a host of social networking sites. (See Case 14.1.) The "Caller ID Spoof" can mimic the caller ID of a bank, cell phone provider or utility company, etc. in an effort to obtain personal information.

The law struggles to keep up with technology, but cases are often difficult to prosecute and prove partly because the stalker frequently operates under a cloak of anonymity. However, clients do have some options they can pursue including but not limited to the following:

- They can take steps to protect themselves by password protecting all accounts on an ongoing basis and having their electronic devices checked by a professional to see if they have been compromised in any way. They can install safety apps on phones. If communications are coming from a free e-mail or social media account, they can file complaints with the companies, report the messages to social media outlets, and block the offender from phone and friends lists. They can consider "going black" and engage in no online activity.

PARALEGAL PRACTICE TIP

To learn more about federal and state-by-state stalking laws, and stalking under Tribal Codes and the Uniform Code of Military Justice, visit the National Center for Victims of Crime site at *www.ncvc.org*.

PARALEGAL PRACTICE TIP

To see forms used by South Dakota courts in Stalking Cases, visit *www.sdjudicial.com*.

Cyberstalking

repeated use of the Internet, text messaging, e-mail, or other forms of electronic communication with the intent to harass, intimidate, torment, or embarrass another person

Cyberharassment

A form of cyberstalking that does not typically involve a credible threat of violence. Rather it is designed to harass the victim through email messages, blog entries and the like.

PARALEGAL PRACTICE TIP

Clients need to be aware of the many ways in which they can be located on the Internet. There are dozens of data-furnishing companies, some free, that supply private records with the click of a mouse!

PARALEGAL PRACTICE TIP

For a compilation of federal, state, tribal, and military stalking statutes, go to *www.victimsofcrime.org* (search stalking statutes). A listing of specific cyberstalking and cyberharassment laws can also be found at *www.ncsl.org*.

PARALEGAL PRACTICE TIP

A recent study by the PEW Research Center found 40% of adult Internet users have experienced harassment online.

- They can assist prosecutors by reporting cyberstalking and providing evidence gathered through use of "stat" or other registry counters that record information about all incoming traffic to social media sites, etc. such as the IP addresses and Internet service providers of individuals viewing the sites. As tempting as it may be to erase all messages of any kind, they can keep and document contacts including screenshots in case the harasser tries to delete them.

- In addition to criminal actions, "civil protection orders are particularly well-suited to address the tactics most often used by stalkers to harass and control their victims. Three-quarters of all stalking victims report receiving unwanted telephone calls, text messages, or other forms of written or spoken correspondence, more than half of all female victims and just under half of all male victims report being approached by their stalkers, and approximately one-third of all victims report being watched, followed, or tracked. Traditional civil protection orders, which include no contact, no harass, and stay away provisions, directly address the behavior perpetrated by stalkers against their victims."[24]

CASE **14.1** *Elonis v. U.S.*, No. 13-983 U.S. Supreme Court (2015)

In December of 2014, the United States Supreme Court heard arguments in this case which involves a young man from Pennsylvania sentenced to 44 months in prison after being convicted under a federal law that makes it a crime to "transmit in interstate or foreign commerce any communication containing any threat to kidnap any person or any threat to injure the person of another." (18 U.S.C. §875(c)) The federal prosecutors treated as actual threats the violent Facebook postings he made (under a pseudonym) against his now ex-wife largely quoting rap lyrics such as the following: "There's no one way to love you but a thousand ways to kill you. I'm not going to rest until your body is a mess, soaked in blood and dying from all the little cuts." Elonis claimed that he was not making "true threats" and that he had no subjective intent to harm his then wife. She, on the other hand, testified "I felt like I was being stalked. I felt extremely afraid for mine and my children's and my families' lives."

The basic issue in the case is whether consistent with the First Amendment right of free speech and *Virginia v. Black*, 538 U.S. 343 (2003) conviction under the federal statute requires proof of the defendant's intent to threaten (the position of the Ninth Circuit and high courts in Vermont, Rhode Island and Massachusetts), or whether it is enough to show that "a reasonable person" would regard the statements as threatening (the position of other federal courts of appeals and state courts). Prosecutions for threats made in the media or "the public square" generally have been confined to "true threats" where the speaker means to communicate a serious expression of an intent to commit an act of unlawful violence to a particular individual or group of individuals. "True threats" do not encompass "political hyperbole" or "vehement, caustic, or unpleasantly sharp attacks."

SIDEBAR

Can social media be a crime scene? Should the court look at the issue of intent in such cases from a subjective perspective focusing on the speaker OR from an

(Continued)

objective perspective focusing on a hypothetical "reasonable person" exposed to the message? The implications of this decision are potentially great for freedom of expression on the Internet generally and for provocative and violent postings online in particular. How do you think the court should address the issue? Read the opinion rendered by the U.S. Supreme Court in June 2015 and see if the Court agreed with your position. You can find the full opinion at *www.pearsonhighered. com/careersresources/* on the companion website for this text in the material related to Chapter 14 under Cases.

Paralegal **Application 14.2**

Battered Woman's Syndrome—A Viable Defense?

Many states permit evidence of a history of abuse to be raised as a defense when a victim finally retaliates and causes injury or death to the abuser. What has come to be known as **battered woman's syndrome** is usually not a complete defense to a crime, but rather may serve to reduce the degree of the crime with which the defendant/victim is charged (from first-degree murder, for example, to second-degree murder or manslaughter) or to mitigate the sentence imposed.

This defense is by no means universally accepted. Many in the criminal justice system agree with commentators who contend it is just one of dozens of potential "abuse excuses" by means of which criminals fail to accept responsibility for their conduct. These critics assert that no prior acts of abuse justify killing or injuring an abuser absent an immediate act of provocation.

Sidebar

Do you believe that evidence of a history of abuse should be admissible in cases where victims of abuse have killed or assaulted their abusers? Should self-defense based on past abuse be a complete defense (resulting in a not guilty verdict) or only reduce the severity of the crime or the sentence? Are there circumstances in which the defense is more appropriate than others? Consider the situation in *Commonwealth v. Rodriquez*, 418 Mass. 1, 633 N.E.2d 1039 (1994), in which the Massachusetts Supreme Judicial Court (SJC) ordered a new trial in a manslaughter case involving a woman who was convicted of fatally stabbing her boy friend during an argument. At trial she claimed she acted in self-defense. The trial court excluded evidence of the long history of physical abuse she had suffered at the hands of the boy friend who had among other acts, tried to strangle her, punched her in the stomach when she was pregnant, thrown bleach in her face, raped her, and held a baseball bat to her head while threatening to kill her. The SJC held that where a claim of self-defense is in issue and there is evidence of a pattern of abuse of the defendant by the victim, expert testimony should be allowed on the effects of battering to aid the jury in determining the reasonableness of the defendant's use of deadly force. Do you agree?

Battered woman's syndrome
the psychological condition of a woman who has been abused for a sustained period of time; sometimes used as a defense to justify the act or mitigate the penalty when the woman attacks her abuser

CIVIL ACTIONS

Historically, the doctrine of interspousal immunity prevented spouses from suing each other in civil actions. The doctrine was designed to serve strong public policies favoring the preservation of marriage and family harmony and the prevention of fraudulent claims between spouses with liability insurance. The doctrine has eroded to a considerable extent, such that most states now permit one spouse to sue the other spouse for intentional or negligent injury to property and for intentional (but not negligent) injury to the person (e.g., assault, battery), especially if the parties are not living together. If a divorce is pending, the courts may require that such claims be raised in the context of that action. The premise is that, if a party receives a greater share of the marital property based on the other party's abusive conduct during the marriage, that party should not be permitted to file a postdivorce tort claim for battery or intentional infliction of emotional distress for injuries that occurred during the course of the marriage, thereby getting a "second bite of the apple."[25]

Although there may be restrictions on if and when tort remedies will be available to divorcing spouses, depending on the facts of each case, actions may be brought by spouses and other victims for tortious conduct such as intentional infliction of emotional distress, assault and battery, or false imprisonment. In addition, some states, including California, recognize domestic violence as a discrete tort.

PROTECTIVE ORDERS

Under civil domestic violence laws of all fifty states and the District of Columbia, a victim of family violence can seek an order of protection if he or she satisfies the threshold requirements regarding standing and qualifying conduct laid out in applicable statutes which vary considerably from state to state.

Standing

Standing to seek protective orders is generally available to individuals involved in spousal, intimate, or other "special" relationships. Depending on the state, this may include individuals who:

- are or were married to each other
- have a child in common or a child *in utero*
- are related by blood or marriage
- are or have been in a substantial dating relationship
- are or have lived together in the same household (this may include couples, parents and children, roommates, etc.)

Several states have gender neutralized their statutes and/or expressly extended standing to individuals involved in same-sex as well as heterosexual intimate relationships. In addition, a growing number of states have amended their abuse prevention laws to allow certain third parties to obtain restraining orders such as individuals assisting victims of domestic violence or present partners of persons abused by former spouses or intimate partners (see, e.g., Texas Stat. Ann. Tit. 4 sec. 71.0021(1)(B) and Okla. Stat. Ann. Tit. 22 sec. 60.1). The decision with respect to who has standing often is ultimately a matter of judicial discretion. For example, the court decides based on the facts of each case whether or not a couple is in a "substantial" dating relationship.

Qualifying Conduct

Some states require that the petitioner have suffered actual or attempted physical harm or have been caused to engage in sexual relations as a result of force or threat of force. In several states, a threat of serious physical harm is sufficient. A limited number of states extend standing when there is serious emotional or verbal abuse or malicious destruction of property, particularly when there is a history of violence on the perpetrator's part clearly evidencing a potential for harm. Typical examples of violent and controlling abusive behaviors considered by the courts include:

- slaps, punches, bites, or "head butts"
- grabbing, choking, pulling hair

- display or use of weapons in an intimidating manner
- intimidation by use of threatening gestures, shouting, driving recklessly, or refusing to allow entry to or exit from a location
- destruction of furniture or other property
- ripping out phone lines, slashing tires, etc.
- threatening to harm the victim's children or take them away to another state or country
- injuring or threatening to injure pets

Procedure for Obtaining a Protective Order

The procedure for obtaining a **protective order** varies somewhat from state to state, but is invariably relatively simple:

- The plaintiff files a Complaint or Petition for a Protective Order requesting a variety of forms of relief. The Complaint usually includes or is accompanied by an **affidavit** in which the plaintiff describes the nature of the abuse that has led to the filing. In some states, such as Indiana, if the petition is made on the basis of the petitioner's information and belief rather than on personal knowledge, the petitioner also must attach affidavits by one or more persons who have personal knowledge of the facts stated within the petition. The victim may request in the Complaint or separately that his or her address be impounded. The U.S. Postal Service will also keep an address confidential when the victim presents a copy of his or her protective order to the appropriate postal office employee, although the address will still be provided to agents of the state or federal government.
- The Complaint is filed in a court with jurisdiction over such matters. Usually several types of courts have **concurrent jurisdiction**, including courts that hear criminal, juvenile, and family matters. Most states do not require a filing fee, and those that do allow the fee to be waived upon proof of inability to pay. In some states, such as Massachusetts, when a complaint for a protective order is filed, the court is required to search a statewide computerized database to determine if the defendant has been charged with a crime, has been involved in domestic or other violence, or has an outstanding arrest warrant. Depending on the circumstances, the court may be required to take further action which can result in the arrest of the alleged abuser.
- At the petitioner's request, the Complaint often is considered by the court initially on an *ex parte* basis (without notice to the defendant).
- A temporary order will be issued if the court believes there is reason to believe that abuse has occurred or is threatened. The extent of relief granted at this initial stage may be limited to **restraining**, **stay away**, or **no-contact orders**.
- The defendant is served with the Complaint and any *ex parte* orders in a manner consistent with local procedure.
- A second hearing is held within a statutorily prescribed period (commonly ten days), at which both the plaintiff and defendant have an opportunity to be heard, and the court decides whether to extend, modify, or vacate the initial order. In some states, this second hearing must be requested by the defendant, and a failure of the plaintiff to appear may result in automatic dismissal.

Protective order
in the context of family violence cases, a court order directing a person to refrain from harming or harassing another person

Affidavit
a written statement of facts based on firsthand knowledge, information, or belief and signed by the affiant under pain and penalty of perjury

Concurrent jurisdiction
two or more courts having simultaneous jurisdiction over the same subject matter

Ex parte
without advance notice to the opposing party; a matter considered and initially ruled on by the court without hearing from both parties

Restraining order
a court order, most commonly issued in domestic violence cases, restricting an individual from threatening and/or harassing another individual or individuals

Stay away order
a court order requiring a person to keep away from another individual wherever he or she may be (home, work, school, etc.)

No-contact order
a court order prohibiting an individual from having contact of any kind with a person he or she has threatened and/or abused in some manner

PARALEGAL PRACTICE TIP

To see a form used in Connecticut to request nondisclosure of information in a case, visit *www.jud.ct.gov.*

PARALEGAL PRACTICE TIP

Defending a client in an action for a protective order can be a challenge. Initial orders are frequently issued *ex parte* and become a matter of record; the rules of evidence are often not strictly observed; little discovery is usually available; and courts tend to err on the side of caution and grant extensive relief to petitioners. Despite an attorney's best efforts, a defendant in such actions may feel, sometimes justifiably, that he or she is being denied due process.

PARALEGAL PRACTICE TIP

To see a Domestic Violence No-Contact Order and a Protected Person's Motion to Modify/Rescind a Domestic Violence No Contact Order, visit *www.courts.wa.gov/forms* (Washington).

PARALEGAL PRACTICE TIP

Paralegals should not contact the opposing party without supervisor approval when a no-contact order against the firm's client is in force. A 2004 New Hampshire case involving a protective order with a no-contact provision illustrates the potential consequences of unauthorized contact in such circumstances. The New Hampshire Supreme Court held that, regardless of the purpose of the contact, the state could prosecute a defendant who, through his attorney, knowingly contacted the alleged victim. See *State v. Kidder*, 150 N.H. 600, 843 A.2d 312 (2004).

- An extended order will contain an expiration date. When that date approaches, if the plaintiff wants the order extended for an additional period, he or she usually must petition the court for an extension.

Because the procedure for obtaining a restraining order is relatively uncomplicated, it usually can be completed by the plaintiff on his or her own or with minimal technical assistance from court personnel. In some cases there is merit to proceeding *pro se*, as filing often represents the first time the victim has ever asserted his or her rights against the abuser. That psychological advantage aside, it may be helpful for the client to have assistance of counsel, particularly with completion of the affidavit, identification of potential forms of relief that may be available based on the parties' circumstances, and representation at court hearings when the defendant may be present.

Types of Relief Available in Protective Orders

Courts may grant a variety of forms of relief tailored to the facts and circumstances of each case. For example, the court may order that the defendant:

- stay away from the plaintiff at home, work, school, or any other place he or she may be (The stay away order may also extend to locations where the plaintiff's child or children may be.)
- have no contact with the plaintiff by any means, including telephone, text messaging, e-mail, U.S. mail, and notes on vehicle doors and windows
- refrain from abusing, injuring, or harassing the plaintiff either directly and/or with the assistance of third parties
- vacate the household (if the parties live together) regardless of who holds title to the property or is responsible for the lease (The court may permit the defendant to collect his or her personal belongings from the property—usually with police supervision.)
- surrender guns, ammunition, license to carry a gun, and Firearm Identification Card (FID)[26]
- pay compensation to the plaintiff for damages, losses, or expenses incurred as a direct result of the abuse (e.g., for repair of destroyed property, installation of new locks, uninsured medical and counseling expenses, loss of time from work, relocation and moving expenses, and costs of staying in a hotel, motel, or shelter). In some states, such as Illinois, offenders convicted of domestic violence are liable by statute for the cost of counseling for children who witnessed their crimes. (See, e.g., 720 ILCS 5/12–3.2.)
- if requested, judges are customarily authorized to make temporary child custody and support awards in the context of protective order cases. Local procedural rules will dictate how custody and child support orders will be handled if there are already existing or pending orders and/or if one or both of the parties subsequently files for divorce, separation, or custody
- in an increasing number of states, the court may order a defendant to stay away from and/or refrain from abusing a pet and may order exclusive possession/custody of the pet to the plaintiff
- some states, including California, explicitly allow the plaintiff to be granted permission to record communications made by the defendant that violate the judge's orders

In addition to other specific forms of relief, a majority of state statutes include a catchall provision authorizing courts to provide whatever relief is appropriate to stop the abuse and protect the victim in a given set of circumstances. For example, in a case in which a defendant is threatening to expose the plaintiff's HIV status, the court may order the defendant not to "directly or indirectly reveal any information about the Petitioner's health status to Petitioner's employer . . . with intent to cause emotional distress or harass the Petitioner. . . ."[27] Although on the surface such a provision may appear to restrain free speech, such orders have been granted and upheld.

Critics often say that restraining orders are "not worth the paper they are printed on," that they create a false sense of security in victims, that they are frequently violated, and that they often exacerbate rather than eliminate abuse. In addition, the U.S. Supreme Court established in the *Gonzales* case that petitioners have no absolute right to enforcement of the orders they obtain. Those criticisms aside, in some instances they serve their intended purpose. The police usually play a major role in serving and enforcing protective orders. Although protective orders are initially civil in nature, violations constitute contempt of court as well as independent criminal offenses potentially punishable by jail sentences and/or fines. In order to prove a violation, a valid order must have issued (counsel should have a certified copy of the order); the defendant must have been served with the order; the order must have been in effect at the time of the violation; and the defendant must have violated the order.

Occasionally a client will intentionally create a situation in which a violation of a protective order is inevitable. What if the "protected" party in effect aids and abets the violation by continually initiating contact with the defendant by phone, mail, or in person? The potential for problems is especially great when the parties have a child in common. For example, assume both parents want to attend their child's basketball game, dance concert, or school play. Further assume that a protective order is in force requiring the defendant to stay at least 500 feet away from the plaintiff. The defendant arrives at the event after the other parent, and the school auditorium is so small that it is impossible to be present without being within 500 feet of the plaintiff. Technically there is a violation even if the defendant makes no effort whatsoever to approach, threaten, or otherwise communicate with the plaintiff. In such a situation, the defendant may be subject to arrest in front of the child and others present if the plaintiff contacts the police.

Most advocates argue that "mutual restraining orders" should be discouraged, particularly in cases where one of the parties strikes out only in self-defense. To issue a restraining order in such circumstances, in effect, relieves the real abuser of responsibility. In addition, when mutual restraining orders are issued, they may create confusion for police trying to enforce them and for judges trying to make custody orders when a prior history of abuse is a relevant factor to be considered. Some states have addressed this topic by statute. Wisconsin's mandatory arrest statute provides that when an officer has reasonable grounds to believe that spouses, former spouses, or other persons who reside together or formerly resided together are committing or have committed domestic abuse against each other, the officer does not have to arrest both persons but should arrest the person whom the officer believes to be the primary aggressor.[28]

Some states also provide for issuance of "domestic relations restraining orders" in the context of divorce and other family law proceedings. However, these

PARALEGAL PRACTICE TIP

The extent to which a plaintiff has a legal "right" to enforcement of an order is not entirely clear. The *Town of Castle Rock v. Gonzales* case (545 U.S. 748, 752, 125 S. Ct. 2796, 162 L. Ed. 2d 658 (2005)) addressed this issue directly. The opinion can be accessed at *www.pearsonhighered.com/careersresources/* in the website material related to Chapter 14 under Cases.

PARALEGAL PRACTICE TIP

This issue is examined by Livia Fritsche in a 2014 article in the Washington and Lee Law Review titled *The Role of Enforcement in a Violation of a Protective Order.*

PARALEGAL PRACTICE TIP

To see how each state treats mutual restraining orders, visit *www.americanbar.org.*

PARALEGAL PRACTICE TIP

It is not uncommon for a client to want to seek a restraining order against his or her opponent for the sole purpose of gaining a perceived advantage in a case. If the complaint is baseless, the attorney has an ethical duty not to support filing of a claim made in bad faith and solely for the purpose of harassing or embarrassing the other party or to gain an unfair advantage in the matter being litigated.

orders are not technically protective orders, and the safety of victims is not their primary intended purpose. They may be included routinely in marital agreements or may issue at the discretion of the court. There is no requirement for abuse to have occurred to obtain a domestic relations restraining order. Essentially, they are designed to serve as reminders to parties that they are not to interfere in each other's lives.

GUARDIANSHIP

Forms of relief such as protective orders reflect what has been termed an "empowerment model of domestic violence," which presumes that a victim of abuse is capable of deciding to leave an abusive relationship, hold the abuser accountable, and move on making use of available resources such as shelters and support groups. However, for some women, these resources are not genuine options. There are cases in which "a battered woman can become coercively controlled—so incapacitated by repeated abuse that she cannot protect herself or escape from her abuser."[29] She has lost her autonomy and must be empowered by forcible removal from the control of an abuser.

"In extreme cases . . . , the state-sanctioned intervention of guardianship is necessary because an abuser has brutally and systematically deprived a woman of her ability to exercise independent judgment."[30] Guardianship has the potential to bridge the gap for a victim between being totally subject to the control of the abuser and becoming independent. The **guardian** is appointed by the court and is granted the authority to act on behalf of the "ward" for some or all purposes until such time as the court determines the ward has the capacity to act on his or her own behalf. The guardian can, for example, make housing arrangements for the ward, pay bills, make decisions regarding counseling and medical treatment, and represent the ward in legal matters.

Recognizing and Responding When Intimate Partner Violence is an Issue in a Case

Many victims are afraid, ashamed, or embarrassed about the abuse they experience and have never reported it to the police or discussed it with counselors, physicians, family, friends, or attorneys. Many perpetrators are aware that their conduct is criminal but they are unwilling to face the consequences of their actions by acknowledging it to others. As surprising as it may seem, some abusers do not even recognize that they are perpetrators, especially when their conduct is culturally condoned, and many victims, particularly those who believe they are responsible for the abuse they suffer, do not perceive themselves as victims. Some clients will directly acknowledge that they are victims or perpetrators, particularly if the abuse is already a matter of public record, documented in police reports, and substantiated by medical records and other evidence such as photographs. More often, however, the abuse will not be revealed by the client at the outset of a case. Members of the family law team need to listen carefully to the client's language and also be sensitive to cues in behavior that suggest the existence of unacknowledged abuse.

PARALEGAL PRACTICE TIP

To see an example of a Petition for Appointment of Guardian of Incapacitated Individual, visit *www .courts.michigan.gov.*

Guardian
an individual appointed by the court to have legal authority over another's person and/or property during a period of minority or incapacitation

Given the potential that a client is either a perpetrator or a victim of family violence, materials often are made available in family law office reception areas regarding resources designed to assist both victims of abuse and perpetrators who might conceivably be motivated to change their behavior or be forced to accept the consequences. Such materials include, among others, hotline numbers, emergency shelter contacts, law enforcement agency numbers, names of victim advocates, instructions and forms for obtaining protective orders, and locations of resource centers, support groups, and batterers' programs. They may also include educational and consciousness-raising materials about what constitutes abuse and techniques for recognizing when someone is a victim or an abuser.

WHEN THE CLIENT IS A VICTIM

The most important issue to address when the client is a victim of family violence is her safety. This is particularly the case if she has made the decision to leave the relationship and, if married, divorce the abusive spouse. She needs to have a plan of action and a supportive safety net in place when the departure occurs and/or the Complaint is served.

> When an abusive partner realizes that the victim truly has made affirmative efforts to leave him, he may feel emasculated. His threats, protestations of love, and domestic terrorism have all proved futile in his efforts to retain control over her. It is at this time that many batterers turn to other devices to exert domination over the fleeing partner. It is at this time that the risk of serious violence in intimate relationships is at its h[e]ight. After the victim has made efforts to escape, the batterer is most likely to seek to retaliate against her by sabotaging the independent life she tries to establish for herself. . . . Victims constantly relay stories of the batterer's false reports to child protective services; false "anonymous" tip-offs to employers about the victim's disloyalty or dishonesty; and calls to employers or family members revealing damaging, . . . information about the victim.[31]

If the client is not yet committed to leaving the relationship, members of the family law team should listen to her patiently, allow her to freely express her feelings, and be sensitive to the many reasons why people remain in such relationships. Team members need to communicate the message that no one deserves to be threatened or beaten, but also be prepared to let the client make her own decision, even if it means not yet being ready to leave the relationship.

One of the reasons why a client may not be prepared to terminate an abusive relationship may be a sense of helplessness and inability to escape the situation. A common tool for helping clients who are victims develop a sense of control is a Safety Plan. Safety plans may be prepared by the victim independently or with the assistance of a family law team member. There are many models of safety plans and they typically address topics such as the following:

- Contact numbers for resources such as the police, hotlines, and shelters
- Locations where the victim can go if forced to leave home
- Suggestions for increasing safety at home, work, and in the community
- Items and documents to take when leaving home
- Strategies for protecting children

PARALEGAL PRACTICE TIP

One model of a Safety Plan is accessible at *www.pearsonhighered .com/careersresources/* in the website material related to Chapter 14 under Resources. Two additional resources for safety planning can be found at *www.ncvc.org* and *www.foxboroughma.gov* (search for "Safety Strategies for Domestic Violence Victims").

WHEN THE CLIENT IS A PERPETRATOR

Abusers rarely self-identify, and, therefore, members of the family law team may never learn of their conduct or, worse, may be taken by surprise by it! Abusers come in all forms and from all backgrounds, and there is no one mold into which they all fit. There are, however, some red flags to watch for, a cluster of characteristics that batterers in particular commonly share. The team should be alert to these indicators. (See Exhibit 14.2.)

EXHIBIT 14.2 Profile of an Abuser

Technically, there is no such thing as a profile of an abuser. However, there are certain traits, attitudes, and behaviors that may be strong indicators. They typically include the following:

- He believes in traditional, rigid, hierarchical sex roles.
- He engages in jealous, possessive, and controlling behaviors.
- He has a two-sided personality—one mild and gentle, the other mean and abusive.
- He believes he is a victim.
- He is hypersensitive to criticism.
- He has a distorted self-image. (It may be in the form of low self-esteem and feelings of inadequacy or an inflated positive self-image.)
- He is self-centered.
- He is manipulative.
- He engages in minimization, denial, blame, and criticism.
- He is overly dependent on his partner and unable to see her as a separate person.
- He has an explosive temper and breaks or throws things when angry and hits, shoves, and kicks his partner and/or children.
- He is cruel to animals.
- He has difficulty expressing feelings appropriately.
- He has a history of bad relationships.
- He was abused as a child in his family of origin (physically, emotionally, and/or sexually).

Much of this Exhibit is based on a series of presentations by Douglas Gaudette, Director of the Family Safety Project at Holy Family Hospital in Methuen, Massachusetts.

If the client is an abuser, alleged or proven, the ethical challenges of representation are magnified. Members of the family law team need to remain as nonjudgmental and emotionally uninvolved as possible in order to serve as zealous advocates. The legal system in this country is based on the premise that every client is entitled to competent representation, no matter how offensive or illegal his or her behavior may be. Perhaps the greatest challenge to the team is to balance the duty to maintain client confidentiality with the responsibility to prevent the commission of a crime that could cause serious physical injury or death to another individual. This sensitive question is discussed in greater depth at the end of this chapter.

Child Victims of Family Violence

THE SCOPE OF THE PROBLEM

PARALEGAL PRACTICE TIP

The annual "Child Maltreatment" report can be accessed at *www.acf.hhs.gov*.

The most comprehensive and authoritative source of data on child abuse and neglect in the United States is generated through the National Child Abuse and Neglect Data System (NCANDS) by the Children's Bureau in the Administration for Children and Families in the U.S. Department of Health and Human Services (HHS). The Bureau collects and analyzes data submitted by the states, the District of Columbia, and Puerto Rico on an annual basis. The data is presented in an annual report, "Child Maltreatment," published each spring since 1990. Major findings of the report for fiscal year 2013 (published 1/1/2015) include the following:

- Approximately 3.5 million referrals involving about 6.4 million children were made to child protective service (CPS) agencies. Of this number, 60.9% were screened in and approximately 15.5% were substantiated. Less than 1% of the reports were determined to be intentionally false.
- About 60% of the reports were made by professionals (legal/law enforcement, educational, medical, and social services personnel) and the remainder by unclassified reporters, including anonymous reporters and nonprofessionals (relatives, neighbors, friends, etc.).
- With respect to types of abuse experienced by confirmed victims, 79.5% suffered neglect, 18% physical abuse, 9.5% sexual abuse, 7.8% psychological maltreatment, and 2.4% medical neglect. 1,484 children reportedly died as a result of child abuse or neglect.
- Approximately half (47%) of the victims were five years old or younger, and the highest rate of victimization was of children younger than one year old.
- Of the child victims, 51% were female and 49% were male.
- 44% of the victims of abuse were white, 22.4% African-American, and 21.2% Hispanic.
- Approximately 91% of the perpetrators of child maltreatment were parents; 53.9% were women, 45% men, 1.1% unknown; 83% were between 18 and 44 years of age; 49.3% were white, 20.1% African American, and 19.5% Hispanic.[32]

Although many abused children grow up to be good parents, studies indicate that about one third become abusers themselves.[33] In addition, according to the National Institute of Justice, being abused or neglected as a child increases the likelihood of arrest as a juvenile by greater than 50%.[34]

Federal Recognition of the Problem

In 1974, Congress passed the first comprehensive federal legislation to address the problem of child abuse and neglect in the United States, the Child Abuse Prevention and Treatment Act (CAPTA),[35] establishing, among other initiatives, the National Center of Child Abuse and Neglect (NCCAN) to serve as a clearinghouse for information on child protection programs and research. Largely in response to CAPTA, all states now have in place child-abuse-reporting laws and comprehensive child protection systems vesting centralized responsibility in a single designated child protection agency, typically a department of child and family or social services.

Types of Child Abuse

According to the summary "Child Maltreatment" report, children in the United States suffer a variety of forms of abuse in the family environment, ranging

PARALEGAL PRACTICE TIP

Approximately 10% experience other forms of abuse, including abandonment and congenital drug addiction. The percentages regarding types of abuse add up to more than 100% because some children suffered more than one form of abuse.

PARALEGAL PRACTICE TIP

To learn more about federal definitions and search for definitions of various kinds of abuse in your state, visit *www.childwelfare.gov.*

from, in the extreme, death at the hands of their parents, siblings, or caretakers to emotional abuse and the potentially devastating effects of witnessing the abuse of other family members. Types of child abuse are defined by both federal and state law. Under CAPTA, child abuse and neglect is defined as:

> . . . at a minimum, any recent act or failure to act on the part of a parent or caretaker, which results in death, serious physical or emotional harm, sexual abuse, or exploitation, or an act or failure to act which presents an imminent risk of serious harm.[36]

The forms of abuse most commonly identified and further defined by the states are:

Neglect.

Physical abuse

Emotional abuse

Sexual abuse

Substance abuse

The states vary with respect to their treatment of **abandonment** as a category of child abuse and neglect. Several states (including Connecticut, Illinois, Kentucky, Louisiana, New Jersey, Texas, and Virginia) include it in the definition of neglect. More than a dozen states (including Indiana, Kansas, Maine, Massachusetts, New Mexico, New York, Ohio, and South Carolina) establish abandonment as a discrete category.

> In general, it is considered abandonment of the child when the parent's identity or whereabouts are unknown, the child has been left by the parent in circumstances where the child suffers serious harm, or the parent has failed to maintain contact with the child or to provide reasonable support for a specified period of time.[37]

Abandonment
occurs when the whereabouts of a child's parent are unknown, the parent has left the child in unsafe circumstances, and/or has failed to maintain contact with or provide support for the child for an extended period of time

NEGLECT

At the federal level, **neglect** is defined as "a type of maltreatment that refers to the failure by the caregiver to provide needed, age appropriate care although financially able to do so, or offered financial or other means to do so."[38] A distinction is made between an inability to provide for a child and a deliberate failure to provide with or without any apparent reason. Neglect usually involves an ongoing pattern of inadequate care falling into one or more categories: physical, emotional, medical, and educational.

- **Physical neglect** is the form most commonly reported. It generally involves inadequate supervision and/or a failure to provide adequate food, shelter, and clothing such that the child's health, safety, growth, and development are endangered.
- **Emotional neglect** generally includes a pattern of rejecting, isolating, and ignoring the child's needs for nurturance, stimulation, and social contact.
- **Medical neglect** involves the failure of a parent or caretaker to provide appropriate health care for a child. Although medical neglect cases tend to be high-profile, they commonly make up less than 5% of cases of child maltreatment. Medical neglect ranges from situations in which caretakers ignore

Neglect
failure by the caregiver to provide needed, age-appropriate care, although financially able to or offered financial or other means to do so

Physical neglect
inadequate supervision and/or a failure to provide adequate food, shelter, and clothing such that the child's health, safety, growth, and development are endangered

Emotional neglect
a pattern of rejecting, isolating, and ignoring a child's needs for nurturance, stimulation, and social contact

Medical neglect
the failure of a parent or caretaker to provide appropriate health care for a child

medical advice in nonemergency situations to circumstances in which a parent refuses medical care for a seriously ill child due to religious beliefs, cultural traditions, or financial limitations. The state will usually intervene in an emergency or when the child has a life-threatening or chronic condition. However, the CAPTA Amendments of 1996 added a provision specifying that the Act does not establish a federal requirement that "a parent or legal guardian provide a child any medical service or treatment against the religious beliefs of the parent or legal guardian."[39] Approximately thirty states and the District of Columbia exempt from the definition of neglect those parents who do not seek medical care for their children on the basis of religious beliefs, and three states (Arizona, Connecticut, and Washington) specifically exempt Christian Scientists. About half of the thirty states authorize the court to intervene and order treatment when warranted by the circumstances.[40]

- **Educational neglect** refers to a parent's failure to use his or her best efforts to ensure that a child of mandatory school age is enrolled in and attends a legally recognized public or private school or participates in a state-monitored program of home schooling. A distinction is usually made when the child is a chronic truant through no apparent lack of supervision or effort on the parent's part.

Educational neglect
a parent's failure to use his or her best efforts to ensure that a child of mandatory school age attends a legally recognized school or program of home schooling

PHYSICAL ABUSE

In general at the federal level, physical abuse is defined as "non-accidental physical injury to the child"[41] that may be caused by behaviors such as punching, striking, kicking, biting, or burning. Although the most visible form of abuse, it is not as common as neglect. Physical abuse cases reflect varying degrees of culpability and involve:

- parents who deliberately and maliciously physically abuse their children;
- parents who administer severe punishment to their children in the good-faith belief that they are acting in the children's best interests;
- parents who have never developed effective parenting skills and who, as a result, are poor disciplinarians; and
- parents who accidentally injure their children.

Investigations of physical abuse also often reveal that alcohol and drug abuse as well as other forms of domestic violence are evident in a physically abused child's home environment.

Child Abuse or Discipline?

Common law recognized a parental privilege to use reasonable force in disciplining children. In describing the privilege, Blackstone commented that a parent "may lawfully correct his child, being under age, in a reasonable manner," and that "battery is, in some cases, justifiable or lawful; as where one who hath authority, a parent or a master, gives moderate correction to his child, his scholar, or his apprentice."[42] The U.S. Supreme Court has also held that parents have a constitutionally protected fundamental liberty interest in directing their children's upbringing.[43] However, the parental right to discipline is not unlimited, and the states have the right to restrict it to protect children from cruel and excessive punishment. (See Case 14.2.)

Although the Supreme Court has not set a fixed rule defining what constitutes unreasonable or excessive corporal punishment under all circumstances, a majority of states have adopted the common law standard of "reasonableness and moderation." For example, Ohio requires a parent's use of force to be "proper and reasonable under the circumstances."[44] In Washington State, "A parent has a right to use reasonable and timely punishment to discipline a minor child within the bounds of moderation and for the best interests of the child."[45] In Rhode Island, "[t]he test of unreasonableness is met at the point at which a parent ceases to act in good faith and with parental affection and acts immoderately, cruelly, or mercilessly with a malicious desire to inflict pain, rather than make a genuine effort to correct the child by proper means."[46] In Wisconsin, "the accepted degree of force must vary according to the age, sex, physical and mental condition and disposition of the child, the conduct of the child, the nature of the discipline, and all the surrounding circumstances."[47]

Occasionally, inappropriate discipline results in a condition called "**shaken baby syndrome**." First identified in the early 1970s, shaken baby syndrome is a condition that results from repeated, vigorous shaking of a baby that causes brain damage and sometimes death. It can result from a single incident or a more prolonged pattern of abuse. "Violent shaking is especially dangerous to infants and young children because their neck muscles are not fully developed and their brain tissue is exceptionally fragile."[48] Caretakers who abuse very young children in this manner often claim that the babies fell but "The force of shaking a child in anger and frustration is 5 to 10 times greater than if the child were simply to trip and fall."[49] Initially, the condition can be difficult to diagnose because the resulting injuries are not always the same and are frequently not externally observable. They usually include brain damage and swelling, mental retardation or developmental delays, loss of sensory functions such as sight and hearing, and sometimes death. Because of its nature and the lack of a national database addressing this specific form of physical abuse, the number of children who are victims of shaken baby syndrome is unknown.

Shaken baby syndrome
a condition that results from repeated, vigorous shaking of a baby that causes brain damage and sometimes death and that can result from a single incident or a more prolonged pattern of abuse

CASE **14.2** *State of New Mexico v. Lefevre*, 138 N.M. 174, 2005 NMCA 101, 117 P.3d 980 (2005)

BACKGROUND

This case involved the father of a twelve-year-old daughter and her younger brother. The father had been divorced from his wife for several years, and their relationship was still contentious at the time of the incident addressed in this case. He visited regularly with their children (the daughter once a month and the son every other weekend and Wednesdays). He had become concerned that he was not receiving copies of "Wednesday Notes," which advised parents of school schedules and special activities. He had told his daughter that her brother had told him that she was removing the "Notes" from his backpack and that was why he was not seeing them. When the father went to school to pick up the children he approached them from the back, and it appeared that the daughter was removing something from her brother's backpack, which the father presumed were the notes he needed to see. He allegedly grabbed and squeezed her hand "really hard" and said, "That's not your backpack." When she said, "Dad, that's not fair," he replied, "I'm sick

(Continued)

of you." The daughter continued to a sports tryout and only later told her mother about the incident. The mother asked if she wanted to speak to the guardian *ad litem*, go to the hospital, or speak to the police about it. The guardian was unavailable and she declined to see a doctor. She did, however, speak with the police. At the father's trial on a battery charge, a police officer testified that he saw a dime-sized bruise on the daughter's hand.

The father was convicted of battery and then appealed the conviction, arguing that the act of grabbing his daughter's hand was privileged under a parental control justification. He argued that: "(1) federal law recognizes a fundamental right of parents to make decisions concerning care, custody, and control of their children; (2) state law recognizes the common law parental control justification as an affirmative defense for offensive acts which would otherwise be punishable under the battery statute; (3) and the district court erred in finding that the touching was unlawful, . . ."

FROM THE OPINION

We hold that, in New Mexico, a parent has a privilege to use moderate or reasonable physical force, without criminal liability, when engaged in the discipline of his or her child. Discipline involves controlling behavior and correcting misbehavior for the betterment and welfare of the child. The physical force cannot be cruel or excessive if it is to be justified. . . .

2. Defendant's Act Fell Within The Parental Privilege

The battery offense of which the Defendant was convicted proscribes "the unlawful, intentional touching or application of force to the person of another, when done in a rude, insolent or angry manner." § 30–3–4. The State had the burden to prove beyond a reasonable doubt all elements of the offense, including unlawfulness. . . . When a parent's behavior falls within the parental privilege, the act is not unlawful. . . . Thus, when a question of parental privilege exists, the State must prove beyond a reasonable doubt that the parent's conduct did not come within the privilege. . . .

In considering whether the State has disproved the justification, the court or jury is entitled to consider such factors as "the age, physical condition, and other characteristics of a child as well as . . . the gravity of the misconduct." Arnold, 543 N.W.2d at 603; . . . there must exist some threshold at which parental physical force in the discipline of children is justified even though, technically, the elements of the battery offense can be proven. . . .

. . . there must exist for parents a harbor safe from prosecutorial interference in parental judgment. See Model Penal Code and Commentaries § 3.08, cmt. 2 (1985) ("So long as a parent uses moderate force for permissible purposes, the criminal law should not provide for review of the reasonableness of the parent's judgment."). In our view, an isolated instance of moderate or reasonable physical force as that in the present case that results in nothing more than transient pain or temporary marks or bruises is protected under the parental discipline privilege. . . .

This protection for parents should exist even if the parent acts out of frustration or short temper. Parents do not always act with calmness of mind or considered judgment when upset with, or concerned about, their children's behavior. . . . A reaction often occurs from behavior a parent deems inappropriate that irritates or angers the parent, causing a reactive, demonstrative act. Heat of the moment must not result in immoderate physical force and must be managed; however, an angry moment driving moderate or reasonable discipline is often part and parcel of the real world of parenting with which prosecutors and courts should not interfere. What parent among us can say he or she has not been angered to some degree from a child's defiant, impudent, or insolent conduct, sufficient to call for spontaneous, stern, and meaningful discipline?

In the present case, no reasonable minds could differ on the legal consequence of Defendant's acts. The district court did not find or determine that Defendant had no legitimate disciplinary purpose whatsoever in mind. Even were a disciplinary purpose questionable or obscure, Defendant's act was an isolated one. He reacted when he saw Daughter with her hand in Son's pack. His demonstrative act, even if an angry touching, resulted in only a temporary dime-sized bruise on Daughter's hand and transient pain. The force was relatively inconsequential; the injury was marginal. Defendant's conduct was not cruel or excessive, and considering the totality of the circumstances, it was moderate and reasonable. "If such acts, ... with no apparent evidence of any aggravating factors, are sufficient to support an assault charge, then any physical contact by a parent with a child that hurts the child may support an assault conviction if the State elects to prosecute." Wilder, 748 A.2d at 456.

We determine that Defendant's conduct did not reach beyond the point of departure from justified parental discipline and was privileged, and that, as a matter of law, the evidence in this case was insufficient to support a determination of guilt on the charge of battery beyond a reasonable doubt.

Conclusion

We reverse Defendant's conviction of battery and remand with instructions to enter a judgment of acquittal.

SIDEBAR

Do you agree with the decision of the appellate court in this case? Explain your response. The full opinion in the *Lefevre* case is available at *www.pearsonhighered .com/careersresources/* in the website material related to Chapter 14 under Cases.

EMOTIONAL ABUSE

All states and territories except Georgia and Washington include emotional maltreatment in their statutory definitions of types of abuse, sometimes referring to it as psychological abuse. As of April 2015, more than twenty states specifically defined emotional abuse.

Typical language used in these definitions is "injury to the psychological capacity or emotional stability of the child as evidenced by an observable or substantial change in behavior, emotional response, or cognition," or as evidenced by "anxiety, depression, withdrawal, or aggressive behavior."[50]

Caretaker behavior that rises to the level of emotional abuse generally encompasses a persistent pattern of the behaviors described earlier under emotional neglect, along with more overt behaviors including verbally assaulting and belittling children, terrorizing them with threats of punishment and abandonment, humiliating and embarrassing them, and exploiting them by involving them in illegal behavior such as theft. It does not include occasional and unintentionally hurtful outbursts that can occur with even well-intentioned parents. It is more likely to occur among parents who were themselves abused as children, who have never had an opportunity to learn or develop effective parenting skills, and who have unrealistic expectations for their children. Whatever the cause, many researchers believe that emotional abuse is a stronger predictor of developmental problems than is physical abuse.

> Although the visible signs of emotional abuse in children can be difficult to detect, the hidden scars of this type of abuse manifest in numerous behavioral ways, including insecurity, poor self-esteem, destructive behavior, angry acts (such as fire-setting and animal cruelty), withdrawal, poor development of basic skills, alcohol or drug abuse, suicide, difficulty forming relationships, and unstable job histories.[51]

SEXUAL ABUSE

Under CAPTA's "minimum definition," sexual abuse includes:

- the employment, use, persuasion, inducement, enticement, or coercion of any child to engage in, or assist any other person to engage in, any sexually explicit conduct or simulation of such conduct for the purpose of producing a visual depiction of such conduct; or
- the rape, and in cases of caretaker or interfamilial relationships, statutory rape, molestation, prostitution, or other form of sexual exploitation of children, or incest with children.[52]

The states define sexual abuse in various ways, but they generally include both touching offenses (such as fondling the child's genitals, penetrating a child's vagina or anus to any extent directly or with an object, or having the child touch the caretaker's sex organs) and nontouching offenses such as exposing a child to sexual acts (masturbation, sexual relations, etc.) or to pornographic materials. They may also include sexual exploitation of children such as engaging them in acts of prostitution or using them as subjects of pornographic materials.

SUBSTANCE ABUSE

CAPTA requires states to have policies and procedures to notify children's protective services of substance-exposed newborns (SENs) and to establish a plan of safe care for those affected by illegal substance abuse or withdrawal symptoms as a result of prenatal drug exposure. The states have chosen to address this requirement in a variety of ways. Some have placed priority on making drug treatment more accessible for pregnant women. For example, Illinois and Minnesota require mandated reporters to report pregnant women they suspect are abusing drugs so that they can be referred for treatment. California, Maryland, and Missouri, among other states, require that when a substance-exposed newborn is identified, an assessment must be done of both the newborn and the child's family so that appropriate services can be arranged.[53]

Some states have attempted to criminalize prenatal substance abuse using a variety of existing statutes such as delivering drugs to a minor (through the umbilical cord), assault with a deadly weapon, corruption of a minor, criminal abuse and neglect of a child, and manslaughter. Still others treat it under civil child abuse laws and view it as a ground for terminating or suspending parental rights. For example, the Wisconsin children's code as amended in 1998 grants that state's juvenile court exclusive jurisdiction over an unborn child when the pregnant mother "habitually lacks self-control" with regard to drugs or alcohol. The statute defines an unborn child as a "human being from the time of fertilization to the time of birth."[54] In the case *In re Baby Boy Blackshear*,[55] the Ohio Supreme Court interpreted that state's civil child abuse law to mean that if a newborn baby tests positive for drug exposure, it constitutes ***per se*** child abuse even though the state's civil child abuse law made no reference to prenatal abuse.

Some states address by statute the harm caused to a child of any age as a result of exposure to illegal drug activity. Approximately half the states do so in their criminal statutes and some (such as Alaska, Kansas, Minnesota, and Missouri) do so in their child endangerment statutes. Some states (California, Mississippi, Montana, North Carolina, and Washington, for example) impose enhanced penalties for the manufacturing of illegal drugs in the presence of a child. Idaho, Louisiana, and Ohio prosecute the manufacture or possession of any controlled substance in the presence of a child as a felony, and others (such as Illinois, Pennsylvania, and Virginia) specifically target the manufacture of methamphetamine in the presence of a child.

Reporting of Child Abuse

Every state identifies individuals who are required to report suspected child abuse or neglect to a designated child protective services agency (usually a state social or human services agency). **Mandatory reporters** customarily include, at a minimum, law enforcement personnel, individuals in the health professions, social workers, teachers, and day care providers. Mandatory/mandated reporters are required to report suspected abuse and neglect or face civil and sometimes criminal penalties. **Permissive reporters** are individuals who may, but are not required to, report suspected abuse. These individuals include, among others, friends, family members, neighbors, store employees, and strangers, who most commonly witness incidents of abuse in public areas, such as playgrounds, malls, and parking lots. Permissive reporters are not liable for reports filed in good faith. However, some states provide a penalty (usually a fine) for knowingly filing a false report. Some states require "all persons" to report child abuse, by implication including attorneys and their employees. For example, the applicable New Jersey statute requires "Any person having reasonable cause to believe that a child has been subjected to child abuse or acts of child abuse shall report the same immediately to the Division of Youth and Family Services by telephone or otherwise."[56] The statute provides immunity to those who file reports.[57] A failure to report constitutes a disorderly person's offense and may constitute evidence of negligence.[58] States provide notice of reports of abuse to both accused and nonaccused parents and sometimes provide guidance with respect to the nature of the process and the parents' rights. See, for example, forms used for this purpose in New Hampshire at *www.courts.state.nh.us.*

Reports are usually made to the state's designated child protection agency. The agency is responsible for:

- receiving reports of abuse or neglect
- promptly investigating reports, usually by making a home visit, interviewing relevant parties, and evaluating the child's living arrangements (An initial visit customarily must be made within twenty-four hours if a child is in imminent danger or, if not, within three to seven days.)
- developing plans for families in need of services
- providing a wide range of services directly or through third parties (counseling, parent education, educational assessments, homemaker services, etc.)
- removing children from homes where they are at risk of immediate serious harm with or without a court order or prior notice to the parent(s)
- scheduling court hearings before or immediately after removal so that parents are given an opportunity to challenge the agency's actions
- arranging for and monitoring appropriate foster care placements in homes or group facilities
- initiating proceedings to terminate parental rights where appropriate and facilitating adoptions or other long-term care
- referring cases involving serious physical injury or child rape to law enforcement authorities for investigation and possible criminal prosecution

When a report of abuse or neglect is received and processed by a child protection agency, the case customarily proceeds along one of four paths:

1. When the report is determined to be false or frivolous, it is deemed invalid.
2. When the agency determines that the report was made in good faith but finds no reasonable cause to believe the child is at risk, the case is designated unsubstantiated and is closed, although the record remains in the department's files.
3. When the report is substantiated, the agency develops a service plan with the parent(s)/caretaker(s). If the abuse is not serious and services are accepted and effectively implemented, the child may remain with the family. If the services are not accepted or successfully implemented, the agency may file a **care and protection petition** seeking temporary removal or removal and **termination of parental rights**, if appropriate.
4. When the agency has reasonable cause to believe that removal is necessary to ensure the child's safety, the agency may immediately remove the child and file a dependency action/care and protection petition for hearing usually within seventy-two hours. The court will determine whether a service plan should be developed and a reunification sought, or the agency should seek to terminate parental rights in anticipation of adoption or some other permanent placement in the best interests of the child.

The U.S. Supreme Court has long recognized the preservation of the family as a priority. It has also afforded constitutional protection to the right of parents to raise their children as they see fit. However, it has also recognized that parental rights must be balanced with the duty of the state to protect children. Removal of a child from his or her home is clearly an extreme measure, but the state has the authority to initiate such action under the legal **doctrine of *parens patriae*,** the

Latin term for "parent of the country." However, it cannot do so arbitrarily, but rather only for good cause, and parents must be afforded due process to protect their parental rights.

The removal of a child from his or her home may be temporary or permanent. Temporary removal may be appropriate in situations where a report of abuse is substantiated and reasonable steps have been taken to keep the child at home, but the child remains at risk because the parents are "temporarily" unable to provide appropriate care. To remove the child on a temporary basis, the agency files a care and protection/dependency action in which it asks a court to find the child dependent or in need of care and protection. The court also must determine that remaining in the home is contrary to the child's best interests, and that the agency has made reasonable efforts to prevent removal. If successful, the agency is granted temporary custody, assumes primary responsibility for the child, and can make an appropriate placement in foster care while the parents complete the requirements of a service plan. If the removal will be permanent, the agency may convince the parents to voluntarily surrender their parental rights or, if that effort fails, may file a petition for involuntary termination of parental rights. A termination of parental rights severs the legal relationship between a parent and his or her biological or adopted child. Given that parental rights enjoy a high degree of constitutional protection, they cannot be terminated without clear and convincing evidence of parental unfitness.

Since the passage of the federal Adoption Assistance and Child Welfare Act of 1980 (CWA),[59] child protective agencies have had a duty to make "**reasonable efforts**" to keep families together before removing children and, if removal is necessary, to make a reasonable effort to eventually reunite the family. This requirement sometimes has resulted in the premature return of children to high-risk family environments or, in the alternative, to lengthy stays in foster care. Partly to address these problems, in 1997 Congress passed the Adoption and Safe Families Act (ASFA), which retained the reasonable efforts requirement but gave considerable discretion to the states with respect to implementing it. The Act gave priority to the child's "health and safety" and also took steps to limit the time children spend in foster care.[60] ASFA requires that a **permanency planning** hearing be held no later than twelve months after a child has been placed in foster care (or sooner in cases in which reunification is an impossible or inappropriate goal, such as when the child has been abandoned, the parent has subjected the child to serious abuse, or the parent has murdered another family member). To further reinforce the policy of permanency planning, with limited exceptions, the state must also initiate proceedings to terminate parental rights if a child has been in foster care for fifteen of the past twenty-two months. This process is discussed further in this text in Chapter 8 on adoption.

Child protection litigation can be costly, dehumanizing, disempowering, and traumatic for the parties and particularly for children who have been removed from their homes and separated from their parents, siblings, and extended families for reasons usually not of their own making. An alternative to litigation is child protection mediation, which may be used at any stage of a child protection case. It is usually initiated by a child protection worker or an attorney. The goal is to jointly develop a case plan to reunify the family or, if necessary, to find the most suitable permanent placement. "Mediated issues often include the services the parents will use, conditions that must be satisfied before the child may return home, alternative options for child care, and parenting practices, including alternative nonviolent

---

PARALEGAL PRACTICE TIP

Removal cases often involve contrasting, and sometimes biased, views about what constitutes a safe and appropriate home for a child. Parents threatened with losing their children are often ill-equipped financially, socially, and otherwise to effectively defend themselves and advocate for their children. Despite this fact, few states offer or require legal representation for indigent parents in abuse and neglect cases.

Reasonable efforts

the effort a child protective agency must make to prevent removal of a child from his or her home, or, if removed, to reunify the family within a specified period of time

PARALEGAL PRACTICE TIP

To see examples of forms relating to Temporary Removal of a Child, visit *www.nycourts.gov* and view an example of a Petition for Termination of Parental Rights, at *www.courts .delaware.gov.*

Permanency planning

planning for the return home of a child following removal or for termination of parental rights within a legally specified period of time in an effort to promote stability for the child

PARALEGAL PRACTICE TIP

To see an example of a Petition for Permanency Planning Hearing, visit *www.courts.state.va.us* (Virginia).

approaches."[63] Statistics indicate that 60% to 85% of such mediations end in agreements and that they promote family progress and increased compliance with court orders.[64]

In some cases, parents will voluntarily seek the assistance of the state with a child who, despite their best efforts, persistently runs away from home, willfully fails to attend school, and refuses to obey reasonable parental rules. When the parents believe they can no longer adequately care for or protect such a child, they may seek to have him or her designated by the court as a child in need of services (CHINS), thereby triggering a host of alternative placement and treatment options under the supervision of the state. To see one state's description of the CHINS process, visit *www.vermontjudiciary.org* and read "Form 116 Booklet for Parents in CHINS Cases" and "Form 117 Youth in CHINS Cases: Understanding the Court Process."

Abuse and Custody Disputes

The Model Code of the National Council of Juvenile and Family Court Judges recommends that in every proceeding where there is a dispute as to the custody of a child, a determination by the court that domestic or family violence has occurred should raise a rebuttable presumption that "it is detrimental to the child and not in the best interests of the child, to be placed in sole custody, joint legal custody, or joint physical custody with the perpetrator of family violence."[67] A report to the American Bar Association has also recommended that, where there is proof of domestic violence, "batterers should be presumed by law to be unfit custodians for their children."[68] Many of the states have adopted such provisions in one form or another. Some statutes require the courts to consider a history of domestic violence before joint custody can be awarded; some require the court to factor domestic violence into the best interests test; and some mandate that the courts not award joint custody where abuse has been demonstrated.

In cases involving severely abused, abandoned, or neglected children, judges often make use of guardians *ad litem* as well as Court Appointed Special Advocates (CASA volunteers). CASA is part of a national volunteer movement that began about three decades ago. It was initiated by a judge in Seattle, Washington, who sought a "voice in court" for abused and neglected children. There are now more than 900 CASA programs nationwide with at least one in every state. CASA volunteers serve as both mentors and advocates. They work with children who have been removed from their homes and placed in foster care. The one-on-one relationship formed with the child is often the only stable relationship he or she has in a world of social workers, attorneys, therapists, and caregivers. It positions the volunteer to provide the judge with information that will help safeguard the child's best interests and facilitate placement in a safe, permanent home.

When the abuse has been interspousal and not actively directed at the parties' children, judges (and sometimes clients and attorneys as well) may fail to appreciate the impact that witnessing a parent's abusive behavior has on a child. Even if the children have not been the direct recipients of this violence, they are victims as a result of exposure to it. "According to reports by battered mothers, 87% to 90% of their children witnessed the mothers' abuse."[69] They may actually see the physical, sexual, and emotional attacks; overhear them; experience the emotional

PARALEGAL PRACTICE TIP

To see a comprehensive state-by-state picture of the relationship between domestic violence and custody in applicable state statutes, visit www.americanbar.org.

tension in the residence; and/or be exposed to the aftermath, including both the mother's physical injuries and the destruction of property (phones ripped from the wall, dishes and chairs broken, etc.).

Children who live in a battering relationship experience the most insidious form of child abuse. Whether or not they are physically abused by either parent is less important than the psychological scars they bear from watching their fathers beat their mothers. They learn to become part of a dishonest conspiracy of silence. . . .

The effects of witnessing domestic violence are often severe and multifaceted. Certainly, not all children are affected by exposure to domestic violence in the same manner or to the same degree. Numerous factors influence the extent to which a child is affected. These factors include: age, gender, race, frequency and severity of the violence witnessed, and the degree of maternal impairment. Nonetheless, all children exposed to domestic violence are affected in some way. Witnessing domestic violence can affect children behaviorally, cognitively, emotionally, physically and socially.[70]

A mother who has been abused by her partner is "damned if she does and damned if she doesn't" fight for custody of her children. Her abuser may threaten to harm her and/or the children, take the children where she "will never find them," or, if the circumstances fit, expose her to some kind of criminal liability or embarrassment as a result of her drug use or immigration status. The court may not believe her allegations of abuse, particularly if they are undocumented, or if her chameleon spouse persuades the judge that her claims are unfounded or grossly exaggerated. In a state that criminalizes exposing a child to domestic violence, the mother may open herself to criminal liability if she fights back in self-defense against her abuser. In some states, permitting one's child to witness spousal abuse itself may constitute grounds for removing the child from the care and custody of both parents.[71]

Paralegal **Application 14.3**

Making the Case for Custody of a Child Who Has Witnessed Family Violence

Parents in abusive relationships do not come into court with equal power and ability to advocate for themselves and their children. The abusive parent's goal is to depict the victimized parent as unfit, immoral, and incapable of having the children.[72] Abusive parents frequently seek custody of their children, and they are often successful.[73] A 2009 study found that 84% of biological father perpetrators of intimate partner violence have ongoing contact with their children.[74] Although victims who have restraining orders against their abusers are more likely to secure custody than victims who never filed for an order,[75] battered women are less likely than non-battered women to be awarded sole legal custody of their children.[76] A client who has been abused and who makes a decision to pursue

custody of her children usually faces an uphill battle, especially when those children have been exposed to her victimization. The family law team and client will need to work together to establish a solid case and to do so in a manner that does not expose the mother to liability and the children to further trauma. Depending on the judge's background and experience dealing with family violence issues, the family law team may need to research the effects on children of exposure to domestic violence. The client will need to assist by suggesting witnesses, documents, and other evidence that will establish how the children have been, or are likely to be, affected by continued exposure to the abuser's violent conduct. Examples of demonstrated effects of children's exposure to domestic violence that may be evident include, but are not necessarily limited to, the following:[77]

- Aggressiveness, acting out, and antisocial conduct, including behaviors such as bullying, assaults, and destruction of property
- Generally lower levels of social competence
- Poor problem-solving skills
- Lower levels of empathy
- Depression, suicidal behaviors, anxieties, fears, and phobias
- Feelings that they are helpless and powerless
- Low self-esteem
- Guilt and self-blaming for the violence or their inability to prevent or stop it
- Anger at both the abuser and the victim

- A pervasive attitude that the use of violence is an appropriate means of expressing anger, solving problems, and intimidating and gaining control over others
- Greater likelihood of abusing a spouse or partner as an adult[78]
- Abuse of drugs and alcohol
- Running away
- Sexual acting out
- Fear for their lives and/or the lives of their parents and siblings
- Lower levels of cognitive and academic functioning
- Poor health, including colds, elevated blood pressure, insomnia, and bed-wetting
- Posttraumatic stress disorder[79]
- Injuries suffered as a result of trying to intervene and protect the abused parent

In abuse cases, a court's custody order ideally should reflect a thoughtful assessment of the particular nature of the abuse experienced and its likely causes and effects. Based on the facts of the individual case, appropriate actions may range from termination of an abuser's parental rights to a plan in which visitation is permitted and a focus is placed on building the parties' skills in effective parenting, problem solving, and conflict management.

In general, when seeking custody on behalf of an abused mother, a proposed custody order needs to be carefully tailored to the facts of the case and designed to protect the safety and welfare of both the children and the mother. It may ask that the court order any one or more of the following conditions, which may be eased over time if the abusive parent remains in compliance and if it is in the best interests of the children.

- Sole legal and physical custody to the mother without visitation, because joint custody fosters continual conflict and gives the abuser an opportunity to continue his abuse, OR sole legal and physical custody to the mother with supervised visitation, preferably at a supervised visitation center that provides a safe location and trained personnel able to intervene if problems arise
- A restraint on the abusive parent's communication with or proximity to the children except in the context of authorized visitation
- A requirement that the abuser not be granted, or not be permitted to continue, visitation unless he participates in and successfully completes a batterer's program or some other long-term treatment option that addresses anger, battering, and control issues in depth
- A requirement that the abusive parent not use alcohol or drugs during and/or within a specified time period prior to a visit
- Designation of a neutral location such as a social services agency, resource center, or police station for drop-off and pickup of the children for visitation
- Impounding of any information revealing the address and phone numbers of the mother and children
- Denial of access to school and other records containing information regarding the residence of the mother and children

- Exemption for the mother from any required state parenting program or, in the alternative, a requirement that the parents attend separate sessions where appropriate safety precautions can be arranged
- A requirement that the batterer be required to pay for counseling/therapy if needed for the mother and/or the children
- An appropriate recourse to address related disputes. Mediation should not be an option for dispute resolution, especially in cases where the dominant form of abuse is coercive control
- Appointment of a parenting coordinator or master to manage recurring child custody disputes (an approach presently in place in several states)
- Exclusion of any "boilerplate" parental cooperation or "friendly parent" language in separation agreements

In high-conflict child custody cases, a **parenting coordinator** can "assist parents in creating, implementing, and monitoring parenting plans. . . . typically parent coordinators make decisions or recommendations about day-to-day matters such as scheduling, activities, transportation, child care, discipline, education, and health care. They generally cannot modify custody, allow relocation, or make any other major changes to court orders."[80]

> In those cases of domestic violence where one parent seeks to obtain and maintain power and control over the other, the role of the PC [parent coordinator] changes to an almost purely enforcement function. Here the PC is likely to be dealing with a court order, the more detailed the better, rather than a mutually agreed upon parenting plan; and the role is to ensure compliance with the details of the order and to test each request for variance from its terms with an eye to protecting the custodial parent's autonomy to make decisions based on the children's best interests and guarding against manipulation by the abusing parent.[81]

The coordinator in some situations may also have an opportunity to model conflict resolution skills.

Criminal Actions Against Abusive Parents

There has been a long-standing, albeit somewhat fading, tradition in this country of viewing family violence and abuse against children as a private family matter in which the state should intervene only when absolutely necessary. And there has been a parallel reluctance to prosecute family members and parents who harm their children except in particularly egregious cases.

> In the context of parenthood and the criminal justice system, family members are still far more likely to be excused for behavior that would be considered criminal if committed by third parties. Examples abound: the extraordinary difficulties prosecutors face in convicting parents on homicide charges in child abuse cases, the lighter sentences imposed on defendants who kill family members, the preferential treatment in some states given to sex offenders who victimize their own children rather than a stranger, and the outcry over prosecuting negligent parents. . . . This preferential treatment for parents persists

PARALEGAL PRACTICE TIP

Some states have "friendly parent" statutes which require judges to consider which parent will "promote relationships and set aside past conflicts" with the ex-spouse when making custody determinations.

Parenting coordinator

an individual, usually appointed by the court, who assists with creation and implementation of parenting agreements and enforcement of decrees in high-conflict cases involving minor children even though young children in particular face far greater risk of danger from their relatives at home than they do from strangers in public places.[82]

Overall, parents generally receive more favorable treatment by the criminal justice system than nonparents. However, research suggests that parents from various socioeconomic groups are treated differently. Parents in blue-collar professions and parents who are unemployed are four times more likely to be prosecuted than parents from wealthier socioeconomic groups.[83] When parents are prosecuted for abusive conduct toward their children, they may be prosecuted under a variety of criminal statutes:

- Statutes ranging from murder and manslaughter in cases involving deaths, to assault, battery, aggravated assault, rape/sexual assault, etc., with imposition of heightened penalties when the crime is committed against a child
- Statutes that address intentional crimes committed against children in particular, such as rape of a child, incest, child endangerment, or use of a child to commit a crime such as production of child pornography
- Statutes that criminalize parental/caretaker neglect

The same offense may be treated differently in different states. For example, some states, such as Utah, treat the commission of an act of domestic violence in the presence of a child as a distinct criminal offense, and others treat it as a more serious degree of assault resulting in an enhanced penalty.

Tort Actions

Under early common law, parents were immune from liability in **tort** for failure to prevent harm to their minor children resulting from the actions of third parties, and there still is little legislation or case law recognizing that parents who have not created the risk of harm have an affirmative duty to intervene to rescue a minor child from actual or potential harm caused by others. But what about situations in which the parents' child hurts others?

Although this is not technically abuse of a child, parents are sometimes sued by third parties, under a theory of negligent supervision, for damages caused by their children. "Under common law, parents can be liable for their children's acts 'where the parents' [own] negligence has made it possible for the child to cause the injury complained of and probable that the child would do so."[84] Section 316 of the Restatement (Second) of Torts provides that the duty of a parent to take reasonable measures to control a child arises when the parent knows or should know of the need to control the child and has both the ability and the opportunity to do so. The cause of action commonly known as **negligent supervision** is based on the premise that parents have a duty to society at large to exercise reasonable care in the supervision of their minor children in order to prevent them from intentionally causing injury to others.

Although parents will not necessarily be held liable for the intentional or malicious acts of their minor children, a majority of states have enacted statutes making parents liable in certain circumstances. Some states legislate parental responsibility laws in specific areas of conduct. For example, a Mississippi statute[85] provides that, subject to some exceptions, a parent may be found guilty of knowingly permitting a child under eighteen to have, own, or carry a concealed weapon, the carrying of which is prohibited by law. (See Paralegal Application 14.4.)

PARALEGAL PRACTICE TIP

Prosecutions for criminal offenses are subject to applicable statutes of limitations, which may vary from crime to crime and state to state. The statutes may also vary in terms of when they begin to run. For example, statutes for crimes relating to sexual abuse of minors usually begin to run when the abuse is first discovered (or recalled) rather than when the injury first occurred.

PARALEGAL PRACTICE TIP

The Utah statute on "Commission of Domestic Violence in the Presence of a Child" can be found at *le.utah.gov* (Code/Constitution/Title/Chapter/Section 76-5-109.1).

Tort
a civil wrong (other than breach of contract) for which a court provides a remedy, usually in the form of money damages; the wrong must involve harm resulting from breach of a legal duty owed to another

Negligent supervision
a cause of action based on parents' duty to society to exercise reasonable care in the supervision of their minor children in order to prevent them from intentionally causing injury to others

Paralegal **Application 14.4**

Was Mom to Blame?

The Facts

At home one evening at 8:00 p.m., Mavis Daniels received a phone call from her employer. While she was on the phone, her fifteen-year-old son, Eddie Smith, left the house without her knowledge. At the time, he was subject to a 7:30 p.m. curfew Sunday through Thursday imposed by the youth court after he'd struck a boy at school. After Eddie left the house, he and two of his friends activated the alarm on a girl's car by hitting it with a ball. When the girl's boyfriend, Johnny Lee Williamson Jr., came out to investigate, Eddie confronted him and, after a verbal exchange, pulled out a gun and shot the unarmed Williamson, leaving him paralyzed from the waist down. Williamson subsequently filed a complaint alleging Eddie's mother was negligent in her supervision of Eddie and that her negligence was the proximate cause of his injuries.

Eddie had been in trouble on several occasions prior to this particular incident: He wounded his uncle in a fight with a knife, knocked a boy unconscious at school, dropped out of school, and was accused of threatening a ten-year-old girl with a pellet gun and being the lookout for a robbery committed by some of his friends. Without his mother's knowledge, he obtained a handgun. Ms. Daniels testified that she had tried to enforce the curfew and attempted to discipline her son by grounding him, taking away his video games, and applying corporal punishment. When he dropped out of school, she took him to work with her at the Head Start agency and had him clean up around the school, where she could keep an eye on him. She also took him to a mental health center for counseling.

In a negligent supervision action, the plaintiff, Williamson, must establish that the mother had a duty of care, that she breached that duty, that her breach was the proximate cause of his injuries, and that damages are warranted to compensate him for his loss. He must show not only that there was negligence and an injury but also that the injury was reasonably foreseeable.

Sidebar

In this case, do you think Mavis Daniels should be held liable for the injury to Williamson? What are the arguments for both sides of the question? Read the case *Johnny Lee Williamson, Jr. v. Mavis C. Daniels*, 748 So. 2d 754 (Miss. 1999), decided by the Mississippi Supreme Court to see if you agree with the court's decision. The full opinion in *Williamson v. Daniels* is available at *www.pearsonhighered.com/ careersresources/* in the website material related to Chapter 14 under Cases.

In this Paralegal Application, Mavis Daniels appears to be a single mother, and the case makes no reference to the existence or identity of the youth's father. If there are two parents in the picture, each of whom plays a considerable role in the child's life, a question may arise as to whether both parents should be liable for negligent supervision or only the parent with primary custody. A Florida appellate court considered this issue as a matter of first impression in that state. The majority held that only the mother (who had primary residential custody) was liable to a school district for her son's malicious destruction of school property. A strong dissent argued that "On the one hand, the father in this case has successfully sought and procured an equal voice and equal participation in all of the major decision-making process involving the rearing of this minor child. . . ." but on the other hand, was not being held accountable for his son's conduct. See *Canida v. Canida*, 751 So. 2d 647 at 652 (Fla. App. 1999). Do you agree with the majority or the dissent?

To Know or Not to Know . . . to Tell or Not to Tell

Domestic violence often permeates many family law cases, whether or not it is revealed to or detected by counsel or other members of the family law team. If the issue does arise, it is often difficult, even frightening, to address. What can be done when a battered spouse is being bullied into a poor property settlement in order to protect her children and herself or when counsel or the paralegal begins to suspect the client is abusing his or her children or partner and will very likely continue to do so? How can the attorney reconcile the ethical duties to maintain client confidentiality and advocate zealously for the client with the duties to prevent a fraud on the court and commission of a crime that could result in serious physical injury or death?

Clearly, family violence poses ethical issues of monumental dimensions for attorneys and their employees, including paralegals. The legal community itself is split between those who believe lawyers should disclose serious threats to third parties and those who believe they should not. For example, some argue that

> in the context of domestic violence cases, lawyers have an affirmative duty to (1) screen battering clients who have indicated a likelihood of harming others, (2) attempt to dissuade them from carrying out planned violent crimes, and (3) warn identifiable abuse victims whom their clients have threatened.[86]

On the other side, it is argued that mandatory child abuse reporting in the context of representing domestic violence victims interferes with confidentiality and open communication, exposes domestic violence victims and their children to harm, subjects victims to state intervention and potential criminal prosecution for abuse or neglect, and discourages victims from seeking legal assistance.[87]

CAPTA essentially leaves confidentiality and disclosure requirements to the discretion of the states. Little clear guidance is provided to attorneys in this area in state reporting requirements, statutes governing the attorney–client privilege, rules of professional responsibility, or occasional guidelines from bar associations and ethics opinions. Rule 1.6 of the American Bar Association Model Rules of Professional Conduct (Model Rules), adopted in many states, provides in part that a lawyer shall not reveal information relating to the representation of a client unless the client gives informed consent, the disclosure is impliedly authorized in order to carry out the representation, or the lawyer believes the disclosure is reasonably necessary to prevent death or substantial bodily harm or to comply with a law or court order. The ABA Model Rules are not binding, however, and the states are not uniform in their disclosure requirements.

- Some states specifically exclude attorneys from mandatory child-abuse-reporting requirements. The applicable Missouri statute provides: Any legally recognized privileged communication, except that between attorney and client or involving communications made to a minister or clergyperson, shall not apply to situations involving known or suspected child abuse or neglect and shall not constitute grounds for failure to report as required or permitted by sections 210.110 to 210.165, to cooperate with the division in any of its activities pursuant to sections 210.110 to 210.165, or to give or accept evidence in any judicial proceeding relating to child abuse or neglect.[88]
- The Model Rules for attorneys in Texas provide that "When a lawyer has confidential information clearly establishing that a client is likely to commit a criminal or fraudulent act that is likely to result in death or substantial bodily harm to a person, the lawyer shall reveal confidential information to the extent revelation reasonably appears necessary to prevent the client from committing the criminal or fraudulent act."[89]

- The relevant Georgia rule is permissive. Georgia Rule 1.6(b)(3) provides: "Before using or disclosing information pursuant to Subsection (1), if feasible, the lawyer must make a good faith effort to persuade the client either not to act or, if the client has already acted, to warn the victim."
- In one of the few ethics opinions on the subject of the attorney's role in reporting abuse, the Ethics Committee in New Jersey stated that an attorney is not required to report past child abuse in a custody action. However, in a supplement to the opinion, the Committee clarified that the privilege does not apply when the client demonstrates a "continued propensity" for abuse.[90]
- In Wisconsin, attorneys are permitted to use discretion with respect to reporting or not reporting child abuse.[91]

Rules that leave disclosure to the discretion of the attorney are perhaps the least helpful of all.

> Discretionary disclosure may . . . place lawyers in the untenable position of choosing preservation of their bar licenses over victim safety as well as expose them to liability in tort. None of the state professional rules protect the attorney from tort liability in the decision to disclose. Mandatory disclosure rules provide greater protection to practitioners, yet most state rules employ permissive language.[92]

Paralegal **Application 14.5**

What Is Your Opinion?

Do you believe members of the family law team should be mandated reporters? Explain your response. What is the attorney's duty in your state? What do you think the paralegal should do if his or her supervising attorney is a mandated reporter who fails to report? To learn about mandatory reporters in your state, visit *www.americanbar.org*. A chart on this topic identifies applicable statutes and mandatory reporters in each state as of the report date. The chart also specifically references the apparent treatment of legal professionals in this context.

CHAPTER **SUMMARY**

Family violence is a painful reality in our society, as the statistics provided in this chapter indicate. Despite its significance, many members of family law teams have a very limited knowledge about family violence: its causes, manifestations, and effects. This chapter provides prospective paralegals with a very basic introduction to this multifaceted topic. It considers it in the contexts of both intimate partner and parent–child relationships. It introduces definitions and cold, hard statistics. It identifies a variety of legal remedies available to victims and their advocates. It reviews some of the subtle legal, psychological, and sociological dimensions of this complex topic. And finally, it raises troubling ethical questions confronting practitioners.

Child abuse and neglect cases in particular clearly involve the balancing of critical and often competing public policies: a parent's right to raise his or her children free from governmental interference and the state's interest in protecting children. Everyone weighs in: parents, children, offenders, victims, judges, social workers, therapists, attorneys, and, of course, the general public. Paralegals may find themselves in the middle of wrenching situations, troubled deeply by what they see parents do to their children but also recognizing that the police and social service agencies sometimes cross constitutional lines based on "good intentions" and insufficient information. Parents, even parents suspected of harming their children, are protected by constitutional rights. Family violence cases are minefields that challenge members of the family law team. They compel us to examine and control our personal biases and our cultural and religious beliefs about what constitutes appropriate behavior. They strain our emotions, our legal skills, and our ethics, and they remind many of us why we have chosen to specialize in family law.

CONCEPT REVIEW AND REINFORCEMENT

KEY TERMS

Abandonment
Affidavit
Battered woman's syndrome
Care and protection/dependency
  proceeding
Concurrent jurisdiction
Coverture
Cyberharassment
Cyberstalking
Educational neglect
Emotional neglect
Evidence-based prosecution

Ex parte
Family violence
Guardian
Interspousal immunity
Mandatory reporter
Medical neglect
Neglect
Negligent supervision
No-contact order
Parens patriae
Parenting coordinator
Per se

Permanency planning
Permissive reporter
Physical neglect
Protective order
Reasonable efforts
Restraining order
Shaken baby syndrome
Stalking
Stay away order
Termination of parental rights
Tort

REVIEW QUESTIONS

1. Discuss the nature and scope of family violence against adults: Who are the victims? Who are the perpetrators?
2. Identify five services supported by the Violence Against Women Act (VAWA).
3. Identify the four primary remedies available to adult victims of family violence.
4. Identify a minimum of five reasons why victims stay in abusive relationships.
5. Define stalking, cyberstalking, and cyberharassment and give at least three examples of how a perpetrator might stalk and/or cyberstalk/harass a victim.
6. Describe the basic procedure for obtaining a protective order, including who can commonly seek one and what kinds of relief can be sought.
7. Explain when it may be appropriate to seek a guardianship in a family violence case.
8. Describe the nature and purpose of a personal safety plan.
9. Identify at least five common characteristics of abusers.
10. Identify and distinguish among the five forms of child abuse and neglect most commonly identified and defined by the states.
11. Distinguish between mandatory and permissive reporters of child abuse.
12. Describe the nature and purpose of "reasonable efforts" and "permanency planning" in the context of child abuse and neglect actions.
13. Explain how abuse and neglect influence decisions about custody and visitation.
14. Explain whether or not members of the family law team have a duty to report suspected child abuse or other forms of family violence.

DEVELOPING YOUR PARALEGAL SKILLS

FOCUS ON THE JOB

In this Focus on the Job, students have an opportunity to explore common characteristics of perpetrators and victims of abuse as evidenced in the context of a family law case.

The Facts

You are a paralegal working for Attorney Sabrina Westcott, a private practitioner who specializes in family law. She has asked you to conduct a series of information-gathering meetings with a client, Sara Frazier, who is seeking a divorce from her husband, Joseph. During the course of your meetings, you have developed a suspicion that Sara is being abused by her husband. There have been several clues:

- She has insisted that she initiate all contact with the office and that no one try to reach her at home or leave e-mail or phone messages for her.
- As the date for filing has approached, she has become increasingly more anxious.
- She has told you that "everyone" says she must "get out of the marriage."

- She is insistent that she "must" have custody of the children and is fearful that she will lose them.
- She does not want to fight for a fair share of the marital property.
- She says she does not know what her husband will do when he is served with the complaint for divorce and wants to be certain she knows exactly when that will take place.
- She has said that she thinks she must be responsible for the failure of the marriage because she is not a good wife. She does not always have the meals prepared on time or have her husband's shirts ironed. Her husband says she is a bad mother as well because she "lets the kids get away with murder" and never disciplines them effectively.

- She says that her husband loves her so much that he worries about her every minute of the day. She and the children are so important to him that he wants them to spend all their time together, to the exclusion of other people.
- She always wears sunglasses and high-collared, long-sleeved shirts even when the weather is quite warm.

The Assignment

You have shared your concerns with your supervisor, and she has asked that you prepare a memo to her explaining why you believe the client is being abused and recommending a course of action.

FOCUS ON **ETHICS**

In this activity, the student will explore the duty of members of the family law team in cases involving domestic violence in his or her jurisdiction.

The Assignment

Assume that you are a female paralegal working for the attorney who represents Sara's husband, Joe, in the above fact pattern, and that Joe has recently been served with Sara's Complaint for Divorce on no-fault grounds. You are not comfortable working with Joe and have repeatedly expressed your discomfort to your supervisor, Attorney Jules Sanchez. Joe never misses an opportunity to make a sexist remark and always tells you that female paralegals should be home, where women belong, making and raising babies. He never wants to meet with a female paralegal and always says he wants to talk with the boss and get a few things straight. He has told you that up until now, he has kept his wife in line and that she will pay in more ways than one for thinking that she can do this to him. He comments that raising children is "woman's work" and that he isn't much of a parent. However, he says he will get the kids anyway. Besides, he says, "A bad father is better than no father at all." Joe admits that he has hit his wife on several occasions and that he believes he has a right to do whatever he wants in the privacy of his own home. He tells you not to worry, though, because there is no record of any abuse.

He has "a friend on the force" who makes sure of that, and he never lets Sara seek medical attention for any injury she claims to have. He says she has gone too far challenging his authority this time. He is "the man of the house" and he intends to make her understand that fact or else. . . .

Based on what you have learned about family violence, you strongly believe that Joe is abusing Sara and that she is presently at greater risk than ever before of being seriously injured or perhaps worse. You have shared your concern with your supervisor, Attorney Sanchez, who finds it all hard to believe. He wants to approach the matter cautiously and asks you to record the reasons for your suspicions and research his legal and ethical duties in this situation. What ethical issues does it raise? What is the attorney's duty in your state, given the facts of this case? Does the paralegal have a role to play? Do you find any guidance in the ethical canons for paralegals promulgated by the National Association of Legal Assistants contained in Appendix A or in any other code of ethics that may govern your conduct? In a two- or three-page internal memorandum to Attorney Sanchez, do the following: (1) describe your suspicions with respect to the client and your reasons for them; (2) describe the results of your research regarding the ethical duties of attorneys and paralegals in your jurisdiction in such situations; and (3) recommend an appropriate course of action.

FOCUS ON **CASE LAW**

In this activity, the student will analyze a case involving family violence using an IRAC format.

The Assignment

Select, read, and analyze one of the following cases using an IRAC format:

1. *Lefebre v. Lefebre*, 165 Ore, App. 297, 996 P.2d 518 (2000). In this case a defendant challenges the

sufficiency of the evidence underlying a restraining order entered against him.
2. *New Jersey Division of Child Protection and Permanency v. Y.N.*, 220 N.J. 165, 104 A.3d 244 (2014). In this case, the New Jersey Supreme Court considers whether a finding of abuse or neglect can be sustained based solely on a newborn's enduring methadone withdrawal.

3. *In the Matter of Brittany T.*, 15 Misc. 3d 606, 835 N.Y.S. 2d 829 (2007). In this case, a New York court considers whether the failure of parents to address the needs of a morbidly obese child constitutes neglect sufficient to warrant placement of the child in state care until the parents demonstrate an ability to provide appropriate care.

4. *In the Interest of S.W.*, 290 N.W.2d 675 (N.D. 1980). This case addresses a situation in which a father lost custody of his fifteen-year-old daughter when he kicked and struck her repeatedly after finding marijuana under her bed.

5. *Huch v. Marrs*, 858 So. 2d 1202 (Fla. App. 2003). This stalking case involves a victim who tried unsuccessfully to escape her stalker by moving from Texas to Florida.

6. *Commonwealth v. Dorvil*, Case No. SJC 11738 decided by the Massachusetts Supreme Judicial Court (SJC) in June 2015. In this case, the SJC established, for the first time in Massachusetts, legal guidelines for the use of physical punishment by parents. The case involved a father who had been convicted of assault and battery on his three-year-old daughter.

7. A case assigned by your instructor decided in your jurisdiction within the past five (5) years involving some aspect of child abuse and neglect such as termination of parental rights, prenatal substance abuse, or the parental privilege.

FOCUS ON **STATE LAW AND PROCEDURE**

In this activity, the student researches the law and procedure governing protective/restraining orders in her or his own state/county.

The Assignment

Describe the procedure used in your jurisdiction to obtain a protective order against an abusive partner. Who is eligible to petition for an order? What forms of relief may be requested? Obtain copies of any documents that must be filed. Information regarding state variations is available on websites identified in this chapter and may be of assistance with this assignment.

FOCUS ON **TECHNOLOGY**

In addition to the links provided throughout the chapter, this activity provides a series of useful websites for reference along with technology-related assignments for completion.

Websites of Interest

www.aardvarc.org

"AARDVARC" stands for Abuse, Rape, and Domestic Violence Aid and Resource Collection. The site contains links to many resources by state, statistical data, and information about warning signs of abuse, safety plans, related immigration issues, etc.

www.abanet.org/domviol

This is the site for the American Bar Association's Commission on Domestic Violence. Among other services, it provides links to statistical reports on the prevalence of various forms of domestic violence, articles, and links to statutory summary charts on topics such as civil protection orders, advocate confidentiality laws, and prohibition of mutual protective orders.

www.acf.hhs.gov

This is the website for the Administration for Children and Families. It is a rich source of information about children and families in general. From its home page you can link (via drop-down menu) to the Administration's programs, including the Children's Bureau. There you will find, among other resources, the full text of the most recent Child Maltreatment report.

www.afccnet.org

This is the website for the Association of Family and Conciliation Courts (AFCC). AFCC promotes collaborative approaches to dealing with family matters in general and those pertaining to the well-being of children in particular. The organization sponsors conferences, training, projects, task forces, and practice standards, all of which appear on the website. It provides resources for parents as well as professionals.

www.ama-assn.org

AMA is the American Medical Association. Its home page provides a search function. Searches on family violence, child abuse, and elder abuse each yield a number of resources, including journal articles relevant to the medical community's roles, responsibilities, practices, and liabilities in these areas.

www.avahealth.org

This is the website for the Academy on Violence and Abuse (AVA). AVA is an educational organization intended for health care professionals and dedicated to "making violence and abuse a core component of medical and related professional education." The website features online educational materials, including video presentations, written articles, literature searches, and links to other sites with relevant information.

www.bjs.gov

This is an excellent source for "official" crime data. Many reports on topics related to the content of this chapter are available at this site, including Shannon Catalano, *Intimate Partner Violence in the United States* (2006).

www.bwjp.org

This is the site for the Battered Women's Justice Project's Criminal and Civil Justice Office. The Project aims to promote change within community organizations and governmental agencies engaged in responding to domestic violence. It serves as a national clearinghouse for information about domestic violence and the policing, prosecuting, sentencing, and monitoring of domestic violence offenders.

www.cdc.gov

This site for the national Centers for Disease Control (CDC) provides links to a wide range of resources in response to a search for information on intimate partner violence.

www.childwelfare.gov

This is the site for the Child Information Gateway, a service of the Children's Bureau of the Administration for Children and Families. It provides a wealth of information on adoption, child abuse and neglect, and child welfare issues. Of particular value are links to statistical information and state laws on many related topics, such as definitions of abuse, grounds for termination of parental rights, infant safe haven laws, and parental drug use as child abuse.

www.findlaw.com

This site provides links to state laws that then can be searched by specific topic.

www.nnedv.orgg

A link to the Family Violence Prevention Fund can be found here. Its mission is to prevent violence in the home and in the community. It seeks to "transform" the way health care providers, police, judges, employers, and others address violence. A number of fact sheets are available on domestic violence and its relationship to topics such as children, teens, guns, housing, immigrants, and the military. Every month, its personal stories section showcases someone who has triumphed over violence in his or her life or who has made a significant contribution toward preventing violence against women and children.

www.gmdvp.org

This is the site of the Gay Men's Domestic Violence Project, a grassroots, nonprofit initiative supporting men in relationships with men who are victims and survivors of abuse. It offers education, advocacy, and direct services.

www.lrcvaw.org

This is the site for the Legal Resource Center on Violence Against Women, funded by a Violence Against Women grant. The primary focus of the Center is on improving legal representation for domestic violence survivors in interstate custody cases and providing technical assistance in such cases. It features links to other national and state resources on topics including crisis lines, abuse later in life, and assistance in battered immigrant cases. It also provides state-by-state links to child custody jurisdictional statutes (UCCJEA), long-arm statutes, and relocation statutes.

www.ncadv.org

The National Coalition Against Domestic Violence is accessed at this site. Among its other resources, it provides both topic- and state-specific fact sheets on domestic violence.

www.ncea.aoa.gov

This is the website for the National Center on Elder Abuse, a national center dedicated to preventing the mistreatment of elders. It is the major source of available statistics on elder abuse, neglect, and exploitation, including abuse in domestic settings. It provides links to resources for locating state statutes, codes, Supreme Court opinions, and case law. It also provides a directory of state resources on elder abuse prevention.

www.ncvc.org

This is the site for the National Center for Victims of Crime. A Stalking Resource Center is available at this site that provides information about federal stalking laws as well as links to state civil and criminal stalking laws. It also provides statistical information and a digest of both federal and state stalking cases. A dating violence resource center is also accessible at this site.

www.ndvh.org

This is the website for the National Domestic Violence Hotline (1-800-799-7233 or 1-800-787-3224), which provides 24/7 access to calls from all states. Translation services are available in 140 languages. Advocates at the Hotline provide intervention, safety planning information, and referrals to agencies in all states.

Assignments

1. Go to *www.childwelfare.gov* and locate the definitions for various kinds of abuse in your state.
2. Using one or more of the sites listed above, learn what you can about civil protective orders in your state.
3. Using one or more of the above sites, locate the stalking/cyberstalking/cyberharassment laws in your state and at least one case addressing the issue of stalking.

PORTFOLIO PRODUCTS

1. Memorandum on signs of an abusive relationship evident in a family law setting
2. Two- to three-page paper on the legal and ethical duties of members of the family law team in a case involving family violence
3. IRAC of case on an aspect of family violence
4. Description of protective order forms and procedures in a specific jurisdiction

Endnotes

Chapter 1

1. The NALA definition has been adopted in whole or in large part by other bodies. See, for example, the North Dakota Rules of Professional Conduct and South Dakota Supreme Court Rule 92–5.

2. For example, the revised Rules of Professional Conduct for New Hampshire Attorneys (effective January 1, 2008) expressly permit lawyers from different firms to share fees if the fees are divided "in reasonable proportion to the services performed or responsibilities or risks assumed by each" or "based on an agreement with the referring lawyer" (sometimes called a naked referral). The client must agree to the fee division in writing, and the total fee cannot be increased as a consequence of the fee division.

3. NY CLS Dom Rel Appx §1400.1 (2007).

4. *Missouri v. Jenkins*, 491 U.S. 274, 109 S. Ct. 2463, 105 L. Ed. 2d 229 (1989). See Footnote 10 in the opinion.

5. *Smith v. Lewis*, 530 P.2d 589 at 596 (Cal. 1975).

6. See *Hendrix v. Page*, 986 F.2d 195 (7th Cir. 1993). In this case, an appellant failed to cite the only case that was on point for the issue under appeal. The court stated that when an attorney knowingly conceals dispositive adverse authority, it constitutes professional misconduct.

7. William D. Farber, J.D., L.L.M., *Legal Malpractice in Domestic Relations*, American Jurisprudence 44 Am. Jur. Proof of Facts, 2d 377 (as of August 2004).

8. *Hodges v. Carter*, 329 N.C. 517, 519, 520, 80 S.E.2d 144, 145,146 (1954).

9. See Debra Levy Martinelli, *Are You Riding a Fine Line? Learn to Identify and Avoid Issues Involving the Unauthorized Practice of Law*, 15 Utah Bar J. 18 (2002).

10. See *United States v. Hardy*, 681 F. Supp. 1326, 1328–29 (N.D. Ill. 1988), as quoted in *Monroe v. Horwitch* et al., 820 F. Supp. 682 (D. Conn. 1993), a case involving a paralegal who advertised her availability to prepare uncontested divorce papers for clients.

11. 5 U.S.C.A. §555 (1967) allows a person appearing before a federal administrative agency to be represented by an attorney or a nonattorney deemed a "qualified representative" if the agency permits.

12. National Federation of Paralegal Associations Model Code (Definitions).

13. *Bates v. State Bar of Arizona*, 433 U.S. 350, 97 S. Ct. 2691, 53 L. Ed. 2d 810 (1977), rehearing denied 434 U.S. 881, 98 S. Ct. 242, 54 L. Ed.2d 164 (1977).

Chapter 2

1. U.S. Census Bureau, 2005 American Community Survey. See also Sabrina Tavernise, *Married Couples Are No Longer Majority, Census Finds*, NY Times, May 26, 2011 at A22, *www.nytimes.com/2011/05/26/us/26marry.html*.

2. America's Family and Living Arrangements: 2010, from the 2010 Current Population Survey.

3. Meg Jay, *The Downside of Cohabiting Before Marriage*, NY Times, April 14, 2012, *http://www.nytimes.com/2012/04/15/opinion/sunday/the-downside-of-cohabiting-before-marriage.html?pagewanted=all&_r=0*.

4. Williams Institute on Sexual Orientation Law and Public Policy. *http://denverpost.com/news/ci.2837520/u-s-supreme-court-says-same-sex-couples*.

5. Pamela Smock, *Cohabitation in the United States*, Annual Review of Sociology (2000).

6. Marsha Garrison, *Nonmarital Cohabitation: Social Revolution and Legal Regulation*, 42 Fam. L.Q. 309 at 313 (2008–2009).

7. Mich. Comp. Laws Ann. 750.335 (Supp 2003).

8. See Hillary Greene, *Note: Undead Laws: The Use of Historically Unenforced Criminal Statutes in Noncriminal Litigation*, 16 Yale L. & Pol'y Rev. 169 (1997), for an extensive discussion of the secondary enforcement of criminal laws that have essentially been abandoned by state criminal prosecutors.

9. *Marvin v. Marvin*, 5 Fam. L. Rep. (BNA) 3077 (Cal. Ct. App. 1979).

10. See *Marvin v. Marvin*, 176 Cal. Rptr. 555 (Ct. App. 1981).

11. Alexander C. Morey and Dixie Grossman, *Property Rights of Unmarried Cohabitants–Nothing New Under the Sun*, 25 J. Am. Acad. Matrimonial Law 87 (2012).

12. See J. Thomas Oldham, *Divorce, Separation and the Distribution of Property § 1.02* (2002) (listing decisions following *Marvin*).

13. *Lozoya v. Sanchez*, 133 N.M. 579, 66 P.3d 948 (2003); overruled on other grounds in *Heath v. Mariana Apartments and Deaber*, 143 N.M. 657 (2008).

14. See, e.g., *Hastings v. Dickinson*, 7 Mass. 153 (1810).

15. Press Release, American Academy of Matrimonial Lawyers, Big Rise in Prenuptial Agreements Says Survey of Nation's Top Divorce Lawyers, Sept. 22, 2010, available at *http://www.aaml.org/about-the-academy/press/press-releases/pre-post-nuptial-agreements/big-rise-prenuptial-agreements-sa*. Fifty-two percent of the lawyers polled noted an increase in women initiating the requests. Thirty-six percent cited a rise in pensions and retirement benefits being included in prenuptial agreements. This trend can be attributed to the increase in people marrying and remarrying later in life.

16. Arline Dubin, *Prenups for Lovers: A Romantic Guide to Prenuptial Agreements*, Random House, p. 15 (1999).

17. Donna Beck Weaver, CFLS, *The Collaborative Law Process for Premarital Agreements*, 4 Pepp. Disp. Resol. L.J. 337 (2004).

18. Ibid.

19. In some states, such as California, the general Statute of Frauds (§1624, subd. (a) of the Civil Code) provides that the requirement that a contract be in writing is subject to an implied exception for "part performance" of the contract's terms, but the Family Code provides that an interspousal transaction that changes the nature of community or separate property is not valid unless made in writing by an express declaration approved by the adversely affected spouse. See *In re Marriage of Benson*, 36 Cal. 4th 1096, 116 P.3d 1152, 32 Cal. Rptr. 3d 471 (2005). In Florida, the statute generally barring any action based on an agreement in consideration of marriage, unless in writing, has been interpreted as permitting oral premarital contracts if performed within one year or if there has been partial performance of the contract. See *O'Shea v. O'Shea*, 221 So. 2d 223 (Fla. 4th DCA 1969). In Massachusetts, the agreement must be in writing, but may consist of an exchange of letters.

20. See Judith T. Younger, *Lovers' Contracts in the Courts: Forsaking the Minimum Decencies*, 13 Wm. & Mary Journal of Women & L. 349 (2007).

21. Cal. Fam. Code § 1615(c)(1)-(3).

22. Ark. Code Ann. § 9-11-406(a)(2)(ii) (West 2013).

23. *In re Estate of Hollett*, 150 N.H. 39, 834 A.2d 348 (2003).

24. *Fletcher v. Fletcher*, 628 N.E.2d 1343 (Ohio 1994).

25. See, e.g., *Spritz v. Lishner*, 355 Mass. 162, 243 N.E.2d 163 (1969), in which the court held that, absent fraud, the contract was binding regardless of whether its terms were understood.

26. See, e.g., *Rabinovich v. Shevchenko*, 941 N.Y.S.2d 173 (App. Div. 2012) in which an agreement presented to the wife was in English which she did not understand, and she did not have sufficient time to obtain a translation or advice of counsel. See also *In re Marriage of Shirella*, 319 Mont. 385, 89 P.2d 1 (2004). The parties' agreement was

found unenforceable based on the facts that the agreement was written in English and the prospective wife spoke only Russian. The attorney provided by the husband did not speak Russian and any advice given was without the benefit of a translator.

27. Joanna L. Grama, *The "New" Newlyweds: Marriage Among the Elderly, Suggestions to the Elder Law Practitioner*, 7 Elder L. J. 379 (1999).

28. See, e.g., *Waton v. Waton*, 887 So. 2d 419 (FLA. APP. 2004).

29. Jonathan E. Fields, *Forbidden Provisions in Prenuptial Agreements: Legal and Practical Considerations for the Matrimonial Lawyer*, 21 J. Am. Acad. Matrimonial Law 413 (2008).

30. See, e.g., *Zummo v. Zummo*, 574 A.2d 1130 (Pa. Super. Ct. 1990), in which the court refused to enforce a verbal provision of a prenuptial agreement stipulating the religious upbringing of children from the marriage on the grounds that enforcement would involve excessive entanglement and encroachment by the state on a fundamental right of religious freedom protected by the First Amendment. But see *Ramon v. Ramon*, 34 N.Y.S.2d 100 (N.Y. Fam. CT. 1942). For further information on questionable provisions, see Jonathan E. Fields, *Forbidden Provisions in Prenuptial Agreements: Legal and Practical Considerations for the Matrimonial Lawyer*, 21 J. Am. Acad. Matrimonial Law 413 (2008).

31. An interesting decision on point is *Avitzur v. Avitzur*, 58 N.Y.2d 108, 459 N.Y.S.2d 572, 446 N.E.2d 136 (1983), Cert. Denied 464 U.S. 817, 104 S. Ct. 76, 78 L. Ed. 2d 88 (1983). In this case, the court enforced an agreement in which the husband agreed that if a civil divorce was obtained, he would appear before a rabbinical court, the Beth Din, so that the wife would be able to marry again under Jewish law.

32. *Favrot v. Barnes*, 332 So. 2d 873 (La. Ct. App. 1976), rev'd on other grounds; *Favrot v. Barnes*, 339 So. 2d 843 (La. 1976).

33. For a comprehensive treatment of this topic, see Joline F. Sikaitis, *A New Form of Family Planning? The Enforceability of No-Child Provisions in Prenuptial Agreements*, 54 Cath. U.L. Rev. 335 (Fall 2004).

34. ERISA requires private pension plans to offer spousal benefits for couples married for at least one full year before retirement or death, absent a written waiver. Waivers of ERISA and REA benefits must meet specific requirements.
    a. An effective waiver of a spouse's interest can be made only after the spouse is in fact married to the participant.
    b. The waiver must be in writing, witnessed by a plan administrator or notary public.
    c. The waiver must designate a different beneficiary or form of benefits, which may not be changed without spousal consent.
    d. The waiver must acknowledge the effect of the election.
    A good case on point is Hagwood v. Newton, 282 F.3d 285 (4th Circ. Ct. App. 2002).

35. See, e.g., Massachusetts General Laws, Chapter 209, Section 26, which requires that to be effective against third parties, a premarital agreement must be recorded at an appropriate Registry of Deeds within ninety days of execution.

36. Under California law, parties to a premarital agreement are not considered fiduciaries and basic contract law will apply. In Maryland, parties to a premarital agreement are considered fiduciaries, and enforcement will be judged on a higher standard of fairness, full disclosure, and voluntary execution. See *Cannon v. Cannon*, 384 Md. 537, 865 A.2d 563 (2005). See also *DeLorean v. DeLorean*, 211 N.J. Super. 432, 511 A.2d 1257 (1986), for an analysis of the choice of law conflict between New Jersey and California (although the enforceability of the DeLorean agreement was held to have been determined in an arbitration proceeding).

37. See, e.g., *MacFarlane v. Rich*, 132 N.H. 608 (1989). New Hampshire RSA 460:2-a invests prenuptial agreements with a presumption of validity that can be rebutted only if one or more of three standards of fairness have not been met.
    a. The agreement was not obtained through fraud, duress, or mistake, or through misrepresentation or nondisclosure of a material fact.

    b. The agreement is not unconscionable.
    c. The facts and circumstances have not changed since the agreement was executed so as to make the agreement unenforceable.

38. Uniform Premarital and Marital Agreements Act, Prefatory Note, 2012.

39. Barbara A. Atwood and Brian H. Bix, *New Uniform Law for Marital and Premarital Agreements*, Volume 46 #3, Family Law Quarterly 2012, pp. 313–344 at 317.

40. See, e.g., *Curry v. Curry*, 260 Ga. 302 (1990).

Chapter 3

1. In 23 Pa, C.S. § 1103, the Pennsylvania legislature provided that "No common law marriage contracted after January 1, 2005 shall be valid." Any common law marriage entered prior to that date remains valid. A more complete break with common law marriage has been unsuccessfully sought in South Carolina.

2. Covenant Marriage: A Fact Sheet, National Healthy Marriage Resource Center, accessed January 2015 at *www.healthymarriageinfo.org*.

3. *Inhabitants of Milford v. Inhabitants of Worcester*, 7 Mass. 48 (1810).

4. *Goodridge v. Department of Public Health*, 440 Mass. 309, 343, 798 N.E.2d 941, 969 (2003) (Marshall, C.J.).

5. *Id.*

6. *Loving v. Virginia*, 388 U.S. 1, 87 S. Ct. 1817, 18 L. Ed. 2d 1010 (1967), citing *Skinner v. Oklahoma*, 316 U.S. 535, 542, 62 S. Ct. 1110, 86 L. Ed. 1655 (1942).

7. *Zablocki v. Redhail*, 434 U.S. 374, 98 S. Ct. 673, 54 L. Ed. 2d 618 (1978).

8. *Salisbury v. List*, 501 F. Supp. 105 (D. Nev. 1980).

9. *Turner v. Safley*, 482 U.S. 78, 107 S. Ct. 2254, 96 L. Ed. 64 (1987).

10. *Palmore v. Sidoti*, 466 U.S. 429, 104 S. Ct. 1879, 80 L. Ed. 2d 421 (1984), appeal after remand 472 So. 2d 843 (Fla. App. 1985).

11. *M.T. v. J.T.*, 140 N.J. Super. 77, 355 A.2d 204 (1976).

12. See, e.g., *Littleton v. Prang*, 9 S.W.3d 223 (Tex. App. 1999).

13. On this topic, see Tom Green, *Common-law Marriage, and the Illegality of Putative Polygamy*, 17 BYU J. Pub. L. 141 (2002). See also Maura Strassberg, *The Crime of Polygamy*, 12 Temp. Pol. & Civ. Rts. L. Rev. 353 (2003).

14. A report of the National Society of Genetic Counselors indicates that the increased risk of significant birth defects in children born to first-cousin unions is only 1.7% to 2.8% above the risk level for the general population. See Robin L. Bennett et al., *Genetic Counseling and Screening of Consanguineous Couples and Their Offspring: Recommendations of the National Society of Genetic Counselors*, 11 Journal of Genetic Counseling 97 (2002).

15. *Johnson v. Johnson*, 104 N.W.2d 8, 14 (N.D. 1960).

16. See, e.g., R.R.S. Neb. § 42–102, which provides, "No person who is afflicted with a venereal disease shall marry in this state."

17. *Meister v. Moore*, 96 U.S. 76, 24 L. Ed. 826 (1877).

18. Cynthia Grant Bowman, ARTICLE: *A Feminist Proposal to Bring Back Common Law Marriage*, 75 Or. L. Rev. 709, 779 (Fall 1996).

19. Immigration Marriage Fraud Amendments of 1986.

20. See, e.g., *Dommer v. Dommer*, 829 N.E.2d 125 (Ind. App. 2005).

21. House Bill 2007 (HB 2007-A) §2 (3) can be found at *www.leg.state.or.us/07reg/measures/hb2000.dir/hb2007.en.html*.

22. See *In the Matter of Adult Anonymous II*, 88 A.D.2d 30, 452 N.Y.S.2d 198 (N.Y. App. Div. 1982). But see *Matter of Robert Paul P.*, 63 N.Y.2d 233, 471 N.E.2d 424, 481 N.Y.S.2d 652 (1984).

23. *Braschi v. Stahl Associates Co.*, 74 N.Y.2d 201, 543 N.E.2d 49 at 55 (1989).

24. American Law Institute, *Principles of the Law of Family Dissolution: Analysis and Recommendations*, 6.03(1).

25. The city of Berkeley, CA, was the first municipality to extend domestic partnership benefits to its employees in 1984. Many other cities across the country followed (such as Boston and Cambridge, MA;

New York City; San Francisco, CA; and Seattle, WA) and extended employee benefits to domestic partners under a policy that recognized them as spousal equivalents and/or because of a nondiscrimination policy encompassing sexual orientation. Most recognized both opposite-sex and same-sex partnerships broadly defined.

26. *Baker v. State*, 170 Vt. 194, 744 A.2d 864 (1999).

27. Lynn Wardle, *The End of Marriage*, 44 Fam. Ct. Rev. 45, 54 (January 2006).

28. Hawaii Revised Statutes § 572–1. The state of Hawaii subsequently enacted "reciprocal beneficiaries" legislation affording some of the rights of marriage to same-sex couples, blood relatives, and housemates and as of 1/1/2012 will permit civil unions.

Chapter 4

1. For example, Cal. Fam. Code §309 provides "If either party to a marriage denies the marriage, or refuses to join in a declaration of the marriage, the other party may proceed, by action pursuant to Section 10345 of the Health and Safety Code, to have the validity of the marriage determined and declared."

2. Tenn. Code Ann. 1 §36–4–101(2) (2011).

3. Internal Revenue Service Publication 504, *Tax Information for Divorced or Separated Individuals*, p. 3. (2011 edition).

4. *Davis v. Davis*, 119 Conn. 194, 175 A. 574 (Conn. 1934).

5. *Irving v. Irving*, 134 P.3d 718 (Nev. 2006).

6. *Brown v. Watson*, 2005 Tenn. App. LEXIS 387.

7. See *Nave v. Nave*, 173 S.W.3d 766 (Tenn. App. 2005), in which a conservator filed a petition to annul the marriage of her ward—her father—on the ground that he was mentally incapable of entering a marriage contract at the time of the ceremony. Before the court rendered its decision granting the annulment, the ward died. A Tennessee Court of Appeals held that the annulment action did not abate at the moment of death, and the conservator was not deprived of standing to continue to pursue the annulment action. The judgment was entered *nunc pro tunc*, making the judgment effective prior to the death.

8. For an interesting unpublished case on this topic, see *Estate of Julia Dominguez, Deceased*, 2002 NY Slip Op 50481U, 2002 N.Y. Misc. LEXIS 1596. In this case, the "husband" in a "sham" marriage entered to assist him with his immigration status sought to be designated as administrator of his wife's estate after she was killed in a plane accident. The deceased wife's daughter also sought to be named administratrix of her mother's estate and to have the alleged husband disqualified as a surviving spouse based on the fact the marriage was a sham.

9. See, e.g., N.C. Gen. Stat. § 51–3 (2006). The statute provides that no marriage followed by cohabitation and the birth of issue shall be declared void after the death of either of the parties for any cause except bigamy.

10. *In re the Marriage of Linda A. and Robert S. Owen*, 2002 Cal. App. Unpub. LEXIS 1500 at 6.

11. See *Fryar v. Roberts*, 346 Ark. 432, 57 S.W.3d 727 (Ark. 2001). In this case, the Arkansas Supreme Court addresses this issue in considerable detail.

12. *Mayo v. Mayo*, 172 N.C. App. 844, 617 S.E.2d 672 (N.C. App. 2005).

13. See, e.g., Hawaii Revised Statutes §572–6 application; license; limitations.

14. See, e.g., *Tagupa v. Tagupa*, 108 Haw. 459, 121 P.3d 924 (Haw. App. 2005).

15. See *M.T. v. J.T.*, 140 N.J. Super. 77, 355 A.2d 204 (1976) and *Kantaras v. Kantaras*, 884 So. 2d 155 (Fla. App. 2004).

16. *Robertson v. Roth*, 163 Minn. 501, 204 N.W. 329 (Minn. 1925).

17. See, e.g., *Meagher v. Maleki*, 131 Cal. App. 4th 1, 31 Cal. Rptr. 3d 663 (2005).

18. See 4 Am. Jur. 2d Annulment §11 (2002). However, the long-standing rule in most jurisdictions is that an annulment will not be granted on the basis of fraud if one partner conceals from the other partner a serious drinking problem for which he or she refuses to seek help even if

it interferes with the parties' sexual relationship. See, e.g., *Schaub v. Schaub*, 71 Cal. App.2d 467, 162 P.2d 966 (1945).

19. *V.J.S. v. M.J.B.*, 249 N.J. Super. 318, 592 A.2d 328 (1991).

20. *Tam v. Chen*, 2004 Cal. App. Unpub. LEXIS 6283.

21. *Adler v. Adler*, 805 So. 2d 952 (Fla. App. 2001).

22. *In re Marriage of Kramer*, 253 Ill. App. 3d 923, 625 N.E.2d 808 (Ill. App. 1993).

23. See, e.g., *Guzman v. Guzman Alvares*, 205 S.W.3d 375 (Tenn. 2006).

24. *Mayo v. Mayo*, 172 N.C. App. 844, 617 S.E.2d 672 (2005), quoting *Weil v. Herring*, 207 N.C. 6, 175 S.E. 836 (N.C. 1934).

25. Gibson's Suits in Chancery, § 42 (4th edition).

26. For a Tennessee case addressing these issues, see *Janna Sheya Falk v. Geary Falk*, 2005 Tenn. App. LEXIS 34.

27. Pursuant to New York Domestic Relations Law §236(B)(2), a court has discretion to make a maintenance award in any "matrimonial" action (including annulment). §141 specifically provides that support can be ordered in an action to annul a marriage based on a party's incurable illness for a period of five years to ensure he or she is cared for and does not become a public charge. See also the Connecticut annulment statute, General Statutes 46b-60.

28. *In re State ex rel. Dep't. of Econ. Sec. v. Demetz*, 212 Ariz. 287, 130 P.3d 986 (Ariz. App. 2006).

Chapter 5

1. Honey Hastings, *Dispute Resolution Options in Divorce and Custody Cases*, New Hampshire Bar Journal, Volume 46, Number 2, Summer, 2005, p. 54. Although this article focuses specifically on the use of alternative dispute resolution options in New Hampshire, it is an excellent and well-researched discussion of the basic nature of several ADR options.

2. See, e.g., *Kelm v. Kelm*, 623 N.E.2d 39 (Ohio 1993).

3. *Williams v. North Carolina*, 317 U.S. 287, 298-299, 63 S. Ct. 207, 87 L. Ed. 279 (1942).

4. *Kulko v. Kulko*, 436 U.S. 84, 98 S. Ct. 1690, 56 L. Ed. 132 (1978).

5. *Burnham v. Superior Ct.*, 495 U.S. 604, 628, 110 S. Ct. 2105, 109 L. Ed. 631, 650 (1990).

6. *Russo v. Russo*, 714 A.2d 466 (Pa. Sup. Ct. 1998).

7. Utah Code Ann. § 30-3-1. (3)(i).

8. See, e.g., *Ricketts v. Ricketts*, 393 Md. 479, 903 A.2d 857 (Ct. App. 2006). In this case, a Maryland appellate court reversed a lower court's dismissal of a complaint for a limited divorce on the ground of constructive desertion based on an alleged denial of marital relations while the parties continued to live under the same roof in separate bedrooms.

9. *Shaffer v. Shaffer*, not reported in S.E.2d, 2003 WL 21739039 (Va. App.).

10. 750 ILCS 5/401 (1).

11. *Verplatse v. Verplatse*, 17 Ohio App. 3d 99, 477 N.E.2d 648 (1984). Also see, e.g., *Hoppes v. Hoppes*, 5 Ohio Misc. 159, 214 N.E.2d 860 (1964).

12. See, e.g., *Routhier v. Routhier*, 128 N.H. 439, 524 A.2d 825 (1986).

13. M.G.L. c.208 §1.

14. O.C.G.A. § 19-5-3 (9) and (12).

15. 750 ILCS 5/401 (1).

16. Md. FAMILY LAW Code Ann. § 7-103 (a)(4).

17. O.C.G.A. § 19-5-3 (8).

18. Orca NN. 3105.01 (4).

19. Va. Code Ann. § 20-91 A.(3).

20. See, e.g., 750 ILCS 5/401 (1).

21. See N.H. Rev Stat. Ann.

22. See, e.g., Conn. Gen. Stat. § 46b-40 (c)(10).

23. Md. FAMILY LAW Code Ann. § 7-103 (a)(7).

24. Utah Code Ann. § 30-3-1 (3)(d).

25. ORC Ann. 3105.01 (F).

26. *In re Hightower*, 830 N.E.2d 862 (Ill App. Ct. 2005), quoting *Quagliano v. Quagliano*, 94 Ill App. 2d 233, 237, 236 N.E.2d 748 (1968).

27. See *Vandevort v. Vandevort*, 134 P.3d 892 (Okla. Civ. App. 2005).
28. 50 U.S.C § 521 (1982).
29. *Long v. Long*, 166 S.W.2d 460 (Tex. App. 2006).
30. See, for example, Mark Chinn, *The Exit Interview*, Family Advocate, Fall 2006, American Bar Association.

Chapter 6

1. See, e.g., Massachusetts Supp.Dom.Rel.P. Rule 410 Mandatory Self-Disclosure of Financial Documents.
2. The content of this segment reflects, in part, observations made in a workshop handout prepared by Hon. Geoffrey A. Wilson, Franklin Probate and Family Court, titled "A Judge's Thoughts on Financial Statements (A Work in Progress)" and reprinted in several publications, including Donald G. Tye et al., Trying Divorce Cases, Volume I, MCLE, Inc. (2005).
3. Gaetano Ferro, Marcus Lawson, and Sarah Murray, *Electronically Stored Information: What Matrimonial Lawyers and Computer Forensics Need to Know*, Journal of the American Academy of a Matrimonial Lawyers, Volume 23, Issue 1 (2010), pp. 1–44.
4. Id at 28.
5. Amanda Showalter, *"What's Yours is Mine": Inadvertent Disclosure of Electronically Stored Privileged Information in Divorce Litigation* [comments], 23 J. Am. Acad. Matrimonial Laws, Issue 1 (2010), pp. 177–198 at 184.
6. See, e.g., *Gallion v. Gallion*, 2011 Conn. Super. LEXIS 2517 (9/30/11 J. Shluger).
7. *Supra* at note 5.
8. Matthew Robertson, *Electronic Evidence: Comment: Why Invisible Electronic Data is Relevant in Today's Legal Arena*, 23 J. Am. Acad. Matrimonial Law (2010), pp. 199–215.
9. *Supra* at note 5.
10. *St. Clair v. Johnny's Oyster and Shrimp, Inc.*, 76 F. Supp.2d 773 (S.D. Tex. 1999).
11. Carolyn Davis, *Divorce Facebook Style*, Philadelphia Enquirer, July 12, 2010.
12. *McMillen v. Hummingbird Speedway, Inc.*, 2010 Westlaw 4403285 (Pa. Ct. Com. Pl. Sept. 9, 2010).

Chapter 7

1. Several courts across the country have held that both parents have a support obligation to a child who is the product of statutory rape. See, e.g., *State of Kansas ex rel. Hermesmann v. Seyer*, 252 Kan. 646, 847 P.2d 1273 (1993).
2. E. Gary Spitko, *Sexual Orientation: Public Perceptions: From Queer to Paternity: How Primary Gay Fathers Are Changing Fatherhood and Gay Identity*, 24 St. Louis U. Pub. L. Rev. 195 at 216 (2005).
3. See Cynthia R. Mabry, *Who Is the Baby's Daddy (and Why Is It Important for the Child to Know)?*, 34 U. Balt. L. Rev. 211 (Winter 2004). Based on the Census data cited, 48% of children not living with their fathers were African American; 25% were Latino. Asian families reported the lowest number of children who lived with their single mothers, 13%.
4. *Nguyen v. Immigration and Naturalization Services*, 533 U.S. 53, 121 S. Ct. 2053, 150. L. Ed. 2d 115 (2001).
5. *Levy v. Louisiana*, 391 U.S. 68 (1968).
6. *Lehr v. Robertson*, 463 U.S. 248, 103 S. Ct. 2985, 77 L. Ed. 2d 614 (1983).
7. *Supra* n.4 at 62.
8. 8 U.S.C.S. §1409.
9. Id. at §1409(c).
10. Id. at §1409(a).
11. See Katharine Baker, *Bargaining or Biology? The History and Future of Paternity Law and Parental Status*, 14 Cornell J. L. & Pub. Pol'y 1 at 6 (Fall 2004), for a comprehensive discussion of the rationale for

and implementation of the duty of paternity support initially in the criminal context as "punishment for fornication and bastardy."

12. Nancy E. Dowd, Essay: *From Genes, Marriage and Money to Nurture: Redefining Fatherhood*, 10 Cardozo Women's L.J. 132 at 138 (Fall 2003). According to U.S. Census Bureau data, an estimated sixteen million children, or about one in five, received food stamp assistance in 2014.
13. Uniform Parentage Act of 2000 (as amended 2002), Article 2 §201.
14. *Barnes v. Jeudevine*, 475 Mich. 696, at 715, 718 N.W.2d 311 (2006) (Markman, J., dissenting).
15. 41 U.S.C. 666(a)(5)(D).
16. 41 U.S.C. 666(a)(5)(D)(i).
17. Gary A. Debele, *Family Law Issues for Same-Sex Couples in the Aftermath of Minnesota's Same-Sex Marriage Law: A Family Law Attorney's Perspective*, 41 Wm. Mitchell L. Rev. 157 (2015).
18. Id.
19. *Principles of the Law of Family Dissolution: Analysis and Recommendations*, American Law Institute, Philadelphia, PA, *www.ali.org*.
20. Niccol D. Kording, *Little White Lies That Destroy Children's Lives—Recreating Paternity Fraud Laws to Protect Children's Interests*, 6 J.L. Fam. Stud. 237, 245 (2004).
21. Alaska Stat. § 25.27.166. Exception: Disestablishment is not permitted if paternity has been acknowledged or admitted or established through genetic testing.
22. O.C.G.A. § 19–7–54.
23. Md. Code Ann., Fam. Law § 5–1038(a)(2)(i)2. Exception: Cannot disestablish paternity if father has previously acknowledged paternity knowing he was not the father.
24. Ohio Revised Code Sections 3119.961 and 3119.962. Exception: Cannot disestablish paternity if father has previously acknowledged paternity knowing he was not the father. Two Ohio courts of appeal have declared the statutes unconstitutional because the legislature, in effect, was dictating to the courts what to do with paternity judgments rendered years before, in violation of the separation of powers doctrine.
25. See, e.g., *Doran v. Doran*, 2003 PA Super 129, 820 A.2d 1279 (2003), in which the court denied a request for an award in the amount of previously paid child support; but see *Denzik v. Denzik*, 197 S.W.3d 108 (Ky. 2006), in which the Kentucky Supreme Court reinstated a jury verdict in a husband's fraudulent misrepresentation action and allowed "restitution, albeit with considerations to limit the rate of payment in order to prevent detriment to the child(ren) supported."
26. *Langston v. Riffe*, 359 Md. 396 at 437, 754 A.2d 389 (Ct. App. 2000).
27. Id. at 416.
28. *Williams v. Williams*, 843 So. 2d 720 at 723 (Miss. 2003).
29. *Godin v. Godin*, 168 Vt. 514 at 523, 725 A.2d 904 (1998).
30. Mabry, *supra* n. 3 at 213, reflecting decisions of courts in New Jersey, Pennsylvania, Kansas, and Delaware.
31. *Betty L.W. v. William E.W.*, 212 W. Va. 1 at 12, 569 S.E.2d 77 (2002) (Maynard, J. dissenting).
32. *www.paternityfraud.com*.
33. Kording, *supra* n. 20, at 237.
34. Bruce Lord Wilder, *Current Status of Assisted Reproduction Technology: An Overview and Glance at the Future*, 39 FAM. L. Q. 573 (at 1) (No. 3 Fall 2005).
35. 750 ILCS 47.
36. N.H. Rev. Stat. §168-B: 9.
37. Mass. Gen. Laws Ch. 112 §12J.
38. 18 Pa. C. S. Ann. §3213(e).
39. Ark. Code Ann. § 23–85–137.
40. Md. Code Ann. §15–810(d) re limits and (b)(1) re mandates.
41. Del.Code Ann. Tit. 13 § 8-703.
42. Nev. Rev. Stat. Ann. § 126.670.
43. 40 N.M. Stat. Ann. § 40-11A-703.
44. Wash. Rev. Code Ann. § 26.26.710.
45. Utah Code Ann. §78B-15-801.

46. N.H. Rev. Stat. Ann. §168-B:13.

47. Va. Code Ann. 20–165 (A)(B).

48. 750 ILCS 47/15.

49. *Hodas v. Morin*, 442 Mass. 544, 814 N.E.2d 320 (2004).

50. See, e.g., Cal. Fam. Code §7630 (f). For an excellent resource on pre-birth parentage orders, see Steven H. Snyder and Mary Patricia Byrn, *The Use of Prebirth Parentage Orders in Surrogacy Proceedings*, 39 Fam. L. Q. 633–662 (No. 3 Fall 2005). The article includes as an appendix a state-by-state list of laws affecting surrogacy and pre-birth order proceedings.

51. *Doe v. Doe*, 710 A.2d 1297 (Conn. 1998).

52. See Cyrene Grothaus-Day, *Criminal Conception: Behind the White Coat*, 39 FAM. L. Q, 707 (2005).

53. *In the Matter of Baby M.*, 109 N.J. 396, 537 A. 2d 1227 (1988).

54. Id. at 441, 442.

55. *Johnson v. Calvert*, 5 Cal. 4th 84, 851 P.2d 776, 19 Cal. Rptr. 2d 494 (1993), Cert. Denied 510 U.S. 874, 114 S. Ct. 206, 126 L. Ed. 2d 163 (1993).

56. Id. at 93.

57. See Charles P. Kindregan and Maureen McBrien, *Embryo Donation: Unresolved Legal Issues in the Transfer of Surplus Cryopreserved Embryos*, 49 Vill. L. Rev. 169 at 170 (2004).

58. See Naomi D. Johnson, *Excess Embryos: Is Embryo Adoption a New Solution or a Temporary Fix*, 68 Brook. L. Rev. 853 (2003).

59. See N.H. Rev. Stat. Ann. § 168-B:13 and La. Rev. Stat. Ann. § 9:129.

60. See generally La. Rev. Stat. Ann. §§9:129.

61. Fla. Stat. Ann. § 742.17.

62. 10 Okla. St. § 556.

63. *Davis v. Davis*, 842 S.W.2d 588 (Tenn. 1992).

64. Id. at 597.

65. Id. at 601.

66. Id. at 602.

67. *Kass v. Kass*, 91 N.Y.2d 554, 696 N.E.2d 174, 673 N.Y.S.2d 350 (N.Y. 1998).

68. Id. at 180.

69. Fla. Stat. §742.17.

70. La. R.S. 9:391.1A.

71. On this topic see Jessica Knouse, *Liberty, Equality, and Parentage in the Era of Posthumous Conception*, 27 J. L. & Health 9 (2014).

Chapter 8

1. U.S. Census Bureau, *Adopted Children and Stepchildren: 2000* (2003), www.census.gov/prod/2003pubs/censr-6.pdf.

2. Elizabeth J. Samuels, *Time to Decide? The Laws Governing Mothers' Consents to the Adoption of Their Newborn Infants*, 72 Tenn. L. Rev. 509, 518 (Winter 2005), referencing Sue Zeidler, *"Internet Transforms U.S. Adoption Process,"* Reuters, May 21, 2004.

3. Intercountry Adoption, Bureau of Consular Affairs, U.S. Department of State, www.state.gov.

4. Peter Selman, *The Rise and Fall of Intercountry Adoption in the 21st Century*, International Social Work, 52 (5): 575–594.

5. U.S. Department of Health and Human Services, Health Resources and Services Administration, Maternal and Child Health Bureau, *Child Health USA 2010,* Rockville, Maryland: U.S. Department of Health and Human Services, 2010.

6. U.S. Department of State Bureau of Consular Affairs, FY (Fiscal Year) 2013 Annual Report on Intercountry Adoption.

7. Intercountry Adoptions from Hague Convention and Non-Hague Convention Countries, www.childwelfare.gov.

8. See, e.g., Colo. Rev. Stat. §25–2–113.5.

9. See, e.g., Massachusetts General Laws, Chapter 210, Section 5D.

10. Ala. Code § 22–9A-12(c); Alaska Stat. § 18.50.500(a); Kan. Stat. Ann. 65-§2423(a); and Or. Rev. Stat. § 432.228(1) (at age 21).

11. Massachusetts General Laws Chapter 210, Section 1.

12. Utah Code Title 78B, Chapter 6, Section 117(3).

13. *Lehr v. Robertson*, 463 U.S. 248 at 262, 103 S. Ct. 2985, 77 L. Ed. 2d 614 (1983).

14. For an interesting New Mexico case addressing whether or not a father's conduct prior to his child's birth can be used to terminate parental rights under a presumptive abandonment statute, see *Helen G. v. Mark J. H. (In re Adoption Petition of Romero)*, 2006 NMCA 136, 145 P.3d 98 (2006).

15. See *In re Adoption of Reeves*, 831 S.W.2d 607 (Ark. 1992).

16. Erin Green, *Unwed Fathers' Rights in Adoption: The Virginia Code vs. The Uniform Adoption Act*, 11 Wm. & Mary J. of Women & L. 267, 273 (Winter 2005).

17. Fla. Stat. Ann. §383.50 (5). For a multistate review of the nature and complexity of safe haven laws, see Dayna R. Cooper, *Fathers Are Parents Too: Challenging Safe Haven Laws with Procedural Due Process*, 31 Hofstra L. Rev. 877 (2003), and Jeffrey A. Parness, *Deserting Mothers, Abandoned Babies, Lost Fathers: Dangers in Safe Havens*, 24 Quinnipiac L. Rev. 335 (2006).

18. Shirley Darby Howell, *Adoption: When Psychology and Law Collide*, 28 Hamline L. Rev. 29, 54 (Winter 2005). For a more extensive discussion of this topic, see Robbin Potz Gonzalez, *The Rights of Putative Fathers to Their Infant Children in Contested Adoptions: Strengthening State Laws That Currently Deny Adequate Protection*, 13 Mich. J. Gender 7 L. 39 (2006).

19. Code of Ala. § 26–10C-1(i).

20. Code of Ala. § 26–10A-9(a).

21. Minn. Stat. § 259.52(8). See also 750 Ill. Comp. Stat. § 50/12.1 (2011).

22. Ariz. Rev. Stat. §8–106.01(F); see also R.S.Mo. §192.016.

23. Utah Code Ann. § 78B-6-110 (2011).

24. See Mo. Ann. Stat. § 192.016(9)(2,3).

25. Utah Code Ann. 78B–6–102 (2011).

26. *G.P. v. State*, 842 So. 2d 1059 (Fla. Dist. Ct. App. 2003), invalidating Fla. Stat. Ann. §§ 63.087, 63.088, commonly known as the Scarlet Letter Provisions, OK.

27. Kimberly Barton, *Who's Your Daddy? State Adoption Statutes and the Unknown Biological Father*, 32 Cap. U.L. Rev. 113 (Fall 2003). See also Jeffrey A. Parness, *Adoption Notices to Genetic Fathers: No to Scarlet Letters, Yes to Good Faith Cooperation*, 36 Cumb. L. Rev. 63 (2005/2006).

28. Kan. Stat. Ann. § 59–2136(c) requires the court to order publication notice of the adoption hearing if no person is identified as the father or a possible father.

29. N.C. Gen. Stat. §§ 48–2–401(c)(3) and 48–2–402(b).

30. 105 P.L. 89, 111 Stat. 2115 (codified as amended in scattered sections of 2 U.S.C. and 42 U.S.C.).

31. Barbara Bennett Woodhouse, *Waiting for Loving: The Child's Fundamental Right to Adoption*, 34 Cap. U. L. Rev. 297, 328 (Winter 2005).

32. See, e.g., Massachusetts General Laws, Chapter 210, Section 2.

33. Samuels *supra* n. 2 at 526, 527.

34. Samuels *supra* n. 2 at 528. For an example of a state statute regarding requirements for effective consents, see the following Vermont Statutes: 15A V.S.A. § 2–405 and 15A V.S.A. § 2–406. For an excellent resource, see Ann McLane Kuster and Marilyn T. Mahoney, *A Practitioner's Guide to Creating a Secure Adoption*, New Hampshire Bar Journal, March 1996.

35. Susan Calkins, *Ineffective Assistance of Counsel in Parental-Rights Termination Cases: The Challenge for Appellate Courts*, 6 J. App. Prac. 179 (Fall 2004). A problem sometimes arises when the adoption of a child is approved while termination of a parent's rights is under appeal. For a discussion of cases involving such situations, see Kate M. Heideman, *Avoiding the Need to "Unscramble the Egg": A Proposal for the Automatic Stay of Subsequent Adoption Proceedings When Parents Appeal a Judgment Terminating Their Parental Rights*, 24 St. Louis U. Pub. L. Rev. 445 (2005).

36. 42 U.S.C.A. §12132.

37. D.C. Code 16–2353(b)(4).

38. 42 U.S.C.A. §1996b.

39. 25 U.S.C.A. §1901.

40. 25 U.S.C.A. §1915(a) codifies this provision of the Indian Child Welfare Act. The Bureau of Indian Affairs has published Guidelines for state courts' implementation of the Act in 44 Fed. Reg. 67, 584. Guideline F.3 provides that good cause may be based on a request of the biological parents, established extraordinary physical or emotional needs of the child, or the unavailability of suitable families for placement after a diligent search. For a case applying this guideline, see *In re Adoption of B.G.J.*, 281 Kan. 552, 133 P.3d 1 (2006), decided by the Supreme Court of Kansas.

41. 25 U.S.C. §1903(4). For examples of cases addressing the requirements and application of the addressing the requirements and application of the Indian Child Welfare Act, see *In re Dependency of T.G.L.* et al., 126 Wn. App. 181, 108 P.3d 156 (2005), and *In the Matter of Baby Boy L.*, 2004 OK 93, 103 P.3d 1099 (2004).

42. See Cal. Fam. Code 9000(b); Conn. Gen. Stat. Ann. 45a-724(a)(3); and Vt. Stat. Ann. Tit. 15A, 1 102(b).

43. *Lawrence v. Texas*, 539 U.S. 558 (2003), is a landmark decision by the United States Supreme Court. In the 6–3 ruling, the Court struck down the sodomy law in Texas and, by extension, invalidated sodomy laws in 13 other states, making same-sex sexual activity legal in every U.S. state and territory.

44. *DeBoer v. DeBoer*, 509 U.S. 1301, 114 S. Ct. 1, 125 L. Ed. 2d 755 (1993).

45. *In re Doe*, 254 Ill. App. 3d 405, 627 N.E.2d 648 at 651–652 (Ill. App. 1 Dist. 1993).

Chapter 9

1. *Garska v. McCoy*, 167 W.Va. 59, 278 S.E.2d at 360 (1981).

2. American Law Institute, Principles of Marital Dissolution, §2.03 (1). The American Law Institute's Principles of Marital Dissolution refer to "allocation of parental responsibilities" rather than to "visitation" and "custody."

3. New Hampshire RSA 461-A:1, 2. Proposed by a Family Law Task Force after a two-year study, the Act went into effect in 2005. Similar to other jurisdictions moving in this direction, it supports "frequent and continuing contact between each child and both parents" and encourages parents "to develop their own parenting plans" and "to share in the rights and responsibilities of raising their children. . . ." RSA 461-A:2. "custody."

4. The Uniform Child Custody Jurisdiction Act, 9(1A) U.L.A. 261 (1968).

5. The Uniform Child Custody Jurisdiction and Enforcement Act, 9(1A) U.L.A. 649 (1997).

6. Federal Parental Kidnapping Act, P.L. 96–611 § 6–10.

7. Convention on the Civil Aspects of International Child Abduction, held at The Hague on October 25, 1980. The language of the Convention can be found in Appendix 2 to the Department of State Notice, 51 FR 10498 March 26, 1986. The federal legislation that makes the terms of the Convention available as a judicial remedy in the United States is the International Child Abduction Remedies Act (ICARA), Sec. 1 of P.L. 100–300, 42 U.S.C.A.11601 *et seq*. The federal regulations that define the state department's role in implementing the Convention are found in 22 C.F.R. 94.4.

8. National Child Search Assistance Act, 42 USC §§ 5779 and 5780.

9. The International Parental Kidnapping Crime Act, 18 USC §1204.

10. The Fugitive Felon Act, 18 USC §1073.

11. The International Child Abduction Remedies Act, 42 USC §11601 *et seq.*

12. *In re Milovich*, 105 Ill. App.3d 596, 434 N.E.2d 811 (1982).

13. See, e.g., *Burchard v. Garay*, 724 P.2d 486 (Cal. 1986.); *Maureen F.G. v. George W.G.*, 445 A.2d 934 (Del. 1982); *Agudo v. Agudo*, 411So. 2d 249 (Fla. Dist. Ct. App 1982); *Rolde v. Rolde*, 12 Mass. App. Ct. 398, 425 N.E.2d 388 (1981); *Maxfield v. Maxfield*, 452 N.W.2d 219 (Minn.

1990); *Riaz v. Riaz*, 789 S.W.2d 224 (Mo. App. Ct. 1990); *Burleigh v. Burleigh*, 650 P.2d 753 (Mont. 1982); *Crum v. Crum*, 505 N.Y.S.2d 656 (App. Div. 1986); *Moore v. Moore*, 574 A.2d 105 (Pa. Super. Ct. 1990); *Pusey v. Pusey*, 728 P.2d 117 (Utah 1986); *Harris v. Harris*, 546 A.2d 208 (Vt. 1988); and *Garska v. McCoy*, 167 W.Va. 59, 278 S.E.2d at (360 1981).

14. See *Pascale v. Pascale*, 140 N.J. 583, 660 A.2d 485 (N.J. 1995).

15. American Law Institute, Principles of the Law of Family Dissolution: Analysis and Recommendations, §208.

16. *Silva v. Silva*, 136 P.3d 371 (Idaho App. 2006).

17. *Kilsing v. Allison*, 343 S.C. 674, 541 S.E.2d 273 (S.C. App. 2001).

18. § 452.375 R.S. Mo.

19. Source: *Custodial Mothers and Fathers and Their Child Support: 2011 Current Population Reports* by Timothy Grall, issued October 2013.

20. Source: U.S. Census Bureau, Current Population Survey, April 1994–2002.

21. MCLS § 722.23.

22. *Garrett v. Garrett*, 527 N.W.2d 213, 221–222 (Neb. Ct. App. 1995).

23. *Hicks v. Hicks*, 2005 PA Super. 58, 868 A.2d 1245 (2005). There are those who might argue that the court violates the Constitution by, in effect, preferring one religion over another. Occasionally, a dispute is about a particular religious practice between two parents who share the same faith. See *Sagar v. Sagar*, 57 Mass. App. Ct. 71, 781 N.E.2d 54 (2003).

24. Ella Callow et al., *Parents with Disabilities in the United States: Prevalence, Perspectives, and a Proposal for Legislative Change to Protect the Right to Family in the Disability Community*, 17 Tex. J. C.L. §C.R. 9 (2011).

25. *Newton v. Riley*, 899 S.W.2d 509 (Ky. Ct. App. 1995).

26. *In re Stopher*, 328 Ill. App. 3d 1037, 263 Ill. Dec. 199, 767 N.E.2d 925 (2002).

27. *Matta v. Matta*, 44 Mass. App. Ct. 946, 693 N.E.2d 1063 (1998).

28. *Taylor v. Taylor*, 345 Ark. 300, 47 S.W.3d 222 (2001).

29. See, e.g., *Boyle v. Boyle*, 12 Neb. App. 681, 684 N.W. 2d 49 (2004).

30. *McGriff v. McGriff*, 140 Idaho 642, 99P.3d 11 (2004). In this case, the Idaho Supreme Court affirmed a lower court's decision conditioning visitation with a homosexual father on his not residing in the same house with his male partner during visits.

31. *Supra* note 21.

32. *Anderson v. Anderson*, 278 Ga. 713, 606 S.E.2d 251 (2004).

33. Ill. Rev. Stat. § 750 ILCS 5/602.

34. *Resigno v. Annino*, 869 So. 2d 741 (Fla. 2004).

35. *In re Julie Anne*, 121 Ohio Misc. 2d 20, 2002 Ohio 4489, 780 N.E.2d 635 (Ohio Com. Pleas 2002).

36. Wyo. Stat. Ann. §20–2–201(a)(iii).

37. But in an Illinois case, the appeals court noted that "Neither the legislature or case law in Illinois has seen fit to set forth a rule of law that the killing of one parent by the other in the presence of the children, no matter what the circumstances, standing alone is sufficient to deprive that parent of his or her children on the basis of unfitness." *Tranel v. Lutgen*, 177 Ill. App. 3d 954, 127 Ill. Dec. 147, 532 N.E.2d 976 (2 Dist. 1988).

38. S.C. Code § 63–15–30 (2008).

39. Nicholas Bala, Rachel Burnbaum, Francine Cyr, and Denise McColley, *Children's Voices in Family Court: Guidelines for Judges Meeting Children*, Fam. L. Q. Volume 47, No. 3, Fall 2013, pp. 379–408.

40. Jacqueline Clarke, *Do I Have a Voice? An Empirical Analysis of Children's Voices in Michigan Custody Litigation*, Fam. L. Q. Volume 47, No. 3, Fall 2013, at pp. 466–467.

41. See, e.g., *Sinicropi v. Mazurek*, 729 N.W.2d 256 (Mich. Ct. App. 2007); *Henderson v. Henderson*, 2008 WL 4599607 Ohio Ct. App. Oct. 10, 2008; and *Holiday v. Holiday*, 2011 WY 12; 247 P.3d 29 (2011).

42. *Bodne v. Bodne*, 277 Ga. 445, 588 S.E.2d 95 (Ga. App. 2002).

43. Rev. Code Wash. (ARCW) § 2609.184.

44. Sometimes innovative strategies are used, such as having parents who cannot talk reasonably with each other in person communicate by writing basic messages in a notebook. *Shenk v. Shenk*, 159 Md. App. 548, 860 A.2d 408 (2004).

45. See, e.g., *Beck v. Beck*, 86 N.J. 480; 432 A.2d 63 (1981).

46. See, e.g., *Cohen v. Cohen*, 162 Md. App. 599, 875 A.2d 814 (2005).

47. *McCoy v. McCoy*, 336 N.J. Super. 172, 764 A. 2d 449 (N.J. Super. App. Div. 2001). See also *McCubbin v. Taylor*, 5 S.W.3d 202 (Mo. App. 1999).

48. Many states have adopted the language of the UMDA in their no-fault statutes. According to the Uniform Law Commission, the states that have adopted the UMDA as of January 2014 include Arizona, Colorado, Georgia, Minnesota, Montana, and Washington.

49. 50 USCS Appx. § 501 *et seq*.

50. See, e.g., *Spahmer v. Gullette*, 113 P.3d 158 (Colo. 2005).

51. *Hawkes v. Spence*, 2005 VT 57, 178 Vt. 161, 878 A.2d 273 (2005).

52. See *Prenaveau v. Prenaveau*, 81 Mass. App. Ct. 479, 964 N.E.2d 353 (2012).

53. William G. Austin, *Relocation Law and the Threshold of Harm: Integrating Legal and Behavioral Perspectives*, 34 Fam. L. Q. 63, 65 (Spring 2000), as quoted in *Fenwick v. Fenwick*, 114 S.W.3d 767 (Ky. 2003). See also *Tibor v. Tibor*, 598 N.W.2d 480, 485 (N.D. 1999), in which the court acknowledges that a "move which benefits the health and well-being of a custodial parent is certainly beneficial to the parent's child, and is consequently in the child's best interest."

54. California Family Code Article 3048; Minnesota Statute Article 518.175; Revised Statutes of Missouri Article 452.377; and CRS 14-10-129.

55. *Morgan v. Foretich*, 546 A.2d 407 (D.C. App. 1988). See also *Morgan v. Foretich*, 564 A.2d 1 (D.C. App. 1989), in which the contempt judgment was overturned.

56. Gupta-Kagan, *Children, Kin, and Court: Designing Third Party Custody Policy to Protect Children, Third Parties, and Parents*, 12 N.Y.U. J. Legis. & Pub. Pol'y 43 at 48 (2008).

57. Maya Manian, *Functional Parenting and Dysfunctional Abortion Policy: Reforming Parental Involvement Legislation*, 50 Fam. Ct. Rev. 241, 246–247 (2012).

58. Some of the states imposing such obligations include Delaware, Hawaii, Iowa, Kentucky, Montana, North Carolina, and North Dakota.

59. See, e.g., *V.C. v. M.L.B.*, 163 N.J. 200, 748 A.2d 539 (2000).

60. *J.A.L. v. E.P.H.*, 453 Pa. Super. 78, 88–89; 682 A.2d 1314, 1319–1320 (1996).

61. Mary Ann Mason and Nicole Zayac, *Rethinking Stepparent Rights: Has the ALI Found a Better Definition?*, 36 Fam. L. Q. No. 2, Summer 2002.

62. Id.

63. In a Michigan case, for example, a court extended parental status to a stepparent, applying the concept of "equitable parenthood" under circumstances in which (1) the husband and child mutually acknowledge a relationship as father and child, or the mother of the child has cooperated in the development of such a relationship over a time prior to the filing of the complaint for divorce, (2) the husband desires to have the rights afforded to a parent, and (3) the husband is willing to take on the responsibility of paying child support. *Atkinson v. Atkinson*, 160 Mich. App. 601, 408 N.W.2d 516 (1987). In the Minnesota case, *Simmons v. Simmons*, 486 N.W.2d 788 (Minn. App. 1992), the court relied on the *in loco parentis* doctrine when it awarded visitation to a stepfather over the mother's objection.

64. Source: U.S. Census Bureau, 2013 American Community Survey.

65. See *Troxel v. Granville*, 530 U.S. 57 at 74 (2000).

66. Sandra Martinez, *The Misinterpretation of Troxel v. Granville: Construing the New Standard for Third-Party Visitation*, 36 Fam. L. Q. No. 3, Fall 2002, at p. 495.

67. The U.S. Supreme Court has recognized the rights of a "mature" minor in some contexts, such as in the making of abortion decisions.

68. Barbara Atwood, *Representing Children: The Ongoing Search for Clear and Workable Standards*, 19 J. Am. Acad. Matrimonial Law (2005).

69. Id.

70. *State of New Mexico ex rel. Children, Youth and Families Department, Petitioner-Appellant, v. IN THE MATTER OF GEORGE F. and FRANK F., Children, Respondents-Appellees,* 125 N.M. 597, 1998-NMCA-119; 964 P.2d 158 (1998).

71. *Lawrence v. Lawrence*, 2004 WI App. 170; 276 Wis. 2d 403, 687 N.W.2d 748 (2004).

72. *Kendall v. Kendall*, 426 Mass. 238, 687 N.E.2d 1228 (1997).

73. Barbara Bennett Woodhouse, *Talking About Children's Rights in Judicial Custody and Visitation Decision-Making*, 36 FAM. L. Q. Number 1, Spring 2002, p. 105 at 129.

74. Jeff Atkinson, *Modern Child Custody Practice*, Volume 1, § 4.1.

75. John DeWitt Gregory, *Family Privacy and the Custody and Visitation Rights of Adult Outsiders*, 36 FAM. L. Q. No. 1, Spring 2002, p. 163 at 168.

Chapter 10

1. 42 U.S.C. §666(a)(5)(D)(ii).

2. *Kirkpatrick v. O'Neal*, 197 S.W.3d 674 (Tenn. 2006).

3. *Rodney P. v. Stacy B.*, 169 S.W.3d 834 (Ky. 2005). The Guidelines will usually be used to determine the level of each parent's obligation. The basic premise is that a parent who has the ability to pay should not be relieved of the duty to do so solely because the child is removed from his or her custody. However, the total payment from the parents should not exceed the actual costs to the agency of caring for the child. See also *In re Katherine C.*, 390 Md. 554, 890 A.2d 295 (Md. 2006).

4. See *In the Matter of the Marriage of Risley Doney and Risley*, 41 Kan. App. 2d 294, 201 P.3d 770 (2009) and Section 25-320, A.R.S.

5. 11 U.S.C. §§ 523(a)(5) and 507(a).

6. Pub. L. No. 93–647, 88 Stat. 2361 (codified as amended at 42 U.S.C. §§651–662).

7. Child Support Enforcement Amendments of 1984, Pub. L. No. 98–378, 98 Stat. 1321 (1984) (42 U.S.C. §667).

8. 42 U.S.C. § 666(a)(5).

9. Pub. L. No. 100–485, 102 Stat. 2343 (1988) as codified in U.S.C. 42 § 667(b).

10. Uniform Interstate Family Support Act, 9(1) U.L.A., 201 (Supp. 1996). First developed in 1992, the act was subsequently revised in 1996, 2001, with additional amendments in 2008. Initially all states adopted the 1996 version pursuant to federal mandate. The 2001 amendments clarified and extended the act without making any fundamental changes in the earlier policies and procedures. As of March 2014, twenty-one states and the District of Columbia had enacted the 2001 version. A 2008 version has been drafted and adopted in twelve states as of March 2015 (Florida, Georgia, Maine, Minnesota Missouri, Nevada, New Mexico, North Dakota, Rhode Island, Tennessee, Utah, and Wisconsin). A primary addition to the 2008 UIFSA is the expansion of international child support enforcement initiatives consistent with the tenets of the new Hague Convention on the Enforcement of Child Support and Other Forms of Family Maintenance signed in 2007.

11. Pub. L. No. 100–485, 102 Stat. 2343 (1988) as codified in U.S.C. 42 § 666.

12. Pub. L. No. 104–193, 110 Stat. 2105 (42 U.S.C. § 601 *et seq.*).

13. 28 U.S.C. § 1738B. This act is similar in structure and intent to UIFSA, and the acts are largely complementary and not contradictory. It was passed before UIFSA was adopted by all states in response to federal mandate.

14. 45 C.F.R. § 302.56.

15. Jo Michelle Beld and Len Biernat, *Federal Intent for State Child Support Guidelines: Income Shares, Cost Shares, and the Realities of Shared Parenting*, 37 Fam. Law Q. No. 2 (Summer 2003).

16. For a discussion of this approach, see *Maturo v. Maturo*, 296 Conn. 80, 995 A.2d 1 (2010).

17. See, e.g., *In re the Marriage of Jack and Cindie Alter*, 171 Cal. App. 4th 718, 89 Cal. Rptr. 3d 849 (2009) and *In re Marriage of Rogers*, 213 Ill.2d 129, 820 N.E.2d 386 (2004).

18. See, e.g., *In re State (Taylor)*, 153 N.H. 700, 904 A.2d 619 (2006).

19. Tori R. A. Kricken, *Child Support and Social Security Dependent Benefits: A Comprehensive Analysis and Proposal for Wyoming*, 2 Wyo. L. Rev. 39 (2002). This article provides an in-depth review of how various states deal with SSDI benefits. The author concluded that Wyoming should adopt the majority position of including the benefit in the obligor's income and subsequently allowing a setoff of his or her support obligations.

20. See, e.g., *Brown v. Brown*, 849 N.E.2d 610 (Ind. 2006); *Metz v. Metz*, 120 Nev. 786, 101 P.3d 779 (Nev. 2004); and *Groenstein v. Groenstein*, 2005 WY 6, 104 P. 3d 765, (Wyo. 2005), which are good examples of cases addressing this topic.

21. 42 U.S.C. §407(a).

22. See, e.g., *In the Matter of Takiyah Massey and David Evans*, 68 A.D.3d 79, 886 N.Y.S.2d 280 (2009).

23. 10 U.S.C.A. §1408 (c), (d), and (e)(1998 and Supp. 2004).

24. La.R.S. 9:315.

25. An excellent case on this topic is *Caplan v. Caplan*, 182 N.J. 250, 864 A.2d 1108 (2005).

26. See, e.g., *In re Bazemore*, 153 N.H. 351, 899 A.2d 225 (2006).

27. 45 C.F.R. §302.56 (c).

28. Office of Child Support Enforcement, *Essentials for Attorneys in Child Support Enforcement*, Chapter 9 (3rd edition, 2002).

29. See *Wilkins v. Wilkins*, 269 Neb. 937, 697 N.W.2d 280 (2005). R.R.S. Neb. § 42-364.16 (2006) establishes that the Supreme Court of Nebraska shall provide child support guidelines by court rules. The language cited in the text is found in Nebraska Supreme Court Rules, Chapter 4, Children and Families, Article 2, Child Support Guidelines, §4-220.

30. *Busse v. Busse*, 141 Idaho 566, 113 P.3d 224 (2005).

31. RSA 461-A:14 V.

32. M.G.L. ch. 208 §28.

33. *In re Marriage of Vannausdle*, 668 N.W.2d 885 (Iowa 2003). See also *Gac v. Gac*, 186 N.J. 535, 897 A.2d 1018 (2006). This is a good case illustrating a court's consideration of factors related to coverage of the costs of higher education.

34. WISC. Admin. Code Chapter DCF 150.

35. ARIZ. REV. STAT. §25-320 (2001).

36. COLO. REV. STAT. ANN. § 14–10–115 (West 1997 & Supp. 1998).

37. 19-A M.R.S. § 2006 (5)(D-1). See *Jabar v. Jabar*, 2006 Me.74, 899 A.2d 796 (2006). In 2003, the state of Maine enacted new child support guidelines that mandated an alternative method for calculating child support when the parties provide "substantially equal care for a child."

38. N.J. Court Rules, R., Appx. IX-A 2006 13.

39. Oklahoma Child Support Guidelines: 43 Okl. St. § 118E.

40. TEX. FAM. CODE §157.008. See, e.g., *In the Interest of A.M.*, 192 S.W.3d 570 (Tex. 2006).

41. N.D. Admin. Code, Section 75-02-04.1-08.2. (2003). Under North Dakota case law, the split custody offset will apply even when one parent assigns his or her right to receive child support to the state. See, e.g., *Simon v. Simon*, 2006 ND 29, 709 N.W.2d 4 (N.D. 2006).

42. An excellent case on this topic is *Gladis v. Gladisova*, 382 Md. 654, 856 A.2d 703 (2004).

43. *Smith v. Freeman*, 149 Md. App. 1, 814 A.2d 65 (Md. Spec. App. 2002).

44. In the case of *Scott-Lasley v. Lasley*, the Georgia Supreme Court held that when "an award of child support is made for several children and the trial court provides for reductions in child support as the children reach majority, the trial court may not reduce the child support on a pro rata per child basis, but must instead do so in accordance with the child support guidelines." *Scott-Lasley v. Lasley*, 278 Ga. 671, 604 S.E.2d 761 (2004).

45. 42 U.S.C.A. §666(a)10).

46. New York State Bar Association Committee on Professional Ethics, Op. 569 (Feb. 7, 1985).

47. See, e.g., *Prisco v. Stroup*, 2004 D.C. Super. LEXIS 23 (2004) and Pub. L, No. 105–187, 112 Stat. 618 (1998) (codified at 18 U.S.C. § 228)—an amendment to the Child Support Recovery Act of 1992; Pub. L. No. 102–521, 106 Stat. 3403.

48. Pub. L. No. 105–187, 112 Stat. 618 (1998) (codified at 18 U.S.C. § 228)—an amendment to the Child Support Recovery Act of 1992; Pub. L. No. 102–521, 106 Stat. 3403.

49. 18 U.S.C.A. § 228.

50. MCL 600.5809(4).

51. MCL 767.24(5). For a related case see, e.g., *People v. Monaco*, 474 Mich. 48, 710 N.W.2d 46 (2005). Note: (5) relates to identity theft. (7) is the "all other" clause into which felony nonsupport falls.

52. 42 U.S.C. § 666(a)(4).

53. 42 U.S.C. §666(a)(7).

54. *Zablocki v. Redhail*, 434 U.S. 374, 98 S. Ct. 673, 54 L. Ed. 2d 618 (1978).

55. *State v. Oakley*, 2001 WI 103, 245 Wis. 2d 447, 629 N.W.2d 200 (Wis. 2001).

56. There are three exceptions to the general rule: (1) The decree or parties' agreement provides that the noncustodial parent is entitled to the deduction 26 U.S.C. §152(e)(2)(A); (2) the noncustodial parent furnishes at least $600 in support, and a pre-1985 instrument provides that the noncustodial parent is entitled to the deduction 26 U.S.C. §152(e)(3)(A); and (3) a multiple-support agreement provides that the child is to be claimed as a dependent by a taxpayer other than the custodial parent 26 U.S.C. §152(e)(5). The exemption gets reduced or even eliminated in the case of taxpayers with higher incomes (I.R.C. §151(d)(3)).

57. I.R.C. §24(b). The child tax credit phases out at a lower income level than does the dependency exemption.

58. See, e.g., *Columbus Bar Ass'n v. Albrecht*, 106 Ohio St. 3d 301, 2005 Ohio 4984, 834 N.E.2d 812 (2005).

Chapter 11

1. The Divorce Act of 1857 20 & 21 Vict. C. 85.

2. Richard Chused, *Married Women's Property Law, 1800–1850*, 71 Georgetown Law Journal 1359 (1983). This article provides an overview of these laws along with passage dates.

3. *Orr v. Orr*, 440 U.S. 268, 279-280, 283, 99 S. Ct. 1102, 59 L. Ed. 2d 306 (1979).

4. See, e.g., *In re Marriage of Thornley*, 361 Ill. App.3d 1067, 838 N.E. 2d 981 (2005).

5. See, e.g., *Austin v. Austin*, 445 Mass. 601, 839 N.E.2d 837 (2005).

6. *Pendleton v. Pendleton*, 5 P.3d 839 (Cal. 2000).

7. *Chappelow v. Savastano*, 195 Misc. 2d 346, 758 N.Y.S.2d 782 (2003).

8. Definitions based on *Black's Law Dictionary*, Abridged 8th Edition, Bryan A. Garner, Editor in Chief, Thomson West (2005).

9. Uniform Marriage and Divorce Act (UMDA) 1970, as amended in 1971 and 1973 (U.L.A.) §308.

10. See Patricia Barbarito, *Standard of Living— What Does It Really Mean?*, New Jersey Lawyer, Trends in Family Law, Volume 14, Number 36, p. A3. This is an interesting article on proving standard of living in New Jersey in particular.

11. See, e.g., *Trs. of the AFTRA Health Fund v. Biondi*, 303 F.3d 765 (7th Cir. 2002).

12. See Christopher Melcher, *Simple Answers to Complex Alimony Questions*, 27 J. Am. Acad. Matrimonial Law 61 (2014/2015) and Jackline Mola, *Overcoming a Client's Reluctance to Pay Alimony*, 20 J. Contemp. Legal Issues 171 (2011/2012).

13. The spousal support rules are located in the Internal Revenue Service Code, 26 U.S.C. §71 (1988).

14. *In re Sorah*, 163 F.3d 397, 401 (6th Cir. 1998).

15. Rachel Biscardi, *Dispelling Alimony Myths: The Continuing Need for Alimony and the Alimony Reform Act of 2011*, 36 W. New Eng. L. Rev. 1 (2014).

16. Richard R. Peterson, *A Re-Evaluation of the Economic Consequences of Divorce*, 61 Am. Soc. Rev. 528, 532 (June 1996).

17. *Bak v. Bak*, 24 Mass. App. Ct. 608 n.14, 511 N.E.2d 625 n.14 (1987).

18. §750 ILCS 5/504.

19. As of 2015, about one-fifth of the states have adopted the act in whole or part.

20. Va. Code Ann. § 20–107.1 (2006) and Utah Code Ann. section 30–3–5 subsection 8 (b) (Supp. 1995); see also *Riley v. Riley*, 2006 UT App 214, 138 P.3d 84 (2006). In the *Riley* case, a Utah appellate court opined that the "Husband's engagement in extramarital affairs and his prolonged deceitful conduct that led to the divorce—present precisely the type of situation where the legislature intended the trial court to consider fault. Indeed, Husband's fault goes a long way in explaining the propriety of a $900 per month alimony award, even though such an award would be too high if only economic factors were considered."

21. See generally Paula Y. Goodman, William D. Mosher, and Anjani Chandra, National Center for Health Statistics, U. S. Department of Health and Human Services, *Marriage and Cohabitation in the United States: A Statistical Portrait Based on Cycle 6 (2002) of the National Survey of Family Growth (2010)*.

22. See, e.g., Edward M. Ginsburg, *The Place of Alimony in the Scheme of Things*, Massachusetts Family Law Journal, Volume 14, Number 5, January 1997. This article proposed guidelines that the author believed would be applicable in the great majority of cases. Now retired, Judge Ginsburg began applying "guidelines" in his alimony cases in western Massachusetts in the late 1970s in hopes of fostering predictability and limiting litigation regarding what constitutes reasonable need and ability to pay. His position was that need is a function of available income and that making an equitable division of available income can prevent the difficulties inherent in an open-ended, case-by-case approach.

23. On spousal support guidelines, see Victoria M. Ho and Jennifer J. Cohen, *An Update on Florida Alimony Case Law: Alimony Guidelines a Part of Our Future*, 77 Fla. Bar J. 85 (2003); Marie Gordon, *Spousal Support Guidelines and the American Experience: Moving Beyond Discretion*, 19 Can. J. Fam. L. 247 (2002); and June Carbone, *The Futility of Coherence: The ALI's Principles of the Law of Family Dissolution, Compensatory Spousal Payments*, 43 J. L. & Fam. Stud. 43 (2002).

24. See, e.g., Marshall Willick, *A Universal Approach to Alimony: How Alimony Should Be Calculated and Why*, 27 J. Am. Acad. Matrimonial Law 153 (2014/2015).

Chapter 12

1. See *Solomon v. Solomon*, 383 Md. 176, 857 A.2d 1109 (2004), for an example of a case in which the court held that a nonequity club membership lacked the fundamental characteristics of property and was, therefore, not part of the marital estate.

2. See, e.g., *In re Marriage of Keedy*, 249 Mont. 47, 813 P.2d 442 (1991). In this case, the Montana Supreme Court upheld a lower court's decision that a baseball card collection consisting of more than 100,000 cards was marital property worth $208,000, less the $5,000 portion the husband brought into the marriage.

3. See *Stageberg v. Stageberg*, 695 N.W.2d 609 (Minn. App. 2005). In this case involving contingent attorney's fees, a Minnesota appellate court upheld a lower court's conclusion that "the portion of a contingent fee for work in progress on the valuation date that is attributable to work done before the valuation date shall be treated as marital property for dissolution purposes."

4. See, e.g., *In re Marriage of Anderson*, 811 P.2d 419 (Colo. App. 1990), finding that the portion of the husband's contract as a professional basketball player paid, but not expended, during the marriage was marital property subject to division.

5. See, e.g., *Campbell v. Campbell*, 213 A.D.2d 1027, 624 N.Y.S.2d 493 (N.Y. App. Div. 1995). This case involves a determination that a spouse's share of lottery winnings on a ticket purchased with ten coworkers was marital property.

6. See the New York case involving two roommates in which the court reached a decision based less on an ownership of property and more on a sentimental, pet-centered best interests custody analysis. *Raymond v. Lachman*, 264 A.D.2d 340, 695 N.Y.S.2d 308 (N.Y. App. Div. 1999). See also *Bennett v. Bennett*, 655 So. 2d 109 (Fla. App. 1995) re supervision problems when "custody" of pets is awarded.

7. See *In re Marriage of Rogers*, 352 Ill. App.3d 896, 817 N.E.2d 562 (2004). In this case, an Illinois appellate court held that Social Security benefits may be considered in calculation of maintenance awards, although they are not subject to division upon dissolution of a marriage. The court noted: "Section 407(a) of the Social Security Act prohibits a beneficiary from transferring or assigning his or her benefits to another and imposes a broad bar against the use of any legal process to reach social security benefits. . . . however . . . Congress has carved out a narrow exception to this rule to allow the collection of past-due child support or alimony (maintenance). . . . A trial court dividing assets in a marital dissolution proceeding should simply not give any consideration to federal social security benefits; those benefits have already been divided by the Congress."

8. See *Brebaugh v. Deane*, 211 Ariz. 95, 118 P.3d 43 (Ariz. App. 2005), a case of first impression in Arizona addressing the issue of whether stock options that had not vested before the petition for dissolution was served can be divided as community property. The court examined approaches taken in other states before holding that unvested stock options received prior to service of the dissolution petition constitute community property based on the employer's intent, to the extent that they compensate the employee for past or present service and not as an incentive for future performance.

9. See *In re Marriage of Schriner*, 695 N.W.2d 493 (Iowa 2005), in which the Supreme Court of Iowa considered as a matter of first impression whether worker's compensation benefits awarded to one spouse during the marriage are divisible property at the time of divorce. After reviewing approaches taken in other jurisdictions, the Iowa Supreme Court held "that workers' compensation benefits received up to the time of the dissolution are property subject to an equitable division to the extent they have been retained and not spent. Benefits received after the divorce constitute separate property of the injured spouse." See also *Drake v. Drake*, 555 Pa. 481, 725 A.2d 717 (1999).

10. See *Landis & Landis*, 200 Ore. App. 107, 113 P.3d 456 (2003). In this case, an Oregon appeals court affirmed a lower court's decision to reopen a case based on the wife's discovery that, in listing his assets, the husband did not mention or account for a $16,687 lump sum payment he had received as a Veteran's Disability Benefit.

11. *Buckl v. Buckl*, 373 Pa. Super. 521, 542 A.2d 65 (1988), quoting *White v. Rairdon*, 52 D. & C. 558, 559 (Delaware County 1944).

12. See, e.g., *Baker v. Baker*, 2004 PA Super 413, 861 A.2d 298 (2004).

13. *In re the Marriage of Graham v. Graham*, 194 Colo. 429 at 432, 574 P.2d 75 at 77 (1978).

14. *DeWitt v. DeWitt*, 98 Wis. 2d 44 at 58, 296 N.W.2d 761 at 768 (1980).

15. See Elizabeth Paek, *Fido Seeks Full Membership in the Family: Dismantling the Property Classification of Companion Animals by Statute*, 25 Hawaii L. Rev. 481 (2003). See also endnote 6 above.

16. S.C. Code Ann. § 20-3-630 (2014).

17. See *Quinn v. Quinn*, 13 Neb. App. 155, 689 N.W.2d 605 (2004).

18. See, e.g., *Conrad v. Conrad*, 216 W. Va. 696, 612 S.E.2d 772 (2005). See also *Villasenor v. Villasenor*, 134 Ariz. 476, 657 P.2d 889 (Ariz. App. 1982), holding that the husband's disability compensation had both a disability component deemed separate property and a retirement component considered community property; *Gay v. Gay*, 573 So. 2d 180 (Fla. App. 1991), holding that disability benefits are separate property because they replace future income; and *Allard v. Allard*, 708 A.2d 554 (R.I. 1998), holding that the disability pension at issue was

separate property to the extent it compensated for lost earning capacity but marital property to the extent it constituted retirement pay earned by the disabled spouse during the marriage.

19. *Huber v. Huber*, 200 W. Va. 446, 490 S.E.2d 48 (W. Va. 1997).

20. See *Abrell v. Abrell*, 236 Ill. 2d 249, 923 N.E.2d 791 (2010). In this opinion, the Illinois Supreme Court provides an excellent review of various approaches taken by courts across the country to classification of accrued vacation and sick leave benefits.

21. See, e.g., *Bacon v. Bacon*, 26 Mass. App. Ct. 117, 524 N.E.2d 401 (1988), a case in which the assets derived from one spouse's family and the appreciation on it was due to inflation and sound investment advice received from that spouse's family. In such cases, courts will usually consider whether the parents intended a gift or a loan, as evidenced by appropriate documentation such as a letter and promissory note.

22. See, e.g., *Wiese v. Wiese*, 46 Va. App. 399, 617 S.E.2d 427 (2005). This is a case of first impression in Virginia that addresses the question of whether refinancing precludes the possibility of tracing separate property or constitutes a transmutation of separate property into marital property. See also *Schmitz v. Schmitz*, 88 P.3d 1116 (Alas. 2004). This case addresses the complexities of appreciation, tracing, transmutation, and commingling issues in a determination of separate and marital property. See also J. Thomas Oldham, *Tracing, Commingling, and Transmutation*, 23 Fam. L. Q. 219 (1989), for a discussion of tracing.

23. See, e.g., *Painter v. Painter*, 65 N.J. 196, 320 A.2d 484 (1974).

24. Wisconsin adopted the Uniform Marital Property Act in 1986 (Wis. Stat. §766.31), which incorporates many community property principles. The IRS subsequently ruled that Wisconsin marital property is the equivalent of community property for income tax purposes. (Rev. Rul. 87–13, 1987–1 C.B. 20.) The Wisconsin Act is different in several respects from other "community property" states, and property division upon divorce can be complex. In case law, the Wisconsin Supreme Court has held that the legislature did not intend, as a general rule, that the Marital Property Act change the state's statutory equitable distribution principles and that classification of property under the Marital Property Act is not necessarily determinative of property division on divorce. *Mausing v. Mausing*, 146 Wis. 2d 92, 429 N.W.2d 768 (1988). The Marital Property Act is concerned primarily with the spouses' ownership of property during the marriage and at their death, not on dissolution. *Kuhlman v. Kuhlman*, 146 Wis. 2d 588, 432 N.W.2d 295 (1988).

25. Alaska Statute § 34.77.030 (2011). Although not generally considered a community property state, the Alaska legislature enacted the Alaska Community Property Act, effective in 1998. The Act essentially adopts the Uniform Marital Property Act as Wisconsin had done in 1986. The Act is unique in that it allows, but does not require, a married couple who are both Alaska residents to elect to classify property as community property in a community property agreement or a community property trust. In addition, under the Act, nonresident spouses may transfer property to an Alaska Community Property Trust (a form of Marital Property Agreement), and the property will be characterized as community property under Alaska law, provided at least one trustee is a "qualified" individual (essentially, a resident of Alaska).

26. Ibid.

27. See J. Thomas Oldham, *Everything Is Bigger in Texas, Except the Community Property Estate: Must Texas Remain a Divorce Haven for the Rich?*, 44 FAM. L. Q. No. 3 (Fall 2010).

28. Wis. Stat. § 766.55.

29. Internal Revenue Code §1041(b)(6). The one exception to this rule is that if separate property is converted to community property within a year of the decedent's death, it will pass back to the donor spouse and not receive a step-up in basis. Sec. 1014(e).

30. See, e.g., RCW 26.16.030 (2011).

31. *In re Estate of Erikson*, 368 N.W.2d 525 (N.D. 1985).

32. Restatement (Second) of Conflicts of Laws, Introduction, and §§ 258, 259.

33. *In re Marriage of Welchel*, 476 N.W.2d 104 (Iowa App. 1991).

34. See, e.g., *Horner v. Horner*, 2004 ND 165, 686 N.W.2d 131 (2004).

35. See, e.g., *Thompson v. Thompson*, 105 P.3d 346 (Okla. App. 2004).

36. *Bratcher v. Bratcher*, 26 S.W.3d 797 (Ky. App. 2000).

37. See Dylan A. Wilde, *Obtaining an Equitable Distribution of Retirement Plans in a Divorce Action*, 49 S.D. L. Rev. 141 (2003). See also Susan J. Prather, *Characterization, Valuation, and Distribution of Pensions at Divorce*, 15 J. Am. Acad. Matrimonial Law, 443 (1998).

38. See, e.g., *Moore v. Moore*, 376 N.J. Super. 246, 870 A.2d 303 (2005). See also *Andrukiewicz v. Andrukiewicz*, 860 A.2d 235 (R.I. 2004), in which the Supreme Court of Rhode Island bound a husband who chose not to retire at "normal retirement age" to the terms of a written property settlement agreement between the parties incorporated in a Qualified Domestic Relations Order. The Agreement provided as follows: "The Husband agrees and acknowledges that the Wife will receive the first $583.00 of the monthly benefit that he will be entitled to receive at the time of his normal retirement date under the Husband's Pension Trust Benefit Plan that he has through the Town of Coventry. . . ."

39. See *In the Matter of Patricia and Warren Preston*, 147 N.H. 48, 780 A.2d 1285 (2001) adopting a "mechanistic" approach and overruling *Fabich v. Fabich*, 144 N.H. 577, 744 A.2d 615 (1999), a case of first impression in New Hampshire on this topic. In *Fabich*, the state Supreme Court adopted a functional approach to determining whether or not a retirement disability pension is divisible marital property after discussing the various approaches applied in other jurisdictions.

40. QDROs are not favored by plan administrators because they create additional "paperwork," or by parties who want their pensions to remain intact. Prior to 1984, companies were not permitted to distribute pension benefits to payees other than the employee participant.

41. See, e.g., *Kazel v. Kazel*, 3 N.Y.3d 331, 819 N.E.2d 1036, 786 N.Y.S.2d 420 (N.Y. 2004). In this case, a New York court of appeals held that "A judgment of divorce and qualified domestic relations order (QDRO) awarding an interest in the husband's pension plan do not automatically include pre-retirement death benefits available under the plan. If the intent is to distribute such benefits, that should be separately, and explicitly stated."

42. *Hardy v. Hardy*, 311 S.C. 433, 429 S.E.2d 811 (S.C. App. 1992).

43. Internal Revenue Code §1041. See generally, Craig D. Bell, *Need-to-Know Divorce Tax Law for Legal Assistance Officers*, 177 Mil. L. Rev. (2003).

44. The *Solomon* case referenced in endnote 1 above includes a good discussion by the court regarding the issue of whether tax liabilities may be considered as "another factor" under the Maryland statute for purposes of distributing a marital property award.

45. See *Keff v. Keff*, 757 So. 2d 450 (Ala. Civ. App. 2000). In this case the court might have adopted the husband's position that his stock options should have been valued as of the date of the divorce, but the appellate court affirmed the lower court's decision, stating, "He cites no authority in support of this contention. An appellant's failure to cite supporting authority for his or her arguments leaves the court with no alternative but to affirm." In an Oregon case, *Timm & Timm*, 200 Ore. App. 621, 117 P.3d 301 (2005), the court remanded a case involving premarital contribution to marital assets, because the parties had relied on authority that was no longer controlling.

46. See, e.g., *Rodrigue v. Rodrigue*, 55 F. Supp.2d 534 (E.D. La. 1999). This case involved a conflict between federal copyright law and the state of Louisiana's community property law concerning certain artworks produced by the husband, in which the wife claimed a copyright interest. See also *Coon v. Coon*, 364 S.C. 563, 614 S.E.2d 616 (2005), in which the South Carolina Supreme Court examined the relationship between federal and state law governing disposable military retirement pay. The court held that under federal law, states may treat disposable retired pay payable to a service member either as property solely of the member or as property of the member and his spouse, provided the award does not exceed 50% of the disposable retirement pay.

The court held that South Carolina had elected to treat it as marital property.

Chapter 13

1. *Dominick v. Dominick*, 18 Mass. App. Ct. 85, 463 N.E.2d 564 (1984).
2. They may also ask that a constructive trust be imposed over the proceeds of the policy received by the new wife.

Chapter 14

1. Richard Gelles, *Intimate Violence in Families*, 3rd Edition, Thousand Oaks, CA, 1997, Sage, as quoted in Henry H. Brownstein, *The Social Reality of Violence and Violent Crime*, Allyn & Bacon, 2000, p. 77.
2. Id.
3. See Anne E. Appel and George W. Holden, *The Co-Occurrence of Spouse and Physical Child Abuse: A Review and Appraisal*, 12(4) Journal of Family Psychology, 578–599 (1998). See also S. M. Ross, *Risk of Physical Abuse to Children of Spouse Abusing Parents*, 20(7) Child Abuse & Neglect, 589–598 (1996) (asserting that intimate partner violence increases the risk of child abuse from 5% after one abusive act to 100% after fifty acts of intimate partner violence).
4. Kathleen Finley Duthu, Feature: *Why Do [We] Need to Know [About] Domestic Violence? How Attorneys Can Recognize and Address the Problem*, 53 LA Bar Jnl. 20 (June, July 2005).
5. Bureau of Justice Statistics Crime Data Brief, *Intimate Partner Violence, 1993–2001*, February 2003. See also the National Intimate Partner and Sexual Violence Survey: 2011, available at *www.cdc.gov*.
6. Patricia Tjaden, *Symposium on Integrating Responses to Domestic Violence: Extent and Nature of Intimate Partner Violence as Measured by the National Violence Against Women Survey*, 47 Loy. L. Rev. 41, 54 (2001).
7. Constance M. Weimann et al., *Pregnant Adolescents: Experiences and Behaviors Associated with Physical Assault by an Intimate Partner*, 4 Maternal & Child Health J. 93 (2000).
8. Pamela B. Teaster et al., 2004 Survey of State Adult Protective Services: Abuse of Vulnerable Adults 18 Years of Age and Older, National Adult Protective Services Association.
9. Id.
10. The American Bar Association's Commission on Domestic Violence provides a comprehensive survey of recent statistics "as a service to legal practitioners and advocates who may find it useful to include current statistical data in their arguments to the court." The survey references a number of resources for data on domestic violence by race and ethnicity.
11. The National Intimate Partner and Sexual Violence Survey: 2010 Executive Summary, CDC.
12. Patricia Tjaden and Nancy Thoennes, National Institute of Justice and the Centers of Disease Control and Prevention, *Extent, Nature, and Consequences of Intimate Partner Violence: Findings from the National Violence Against Women Survey* (2000).
13. Shannon Catalano, Bureau of Justice Statistics, *Intimate Partner Violence in the United States*, December 2007.
14. Hilary Mayell, *Thousands of Women Killed for Family Honor*, National Geographic News, February 2, 2002.
15. See Leila Abolfazli, *Violence Against Women Act*, 7 Geo. J. Gender and L. 863 (2006), for a description of the provisions of the first three VAWA acts.
16. See Erin L. Han, *Mandatory Arrest and No-Drop Policies: Victim Empowerment in Domestic Violence Cases*, 23 B.C. Third World L.J. 159, 176 (2003).
17. Laurie S. Kohn, *Why Doesn't She Leave? The Collision of First Amendment Rights and Effective Court Remedies for Victims of Domestic Violence*, 29 Hastings Const. L.Q. 1 at 5. ("Literature examining same-sex battering routinely refers to the fear of HIV 'outing' as being a primary cause of the secrecy that characterizes same-sex domestic violence.") ("Fearing homophobic responses, gay men and women often hide their sexual orientation from employers and family members. This fear gives batterers a manipulative tool to force victims to endure additional abuse. As long as a victim knows that a batterer intends to publicize this information and finds his threats credible, he may well stay in an abusive relationship rather than face the potential repercussions, which could include loss of child custody, employment, and family and personal relationships.")
18. Black, M. et al., The National Intimate Partner and Sexual Violence Survey (NISVS): 2010 Summary Report.
19. Katrina Baum et al., *Stalking Victimization in the United States* (Washington, DC, Bureau of Justice Statistics, 2009).
20. Patricia Tjaden and Nancy Thoennes, *Stalking in America: Findings from the National Violence Against Women Survey*, U.S. Department of Justice, National Institute of Justice, Washington, DC, as reported on the website of the National Center for Victims of Crime Stalking Resource Center in a fact sheet titled "Stalking in America—National Violence Against Women Survey (NVAW)."
21. Judith McFarlane et al., *Stalking and Intimate Partner Femicide*, Homicide Studies 3, no. 4 (1999).
22. *Supra* at n. 20.
23. Patricia Tjaden, and Nancy Thoennes, *Stalking in America: Findings from the National Violence Against Women Survey*.
24. Report of the American Bar Association Commission on Domestic and Sexual Violence, Angela Vigil, Chair, February 2015.
25. See, e.g., *Heacock v. Heacock*, 402 Mass. 21, 520 N. E. 2d 151 (1988), and *Heacock v. Heacock*, 30 Mass. App. Ct. 304, 568 N. E. 2d 621 (1991). (The Superior court dismissed a wife's tort action for unreasonable delay in serving process. In an effort to gain a tactical advantage in the parties' divorce action, the wife filed a tort action relating to an event that allegedly occurred during the marriage but did not attempt to serve it prior to the divorce, in order to avoid alerting her husband to the pending claim. The Appellate Court affirmed. The Supreme Court transferred the case from the Appellate Court and reversed on other grounds.)
26. See the Federal Gun Control Act of 1968 as amended codified at 18 U.S.C. §922 (g)(8).
27. Kohn *supra* n. 17 at pp. 10–11. This article provides an excellent discussion of the constitutionality of such speech restrictions in protective orders. ("Although at least one court has granted such a restriction, none has resulted in an appellate decision. Because privacy invading speech in a domestic violence context does not fall into one of the predetermined categories of unprotected speech, the court would therefore engage in balancing, weighing the value of the speech against the countervailing interests to be protected by the injunction.")
28. See Wis. Stat. 968.075(3)(a)1.b.
29. Ruth Jones, *Guardianship for Coercively Controlled Battered Women: Breaking the Control of the Abuser*, 88 Geo. L.J. 605, 612 (April 2000).
30. Id. at 509.
31. *Supra* n. 17 at 59.
32. Child Maltreatment Report for Fiscal Year 2013, published January 1, 2015, HHS Department of Children and Families.
33. Daniel Goldman, *The Sad Legacy of Abuse: The Search for Remedies*, NY Times, January 24, 1989.
34. Cathy S. Wadom et al., *An Update on the Cycle of Violence Research in Brief*, Washington, DC, U.S. Department of Justice, National Institute of Justice, February 2001, NCJ 184894. See also Janet Currie and Erdal Tekin, *Does Child Abuse Cause Crime?*, The National Bureau of Economic Research, NBER Working Paper No. 12171.
35. The Child Abuse Prevention and Treatment Act of 1974 (CAPTA) codified at 42 U.S.C. 5101 through 5107 as most recently amended by the Keeping Children and Families Safe Act of 2003.
36. 42 U.S.C.A. 5106(g)2.
37. *Definitions of Child Abuse and Neglect: Summary of State Laws*, Child Information Gateway, accessed May 2012 at *www.childwelfare.gov*.

38. Definitions of various types of neglect are provided in the National Child Abuse and Neglect Data Collection System.

39. 42 U.S.C. § 5106i.

40. *Supra* n. 37.

41. *Supra* n. 37.

42. *State v. Wilder*, 2000 ME 32, 748 A.2d 444, 449 n.6 (Me. 2000) (quoting William Blackstone, *Blackstone's Commentaries on the Laws of England 440* (Oxford reprint 1966), and William Blackstone, *Blackstone's Commentaries on the Law of England 120* (1768)).

43. *Wisconsin v. Yoder*, 406 U.S. 205, 213–215, 92 S. Ct. 1526, 32 L. Ed. 2d 15 (1972); *Pierce v. Society of Sisters*, 268 U.S. 510, 534–535, 45 S. Ct. 571, 69 L. Ed. 1070 (1925).

44. *State v. Adaranijo*, 153 Ohio App. 3d 266, 2003 Ohio 3822, 792 N.E.2d 1138, 1140 (2003).

45. *State v. Singleton*, 41 Wn. App. 721, 705 P.2d 825, 827 (Wash. App. 1985).

46. *State v. Thorpe*, 429 A.2d 785, 788, (R.I. 1981).

47. *State v. Kimberly B.*, 2005 WI App 115, 283 Wis. 2d 731, 699 N.W.2d 641 at 650 (Wis. App. 2005).

48. American Humane Association, *Shaken Baby Syndrome*, accessed May 2011 at *www.americanhumane.org*.

49. Id.

50. *Supra* n. 37.

51. American Humane Association, *Emotional Abuse*, accessed May 2012 at *www.americanhumane.org*.

52. 42 U.S.C.A. § 5106g(4).

53. *Parental Drug Abuse as Child Abuse: Summary of State Laws*, Child Welfare Information Gateway, available online at *www.childwelfare.gov*.

54. Wis. Stat. §§ 48.02 and 48.133.

55. *In re Baby Boy Blackshear*, 90 Ohio St. 3d 197, 2000 Ohio 173, 736 N.E.3d 462 (2000).

56. N.J. Stat. Ann. §9:6–8.10.

57. Id. at Article 9:6–8.13

58. Id. at Article 9:6–8.14. See Lauren E. Parsonage, *Note: Caught Between a Rock and a Hard Place: Harmonizing Victim Confidentiality Rights With Children's Best Interests*, 70 Mo. L. Rev. 863 (Summer 2005).

59. Pub. L. No. 96–272, 94 Stat. 500 (codified at 42 U.S.C. §§620-628 and 670–679).

60. See Kathleen Bean, *Reasonable Efforts: What State Courts Think*, 36 U. Tol. L. Rev. 321 (Winter 2005), for a comprehensive discussion of the federal reunification requirements and the states' interpretations and applications of those requirements.

61. *DeShaney v. Winnebago Department of Social Services*, 489 U.S. 189, 109 S. Ct. 998, 103 L. Ed.2d 249 (1989).

62. For an argument favoring imposition of liability on state actors for failure to protect victims of domestic violence and child abuse, see G. Kristian Miccio, *Notes from the Underground: Battered Women, the State, and Conceptions of Accountability*, 23 Harv. Women's L.J. 133 (Spring 2000).

63. Alicia Hehr, *A Child Shall Lead Them: Developing and Using Child Protection Mediation to Better Serve the Interests of the Child*, 22 Ohio St. J. on Disp. Resol. 443 at 455–456 (2007).

64. Id. at 457–458.

65. 25 U.S.C. § 1901 *et seq.*

66. See, e.g., California Rules of Court, rule 1439(f); RCW 13.34.070 (Washington); and Title 10 O.S. 20 §40, the Oklahoma Indian Child Welfare Act, which essentially codifies the holding in *Mississippi Band of Choctaw Indians v. Holyfield*, 490 U.S. 30, 109 S. Ct. 1597, 104 L. Ed. 2d 29 (1989).

67. National Council of Juvenile and Family Court Judges, Family Violence: Model Code on Domestic and Family Violence, Chapter 4, Section 401 (1994). The Council has published a useful resource for judges entitled *Navigating Custody & Visitation Evaluations in Cases with Domestic Violence: A Judge's Guide.*

68. Nancy Ver Steegh, *Differentiating Types of Violence: Implications for Child Custody*, 65 La. L. Rev. 1379 at 1477 (Summer 2005), referencing Howard Davidson, *The Impact of Domestic Violence on Children, a Report to the President of the American Bar Association 13* (1994).

69. Laurel Kent, *Comment: Addressing the Impact of Domestic Violence on Children: Alternatives to Laws Criminalizing the Commission of Domestic Violence in the Presence of a Child*, 2001 Wis. L. Rev 1337 at 1342, referencing K. J. Wilson, *When Violence Begins at Home: A Comprehensive Guide to Understanding and Ending Domestic Abuse*, p. 31 (1997), and Honore Hughes, *Impact of Spouse Abuse on Children of Battered Women: Implications for Practice*, Violence Update, Aug. 1992, at 1.

70. Id. at 1342.

71. This practice is not universally accepted. For example, in *Nicholson et al. v. Scopetta*, 3 N.Y.3d 357, 820 N.E. 2d 840 (N.Y. 2004), New York's high court held that it is inappropriate to remove children from a parent based solely on the ground that they have been exposed to a parent's domestic violence. The victim's "failure to protect" the child must be understood in context before a determination of neglect can be reached. See Justine A. Dunlap, *Sometimes I Feel Like a Motherless Child: The Error of Pursuing Battered Mothers for Failure to Protect*, 50 Loy. L. Rev. 565 (Fall 2004).

72. Prentice L. White, *You May Never See Your Child Again: Adjusting the Batterer's Visitation Rights to Protect Children From Future Abuse*, 13 Am. U.J. Gender Soc. Pol'y & L. 327, 334 (2005).

73. See American Judges Foundation, *Domestic Violence and the Court House: Understanding the Problem . . . Knowing the Victim*, available at *aja.ncsc.dni.us/domviol* (indicating that such abusive fathers are successful approximately 70% of the time).

74. Johnson, N., Saccuzzo, D. and Koen, W, *Child Custody Mediation in Cases of Domestic Violence: Empirical Evidence of a Failure to Protect*, Violence Against Women, 11(8) 2005.

75. Rosen. L. and O'Sullivan, C., *Outcomes of Custody and Visitation Provisions When Fathers are Restrained by Protective Orders: The Case of the New York Family Courts*, Violence Against Women. 11(8) 2005.

76. Israel, E. and Stover, C.S., *Intimate partner Violence: The Role of the Relationship Between Perpetrators and Children Who Witness Violence*, Journal of Interpersonal Violence (2009).

77. A majority of the effects identified in this application are commonly accepted and well documented in Laurel A. Kent, *supra* n. 69. The content draws on additional sources, including Dawn Bradley Berry, *The Domestic Violence Sourcebook* 8 (1998); Laura Crites and Donna Coker, *What Therapists See That Judges May Miss: A Unique Guide to Custody Decisions When Spouse Abuse Is Charged*, 27 Judges' J. (Spring 1988); John W. Fantuzzo and Wanda Mohr, *Prevalence and Effects of Child Exposure to Domestic Violence*, 9 Future of Children 21 (1999); K. J. Wilson, *When Violence Begins at Home: A Comprehensive Guide to Understanding and Ending Domestic Abuse* (1997).

78. "Research indicates that children who witness or experience abuse are one thousand times more likely to abuse a spouse or partner than children from non-violent homes." Kent, *supra* n. 69 at 1345, referencing Dawn Bradley Berry, *The Domestic Violence Sourcebook* at 121 (1998).

79. "Studies assessing children living in domestic violence shelters for posttraumatic stress disorder have found incidence rates ranging from 13% to more than 50%." Hon. Donna J. Hitchens and Patricia Van Horn, Ph.D., J.D., *Courts Responding to Domestic Violence: The Court's Role in Supporting and Protecting Children Exposed to Domestic Violence*, 6 J. Center for Fam. Child. & Cts. 31 at 33 (2005).

80. Ver Steegh *supra* note 68 at 1412. See Association of Family and Conciliation Courts (AFCC) Task Force on Parenting Coordination, *Parenting Coordination: Implementation Issues*, 41 Fam. Ct. Rev. 533 (2003).

81. Id. at 1413–1414 referencing Christine A. Coates et al., *Parenting Coordination for High Conflict Families*, 42 Fam. Ct. Rev. 246, 247 (2004).

82. Jennifer M. Collins, *Crime and Parenthood: The Uneasy Case for Prosecuting Negligent Parents*, 100 Nw. U.L. Rev. 807, 810–811 (Winter 2006).

83. Id. at 809.

84. *Dempsey v. Frazier*, 119 Miss. 1, 80 So. 341, 342 (1918).

85. Miss. Code. Ann. §§97–37–14 and 15.

86. Sara Buel and Margeret Drew, *Do Ask and Do Tell: Rethinking the Lawyer's Duty to Ward in Domestic Violence Cases*, 75 U. Cin. L. Rev. 447 (Winter 2006). This article provides a detailed survey of disclosure rules in various states.

87. See Adrienne Jennings Lockie, *Salt in the Wounds: Why Attorneys Should Not Be Mandated Reporters of Child Abuse*, 36 N.M.L. Rev. 125 (Winter 2006).

88. Mo. Rev. Stat. § 210.140 (2000).

89. Tx. R. Prof. Conduct 1.05(e).

90. Opinion 280, 97 N.J.L.T. 362 (1974).

91. Wis. Stat. 48.981(2)(c).

92. Buel and Drew *supra* at n. 86 at pp. 450–451.

NATIONAL ASSOCIATION OF LEGAL ASSISTANTS (NALA) CODE OF ETHICS AND PROFESSIONAL RESPONSIBILITY

First adopted by the NALA membership in May of 1975, the Code of Ethics and Professional Responsibility is the foundation of ethical practices of paralegals in the legal community.

A paralegal must adhere strictly to the accepted standards of legal ethics and to the general principles of proper conduct. The performance of the duties of the paralegal shall be governed by specific canons as defined herein so that justice will be served and goals of the profession attained. (See Model Standards and Guidelines for Utilization of Legal Assistants, Section II.)

The canons of ethics set forth hereafter are adopted by the National Association of Legal Assistants, Inc., as a general guide intended to aid paralegals and attorneys. The enumeration of these rules does not mean there are not others of equal importance although not specifically mentioned. Court rules, agency rules and statutes must be taken into consideration when interpreting the canons.

Definition: Legal assistants, also known as paralegals, are a distinguishable group of persons who assist attorneys in the delivery of legal services. Through formal education, training and experience, legal assistants have knowledge and expertise regarding the legal system and substantive and procedural law which qualify them to do work of a legal nature under the supervision of an attorney.

In **2001**, NALA members also adopted the ABA definition of a legal assistant/paralegal, as follows:

A legal assistant or paralegal is a person qualified by education, training or work experience who is employed or retained by a lawyer, law office, corporation, governmental agency or other entity who performs specifically delegated substantive legal work for which a lawyer is responsible. (Adopted by the ABA in 1997)

Canon 1

A paralegal must not perform any of the duties that attorneys only may perform nor take any actions that attorneys may not take.

Canon 2

A paralegal may perform any task which is properly delegated and supervised by an attorney, as long as the attorney is ultimately responsible to the client, maintains a direct relationship with the client, and assumes professional responsibility for the work product.

Canon 3

A paralegal must not: (a) engage in, encourage, or contribute to any act which could constitute the unauthorized practice of law; and (b) establish attorney-client relationships, set fees, give legal opinions or advice or represent a client before a court or agency unless so authorized by that court or agency; and (c) engage in conduct or take any action which would assist or involve the attorney in a violation of professional ethics or give the appearance of professional impropriety.

Canon 4

A paralegal must use discretion and professional judgment commensurate with knowledge and experience but must not render independent legal judgment in place of an attorney. The services of an attorney are essential in the public interest whenever such legal judgment is required.

Canon 5

A paralegal must disclose his or her status as a paralegal at the outset of any professional relationship with a client, attorney, a court or administrative agency or personnel thereof, or a member of the general public. A paralegal must act prudently in determining the extent to which a client may be assisted without the presence of an attorney.

Canon 6

A paralegal must strive to maintain integrity and a high degree of competency through education and training with respect to professional responsibility, local rules and practice, and through continuing education in substantive areas of law to better assist the legal profession in fulfilling its duty to provide legal service.

Canon 7

A paralegal must protect the confidences of a client and must not violate any rule or statute now in effect or hereafter enacted controlling the doctrine of privileged communications between a client and an attorney.

Canon 8

A paralegal must disclose to his or her employer or prospective employer any pre-existing client or personal relationship that may conflict with the interests of the employer or prospective employer and/or their clients.

Canon 9

A paralegal must do all other things incidental, necessary, or expedient for the attainment of the ethics and responsibilities as defined by statute or rule of court.

Canon 10

A paralegal's conduct is guided by bar associations' codes of professional responsibility and rules of professional conduct.

appendix B

WEBSITES OF GENERAL INTEREST

Note: The World Wide Web offers a wealth of freely accessible and rapidly changing information that may be immensely useful, but it should be verified when appropriate. The following URLs were all operational as of November 2015.

GOVERNMENT SITES

www.acf.hhs.gov

This is the site for the Administration for Children and Families (ACF). It provides links to a number of topics related to family law, including adoption and foster care, child abuse and neglect, and child support.

www.acf.hhs.gov/programs/cse

This is the website for the federal Office of Child Support Enforcement (OCSE). There is a wealth of material available on this website, including the publication, "Essentials for Attorneys in Child Support Enforcement." It also includes a list of, and links to, child support (IV-D) agencies in each state.

www.bioethics.gov

Sponsored by the President's Council on Bioethics, this site offers a rich variety of sources, including transcripts, reports, background materials, and books. The reports may either be downloaded or ordered in print form.

www.cdc.gov

This is the site for the Centers for Disease Control and Prevention National Center for Health Statistics. It provides an alphabetical directory to offices of vital records in the individual states and territories. A variety of useful statistical reports are available at this site on topics such as abuse and intimate partner violence.

www.census.gov

A number of statistical reports relevant to family law topics are available on this government site.

www.childwelfare.gov

This is the website for the Child Information Gateway, previously known as the National Adoption Information Clearinghouse, an activity of the Department of Health and Human Services. This site contains links to federal and state laws, fact sheets, statistics, and publications on a variety of child-related topics, including adoption, types of abuse, grounds for termination of parental rights, infant safe haven laws, and parental drug abuse. The text of the most recent Child Maltreatment Report is available at this site.

www.dol.gov/ebsa

This is the Department of Labor's site for the Employee Benefits Security Administration. Available at this site is an informative forty-eight-page publication on

QDROs produced by the U.S. Department of Labor. Extensive information is also available at the DOL site on occupational statistics and labor market trends.

www.irs.gov

This is the home page of the Internal Revenue Service, which provides access to general tax information, forms, and specific treasury regulations.

www.ncea.aoa.gov

The National Center on Elder Abuse (NCEA) is the major source of available statistics on elder abuse, neglect, and exploitation in the United States, including abuse in family settings. The website provides links to resources for locating state statutes, codes, and case law.

www.ojp.usdoj.gov

This is the foremost site for "official" crime statistics.

TOPICAL SITES

Adoption

www.adoptioncouncil.org

This is the website for the National Council for Adoption, a not-for-profit organization that engages in research, education, and advocacy for adoption. The 2007 Fact Book available at this site provides facts, statistics, and an analysis of state adoption laws.

www.adoptionattorneys.org

This is the site for the American Academy of Adoption Attorneys.

www.adoptioninstitute.org

This is the website for the Evan P. Donaldson Adoption Institute. It provides links to state putative father registries, open records information, state registries, and confidentiality statutes. It provides reports on the effectiveness of safe havens and the rights of all parties interested in the adoption process.

Assisted Reproductive Technology

www.asrm.org

This is the site for the American Society for Reproductive Medicine. It provides links to articles and websites on virtually every form of ART.

Child Advocacy

www.casaforchildren.org

This is the website for the National Court Appointed Special Advocates for Children (CASA) Association. The site provides links to state CASA programs.

www.childrensdefense.org

This is the site for the Children's Defense Fund, an advocacy organization for children. Among other things, the site provides data links and fact sheets on grandparents raising children.

www.crckids.org

This is the site for the Children's Rights Council. Available at this site are links to state codes, contact numbers for legislators, information on pending legislation, etc.

www.cwla.org

This is the site for the Child Welfare League of America.

Child Support

www.supportguidelines.com

This is a comprehensive resource on child support guidelines in the United States. It provides a number of useful resources and links to state material. It addresses additional topics relating to divorce and custody in particular.

Courts

www.ncjfcj.org

This is the site for the National Council of Juvenile and Family Court Judges.

Custody

www.ancpr.com

This is the site for the Alliance for Non-Custodial Parents' Rights, an organization that provides assistance to noncustodial parents on issues related to child support, custody, and visitation. It provides information about legal resources, UIFSA, recent cases, and obtaining school records. It also offers a "Winning Strategies Handbook" for sale.

www.coloradodivorcemediation.com

This is a court-sponsored site providing information about the psychological effects of divorce on children who are not physically close to their noncustodial parent. It offers age-specific suggestions on fostering the parent-child relationship through long-distance parenting.

www.deltabravo.net

The stated goal of this site is to ensure that children of divorce have access to both parents regardless of marital status. It offers links to a variety of resources, including one featuring an online parenting-plan generator.

www.stepfamily.org

This is the site for the StepFamily Foundation.

Domestic Violence/Child Abuse

www.bwjp.org

This is the site for the Battered Women's Justice Project Civil and Criminal Justice Office. This project serves as a national clearinghouse for information about domestic violence and the policing, prosecuting, sentencing, and monitoring of domestic violence offenders. The site provides links to state domestic violence coalitions.

www.childfindofamerica.org

This site provides facts and statistics and offers free investigation and location services, kidnap prevention programs, and referral, media, and support services in parental abduction cases.

www.ncadv.org

This is the site for the National Coalition Against Domestic Violence.

www.ncmec.org

This is the website for the National Center for Missing and Exploited Children. This site provides resources in English and Spanish for parents, grandparents, childcare providers, law enforcement personnel, and attorneys.

www.victimsofcrime.org

This is the site for the National Center for Victims of Crime. Available at this site is a stalking resource center that provides links to federal and state stalking laws and a digest of relevant cases. A dating-violence resource center is also available at this site.

www.thehotline.org

This is the site for the National Domestic Violence Hotline (800-799-SAFE; 800-787-3224). The line provides 24/7 access for calls from all states with translation services available in 140 languages.

www.lrcvaw.org

This is the site for the Legal Resource Center on Violence Against Women (funded by VAWA). The primary focus of the Center is on improving legal representation for domestic violence survivors particularly in interstate custody cases. It features links to national and state resources on topics including crisis lines, abuse later in life, and immigration issues. It also provides state-by-state links to child custody jurisdictional statutes, long-arm statutes, and relocation statutes.

Ethics

www.legalethics.com

This site abstracts and provides links to recently published articles on a number of topics related to legal ethics. It also provides links to other ethics-related sites.

Gender-Based Issues

www.feministmajority.org

This is the website for the Feminist Majority Foundation.

www.lambdalegal.org

This is the site for Lambda Legal's National Headquarters. The site provides extensive information regarding states, municipalities, and other entities offering domestic partnerships and civil union benefits. It also provides information on hot topics related to divorce, marriage, relationships, and family law.

www.mensdefense.org

This is the site for the Men's Defense Organization, which provides Web assistance to men, particularly fathers.

www.now.org

This is the site for the National Organization for Women.

www.thetaskforce.org

This is the site for the National Gay and Lesbian Task Force.

Legislation

www.ncsl.org

This site for the National Conference of State Legislatures provides summaries of enacted and proposed legislation in the various states.

www.uniformlaws.org

This is the site for the National Commission on Uniform State Laws. It provides copies of various iterations of uniform state laws and indicates which state(s) have adopted each act in whole or in part.

Nonmarital Families

www.unmarried.org

This is the site for Unmarried Equality, a national nonprofit organization advocating for equality and fairness for unmarried persons. It contains information and statistics on cohabitation, living single, domestic partner benefits, common law marriage, etc., as well as information on current news events, statistics, and advocacy efforts.

www.palimony.com

This is the site for Unmarried Couples and the Law.

Paralegal Organizations/Associations

www.nala.org

This is the website for the National Association of Legal Assistants (NALA). In addition to providing links to NALA-affiliated paralegal/legal assistant associations in thirty-five states, this site also contains the NALA Model Standards and Guidelines for Utilization of Legal Assistants. The Addendum to the Guidelines includes case references on a variety of ethical issues, including Unauthorized Practice of Law (UPL).

www.paralegals.org

This is the website for the National Federation of Paralegal Associations (NFPA).

www.nationalparalegal.org

This is the website for the National Paralegal Association (NPA).

Parental Rights

www.acfc.org

This is the site for the American Coalition for Fathers and Children.

Professional Organizations

www.aaml.org

This is the site for the American Academy of Matrimonial Lawyers. It provides links to family law organizations, courts and cases, the IRS, relevant federal statutes, and sites addressing topics such as ADR, divorce, adoption, custody, and parental kidnapping.

www.americanbar.org

This is the site for the American Bar Association (ABA). The ABA has several sections and centers that offer helpful information, such as the ABA Juvenile Justice Center, Commission on Domestic Violence, and the Family Law Section. Of particular assistance are the Tables produced by the ABA each year on various aspects of family law in the fifty states, for example, alimony/spousal support, custody, child support, grounds for divorce, property division, and third-party visitation.

www.socialworkers.org

This is the website for the National Association of Social Workers.

Research

www.alllaw.com

This site provides articles on many aspects of family law. It includes a generic child support guidelines calculator feature.

www.divorcelinks.com

A divorce and child custody law site with direct links to state and federal divorce laws by topic. As of December 2015, the site placed a heavy emphasis on parenting plans.

www.divorcenet.com

This site contains information on a number of family law topics. Search by topic and/or by state. This site offers links to state divorce laws and provides statutory references and brief narratives on topics such as grounds for divorce, approaches to division of property, alimony, and child custody, visitation, and support.

www.divorceonline.com

This site provides a wide range of articles and information on various aspects of divorce along with links to state divorce laws.

www.findlaw.com

In Findlaw's "Family Law Center," the user can search specific topic areas and narrow down and focus research. The Center provides generic articles as well as state-by-state links to laws relating to virtually every family law area, including, among others, marriage, divorce, child custody, adoption, abuse, surrogacy, paternity, support, and parental liability. Some of the links it provides to divorce forms by state contain sample separation agreements and parenting plans. Findlaw's Legal Technology Center has an Electronic Discovery Rule Wizard, an online interactive tool to help legal professionals understand the amended Federal Rules of Civil Procedure and improve their use of e-discovery methods and procedures.

www.law.cornell.edu

This is the site for Cornell Law School. It provides a variety of links to federal and state codes. For example, see *www.law.cornell.edu/wex/table_marriage* on state marriage laws. The master topic list includes adoption, divorce, emancipation of children, and marriage.

www.library.law.emory.edu

This Law Library resource provides links to state codes and selected cases. It also provides an Internet legal research guide.

www.lectlaw.com

Among other resources, this site provides articles on a range of topics related to marriage and divorce, custody and support, etc.

appendix C

STATE WEBSITES FOR FORMS AND STATUTES

State	Statutes	Forms
AL	www.legislature.state.al.us	eforms.alacourt.gov
AK	www.alaska.gov	www.courts.alaska.gov
AR	portal.arkansas.gov	courts.arkansas.gov
AZ	www.azleg.gov	azcourts.gov
CA	www.leginfo.ca.gov/calaw.html	www.courts.ca.gov
CO	www.lexisnexis.com	www.courts.state.co.us
CT	www.cga.ct.gov	www.jud.ct.gov
DC	www.lexisnexis.com	www.dccourts.gov
DE	www.delcode.delaware.gov	www.courts.delaware.gov
FL	www.leg.state.fl.us	www.flcourts.org
GA	www.legis.ga.gov	www.georgiacourts.org
HI	www.capitol.hawaii.gov	www.courts.state.hi.us
ID	www.legislature.idaho.gov	www.courtselfhelp.idaho.gov
IL	www.ilga.gov	www.cookcountyclerkofcourt.org
IN	www.in.gov	www.in.gov
IO	www.legis.iowa.gov	www.iowacourts.gov
KS	www.kslegislature.org	www.kscourts.org
KY	www.lrc.ky.gov	courts.ky.gov
LA	www.legis.louisiana.gov	www.familycourt.org
MA	www.malegislature.gov	www.mass.gov
MI	www.legislature.mi.gov	www.courts.mi.gov
MD	www.lexisnexis.com	www.courts.state.md.us
ME	www.legislature.maine.gov	www.maine.gov
MN	www.revisor.mn.gov	www.mncourts.gov
MO	www.moga.mo.gov	www.courts.mo.gov
MS	www.lexisnexis.com/hottopics/mscode/	(commercial sites only for non-Bar members)
MT	courts.mt.gov	courts.mt.gov
NC	www.ncga.state.nc.us	www.nccourts.org
ND	www.legis.nd.gov	www.ndcourts.gov (only for pro se)
NE	nebraskalegislature.gov	www.supremecourt.ne.gov
NH	www.nh.gov	www.courts.state.nh.us
NJ	www.njleg.state.nj.us	www.judiciary.state.nj.us

(Continued)

State	Statutes	Forms
NM	www.nmlegis.gov	supremecourtlawlibrary.org
NV	www.leg.state.nv.us	lawlibrary.nevadajudiciary.us
NY	assembly.state.ny.us	www.nycourts.gov/forms
OH	codes.ohio.gov	www.ohiolegalservices.org (not a government site)
OK	www.oklegislature.gov	(commercial sites only for non-Bar members)
OR	www.oregonlegislature.gov	courts.oregon.gov
PA	www.legis.state.pa.us	http://www.pacourts.us
RI	www.rilin.state.ri.us	www.courts.ri.gov/PublicResources/forms
SC	www.scstatehouse.gov	www.judicial.state.sc.us
SD	legis.state.sd.us/statutes	www.ujs.sd.gov/forms
TN	www.lexisnexis.com	www.tncourts.gov
TX	www.statutes.legis.state.tx.us	www.txcourts.gov/rules-forms
UT	www.le.state.ut.us	www.utcourts.gov
VA	Leg1.state.va.us	www.courts.state.va.us
VT	www.lexisnexis.com	www.vermontjudiciary.org
WA	apps.leg.wa.gov/rcw	www.courts.wa.gov/forms
WI	www.legis.wisconsin.gov	www.wicourts.gov
WV	www.legis.state.wv.us	www.courtswv.gov
WY	www.lexisnexis.com	www.courts.state.wy.us/forms

Note: All URLs operational as of November 2015.

GLOSSARY

Note: This Glossary defines terms as they are applied in the family law context.

A

Abandonment   a fault ground for divorce in some states; the plaintiff must show that the defendant deliberately and without consent left the marital relationship with no intention to return, and that the absence has continued for a specified continuous period of time (customarily a year or more); in child abuse context, occurs when the whereabouts of a child's parent are unknown, the parent has left the child in unsafe circumstances, and/or has failed to maintain contact with or provide support for the child for an extended period of time

Absolute divorce   a total divorce of husband and wife that dissolves the marital bond; frees the parties to remarry. See also *Divorce a vinculo matrimonii*.

Abuse   the causing of harm to another, often in the family setting; may include physical, emotional, sexual, and other forms of abuse

Abuse of discretion   the failure of a court to exercise sound, reasonable, and legal decision making

Acceptance of service   acceptance and acknowledgment of receipt of a summons and complaint or other legal document

Acknowledgment of paternity   a voluntary acknowledgment of paternity by the father of a child in a sworn (notarized) affidavit of parentage; sometimes a joint acknowledgment with the child's mother

Active appreciation   increase in the value of an asset that results from effort rather than simply market forces or the passage of time

Actual service of process   actual delivery of notice to the person for whom it is intended

Actuary   a statistician who determines the present value of a future event; one who calculates insurance and pension values on the basis of empirically based tables

Adjudication of paternity   a judicial decision declaring a man to be the legal father of a child

Adjusted gross income   income after nonvoluntary deductions are taken out, such as federal and state tax obligations, social security withholding, union dues, and wage assignments related to prior support orders

Adoptee   the individual who is adopted

Adoption   the judicial process by which a new parent–child relationship is created and an adoptive parent assumes the legal rights and duties of a biological parent

Adoption abrogation   an annulment, repeal, or undoing of an adoption

Adoption reunion registry   a vehicle available in some states that allows adoptees after a certain age (usually eighteen) to try to contact their biological parents and siblings

Adoptive parent   a person who, by means of legal process, becomes a parent of a child to whom he or she is biologically unrelated

Adultery   voluntary sexual intercourse between a married person and a person other than his or her spouse; a fault ground for divorce recognized in some states

Affidavit   a written statement of facts based on firsthand knowledge, information, or belief and signed by the affiant under pain and penalty of perjury

Affidavit of competency   an affidavit from a physician that an individual is competent to perform a particular act

Affinity   relationship by marriage (i.e., the relationship a spouse has to the blood relatives of the other spouse)

Age of consent   the age at which a person becomes eligible to consent to his or her marriage without parental permission

Age of majority   the age, usually eighteen, at which a person attains adulthood and associated legal rights. The age varies from state to state

Agency adoption   an adoption facilitated by an agency licensed by the state

Alimony   See **Spousal support**.

Alimony in gross   alimony ordered payable in the form of a definite sum, usually in a single or limited number of installments; usually not subject to modification

Alimony *pendente lite*   [Latin: while the action is pending] support awarded to a dependent spouse in order to maintain the status quo as to financial circumstances while a marital action is pending

Alimony recapture rule   the IRS rule that the government can recover a tax benefit (such as the prior claiming of a deduction for payment of alimony) by taxing the income that no longer qualifies for the benefit

All property states   states in which divorce courts may reach all property however acquired without distinguishing between separate and marital property if necessary to achieve an equitable distribution. Some describe this approach as "dipping into" separate property to achieve a fair division of property

Alternate payee   a recipient of a pension payment other than the plan participant

Alternative dispute resolution (ADR)   a procedure for settling a dispute by means other than litigation, such as mediation or arbitration

Annulment   the legal procedure for declaring that a marriage is null and void because of an impediment existing at its inception

Answer   a pleading filed by a defendant in response to a plaintiff's complaint, setting forth the defendant's defenses and counterclaims

Antenuptial agreement   See **Premarital agreement**.

Anti-Heartbalm Statutes   state laws that abolish the cause of action for breach of promise

Appearance   a document filed with the court by an attorney, indicating that he or she will be representing a specific party in a matter before the court

Appellant   the party bringing an appeal of a lower court's judgment

Appellee   the party against whom an appeal is brought

Appreciation   an increase in value

Approximation Rule   the rule that the custodial responsibilities of the parents at dissolution should be allocated in a manner that approximates the proportion of time each parent spent caring for the child when the family was intact

Arbitration   a process in which one or more neutral third persons who are trained arbitrators hear arguments, review evidence, and render a decision with respect to the issues selected for arbitration by the parties involved in a dispute

Arrearage   a payment that is due but has not been made

Artificial insemination   the process of inseminating a woman by means other than sexual intercourse

Assisted reproductive technology (ART)   treatment or procedures designed to make parenthood possible for persons with fertility problems or individuals who are otherwise unable or personally unwilling to reproduce

At-risk adoption   an adoption that is at risk of being challenged at a later date because the rights of one or both biological parents have not been terminated; an alternative to permanent foster care

Attorney-client privilege   the client's right to refuse to disclose and to prevent the attorney from disclosing confidential communications between the client and the attorney unless the communication concerns future commission of a serious crime; the privilege is established by statute and/or rules of evidence. See also **Rule of attorney-client confidentiality**

B

Bankruptcy   a legal proceeding in which a party seeks to be relieved of responsibility for paying his or her debts

Basis   the value assigned by the IRS to a taxpayer's investment in property

Battered woman's syndrome   the psychological condition of a woman who has been abused for a sustained period of time; sometimes used as a defense to justify the act or mitigate the penalty when the woman attacks her abuser

Beneficiary   the person named in a document (such as a will, trust, or insurance policy) to receive property, money, or some other benefit

Best interests of the child   the legal standard for resolving custody disputes that focuses on the needs of the child over the rights or wishes of the parents

Best interests of the child test   the position that determinations of legal parentage in surrogacy cases should be based upon who is best able to fulfill the social and legal responsibilities of parenthood

Bifurcated divorce   a divorce in which the dissolution of marriage is resolved in one proceeding, and all other issues, such as property division and child custody, are resolved in one or more later, separate proceedings in the same or another state

Bigamy   the act of entering a subsequent marriage while a prior marriage of one or both of the parties is still in effect; in most states constitutes a criminal offense if committed knowingly; a ground for annulment and/or divorce in all states

Binding arbitration   arbitration in which the parties agree to abide by the arbitrator's decision as final and unappealable

Biological parent   a blood-related parent who contributes half of a child's genetic material by means of a reproductive cell (egg or sperm); sometimes called a genetic or natural parent

Biology-plus rule   the rule that an unwed father's parental rights are worthy of constitutional protection if the father grasps the opportunity to develop a relationship with and accept responsibility for his child

Black market adoption   an adoption brokered by an individual who collects a substantial fee for locating a child who is transferred from one person or couple to another without proper legal process

Blog (web log)   a website feature in which an individual maintains a chronicle—frequently on a single topic

Boilerplate   standard language that is commonly used in a particular kind of document and that usually does not require negotiation

Bottom line   the limit beyond which a party will not go in a negotiation

Breach of promise   under common law, the breaking of an engagement without justification, entitling the innocent party to damages

Burden of proof   the requirement that a party prove a disputed assertion or charge

C

Canon law   church law; the body of law developed within a particular religious tradition

Capacity   the legal power to perform a particular act and to understand the nature and effect of that act

Capital gains tax   a tax on income derived from the sale of a capital asset as defined by the Internal Revenue Code

Care and protection proceeding   a court proceeding in which the state seeks custody of a child and termination of parental rights if warranted

CASA Program   a national program that trains court-appointed volunteer advocates to work one on one with abused and endangered children; CASA volunteers provide objective recommendations to the court concerning the environment that will best ensure a particular child's safety and well-being

Case law   the body of law contained in court opinions

Case of first impression   a case involving an issue being addressed for the first time in a given jurisdiction

Case registry   a federally mandated statewide database containing basic information on all child support orders issued by courts within the state; there exists a federal case registry as well

Cause of action   the fact or combination of facts that gives a person the right to seek judicial redress or relief against another; a legal theory on which a lawsuit can reasonably be based, given a particular set of facts

Ceremonial marriage   a marriage that complies with statutory requirements, such as obtaining a license and having the marriage performed by an authorized person

Child support   the payments made by a parent to meet his or her legal obligation to contribute to the economic maintenance of a child until the age of majority or emancipation or some other time or circumstance set by a court

Child support guidelines   guidelines developed by states in response to federal mandate that are presumed to generate an appropriate amount of child support, given a particular set of assumptions and circumstances

Chose in action   a pending right to recover something in a lawsuit, such as an action for wrongful termination

Civil contempt   a sanction for failure to obey a court order issued for another's benefit; a civil contempt proceeding is remedial in nature and its purpose is to promote compliance with the order. See also **Criminal contempt**.

Civil law   one of the two primary legal systems in the Western world, originating in the Roman Empire and influential in several parts of the world and a small number of states

Civil union   a formal legal status that provides a same-sex couple with the rights, benefits, protections, and responsibilities that a married heterosexual couple has under state but not federal law

Clear and convincing evidence   a standard of proof requiring that the evidence show that it is highly probable or reasonably certain that an alleged fact is true or false as claimed; a greater burden than preponderance of the evidence, but less than evidence beyond a reasonable doubt, the standard for criminal trials

Cloning   the genetic replication of a living organism

Closed adoption   an adoption in which biological and adoptive parents essentially know nothing about each other, and adoptees have no access to their original birth certificates or identifying information about their biological parents

Cloud   a communications network; the word "cloud" usually refers to the Internet and to software and data storage on an Internet site or network of sites

Cloud computing   Internet-based computing in which both the software and the data storage reside on an Internet site or network of sites

Cohabitation   two unmarried people living together, commonly in an intimate relationship

Cohabitation agreement   an agreement between two unmarried individuals who live or intend to live together, defining their intentions, rights, and obligations with respect to one another while living together and upon termination of their relationship

Collaborative law   an approach to reaching agreements and resolving differences that stresses cooperation, joint problem solving, and the avoidance of litigation

Collusion   a determination by the court that the parties should not be granted a divorce because they jointly deceived the court as to the true nature and purpose of the action

Comity, doctrine of   the practice of giving effect to the laws and judicial decisions of another jurisdiction (e.g., nation or state) out of mutual respect even if not legally obligated to do so

Commingling   mixing together a spouse's separate property with marital property, or mixing together the separate property of both spouses

Common law   judge-made law; the legal system that originated in England based on evolving case law and statutes

Common law marriage   a form of marriage created by the conduct of the parties rather than in a formal ceremony; usually requires capacity and intent to marry, cohabitation, and a holding out to the public as husband and wife; recognized in a limited number of states

Common law property state   a state in which a spouse's interest in property held by the other spouse does not vest until a divorce or death of the other spouse; with limited exceptions, property acquired during the marriage is divided equitably upon divorce in common law property states

Community property   assets owned in common by a husband and wife as a result of having been acquired during the marriage by a means other than an inheritance or a gift to one spouse, each spouse generally holding a one-half interest in the property no matter in whose name it is held; usually divided equally between the parties upon dissolution of the marriage absent an agreement to the contrary

Community property states   states in which a husband and wife hold property acquired during the marriage (exclusive of gifts and inheritances) in common, with each spouse entitled to a one-half interest in the property upon divorce

Comparative rectitude, doctrine of   in the divorce context, the granting of a divorce to the party who is least at fault when both parties have committed marital wrongdoing

Compensatory damages   damages sufficient to compensate an injured person for a loss suffered

Complaint   the main pleading in a case that sets forth the nature of the action and the request for relief

Complaint for contempt   a complaint to obtain compliance with a court order or to punish a person for noncompliance

Complaint for modification   a complaint seeking an alteration in an existing order based on a change of circumstances

Conclusions of Law   statements as to how governing law applies to a case

Concurrent jurisdiction   two or more courts having simultaneous jurisdiction over the same subject matter

Condonation   the forgiveness of a matrimonial offense

Conflict of interest   a situation or circumstance that interferes with the attorney's or a paralegal's duties of zealous advocacy and loyalty to a client

Conflict of law   a conflict arising out of a difference between the laws of two jurisdictions, such as two states or two nations

Connivance a traditional defense in which the defendant alleges the plaintiff consented to, or participated in, the act complained of in the complaint

Consanguinity a blood relationship between individuals

Consent the approval, permission, or assent to some act or purpose, given voluntarily by a competent person, as in consent to an adoption

Consideration a bargained-for exchange or mutual promises underlying the formation of a contract

Consortium companionship, affection, and, in the case of spouses, sexual relations, that one receives from another based on existence of a legal relationship (e.g., husband-wife, parent-child)

Constructive desertion a situation in which a spouse's objectionable conduct is so abusive or otherwise intolerable that it renders continuation of the marital relationship impossible and forces the "innocent spouse" either to move out or move into a separate area within the marital residence in order to maintain his or her health, safety, or self-respect

Constructive trust a trust imposed by the court on an asset of a party who improperly or wrongfully acquired the property

Consummation making a marriage complete by engaging in sexual intercourse

Contingent fee the payment of a certain percentage of the amount recovered by the client in a settlement or court judgment (plus fees and costs) based on results obtained; common in personal injury cases but generally not permitted in divorce cases except in limited circumstances such as collection of past-due child support

Continuing jurisdiction when a court has acquired proper jurisdiction (as in a child custody case), the retention of that jurisdiction over the matter to the exclusion of other courts for purposes of modification, etc.

Contract an agreement that establishes legally enforceable rights and obligations between two or more parties

Co-parent a person who is engaged in a nonmarital relationship with the legal parent of a child and who regards himself or herself as a parent rather than as a legal stranger to the child; a person who shares childrearing responsibilities with a partner with or without benefit of a legally recognized relationship

Co-respondent a person alleged to have had sexual intercourse with a defendant charged with adultery

Counterclaim a defendant's claim against the plaintiff

Court of equity a court that has authority to decide controversies in accordance with rules and principles of equity (principles of fairness)

Covenant marriage a type of marriage that emphasizes the permanence of marriage; a kind of marriage in which the parties participate in counseling prior to the marriage, accept marriage as a lifelong commitment, and agree not to seek a divorce absent a total and complete breach of the marriage covenant

Coverture (archaic, "couverture") the legal doctrine that upon marriage, a husband and wife become one person (the husband), and the wife loses many of the legal rights she possessed prior to marriage

Criminal contempt a punishment for failure to comply with a court order; a criminal contempt proceeding is punitive in nature and designed to punish an attack on the integrity of the court

Criminal conversation a tort action for adultery brought against a third party who has sexual intercourse with another's spouse; abolished as a cause of action in most jurisdictions

Cruel and abusive treatment a fault ground for divorce available in some states; conduct that is so physically or mentally damaging that it endangers the spouse's health, safety, or reason

Cryopreservation freezing and storage of genetic material for later use in procreation or research

Curtesy at common law, the right of a husband to lifetime use of land owned by his deceased wife during the marriage if children were born of the marriage

Custodial parent the parent with whom the child primarily resides; the parent who has the right to have the child live with him or her

Cut-off rule the rule requiring that a biological parent's rights to his or her child be terminated prior to adoption of the child by a third party; does not apply to the custodial biological/legal parent who remains in the new family unit

Cyberharassment a form of cyberstalking that does not typically involve a credible threat of violence. Rather, it is designed to harass the victim through email messages, blog entries, and the like

Cyberstalking repeated use of the Internet, text messaging, e-mail, or other forms of electronic communication with intent to harass, intimidate, torment, or embarrass another person

D

Decree *nisi*   [Latin: unless] an interim decree; a decree that is not final

Declaratory judgment   a binding adjudication that establishes the rights, status, or other legal relations between the parties

De facto **adoption**   [Latin: in point of fact] an adoption that does not meet formal statutory requirements but is considered an adoption based on the conduct of the parties and the surrounding circumstances; sometimes called an equitable adoption or adoption by estoppel

De facto **parent**   [Latin: in point of fact] an individual who performs a caretaking role without compensation for an extended period knowing he or she is not a child's legal parent; often with the consent of the legal parent(s)

Default judgment   a judgment entered against a defendant who fails to respond to a complaint or otherwise defend the action

Defense   a defendant's stated reason why a plaintiff has no valid claim or why the court should not grant the relief requested

Defense of Marriage Act (DOMA)   a federal law restricting the definition of marriage to the union of one man and one woman for purposes of federal law and allowing the states to deny full faith and credit to same-sex marriages valid in a sister state

Defined-benefit plan   a retirement plan in which the amount of the benefit is usually determined according to a formula based on the participant's earnings, length of service, or a target monthly benefit

Defined-contribution plan   a retirement plan funded by the employee's contributions and the employer's contributions (usually in a preset amount) in which the eventual benefit is based on the amount of contributions and investment earnings in the years during which the employee is covered by the plan

Dependency exemption   a deduction a taxpayer may take for a person principally dependent on him or her for support; in the custody context, usually taken by the parent with primary physical custody of a child, although the parties may agree otherwise

Dependency proceeding   See **Care and protection proceeding**.

Deponent   the individual who is asked to respond under oath to questions asked in a deposition

Deposition   a method of pretrial discovery in which one party questions the other party or a third person under oath; responses to oral or written questions are reduced to writing for possible later use in a court proceeding

Desertion   See **Abandonment**.

Directory of new hires   federally mandated databases maintained by both the state and federal governments and containing basic information from employers regarding all newly hired employees and applicants for unemployment

Discharge   to extinguish a legal obligation

Discharge a debt   to relieve an obligor of the legal obligation to pay a debt; the method by which a legal duty to pay a debt is extinguished

Discovery   the process of gathering information relevant to a matter at issue; includes both formal and informal methods

Disestablishment of paternity   a court order vacating an earlier paternity judgment or acknowledgment based on evidence the man is not the child's father, in effect disestablishing a previously existing father–child relationship

Dissipation   the use of an asset for an illegal or inequitable purpose, such as when a spouse uses or expends marital property for personal benefit when a divorce is pending

Divisible divorce   See **Bifurcated divorce**.

Divorce   a judicial determination that a marriage is legally terminated

Divorce *a mensa et thoro*   [Latin: divorce from bed and board] a legal separation

Divorce *a vinculo matrimonii*   [Latin: from the chains or bonds of marriage] an absolute divorce that frees the parties to marry

DNA (deoxyribonucleic acid) test   a test used to determine inherited characteristics and establish parentage

Docket number   the number assigned to a case by the court for organizational and reference purposes; the number appears on all papers filed in the case; sometimes called a calendar number

Domestic partnership   a status granted to an unmarried couple who live together and receive a variety of economic and noneconomic benefits customarily granted to spouses

Domestic violence   See **Family violence**.

Domicile a person's legal residence; the place one considers his or her permanent home and to which he or she intends to return when away

Donee the one to whom a gift is made

Donor the one who gives a gift; in ART, a person who donates genetic material

Dower a widow's right to lifetime use of one-third of the land owned by her deceased husband during the marriage

Dual divorce a divorce granted to both parties

Dual property states states that distinguish between marital and separate property for distribution purposes and permit only marital property to be divided and distributed at divorce

Due process the constitutional requirement that legal proceedings be conducted according to established rules and principles, including notice and the right to a fair hearing

Durable power of attorney a document that grants someone authority to act in the grantor's stead for convenience and/or in the event of incapacity; the authority survives incapacity but terminates on the death of the grantor

Duress a threat of harm made to compel a person to do something contrary to his or her free will or judgment

E

Ecclesiastical law (syn. **Canon law**) the law governing the doctrine and discipline of a particular church

Educational neglect a parent's failure to use his or her best efforts to ensure that a child of mandatory school age attends a legally recognized school or program of home schooling

Electronic discovery discovery of information created, stored, or best utilized with computerized technology of any sort

Emancipation the point at which a child is considered an adult and granted adult rights; the age, act, or occasion that frees a child from the control of a parent and usually the parent from a child support obligation unless otherwise ordered or agreed; usually occurs at the age of majority or upon the occurrence of certain acts or events such as marriage or entering the armed services

Emergency jurisdiction jurisdiction based on a child's physical presence in a state and need for emergency protection

Emotional neglect a pattern of rejecting, isolating, and ignoring a child's needs for nurturance, stimulation, and social contact

Employee Retirement Income Security Act (ERISA) a federal statute designed to protect qualified employee pensions in the event an employer goes out of business or declares bankruptcy; ERISA governs retirement plans that do not discriminate in favor of highly compensated employees.

Equal protection constitutional protection provided by the Fourteenth Amendment that prevents states and the federal government from imposing arbitrary and discriminatory legislative classifications that treat citizens unfairly or unequally based on race, religion, disability, sex, age, or national origin

Equitable adoption/adoption by estoppel refers to a situation in which prospective adoptive parents accept a child into their home and raise the child as their own without ever formally finalizing the adoption; treated by some courts as an adoption to promote fairness and serve the ends of justice

Equitable division/distribution the legal concept that upon divorce property accumulated during a marriage should be divided between the parties equitably, but not necessarily equally, based upon principles of fairness

Equitable estoppel preventing a party from asserting a claim or a defense because it would be unfair to an opposing party to do otherwise

Equitable parent doctrine a doctrine used to extend parenthood to an individual who is willing and able to assume parental rights and responsibilities and/or who has done so in the past

Equitable parenthood parenthood established on the basis of equitable principles of fairness rather than on biological connection

Equity in real estate law, the fair market value of a property less any encumbrances (mortgages, loans, tax liens, etc.)

Equitable remedy a remedy used by a court to achieve a just and fair result in situations not covered by existing laws

Error of law a mistake made by a court in applying the law to the facts of a case

Estoppel the doctrine that a person should be prevented by his or her prior conduct from claiming or denying the right of another person who has reasonably relied on that conduct

Escalation clause a provision in an agreement that provides for an automatic increase in an amount owed, such as in an alimony payment

Ethical wall   a screening mechanism designed to protect a client from a conflict of interest by preventing one or more lawyers (or paralegals) within a firm from participating in any legal matter involving that client

Ethics   the standards or rules of conduct to which members of a profession are expected to conform

Evidence-based prosecution   prosecution of a defendant that relies on physical evidence and testimony of persons other than the victim, such as police officers; formerly called "victimless" prosecutions

Exhibit notebook   a notebook, prepared for the convenience of the court and counsel, containing all exhibits to be introduced at trial by either or both parties

Ex parte   without advance notice to the opposing party; a matter considered and initially ruled on by the court without hearing from both parties

Ex parte **motion**   [Latin: from the part] a motion made without advance notice to the opposing party; a motion considered and initially ruled on by the court without hearing from both parties, based on the urgency of the matter or the harm that might otherwise result

Expectation damages   compensation awarded for the loss of what a person reasonably anticipated from a contract or transaction that was not completed

Expert   a person who, through education or experience, has developed special skill or knowledge in a particular subject

Express contract   a contract that is created by an actual articulated agreement of the parties as to certain terms of their relationship expressed orally or in writing

Extraordinary expense   an unusual, unanticipated childrearing expense that is substantial in amount and/or duration

F

Fair market value   the price a willing buyer would pay a willing seller in an arm's-length transaction (e.g., not between friends or family members) when neither party is under any compulsion to buy or sell

Family law   the body of law that governs the rights and responsibilities of individuals in the formation, continuation, and dissolution of marriages and other "family" relationships

Family violence   a pattern of coercive behavior designed to exert power and control over a person in a familial relationship; sometimes called domestic or intimate partner violence

Fault grounds   grounds for divorce based on the fault of one of the parties

Federal Parent Locator Service (FPLS)   a service operated by the Office of Child Support Enforcement (OCSE) for the purpose of locating parents delinquent in meeting their child support obligations when multiple states are involved

Fee agreement   a contract between an attorney and a client regarding payment for the attorney's professional services

Fiduciary   a person who owes another a duty of good faith, trust, loyalty, and candor

Fiduciary duty   a duty of good faith, trust, loyalty, and candor owed by one person to another based upon the existence of a special relationship

Filius nullius   [Latin: the son of no one] the child of no one

Final Judgment/Judgment Absolute   the court's final decision determining the rights of the parties and issues in dispute

Financial statement   a party's statement of his or her assets and liabilities signed under pain and penalty of perjury; sometimes called a financial affidavit or case information statement (CIS)

Flat fee   a fixed dollar amount charged to handle a specific legal matter, such as the negotiating and drafting of a cohabitation agreement

Foreign divorce   a divorce obtained in another state or country

Forensic   gathered as potential evidence in a lawsuit

Forensic accountant   an accountant who applies accounting principles and analysis to gather and present evidence in a lawsuit

Formal discovery   discovery methods that are subject to procedural and court rules

Forum   a location where disputes are heard and decided; a website feature in which a thread (specific topic within a subject area) or multiple simultaneous threads can be discussed

Forum *non conveniens*   [Latin: an unsuitable court] the forum in which an action is filed is not convenient for one or both of the parties, and the court, in its discretion, may find that justice would be better served if the matter is heard in another court

Forum shopping   seeking a court in a jurisdiction that will provide the most favorable ruling in a case

Foster parent   a person or persons who provide a temporary home for a child when his or her parents are temporarily unwilling or unable to do so, usually through a child welfare agency for a modest payment

"Four corners"   the face of a written instrument

Fraud   a false statement of a material fact with intent that another rely on the statement to his or her detriment

Front loading   the making of substantial payments to a former spouse shortly after a divorce in an effort to disguise a property division as deductible alimony

Full faith and credit   the recognition, acceptance, and enforcement of the laws, orders, and judgments of another jurisdiction

G

Genetic parent   a biological parent who is genetically related to the child

Genetic test   the position taken in parentage determinations that the individuals who contribute a child's genetic material should be considered his or her legal parents

Gestational mother   a woman who carries and gives birth to a child; the woman may or may not be biologically related to the child

Gestational surrogacy   involves harvesting eggs from either an intended mother or a third party donor and then fertilizing them outside of the gestational carrier's womb with sperm of the intended father or a third party donor (*in vitro* fertilization) for implantation in the surrogate mother's uterus

Gestational test   the position taken in maternity determinations that the woman who carries and gives birth to a child should be deemed the child's legal mother

Get   a "bill of divorce" in the Jewish religion

Green card   a document (registration card) evidencing a resident alien's status as a permanent resident of the United States; a "green card marriage" is a sham marriage in which a U.S. citizen marries a foreign citizen for the sole purpose of allowing the foreign citizen to become a permanent U.S. resident

Gross income   total income from all sources before any deductions are made

Ground for divorce   the reason for filing the action, the basis on which relief is sought in a divorce action; may be a fault or no-fault ground

Guardian   an individual appointed by the court to have legal authority over another's person and/or property during a period of minority or incapacitation

Guardian *ad litem*   [Latin: for the suit] a person, usually a lawyer, appointed by the court to conduct an investigation and/or represent a party who is a minor or otherwise unable to represent himself or herself in a legal proceeding; the guardian's role may be limited to investigation of a particular matter, such as custody

H

Health care proxy   a document granting another person the authority to make health care decisions for the grantor in the event of his or her incapacity

Hold harmless (indemnity) provision   a provision specifying that a particular spouse will be solely responsible for payment of certain debts and that the other spouse shall be free and clear of any obligation regarding those debts and will be indemnified by the debtor spouse if forced to pay them

Home state   under UIFSA, the state where the child has lived for six consecutive months prior to the filing or since birth if the child is less than six months old

Home state jurisdiction   jurisdiction in custody matters based on where the child has lived for a specified period of time

Home studies   assessments of prospective adoptive parents and home environments, customarily conducted by social workers licensed by the state

I

Ignorantia legis non excusat   [Latin: ignorance of the law is not an excuse]

Illegal adoption   See **Black market adoption**.

Illegitimate child   a child born to unmarried parents; a term abandoned in most states

Impediment   a legal obstacle to formation of a valid marriage or contract

Implied-in-fact contract   a judicially created contract, the existence of which is inferred from the conduct of the parties

Implied partnership/Joint venture   a judicially created partnership, the existence of which is inferred from the conduct of the parties

Impotence   lack of capacity to procreate due to inability to have sexual intercourse or to incompetent sperm or ova

Impounded   kept in the custody of the court and not available to the public, and, in some instances, to other parties

Imputed income   income that is attributed to a party based upon his or her earning capacity rather than on actual earnings

In camera   in the judge's chambers

Inception of title theory   a theory that fixes ownership of property at the time it is acquired and holds that postmarital contributions are of no effect

Incest   sexual intercourse between two people who are too closely related for some purpose as defined by civil and criminal statutes; a term used in some states to describe prohibited degrees of consanguinity and affinity in the marriage context

Income withholding   an automatic deduction of child support from an obligor's paycheck

Incompatibility   a no-fault ground for divorce that exists when there is such discord in the marriage that the parties are unable to live together in a normal marital relationship

Incorporation by reference   adoption by reference; made a part of the agreement by including a statement in the agreement that the Exhibits are to be treated as if they are part of the agreement

Independent adoption   an adoption usually facilitated by a third party such as a physician or attorney, rather than by a licensed state agency; sometimes called private, designated, or identified adoption

Independent legal significance   a contract that is legally binding in its own right

Informal discovery   information gathering not governed by specific procedural rules, such as researching public records and locating *Bluebook* values

In loco parentis   [Latin: in the place of the parent] taking on some or all of the responsibilities of a parent

Innocent spouse   a spouse who may be relieved of liability incurred if the other spouse prepared the tax forms, controlled the information that went into them, and is solely responsible for errors, omissions, and/or fraud that resulted in imposition of significant taxes, interest, and penalties

In rem jurisdiction   [Latin: against a thing] the authority a court has over a property or thing (rather than over persons) located within its jurisdictional borders

Intangible property   property that has no physical presence or form, such as legal claims, patents, and trademarks

Intended parent   a person or couple who intend to take custody of and assume all parental rights and responsibilities for a child as a result of an adoption, a surrogacy arrangement, or some other technique of assisted reproduction; an intended parent may or may not be genetically related to the child

Intent test   the position taken in parentage determinations that the individual(s) who set the procreative process in motion with the intent of raising any resulting children should be deemed the legal parent(s) of those children

Interlocutory order or decree   an interim decree; a decree that is not final

International adoption   an adoption in which a child residing in one country is adopted by a resident of another country

Interrogatories   a method of discovery in which one party submits a series of written questions to an opposing party to be responded to in writing within a certain period of time under pain and penalty of perjury

Interspousal immunity   a doctrine preventing spouses from suing each other in civil actions

Intestacy laws   the laws governing distribution of property when a decedent dies without a valid will

Intestate   dying without leaving a valid will

In vitro fertilization   [Latin] a technology that involves retrieval of eggs from a female to be fertilized in a laboratory by sperm from a male

Irreconcilable differences   a no-fault ground for divorce, the essence of which is that the marriage has irreparably broken down due to serious differences between the parties

Irremediable breakdown   See **Irreconcilable differences**.

IV-D agency   the state agency charged with responsibility for enforcing child support obligations

J

Joint award   an award made to both parents; may apply to legal or physical custody

Joint custody   an arrangement in which both parents share in the responsibility for and authority over the child at all times, although one parent may exercise primary physical custody

Joint petition for adoption   a petition to adopt a child that is brought by both parties to a marriage (or by co-parents)

Joint physical custody   a custody arrangement in which a child spends a more-or-less equal amount of time living with each parent

Joint tenants with right of survivorship a form of ownership of property by two or more persons in which each tenant owns an identical interest in the property, and each joint tenant has a right of survivorship in the other's share

Joint venture an express or implied agreement to conduct a common enterprise in which the parties have a mutual right of control

Judicial estoppel an equitable doctrine designed to prevent a party from gaining an unfair advantage over another party by making inconsistent statements on the same issue in different lawsuits

Judicial notice a court's acceptance of a well-known fact without requiring proof

Jurisdiction (1) a geographical area in which a certain law or procedure is governing; (2) the authority of a court to issue enforceable orders concerning a particular type of legal matter, person, or thing

L

Laches unreasonable delay in pursuing a right or claim that prejudices the other party's rights

Laws of descent and distribution the laws governing inheritance of property by heirs when a decedent dies without leaving a valid will. Usually, a surviving spouse will inherit the entire estate or will receive half of it, with the other half being distributed to any surviving children in equal shares. If the spouse dies testate (with a will) and the will largely disinherits or fails to make adequate provisions for the surviving spouse, some states allow him or her to "waive the will" and claim a "forced share" of the estate as set by statute

Lay witness a witness who is not an expert on a matter at issue in a legal proceeding, who testifies as to opinions based on firsthand knowledge

Legal custody custody relating to decision-making authority with respect to major issues affecting a child; may be sole or joint

Legal parent a person who is recognized as a child's parent under state and/or federal law

Legal separation a judicial determination that allows the parties to live separate and apart without dissolving their legal relationship as husband and wife; sometimes called a limited divorce

Letter of engagement a letter from an attorney to a client confirming that the attorney agrees to represent the client in a particular legal matter

Letter of nonengagement a letter from an attorney to an individual confirming that the attorney will not be representing that individual with respect to a particular legal matter

Letters rogatory documents issued by a court in one state to a court in another state requesting that the "foreign" court serve process on an individual within the foreign jurisdiction

Liabilities legal obligations, responsibilities, and debts

Lien an encumbrance on the property of another that operates as a cloud against clear title to the property

Limited-scope agreement an agreement between an attorney and a client that specifically limits the nature and extent of the professional representation to be provided

Liquidated damages an amount agreed to in a contract as the measure of damages to be paid by the breaching party to the nonbreaching party

Living separate and apart a no-fault ground for divorce based on the fact that, due to a breakdown of the marriage, the parties have lived apart from each other for a requisite period of time

Long-arm jurisdiction jurisdiction over a nonresident defendant on the basis of his or her contacts with the state that is seeking to exercise personal jurisdiction

Long-arm statute a statute setting forth the circumstances in which a state may exercise personal jurisdiction over a nonresident defendant; identifies the minimum contacts a defendant must have with the state where the statute is in effect

Lord Mansfield's rule the evidentiary rule that prohibited either spouse from testifying as to a husband's access to his wife at the time of conception if the testimony would tend to render the child illegitimate

Lump-sum alimony See **Alimony in gross**.

M

Malpractice intentional or negligent professional misconduct of an attorney that may occur in the form of a failure to properly supervise a paralegal

Mandatory reporter an individual who, by virtue of his or her employment as a police officer, nurse, etc., is required to report suspected child abuse and neglect

Mandatory self-disclosure   material specified by statute or court rule that each party in a particular legal action must provide to the other party within a certain period after filing and service of a summons and complaint

Marital communications privilege   the privilege that allows a spouse to refuse to testify, about confidential communications between spouses during their marriage; does not apply in certain contexts, such as cases involving child custody and/or abuse

Marital debt   debt incurred during the marriage for the benefit of the marital enterprise regardless of which party incurred the obligation

Marital estate   See **Marital property**.

Marital presumption   the presumption that when a woman gives birth to a child while married or within 300 days of termination of the marriage, her husband is presumed to be the child's legal father

Marital property   property that is acquired by either or both parties during the marriage, other than by gift or inheritance, that is subject to division at the time of dissolution

Marriage   a government regulated and approved legal status that two consenting adults attain by entering a contract with each other which confers rights, benefits and obligations; a civil contract between a man and a woman or between two same-sex partners

Marriage Evasion Statutes   laws designed to prevent a resident of State A from going to State B to get married if the marriage would have been illegal in State A. State A may elect to not recognize the marriage.

Marriage restriction laws   state laws that prevent certain persons from marrying each other, such as persons closely related by blood

Married Women's Property Acts   state statutes that extended to women various property rights denied them under common law, including ownership and control of property

Material change in circumstances   a change in the physical, emotional, or financial condition of one or both of the parties sufficient to warrant a change in a support order; a change that, if known at the time of the divorce decree, would have resulted in a different outcome

Maternal preference   the concept that custody should be awarded to a mother over a father, provided she is fit

Mediation   an approach to resolving differences in which a neutral third person helps the parties identify their differences, consider their options, and structure a mutually acceptable agreement

Medical neglect   the failure of a parent or caretaker to provide appropriate health care for a child

Meeting of the minds   a shared understanding with respect to the terms and conditions of a contract

Memorandum of *lis pendens*   [Latin: a pending lawsuit] a notice that ownership and disposition of certain real property is subject to a pending legal action, and that any interest acquired during the pendency of that action is subject to its outcome; usually filed in a Registry of Deeds where the property is located

Meretricious sex   unlawful or illicit sexual relations, such as prostitution or sex outside of marriage

Merge   the process by which a separation agreement is incorporated in a divorce judgment and does not survive but rather loses its identity as a separate and independent contract

Metadata   information that is stored or transmitted electronically together with a file or message that describes the file or message

Military affidavit   an affidavit submitted by a party stating under pain and penalties of perjury that an absent party is not currently serving in the armed services

Minor child   a child who has not reached full legal age

Modification   a change in a court's order or judgment based on a change in circumstances; customarily sought by motion of one of the parties

Motion   a written or oral request that a court issue a particular ruling or order

Motion to Dismiss   a request that the court dismiss the case because of some procedural or other defect, such as lack of jurisdiction or failure to state a claim on which relief can be based

Motion to Vacate the Judgment   a motion requesting the court to nullify or cancel a judgment before it becomes final

Motion *in limine*   [Latin: at the outset] a motion asking the court to exclude or limit the use of certain evidence at trial

N

Natural parent   biological (genetic) parent of a child

Necessaries   things that are indispensable to living, such as food, clothing, and shelter

Necessaries, doctrine of   under common law, a husband's duty to pay debts incurred by his wife or children for "necessaries" indispensable to living, such as food, shelter, and clothing

Neglect   failure by the caregiver to provide needed, age-appropriate care, although financially able or offered financial or other means to do so

Negligence   a failure to exercise reasonable care that results in harm to a person to whom one owes a duty of care

Negligent supervision   a cause of action based on parents' duty to society to exercise reasonable care in the supervision of their minor children in order to prevent them from intentionally causing injury to others

Net income   total income from all sources minus voluntary and nonvoluntary deductions

Neutral case evaluation   a process in which a neutral third party, usually an experienced trial attorney or judge, listens to the parties' positions and offers an opinion about settlement potential and the likely outcome if the matter proceeds to trial

Nexus   a connection or link; in the custody context, a requirement that there be a connection between parental conduct and a detrimental effect on a child before the conduct will be considered by the court

No-contact order   a court order prohibiting an individual from having contact of any kind with a person he or she has threatened and/or abused in some manner

No-fault divorce   divorce based on an irremediable breakdown of the marital relationship rather than on the fault of one or both of the parties

No-fault grounds   grounds for divorce based on an irremediable breakdown of the marital relationship rather than on the fault of one or both of the parties

Nonage   below the minimum age established by law to perform a particular act

Nonbinding arbitration   arbitration in which the parties are free to accept or reject the arbitrator's decision

Noncustodial parent   a parent who does not have sole or primary physical custody of a child but who is still a legal parent with enforceable rights and responsibilities

Notice of Deposition   the notification sent to an opponent (or his or her attorney, if represented) of an intention to depose him or her at a certain date, place, and time

O

Obligee   a person to whom a debt is owed

Obligor   a person who owes a legal duty; in the child support context, the parent who owes the duty of support

Open adoption   an adoption in which biological parents, adoptive parents, and the adoptee have varying degrees of contact with each other

Operation of law   a result that occurs automatically because the law mandates it regardless of whether or not a party agrees or intends that result; a party does not need to take any further action to bring about the result

Order to Show Cause   an order directing a party to appear in court and explain why he or she took, or failed to take, some action and why relief should not be granted

P

Palimony   a term that originated in the media; palimony refers to a court-ordered allowance paid by one cohabitant to the other after their relationship terminates; recognized in some states by case law, but generally not by statute

***Parens patriae* doctrine**   [Latin: parent of the country] the doctrine holding that the government, as parent of the country, has standing to act on behalf of a citizen, particularly one who is a minor or under a disability

Parentage   the identity and origins of one's parents

Parenthood   the position, function or standing of being a parent; the state of being or acting as a co-parent with all of the associated responsibilities

Parent locator service (PLS)   a federal or state government program that helps locate parents, particularly those who are delinquent in child support payments

Parental alienation syndrome   a condition in which a child involved in a custody dispute comes to idealize one parent and demonize the other parent as a result of the former parent's pressure and manipulation

Parental responsibility law   a statute that imposes vicarious liability on parents for the torts committed by their children

Parent by estoppel   essentially provides that a person may be designated the legal parent of a child if he or she has held himself or herself out as the child's parent and has supported the child emotionally and financially; a theory used to establish parenting rights that asserts a legal parent should not be permitted to deny a co-parent's parental status based on a prior agreement with the legal parent, on which the co-parent relied, to raise a child together; parenthood based on the fact an individual has functioned as a parent with the approval of a child's legal parents

Parenting coordinator   an individual, usually appointed by the court, who assists with design and implementation of parenting agreements and enforcement of decrees in high-conflict cases involving minor children

Parenting plan   a written agreement in which parents lay out plans for taking care of their children postseparation or postdivorce

Parol evidence rule   the rule that when a writing is intended to embody the entire agreement between the parties, its terms cannot later be varied or contradicted by evidence of earlier or contemporaneous agreements

Passive appreciation   increase in the value of an asset that results without effort and as a result of market forces and the passage of time

Paternal preference   the common law doctrine that fathers had an absolute right to the care and custody of their children

Paternity fraud   fraud in which a mother has intentionally misled a man into believing he is the father of a child to whom he is genetically unrelated

Pendente lite   [Latin: while the action is pending]

Pension   a job-related retirement benefit acquired by an employee and funded through contributions by the employer, the employee, or a combination of both

Permanency planning   planning for the return home of a child following removal or for termination of parental rights within a legally specified period of time in an effort to promote stability for the child

Permanent alimony   alimony usually payable in weekly or monthly payments either indefinitely or until a time or circumstance specified in a court order

Permissive reporter   an individual who may, but is not required to, report suspected child abuse

Per se **invalid**   invalid in and of itself, standing alone, without reference to any additional facts or circumstances

Per se **rule**   [Latin: by itself] without reference to any additional facts or circumstances

Personal jurisdiction   the authority of a court to issue and enforce orders binding a particular individual; sometimes called *in personam* jurisdiction

Personal property   any movable or intangible thing that is subject to ownership and is not classified as real property

Physical custody   custody relating to where and with whom the child resides; can be either sole or joint

Physical neglect   inadequate supervision and/or a failure to provide adequate food, shelter, and clothing such that the child's health, safety, growth, and development are endangered

Pleading   a document in which a party to a legal proceeding sets forth or responds to a claim, allegation, defense, or denial

Polyandry   the practice of a woman having more than one husband at the same time

Polygamy   the state of having more than one spouse at the same time

Polygyny   the practice of having more than one wife at a time

Posthumous reproduction   reproduction that occurs after the death of one or both of the gamete donors

Postmarital agreement (postmarital contract, postnuptial agreement)   an agreement made by two people already married to each other who want both to continue their marriage and also to define their respective rights upon separation, divorce, or death of one of them

Precedent   a higher court's decision regarding a question of law that provides a basis for determining later cases that involve similar facts or issues in a given jurisdiction

Premarital agreement   an agreement made by two persons about to be married defining for themselves their respective rights, duties, and responsibilities in the event their marriage terminates by death, annulment, separation, or divorce

Preponderance of the evidence   a standard of proof requiring that the evidence show that it is more likely than not that an alleged fact is true or false as claimed

Presumed father   a man who is presumed to be the father of a child who is conceived/born during the course of his marriage to the mother (or within a certain period thereafter)

Presumption an assumption of fact that can reasonably be drawn based on other established facts

Presumptive child support guidelines See **Child support guidelines**.

Prima facie **showing** [Latin: first face] a legally rebuttable showing

Primary authority authority created by a governmental body such as a legislature or court—includes statutes, constitutions, and case law

Primary caretaker the individual who has performed most of the significant parenting tasks for the child since birth or in the years preceding the divorce

Privilege a legal right or exemption granted to a person or a class of persons not to testify in a legal proceeding; generally based on the existence of a special relationship

Pro rata **theory** [Latin] See **Source of funds theory**.

Pro se [Latin: for himself or on his or her own behalf] [adj. or adv.] representing one's self in a legal proceeding without the aid of an attorney

Procedural fairness fairness in the negotiation and execution of an agreement

Procedural law the technical rules for bringing and defending actions before a court or administrative agency, e.g., the steps to be followed in seeking child support

Property division the distribution upon divorce of property accumulated during the marriage; if not agreed upon by the parties, the division will be based on community property or equitable distribution principles depending on the jurisdiction

Proposed Findings of Fact facts that a party asks a court to accept as true

Protective order a court order restricting or prohibiting a party from unduly burdening an opposing party or third-party witness during the discovery process; in the context of family violence cases, a court order directing a person to refrain from harming or harassing another person

Provocation a traditional defense claiming that the plaintiff provoked the conduct alleged in the complaint and therefore should be denied relief

Proxy marriage a marriage ceremony in which a designated agent stands in for and acts on behalf of one of the absent parties (prohibited in most states)

Psychological parent the individual who has the strongest "parental" bond with the child, who has provided the most significant care in quality and quantity, and whom the child often regards as the "parent"

Public assistance programs government programs providing financial and other forms of assistance to poor and low-income families

Public charge a person dependent on public assistance programs for necessaries

Public policy an idea or principle that is considered right and fair and in the best interest of the general public

Putative father a man who is reputed or believed to be the father of a child but who was not married to the mother when the child was born and whose paternity has not yet been established by legal process

Putative father registry a vehicle available in several states that is designed to protect a putative father's parental rights by giving him notice of a pending adoption proceeding without his having to rely on the birth mother or prospective adoptive parents for such information

Putative spouse a person who believes in good faith that his or her invalid marriage is legally valid

Q

Qualified Domestic Relations Order (QDRO) a court order directing the administrator of a pension plan to pay a specified portion of a current or former employee's pension to an alternate payee to satisfy a support or other marital obligation

Qualified Medical Child Support Order (QMCSO) a court order requiring provision of medical support or health benefits for the child of a parent covered by a group insurance plan

Quantum meruit [Latin: as much as he deserved] a basis for establishing damages or providing relief based on the reasonable value of services one person has provided to another

Quasi-community property [Latin, *quasi*: as if] property acquired during a marriage in a non-community-property state that would be marital property if acquired in a community property state

Quasi-contract/Implied-in-law contract [Latin, *quasi*: as if] a contract imposed by a court to prevent unjust enrichment of one party at the expense of the other

Quasi-**marital property**   [Latin, *quasi:* as if] property treated as if it was acquired by the parties during the marriage even though the marriage was never valid

Quid pro quo   [Latin: this for that] an action or thing exchanged for another action or thing of relatively equal value

R

Ratification   acceptance or confirmation of a previous act thereby making it valid from the moment it was done

Real property   land and anything growing on, attached to, or erected on it, excluding anything that may be severed without injury to the land

Reasonable efforts   the effort a child protective agency must make to prevent removal of a child from his or her home, or, if removed, to reunify the family within a specified period of time

Rebuttable presumption   an inference drawn from certain facts that can be overcome by the introduction of additional or contradictory evidence

Recapture rule   the IRS rule that provides for the government's recovery of a tax benefit (such as a claimed deduction or credit) by taxing income or property that no longer qualifies for the benefit

Reciprocal beneficiaries   a nonmarital family status, available in a limited number of states, in which two adults residing together may register for certain benefits available to married persons

Recrimination   a defense raised when the defendant alleges the plaintiff has also committed a marital wrong and therefore should not be granted a divorce

Rehabilitative alimony   alimony designed to assist a divorced person in acquiring the education or training required to find employment outside the home or to reenter the labor force; sometimes called limited or transitional alimony

Reimbursement alimony   See **Restitution alimony**.

Reliance damages   damages awarded to a plaintiff for losses incurred from having acted in reliance on a contract that was breached by the other party

Relocation   moving from one place to another

Request for Admissions   a discovery method in which a party makes written requests to an opposing party, calling for an admission or denial of specific facts at issue or verification or denial of the genuineness of documents relevant to the case

Request for Physical or Mental Examination   a method of discovery in which one party requests that the court order the other party (or, in some instances, a third party) to submit to a physical or mental examination

Request for Production of Documents or Things   a method of pretrial discovery in which a party makes a written request that the other party, or a third person, produce specified documents or other tangible things for inspection and/or copying

Res judicata   [Latin: a thing adjudicated] an issue that has been definitively settled by judicial decision; the three essential elements are: (1) an earlier decision on the issue, (2) a final judgment on the merits, and (3) the involvement of the original parties

Rescission   the cancellation or unmaking of a contract for a legally sufficient reason

Respondeat superior, **doctrine of**   [Latin: let the superior make answer] the doctrine under which an attorney is held vicariously liable for the acts of his or her employees performed within the scope of employment

Restitution alimony   alimony designed to repay a spouse who made financial contributions during the marriage that directly enhanced the future earning capacity of the other spouse; sometimes called reimbursement alimony

Restraining order   a court order, most commonly issued in domestic violence cases, restricting an individual from threatening and/or harassing another individual or individuals

Resulting trust   a trust created by the court when one party contributes funds or services toward the acquisition of property and the title to that property is held in the name of the other party

Retainer   used in general to describe a form of contract between an attorney and a client, particularly with respect to fees; most commonly, the client advances a lump-sum payment to an attorney for deposit in a client trust fund account, the attorney withdraws funds from the retainer as the client incurs fees and costs, and any unused portion of a retainer is returned to the client at the conclusion of the representation

Right of survivorship   the right of surviving joint tenants to succeed to the whole estate upon the death of one or more of the other joint tenants

Rule of attorney-client confidentiality   the duty of an attorney not to reveal any information relating to representation of a client; the rule is an ethical rule established in codes of professional conduct

S

Safe haven law   a law that allows a parent, or an agent of a parent, of an unwanted newborn to anonymously leave the baby at a safe haven center, such as a hospital emergency room, without fear of legal charges of abandonment or child endangerment, etc., provided there is no evidence of abuse

Safety plan   a plan prepared by a victim of family violence (sometimes with assistance) outlining actions to be taken in the event the victim needs to protect herself or himself and/or escape from the presence of the abuser

Sanctions   penalties imposed by a court when, for example, a party fails to comply with court rules or orders

Second look doctrine   an approach to determining enforceability of premarital agreements adopted by some courts that involves examining the terms of a premarital agreement for fairness at the time of performance as well as at the time of execution

Secondary authority   publications that discuss but do not establish law including, for example, treatises, annotations, and law review articles

Separate maintenance   court-ordered spousal support while the parties are living separate and apart but not divorced

Separate property   property that a spouse owned before marriage or acquired during the marriage by inheritance or gift from a third party; may include property acquired during marriage in exchange for separate property

Separate support   See **Separate maintenance**.

Separation agreement   an agreement made between spouses in anticipation of divorce or legal separation concerning the terms of the divorce or separation and any continuing obligations of the parties to one another

Service of process   delivery of a summons and complaint to a defendant in a manner consistent with state and federal law; usually accomplished by personal "in-hand" service by an authorized individual such as a sheriff or by publication in a newspaper and mailing to the defendant's last known address

Service plan   a plan developed by a child protection agency outlining services to be provided to parents to help them care for their children and identifying obligations the parents must perform in order for their children to remain in or be returned to the home

Shaken baby syndrome   a condition that results from repeated, vigorous shaking of a baby that causes brain damage and sometimes death and that can result from a single incident or a more prolonged pattern of abuse

Sham marriage   a marriage in which one or both of the parties has no intention of fulfilling the responsibilities of marriage

Significant connection jurisdiction   jurisdiction based on the existence of substantial evidence in a state concerning a child

Social network   a collection of people connected electronically by something they have in common

Social networking sites   Internet-based services that promote the formation of social networks by providing a means for people to describe (profile) themselves and to search for others whose public profiles match theirs in some respect

Sole award   an award made to one parent only; may apply to legal or physical custody

Sole legal custody   an arrangement by which one parent has full control and sole decision-making responsibility—to the exclusion of the other parent—on matters such as health, education, religion and living arrangements; sole custody can also apply to physical custody awards

Source of funds theory   a theory that bases ownership of property on contribution; an asset may be characterized as both separate and marital in proportion to the respective contributions of the parties

Specific performance   a court-ordered remedy for breach of contract requiring that the terms of a contract be fulfilled as fully as practicable when money damages are inappropriate or inadequate

Split custody   a custody arrangement in which each parent has legal and/or physical custody of one or more of the parties' children

Spousal support   an allowance for support and maintenance that one spouse may be ordered by a court to pay to the other spouse while they are divorced or living apart; also called alimony, maintenance, or separate support depending on the circumstances and the jurisdiction

Stalking   a knowing and willful course of conduct intended to cause another substantial emotional distress or fear for his or her safety; includes behaviors such as following, telephoning, or watching a person's place of residence or employment

Standing   an individual's right to bring a matter before the court and seek relief based on a claim that he or she has a stake in the outcome of the case

Stare decisis   [Latin: let the decision stand] the doctrine that requires a lower court to follow the precedent of a higher court in its jurisdiction (e.g., application of earlier case law to current cases)

State Case Registry   See *Case registry*.

State Directory of New Hires   See **Directory of New Hires**.

State Parent Locator Service (SPLS)   See **Parent Locator Service**.

Statute of frauds   the requirement that certain types of contracts be in writing, such as a contract that by its terms cannot be completed within a year, a contract in consideration of marriage, or a contract for the sale of land

Statute of limitations   a statute that bars a certain type of claim after a specified period of time

Stay away order   a court order requiring a person to keep away from another individual wherever he or she may be (home, work, school, etc.)

Stepparent   a parent by virtue of marriage to a child's legal parent

Stipulation   an agreement between the parties concerning some matter; may be filed with the court to be entered as an order

Subject matter jurisdiction   the authority of a court to hear and decide a particular type of claim or controversy

Subpoena   a document ordering a witness to appear and provide testimony in a legal proceeding, such as a deposition, court hearing, or trial

Subpoena *duces tecum*   [Latin: bring with you] a subpoena ordering a witness to appear in a legal proceeding such as a deposition, court hearing, or trial and to bring with him or her specified documents, records, or things

Substantive fairness   fairness in the specific terms of an agreement

Substantive law   laws that relate to rights and obligations/duties rather than to technical rules and procedures

Summons   a formal notice from a court informing a defendant of an action filed against him or her and ordering the defendant to respond and answer the allegations of the plaintiff within a certain period or risk entry of a default judgment

Surrender   a formal document in which a legal (usually biological) parent gives up his or her parental rights to a specific child

Surrogate mother   a woman who agrees to carry and deliver a baby with an understanding that she will surrender the child to the intended parents at birth or shortly thereafter; she may or may not be biologically related to the child

Surviving agreement   an agreement of the parties incorporated in a court's divorce decree that also retains its existence as an independent contract enforceable under basic principles of contract law

T

Talak   an Arabic word that means to release or divorce

Tangible property   property that has a physical form capable of being touched and seen

Temporary alimony   See **Alimony *pendente lite***.

Temporary orders   orders designed to protect the parties and maintain the status quo while a matter is pending before the court

Tender years doctrine   the doctrine holding that custody of very young children should be awarded to the mother rather than the father unless she is found to be unfit

Term alimony   alimony payable in weekly or monthly payments that continue for a set period of time or until a condition specified in a court order or agreement

Termination of parental rights   a judicial severing of the legal relationship between a parent and a child; may be voluntary or involuntary based on clear and convincing evidence of unfitness

Third-party beneficiary   a person who, though not a party to a contract, benefits from performance of the contract

Tort   a civil wrong (other than breach of contract) for which a court provides a remedy, usually in the form of money damages; the wrong must involve harm resulting from breach of a duty owed to another

Tracing   the process of tracking ownership of a property from the time of inception to the present

Traditional surrogacy   occurs when a woman is artificially inseminated with the sperm of a man other than her husband for the purpose of carrying a child to term for another woman, a man, or a couple who intend to raise the child as their own

Transitional alimony   the periodic or one-time payment of support for the purpose of transitioning the recipient to an adjusted lifestyle or a new location as a result of the divorce

Transitional Assistance to Needy Families Program (TANF)   a federal block grant program that provides support to poor families subject to certain conditions; replaced the former Aid to Families with Dependent Children Program

Transmutation a change in the classification of an asset from separate to marital or marital to separate

Trial notebook a term used loosely to describe the organizational system used by an attorney to assemble all of the materials needed for a trial

Trust a legal construct in which legal title to property is held by one or more persons (trustee(s)) for the benefit of another (the beneficiary)

Trustee process a legal process by which a third party holds the property of a party in trust at the direction of a court

U

Unallocated support support payments made to a former spouse that do not distinguish between alimony/spousal support and child support

Unauthorized practice of law (UPL) engaging in the practice of law without a license

Unconscionable so substantially unfair in terms or result as to shock the conscience

Unclean hands the principle that a party should not be granted relief if he or she has acted unfairly, wrongfully, or illegally

Undue influence the improper use of power or trust in a way that deprives a person of his or her free will and substitutes another's purposes in its place

Unearned income income derived from investment rather than labor

Uniform Interstate Family Support Act (UIFSA) a model act designed to facilitate establishment and enforcement of interstate child support orders

Uniform Law an unofficial law proposed as legislation by the National Conference of Commissioners on Uniform State Laws for adoption by the states as written in the interest of promoting greater consistency among state laws such as the Uniform Marriage and Divorce Act (UMDA)

Uniform Premarital and Marital Agreement Act (UPMAA) The National Conference of Commissioners on Uniform State Laws approved the UPMAA in 2012 and has recommended it for adoption in all the states. It is designed to bring greater consistency to the enforcement of both premarital and postmarital ("marital") agreements across the country.

V

Vacuum/last resort jurisdiction jurisdiction based on the fact no other state is willing or able to exercise jurisdiction, and it is in the child's best interest for a state to do so

Valuation the process of assessing the financial worth of property, real or personal

Venue refers to the geographical location within which a particular action should be filed

Vest to give a person an immediate, fixed right of ownership and present or future enjoyment; a vested interest is fixed or accrued and is usually unable to be taken away by subsequent events or circumstances

Virtual visitation communication between parents and children through the use of technology

Visitation a noncustodial parent's period of access to a child

Void invalid and of no legal effect

Void *ab initio* [Latin: from the beginning] of no legal effect from the outset; a contract is void *ab initio* if it violates a law or a strong public policy

Voidable marriage a marriage capable of being nullified because of a circumstance existing at the time it was established; the marriage remains valid unless and until it is declared invalid by a court of competent jurisdiction

W

Wage assignment/withholding an order directing a support obligor's employer to take support payments directly out of that person's paycheck for the benefit of the obligee

Waiver the giving up of a right or privilege

Work product written or oral material prepared for or by an attorney in preparation for litigation, either planned or in progress

Writ *ne exeat* [Latin: that he not depart] a court order restraining a person from leaving the jurisdiction until the petitioner's claim has been satisfied

Wrongful adoption a tort action that an adoptive parent can bring against an adoption agency for failure to provide accurate and sufficient information regarding an adoptive child prior to adoption

INDEX